1995

New Foundations for Scientific Social and Behavioral Research

The Heuristic Paradigm

KATHERINE TYSON

Loyola University of Chicago

ALLYN AND BACON

Boston   London   Toronto   Sydney   Tokyo   Singapore

This book is dedicated to my students, who by sharing with me their search for knowledge in the context of its practical applications in social work have offered me a constant challenge and reward.

Each one of us, whether we specialize in administration, community organization, treatment, or public policy, can and, hopefully, will have a simultaneous identity as a researcher, because each one of us is capable of exercising judgment and creativity in our area of interest so as to advance our knowledge about the important problems that we encounter daily.

—Martha Heineman Pieper (1989), "The Heuristic Paradigm: A Unifying and Comprehensive Approach to Research," *Smith College Studies in Social Work*, 60, p. 29.

Editor: Linda James Scharp MSW
Production Editor: Louise N. Sette
Text and Cover Designer: Jill E. Bonar with Janice Hovey, Boldface Design
Production Manager: Deidra Schwartz
Electronic Text Management: Marilyn Wilson Phelps, Matthew Williams,
    Jane Lopez, Karen L. Bretz

LIBRARY OF CONGRESS CATALOGING-IN-PUBLICATION DATA
New foundations for scientific social and behavioral research : the
heuristic paradigm / [edited by] Katherine Tyson.
        p.   cm.
    Includes bibliographical references (p.   ) and index.
    ISBN 0-02-421901-0
        1. Social service—Research. 2. Social service—Methodology.
3. Heuristic. I. Tyson, Katherine Bronk, 1953–   .
    HV11.N49   1995
    361—dc20   94-142
                                                                                 CIP

Printed in the United States of America

10 9 8 7 6 5 4 3 2 1   99 98 97 96 95 94

Brief Contents

Contents

II
Applying the Heuristic Paradigm   221

Editor's Introduction

What is truth? How do you and I discover and/or know what is true?

These are among the oldest questions that human beings have asked of themselves and each other. Often such questions have been viewed as the domain of philosophers, not scientists. Yet every scientist pursues knowledge only in the context of having responded to these questions. Sometimes the scientist explicitly articulates the responses; often the responses are implicit and assumed, yet they inform everything the scientist does. This book examines contemporary assumptions about scientific knowledge in the social and behavioral sciences, looks at some of the traditions that have shaped our beliefs about scientific knowledge, and introduces some up-to-date, nonrestrictive ideas about scientific truths and ways of knowing those truths. The book builds on the foundations developed by the leading scholars in the philosophy of the social and behavioral sciences today, and so includes selections from their work.

The Introduction is by Ann Hartman, who has been recognized as one of the most eminent contemporary social workers. She is the Dean of the Smith College School for Social Work and also the Editor-in-Chief of *Social Work*, the journal of the National Association of Social Workers. She has contributed research about family therapy and the history of the social work profession. She has always used research in the service of advocating for social justice, and as her introduction emphasizes, she has inspired us to recognize how knowledge shapes both our inner subjective experience and our wider social reality.

The Preface is by Martha Heineman Pieper, a psychotherapist, consultant, and researcher in Chicago, Illinois. Heineman Pieper's trailblazing papers advancing the heuristic paradigm, included in Chapter 3, opened up new avenues for social work researchers to generate scientific knowledge and to fulfill their commitment to the humanistic values that motivate most social and behavioral scientists. In the Preface, she carves out a naturalistic approach to social and behavioral research that, when applied to clinical practice, has the important aim of preserving the integrity of the therapeutic process while generating scientific knowledge. Heineman Pieper has recently used naturalistic methods to develop a new psychology and philosophy of mind, called *intrapsychic humanism* (Pieper & Pieper, 1990), which has already yielded very promising applications to clinical practice, including ways of helping people whose difficulties previously were considered untreatable (see Chapter 8).

Many other research texts discuss the implementation of specific methods for gathering and analyzing data. This book addresses the assumptions that underlie every social and behavioral scientist's decisions about designing a research study, specifically, assumptions about (1) formulating research problems; (2) choosing theories to guide the research; (3) planning data gathering; and (4) deciding how to analyze the data. One of the central ideas in the heuristic approach to scientific research advanced in this book is that all ways of knowing are heuristics, and that no one way of knowing is inherently superior to any other for generating scientific knowledge. When designing research, researchers who adopt the heuristic paradigm evaluate the usefulness of ways of knowing in relation to their assumptions about reality and the problem they want to solve.

The term *heuristic* is from the Greek word *heuriskein*, which means to discover or to find. Heineman Pieper, following the work of the noted philosophers of science Herbert Simon and William Wimsatt, uses the term to mean "any problem solving strategy that appears likely to lead to relevant, reliable, and useful information" (1989, p. 8).

One of the most important challenges that the field of social work and the other social and behavioral sciences face today is how to generate knowledge that actualizes humanistic values, contributes to solving social problems, and is also rigorous and systematic. For example, clinicians often uncover useful ways to understand and help clients. If they can conceptualize their discoveries and communicate them so that other practitioners can apply those discoveries in their own work, the discoveries can be extraordinarily helpful. If clinicians say that their work is derived only from "hunches" or "intuition," no one else can understand their thought process and benefit from that knowledge. Scientific rigor has the very important aim of fostering communication and collaboration so that we can mutually enrich each other's insights and advance knowledge in our field. Although approaches to social and behavioral knowledge derived from a philosophy of research called positivism (see Chapter 1) emphasize that rigor should be obtained by the application of particular research methods, such a view of rigor has been unnecessarily confining and also confounding for the social and behavioral sciences. No single research method can guarantee rigorous knowledge, because every step in planning research, including choices about data collection and data analysis, introduces a form of bias. To generate truly rigorous knowledge, systematic conceptual analysis must anchor carefully executed research strategies. Another reason why it is important to understand the ideas about scientific knowledge set forth in this book is that recognizing how heuristics and biases operate makes it possible to regulate the inevitable biases that inform the research process. The heuristic approach to research advanced in this book offers a postpositivist* conceptual framework that social and behavioral researchers can use to generate rigorous, relevant scientific knowledge that also fulfills their value commitments.

The heuristic approach is presented in the context of other beliefs about knowledge so that the reader can understand competing philosophies of research as well. Part 1 introduces the heuristic paradigm and places it in historical context. Chapter 2 presents a history of the approaches to research in the field of social work and also illustrates how historical research can be conducted within the heuristic paradigm. The history provides a context for contemporary debates about knowledge generation and illuminates some important implications of a discipline's choice of research paradigm. In addition, the history includes a focus on the contributions of the early women social work researchers, which were overlooked or depreciated in many prior histories of the social work profession. Chapter 3 presents Martha Heineman Pieper's ground-breaking papers, in which she critiques the positivist approach to social and behavioral research and advances the heuristic paradigm. Selections from the debates among social work researchers that occurred in response to her work are presented so that the reader can examine the controversy about the philosophy of social and behavioral research from various perspectives. Part 2 focuses on applying the heuristic paradigm. Chapter 4 provides an overview of how the heuristic paradigm can be used to design social and behavioral research. To further illustrate how the heuristic paradigm can be used to design research, elements of a sample research project are presented in Chapters 4–6. Chapter 5 includes papers by leading contemporary postpositivist philosophers of science (Hull, Scriven, Simon, Wimsatt, and Bhaskar) that critique the logical positivist metatheory and also propose alternative approaches to understanding knowledge. Social and behavioral scientists in decision theory, psychology, education, linguistics, and anthropology have joined the discussions about the conceptual foundations of scientific knowledge; some of the most notable contributions are included in Chapters 5 and 6 (by Manicas and Secord, Tversky and Kahneman, Whorf, and Gadlin and Ingle). Also in Chapter 6, Richard Lewontin, a leading evolutionary biologist, presents some of the most fundamental issues involved in using a common form of inferential statistical analysis called analysis of variance. The references for the selections that do not use footnotes for citations are in a common list at the back of the book. All selections are preceded by introductions, discussion questions, and key terms that further describe central concepts in the philosophy of social and behavioral research and that take a closer look at issues in designing research using the heuristic paradigm. The reader will find definitions of the key terms in the glossary. Because one of the most enduring problems in social and behavioral research has been how to evaluate practice systematically

---

*Editor's Note: Postpositivist refers to beliefs about scientific knowledge that have evolved following critiques of logical positivism and includes social constructionism (Gergen, 1986; Lincoln, 1990), critical or transcendental realism, as formulated most notably by Roy Bhaskar (1989a, 1989b, 1991), and many types of scientific realism (Leplin, 1984; Wimsatt, 1987). Postpositivist, as used here, does not refer to derivatives of logical positivism, a more narrow meaning of the term as used by Phillips (1990). Unless the context indicates otherwise, the terms positivist and positivism refer to the constellation of ideas about scientific knowledge that derive from the philosophy of science termed logical positivism.

without distorting that practice for research purposes, Chapter 7 describes a naturalistic approach to evaluating practice that is based on the conceptual foundations of the heuristic paradigm. In Chapter 8, Martha Heineman Pieper and William Joseph Pieper use a naturalistic approach to clinical research to study the application of their pioneering treatment approach—intrapsychic humanism—to violent teenage wards of the Illinois Department of Children and Family Services. Their study exemplifies how naturalistic clinical research can be conducted within the conceptual framework of the heuristic paradigm; it also indicates how the new avenues for scientific research opened up by the heuristic paradigm facilitate the discovery of promising solutions to our pressing social problems. The Appendix contains selections from two philosophers of science (Percy Bridgman and Moritz Schlick), who advanced ideas associated with logical positivism, and a selection by Karl Popper, who disagreed with many aspects of logical positivism but also sought to construct a philosophy with many of the same aims.

REFERENCES

Pieper, M. Heineman. (1989). The heuristic paradigm: A unifying and comprehensive approach to social work research. *Smith College Studies in Social Work, 60,* 8–34.

Pieper, M. Heineman, & Pieper, W. J. (1990). *Intrapsychic humanism: An introduction to a comprehensive psychology and philosophy of mind.* Chicago, Falcon II Press.

Introduction

Ann Hartman

There is nothing more crucial in shaping and defining the social work profession and its practice than that profession's definition of "the truth." Further, the processes through which truth is defined and the methods of truth seeking selected are highly political. As French philosopher Michael Foucault has taught us, knowledge is power and power is knowledge. He writes, "We are subjected to the production of truth through power and we cannot exercise power except through the production of truth" (1980, p. 93). Although some truths are privileged and some are not, Foucault points out that it is not the privileging of specific ideologies in that process that is most important, but rather the

> production of effective instruments for the formulation and accumulation of knowledge—methods of observation, techniques of registration, procedures for investigation and research, apparatuses of control. All this means that power, when it is exercised through these subtle mechanisms, cannot but evolve, organize and put into circulation a knowledge, or rather apparatuses of knowledge, which are not ideological constructs. (1980, p. 102)

Power becomes invested in the specific strategies of knowledge. It is thus that we can understand the intensity of the arguments, painstakingly presented in this volume, concerning what is the proper, the appropriate path to the discovery of "truth." Those who guard that path have control of, in Foucault's term, knowledge-power, a position not cheerfully relinquished.

Katherine Tyson, in this informative and provocative volume, offers an alternative route to knowledge, a route that challenges the hegemony of positivistic epistemology. As our guidepost on this journey, she offers the "heuristic," defined as "any problem solving strategy that appears likely to lead to relevant, reliable, and useful information" (Heineman Pieper, 1989, p. 8). Clearly, the heuristic approach broadens the concept of "research" and gives credence not only to quantitative methods of data gathering and analysis, but also to the findings of any thoughtful, careful observer-practitioner who is close to the data, to what Geertz would call "local knowledge" (1983). To establish a context for the presentation of the heuristic paradigm, the author presents a fascinating and original history of the social work profession's relationship with knowledge development. This history includes a review of the social processes that organized and guided the development of social work knowledge, but also performs a critical analysis of the underlying philosophical and value assumptions embedded in knowledge-development efforts. The story of these efforts reminds us of our ancient professional tradition of bearing witness, of bringing the social worker's "experience-near" knowledge of those on the margins of society to bear on the understanding and solution of social problems.

It also takes us through our forebears' efforts to gain recognition for social work as a responsible, viable, and knowledgeable profession. Without that recognition, the profession would not be taken seriously. The route to professionalization, even in the early days, was thought to be through a close association with science, however science was defined in the current discourse (Germain, 1970). For Mary Richmond, a daughter of nineteenth-century epistemology, knowledge came through the painstaking gathering, categorizing, and assessment of an enormous amount of detailed data, carefully noted in a tidy hand on five-by-eight cards and later published in her classic, *Social Diagnosis* (1917). The leaders of the settlement movement followed suit with careful hands-on surveys of the socioeconomic conditions of the poor.

In spite of the Charity Organization and settlement workers' efforts to develop a professional knowledge base, Abraham Flexner, a powerful definer of privileged discourse, studied the fledgling occupation and concluded, in 1915, that social work was not a profession. He reasoned this was the case in part because he thought we had no clearly defined knowledge base. Social workers were borrowers, not originators, of knowledge. Implicit in Flexner's views—so reminiscent of the current discussions around the sources of "truth"—was that local knowledge, the wealth of "experience-near" information gathered by social work practitioners, was not "scientific" and, thus, that social work was not a profession.

Tyson traces social workers' efforts to develop research methods that would be both scientific and tap the required level of information about the complexities of the individual and family in their social world. The detailed case study of individual or community continued to be a major model of research. This model, not unlike that of the Charity Organization Societies and the Settlement Movement, but encompassing a more sophisticated analysis of social and psychological factors, is demonstrated in the work of the theory builders and leaders of the 1930s, 1940s, and 1950s, such as Bertha Reynolds's study of short-term contacts (1932), Annette Garrett's (1941) "Casework Treatment of a Child," and Florence Hollis's early doctoral dissertation, *Social Casework in Practice: Six Case Studies* (1939) and her *Women in Marital Conflict* (1949).

The unity of power and knowledge was again illustrated in the development in the 1950s of the Social Work Research Group, which took the lead in redefining knowledge-development efforts in the profession. Taking what Foucault terms a "global, unitary view," the group's expressed purpose was "to formalize a new systematic approach to social work research for the entire profession" (see Chapter 2). The group, like Flexner, challenged the accumulated experience-based knowledge of the profession. For example, Ernest Greenwood said,

> Social work practice theory was not developed via systematic research which converted social science laws into principles. It was constructed by social work practitioners who were untutored in the cannons (sic) of scientific inquiry and who relied upon the richness of their insight and the wisdom derived from their day to day experience on the job. (1955, p. 28)

This volume describes the complex social and political processes that gradually concentrated knowledge-power in the hands of primarily university-based researchers, and how as positivist discourse about the nature of "truth" became increasingly privileged, other knowledge, other ways of knowing were discredited or subjugated. This shift in social work's epistemological stance, resulting in the development of a dominant discourse and the subjugation of other discourses, is reminiscent of Foucault's (1980) analysis of the history of systems of thought since the seventeenth century.

As in Foucault's (1980) analysis, the privileging of the methods of science has led to the subjugation of both previously established erudite knowledge and local popular or indigenous knowledge, located on the margins, "exiled from the legitimate domains of the formal knowledge" (White & Epson, 1990, p. 26). Foucault argues for the insurrection of the subjugated knowledge against the institutions and against the effects of the knowledge and power that invest scientific discourse (1980, p. 84). It is through this insurrection, through the emergence of disqualified knowledge, that dominant knowledge and privileged epistemologies may be critiqued.

In 1981, Martha Heineman Pieper, joined by others uncomfortable with the positivist discourse that defined the acceptable methods of knowledge development, began an insurrection. A story of this insurrection and of the response to it is presented in this volume. It makes exciting reading.

Happily, it is not summarized or interpreted but presented in the words of the protagonists in the original documents. The reader can follow the lively argument and then turn to a fascinating selection of related readings from social scientists and philosophers whose views form the basis of or elaborate the discussion. The volume offers readers the opportunity to experience the conversation first-hand, to reflect on it, and to critique all positions. In a sense, much of this volume is background, providing a historical and current context that prepares readers to consider the heuristic paradigm, and under that broad umbrella, to consider a variety of options in the process of discovery. The demanding and fruitful intellectual journey includes an extensive application of the heuristic paradigm in naturalistic approaches to research about practice. This helps readers apply the principles of the paradigm, asking the questions that must be asked of any research endeavor, identifying the heuristic choices that are to be made and identified, to ensure consistency between research method and the worker's identified epistemology and ontology and to ensure the production of useful information.

This impressive work offers a vision of our competing epistemologies presented in the words of the passionate advocates of the different positions. It challenges readers to review and reflect on the social work profession's engagement in knowledge building. The volume also offers a broad and flexible heuristic research paradigm that may well have the potential to make room for all of our varied knowledge-building efforts.

REFERENCES

Flexner, A. (1915). Is social work a profession? *Proceedings of the National Conference of Charities and Corrections*, pp. 576– 590. Madison, WI: Midland Pub. Co.

Foucault, M. (1980). *Power/knowledge: Selected interviews and other writings 1972–1977*. (C. Gordon, Ed.; C. Gordon, L. Marshal, J. Mepham, & K. Soper, Trans.). New York: Pantheon.

Garrett, A. (1941). *Casework treatment of a child*. New York: Family Welfare Association of America.

Geertz, C. (1983). *Local knowledge: Further essays in interpretive anthropology*. New York: Basic Books.

Germain, C. (1970). Casework and science: A historical encounter. In R. Roberts and R. Nee (Eds.), *Theories of social casework*. Chicago: University of Chicago Press.

Greenwood, E. (1955). Social science and social work: A theory of their relationship. *Social Service Review, 29*, 20–33.

Hollis, F. (1939). *Social casework in practice: Six case studies*. New York: Family Welfare Association of America.

Hollis, F. (1949). *Women in marital conflict: A casework study*. New York: Family Welfare Association of America.

Heineman [Pieper], M. (1981). The obsolete scientific imperative in social work research. *Social Service Review, 55*, 371–397.

Pieper, M. Heineman. (1989). The heuristic paradigm: A unifying and comprehensive approach to social work research. *Smith College Studies in Social Work, 60*, 8–34.

Reynolds, B. C. (1932). An experiment in short-contact interviewing. *Smith College Studies in Social Work, 3*, 3–107.

Richmond, M. (1917). *Social diagnosis*. New York: Russell Sage.

White, M., & Epson, D. (1990). *Narrative means to therapeutic ends*. New York: W. W. Norton.

Preface

Martha Heineman Pieper

One of the exciting implications of the postpositivist, heuristic paradigm of scientific investigation is that it allows social and behavioral researchers and practitioners simultaneously to uphold their ideals of doing genuine science and to harness the robust possibilities of naturalistic research to study the full complexity of clinical practice.[1] The heuristic paradigm conceptualizes science broadly as a systematic inquiry into some aspect of reality that is communicated in a way that will allow an interested person to make an informed evaluation of the process of inquiry and its conclusions. The heuristic paradigm recognizes that not all scientists will be able to agree on the precise meaning of words such as *systematic, reality, communicated, informed,* and *evaluation* (Manicas & Secord, 1983).

Although naturalistic research has unique strengths and has as much scientific warrant as interventionist research, it has been overlooked and underutilized due to the positivist prejudices that have colored the thinking of social and behavioral researchers and practitioners since the 1950s. *Naturalistic research* entails the systematic study of clinical practice that is not intentionally altered for research purposes.[2] The contrast between naturalistic and interventionist research in no way implies the naive view that the subject can be studied apart from interactional researcher effects (LeCompte & Goetz, 1982). Rather, the categories of naturalistic and interventionist research refer only to the intentions and practices of the researcher. The interventionist researcher intentionally alters clinical practice for research purposes. In contrast, the naturalistic researcher is a practitioner who aims to minimize research intrusiveness into practice. The focus here is on research into clinical practice, which is why the researcher is referred to as a practitioner. In naturalistic research on an organization, a culture, or a subculture, the naturalistic researcher would be a member of the group under study—not an outsider. Research done by outsiders, no matter how skilled in minimizing research intrusiveness, is always interventionist. Naturalistic research on treatment excludes methodologies that for research purposes dictate, for example, that the client take personality inventories or fill out questionnaires before and during the treatment process, that the treatment process should be artificially shortened or lengthened, or that the therapeutic relationship should be recorded by third-party observers or electronic recording devices. Data gathering in naturalistic research takes the form of anamnestic process recording.

The unwarranted and largely categorical dismissal of naturalistic methods by positivist researchers is fueled in part by a pervasive category mistake whereby issues of qualitative versus quantitative data and group versus single-organism designs have been conflated with the more fundamental distinction between naturalistic and interventionist research, with the result that this distinction has been obscured and neglected (Allen-Meares & Lane, 1990; Cook & Reichardt, 1979; Lincoln & Guba, 1985). Qualitative research frequently is equated erroneously with new (postpositivist) research paradigms, while quantitative research is used mistakenly as a synonym for the standard (positivist) research paradigm (Allen-Meares & Lane, 1990; Taylor & Bogdan, 1984). This conceptual error occurs when issues that pertain to data analysis are confused with issues that relate to data gathering. To illustrate, just as interventionist methods can produce qualitative data (an example is the videotape of a family therapy session), naturalistic designs can generate quantified data (for example, anamnestic process can be coded for the purpose of executing a chi-square test). Moreover, many single case designs, such as experimental designs and most change process designs, are deemed naturalistic, when they should be categorized as interventionist because they involve manipulations of the treatment process (Berlin, Mann, & Grossman, 1991; Bloom & Fischer, 1982; Davis & Reid, 1988).

I would emphasize that most authors mistakenly define naturalistic research to include interventionist strategies, such as research-driven data gathering by self-report instruments, personality inventories, electronic recording devices, and/or third-party observers (Lincoln & Guba, 1985). This mislabeling rests on the unrealistic notion that participants forget or adjust to research-determined interventions and behave as if they were not there. The fact that subjects do not complain or comment should not be taken to indicate that they are behaving exactly the way they would in the absence of research-determined instruments of observation or inquiry (Bronfenbrenner, 1979).

One consequence of the failure to consider the interventionist nature of electronic recording devices, third-party observers, questionnaires, research-motivated adjustments to the therapeutic process, etc., is that the ethical questions raised by research-motivated interventions are rarely if ever considered. By definition, research-motivated interventions introduce nontherapeutic motives and experiences into the treatment relationship and, therefore, always reduce the quality of the service being offered.[3] An example is when limits are placed on client visits for the sole purpose of standardizing the treatment for research purposes. The lowering of treatment quality to serve research purposes should be done only after a careful consideration of ethical issues and a weighing of competing values, especially because clients whose treatments are adversely affected are usually both desperate and disadvantaged, and lack the means to avoid research protocols by choosing among private service providers. Ethical issues are also raised by so-called unobtrusive measures, such as hidden cameras, which depend on deception and conflict with both humanistic and professional values. In contrast to interventionist research, naturalistic research raises neither ethical nor privacy issues, because the quality of service is not affected and deception is not an issue.

The position that the only incontrovertibly scientific way to study clinical process is by manipulating that process not only raises ethical questions, but also is conceptually flawed because of its unwarranted claim of privilege for its positivist ontology (theory of reality) and its positivist epistemology (theory of how to know that reality). The positivist view is that the researcher (or her or his electronic surrogates) but not the practitioner can make unbiased observations of events (facts), and that these observations can then serve to confirm or disconfirm theories. Beginning about 1950, the social work research literature repeatedly advocates empirical, atheoretical, and grounded research, and condemns naturalistic social work research, which is deemed old-fashioned, anecdotal, soft, and unscientific. This view reflects the misuse of the word *empirical* by social workers and other social and behavioral researchers, and it explains why positivist authors have mislabeled my position "anti-empiricist" (Glisson & Fischer, 1987, p. 51). The terms *empirical* and *empiricism* traditionally refer to knowledge arising from experience that originates extracranially. The positivists fallaciously apply these terms only to data collected in a manner compatible with the positivist paradigm. In fact, a comparison of theories, a recollected process recording, and a client's self-report are just as empirical as the data brought to us by a video camera. Contributing to the confusion is the conflation of a misleading definition of accuracy with the term empirical. Certain methods of data gathering, such as the electronic or third-party recording of a subject's words and gestures, are considered accurately to mirror reality and, therefore, to be free from subjectivity. Data that fit this erroneous definition of accuracy are assumed to exhaust the category of empirical. The problem, of course, is that accuracy is a construct that reflects a heuristic choice of data rather than an unalterable, one-to-one, uncontaminated correspondence with reality. Therefore, not only are there many viable types of accuracy, but the choice and pursuit of one kind of accuracy makes other kinds of accuracy more difficult or impossible to attain. For example, in order to obtain an accurate recording of the exact sequence and details of a client's speech and behavior, one sacrifices an accurate knowledge of what the client would say or do without the research intervention that introduces an electronic recording device or third-party observer. There is an ostrich-like quality to the definition of "unobtrusive" measures as data gathering that requires "observers to be inconspicuous in their observing role and to guard against disclosing to subjects the specific nature of the data collected" (Allen-Meares & Lane, 1990). Those who argue that clients soon "forget" about electronic devices or observers depreciate the intelligence of their participant/subjects and mistake compliance for habituation.[4]

In addition, the focus on a single type of accuracy blinds researchers to the biases introduced by their preferred methodologies. For example, references to taping or the presence of third-party observers are made only in passing, and the effects on clients of being subjected to numerous rating scales and to repeated evaluations of their treatments are dismissed or never mentioned. When clients do express concern about research intrusiveness into their treatment, positivist researchers do not take these concerns seriously. In a recent article, a client's anxiety about having her symptoms tape-recorded is dismissed as a psychopathological "dysfunctional assumption" that needs correcting (Berlin et al., 1991, p. 10).

Similarly, because positivist researchers are unaware that there are many different but equally useful types of accuracy, they dismiss other methodologies, such as anamnestic process recordings, as less accurate and, therefore, less desirable than their preferred methods of data gathering. The authors of the influential *Nonreactive Measures in the Social Sciences* depreciate humans as "low-fidelity observational instruments" (Webb, Campbell, Schwartz, Sechrest, & Grove, 1981, p. 241). Anamnestic recordings are dismissed as anecdotal, and data that are recorded or gathered through structured instruments are praised as objective.[5] However, because in actuality each method of data gathering has its own strengths and limitations, a tape recorder or third-party observer is inherently no more able to render an accurate version of reality than the trained clinician. Clearly, tape recorders introduce bias.

Akin to the positivists' overly restrictive use of the construct of accuracy is their overvaluation of reliability, which is the precept that a practitioner-researcher's perceptions about a client or treatment process lack scientific value unless they can be correlated with another qualified person's perceptions about the same or a similar client or process (McVicker Hunt, 1959). I suggest that it is more meaningful to focus on credibility than on reliability. Reliable observations are not necessarily credible; no matter how many people tell us they saw the same flying saucer, we are unlikely to find them credible. Clinical credibility—our conviction of the scientific value, i.e., fundamental correctness, of the practitioner-researcher's interventions and theoretical understanding—can rest on the comprehensive, detailed, well-conceptualized presentation by a single practitioner of her or his conduct and understanding of a specific treatment process.

Researchers who confuse reliability and credibility tend to adopt the absurd position that it is acceptable to trust clients' lives and well-being to trained practitioners but that the judgments of these same practitioners about their clients lack scientific merit. Because it has been amply demonstrated that there are no truly neutral measures—that all methods of gathering data introduce their own biases—we are free to reintroduce, that is, to depend on, the practitioner's informed judgment. In fact, an experienced clinician's understanding of her or his treatment process will contribute meanings that will be absent from the observations and conclusions of a researcher/observer who has no prior knowledge of the client, and who has a professional identity that is antithetical to the development of therapeutic involvement with the client. If experience and involvement count for something in real-life clinical situations, they should also be worthwhile in research situations.

In addition to the conceptual difficulties with portraying the researcher as a passive recorder of unproblematic data, there is the practical consequence that this depiction of the researcher is antithetical to the erstwhile role of the researcher as the handmaiden of social change, and it is largely responsible for the split in social work and the other social and behavioral sciences between advocate and researcher. The positivist researcher belittles the advocate for being too involved with her/his clients and, thereby, for falling prey to an unscientific subjectivity. Once researchers recognize that the ideal of the value-free, atheoretical, neutral researcher both is an impossible fiction and also exalts only one of many competing values, researchers are free to ally themselves with advocates and unapologetically to gather facts with the aim of supporting and furthering the traditional humanistic concerns of social work and the other social and behavioral sciences.

Finally, I would like to take this opportunity to address one of the most frequent misunderstandings of the heuristic paradigm, namely that by adopting the position that no single methodology is inherently superior to any other at producing useful, scientific knowledge, the heuristic paradigm endorses relativism, which is a type of epistemological skepticism. Relativists argue that the untenability of the claim of superiority for any one methodology results from the impossibility of a well-founded conviction that a mind-independent reality exists. Consequently, relativists abandon the pursuit of knowledge that reflects or corresponds to reality and instead aim at explanatory coherence. An example is the increasingly popular use of narrative coherence as a therapeutic tool. Advocates of a focus on narrative structures believe that the client lacks and needs a coherent self-narrative, and that the curative element is the coherence of the narrative, not the knowledge of the primary causes of the client's psychological dynamics, which they believe to be unattainable. In contrast, the heuristic paradigm's assertion that the positivist ontology and the positivist epistemology are heuristic choices rather than privileged objects of study and privileged ways of knowing is not synonymous with an endorsement of relativism. Both relativism and realism[6] are heuristic choices and, as such, are encompassed within the heuristic paradigm, although they neither define nor exhaust it.

Although the heuristic paradigm does encompass any ontology whose adherents are engaged in doing science, as I have made clear elsewhere (see, for example, Heineman Pieper, 1987, in Chapter 3), my own preferred ontology is a qualified realism. That is, I adopt the position that external reality exists and can be known, even though this knowledge will always be partial, imperfect, and colored to some extent by the researcher's heuristics (Bhaskar, 1989).

In summary, if social work and the other social and behavioral sciences adopt the heuristic paradigm, researchers will cease the single-minded pursuit of the chimerical goal of neutral, value-free science, and will be able to integrate the more attainable values of the recognition and regulation of bias with their traditional humanistic values (e.g., respect for the client's self-experience, sensitivity to gender and racial discrimination, and concern with social injustice) into their scientific activities.

Further, both the effort of critiquing the positivist claim for the superiority of interventionist research and the concomitant argument for the scientific standing of naturalistic social and behavioral research are matters of great concern, because for so many years unwarranted positivist strictures have limited the range of data that are considered legitimate, which in turn restricts social and behavioral researchers' ability to study clinical practice in all its complexity and to be effective advocates for social reform. To illustrate, one researcher makes the frightening assertion that, "If you cannot measure the client's problem, it does not exist" (Hudson, 1978, p. 65).

Naturalistic research is just as scientifically respectable and able to produce legitimate, helpful, relevant, generalizable knowledge as interventionist research. If the social and behavioral sciences were to embrace the heuristic paradigm, one significant consequence would be that research-motivated interventions in clinical services, such as the introduction of third-party observers, electronic recording devices, and client instruments, would no longer be misperceived as nonreactive and unobtrusive. These service manipulations would cease to be implemented unthinkingly, but would have to be justified both in relation to their potential to contribute significantly to the research being undertaken, and also in terms of the negative effects they may have on a particular service modality and the degree of their compatibility with the broad spectrum of professional values.

Some of the advantages of naturalistic clinical research are that the values of putting the client's interest first and of doing no harm are respected, that treatment is studied in an undisturbed form from an experience-near perspective, and that the practitioner's trained understanding and assessment of the treatment process are highlighted. The resurrection of naturalistic research will encourage practitioners to leave the sidelines and to participate comfortably in relevant, significant, helpful, humanistic, *science* (Sherman, 1987). Practitioners, who for the last forty years have unjustly been made to feel that their experienced and educated judgments are unscientific and, therefore, unimportant, can join the effort to devise creative and productive ways to study and shed light on the complex, multifactorial, overdetermined problems that plague us all.*

NOTES

1.   This Preface is abstracted and adapted from the Keynote Address at the Conference on Qualitative Methods in Social Work Practice Research, State University of New York at Albany, August 23, 1991. A full-length version of the address is published in E. Sherman and W. J. Reid (Eds.), *Qualitative Research in Social Work* (New York: Columbia University Press, 1994).

2.   Naturalistic research is distinguished from *naturalism*, which is the philosophical notion that the human sciences can best be studied by the methods of the natural sciences (Bhaskar, 1989).

3.   Sometimes authors confuse therapeutic and research aims and argue that research-motivated interventions are helpful to clients, but this argument is irrelevant to the ethical questions raised by the use of interventions that are introduced purely for research purposes. When a given practice theory prescribes ongoing testing or mechanical recording for diagnos-

Editor's Note: Because the Preface contains many ideas that are discussed further in the text, it may be helpful in integrating this material to read the Preface again after reading the text.

tic or therapeutic purposes (e.g., allowing clients to see themselves on videotape), then naturalistic research would obviously encompass use of the data produced by these therapeutically motivated instruments and recording devices. Complications arise, however, because some social work treatment modalities have been developed precisely because they were "researchable," and these models consider interventions therapeutic because they are research-driven (Reid, 1983; Reid & Epstein, 1972). For this reason, I would argue that research on these practice modalities is interventionist rather than naturalistic, even though the research imposes no additional data collection measures.

4. Even after he spent an entire school year in a California classroom, Philip Jackson noted that he remained enough of an outsider that when he happened to sneeze, members of the class turned around, whereas the sneezes of teacher and students went unremarked (1990).

5. Kazdin typifies the positivist approach to anamnestic process. He concludes that "scientific inferences are difficult if not impossible to draw from anecdotal information. Indeed, it is the anecdotal information that is the problem rather than the fact that an individual case is studied" (1981, p. 185).

6. Realism is the view that there are sound grounds for positing a mind-independent reality, which is amenable to study.

REFERENCES

Allen-Meares, P., & Lane, B. (1990). Social work practice: Integrating qualitative and quantitative data collection techniques. *Social Work, 35,* 452–458.

Berlin, S., Mann, K., & Grossman, S. (1991). Task analysis of cognitive therapy for depression. *Social Work Research and Abstracts, 27,* 3–11.

Bhaskar, R. (1989). *The possibility of naturalism: A philosophical critique of contemporary human sciences* (2nd ed.). New York: Harvester Wheatsheaf.

Bhaskar, R. (1991). *Philosophy and the idea of freedom.* Oxford: Basil Blackwell.

Bloom, M., & Fischer, J. (1982). *Evaluating practice: Guidelines for the accountable professional.* Englewood Cliffs, NJ: Prentice-Hall.

Bronfenbrenner, U. (1979). *The ecology of human development: Experiments by nature and design.* Cambridge, MA: Harvard University Press.

Cook, T., & Reichardt, C. (1979). *Qualitative and quantitative methods in evaluation research.* Beverly Hills, CA: Sage.

Davis, I., & Reid, W. J. (1988). Event analysis in clinical practice and process research. *Social Casework, 69,* 298-306.

Gergen, K. J. (1986). Correspondence versus autonomy in the language of understanding human action. In D. W. Fiske & R. A. Shweder (Eds.), *Metatheory in social science* (pp. 136–162). Chicago: University of Chicago Press.

Glisson, C., & Fischer, J. (1987). Statistical training for social workers. *Journal of Social Work Education, 23,* 50–58.

Hudson, W. (1978). First axioms of treatment. *Social Work, 23,* 65–66, 518–519.

Jackson, P. (1990). *Life in classrooms.* New York: Teacher's College Press.

Kazdin, A. (1981). Drawing valid inferences from case studies. *Journal of Consulting and Clinical Psychology, 49,* 183–192.

LeCompte, M. D., & Goetz, J. P. (1982). Problems of reliability and validity in ethnographic research. *Review of Educational Research, 52,* 31–60.

Leplin, J. (Ed.). (1984). *Scientific realism.* Berkeley: University of California Press.

Lincoln, Y. S. (1990). The making of a constructivist: A remembrance of transformations past. In E. Guba (Ed.), *The paradigm dialog*. Newbury Park: Sage.

Lincoln, Y. S., & Guba, E. G. (1985). *Naturalistic inquiry*. Newbury Park: Sage.

Manicas, P. T., & Secord, P. F. (1983). Implications for psychology of the new philosophy of science. *American Psychologist, 38*, 399–413.

McVicker Hunt, J. (1959). On the judgment of social workers as a source of information in social work research. In A. Shyne (Ed.), *Use of judgments as data in social work research* (pp. 38–54). New York: National Association of Social Workers.

Phillips, D. L. (1990). Postpositivistic science: Myths and realities. In E. Guba (Ed.), *The paradigm dialog*. Newbury Park, CA: Sage.

Reid, W. J. (1983). Developing intervention methods through experimental designs. In A. Rosenblatt & D. Waldfogel (Eds.), *Handbook of clinical social work*. San Francisco: Jossey-Bass.

Reid, W. J., & Epstein, L. (1972). *Task-centered casework*. New York: Columbia University Press.

Sherman, E. (1987). Hermeneutics, human science, and social work. *Social Thought, 13*, 34–41.

Taylor, S. J., & Bogdan, R. (1984). *Introduction to qualitative research methods: The search for meanings* (2nd ed.). New York: Wiley.

Webb, E. J., Campbell, D. T., Schwartz, R. D., Sechrest, L., & Grove, J. B. (1981). *Nonreactive measures in the social sciences* (2nd ed.). Boston: Houghton Mifflin.

Wimsatt, W. C. (1987). False models as means to truer theories. In M. H. Nitecki & A. Hoffman (Eds.), *Neutral models in biology* (pp. 23–55). New York: Oxford University Press.

DISCUSSION QUESTIONS

1. How does Heineman Pieper conceptualize science, and what allowance does she make for different points of view about her definition of science?

2. How is Bhaskar's definition of naturalism different from naturalistic research?

3. When Heineman Pieper conceptualizes naturalistic and interventionist research, she makes an original and extremely important distinction between two types of social and behavioral research.

   a. What is naturalistic research?

   b. What is interventionist research?

   c. Why is that distinction important to social and behavioral researchers?

4. What common psychotherapy research strategies are *not* included in the category of naturalistic research?

5. Summarize the distinctions Heineman Pieper makes between accuracy, credibility, and reliability.

6. Many researchers say that tape recorders are naturalistic research. What is Heineman Pieper's argument that they are interventionist?

7. In naturalistic research, who can be the researcher? What are some implications of the decision about who is the researcher?

▼ ▼ ▼ ▼ ▼ ▼ ▼ ▼ ▼ ▼ ▼ ▼

ACKNOWLEDGMENTS

This book would not have been possible without the contributions of colleagues; the magnitude of their support can be only dimly reflected in the following acknowledgments. William Wimsatt provided extremely insightful comments on conceptualization, as well as sharing his inspiring teaching materials. Edward Hamburg generously volunteered his guidance with the statistical analysis, as well as his cogent reflections about the reader's experience. Beth Bradfish, Robert Carroll, Emily Carroll, Stuart Glennan, Catherine Friedman Kleinmuntz, Don Kleinmuntz, Katherine Knight, Richard Sanders, Mark Steinberg, and Patricia Walker all offered supportive and insightful suggestions on various aspects of the manuscript. Martha Heineman Pieper and William Joseph Pieper offered valuable assistance with regard to the conceptual framework. Mimi Abramovitz, Robert Bogdan, Clarke Chambers, Charles Garvin, Gerd Gigerenzer, Howard Goldstein, David Harrison, Chris Ross, Ann Weick, Stan Witkin, and Deborah Zuskar all contributed helpful suggestions.

Colleagues at Loyola generously paved the way for me to teach this material in its nascent form, in particular, Charles OReilly, Joseph Walsh, and Stanley Piwowarski. Randy Lucente, Gloria Cunningham, and Tom Meenaghan also offered especially meaningful reflections.

Many students offered thought-provoking dialogue and stimulating questions; they cannot all be named here but include Terry Ann Rosander, Jill Feldman, Dan Grohens, and Susan Kaplan. Others who helped with many aspects of the research and practical aspects of preparing the manuscript include Ellen Feldman, Mark Gordon, Lisa Grant, Julia Huberty, Cheryl Krueckeberg, Mary Leas, Lisa Maroski, Terry Myers Quirini, Miki Rukin, Emily Stein, and Deborah Strauss. Leo Bourneuf, Mary Frazier and Deborah Major offered especially comprehensive assistance and comments about this material and its relevance for students. Janice Hovey's skill with the graphic designs is greatly appreciated.

Archivists and librarians at several locations were extremely helpful, especially the library staff at Loyola University of Chicago and Professor David Klaassen, archivist with the Social Welfare History Archives. I also thank the archivists of the Departments of Special Collections at the University of Chicago, Smith College, and the University of Illinois for their assistance.

The following authors and publishers have generously given permission to reproduce the articles selected in this book:

University of Chicago Press:

Brekke, J. (1986). Scientific imperatives in social work research: Pluralism is not skepticism. *Social Service Review, 60,* 538–544.

Brekke, J. (1987). Author's reply. *Social Service Review, 61,* 370–373.

Geismar, L. L. (1982). Comments on "The obsolete scientific imperative in social work research." *Social Service Review, 56,* 311–312.

Gyarfas, M. (1983). The scientific imperative again. *Social Service Review, 57,* 149–150.

Heineman (Pieper), M. (1981). The obsolete scientific imperative in social work research. *Social Service Review, 55,* 371–397.

Heineman (Pieper), M. (1982). Author's reply. *Social Service Review, 56,* 146–148.

Holland, T. (1983). Comments on "Scientific imperatives in social work research and practice." *Social Service Review, 57,* 337–339.

Hudson, W. (1982). Scientific imperatives in social work research and practice. *Social Service Review, 56,* 246–258.

Hudson, W. (1983). Author's reply. *Social Service Review, 57,* 339–341.

Lewontin, R. C. (1974). The analysis of variance and the analysis of causes. *American Journal of Human Genetics, 26,* 400–411.

Peile, C. (1988a). Author's reply. *Social Service Review, 62,* 708–709.

Peile, C. (1988b). Research paradigms in social work: From stalemate to creative synthesis. *Social Service Review, 62,* 1–19.

Pieper, M. Heineman. (1982). Author's reply. *Social Service Review, 56,* 312.

Pieper, M. Heineman. (1987). Comments on "Scientific imperatives in social work research: Pluralism is not skepticism." *Social Service Review, 61,* 368–370.

Pieper, M. Heineman. (1988). Comments on "Research paradigms in social work: From stalemate to creative synthesis." *Social Service Review, 62,* 535–536.

Schuerman, J. (1982). The obsolete scientific imperative in social work research. *Social Service Review, 56,* 144–146.

Wimsatt, W. (1986). Heuristics and the study of human behavior. In D. W. Fiske & R. A. Shweder (Eds.), *Metatheory in social science: Pluralisms and subjectivities* (pp. 293–314). Chicago: University of Chicago Press.

Verso Publications:

Bhaskar, R. (1989). On the possibility of social scientific knowledge and the limits of naturalism. From *Reclaiming reality: A critical introduction to contemporary philosophy.* London: Verso.

Macmillan:

Bridgman, P. (1927). Broad points of view. In *The logic of modern physics* (pp. 1–32). New York: Macmillan.

American Psychological Association:

Gadlin, H., & Ingle, G. (1975). Through the one-way mirror: The limits of experimental self-reflection. *American Psychologist, 30,* 1003–1009.

Manicas, P. T., & Secord, P. F. (1983). Implications for psychology of the new philosophy of science. *American Psychologist, 38,* 399–413.

National Association of Social Workers:

Goldstein, H. (1986). Toward the integration of theory and practice: A humanistic approach. *Social Work, 31,* 352–357.

Smith College Studies in Social Work:

Pieper, M. Heineman. (1989). The heuristic paradigm: A unifying and comprehensive approach to social work research. *Smith College Studies in Social Work, 60,* 8–34.

Basic Books:

Popper, K. R. (1959). A survey of some fundamental problems. In *The logic of scientific discovery* (pp. 27–42) (original title, *Logik der Forschung,* trans. author). New York: Basic Books. (Original work published 1934)

Johns Hopkins Press:

Scriven, M. (1969). Logical positivism and the behavioral sciences. In P. Achinstein & S. Barker (Eds.), *The legacy of logical positivism: Studies in the philosophy of science* (pp. 195–209). Baltimore: Johns Hopkins University Press.

University of Pittsburgh Press:

Simon, H. (1966). Scientific discovery and the psychology of problem solving. In R. Colodny (Ed.), *Mind and cosmos: Essays in contemporary science and philosophy* (pp. 22–40). Pittsburgh: University of Pittsburgh Press.

American Association for the Advancement of Science:

Tversky, A., & Kahneman, D. (1981). The framing of decisions and the psychology of choice. *Science, 211,* 453–458.

Massachusetts Institute of Technology Press:

Whorf, B. (1956). Science and linguistics. In J. B. Carroll (Ed.), *Language, thought and reality: Selected writings of Benjamin Lee Whorf.* New York: MIT Press and John Wiley & Sons.

Society of Systematic Zoology:

Hull, D. (1968). The operational imperative: Sense and nonsense in operationism. *Systematic Zoology, 17,* 438–457.

Kluwer Academic Publishing Group, Dordrecht, Holland:

Schlick, M. (1979). Meaning and verification. In H. L. Mulder & B. van de Velde-Schlick (Eds.), *Philosophical papers* (Vol. 2, 1925–1936, pp. 309–312, 361–369). Boston: D. Reidel. (Original work published 1938)

Pieper, Martha H., & Pieper, William J.:

Pieper, M. Heineman, & Pieper, W. J. (May, 1992). *Treating violent "untreatable" adolescents: Applications of intrapsychic humanism in a state-funded demonstration project.* Paper presented at the Alumni Centennial Invitational Lecture Series, University of Chicago, School of Social Service Administration.

Witkin, S. L. (1993). *Making social work scientific: Analysis and recommendations.* Unpublished manuscript. University of Vermont.

All authors whose work was excerpted were given the opportunity to review and revise the excerpt.

The Heuristic Paradigm:
Evolution and Debate

The Power of Ideas

Jane Addams, who was awarded a Nobel Prize in 1931 for her extraordinary accomplishments as a social worker, described the following incident, which took place shortly after she founded the Chicago settlement house community, Hull House, in 1889,

> I remember one night when I addressed a club of secularists, which met at the corner of South Halsted and Madison Streets, a rough looking man called out: "You are all right now, but, mark my words, when you are subsidized by the millionaires, you will be afraid to talk like this." The defense of free speech was a sensitive point with me, and I quickly replied that while I did not intend to be subsidized by millionaires, neither did I propose to be bullied by workingmen, and that I should state my honest opinion without consulting either of them. To my surprise, the audience of radicals broke into applause, and the discussion turned upon the need of resisting tyranny wherever found, if democratic institutions were to endure. (1910/1990, p. 110)

This courageous response is only one example of how Addams advanced the humanistic values she believed were a foundation for bringing about a more just and nurturing society. Addams recognized that tyranny can come about through ideas as well as through political systems, and she wanted to use the power of ideas to improve society. Addams was a dedicated scholar; she contributed relevant, innovative social research about the most pressing social problems of her time. To help to bring about a more just society, researchers today also need to be informed about the most current ideas in the social and behavioral sciences. Many of you may have chosen the social and behavioral sciences because it is potentially very challenging and rewarding to understand people, their relationships, how society can be organized, and how individuals and communities can be helped to solve contemporary problems. The purpose of this book is to set forth conceptual foundations you can use to plan research that will help solve the social problems you see as important and that will contribute to scientific knowledge about issues that interest you.

WHAT IS A PHILOSOPHY OF RESEARCH?

While learning new ideas about society and human behavior, you may wonder, How does this scientific knowledge develop, how do people create it, and how can I contribute to it? There are many different aspects of knowledge in the social and behavioral sciences: methods of clinical practice, professional values, theories of human development, ways to collect data, and strategies for analyzing data. All of these aspects of scientific knowledge are based on beliefs about the nature of knowledge itself. For example, values are one aspect of beliefs about scientific knowledge. One of the social work profession's most important values is respect for the client's right to self-determination. Many social work researchers built their practice theories around the value of self-determination, because they believed that social work theories should reflect the values of the social work profession. Similarly, when we create or evaluate any knowledge, we do so based on our beliefs about scientific knowledge. You may have learned that scientists should be objective, or neutral and value-free, and so you may be concerned that if you care deeply about clients, or about remedying a social problem, you cannot be objective and scientific. Many contemporary social and behavioral scientists, however, recognize that values underlie all knowledge (Bixenstine, 1976; Howard, 1985; Scriven, 1983) and that caring is not incompatible with a scientific attitude. Further, modern scholars know that objectivity has been defined in many different ways. A contemporary view of scientific knowledge recognizes that everyone necessarily chooses a perspective from which to know anything and that objectivity entails understanding an issue from diverse perspectives. You may find that the more committed you are to understanding an issue, the more you explore different points of view about it, and so the more objective you can be.

Another example of the impact of beliefs about knowledge is that as you master new knowledge, you evaluate it using various criteria. Perhaps you find some of the theories that you are learning more interesting and useful than others. Some ideas may change how you see yourself and your relationships and how you plan to help bring about a nurturing, humane society; other knowledge may seem of questionable value to you. Some theories may correspond with your experience, while other theories may seem foreign. Your beliefs about scientific knowledge influence how you evaluate theories as well as other aspects of research. To illustrate, you may believe that the social and behavioral sciences should correct rather than perpetuate prejudices based on race, gender, class, or sexual preference, and you may use that value as one standard in evaluating knowledge in the social and behavioral sciences. Just as you bring beliefs about knowledge to your education, your education may change your beliefs about knowledge. An understanding of the metatheories of knowledge set forth in this book will help you to contribute new ideas that will change how others think about knowledge as well.

Beliefs about the nature of scientific knowledge can be articulated in a metatheory, or philosophy of research. Certain key issues in any philosophy of research concern the degree of certainty possible in scientific knowledge, such as how knowable reality is, how sure facts are, and the degree of universality possible in any knowledge. To illustrate, Will a fact that you perceive today—such as that children with mental disorders often have been physically or emotionally abused—be recognized by someone 100 years from now? If so, will she or he explain that fact the same way you do? Almost 100 years ago, many researchers assumed that a child with behavioral symptoms had a "defect in moral consciousness," and physical punishment was often recommended as a potential remedy (Still, 1902). By contrast, today, many people recognize that physical punishment not only does not remedy but often exacerbates psychological symptoms.

Any philosophy of research includes an assumption about the role of values in the research process; even the notion that research can be value-free represents a value position (Bixenstine, 1976; Scriven, 1969). A value can be defined as "the subjective response of a human being to an event" (Bixenstine, 1976, p. 40; Heineman Pieper, 1981).[1] You may have learned that discussions of values occur in philosophy rather than in science. Yet scientists in many disciplines, as well as most contemporary philosophers of science, recognize that the scientist's values inform every aspect of their research, so that neither scientists nor their knowledge can be value-free (Kuhn, 1970; Scriven, 1969; Sperry, 1983). Accordingly, all knowledge is inherently evaluative; facts are not value-free, and the observations to which scientists accord the status of "facts" derive, in part, from the values of the scientists' research community (Bixenstine, 1976; Riger, 1992; Scriven, 1969, 1983). One illustration of how even very common facts are value-laden is that an IQ test score previously was accepted as a relatively nonproblematic statement about an individual's intelligence. More recently, however, researchers have shown that both the measure that yields the IQ score and the use of the IQ score as an indicator of intelligence reflect cultural values (Block & Dworkin, 1974; Gould, 1981).

Another issue in a metatheory of knowledge concerns the relationship between theories and observations. To illustrate, do you think your theories about human beings and their relationships affect the observations you make and your actions toward others, both in your personal life and as a social and behavioral scientist? Can you make new observations when you apply a new theory? Do your observations change the theories in which you believe? You may wonder how people appraise the utility and veracity of scientific theories, another important issue in any philosophy of research. For example, why did people five hundred years ago believe in some scientific theories that we now know to be false, such as that the sun circles the earth? Why is it that even the best scientific theories today have tenets that are logically inconsistent, or not in accord with some observations? It is widely known, for instance, that aspects of the theory of relativity and the theory of quantum mechanics contradict each other, yet physicists accept both theories as important and valid contributions. You may also wonder how people change their theories and create or adopt new ones. For example, until the nineteenth century, physicians commonly prescribed bloodletting, often using leeches; and many different theories offered rationales for the practice. Such interventions are rarely used today. What made it possible for those physicians to question their theories and to recognize that blood-letting was not helpful? To begin to answer such questions, contemporary historians and philosophers of science have explored how scientific theories change. The history in Chapter 2 will explore how the social work profession's beliefs about scientific social work research have changed over time.

One more critical aspect of a metatheory of social and behavioral research concerns the nature of the relationships between those who participate in research as researchers (participant/researchers) and those who participate in the research as subjects (participant/subjects). For example, Kurt Danziger describes how psychologists in the late 1800s often conducted their experiments on their colleagues. Being a "subject" in psychological research was highly esteemed, and the uniqueness and complexity of participant/subjects' experiences were valued and reported in psychological research (Danziger, 1979, 1988a). In this century, however, a model of the psychological experiment began to develop in which "subjects" were presented anonymously in research papers. Such participant/subjects were generally not the researcher's peers but were of lower socioeconomic status than the participant/researcher; participant/subjects' individualities were de-emphasized because participant/researchers wanted to find common characteristics that they could use to generalize about the participant/subjects as a group (Danziger, 1979, 1988a; Kidder, 1982). More importantly, many participant/researchers came to believe that it was necessary for participant/subjects to be ignorant, or even deceived, about the nature of research rather than full participants in it.

As you can see from the preceding examples, scientific theories and methods have varied considerably over time. Metatheories about knowledge have varied, too. Some metatheories have been more restrictive than others. Galileo was persecuted during the Inquisition when he challenged Ptolemy's view that the sun revolved around the earth, because he was challenging the belief that the earth was the center of the universe. In effect, he studied questions that were heretical according to the Inquisitors' metatheory of research. The Inquisitors believed that the Church's dogma encompassed reality and that any knowledge that appeared to contradict it was the devil's work and should be eradicated. The example of Galileo also illustrates how a change in scientific theories or metatheories often involves conflict. Kuhn has described such changes as paradigm shifts, or scientific revolutions (1970). Heated debates about the field of social work's philosophy of research are now occurring. A paradigm shift is also taking place in the other social and behavioral sciences (Gergen, 1991; Guba, 1990; Manicas, 1987). This book introduces the ideas that are the focus of the revolution in social and behavioral research.

In summary, a metatheory or philosophy of research addresses beliefs about what constitutes scientific knowledge (as opposed to other intellectual products, e.g., poetry). It includes such concerns as the role of values in research, how one appraises scientific theories, the relationship between theories and observations, and the relationship between participant/researcher and participant/subject. The beliefs that comprise the social and behavioral sciences' philosophy of research contribute to important decisions that affect all researchers, including how scientific knowledge is applied in social programs, what knowledge is published in scientific journals, and what kinds of research students are allowed to pursue. A metatheory of knowledge often operates implicitly; that is, we may make assumptions about the nature of knowledge without realizing it. One reason why the contemporary debates about the social and behavioral sciences' philosophy of research are so important is because they shed light on previously implicit assumptions about how we generate and appraise knowledge.

POSITIVISM AND LOGICAL POSITIVISM

Many of you probably chose to learn more about the social and behavioral sciences because you have certain values about how you want society to treat people, such as social justice and respect for the dignity and humanity of every individual. Yet most research textbooks in the social and behavioral sciences today do not advance an approach to research that emphasizes how research can be used to improve client care or how research can promote social justice. These omissions are striking, particularly because when the social and behavioral sciences were founded, research often was conducted expressly and explicitly for the purpose of improving client care and effecting social change. The research of the social workers and sociologists at the turn of the century led to substantive social changes, such as the founding of the Juvenile Court in Chicago to provide special services for abused, neglected, and "delinquent" children, and enacting legislation to protect workers. William James, one of the first American psychologists and a colleague of Jane Addams, emphasized that research was meaningless unless it led to specific improvements in human well-being (James, 1970). Over the course of this century, however, researchers in the fields of social work, psychology, education, and sociology relinquished those early beliefs about science and increasingly adopted beliefs about scientific research derived from a philosophy called *logical positivism*. How did the social and behavioral sciences adopt a philosophy of research that uncoupled the activity of generating scientific knowledge from the activities of social change? Chapter 2 of this book begins to answer that question by looking at the history of the approaches to research developed by social workers.

Positivist beliefs about science have evolved and varied over time. Positivism drew from ideas that have been advanced since antiquity and were also described by British empiricist philosophers, such as David Hume (1711–1776). As a specific philosophy, positivism was first formulated by the French philosophers Claude-Henri, Comte de Saint-Simon (1760–1825) and, most notably, Auguste Comte (1798–1857). Positivism reflected an optimism about social progress that was a response to the advances in technology that began the nineteenth-century industrial revolution. As Comte formulated it, positivism did not focus on the limitations of the validity of scientific knowledge but instead exalted science. Comte believed that scientific understanding could be used to ameliorate social problems. Positivists regard the aim of science as being to describe observed phenomena and to organize such observations under general laws. Those laws then would be used to make predictions and thereby enhance human capability. Comte's ideas were very influential and were used as a touchstone by many philosophers in France, Great Britain (including John Stuart Mill and Karl Pearson), and Germany (including Ernst Mach and the logical positivists). One implication of the positivist view of human nature is represented in John Stuart Mill's formulation, "If we knew the person thoroughly, and knew all the inducements which are acting upon him, we could foretell his conduct with as much certainty as we can predict any physical event" (Mill, 1974, Book 6, p. 837). Mill's comment also illustrates how positivist philosophers of science prioritized prediction in their beliefs about scientific explanation.

As the logical positivist philosophers began to reformulate positivist ideas in Vienna between the two World Wars, they "assumed that there was a certain rock bottom of knowledge, the knowledge of the immediately given, which was indubitable. Every other kind of knowledge was supposed to be firmly supported by this basis and therefore likewise decidable with certainty" (Carnap, 1963/1991a, p. 57). You may have learned some of the concepts of a logical positivist view of scientific research if you were taught that scientists can and should be neutral or value-free, or that scientists can observe facts without their perceptions being influenced by the theories they espouse. The logical positivists advanced criteria for scientific meaningfulness; specifically, to be scientifically meaningful, theoretical propositions must be either analytic (logically derived from accepted premises as in mathematical theorems) or verifiable using the methodological guidelines the logical positivists advanced. They believed such restrictions would yield a superior form of scientific knowledge and make the philosophy of science more productive by cleansing it of statements they deemed metaphysical. In their view, metaphysical statements included statements about religious beliefs, values, and introspected psychological experiences, such as motives (Carnap, 1963/1991a; Hanfling, 1981a, 1981b; Schlick, 1938/1979; Suppe, 1977). Positivist philosophers admired the ways of knowing implemented in the natural sciences and believed the human sciences should emulate them; the logical positivists in particular believed that all scientific statements could be formulated in a common language with a common set of observation terms, namely, the language of physics (Carnap, 1963/1991a). A central implication of this position was that psychological terms could be defined on the basis of physical observation statements without a loss of meaning (Carnap, 1963/1991a). Carnap recommended that to make a scientifically meaningful statement, one should describe another person's feelings in terms of her or his observable behavior (1963/1991a). For instance, one would say, "he is crying" rather than "he feels sad." The logical positivists' formulations did not withstand the criticism they aroused; in response, they quickly abandoned their most stringent restrictions (Carnap, 1963/1991a; Hanfling, 1981a, 1981b).

American social and behavioral scientists, however, adopted many of the stringent logical positivist views, often without recognizing them as logical positivist (Boring, 1929/1950; Danziger, 1979, 1990). Beginning in 1949, social work researchers formulated an approach to research derived from logical positivist beliefs about science. One consequence of that formulation was that social work researchers rejected the research contributions of early social workers such as Jane Addams. The approach to social work research that was derived from logical positivism unduly restricted the ways of knowing that would produce scientifically meaningful knowledge and thereby circumscribed the topics that could be studied. So, for example, positivist social work researchers advanced a hierarchy of research designs. According to this hierarchy, the most valuable research uses a variant of the experimental design advanced by positivist social researchers (D. T. Campbell & Stanley, 1963; Polansky, 1960/1975; Reid & Smith, 1989; Tripodi, 1981). Experimental design, however, is not the design of choice for all topics. For example, to investigate the movements of the stars, or how a species evolves in a particular environment, scientists do not apply experimental design as it has been advanced by positivist social researchers. In the version of experimental design advanced by positivist social researchers, the scientist introduces an experimental "independent" variable, and observes and compares its effects on another variable, called the "dependent" variable, with a "control group," which did not experience the experimental variable. Further, often it is unethical to use control groups, such as when establishing a control group entails depriving people of help or treatment. To illustrate, it would be unethical to test the value of preschool by setting up a control group of children who were kept at home. Positivist social and behavioral researchers who wanted to study such topics either changed the topic so that it could be studied using experimental designs or collected data in different ways, used alternative strategies for data analysis, and produced knowledge that the positivist approach to social and behavioral research classified as inherently inferior, for example, "soft," "exploratory," or "unconfirmed" (D. T. Campbell & Stanley, 1963; Cook & Campbell, 1979; Reid & Smith, 1989). Social workers who espoused the positivist philosophy of research typically did not call themselves or their philosophy "positivist." Instead, they incorrectly used the term "empiricist" to describe their views. That usage is incorrect because it unjustifiably limits the category of empirical knowledge to that obtained via the ways of knowing that positivism regarded as producing scientifically meaningful knowledge. In fact, "the terms *empirical* and *empiricism* traditionally refer to knowledge arising from experience that originates extracranially" (Heineman Pieper, Preface; see also Glossary). Positivism, as it has been adapted in the social and behavioral sciences, has included other tenets such as the following:

1. Observations can be made independently of theories.
2. Social and behavioral science should give priority to the justification or testing of theories over discovery.
3. Theoretical concepts should be defined in quantifiable, observable terms (operationism).*

Since the early 1980s, social workers have become increasingly dissatisfied with the positivist philosophy of research and have begun to develop alternatives. Other social and behavioral scientists have been criticizing positivism and endorsing alternative philosophies of research for some time (Cronbach, 1975; Margenau, 1966; Mishler, 1979; Scriven, 1969).

Roy Bhaskar points out two implications of logical positivism that are especially relevant for research in the social and behavioral sciences: (1) the assumptions about reality that stem from logical positivist prescriptions, and (2) the sociology (or theory

---

*Editor's Note: *Operationism* is also called the *"operational point of view"* (e.g., in the 1927 selection by Percy Bridgman included in the Appendix) or *operationalism,* and is often indicated in such terms as *operationalize* or *operational definitions.*

of human nature, human social institutions, and human relationships) that is inherent in the positivist metatheory of knowledge (Bhaskar, 1978, 1989a, 1989b, 1991). Any metatheory of knowledge presupposes an ontology, a theory about what is real, in that it assumes "that the world is such that it could be the object of the knowledge of the specified type" (Bhaskar, 1989b, p. 49). Any metatheory of knowledge also includes an epistemology, or theory about how to know reality. Logical positivism proscribes from the domain of scientific inquiry the study of "reals" that cannot be researched according to the ways of knowing that logical positivism regards as acceptable for generating scientifically meaningful knowledge. In other words, the beliefs about ways of knowing (epistemological assumptions) of logical positivism restricted how a researcher could generate scientifically meaningful knowledge and, in doing so, restricted what the scientific researcher could study. So, for example, Rudolf Carnap, one of the founding logical positivists, asserted that all psychological terminology could be reduced to "sense data" or "perception" terms and that any talk of something beyond that, such as an introspected experience of anger, is scientifically meaningless (Carnap, 1936, pp. 463 ff.; Hanfling, 1981b, p. 119). One aspect of the unjustifiably restrictive nature of logical positivism is the belief that values can and should be separated from both the generation and appraisal of scientific knowledge.

As Bhaskar points out, a metatheory of knowledge also "presupposes a sociology" by assuming that "the nature of human beings and the institutions they reproduce or transform is such that such knowledge could be produced" (Bhaskar, 1989b, p. 49). For example, some psychological theories built on logical positivist beliefs, such as behaviorism, rest on an assumption that one cannot study scientifically how a person's conduct may be regulated by unobservable factors such as that person's values. Further, Bhaskar points out that positivism regards people as "passive sensors of given facts" and "recorders" of constant patterns of events. In addition to assuming that humans do not affect their sensory perceptions, positivism is biased toward studying people and events in the simplest, most discrete, and least interactive terms (Bhaskar, 1989b, pp. 49–50). As Bhaskar indicates in Chapter 5, the positivist assumption that knowledge could be generated and analyzed in a purely individualistic way discouraged recognition of how much human knowledge is both informed by and also influences patterns of human relationships. It also discouraged an appreciation of the potential role of research in social change. The innovative views of philosophers such as Roy Bhaskar, Herbert Simon, and William Wimsatt, as well as findings from physics and cognitive, cultural, and linguistic studies, have caused researchers to grow increasingly critical of logical positivist beliefs about the social and behavioral sciences. Researchers have begun to formulate alternatives. For example, Chapter 5 includes an article by Peter Manicas and Paul Secord that describes some implications of Bhaskar's ideas for psychology.

THE CONTEMPORARY SHIFT IN SOCIAL WORK RESEARCH PARADIGMS

In her landmark 1981 paper, "The Obsolete Scientific Imperative in Social Work Research," Martha Heineman Pieper ignited debates in the social work profession about the beliefs that constitute scientific social work knowledge. Other researchers had offered critiques of some aspects of the prevailing approach to research in the field of social work (Saleebey, 1979; Salomon, 1967; Vigilante, 1974). Heineman Pieper, however, was the first to evaluate comprehensively the foundations of the logical positivist approach to social work research and at the same time to import unifying concepts for a new philosophy of scientific social work research. Positivist social work researchers had to stretch, twist, and distort the practice problems they wanted to study in order to conform to their beliefs about knowledge generation. Researchers often found they were no longer studying what they had wanted to study in the first place (Beckerman, 1978; Imre, 1991b). Other researchers' work was ignored or depreciated because it did not conform to positivist standards; some social work faculty was denied tenure for the same reasons (Hartman, 1990; A. Weick, 1992). Among Heineman Pieper's central points was that the prevailing philosophy of research in the field of social work was derived from the logical positivist philosophy of science. It was unjustifiably restrictive and led to research that was largely irrelevant to practice. The alternative philosophy of research she proposed for social work, which she termed the *heuristic paradigm*, incorporates contemporary philosophy of science as well as up-to-date findings from physics and cultural, cognitive, and linguistic studies. It provides conceptual foundations for generating social work knowledge that is important and relevant to practitioners (Heineman Pieper, 1981, 1985, 1989, 1994).[2] As Heineman Pieper says in the preface to this book,

> the heuristic paradigm conceptualizes science broadly as a systematic inquiry into some aspect of reality that is communicated in a way that will allow an interested person to make an informed evaluation of the process of inquiry and its conclusions. The heuristic paradigm recognizes that not all scientists will be able to agree on the precise meaning of words such as systematic, reality, communicated, informed, and evaluation.

DISCUSSION QUESTIONS

1. What kinds of knowledge have you found useful and helpful in understanding and trying to find solutions for the social problems that you are most concerned about?

2. When you have wanted to study a social problem in the past, what has that study process been like for you? Did you enjoy it, or was it frustrating or uncomfortable? If it was unpleasant, why? What did you like about it?

3. Do you read the professional journals in your discipline now? If yes, what kinds of articles have you found useful? If not, can you say why you don't find the knowledge in the journals useful?

4. If you've had prior research courses, how well did they translate into your desire to study practice?

5. a. What are some of the issues addressed in a metatheory of research?

   b. How is a metatheory of research different from a way of collecting data?

6. a. What are the two major metatheories of research in the social and behavioral sciences today?

     b. Where did the ideas inherent in the positivist approach to social and behavioral research come from?

     c. Where did the ideas inherent in the heuristic approach to social and behavioral research come from?

7. What are some of the ways that scientists' choice of a metatheory of research influences:

     a. the knowledge that the scientists' discipline generates?

     b. the other members of the scientists' discipline?

     c. others outside the scientists' discipline?

CHAPTER 2

A History of the Approaches to Research in the Field of Social Work

The history of social experimentation . . . is of first-rate importance because experiments involving the lives of human beings are very costly and ought never to be unnecessarily repeated. Moreover, it is only by building on the knowledge of the past that we shall go forward and not backward. (Edith Abbott, 1931, p. 55)

Topics having to do with historiography . . . while perhaps less urgent than some current public policy matters, remain topical and even relevant in any honest quest for a better social order. This is what provides enormous satisfaction to this historian who seeks to mine the various quarries of the past in the belief that good history is a good foundation for a better present and future. (John Hope Franklin, 1989, p. x)

INTRODUCTION: PURPOSE AND RESEARCH DESIGN

Purpose

Contemporary researchers build their approaches to research in part by reflecting on conceptual foundations laid by previous researchers. Thus, the history of social and behavioral research provides a cornerstone on which contemporary social and behavioral scientists can build knowledge for the future. This history describes how the members of one discipline, social work, have approached the generation of knowledge. Although recent debates about their approaches to research have prompted social workers to examine many of their beliefs about social work knowledge, there are still unexamined assumptions about the historical facts of social workers' approaches to research. One such assumption is that the social workers who founded the profession at the turn of the century produced knowledge without developing reflective standards for social research.[3] Another way that assumption has been articulated is that the early social workers' research methods and the knowledge generated were unscientific.[4] A second and similarly unexamined assumption about the history of social workers' approaches to research is that the profession's adoption of the Social Work Research Group's (SWRG's) beliefs about research in the 1950s represented a new commitment to scientific knowledge, which the SWRG often called "basic science" (e.g., W. E. Gordon, 1951). By definition, "basic science" was value-free or neutral with regard to sociopolitical conflicts.[5] Although these assumptions have informed contemporary approaches to research, and although they have powerful implications for social workers' views of the profession and its knowledge base, they have never been subjected to critical historical analysis.[6] This study examines these assumptions by beginning to explore the vast and fertile field of the history of social workers' approaches to research.

The assumptions described above have had unfortunate consequences for social workers' understanding of their profession and its knowledge base. Some researchers who adopted the SWRG's beliefs about scientific knowledge concluded that the knowledge generated by the early social workers was inherently unsound.[7] Further, based on inaccurate versions of the history of social workers' approaches to research, some social work researchers have drawn depreciating conclusions about social workers' interest in and capacity to generate useful scientific knowledge. For example, in 1979 Briar wrote, "One of the more striking paradoxes in social work is that although it is predominantly a profession of clinicians, and although it has long claimed to be one of the scientifically based professions, it has not produced more than a handful of clinical scientists" (p. 132).[8] Other researchers who claimed that social workers' approaches to research before 1950 were unscientific also depreciated social workers' interest in generating scientific knowledge because they concluded that the field of social work was not a science. For example, Norman Polansky, a prominent member of the SWRG who authored several influential works on social work research, including a commonly used textbook, stated:

> A science is patently dedicated to acquiring information, ordering it into verifiable laws, and disseminating it. Social work, however, is not a science; it is a service profession. The practitioner involved in trying to help clients is at most a scientist coincidentally. He does not value knowledge for its own sake, and this stance seems quite appropriate. (1971, p. 1098)

Polansky had adopted logical positivist beliefs about science, such as that actualizing the values associated with helping clients is incompatible with scientific aims. From the standpoint of those beliefs about science, he concluded that social work knowledge was not scientific.

Every historian, like every scientist, necessarily begins with a philosophy of research, including premises about human nature and society: "history has no argument, but historians do" (Richards, 1987, p. 11; see also J. Scott, 1989; Scriven, 1959). Ideally, the historian articulates those premises and the biases they introduce (Abramovitz, 1988; Bronfenbrenner, Kessel, Kessen, & White, 1986; Danziger, 1979, 1987; Fay, 1988; Higham, 1954; Himmelfarb, 1989, 1992; D. Kelley, 1990; O'Donnell, 1979). In constructing this history, I drew from the premises of the heuristic paradigm (e.g., scientific knowledge does actualize value commitments).

Accordingly, this chronicle is not based on the logical positivist beliefs about science that, when used by many prior historians, have cast a depreciating pall over the contributions of the social work researchers of the past. This chapter describes how the significant events in the history of social workers' approaches to research are connected and how they influenced subsequent events. By interpreting the history of social workers' approaches to research based on the assumptions of the heuristic paradigm, this history aims to improve the foundation for contemporary approaches to generating knowledge for the social and behavioral sciences.

The researcher who adopts the heuristic paradigm recognizes that bias informs any act of knowing and aims to regulate bias by understanding its impact on knowledge. Accordingly, a first step in studying the history of social workers' approaches to research was to identify salient biases that informed prior histories of the field of social work.

First, logical positivist assumptions skewed the way in which many prior historians treated social work knowledge. When historians used logical positivist beliefs about science and concluded that the knowledge base of the field of social work was never scientific—indeed, could not be by definition (Austin, 1978; Ehrenreich, 1985; Grob, 1983)—they imposed their own beliefs about science on the past, creating inaccurate histories.[9] By contrast, contemporary historians of science recognize that their challenge is to "maintain connection with a particular historical moment in order to understand people and their behavior on their own terms" (Brumberg, 1988, p. 3; see also Himmelfarb, 1992), and accordingly to understand the work of past researchers according to those researchers' own standards (I. B. Cohen, 1977; Kuhn, 1977; Richards, 1981, 1987). The first step in this process is unearthing those standards.

Second, although it is widely recognized that most social workers have been women (Dressel, 1987; Mason, 1992; Sancier, 1992b), many historians did not address the impact of bias against women on the evolution of the social work profession. Brumberg and Tomes commented:

> Although gender is obviously an important factor in structuring occupational hierarchies, it has not been considered in any substantive way in the historical analysis of the professionalization process. The primary actors in the standard works are inevitably male. The working definition of "profession," in sociology as well as history, excludes fields dominated by women because they seem to lack the qualities of autonomy and expertise central to professional power. Even in those historical works that have examined a predominantly female profession, such as social work or education, the issue of gender is overlooked. (1982, p. 275)

Bias against women has often taken the form of beliefs, held by both women and men, that women's intellectual and creative capabilities are inherently inferior to those of men (Pieper & Pieper, 1992b; Sancier, 1992a; Star, 1979). Accordingly, bias against women might influence the treatment of research conducted by women (Fish, 1983; Riger, 1992). Feminist historians have described discriminatory practices that denied women access to educational resources and career opportunities; they also have noted how bias against women caused the intellectual and creative contributions of women to be depreciated or ignored altogether (Abramovitz, 1988; Brumberg & Tomes, 1982; Furumoto, 1987; Heilbrun, 1991; R. Rosenberg, 1982; Rossiter, 1982; S. Rothman, 1978; Sancier, 1992a; Sklar, 1985). As feminist historians have pointed out, many historians have ignored the impact of the women's rights movement on the history of the social work profession and have overlooked the pervasive discrimination the first women social workers encountered (Deegan, 1986; Muncy, 1991; Sklar, 1985; D. Smith, 1974; Westkott, 1979).[10] For example, when Gerald Grob alluded to how psychiatric social workers were undervalued and their professional functions circumscribed by many physicians, he concluded that social workers' problems with status derived from their primarily female membership and from psychiatric social workers' "rejection of a service function"; he did not recognize the role of misogyny in psychiatric social workers' low status (1983, p. 257). Recently, historians have begun to correct for such biases by revealing the discrimination that the early social workers sought to change as well as by chronicling their accomplishments (Chambers, 1986a, 1986b; Costin, 1983a, 1983b; Muncy, 1991; Sklar, 1985).

Logical positivist assumptions and bias against women have resulted in a third kind of problem in prior histories of the field of social work: the oversimplification of the complexity of clinical practice and clinical research. Most historians who examined the field of social work have not systematically studied social workers' clinical research or explored clinical practice using, for example, casework records. When historians assumed they could draw accurate conclusions about social work practice based only on studies of the social work literature, inaccurate histories resulted (Field [Heineman Pieper], 1979, 1980). Following both the logical positivist bias toward oversimplification and the depreciation of women's work that is one hallmark of discrimination, some historians made sweeping generalizations about practitioners, such as that the early social workers were ineffective, judgmental, and unempathic with their clients (Briar & Miller, 1971; Grinker, MacGregor, Selan, Klein, & Kohrman, 1961; Trattner, 1989). When Heineman Pieper studied records of casework practice systematically, she contributed radically new insights about the history of social work practice. She found that the "deluge" of psychodynamic theory that infused the social work literature during the 1920s and 1930s was not evident in practitioner formulations at a representative child placing agency as late as 1939; even in 1949, psychodynamic theory had not been fully integrated into the agency's practice (Field [Heineman Pieper], 1979, 1980). Another researcher who investigated casework records, Margo Horn (1984), found that practitioners in child guidance clinics often were supportive and respectful of clients. Her findings suggest that those historians who assumed clients were controlled and oppressed by social workers underestimated clients' assertive contributions to the clinical relationship.[11] Another consequence of historians' failure to examine clinical practice and clinical research is that important issues in the history of social work have been overlooked. For example, some histories do not address the influence of changes in the contexts of casework practice on social workers' approaches to clinical research (e.g., Ehrenreich, 1985; Trattner, 1989; Wagner, 1986). By focusing on clinicians' descriptions of their practice and research, and by drawing from those historians who did study clinical practice, this study begins to amend the oversimplification of clinical practice and clinical research in histories of the social work profession.

In sum, because understanding the origins of ideas about social and behavioral research is important for developing contemporary approaches to research, I conducted this study to unearth social workers' approaches to research, to trace how those approaches have changed over time, and to examine factors that might account for those changes, including the events that social work researchers themselves viewed as important influences on their approaches to research. Because it is based on the conceptual foundations of the heuristic paradigm, this study can begin to compensate for the biases produced when logical positivist beliefs about scientific knowledge regulated prior histories of the field of social work. To begin to remedy the impact of bias against women on the history of social work, this analysis includes a focus on women researchers' contributions to social workers' approaches to research. It considers how the roles of women and men in the social work profession were influenced by (and sometimes contributed to) societal attitudes toward the roles of women and men.

Research Design

Historians concur that the professionalization of social work practice began at the turn of the century, when social workers planned and founded schools of social work that accelerated the generation of social work knowledge and trained social workers in the principles of social work research. Accordingly, the point of departure for this history is 1900. This chronicle focuses on the period between 1900 and 1960, because the major trends in social workers' approaches to research through 1981 were entrenched by 1960. Also, changes in social workers' philosophy of research after 1960 are discussed in the remainder of this volume. Further, by focusing on the period 1900 to 1960, I could more completely describe the distinctive approaches to research that developed from 1900 through 1930 and comprehensively analyze the significant shift that took place in social workers' approaches to research during the 1950s.

The sources of data for this history follow:

1.   A survey of the published social work literature in which researchers described the principles that regulated the conduct and appraisal of social work research. This included a systematically selected sample of 2,884 studies published in the three leading social work journals—*Social Service Review*, *Social Casework* (originally entitled *The Family* and very recently renamed *Families in Society*), and *Social Work* from their inception through 1989.

2.   Archival resources that provide further information about how social workers thought about and developed their approaches to research.

3.   Secondary accounts, primarily histories of the field of social work and the social and behavioral sciences, as well as histories of women and feminism.

The combination of sources ameliorates the biases introduced by a reliance on any one source of data.[12] I analyzed the data using qualitative analysis as developed by historians of ideas and using a content analysis with descriptive statistics and a chi-square test.

The History of Ideas

In addition to the canons for historical analysis that were described previously, post-positivist historians of the social and behavioral sciences have contributed precepts for understanding the evolution of scientific ideas. Although space does not permit a complete discussion of those contributions, the following precepts are most relevant for this chapter. Gail Hornstein notes that intellectual histories have tended to omit researchers' debates. Although this omission generates an apparently more coherent narrative, its effects can be described as follows:

> [S]cientific perspectives become stripped of the social, political, and economic contexts in which they were created. This process of deletion renders scientific approaches static and ahistorical, thereby obscuring the ways in which they represent attempts at solving particular technical or definitional problems facing a discipline at a given moment in its development. (Hornstein, 1988, p. 3)

Postpositivist historians and sociologists of science increasingly recognize that debate among researchers is an inevitable, and often desirable, catalyst for knowledge development (Hull, 1988; Latour, 1987; Richards, 1981, 1983, 1987). Therefore, I made a deliberate attempt to describe the controversies regarding approaches to generating social work knowledge.

Some sociologists of science, recognizing the impact of sociocultural factors on scientific knowledge, claim that sociological explanations can account completely for scientists' beliefs and changes in those beliefs (e.g., Bloor, 1976). However, to view social context as the determinant of scientific beliefs implies a reductionistic concept of human nature in which human agency is regulated entirely by sociocultural forces. Sociohistorical context clearly influences factors such as the scientist's choice among competing theories (Richards, 1987). For example, one cannot apply a theory that has not yet been developed. Also, the scientist's educational experiences profoundly influence the direction of her or his thought (Kuhn, 1970). On the other hand, scientists develop new theories in response to their dissatisfaction with existing theories, and they use diverse criteria, only some of which may be social in nature, in choosing among theories (Laudan, 1981, p. 196, 1984; Richards, 1981, 1987). Further, Shapere emphasized that scientists often articulate rational criteria for choosing the beliefs they adopt, "context is not monolithic; nor is it all-determining. Even background beliefs can be rejected, and for reasons" (1989, p. 435).[13] Accordingly, although I have examined sociocultural factors as important influences on social workers' approaches to research, I have also focused on social work researchers' explanations about why they adopted their beliefs about research.

Content Analysis

A strategy for data analysis called *content analysis* enables a historian of ideas to discern trends in the frequency of occurrence of events over time as well as the frequency of associations between those events. Content analysis of social work journal articles has been used as one indicator of trends in the profession's knowledge base (Howe & Schuerman, 1974; Weinberger & Tripodi, 1969). Content analysis is used here to determine whether some potentially sensitive indices of the impact of social workers' approaches to research manifest changes over time and, if so, whether those changes correspond to changes in social workers' philosophy of research. Content analysis generates a bias by decontextualizing the phenomena it studies; the historical narrative provides a context to correct for that bias.[14]

Although other researchers have conducted content analyses of social work journal articles, coding categories in prior analyses have reflected logical positivist beliefs about research. One consequence of the restrictive assumptions of positivism is that a significant proportion of social work articles were excluded from the category of "research." For example, Taber and Shapiro (1965) coded "empirical" and "nonempirical" references. They defined "empirical" statements as those "based on experience of observation or data pertaining to or founded on experiment," whereas "nonempirical" statements included "value preferences, recommendations for action, or statements about phenomena supposed to exist but not directly observable" (p. 102). In their view, only knowledge they mislabeled as exhausting the category of "empirical" counted as research, an exclusionary definition of research that led them to conclude that only 8 of the 124 social work studies were "research reports" (p. 106). Weinberger and Tripodi (1969) also analyzed the periodical literature, beginning with the premise that only 332 out of 1,894 studies published between 1956 and 1965 were "research" (p. 445). When they further divided the category "research" using their definitions of "empirical" and "nonempirical," they were left with only 176 examples of "empirical" research (9% of all the articles in their sample).

A content analysis of the social work journal literature that builds on the premises of a postpositivist philosophy of research has not been conducted before. The ideas that comprise a metatheory of knowledge are distinct from, but also have a regulatory impact on, a researcher's decisions about data collection and data analysis. In concert with the nonrestrictive emphasis of the heuristic paradigm, I designed this content analysis to include all the methods that social workers have used to collect and analyze data. In addition, to apply the postpositivist recognition that scientific knowledge reflects sociocultural trends, I analyzed a substantial time period and also a variable that may be particularly responsive to changes in sociocultural values: the gender of the first author of the research.

A researcher makes several decisions in designing a research study, including decisions about how to collect and analyze data. The heuristic approach does not prescribe or proscribe any specific research decisions. By contrast, as Heineman Pieper pointed out (Pieper, 1989, p. 10), one of the salient tenets of the positivist approach to social work research is that some research designs are better than others for testing theories, in particular, that experimental design is a privileged test of theories (Fischer, 1980–1981; Reid & Smith, 1989; Tripodi, 1981). In addition, positivist social researchers claim that quantifying data results in findings that are "harder," or more free of bias than when data are analyzed qualitatively (Grinnell, 1988; Reid & Smith, 1989; Thyer, 1991). Accordingly, I hypothesized that after 1950, as social work researchers increasingly adopted the logical positivist philosophy of research, authors of articles published in social work journals would increasingly choose experimental designs and quantify their data. To test that hypothesis, I developed a set of coding categories for the content analysis that addressed the studies' designs. For the coding categories, I regarded the decisions a researcher makes in designing a study as setting up a heuristic to solve the research problem. An examination of social work journal articles over time yielded seven broad types of research design heuristics. Accordingly, each journal article was coded as having implemented one of the following design heuristics:

1. Review and commentary: descriptive and conceptual articles, for example, reporting current events or innovations in practice, or critiquing a developmental theory;

2. History;

3. Single case studies describing casework practice with individuals, families, or groups in which the researcher analyzed data qualitatively and did not quantify data;

4. Large-scale qualitative analyses that reflect interviews with several informants, such as compilations of several qualitative case studies, or ethnographies, in which the researcher analyzed data qualitatively and did not quantify data;

5. Large-scale studies in which the researcher quantified the data, such as content analyses or multiple regression analyses;

6. Single case studies describing casework practice with individuals, families, or groups in which the researcher quantified the data;

7. Experimental designs; in the articles reviewed for this analysis, the researchers who conducted experimental studies quantified their data.[15]

Studies were included in categories 3 or 4 only if the researcher relied solely on qualitative data to support her or his conclusions. Accordingly, studies that relied on both qualitative and quantified data were coded in categories 5 and 6. Other coding categories used for exploratory and descriptive purposes follow:

a. The gender of the first author;[16]

b. Whether or not the topic of the article included evaluation of social work practice or one or more social work programs;

c. If the article did address evaluation, the aim of the evaluator's research.[17]

The findings with regard to evaluation are summarized in Chapter 7.

To compose the sample of articles, all the studies in every third issue of *Social Work*, *Social Casework*, and *Social Service Review*, from the inception of the journal through 1989, were coded.[18] *Social Casework* began in 1920, *Social Service Review* in 1927, and *Social Work* in 1956, producing a sample of 2,884 articles spanning the years 1920 through the present. The sample covers a longer time frame and is substantially larger than previous content analyses of the social work journal literature.[19]

The number of research articles in the sample from *Social Service Review* was 645; from *Social Work*, 847; and from *Social Casework*, 1,392. The preponderance of articles from *Social Casework* reflects that journal's early start, as well as its tendency to publish more articles per year than the other two journals.

The analysis of the 2,884 articles showed that over the 70-year period, the majority (57%) of social work researchers used a review–commentary design (Figure 2–1). In such articles they reported and analyzed current events or examined the literature on a particular topic. Social workers' extensive interest in reviews and commentaries indicates the profession's enduring, substantial commitment to reflect on and debate the significance of contemporary events and to examine new ideas and their applications to the field of social work. Positivist social work researchers, however, did not accord such reviews and commentaries the status of "research" (Taber & Shapiro, 1965; Weinberger & Tripodi, 1969), although positivist social researchers

Figure 2–1
Distribution of seven research design heuristics in social work journal articles, 1920 to 1989

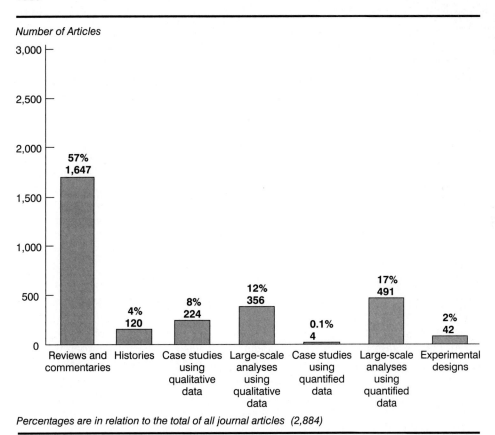

Percentages are in relation to the total of all journal articles (2,884)

wrote reviews and commentaries to advance their opinions (e.g., Blenkner, 1950; W. E. Gordon, 1951; Greenwood, 1955). Next to reviews and commentaries, authors of journal articles most often conducted large-scale analyses with quantified data. Researchers quantified their data in only a very small number of single case studies (only 4 of 2,884 studies, or 0.1%). This observation does not support the belief that a revolution occurred in which researchers adopted the behaviorist single case designs with quantified data, often viewed as the hallmark of the "empirical clinical practice model" (Fischer, 1981, 1984).[20] Researchers who conducted case studies almost invariably used qualitative analysis; they also compiled qualitative case studies into larger-scale qualitative analyses.

THE EARLY SOCIAL WORKERS' APPROACHES TO RESEARCH

Historians and sociologists of science have shown that scientific traditions always develop in the context of research communities that encourage new discoveries, critical analysis, and debate (I. B. Cohen, 1963; Danziger, 1987; Hull, 1988; Knorr-Cetina, 1981; Kuhn, 1970; Latour, 1987; Richards, 1981, 1983, 1987; Woolgar, 1976). In the first 25 years of the twentieth century, there were three distinctive kinds of social work research communities: settlement houses, charity organization societies, and psychiatric social work groups, which often included members of other disciplines (e.g., psychiatrists and psychologists) in settings such as hospital social service departments and child guidance clinics. Each of the communities developed distinctive models of clinical practice. Although the three communities differed in their conduct and use of research (e.g., Addams, 1897), they also shared some beliefs about scientific social work research.

In the following discussion, examples of research contributions from each of the three communities will be provided, and then their common beliefs about social research will be summarized. Finally, social work researchers' adoption of logical positivist beliefs about research in the 1950s will be described, showing that the positivist approach to social work research represented a significant departure from the approaches to research formulated by the early social workers.

The social workers who founded the profession in the first 25 years of the twentieth century drew from and adapted beliefs about scientific research from diverse philosophical traditions. Jane Addams read the writings of Auguste Comte, admired his vision of a religion that celebrated humanity, and explored the work of Comte's followers during her travels to England (Addams, 1910/1990). She did not, however, adopt Comte's positivist views about science, which had become outdated. Instead, in formulating beliefs about social science, she collaborated with the American pragmatist philosophers William James (1842–1910) and John Dewey (1859–1952). One of the leading researchers about social work practice in the charity organization societies, Mary Richmond, and two leading psychiatric social work researchers, Jessie Taft and Virginia Robinson, also drew from Dewey and James in developing their beliefs about research (Richmond, 1922; Robinson, 1962; see also Young, 1939).

Although they differed on many points, Dewey and James espoused an approach to scientific research that was not methodologically restrictive (Dewey, 1938; W. James, 1970). For example, they recognized that hypothesis testing through "experimentation" was a major component of scientific research, but did not limit an experiment to any particular research design. They recognized that all research is value-laden. Dewey rejected the positivist view that science aims to generate universal laws. He regarded scientific research as a variant of, rather than distinct from, commonsense problem solving and described the purpose of scientific research as generating workable solutions for human problems (Copleston, 1966/1985; Dewey, 1938, 1900–1901/1970; M. White, 1963).[21]

Dewey taught at the University of Chicago and then at Columbia University, in close proximity to the first schools of social work. Dewey and Jane Addams were life-long friends. Dewey's daughter was named after Addams. When his eight-year-old son died during one of Dewey's trips abroad, Addams presided over the memorial service, which was held at Hull House (A. F. Davis, 1973). Addams turned to Dewey on several occasions for advice regarding research and educational activities at Hull House (Addams, 1910/1990).

Addams also was very familiar with William James's work, and often they lectured together about pacifism (A. F. Davis, 1973). In describing an ideal that guided her explorations of the inner life of elderly women in *The Long Road of Woman's Memory*, Addams commented, "while I may receive valuable suggestions from classic literature, when I really want to learn about life, I must depend upon my neighbors, for, as William James insists, the most instructive human documents lie along the beaten pathway" (1916, p. xi). James also admired Addams's work. For example, in response to her book *Newer Ideals of Peace* (1907) he wrote, "I find it hard to express the good it has done me in offering new points of view and annihilating old ones. New perspectives of hope! . . . Yours is a deeply original mind . . . yet revolutionary in the extreme, and I should suspect that this work will act as a ferment through long years to come" (1907).

In addition to pragmatism, other beliefs about research informed the American social and behavioral sciences at the beginning of the twentieth century. Although most early social workers did not draw from positivist ideas, some social and behavioral scientists (who were not social workers) had been trained in German universities, visited or corresponded with British social scientists and philosophers, and were greatly influenced by the positivist philosophers such as Auguste Comte, the physicist Ernst Mach, and the British positivists John Stuart Mill and Karl Pearson (Manicas, 1987). When those social and behavioral scientists returned to this country, they imported the tenets of positivism into other social and behavioral sciences such as sociology and psychology (Danziger, 1987, 1990; Manicas, 1987; Morawski, 1988). Not until the 1950s, however, did social work researchers adopt the tenets of the more stringent offshoot of positivism commonly known as logical positivism.

The early social work research communities developed in the context of massive social changes, prompted largely by industrialization. People migrated from rural to urban areas to seek work, and there was significant migration from the rural Southern states to Northern cities. Many people emigrated from Ireland, Italy, Russia, and Eastern Europe, settling primarily in cities. Business empires expanded rapidly, and the disparity between rich and poor became more evident. One of the most important social changes that strongly influenced the social work profession was the growth of what was termed the "woman movement." At the turn of the century, women who pursued social research were committed almost uniformly to social reform. Yet, the cultural context in which they worked was inimical to women's intellectual achievements (Furumoto, 1987; Muncy, 1991; Rossiter, 1982; S. Rothman, 1978; Sklar, 1985). It was widely believed throughout the Victorian era that development of a woman's intellect would harm her reproductive capacities (R. Rosenberg, 1982; S. Rothman, 1978). Even during the Progressive era (beginning in the late 1890s), when social workers began to organize as a profession, those Victorian concepts of womanhood continued to define both the treatment of women and the way women understood themselves (S. Rothman, 1978). At the turn of the century, women could not vote; they were excluded from many colleges and most graduate schools; and the few women who entered the professions "encountered blatant discrimination in education, hiring, promotion, and salaries" (Muncy, 1991, p. xxiii; see also Chambers, 1986b; Furumoto, 1987; J. W. James, 1979; V. Smith, 1891). The "doctrine of separate spheres" held that women's natural milieu was the private world of the home; men alone ruled the public world (R. Rosenberg, 1982). Prominent social and behavioral scientists actively endorsed such views (Rossiter, 1982). Albion Small, the first president of the American Sociological Association, wrote, "Equal pay for equal work is simple justice. But at best social ideals that train women to be competitors with men are like poisons administered as medicine" (quoted in Deegan, 1981, p. 15). In many states, when a woman married she lost her right to choose her place of domicile. Moreover, her funds (including earnings from her employment) and her property were transferred to her husband (Abramovitz, 1988; Breckinridge, 1930). Some states had retained outlandish statutes, such as that knowledge about contraception was illegal (Reed, 1979). Although by the 1920s some states had begun to repeal or revise such laws, in 1930 a woman still could not legally choose to live apart from her husband, if, for example, she received an important professional appointment in another city (Breckinridge, 1930).[22]

The "woman movement" in the United States and Great Britain steadily gathered influence following events such as the Seneca Falls Convention, organized by Lucretia Mott and Elizabeth Cady Stanton in 1848 (DuBois, 1992; Schneir, 1972). Feminists voiced diverse theories about how gender influences personality and how the social roles of men and women should be revised. They united around working for women's rights, especially the right to vote (S. Evans, 1989; S. Rothman, 1978). African-Americans such as Frederick Douglass and Sojourner Truth were outspoken advocates of women's rights (Schneir, 1972). Charlotte Perkins Gilman (1860–1935), in her books *Women and Economics* and *Our Androcentric Culture*, advocated changes in domestic roles, such as that housekeeping chores should be treated as a form of paid labor, analogous to work outside the home (Schneir, 1972, p. 230). Social workers such as Jessie Taft read and used Gilman's work. From the turn of the century through the beginning of World War I, the movement for women's suffrage steadily gained both supporters and publicity. In Great Britain, feminists led by the Pankhursts brought women's suffrage to public attention through such strategies as disrupting political meetings by asking the candidates about their positions on women's rights. The Pankhursts and their followers often were jailed, and when they engaged in hunger strikes they were commonly force-fed, a torturous practice that often had permanently harmful consequences (Schneir, 1972). Some suffragists in the United States began to adopt the Pankhursts' methods and experienced similarly violent retaliations.

Many of the leading social workers, including Jane Addams, Florence Kelley, Sophonisba Breckinridge, Edith and Grace Abbott, Virginia Robinson, and Jessie Taft, were deeply influenced by the women's movement and worked for women's suffrage (E. Abbott, 1910; G. Abbott, 1909; Breckinridge, 1930; F. Kelley, 1905/1969; V. Robinson, 1962; Taft, 1915). Jane Addams was one of the leaders of the women's suffrage movement. Florence Kelley described how her great-aunt, Sarah Pugh, introduced her to the women's movement during childhood (F. Kelley, 1986). Pugh was a close friend of Lucretia Mott and accompanied Mott on her speaking engagements on behalf of women's rights (F. Kelley, 1986). Jessie Taft (1915) regarded awareness of issues addressed by the women's movement as one attribute of "self-conscious" individuals, and she believed remedying discrimination against women was necessary for a just society. Grace Abbott's master's thesis at the University of Chicago in 1909, "The Legal Position of Married Women in the United States," began by stating:

> Under the common law upon marriage a woman lost her rights, her responsibilities and even her identity—Whether the Courts in formulating the rules which governed her were acting upon the theory that the husband was the guardian or master of his wife, or that, because of the unity of married people, the wife's legal status became merged and lost in that of her husband, her position was most unequal and unjust. (p. 1)

She concluded, "what is most needed to complete the revolution [in women's rights] which is already well started is to give her [the contemporary woman] political responsibility for the laws under which she lives and works" (p. 43). These feminists believed that, to significantly change discriminatory practices, women had to obtain political power, draft legislation, and implement social programs. For example, Breckinridge wrote with regard to the process of revising repressive marital statutes, "women should both direct its movement and so far as possible determine the rate of progress" (1930, p. 51).

Women united and directed their efforts for social reform through dynamic, activist organizations such as the Illinois Women's Alliance and the Indiana Association of Colored Women's Clubs (Jackson, 1978; S. Rothman, 1978; Stetson, 1983; Sklar, 1985, p. 665). They also used research to combat misogynist views. For example, Marion Talbot was denied admission to Harvard, in part because the president of the university believed that scholarship would interfere with women's health, especially their reproductive organs. After obtaining her degree elsewhere, Talbot conducted a study demonstrating that college-educated women bore children at the same rate as women who did not have a college education (R. Rosenberg, 1982). Talbot and Breckinridge were influential members of the American Association for University Women, which sponsored much research, including, at Breckinridge's suggestion, an investigation into how to rectify the problem that women were being paid less than men for the same work (Talbot & Rosenberry, 1931).

The discrimination that white women encountered was multiplied several times for members of racial minority groups (Carlton-La Ney, 1983; Jackson, 1978), especially for female members of minority groups (Abramovitz, 1988; Muncy, 1991). Racist theories pervaded the biological and social and behavioral sciences (Cravens, 1985). When Ida B. Wells-Barnett brought lynching to public attention in 1892, racist vigilantes destroyed her press in Tennessee. To save her life, she moved to the East Coast and then to Chicago, where she enlightened Jane Addams about the problem of lynching and prompted Addams's support for her campaign against segregation in Chicago schools (Peebles-Wilkins & Francis, 1990). Wells-Barnett and Mary Church Terrell (who was known internationally for her writing and speeches advancing women's suffrage and the need for racial integration and equality in the United States) helped to found the National Association for the Advancement of Colored People in 1910 (Peebles-Wilkins & Francis, 1990). Both Wells-Barnett and Terrell used research to advance public awareness of racism and misogyny and to stimulate reform (Peebles-Wilkins & Francis, 1990). Similarly, through his scholarship, W. E. B. DuBois stimulated resistance to the Jim Crow laws that were systematically disenfranchising African-Americans (J. H. Franklin, 1989). George Edmund Haynes, an African-American who was among the first students to earn a doctorate at the New York School of Philanthropy, conducted a comprehensive survey of African-American New Yorkers and subsequently became a cofounder of the National Urban League (Carlton-La Ney, 1983).

Hull House and the Settlement Houses: Developing the "Great Science" of Social Welfare

Research was an inherent aspect of the settlement house movement as Jane Addams pioneered it in this country (Addams, 1910/1990).[23] Addams founded Hull House in 1889 in a disadvantaged, multicultural Chicago urban community. Many of the neighbors were immigrants who worked in the factories that surrounded the neighborhood. Hull House grew rapidly, from one house staffed by Addams and her colleague, Ellen Gates Starr, until it served over 1,500 people; by 1921 there were over 45 residents (or settlers), and its buildings spread over an entire city block (Hull House Residents, 1906–1935). In the two decades following the founding of Hull House, settlement houses grew rapidly in many major cities, including the Chicago Commons in Chicago (G. Taylor, 1936; L. Taylor, 1954) and the Henry Street Settlement (Wald, 1915) and Greenwich House in New York (Simkhovitch, 1938). Women led the settlement movement, and in 1910 the majority (66%) of the directors of settlement houses were women. Although for some time women continued to lead settlements, by the 1950s, more men than women were leaders of settlements (Trolander, 1987), consistent with similar trends in the social work profession as a whole, which will be described later.

Knowledge about principles of practice in settlement houses grew because the settlers wrote about their practice and read, responded to, and debated each other's work. A survey of fourteen settlement houses at the turn of the century indicated that the residents had published forty-five books (Trolander, 1987). Narrative in style and rich with examples, their publications brought to public attention the strengths and needs of people in disadvantaged circumstances. Through their research, many settlers mobilized support for new legislation to combat social inequalities, and they influenced social policy at the national level. For example, Lillian Wald and Florence Kelley worked to establish the Children's Bureau to study and remedy problems afflicting children and families (Addams, 1935b; Muncy, 1991).

Hull House was generally regarded as the leading settlement. Hull House founders included Julia Lathrop, Florence Kelley, and Edith and Grace Abbott, who became leaders in social research and social work education (Costin, 1983a, 1983b). Therefore, illustrations in this text of the research approach developed in the settlement communities are drawn primarily from Hull House.[24]

Because the settlers lived in the disadvantaged communities they sought to understand and aid, they became very familiar with the strengths and needs of their neighbors. They developed resources and advocated for reforms that ranged from adequate sanitation to legal protections for workers. Many settlers used research to investigate, publicize, and develop responses to the problems that they identified and that their neighbors brought to their attention (e.g., E. Abbott, 1915, 1936; Addams, 1935b; Breckinridge, 1913; Breckinridge & Abbott, 1912; F. Kelley, 1905/1969; Lathrop, 1905). In contrast to the authoritarian relationship between researchers and those who participated as subjects that characterized later twentieth-century approaches to psychological research (Danziger, 1988a), Addams recognized she needed the neighbors to correct her possible misperceptions:

> I never addressed a Chicago audience on the subject of the Settlement and its vicinity without inviting a neighbor to go with me, that I might curb any hasty generalization by the consciousness that I had an auditor who knew the conditions more intimately than I could hope to do. (1910/1990, p. 58)

The problems the Hull House settlers addressed both in research and practice were identified by settlers and neighbors. To illustrate, to remedy the complete lack of day-care resources, one of the first activities at Hull House was providing day care and a kindergarten. Almost as soon as Addams and her colleague Ellen Starr moved into Hull House, women knocked on the door to request help caring for their children while they were at work. Jane Addams and Julia Lathrop delivered the baby of a woman who had been shunned because she was giving birth out of wedlock (Addams, 1910/1990). The Hull House settlers set up classes that responded to the interests of neighbors, covering subjects that ranged from sewing to music. They arranged athletic contests and sponsored concerts and dramatic performances by the neighbors that expressed the neighbors' diverse cultural traditions. They researched children's reading levels, rates of tuberculosis among schoolchildren, the transmission of typhoid infections, the educational and domestic status of newsboys (who were not protected by the Illinois Child Labor Law), and sanitation practices (Addams, 1910/1990).[25] They affirmed cultural values that were depreciated in the wider society (Addams 1910/1990; Leighninger, 1975), and they recognized and sought to change discriminatory practices (W. E. B. DuBois cited in Aptheker, 1966; Diner, 1970; Jackson, 1978; Mohl & Betten, 1974). Breckinridge (1913), for example, investigated racial discrimination in Chicago housing. She documented how African-American families had to pay higher rents for poorer-quality housing and were forced to live in segregated neighborhoods where they were denied basic community resources such as police protection.

The Hull House settlers were courageous in many respects. As part of their efforts to combat a smallpox epidemic that followed the Columbian Exposition of 1893 in Chicago, Florence Kelley and Julia Lathrop went to sweatshop factories and homes to prevent people from sending disease-infected garments into the community:

> I saw these two women do that which the health department of the great city of Chicago could not do. The authorities were afraid not only of personal contagion but of damage suits if they destroyed the infected garments. They therefore said that there was no smallpox in Chicago. Later as the result of a joint attack by Miss Julia Lathrop and Mrs. Florence Kelley they were induced to act and they destroyed thousands of dollars worth of clothing. That attack illustrates the difference between these two tremendously useful women. Julia Lathrop, the diplomat, reasoned and cajoled. Mrs. Kelley, the fighter, asked me to file a mandamus suit to compel action. Each acted in her own way, but each fought for the same cause and each risked her life in the same conflict. Working together, they saved hundreds, perhaps thousands of human lives. (Judge Bruce quoted by Addams, 1935b, p. 118)

Many of these early social workers, the Hull House settlers in particular, recognized that they were contributing to the new and burgeoning social and behavioral sciences. Following the lead of the New York Charity Organization Society,* which sponsored a six-week summer course on philanthropy in 1898 and began to offer year-long courses in 1904, Julia Lathrop of Hull House and Graham Taylor of the Chicago Commons Settlement House founded the Institute of Social Science. The Institute became the Chicago School of Civics and Philanthropy in 1908 and later became the School of Social Service Administration at the University of Chicago (Lubove, 1965). The Russell Sage Foundation was an extremely important source of support and funding for social work research after it was founded in 1907, and it provided grant funds that helped the Chicago school to establish a research department led by Julia Lathrop and Sophonisba Breckinridge (Lubove, 1965, p. 141). Because they saw that the new profession needed a scientific knowledge base, Edith Abbott (who became the dean of the School of Social Service Administration at the University of Chicago) and Breckinridge (one of the first women professors at the University of Chicago) founded the journal *Social Service Review* to facilitate the dissemination and critique of new social work knowledge. Breckinridge authored one of the first textbooks used to teach social work practice (E. Abbott, 1923; Breckinridge, 1924; Costin, 1983a, 1983b).[26]

Editor's Note: Charity Organization Societies were established by philanthropists to provide "outdoor relief" or funds for needy families; the relief was administered largely by "friendly visitors."

In addition to the growing numbers of social workers, Chicago was an active center for other social researchers at the turn of the century. The first department of sociology in the United States was founded at the University of Chicago in the 1890s, and some sociologists, such as George Herbert Mead, worked closely with Jane Addams on several Hull House projects. Mead lectured at the Chicago School of Civics and Philanthropy and was one of the committee members for Jessie Taft's dissertation. Both Mead and Dewey rejected Victorian gender stereotypes, supported feminism, and actively encouraged women students' intellectual and career development (R. Rosenberg, 1982).

Abbott called the field of social work a "new science." She emphasized that the methods and theories of both social treatment and public welfare administration needed to be evaluated comprehensively so that social workers could learn from prior efforts (E. Abbott, 1931; Costin, 1983a, 1983b). As part of developing the ideas of the "new science," the Hull House community offered residents and neighbors ongoing opportunities to learn new ideas and refine their own views. Addams established discussion groups at Hull House in which the most influential scholars, social scientists, and reformers (including John Dewey and W. E. B. DuBois) spoke and interacted with the neighbors. The Working People's Social Science Club, for example, was developed to advance scientific knowledge about the origins of social problems and ways to remedy them. Participants debated social issues from the standpoint of diverse political perspectives, including anarchism, socialism, liberalism, and feminism (Addams, 1910/1990). Hull House residents described how much they enjoyed the ongoing intellectual debates (Addams, 1935a; E. Abbott, 1952). Julia Lathrop and Florence Kelley, although friends and allies in many projects, had a long-standing disagreement about ways to use the legal system to accomplish social change (Addams, 1935b, pp. 120–121). The Hull House settlers' very different backgrounds appear to have enriched the ongoing interchange; one woman who said that she felt completely at home with the intellectual debates at Hull House was "one of the early Russian Revolutionists who had escaped from Siberia and had come to Hull House" (E. Abbott, 1952, p. 337).

Although some historians said that settlers, including the Hull House activists, were patricians who were insensitive to the differential impact of social class on social problems and their solutions (Platt, 1978; Wagner, 1986), the work of Hull House researchers contradicts that conclusion (Leighninger, 1975). For example, Edith Abbott's 1910 book, *Women in Industry*, was a comprehensive survey of the economic history of working women that analyzed both qualitative and quantified data. The book was specifically directed to redress the problem that working-class women had not been sufficiently represented in the "woman movement" of the time. Abbott wrote:

> While the problems of all gainfully employed women, whether professionally trained and educated or untrained and unskilled, are fundamentally interdependent, yet for many purposes they must be considered separate questions; and the working woman has undoubtedly been wronged in the past because of the pseudo-democratic refusal to recognize class distinctions in discussions of the woman question. Moreover, a failure to see

important points of unlikeness has led, at times, to confusion in theory and to unfortunate practical results. (p. 8)

She elaborated:

> It has, finally, been too often assumed that the conspicuous broadening of the field of opportunities and activities for educated women during the latter half of the nineteenth century has been a progress without class distinctions in which all women have shared alike. But the history of the employment of women in professional and industrial life has been radically different, and the fruits of that long struggle of the last century for what is perhaps nebulously described as "women's rights" have gone, almost exclusively, to the women of the professional group. (p. 9)

In her analysis of women in industry from colonial times through 1910, Abbott included women who worked in the home, in mills and factories, in the cotton industry, and in the printing industry. She concluded the study by emphasizing that, whereas in 1910 the educated woman faced a world of expanded opportunities, "the woman of the working classes finds it, so far as her measure of opportunity goes, very much as her great grandmother left it" (1910, p. 323). The concern for women workers expressed in Abbott's research was reflected in the Hull House community's research and activism to improve working conditions (Amsterdam, 1982; F. Kelley, 1986; Sklar, 1985). The Hull House social workers sought to help individuals and the immediate community. They also believed that new legislation and social programs at the state and federal levels were needed to bring about enduring change in oppressive conditions.

Addams and her colleagues recognized that disseminating information about social problems was not sufficient to accomplish change. The Hull House settlers' advocacy of legislation protecting workers illustrates how they combined research with lobbying, public education, and mobilizing grass-roots support. The Hull House settlers quickly saw how their neighbors, especially women and children, were exposed to dangerous and brutal working conditions. Florence Kelley, who translated Engels's massive study of the conditions of British workers into English, "suggested to the Illinois State Bureau of Labor that they investigate the sweating system in Chicago with its attendant child labor" (Addams, 1910/1990, p. 119). Having been engaged by those public officials, Kelley conducted the investigation (F. Kelley, 1905/1969) and presented it to the Illinois legislature, which subsequently set up a special commission to conduct further investigations. That committee then recommended legislation that became the first Factory Law of Illinois. The Hull House proposals were opposed by some business leaders, who tried to bribe Addams by offering to contribute funds to the settlement if she would curtail the settlers' efforts to improve working conditions (Addams, 1910/1990). Despite such opposition, the Hull House residents mobilized grass-roots support for the new legislation through speaking engagements with prospective opponents of the legislation as well as its supporters.

When the law was passed, Kelley was appointed the first factory inspector.[27] Working out of an office across the street from Hull House, she enforced the law with the help of twelve deputies. In some cases she prosecuted factory managers for violations. Kelley collected statistics about the law's impact; for example, she notified the Board of Education of sixty-five children under the age of fourteen who had been working in factories, and found that those children were subsequently returned to school or engaged in other occupations under safer conditions (Sklar, 1985, p. 673). In 1899, Kelley helped to found and became general secretary of the National Consumers League in New York City, an organization that conducted investigations and continued to draft protective legislation, which was enacted in thirteen states and the District of Columbia. The battle over the constitutionality of legislation protecting workers (including child workers) continued for some time. Kelley argued that "judicial nullification of beneficent legislation on the ground of unconstitutionality set a distinct limitation to the experiments through which the nation might increase its fund of social knowledge and that it curtailed the opportunity for utilizing experimentation as a method for progressive government" (Addams, 1935b, p. 120). Although the Supreme Court decided that the states' legislation protecting workers was unconstitutional, Justice Holmes supported Kelley's argument in his minority opinion (Addams, 1935b, p. 120). The historian Richard Hofstadter concluded:

> Even when much allowance is made for spottiness in administration and enforcement, and for the toll that judicial decisions took of them, the net effect of these laws in remedying the crassest abuses of industrialism was very considerable. Today it is perhaps necessary to make a strong effort of the imagination to recall the industrial barbarism that was being tamed—to realize how much, for instance, workmen's compensation meant at a time when every year some 16,000 or 17,000 trainmen (about one out of every ten or twelve workers so classified) were injured. (1955, p. 240)[28]

The members of the Hull House community worked to establish the Juvenile Court in Chicago (Breckinridge, 1938). In 1912, Breckinridge and Abbott coauthored a large-scale study of over 800 delinquent children who were referred to the Juvenile Court of Chicago. Breckinridge and Abbott conducted in-home assessments, analyzed court records, and compiled a statistical analysis of the factors that led to juvenile delinquency. Social workers then used that knowledge to plan interventions with children and families referred to the Juvenile Court (Breckinridge, 1938). Addams also used their findings to design Hull House activities. For example, Breckinridge and Abbott found that many of the youngsters referred to the Juvenile Court for delinquency were the oldest children in their families. Many were forced to curtail their education prematurely to work and support their families; they then lacked adequate skills to advance in the workplace. Hull House began to offer classes that would provide the teenagers with supplemental skills (Addams, 1910/1990).

The establishment of the Children's Bureau is another important example of how the Hull House community used research to investigate specific social problems and then advocate for programs that would address those problems. The Hull House settlers, most notably Julia Lathrop, conceptualized the Children's Bureau as a clearinghouse for information, conducting research, and publicizing expert advice.

The agency generated public support for its own recommendations on behalf of women and children (Muncy, 1991, p. 104). Establishing the Children's Bureau was a significant move to gain political power that required extensive lobbying by, among others, Addams, Lathrop, and Edith and Grace Abbott.[29] The Bureau was signed into law in 1912. Lathrop, who was appointed director, made one of her first activities setting up a research project to survey infant-care practices and the problem of infant mortality. When she wanted to educate the public about better infant care, rather than hiring (predominantly male) physicians to write the pamphlets she planned to distribute, she hired a woman, Mary Mills West. The pamphlets were so useful that over a million and a half were distributed between 1914 and 1921. The Children's Bureau staff also sponsored a study about the care of children with learning problems; they were successful in achieving improvements in understanding and service provision in many states (Muncy, 1991). Lathrop also drafted a maternity and infancy bill, which provided for the federal government to give grants-in-aid to states for financial assistance to mothers and children. The lobbying efforts of the Hull House community and other women reformers on behalf of the maternity and infancy bill were so influential that by 1921, one legislator said, "I think every woman in my state has written to the Senator" (quoted in Muncy, 1991, p. 105). One "opponent accused Lathrop of having built up 'a political machine'" (Muncy, 1991, p. 105). Called the Sheppard-Towner Maternity and Infancy Act, the bill was passed in 1921, in part because the vote was public and politicians wanted the support of their newest constituency—women voters.

Although settlers often disagreed with members of the charity organization societies about ways to respond to people in need (Addams, 1897; D. Franklin, 1986; Germain & Hartman, 1980; Richmond, 1897a), there was frequent interchange between the two communities, and there were areas of agreement as well. Both the settlement houses and the charity organization societies conducted large-scale surveys of community problems. For example, the Pittsburgh Survey was initiated largely through the influence of Edwin Devine. Devine, who had been an educator in the Midwest, moved to New York, where he was professor of social economy at Columbia University, general secretary of the New York Charity Organization Society, and founder of a Charities Publications Committee that included Jane Addams (Kellogg, 1914). He also edited the journal *Charities and the Commons*, a merger of the Chicago Commons settlement publication *The Commons* and the New York Charity Organization Society publication *Charities*. Research on social problems presented in the journal inspired Pittsburgh citizens and social workers to ask that the Charity Publications Committee study Pittsburgh's social problems in 1907 (Zimbalist, 1977). The Pittsburgh Survey included a comprehensive description of services provided in Pittsburgh's children's institutions as well as documentation of working conditions in the steel mills, including the numerous industrial fatalities (Kellogg, 1914; Young, 1939). Paul Kellogg sought out and used women reporters and scholars in the research, and women authored four of the six volumes of the survey (Chambers, personal communication, April 28, 1992). Some social workers said that the survey's shocking findings and eloquent, forceful presentation prompted the passage of workmen's compensation legislation (Mary Van Kleeck cited in Zimbalist, 1977, p. 126).

Although some historians have described the settlement houses' commitment to research (e.g., Chambers, 1963/1980), most have not highlighted the ways in which the settlement communities' organization enabled them to use research to advance social reform. Addams viewed the intellectual freedom of Hull House as hinging directly on the settlement's financial and organizational autonomy. Not only did she reject the enticements of those who sought to quell Hull House's reform efforts, but she also turned down an offer from the University of Chicago to provide permanent support for Hull House. Her rationale was that the integrity of Hull House's critical reflection on social problems depended largely on its autonomy (Addams, 1895). To fund the settlement, she depended on individual benefactors and proceeds from the settlers' writings and other efforts. In other words, to conduct research that could adequately explain social inequalities and advocate for social reforms, Addams recognized that the researchers had to have a supportive community based on alternative values. Moreover, in the context of the discrimination against women and members of ethnic minority groups that pervaded many institutions (including universities, Talbot & Rosenberry, 1931), Addams emphasized that the support of a strong, autonomous community was necessary for the settlers to conceptualize, study, and advocate for social reforms.

The Charity Organization Societies: Mary Richmond's Formulation of "Scientific Charity"

Designed to administer relief funds and to counsel poverty-stricken individuals and families, the charity organization societies also were communities within which social workers developed casework methods (Richmond, 1899/1912). Many social workers who became leaders in the new profession of social work during the first decade of the twentieth century formed their concepts of social work practice in charity organization societies. For example, Porter Lee, who in 1912 became the first director of the New York School of Philanthropy, was introduced to and trained in social work methods in the Buffalo Charity Organization Society. Lee's famous 1929 address, "Social Work as Cause and Function," articulated how professionalization enabled social workers to see their role as advancing social reform as well as organizing and providing human services (1929/1937a).

One of the most prominent charity organization society researchers was Mary Richmond. Her work will be used to exemplify the principles used to guide research about casework practice with individuals and families in the charity organization societies. Richmond's work was based not only on her clinical experience but also on her extensive experience as a manager and educator. Richmond built on the methods that "friendly visitors"* developed during the 1880s and used research to

---

Editor's Note: Richmond said about the role of the "friendly visitor": "The term 'friendly visitor' does not apply to one who aimlessly visits the poor for a little while, without making any effort to improve their condition permanently or to be a real friend to them. Friendly visiting, as distinguished from district visiting, originated with the charity organization societies, some of which are indefatigable in training volunteers to do effective work in the homes of the poor" (1899/1912, p. v).

advance knowledge about the casework process (Richmond, 1899/1912, 1922). She began developing her contributions to social science knowledge in the 1890s, while serving as a friendly visitor for the Baltimore Charity Organization Society (Richmond, 1899/1912), where she also worked with colleagues such as the psychologist G. Stanley Hall (Drew, 1983; Germain, 1970). As it was for many women at the time, for Mary Richmond social work was a pathway by which she could begin to actualize both her aspirations for fulfilling, self-supporting employment and her desires for a more just society.[30] She wrote:

> It seemed to me, in those first years with the Baltimore COS, that I had never lived before . . . everywhere it [social work] has opened a wonderful door of opportunity for the victims of routine, for the people who have failed to find elsewhere the means of complete self-expression. (Richmond to John M. Glenn, August 11, 1911, quoted in Drew, 1983, p. 6)

After organizing the Baltimore Charity Organization Society, Richmond became the first woman director of the Philadelphia Charity Organization Society, an extensive bureaucracy that had always had male directors despite the fact that its 763 caseworkers were all women (Rauch, 1975, p. 243). After Richmond began directing the program, "the superintendency was almost wholly feminized" (Rauch, 1975, p. 255). In 1909, she became the director of the charity organization department of the very influential Russell Sage Foundation; in that position she had a far-reaching impact on casework practice and research until her death in 1928. She collected and gathered case histories that were disseminated to practitioners through the departmental *Bulletin* (Lubove, 1965, p. 46). Richmond was among the first social workers to articulate the need for a "training school in applied philanthropy" (Richmond, 1897b). She led training institutes for caseworkers and supervisors at the New York School of Applied Philanthropy that were well-attended and extremely influential (Lubove, 1965; Watts, 1964). Although she did not ally herself with the organized women's movement, Richmond recognized the problem of discrimination against women and advised her colleagues to avoid those charity organizations that did not include women in management positions (Richmond, 1930, p. 53).

Richmond's research indicates the very wide range of her scholarly and professional interests (Pumphrey, 1957; Richmond, 1922). Although M. Fraser, Taylor, Jackson, and O'Jack (1991) state that Richmond derived her views from a positivist philosophy of science, their definitions of positivism and postpositivism are inaccurate. Furthermore, they do not support their claim about Richmond with documentation from Richmond's work. In fact, as discussed later, many aspects of Richmond's approach are incompatible with the tenets of a positivist approach to social research. She read very widely in psychology, philosophy, and sociology, including the works of William James, George Herbert Mead, Josiah Royce, James Mark Baldwin, William Healey, Augusta Bronner, and the moral philosophers of the Scottish Enlightenment; she also read and responded to the work of her colleagues, such as Edith Abbott, Francis McLean, and Jane Addams (Germain & Hartman, 1980; Pumphrey, 1961; Richmond, 1899/1912). Her accomplishments are all the more striking given that she lacked the resources for education as a young woman, was almost entirely self-educated (Pumphrey, 1961), and began her research at a time when women were excluded from most graduate schools and could not even vote.

The principles that guided Richmond's approach to research about social work practice are stated clearly in *Social Diagnosis* (1917) and *What Is Social Casework?* (1922). Her approach to research was not proscriptive: She did not exclude from scientific inquiry any aspects of human experience or relationships. To represent various cultural groups and their values, she deliberately studied clients from diverse cultural backgrounds and nationalities. One of Richmond's primary goals was to use caseworkers' documentation of the needs of individuals and families, and the ways clients and caseworkers met those needs, for generating larger-scale social reforms. She emphasized a collaborative definition of the client's problem, as it was perceived by both the client and the caseworker. She also recognized that in using and discussing case records she had to protect the client's right to confidentiality (Richmond, 1922).

Richmond saw that "untested assumptions" were among the major impediments to valuable research and practice (1917, p. 94 ff.). Her approach to research reflects her efforts to continually recognize and evaluate her assumptions. For example, despite the moralistic climate of the Prohibition, Richmond's practice experience showed her that a client's "intemperance" was potentially due to many different causes, including deficient resources in the community. She emphasized that the caseworker could help individuals only by understanding the unique causes of their problems. A scientific approach to the helping process, as Richmond saw it, recognized the importance of the client's subjective experience, particularly the client's experience of the relationship with the social worker, as well as social relationships and resources. Although she was very influenced by her collaboration with physicians in medical social work and adopted some aspects of their "diagnostic" approach (Richmond, 1917), she resisted the tendency to categorize by problem types or situations. Diagnostic categorization had the apparent advantage of generating broadly applicable principles about helping, but Richmond believed that in practice such principles could not be effective, because "people in like circumstances are never so much alike as they appear to be" (Richmond, 1922, p. 157). If others used the social history questionnaires she provided without reference to their clients' unique interests and strengths, she viewed it as a misapplication of her principles (Richmond, 1930).

Richmond also examined the process of inference in social work practice, recognizing that one of the major challenges for social workers (and all decision-makers) is the effect of assumptions on judgment. While recognizing the problem of "untested assumptions" in practice, she respected the practitioner's informed judgment (1917, p. 94 ff). For example, she described how some agencies tried to address the issue of workers' implicit assumptions by instructing the workers to

> enter upon case records "nothing but the facts," reporting each of these colorlessly, "as it happened." Workers who attempted to follow this rule produced records which have been likened to unstrung beads; in the attempt to eliminate all prejudice, they eliminated the judgment and discernment which would have given to the whole investigation unity and significance. (1917, p. 94)

Richmond found that a better strategy was to incorporate into her research the dialogue between practitioner and supervisor, and between practitioner and researcher, because such feedback helps both practitioners and researchers to become aware of their assumptions: "It is the worker's very awareness of his special predisposition on which depends the reliability of his observation and judgment. Once he brings a prejudice into the light of day, he can offset its influence on his thinking" (1917, p. 94).

Most of the casework that Richmond studied in *What Is Social Casework?* and *Social Diagnosis* was conducted by other practitioners, so her approach to that research also illustrates her view of the relationship between researcher and practitioner. She regarded the practitioner both as a resource for invaluable information and as uniquely qualified to validate the accuracy and usefulness of the research findings. For the research that led to *What Is Social Casework?*, Richmond read practitioners' case reports extensively; questioned practitioners about their methods, thought process, and findings; wrote up her analyses of the caseworkers' methods, rationale, and the case outcome; and then resubmitted her work for revision by the practitioners. In *Social Diagnosis*, Richmond targeted her research to address different aspects of the "beginning processes" of casework and also used diverse approaches to gathering and analyzing data. She included a statistical survey of fifty-six social agencies in three cities to ascertain the outside sources that caseworkers consulted in the assessment phase of casework. She conducted extensive qualitative analyses of case records. She supervised two social workers who assisted her with the research, and they read case records in five different cities for a year: "Our aim was to bring to light the best social work practice that could be found, provided it was actually in use and not altogether exceptional in character. In addition these case readers held many interviews with case workers, all of which were carefully reported" (1917, p. 7). Richmond prefaced *Social Diagnosis* with a request that the practitioners reading the volume send her their comments so that she could revise the work to improve its usefulness and accuracy. In short, in the approach to research that Mary Richmond enacted, practitioners evaluated the validity and utility of research, and researchers responded to practitioners' conclusions.

Two further examples from Richmond's work illustrate her approach to issues that contemporary clinical researchers also consider in planning research. In *What Is Social Casework?* Richmond sought to elucidate how the caseworker helps clients to change. To demonstrate that the client had indeed changed, Richmond thought it was important to use several indicators. In the case of Maria Bielowski, Richmond's documentation that the casework had been helpful included the following:

1. Observed changes in one or more of the client's problems (e.g., the girl, who habitually stole, stopped stealing altogether), as reported by several observers;
2. The client's own responses that she felt the casework was helpful;
3. The caseworker's perceptions about how helpful the process was;
4. Richmond's own conclusions about whether or not the client had changed, based on her review of the case records.

Richmond used her study of casework processes to formulate how those caseworkers who helped their clients thought through their interventions, so that those insights could be applied by other caseworkers. She termed one element of the effective caseworker's thinking "imaginative sympathy" and elaborated its components. *Imaginative sympathy* included understanding the world and relationships from the client's perspective, treating the client with respect and warmth, refraining from denying the client's requests unless absolutely necessary, sharing the rationale for one's actions openly with the client so that the worker's behavior would not seem arbitrary to the client, and being honest with the client.[31] Although the assumptions about human nature that undergirded Richmond's thinking cannot be detailed further here, she regarded articulating such assumptions as a necessary part of setting forth her approach to casework.

Richmond's research was an influential, enduring contribution to social work knowledge. She was awarded an honorary Master of Arts by Smith College School for Social Work, at which time her work was praised as having provided "the scientific basis of a new profession" (cited in Drew, 1983, p. 41). More than thirty years later, Charlotte Towle hailed Richmond's work as a landmark and said that her work continued to be a foundation that caseworkers used in their practice (1958, p. 2). Some of the principles that Richmond used to generate research can still be helpful to social workers today. In particular, Richmond's formulation of nonhierarchical, collaborative roles for researchers and practitioners can provide contemporary social workers with a model for closing the gap between researchers and practitioners. Her work reflects her respect for the practitioners with whom she collaborated. While frankly critiquing what she viewed as mistakes in their work so that others could learn from them, she also elaborated what she learned from them about the elements of helpful, effective casework. Her goal was to produce knowledge that would be useful for social workers in remedying both individual difficulties and large-scale social problems. She recognized that the dialogue that can occur between practitioners and supervisors, and between practitioners and researchers, was indispensable in helping both practitioners and researchers to become aware of their assumptions and to test them. She incorporated that dialogue in her research process to improve both practice and research. Finally, Richmond made significant contributions by studying caseworker–client interactions as they occurred naturally rather than by imposing irrelevant beliefs about research on the casework process.

Social workers in settlement houses and the charity organization societies sought to establish the profession of social work (American Association of Social Workers, 1929/1931). Bias against women was one of their biggest obstacles. Abraham Flexner's 1915 address at the National Conference of Charities and Corrections is one example of the opposition they faced. Flexner, one of the leaders in organizing the medical profession, claimed in his address that the field of social work did not have the characteristics of a profession, such as a knowledge base. Many historians of the social work profession speak positively of Flexner, mistakenly claiming that Flexner stimulated social workers to develop a knowledge base (Austin, 1983; Briar & Miller, 1971; Ehrenreich, 1985; M. Fraser et al., 1991; Trattner, 1989; Wagner, 1986).[32] However, Flexner's comments were incorrect, because, as noted previously, social workers had been developing both their knowledge base and professional training schools for several years before Flexner's 1915 address. In addition, those historians overlooked the fact that Flexner himself twice admitted that he had such a "distinctly limited" familiarity with the field of social work and its research that perhaps his comments were unfounded (1915, p. 576).

Finally, historians who assert that Flexner's comments were respected by leading social workers ignore the comments of those social workers who recognized that Flexner's remarks were both unscholarly and served political aims. Flexner's views about the primarily female professions of nursing and social work reflect the misogynist emphasis on the subordination of women, especially the denigration of women's intellectual abilities. For example, when speaking about nursing (another group gaining professional status that he claimed was not a profession), Flexner said that the trained nurse

> may be described as another arm to the physician or surgeon . . . it is the physician who observes, reflects, and decides. The trained nurse plays into his hands; carries out his orders; summons him like a sentinel in fresh emergencies; subordinates loyally her intelligence to his theory, to his policy, and is effective in precise proportion to her ability thus to second his efforts. Can an activity of this secondary nature be deemed a profession? (1915, p. 583)

Flexner compared social workers to nurses and said that social workers also did not exercise informed professional judgment. In her characteristically ironic and incisive style, Mary Richmond said that many social workers recognized that Flexner's comments were specious. In an address she presented in 1917 at the National Conference of Social Work, she acknowledged that although at times social workers might appear to be simply making referrals rather than exercising informed professional judgment and analysis,

> as we listened to Mr. Flexner we were more or less aware that quietly and behind his back, apparently, there was developing a skill quite different in method and in aim from the work that he described. We were not all behaving like the telephone girl at the switchboard who pulls out one plug and pushes in another; many of our social agencies were something better than animated clearing-houses, we felt. In fact, the distinguishing marks of their work were, first, skill in discovering the social relationships by which a given personality had been shaped; second, ability to get at the central core of difficulty in these relationships; and third, power to utilize the direct action of mind upon mind in their adjustment. (1930, p. 399)

In addition to serving misogynist political aims, Flexner's critical comments about the field of social work served his own explicit desire to moderate social workers' reform initiatives. By 1915, when he gave his address, the work of the settlement house communities, especially the Hull House community, had begun to influence social policy at the national level through labor reforms and the contributions of the Children's Bureau. Yet from Flexner's perspective, social workers were "too self-confident." As a result, he claimed,

> social work has suffered . . . [from] excessive facility in speech and in action. Let us suppose for a moment that our reflection on the differences between the accepted professions and social work reminds the social worker at crucial moments that he is, as social worker, not so much an expert himself as the mediator whose concern is to summon the

expert: will not his observation be calmer, his utterance more restrained, be the difficulty he encounters economic, educational, or sanitary? He will, I mean, be conscious of his dependence, and this consciousness will tend to induce caution, thoroughness, and moderation. For if social work is not definite enough to be called a profession, the social worker will at least be less cock-sure than the professional man whom he calls in. Is it not possible that part of the vast army of reaction is made up of those needlessly terrified by the occasionally reckless—and perhaps somewhat baseless—confidence of the reformer? If so, failure to realize the limitations of social work from the professional point of view is not without practical consequences. (Flexner, 1915, p. 588)

Edith Abbott responded politely to Flexner's comments at the convention, but she concluded firmly that the field of social work was a profession (1915). In a 1931 paper, Abbott, who was then dean of the School of Social Service Administration at the University of Chicago, advanced ideas about social work knowledge that controverted Flexner's fallacious assertions. Whereas Flexner had claimed that the knowledge social workers generated was not scientific, Abbott argued that standards of scientific research were not incompatible with the social work profession's commitment to involvement with clients as well as to large-scale social change. She quoted Flexner's statement that the humanitarian involvement of physicians with their patients was not only compatible with but necessary for the development of scientific knowledge in professions such as medicine. She described how disagreements had developed between those social scientists who pursued forms of social treatment and reform and those who did not. She noted that those who eschewed social change tended to claim that the field of social work was not a science but simply a collection of change "techniques," to which she retorted:

It is true that some of our social scientists, courageous as you might expect them to be, are a little afraid of us, and a timid few insist that we cannot be scientific because we are trying to find a remedy for the evils with which society has to deal. But if it is unscientific to do this, to follow diagnosis by curative treatment, then we should be quite willing to be called by another name. We ought not, however, to fail to remind our friends that if finding a remedy is unscientific, then the great physicians must also be excluded from the scientific ranks. (1931, pp. 71–72)

Psychiatric Social Work

Most historical accounts of the development of psychiatric social work have been based on the misconception that social work practice was "deluged" with psychodynamic theory during the period between the First and Second World Wars. Heineman Pieper corrected this misconception when she investigated the extent to which psychodynamic theory informed practice in a representative Midwestern child-placing agency (Field [Heineman Pieper], 1979, 1980). Her findings "directly contradicted the consensus among historians of the field of social work and primary source authors that a 'psychiatric deluge' inundated casework practice during World War I and had thoroughly transformed it by 1930" (Field [Heineman Pieper], 1979, p. 203). Although psychodynamic theory did indeed pervade the social work literature during that period, Heineman Pieper's analysis of the casework and personnel records of the Illinois Children's Home and Aid Society revealed that, before 1938 ICH&A administrators and supervisors neither expected workers to possess psychodynamic skills nor were themselves psychodynamically oriented. Although administrative and supervisory staff adopted an increasingly psychodynamic approach in the 1940's and attempted to require the line staff to follow suit, the transition occurred as a painful, slow, creaky process of wresting workers away from longstanding habits of practice rather than as a sudden "deluge." Even when repeated evaluations made clear that their jobs depended on their ability to adopt the new approach, many workers could not change and had to be let go. (Field [Heineman Pieper], 1979, p. 202)

Even as late as 1949, the agency practitioners had not integrated psychodynamic theory into their practice. Therefore, in the context of the profession as a whole, the psychiatric social work research community described below can be regarded as a relatively small but prolific group of practitioner–researchers.

In the settlement houses and charity organization societies, social workers directed both practice and research. By contrast, the psychiatric social work research community developed in an interdisciplinary context in which psychiatrists and psychologists often played leading roles. William Healey, a psychiatrist, taught the first course with psychiatric content at the Chicago School of Civics and Philanthropy in 1908. As the profession increasingly adopted psychodynamic theory, psychiatrists and psychoanalysts such as Marion Kenworthy and Otto Rank taught courses in schools of social work. One of the first casebooks used to teach psychiatric social work was coauthored by E. E. Southard, a psychiatrist (who had been a student of William James, per Borenzweig, 1971), and Mary Jarrett, one of the first psychiatric social workers (Southard & Jarrett, 1922; see also Lee & Kenworthy, 1929).

The psychiatric social work community developed in response to a nationwide, multidisciplinary effort to improve mental health care, which was spurred on by leaders such as Clifford Beers, Julia Lathrop, Jessie Taft, and William Healey (Addams, 1935a, 1935b; Deutsch, 1937). Mary Jarrett described the psychiatric social workers' definition of their role in the new movement: "We would claim to have created the part that the social worker is to play in the mental hygiene movement and to have given it a name—psychiatric social work" (Southard & Jarrett, 1922, p. 521). In 1910, Jarrett, who was the director of the social services department at the Boston Psychopathic Hospital, founded a group to develop principles of psychiatric social work.[33] The group's members collaborated with a "half a dozen" psychiatric social workers in New York, Baltimore, and Chicago, including Jessie Taft; they rapidly began to explore applications of psychoanalytic theory to social work practice (Lubove, 1965; V. Robinson, 1962, p. 57). During World War I, physicians increasingly recognized that social workers could help veterans of war trauma to readjust to civilian life (Southard & Jarrett, 1922, p. 521). In 1918, the National Committee on Mental Health funded courses at Smith College to train social workers to treat returning soldiers; it subsequently provided some financial support for the Smith College School for Social Work.

The psychiatric social work community expanded as students were trained in the new psychiatric ideas (Jarrett, 1927). The membership of the American Association of Psychiatric Social Workers grew from 36 members in 1915 to 216 members in 1937. Most psychiatric social workers were employed in child guidance clinics and mental hygiene clinics, but some worked as supervisors and caseworkers in child welfare agencies. "In 1936 well over half the graduates who prepared for psychiatric social work entered the family and child welfare fields" (L. French, 1940, p. 106).

In 1926 Jessie Taft regarded the birth of the psychiatric social work part of the mental hygiene movement as an "epoch-making event" (Taft cited in V. Robinson, 1962, p. 56). Taft was strongly influenced by the Hull House community during her doctoral studies at the University of Chicago. In her dissertation research, she addressed the discriminatory practices that inhibited women's intellectual fulfillment in education and the workplace, and she described how a transformation in individual self-understanding was a necessary part of large-scale social reforms (Taft, 1915, p. 57). After receiving her doctorate, Taft moved to New York City, where she was an assistant superintendent at the New York State Reformatory for Women. She then began clinical practice in a child guidance clinic, first in New York, then in Philadelphia, where she applied new insights from psychodynamic theory to her clinical research and practice. Taft and other psychiatric social workers regarded the National Conference of Charities and Correction in Atlantic City in 1919 as the occasion when other social workers began to notice the work of the psychiatric social workers: "Social workers crowded a hall to overflowing to hear Mary Jarrett, Jessie Taft, Dr. Spaulding, and Dr. Glueck talk on the psychiatric worker and her preparation" (V. Robinson, 1930/1934, p. 54). Social workers debated whether psychiatric social work was a specialty within the profession or whether psychiatric principles were, as Jarrett argued, a conceptual basis for all social work practice (Jarrett, 1919).

Although some historians portrayed psychiatric social workers as an "elite" (Ehrenreich, 1985; see also Lubove, 1965), the facts about the working conditions of the psychiatric social workers do not support such a view. Even as late as 1937, long after the mental hygiene movement began, the ratio of patients per psychiatric social worker in state mental hospitals ranged from 775 to 1,600 patients to one worker; many mental hospitals required that the psychiatric social workers reside where they were employed (L. French, 1940). The salaries for psychiatric social workers did not differ from the salaries of social workers in family and child welfare agencies. Mary Jarrett expressed concern that most psychiatric social workers were so overburdened by high case loads that it was very difficult for them to conduct research (1925). During the Depression, psychiatric social workers suffered salary decreases as the budgets of many child guidance and mental hygiene agencies were cut (L. French, 1940).

The psychiatric social workers' adoption of psychodynamic theory can be understood in the light of a developmental process that Kuhn observed in other sciences: When scientists begin to solve one set of problems, they then notice other sets of problems (Kuhn, 1970). Many of the leading psychiatric social workers increasingly recognized that although they could provide environmental resources to their clients, some clients would not use those resources. They recognized that the resource provision that was a major feature of practice models in charity organization societies and settlement houses was necessary but not sufficient help for some clients. The social workers wanted to understand how to help people with apparently irrational, self-defeating patterns of behavior (Garrett, 1949; V. Robinson, 1930/1934, 1962). Psychodynamic theory provided an explanation for why clients might not use resources; it also offered a conceptual framework for developing ways to help people to change. In her reminiscences, Bertha Reynolds commented:

> [W]e learned about the working of the subconscious, and many things in everyday life became clear to us. We saw fears displaced from childhood, jealousy displaced from other persons, hostility disguised as solicitude, desire as fear, and wish as certainty. No wonder we felt that we had been fooled by appearances all our lives and that we now had the key to wisdom in human relations. (quoted in Field [Heineman Pieper], 1979, p. 29)

Charlotte Towle expressed the views of many practitioner–researchers when she said that psychodynamic theory was humanizing and gave social workers' research scientific validity (Towle, 1958; see also Perlman, 1957; Reynolds, 1965; Taft cited in V. Robinson, 1962).

Annette Garrett (1949) described how at first psychiatric social workers had circumscribed responsibilities, consisting largely of responding to psychiatrists' requests. Initially, psychiatric social workers who worked in child guidance clinics arranged for the child's parents to bring the child to appointments with the psychiatrist. Psychiatric social workers, however, soon expanded their role. Because they also wanted to provide therapeutic help for the parents, they began to develop treatment principles (Lee & Kenworthy, 1929). Because social workers emphasized family and community relationships, they had "a total picture of the family constellation" and thus conceptualized the individual's needs and strengths within a broader social context (Garrett, 1949, p. 226). Their approaches to treatment ranged from attitude therapy (following the psychiatrist David Levy) to relationship therapy (the hallmark of the functionalist approach) (Lowry, 1939; V. Robinson, 1930/1934).

Some historians mistakenly characterized the psychiatric social workers as ignoring the importance of evaluating and improving practice (Briar & Miller, 1971). However, the psychiatric social work researchers reported that

> the causes of failure to respond to treatment, and the concentration upon techniques for handling such resistance, became of absorbing interest. Progress is revealed in increased understanding of causes for such resistance, definite adaptations in procedure, and a changing philosophy of the relationship between client and worker. (L. French, 1940, p. 212)

Psychiatric social workers developed their knowledge in two primary phases. First, during the 1920s, they focused on interview techniques, as "the prevailing belief seemed to be that results could be obtained with these baffling situations if only the worker could develop sufficient skill in changing attitudes," and workers studied the interviews with a focus on finding different approaches (L. French,

1940, p. 213). Then, with the contributions of the functionalist theorists* in the 1930s, they began to focus on "the patient's emotional responses in his relationships" (L. French, 1940, pp. 212–213; see also Aptekar, 1941; Taft, 1937).

Many psychiatric social workers regarded their research as a scientific approach to developing new insights into clinical practice (V. Robinson, 1930/1934; Taft, 1937; Towle, 1941b). They reconceptualized terms traditionally associated with social and behavioral science, such as "objectivity" and "bias." For example, Virginia Robinson—who synthesized many of the new psychiatric ideas in her influential dissertation research, *A Changing Psychology in Social Casework* (1930/1934) and who became one of the most prominent theorists of the functionalist school of casework practice—said that objectivity was an ideal toward which the worker should strive. She defined *objectivity* as "detachment from a personal stake in the client's problem. The worker does not have to take over the problem but can let the other solve it in his own way and time" (1930/1934, p. 159). It was extremely difficult for social workers to integrate psychodynamic theory into their clinical practice and research (Field [Heineman Pieper], 1979, 1980); some social workers sought psychoanalytic help in an effort to attain the new scientific ideals, such as the "objectivity" that Robinson described (1930/1934, p. 160).

Psychiatric social workers wanted their research to reflect each client's uniqueness and the complexity of clients' relationships with the caseworker and with others. They needed research designs that would allow for individual variations and afford a comprehensive view of the casework process, both for developing practice theories and for educational purposes. Following in the tradition of Mary Richmond as well as of Freud and dynamically oriented psychiatrists, psychiatric social workers often conducted qualitative case studies. Fourteen percent of the social work journal articles from the 1920s surveyed for this study were qualitative case studies (as shown later, in Table 2–2). In 1918, Jessie Taft presented an intensive case study at the first Smith College courses in psychiatric social work (V. Robinson, 1962). Mary Jarrett emphasized that some researchers mistakenly held a narrow view of experimentation, one confined to the laboratory; she claimed that a qualitative single case study also constituted an experiment and was a promising way to advance knowledge in psychiatric social work (Southard & Jarrett, 1922). Researchers compiled the case studies into larger-scale qualitative studies. The larger-scale analyses advanced treatment techniques for clients suffering from psychiatric disorders such as dementia praecox (later called *schizophrenia*) and for clients who manifested particular social problems such as delinquency (Odencrantz, 1929).

Editor's Note: The functionalist theorists drew from Rank's psychology to elaborate an approach to social work treatment that Jessie Taft termed "relationship therapy." Following is one of Taft's initial descriptions of "relationship therapy": "An opportunity to experience more completely than is ordinarily possible the direction, depth, and ambivalence of the impulses which relate the self to the other, to outer reality, and to discover first-hand the possibility of their organization into an autonomous, creative will." (1933/1962, pp. 288–289)

In chronicling the profession's focus during the 1920s, some historians have described social workers as turning away from social reform, claiming that the adoption of psychodynamic theory was a major reason for that shift (Ehrenreich, 1985).[34] For example, Floyd Matson wrote that "possibly the most crucial factor contributing to the individualist orientation of social casework in the 1920s was the influence of Freudian psychology" (cited by Field [Heineman Pieper] when she criticized his conclusion, 1979, pp. 19–20). Others accused those psychiatric social workers who adopted psychodynamic theory of betraying their commitment to the poor and disadvantaged (Richan & Mendlesohn, 1973). There are several errors in these versions of the history of the field of social work. First, as Heineman Pieper pointed out, valid conclusions about social work *practice* cannot be drawn from surveying only the social work *literature* (Field [Heineman Pieper], 1979, 1980). Most historians who concluded that psychodynamic theory led practitioners to withdraw from advocacy for social reform surveyed the social work literature and did not investigate casework practice. Practitioners adopted psychodynamic theory only with great difficulty and quite unevenly, so that, even as late as 1949, many practitioners in the agency Heineman Pieper surveyed still had not integrated psychodynamic theory. Accordingly, psychodynamic theory cannot be regarded as an influence that pulled social workers away from social reform. Moreover, the view that the psychiatric social workers who adopted psychodynamic theory abandoned the disadvantaged relies on the assumption that those clients who suffer from mental disorders are not themselves disadvantaged and in need of both advocacy and better mental health care. In fact, the mental hygiene movement was born in part because at the turn of the century treatment conditions for the mentally ill (especially children) were woefully inadequate and often inhumane (Addams, 1935a, 1935b; Grob, 1983; D. Rothman, 1971). Psychiatric social workers worked to humanize and improve the quality of care provided to those who sought outpatient care as well as psychiatric inpatients.

Finally, the assumption that social workers' diminished capacity to accomplish social reform was caused primarily by influences within the profession (e.g., the theories the profession's leaders espoused) reflects a bias against recognizing the impact of nationwide political forces. Examination of the wider social context during the 1920s indicates the nation turned against social reform efforts (Chambers, 1963/1980). When the United States entered World War I and the country became more aggressively militant, Jane Addams, who previously had been extremely influential and respected, was attacked for her pacifist views and activities; many viewed her as a traitor (A. F. Davis, 1973). The "woman movement," which often had been a springboard for social reforms other than women's suffrage, began to unravel after women obtained the vote, for reasons that feminist historians are still exploring (S. Evans, 1989; R. Rosenberg, 1982). After 1919, politicians warned Americans about the threat of Bolshevism, and government employers fired individuals suspected of communism (Schlesinger, 1956, p. 360; Wexler, 1984). Archibald Stevenson, a New York lawyer employed by the military intelligence division of the War Department, testified before a Senate subcommittee and named sixty-two people who he believed espoused dangerous and destructive political views and who had been under government surveillance for some time. The people on the list included most of the social reformers and pacifists of the time, including Jane Addams and Lillian Wald. Addams, as well as Paul Kellogg and many other social workers, protested both the charges and the surveillance.[35] The Secretary of War eventually denounced the surveillance, but Stevenson's actions voiced the opinions of many and represented the increasingly conservative and oppressive climate of the country (Chambers, 1963/1980; A. F. Davis, 1973, p. 252; Wexler, 1984). During the 1920s, national income and corporate profits boomed, but farm income and housing construction were depressed; social inequalities increased as the wealthiest individuals amassed greater fortunes, whereas disposable per capita income rose only slightly. Despite the increased prosperity of the wealthy, pervasive suspicion of social reform movements made it more difficult for settlement houses and other reform efforts to obtain funding (Chambers, 1963/1980).

The writings of psychiatric social workers show that many did not repudiate social reform (Lee, 1935/1937b; Lowry, 1939). Some of the leading psychiatric social workers, such as Bertha Reynolds, espoused controversial and radical political views. Others regarded individual change as one enduring path toward social change (V. Robinson, 1930/1934; Taft, 1933/1962). Helen Harris Perlman said that when psychiatric social workers emphasized values such as client self-determination, they saw themselves as combating the erosion of civil liberties in the United States as well as the atrocities perpetrated under Nazism during the 1930s and 1940s (Perlman, 1989). Further, the psychiatric social workers' emphasis on helping increasingly set them apart from other social and behavioral scientists, who had begun to adopt positivist beliefs about social research and who often prioritized gathering "objective" data over helping people. For example, when the historian Kathleen Woodroofe asked Charlotte Towle why the field of social work broke ranks with sociology in the 1920s, Towle offered several explanations. First, she said that social work programs subsumed within departments of economics and social sciences "were not faring well" (Towle, 1958, p. 3). Second, social workers had recognized that some patterns of family life "cut across socio-economic levels and ethnic groups, to produce common problems related to family pattern rather than to economic levels or nationality. This rendered them receptive to Freudian concepts on dynamics of family life" (Towle, 1958, pp. 3–4). Finally,

> social workers found the sociologist's conduct of research incompatible. His approaches to people and his inferences seemed naive. They also seemed ruthless. His disregard for what he did to people while studying them antagonized social workers and his indifference to the problems perceived infuriated social workers. (Towle, 1958, p. 4)

Towle used a fictional sociologist in one of Richard Wright's novels as an example. She said that Wright's portrayal

> typifies many of our experiences in which the social scientist befriended the delinquent boy in order to observe him and sat by, never lifting a wrist to put him in helping hands, while he watched him proceed to the electric chair. The Clifford Shaw group of sociologists sat by and wrote "Jack Roller" accounts and were loath to refer individuals for help lest they interfere with their research findings. Unlike the medical group they separated

study and treatment and did not use social caseworkers to treat individuals in their hour of need. Instead they were focussed on eventually making social ills known in order that broadside program planning might occur. The individual of the moment was not their responsibility even to refer for help. Inevitably social caseworkers saw them as ruthless and perceived that in hobnobbing with individuals to study them, they were exploiting them and often affording a corruptible relationship to those who confided in them. (Towle, 1958, p. 4)

As Towle's comments illustrate, because psychiatric social workers prized helping people over treating them as objects for study, the workers allied themselves with physicians' therapeutic aims. Further, many psychiatrists clearly were supportive and encouraged psychiatric social workers' clinical practice and research (Hale, 1971). For example, George Stevenson, the medical director of the National Committee for Mental Hygiene, introduced Lois French's book *Psychiatric Social Work* with the comments, "Almost every psychiatrist can recall patients whose difficulties might have been better understood and relieved if the circumstances of their daily lives at home and at work could have been studied" (1940, p. ix). He defined the purview of the psychiatric social worker generously as "the study and interpretation of community conditions and the reactions of an individual to them . . . the halting of the progress of mental disease . . . ensuring the return of sick people to an effective and satisfying place in society, and . . . the forestalling of the breakdown itself" (1940, p. x). His standpoint was not territorial: "the fact that such aims are shared by other groups does not alter the particular contribution or opportunity of psychiatric social work" (1940, p. xi).

The psychiatric social workers' alliance with physicians presented some disadvantages, however. The writings of psychiatric social workers often include the recognition that, especially initially, psychiatrists diagnosed all patients, formulated treatment plans, and treated the "more difficult" cases (Odencrantz, 1929). In research projects conducted by psychiatric social workers, physicians often directed the research (Odencrantz, 1929). The hierarchical role structure distinguished psychiatric social workers from social workers in the charity organization societies and settlement houses, who directed their own practice and research. Some psychiatric social workers recognized the value of autonomous practice and the education of caseworkers by caseworkers (Garrett, 1949). Even so, the role of psychiatric social workers often was defined as subservience to psychiatrists. The comments of an influential psychiatrist, Jacob Kasanin, exemplify the discriminatory attitude of some physicians toward psychiatric social workers:

The psychiatrist is quite suspicious about the trend toward therapy in social work because he wonders whether psychotherapy is not just another panacea for solving human ills. Social work, not being an independent discipline and being essentially a woman's profession, has tended to look for some remedy for its problems. At one time it was legislation, then it was social reform, then it was education, then it was medicine itself, and now it is psychiatry. No wonder psychiatry is suspicious of this surrender which, complete as it may seem, has no earmarks of permanency—it is too rapid, too sweeping, and perhaps too emotional. (1935, p. 37)

Such an overt expression of bias was apparently not uncommon at the time, as Kasanin's comments were published in *The Family*.

The psychiatric social workers also differed from the other research communities in their beliefs about clinical practice and research. The researchers in the charity organization societies and settlement houses regarded their research as inherently scientific. By contrast, some psychiatric social workers adopted positivist beliefs about science and then took the extreme position that the field of social work could not be a science but only an art (Witmer, 1930, 1943). To illustrate, when Edith Abbott described the field of social work as a science, Helen Witmer, director of research at Smith College School for Social Work and editor of *Smith College Studies in Social Work*, stated in the editorial to the first issue of that journal that social workers could use scientific knowledge but that fundamentally social workers were artists rather than scientists and that social work practice was an art, not a science (Witmer, 1930). Witmer cited the British positivist Alfred North Whitehead as an influence on her beliefs about scientific research.[36] Similarly, Maurice Karpf (1931) concluded his survey of social work research and practice by saying that social work knowledge was "unscientific." He drew his beliefs about science from the positivist philosophers Morris Cohen and Ernest Nagel.[37] Why, after developing a knowledge base for the practice of psychiatric social work, did some psychiatric social workers regard their work as an art rather than a science? Perhaps their use of that label reflected the acceptance of an inferior position in relation to psychiatry, which was viewed as scientific. Further, Freud's views influenced the psychiatric social workers. Freud had been very concerned with positivist ideals, and the assumptions of positivism pervaded psychoanalytic theory (S. Freud, 1895/1953–1974; Gay, 1988; Pieper & Pieper, 1990). Finally, the psychiatric social workers did not explicitly critique the misogyny in Freud's theories (L. Gordon, 1989), and Freud's derogatory opinions about women's intellectual abilities may have compromised the esteem with which many psychoanalytically trained social workers regarded a woman's pursuit of intellectual interests through research.[38]

Shared Tenets of All Three Approaches

Although the social workers in the settlement houses, charity organization societies, and psychiatric settings who developed approaches to social work research had many distinctive ideas about social work knowledge, they also shared the following beliefs about generating social work knowledge:

1. Methodological pluralism;
2. A nonrestrictive approach to the variables that could be studied scientifically;
3. Social work research actualizes values.

Methodological Pluralism

All three communities implemented diverse research designs without prescribing any one as inherently superior to the others for testing social work theories. Clyde

White quoted Karl Pearson and said that anyone "'who classifies facts of any kind whatever, who sees their mutual relations and describes their sequences, is applying the scientific method'" (R. C. White, 1930, p. 261). There were methodologically oriented debates, as Clyde White described in 1930:

> A discussion, bordering on controversy, has for a number of years been going on between those who believe in the case study method and those who believe in the statistical method in social research. It is important for the future of social research that the two methods be clearly understood. (p. 259)

White concluded, however, that both designs were equally useful for generating scientific social work knowledge. His conclusion was accepted by many social workers (American Association of Social Workers, 1929/1931; Hurlin, 1941), as is illustrated by Clague's 1935 description of social work research in the *Social Work Year Book:*

> The most striking development of recent years has been the rapid increase in the use of statistical methods, but statisticians themselves would be the last to insist that theirs is the only method of research. Clinical observation—the detailed analysis of the individual case—can be just as truly research as the statistical questionnaire covering 10,000 cases. (p. 422)

Even the minority who claimed that the field of social work was not scientific adopted John Dewey's broad definition of a social science experiment (Jarrett, 1925; Karpf, 1931). Dewey explicitly critiqued logical positivist beliefs about science and regarded an "experiment" as characterized primarily by the scientist's formulation of hypotheses and observations of facts in support of or contrary to the hypotheses. His definition was sufficiently broad that he considered social policies to be a form of experiment. For example, he said that social welfare policies could be formulated with explicit hypotheses and the policies' consequences could be carefully observed (Dewey, 1938, p. 509). Like Dewey, the early social workers believed they could implement a variety of research design heuristics as experiments to test social work theories.

A Nonrestrictive Approach to the Variables that Could Be Studied Scientifically

None of the communities endorsed a restrictive stance toward the variables that could be examined to generate scientific knowledge.[39] Instead, researchers emphasized that to advance social work knowledge, social workers needed to obtain data using their own introspective experience as well as the client–worker relationship and larger-scale social problems (American Association of Social Workers, 1929/1931; Breckinridge, 1931). The "Report of the Milford Conference," an extremely influential and comprehensive analysis produced by several leading social workers who met annually from 1923 to 1928, stated:

> The future growth of social case work is in large measure dependent upon its developing a scientific character. Its scientific character will be the result in part of a scientific attitude in social case workers towards their own problems and in part of increasingly scien-

tific adaptations from the subject matter of other sciences. (American Association of Social Workers, 1929/1931, p. 27)

Many of the early social workers (including Richmond, Robinson, and Addams) were familiar with behaviorism's atomistic, overly reductionistic approach to studying humans (e.g., Watson, 1913), but they did not adopt behaviorist assumptions.[40] The early social workers paid detailed attention to clinical interactions, as described in interview process recordings, to understand both how to approach the casework relationship and how to help individuals to change during casework treatment. As Virginia Robinson said in describing the history of theories of casework,

> This refusal to accept classifications prematurely was the saving grace of social case work in that it preserved its identification with the moving changing flow of its human living material until that content became rich enough to risk some tentative classifications. (1930/1934, p. 64)

Social Work Research Actualizes Values

In the views of the leading early social workers, scientific research aimed to find workable solutions to very specific problems facing individuals or communities (E. Abbott, 1931; Breckinridge, 1931; Lee, 1935/1937c). These social workers regarded research as actualizing values about how the researcher should relate with clients and also as a way to advance large-scale social reforms (Breckinridge, 1931; Richmond, 1922; Taft, 1937). Clients as well as practitioners defined the problems that researchers addressed. Settlers such as Jane Addams turned to their neighbors to understand what problems were most important to investigate. Breckinridge summarized the role of research in 1931:

> Research activities in the program of the family welfare agency or of any social agency should, in my opinion, be judged with reference to the light thrown on five possible questions: First, who are our clients and how can we better serve them? Second, how can wise decisions in the development of the agency itself be reached? Third, what suggestions as to services of which the agency stands in need, but cannot itself supply, are to be obtained? Fourth, what light can be thrown on general community organization? Fifth, what possible contribution to programs of fundamental social readjustment can be hoped for from them? (p. 223)

Breckinridge's comments also illustrate how the early social workers conceptualized the relationships between practitioners and researchers as collaborative. In her conclusion she emphasized, "the research agency should be the servant of the family welfare society" (Breckinridge, 1931, p. 231). Similarly, Edith Abbott believed that social work research was, by definition, designed to be relevant to the needs of practitioners and that "every social worker ought to be a research worker" (as also was recommended by the American Association of Social Workers, 1929/1931, and Breckinridge, 1931). Researchers such as Mary Richmond asked practitioners to evaluate the utility and validity of their research.

In summary, as of 1929, most social workers concurred with Edith Abbott's assertion that the field of social work, with its commitment to social reform, was a new science (American Association of Social Workers, 1929/1931). In the other social and behavioral sciences, however, the alliance between social research and the value of social reform was short-lived. The split that occurred in the field of social work in the 1950s was prefigured by a split in sociology in the late 1920s.[41] To illustrate, William Ogburn, who joined the University of Chicago department of sociology in 1928, concluded his presidential address to the American Sociological Society with these chilling remarks:

> Sociology as a science is not interested in making the world a better place in which to live, in encouraging beliefs, or in spreading information, in dispensing news, in setting impressions of life, in leading multitudes, or in guiding the ship of state. Science is interested directly in one thing only, to wit, discovery of new knowledge. (quoted in Manicas, 1987, p. 226)

The Impact of the Depression and the New Deal Programs, 1929 to 1948

The Depression and the accompanying social unrest increased public awareness of the long-standing problems of poverty and economic inequality. The moralistic censure with which many Americans had traditionally responded to economically disadvantaged people was mitigated somewhat as people found themselves, their friends, and their neighbors suddenly among the poor. The Hull House social reformers as well as other social workers had advocated more federal responsibility for ensuring an adequate standard of living for all, and their ideas influenced the new legislation. Roosevelt's secretary of labor, Frances Perkins, the first woman cabinet member, had been a resident of Hull House. Harry Hopkins, a social worker, was in charge of the Federal Emergency Relief Administration under the First New Deal (McJimsey, 1987); other social workers, such as Josephine Chapin Brown, worked with him (Martinez-Brawley, 1987). Eleanor Roosevelt was strongly influenced by her work with Lillian Wald, who founded and directed the Henry Street "visiting nurses" settlement in New York City (Schlesinger, 1956; Wald, 1915).

Because the New Deal programs called for a tremendous expansion of social services, the demand for social workers quickly exceeded the supply of trained workers. It was a time of great challenge and growth for the young profession. The early social workers' advocacy for federal financial assistance and health-care programs began to be actualized in the New Deal, and the influx of public interest and support had an electrifying effect on the profession's leaders:

> Those of us who are here, even the new and young members of our group, have had the rare opportunity such as comes to a profession about once in any generation, of seeing great steps being taken in a progressively forward direction and as yet no sign that we must go backward. The national calamity has increased the need for social workers and the public understanding of their work; it has convinced many formerly half-hearted and doubting friends of public social work of the need of men and women with the best professional training and disciplined intelligence in this field. (E. Abbott, 1930–1933, pp. 21–22)[42]

Even before the worst of the Depression, the social work staffs of the juvenile courts, which by 1930 existed in every city of 1,000 or more people, were overloaded (Oppenheimer, 1930, p. 18). In 1935 there were 5,296 registered students in the schools of social work—880 men and 4,416 women; in 1936 there were 30 schools in the Association for Schools of Social Work. However, "these are few, compared with the increased personnel recently called for by the emergency relief service" (Breckinridge, 1936, p. 447; see also Lee, 1935/1937c). In addition to expanding their full-time degree programs, schools of social work provided part-time supplementary classes for the new and often untrained caseworkers hired by the overtaxed agencies (E. Abbott, 1930–1933; Lee, 1935/1937c). To illustrate, Edith Abbott wrote to the president of the University of Chicago, "The depression greatly increased the demands on social workers and the funds of the social agencies of Chicago were not adequate to meet the needs. At the request of the Council of Social Agencies the School offered four different courses for women who might give volunteer assistance during the emergency" (Abbott, 1930–1933, p. 10). To compensate for the shortage of trained social workers, public relief agencies sent 1,133 Federal Emergency Relief Administration workers to social work schools.[43] Private social work agencies closed as the business leaders who had provided funds could no longer support them; new public agencies hired the experienced family welfare and psychiatric social workers in supervisory positions. The Depression and New Deal programs led to another change in the social work profession, which Charlotte Towle described: "Social caseworkers became divided in two groups and social casework split into two levels of operation. Roughly, the focus was on attending to the external social circumstances of man versus attending to his inner psychological needs and problems. Social services versus psychotherapy emerged" (1958, p. 5).

The New Deal did not resolve pervasive inequalities between women and men or among racial, ethnic, and class groups. Because they were discriminatory, the New Deal programs actively inhibited women's advances in employment (Rossiter, 1982; Strom, 1983). For example, "the 1933 National Industrial Recovery Act (NIRA) minimum wage codes sanctioned lower pay rates for women workers than for men in the same occupations" (Strom, 1983, p. 361). Women were excluded from the first Civilian Conservation Corps camps; when they were included later, they were paid one half of what men were paid. In public perceptions, the lack of employment opportunities for men was often attributed to increased numbers of women working (Strom, 1983). Discrimination against women within the social work profession had always been reflected in ranking and salary scales, but by the late 1930s, the profession's founders' advances towards equality had seriously eroded (Chambers, 1986b).[44]

Some African-Americans emphasized that the New Deal was better than previous conditions. The *Baltimore Afro-American* testified that although "relief and WPA [Works Progress Administration] are not ideal, they are better than the Hoover bread lines and they'll have to do until the real thing comes along" (cited in Wolters, 1975, p. 210). However, many African-American leaders, such as Francis Rivers, criticized the New Deal policies; they predicted that reliance on relief could lead to "political and economic serfdom," and that without full integration in employment, there would be no lasting solution to the economic plight of African-Americans (Rivers cited in Wolters, 1975, p. 210). Although the public housing and work programs diminished some of the problems created by the Depression, as Wye noted, "they also contributed to the preservation of perhaps the two salient components which combine to produce a caste-like Negro social structure—residential segregation and a distinctly racial occupational pattern" (1972, p. 639). Racial prejudice continued to infuse every profession and most academic institutions, including the field of social work (Blackwell, 1981), and continued to bias social research as well (Billingsley, 1970; O'Reilly, 1969).

In brief, the New Deal was aimed at the disadvantaged whose circumstances, although difficult, had not shorn them of their capacity to use opportunities for rehabilitation through the New Deal employment or income maintenance programs. However, the difficulties of whole segments of the population were not addressed under the New Deal. Many continued to suffer discrimination and disenfranchisement, including members of ethnic minority groups, women, and those who, as a result of handicaps or protracted disadvantage, required more sustained and individualized rehabilitative support than the New Deal provided.

As the inadequacies of the New Deal became more apparent, social workers debated about how the profession should respond to continuing social inequalities (E. Abbott, 1930–1933; Lee, 1935/1937b; Van Kleeck, 1934). In 1940, Edith Abbott criticized Roosevelt for not keeping his promises to help all the poor and described the inadequacies of the New Deal programs. According to the American Public Welfare Association, one million people were still on the WPA lists, and many local communities "have refused to accept any responsibility for the men who are able to work, and there has been a cruel community indifference regarding the needs of the families of these men" (Abbott, 1940, p. 439). Abbott described how some WPA programs had used relief workers in place of regular municipal workers if funds were not available for the regular workers. In effect, then, the WPA displaced people from jobs: "this means that a method of unemployment relief has been used to relieve the city budget by putting their regular workers on relief lists and then pretending to be charitable by requiring them to work for relief. This is surely the finest kind of irony" (1940, p. 441). In an address she delivered at the 1940 National Conference of Social Work in Grand Rapids, Michigan, Abbott described her proposals for more extensive federal responsibility to ensure adequate income for all the economically disadvantaged. When she made those recommendations at the American Public Welfare Conference, social workers not only voted her down but she was "shouted down" (1940, p. 452); at the Public Assistance Committee of the White House Conference, she again was voted down. Finally, the American Association of Social Workers agreed to consider her proposal.

In addition to researchers and educators such as Edith Abbott, a new group of practitioners, called the rank and file movement, advocated a more adequate remedy for massive social inequalities. Most of the members of the rank and file movement lacked a formal social work education and had been hired to implement the new public welfare programs, although many, in New York City especially, were highly trained professionals (Chambers, personal communication, April 28, 1992). They founded the journal *Social Work Today* to advance "an interest in the fundamental reorganization society must undergo to provide security for all and to support labor's struggle for a greater measure of control as the basic condition for that reorganization" (Reynolds cited in Straussner & Phillips, 1988, p. 113). Other social workers, such as Mary Van Kleeck of the Russell Sage Foundation, criticized the New Deal from the standpoint of the political left. She recommended reform of America's economic structure and emphasized that social workers should ally themselves with the working class rather than accept the government's position that a system of chronic unemployment and relief was inevitable (Van Kleeck, 1934).

The new and overloaded public social service programs dramatically changed the context within which approaches to social work research developed. As Ogburn's comments indicate, positivists in other social and behavioral sciences idealized the view that scientific knowledge should be developed for its own sake and not to solve social problems, but many social workers at the time did not agree: "the administrator in the field of social welfare comes to realize fully that there neither is nor can be such a thing as purely 'theoretical research,' or, as it is often erroneously termed, 'research for research's sake'" (Keith, 1941, p. 328). Some social workers regarded the "research attitude" as a problem-solving process that all practitioners could adopt rather than as a characteristic of a professional subspecialty:

> Every member of our staff [in this example, the Wisconsin Department of Public Welfare], I hope, constantly employs the research attitude in his or her work. More often than not it is the individual member of the staff . . . who raises questions needing solution and, more important, offers the solution . . . every worker in our field, from the visitor to the administrator, to be effective must have a research attitude towards his work. (Keith, 1941, p. 335)

Social workers believed that the aim of research was to yield findings that could be useful to agency administrators as well as to practitioners (Geddes, 1941). Although social work researchers gathered qualitative data and also quantified their data, social workers' use of large-scale analyses with quantified data increased in social work journals during the 1930s (as shown later, in Table 2–2). This increase probably reflects how social researchers sought to compile and systematize the flood of diverse client needs.

In direct contrast to the positivist view that caseworkers' commitment to help clients compromised their capacity to produce scientific knowledge, Charlotte Towle stated:

> The case worker early learns that he gets valid diagnostic material in so far as he is therapeutic in his approach to people. The specialist in social research frequently has not learned this to the same extent as has the case worker. In this area the field of case work has much to offer the field of social research. (1941b, p. 75)

Towle cited William James in support of her emphasis that the caseworker's therapeutic involvement with clients does not inherently compromise the quality of the knowledge the caseworker can generate, "If you want an absolute duffer in an investigation, you must, after all, take the man who has no interest whatever in its results; he is the warranted incapable, the positive fool" (James quoted in Towle, 1941b, p. 74). She recognized that inductive reasoning is inherent in scientific thinking and advised educators to use case studies to help their students look for "the universal elements which permeate the unique whole" (1941b, p. 79; see also Towle, 1954). In response to the argument that the field of social work could not be a science because social workers had to discover answers and act based on incomplete knowledge, Towle said:

> If caseworkers consciously make decisions on the basis of partial knowledge and in accordance with hypotheses that cannot yet be tested adequately, with full awareness of the tentativeness of their thinking and with a readiness to revise thinking and action as the case situation unfolds, then their work is not necessarily unscientific. It may be experimental but scientifically so. Furthermore, this difference would not be acknowledged by many scientists who maintain that valid research does seek answers and that it becomes a futile end in itself when it has no focalized quest. (1941b, p. 74)

Towle defined the "scientific method," which she believed was the basis for research as well as for practice, as a systematic, reflective conceptual process:

> 1) observation and gathering of facts; 2) scrutinizing the facts in the light of certain knowledge; 3) formulation of a tentative hypothesis; 4) testing of the hypothesis through further inquiry and sometimes also through emergent action which has been guided by the initial tentative thinking; 5) formulation of an interpretative or diagnostic statement; 6) action recommended or taken on the basis of the diagnosis which is tested further and revised in accordance with the results of the action; 7) throughout the process a continuous self-appraisal by the worker to discount his own bias. (1948, pp. 318–319; see also Towle, 1954)

Towle's approach differed from the views of some of her contemporaries, who by 1949 had begun to adopt logical positivist beliefs about science (e.g., Maas & Varon, 1949). For example, Towle did not prescribe that quantified measurement was necessary for a research method to be scientific. However, following Sidney and Beatrice Webb, influential British social scientists,[45] Towle claimed (1941b) that "facts" could be perceived or experienced independently of "theories." This claim reflected the positivist belief that observations attained through experimentation can be theory-free and used as independent tests of the validity of scientific theories.

Despite the leading social workers' aspirations for all social workers to contribute research, many practitioners' writings indicate that those aims were extremely difficult to realize. As social work programs became more bureaucratized in the context of the public agencies, social workers had to conform to agency mandates (with which they may or may not have agreed), which often included unrealistic case loads, low pay, and insecure working conditions. Although caseworkers may have entered the field because they wanted to help clients, limited resources often made it difficult for them to respond to client needs. It was not uncommon for the workers who handled the most disadvantaged clients with the most complex and serious problems to have had the least training and to work for the most overburdened agencies (Cullen, 1983; J. Fisher, 1936/1990).[46] Social workers saw hungry, disadvantaged clients, many of whom they did not have adequate resources to serve. Given their unstable working conditions and low pay, the social workers themselves were separated from the plight of their clients by only a very fragile line (Cullen, 1983). In some agencies, researchers were paid even less than caseworkers (Geddes, 1941).

Although during the early years of the century, settlers designed services and then obtained funding to implement their programs, as social workers implemented the new public programs, they had to conform to state and federal guidelines. The social work profession was no longer an autonomous community based on alternative values. Instead, many social workers saw their role as to "express the will of society or of some group in that society" (Perlman, 1957, cited in Steinberg, 1988, p. 13). Practitioners described how this problem of professional autonomy affected the quality of services that social workers could provide (Steinberg, 1988). In effect, those social workers who had direct experience of the need for research to promote empowerment and advocacy for disadvantaged clients were themselves disempowered within their own professional contexts. Those restrictive contexts had an important regulatory impact on the direction of social work research and on the conceptualization of the philosophy of social work research. Most important, whereas early social work leaders such as Richmond and Addams were researchers as well as practitioners, the new bureaucratic constraints made it more difficult for social workers to perpetuate the alliances among research, practice, and reform that had helped to create the profession's knowledge base.

The Diagnostic and Functionalist Debates: The Problem of Incompatibility between Casework Theories

In the 1930s and 1940s, an important controversy arose within psychiatric social work between proponents of what were called the *diagnostic* and the *functionalist approaches* to clinical practice. The New York School of Social Work and the Smith School for Social Work became the geographical centers of the diagnostic school, while the Pennsylvania School of Social Work, where Jessie Taft and Virginia Robinson were on the faculty, became the locus of the functionalist school. The diagnostic approach melded classic Freudian psychoanalytic principles and the person-in-situation emphasis advanced by Mary Richmond. In 1929, Porter Lee, director of the New York School, and Marion Kenworthy, a psychoanalyst on the faculty at the New York School, published *Mental Hygiene and Social Work*, the first practice text based on Freudian principles and one of the leading texts of the diagnostic school. Gordon Hamilton, also on the faculty of the New York School, was another major diagnostic theorist and drew heavily from the work of her friend Mary Richmond (Hamilton, 1947).

The functionalist theorists were influenced strongly by Otto Rank (see, e.g., Aptekar, 1941). They explicitly distinguished their clinical theory from Richmond's, viewing hers as "sociological" and the functionalist approach as "psychological" (V. Robinson, 1930/1934). Jessie Taft had heard Otto Rank speak and invited him to give a commencement address at the Pennsylvania School of Social Work in 1924.

She experienced a brief psychoanalysis with Rank, attended the courses he gave in New York on his approach to treatment, and translated two of his works into English (Rank, 1936, 1936/1978). Rank gave several courses at the Pennsylvania School of Social Work (Dore, 1990; V. Robinson, 1960, 1962; Ross & Johnson, 1946; Taft, 1933/1962, 1937).

Functionalist social workers such as Robinson and Taft rejected Freud's premises. Instead, following Rank, they conceptualized the crux of psychological treatment as a "clash of wills" between therapist and client. Taft (1937) developed the functionalist approach in part as a response to the increasing bureaucratization of services during the Depression; she also felt that the profession should conduct more in-depth study of the helping process. Like theoreticians from the diagnostic school, such as Charlotte Towle, Taft (1937) regarded the social worker as a scientist and believed that social workers should see the helping process itself as a scientific experiment.

The functionalist approach, as Taft and Virginia Robinson described it, was "relationship therapy." Reflecting the severe limitations of agency-based services in the face of Depression-era needs, Taft emphasized that a central feature of human existence is the struggle with limitations, such as time and mortality. The functionalist social workers conceptualized the casework relationship as an opportunity for clients to discover their own ways of responding to such limitations. The social worker was not to guide or direct clients; instead, using "passive" attention, the worker would allow clients to discover their own answers to those existential dilemmas. The functionalist theorists studied the relationship process itself, a focus that became their hallmark: "there is one common quality underlying the attitudes of clients seeking case work help: the active search for a relationship in which to solve a problem" (V. Robinson, 1930/1934, p. 151; see also Aptekar, 1941). The functionalists recognized that all aspects of the data from the casework process were inseparable from and regulated by the relationship with the social worker. For example, Taft (1937) said that clients discovered their own needs only from what they experienced in the helping process.

The diagnostic and functionalist approaches led to markedly different casework interventions. Although the practice implications cannot be analyzed in depth here, the differences between the two approaches are immediately apparent if one compares the interviewing procedures in Jessie Taft's case studies (1933/1962) with those of the social workers who espoused the viewpoint of the diagnostic school (e.g., Towle, 1940). Some psychiatric social workers accepted the different theoretical formulations as an opportunity and recognized that debates are part of the process of generating scientific knowledge. Robinson emphasized, "I am convinced that case work theory must progress as other scientific theory has progressed, by the frank expression of difference, by discussion, argument, controversy" (1930/1934, p. xv). Others were less tolerant. One practical consequence of the theoretical controversy was a major schism between practitioners. Adherents of one approach found it difficult to obtain employment at an agency that supported the other approach (Herzog & Frings, 1952). Throughout the 1940s, the diagnostic–functionalist controversy was debated hotly and was one of the primary intradisciplinary problems that social workers wanted to solve.

The debates brought to the fore a problem that any approach to research would have to address: whether the approach to research can accommodate more than one theory. Robinson quoted an early social worker's observation that different interview approaches yield different data:

> The traditions and training of the observer more or less condition the nature of the fact-items that make their appearance. Two visitors who know the same girl may, through their different personalities, bring out and become cognizant of quite different facts in her experience. In this sense the subject matter of much social study is unstable. Not only do two students perceive different facts, they actually in a measure make different facts to be perceived. (Mrs. Sheffield, quoted in V. Robinson, 1930/1934, p. 65)

The preceding comments illustrate a sophisticated awareness that clinical observations cannot be divorced from the clinician's approach to practice. The crucial problem for clinical research was the following: Clinical researchers who use different theories work with different data, and how can a single approach to research help social workers to study diverse casework theories and processes systematically? This problem remained unsolved until Heineman Pieper advanced the heuristic paradigm in 1981. During the 1950s, as social work researchers adopted a logical positivist approach to research, they sought to solve the problem of diverse clinical practice models by adopting and prescribing a single theory, a derivative of behaviorism they mislabeled "empirical" clinical practice (Bloom & Fischer, 1982; Blythe & Briar, 1985). Contemporary social workers have increasingly critiqued that practice model as severely limited in many respects (Goldstein, 1990; Heineman Pieper, 1981, 1985, 1989; Witkin, 1991). As discussed in the remainder of this volume, because the heuristic paradigm does not restrict the tenets of any casework model, clinical researchers can use the heuristic paradigm to systematically investigate diverse clinical theories.

In 1947, the Family Service Society of America established a commission to study the diagnostic and functionalist points of view and to resolve the controversy. However, the commission could not choose one theory over the other and also concluded the theories could not be melded (Herzog & Frings, 1952). In their discussions of the commission's findings, practitioners articulated the dilemma facing clinical researchers, "it is increasingly recognized that the line between fact and theory is elusive and fuzzy, a product of the viewing eye as well as of the matter under analysis" (Herzog & Frings, 1952, p. 143). At the same time, however, Herzog and Frings voiced the contemporary logical positivist belief that the impact of clinical theory on clinical observations could be prevented, "part of this task would be the setting up of safeguards against the distortion of fact by theory and by subjective interpretation" (1952, p. 143). Herzog and Frings said that the task of identifying and controlling bias would be the special province of researchers:

> It is the explicit and accepted responsibility of the research worker to recognize sources of distortion and bias, to avoid them as much as possible, and where feasible to compensate or allow for them. We have outgrown belief in the mythical quality of complete objectivity, and in doing so we have increased our ability to set up mechanisms designed to control, to counterbalance, or at least to identify and state them. (1952, p. 143)

Finally, Herzog and Frings implied that a practitioner's expertise with a specific clinical theory was a disadvantage rather than an asset for clinical research: "The fact that research methods would be utilized would help to diminish subjective judgment because of the character of research training and also because in the nature of things most researchers are not so strongly committed to one casework approach as are many practitioners" (p. 146). By assigning a new, distinctive role to researchers that assumed researchers would be freer of subjectivity and bias than practitioners, the conclusions of Herzog and Frings reflected the logical positivist beliefs that by 1952 had already begun to influence social work. In the following pages, those logical positivist assumptions are elaborated.

THE FORMULATION OF A LOGICAL POSITIVIST APPROACH TO SOCIAL WORK RESEARCH

The Cultural Context in which Social Work Researchers Adopted Logical Positivism

American society was transformed by the mobilization of resources for World War II. Scientific research became enormously important: "During World War II the research effort that produced radar, the atom bomb, and penicillin persuaded even the skeptical that support of science was vital to national security" (Starr, 1982, p. 335). Americans understandably attributed the preeminence of the United States after World War II to superior technology,

> The United States emerged from the Second World War as the major economic and military power in the world. European economies were devastated while American industrial production and national income more than doubled during the war. In 1947 the United States produced more than half the world's manufactured goods, 62 percent of its oil, and 80 percent of its automobiles. It was also producing a larger share of the world's science than ever before (with the help, to be sure, of European scientists who had fled from the Nazis). Spokesmen for American science pointed out that it would be neither wise nor possible for the United States to depend any longer on European, much less German, scientific achievement. And in the cold war, science assumed a symbolic as well as a practical function in maintaining America's position as "leader of the free world." (Starr, 1982, p. 336)

The massive investment in scientific research continued as the Cold War with the Soviet Union began, the United States entered the Korean War, and the National Science Foundation was established (Roland, 1985).

The Cold War not only influenced public investment in science but also dramatically affected the domestic political climate. Civil liberties were steadily eroded after World War II, and social workers, like others who were dedicated to social reform, were threatened and, often, persecuted. The passage of the Internal Security Act permitted suspected communists to be detained without trial. Ethel and Julius Rosenberg were accused of being communists and were executed on the charge that they had given key A-bomb information to the Soviet Union, despite worldwide efforts on their behalf. Many social workers protested their conviction and execution. Most members of the U.S. Communist Party were either hiding or in jail. Teachers, journalists, newspaper reporters, screenwriters, and government workers lost their jobs for refusing to cooperate with government investigatory committees. College professors were particularly vulnerable to the harassments of McCarthyism; between 10% and 16% of university faculty in the social sciences lost their jobs because of suspected communist sympathies (Caute, 1978). Bertha Capen Reynolds, an influential social worker and leader of the Union for Maritime Workers, lost her job as a result of her membership in the Communist Party. Reynolds wrote several pamphlets voicing her controversial protests against the repressive government activities of the time: "The Press Lies about Relief," "Fear in Our Culture," and "McCarthyism versus Social Work" (Cullen, 1983, pp. 67–68). Included among the prominent signers of an "Open Letter to the President and the Congress" urging an end to the Cold War were Harry Lurie, Wayne McMillen, Bertha Reynolds, and Mary Van Kleeck, all of whom were social workers (Schriver, 1987). The social work profession, which the federal government sought out to administer the new social services during the Depression, was now often suspect. Some social workers were actively harassed:

> Hundreds of social workers had job problems, were harassed by the FBI, called before the HUAC [McCarthy's committee]; but few of these reached the public eye and for good reasons. It was not to the individual's advantage to publicize this. So it became public knowledge only when the press got hold of such incidents. (Verne Weed quoted in Cullen, 1983, p. 66)

Charlotte Towle described the social work profession as the "conscience" of the nation. In an era that was not oriented toward social reform, the traditional mission of the social work profession was in opposition to the values of the wider society (Towle, ca. 1950s; see also Towle, 1961). In 1956, the president of the National Association of Social Workers voiced his concern that "the poison of McCarthyism is still in our system. The real threat to the future of our democracy is the pattern of conformity it has created in our institutions which deal with education for effective living" (N. Cohen, 1956, p. 13).

One of the most famous episodes in the history of the social work profession during the 1950s entailed a clash between research that reflected the social work profession's humanistic values and the repressive practices of McCarthyism. It came to be known as the "Common Human Needs affair." In 1945 Charlotte Towle had written a book entitled *Common Human Needs* (1945/1987), which was designed to "get the psychological into the social through helping workers in public assistance programs see the emotional import, in fact the ego development implications, of administration policies, statutory regulations and social service procedures" (Towle, 1958, p. 6). Many people praised the book for its insights and usefulness. In 1951, however, the president of the American Medical Association interpreted one sentence in Towle's book as advocating socialism.[47] He then accused the administrator of the Federal Security Agency, which had published the book, of promoting socialist attitudes. The Federal

Security Agency ordered the Government Printing Office to destroy all of its copies, which it did, despite the protests of the social work profession and many civil libertarians. The book was later republished by the National Association of Social Workers, received wide circulation, and ultimately was translated into at least nine languages. In 1953 Towle was invited to spend a year as a senior Fulbright scholar at the London School of Economics, serving as an educational consultant to English social work faculty (Posner, 1986; Sutter, 1980). Her passport was temporarily withheld, however, because she was suspected of "communist leanings," based on her membership in two alleged "front" organizations and the fact that she had signed a clemency petition for the Rosenbergs (Posner, 1986). "She again became a cause célèbre in her profession and beyond" (Sutter, 1980, p. 5). Eventually, her passport was granted.

While social workers were often in an adversarial relationship with the prevailing cultural norms, the medical profession grew into a major institutional power:

> From modest prewar beginnings the United States built up an immense medical research establishment. It enlarged and equipped the most scientifically advanced hospitals in the world and created an entirely new network of community mental health centers. Between 1950 and 1970, the medical work force increased from 1.2 to 3.9 million people. National health care expenditures grew from $12.7 billion to $71.6 billion (up from 4.5 to 7.3 percent of the GNP [gross national product]), and medical care became one of the nation's largest industries. (Starr, 1982, p. 335)

Quantum leaps took place in technologies that investigated physiological variables, such as the electroencephalogram for assessment of neurological functioning, as well as in psychopharmacologic research. Psychiatric research became more focused on neurological variables and psychopharmacologic interventions and adopted the prioritizing of experimental designs that was a hallmark of positivist social and behavioral research. Psychiatry switched its emphasis from the care of the insane to advocacy for individual mental health, which "took on an evangelistic fervor. With the collapse of the left as a political force, social reformers increasingly appropriated the language of clinical medicine. Psychiatrists were in the vanguard of this movement to redefine social problems in medical terms" (Starr, 1982, p. 337; see also Romano, 1975).

In a climate where social reform was suspect and technological development was emphasized, other social and behavioral sciences increasingly adopted logical positivist approaches to research that advanced methodological solutions to the problem of creating systematic and rigorous knowledge. For example, one of the most common methodological prescriptions to psychological researchers was for a variant of experimental design that used random samples and control groups and presented the findings in terms of generalizations about anonymous groups of "subjects" (Boring, 1929/1950; Danziger, 1985, 1987; Hearnshaw, 1987; Morawski, 1988). Although many researchers, especially in psychology, had been aware of behaviorism (a psychological theory that had been developed to conform to positivist beliefs) since John Watson's book on the subject was published in 1912, more clinicians adopted behaviorism during the 1950s (Buckley, 1989; Ehrenwald, 1976; Hearnshaw, 1987); social workers began to do so as well.[48] In the 1950s, the scientific stature of psychoanalysis was contested (Hempel, 1965b; Hook, 1959; Meier, 1951), which called into question the models of social work practice that were based on psychoanalytic theory.

Numerous changes within the profession also influenced the social work profession's approach to research. One of the legacies of the Depression-era recruitment of caseworkers with little or no formal education was that in 1951 most practitioners in public social services still lacked a professional social work education (E. Hollis & Taylor, 1951; SWRG, *Newsletter*, No. 9, Nov. 1951). In 1956, Nathan Cohen, the president of the National Association of Social Workers, said that 84% of social workers who were members of that organization had not completed graduate training. The field of social work had always been associated with the poor and mentally ill, and social workers had often been devalued in relation to other professionals, which only exacerbated social workers' concerns about their status. In an increasingly competitive professional environment, and with so many social workers lacking professional training and credentials, social workers were even more vulnerable to insecurities about their status (W. E. Gordon, 1951).

The early social workers regarded advocacy as compatible with scientific aims. In the 1950s, however, social work researchers' adoption of a logical positivist approach to social research meant social workers had to choose between advocacy for social justice and conformity with logical positivist beliefs about science. Despite a climate inimical to reform, the seeds of a different attitude were sown as one of the most powerful social movements of the century gathered momentum—the civil rights movement led by Dr. Martin Luther King, Jr. Although the ravages of the Depression receded during World War II, massive social inequalities persisted. Racial discrimination remained pervasive, as was exemplified by the Jim Crow laws and enforced segregation in many Southern states. The growth of the civil rights movement challenged social workers to examine their commitment to social justice and cultural pluralism. In 1954, the same year the Supreme Court decided against segregated education in *Brown v. Board of Education*, the Council on Social Work Education began to require that schools of social work enforce nondiscriminatory practices in student admissions, setting a standard that was unique among the professions at the time (Blackwell, 1981). Even so, incoming students who were members of ethnic and racial minority groups criticized educators because the curriculum lacked knowledge relevant to minority groups' histories and contemporary priorities.

Although public awareness about racial discrimination began to grow, discrimination against women remained both pervasive and largely ignored throughout the 1950s and well into the 1960s (Abramovitz, 1988; S. Evans, 1989; S. Rothman, 1978; Stricker, 1976; Westkott, 1979). Whereas during World War II women were encouraged to become leaders in the labor force to produce resources for the war effort, when soldiers returned home, women workers often were viewed as competitors who could rob a family's breadwinner of employment (S. Evans, 1989). Unemployment rose even among single women, and women members of minority groups suffered dual discrimination based on gender as well as ethnicity and/or race (Abramovitz, 1988, p. 320). Discrimination in the workplace was rampant, and exhortations to women to stay at home proliferated in the lay press:

> Women who went to the U.S. Employment Service were incredulous to discover that the only jobs available to them paid only half what they had made in war industries. Skilled industrial jobs were no longer open to them. One union organizer reported that

the U.S.E.S. in her area told women, "No, these jobs are for men; women can't do them." (S. Evans, 1989, p. 231)

Even so, the baby boom,[49] combined with the lack of adequate day care, meant that many women had to work or become dependent on the new Aid to Dependent Children (ADC) programs (Abramovitz, 1988).

The social work profession underwent changes in membership as the composition of the work force changed. During the 1940s, while many men were overseas at war, women increasingly entered the work force and held leadership positions (S. Evans, 1989). When men returned from World War II, many entered the social work profession under the G.I. bill (N. Cohen, 1956). Male graduates from social work masters' programs increased from 5% in 1944 to 39% in 1950 (National Association of Social Workers [NASW], 1983–1984).[50] Given the gender-role expectations of the times, female social workers' commitment to their careers often was tempered by family responsibilities, whereas male social workers could devote themselves full-time to career advancement (Steinberg, 1988). Furthermore, male social workers did not experience the discrimination that women social workers did. Consequently, men tended to advance more rapidly than women into higher-paying and more authoritative positions in the social work profession (Andrews, 1990; L. Davis, 1985; Dressel, 1987; A. Schwartz, 1967).[51] Because few programs offered doctoral degrees in social work,[52] men who wanted doctorates often studied in other disciplines such as sociology, anthropology, or social psychology. They frequently focused on research, which the academic community tended to value more highly than direct practice (Broadhurst, 1982). These trends persisted throughout the 1950s, so that in the 1960s and 1970s, men, many of whom had learned beliefs about research in disciplines other than social work, held most of the positions of authority and influence in the social work profession (Dressel, 1987; A. Rosenblatt, Turner, Patterson, & Rollosson, 1970; Ruel, 1972; Sancier, 1992a).

As more men entered the field, their contributions to research increased as well. From 1920 to 1949, the great majority of first authors of social work journal articles were female (Figure 2–2 and Table 2–1). In fact, women were first authors of almost twice as many articles as men from 1920 to 1929 and again from 1940 to 1949. During the 1950s, however, an almost equal number of men and women were first authors. In the 1960s and 1970s, men were first authors of many more social work articles than women. During the 1970s, many social workers began to protest the bias against women in the profession (Davenport & Reims, 1978; Kravetz, 1976; Ruel, 1972; Sancier, 1992a; Scotch, 1971; M. C. Schwartz, 1973), which nurtured the changes of the 1980s. When the debates about the philosophy of social work research began in the 1980s, the proportions of male and female first authors were again almost equal (see Figure 2–2). In sum, it has often been assumed that social work researchers' adoption of the positivist approach to social and behavioral research in the 1950s reflected only a commitment to "science." However, changes in the profession's membership—specifically, shifts in the proportion of women and men in the profession and in the proportion of women and men in leading roles in the profession—clearly accompanied the major shifts in approaches to social work research.

Figure 2–2
Distribution by decade of the number of articles first-authored by women and by men, 1920 to 1989

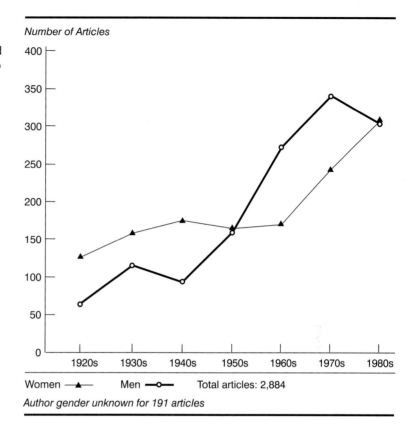

Number of Articles

Women —▲— Men —○— Total articles: 2,884
Author gender unknown for 191 articles

The Organization of the Social Work Research Group

In the context of the idealization of technological scientific research, persecution of advocates for social reform, and intensified discrimination against women, social workers began to scrutinize the scientific status of social work knowledge. The SWRG was organized following a 1948 workshop on social work research at Case Western Reserve University. The SWRG's express purpose was to formulate a new, systematic approach to social work research for the entire profession (Maas & Varon, 1949; Zimbalist, 1977). The SWRG, however, was a voluntary rather than an elected or representative group. Despite its explicit aim to unify social work research, leading clinical researchers such as Charlotte Towle and Gordon Hamilton were not represented on the SWRG's steering committee. Many members of the steering committee had received their doctorates in, and were associated with, other social and behavioral science disciplines, such as anthropology, psychology, and sociology.[53] The SWRG prized the approach to research increasingly advanced in those other disciplines—a derivative of logical positivism—and wanted social work researchers to accept those standards.

SWRG members frequently stated that a primary problem the organization wanted to address was that social work's approach to research was not scientific (as

Table 2–1

Distribution and Percentages of Seven Research Design Heuristics by First-Author Gender and by Decade, 1920 to 1989

Women First Authors

Research Design Heuristics	1920s		1930s		1940s		1950s		1960s		1970s		1980s	
	#	%	#	%	#	%	#	%	#	%	#	%	#	%
Reviews and commentaries	75	60	87	56	90	51	105	66	85	50	120	49	142	46
Histories	14	11	7	5	3	2	9	6	6	4	7	3	10	3
Case studies - Qualitative data	18	14	24	15	23	13	17	11	15	9	12	5	23	8
Large-scale analyses - Qualitative data	6	5	18	12	50	29	21	13	40	24	49	20	43	14
Case studies - Quantified data	0	0	0	0	0	0	0	0	0	0	1	0	1	0
Large-scale analyses - Quantified data	14	11	20	13	9	5	5	3	22	13	49	20	85	28
Experimental designs	0	0	0	0	0	0	3	2	1	1	8	3	3	1
Totals	127	101	156	101	175	100	160	101	169	101	246	100	307	100

Men First Authors

Research Design Heuristics	1920s		1930s		1940s		1950s		1960s		1970s		1980s	
	#	%	#	%	#	%	#	%	#	%	#	%	#	%
Reviews and commentaries	46	72	74	64	59	62	102	65	152	56	210	61	174	57
Histories	5	8	5	4	8	8	7	4	18	7	8	2	5	2
Case studies - Qualitative data	2	3	10	9	8	8	10	6	17	6	12	4	17	6
Large-scale analyses - Qualitative data	0	0	5	4	10	11	17	11	35	13	26	8	22	7
Case studies - Quantified data	0	0	0	0	0	0	0	0	0	0	2	1	0	0
Large-scale analyses - Quantified data	11	17	22	20	10	11	21	13	41	15	77	22	79	26
Experimental designs	0	0	0	0	0	0	1	1	9	3	8	2	8	3
Totals	64	100	116	101	95	100	158	100	272	100	343	100	305	101

Gender of First Author Unknown

Research Design Heuristics	1920s		1930s		1940s		1950s		1960s		1970s		1980s	
	#	%	#	%	#	%	#	%	#	%	#	%	#	%
Reviews and commentaries	39	65	20	65	11	55	13	68	24	86	13	62	6	50
Histories	4	7	2	7	1	5	1	5	0	0	0	0	0	0
Case studies - Qualitative data	14	23	1	3	0	0	1	5	0	0	0	0	0	0
Large-scale analyses - Qualitative data	2	3	1	3	4	20	2	11	2	7	2	10	1	8
Case studies - Quantified data	0	0	0	0	0	0	0	0	0	0	0	0	0	0
Large-scale analyses - Quantified data	1	2	7	23	4	20	2	11	2	7	5	24	5	42
Experimental designs	0	0	0	0	0	0	0	0	0	0	1	5	0	0
Totals	60	100	31	101	20	100	19	100	28	100	21	101	12	100

Percentages have been rounded and so may not add up to 100 in some cases.

they defined it), and that in an increasingly technological age in which competition among the sciences and scientists was accelerating rapidly, the social work profession would be left behind if it did not develop a more "scientific" approach to research: "To be unscientific is not wrong, either in the moral or statistical sense. To be unscientific and proud of it, however, has little status value in our present culture and is a luxury which we can ill afford from here on" (W. E. Gordon, 1951, p. 9).[54] The SWRG was acutely aware of the status problems that had always plagued social workers, and SWRG members were concerned that the academic community regarded social work as an inferior discipline. Even as late as 1961, Werner Boehm, a prominent member, described the social work profession as still "perceived as somewhat out of place or as an awkward guest in the university milieu" (1961, p. 149).

At its inception, the SWRG group was small; it worked assiduously to gain recognition and adherents. The fact that social work researchers often were no longer practitioners may have made it more difficult for the SWRG to gain influence in a practitioner-oriented profession. For example, in 1950 several social work organizations were planning to join together into the National Association of Social Workers. The SWRG wanted to be included in the discussions, but two practitioner groups were not in favor of including representatives from the SWRG (SWRG, 1951b). In reminiscing, Henry Maas commented that the differences involved both role definitions and values:

> In the mid-1940s a new breed of social workers emerged, soon organized into a nationwide association. Its membership was committed to the use of empirical research and social science theory in the development of what Alfred Kahn called "social work knowledge" and Alfred Kadushin labeled "the knowledge base of social work." (1991, p. 20)[55]

Even so, at its inception the SWRG drew from the momentum of social workers' long-standing commitment to research. The *Newsletter* reported that there was a great deal of enthusiasm and a wave of interest in research at the 1950 National Conference of the American Association of Social Workers (SWRG, *Newsletter*, No. 3, April 1950; No. 4, June 1950). When the SWRG canvassed practitioner organizations in 1950, they found that those organizations felt that "the lack of scientific research hampers their efforts" and that practitioners were eager to conduct research but lacked funds for trained staff (SWRG, *Newsletter*, No. 5, Nov. 1950, p. 1). This illustrated the continuing priority that social workers accorded to research, which also was reflected in the standards of the Council on Social Work Education and in curricula (see also E. Hollis & Taylor, 1951).[56] It also illustrated the ongoing difficulty that agency-based social workers had in acquiring resources and time for conducting research.

Within a few years, over half of all social work researchers from both academic and agency settings were members of the SWRG, and the membership spanned the entire country. The SWRG had gained influence quickly within the profession, as William Gordon noted in the SWRG *Newsletter* in 1953:

> With the usual vigor and enthusiasm of a youthful organization, the SWRG has moved quickly to a position of importance and influence in social work. Increase in strength and

influence also brings increase in responsibility for crucial decisions affecting research program, practice, organization and education in social work. (No. 13, p. 10)

Researchers enjoyed the opportunity for interchange at conferences, where the SWRG had an increasingly influential role. As a new member, Gloria Roman from Los Angeles, wrote, "I suppose everyone is excited about their first conference and I was no exception. What struck me most was that social work researchers are awfully nice people, something I had suspected before. But it was a hypothesis I hadn't fully tested" (SWRG, *Newsletter*, No. 18, Aug. 1954, p. 5).

The SWRG *Newsletter* provides a window to the contemporary events that members regarded as most influential for social work research. The first edition reported that "when Congress reconvenes in January it is expected to complete action on a number of bills aimed at expanding federal research funds, facilities, and resources," including "a grants-in-aid program for research in child life and bills authorizing a number of special studies and surveys," and establishing the National Science Foundation (SWRG, *Newsletter*, No. 1, 1949, p. 1). The Mid Century White House Conference on Children, which was scheduled to take place on December 3, 1949, was led by social workers (SWRG, *Newsletter*, 1949). In 1950, the *Newsletter* said that the field of social work was being influenced by several socioeconomic trends: "present levels of unemployment," the "continued baby boom," an "increasing proportion of young people who are going to college," the "rising proportion of older people coupled with the lessening possibility of work for them," and "the increasing complexity of our economy" (SWRG, *Newsletter*, No. 4, June 1950, p. 4). The *Newsletter* alluded to the repressiveness of the McCarthy hearings, noting that researchers who wanted to study the impact of loyalty and security measures on federal employees had received funding for their work (No. 13, 1953, p. 4). The *Newsletter* advocated methods for analysis of quantified data, such as regression analyses and analysis of variance (ANOVA). At that time, statistics were not taught at 75% of the liberal arts colleges in this country (*American Sociological Review* cited in SWRG, *Newsletter*, No. 2, 1950, p. 8); even so, SWRG members evaluated the social work profession as being especially behind the times in using statistical approaches to analyzing data (SWRG, *Newsletter*, 1950; Blenkner, 1950, Part I). In 1954, the *Newsletter* praised a textbook on statistics for social workers, authored by Wayne McMillen of the School of Social Service Administration at the University of Chicago, as a much-needed contribution.

As the new cadre of researchers increasingly carved out a niche, they identified themselves with the view that research and practice should be separate. According to Maas and many other SWRG members, social work research was a "science," whereas those who espoused the humanistic values represented by the work of practitioners created knowledge that was an "art" (1991, p. 20). This sharp demarcation was not just conceptual; some positivist social researchers commented that there were increasing rifts between practice and research faculty in schools of social work as well (Greenwood, 1958; Maas, 1991). Willard Richan and Alan Mendlesohn said that "when social scientists began invading social work faculties in the late 1950's and early 1960's, the turmoil they unleashed was predictable. Established senior faculty members [many were practice theorists who used variants of psychodynamic theory] suddenly found the ground underneath them shifting" (1973, p. 169). According to Maas, practice theorists and proponents of what was then the new approach to social work research rarely read each others' work. Maas commented, "in retrospect, it seems unfortunate for social work's development that researchers and practice theorists made so little mutual use of each other's thinking. Exceptions were rare" (1991, p. 21).[57] Some SWRG members overtly disparaged practitioners and their knowledge base. Greenwood, for example, wrote, "Social work practice theory was not developed via systematic research which converted social science laws into principles. It was constructed by social work practitioners who were untutored in the cannons [sic] of scientific inquiry and who relied solely upon the richness of their insight and the wisdom derived from their day-to-day experiences on the job" (1955, p. 28).

As a consequence of the growing chasm between research and practice and of the different heuristics that positivist social researchers and practitioner–researchers used, the two groups often worked with very different data. Whereas practitioners had multiple daily experiences of complex and intimate casework relationships, researchers who were not practitioners had difficulty obtaining access to data that directly detailed clinical processes because of such issues as confidentiality. The standards the SWRG advocated further distanced researchers from clinical data. The SWRG began to collect and disseminate abstracts of social work research, a project that developed into the journal *Social Work Research and Abstracts*. For inclusion of a study in their abstracts, the SWRG required that the data used in the studies be available for other researchers to examine. Because data from casework treatment were confidential and could not be circulated to other researchers, studies based on such data were excluded from the project (SWRG, 1951c). Some researchers tried to compensate for the lack of access to clinical data by studying social work students in simulated practice situations, imitating the laboratory approach to research that was increasingly prevalent in psychology (Blenkner, 1959; Miller, 1958; Reid, 1966). Such studies, however, had limited applicability for understanding social work treatment. For example, studies of student practitioners could not examine one of the most important variables in the treatment process—the impact of professional experience on the clinician's judgment. By contrast, researchers who were also clinicians used data from their own practice to study social work treatment.

Pressures on social workers to adopt a positivist approach to research not only were due to the profession's desire for status, they also stemmed from the directives of funding sources about how the effects of services should be demonstrated. Governmental agencies, such as the Department of Defense, issued statements about their criteria for funding studies that relied on positivist assumptions about knowledge generation (cited in House, 1983; see also D. G. French, 1952).[58] In describing agency-based evaluations of services for children, Beck commented that

> under the stimulus of pressure from financial supporters for clear and objective evidence of the effectiveness of service, figures are provided wherever possible on the percentage of cases improved after casework contact. Usually the only available source for such figures are the judgments of caseworkers involved or of trained case readers. (1958, p. 111)

Beck said "a few penetrating questions [from representatives of funding sources] rapidly submerge one in deep water," and she described how their methodological requirements conflicted with practitioners' values:

> Some require the experimental variation of case type or treatment method. Others cannot be answered without control groups. Although none of these requirements can be easily met under usual practice conditions, the provision of a control group is perhaps the most difficult and elusive of the requirements. The problem arises mainly because of the conflict between the needs of research and ethical objections to the direct refusal of service. (1958, p. 111)

Tenets of the Approach to Research Advanced by the Social Work Research Group

Members of the SWRG held prominent academic positions and published prolifically on the subject of an approach to social work research. Probably the single most important reference about the SWRG's approach to research is *The Function and Practice of Research in Social Work* (SWRG, 1955). This document, the fruit of three years of discussion and debate among the leaders of the SWRG, reflects the members' varying viewpoints (see esp. pp. 30–32). The SWRG never called their approach to research "positivism," perhaps because they did not use extant critiques of logical positivism and the postpositivist alternatives that were developing rapidly (e.g., Hanson, 1958; Quine, 1948; Scriven, 1959; Toulmin, 1953). For example, in a 1959 address attended by leading members of the SWRG, Martin Loeb (1960) cited an early book by Herbert Simon, whose later formulation of heuristics was adopted by Martha Heineman Pieper in 1981 as a conceptual foundation for the heuristic paradigm. With regard to Simon's *Models of Man: Social and Rational* (1957b), Loeb said that Simon was a mathematician and that "most social scientists are not yet prepared to be so specific [as mathematicians]" (p. 9). The SWRG and its followers adopted ideas that were central to the logical positivist philosophy or closely allied with the logical positivist philosophy or its immediate derivatives (Hoffman, 1952, cited Bridgman, 1927; McVicker Hunt, 1959, cited Reichenbach, 1938; R. C. White, 1956, cited Rescher & Oppenheim, 1955). To illustrate, Martin Loeb, having already stated the logical positivist assumption that "the criterion of science is the physical sciences" (1960, p. 5), adopted the prescription of a prominent philosopher who pursued many of the aims of the logical positivists, Karl Popper: "Karl Popper has made a plea for a 'technological social science' which will have as its focus 'problems' rather than 'subject matter' or 'disciplines.' Social work can be an essential part of this 'technological social science'" (Loeb, 1960, p. 12; see the selection by Popper in the Appendix).

The members of the SWRG were introduced to logical positivist ideas through many avenues; their work is full of references to collaborative work with social and behavioral scientists from other disciplines who were applying ideas about social and behavioral research derived from logical positivism (D. G. French, 1952; G. Hearn, 1958; Klein & Merriam, 1948; Kogan, 1960; McVicker Hunt & Kogan, 1950). Most notably, the work of two prominent philosophers of science, Carl Hempel and

Rudolf Carnap, was promulgated throughout the 1940s and 1950s. Hempel and Carnap emigrated to this country in the late 1930s. They called their philosophy "logical empiricism" after logical positivism prompted considerable criticism, and they were very interested in the implications of their philosophy for the social and behavioral sciences. They held influential and prominent academic positions (Hempel was at Princeton for much of his career, and Carnap was at the University of Chicago and then at the University of California at Los Angeles) and authored many papers and addresses while members of the SWRG were formulating their ideas about research (Carnap, 1963/1991a; Hempel, 1965b). Hempel applied his ideas to psychiatric classification at a conference sponsored by the American Psychopathological Association in 1959, and Carnap was a member of a cross-disciplinary study group for scientists and philosophers at the University of Chicago. The dominant tenets of the SWRG's approach to research, which mirror the tenets of the logical positivist philosophy of science, follow:

1. A methodologically based demarcation of scientific from nonscientific knowledge;
2. A focus on the verification of theories as opposed to discovery;
3. The belief that scientific explanations must be predictions, a belief that in turn led to prioritizing experimental design over other research designs;
4. Operationism;
5. The belief that scientific research can and should be value-free.

A Methodologically Based Demarcation between Scientific and "Nonscientific" Knowledge

The SWRG defined scientific research in a way that excluded many forms of social work knowledge. Their aim of omitting some forms of social work knowledge from the category of research was consistent with the overriding aim of the logical positivist philosophers of science: to define how scientifically meaningful propositions could be distinguished from other statements that the logical positivists deemed scientifically meaningless or "metaphysical" (Carnap, 1936, 1963/1991a; see also Bridgman and Schlick in the Appendix). To effect this demarcation, the logical positivists advanced methodological criteria. Schlick, for example, said, "the meaning of a proposition is its method of verification" (see Appendix). Similarly, the SWRG used methodological criteria to outline the projects they defined as "scientific research." Only studies that used the experimental designs and quantified data that they prized were accorded the status of scientific research. The SWRG's restrictive, methodologically based definition of scientific research excluded the substantial conceptual and descriptive literature on practice as well as the many social surveys social workers used to understand social problems (Blenkner, 1950; Greenwood, 1955).[59] To illustrate, when considering whether descriptive studies (e.g., "a study of unit cost of service in an agency") "represented research," the SWRG concluded that "a study of unit costs alone is essentially a fact-finding undertaking and as such does not qualify as research" (SWRG, 1955, p. 14).[60]

Focus on Theory Verification Rather than Discovery

The pragmatist philosophers John Dewey and William James defined science as a systematic, practical problem-solving process, and many early social work researchers agreed with that conception. The SWRG adopted a different definition of science. One of the leading members of the SWRG, Ernest Greenwood, defined science as "a system of descriptive propositions about some aspect of nature" (1955, p. 21). Greenwood described how the propositions, or "scientific laws," are generated:

> The descriptive propositions of every science, the social sciences included, possess a generalizing character. Scientists are uninterested in single and completely unique events per se. . . . around a discovered uniformity a logical class is constructed; about the class and its observed pattern a descriptive generalization is formulated. . . . It is through such interlocking and pyramiding of its generalizations that a social science achieves a system of interrelated propositions, which, with all their elaborations, ramifications, and rationalizations, constitute its body of knowledge. (1955, p. 21)

Greenwood's definition is almost a paraphrase of the logical positivist philosophers' definition of scientific knowledge (which some scientists had criticized as inaccurate, e.g., Einstein, 1934/1959).[61] For instance, Moritz Schlick defined science as "a connected system of propositions which form the result of patient observation and clever combination" (see the selection by Schlick in the Appendix; see also Hempel & Oppenheim, 1948; Salmon, 1989). As early as 1943, Helen Witmer, director of research at Smith College School for Social Work and a prominent member of the SWRG, said that scientific knowledge is deductive and uses statistical generalizations; she formulated methodological criteria for appraising the scientific value of research (Witmer, 1943, p. 224).

According to the SWRG, the purpose of research was to test propositions so as to yield a system of confirmed propositions. Thus, the SWRG's definition of a research study was much more restrictive than the definition set forth by the early social workers. In particular, the SWRG defined the purpose of research as the testing of social work theories (D. G. French, 1952; Klein & Merriam, 1948). For example, Greenwood said, "The function of research in the service of a social science is to test the accuracy of its theoretical models, so as to bring about maximum correlation between these descriptive formulations and the social phenomena thus described" (1955, pp. 21–22). The SWRG's formulations imported into social work research the untenable logical positivist delineation between the verification or confirmation of theories and their discovery (following the distinction made by Reichenbach, 1938;[62] see also Carnap, 1936; Hempel, 1965b; and Popper, see the Appendix). In an influential address at a conference held by the SWRG in 1958, J. McVicker Hunt demonstrated how positivist social researchers used logical positivist ideas to disallow the scientific merit of (1) the theories of practice that had been generated by prior social workers and (2) of practitioner judgments:

> . . . how useful clinical observations and judgment can be in testing the beliefs they have helped to form is a question. In making this point, let me emphasize strongly the distinction between hypothesis- or belief-finding on the one hand, and hypothesis- or belief-testing on the other. This is a distinction that Reichenbach [1938] has made between

what he called "the context of discovery" and the "context of justification." We have derived a great many beliefs from our clinical experience. We are fond of these beliefs; but are they true and can clinical judgment serve in testing them? (1959, p. 38)

The logical positivists initially advanced Carnap's stringent requirement of "testability" as a procedure for confirming theories, which Carnap later paraphrased as "a sentence which is confirmable by possible observable events is . . . testable if a method can be specified for producing such events at will; this method is then a test procedure for a sentence" (Carnap, 1963/1991a, p. 59). Testability was associated with an extreme version of reductionism—the assumption that all terms in the social and behavioral sciences could be reduced to "physicalist" language without a loss of meaning (Carnap, 1963/1991a).* In response to criticism, the logical positivists abandoned the more stringent requirement of testability. Instead, they emphasized that theoretical propositions can and should be confirmed or disconfirmed and that such processes of confirmation were at the heart of any science's development (Carnap, 1963/1991a; Hempel, 1965a). Even that modification, however, was subsequently recognized to be untenable: It did not conform with many historians' findings about the growth of sciences, and (as Popper says in the 1934 selection included in the Appendix) a theory can never be confirmed conclusively.

Despite the preceding developments, the SWRG did not question or revise their assumptions about theory testing and confirmation to keep pace with prior and extant critiques of the logical positivist requirements for testability and confirmation. One notable exception occurred when, in 1952, in Social Casework, one social work researcher, Sidney Zimbalist, asked a crucial question: "what test shall be applied to the test itself?" (p. 3). He emphasized that the social and behavioral sciences offered diverse approaches to conducting research and that social workers' approach to research was becoming too narrowly focused. For the most part, however, the writings of the SWRG reflect their view that the purpose of research was to test, not to generate, social work practice theories, and they emphasized that only some methods could be scientific tests of theories.

Prescriptions for Scientific Explanations and Theory Testing

One of the hallmarks of the approach to research advanced by the SWRG was the hierarchical ranking of research methods (D. G. French, 1952; Levitt, 1959; R. C. White, 1956), which stemmed from their view that the verification of theories required the use of experimental designs as they defined them. For example, Isaac Hoffman said scientific knowledge was knowledge that had been confirmed by experimentation (1956; see also Greenwood & Massarik, 1950; Polansky, 1952). Heineman Pieper points out, "The requirement that a hypothesis be 'testable' by controlled experiment is merely a statement of the viewpoint that any valuable explanation is in the form of a prediction" (1981, p. 376), which in turn derives from the logical positivists' "symmetry thesis" (see Heineman Pieper's 1981 article in Chapter 3; see also Hempel & Oppenheim, 1948; Salmon, 1989). As advanced by the logical positivists, the symmetry thesis "asserted that explanation and prediction were formally the same" (Heineman Pieper, 1981, p. 376). The SWRG's adaptation

*Editor's Note: See Chapter 1 for further information about this aspect of logical positivism.

of the symmetry thesis had long been adopted in experimental psychology: the deduction of a predictive hypothesis from initial conditions and theory and the use of an experiment to test the hypothesis and thereby the theory (see Miller, 1958, for a good example).

The SWRG consigned practitioner knowledge derived from the examination of casework processes to a separate category of knowledge that required "verification" before it could be considered "scientific" knowledge. Gloria Roman commented in the SWRG *Newsletter:*

> The practitioner's insight derived from experience is a candidate for theory. If the concepts and assumptions on which this insight is based are analyzed and explicated, the insight becomes a bit of speculative theory. When this bit of speculative theory is studied empirically and the conditions under which it holds are stated, it becomes communicable knowledge from which determinate predictions can be made. When theory-development is admitted to the research process, the relationship among "fact", "generalizations", [sic] and "theories" becomes clearer. We can say that theory is a formal structure of concepts and statements about concepts. Research is concerned with relating this formal structure to the empirical world. As this is done, "facts" and "generalizations" are uncover [sic] which are empirically sound. (No. 13, 1953, p. 12)[63]

Roman's comments also illustrate the logical positivist belief that theories and observations can be sharply distinguished, and that observations, or facts, are theory-free and then can serve as independent tests of theories (Heineman Pieper, 1981, 1989, Chapter 3; see also, e.g., Hempel, 1945). This positivist belief about facts and observations was in direct opposition to some early social workers' recognition that every clinical observation is regulated by the theoretical precepts that the caseworker implements in interviewing the client and hence obtaining data (e.g., V. Robinson, 1930/1934). The SWRG also used methodological criteria for determining whether or not social workers met ethical standards in helping clients. They prescribed that an ethical social worker should use knowledge derived from research that implemented an experimental design rather than "practice wisdom," because they mistakenly believed experimental design was a privileged test of theories (D. G. French, 1952). The verification of knowledge was then conflated with the value of providing effective service: "The function of research in a helping profession is to provide a body of verified knowledge directed toward increasing and extending the effectiveness of service to client and community" (SWRG, 1955, p. 33). In contrast to Richmond's approach to research, which built practitioners' appraisals of the utility of knowledge into the research process and the definition of research, the SWRG assumed that knowledge would be useful to practitioners only after it had been verified by researchers.

Mary MacDonald, one of the leading research faculty members at the School of Social Service Administration at the University of Chicago, described the implications of the hierarchical ranking of research methods for the status of social workers' knowledge base:

> Except as hypotheses are systematically tested, the process of research—that is the application of scientific method—is essentially incomplete. Relatively few such studies

have been made in social work. Exploratory and descriptive studies are necessary antecedents to hypothesis-testing but they fail in this purpose unless they are planned with this end in view and with reference to other studies. (1957, p. 491)

Greenwood said theory testing "means conducting the observations, where possible, under experimental conditions and with mensurative devices" (1955, p. 22). Margaret Blenkner said that because social workers had not used experimental designs to generate their knowledge about practice, social work had yet to "establish its own scientific base" (1950, Part II, p. 105).

The SWRG's emphasis on an overly restrictive version of experimental design—one that required quantified data as well as control groups—distanced practitioners from the research process as the SWRG defined it. The experimental group designs obscured the individual variations in clients and in treatment processes that clinical researchers had valued since Richmond's time. Practitioners often found experimental designs impracticable or unethical ways to study the treatment process for many reasons (see the Preface to this volume by Heineman Pieper). The belief that social work theories could be tested only in that way meant that much social work knowledge would be consigned to the depreciated realm of "untested" or, as later researchers termed it, "soft" knowledge. Further, the knowledge produced by such experiments would already be a step removed from the knowledge that practitioners would use.

Operationism

Terms associated with operationism (e.g., "operationalize," "operational definitions") did not appear in the social work literature before the 1950s. In the 1950s many positivist social work researchers prescribed operational definitions (e.g., Greenwood, 1955; MacDonald, 1959; R. C. White, 1956). The extent to which social work researchers adopted operationism[64] during the 1950s is illustrated by a playful comment in the SWRG *Newsletter:* "Researchers who are interested in operational definitions (and which researcher isn't?) will want to look at a delightful little book called *A Hole is to Dig*" (No. 13, 1953, p. 6).

As it was initially formulated by Percy Bridgman in 1927, *operationism* was the view that the meaning of a theoretical concept is "synonymous with the corresponding set of operations" (see the selection by Bridgman, Appendix). Bridgman's operationism aimed to tie each scientific concept to particular methods of observation, which he hoped would both facilitate communication among scientists and improve the accuracy of scientific concepts. He used the measurement of length as an example of an operational definition. The logical positivist Rudolf Carnap said that Bridgman's operationism was similar to his concept of "testability" as a criterion for scientific meaningfulness (1936; see also Hempel, 1965b). The logical positivists had thought that all scientific statements could ultimately be reduced to a single system of propositions using the logical and mathematical language of physics (see the Appendix and Carnap, 1963/1991a). As noted previously, however, the logical positivists' prescriptions could not weather the storm of criticism they provoked, and Carnap revised his concept of "testability" shortly after he advanced it because he recognized that it was flawed (1963/1991a). Bridgman himself concluded that a flaw in the operational point of view was that it was impracticable. Subsequently, postpositivist philosophers such as David Hull (see the selection by Hull in Chapter 5) pointed out several flaws in operationism. For example, operationism was based on the invalid argument that a concept is equivalent to a set of operations. Furthermore, operationism represented the unwarranted assumption that theories and observations can and should be sharply demarcated (see also Heineman Pieper in Chapter 3).

Positivist social work researchers' adaptation of operationism had two central ramifications. First, theoretical or conceptual terms must be rendered in terms of "sense data." One consequence of that requirement was that theoretical concepts that referred to phenomena that could not be observed directly, such as unconscious motives, were not considered researchable using methods that positivist social work researchers deemed scientific. For example, Clyde White—who in 1930 believed that case studies were legitimate sources of scientific knowledge—in 1956 criticized Gordon Hamilton and Virginia Robinson's case study-based theoretical contributions for being "descriptive" and failing to operationalize their concepts (R. C. White, 1956). Greenwood and Massarik said that "the researcher must invariably recast the practitioner's formulation into operational terms to render the problem empirically manageable. That is, he must anchor the problem to a number of objective, empirically ascertainable referents so that he might deal effectively with it" (1950, p. 549). Second, data must be quantified. Although Bridgman's (1927) original definition had not explicitly equated operationism with gathering quantified data, as operationism was imported into social work in the 1950s, it often was reformulated as a prescription that data must be quantified to yield "scientific" knowledge. William Gordon said that the contemporaneous emphasis on quantified measurement was a needed and natural development (1951, p. 7; see also D. G. French, 1952; McVicker Hunt, 1948). Margaret Blenkner said that scientific research required quantified measurement (1950, Part II). She regarded the prescription for quantified measurement as an improvement in scientific standards and emphasized that "scientific" researchers analyze their data using inferential statistics: "the standards of scientific evidence have been raised and . . . the spirit of statistical probability is abroad in the land" (1950, Part I, p. 60).

Although many important practice issues could not be studied using operational definitions, or they had to be changed so much that they no longer reflected what the researcher originally wanted to study, positivist researchers attributed such problems to the insufficiencies of casework theories rather than to flaws in operationism: "Research on the casework process is particularly difficult because the present formulations of principles and processes in casework are not readily amenable to research. The casework method is difficult to partialize and define operationally, and much of the wisdom applied in practice has not been explicated" (Shyne, 1967, p. 469). One proposed solution to the problems in clinical research was to develop standardized instruments, or ready-made operational definitions, that generally gathered data in quantitative form and were believed to "objectify observations and reduce the error due to observer differences" (Shyne, 1959, p. 8; see also Blenkner, Part II, 1950; Klein & Merriam, 1948, p. 20; McVicker Hunt, 1948).[65]

The Belief that Research Should Be Value-Free

As Maas (1991) suggests, the SWRG's approach to research abjured the place of values in social work research and thereby also the role of research in relation to social reform. A distinctive feature of the logical positivist program was the claim that statements about values were "metaphysical" or scientifically meaningless (Carnap, 1963/1991a). The logical positivists believed that a system of value-free scientific knowledge could be developed (see the selection by Scriven in Chapter 5).

The belief that researchers could and should be neutral or value-free was one of the distinctions between the basic and applied sciences as the SWRG defined them.[66] "Basic research" about social work aimed "to expand the body of practice theory that guides the social worker, to develop measuring devices for use in refining diagnosis and treatment, and to achieve understanding of the evolution, values, and culture of social work" (Greenwood, 1958, p. 160). Applied or "operational" research was concerned with solving agency or practitioner problems (D. G. French, 1952; SWRG, 1955). The SWRG did not explicitly reject the values of the social work profession; in fact, many members believed that a focus on "verified," "basic" knowledge was an ethical improvement, because they thought that the generalizations or laws that would compose basic science would provide a better foundation for good practice decisions. For example, Greenwood concluded, "For decades, social work research has been almost exclusively operational in nature, dominated by the planning and administrative needs of agencies. The consequence has been neglect of some of the most basic problems, the solutions of which carry long-range implications for the profession" (Greenwood, 1958, p. 161). However, the primary aim of basic research—the most valuable research according to the SWRG—no longer was to investigate specific client and community problems and work toward their solution. So, for example, Alfred Kahn, an influential member of the SWRG, described the scientist as someone who is silent on basic issues (1954, p. 199; see also Klein & Merriam, 1948). In another reversal of the early social workers' value of conducting research to serve agency administrators and practitioners, an SWRG participant defined "scientific researchers" in part as those who did *not* allow research issues as formulated by an agency or practitioners to influence their research:

> The research worker in an operating agency is frequently given a problem which is formulated for him either by an administrator or possibly by a legislative committee. He is not always free to consider alternative solutions to the problem presented him but must usually present his answer in the terms that have been formulated for him. In such instances he may be considered as doing engineering research, in contrast to scientific research. (SWRG, 1955, p. 14)

The SWRG's distinction between "research" and other forms of knowledge also set up a hierarchy among social workers. Many SWRG members recommended that practitioners give their "hunches" (and often, their data, per Maas & Varon, 1949) to a researcher, who would implement the designs positivist researchers prized and then inform practitioners whether or not they were correct in their perceptions of the clinical treatment process they were conducting (Greenwood, 1955; Miller,

1970). Some SWRG members disparaged practitioners' knowledge base. Margaret Blenkner, for example, said that researchers might glean some valuable information from practitioner "lore," although she thought researchers could disregard practitioners' explanations of *why* certain events occurred in the treatment process (1959).[67] Alfred Kahn said that social work knowledge was composed of "doing," not "science" (1954). Isaac Hoffman (1952) set up his "logic of research in social work" based on two "universes": a "Universe of Thought" to which the "scientist" belonged and a "Universe of Action" to which the practitioner belonged. One of the functions of the "scientist," according to Hoffman, was to test the knowledge produced by the practitioner.[68] This conceptualization of the roles of researchers and practitioners promoted a specialized role within the social work profession—that of the researcher—and used "science" to accord to researchers a higher status than that attributed to (predominantly female) practitioners.

The impact of the SWRG's prescription that practitioner knowledge needed to be tested by researchers to be scientific was immediately evident in a change in the *Social Work Year Book*. In 1947, Fletcher's definition of research was focused on practice:

> The social worker in his daily practice becomes increasingly aware of common denominators which form distinguishable patterns in certain types of situations. It is the task of social work research to study these phenomena and to reduce them, if possible, to well-defined and usable generalizations in order to increase the effectiveness and economy of practice. The key person in social work research is thus the social worker, who furnishes the hypotheses for research and utilizes the results. Research in social work does not, of course, furnish the entire scientific basis upon which the practice of social work is established. (p. 439)

Social work research as defined in 1947 had four aims:

1. Improving casework diagnosis and treatment;
2. Enhancing agency efficiency;
3. Appraising community needs for services and determining how those needs could be met;
4. Adding to understanding about the cause of "social pathology" to assist preventive services (Fletcher, 1947, pp. 439–440).

In 1949, by contrast, after describing the founding and initial mission of the SWRG, Fletcher said, "research in social work is the scientific testing of the validity of social work function and method" (Fletcher, 1949, p. 435). Finally, whereas the early social workers had advanced the ideal of the social worker as a practitioner–researcher, the SWRG's definition of valuable research led them to conclude, "competence in research design calls for a degree of specialization which most practitioners cannot be expected to achieve" (1955, p. 13).

SOME IMPLICATIONS OF THE FORMULATION OF A LOGICAL POSITIVIST APPROACH TO SOCIAL WORK RESEARCH

Researchers Espoused Different Priorities for Research Design

Substantial changes in social work research accompanied the adoption of the positivist approach to social work research advanced by the SWRG. As described previously, to investigate the trends and changes in social work research, I examined a systematic sample of 2,884 articles published in *Social Service Review, Social Casework,* and *Social Work* from 1920 to 1989. The articles were coded for research design heuristic, first-author gender, year of publication, and approach to evaluation. As a first step toward testing my hypothesis that when social work researchers adopted a positivist approach to social and behavioral research, researchers increasingly used experimental designs and quantified data, I combined the seven research design heuristics into three groups, according to the type of data the researcher gathered.

First, I grouped the studies by whether or not the researcher gathered her or his own data directly from clients or participant/subjects in the research. Studies based on data that were relatively distant from informants included those in which the researcher gathered data about events in the distant past (histories), other researchers' conceptualizations (reviews), or reports about current events (commentaries). Studies based on data that were gathered more directly from clients and informants included those in which the data were drawn from contemporaneous human services (e.g., case studies or compilations of characteristics of public welfare applicants) or from the researcher's relationship with participant/subjects in research who were not clients (e.g., unstructured interviews about informants' childhood experiences).

The second and third groups of studies (those using data gathered directly from clients and informants) were differentiated according to whether or not the researcher quantified her or his data. The studies in the sample that used experimental designs all also used quantified data. The recombination resulted in three groups of studies:

1. Reviews, commentaries, and histories;
2. Qualitative case studies and large-scale qualitative analyses;
3. Experimental designs, case studies with quantified data, and large-scale analyses with quantified data.[69]

The years covered were also combined into decades (1920 to 1929, 1930 to 1939, etc.). Figure 2–3 shows the distribution that resulted from the recombination into the three groups of studies. A look at the sample as a whole, over the total 70-year period, indicates that researchers had a marked preference (61%) for reviews, commentaries, and histories, and that they chose qualitative data and qualitative analyses (20%) slightly more often than they chose to quantify their data (19%).

Figure 2–3

Distribution of research design heuristics using three types of data in social work journal articles, 1920 to 1989

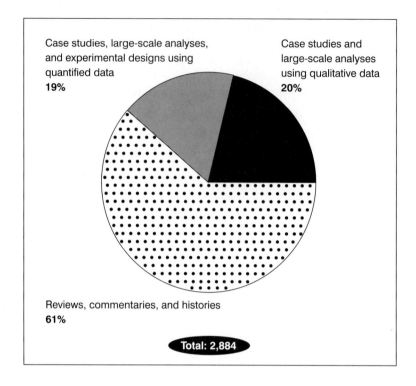

Case studies, large-scale analyses, and experimental designs using quantified data
19%

Case studies and large-scale analyses using qualitative data
20%

Reviews, commentaries, and histories
61%

Total: 2,884

The findings of the content analysis support my hypothesis that researchers increasingly used experimental designs and quantified data following the adoption of the positivist approach to social work research (Table 2–2, Figure 2–4). The data in Table 2–2 and Figures 2–4 through 2–6 indicate that the 1950s was a decade of transition. During the 1950s, 70% of articles were review/commentary/historical studies (an increase from 59% in the 1940s). The many commentaries included articles

Table 2–2

Distribution and Percentages of Seven Research Design Heuristics within Each Decade, 1920 to 1989

Research Design Heuristics	1920s		1930s		1940s		1950s		1960s		1970s		1980s	
	#	%	#	%	#	%	#	%	#	%	#	%	#	%
Reviews and commentaries	160	64	181	60	160	55	220	65	261	56	343	56	322	52
Histories	23	9	14	5	12	4	17	5	24	5	15	3	15	2
Case studies - Qualitative data	34	14	35	12	31	11	28	8	32	7	24	4	40	6
Large-scale analyses - Qualitative data	8	3	24	8	64	22	40	12	77	16	77	13	66	11
Case studies - Quantified data	0	0	0	0	0	0	0	0	0	0	3	<1	1	<1
Large-scale analyses - Quantified data	26	10	49	16	23	8	28	8	65	14	131	22	169	27
Experimental designs	0	0	0	0	0	0	4	1	10	2	17	3	11	2
Totals	251	100	303	101	290	100	337	99	469	100	610	101	624	100

Percentages have been rounded and so may not add up to 100 in some cases.

advancing positivist approaches to social research (e.g., Blenkner, 1950; W. E. Gordon, 1951; Greenwood, 1955; Hoffman, 1956).

From the 1950s through the 1980s, a steadily growing percentage of researchers quantified their data (see Figure 2–4). In the 1940s, 8% of the articles used quantified data, and the percentage increased steadily to 29% in the 1980s. The emphasis on experimental designs and quantified data after the 1950s was accompanied by a decreasing percentage of qualitative analyses. Whereas in the 1940s 33% of researchers conducted case studies or large-scale qualitative analyses, only 20% used those research design heuristics in the 1950s, and the percentage shrank to 17% in the 1970s and 1980s (see Figure 2–4). The shift that began in the 1950s is even more evident when the percentage of articles with quantified data is calculated in relation to the total number of articles with either quantified or qualitative data (see Figure 2–5). In other words, of the studies in which the authors chose to gather their data directly from the participant/subjects in the research, the percentage of studies in which authors quantified their data increased dramatically with the adoption of positivist beliefs about research (see Figure 2–5).

Researchers first began to use experimental designs during the 1950s. The percentage of experimental designs, although slight overall, increased from 1% in the

Figure 2–4

Distribution of three research design heuristics in social work journal articles, by decade, 1920 to 1989

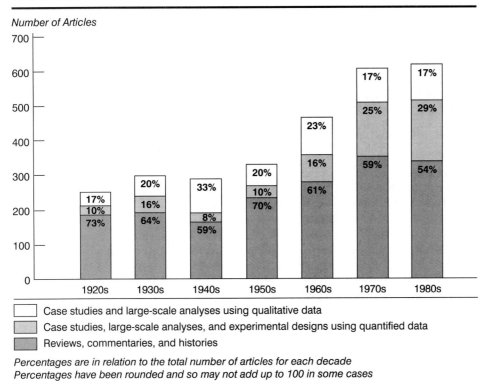

Percentages are in relation to the total number of articles for each decade
Percentages have been rounded and so may not add up to 100 in some cases

Figure 2–5
Articles that used quantified data in relation to the total number of articles that used qualitative or quantified data, by decade, 1920 to 1989

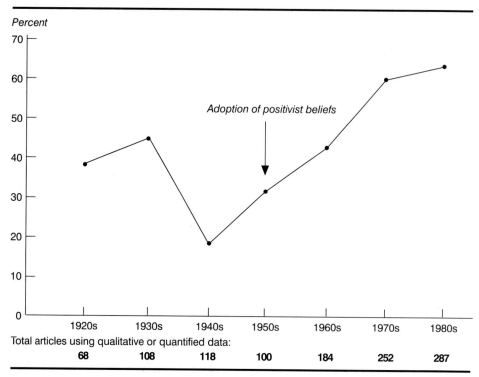

Total articles using qualitative or quantified data:

1920s	1930s	1940s	1950s	1960s	1970s	1980s
68	108	118	100	184	252	287

1950s to 3% in the 1970s (see Table 2–2). The prescription for experimental designs that began in the 1950s is exemplified by an article published in 1959 in *Smith College Studies in Social Work*, a journal that since its inception in 1930 had published a great many qualitative case studies:

> Research which does not follow the accepted methodology [a variant of experimental design using operational definitions] cannot lead directly to scientific facts . . . the case study, as well as many studies of groups of individuals, do not conform to the requirements of scientific investigation. (Levitt, 1959, p. 63)

Further, Mary MacDonald observed in the *Social Work Year Book* in 1960 that although "relatively few experimental studies have yet been made in social work, the trend appears to be toward more rigorously designed research" (1960a, p. 508). She then described the recent use of experimental simulations of practice situations to study practitioner responses. The members of the SWRG applied experimental designs to different problems. For example, Margaret Blenkner compared the status of one group of elderly clients who received casework treatment with another group who did not receive services (1962). Otto Pollak compared findings from measures of outcomes for the treatment of marital partners conjointly with measures of the outcome of individual treatment of marital partners (1963). Roger Miller tested a prediction derived from Reik's theory about therapists' use of free-floating attention on two groups of students. He regarded one group as oriented toward diagnosis and another group as oriented toward empathy. He concluded that "the students who used more than average free floating attention also gave evidence of a superior grasp of the client . . . similarly, the observers who directed more than an average amount of their attention internally demonstrated superior psychological comprehension" (1958, p. 102). His conclusions illustrate how experiments were regarded as premier tests of casework theories: "this experiment indicates that the model proposed by Reik may continue to be entertained as a fruitful explanation for the process of observation in casework interviewing" (p. 102). Miller's comment also indicates that these researchers believed that the findings from experimental designs should be used to regulate how practitioners understand practice.

To take a closer look at the data obtained by analyzing the 2,884 articles, I used the chi-square analysis (Norusis, 1988, p. 242) to test whether there is a statistically significant departure from how one would expect the variables of research design heuristic and decade of publication to be related if chance alone were operating.[70]

Figure 2–6

Chi-square analysis of the distribution of research design heuristics in social work journal articles, by decade, 1920 to 1989: Adjusted standardized chi-square residuals

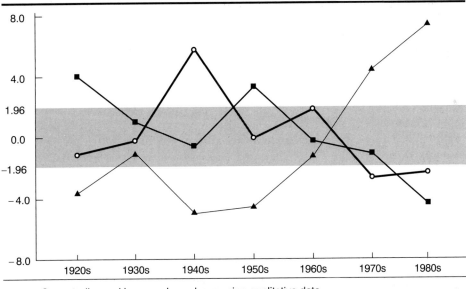

—○— Case studies and large-scale analyses using qualitative data
—▲— Case studies, large-scale analyses, and experimental designs using quantified data
—■— Reviews, commentaries, and histories

Chi Square: 143.72   Significance: p< .00005   Total articles: 2,884

Figure 2–6 shows the results of the chi-square test. Over the 70-year period, the relationship between research design heuristic and year of publication is much stronger than one would expect given the influence of chance alone. The chi-square statistic[71] is 143.72, and the probability that these relationships would occur given chance alone is less than .00005. The adjusted standardized residuals, plotted in Figure 2–6, allow one to examine particular instances in the relationships between the variables tested in the chi-square. The adjusted standardized residuals show whether or not the presence of a particular variable is more or less than an expected presence of a particular variable; in this case, one of the research design heuristics in a given decade. If the residual is 0, that variable is present as one would expect it, given chance variations alone; if it is negative, it appeared less often than one would expect; and if it is positive, it is present more often than one would expect. When the adjusted standardized residuals are greater than $+1.96$ or less than -1.96, the relationship is statistically significant.[72] During the 1920s and 1940s, articles with quantified data were written much less frequently than would be expected given chance alone, perhaps because at that time compiling quantified data was exceedingly tedious. In the 1940s, articles with qualitative data were authored much more often than would be expected given chance alone. In the 1970s and 1980s, however, articles relying solely on qualitative data were authored much less, and articles with quantified data were authored much more, than would be expected given chance alone. One way to interpret the results of the chi-square test is that researchers' decisions about research design, far from being "neutral," "bias-free," or independent of sociohistorical influences, are deeply wedded to forces at work in the researchers' cultural milieu, including the hegemonic metatheory of research.

In addition to the SWRG's approach to research, other trends during the 1950s and after may have encouraged social work researchers to quantify their data. The largest surge in research design heuristics using quantified data occurred in the 1970s, coinciding with the increasing sophistication and accessibility of computer technologies. Researchers often find new technologies fascinating and are inclined to plan research so they can try out the new tools (Latour, 1987; Purpura & Reaser, 1974; C. Rosenberg, 1961/1976). Social work researchers may have enjoyed the rapidity of data compilation and new variations in data analysis that computers offered, which encouraged them to explore statistical analyses using quantified data. Another reason for the surge of studies using quantified data in the 1970s is the publication during that decade of many large-scale program evaluations conducted during the War on Poverty (Rossi & Wright, 1984). Finally, by the 1970s researchers taught in the 1950s by a generation of positivist social researchers had become leaders in social work research.

As indicated previously (see Figure 2–1 and Table 2–2), experimental designs were used in only 42 of 2,884, or 2%, of published studies in this sample. It is striking that the research design heuristic that was virtually impracticable for most social workers was the design that positivist social researchers most prized. In 1973, Joel Fischer epitomized how positivist social work researchers enshrined their version of experimental design when he used a compilation of eleven experimental studies of casework to address the question of the effectiveness of social casework as a whole. Like other positivist researchers (e.g., Hanrahan & Reid, 1984), Fischer

(1980/1981) believed that experimental design was, in itself, such a powerful test of theories that conclusions drawn from a tiny minority of studies using experimental designs were superior to the conclusions of the great majority of research on casework based on other design heuristics.[73]

A Gulf Widened between Practitioners and Researchers

In the 1950s, social work authors steadily reported a widening gulf between researchers and practitioners (Kogan, 1960). Several blows widened that gulf. Members of the SWRG denigrated social work practitioners' judgments as unreliable (Blenkner, 1950; McVicker Hunt, 1959). Blenkner said that caseworkers' observations were full of "pitfalls" and that "wherever possible, they must be checked by non-participant observers" (1950, Part II, p. 100). She hailed the newly developed electronic recording devices and hoped that "photographic" records of treatment sessions would become available. Although practitioners voiced reservations about using intrusive recording devices for third-party monitoring, Blenkner dismissed clinicians' reservations as psychopathological: "mention of such tools raises in the caseworker's mind connotations of wire-tapping and Peeping Toms. How much of this is due to genuine ethical considerations and how much to the caseworker's own insecurity is difficult to determine but one cannot help speculate that the latter factor plays a substantial role" (1950, Part II, p. 101). Blenkner concluded that "one cannot, however, meet the criteria of scientific measurement with such an instrument [caseworkers' judgments] without some calibration. Methods must be developed for objectifying, validating, and standardizing caseworker judgments if they are to lay a base for scientific evidence and conclusions" (1950, Part II, p. 101).

SWRG members attributed practitioner reservations about the SWRG's approach to research to flaws in practitioners' motivation to produce scientific knowledge and *not* to the SWRG's assumptions about social work research. Blenkner criticized clinical researchers such as Charlotte Towle because Towle, like some other clinical theorists, had not "conceded either the dearth of it [clinical research] or the unsatisfactory nature of much that has been done" (1950, Part I, p. 55). Further, Blenkner dismissed practitioners' concerns about research, "the recurrent theme is always the same—caseworkers need such research, they must do it themselves, they are just on the verge of doing it, but they have not quite managed to get around to it" (1950, Part I, p. 55). She believed that caseworkers and researchers were cut from entirely different cloth. She said that a good caseworker has an "intuitive, imaginative mind and a capacity for deep identification with others . . . coupled with a strong drive to succor the person in distress" (1950, Part I, pp. 55–56). On the other hand, the "good scientific worker . . . must have traits of a different order: a conceptual, analytical approach to phenomena and a drive to arrive at conclusions through rational induction or objective deduction from explicit principles" (1950, Part I, p. 56). Greenwood said that "to apply to a practitioner the term 'scientist' (qualified though it be by the adjective 'applied') is to distort the meaning of that term" (1955, p. 27). He said that practitioners did not contribute to scientific theory but only applied what was already known; further, the practitioner could not be a scientist because she or he must rely on "intuition" when lacking "scientific guides" (Greenwood, 1955). Samuel Mencher, who was commissioned to examine how the SWRG's approach to research could be taught in schools of social work, concluded that practitioners in master's programs might not be able to learn to do research as the SWRG defined it (1959).[74]

The gulf between researchers and practitioners reflected not only beliefs about social work knowledge but also differences between the authority and status of women and men in the social work profession. More women were in direct practice, whereas more men held management, research, and faculty positions (Dressel, 1987; Kadushin, 1976; A. Schwartz, 1967; Steinberg, 1988). Selma Fraiberg summarized how the practitioner–researcher schism was infused by restrictive gender roles when she said, "the clinician has taken to minding the pots in the kitchen and the researcher is conducting an affair with a computer" (1970, p. 101). The gender-related schism between researchers and practitioners, in which practitioners occupied lower-paid and lower-status positions in the hierarchy, mirrors what Brumberg and Tomes observed about the development of other professions during the twentieth century: Women generally occupied lower-status positions with more direct client contact and were regarded as "intellectually inferior but altruistically superior" to men (Brumberg & Tomes, 1982, p. 288; Furumoto, 1987).[75]

The data from the content analysis also indicate profound gender-related trends in social work journal articles. The relative preeminence of women and men as first authors of journal articles shifted dramatically from the 1940s to the 1950s. In the 1940s, almost twice as many women as men were first authors of journal articles (175 and 95, respectively), whereas in the 1950s, the number of female first authors decreased and the number of male first authors increased until they were almost equal (160 women and 158 men, see Table 2–1 on p. 64). Those changes are all the more striking because with the introduction of the new journal *Social Work* in 1956, the overall number of social work journal articles increased from 290 in the 1940s to 337 in the 1950s and 469 in the 1960s. Men's dominance as first authors continued to increase, so that substantially more men than women were first authors in the 1960s and 1970s (36% women, 58% men in the 1960s; 40% women, 56% men in the 1970s). That trend began to shift only in the 1980s, when the proportion of women and men first authors was restored to equality (see Table 2–1).

Another noticeable trend is that women and men made very different choices of research design heuristics (Figure 2–7). Over time the total numbers of women and men first authors were almost equal. A greater percentage of men, however, authored reviews, commentaries, and histories (65%), and studies using quantified data and/or experimental designs (21%). A greater percentage of women than men chose research design heuristics that used qualitative data (27% vs. 14%, respectively).[76] During the 1940s, when most first authors were female, there was a corresponding surge in the use of research design heuristics relying on qualitative data (see Figures 2–4 on p. 79 and 2–6 on p. 81). The changes in the 1950s affected women's and men's pursuit of qualitative research very differently. Although the percentage of men who authored qualitative studies held relatively constant from the 1940s to the 1950s (19% and 17%, respectively, Figure 2–8 a and b), the percentage of women who published qualitative studies in the 1940s was reduced by almost a half during the 1950s (42% in the 1940s and 24% in the 1950s, Figure 2–8

Figure 2–7
Research design heuristics used in articles first-authored by women and by men, 1920 to 1989

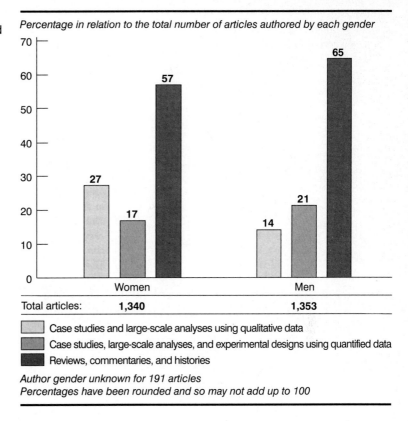

Percentage in relation to the total number of articles authored by each gender

Total articles: Women **1,340** Men **1,353**

Case studies and large-scale analyses using qualitative data
Case studies, large-scale analyses, and experimental designs using quantified data
Reviews, commentaries, and histories

Author gender unknown for 191 articles
Percentages have been rounded and so may not add up to 100

a and b). However, the conclusion that beliefs about research are simply a function of gender is not warranted because:

1. Over time, women researchers also increasingly quantified their data (see Table 2–1 on p. 64);

2. Choice of research design heuristic is not synonymous with beliefs about research;

3. Many women espoused logical positivist beliefs (e.g., Margaret Blenkner, 1950, and Mary MacDonald, 1960b),[77] while many men advocated alternatives (e.g., Joseph Vigilante, 1974, and Dennis Saleebey, 1979).

In the context of the social work profession, the differences between women and men with regard to their choice of research design heuristics may reflect women's and men's different roles. The great majority of social work practitioners have always been women (A. Schwartz, 1967), and men more often held management and faculty positions, a trend that persists (Dressel, 1987; Garvin & Reed, 1983; Steinberg, 1988). Many researchers have noted that qualitative data are particularly helpful for investigating many important problems in social work practice,

Figure 2–8a

Research design heuristics used in articles first-authored by women and by men, 1940s

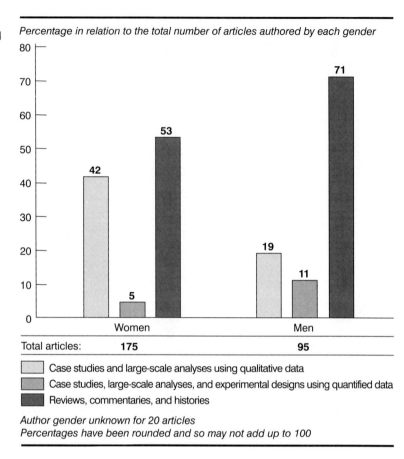

Percentage in relation to the total number of articles authored by each gender

	Case studies and large-scale analyses using qualitative data
	Case studies, large-scale analyses, and experimental designs using quantified data
	Reviews, commentaries, and histories

Author gender unknown for 20 articles
Percentages have been rounded and so may not add up to 100

such as the unique complexities of client–worker relationships. Therefore, women's preferences for research design heuristics relying on qualitative data may reflect practitioners' commitment to conducting research about practice. This explanation is further supported by the finding that women were much more likely than men (46% and 33%, respectively) to author evaluative studies about social work practice, educational processes, or social programs (see Chapter 7). Further, as social work adopted positivism in the 1950s, the qualitative studies that practitioners had traditionally used to examine and discuss their clinical work were depreciated by comparison with studies using quantified data. Women, who were more likely to be practitioners and to author qualitative studies, may have found that their interests were likely to be devalued during the shift to positivist beliefs, accounting for the reduction in the proportion of women who published qualitative studies from the 1940s to the 1950s.

The time-related patterns of gender and research design heuristic noted previously also were reflected in the social work journals (Figures 2–9 and 2–10, Table 2–3). *Social Casework,* the journal traditionally devoted to studies of practice, published three times as many qualitative studies (30%) as articles using quantified data

(10%, see Figure 2–9). *Social Work*, the journal founded by the National Association of Social Workers in 1956, reflected positivist social work researchers' preference for quantified data. In *Social Work*, only 15% of the articles had solely qualitative data, whereas 25% of the articles used quantified data (see Figure 2–9). Even more striking, only 6% of *Social Service Review's* articles were qualitative, as compared with 29% that used quantified data. Perhaps *Social Casework's* emphasis on qualitative studies reflected practitioners' common preference for qualitative data for investigating the complexities of practice. From these data, I conclude that journals are not neutral disseminators of scientific research: Editorial policy varies strongly among journals, reflects preferences for particular research methods, and also reflects changing sociohistorical influences and priorities.

Social Casework was more likely to have published an article by a female first author than the other journals; 55% of articles in that journal were first-authored by women, by comparison with 40% in *Social Work* and 37% in *Social Service Review* (see Figure 2–10). This may be because the various emphases of the journals corresponded to other differences within the profession, which in turn corresponded to gender. For example, as noted, historically, most social work practitioners have been

Figure 2–8b
Research design heuristics used in articles first-authored by women and by men, 1950s

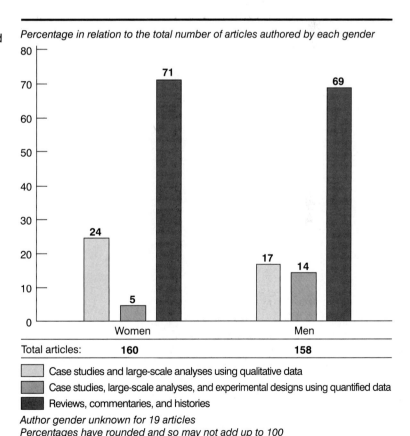

Percentage in relation to the total number of articles authored by each gender

Total articles: 160 (Women), 158 (Men)

☐ Case studies and large-scale analyses using qualitative data
▨ Case studies, large-scale analyses, and experimental designs using quantified data
■ Reviews, commentaries, and histories

Author gender unknown for 19 articles
Percentages have rounded and so may not add up to 100

women, a trend that persisted despite the substantial influx of men into the profession in the late 1940s and early 1950s (Dressel, 1987; Garvin & Reed, 1983; Steinberg, 1988). *Social Casework* traditionally has focused on publishing studies of social work practice using qualitative data, which may account for why it was more likely to have published a study authored by a woman. A more disturbing implication of these findings is that because some editorial policies reflected ideological biases against relying solely on qualitative data, and because women were more inclined than men to author qualitative analyses, those editorial policies may have had the effect of reinforcing discrimination against women researchers.

Some researchers and practice theorists of the 1950s expressed concern about the implications of the developing schism between practitioners and researchers (Coyle, 1952). For example, in 1952, Zimbalist elaborated what he termed the difference between "organismic casework" and "partialistic research." He was con-

Figure 2–9
Research design heuristics used in articles published in three social work journals, 1920 to 1989

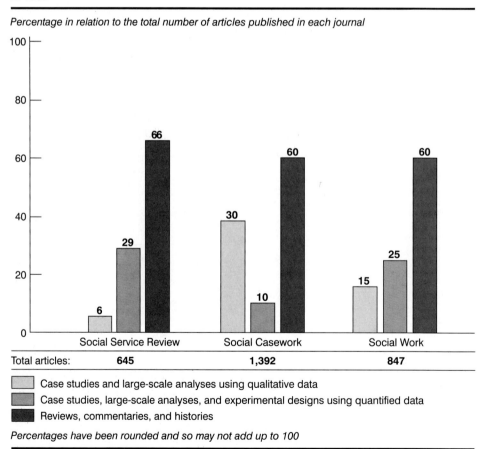

Percentage in relation to the total number of articles published in each journal

	Social Service Review	Social Casework	Social Work
Total articles:	**645**	**1,392**	**847**

☐ Case studies and large-scale analyses using qualitative data
▨ Case studies, large-scale analyses, and experimental designs using quantified data
■ Reviews, commentaries, and histories

Percentages have been rounded and so may not add up to 100

Figure 2–10
Articles first-authored by women and by men in three social work journals, 1920 to 1989

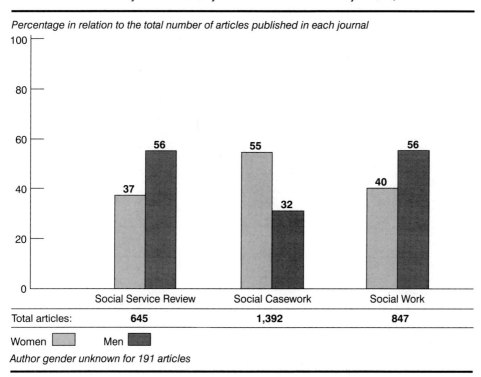

Percentage in relation to the total number of articles published in each journal

| Total articles: | 645 | 1,392 | 847 |

Women ☐   Men ◼
Author gender unknown for 191 articles

cerned that the "partialistic" approach to research would impede the development of social work's knowledge base. He hoped that social workers could join other social scientists in "working toward a whole-centered science of human relationships. In these ways, social work may be able to contribute its proper share to the long-awaited 'humanizing' of research in the social sciences, as well as in its own field" (Zimbalist, 1952, p. 10).

Others debated Zimbalist's conclusions, stating that "the problem of research lies in the absence of a theory of basic research in social work rather than in the fact that a theory exists which is part-centered" (Berkman, 1952, p. 164). Gallagher agreed with Zimbalist, saying that clinicians had begun to "distrust research as being unreliable and of little use to them" (1952, p. 255). Consonant with the methodological and technological emphasis of the SWRG, however, Gallagher believed the "major problem . . . lies in obtaining the proper techniques with which to measure these elusive factors [in casework] . . . to generalize from data, one must use mathematics in one form or another" (1952, p. 256). Gershonson, MacDonald, Perlman, and Ripple wrote a letter in response to Zimbalist, claiming, "If research in social work is to be meaningful, the social work practitioners must become articulate about the problems that are important to them and insistent that these be the problems to which social work research address itself" (1952, p. 258).

Table 2–3

Distribution and Percentages of Seven Research Design Heuristics by Social Work Journal and by Decade, 1920 to 1989

Social Service Review

Research Design Heuristics	1920s		1930s		1940s		1950s		1960s		1970s		1980s	
	#	%	#	%	#	%	#	%	#	%	#	%	#	%
Reviews and commentaries	14	47	63	58	72	70	53	60	63	59	41	42	43	39
Histories	4	13	11	10	8	8	15	17	14	13	11	11	12	11
Case studies - Qualitative data	2	8	2	2	5	5	3	3	3	3	0	0	1	1
Large-scale analyses - Qualitative data	0	0	4	4	4	4	3	3	5	5	1	1	3	3
Case studies - Quantified data	0	0	0	0	0	0	0	0	0	0	3	3	0	0
Large-scale analyses - Quantified data	10	33	28	26	14	14	13	15	17	16	37	38	47	43
Experimental designs	0	0	0	0	0	0	2	2	5	5	5	5	4	4
Totals	30	101	108	100	103	101	89	100	107	101	98	100	110	101

Social Work

Research Design Heuristics	1920s	1930s	1940s	1950s		1960s		1970s		1980s	
				#	%	#	%	#	%	#	%
Reviews and commentaries				55	68	122	63	176	58	148	55
Histories				1	1	1	1	2	1	2	1
Case studies - Qualitative data		*Publication Began in 1956*		7	9	15	8	11	4	15	6
Large-scale analyses - Qualitative data				11	13	28	14	28	9	15	6
Case studies - Quantified data				0	0	0	0	0	0	1	0
Large-scale analyses - Quantified data				6	7	27	14	79	26	81	30
Experimental designs				2	2	2	1	7	2	5	2
Totals				82	100	195	101	303	100	267	100

Social Casework

Research Design Heuristics	1920s		1930s		1940s		1950s		1960s		1970s		1980s	
	#	%	#	%	#	%	#	%	#	%	#	%	#	%
Reviews and commentaries	146	66	118	61	88	48	112	68	76	46	126	60	131	53
Histories	19	9	3	2	4	2	1	1	9	5	2	1	1	1
Case studies - Qualitative data	32	15	33	17	26	14	18	11	14	8	13	6	24	10
Large-scale analyses - Qualitative data	8	4	20	10	60	32	26	16	44	26	48	23	48	19
Case studies - Quantified data	0	0	0	0	0	0	0	0	0	0	0	0	0	0
Large-scale analyses - Quantified data	16	7	21	11	9	5	9	5	21	13	15	7	41	17
Experimental designs	0	0	0	0	0	0	0	0	3	2	5	2	2	1
Totals	221	101	195	101	187	101	166	101	167	100	209	99	247	101

Percentages have been rounded and so may not add up to 100 in some cases.

Early Social Work Researchers' Contributions Were Evaluated as "Unscientific"

In her denunciations of prior approaches to research, Margaret Blenkner said about social work practice, "there has been too much talk of love and kindness—an oversimplification of the job" (1950, Part I, p. 57). Recognizing that social work practitioners at the time were in an adversarial position with regard to the values of the wider society, Blenkner attributed responsibility for the problem to social workers:

> Because caseworkers have not yet done the research job necessary fully to expose and interpret the complexities of their job and the difficulties and failures involved, the caseworker's art . . . is still in that immature and unhappy state where critical editors and news reporters, and economy-minded budget committees are only too happy to pounce on them as befuddled sentimentalists. (1950, Part I, p. 57)

As Blenkner's statements illustrate, some social work researchers sided with opponents of the profession's traditional humanistic aims. The SWRG's statements about social workers and clinical research appear extremely harsh, especially because the SWRG's critiques were grounded in an approach to research deemed unwarranted according to many contemporaneous beliefs about scientific research. Nonetheless, the SWRG was profoundly influential for some time. As Zimbalist noted:

> By 1959, its membership numbered approximately 600, and local sections were functioning in 11 N.A.S.W. chapters. Later, with the restructuring of the N.A.S.W. in 1963, the Section became its Council on Social Work Research. The impact of these organizational developments on the growth and visibility of social work research over the years has been extensive and crucial to the strengthening of this special component of the field, and to its clarification. (1977, pp. 22–23)

Members of the SWRG authored the definitions of research in the *Social Work Year Book* (MacDonald, 1957) and in the *Encyclopedia of Social Work* (Polansky, 1971). They founded the journal *Social Work Research and Abstracts* and were members of the editorial boards of the most prominent social work journals. The impact of the SWRG's ideas on the assessment of the early social workers' research was evident when *Social Work Research and Abstracts* opened with an editorial that stated: "Only a fraction of the knowledge that actually informs social workers can be considered to have scientific underpinnings" (Reid, 1977a, p. 2).

By the 1960s, the logical positivist beliefs about research promulgated by the SWRG were well entrenched in social work research. For example, in 1967 Elizabeth Salomon wrote that "positivism is the dominant philosophy in the world today." She warned that "this method of generating knowledge explicitly denies value" (p. 27; see also Back, 1969). In their 1965 content analysis of the social work literature, Taber and Shapiro stated that although there was a substantial knowledge base in social work, "a more rigorous definition of knowledge is generally accepted," and in that context, "facts, reports of experience, and concepts in a field contribute to its knowledge base only as they are used to develop relatively well-confirmed theory" (p. 106).[78] The impact of the SWRG's formulation of a "scientific" approach to social work research continues to this day (Maas, 1991). As recently as 1991, Margaret Blenkner's (1962) suggestion that caseworkers offer "placebo" treatments to set up control groups for experimental designs (e.g., that social workers deceive their clients by pretending to treat them) was cited as one solution to contemporary problems in research about casework practice (Thyer, 1991). In 1991, a Task Force that was appointed by the National Institute of Mental Health to advance social work research completed a report that virtually ignored the contemporary debates about the appropriate paradigm for social work research, despite the fact that many social work educators had voiced their concern about the irrelevance of positivist social work research directly to members of the Task Force and despite the Task Force's stated mission to survey and represent contemporary social work research. Furthermore, two prominent ways in which the Task Force manifested its positivist bias were in its definition of "empirical research" and in its criticism of published social work research as lacking in scientific merit because it was not based on the "scientific methods" of experimental and quasi-experimental designs.[79]

Research No Longer Had the Explicit Purpose of Advancing Social Reform

Another eventual consequence of the adoption of positivism was that some accounts of the history of social work research erased the approaches to research espoused by the early social workers. When the SWRG conceptualized the primary role of researchers as testing and validating the usefulness of what practitioners did, they uncoupled the partnership of research and practice that early social workers such as Abbott, Richmond, and Addams had forged.[80] This uncoupling had unfortunate consequences. It fostered the generation of knowledge that practitioners found unusable and alienated practitioners from research (Miller, 1970); it also discouraged the use of research for social change (Goldstein, 1963). A version of social work history developed that overlooked the early social workers' use of research for social reform (Chambers, 1986a), as the following comments by Polansky illustrate:

> Most community surveys were initiated in the hope that once the facts were compiled and artfully presented, the local leadership would be inspired to act. . . . Experience in this country, alas, was that knowledge of needs did not guarantee incentive to meet them. Few were as successful as Dorothea Dix. (Polansky, 1971, p. 1102)

Such historians ignored the impact of the early social workers on social institutions, such as changes in labor legislation and rights for women; the establishment of the Children's Bureau; the Shepphard-Towner Maternity and Infancy Act, which initiated federal financial assistance for disadvantaged women and children; and the Social Security Act.

The uncoupling of the metatheory of social work research from the value of social reform had powerful effects on the conduct of social work research. Aronson and Sherwood described a common problem that occurred when War on Poverty programs were evaluated by positivist social researchers:

> Any program designer or practitioner ought to want to know what effects the program is trying to produce, but the research responsibility of a demonstration program cannot be fulfilled unless these outcomes are defined in terms that can be operationalized and measured. It was not always possible to get the [program] designers to define the goals; researchers frequently had to suggest what the goals were and attempt to get the designers to go along. (1967, p. 91)

Anderson and Sherwood described how practitioners did not like positivist social and behavioral researchers' prescriptions (e.g., the use of control groups), criticized such approaches as dehumanizing, and often protested, "'when are you going to stop experimenting with people and let us start helping them?'" (1967, p. 92). Further, many of the studies of social work practice that implemented experimental designs were not conducted with middle-class psychotherapy "patients" as participant/subjects but rather were conducted with the clients of agencies serving the poor, the elderly (Jahn & Blenkner reported in Blenkner, 1962), and children or adolescents (Powers & Witmer reported in D. G. French, 1952; Rossi & Wright, 1984). In other words, those who most often filled the anonymous, nonparticipatory role of the "subject" in positivist social and behavioral researchers' versions of experimental design were disadvantaged clients who could not turn elsewhere for services, and whose unique strengths, values, and needs were, for the most part, already ignored by the wider society.

CONCLUSIONS

To improve the conceptual foundations for contemporary social work research, this history has explored prior approaches to research in the field of social work. Although previous historians have not focused on approaches to social work research, in discussing the history of the social work profession most have made two assumptions about social work research. This study has examined those assumptions. The first assumption was that the knowledge generated by the social workers who founded the profession at the turn of the century was unscientific. Those historians thought that the early social workers did not develop principles to systematically guide their research. However, the historical data do not support that assumption. In fact, at the beginning of this century, three social work research communities generated principles for the conduct of social work research: the settlement houses, the charity organization societies, and psychiatric social work researchers in hospitals and mental hygiene clinics. The early social work researchers drew from the approach to scientific research advanced by the pragmatist philosophers and developed an approach to research that aimed to advance social justice, understand social problems, and offer specific and workable solutions to those problems to improve human well-being. The second assumption about the history of social work research that has pervaded prior histories is that the profession's adoption of the SWRG's approach to research in the 1950s represented a new commitment to "basic" science. By definition, "basic" science was value-free, or neutral, with regard to sociopolitical conflicts. The second assumption also does not hold up under scrutiny. Rather than being value-free, the SWRG's positivist approach to research represented different values, as summarized next.

Many of the early social workers regarded research as a way to work for solutions for the most pressing problems of their time. They were influential advocates for women's rights, better mental health care, more humane working conditions, and improved services and financial support for families. They did not divorce the goals of generating knowledge from the goals of helping individuals and society. To the contrary, the early social work researchers sowed the seeds for and led several extremely important movements for social change. Some other research principles advanced by the early social workers follow:

1. Methodological pluralism—no one research design was regarded as inherently superior to any other design for testing theories;

2. A commitment to the values of using research to advance social justice through advocacy for specific social reforms;

3. A nonrestrictive approach to those subjects that could be legitimate topics for research (e.g., they included the study of variables such as introspected feelings within the domain of scientific research);

4. A nonhierarchical role structure for the relationships between researchers and practitioners and between researchers and agency administrators (e.g., researchers wanted practitioners to evaluate the utility and validity of research findings, and researchers respected the judgments of practitioners);

5. A collaborative relationship between the researcher and the participant/subject in the research, in which the participant/subjects' formulations of the problems to be addressed in research, as well as their evaluations of solutions, were respected.

In the 1950s, the SWRG adopted overly restrictive beliefs about science that were derived largely from the logical positivist philosophy of science, although the SWRG did not call their beliefs positivist. The major tenets of the SWRG's approach to research follow:

1. An overly restrictive definition of social work research that relied on methodological criteria to demarcate social work research from other forms of social work knowledge;

2. The belief that the purpose of research is to generate a reservoir of "confirmed" knowledge, in contrast with practitioner knowledge, which the SWRG regarded as unconfirmed "lore";

3. A hierarchy of research methods, based on the assumption that the version of experimental design preferred by the SWRG was a privileged test of social work theories;

4. The requirement that research problems be operationalized, which was commonly implemented as a preference for quantified data;

5. The belief that research could and should be value-free and neutral with regard to sociopolitical conflicts.

Using the preceding standards, members of the SWRG evaluated the knowledge contributed by the early social work researchers as unscientific.

Several contextual influences encouraged social workers to define social work research using logical positivist ideas about science. During the beginning of the Cold War, when many social workers who advocated social reform were subjected to intimidation and/or persecution, the positivist view that social researchers could not simultaneously be scientists and advocates conformed with McCarthy-era dictates. The SWRG, which in the 1950s took it upon itself to articulate the function of social work research, defined the problem facing the social work profession as the need to maintain its status in an increasingly technological society. The early social work researchers' commitments to rectify social inequalities and to understand the complexity and intimacy of caseworker–client relationships did not correspond to those technological images of "science." Other social and behavioral sciences with higher status than the social work profession had adopted logical positivist ideas. For instance, psychologists had increasingly prescribed that, to generate scientific knowledge, researchers should use experimental design (Danziger, 1988a, p. 44; Morawski, 1988). Members of the SWRG said they wanted to increase their status in relation to the other disciplines. By adopting the positivist approach to social and behavioral research, researchers also carved out a specialized role for themselves that increased their stature in the academic community and distanced them from caseworkers (Karger, 1983), who were a socially depreciated group during the 1950s (A. Schwartz, 1967; Towle, 1961; Sanders, 1957, exemplifies that depreciation).[81] The positivist belief that theories could be tested definitively by experimental designs promised to yield certain "facts" in a field that was full of uncertainty. The debates between diagnostic and functionalist social work theorists had broken some alliances among practitioners; the logical positivist premise that sufficient methodological rigor could confirm scientific theories conclusively may have seemed to offer a resolution to the controversy.

Another factor that may have furthered the SWRG's adoption of a positivist approach to research, and its depreciation of the work of the early social workers (most of whom were women), was that discrimination against women was marked in the country as a whole in the 1950s. After the 1950s, most historians of social work cloaked the early social workers' research accomplishments in the invisibility that is one hallmark of racial discrimination and misogynist bias (Sancier, 1991, 1992a). The way social work research was conceptualized and presented in research texts reflected the bias against the early social workers' research (Grinnell, 1988; Reid & Smith, 1989; Rubin & Babbie, 1989). Although serious consideration of the work of the founders of the profession might have led social workers to reject positivist beliefs about science, bias against women accelerated the profession's depreciation of its knowledge base under the banner of positivist beliefs about science.

A shift in the membership of the profession accompanied the adoption of a logical positivist approach to research. One of the most important findings of this study was the powerful relationship between the roles of women and men in social work and trends in approaches to social work research. For instance, the content analysis of social work journal articles presented earlier shows a noticeable association between the proportions of women and men as first authors and the major shifts in philosophies of social work research. From 1920 to 1949, women were the first authors of the majority of published articles, and in the 1940s in particular, women's inclination to author qualitative analyses predominated in published journal articles. Those trends in research corresponded to gender-based social roles. Although women had assumed positions of authority in social agencies while men were overseas fighting during World War II, when men returned from the war and throughout the 1950s, settlement houses, schools of social work, and national organizations increasingly were led by men (NASW, 1983–1984). During the 1950s, men chose the experimental designs and quantified data prioritized under the positivist approach to research more often than women, a trend that persisted through 1970. This suggests that the movement to implement positivist beliefs about research may have been led primarily by male social work researchers. In the 1960s and 1970s, when positivism was entrenched in social work research, the majority of first authors were men. In the 1980s, when social workers began to question the positivist approach to social work research, again almost equal numbers of women and men were first authors. However, adherence to a particular approach to research cannot be simply related to gender, because the researchers' work shows that some women advanced logical positivist ideas about research and depreciated the work of the early social workers, and some men criticized positivist formulations.

This study contradicts a common assumption about the different contributions of women and men to published social work research. Overall, women and men have been first authors of social work journal articles in almost equal proportion, which provides an antidote to claims about the "greater intellectual productivity of men" based on the "predominance of male authors in social work publications" (A. Rosenblatt et al., 1970, p. 421). These claims were based on the analysis of a limited time period, 1964 to 1968, when, as the authors noted, the great majority of the positions of leadership in the profession were held by men, despite the fact that two thirds of the members of the NASW were women (p. 421). Because the authors did not attempt a historical study, they did not see that their findings were time-bound. Moreover, they did not see that their study reinforced the misogynist tendency to ignore the significant intellectual contributions of women social workers. In fact, the period when men were preeminent as first authors of social work journal articles (the 1960s and the 1970s) was an unusual time for the social work profession.

Even though women authors have published more social work research than has previously been thought, women did not author journal articles in proportion with their representation in the profession as a whole. One reason for this underrepresentation may be that women did not hold the positions of authority that typically confer more control over resources and allocation of professional time for research (Ruel, 1972; Sancier, 1992a; Steinberg, 1988). Even though women had less authority than men and experienced other obstacles that were due to discrimination (Chambers, 1986a), it is striking that the numbers of female and male first authors were roughly equal. This finding begins to correct misogynist stereotypes that women cannot be productive leaders in research (see also Furumoto, 1987; Rossiter, 1982).

Not only did the SWRG's adoption of a positivist approach to research fail to solve the profession's problems, it generated new ones. Logical positivist researchers classified values as belonging to philosophy rather than as inherent in all science; they regarded research as unscientific if it was explicitly value-based, such as aimed at remedying social inequalities. Although during the founding of the profession, researchers aimed to advocate clients' needs and to advance social justice, once positivism was adopted in the 1950s, positivist social work researchers backed away from the value of using research to advance social reform. Prominent members of the SWRG also regarded practitioner judgments as inherently more biased than the judgments of researchers, depreciated practitioner knowledge as unscientific unless it was tested by experimental design, and prescribed that practitioners should modify their interventions to conform to positivist research requirements. Most practitioners disliked the approach to research advanced by the SWRG, and a gulf widened between social work researchers and practitioners (Karger, 1983). By the 1960s, the irrelevance of social work research for most social workers had become such a problem that in 1968 the Council on Social Work Education deleted the research requirement from its standards in the hope that educators would find ways to integrate research into other content areas (Rubin & Zimbalist, 1981). Many social work educators, however, have agreed that the effort has not succeeded (Casselman, 1971; Rubin, Franklin, & Selber, 1992). Further, in the 1970s, women and members of ethnic minority groups emphasized (1) that their voices, and the voices of other disadvantaged groups, had been excluded from social and behavioral science and (2) that racist and misogynist stereotypes infused social and behavioral knowledge (Billingsley, 1970; Hill, 1980; Westkott, 1979). Those groups increasingly showed that research always plays a role in social conflict and that unless research is designed for empowerment it will be used for social oppression.

A full-scale critique of and challenge to the positivist philosophy of social work research did not begin until Martha Heineman Pieper published her 1981 article "The Obsolete Scientific Imperative in Social Work Research." One reason positivism remained entrenched in social work research may be that positivist researchers regarded conceptual critiques as philosophy rather than science, because such critiques did not derive from the experimental testing of propositions (Bhaskar, 1989b). Accordingly, positivist social work researchers did not regard conceptual analyses of approaches to social work research as research (e.g., Hudson, 1986). As social work students imbibed the positivist philosophy of social work research, they also were taught to devalue the legitimacy of the reservations they may have had about it.

Approaches to research in the field of social work have been profoundly influenced by the sociohistorical contexts in which they have been generated, and they have served political values. Those political values have aimed either to advance social justice or to discourage social reform; over time, approaches to social work research oscillated between the two. One of the most unfortunate consequences of positivism for social work was that the belief that research can be value-free caused social workers who adopted or were influenced by positivism to ignore the effects of a philosophy of research on human well-being (Bhaskar, 1989b, 1991; I. Shapiro, 1982, p. 572). When researchers believed they could be neutral with regard to contemporary social conflicts, they contributed to how those social conflicts were resolved.

It is extremely challenging for social workers to develop an approach to research that suits their profession's commitments and aspirations. To do so, history suggests social workers need to create a community within which they can test out their ideas with each other and critically evaluate their assessments of problems and potential solutions, a community that affords professional authority and autonomy and that appreciates the opportunities inherent in a diversity of theoretical perspectives. The social workers who founded the profession used research to advance a more just and humane society. Now social workers can draw from that heritage and use the heuristic paradigm to build an approach to research that advances social work knowledge and carries on the social work profession's long-standing commitment to human liberation.

DISCUSSION QUESTIONS

1. What were the shared tenets of the approaches to research developed by the three research communities of the founding social workers?

2. What were the tenets of the approach to research adopted by the Social Work Research Group?

3. Look at the approach to research and advocacy developed by the Hull House community. Take one of the examples of research and activism (e.g., on behalf of workers' or women's rights) and briefly describe how they:

    a. analyzed a social problem from the standpoint of those who were disadvantaged and powerless;

    b. voiced the concerns of the powerless group;

    c. considered the social services or new legislation needed to redress the problem;

    d. disseminated their research, lobbied, and educated the public as to how the problem might be remedied.

4. What was the subject of the debates between the proponents of the diagnostic and functionalist approaches to casework? Are there similar debates in the field of social work today? If so, what are the different theories about which social workers are debating?

5. a. What is the approach to quantifying data that is used in this history? What statistical methods were used to analyze the quantitative data?

    b. What guidelines were used for collecting qualitative data in this history?

6. Take a social problem that concerns you, either an individual or a larger-scale problem. Imagine that you are a researcher in the Hull House community and

are talking with Jane Addams, Edith Abbott, and Sophonisba Breckinridge about the problem. What perspectives might they take on the problem? What possible solutions might they offer?

7. Choose a puzzling moment from your experience as a social work practitioner (if you have not yet had any experience as a professional social worker, choose an experience during an interaction with someone you helped that puzzles you). Imagine you are with Mary Richmond and that you are discussing how you could look into this problem. What suggestions do you think she might have for you?

8. What problem did the diagnostic–functionalist debates bring to social workers' attention? How did the positivist approach to social work research address that problem? (Chapters 3 to 5 and 7 discuss the heuristic paradigm's approach to that problem.)

9. How are both ways of analyzing data used in this history heuristics that focus the research in a particular direction? How do they also set up specific biases?

10. Roy Bhaskar quotes Thomas Kuhn's famous statement that "though the world does not change with a change of paradigm, the scientist afterwards works in a different world" (Kuhn, 1970, p. 121). He then revises Kuhn's statement to read: "though the (natural (or object)) world does not change with a change of paradigm, the scientist afterwards works in a different (social or (cognitive)) world" (1991, p. 10). How did the world within which social work practitioners–researchers worked change when the Social Work Research Group advanced logical positivist guidelines for social work research?

CHAPTER 3

Debates about a Philosophy of Research for the Field of Social Work

Introduction to "The Obsolete Scientific Imperative in Social Work Research" and the Debates in Response

This chapter presents two of Martha Heineman Pieper's landmark papers. Also presented are key debates among social work researchers in response to Heineman Pieper's critiques of the logical positivist approach to social work research and in response to the alternative approach she has imported into the field of social work, termed *the heuristic paradigm.*

The selections by Heineman Pieper, Schuerman, Geismar, and Gyarfas present the first round of the debates about the heuristic paradigm. From our vantage point more than 12 years later, we can see that Heineman Pieper's 1981 article has had a revolutionary impact on social work research. In that article, she called attention to the need both to examine the assumptions regulating research and to integrate advances made in other disciplines (philosophy of science, physics, sociology, and cognitive, cultural and linguistic studies) into social work's philosophy of research. The debates in response to her article were published in two major journals: in *Social Service Review,* beginning with "The Obsolete Scientific Imperative in Social Work Research" in 1981, and in *Social Work Research and Abstracts,* beginning with "The Future of Social Work Research" in 1985 (Heineman Pieper, 1985, 1986a, 1986b; Hudson, 1986; Thyer, 1986). John Schuerman, Ludwig Geismar, and Mary Gyarfas authored the responses following Heineman Pieper's article. Heineman Pieper's replies are included as well. Within a few years, the controversy about the philosophy of social work research could be found in articles in every major social work journal (Geismar & Wood, 1982; Haworth, 1984; Imre, 1984; Ruckdeschel & Farris, 1982).

In this article, Heineman Pieper (1) comprehensively summarizes the logical positivist philosophy of research and its flaws; (2) describes how logical positivist ideas had infused the prevailing approach to social work research; and (3) advances an alternative approach to research, the heuristic paradigm, which draws from the work of postpositivist philosophers of science (most notably, William Wimsatt, Herbert Simon, and Roy Bhaskar). Mastering the concepts presented in this article may be difficult, but it will give you an especially helpful foundation for understanding both logical positivism and the heuristic paradigm. Further, the ideas Heineman Pieper discusses have vital relevance for practitioners in the social and behavioral sciences, because ultimately our beliefs about how to generate social and behavioral knowledge regulate the knowledge we create, apply, and appraise.

It is important to understand logical positivist and postpositivist beliefs about the relation between theories and observations. In 1981, a common requirement for the most valuable social work research was that data be quantified. Heineman Pieper describes how such a requirement rests on the assumption that "observed and theoretical entities can and should be sharply distinguished" (1981, p. 372). To elaborate, the logical positivist philosophers of science assumed that observations could reflect reality directly. Measurement procedures were assumed to record reality without affecting it in the course of the measurement process. Thus, the logical positivists prescribed that, to be scientifically meaningful, theoretical concepts had to be tied to measurement procedures, which they also called "operational definitions" (see Percy Bridgman in the Appendix). Positivist social and behavioral researchers based much of their work on the assumption that theories and observations could be sharply distinguished. For example:

1. They prescribed that a single method of collecting data (i.e., quantification) was, in itself, a guarantor of scientifically superior knowledge.
2. They claimed that observations could be "atheoretical."
3. They regarded measurement as a way to reduce bias, as when Schuerman stated in his response to Heineman Pieper that "the assessment of error requires repetition of measurement" (1982, p. 145).

Philosophers of science no longer rely on those logical positivist prescriptions, because it is widely recognized that observations cannot simply mirror reality. Any act of knowing organizes reality according to heuristics that help us to focus on some variables and disregard others. For example, what do you see in Figure 3–1? You do not see only black marks on the page, but you automatically add something to them that makes them meaningful to you. Similarly, researchers record those facts that their theories cause them to look for, and they report and integrate facts according to the heuristics they use. Accordingly, facts inevitably reflect the researcher's theory and choice of observational method. Further, perception itself is regulated by the knower's heuristics. For example, visual cues help us to organize our visual perceptions. We usually do not recognize how our visual heuristics work until we are faced with an unusual visual experience such as an optical illusion. The belief that observations can be theory-free only encourages a researcher to overlook the percep-

Figure 3–1
The impact of theories on perception

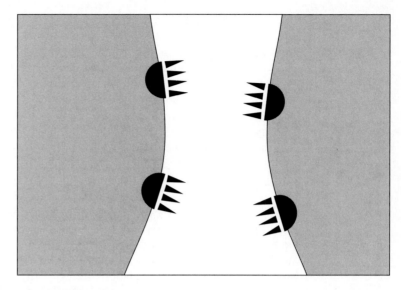

Source: Adapted from the work of Norwood Russell Hanson with the permission of Mrs. Fay Hanson.

tual and cognitive heuristics and theoretical assumptions that do regulate the investigative process.

Some researchers misread Heineman Pieper as debunking the use of standards for appraising research (e.g., Schuerman, 1982). However, recognizing that observations and facts are both theory- and value-laden does not have to lead to the conclusions that we cannot appraise how well theories explain our experience or that there is no mind-independent reality. To the contrary, when researchers recognize the theory- and value-ladenness of all research, they can look for the theoretical assumptions and values that underlie research, and they can improve how they appraise and generate knowledge. Finally, as Heineman Pieper points out in her response to Schuerman, the major problem she addresses is not the usefulness of experimentation or measurement for studying some social problems, but rather that "just as the logical empiricists do, social work researchers apply certain principles so restrictively that important questions, methods, and data are excluded from scientific activity, even though the principles being used restrictively are themselves too problematic to be infallible or exclusive roads to truth" (Heineman Pieper, 1982, p. 146).

Another of the most important concepts to understand in Heineman Pieper's 1981 paper concerns scientific explanation. The theory of scientific explanation is complex and has evolved considerably since the 1920s. These complex ideas and their development cannot be elaborated here. For readers interested in more information, Wesley Salmon's *Four Decades of Scientific Explanation* (1989) is an excellent reference. The following discussion highlights several issues that Heineman Pieper raises in relation to the theory of scientific explanation.

Philosophers of science have long recognized that one of the most important problems in scientific explanation is the problem of induction. Two essential points about induction can be briefly summarized as follows. First, given an event or observation that the scientist wants to explain (the explanandum), the scientist always chooses an explanation (or explanans) from among the countless, diverse possible explanations for that event. The scientist necessarily uses inductive reasoning to decide which explanans to use. Any single explanans cannot be confirmed for many reasons, one of which is that other explanations are always possible. For instance, scientists thought that the best explanation for the observation that the sun rises every morning was that the sun revolves around the earth, until the alternative, heliocentric, theory of the solar system was developed. An example from social and behavioral research is that some researchers might predict that if a hyperactive child is given medication, he will remain seated longer. The child's staying seated is the explanandum. We can never be sure, however, that if he does remain seated, there is no other explanation (or explanans) for the event (e.g., the class is studying different lessons that the child finds more interesting). Methodological prescriptions are inadequate responses to the problem of induction in part because, in implementing any method, one necessarily uses inductive reasoning, conceptual analysis, and informed judgment. For example, to control for alternative explanations for why a hyperactive child remains seated, a behaviorist might want to rule out the possibility that other children stopped encouraging the child's noncompliance. By contrast, a researcher who believes that food coloring causes hyperactivity might choose to control for elements of the child's diet.

A second important aspect of the problem of induction is that if one induces an explanation from observations, one cannot be sure the explanation will hold for all cases, because contradictory observations that are not yet known may exist. In discussing this problem, Karl Popper gives the well-known example that if a scientist makes the claim that "all swans are white," based on having seen many white swans, the possibility always remains that the scientist may find a black swan (see the article by Popper in the Appendix).

The logical positivists and their followers sought to resolve the problem of induction in many ways. One was to try to eliminate induction from the process of scientific reasoning altogether, as Popper attempts to do in presenting falsification and the deductive model of theory testing (see the Appendix). Hempel and Oppenheim, perhaps the most important architects of the logical empiricist approach to scientific explanation, described a model of scientific explanation that was regarded as expressing a consensus that emerged among philosophers of science in the first part of this century (1948). One of Hempel and Oppenheim's key points was that the explanans must contain a statement of "at least one general law that is essential to the validity of the argument" (Salmon, 1989, p. 8; this is the "covering law model"). The explanandum is logically entailed by the explanans. The explanandum may be a single event; it also may be a class of events, whose occurrence is covered by a probability distribution, in which case the explanation is a derivative termed the *deductive-statistical model*. Those responses to the problem of induction do not work, because, for the reasons noted here, induction cannot be eliminated from the process of generating scientific knowledge.

Yet another positivist response to the problem of induction was an extension of the deductive-nomological model of explanation termed the *symmetry thesis*—the belief that scientific "explanation and prediction were formally the same" (Heineman Pieper, 1981, p. 376). According to the symmetry thesis, a scientific explanation for a predicted event is "the conclusion of a deductive argument of the syllogistic form: (1) If X (initial conditions), then Y (event to be predicted); (2) X is present; (3) therefore Y (the predicted event) must occur" (Heineman Pieper, 1981, p. 376). The logical positivists believed that an experiment that tested a prediction could provide relatively nonproblematic support or disconfirmation of the hypothesis and that a series of such experiments would confirm or disconfirm a theory.

Researchers who adopted positivist beliefs often used those beliefs to demarcate scientific and unscientific explanations in the social and behavioral sciences. For example, positivist social and behavioral researchers regarded experimental designs as privileged tests of theories (D. T. Campbell & Stanley, 1963; Tripodi, 1981). They believed that research designs that were not based on prediction but instead led, for example, to retrospective or ex post facto explanations of events were inferior (Heineman Pieper, 1981, p. 382). The prescription that to be scientific an explanation must be in the form of a prediction was particularly irrelevant for social and behavioral researchers, who, as Bhaskar points out, work with open and continually changing systems that are inherently unpredictable. For example, clinicians generally cannot predict a client's behavior using knowledge of initial conditions and deduction from universal laws, as the symmetry thesis requires.

Clinicians, however, often can explain a client's behavior in retrospect (or ex post facto); positivist social and behavioral researchers evaluated such explanations as inherently unscientific.

As Heineman Pieper points out, postpositivist philosophers have described several problems with the logical positivist models of scientific explanation (Kim, 1964; Salmon, 1989). Citing especially Michael Scriven, Salmon maintains that many valuable scientific explanations are not, in fact, predictive, for example, Darwin's theory of natural selection. Heineman Pieper refers to Wesley Salmon and Stephen Toulmin, who emphasize that explanation and prediction serve different purposes and that it is often much more useful to know why or how something happened, rather than to be able to predict its occurrence. Some researchers tried to rescue the deductive-nomological model of scientific explanation by talking about probabilities rather than certainties. Following Jeffrey, Salmon criticized researchers' reliance on estimates of probability as a major criterion for evaluating hypotheses and generating explanations because "showing that the outcome is highly probable, and that it was to be expected, has nothing to do with the explanation" (1989, p. 62). He gives examples of explanations that are highly probable and yet not explanatory because the variables included in the explanation are irrelevant to understanding the occurrence of the event. His examples include the explanation that table salt dissolves in water because a spell has been put on it (following Kyburg) and that loud noises will cause the moon to reappear after an eclipse (1971a, pp. 33–35). Finally, given that social systems are complex and open, they change continuously. Social researchers often find explanations that "can tell us how to operate under changing conditions" to be more relevant than predictions (Heineman Pieper, 1981, p. 382).

Salmon, with others and notably Coffa, proposes an alternative, "ontic" model of explanation (1989), which includes understanding the (frequently unobservable) mechanisms that cause the phenomena one wants to explain. Salmon's model also includes the criterion of "statistical relevance," which he defines as follows: "An explanation of a particular fact is an assemblage of facts *statistically relevant* to the fact-to-be-explained *regardless of the degree of probability* that results" (Salmon, 1971b, p. 11). An explanation shows "what sorts of expectations would have been reasonable and under what circumstances it was to be expected" and how the explanation helps us to expect that the event to occur can be "translated into practical predictive behavior such as wagering on it" (Salmon, 1971a, p. 79). One of the implications of Salmon's account of explanation in terms of statistical relevance is that "there is no rule that tells one when to accept an hypothesis or when to reject it; instead, there is a rule of practical behavior that prescribes that we so act as to maximize our expectation of utility" (1971a, p. 77). Salmon's reformulation of scientific explanation emphasizes that when evaluating a scientific explanation, one cannot replace researchers' informed judgment with methodological rules (e.g., statistical significance testing).

The authors who respond to Heineman Pieper's 1981 article raise several topics that become the focus of subsequent debates. The first topic, raised by Schuerman and Geismar, is the claim that logical empiricist concepts do not influence social work research. In her response to Geismar, Heineman Pieper points out that Geismar does not support his claim with citations from social work research. The second topic, presented in Schuerman's reply, is that the philosophy of science is irrelevant to planning and evaluating social research. Schuerman, however, also advances standards for good science, which are based on his beliefs about reality and how one can know that reality. Thus, his views are informed by his philosophical assumptions. The third topic, also raised by Schuerman, is that Heineman Pieper is debunking all standards for science. Others who bring up that theme (e.g., Hudson and Brekke later in this chapter) also view scientific standards as equivalent to logical positivist beliefs about science; they then conclude that Heineman Pieper renounces standards for good science. In fact, as she says in this article and in her replies, the scientific standards of the heuristic paradigm are more up-to-date and relevant to the mission of the social work profession. Finally, Mary Gyarfas writes that neither side of the debate hears the other side, implying that the two perspectives can be synthesized or reconciled and that the problem is misunderstanding on both sides. However, the positivist approach to social and behavioral research and the heuristic approach cannot be conjoined, because they represent mutually contradictory ideas.

KEY TERMS

Empiricism	Epistemology
Heuristic	Logical empiricism
Ontology	Paradigm

DISCUSSION QUESTIONS

1. What is the birthright that Heineman Pieper says social work researchers have turned away from when they prescribed a research paradigm based on logical positivist beliefs?

2. a. What is an example of how one cannot make a sharp separation between theories and observations?

   b. How has the belief that there can be a sharp separation between theories and observations been manifested in positivist approaches to social and behavioral research?

   c. Why is this issue important to the researcher?

3. What are some examples of heuristics in

   a. clinical practice?

   b. community organizing?

   c. program management?

   d. social policy and planning?

   Why does a heuristic inevitably set up systematic biases? Can there be practice or research without heuristics?

4. Norwood Hanson is a philosopher of science who contributed significantly to the postpositivist movement. In illustrating how any argument about causation is inherently theory-laden, Hanson stated,

   > Seeing the cause of the movement of the stars, or the coolness of the night air, is less like seeing flashes and colors and more like seeing what time it is, or seeing what key a musical score is written in, or seeing whether a wound is infected, or seeing if the moon is craterous. (1958, p. 54)

   a. Why does Hanson say the cause of the movement of the stars is *less* like seeing flashes and *more* like seeing what time it is?

   b. How is it possible to argue that any model of causation is in itself theory-laden, or is a heuristic, as Hanson emphasizes in the preceding quote?

5. Review the sections in which Heineman Pieper discusses the symmetry thesis and criticisms of the symmetry thesis.

   a. Summarize the criticisms of the symmetry thesis.

   b. Deduce a prediction from a theory that interests you. Now show how you might explain the event you have predicted and how the prediction itself will not suffice as an explanation of that event.

   c. Clinicians are asked repeatedly to explain events and sometimes to make predictions (e.g., will this child become suicidal as a teenager? will this client hurt someone?). How can Heineman Pieper's discussions of causality, prediction, and explanation help you think about how you can answer questions in which you are asked to make clinical predictions?

   d. Compare your answer to "c" with the implications of the symmetry thesis for clinical explanations.

   e. Some of the greatest scientists have used diverse criteria in evaluating scientific explanations, in addition to the criterion of whether the explanation yields predictions of observations. To illustrate, Einstein's general relativity theory predicts that "light should be bent by gravitational fields" (Hawking,

1988, p. 31). Light from the sun, however, hinders our ability to observe test cases, such as how the light from stars near the sun is bent by the sun's gravitational field. Einstein proposed his theory several years before his 1915 prediction of light deflection could be tested by observations. It was not until 1919 that a British expedition led by Sir Arthur Eddington observed an eclipse in West Africa and obtained measurements that "showed that light was indeed deflected by the sun" (Hawking, 1988, p. 32). When he was shown the measurements obtained by the expedition, Einstein "gave them little weight as evidence for his theory," and he remarked to his student, Ilse Rosenthal-Schneider,

> "But I knew that the theory is correct." When she asked what he would have done if the prediction had not been confirmed, he said, "Then I would have been sorry for the dear Lord—the theory is correct." Later he wrote, "I do not by any means find the chief significance of the general theory of relativity in the fact that it has predicted a few minute observable facts, but rather in the simplicity of its foundation and in its logical consistency." (quoted in Brush, 1989, p. 1125)

A later re-examination of the expedition's measurements indicated that "the errors were as great as the effect they were trying to measure. Their measurement had been sheer luck, or a case of knowing the result they wanted to get, not an uncommon occurrence in science" although "the light deflection has . . . been accurately confirmed by a number of later observations" (Hawking, 1988, p. 32). Following Einstein, what criteria, aside from predictive power, might you use in evaluating social and behavioral theories?

6. What does Schuerman offer as precepts for scientific research? What philosophy of research do those precepts reflect?

7. Why is it important to examine one's philosophy of research?

The Obsolete Scientific Imperative in Social Work Research

MARTHA BRUNSWICK HEINEMAN   *Chicago, Illinois*

ABSTRACT: In a misguided attempt to be scientific, social work has adopted an outmoded, overly restrictive paradigm of research. Methodological rather than substantive requirements determine the subject matter to be studied. As a result, important questions and valuable data go unresearched. The assumptions and postulates of this prevailing "scientific" model of research and evaluation are examined: their roots in the logical empiricist tradition are described; criticisms of these assumptions are discussed; and alternative, less restrictive approaches to research are suggested.

Over the last three decades the profession of social work has increasingly declared its traditional model of research to be insufficiently scientific and has replaced it with discrete canons of scientific acceptability, which are used to evaluate service models and research findings.[1] Although the assumptions underlying these changed criteria for service models and research have been abandoned by most philosophers of science, they are rarely examined or criticized in the social work literature.[2] This paper examines the major assumptions of the prevailing "scientific" model of research and evaluation, describes their roots in the logical empiricist[3] tradition, presents some of the criticisms of these assumptions which have been advanced by philosophers of science, and suggests an alternative approach to the design and evaluation of social work research.

Because the requirements of logical empiricism have been used prescriptively to limit the permissible range of research questions and data and to define service effectiveness, the issue of their validity is crucial for social work and the social sciences in general. Winifred Chambers describes "the hold of some of the more positivistic demands on the social sciences" and concludes, "While some social scientists have tended to give up hopes of being scientific in the face of these strictures, others have gravitated toward statistics, extreme behaviorism, and purely descriptive studies in an unquestioning effort to meet the rigor and precision of [logical empiricist] standards for a science—at the expense, frequently, of simplifying the issues or narrowing the range of significant inquiries."[4] In his 1975 presidential address to the American Sociological Association, Lewis Coser warns that "preoccupation with method largely has led to neglect of significance and substance. And yet, our discipline will be judged in the last analysis on the basis of the substantive enlightenment which it is able to supply. . . . If we neglect that major task, if we refuse the challenge to answer these questions, we shall forfeit our birthright and degenerate into congeries of rival sects and specialized researchers who will learn more and more about less and less."[5]

Source: "The Obsolete Scientific Imperative in Social Work Research" by M. B. Heineman, 1981, *Social Service Review*, 55, pp. 371–397. Copyright 1981 by The University of Chicago. Reprinted by permission.
Social Service Review (September 1981). © 1981 by The University of Chicago. 0037–7961/81/5503–0006$01.00

Social work has yet to begin the critical examination of logical empiricist assumptions and methodology which is increasingly found in the literature of psychology and sociology.[6] One prevalent assumption is that certain methods of data gathering are "objective," that is, distortion free, and therefore able to generate data which accurately reflect reality. For example, tape recorders, videotapes, and observers not involved in the planning of research or the execution of treatment are often asserted to yield value-neutral, generally truthful data about social interactions. William Reid, for example, says that "the trend toward greater use of direct and electronic observation of program operations, such as individual and group counseling services, can be expected to continue, in response to the need for the most accurate data possible. Most researchers have regarded with skepticism practitioners' records of program events, but until recently little else was available."[7] In this model, data must be observable in certain restricted ways, specifically, they must be converted to measurable form.[8] Behind the requirement of quantification lies the more fundamental assumption that observed and theoretical entities can and should be sharply distinguished. In an article proposing "Criteria for Evaluating Research," Harris Goldstein instructs the reader to "note whether or not the researcher has clearly separated his theoretical concepts from his empirical ones and whether or not he has indicated directly which are which."[9] Similarly, in an article setting forth "Principles of Measurement," Kogan asserts that "the researcher shuttles between the real world and the world of concepts. The real world provides his empirical evidence, the world of concepts a scheme or map for 'making sense' out of the portion of the real world which he is seeking to account for, explain, or predict. The conceptual scheme or map is known as a theoretical model."[10]

According to the prevailing model of social work research, data which are assumed to be "empirical" or "objective," that is, thought both to mirror reality and to appear similar to all normal people, straightforwardly "ground" theoretical constructs in reality.[11] In consequence, atheoretical research is said to be both possible and desirable. For example, in an article on "Evaluating One's Own Effectiveness and Efficiency," Bloom and Block say, "In the approaching era of ecumenical therapeutic practices, it would seem preferable to have a theory-free measurement procedure. All practitioners, regardless of their theoretical orientation or the specific techniques they use, require objective evaluation to help them attain the goal of their intervention, however defined."[12] In her study of social work outcome research, Katherine Wood asserts that practitioners who bring a preexisting theoretical orientation to their work are unethical: "The worker may not, professionally or ethically, force the data into a preconceived theoretical orientation focused on only one of the [intrapersonal, interpersonal or systems] dimensions—as the researchers and practitioners in many of the studies appear to have done."[13] Wood does not, however, discuss the effects on research and practice of the unquestioned adherence to a rigidly controlling methodology.

A related postulate is that, although research cannot proceed without an attempt to organize these "empirical" data into concepts, these concepts are meaningless unless their direct link to the data from which they derive can be manifested by specific operations or measurements. The very meaning of the concepts is often thought to be synonymous with these operations. According to this postulate, theories and concepts which do not lend themselves to definition by measurement operations cannot be studied fruitfully. Kogan, for example, says that if a theoretical model is to be useful, "there is the necessity of specifying rules connecting at least some part of the conceptual system with the world of reality."[14] Goldstein posits that "scientific methods indicate a preference for concepts which can be defined operationally."[15] This requirement that concepts be definable by quantitative measurement operations has significantly restricted the scope and nature of the questions studied in current social work research. For example, broad treatment and program goals have been criticized as hard to define operationally and, therefore, deemed inferior or unacceptable—an example of the use of methodology to beg a substantive question.[16]

In addition to the assumptions of the unproblematic nature of observation and the need to define concepts in terms of these "reality-based" perceptions, a third important assumption is that good science inherently involves predictions.[17] Norman Polansky, for example, says, "The whole aim of research in the profession, therefore, is to improve our feeble ability to predict the course of events. Our concern is with knowledge for use; foresight is crucial to effective practice. It is no wonder that successful prediction is the major criterion of whether a law one thinks he has discovered is 'valid.' This is as true for science in general as it is for each profession."[18] Edward Mullen asserts that prediction is even more important than explanation. He criticizes social work practice models for having "too often elevated the goal of explanation over the goal of prediction" and says that, given the imperfect state of our knowledge, we should choose models "that have a good probability of guiding us toward predictable results with our clients, even though these models may not be very satisfying when it comes to understanding causation or the complexities of the interactions we are working with."[19]

Thus the prevailing model of social work research posits a hierarchy of research designs which runs the gamut from least to most scientific and is ordered by the extent to which the criterion of prediction and its concomitant requirements—such as experimental manipulation, control groups, and randomization—are satisfied. As a result, ex post facto research is considered less rigorous than a "true" experimental design and is relegated to exploratory endeavors.[20] Similarly, studies in which the experimental variable cannot be manipulated for other reasons, such as ethical considerations, are not considered good science. The social work research literature is replete with statements to this effect. As early as 1950, Blenkner said that without prediction and experimental manipulation, "nothing is really established except that one has done a more or less adequate job of describing one's sample."[21]

The problem is not that these assumptions about what constitutes good science and hence good social work research never lead to useful knowledge, but, rather, that they are used normatively, rather than descriptively, to prescribe some research methodologies and proscribe others. An example is Reid's prescription for "empirical" models of practice, that is, "models whose general development and case applications are substantially based on 'hard' data, such as measurements of observed behavior. . . . An essential characteristic of these models is their emphasis on phenomena that can be observed and specified with considerable objectivity and precision."[22] Reid's requirement that these models be "testable" makes normative the assumptions of value-free data, operational definitions to connect these data to conceptualizations, and prediction as equivalent to explanation. He describes "testable models" as those "whose targets for change, interventions and outcomes can be operationalized in terms of indicators that can be reliably and validly measured. Such models should also incorporate procedures for obtaining accurate data. To facilitate an understanding of the connection between input and outcome, practitioners' activities must be capable of producing some change within a limited period of time."[23] The prescriptive nature of current social work conceptualizations of science is exemplified by Reid's suggestion that, rather than have practice determine the form of scientific inquiry, the demands of science, as he perceives them, should determine the nature of practice: "In short, testability should be made an important criterion in determining what social workers should do. Practitioners have always taken the position that the requirements of science should be adapted to existing forms of practice, no matter how difficult it might be to apply scientific methods to the study and improvement of that practice. The author is suggesting that this position be reversed and that service models be adapted to scientific requirements wherever feasible."[24]

LOGICAL EMPIRICISM

The conceptualizations of science which shape the prevailing model of social work research derive most directly from the logical empiricist philosophy of science, which flowered in Vienna in the 1920s and was most in vogue between 1920 and the mid-1950s.[25] The logical empiricists participated in the quest for certainty that characterizes much early twentieth-century philosophy.[26] They hoped to establish epistemological guarantees for science in order to ensure that scientific findings would reflect a reality uncolored by the preconceptions or biases of the human mind.[27] A cornerstone of this effort was the logical empiricists' mistrust of theory and their belief that perceptions of the observable properties of material things were incontrovertible because they directly mirrored reality. Theoretical concepts were considered meaningless unless they were connected to physical observations by logical structures; these structures were understood to be truth preserving, that is, they organized experience without adding to it. Thus the only meaningful statements were either observational or logical. All other propositions, for example, propositions about hidden causes of observables, were considered metaphysical and, therefore, meaningless. From this point of view theories are nothing more than abbreviations for physical observations.

From these epistemological assumptions the logical empiricists derived a number of prescriptions for meaningful scientific inquiry. The most important of these will be summarized briefly.

Correspondence rules (operational definitions).—Because of the belief that, in order to preserve the truth inherent in physical observations, concepts and definitions (theory) must be tied to these observations by logical operations, the logical empiricists embraced Percy Bridgman's correspondence rules. In 1927 in *The Logic of Modern Physics* Bridgman said, "*The concept is synonymous with the corresponding set of operations.*"[28] Thus operational definitions had three functions in the logical empiricist program: (1) They were thought to define theoretical terms in a truth preserving way by combining observations and logical (mathematical) manipulations; (2) therefore, they were supposed to guarantee the meaningfulness of theoretical terms, and (3) they specified the admissible experimental procedures for applying a theory to phenomena.[29]

The symmetry thesis.—The symmetry thesis asserted that explanation and prediction were formally the same. A scientific explanation was the prediction (deduction) of an event from applicable hypotheses (general laws) plus specific experimental (initial) conditions. The predicted event was thus supposed to be the conclusion of a deductive argument of the syllogistic form: (1) If X (initial conditions), then Y (event to be predicted); (2) X is present; (3) therefore Y (the predicted event) must occur. In a later development, statistics were used to show that, although it might not be possible to demonstrate that an event was necessitated by deductive logic, it could be shown to be highly probable.[30]

The requirement that a hypothesis be "testable" by controlled experiment is merely a statement of the viewpoint that any valuable explanation is in the form of a prediction. The insistence that prediction is the only valid type of explanation assumes, of course, that the universe is governed by causality, that is, that a state is methodologically necessitated by former states and that this necessity is made possible by a law of nature.[31]

The business of science is the justification, not the discovery, of theories.—The logical empiricists argued that scientific logic was deductive logic because deductive logic preserved truth. The only nondeductive part of the scientific enterprise was supposed to be the discovery of hypotheses, which was not considered a process of logic but of psychological creativity. The business of science was to justify theories (test hypotheses by prediction), not discover them; logical empiricists considered the context in which those hypotheses were generated irrelevant. As Carl Hempel, an early member of the Vienna Circle, said, "Although no restrictions are imposed upon the *invention* of theories, scientific objectivity is safeguarded by making their *acceptance* dependent upon the outcome of careful tests. These consist in deriving, from the theory, consequences that admit of observational or experimental investigation, and then checking them by suitable observations or experiments."[32] The emphasis on science as an enterprise of justification had some important consequences. In the first place, the result of the logical empiricists' exclusive focus on the justification rather than the discovery of theories was that their philosophy of science was normative and prescriptive. It legislated standards for good science which were not and are not met by ongoing scientific work. These standards have been used to criticize practicing scientists rather than to describe actual scientific practice. Second, the history of science was ignored by the logical empiricists, who thought that, because there could be no logic of discovery, the processes by which science advances are the province of the psychologist and the sociologist rather than the philosopher of science.[33]

Reductionism.—If the logic of science is deductive and if theories are merely abbreviations for observations, it follows that complex theories should reduce into simpler ones that are closer to basic observations. William Wimsatt defines the logical empiricist postulate of reductionism as the belief that upper-level (more complex) entities, properties, theories, and laws must be deducible in terms of the properties, laws, and relations of the lower-level (less complex) theory. Upper-level entities are thus seen as "nothing more than" collections of lower-level entities, and upper-level laws and causal relations are understood as "nothing more than" abbreviations for and results of lower-level laws and causal relationships.[34] The belief that social work models can and should be reduced to simplified, quantified, time-limited, experimentally "testable" models without any loss of valuable information is an example of the influence of the logical empiricist belief in reductionism on social work research.

CRITICISMS OF LOGICAL EMPIRICISM

Although the social work research literature continues generally to embrace logical empiricist assumptions and postulates, philosophers of science have long aban-doned them as universal principles. Frederick Suppe, who moderated a major conference on the philosophy of science and logical empiricism, concludes,

> Consider the classical philosophical theses that an absolute causal account can be given of phenom-ena, that ultimate laws of a deterministic sort can be gleaned from natural phenomena, and that some rockbed of perceptual certainty is necessary to gain a firm knowledge of the world. All three of these theses are false and hopelessly out of date in terms of the kinds of theories now coming to dominate science. . . . It is from ancient antecedents in reli-gion and philosophy, not from ordinary experience, that these fallacious doctrines have been drawn and have received sanction for so long a time.[35]

Similarly, Wimsatt says, "Many of the philosophical assumptions on which the emphasis on statistical and quantitative methodology have been based have been challenged and often given up by many recent philoso-phers of science. These challenges do not deny the usefulness of such approaches, or even their necessity to answer some kinds of questions, but rather chal-lenge the idea that any useful research must conform to these methodological constraints."[36]

Criticisms of the theory-observation distinction.— The logical empiricist attempt to guarantee the truth-fulness of science by positing a sharp distinction between theory and observation and taking physical observations to be unimpeachable representations of reality has been attacked by most contemporary philosophers of science (and even abandoned by one of the architects of logical empiricism, Carl Hempel). The most common argument against the existence of inherently truthful observations is that there can be no direct or untainted perceptions because all observation is shaped by theory.[37] The weltanschauung philoso-phers of science[38] argue that all science proceeds from one's world view and, therefore, "one's knowledge and beliefs may influence what facts one is able to deter-mine observationally. Persons accepting different theo-ries for a given range of phenomena thus may be able to observe different facts, and so may disagree on what the facts are which a theory must accommo-date."[39] People holding different theories about the same object do not even see the same thing. Norwood Hanson suggests that at dawn Tycho Brahe would

believe the sun rose and Kepler would think the earth moved so the sun came into view. If perception is the-ory dependent, observation is not epistemologically "safe." As David Hull points out, "No 'fact' is suffi-ciently brute and pristine to be infallibly insulated against the possibility of error. For example, no obser-vation seemed more direct and free from interference than the observation that the earth did not move."[40] Anthropologists and psychologists call the belief in the validity of sense data "phenomenal absolutism," which they define as "one ubiquitous and misleading attribute of naive conscious experience, namely, that the world is as it appears,"[41] either to the unaided human perceptual apparatus or through the most elab-orate of instruments. Optical "illusions" are cited as proof that the experiences of objectivity and certainty which accompany visual perception are often mislead-ing and also give no clues to the inferences on which they rest.[42] Anthropologists, linguists, and psycholo-gists have documented cultural differences in percep-tion.[43] Also, studies have shown that when people blind since birth have their sight restored as adults, they cannot comprehend but must learn to interpret visual stimuli.[44]

The logical empiricists postulated that theory and observation could be sharply differentiated, but philosophers now argue that this distinction, too, is theory dependent and untenable. For example, the observation language of one epoch of physics is the theoretical language of another: Rigid bodies are observable entities in classical physics and theoretical entities in relativity theory. Subjective states are observable entities to psychodynamically oriented investigators and theoretical (even metaphysical) enti-ties to methodological behaviorists. Furthermore, the-ory determines what is to count as an instrument of observation, and, as new instruments of observation are acknowledged or old ones are discarded, the cate-gories of observation and inference expand and con-tract accordingly. Jerry Fodor says,

> The line between observed and inferred entities is just as hard to draw as the line between observa-tion and inference. It is, indeed, the same line. I think that there is a strong temptation to say that the larger viruses are not inferred entities any more—specifically because of the electron micro-scope. Yet it is possible to maintain that the argu-ment from shadows on the plate to viruses on the

slide is fully as complex as the argument from spectroscopic results to vegetation on Mars. What we decide to call an observation is in part determined by what we feel comfortable about calling an instrument of observation.[45]

Some psychologists and social workers reject empathy as a valid instrument of observation, while other investigators in their fields argue that empathy yields important and reliable information.

In modern physics, as the physicist-philosopher David Bohm emphasizes, even the distinction between instrument and observed entity is problematic: "The 'quantum' context calls for a new kind of description which does not make use of the potential or actual separability of 'observed object' and 'observing apparatus.' Instead, the form of the experimental conditions and the content of the experimental results have now to be one whole, in which analysis into disjoint elements is not relevant."[46] An eminent contemporary physicist, Arthur Eddington, concludes, "We have found that where science has progressed the farthest, the mind has but regained from nature that which the mind has put into nature. We have found a strange footprint on the shores of the unknown. We have devised profound theories, one after another, to account for its origin. At last we have succeeded in reconstructing the creature that made the footprint. And Lo! It is our own."[47]

One implication for the social sciences is that sharp distinctions between data and data gatherer may be impossible. As psychologists are beginning to recognize, participant observers in the field are not inherently any more unreliable than "disinterested" researchers in the laboratory.[48] The question becomes which kind of observer will produce more fruitful information about a particular problem or theory.

The abandonment of the assumptions (1) of the unimpeachability of physical observations, (2) of a sharp distinction between theory and observation, and (3) of a sharp distinction between observer and observed has far-reaching consequences for the prevailing model of social work research. In an ironic attempt to make social work research more scientifically acceptable, many authors have unquestioningly embraced as doctrine presuppositions that the "hard" sciences abandoned years before. For example, it has been clear since 1927 that quantum theory cannot be understood in terms of observable entities.[49]

Social work's attempt to establish a dichotomy between values and knowledge, between what William Gordon calls a picture of the world "as it *is*," "derived from the most rigorous interpretation [one] is capable of giving to the most objective sense data he is able to obtain," and a picture of the world as we "wish or fantasy or prefer it to be"[50] is based on the now discredited belief that certain sense data are epistemologically privileged. Contemporary philosophers see values, or subjective responses to events, as an inherent part of knowing or science. If what the logical empiricists call facts are reports rather than direct representations of physiological experiences,[51] then "objectivity" can be seen to be a particular species of report or viewpoint in which the observer is regarded as a constant. The "objective researcher" is thus as much a fiction as is value-free knowledge. Electronic and similar observational means accomplish a high level of reproducibility, but this is not equivalent to truth. It is frequently asserted that verification of factual assertion rests on a high degree of observer consensuality, but, as Edward Bixenstein points out, "This is tautological if verity is a matter of what humans are persuaded, and does not inhere in events."[52] Thus replication is not the safeguard many authors have supposed, particularly in the usual case in which the replicators have the same expertise and interests. Robert Rosenthal, a psychologist who has done pioneering studies of the biases inherent in the experimental method, says, "Within any area of behavioral research the experimenters come precorrelated by virtue of their common interests and any associated characteristics. Immediately, then, there is a limit placed on the degree of independence we may expect from workers or replicators in a common vineyard."[53] A contemporary definition of objectivity is suggested by Paul Schmidt, who says, "Relative to some chosen frame of reference identical empirical descriptions will be given by trained scientists. . . . Objectivity does not refer to how nature really is but to how scientists find it in a given context."[54]

The "objective" recording of behavior is a convention in which not only is the researcher regarded as a constant, but also the subject matter and the method of investigation are seen as separate. However, social facilitation researchers like Gadlin and Ingle have found that "the experimenter, whether physically present or electronically represented, functions as an audience (spectator) who influences the behavior of his or her subject in ways that extend well beyond the structure of the experiment and the manipulation of variables."[55] Other sources of experimenter effects include biosocial characteristics (such as age, sex, or race), attributes (such as anxiety, hostility, warmth, and status) and the experimenter's expectation (hypothesis). For example, one study demonstrated the power of experimenter expectation by presenting subjects with nonsensical geometric figures to which "correct" and "incorrect" labels had randomly been assigned. Experimenters had the key but were warned not to let this influence their presentation. To a significant degree the subjects chose the items marked "correct" on the key.[56]

If the convention of assigning the researcher a constant function is misunderstood as reality, not only will significant bias go unnoticed, but a fruitful source of knowledge, the inevitable interaction between researcher and client, will go unstudied.[57]

Criticisms of operationalism.—The logical empiricists thought that the primary function of operational definitions was to connect observed and conceptualized (inferred) entities so as to guarantee that concepts preserved the truth inherent in physical observation.[58] Therefore, the entire rationale for defining concepts operationally falls with the abandonment of the belief in theory-free and value-free observation. In addition, philosophers have leveled other, more specific criticisms against the requirement of operationalism. If, as Bridgman said, "the concept is synonymous with the corresponding set of operations,"[59] the number of concepts is multiplied beyond all reason. We certainly do not want to say that weight is one concept when measured with a balance scale and another when measured with a spring scale.[60] Also, it takes theory to decide when an operation is the same and when it is not: Is an IQ test taken with 200 people the same operation as one taken by oneself with an examiner? Ned Block and Gerald Dworkin explain that "operationalism goes wrong in construing as a linguistic stipulation a theoretic inference that a particular interaction between a thing and a device is a measurement."[61]

Given the impossibility of establishing epistemological guarantees for science, the restrictions required by operationalism guarantee nothing and proscribe much potentially fruitful inquiry. As David Hull puts it, "Operationalism was intended as a cathartic to purge physics of all non-empirical wastes, but it proved to be so strong that the viscera were eliminated as well."[62]

Criticisms of the symmetry thesis.—Contemporary philosophers have roundly attacked the logical empiricist doctrine that explanation and prediction are formally the same and, therefore, that there is no true scientific explanation without prediction. Jaegwon Kim, Stephen Toulmin, and others point out that, although prediction and explanation share the same form, they have very different functions: prediction proves the existence of an event, whereas explanation helps us understand it. Explanation, Toulmin argues, is a much more important scientific undertaking than prediction. Although theories are used to predict, their main function is to provide explanations of recognized regularities. Prediction or forecasting "is a craft or technology, an application of science rather than the kernel of science itself."[63] The Babylonians were able to predict certain natural events with astounding accuracy, even though their explanations of these events were thoroughly inaccurate.[64] Also, explanation is more useful than prediction, because only explanation can tell us how to operate under changing conditions.[65]

One implication of recognizing the different functions of explanation and prediction is that ex post facto designs are no longer deemed inherently inferior. Many sciences achieve understanding without prediction or retrodiction. For example, in evolutionary theory the object of scientific inquiry is not an event (such as the extinction of a species) but the search for relevant premises. Many scientific explanations inherently lack the power to predict—such as explanations of the occurrences of earthquakes, the emergence of a new biological species, or the phenotype of second generation pea plants—but once the event occurs it can be explained.[66] The behavioral sciences are often taken to task because human behavior does not lend itself to specific predictions. But behavioral science theory may provide valuable explanations for individual or group behavior without necessarily being able to predict the exact timing or nature of this behavior.

Another shortcoming of the symmetry thesis is its dependence on an outmoded notion of causality. In other words, prediction is not explanatory if the predicted event cannot be shown to be caused by the experimental conditions. However, neither causality nor noncausality can ever be proved because we can never be sure we have exhausted all possible explanations. Henry Margenau describes causality as "a methodological, nonempirical regulative maxim which belongs to the metaphysical domain."[67] In the eighteenth century, David Hume concluded that causality was a projection of our conditioned expectations,[68] and contemporary philosophers like Norwood Hanson agree that causality, like observation, is theory dependent: "Causes certainly are connected with effects, but this is because our theories connect them, not because the world is held together by cosmic glue."[69] Einstein wanted to believe that "God does not play dice."[70] Stephen Hawking, whose work on black holes has made him one of the most respected contemporary physicists, asserts that "not only does God throw dice, He throws them where they cannot be seen."[71] Furthermore, prediction is impossible in much of modern physics, a development which has drastically eroded classic notions of causality. Hanson says that elementary-particle theory "requires that the nucleus of every unstable isotope be identical with every other nucleus of that type. . . . But these nuclei decay in an unpredictable way (another part of the theory requires that); so the decay cannot be conceived of as a caused event. . . . This leads physicists to say unrepentant things about the collapse of the law of causality in modern science."[72] Quantum mechanics thus elevates chance to the status of a fundamental principle of nature and introduces a new kind of causality which does not allow the prediction or entail the predetermination of one event on the basis of another but, rather, couples probability distributions of whole aggregates of events. The name of this new relation is stochastic or statistical causality.[73]

One final criticism of the symmetry thesis is that it does not correspond to the way in which scientific theories actually evolve. For example, if practicing scientists had embraced prediction as the only adequate form of explanation, Einstein's equation of mass and energy ($E = mc^2$) would not have been accepted until the atom was split in 1932.[74]

As the classic notion of causality becomes less and less tenable, logical empiricists such as Hempel have tried to salvage the symmetry thesis by demanding that, if an explanation did not necessitate an event, it must at least predict it with a high degree of probability (usually the probability has to be greater than .95). Wesley Salmon persuasively argues that since prediction and explanation have different functions, statistical probability, no matter how high, will not necessarily turn a prediction into an explanation. Salmon's examples include the highly probable but nonexplanatory predictions that if we bang pots and pans, the tigers will stay out of Times Square, and that if a man takes his wife's birth control pills, he will not become pregnant. He suggests that statistics be evaluated by

the criterion of statistical relevance: "Statistical explanations need not be regarded as inductive arguments, and . . . a high probability is not required for a correct statistical explanation. If a high probability is not the desideratum, what can we offer as a substitute? The answer is statistical relevance. . . . To say that a certain factor is statistically relevant to the occurrence of an event means, roughly, that it makes a difference to the probability of that occurrence—that is, the probability of the event is different in the presence of that factor than in its absence."[75]

Criticisms of the emphasis on justification.— Another tenet of logical empiricism which has been generally abandoned by contemporary philosophers is that science should be concerned only with the justification, not the discovery, of theories because there is a logic of verification but no "logic of discovery." However, the logic of science is not a purely deductive process in which consequences are deduced from hypotheses and checked against observation. When we assert that observational evidence supports a hypothesis, the hypothesis is a conclusion, not a premise. As Salmon says, "The inference *from* observational evidence *to* hypothesis is surely not deductive. If this point is not already obvious it becomes clear the moment we recall that for any given body of observational data there is, in general, more than one hypothesis compatible with it."[76] Thus all scientific activity, including hypothesis testing, can be shown to embody induction. Induction itself is no guarantee of truth, as evidenced by the ever-present possibility that a counter example will falsify a generalization.

Karl Popper attempts to dispense with the problem of induction by substituting falsifiability rather than confirmation of hypotheses as a method of verification that will be entirely deductive. However, deductive inferences are specific and descriptive rather than generalizable, so that the moment Popper begins to choose between unfalsified hypotheses by turning to evidential corroboration, he necessarily employs induction rather than deduction. Salmon concludes, "The basic trouble with the hypothetico-deductive inference is that it always leaves us with an embarrassing superabundance of hypotheses. All of these hypotheses are equally adequate to the available data from the standpoint of the pure hypothetico-deductive framework. Each is confirmed in precisely the same manner by the same evidence."[77]

Other philosophers attack the assumption that it is possible to make sharp distinctions between discovery and justification. Brown, for example, says that "when we credit Galileo or Newton or Einstein or Bohr with having made scientific discoveries, we only consider those hypotheses which they had good reasons for entertaining to be discoveries. The context of justification is thus part of the context of discovery and no sharp line can be drawn between discovery and justification."[78]

Criticisms of reductionism.—Wimsatt argues that the logical empiricist postulate of reductionism not only ignores the scientist as decision maker and problem solver but also sets in place a series of biases that are very difficult to detect because they are built into its assumptions. He identifies what he calls biases of conceptualization, in which the world is divided into the system being studied and external forces in accordance with interest, intuition, or jurisdictional criteria (a molecular geneticist is unlikely to consider social forces as part of the subject matter of his discipline). He says that the impossibility of analyzing exhaustively or exactly the behavior of the system in its environment and the consequent need for simplifying assumptions result in biases of observation and experimental design and also in biases of model building and theory construction. A reductionist is thus led to understand the behavior of his system in terms of the interaction of its parts as he conceives them.[79] These biases are perpetuated by inertia, perceptual focus, and perceptual reinforcement. "Inertia" refers to the fact that some assumptions are so common that they are not examined, particularly because these assumptions are likely to result in increased analytic tractability.[80] Perceptual focus is described by Wimsatt as follows:

Model-building activity is performed against a background of presumed mechanisms operating in the interaction of presumed units. If the presumed units are very well entrenched in a given area, there is a strong tendency to describe and to think about even phenomena at other levels of organization in terms of these units. In traditional evolutionary theory and even at present, the most obvious unit is the individual organism—the unit which our everyday thought and our perceptual apparatus naturally predisposes us to consider. . . . Consequently, there is a strong tendency to see, and to talk about groups of organisms as *collections of individuals, rather than as unitary entities.* This is true even for

colonies of social insects, whose interdependencies extend even to reproductive specialization, making the metaphor of the colony as an organism perhaps more revealing in evolutionary terms than the view of it as a collection of organisms.[81]

Wimsatt also identifies perceptual reinforcement, the phenomena that "one bias may act in such a way as to hide the fact that another bias is a bias, and conversely."[82]

The assumption that complex models should be translated into simpler ones for research purposes is made by social work authors who propose that complex treatment models and situations can be simplified or reduced to time-limited treatment situations and quantifiable indicators of complex psychological events without a substantial loss of information or a significant change in the subject under study. However, as Hanson points out, "Complexity is not confusion. When analysis results in destroying complexity in the name of clearing up confusions, to that extent it destroys the concept in question."[83] Wimsatt concludes, "Now for pragmatic as well as for theoretical reasons, reduction in science is better seen as the attempt to understand the explanatory relations between different levels of phenomena, each of which is taken seriously in its own right, than as an unending search for firm foundations at deeper and deeper levels in which, as Roger Sperry so aptly put it, ' . . . eventually everything is explained in terms of essentially nothing.'"[84]

In his 1979 presidential address to the American Association of Sociologists, H. M. Blalock cautions against "an important kind of temptation, namely that of substituting relatively simple operational indicators for theoretical constructs without paying careful attention to the underlying measurement model and required simplifying assumptions,"[85] and concludes that "I do not believe we can simultaneously achieve generality, accuracy, and simplicity. Therefore we must give up one or another of these desirable characteristics. If we opt for simplicity, and if social reality is in fact complex, we shall inevitably be misled."[86]

Prescriptions and proscriptions.—The normative tone of much research literature derives from the logical empiricist belief that its methodology could provide a truth guarantee for scientific results and weed out unscientific (nonwarrantable) results. However, the logical empiricist model is itself not open to test because, claiming to be prescriptive rather than descriptive, it disallows actual examples from the history or current practice of science as falsifying instances of the model. Wimsatt argues that "models of scientific activity, even normative ones, should be subjected to empirical tests like any other scientific hypotheses, in this case by detailed analysis of cases from the history of science and from current science."[87] When this has been done, the logical empiricist model shows little or no relationship to how scientists actually work. According to Herbert Simon, concerns with how scientists ought to proceed are "interesting questions of philosophy, but they turn out to have relatively little relation to the actual behavior of scientists—and perhaps less normative value than has been supposed."[88] Similarly, Wimsatt suggests that we must "follow the Kantian maxim: 'Ought implies can.'"[89] If a model of scientific endeavor requires computational power far beyond our means, such a model cannot be accepted as having normative import because it would be irrational to follow it. Any acceptable normative model must provide a more accurate description of scientific capability.

In addition, because of the problems with "objectivity" described above, no single epistemology or methodology can guarantee truth in science. Michael Scriven insists that "there is no possibility that the social sciences can be free either of value claims in general or of moral value claims in particular, and the arguments which suggested that, for their own good they should be, were themselves metascientific value claims."[90]

The social work research literature has generally embraced the prescriptive approach of logical empiricism. Instead of recognizing that each body of knowledge has its own problems and that a good design for one is not necessarily the best for another, many social work authors have prescribed unitary standards for good science.[91] This approach has arguably inhibited social work from developing a discipline-specific body of knowledge. A similar retardation in theory development has occurred in sociology[92] and, as Jerry Fodor points out, in psychology:

Psychological metatheory has remained seriously underdeveloped. With a few important exceptions, its history during the second quarter of this century has been an attempt to work out a variety of behaviorism that would satisfy the constraints imposed on psychological explanation by an acceptance and application of empiricist (and particularly operationalist) views of general scientific method. The better known accounts of psychological explanation have thus often failed to reflect the most important movement in current philosophy of science: the attempt to determine the consequences of rejecting key features of the empiricist program. . . . These have recently come into question among philosophers of science who have realized that these doctrines are by no means indispensable to characterizations of scientific explanation and confirmation and that philosophical accounts that exploit them may in fact seriously distort the realities of scientific practice. Yet it is upon precisely these views that much of the implicit and explicit metatheory of American experimental psychology appears to rest.[93]

Both the failure of practitioners to utilize research and the tension between researcher and practitioner, the subject of numerous articles,[94] are products of this normative approach. Rather than advocate that research be tailored to actual practice, authors have demanded "objectivity," "hard" data, time-limited treatment, simplified models, and predictive designs, with the result that there has in fact developed a genuine, though unnecessary, conflict between service and research goals.

ALTERNATIVES

Numerous alternatives to the logical empiricist view of science have been suggested, all of which reject the logical empiricist assumption that the truthfulness of scientific results can be guaranteed. Consequently, contemporary philosophers concentrate on the practicing scientist as decision maker and problem solver rather than on the derivation of absolute prescriptions for all science. Wimsatt says, "We cannot have an adequate philosophy of science without putting a realistic model of the scientist as decision maker and problem solver back into our model of science."[95] The focus should be functional and dynamic rather than normative and, as Chambers says, "move away from the simple question of whether to apply or withhold the term 'scientific' and place it more appropriately on issues as to what kinds of insight . . . sciences can offer us and how their investigations can be furthered."[96] Thus the primary consideration is not whether or to what extent a theory is correct but whether it is an improvement—not whether this theory is better confirmed but whether it is better.[97]

An alternative approach which embraces and accounts for such complexities has been developed by Herbert Simon, who won a Nobel Prize for his work. Simon concludes that "scientific discovery is a form of problem solving,"[98] and, using computer analogs, he shows that very few problems of interest to scientists are amenable to formal procedures, that is, to algorithms (ways of systematically finding the solution that is best or maximal by some criterion).[99] He suggests a "principle of bounded rationality" which asserts that almost all significant problems are of such complexity that we cannot solve them exactly, and that, therefore, in order to find workable solutions, we introduce various simplifying and approximate techniques which he calls "heuristics":[100] "Problem-solving searches are selective in that they generally explore only a minuscule fraction of the total (and usually immense) number of possibilities. In most cases of interest, the selection of the paths to be searched is not governed by foolproof, systematic procedures, but by rules of thumb we call *heuristics*."[101] Examples of heuristics include the decisions to employ only data which are quantitatively measurable and to consider motor behavior superior to verbal behavior as a validating criterion of constructs.[102]

Unlike the logical empiricists, Simon includes "unmanageable" problems in his view of science by concluding that they can be resolved even though they are not formally solvable: "In most problem-solving domains of everyday life, however, and even in many formal ones, like chess . . . a modest number of possible solutions can be considered, and there is no way of telling whether a given solution is the best, since many other possibilities must, perforce, go unexamined. In these domains, human problem solvers and the computer programs that simulate them do not search for the 'best' solution, but for a solution that is 'good enough' by some criterion. Heuristics that proceed on this basis are sometimes called 'satisficing' heuristics."[103] Because the failures and errors producing any heuristic are not random but systematic, once a heuristic is understood, it can be made to fail: "Given this knowledge of the heuristic procedure, we can construct classes of problems for which it will always fail to produce an answer, or for which it will always produce the wrong answer. This property of system-

atic production of wrong answers will be called the bias(es) of the heuristic."[104] Modern philosophers of science recognize that these biases are inevitable and, consequently, concentrate on reducing rather than eliminating them. Wimsatt says, "There is no cookbook way of removing, detecting, or correcting sources of bias. One can lie with statistics as easily (and often, unfortunately, far more convincingly!) as without them, and major studies by the best people in the field (whatever the field) still turn up with their share of flaws. Science cannot be made error-free. The most we can hope for is the kind of critical interaction among people with different biases that will make each of us better aware of our own biases."[105]

Levins suggests that bias can be reduced by the "search for robust theorems." To counteract biases in any given model, he proposes building families of alternative models of a given phenomenon based on different simplifying assumptions. Because of their different assumptions, these models will produce different consequences and predictions, but there may be consequences which are true for all models. Levins calls those results that appear independently of the details of any particular model "robust theorems" and concludes that "our truth is the intersection of independent lies."[106] Wimsatt points out that two disadvantages with Levins's approach to reducing bias are, first, that we may be in a situation in which not even one model is available, and, second, when a number of models make a well-disguised assumption, it is not always possible to tell if models are in fact independent.[107]

Wimsatt suggests that another way of reducing scientific bias is "multilevel reduction analysis," in which, because the system-environment boundary is changed in going from one level to another, the biases of the same heuristics will lead to different simplifications when applied to a system at different levels of abstraction and organization.[108] For example, in the kind of "objective" data gathering advocated in the current social work literature, the generally unrecognized heuristic is the view of the researcher or his electronic agent as a constant and the client and his world as the only object of study. While this heuristic is valuable for certain purposes because it is designed to enhance reproducibility, never to expand the system-environment boundary to include the researcher-client relationship is to deprive social work of much valuable data and an important corrective to the bias inherent in the "experimental" heuristic. Because of social work's historic emphasis on the person in his situation, it is particularly ironic that more attention has not been paid to the psychosocial processes of the investigator-client relationship—not, it should be emphasized, with an eye to eliminating bias therefrom but for the purpose of gleaning new and significant knowledge about social treatment or planning. Practitioners are not inherently any more biased in their description of treatment processes than are tape recorders or observers. Practitioners and tape recorders introduce different biases, and for many evaluative purposes, the bias accompanying electronic recording may be much more detrimental to our understanding than that resulting from a practitioner's reports.

Psychologists concerned with this issue have stressed the valuable information that can be gained by treating clients as informants rather than as uninformed subjects.[109] Martin Orne, an investigator who has extensively studied subjects' conscious and unconscious attempts to respond to what they perceive as the demands of the experimental situation, concludes, "It never fails to amaze me that some colleagues go to the trouble of inducing human subjects to participate in their experiments and then squander the major difference between man and animal—the ability to talk and reflect on experience."[110]

It should be clear that the belief that theories can easily be compared because everyone is talking about the same data in the same language cannot be universally assumed. Suppe shares the pessimism of the weltanschauung philosophers about the possibility of assessing the merits of competing theories: "The proponents of two competing theories will be unable to agree on which facts the competing theories must accommodate if they are to be adequate. . . . Which facts are relevant to assessing the adequacy of a theory will be a function of which aspects of the phenomena the theory describes and which questions it is committed to answering. It is perfectly conceivable that the proponents of different competing theories may disagree on what sorts of questions ought to be answered by an adequate theory for a particular range of phenomena."[111]

CONCLUSION

A crucial difference between the logical empiricists and contemporary philosophers of science is that, while the former tried to reduce scientific problems and methodology to simplified and supposedly "safe" proportions, the latter try to reduce inevitable bias by studying as many aspects of a problem from as many vantage points as possible (by comparing the work of different individuals, focusing on different levels of abstraction or different environment-system boundaries, or employing different theoretical models, etc.). If scientific objectivity is inherently impossible, contemporary models, which attempt to account for biases in the context of recognizing and including complexities, seem obviously superior to the logical empiricist attempt to solve epistemological problems by simply declaring much of the work of practicing scientists unscientific. Blalock stresses that sociologists must stop trying to eliminate bias and instead recognize that "the essential point is not that assumptions can or should be avoided but that they need to be made explicit. . . . Each measurement strategy requires the use of theoretical assumptions, only some of which can be tested."[112]

This paper has described the extent to which social work and behavioral science authors who insist on accepting as truly scientific only that research comprised of "hard" data, "objective" measurements, operational definitions, and experimental (predictive) designs base their prescriptions on logical empiricist assumptions and postulates. The adoption of the logical empiricist view of science has had the grave consequence of prohibiting researchers from studying many important questions, using much valuable data, and researching social interactions in all their complexities. If current alternatives to the logical empiricist program are adopted, such as those being developed by Mitroff, Salmon, Simon, Wimsatt, or the weltanschauung philosophers, social work and other behavioral science researchers will no longer try to meet logical empiricist requirements for science by studying only those problems and theories which meet these requirements. Rather, they will select research questions because of their importance to the field and will determine appropriate data and methods of data gathering not on the basis of unquestioned assumptions about "objectivity," but on their rational relation to the theory or problem under study. Explanation will be recognized as having a separate function from prediction, and criteria for prediction will not be applied to explanation. Therefore experimental (predictive) designs will not be regarded as inherently superior and ex post facto designs as inherently inferior; rather, designs will be adapted to the theory or problem in question, and the value of a design will be determined by whether it provides a useful explanation of significant phenomena. Statistics will be used to explain,not "prove," an event; therefore the test of whether statistics are significant will not be high probability but "statistical relevance"—whether a factor makes a difference in the probability that an event will occur.

Furthermore, rather than prescribe a single acceptable methodology in a quixotic attempt to eliminate bias, researchers will embrace different theories, methodologies, levels of focus (macro or micro), and kinds of data and data gathering. This will reduce inevitable bias by rotating the perspective on the system under investigation.[113] Finally, research will be conceptualized descriptively and functionally rather than normatively—it will adapt to relevant problems rather than dismember them to fit notions of good research.

Because of its failure to promise bias-free results, this alternative to the logical empiricist view may make some researchers uncomfortable. In the face of the findings of the last two decades of the philosophy of science, however, the desire to cling to logical empiricist theories and methodology can be understood psychologically as the wish for a certain, knowable world but should not be mistaken for proof that such a world exists. Like physics, genetics, and mathematics, social work and the other behavioral sciences must accept that reality cannot be perceived either directly or in its full complexity and, therefore, that science represents our best efforts at solving important problems for which there can be no guaranteed or permanent solutions. In Margenau's words, "If the history of science teaches anything at all it is that there are no eternal verities which man can grasp and hold forever."[114] We must learn to live with and use rather than continue to deny the complexities and ambiguities inherent in scientific activity.

NOTES

1. See, e.g., Joel Fisher, "Evaluating the Empirical Base of Clinical Practice" (Occasional Paper no. 1, Jane Addams College of Social Work, Chicago, 1979), pp. 7–8; Mary Macdonald, "Social Work Research: A Perspective," in *Social Work Research*, ed. Norman Polansky (Chicago: University of Chicago Press, 1960), pp. 1–23; and Helen Witmer, "Science and Social Work," *Smith College Studies in Social Work* 14 (1943): 222–30.

2. Although these assumptions are widely accepted, some social work authors have questioned them. See, e.g., Aaron Beckerman, "Differentiating between Social Research

and Social Work Research," *Journal of Education for Social Work* 14 (1978): 9–15; John Crane, "Utilizing the Fundamentals of Science in Educating for Social Work Practice," *Journal of Education for Social Work* 2 (1966): 22–29; Samuel Finestone and Alfred Kahn, "The Design of Research," in *Social Work Research*, ed., rev. ed. Norman Polansky (Chicago: University of Chicago Press, 1975); Henry Maas, "Research in Social Work," *Encyclopedia of Social Work*, 17th ed. (Washington, D.C.: National Association of Social Workers, 1977), 2:1183–93; Martin Rein and Sandra Tannenbaum, "Social Science Knowledge and Social Work Practice," in *Sourcebook on Research Utilization*, ed. Allen Rubin and Aaron Rosenblatt (New York: Council on Social Work Education, 1979), pp. 189–219; and Joseph Vigilante, "Between Values and Science," *Journal of Education for Social Work* 10 (1974): 107–15.

3. Logical empiricism derives from empiricism, the belief that all certain knowledge comes from experience, and from logicism, whose central tenet is that propositional logic (which includes mathematics) is truth preserving (Harold Brown, *Perception, Theory and Commitment: The New Philosophy of Science* [Chicago: University of Chicago Press, 1977], pp. 15–29). The term "logical empiricism" has been chosen over "logical positivism" because it is more inclusive. Logical positivism refers specifically to an early and even more extreme form of logical empiricism, whose major doctrine is the verification theory of meaning—the thesis that a proposition is meaningful only if it can be empirically verified, that is, if there is an empirical method for deciding if it is true or false. The difficulty is that "scientific laws, which are formulated as universal propositions, cannot be conclusively verified by any finite set of observation statements" (ibid., p. 23). The logical positivists who became logical empiricists gave up the strict verificationist theory of meaning and instead adopted the requirement that all meaningful propositions had to be tested by observation and experiment (ibid., p. 23).

4. Winifred Chambers, "Clinical Interpretations and the Debate over the Scientific Acceptability of Psychoanalysis," (Ph.D. diss., University of Chicago, 1975), pp. 2–3.

5. Lewis Coser, "Presidential Address: Two Methods in Search of a Substance," *American Sociological Review* 40 (1975): 698.

6. E.g., see James K. Cole, ed., *Nebraska Symposium on Motivation*, vol. 23 (Lincoln: University of Nebraska Press, 1976); Daryl Bem and Andrea Allen, "On Predicting Some of the People Some of the Time: The Search for Cross-situational Consistencies in Behavior," *Psychological Review* 81 (1974): 506–20; Roy Bhaskar, "On the Possibility of Social Scientific Knowledge and the Limits of Naturalism," *Journal for the Theory of Social Behaviour* 8 (1978): 1–28; Edward Bixenstein, "The Value-Fact Antithesis in Behavioral Science," *Journal of Humanistic Psychology* 16 (1976): 35–57; H. M. Blalock, "Presidential Address: Measurement and Conceptualization Problems," *American Sociological Review* 44

(1979): 881–94; Coser; Howard Gadlin and Grant Ingle, "Through the One-way Mirror: The Limits of Experimental Self-Reflection," *American Psychologist* 30 (1975): 1003–9; Michael Gorman, "Towards a Unification of Physics and Psychology," *Etc* 35 (1978): 400–407; Patrick Horan, "Is Status Research Atheoretical?" *American Sociological Review* 43 (1978): 534–41; Russell Keat, "Positivism, Naturalism, and Anti-Naturalism in the Social Sciences," *Journal for the Theory of Social Behaviour* 1 (1971): 3–17; Brian Mackenzie, "Darwinism and Positivism as Methodological Influences on the Development of Psychology," *Journal of the History of the Behavioral Sciences* 12 (1976): 330–37; Ian Mitroff, "Psychological Assumptions, Experimentation, and Real World Problems," *Evaluation Quarterly* 2 (1978): 235–59; Thomas Olshewsky, "Dispositions and Reductionism in Psychology," *Journal for the Theory of Social Behaviour* (1975): 129–44; Joseph Royce, "Psychology Is Multi," in Cole, ed., pp. 1–63; Duane Schultz, "Psychology: A World with Man Left Out," *Journal for the Theory of Social Behaviour* 1 (1971): 99–107; Laurie Wiseberg, "The Statistics Jungle: Measuring War, Plague, Fire and Famine," *Society* 12 (1975): 53–60.

7. William Reid, "Developments in the Use of Organized Data," *Social Work* 19 (1974): 590; see also Anne Shyne, "Casework Research: Past and Present," *Social Casework* 43 (1967): 467–73. The point here is not that electronic or third-party observation is never valuable but that it is erroneously asserted to be the only credible source of therapeutic observation. Interestingly, although the methodological behaviorists followed the logical empiricists in eliminating subjective experiences from the scope of science, the radical behaviorists are moving toward a recognition of the need to include subjective experiences and perceptions in scientific accounts of human behavior; see, e.g., John and Janet Baldwin, "Behaviorism on Verstehen and Erklaren," *American Sociological Review* 43 (1978): 335–47.

8. See, e.g., John Schuerman, "On Research and Practice Teaching in Social Work," in Rubin and Rosenblatt, eds. p. 145; Jerry Turem, "Research Priorities in Social Work Education: A Communication to Colleagues," in ibid., pp. 33–35; and Katherine Wood, "Casework Effectiveness: A New Look at the Research Evidence," *Social Work* 23 (1978): 451.

9. Harris Goldstein, "Criteria for Evaluating Research," *Social Casework* 43 (1962): 476.

10. Leonard Kogan, "Principles of Measurement," in Polansky, ed., rev. ed. (n. 2 above), pp. 71–72.

11. Stuart Kirk and Joel Fischer, "Do Social Workers Understand Research?" *Journal of Education for Social Work* 12 (1976): 63. See also Harry Butler, Inger Davis, and Ruth Kukonnen, "The Logic of Case Comparison," *Social Work Research and Abstracts* 15 (1979): 4.

12. Martin Bloom and Stephen Block, *Social Work* 22 (1977): 130. An example from the sociological literature is the claim that status attainment research is theory free. For a good discussion and rebuttal see Horan (n. 6 above).

13. Wood, p. 453. See also Lillian Ripple, "Problem Identification and Formulation," in Polansky, ed. (n. 1 above). pp. 24–47. For an example from the psychological literature on the belief that operational ("response invariant") variables are value free, see Lois Shawver, "Research Variables in Psychology and the Logic of Their Creation," *Psychiatry* 40 (1977): 1–16.

14. Kogan, p. 72.

15. Harris Goldstein, "Making Practice More Scientific through Knowledge of Research," *Social Work* 7 (1962): 110.

16. E.g., see Wood; and Martin Kushler and William Davidson II, "Using Experimental Designs to Evaluate Social Programs," *Social Work Research and Abstracts* 15 (1979): 27–32. For a critique of this viewpoint, see Ian Mitroff and Thomas Bonoma, "Psychological Assumptions, Experimentation, and Real Life Problems," *Evaluation Quarterly* 2 (1978): 235–59; and Robert Weiss and Martin Rein, "The Evaluation of Broad-Aim Programs: Experimental Design, Its Difficulties, and an Alternative," *Administrative Science Quarterly* 15 (1970): 97–109.

17. See, e.g., Harris Goldstein, *Research Standards and Methods for Social Workers*, rev. ed. (Wheeling, Ill.: Whitehall Co., 1969), p. 7, and Norman Polansky, "Research in Social Work: Social Treatment," in *Encyclopedia of Social Work*, 17th ed., 2:1206.

18. Norman Polansky, "Introduction: Social and Historical Context," in Polansky, ed., rev. ed., p. 2.

19. Edward Mullen, "The Evaluation of Social Work Progress" (Occasional Paper no. 1, Jane Addams College of Social Work, Chicago, 1979), pp. 24–25.

20. See, e.g., Richard Stuart, "Research in Social Work: Social Case Work and Social Group Work," in *Encyclopedia of Social Work*, 17th ed., vol. 2; Peter Rossi, "Research in Social Work: Social Policy," in ibid., 2:1204; Francis Caro, "Research in Social Work: Program Evaluation," in ibid., 2:1201; David French, *An Approach to Measuring Results in Social Work* (New York: Columbia University Press, 1952); and Kushler and Davidson, pp. 27–32. When a social work author recommends a "quasi-experimental" design, it is nearly always because a "scientific," i.e., "experimental," design cannot be used for some logistical reason or because the state of a particular body of knowledge is not considered sufficiently developed for "rigorous" testing, rather than because the author doubts the hierarchical ordering of research designs (see, e.g., Ann Shyne, "Evaluation in Child Welfare," *Child Welfare* 55 [1976]: 5–18). Mitroff and Bonoma make the same point about Campbell and Stanley's discussion of quasi-experimental designs (pp. 246–48).

21. Margaret Blenkner, "Obstacles to Evaluative Research In Casework: Part II," *Social Casework* 31 (1950): 99. See also Aaron Rosen and Enola Proctor, "Specifying the Treatment Process: The Basis for Effectiveness Research," *Journal of Social Service Research* 2 (1978): 25–26.

22. Reid (n. 7 above), p. 589.

23. William Reid, "Social Work for Social Problems," *Social Work* 22 (1977): 377.

24. Ibid., p. 378.

25. See n. 3 above.

26. E.g., Bertrand Russell, Alfred North Whitehead, Gottlob Frege, the phenomenologists, the early Ludwig Wittgenstein, and Alfred Ayer all sought unsuccessfully a certainty that would solve the epistemological ambiguities stemming in most troublesome form from the Kantian paradigm that true reality can never be known because sense perceptions are invariantly distorted by the imposition of innate mental categories. For a good summary, see W. T. Jones, ed., *A History of Western Philosophy* (New York: Harcourt Brace Jovanovich, Inc.), vol. 4, *Kant to Wittgenstein and Sartre*, 2d ed. (1975).

27. Bixenstein (n. 6 above), p. 38.

28. P. W. Bridgman, *The Logic of Modern Physics* (New York: Macmillan Co., 1927), p. 5.

29. Frederick Suppe, "The Search for Philosophic Understanding of Scientific Theories," in *The Structure of Scientific Theories*, ed. Frederick Suppe (Urbana: University of Illinois Press, 1974), p. 17.

30. Brown (n. 3 above), pp. 58–60.

31. Henry Margenau, "The Philosophical Legacy of Contemporary Quantum Theory," in *Mind and Cosmos*, ed. Robert Colodny (Pittsburgh: University of Pittsburgh Press, 1966), p. 353.

32. Carl Hempel, "Recent Problems of Induction," in Colodny, ed., 116.

33. Dudley Shapere, "Meaning and Scientific Change," in Colodny, ed., p. 46.

34. William Wimsatt, "Reductionistic Research Strategies and Their Biases in the Units of Selection Controversy," in *Scientific Discovery: Case Studies*, ed. Thomas Nickles (Hingham, Mass.: D. Reidel Publishing Co., 1980), p. 214.

35. Suppe (n. 29 above), p. 283; see also Suppe, "Theory Structure," in *Current Research in Philosophy of Science*, ed. Peter Asquith and Henry Kyberg (East Lansing, Mich.: Philosophy of Science Association, 1979), pp. 317–38; and Gunther Stent, "Limits to the Scientific Understanding of Man," *Science* 187 (1975): 1052–57.

36. Wimsatt to Edward Mullen, spring 1978, School of Social Service Administration, University of Chicago.

37. Norwood Hanson, "Logical Positivism and the Interpretation of Scientific Theories," in *The Legacy of Logical Positivism*, ed. Peter Achinstein and Stephen Barker (Baltimore: Johns Hopkins University Press, 1969), p. 74. Some social work authors disclaim the existence of pristine observations while they simultaneously embrace logical empiricist tenets based on the assumption of theory-free observation; see, e.g., Goldstein, *Research Standards and Methods for Social Workers* (n. 17 above), p. 17.

38. This group includes Thomas Kuhn, Paul Feyerabend, and Norwood Hanson. For a discussion of this viewpoint see Suppe, ed., pp. 125–90.

39. Suppe, "The Search for Philosophic Understanding of Scientific Theories," p. 212.

40. David Hull, "The Operational Imperative: Sense and Nonsense in Operationalism," *Systematic Zoology* 17 (1968): 445.

41. Marshall Segall, Donald Campbell, and Melville Herskovits, *The Influence of Culture on Visual Perception* (Indianapolis: Bobbs-Merrill Co., 1966), p. 4.

42. Ibid., p. 6.

43. Ibid., see also Benjamin Whorf, "Science and Linguistics," in *Psycholinguistics: A Book of Readings*, ed. Sol Saporta (New York: Holt, Rinehart & Winston, 1961), pp. 460–67.

44. Ibid., p. 79.

45. Jerome Fodor, "Materialism," in *Materialism and the Mind-Body Problem*, ed. David Rosenthal (Englewood Cliffs, N.J.: Prentice-Hall, Inc., 1971), p. 132.

46. "Science as Perception-Communication," in Suppe, ed., p. 382.

47. Quoted in Morris Kline, *Mathematics: The Loss of Certainty* (New York: Oxford University Press, 1980), p. 341.

48. See, e.g., Robert Rosenthal, *Experimenter Effects in Behavioral Research* (New York: Appleton-Century Crofts, 1966). See also n. 55 below.

49. Margenau, p. 351. See also Harold Morowitz, "Rediscovering the Mind," *Psychology Today* 14 (1980): 12–19; and Steven Rosen, "Toward a Relativization of Psychophysical Relativity," *Perceptual and Motor Skills* 42 (1976): 843–50. For an excellent nontechnical summary of recent developments in physics and their philosophical implications, see Gary Zukav, *The Dancing Wu Li Masters: An Overview of the New Physics* (New York: William Morrow & Co., 1979).

50. William Gordon, "Knowledge and Value: Their Distinction and Relationship in Clarifying Social Work Practice," *Social Work* 10 (1965): 34.

51. Bixenstein (n. 6 above), p. 35.

52. Ibid, p. 50. See also, Albert Scheflen, "Classical Biases and the Structural Approach to Research," *Etc* 34 (1977): 290–313.

53. Rosenthal, p. 324. See also Rosenthal, "Interpersonal Expectations: Effects of the Experimenter's Hypothesis," in *Artifact in Behavioral Research*, ed. Robert Rosenthal and Ralph Rosnow (New York: Academic Press, 1964): 182–279; and Rosenthal, "Biasing Effects of Experimenters," *Etc* 34 (1977): 253–64.

54. Paul Schmidt, "Models of Scientific Thought," *American Scientist* 45 (1957): 148.

55. Gadlin and Ingle (n. 6 above), p. 1007. See also Leo Goldman, "A Revolution in Counseling Research," *Journal of Counseling Psychology* 23 (1976): 543–52; Milton Rosenberg, "The Conditions and Consequences of Evaluation Apprehension," in Rosenthal and Rosnow, eds., pp. 280–350; Schultz (n. 6 above); Paul Wachtel, "Psychodynamics, Behavior Ther-

apy, and the Implacable Experimenter," *Journal of Abnormal Psychology* 82 (1973): 324–34; and Wachtel, "Investigation and Its Discontents," *American Psychologist* 35 (1980): 399–408.

56. Rosenthal, *Experimenter Effects in Behavioral Research*, p. 135.

57. Ibid., p. 401.

58. See, e.g., Hull (n. 40 above), pp. 438–57.

59. Bridgman (n. 28 above), p. 5.

60. This extreme version of operationalism is often modified so that different operations need not always result in different concepts, but this attempt to salvage operationalism merely introduces the kind of theoretical judgments it was supposed to eliminate, such as those necessary to decide which operations measure the same concepts; see, e.g., Norman Polansky, "Introduction: Social and Historical Context," in Polansky, ed., rev. ed., pp. 23–24.

61. Ned Block and Gerald Dworkin, "IQ: Heritability and Inequality," *Philosophy and Public Affairs* 3 (1974): 352.

62. Hull, p. 440.

63. Stephen Toulmin, quoted in Suppe, ed. (n. 29 above), p. 128.

64. Stephen Toulmin, *Foresight and Understanding* (New York: Harper Torchbooks, 1961), p. 30.

65. William Wimsatt, Seminar at the School of Social Service Administration of the University of Chicago, 1978.

66. Jaegwon Kim, "Inference, Explanation, and Prediction," *Journal of Philosophy* 61 (1964): 365.

67. Margenau (n. 31 above), p. 340.

68. David Hume, *On Human Nature and the Understanding*, ed. Antony Flew (New York: Collier Books, 1962), pp. 76–91.

69. Norwood Hanson, *Patterns of Discovery: An Inquiry into the Conceptual Foundations of Science* (Cambridge: Cambridge University Press, 1958), p. 64.

70. Quoted in Nigel Calder, *Einstein's Universe* (New York: Viking Press, 1979), p. 141.

71. Quoted in *Science News* 117 (February 16, 1980), p. 104.

72. Hanson, p. 92.

73. Margenau, p. 353.

74. Calder, p. 14.

75. Wesley Salmon, *Statistical Explanation and Statistical Relevance* (Pittsburgh: University of Pittsburgh Press, 1971), pp. 10–11.

76. Wesley Salmon, "The Foundations of Scientific Inference," in Colodny, ed. (n. 31 above), p. 153. See also Clyde Noble, "Philosophy of Science in Contemporary Psychology," *Psychological Reports* 35 (1974): 1239–46.

77. Ibid., pp. 249–50. For a thoroughgoing critique of falsifiability, see Hilary Putnam, "The 'Corroboration' of Theories," in *Philosophy As It Is*, ed. Ted Honderich and Myles Burnyeat (New York: Penguin Books, 1979): 349–80; and Ian Mitroff, "Systems, Inquiry and the Meanings of Falsification," *Philosophy of Science* 40 (1973): 255–76.

78. Brown (n. 3 above), p. 130.

79. Wimsatt, "Reductionistic Research Strategies and Their Biases in the Units of Selection Controversy" (n. 34 above), pp. 230–35.

80. Ibid., p. 248.

81. Ibid., p. 249.

82. Ibid., p. 250.

83. Hanson (n. 37 above), p. 77. The issue of reduction is an important one in sociology because the question of whether sociology can or should be reduced to psychology is obviously a critical one; see Murray Webster, "Psychological Reductionism, Methodological Individualism, and Large Scale Problems," *American Sociological Review* 38 (1973): 258–73.

84. Wimsatt, "Reductionistic Research Strategies and Their Biases in the Units of Selection Controversy," p. 252.

85. Blalock (n. 6 above), p. 883.

86. Ibid., p. 882.

87. William Wimsatt, "Reduction and Reductionism," in Asquith and Kyberg, eds. (n. 35 above), p. 7. See also Ian Mitroff and Tom Featheringham, "On Systemic Problem Solving and the Error of the Third Kind," *Behavioral Science* 19 (1974); 383–91.

88. Herbert Simon, "Scientific Discovery and the Psychology of Problem Solving," in Colodny, ed., p. 23. When it is taken into account, the history of science indicates that scientific methodology, including definitions of logic and rigor, are time and culture dependent; see Kline (n. 47 above) and Larry Laudan, "Historical Methodologies: An Overview and Manifesto," in Asquith and Kyberg, eds., pp. 40–54.

89. Wimsatt, "Reduction and Reductionism," p. 7.

90. Michael Scriven, "Logical Positivism and the Behavioral Sciences," in Achinstein and Barker, eds., p. 201.

91. See n. 21 above.

92. Coser (n. 5 above), pp. 691–700.

93. Jerry Fodor, *Psychological Explanation: An Introduction to the Philosophy of Psychology* (New York: Random House, 1968), pp. xiv–xv.

94. See, e.g., Sidney H. Aronson and Clarence C. Sherwood, "Research vs. Practitioner," *Social Work* 12 (1967): 89–96; Scott Briar, "Toward the Integration of Practice and Research," in *Future of Social Work Research*, ed. David Fanshel (Washington, D.C.: National Association of Social Workers, 1980): 31–37; Francis Caro, "Evaluative Researchers and Practitioners: Conflicts and Accommodation," *Journal of Research and Development in Education* 8 (1974–75): 55–62; Reid, "Social Work for Social Problems" (n. 23 above), p. 378; Frederick Seidl, "Making Research Relevant for Practitioners," in Fanshel, ed., pp. 53–62; and Edwin Thomas, "Research and Service in Single-Case Experimentation: Conflicts and Choices," *Social Work Research and Abstracts* 24 (1978): 20–31.

95. Wimsatt, "Reduction and Reductionism," p. 8.

96. Chambers (n. 4 above), p. 3.

97. Wimsatt, seminar (n. 65 above).

98. Simon, p. 22.

99. Herbert Simon, "Thinking by Computers," in Colodny, ed., p. 15.

100. Wimsatt, "Reductionistic Research Strategies and Their Biases in the Units of Selection Controversy," p. 220.

101. Simon, "Thinking by Computers," p. 12. See also Amos Tversky and Daniel Kahneman, "The Framing of Decisions and the Psychology of Choice," *Science* 211 (1981): 453–58.

102. In the behavioristic heuristic, intentionality is not considered, and the fact that we can lie with gestures as well as with words is rarely mentioned: see Else Frenkel-Brunswick, "Psychoanalysis and the Unity of Science," *Proceedings of the American Academy of Arts and Sciences* 80 (1954): 271–347 and Olshewsky (n. 6 above).

103. Simon, "Thinking by Computers," p. 16.

104. Wimsatt, "Reductionistic Research Strategies and Their Biases in the Units of Selection Controversy," p. 220.

105. Wimsatt to Mullen (n. 36 above).

106. Quoted in Wimsatt, "Reductionistic Research Strategies and Their Biases in the Units of Selection Controversy," p. 251.

107. Ibid., pp. 251–52.

108. Ibid., p. 252.

109. Gadlin and Ingle (n. 6 above), p. 1008.

110. Martin Orne, "Demand Characteristics and the Concept of Quasi-Controls," in Rosenthal and Rosnow, eds. (n. 53 above), p. 153.

111. Suppe, ed., p. 211.

112. Blalock, p. 888.

113. C. W. Churchman and Ian Mitroff, among others, have attempted to systematize and conceptualize different perspectives on scientific inquiry. They suggest at least five different approaches to science, each of which has its particular strengths and weaknesses; see, e.g., Churchman, *The Design of Inquiring Systems* (New York: Basic Books, 1971); and Mitroff, "Systems, Inquiry, and the Meanings of Falsification" (n. 77 above).

114. Margenau (n. 31 above), p. 355.

Debate with Authors

THE OBSOLETE SCIENTIFIC IMPERATIVE IN SOCIAL WORK RESEARCH

JOHN R. SCHUERMAN *University of Chicago*

Martha Brunswick Heineman's article on the bases of social work research (*Social Service Review* 55, no. 3 [September 1981]: 371–97) is a fascinating and challenging piece. The point of view she presents is not new but has rarely been presented in such a scholarly way within social work. I want to discuss two aspects of the article, its rhetoric and its substance.

With regard to the rhetoric, Heineman begins with quotations from a number of social work researchers. She then recites several principles of "logical empiricism," a set of methodological prescriptions based on but less rigid than classical logical positivism. She proceeds to attack these principles using, for the most part, well-known arguments of "post-logical positivist" philosophers. Having presumably demolished certain elements of logical empiricism, she assumes that she has also discredited the views of the quoted social work researchers, views she believes are derived from logical empiricism.

While it may be good rhetoric, Heineman has committed the classic logical error of affirming the consequent. The argument might be schematized as follows: Logical empiricism implies that social work researchers are correct; logical empiricism is wrong; therefore, social work researchers are wrong. At least

from a logical standpoint. Heineman has proved nothing about the views of social work researchers in going after the theories of logical empiricists. (If L implies R then not-R implies not-L, and showing that not-L is true says nothing about the truth of not-R.)

Perhaps more serious is the assumption that the views of social work researchers are derived from logical empiricism. Social work research uses a wide variety of methodologies with varying intellectual roots. It is a gross oversimplification to assert that the principles used by social work researchers are derived from logical empiricism, although they may be consistent in some respects. Most of these principles have roots that far predate the Vienna circle. The principle of parsimony in conceptualization and theorizing was explicated by Ockham in the fourteenth century. The idea of experimentation, that is, manipulating things to see what will happen, is at least as old as mankind. The use of experimentation to establish general laws was advocated by Francis Bacon in the sixteenth century. The use of contrast groups to deal with variability of subjects' responses to experimental conditions was anticipated by Boylston in the investigation of smallpox vaccine in the early eighteenth century and was

Source: "The Obsolete Scientific Imperative in Social Work Research" by J. R. Schuerman, 1982, *Social Service Review, 56,* pp. 144–146. Copyright 1982 by The University of Chicago. Reprinted by permission.
Social Service Review (March 1982). © 1982 by The University of Chicago. All rights reserved.

given a statistical underpinning in the late nineteenth century.

Furthermore, it is interesting that Heineman herself observed that the philosophy of science has little impact on the way science is conducted. I agree with that observation; it is certainly true of social work researchers. Philosophers of science have long set down various methodological canons only to have them ignored or violated by practicing scientists. Sometimes the violations are accompanied by guilt. At other times, quite competent scientists are blithely unaware of current philosophical positions, with no perceptible negative effects on their contributions. Apparently this is true in all disciplines.

So much for rhetoric; I turn now to substance. Much of the substance of Heineman's arguments could be disputed. However, I want to focus on what I consider the most troubling parts of her argument. These have to do with the relationship between theory and observation, with operationalism, the nature of data, and the role of replication.

It should be observed at the outset that Heineman describes a form of operationalism that is extreme, has never been followed by actual researchers, is easily disputed, and was abandoned early on by philosophers. Heineman is correct in pointing out that it is not possible for us to achieve measurements that are fully atheoretical. All observation is biased. To begin with, observation is biased because it is selective; not all sensory experiences can be recorded.

But as Heineman also clearly demonstrates, science is very much a social enterprise. We need to communicate our observations and our theories, and we need to have our observations and our theories criticized by others. Such communication requires conventions. At the very least it requires the conventions of language. Communication requires that we be clear about the meanings of important terms. We cannot share fully any experience with another individual, and we cannot fully make known to another person the contents of our minds. Thus we must define the meanings of words in terms of the thing we come closest to having in common, sensory experiences, realizing that our communication will be limited by the fact that one person's sensory experience will not be exactly that of another.

Beyond such social and linguistic considerations, there are, of course, other reasons for clearly specifying at least some of our concepts in terms of observables. One is the desirability of consensual validation

and replication, both of which Heineman derides as old-fashioned ideas. There are many examples of scientific "findings" that turned out to be flukes or hoaxes when replication was attempted. Besides that, scientists have long accepted the inevitability of error in observation. Heineman herself points out the common occurrence of error arising out of experimenter expectations and other biases. Given the inevitability of error, we are left with the necessity of evaluating its extent in any given research and its impact on the conclusions that can be drawn. Ordinarily, the assessment of the extent of error requires repetition of measurement, which in turn requires definitions of concepts in terms of observables.

I do not mean by "replication" the repetition of observation under exactly the same conditions. That is impossible in the social sciences and probably impossible in the physical sciences. That fact is not a limitation but an advantage; in fact, it is desirable that a replication be a repetition with a difference. In that way, successful replications contribute not only to increased confidence in the findings but also to making the findings more general. Unlike strict operationalists, we do not want our conclusions to be specific to particular measurement procedures or to other specifics of the study.

After all of Heineman's dissection of the errors of researchers, one must ask what she would suggest as an alternative view of social work research and what criteria she would propose for evaluating research. The conclusion to her paper is notably lacking in such suggestions. I take it that the response would be to refuse to answer that question directly on the grounds that it is inappropriate to prescribe research methods, beyond insisting that the procedures should be open. We should judge each piece of research on its own terms and within its own context.

I would be quite happy if philosophers of science would get out of the business of prescribing scientists' behavior and criticizing their methods. I think it is fine if they want to get back to pure descriptions of science. However, that will not do for members of the research profession. We have the responsibility to evaluate and criticize our colleagues' work, as do social work practitioners. Surely we cannot take the position that anything goes. To judge research solely in its own context would result in hopeless relativism. Furthermore, it seems to me that if Heineman were to make judgments of research studies, she would not be able to hold for long to a purely relativistic stance. After all, no observation is purely atheoretical. Eventually, at least some criteria would be evident in her judgments.

AUTHOR'S REPLY

MARTHA BRUNSWICK HEINEMAN   *Chicago, Illinois*

John Schuerman's negative remarks about "The Obsolete Scientific Imperative in Social Work Research" (*Social Service Review* 55 [September 1981]: 371–97) are groundless in that he neither accurately represents the content of the article nor addresses the issues raised.

In taking issue with the assertion that the current regulative principles of social work research derive in important ways from logical empiricism, Schuerman misreads the article. It states only that the prevalent principles of social work research derive most directly from logical empiricism, and it certainly neither says nor implies that the logical empiricists invented the principle of parsimony, the idea of experimentation, or the use of contrast groups. Furthermore, the article emphasizes that, taken on a constitutive rather than a regulative level, the value of empiricism or experimentation is not in question. Rather, the problem is that, just as the logical empiricists do, social work researchers apply certain principles so restrictively that important questions, methods, and data are excluded from scientific activity, even though the principles being used restrictively are themselves too problematic to be infallible or exclusive roads to truth.

Schuerman's exegesis on the logical error of affirming the consequent should have been obviated by an alert reading of the article, which clearly demonstrates that both the prescriptive tone and also many of the specific criteria for acceptable research advanced by social work researchers are identical with the prescriptive tone and criteria advanced by the logical empiricists. Thus the logic of the argument is actually in the paradigmatic form: A equals B; not A; then not B (where A represents the major tenets of logical empiricism and B represents major tenets of contemporary social work research).

Schuerman's statement that I describe an extreme form of operationalism is puzzling in that my note 60 clearly states that, although operationalism is often applied less restrictively than it was originally, this more relaxed use of operationalism (which permits different operations to measure the same concept)

merely reintroduces the theoretical judgments operationalism was supposed to eliminate, such as which operations measure the same concept. Schuerman never responds to the assertion that there are fatal defects inherent in the concept of operationalism.

The remainder of Schuerman's objections either continue to avoid the issues raised in the article or hit hard at straw men. For example, he reads the article to say that I am against clarity of meaning, definitions based on sensory experience, consensual validation, and replication. These sentiments are expressed nowhere, and, in fact, I am all for these scientific shibboleths as ideals or Platonic forms. However, as the article says, in the real world these research ideals are problematic in that there is no possibility of an unambiguous, unchanging definition of, say, an observable or a sensory experience and thus no possibility that following Schuerman's particular definition of observable or his criteria for adequate replication will guarantee anything except probable agreement with those researchers who happen to see the world and define things the way he does. The question that arises is, Why should Schuerman's particular definitions or criteria control what other social work researchers can do? This is the main issue raised by the paper— namely, why the social work profession allows certain researchers to use discredited scientific criteria to proscribe or restrict research questions, data, or methods which other social work researchers believe will significantly enhance the knowledge base and clinical tools of social work. Unfortunately, Schuerman never addresses this central issue or even acknowledges that it was raised.

Schuerman's final objections are, first, that the position that there are no scientific definitions or procedures that can guarantee bias-free results is untenable because it leads to "hopeless relativism" and, second, that I suggest no alternatives to the current program of social work research. Again, he seems not to have read the article carefully, because the last section and conclusion of the article are devoted to the discussion of alternatives, that is, ways in which inevitable bias can be reduced without excluding com-

Source: "Author's Reply," by M. B. Heineman, 1982, *Social Service Review*, 56, pp. 146–148. Copyright 1982 by The University of Chicago. Reprinted by permission.
Social Service Review (March 1982). © 1982 by The University of Chicago. All rights reserved

plexities or important problems. It seems to me that a "hopeful relativism" such as I am espousing is superior to the unquestioning adherence to a discredited set of principles that proscribe much potentially fruitful research on the promise of a certainty they cannot deliver. In conclusion, I would like to quote briefly from an applicable passage in the article: "Because of its failure to promise bias-free results, this alternative to the logical empiricist view may make some researchers uncomfortable. In the face of the findings of the last two decades of the philosophy of science, however, the desire to cling to logical empiricist theories and methodology can be understood psychologically as the wish for a certain, knowable world but

should not be mistaken for proof that such a world exists" (p. 391).*

When I wrote "The Obsolete Scientific Imperative in Social Work Research," I hoped that it would stimulate a much-needed dialogue about the current regulative principles of social work research. Unfortunately, Schuerman, instead of contributing to such a dialogue, both misreads the article and merely reiterates the prevalent view of social work research without either addressing or acknowledging the criticisms of that view advanced in the article.

---

*Editor's Note: See p.121 in this text.

Debate with Authors

COMMENTS ON "THE OBSOLETE SCIENTIFIC IMPERATIVE IN SOCIAL WORK RESEARCH"

LUDWIG L. GEISMAR   *Rutgers University*
I have read with interest Martha Brunswick Heineman's criticism of research approaches giving primacy to methodological rather than substantive requirements ("The Obsolete Scientific Imperative in Social Work Research," *Social Service Review* 55 [September 1981]: 371–97). I wondered, however, why Heineman zeroed in on logical empiricism as the culprit for the kind of research ritualism she was describing.

Logical empiricism, as the author herself pointed out, flowered between the 1920s and 1950s and contributed greatly to the growth of empirical social science, which heretofore had lacked a broad philosophic formulation. It is hard to say whether the contemporary philosophy of science that Heineman speaks of arose in opposition to or was inspired by logical empiricism.

The fact is that such empiricist excesses as absurd reductionism or phenomenal absolutism are not the stuff that social work research is presently made of, nor do social work researchers as a group affirm these days that explanation and prediction are synonymous. The declaration that "complex treatment models and situations can be simplified or reduced to time-limited treatment situations . . ." (p. 385) is neither logical empiricism nor any kind of research methodology but just another form of treatment faddism which pervades the field at the present time.

This reader was particularly puzzled by Heineman's statement that social work research is characterized by "discrete canons of scientific acceptability, which are used to evaluate service models and research findings" (p. 371) embodied in the work of two writers. She must surely be aware of the fact that social work research, whether it be in the form of "how to do it" writings or substantive inquiries, covers a wide spectrum of approaches. These range from the narrowly behavioristic to the qualitative-comparative. None of these has a monopoly on the social work research market or can claim to best represent the research enterprise.

Heineman's attack on logical empiricism is less a critique of social work research than it is a game of putting up and shooting down straw men. Her "alternatives," which include the views that a good theory is a better explanation rather than the only correct one or that electronic data-gathering devices can introduce different data biases, represent widely accepted mainstream thinking among social science and social work

Source: "Comments on 'The Obsolete Scientific Imperative in Social Work Research'" by L. L. Geismar, 1982, *Social Service Review*, 56, pp. 311–312. Copyright 1982 by The University of Chicago. Reprinted by permission.
Social Service Review (June 1982). © 1982 by The University of Chicago. All rights reserved.

researchers. To depict the author's alternatives as the antithesis to an orthodox, obsolete philosophy (where does one find it nowadays?) does little to further the movement toward more effective models of social work research.

AUTHOR'S REPLY

MARTHA HEINEMAN PIEPER* *Chicago, Illinois*
I was most interested to learn from Ludwig Geismar that the field of social work research is so eclectic and up to date that my article merely brought coals to Newcastle. Unfortunately, since Geismar cites no authors, books, articles, or statistics in support of his contentions, it is impossible to know on what he bases his optimism. On the other hand, my conclusions about the current state of social work research are supported by citations of the work of over thirty of the most prolific and prominent social work researchers. Geismar's assertions that my conclusions are both unfounded and also based on the work of only two authors is thus most puzzling. In his desire to dismiss my argument as the setting up and demolishing of straw men, Geismar also neglects to mention that I described a prevailing stance toward research, not a monolithic one (see my article, p. 391–92, n. 2).**

Since Geismar indulges in unsupported impressions, I would like to add one or two of my own. In my experience, social workers who submit articles to the leading journals for publication, try to get dissertations approved, or apply for research grants, jobs, or tenure do not, in fact, find the field of social work hospitable to research methodologies or interests which are not consonant with the assumptions of logical empiricism. On the contrary, a perusal of dissertation abstracts and the articles selected for publication in research journals indicates not only the continued hegemony of positivist assumptions and prescriptions but also a distressing absence of critical and analytic discussion of the foundations of social work research.

Source: "Author's Reply" by M. Heineman Pieper, 1982, *Social Service Review*, 56, p. 312. Copyright 1982 by The University of Chicago. Reprinted by permission.
Social Service Review (June 1982). © 1982 by The University of Chicago. All rights reserved.
*Formerly Martha Brunswick Heineman.
**Editor's Note: See p.121 in this text.

Debate with Authors

THE SCIENTIFIC IMPERATIVE AGAIN

MARY GORMAN GYARFAS   *Evanston, Illinois*
It is both exciting and sad to read the exchange between Martha Brunswick Heineman (now Martha Heineman Pieper) and John R. Schuerman about the state of research in social work (*Social Service Review* 56, no. 1 [March 1982]: 144–48). Exciting because an important controversy that has shaped social work development has found its way into print; sad because, in a way, the dialogue epitomizes the troubles that beset social work. Both writers represent their points of view aptly, but neither really "hears" the other.

Schuerman never responds to the point that most social work problems and processes are too complicated to lend themselves to experimental designs. Pieper, on the other hand, does not adequately acknowledge the problems of reliability and validity that continue to plague social work research. In short, although both writers make important points, neither really addresses the other's position.

Schuerman appears to represent a point of view that does not distinguish between the necessity for consensually validated behavioral criteria in social work research and for behaviorism as a treatment method. Behavioral definitions of problems and processes are necessary and desirable, but to limit social work problems and processes to those considered respectable by behaviorally oriented therapists is to succumb to a theoretical bias that has had the effect of ignoring most of the real world of social work practice, where (even if it were their goal to do so) neither practitioners nor clients are in a position to control the consequences of behavior—a sine qua non of behavioral therapy.

Most social work concepts and activities, although complicated, can be "operationalized" in observable behavioral terms, thereby meeting Schuerman's requirement. However, in recent years only some concepts and activities (variants on the theme of behaviorism) have been considered respectable and therefore worth testing. Social work practitioners and researchers need to understand the issues that Pieper so aptly summarizes in her paper so that they can get to work to solve the basic problems confronting social work research at practical as well as epistemological levels.

In recent years, the tendency to limit social work practice and research to one-dimensional experimental designs considered acceptable by behaviorists has had the effect of devaluing a rich body of social work knowledge, thereby impoverishing the profession as a whole. Concepts that should have been refined and tested in complicated, sophisticated research designs have been thrown out like the proverbial baby in the bath water because we lacked the research technology at the time to examine them rigorously.

Now that the controversy between behaviorists and nonbehaviorists has begun to surface, it would be nice if the protagonists allowed themselves to listen and learn from each other. In short, behaviorally oriented researchers could help nonbehaviorists learn to define their concepts in observable measurable terms, while the latter could teach the former something about the multiplicity of variables that must be accounted for in valid social work research. Both could profit from the exchange of information.

Perhaps this is not too much to hope for in a new generation of social workers who are clearly better prepared to argue their positions publicly than were their elders. By publishing Martha Heineman Pieper's excellent paper, the *Social Service Review* has taken a significant step in that direction.

Introduction to "Scientific Imperatives in Social Work Research and Practice" and the Debates in Response

Walter Hudson's central contribution to social work was the development of a model of social work practice that drew heavily from behaviorism. Behaviorism, as it was developed by Thomas Watson and then B. F. Skinner, was designed to conform to positivist standards for good science. An example of Hudson's prescriptions for social work treatment is the axiom "if you can't measure the client's problem, it doesn't exist" (Hudson, 1978, p. 65). In the conclusion of this paper, Hudson sets forth what he regards as "basic tenets of science." Comparison of Hudson's beliefs about science with those promulgated by the Social Work Research Group (SWRG) during the 1950s shows the historical origins of Hudson's beliefs.

A paradigm shift entails a radical change of beliefs about what is real (ontology) and how to know that reality (epistemology). Scientists who advance a new paradigm typically reformulate the central problems to be explored in their field:

> Paradigms provide scientists not only with a map but also with some of the directions essential for map-making. In learning a paradigm the scientist acquires theory, methods, and standards together, usually in an inextricable mixture. Therefore, when paradigms change, there are usually significant shifts in the criteria determining the legitimacy both of problems and of proposed solutions. (Kuhn, 1970, p. 109)

Because the criteria for appraising all aspects of scientific research change so radically with a new paradigm, adherents of an old paradigm often have great difficulty understanding the tenets of the new paradigm. At the same time, participating in a paradigm shift can be liberating. The explosive significance of a paradigm shift for a field is captured by Donald Campbell, as he described such a shift in the philosophy of science. He says that Thomas Kuhn was among the leaders of the movement within the philosophy of science who generated "effective critiques (concentrated in the years 1958 to 1962) that toppled the establishment" (which had been positivism) (quoted in Callebaut, 1993, p. 43). Campbell describes how he believes Kuhn was, in turn, influenced by Quine's "Two Dogmas of Empiricism" (1948), which was widely regarded as a landmark paper that pointed out that logical positivism and its derivatives were fatally flawed as a philosophy of science. In Campbell's view, Quine's paper was "tremendously emancipating" (cited in Callebaut, 1993, p. 43) for philosophers of science. Regarding the influence of the postpositivist philosophy of science on her work as a sociologist of science, Karin Knorr Cetina writes, "Kuhn has encouraged us, he has somehow *empowered* us [italics in original], made it possible for us to go into the laboratory and look at the content of science. I don't believe one would even have considered that as reasonable before Kuhn. It took Kuhn to make that obvious to us" (quoted in Callebaut, 1993, p. 43). The debates within the field of social work provide another example of exchange between scientists during a paradigm shift.

KEY TERMS

Mentalism   Syllogism

DISCUSSION QUESTIONS

1. One of Hudson's points about scientific research is that "if scientists cannot define or observe" a posited entity (or construct), "they conclude that it does not exist." He also believes that "science is a self-corrective process that develops and validates knowledge through reliance on imperfect observations of observable entities."

    a. Do scientists conclude that entities they cannot define or observe do not exist? (You might consider, e.g., the discovery of new planets, and the study of hidden fault lines, gravity, and magnetism.) What would happen to the process of scientific discovery and research if scientists conducted research as Hudson believes they do?

    b. Hudson's application of the preceding belief about scientific research led him to conclude that "if you can't measure a client's problem, it doesn't exist." (1978, p. 65)

        i.   Would you want to apply that as a precept for clinical practice with clients? Why or why not?

        ii. Would you want to apply it as a precept in developing policy solutions to social problems? Why or why not?

    c. Extra-credit question: Dudley Shapere, a noted postpositivist philosopher of science, says,

        the very distinction between actuality and possibility, between reality and unreality, does not fit the kind of "entity" that we have in quantum field theory. In other words, the content of what we are learning even about the word "about" has to be learned in the development of science; and we are still learning what it means "to exist." (quoted in Callebaut, 1993, p. 175)

    A postpositivist critique of a logical positivist approach to social and behavioral research is that its epistemological assumptions unjustifiably restricted the ontological assumptions that social and behavioral scientists could use in their research. How does Hudson's statement (quoted previously) illustrate that problem?

2. Compare Hudson's definition of *objectivity* with Heineman Pieper's.

3. Take the nine points in Hudson's conclusion and see how they draw from ideas set forth by logical positivist philosophers of science, as exemplified in the selections in the Appendix.

    a. Compare statements 3 and 4 with Schlick's definition of *scientific meaningfulness*.

    b. Compare statement 5 with Bridgman's definition of *operationism*.

    c. Compare statement 7 with Popper's concept of *falsification* as a criterion to demarcate scientific from other forms of knowledge.

4. Holland raises the important issue of what constitutes a legitimate subject of scientific inquiry. What topics of inquiry does Holland say Hudson's assumptions "eviscerate" from social work research?

5. In his "Author's Reply," Hudson claims that Heineman Pieper advances an approach to research that lacks scientific standards. What are the standards that Heineman Pieper advances?

Scientific Imperatives in Social Work Research and Practice

Walter W. Hudson   *Florida State University*

ABSTRACT: This article examines recent assertions regarding shortcomings of method and prescription alleged to occur within the field of social work research. It attempts to clarify misinterpretations of scientific thought and to correct misinformation presented in a recent article in this journal. The major purpose of this article is to set forth, in this author's opinion, a sounder view of the use of scientific imperatives in the conduct of social work research and practice.

In a recent article, Heineman[1] claimed that "social work has adopted an outmoded, overly restrictive paradigm of research" which has caused "important questions and valuable data to go unresearched." She further claims that "the social work research literature has generally embraced the prescriptive approach of logical empiricism" and that "the requirements of logical empiricism have been used prescriptively to limit the permissible range of research questions and data and to define service effectiveness." According to Heineman, "this approach has arguably inhibited social work from developing a discipline-specific body of knowledge." These are very serious accusations, indictments, or concerns; it is, therefore, important to examine Heineman's assertions in some detail.

It is the thesis of this article that Heineman has set forth a number of fallacious conclusions which she arrived at through the use of faulty logic, misinformation, and a basic failure to understand the fundamental tenets of scientific thought and behavior. The concern of this article is not that Heineman is misled as an individual, but that her arguments and conclusions could severely mislead others who may give some credence to her thesis through a hasty and uncritical review of it. In order to reduce the risk of such an occurrence, it is therefore necessary to examine and disclose at least the basic flaws in her analysis.

LOGICAL EMPIRICISM

The fundamental thesis of Heineman's article is that social work has adopted "logical empiricism" as a model of science, and a substantial portion of her article is devoted to the task of showing that logical empiricism is an outmoded paradigm. Logical empiricism is defined by Heineman in her note 3, where she says that it derives from empiricism and logicism. Heineman defines empiricism, in the same note, as the belief that "all *certain* knowledge comes from experience" (emphasis added), and she states that the central tenet of logicism is that propositional logic is truth preserving.

I can see four aspects of logical empiricism, as represented by Heineman, that one might regard as being objectionable: (1) that knowledge is certain and unchangeable; (2) that knowledge comes from experi-

Source: From "Scientific Imperatives in Social Work Research and Practice" by W. Hudson, 1982, *Social Service Review*, 56, pp. 246–258. Copyright 1982 by The University of Chicago. Reprinted by permission.

Social Service Review (June 1982). © 1982 by The University of Chicago. All rights reserved. 0037–7961/82/5602–0008$01.00

ence; (3) that one might use propositional logic; and (4) that propositional logic is truth preserving. Much of what we think we know simply cannot be regarded as certain, and the history of science clearly demonstrates that our understanding of the world and the universe changes as new information about them is obtained. The history of empirical science has also taught us to be very wary[2] of any propositional logic (including mathematics) whose nouns are not tied firmly to real-world referents.[3] The suggestion that any logic is truth preserving is risky because such a statement implies the existence of some absolute truth in the Platonic sense. Yes, these three aspects of Heineman's logical empiricism are highly objectionable. But what about the modified assertion that "all . . . knowledge comes from experience"? Whether Heineman would reject that assertion is not clear from anything she presents in her article.

Except for the business of experience,[4] it does appear that logical empiricism is a flawed model of science—and it was experience that so taught us. Even so, logical empiricism is a fairly harmless brute unless and until it amasses a following of social work researchers, and that is a matter of grave import to Heineman's entire thesis.

Over the past twenty years or so I have had occasion to speak, often at length, with a rather large number of social work researchers. My general experience has been that (1) none of them has ever expressed the conviction that our knowledge of the world is certain and unchangeable; (2) they indeed seem to reject the use of propositional logic that is not grounded by real-world referents; and (3) I never hear them advocating the pursuit of some ultimate Platonic truth. In short, I do not see a long train of social work researchers following dutifully behind the logical empiricism villain. In all candor, the social work researchers I have known and talked with *do* act as though they believe that an understanding of how the world works can be obtained from experience, that is, they claim that it is very difficult to acquire an understanding of the world through the use of nonexperience!

THE HEINEMAN SYLLOGISM

Actually, Heineman never pointed to any specific researcher and then claimed that he or she follows the three evils of logical empiricism: pursuit of certain and unchangeable knowledge, use of propositional logic that is not grounded by real-world referents, and pur-

suit of some absolute Platonic truth. What she did do was accuse social work research of doing so. I have not met social work research or shaken its hand, but according to Heineman it is clearly social work who is the principal actor and who "has adopted an outmoded, overly restricted paradigm of research." The important point here is that "social work" is merely a label, a term, to attach to an ever-changing collection of entities who call themselves social workers, but social work is not an entity that has adopted anything. Nonetheless, Heineman personified social work and then, in effect, advanced a common Aristotelian syllogism.[5]

A substantial part of Heineman's article is devoted to the argument that logical empiricism is an obsolete paradigm of science, and that is the major premise of her syllogism. Her minor premise, generally stated, is that social work research has adopted the approach of logical empiricism, and the conclusion of her syllogism is that, therefore, social work research is based on an outmoded paradigm of science. It might well be possible to grant the major premise because it has some things that just do not measure up—to experience? However, the minor premise is simply untenable. It rests on the law of the excluded middle and relies on a personification of social work and social work research—which are not acting entities capable of adopting anything. . . .

STRICTURES ON PRECIOUS DATA

Heineman asserted in her article that social work has caused important questions and valuable data to go unresearched and that logical empiricism has been used to limit the permissible range of research questions. There are several points to consider in this regard. First, Heineman did not identify even one researchable question that social work researchers are preventing from being addressed. Presumably there were several that she had in mind, but she did not name them. Second, she never once indicated how these social work researchers are going about the business of actively suppressing the study of valuable data. A third point to consider is the simple fact that Heineman never identified what was contained in all those valuable data that are being suppressed, nor did she indicate what criteria were used in judging their value. Actually, she levied these charges against, not researchers, but social work—a personified nonentity. Heineman did complain that not much research has been devoted to the client-practitioner relationship. In that she is simply wrong. There is a large literature devoted to that topic. Perhaps she wants more, or perhaps she feels that what has been done is simply worthless. Whatever she had in mind, her claim that not much has been done is simply an uninformed assertion. . . .

PHILOSOPHY VERSUS SCIENCE

Throughout her article, Heineman complains about science and turns to the philosophers for solutions. She complains about social work research being prescriptive while writing an intensely prescriptive article. Her prescription is that social work research turn to the modern philosophers and learn from them how to proceed. Heineman should read Heineman, who says, quoting Simon, that "concerns with how scientists ought to proceed are 'interesting questions of philosophy, but they turn out to have little relation to the actual behavior of scientists.' "[7]

If there is anything that history has taught science (my personification), it is to be wary of philosophers. The lesson should not be abandoned. It was the emergence of science in terms of brutish empiricism that so long ago finally solved Zeno's paradox.[8] It was none other than Hegel who claimed on philosophical grounds alone that it was not possible to find any new celestial bodies in the solar system. He did that one year before astronomers discovered the asteroid, Ceres.[9] Heineman (p. 379) quotes Fodor as saying, "I think that there is a strong temptation to say that the larger viruses are not inferred entities any more—specifically because of the electron microscope. Yet it is possible to maintain that the argument from shadows on the plate to viruses on the slide is fully as complex as the argument from spectroscopic results to vegetation on Mars." Now, I do submit that, given this argument, a clever mind is probably very capable of "proving" that (1) large viruses do not exist; (2) vegetation, full-blown, does exist on Mars; and (3) possibly both! One can do truly wondrous things with the mind and to the universe when one is permitted to use only argument. That is the key. The scientist does not live by argument alone but by evidence; raw, brutish empiricism—experience. What that means is that one must relate argument to the real world as experienced by poor, hapless, fallible *Homo sapiens* in order to settle arguments about the real world. Arguments, taken alone, do not and cannot settle other arguments about the real world.

To the extent that we engage in arguments about other arguments, we engage in philosophy. To the extent that we engage in arguments and settle them in terms of experience, we engage in science.[10] . . .

When social work researchers are told (or conjure up in their own heads), for example, the notion (theory) that mental disease is something that exists somewhere or somehow within the victim, they set about to find it. They do that by trying to define it with sufficient precision that they can then observe it. If they can define it and if they can observe it, there is a good chance that they can measure it. The purpose of measuring it is then to be able to describe it in a systematic way and with greater precision. However, if the method used to measure the disease does great violence to the definition of it, the measurements will not do a good job of representing the very thing they want to study. So, they call their measurements an operational definition, and they call the original definition a construct. In order to determine whether reasonable people can agree that the measurements do a good job of representing the original definition, scientists claim, as did Goldstein (whom Heineman criticized), that it is important to distinguish and compare the operational and construct definition of "disease."

Now, scientists sometimes engage in tremendously strange behaviors at this point. If they find they cannot define or observe this construct called mental disease, they conclude that it does not exist, and they give it back to the philosophers with a new name. They call it a mentalism. The philosopher may choose to play with the mentalism for eons but the scientists turn their attention back to observable entities. It was this kind of thinking that led this author to state elsewhere that "if you cannot measure a client's problem it does not exist," and "if you cannot measure a client's problem you cannot treat it."[13] It was this kind of thinking that also led Gingerich to claim that "if you cannot measure your treatment it does not exist," and "if you cannot measure your treatment you cannot administer it."[14]

OBJECTIVITY, MEASUREMENT, AND ERROR

Heineman's article deals at length with the notion of objectivity. She says that social work somehow or other assumes objective data to be distortion free; "objectivity can be seen to be a particular species of report"; "objectivity does not refer to how nature really is but to how scientists find it in a given context" (as quoting Schmidt); and "objectivity is inherently impossible."

I do not know who in social work Heineman has spoken with about the use of objective data, but none of the researchers I have talked with has ever told me that he has distortion-free data of any kind. If one dared to propose such a thing in the classroom, even our beginning students would simply laugh him out of the room. As for objectivity being some species of report, she is simply dead wrong. Objectivity is a prescription or a result, depending on context. The prescription is that one produce definitions and descriptions of procedures and methods with sufficient clarity that other researchers will be able to reproduce (replicate) the study. If the effort to be objective is such that other researchers will be able to (and do) replicate the study, then objectivity is a result—one has conducted an objective investigation.[15] If, in addition to the use of objective methods and procedures, the replicating scientists are also able to obtain highly similar findings, we can then say that we have objective evidence to support the original scientist's statements about the findings. Moreover, the two scientists (or more) do not have to agree on world views. If a psychoanalytic researcher has conducted an objective study in the sense described above, a behaviorist can replicate the study faithfully—and vice versa. They might even get the same results, although differences in world view might cause them to render different interpretations of those results.

Objectivity does not correspond to how scientists "find" nature at all. It merely characterizes the extent to which others can understand what they do and how they proceed. Heineman's assertion that "objectivity is inherently impossible" is simply incorrect—or it has validity in the realm of some nonexistent Platonic idealism. If we follow Heineman's prescription that we seek "satisficing" solutions rather than purist ideals, it is quite accurate to say that scientists do regularly achieve a highly satisficing degree of objectivity! . . .

Heineman complains a great deal about the use of tape recorders, objective data, and the prescription that we use "indicators that can be reliably and validly measured."[18] What are the alternatives?—to use unobjective, invalid, and unreliable measurements or descriptions of the phenomena that concern us and about which we wish to learn and understand? Is this the model of science that Heineman would have us

subscribe to in order to create a viable basis for practice? Quite the opposite, I should hope, and a careful review of the research literature in our field does strongly suggest that our knowledge has been greatly impeded in proportion to our refusal or inability to develop objective, reliable, and valid measurements (descriptions) of the variables we must work with and understand as researchers and as practitioners.

TESTABLE MODELS

A major complaint in Heineman's article had to do with the prescription that we use testable models in social work research and practice. She complained of Reid's "prescription" that we use "testable models . . . whose targets for change, interventions and outcomes can be operationalized in terms of indicators that can be reliably and validly measured." She labels Carl Hempel as a logical positivist (as a "bad" thing) and then complains of his statements: "Although no restrictions are imposed upon the invention of theories, scientific objectivity is safeguarded by making their acceptance dependent upon the outcome of careful tests. These consist in deriving, from the theory, consequences that admit of observational or experimental investigation, and then checking them by suitable observations or experiments."

Hempel may well have subscribed to some of the evils of logical positivism or logical empiricism—I frankly do not know. If he did, he erred. However, it is a most extreme error to discard everything the man said merely because he was one of them.[19] The consequences of rejecting Hempel's and Reid's prescriptions are grave and enormous. Their rejection implies that we freely generate theories about the workings of the world, and that we avoid the painful or difficult task of determining whether, in terms of experience, they are even plausible. For social work practice, this implies that we be permitted to use untested theories of practice, intervention strategies that may do no one any good, and even that we use unreliable and invalid data or observations. The rejection of Reid's and Hempel's prescriptions will very possibly lead to the adoption of witchcraft, sorcery, and astrology as models of social work practice.[20] . . .

CONCLUDING REMARKS

As I said at the beginning of this article, it matters little whether Heineman as an individual is correct or not. What does matter is that she may well have misled some readers into believing a set of unfounded conclusions in support of which she provides not one shred of evidence. Worse yet, the form and structure of many of her arguments suggest that social workers do not need or require the development of empirically validated models of practice, and that prescriptions to develop and use reliable and valid observations about the real world could well be a set of misled objectives.

Heineman was quite willing to interpret the psychology of scientists as a "wish" for a certain, knowable world. She is quite right that the wish for such a world is not proof of its existence—that was the essential point behind William Gordon's statement which she criticized. I think Heineman is correct in suggesting that scientists do wish for a dependable and knowable world. Although they have learned much about the risks of claiming or pursuing certainty in some absolute Platonic sense, the wish for or belief in a knowable world does not appear to be an unreasonable one. Moreover, scientists have shown that ours is a knowable world. After all, our species has climbed out of the slime of our terrestrial history and developed a complex body of validated knowledge about the world in which we live. It has done that by systematically observing—experiencing—that world. Nothing more.

None of this is to suggest that Nature gives up her secrets easily. She does not. Those secrets have been extracted by a wondrous tool we call science. The basic tenets of science are routinely offered to our students, and they are routinely used by those who do social work research. Even so, a few are offered below which I believe will help to advance and validate the knowledge base of our profession.

1. All knowledge is ultimately based on experience.
2. A basic purpose of science is the study and description of relationships among variables.
3. A fundamental aim of the scientist is to generate propositional statements about how the real world operates and to test the veracity of those statements against systematic observation and experimentation by using observable entities.
4. Logical systems that are not grounded by real-world referents are of no use to science.
5. Constructs that cannot be defined, operationalized, and then measured are mentalisms that are useless to an understanding of the world in which we live.

6. The development and validation of testable models of how the world operates (including the world of social work practice) are essential to the development of new knowledge.
7. The validity of any theory (including theories of social work practice) cannot be established if it is not capable of refutation through experience.
8. Our understanding of how the world and the universe operate will improve with new observation and new experiment.
9. Science is a self-corrective process that develops and validates knowledge through reliance on imperfect observations of observable entities.

NOTES

1. Martha Brunswick Heineman, "The Obsolete Scientific Imperative in Social Work Research," *Social Service Review* 55 (1981): 371–97.

2. Perhaps "caution" would be a better word here, at least in the sense of asking to what extent there can be demonstrated a one-to-one correspondence between observable entities and the nouns and verbs of the logic system.

3. In a wonderful little book, first published in 1938, Stuart Chase (*The Tyranny of Words* [New York: Harcourt, Brace & Co., 1959]) presented a popularization of the then emerging field of general semantics and drew heavily on the staggering contribution of Alfred Korzybski's *Science and Sanity* (Lakeville, Conn.: Institute for General Semantics, 1933). Although heavily influenced by logical positivism (there was not much else that was "better" at the time), Chase's book presents a penetrating and convincing discussion of the value of tying nouns of language to observable entities—the latter he and Korzybski refer to as "real-world referents."

4. Actually, Heineman has derogated the definition of "empirical" by injecting the term "certain" and hence the implication that empiricism involves the pursuit of absolute Platonic truths. A much better definition, I think, is in the 1980 *Webster's New Collegiate Dictionary*, s.v. "empiricism," which describes empiricism as "the practice of relying on observation and experiment . . ." Here and in the remainder of this paper I equate the word "experience" with this definition of empiricism.

5. I am acutely aware of my own personifications, such as "the history of science has taught us . . ." and perhaps I should have said that "we have learned from experience over long periods of time . . ."

. . . . .

7. This is a point well argued by Martin Goldstein and Inge F. Goldstein in their book, *How We Know: An Explo-*

ration of the Scientific Process (New York: Plenum Press, 1978). Goldstein and Goldstein also present a superb case for the role of art in science.

8. Chase (n. 3 above), pp. 152–55. Carl Sagan (*Broca's Brain* [New York: Ballantine Books, 1979], pp. 49–172) presents a very useful discussion of the nature of paradoxers and their role in the development of knowledge.

9. Ibid., p. 235.

10. One might here ask, "What is argument about whether the argument is settled by experience?" One might answer, "Philosophy!" Such a question is commonly regarded as a form of metalanguage. Philosophers might well debate the question endlessly, but scientists must get on with the business of doing science. In doing so, they seem to have settled the question by returning to experience, and they are likely to depend on that answer unless and until some equally good or better one is provided.

· · · · ·

13. Walter W. Hudson, "First Axioms of Treatment," *Social Work* 24 (January 1978): 65–66.

14. Wallace Gingerich, "Measuring the Process," *Social Work* 24 (March 1978): 251–52.

15. If this is what Heineman meant as a "species" of report, it would have been clarifying and helpful for her to have so indicated. If she had some other meaning in mind, it also would have been clarifying had she revealed that.

· · · · ·

18. Heineman attempts to soften her textual assertions by her comments in her n. 7 (p. 392). However, even there she underplays the enormous value of obtaining or producing reliable and valid data. Moreover, she implies in this note that Reid, and perhaps other researchers as well, are guilty of advocating such tools under the belief that they provide the only credible source of therapeutic observation. Her implicit statement is simply inaccurate.

19. It is very difficult to resist regarding such a behavior as a form of intellectual racism. In some social work circles, e.g., a person is often discredited these days by merely being labeled as a behaviorist or Freudian. Let us test ideas rather than sling discrediting labels such as logical positivist or (now a new one) logical empiricist.

20. By refusing to employ and require the prescriptions of Reid and Hempel, we have come to the point where just about anything can now pass for "therapy" (music, dance, basketball, jogging, surfing, etc.), and just about anyone who chooses to do so can call himself or herself a "therapist." Little or no evidence of effectiveness is required, little or no concern is exercised with respect to the possibility of harmful side effects, and we too often lack the courage to even confront a blatant charlatan who wants to merely converse with clients and charge them money for that. See Thomas Szasz, *The Myth of Psychotherapy* (Garden City, N.Y.: Doubleday & Co., Anchor Books, 1979).

Debate with Authors

COMMENTS ON "SCIENTIFIC IMPERATIVES IN SOCIAL WORK RESEARCH AND PRACTICE"

THOMAS P. HOLLAND   *Case Western Reserve University*

In the June 1982 issue of *Social Service Review* ("Scientific Imperatives in Social Work Research and Practice," *Social Service Review* 56 [June 1982]: 246–58), Walter Hudson made some interesting comments regarding the nature and basis of social work research. As a participant in the efforts to develop the knowledge base of our profession, I was intrigued by some of Hudson's statements and puzzled by others.

After asserting the distinctiveness of his own position from that of logical positivism, Hudson made some assertions that seem inexplicable without some reference to the latter philosophical perspective. For example, he maintains, "If you cannot measure a client's problem, it does not exist" (p. 252). Experience is our only source of knowledge, he points out. Then, with a summary dismissal of "mentalisms," he seems to constrain his meaning of experience to direct sensory observations. Apparently, Mr. Hudson's position is that anything that cannot be directly observed is meaningless or, at any rate, unreal. My discomfort is prompted by what seems to be a severely prescriptive exclusion of vast domains of human experience.

His position must have surprised many *SSR* readers inasmuch as it would appear to rule out most of what human beings consider important in life—love, courage, hope, faith, commitment, and so forth. I hope that my concerns arise from misunderstanding Hudson's remarks, clouded as they were with ambiguities, oversimplifications, and gratuitous sarcasm toward Martha Heineman Pieper. But, on the off chance that he indeed meant what he seemed to be saying, let us examine the position for a moment. Should our concerns be unwarranted or based upon misunderstanding, perhaps Hudson will resolve our apprehensions by further clarification.

At first glance, it would appear that Hudson has set up a principle or criterion for knowledge that his own position cannot meet. If it is true that knowledge is obtained only via sense perceptions, then by means of what sense perceptions did Hudson gain this very conclusion? When, where, and how does anyone encounter the observations that provide the basis for concluding that any other dimensions of knowledge are mere illusions?

The principle Hudson seems to be invoking is really an a priori assumption, a rule set forth prior to any specific sensations, not a conclusion from them at all.

Source: "Comments on 'Scientific Imperatives in Social Work and Practice'" by T. Holland, 1983, *Social Service Review, 57,* pp. 337–339. Copyright 1983 by The University of Chicago. Reprinted by permission.
Social Service Review (June 1983). © 1983 by The University of Chicago. All rights reserved.

As such, it would fall within his category of mere "mentalisms," which he so disdainfully casts aside as useless.

A profession so soundly criticized for allowing its status desires to lure it into an affair with psychoanalytic theory should beware of the rewards apparently offered now in the name of science, if only we give up some minor illusions—our incidental mental experiences of dread, courage, fear, hope, guilt, love. By insisting that any experiences that cannot be operationalized, observed, and measured are meaningless, Hudson's extreme position would seem to the casual observer to eviscerate not only most of what the profession of social work deals with, but also much of what humanity has deemed most important. Can we really accept such a direction?

The development of knowledge about our social world does proceed through processes of controlled inference and must be formulated in propositions that may be assessed by anyone who cares to take the trouble to do so. However, the process of assessment need not rely exclusively on sense perceptions. Hudson appears to be trapped in his own form of positivism, perhaps assuming that the only alternative to such an extreme position is subjective, uncontrollable, unverifiable introspection. However, our knowledge of social reality is a complex pattern of shared meanings, communicated by language and transmitted by socialization. Taking cognizance of the meanings, goals, purposes, and values people attach to their actions is essential to developing an adequate understanding of social reality, including that of a scientist. This does not mean that we are limited to subjective introspection, uncontrolled by the experiences of others. Rather, our efforts to understand meanings are controllable at least to the same extent as the individual sensory perceptions of one observer are checked by another.

Empiricism or positivism takes for granted our intersubjective, shared reality. They assume a solution to the problem of social research before the inquiry ever begins. Rather than taking such a leap and denying that he is doing so, the social scientist should begin with careful attention to the variety of human experience and the meanings, values, and patterns people attach to them. Theories that relate these components can be evaluated on the basis of their logical consistency and their explanatory adequacy. Aspects of the theories may then be experimentally varied and predicted changes assessed for their accuracy. All such steps rely on experience, provided we do not unnecessarily constrain ourselves exclusively to sensory perceptions of external events or objects but include an understanding of human actions in terms of their underlying motives, goals, and meanings.

Actually, "it matters little whether [Hudson] as an individual is correct or not. What does matter is that [he] may well have misled some readers into believing a set of unfounded conclusions in support of which [he] provides not one shred of evidence" (p. 255). Worse yet, the form and structure of many of his arguments suggest that social workers discard their own experiences for a viewpoint that would not only undermine research but eviscerate practice.

But perhaps my mentalisms about Hudson's intentions are based on mistaken perceptions. In lieu of direct observation of his behavior, perhaps he could communicate to us a valid mental understanding of his intended meanings. My hope for that is what motivated the behavior of preparing these comments.

AUTHOR'S REPLY

WALTER H. HUDSON   *Florida State University*
Professor Thomas P. Holland tells us that he is puzzled by some of the statements in my article ("Scientific Imperatives in Social Work Research and Practice," *Social Service Review* 56 [June 1982]: 246–58). I am puzzled by some of the statements in his letter. For example, Holland implies that I argue for exclusive use of direct observation. Nowhere in my article did I assert or imply such a thing. Holland seems to have read something that was not even there. Indeed, I did not, do not, and will not advocate such an absurd position.

The greatest puzzlement for me arises from Holland's implicit rejection of the thesis that "knowledge is obtained *only* via sense perception." I should like Holland to explain to us by what mechanisms of "nonsense" perception he and others produce new knowledge? Surely he is not urging the use of "extra"-sensory perceptions as a basis for developing and validating the knowledge base of our profession.

Holland says that my position (of using experience and asking for empirical evidence to support our

Source: "Author's Reply" by W. Hudson, 1983, *Social Service Review*, 57, pp. 339–341. Copyright 1983 by The University of Chicago. Reprinted by permission.
Social Service Review (1983). © 1983 by The University of Chicago. All rights reserved.

claims) "would appear to rule out . . . love, courage, hope, faith, commitment, and so forth." How he could arrive at such a conclusion is beyond me. Surely Holland knows that people regularly experience love, courage, hope, and so forth. He surely must know also that scientists can directly observe behaviors that seem to reflect such experiences, but they cannot directly observe those experiences in others. What they can directly observe in others is the acts of reporting that those experiences occur (a form of indirect observation).

Holland seems distressed over my "summary dismissal of mentalisms." I would hope that he is not advocating retention and use of mentalisms of the sort described and illustrated in my article.

Holland says, "The development of knowledge about our social world does proceed through processes of controlled inference and must be formulated in propositions that may be assessed by anyone who cares to take the trouble to do so." Granted, but I suggest we pay little heed to those who minimally trouble themselves in their assessments (like those who merely read tea leaves) and attend more to the findings and methods of those who trouble themselves greatly by conducting controlled, replicable assessments through empirical testing.

Professor Holland suggests that his "mentalisms" about my article arise from his own mistaken perceptions. He is, of course, correct in that, but his misconstructions about my article are not the heart of the matter. The heart of the matter is that the article by Martha Heineman Pieper ("The Obsolete Scientific Imperative in Social Work Research," *Social Service Review* 55 [September 1981]: 371–97) was not a construction but a destruction. It was not an attack on logical empiricism but on empiricism. Her article and another by Roy A. Ruckdeschel and Buford E. Farris ("Assessing Practice: A Critical Look at the Single Case Approach," *Social Casework* 62 [September 1981]: 413–19) are examples of a body of thought that seeks permissive freedom to render uncontrolled and even unverifiable assertions about social reality in general, and in social work practice specifically. Such authors seek to establish a basis for that permissive freedom by first attacking, and they hope rendering inoperable, the devices that we use to test, validate, or invalidate propositions about social reality and social work practice.

In the early 1970s our profession was severely embarrassed because we had to report that precious little evidence was available to support our claims of practice effectiveness. To our credit, we sought remedy by adopting new methods of assessment, and an increasing number of schools of social work are now routinely providing a type of training that enables practitioners to regularly validate the effectiveness of our interventions and to modify constructively those found wanting. In the space of a single decade we have built a rather large literature around an emerging practice modality that quickly demonstrated high promise. It is the high promise of providing more effective service to our clients in virtually every arena of social work practice. It is the high promise of being able to demonstrate to ourselves and our constituents that we do know what we are talking about.

Of course, the final chapter is not in. It has only begun to be written. Unfortunately, in the midst of making rapid and large progress we find some who speak against validating our practice effectiveness and argue against the use of the very tools that seem to account for it. They speak against the use of controlled testing of propositions, reliable and valid information, and replication of research. They offer a set of unclear alternatives that are poorly articulated. They thereby fail to offer more effective or efficient means of developing or validating our knowledge base. By their constructions and destructions they move us backward in time when our principle modes of "knowing" consisted of authority, intuition, and insight. It is a plea to avoid accountability.

One of the fundamental targets of the detractors is the introduction and use of single-subject or time-series designs in social work practice. However, any advocacy for the use of that technology must avoid excesses of zeal, and the response by Ludwig L. Geismar and Katherine M. Wood ("Evaluating Practice: Science as Faith," *Social Casework* 63 [May 1982]: 266–75) provides a superb statement of perspective in that regard. On the other hand, idle and poorly argued logicism does not provide a sound basis for abandoning the use of rapidly emerging tools that seem to be bringing about rapid progress. Had Pieper or Ruckdeschel and Farris conducted carefully controlled studies to show, for example, that the use of $N = 1$ designs are not what they are cracked up to be, that would be a solid contribution to which many would have attended constructively.

No, Professor Holland, we cannot and must not ignore the uncontrolled observations or theoretical assertions of our practitioners or our scholars. The theorist and empiricist desperately need each other. When the former gains ascendency, we create, in the extreme, forms of myth and magic that produce charlatans who rely on authority to retain their status. When the latter gains ascendency, we create, in the extreme, a group of inhuman mechanists who are equal charlatans by dint of their colossal simplifications. We need the theorist who creates or advocates new models of practice. We also need the empiricist who will test those models. Finally, we need a set of models that has been tested and that by virtue of having passed some rigorous tests of evidence do provide some assurance that we in fact serve when we claim to do so. In past years, we had clear excesses of theorizing and clear deficits of empirical testing. Today we have a much improved balance between them. If we choose to retain and strengthen that balance, the prospects for our continued growth and development as a profession appear to be promising.

Introduction to "Toward the Integration of Theory and Practice: A Humanistic Approach"

In this 1986 paper, Howard Goldstein contributed to the debates about a metatheory of research for the field of social work by questioning positivist assumptions about social work practitioners. He underscored the opinions and concerns of a growing number of social workers at the time (Haworth, 1984; Imre, 1984; Ruckdeschel & Farris, 1982; Saleebey, 1979). For example, in her 1984 editorial in *Social Work*, Carol Meyer, the editor-in-chief, said:

> In the last decade, there has been a tipped balance [between research and practice]; not only has research "taken off," it has occasionally landed heavily on practitioners who are going about their daily chores. Thus, an unpleasant "town and gown" tension has developed, in which academics who specialize in research have sometimes assumed an elitist attitude toward practitioners, whom they patronize as "doers." Neither the attitudes of researchers nor those of practitioners who persist in viewing themselves merely as "doers" contribute to the values of congeniality among professionals and the sharing of concerns. There is no contradiction in working in the vineyards as practitioners and doing so as rigorously as possible. (p. 323)

Meyer also described how positivist approaches to problem formulation are incompatible with most social work practice models:

> Most of the research methodology in use today requires the kind of narrow definition of problems and specification of variables that only behaviorist practice can provide concretely; thus, it is all but impossible for practitioners who work in different modes to participate in research. (p. 323)

Research indicated that practitioners did not use findings from positivist social work research. Positivist social work researchers then concluded that social work practitioners do not plan their interventions rationally, and they prescribed that practitioners should plan practice by deriving interventions from knowledge developed through "basic" science. Goldstein disagrees with that positivist prescription. Moreover, he notes that assuming practitioners do not plan interventions rationally has *not* been useful for understanding how social workers use knowledge in their practice, and it ignores how the social worker is a "theory-developer" as much as a "theory-consumer" (1986, p. 355). Although some positivist social work researchers claim that practitioners are not guided by theoretical principles, Goldstein says such charges are unfounded. He emphasizes that "until it can be shown that this is indeed the case, one must assume that most social workers are guided in their practice by some kinds of principles" (1986, p. 352). These principles, Goldstein emphasizes, include the values of the social work profession. In Goldstein's alternative view, practitioners are cognizant that the client's well-being is entrusted to the worker both by the client and by society. Furthermore, practitioners need not view their commitment to regulated involvement with and advocacy for clients as conflicting with a commitment to the generation of practice theories.

Goldstein emphasizes that practitioners *do* develop theories in the course of practice. He prioritizes the study of the client's experience of meaning, which, he suggests, has been depreciated because of the biases introduced by positivism— biases ingrained both in psychoanalysis and in behaviorism. Goldstein explains that rather than requiring clients to define their problems in the positivist social worker's terms (e.g., requiring clients to describe their problems in measurable, observable terms), the worker can focus on understanding clients' definitions of their difficulties. The worker can gain knowledge about clients' subjective experiences in the way and at the pace clients prefer. Practice models derived from positivist research principles (e.g., worker-determined time limits for the intervention) customarily impose the worker's meanings and pace on the client. Goldstein emphasizes, "Understanding begins with the unchallenged narrative, because it contains the first vestige of meanings held by the client, created out of the miscellany of his or her life" (1986, p. 355).

Other social workers, such as Ann Weick, increasingly have emphasized that practice models should be developed in accordance with the traditional values of the social work profession rather than made to fit outmoded models of science. In concert with those values, Weick has advanced a holistic orientation to practice that focuses on the client's strengths and health (1983a, 1986, 1987).

DISCUSSION QUESTIONS

1. Goldstein describes how the traditional division between "basic" or "pure" science, and "applied" science is becoming less relevant as a way to understand contemporary social work practice. What is your experience of the relationship between the knowledge you learn in the classroom and your application of that knowledge in practice?

2. a. Goldstein suggests that the positivist view of the scientist affects the structure of the practitioner's relationship with clients. What are some implications of the positivist view of the scientist for the practitioner–client relationship?

   b. In the last section of his paper, Goldstein states that, when practitioners conceptualize their role based on precepts that Goldstein elaborates, they will relate differently with clients. Summarize some of the characteristics of the practitioner–client relationship that Goldstein suggests.

3. In 1989, Dennis Saleebey emphasized that the positivist approach to research led to an estrangement between "knowing" and "doing" in the field of social work. How might the assumptions of positivism lead to that estrangement?

4. Consider the practice theories you have been learning. Use the categories shown in Figure 3–2 to compare the assumptions of each theory or heuristic. Look at some of the biases that each heuristic sets up when you apply it in interviewing clients. Describe some of the biases set up by a practice heuristic of your choice.

Figure 3–2

Model for comparing assumptions that underlie theories of clinical practice

Theory:
_____

What is the "real" for this theorist? (ontological assumptions)
_____

How does the theorist know that "real"? (epistemological assumptions)
_____

What are the interviewing methods used in this model?
_____

How does this theory draw the line between normal and pathological?
_____

According to this theory, what causes the client's problem?
_____

How is the change process conceptualized?
_____

What are the long-term goals of the intervention?
_____

How is change maintained?
_____

What does the practitioner do?
_____

What does the client do?
_____

What is the duration of intervention and how is that determined?
_____

To what extent is the practitioner involved outside the practitioner-client relationship?
_____

Toward the Integration of Theory and Practice: A Humanistic Approach

HOWARD GOLDSTEIN

An acrid cloud of self-doubt and recrimination seems to settle over the profession of social work when faddish articles and books raise such poignant questions as "Is casework effective?" or "Can social work survive?"[1] Although this article deals with a question bearing on the effectiveness of social work practice, the author's purpose is to try to clear the air rather than add to the existing miasma.

There is a growing body of opinion and evidence suggesting that what many social workers *do* often has little connection with what they *know* in theoretical terms. Workers are sometimes pictured as unimaginative doers who either ply their routine techniques or merely react to whatever happens to arise in their exchange with clients—either way, without the benefit and support of a sound rationale or theory. Sheldon, for example, had doubts that social workers know how to make other than random or subjective choices from the available range of theories.[2] Sainsbury found that the difficulty social workers have in relating practice to theory leads them "sometimes to produce casework which, from the perspective of participants, is aimless, muddled and deleterious to morale."[3] Kolevzon and Maykranz's study of almost 700 clinical educators discovered a very weak fit between the educators' theoretical orientations and their choices of interventive strategies. These authors expressed their concern that practice would, as a result, "become more idiosyncratic, random, and unpredictable."[4] A similar study by Carew, confirming that social workers make minimal use of theory, dis-

mally concluded that "there is something questionable about the whole exercise of theory building in social work. It seems to be an exclusively academic exercise."[5] . . .

Given the persuasive evidence of these findings, one needs to consider why the discrepancy between theory and practice seems so pervasive and, more important, what it means. The discrepancy cannot be the result of indifference on the part of educators or practitioners: The weight that is given to the teaching of theoretical foundations in educational programs and the profusion of articles, seminars, and conference papers on theoretical approaches to practice signify a commitment to the idea that sound theory and good practice are inseparable partners. Nor can the discrepancy be the result of workers' indifference to their clients' problems, because if they were practicing without reference to some sort of theoretical grounding, would this not be tantamount to their having relinquished a measure of moral obligation?

Social work is primarily a moral and ethical enterprise if only because its locus is the intimate confines of the lives of people we social workers call clients. Obviously, what we do or, for that matter, fail to do

Source: From "Toward the Integration of Theory and Practice: A Humanistic Approach" by H. Goldstein, 1986, *Social Work, 31*, pp. 352–357. Copyright 1986 by the National Association of Social Workers. Reprinted by permission.
CCC Code: 0037–8046/86 $1.00 © 1986. National Association of Social Workers, Inc.

has some influence on the course of our clients' existence. An even greater moral obligation flows out of the kind of power that workers wield—the ascribed power to intervene, which is part of the workers' social and institutional role—or the power that clients themselves grant to workers. In the latter instance clients are especially vulnerable. Typically, clients who grant workers the right to influence their lives, relationships, and futures do so without much certainty or information about workers' professional competence. Rather, clients' endowment of this right is an expression of trust that workers care about their well-being and will do what is right in the helping role.[6] The profession would be in deep trouble if workers were indeed abusing this trust by meddling in clients' lives in an undisciplined and groundless fashion. Until it can be shown that this is indeed the case, one must assume that most social workers are guided in their practice by some kinds of principles.

It would seem that the question is not *whether* practitioners' interventions are guided by dependable principles, but *how* they are guided and by *what kind* of principles. The author's premise is that what appears to be the disengagement of practice from classical theory is really an indication of some mistaken assumptions about the relationship of one to the other. As educators and practitioners (and as products of 300 years of Western thought and ideas about education), we have unquestioningly accepted some prevalent assumptions about the nature of knowledge. These include the positivistic-empirical convictions that the world is objective, stable, and subject to a proper and particular form of scientific investigation. In other words, the use of the scientific method should enable us to establish certain laws and principles that, in turn, should help to explain the cause and predictable nature of the things we want to comprehend. This knowledge, it is supposed, then arms us with the practical methods that can be applied to the personal and social problems that fall within our domain of expertise. Generally speaking, this is the accepted rationale for the structure of education for professional practice. As Schön put it, the idea that *basic science yields applied science* has three components: (1) there is an underlying foundation of knowledge upon which practice rests [basic theory courses]; (2) this foundation generates an applied science component [methods/practice/casework courses]; (3) these applied procedures are employed in the active development of skills and attitudes [the practicum].[7]

A historical review shows that although these beliefs have played an increasingly dominant role in the development and refinement of social work practice and theory, the results have not succeeded in creating a useful merger of knowledge and action. Thus, the "pure" sciences that first offered this traditional model of knowledge and education (that is, "basic science yields applied science") are themselves giving serious question to the assumptions on which this model was founded. This leads to the consideration of other alternatives, other modes of understanding that have a more commonsense and humanistic nature and that, therefore, are more suited to the attempt to make sense of and respond to the enigmatic human situation. . . .

[M]any of the assumptions about and commitments to rationality, objectivity, scientism, and realism are being called into question—oddly enough, by the so-called hard scientists who once epitomized the purity of positivistic thinking. A few examples, somewhat relevant to the knowledge foundations of social work, illustrate the challenge to the traditional metatheoretical perspective.

In the field of neuroscience, Sir John Eccles, the distinguished neurobiologist and Nobel Prize laureate, observed that it is wrong to assume that traditional scientific methods tell anything useful about consciousness or mind—the unique source of selfhood and personhood. In fact, according to Eccles, these methods blind one to the actual nature and meaning of human consciousness and mind:

> The principal trouble with mankind today is that the intellectual leaders are too arrogant in their self-sufficiency. We must realize the great unknowns in the material makeup and operation of our brains, in the relationship of brain to mind, in our creative imagination, and in the uniqueness of the psyche. *When we think of these unknowns as well as the unknown of how we come to be in the first place, we should be much more humble.* [Emphasis in the original.][10]

With regard to the long-standing theories of nature, nurture, and human development, genetic biologists have demonstrated that former certainties about how the "biological," "psychological," and "social" dimensions of human behavior interact with one another are now in great doubt. For instance, Lewontin, Rose, and

Kamin noted that prevailing theories are merely reductionist myths about nature and nurture, which, in futile ways, strive to measure how a certain percentage of nature affects nurture and vice versa.[11] Although interpenetration of one by the other is constantly in process, this process is not subject to empirical investigation. The best that can be hoped for is the attainment of subjective meaning rather than positivistic truths. Thus, one would consider the meaning of being a biological as well as a psychological person.

Open and modest perspectives on mind, body, and environment are expressions of the radical scientific point of view that accompanied the emergence of modern quantum physics early in this century.[12] The Nobel Prize laureate in thermodynamics, Ilya Prigogine and his colleague, Stengers, asserted that the sciences have rid themselves of the conception of reality as objective, as a closed system of knowledge that denies novelty and diversity. The authors stated that "They [the sciences] are now open to the unexpected, which they no longer define as the result of imperfect knowledge or insufficient control."[13]

These ideas are not entirely foreign to some thinkers in the social and behavioral sciences; many voices question whether scientific methods can penetrate or quantify the opaque and multiplex nature of the human state. In his recent work, the eminent social psychologist Kenneth Gergen summed up the argument for reformulating the dominant scientific model of the behavioral sciences as follows:

> . . . during the past century the socio-behavioral sciences have participated in one of humankind's greatest intellectual adventures . . . the pursuit of . . . certain knowledge. . . . Early in this century, it appeared that the means had been discovered for gaining certainty in the behavioral sciences. Yet subsequent examination has found such means sadly wanting. The search for certainty is a child's romance, and like most, one holds fast to even the most fragile shard attesting to continued life. The question that must now be confronted is how to pass successfully into the maturity of the second century. A new romance is required to extinguish the old, and it appears that the overtures are at hand.[14]

In social work, there is a small but growing interest in cognitive theory and practice, an orientation that does not depend on deductive or reductionist theories about human behavior. Rather, this orientation attempts to fathom the nature of the individual's subjective reality and the constructs on which the client relies for defining and locating his or her place in the world.[15] In addition, the increasing number of articles (and the occasional book) on the moral and ethical dimension of human interaction seems to indicate the promise of moral philosophy becoming an immensely valuable source of understanding.[16] And, in the field of social research, one may see the infrequent article that challenges the positivistic ideals of current teaching and investigation.[17]

These are, however, only minor tremors in an otherwise firm body of knowledge and practice. The great majority of publications, articles, and reports: the composition of curricula in educational programs: and the gist of professional conferences suggest that academics as well as practitioners persist in the "pursuit of certain knowledge" to which Gergen referred.

ARE THERE ALTERNATIVES?

The alternative proposed here may appear to threaten the scientific posture that is so well cherished by the profession. In reality, however, the alternative closely represents the ideas about knowledge development, understanding, and reflective problem solving that are emerging from the natural and cognitive sciences. The alternative also may correspond more closely with what day-to-day professional practice actually entails. It proposes a more open-ended approach to understanding and practice—one that is centered on the subjective nature of the human and helping experience and on the reflective talents that create access to this subjectivity. In this view, the worker is far more of a theory-developer than a theory-consumer.

Because social workers typically are involved in something as enigmatic and elusive as "problems of living," should they not be more concerned with subjective meanings than with objective facts? This is not to say that most workers, in the course of their everyday activities, do not come face-to-face with many serious and troubling facts, such as the painful realities of deprivation and the consequences of illness, abuse, depression, poverty, and other kinds of suffering. Certainly, as professional caregivers, we can stand back and intellectually attempt to explain or generalize about these conditions. If we truly wish to understand the conditions and to know their real pathos and significance, however, it is necessary to be open to the *meaning* of these conditions in the lives of those people suffering. Only when we ask, "What is it really like for you?" and gain some sense of our clients' experiences can we join with our clients in the search for greater understanding, for new learning, for creative solutions that perhaps will restore morale and dignity, and in the end, for the ability to take responsibility for one's life. No matter how severe the plight of our clients may be, any solution would be meaningless if it did little to generate these vital qualities.

The importance of theory as a basis for practice is not denied by this approach. Indeed, the approach suggests that the "best" theory is an analogue of the circumstances that we attempt to deal with. Thus, when we use this theory to guide our response, there is a greater probability that it will fit, or be relevant to, those circumstances. If theory does not fit, we will know immediately that rethinking is necessary. In this way, we can avoid the consequences of applying, by trial and error or by force fitting, a generalized concept to a specific situation. . . .

A guiding theory emerges with the worker's openness to the client's own story.[18] Understanding begins with this unchallenged narrative, because it contains the first vestige of meanings held by the client, created out of the miscellany of his or her life. The worker is not privy to verifiable truth or facts, because by its very nature, the client's story or autobiography is a fiction of sorts, told at a particular point in time, and for a particular purpose. What the worker hears is the client's "I" weaving together a narrative of how things came to be and, from the client's perceptions, how things really are, and who the "I" might be. Altogether, this is a uniquely personal account that strives to make sense of living, that clings to a trace of dignity, and that, above all else, tries to maintain sanity and order.

The orientation presented here is conspicuously similar to the ordinary commonsense ways by which we practitioners go about making sense of and dealing with our everyday relationships with people. After all, in the ordinary course of living, when we run into novel circumstances or confront certain crises or exigencies, do we not find it necessary to reflect on our state and construct a theory (ad hoc though it may be) so as to explain the event to ourselves as a basis for

action? Are not these cognitive skills—the ability to reason, judge, recall, compare, and recognize our emotions—measures of competency and security? Ultimately, are they not the abilities we wish to help our clients develop?

Obviously, the difference between this orientation and the commonsense life approach is regulated by the professional qualities of the helping relationship. It is the worker's responsibility to create a climate that allows this process to unfold and to be perceptive to the special demands of each client's unique circumstances and needs. A commitment to the client's subjective world also draws the worker into the ethical realm of the helping process, which is concerned with the deeply held normative and spiritual beliefs of both the client and the worker. At every point in the unfolding process, acute questions and dilemmas of a moral and ethical character are bound to surface. Formal theories—the espoused values of the profession, or for that matter, a higher order code of ethics—cannot resolve these questions and dilemmas. Practitioners may turn to these systems for support, but the systems cannot prescribe how we ought to work out the tensions that arise regarding the client's rights, freedoms, and obligations; the extent of our right or obligation to intervene; and the differences between the client's and our moral outlooks. Nor can the theories or code of ethics prescribe how to resolve intermittent moral conflicts of daily living or painful uncertainties regarding questions of divorce, abortion, abuse, and not the least, the choice to live or die.

Undoubtedly, some readers will exclaim that this model presents nothing new, that many social workers already follow this model in their work with clients. These readers would probably be correct. However, this natural, reflective, and truly client-centered and problem-solving approach may be disparaged by many other social workers, because it is not "scientific" and, even worse, because it has a seat-of-the-pants or intuitive connotation. Still others may protest that the model described here is not "professional" practice but is something that a caring friend or relative could do as well. And, indeed, most people do succeed in getting the help and support they need from sources other than professional caregivers. This protest misses the point being made: rather than attempting to force-fit this natural human dialogue into facile theories or methods or pretending that we practitioners use some sort of scientific technology, we ought to study and maximize the special nature of our reflective talents and knowledge that make the difference in interpersonal helping.

A HUMANISTIC APPROACH

According to the strictures of modern positivism, the alternative model proposed here is certainly less "scientific." But it is no less rigorous in its pursuit, with the client, of meaning and understanding. The model calls for workers to develop their reflective, theory-building talents and be able to fathom the subjective worlds of their clients. In so doing, it does not advocate the discarding of the existing body of knowledge and theory; rather, such knowledge is but one aspect of understanding that may help enrich awareness. This commonsense humanistic orientation draws from the new knowledge of the cognitive sciences about the way people ordinarily go about the task of coping and problem solving. Within this perspective, social work practice cannot be divorced from theory: Knowing and acting have an interdependent relationship in the real-life nature of the helping experience. One might speculate that perhaps some social workers who do not or cannot articulate their theoretical rationale use this approach to practice "naturally." At least two persuasive studies, one by Maluccio, the other by Schön, support this possibility.[19]

Perhaps the ethical dimension of practice offers the most compelling argument for an orientation to social work practice that is not rooted in notions of objective certainty and scientific method. Consider that an empirical-positivistic orientation retains its authority only as long as either of two conditions are met: (1) it can *ignore* the subjectivity of the client's ethical, moral, value, or spiritual beliefs or (2) it can *convert* or *reduce* these subjective beliefs into objective and explanatory psychological categories, such as, traits, defenses, learned or conditioned responses, and so on. . . .

So far, little has been said about the implications for education of an approach that is humanistic, reflective, and subjective. In this regard, education for reflective practice would be equally as rigorous as or more rigorous than current models. Students would need to develop and refine the inductive skills necessary for theory building rather than the rote skills currently required for theory learning. Creative, imaginative practice would take the place of the development of technique. And, educational programs would include a strong foundation of moral philosophy and ethical reasoning to enable students to grapple with both social and personal ethical dilemmas. Moreover, teachers would assume more of a collegial rather than an expert role with their students as they work together in a reflective, learning, and problem-solving venture.[20]

The basic intent, after all, is to educate social workers, not to train them. The skills and facts that are accumulated in training may well be forgotten over time or with disuse. The knowledge, wisdom, and guiding principles that are absorbed in a humanistic and reflective approach to education cannot be easily lost, because they become an integral part of the total self.

Howard Goldstein, DSW, is Professor of Social Work, School of Applied Social Sciences, Case Western Reserve University, Cleveland, Ohio.

NOTES AND REFERENCES

1. See for example, J. Fischer, "Is Casework Effective?" *Social Work*, 18 (January 1973), pp. 5–20; and C. Brewer and J. Lait, *Can Social Work Survive?* (London, England: Temple Smith, 1980), among many articles.

2. B. Sheldon, "Theory and Practice: A Reexamination of a Tenuous Relationship," *British Journal of Social Work*, 8, No. 1 (January 1978), pp. 1–25.

3. E. Sainsbury, "Research and Reflection on the Social Work Task," *Social Work Service*, 23 (1980), p. 13.

4. M. S. Kolevzon and J. Maykranz, "Theoretical Orientation and Clinical Practice: Uniformity versus Eclecticism?" *Social Service Review*, 56 (March 1982), p. 127.

5. R. Carew, "The Place of Knowledge in Social Work," *British Journal of Social Work*, 9, No. 3 (Autumn 1979), pp. 349–363. For additional discussion of this problem, see also M. Siporin. "Practice Theory and Vested Interests," *Social Service Review*, 52 (September 1978), pp. 418–436; and D. Howe, "Inflated States and Empty Theories in Social Work," *British Journal of Social Work*, 10, No. 3 (Fall 1980), pp. 317–340.

6. For an excellent discussion of moral responsibility in practice, see M. Whan, "Tricks of the Trade: Questionable Theory and Practice in Family Therapy," *British Journal of Social Work*, 13 (1983), pp. 321–337.

7. D. Schön. *The Reflective Practitioner: How Professionals Think in Action* (New York: Basic Books, 1983), p. 23.

. . . . . .

10. Sir J. Eccles and D. Robinson. *The Wonder of Being Human: Our Brain and Our Mind* (New York: Free Press, 1984), p. 178.

11. R. C. Lewontin, S. Rose, and L. Kamin, *Not in Our Genes: Biology, Ideology, and Human Nature* (New York: Pantheon Books, 1984).

12. See, for example, W. Heisenberg, *Physics and Philosophy: The Revolution in Modern Science* (New York: Harper & Bros., 1958).

13. I. Prigogine and I. Stengers, *Order Out of Chaos: Man's New Dialogue with Nature* (New York: Bantam Books, 1984), p. 306.

14. K. Gergen. *Toward Transformation in Social Knowledge* (New York: Springer-Verlag, New York, 1982), p. 209.

15. See, for example, H. Goldstein, *Social Learning and Change: A Cognitive Approach to Human Services* (Columbia: University of South Carolina Press, 1981); Goldstein, *Creative Change: A Cognitive-Humanistic Approach to Social Work Practice* (New York/London: Tavistock, 1984); H. Werner, *Cognitive Therapy* (New York: Free Press, 1981); and S. L. Witkin, "Cognitive Processes in Clinical Practice," *Social Work*, 27 (September 1982), pp. 389–396.

16. See, for example, R. Plant, *Social and Moral Theory in Casework* (London, England: Routledge & Kegan Paul, 1970); F. G. Reamer, "Ethical Dilemmas in Social Work Practice," *Social Work*, 28 (January–February 1983), pp. 31–36; Reamer, "Fundamental Ethical Issues in Social Work: An Essay Review," *Social Service Review*, 53 (June 1979), pp. 229–243; M. Siporin, "Moral Philosophy in Social Work Today," *Social Service Review*, 56 (December 1982), pp. 516–538; and N. Timms and D. Watson, eds., *Philosophy in Social Work* (Boston: Routledge & Kegan Paul, 1978).

17. M. Heineman. "The Obsolete Scientific Imperative in Social Work Research," *Social Service Review*, 55 (September 1981), pp. 371–397.

18. For a more thorough discussion of the "client's story," see M. Whan, "Accounts, Narrative, and Case History," *British Journal of Social Work*, 9 (1979), pp. 488–499.

19. See A. Maluccio, *Learning from Clients* (New York: Free Press, 1979) for a study of workers' and clients' perceptions of interpersonal helping that found that a reflective dialogical process, *not consciously or systematically used*, was related most critically to successful helping. In this process, workers were constantly attuned and responsive to their clients' expectations, roles, perceptions, goals, and other subjective states. Also, see Schön, *The Reflective Practitioner* for a study of the actual practices of not only psychotherapists but also architects, city planners, engineers, and other professionals. Most professionals approach each problem as a unique case and, although their approach is effective, they cannot state the criteria for their judgments and procedure.

20. For a more intensive exploration of the challenge to education for reflective practice, see Schön, *The Reflective Practitioner*.

Accepted April 18, 1985

Introduction to "Scientific Imperatives in Social Work Research: Pluralism Is Not Skepticism"

In this article, John Brekke continues the debates in response to Heineman Pieper's 1981 paper. Brekke focuses on an important problem that the logical positivist philosophers also emphasized: how to appraise scientific knowledge and, more specifically, how to demarcate scientific and nonscientific knowledge. Consider, for example, why using a crystal ball is not currently considered a scientific way of predicting a client's potential for violence. Like Heineman Pieper, Brekke does not believe that prescribing particular research methods is the way to demarcate scientific and nonscientific knowledge; also like Heineman Pieper, he advocates methodological pluralism as a tenet of a metatheory of social work research. He recognizes that methodological pluralism does not have to mean abandoning standards for good science (an extreme version of skepticism), but he misunderstands Heineman Pieper in that he believes that, in the heuristic paradigm, methodological pluralism does lead to skepticism.

Brekke misreads Heineman Pieper as abandoning standards for appraising the correctness of scientific knowledge and endorsing the philosophical position of skepticism. Brekke assumes Heineman Pieper takes a skeptical position partly because he confuses relativism and skepticism. Skeptics claim that, because all knowledge is biased, one cannot advance rational standards for justifying and appraising knowledge. Relativism has many variants, including cultural, ethical, ontological, and epistemological. With regard to the conceptual foundations for scientific knowledge, relativism is typically understood to be the position that, because all knowledge is inherently biased, the claim that a reality independent of our awareness can serve as a standard for the veracity of theories has no sound grounds. Accordingly, instead of aiming for "truer" theories, relativists focus on other criteria in theory appraisal, such as coherence. Rorty provides a contemporary example of an epistemic aim compatible with relativism in stating, "edifying philosophy aims at continuing a conversation rather than at discovering truth" (1979, p. 373) or "the point of edifying philosophy is to keep the conversation going rather than to find objective truth. Such truth, in the view I am advocating, is the normal result of normal discourse" (1979, p. 377). Social constructionism is a contemporary, relativist theory of social and behavioral knowledge.* Roy Bhaskar is one of the postpositivist realist philosophers of science who have critiqued relativism. Bhaskar says that relativism is based on the "epistemic fallacy," the assumption that one can define what is in terms of what one can know (1989a, 1989b). Brekke mistakenly characterizes Heineman Pieper as "antirealist." In fact, in her reply, Heineman Pieper emphasizes that she is a realist in that she believes that "the objects of knowledge exist independently of our awareness" (1987, p. 369).** Brekke's critiques suggest that he also endorses a realist position; Brekke and Heineman Pieper therefore agree in their ontological assumptions.

---

*Editor's Note: Social constructionism has many variants and is also known as constructivism (see Witkin in this chapter and also Gergen, 1986, and Lincoln, 1990).
**Editor's Note: See p. 172 in this text.

Brekke wants to make standards for appraising knowledge rule-based or normative (a position Heineman Pieper has criticized). In her reply to Brekke, Heineman Pieper emphasizes that although she is arguing for methodological pluralism, she is not a skeptic and she does believe there are nonprescriptive ways to appraise and improve scientific knowledge. Brekke confuses Heineman Pieper's rejection of a prescriptive approach to appraising knowledge with the skeptic's rejection of standards for appraising knowledge. The position that prescription is unjustified is not the same as the position that one cannot appraise or improve scientific knowledge.

While Heineman Pieper suggests some promising ways to recognize bias and some alternative standards for appraising knowledge, she strongly opposes the view that prescribing norms or rules is the way to improve and appraise scientific knowledge. Heineman Pieper appraises the validity of the logical positivist metatheory of research. She sets forth some promising ways to appraise scientific knowledge using the heuristic paradigm, such as bias recognition. Her work exemplifies her belief that it *is* possible to appraise and improve knowledge claims. Such a position does not necessarily lead to Brekke's conclusion that prescribing norms or rules is the best way to ensure that the correctness of knowledge can be evaluated. In other words, we can find and suggest ways to appraise and improve scientific knowledge without requiring that others agree with our methods and adhere to our preferences. The assumption that prescribing rules can lead to a superior form of scientific knowledge was one hallmark of logical positivism, and that prescriptive approach to knowledge generation and appraisal has had unfortunate consequences, as Heineman Pieper points out.

Because she does not endorse his prescriptive approach, Brekke misunderstands Heineman Pieper as saying that "science has failed as an epistemology" (Brekke, 1986, p. 542).* In fact, Heineman Pieper emphasizes that the logical positivist philosophy of science has failed as an epistemology (an assertion that is widely accepted, as she notes) and that an alternative philosophy of science will provide superior conceptual foundations for a philosophy of social and behavioral research. Brekke continues to view the prescriptive approach advanced in the positivist metatheory as a method of determining whether knowledge is "correct" (p. 541).** This view suggests that he, like Hudson (earlier in Chapter 3), assumes that Heineman Pieper abandons standards for science because she criticizes the positivist prescriptions that he equates with science. To illustrate, one norm Brekke advances for evaluating scientific knowledge is Popper's concept of falsification (see Popper in the Appendix). Drawing on postpositivist philosophers of science, Heineman Pieper points out how falsification does not work as a standard for appraising scientific knowledge. Heineman Pieper suggests we can appraise and improve scientific knowledge by ensuring that ontological and epistemological assumptions are conceptually coherent (discussed further in the following articles and their introductions) and by recognizing bias.

Heineman Pieper and Brekke define the term *bias* differently. According to Brekke, Heineman Pieper says that, because measurement inevitably entails bias and because quantified data are not inherently superior to other forms of data, there are no standards for appraising scientific knowledge. However, Heineman Pieper says that bias occurs in many other aspects of research besides data collection. Brekke's

---

*Editor's Note: p.. 163 in this volume.
**Editor's Note: p.. 162 in this volume.

use of the term *bias* reflects the assumptions of the positivist research paradigm; that is, he believes that bias occurs primarily as a consequence of the researcher's method and that scientific knowledge can reasonably aim to eliminate bias. Heineman Pieper says that bias occurs the moment the researcher

1. Formulates the problem one way as opposed to another way;
2. Chooses a "real" to study;
3. Selects an epistemology, or a way to know that reality;
4. Draws the environment–system boundary (see Heineman Pieper, 1989, for elaboration).

All of the preceding decisions generate biases before the researcher selects methods to collect and analyze data. Furthermore, as Heineman Pieper points out, contemporary philosophers of science show how other factors set up pervasive, unavoidable biases in all knowledge. These factors include the theory-ladenness of all knowledge; researchers' unavoidable dependence on language and perception, which are inevitably biased by culture (see Whorf in Chapter 6); and the influence of sociohistorical factors on research priorities, procedures, and interpretation of findings (Shapin, 1982). As Wimsatt describes, such biases occur in every aspect of the scientific endeavor and cannot be eliminated (see Wimsatt in Chapter 5).

Brekke draws from two philosophers of science, Popper and Lakatos,* as alternative metatheories (see Popper in the Appendix). Popper distinguished his views from those of the logical positivists, but he sought to accomplish many of the same aims. Although Lakatos embraced some of the tenets of a postpositivist approach to science, he retained some positivist ideas. For example, Nickles (1987a) points out that Lakatos supported Popper's view that a scientific theory is supported empirically by a successful, novel prediction derived from that theory. Heineman Pieper says the problem with such an approach to theory testing is that restricting valuable explanations to predictions is not only untenable but is especially irrelevant for the open systems that are the objects of social and behavioral inquiry. In fact, scientists use many methods to test and support their theories. A more relevant, postpositivist approach to appraising a scientific theory is to examine how well the theory explains the complex and changing situations that social and behavioral scientists frequently encounter (see, e.g., Bhaskar, 1989b, 1991).

KEY TERMS

Instrumentalism	Realism
Relativism	Skepticism

---

*Editor's Note: Imre Lakatos, a Czechoslovakian postpositivist philosopher of science, is probably best known for his book *Methodology of Scientific Research Programmes* (1978). Lakatos studied historical examples of advances in science, particularly physics. He co-edited a book—*Criticism and the Growth of Knowledge* (1970)—that reported on a famous conference in response to Kuhn's work. Lakatos conceptualized a "research programme" as consisting of a central core of theory that scientists adhere to as they refine the corollaries of the heuristic. He emphasized that scientists necessarily ignore anomalies to adhere to the theory that best explains currently accepted findings.

DISCUSSION QUESTIONS

1. How does Brekke formulate the central problem in developing a philosophy of social work research? Compare Brekke's formulation with Heineman Pieper's formulation.

2. First, summarize some of the key arguments in support of the positivist belief that prescriptions will yield superior scientific knowledge. Then, summarize some of the key arguments against that belief in prescriptiveness.

3. Why do positivists assert that scientific knowledge must be distinguished from other forms of knowledge? Look at Heineman Pieper's definition of scientific knowledge in the Preface to this volume. How might a researcher who adopts the heuristic paradigm distinguish scientific knowledge from other forms of knowledge?

4. Some positivists might respond to Heineman Pieper by saying, "We don't believe our research leads to findings that are certain. No one does anymore. But we want to reduce bias in scientific theories, and the best way to do that is through the experimental method."

   a. What is bias? How might positivist researchers and Heineman Pieper define this term differently?

   b. How does Heineman Pieper's definition of bias lead her to take issue with the argument that the experimental design is the best way to reduce bias?

5. Notice that Brekke reads the "logical conclusion" of Heineman Pieper's argument as "antirealism" or "elitism" (1986, p. 539).* The concept of elitism, as Kuhn (1970) elaborates it, is much more complex than Brekke suggests. Although Kuhn does emphasize how political factors (e.g., the structures of authority in educational and research institutions) influence the development of scientific traditions, he also shows how the problem-solving efficacy of a new paradigm will attract adherents, who will then comprise a new "elite."

   a. Contrary to Brekke's claim that she is elitist, Heineman Pieper explicitly states that antirealism and elitism are incompatible with the heuristic paradigm. Can you say why?

   b. Do you agree with Brekke's assumption that without criteria that prescribe and proscribe epistemological assumptions, one is necessarily "antirealist"? Why or why not?

6. Which six of Brekke's seven recommendations do you think Heineman Pieper agrees with? (Hint: see her "Author's Reply.")

7. Consider the three possible philosophical orientations discussed in the debate between Brekke and Heineman Pieper (realism, relativism, and skepticism). Divide the class into three teams, and have each team choose a position, find out more about the philosophers who have advanced that position, and then debate its merits.

---

*Editor's Note: p. 162 in this volume.

8. Why are predictions based on looking into crystal balls not currently considered to be scientific? What information would it take to make them scientific?

9. Do the following statements best illustrate realism, relativism, or skepticism?

    a. From Nietzsche,

    Man is not the effect of some special purpose, of a will, an end; nor is he the object of an attempt to attain an "ideal of humanity" or an "ideal of happiness" or an "ideal of morality." It is absurd to wish to devolve one's essence on some end or other. We have invented the concept of "end": in reality there is no end. (1888/1972, p. 500)

    b. From Shakespeare,

    There are more things in heaven and earth, Horatio,
    Than are dreamt of in your philosophy. (*Hamlet*, act I, sc. 5, ll. 166–167)

    c. From Wallace Stevens,

    The blackbird whirled in the autumn winds.
    It was a small part of the pantomime.

    .   .   .   .   .

    I know noble accents
    And lucid, inescapable rhythms;
    But I know too,
    that the blackbird is involved in what I know.
    (From "13 Ways of Looking at a Blackbird," 1971)

    d. Polonius to Hamlet's mother:

    My liege and madam, to expostulate
    What majesty should be, what duty is,
    Why day is day, night night, and time is time,
    Were nothing but to waste night, day, and time.
    Therefore, since brevity is the soul of wit,
    And tediousness the limbs and outward flourishes,
    I will be brief. Your noble son is mad.
    Mad call I it, for to define true madness,
    What is't but to be nothing else but mad?
    (*Hamlet*, act II, sc. 2, ll. 86–95).

Scientific Imperatives in Social Work Research: Pluralism Is Not Skepticism

JOHN S. BREKKE   *University of Southern California*

ABSTRACT: It is argued in this paper that Martha Heineman ("The Obsolete Scientific Imperative in Social Work Research," *Social Service Review* 55 [September 1981]: 371–95) conflates pluralism and skepticism in science and dismisses any attempt to meet the aims of positivism through other rational means. A critique of her analysis, and responses to it, are used to explore the postpositivist dilemmas of social work research, especially the challenge to rationality in science. The work of Karl Popper and Imre Lakatos on the construction and testing of scientific knowledge is discussed. Recommendations for social work research and education are offered.

There appears to be a growing awareness among social work researchers that the philosophical basis of our knowledge building and testing deserves scrutiny. Many people believe that these issues have far-reaching implications for our discipline as it strives to develop a knowledge base of its own.[1] Martha Heineman is to be applauded for beginning this sorely needed dialogue within social work. In a recent article she argues that social work research is in the grip of outmoded positivist tenets that limit our knowledge building and that incorrectly restrict our notions of what constitutes acceptable science.[2] Unfortunately, her paper has not served as a catalyst for lively debate. Responses to her article suggest that these issues are best ignored, misunderstand her altogether, or advocate a positivist retrenchment.[3]

The purpose of this article is to provide a critique of Heineman's analysis and to use it as a springboard from which to survey the postpositivist dilemmas of the social work researcher. The major focus of this survey will be on the recent work of Imre Lakatos and Karl Popper.[4] Their writings provide a formal solution to the issues of knowledge building and testing that Heineman obscures and that positivism fails to resolve but that have not diminished in importance. They also address the challenge to rationality in science that has been raised by two other recent philosophers of science, namely, Thomas Kuhn and Paul Feyerabend.[5] Finally, a set of recommendations will be offered to operationalize practically the implications of this discussion for social work researchers and educators.[6]

HEINEMAN ON SCIENCE: BACKGROUND ISSUES AND CONFUSIONS

Heineman's analysis of the failures of positivism itself renders the responses to her article unsatisfactory;

Source: "Scientific Imperatives in Social Work Research: Pluralism Is Not Skepticism" by J. Brekke, 1986, *Social Service Review*, 60, pp. 539–544. Copyright 1986 by The University of Chicago. Reprinted by permission.
Social Service Review (December 1986). © 1986 by The University of Chicago. All rights reserved. 0037-7961/86/6004-0008$01.00

however, her presentation contributes to justifiable confusion in several ways. In criticizing positivist thinking, she deals parenthetically and inconsistently with profound issues concerning the construction and testing of scientific knowledge that positivism has been unable to resolve and that she sets out to address. Specifically, she appears to dismiss any rational attempt to deal with two seminal problems that positivism discusses and that are central to the scientific endeavor: (1) how to assess the progress of scientific knowledge and (2) how to prescribe rules for the construction and evaluation of science that will allow it to be differentiated from other forms of knowledge such as religion or mysticism.[7]

Similarly, her conclusions and posited alternatives suffer from two shortcomings: (1) a focus that is largely limited to the issue of measurement and (2) a premature rejection of the notion of scientific realism (i.e., the attempt to understand reality correctly) in favor of a form of consensual relativism, or elitism, that contradicts her central thesis. In sum, in dismissing positivism Heineman rejects any attempt to approach the aims of positivism through other rational means.

It is not surprising, then, that her article has been responded to with conservative fervor, for, if Heineman's argument is followed to its logical conclusion, one must decide that there is no way to evaluate the correctness of scientific knowledge (an "antirealist" notion) or to establish rules for demarcating science from other forms of knowledge other than by relying on scientists to do this via decree (an "elitist" notion). The solution, however, is not to ignore these issues or to retreat to a positivist position, as some of her critics have suggested. Furthermore, without resolving these issues, the social work researcher is left without any rational criteria for knowing when he or she is practicing science and is not able to evaluate rationally the products of social work research. In sum, in dismissing these issues, as Heineman does, it becomes difficult to avoid, as Schuerman states, "hopeless relativism" in the methods and evaluation of science.[8]

The perspective presented here is built on an examination of the shortcomings of Heineman's argument and on a review of the positions of Popper and Lakatos on the issues of (1) discriminating science from nonscience (i.e., does science have any epistemological distinction from, say, mysticism or table talk?); (2) realist knowledge building (i.e., can science offer or approximate correct explanations of reality?); and

(3) testing scientific knowledge (i.e., is there any way to provide a set of rational criteria for evaluating scientific knowledge?). All these issues are central to the rational scientific epistemology that Heineman refers to directly or by implication but fails to explicate.[9]

HEINEMAN'S PRESCRIPTIVE PARADIGM

The bulk of Heineman's paper is devoted to a lucid presentation of positivist positions and their now well-documented shortcomings.[10] However, her shorter treatment of alternatives to positivism is based on one paragraph of pronouncements that quickly raises profound issues in the philosophy of science and that then truncates them, leading the reader to believe that the stage has been set for her conclusions. Among her statements are that "[n]umerous alternatives to the logical empiricist view of science have been suggested, all of which reject the logical empiricist assumption that the truthfulness of scientific results can be guaranteed. Consequently, contemporary philosophers of science concentrate on the practicing scientist as decision maker and problem solver rather than on the derivation of absolute prescriptions for all science. . . . Thus the primary consideration is not whether or to what extent a theory is correct but whether it is an improvement—not whether this theory is better confirmed but whether it is better."[11] These are confusing statements for several reasons, but, before attempting to provide some illumination, a correction must be offered. As will be discussed, not all contemporary philosophers of science reject absolute prescriptions for all science.

The confusion of Heineman's prescriptions arises in two ways. First, all practicing scientists (even positivists) are decision makers. They make decisions on many levels, for example, what, when, and how to investigate. Positivism, however, offers the scientist a way to decide whether what he or she is doing is indeed science and not, for example, religion and, furthermore, whether the knowledge generated is correct.[12] Heineman instructs scientists to be decision makers but not to concern themselves with the correctness of their explanations or predictions—only with whether they are better explanations or predictions. But better than what? And what is better? Do we have any way of telling when we get there? Perhaps Heineman is advocating that we cease metatheoretical discussion altogether and free the scientist's decision making from rational scrutiny.

Second, there seem to be two reigning attitudes toward the potential truth value of science, namely, realism and instrumentalism.[13] These are complex issues that encompass a vast range of philosophical terrains, but, put simply, realism suggests that science is a method that can progressively approximate a correct understanding and explanation of a reality that is separate from our perception of it. Instrumentalism, on the other hand, skirts the issue of whether reality can be known. It suggests that the scientist's only concern should be with whether his or her predictions work and not with whether the theoretical explanations of reality that are offered are correct or are in any way true.

Heineman appears to advocate instrumentalism without making the implications of this position clear. At one point she argues that accurate explanation "is more useful than prediction" but later states that better theories, not more correct ones, are the primary concern.[14] Perhaps she is suggesting a distinction between accurate explanation and correctness. What is clear, however, is that Heineman's position presents a rational dilemma: there are no rules for evaluating the correctness of scientific knowledge, but, nevertheless, some theories are better than others.

In the same vein, Heineman appears to argue that, since the positivist rules for producing and testing scientific knowledge no longer work, then no rules can exist, for, as she states, "research will be conceptualized descriptively and functionally rather than normatively."[15] It is on this basis that she calls for methodological pluralism—the prescription that scientists use an undogmatic approach to design and unrestricted data-gathering procedures in their research.[16] This is a serious error, for one must not conflate arguments for methodological pluralism with arguments for epistemological skepticism, which is the position that science can be no more correct in its understanding of reality than can any other system of knowledge and that there are no rules for assailing the progress of scientific knowledge.[17]

It appears that in advocating methodological pluralism Heineman has taken a position of epistemological skepticism that is not in any way related to her fundamental concern, nor does it need to be. Moreover, by calling the positivist imperatives obsolete and then offering her own undeveloped prescriptions for science, she leaves the impression that all imperatives are

obsolete, unattainable, or unscientific. This line of reasoning is pursued by Imre, who avers that, since positivism has failed, much of what social work practitioners do is outside the purview of empirical science.[18] The problem with these works is not in their statement that positivism no longer suffices but rather in the ensuing implication that science has failed as an epistemology, a view based largely on a misunderstanding of recent developments in the philosophy of science.

The work of Popper and Lakatos represents a solution to this dilemma and offers prescriptions for demarcating science from nonscience, for building realist knowledge, and for testing scientific theory, all of which are scientific imperatives and none of which is obsolete. While these issues are clearly interrelated, they will be discussed in separate sections below. In addition, Lakatos argues that his work is largely an outgrowth of Popper's.

DISCRIMINATING SCIENCE FROM NONSCIENCE

The notion of inductive justificationism is a hallmark of logical positivist thought.[19] This tenet states that our scientific hypotheses and theories can be constructed—and the truth of them tested—within the rules of inductive logic. This is done by using facts (as propositions) generated from pure (or theory-free) experience and observation and then inducing theory from these facts.[20] Positivists argue that by using this method it is possible to prove the truth or the falsity of scientific knowledge. However, the demise of this notion places the verifiability of scientific knowledge at a crisis point.[21]

Both Popper and Lakatos acknowledge the failure of positivist induction but offer different solutions to the problem of science as knowledge. Popper dismisses the problem, while Lakatos concludes that all scientific theories are equally improbable, equally unprovable, and equally impossible to disprove.[22] While this may seem to be a startling conclusion for a philosopher who is trying to build a scientific epistemology, he bases it on four tenets. (1) Induction fails—one cannot logically induce theory from fact, for the laws of induction do not preclude any inducible state of affairs; hence, logic alone cannot be used to increase the content of a scientific theory. (2) No psychological demarcation exists between theory and fact, and, as such, facts are theory laden. (3) On the basis of the work of Wittgenstein, we can conclude that there is no neutral language for describing the world without at the same time interpreting it. (4) Propositions (theoretical statements) can be derived only from other propositions and not from facts. These four notions form part of Lakatos's trenchant rejection of the positivist philosophy of science and provide the suppositional foundation for his own method.[23] The conclusion is that scientific knowledge cannot be logically verified.

What then should be our course as scientists? Should we encourage wild speculation and perhaps end up not being able to distinguish science from hallucination? Moreover, do we conclude that science has little to do with the world apart from our thoughts about it? And then, how do we go about constructing and rationally testing scientific knowledge? Before reaching premature conclusions about science as a method of knowing, it will be valuable to examine at some length the contemporary dilemma over appraising scientific theories (i.e., discriminating science from nonscience and good science from poor), which will put into perspective Heineman's offering, its failings, the controversy surrounding it, and the perspective of the present analysis. Pertinent to this examination is Lakatos's identification of three schools of thought concerning the issue of science as knowledge, namely, skepticism, demarcationism, and elitism.[24] What follows is a brief sketch of each school.

Skepticism, or cultural relativism, gives scientific belief systems no epistemological superiority over any other belief system. One system cannot be more "right" than any other, although some systems may have more "might," or influence, than have others. Implicit in this position is the notion that there can be changes in knowledge systems but no progress in terms of their correctness or truth. Thus the skeptic denies the possibility of finding any acceptable solution to the problem of appraising scientific theories. The skeptic's code of intellectual honesty is to "do your own thing," and as a philosophy of science it is best represented by the work of Feyerabend, who states that "[s]cience is an essentially anarchistic enterprise: theoretical anarchism is more humanitarian and more likely to encourage progress than its law-and-order alternatives."[25]

The remaining two schools—demarcationism and elitism—both posit that there is a solution to the problem of appraising scientific theories, but, while the former searches for universal criteria of appraisal, elitism presupposes that no universal criteria are available. More specifically, demarcationism's fundamental problem is to differentiate, or demarcate, science from pseudoscience or nonscience and to provide universal criteria for doing so. To understand this school, one must grasp the seminal distinction between the three worlds to which demarcationists commonly refer.[26]

First, there is the world of physical things; second is the world of consciousness, of mental states and beliefs; and third is the Platonic world of objective spirit, or the world of ideas. The three worlds are autonomous, but they interact. The products of knowledge—propositions, theories, systems of theories, problems, and so on—live and grow in the third world; the producers of knowledge—in this case, scientists—live in the second world. According to this school, the knowledge generated in the second world can be appraised and compared on the basis of universal criteria, theories of which constitute "methodological knowledge" that lives and grows in the third world of logical truth and logically valid inference.[27]

Demarcationists disagree on many points, but they concur on others.[28] There is agreement that the truth value of a theory has no relation to the psychological influence that it might have on people's minds, and the value of it is independent of the mind(s) that created it. Second, there is critical respect for the articulated theory as the hallmark of rationality and rational appraisal. Third, there is immanent respect for the layperson, in that, given the criteria of the demarcationist, anyone ought to be able to judge rationally the products of science. Finally, the delineation of the demarcationist criteria (Lakatos's criteria will be presented later) is seen as an evolving rational activity and, as such, has a historical character.[29]

Elitism, the final category, is presently the most influential approach to the appraisal of scientific theories. Elitists such as Brown and Kuhn claim that good science can be distinguished from bad science and that scientific progress can be attained but that no universal criteria can be developed to validate these judgments.[30] Instead, this school claims that a large part of what constitutes scientific knowledge is inarticulable and belongs to a tacit dimension that is understandable only to scientists. Hence the judgment of science belongs to the jury of scientists, a jury of the elite. It is this position that Heineman appears to advocate, although it leads to a contradiction in her argument.

BASES FOR THEORY BUILDING

In surveying the dilemma of appraisal, Lakatos states that demarcationism is the central problem for a contemporary philosophy of science. He argues, with others, that the views of both skeptics and elitists ultimately result in irrationality and relativism.[31] Furthermore, he sees his work as an outgrowth of Popper's, and to understand Lakatos's positions fully one must examine the similarities and differences between the two thinkers.

Common to both Lakatos's and Popper's demarcationism is the proposition that the nature of a fact must be conventionally agreed on by scientists or observers. In both systems, then, there is an acceptance of the theory ladenness of perception, but in neither does this imply skepticism (a distinction that Heineman fails to appreciate). They also agree that for a theory to be scientific it must specify falsifying, as opposed to verifying, circumstances and pass rigorous empirical tests. But for Popper this falsification rests largely on the procedures of deductive logic, whereas for Lakatos it rests also on the notion of a "research program," or a series of theories.[32]

To understand the importance of this distinction between the two positions and its relation to theory building, it is necessary to point out that Popper eschews epistemology.[33] He argues that, given the failure of inductive methods in science, we cannot know if a theory is true. We can know, however, if it is false, and we can do this instantly and conclusively by subjecting a theory to the modus tollens of deductive logic: hypothesis "a" (from theory "A") implies fact "b"; if not "b," then not "a." Furthermore, Popper suggests that, if the predictions (hypotheses) from our theories are falsified, so is the theory, and no other way exists to go about it since our theories are untestable in toto.

Concerning theory building, Lakatos's view is that Popper's rejection of epistemology leaves scientists in the position of learning without knowing; that is, we cannot know if something is true but only if it is false. "To put it more sharply: Popper's demarcation criterion has nothing to do with epistemology. It says nothing about the epistemological value of the scientific game . . . [or] that the scientific game produces propo-

sitions ever nearer to the truth."[34] To address this dilemma, Lakatos suggests a synthetic metaphysical inductive principle to guide scientific activity and to become the basis of scientific knowledge building.[35]

In short, this principle instructs the scientist to begin with ideas or laws about how the world works (metaphysical ideas), to formalize them into theories, and to test them empirically. (Bunge provides an operationalization of this procedure and cogently addresses the issues of testability that Hudson raises.)[36] Lakatos justifies this approach by arguing that, if facts are really "facts" (agreed on conventionally) and if the background knowledge of science is based on an accumulation of "facts," then why not accept metaphysical statements (e.g., the world works like a clock) as guiding heuristics and surround them with theories that predict and explain phenomena? Clearly, these metaphysical assumptions cannot be empirically tested directly (although Bunge maintains that they can be tested indirectly), but the surrounding group of theories, which Lakatos calls the "protective belt" of theories, can be subjected to the falsificationist method of modus tollens. In this way it is possible to have both learning and knowing.

Consider an example. Studying human development throughout the life span is a fundamental aspect of social work education, and to illustrate Lakatos's method, two approaches to studying human cognitive development will be compared, namely, the structuralist stage model of Piaget and the learning model of Skinner. Both approaches have well-defined assumptions and have generated a significant amount of research.[37]

A central issue in the debate between Skinnerians and Piagetians is whether human cognitive development progresses through successive stages and whether these stages in fact exist. Without belaboring the complex of definitional issues involved, it is clear that both models accept fundamental assumptions that permeate their research efforts. One of these assumptions involves whether the human organism actively constructs the nature of reality or whether it merely reflects it.[38]

Piagetians assume that people are active creators of what constitutes their known reality. For example, at various stages of cognitive development, it is argued that the child perceives his or her world very differently (e.g., the well-known Piagetian task concerning the child's judgment of space and volume). The perceptual shifts that this task reveals are based on cognitive structures that define the parameters of the child's reality and that the child uses in creating reality. Furthermore, these perceptions change only after the cognitive structures shift as a result of moving into a new developmental stage, and this movement is independent of any amount of evidence that the child receives concerning the "inaccuracy" of his or her perception. In this model, then, the individual's perception of the world is based on the structure of his or her consciousness and cognitive processes; hence, it is more meaningful to speak of the structure of consciousness than of the structure of the world.

Skinnerian models, on the other hand, are based on the assumption that people have an immanently passive relationship with their environment. What a person becomes is dependent on external forces that have impinged on and molded his or her experience; therefore, the child's perception is a reflection of the structure of reality and not of the structure of consciousness. In this model, human beings are the sum of a vast storage system of learning experiences provided by the environment, and stages of development play no part in learning. Hence children ought to be able to master the Piagetian tasks with practice at any age.

According to Lakatos, the Piagetian assumption of activity and the Skinnerian assumption of passivity form part of the metaphysical hard core of each of the research programs. As such, they are empirically irrefutable and inductively unprovable. Nevertheless, they form the bases for knowledge building and testing, in that a protective belt of theories is developed from them and is tested with the modus tollens method.[39] Lakatos calls the theories that are generated from and that surround the metaphysical hard core a "protective belt" because the falsification process never directly challenges the assumed verity of the hard core—it remains untouched. Its validity can, however, be rationally appraised using a method that will be described in the next section.

Lakatos maintains that all scientific theories have this metaphysical hard core, which is used to generate theories and theoretical assumptions that then constitute the positive heuristic of the research program. These varying assumptions are intertwined with different theoretical positions and problems. For example, developmental learning theorists posit quantitative and continuous change in behavior or perception, the reductionistic organization of organisms, and efficient causality. Piagetian theorists, on the other hand,

focus on qualitative and discontinuous changes in perception, emergent organization, and structural or formal causation. However, Lakatos maintains that, while we can never say that the Piagetian hard core is true or that the Skinnerian hard core is not, we can begin to "recognize progress. This can be easily done by an inductive principle which connects realist metaphysics with methodological appraisals, verisimilitude with corroboration, which reinterprets the rules of the 'scientific game' as a conjectural theory about the signs of the growth of knowledge, that is, about the signs of growing verisimilitude of our scientific theories."[40]

In summary, scientific realism is not dead. Lakatos has based his realism on metaphysics and thereby presents a powerful solution to the problem of science as epistemology. The analysis of the metaphysical core of theories has been applied to the study of human life-span development and personality as well as to psychology and physics more generally.[41] This work in the social sciences has been based on the root-metaphor method of Stephen Pepper, who has outlined four discrete world hypotheses, or coherent metaphysical systems, concerning how the world works.[42] As will be discussed, the methodological implications of this analysis have also been presented and have particular relevance to social work.[43]

KNOWLEDGE TESTING

Even if we can know (via metaphysics) and learn (via falsification), a second question arises: How does the scientist choose one theory over another? Heineman argues that one theory is chosen over another when one is better than the other—not more correct, but better. What, then, is "better"?

Much of Popper's brand of falsification was conceived in reaction to the Duhem-Quine thesis that, given enough imagination on the part of the scientist, any theory can be saved from refutation.[44] This can be done by making adjustments to the background knowledge in which a theory is embedded, that is, that which has been accepted as fact. Clearly, Popper realized that two elements of conventionalism or consensus are necessarily present in any theory testing, namely (1) the ceteris paribus clause (the experimental conditions) and (2) the unproblematic background knowledge, which is everything that has been accepted as "fact" up to the time of the experiment. But to have no rules for eliminating a theory would be to give up hope for a rational criticism of science.

Hence, as Lakatos relates, "Popper set out to find a criterion which is both more objective and more hard hitting."[45]

Popper's discussion is comprehensive and complex (too much so for a complete presentation here), but it offers criteria for determining the acceptability and status of a scientific theory. A theory is acceptably scientific if it is experimentally falsifiable, that is, if it posits an "empirically" nonverifying instance ("empirically" meaning within the methodological constraints conventionally agreed on by scientists). A theory is falsified if it contradicts a corroborated or conventionally accepted observational statement (a "fact"). In this way it is possible to demarcate science from nonscience and to test theories in an instantly rational fashion: if a theory fails the test, it is discarded. (This discussion will not include Popper's observations on scientific and pseudoscientific adjustments to theory; the interested reader will have to forage through that on his or her own.)[46]

Lakatos built on the falsificationist method but argued that "any scientific theory has to be appraised together with its auxiliary hypotheses, initial conditions, etc., and especially together with its predecessors so that we may see what sort of change was brought about. Then of course, what we appraise is a series of theories rather than isolated theories."[47] This notion of a series of theories, or the research program, is a hallmark of Lakatos's thought, and with it he introduces a historical character to the evaluation of science. This historical character is evident in his rules for determining the acceptability and the status of a scientific theory.

To Lakatos, a theory is scientifically acceptable if it has corroborated empirical content in excess of its predecessor or rival, that is, if it leads to the discovery of novel facts. A theory (T) is falsified if and only if another theory (T') has been proposed with the following characteristics: (1) T' has excess empirical content over T, in that it predicts facts that are novel, improbable, or forbidden in light of T; (2) T' explains the previous success of T, and the unrefuted content of T is included (within the limits of observational error) in the content of T'; and (3) some of the excess content of T' is corroborated.[48]

Returning to an example in human development, if a learning theory (or series of them) is proposed that accounts for or explains in its own terms all the empirical and theoretical success of a stage/structuralist theory and, in addition, continues to generate and explain new knowledge, then that learning theory will have superceded the stage theory. However, since any program consists of numerous assumptions or theories, this process of elimination can take a considerable amount of time. The point is that the Piagetian and learning programs are made up of many hard-core assumptions and protective theories; hence, no single experiment or series of them can dismantle either program, and a challenging program must appear and meet the Lakatosian criteria.

From this cursory examination of Lakatos's adjustments to Popperian thought, it can be seen that Lakatos's falsificationism strives for absolute prescriptions for all science and, with the notion of the research program, introduces a historical character to the evaluation of scientific theories, that is, a historical rationality as opposed to a Popperian instant rationality. In sum, Lakatos provides a solution to the issues of science as epistemology and to the evaluation of scientific theories. Given the historical nature of his solution, however, another problem arises. When does the practicing scientist stop working on a degenerating series of theories (i.e., one that no longer anticipates or explains novel facts)?

Lakatos himself admits that luck or ingenuity can turn a degenerating program into a generating one.[49] But when does the scientist stop being ingenious or stop waiting for luck? The only answer seems to be when he or she runs out of steam, not when a certain number of experiments or empirical tests fail, for, given the historical nature of Lakatos's criteria, no such number can be generated. Instead, it is when he or she is no longer able to face the prospect of deciding between problematic theories or problematic facts. This may seem to be a flaw in Lakatos's argument, but this is the point at which the scientist as a decision maker must intercede, and Lakatos's criteria are a guiding framework for these decisions. Still, it is clear that the decisions must be made in a theoretical context, that is, the context of many theories.

HEINEMAN AND BEYOND

Returning to Heineman's argument, her prescription for an undogmatic approach (methodological pluralism) to measurement and design seems warranted. As she states, "[R]ather than prescribe a single acceptable methodology in a quixotic attempt to eliminate bias researchers will embrace different theories, methodologies, levels of focus (micro or macro), and kinds of data and data gathering."[50] This is similar to Lakatos's proposition stating that "the honesty of sophisticated falsificationism demands that one should try to look at things from different points of view, to put forward new theories which anticipate novel facts, and to reject theories which have been superceded by more powerful ones."[51]

However, Heineman's lengthy explication of the scientist's inability to remove bias (or theory ladenness) from their observations is not the central issue. Positivism does presume a resolution to this issue that is no longer tenable, but Heineman's rejection of absolute prescriptions for all science because of the impossibility of removing bias from scientific measurement is fallacious. Moreover, she promotes a solution to this prescriptive dilemma—elitism—that is not presented in a lucid perspective. In fact, to reject absolute prescriptions for all science and also to argue for the existence of scientific progress (some theories are better than others) is to posit an elitist position. Yet Heineman states that the central thesis of her article is that "the social work profession allows certain researchers to use discredited scientific criteria to prescribe or restrict research questions, data, or methods which other social workers believe will significantly enhance the knowledge base and clinical tools of social work."[52] If her central thesis is as antielitist as it seems to be, she contradicts herself. Perhaps it is a changing of the guard that she is advocating and not a new castle. If this is the case, she must address herself to the skepticism that is implicit in her argument so that she can convince her critics that she is not dismantling rationality in science altogether.

She is correct, however, that all scientists are decision makers. But these decisions are made within a theoretical context that is rationally assailable via rules, however slowly they are evolving. As has been shown, Lakatos provides such a set of rules that does not assume a bias-free science and that does not retreat to epistemological skepticism or irrationality in science.

RECOMMENDATIONS

It is the position of this paper that social work has been and still is in the grip of a crippling epistemological dogma that is no longer tenable. We need to learn from the debate over these issues that is prevalent in other disciplines. In developmental psychology, for example, questions that involve determinism and the unity of science are being intensively considered.[53] It is only by participating in or becoming informed by these discussions that we will be able to make reasonable theoretical and methodological judgments and to address the issues of central importance to our discipline. To bury our heads in philosophical disgust or fear is to invite the grip of dogma and to limit needlessly the potential of social work as a knowledge-building and knowledge-testing endeavor.

Furthermore, even given that Heineman is right in arguing that science may not be able to promise bias-free results, it is far too early to close the issue of scientific realism[54] or to abandon the effort to formulate prescriptive rules for science as an epistemological endeavor (or, worse, to retrench ourselves in positivism, as Hudson advocates).[55] On the basis of the present analysis, the following recommendations are offered.

1.   Research education in social work ought to encourage a reasoned approach to the breadth of questions and thought that exists on the issues of knowledge building and testing in science. If we are to encourage consumption and production of knowledge, the emphasis should be on addressing the issues, not on assuring allegiance to outmoded approaches to science.

2.   An atheoretical approach to science is untenable. To suggest that the collection of theory-free (sometimes called "hard" or empiricist) data will allow us to construct or to use the most correct theory is to assume resolution of issues that are tenacious in their resistance to solution. A greater mistake, however, is to meet the existing controversies by skirting theoretical issues altogether and assuming that, if enough data is collected, the problem will disappear. One solution is to use a clearly delineated theoretical model when collecting and analyzing data and multitheoretical approaches in assessing the adequacy of the approach and of the data collected.

3.   The notion of eclecticism needs to be reconsidered. In fact, one can argue that eclecticism rests on a faulty assumption: that there is one world (reality) and many lenses (theories) to use; hence, one just picks and mixes. From the present discussion it is clear that theories define or determine the world that we observe. Therefore, it is not possible, for example, to understand and assess clinical phenomena psychoanalytically and then treat them behaviorally. If one wants to treat behaviorally, one must do a behavioral assessment, that is, define the problem in theoretically rele-

vant terms and utilize treatment mechanisms that reflect the theoretical understanding of the problem. In research as well, one does not define a problem in one theoretical language and then explain it in another. Clearly, different lenses can and ought to be used, but, when they are, we must understand that the problems will be defined differently and that our understanding of causes and effects will also change.

4. More than a multitheoretical perspective is required. A metatheoretical approach is needed to examine the presuppositions (the metaphysics) of our theories. Pepper has outlined such a categorization of metaphysical theories, or world hypotheses.[56] It is only through such examinations that social work researchers will be able to determine rationally the limitations of and needs for relevant data collection procedures and theoretical development. Data and design decisions should be made on the basis of clear knowledge of what our research questions imply, not on a priori notions of which data are acceptable. For example, the person-environment paradigm in social work raises profound methodological and theoretical issues that have been addressed for some time in the literature of the psychology of personality and of developmental psychology.[57] It should not be assumed on the basis of this literature that qualitative, contextualistic, organismic, or dialectical approaches have no legitimate position within our discipline. It is only by thoroughly examining the presuppositions of our research that we can reasonably assess our research questions and the methodological and theoretical dilemmas they contain.

5. The above theoretical approach to decision making must also be extended to the arena of statistical significance testing. This dilemma has been discussed in psychology and sociology,[58] and a solution to the failings of the point-null-hypothesis test has been suggested by Serlin.[59] The procedure incorporates a calculation of significance levels based on theoretical estimates of effect size and represents a profound advance in the use of statistics and knowledge testing for social scientists.

6. It should not be assumed that the present discussion has implied a rationale for less rigorous approaches to social work research. To the contrary, the approach suggested implies that empirical rigor must not be forsaken but that this rigor must be based on and extended to an examination of the theoretical and suppositional roots of our research rather than simply of the methodologies used. Clearly, positivistic notions of rigor have failed and do not merit the status of certainty or completeness.

7. Finally, the philosophy of science must be recognized as a legitimate and critical arena wherein complex issues will continue to be discussed and wherein progress can and will be made. Contrary to Schuerman's and Hudson's contentions, philosophers of science are not the creators of the muddle; they are necessary to make us confront what we as scientists often are unwilling or unable to examine.

NOTES

1. Herbert Bisno and Allan Boroski, "The Social and Psychological Context of Research," in *Social Work Research and Evaluation*, ed. R. Grinnell (Itasca, Ill.: F. E. Peacock Publishers, 1985), pp. 83–101.

2. Martha B. Heineman, "The Obsolete Scientific Imperative in Social Work Research," *Social Service Review* 55 (September 1981): 371–95.

3. See John R. Schuerman, "Debate with Authors: The Scientific Imperative in Social Work Research," *Social Service Review* 56 (March 1982): 144–46; Mary G. Gyarfas, "Debate with Authors: The Scientific Imperative Again," *Social Service Review* 57 (March 1983): 149–50; and Walter H. Hudson, "Scientific Imperatives in Social Work Research and Practice," *Social Service Review* 56 (June 1982): 246–58.

4. Imre Lakatos, "Falsification and the Methodology of Scientific Research Programmes," in *Philosophical Papers: The Methodology of Scientific Research Programmes, Vol. 1*, ed. John Worral and Gregory Currie (New York: Cambridge University Press, 1980), pp. 8–101; and Karl R. Popper, *Objective Knowledge* (Oxford: Clarendon Press, 1972).

5. Paul Feyerabend, *Against Method* (London: Trowbridge and Esher, 1975); Thomas Kuhn, *The Structure of Scientific Revolutions* (Chicago: University of Chicago Press, 1970).

6. Not covered will be the work of Larry Laudan, *Progress and Its Problems* (Berkeley: University of California Press, 1977) and *Science and Values* (Berkeley and Los Angeles: University of California Press, 1984). In many ways, he is within the intellectual tradition of Popper and Lakatos, and, while presenting his ideas would make this analysis more complete, it would not alter its major premises.

7. Lakatos, "Falsification and the Methodology of Scientific Research Programmes," pp. 8–101.

8. Schuerman, p. 145.

9. Lakatos, "Falsification and the Methodology of Scientific Research Programmes," pp. 8–101.

10. Harold I. Brown, *Perception, Theory and Commitment* (Chicago: University of Chicago Press, 1979), pp. 13–51.

11. Heineman, p. 387.

12. Brown, pp. 21–23.

13. Lakatos, "Falsification and the Methodology of Scientific Research Programmes," pp. 102–38.

14. Heineman, p. 391.

15. Ibid.

16. Ibid.

17. Imre Lakatos, "The Problem of Appraising Scientific Theories: Three Approaches," in *Philosophical Papers: Mathematics, Science and Epistemology, Vol. 2*, ed. John Worral and Gregory Currie (New York: Cambridge University Press, 1980), pp. 107–20.

18. Roberta Wells Imre, "The Nature of Knowledge in Social Work," *Social Work* 29, no. 1 (January/February 1984): 41–46.

19. For a detailed discussion of the failings of logical positivism and empiricism, see Brown, pp. 15–76.

20. Herbert Fiegl, "The Orthodox View of Theories," in *Minnesota Studies in the Philosophy of Science*, ed. Michael Radner and Stephen Winokur (University of Minnesota Press, 1970).

21. Lakatos, "Falsification and the Methodology of Scientific Research Programmes" (n. 4 above).

22. Ibid., pp. 8–101.

23. Ibid., pp. 12–20.

24. Lakatos, "The Problem of Appraising Scientific Approaches," pp. 107–20.

25. Feyerabend (n. 5 above), p. 17.

26. Karl R. Popper and John C. Eccles, *The Self and Its Brain* (New York: Springer International, 1981), pp. 36–50.

27. Lakatos, "The Problem of Appraising Scientific Approaches," (n. 17 above), pp. 109–11; Tom Settle, "Comments on Farr's Paper (III): Is Popper's World 3 an Ontological Extravagance?" *Philosophy of the Social Sciences* 13 (June 1983): 195–202.

28. Lakatos, "The Problem of Appraising Scientific Approaches" (n. 17 above), p. 109.

29. Lakatos, "Falsification and the Methodology of Scientific Research Programmes" (n. 4 above).

30. Lakatos, "The Problem of Appraising Scientific Approaches" (n. 17 above), pp. 111–12.

31. Ibid., p. 119.

32. Lakatos, "Falsification and the Methodology of Scientific Research Programmes" (n. 4 above), p. 33.

33. Ibid., p. 156.

34. Ibid.

35. Ibid., pp. 154–67.

36. Mario Bunge, *Method, Model and Matter* (Cambridge, Mass.: Harvard University Press, 1973), pp. 27–43.

37. Jonas Langer, *Theories of Development* (New York: Holt, Rinehart & Winston, 1969).

38. Ibid., pp. 148–56.

39. For the Piagetians this protective belt is evidenced in the work of Werner, Chomsky, and Kohlberg, and, for the learning theorists, in the work of Bijou, Berlyne, and Baer.

40. Lakatos, "Falsification and the Methodology of Scientific Research Programmes" (n. 4 above), p. 156.

41. D. Magnusson and N. Endler, *Personality at the Crossroads: Current Issues in Interactional Psychology* (New York: Lawrence Erlbaum Associates, 1977); Barry Gholson and Peter Barker, "Kuhn, Lakatos, and Laudan: Applications in the History of Physics and Psychology," *American Psychologist* 66 (July 1985): 755–69.

42. Stephen Pepper, *World Hypotheses* (Berkeley: University of California Press, 1970).

43. W. F. Overton and H. W. Reese, "Models of Development: Methodological Implications," in *Lifespan Developmental Psychology: Methodological Issues*, ed. J. R. Nesselroade and H. W. Reese (New York: Academic Press, 1972), pp. 65–86.

44. W. V. O. Quine, *From a Logical Point of View* (Cambridge, Mass.: Harvard University Press, 1953).

45. Lakatos, "Falsification and the Methodology of Scientific Research Programmes" (n. 4 above), p. 22.

46. Popper (n. 4 above), secs. 19–20.

47. Lakatos, "Falsification and the Methodology of Scientific Research Programmes" (n. 4 above), p. 33.

48. Ibid., p. 32.

49. Ibid., p. 99.

50. Heineman (n. 2 above), p. 391.

51. Lakatos, "Falsification and the Methodology of Scientific Research Programmes" (n. 4 above), p. 37.

52. Martha B. Heineman, "Author's Reply," *Social Service Review* 56 (March 1982): 147.

53. Dale B. Harris, "Problems in Formulating a Scientific Concept of Development," in *The Concept of Development*, ed. Dale B. Harris (Minneapolis: University of Minnesota Press, 1978).

54. Geoffrey Hellman, "Realist Principles," *Philosophy of Science* 50 (1983): 227–49.

55. Hudson (n. 3 above).

56. Pepper (n. 42 above).

57. Harris; Langer (n. 37 above); Overton and Reese (n. 43 above); and Magnusson and Endler (n. 41 above).

58. See D. Bakan, "The Test of Significance in Psychological Research," *Psychological Bulletin* 66 (1966): 423–37; D. Lykken, "Statistical Significance in Psychological Research," *Psychological Bulletin* 70 (1968): 151–59; and Paul Meehl, "Theoretical Risks and Tabular Asterisks," *Journal of Consulting and Clinical Psychology* 46 (1978): 806–34.

59. Ronald Serlin and Daniel Lapsley, "Rationality in Psychological Research: The Good-enough Principle," *American Psychologist* 40 (January 1985): 73–84.

Debate with Authors

COMMENTS ON "SCIENTIFIC IMPERATIVES IN SOCIAL WORK RESEARCH: PLURALISM IS NOT SKEPTICISM"

Martha Heineman Pieper   *Chicago, Illinois*

I am quite perplexed by John Brekke's article "Scientific Imperatives in Social Work Research: Pluralism Is Not Skepticism" (*Social Service Review* 60 [December 1986]: 539–44), which is largely an attempt to critique an earlier article I published, "The Obsolete Scientific Imperative in Social Work Research" (*Social Service Review* 55 [September 1981]: 371–95). To begin, while Brekke's premise is that he disagrees with me (see his abstract), six out of seven of his final recommendations are completely consonant with the conclusions I reach in my article (a fact he never mentions). Further, the criticisms Brekke does make consist of setting up a straw person and then demolishing it, an exercise I fail to understand given the plethora of fascinating and crucial issues in the philosophy of research that await serious discussion.

Brekke's criticisms of my article are based on various types of faulty reasoning. For example, (1) he asserts that I took positions I never adopted; (2) he redefines philosophical terms idiosyncratically, inaccurately labels my views on that basis, and then criticizes the position represented by the labels; (3) he incorrectly extrapolates what I did say and attacks the extrapolations; (4) he never discusses the points I

make in my article that bear on his critique; and, (5) most amazingly, he complains that I did not write a different article.

An example of the last point is Brekke's criticism that I spend too much time discussing issues of measurement and that I truncate the presentation of alternatives to the logical empiricist philosophy of science (p. 540).* Six years ago, when my article was published, the prevailing philosophy of research in social work was logical empiricism. This outmoded view was severely restricting research design and data gathering and, in consequence, was severely limiting the breadth of articles accepted by the leading social work journals, the diversity of dissertations accepted by social work schools, and the research being done by practitioners. Furthermore, no significant discussion of the logical empiricist assumptions underlying the prevailing ideal of social work research had ever been published in a social work journal. Therefore, my article necessarily focused on an exegesis and critique of logical empiricist assumptions and only secondarily attempted to present alternatives. I devoted much more space to alternatives to the logical empiricist

---

Source: "Comments on 'Scientific Imperatives in Social Work Research: Pluralism Is Not Skepticism'" by M. Heineman Pieper, 1987, *Social Service Review, 61*, pp. 368–370. Copyright 1987 by The University of Chicago. Reprinted by permission.
Social Service Review (1987). © 1987 by The University of Chicago.
*Editor's Note: p. 162 in this volume.

approach to research in a subsequent article published in December 1985,[1] to which Brekke never refers. Using a very peculiar logic, Brekke concludes from the fact that, in my 1981 article, there was no space for a thorough discussion of alternatives; that, therefore, I offered "undeveloped prescriptions for science"; and that, in consequence, I left "the impression that all imperatives are obsolete, unattainable, or unscientific" and that "science has failed as an epistemology, a view based largely on a misunderstanding of recent development in the philosophy of science" (p. 542).* Interestingly, one of the two people Brekke cites as representative of recent developments in the philosophy of science, which he says I misunderstand, is Popper, whose work on falsification is in fact not recent at all. Also, although in my 1981 article I offer a critique of Popper's program for theory construction and evaluation, Brekke fails to mention or discuss this critique.

A good example of Brekke's idiosyncratic use of philosophical terms to incorrectly label my position is his definition of the term "realism." He says that I offer a "premature rejection of the notion of scientific realism," which he defines as "the attempt to understand reality correctly" (p. 539).** However, realism is most commonly defined as the view that the objects of knowledge exist independently of our awareness. By this definition I am most certainly a realist. I have never seen any definition of realism that corresponds to Brekke's statement that in order to qualify as a realist one has to believe one can get to a *correct* view of external reality. Thus, rather than discuss what I did say, Brekke labels my thinking incorrectly (as antirealist) and then proceeds to attack the position represented by his label.

Brekke compounds this specious reasoning by asserting that, since by his definition I am not a realist, it follows that (1) I do not believe there is any rational means to approach the aims of positivism, (2) I think there is no way to evaluate the correctness of scientific knowledge, and (3) I think there is no way to demarcate science from religion (p. 539). This reasoning is so absurd that it is almost impossible to untangle. Rather than try, I merely state what was clear in my article, namely, (1) that I believe there is a world to be understood apart from my mind, (2) that I believe in rational approaches to knowledge building and evaluation, and (3) that I believe science and religion can be distinguished. For example, I say "rather than prescribe a single acceptable methodology in a quixotic attempt to eliminate bias, researchers will embrace different theories, methodologies, levels of focus (macro and micro), and kinds of data and data gathering. This will reduce inevitable bias by rotating the perspective on the system under investigation."[2] Brekke never bothers to discuss the rational approaches to knowledge building and evaluation that I suggest as interesting avenues for exploration, all of which concentrate on ways of trying to understand, reduce, and account for inevitable bias. Brekke does not seem to realize that recognizing and accounting for bias is not the same as disparaging rationality or embracing a transcendental approach to science. Some of the rational approaches to bias reduction I cited are Herbert Simon's concept of heuristics, Levins' search for robust theories, and Wimsatt's multilevel reduction analysis. Brekke never discusses any of these alternatives to the logical empiricist approach. Rather, he perversely concludes that "Heineman instructs scientists to be decision makers but not to concern themselves with the correctness of their explanations or predictions—only with whether they are better explanations or predictions. . . . Perhaps Heineman is advocating that we cease making metatheoretical discussion altogether and free the scientist's decision making from rational scrutiny" (p. 541).*** It is clearly illogical to take my (by now mundane) statement that some bias is inevitable in scientific activity and conclude that I am saying that scientific activity should be immune from rational scrutiny. In fact, the entire purpose of my article is rational scrutiny of scientific decision making. One important source of Brekke's confusion seems to be his failure to distinguish between (1) the position that there are *no* workable rules for arriving at absolute truth and, therefore, that a normative approach to science is restrictive without being heuristic and (2) the position that there *are* rational rules (in the sense of guidelines) that can help reduce bias and, therefore, lead to a closer approximation of relevant truths. It is his failure to understand this distinction that leads Brekke to say over and over that I "dismiss" or "reject" rational approaches to the construction and evaluation of scientific theories.

The most astounding instance of Brekke's asserting that I adopted a stance I never took and then criticizing me for it is embodied in his subtitle "Pluralism Is Not Skepticism." He says that my argument for methodological pluralism is "a serious error, for one

---

*Editor's Note: p. 163 in this volume.
**Editor's Note: p. 162 in this volume.

***Editor's Note: pp. 162-163 in this volume.

must not conflate arguments for methodological pluralism with arguments for epistemological skepticism, which is the position that science can be no more correct in its understanding of reality than can any other system of knowledge and that there are no rules for assailing [sic] the progress of scientific knowledge. It appears that in advocating methodological pluralism Heineman has taken a position of epistemological skepticism" (p. 541).* It is clearly specious to maintain that methodological pluralism cannot exist without epistemological skepticism and that, if one believes that absolute truth is an unattainable goal, one is an epistemological skeptic. Similarly, Brekke says that "Heineman fails to appreciate" the distinction between the theory ladenness of perception and skepticism (p. 545).** Since I nowhere advocate or endorse skepticism, it is hard to understand the source of Brekke's comments unless, of course, he believes that anyone whose view of science is different from his is a skeptic. Brekke's article would have been much more logical and productive if he had discussed what I actually said.

In summary, Brekke's article seems to consist mainly of mislabeling my arguments and then attacking the position represented by the label he has incorrectly attached. Nowhere does he seriously address the issues I raised, the alternatives I suggested, or the position I really adopted. This failure is unfortunate because a genuine, fruitful dialogue on the fundamental issues relevant to the philosophy of research is both possible and desirable.

NOTES

1. Martha Heineman Pieper, "The Future of Social Work Research," *Social Work Research and Abstracts* 21 (Winter 1985): 3–11.
2. Martha Heineman [Pieper], "The Obsolete Scientific Imperative in Social Work Research," *Social Service Review* 55 (September 1981): 391.

AUTHOR'S REPLY

JOHN S. BREKKE   *University of Southern California*

Heineman Pieper's response to my critique states that my arguments and reasoning are specious, absurd, idiosyncratic, and, worst of all, perverse. In the spirit of genuine and fruitful dialogue I shall respond to these charges in turn.

First, I do not "complain" that Heineman Pieper spends too little time discussing alternatives to a positivist philosophy of science. It was her choice to make a limited presentation—it will be judged, nonetheless, on its coherence and accuracy. Second, I acknowledge the lucidity of her presentation on the failings of positivism. Third, it was not my logic that led to confusions in Heineman Pieper's positions, as I will now discuss.

Concerning the charge of idiosyncrasy in my definition of scientific realism, I offer two of the mainstream definitions that Heineman Pieper may not have seen:

"By 'scientific realism' philosophers ordinarily mean the doctrine that non-observable terms in scientific theories should typically be interpreted as putative referring expressions, and that when the semantics of theories is understood that way ("realistically"), scientific theories embody the sorts of propositions whose (approximate) truth can be confirmed by the ordinary experimental methods which scientists employ."[1]

"Realists propose that there is a relation between the observational and theoretical vocabulary that is strong enough to support ontological claims using that theoretical vocabulary."[2]

My definition does not differ from these. In fact, while Heineman Pieper offers no references, I have not found a definition of scientific realism that does not in some way discuss the relation between epistemology and ontology as an essential feature. A moment's thought will suggest the foolishness of being essentially concerned with a world separate from our perception of it if our best models of knowledge cannot capture it more and more correctly over time. Why, then, not be a skeptic? There are, of course, sometimes great variations in the positions of scientific realists, from the metaphysical brand of Lakatos or Boyd to a brand that equates epistemology and ontology in the work of Hilary Putnam. However, they are all concerned with science as a truth producing or approximating endeavor, and truth by most definitions is correct. As I

---

*Editor's Note: p. 163 in this volume.
**Editor's Note: p. 165 in this volume.

Source: "Author's Reply" by J. S. Brekke, 1987, *Social Service Review,* 61, pp. 370–373. Copyright 1987 by The University of Chicago. Reprinted by permission.

pointed out, Heineman argues against the concern with the correctness of science. As such, my criticism of her position as implicitly antirealist stands.

Concerning her suggestion that I should have read her second article before writing my critique, her second article was not available before I submitted my critique for publication. But, having since read it, I would have changed none of my main points. In fact, Mullen's thoughtful review of her second piece raises many of the same issues I do.[3] Further, I assume we must all be accountable for what we write.

Concerning my failure to comment on her paragraph discussing a flaw in Popper's falsificationist method, Brown makes a similar argument,[4] and it is a good one. Lakatos's brand of falsificationism is an attempt to correct this flaw, and the jury is out as to whether he succeeded. And, yes, some of my recommendations concur with Heineman Pieper's. We are, after all, arguing against the same philosophy. However, the bulk of my analysis illustrates that we are arguing for very different positions. Also, I did not comment on the notions of Simon, Wimsatt, and Levins because I was less concerned with them than I was with Heineman Pieper's characterization of them and with her misrepresentation of the contemporary philosophy of science in general.

On the charges of speciousness and absurdity, I suppose that other thoughtful readers will have to judge. However, I do not argue that, because Heineman Pieper's position is antirealist on an essential concern, she therefore disparages rationality, truthfulness, or demarcationism. Heineman Pieper openly disparages correctness as a criterion for evaluating science (even though her response now indicates that her original statement was mundane). It is her antirealism in combination with her position that the criterion for evaluating science should be conceptualized nonnormatively that results in my characterization of her position as skepticism. Her lambasting of my reasoning is puzzling since she describes her own position as one of "hopeful relativism."[5] But hope is not enough to turn a relativist into a nonskeptic.

I am pleased, however, that Heineman Pieper now states that she believes in a world separate from her perception, in rational approaches to knowledge building and evaluation, and also in demarcationism. These are critical issues, but these positions cannot be found in her article. An essential issue here, as I argue, concerns the criteria that should be used in evaluating the epistemological character and progress of scientific knowledge. Mullen raises the same issue with regard to Heineman's second, more developed analysis. Perhaps it is the term "rational" that is at issue, and it is a fascinating one.[6] My position on that is clear as well. Rationality in science does imply rules, and rational rules are normative. Lakatos's rules are seen as belonging to a body of internally consistent and logically valid inference that is not subject to the whims of taste or personal preference—or, as he puts it, the vagaries of mob psychology—to establish their verity. In her article Heineman Pieper is clear: our criteria should not be normative and should remain unconcerned with the correctness of scientific knowledge. This, as anyone slices it, is skepticism and is instrumentalistic.

Again the issue of removing bias from our measurement or modeling strategies is not the essential issue. As I argue, the more central concern is what we are left with after we have employed these strategies and how to evaluate it. Perhaps Heineman Pieper advocates the "sociology of knowledge" position in the philosophy of science[7]; it is difficult to tell. But the issue of whether the sociology of knowledge is skepticism raises extremely interesting issues,[8] none of which has yet been discussed.

Concerning the two positions that Heineman Pieper argues I have failed to distinguish, my argument throughout is that she embraces the first position and dismisses the second. I see nothing in her response to challenge this argument other than her own vitriolic testimonial. Furthermore, I show that Lakatos provides a position that is normative, rational, accepts the theory ladenness of perception, and is pluralistic and heuristic. (There are, of course, arguments about the consistency and usefulness of Lakatos's position, and I hope this discussion continues.)

Heineman Pieper was most astounded by "my" argument that pluralism cannot exist without skepticism. I do not know where she read this, for a central thesis of my article is that the two positions are distinct and that one in no way implies the other. If Heineman Pieper had finished reading the sentence that she quotes only half of, she would have seen one example of this.

Finally, if Heineman Pieper has discovered rational criteria for evaluating scientific knowledge that are nonnormative and that are also nonskeptical, I do not find them in either of her articles. It is not perverse to be a skeptic. It is, however, seriously misleading to be a skeptic (or an elitist) in realist's clothing. We could also summarily dismiss these issues as meaningless, but I agree with Scriven, who states that we do so at our own peril.[9]

In sum, I did not create a straw person for demolition or extrapolate positions that were not evident in Heineman Pieper's analysis. I would submit that her discussion and the positions she explicitly or implicitly takes were contradictory and misleading on crucial issues in the philosophy of science. In any case, my hope is that we will all stand to be corrected by a long and meaningful dialogue on these issues in social work.

NOTES

1. Richard Boyd, "Scientific Realism and Naturalistic Epistemology," vol. 2 (East Lansing, Mich.: Philosophy of Science Association, 1980). For a more detailed explication, see Richard Boyd, "On the Current Status of the Issue of Scientific Realism," *Erkenntnis* (May 1983), pp. 45–90.

2. Barry Gholson and Peter Barker, "Kuhn, Lakatos and Laudan: Applications in the History of Psychology and Physics," *American Psychologist* (July 1985), pp. 755–69.

3. E. J. Mullen, "Methodological Dilemmas in Social Work Research," *Social Work Research and Abstracts* (December 1985), pp. 12–21.

4. Harold I. Brown, *Perception, Theory and Commitment* (Chicago: University of Chicago Press, 1979), pp. 67–76.

5. Martha Brunswick Heineman [Pieper], "Author's Reply," *Social Service Review* 56 (March 1982): 147.

6. See, e.g., A. Lugg, "Explaining Scientific Beliefs: The Rationalist's Strategy Reexamined," *Philosophy of the Social Sciences* (March 1982), pp. 71–75.

7. See, e.g., John Wettersten, "The Sociology of Knowledge vs. the Sociology of Science: A Conundrum and an Alternative," *Philosophy of the Social Sciences* (September 1983): 325–35; W. Schmaus, "Reasons, Causes, and the 'Strong Programme' in the Sociology of Knowledge," *Philosophy of the Social Sciences* (June 1985), pp. 189–97; R. Morrow, "The Sociology of Knowledge Dispute Revisited: Implications of a Failed Theoretical Debate," *Philosophy of the Social Sciences* (December 1985), pp. 507–13.

8. Paul Tibbetts, "The Sociology of Scientific Knowledge: The Constructivist Thesis and Relativism," *Philosophy of the Social Sciences* (May 1985), pp. 39–59.

9. Michael Scriven, "Evaluation Ideologies," in *Evaluation Models: Viewpoints on Educational and Human Services Evaluation*, ed. G. F. Madaus et al. (New York: Kluwer-Nijhoff Publishing, 1983).

Introduction to "Research Paradigms in Social Work: From Stalemate to Creative Synthesis"

In this essay, Peile begins by describing the "empiricist" and "normative" viewpoints, which he regards as the opposing sides in the ongoing debate about a philosophy of research for the field of social work. He believes the debate is currently in a "stalemate" and that a synthesis of metatheories can potentially lead to a new direction for social work knowledge. He offers three potential syntheses: the "critical paradigm," the "new paradigm research approach," and his preferred synthesis, the "creative paradigm." In her responses to Peile, Heineman Pieper agrees that a unifying metatheory is needed, but she emphasizes that Peile's description of the heuristic paradigm is inaccurate, that Peile's subsumption of the heuristic paradigm under "normativism" misrepresents the heuristic paradigm, and that the heuristic paradigm responds to the field of social work's need for a unifying approach to research.

One of Peile's most fundamental assumptions is that all the ideas proposed for a metatheory of social work research should be preserved and then synthesized. Peile's proposal for resolving the debate about an approach to social work research is similar to Gyarfas's proposal in responding to Schuerman in 1983 and reflects a common response to conflict. Peile suggests that the conflict is unfounded and recommends that the opposing sides unite. Peile says, "It is the search for these unifying features, to connect what appears disconnected, that is the basis of my approach" (1988a, p. 708).* Peile, however, overlooks the most important regulatory principle of the heuristic paradigm—that logical positivism's prescriptive and proscriptive approach to generating knowledge is unwarranted. Because the belief that prescriptions and proscriptions will generate better scientific knowledge no longer holds up under scrutiny, social workers and behavioral scientists have no basis for preserving the restrictiveness of the logical positivist metatheory. In short, Peile assumes that all the ideas inherent in the metatheories he presents are worth keeping. A more fundamental issue, however, is to consider which ideas are worth keeping in a metatheory of research, and why.

Peile's "Author's Reply" to Heineman Pieper once again raises the question of how the heuristic paradigm offers a unifying metatheory. When Heineman Pieper describes the heuristic paradigm as unifying, she is not referring to a synthesis of positivist and postpositivist metatheories. The heuristic paradigm is unifying because it offers a nonrestrictive, up-to-date metatheory of scientific knowledge that resolves many contemporary dilemmas in generating social and behavioral knowledge. To illustrate, the heuristic paradigm does not proscribe the ontological or epistemological assumptions of any theory, so practitioners using diverse clinical theories can use the heuristic paradigm. Because the heuristic paradigm does not privilege any one research method, those who prefer qualitative methods of data gathering and analysis as well as those who prefer quantified data and ways of analyzing quantified data can use the heuristic paradigm. Heineman Pieper emphasizes that the

---

*Editor's Note: p. 190 in this volume.

heuristic paradigm "is in opposition to no rational methodology, but only to an inauthentically restrictive and outmoded ontology and epistemology" (1988, p. 536).*

Peile regards the debates about a philosophy of research for the field of social work as highly political. He recognizes that positivism's "value-free stance implicitly supports the dominations of the established order" (see Peile's Table 2). Peile, however, misreads the heuristic paradigm; he groups it under the "normative" approach and assumes that the researcher who uses the heuristic paradigm manifests "disinterest in ethical issues or anarchistic individualism" (p. 7).**

Heineman Pieper, however, has emphasized consistently that the heuristic paradigm offers social workers a way to generate scientific knowledge that is founded on and compatible with the humanistic values of the social work profession, including advocacy. Researchers who adopt the heuristic paradigm can recognize that discourse shapes the conceptualization and creation of society (see also Bhaskar, 1989b, 1991; Hartman, 1991; Levins & Lewontin, 1985; Richardson, 1984; Shapiro, 1982). The ideas in a metatheory of research guide the development of scientific knowledge and have significant effects on human lives (see also Bricker-Jenkins & Hooyman, 1986; Fee, 1983; Hartman, 1991; Messing, 1983; Outhwaite, 1987). Women, members of ethnic and racial minority groups, and gays and lesbians have increasingly described how social and behavioral research that developed under the dominance of positivism has incorporated and disseminated oppressive ideologies based on race, class, gender, and sexual preference (Bernard, 1973; Billingsley, 1970; Bricker-Jenkins & Hooyman, 1986; L. Davis, 1986; Hartman, 1991; Hill, 1980; MacKinnon, 1985; Reinharz, 1992; Stanley & Wise, 1983; see also Bronfenbrenner, 1979a; Reisch, 1986). Increasing our awareness of how scientific knowledge both is informed by and also influences political aims can help us to recognize the sociopolitical consequences of the choices we make in designing research (Garvin & Reed, 1983; Richardson, 1984; Star, 1979; Suzuki, 1986). Finally, following Roy Bhaskar, a researcher adopting the heuristic paradigm can aim to ask,

> to what extent are enduring structures being reproduced in novel forms and to what extent are they being transformed? "Reality" must be "reclaimed" in two senses. First, the concept must be reclaimed from philosophical ideologies which usurped or denied it—reclamation in the sense of lost property. Second, reality itself must be rescued from the effects of those ideologies that have, like stagnant and muddy water, covered it up—reclamation in the sense of land reclamation. What should be done with reality once it is reclaimed? It should, I suggest, be used, nurtured and valued in an ecologically sustainable and humane way for human emancipation, happiness, and flourishing. (1991, p. 144)

KEY TERMS

Ideology   Normative

DISCUSSION QUESTIONS

1. What does Peile's combination of "empiricism, positivist or scientific" imply about how Peile defines "scientific"?

---

*Editor's Note: p. 190 in this volume.
**Editor's Note: p. 183 in this volume.

2. Peile implies that only the supporters of a logical empiricist approach to research regard observation as "a sound basis for research." Is that an accurate reading of the tenets of the heuristic paradigm?

3. Peile says that the trend in social work research at the time (1988b) was toward a "pragmatic" definition of empiricism that responds to the problem of bias in observation by "standardizing research procedures and avoiding constructs that cannot be operationalized and measured." Do you agree with Peile that such a response is "pragmatic"? Why or why not?

4. What are the attributes that Peile ascribes to the "empiricist" view that Heineman Pieper includes in the heuristic paradigm?

5. What are some of the political consequences of a profession's choice of a philosophy of research?

6. Peile says that "relativism is certainly one of the paradigmatic assumptions that can provide a basis for the sort of synthesis she [Heineman Pieper] advocates." How is Heineman Pieper not a relativist?

7. Find the articles in *Social Casework*, cited in Peile's article, in which Ruckdeschel and Farris (1982) and Geismar and Wood (1982) debate the merits of the positivist approach to single-case design and an alternative, postpositivist approach to the qualitative case study. Summarize the points of view represented by both positions. Is it possible to synthesize them and still accurately represent each one? If so, how? If not, why not?

Research Paradigms in Social Work: From Stalemate to Creative Synthesis

COLIN PEILE   *Queensland, Australia*

ABSTRACT: For the last 5 years, four American journals have been the venue for a vigorous debate concerning the appropriate research method for social work. The issues underlying the debate extend well beyond methodology and reflect a broader paradigmatic debate between empiricism and normativism. This debate is extremely important to the future direction of the profession. While the debate remains unresolved in these journals, some movement toward constructive syntheses is possible. Three syntheses are briefly discussed. They are the critical, new paradigm, and creative paradigms.

There is considerable agreement among social work writers that there is a significant trend toward an empirical, positivist, or scientific approach in social work research.[1] The question whether this trend benefits social work has been the focus of a heated debate between the supporters of the empirical and normativist paradigms. The purpose of this article is not to rekindle the conflict but rather to try to understand the issues that lie behind the debate, in order to encourage a more constructive resolution of the conflict.

My discussion of the debate is based on the contributions that have appeared in four journals, *Social Casework, Social Work, Social Work Research and Abstracts,* and *Social Service Review.* Authors involved in the debate include Heineman (presently Heineman Pieper),[2] Hudson,[3] Geismar,[4] Fischer,[5] Gordon,[6] Ruckdeschel and Farris,[7] Geismar and Wood,[8] Rein and White,[9] Schuerman,[10] Holland,[11] Gyarfas,[12] Karger,[13] Imre,[14] Haworth,[15] Ruckdeschel,[16] Gambrill,[17] Mullen,[18] and Thyer.[19] I will consider the literature as a whole as I attempt to identify common patterns and themes that occur in how knowledge is, and should be, developed in social work, and in the actual process of the debate. The debate itself is, of course, one example of how knowledge is developed in social work.

There is a surprisingly similar pattern of debate in each journal. Common elements include the method of criticizing and the style of defending empiricism, the nature and clarity (and criticism) of proposed alternatives to empiricism, the understanding of opposing viewpoints, and the personalization of the debate. Each of these areas is considered in turn.

THE CRITICISM AND DEFENSE OF EMPIRICISM

Those questioning the empiricist influence among social workers tend to define this influence narrowly and in a rigid way compared to those promoting empiricism. The critics argue that the tenets of empiricism are methodologically inadequate, outdated, and overly restrictive for social work research.

Source: From "Research Paradigms in Social Work: From Stalemate to Creative Synthesis" by C. Peile, 1988, *Social Service Review, 62,* pp. 1–19. Copyright 1988 by The University of Chicago. Reprinted by permission.
Social Service Review (March 1988). © 1988 by The University of Chicago. All rights reserved. 0037–7961/88/6201–0001$01.00

179

Those promoting empiricism define it more broadly and pragmatically to avoid some of these criticisms.

The trend toward empiricism is variously defined by the critics as a movement toward logical empiricism,[20] rank empiricism,[21] neopositivism,[22] and logical positivism.[23] The supporters define the trend as moving toward science,[24] scientifically based practice,[25] and scientific inquiry.[26] Using the narrow definition of empiricism, the critics suggest that this approach to research is too restrictive for social work, because it limits the sorts of problems that can be studied.[27] A common concern is that only those aspects of a situation that are measurable and that can be defined operationally are meaningful and available for research.[28] For example, Holland[29] points to such concepts as love and faith that are crucial to social work practice and yet cannot be fully operationalized.

Drawing heavily on literature from the philosophy of science, where in some quarters empiricism has come under strong attack,[30] the critics claim that the empiricist approach is outmoded.[31] Heineman Pieper provides a useful overview of this attack. It includes criticism of the theory-observation distinction, operationalism, the symmetry thesis, the emphasis on justification, reductionism, and the prescriptiveness of empiricism.[32]

Defending the empirical approach, Schuerman and Hudson both question the relevance of philosophy, drawing a sharp distinction between philosophy and science. Schuerman suggests that philosophy has little effect on the practice of science,[33] while Hudson goes farther and suggests that scientists should be wary of philosophers.[34]

The relevance of philosophy aside, most supporters of empiricism accept the validity of criticism with respect to the narrower views of empiricism. Hudson,[35] Schuerman,[36] and Geismar[37] agree that logical empiricism is a flawed model of science, but they argue that this model is not an important influence in social work research. They promote a more pragmatic empiricism and claim that this is, and should be, the major influence.[38] This enables them to avoid criticism specific to logical empiricism. For example, both sides recognize that observation is unavoidably biased. The difference is in how each tries to overcome the problem.

The critics resolve the problem of bias in observation by discarding the empiricist model. This could be labeled a "revolutionary" response. Supporters, taking a contrary position, offer pragmatic "reform." They suggest that, although observation is biased, it is still a sound basis for research, since people make remarkably similar observations.[39] Supporters seek to minimize their bias by standardizing research procedures and avoiding constructs that cannot be operationalized and measured.[40] This more pragmatic position is harder to attack methodologically.

The other prong of the critics' attack that relates to restrictiveness is avoided in a similar way. Geismar and Wood circumvent the problem by suggesting the importance of qualitative and alternative research in the preliminary work of establishing operational definitions.[41] Though such an approach opens up more methodological choice, qualitative or nonempirical research is still endowed with inferior status, while experimental research remains the most powerful method.[42] Geismar and Wood's argument is still unsatisfactory to the critics as it is this hierarchy of methods that they wish to reverse.[43]

While real differences exist between the views of critics and supporters, the exact nature of the difference is confused by varied claims about the nature of the trend from logical to pragmatic empiricism in social work research. Each side shifts the ground of the debate to launch counterattacks and to defend its own position. Both sides are, in effect, criticizing and defending very different points of view.

If the trend in social work research is toward the more pragmatic definition of empiricism and positivism rather than toward the more extreme logical empiricist or logical positivist position,[44] many of the concerns of the critics are minimized, and a common ground is established that is not obvious at first sight. The critics acknowledge the importance of experience,[45] while the supporters acknowledge the problems of observational objectivity.[46] The real difference is not so much the awareness of the problems of empiricist approaches as it is the dilemma whether to reform or to revolt in the face of these problems.

The characterization of the debate as a battle between the reformers and the revolutionaries is not a metaphorical one, since it captures the political nature of the conflict. The specific nature of this battle will become clearer after consideration of the character of the alternatives to empiricism.

THE REVOLT—ALTERNATIVES TO EMPIRICISM

A second pattern evident in the literature is one in which the critics of empiricism tentatively offer alternatives to overcome or to take into account the problems identified. These alternatives are considered to be much more consistent with social work concerns and practice,[47] though the supporters of empiricism commonly argue that they are inadequate, vague, or are already part of established practice.[48]

Alternatives are offered, but consistencies are identifiable in them. The characteristics of the alternatives offered by Heineman, Ruckdeschel and Farris, Ruckdeschel, and Imre are brought together in table 1. The collective characteristics of the alternatives[49] show strong similarities to what Lecomte has labeled the normative approach to research,[50] described by others as qualitative.[51] Given this similarity in the alternative approaches, I will refer to them collectively as the normative approach. . . .

METAVIEW OF THE DEBATE

Karger,[63] Rein and White,[64] Haworth,[65] Imre,[66] and Mullen[67] have, in different ways, attempted to provide a fresh perspective on the debate. Karger focuses on the political-structural issues of research. Rein and White focus on the institutional context of knowledge development, and Imre focuses on the philosophical perspective. Haworth reviews the current research trends in other fields, and Mullen looks at the methodological dilemmas faced by both sides. Each, however, provides only a partial perspective that does not take into account the valuable insights available through other partial views. My intention here is an inclusive one, that is, to try to build a wholistic picture of the research process that is consistent with, or can explain, all these valuable insights.

The presentation in table 1 of the empirical and normative characteristics as a series of contradictions is not my own construction, but it reflects the way both approaches are related in the literature.[68] The alternatives described follow criticism of empiricism and they are defined in contradiction to particular empiricist beliefs. The empiricists in their own defense follow a similar pattern. These contradictions represent the points at which empiricist and normative paradigms come into conflict within the focus of social work research. They are not simply points of difference. Many of the characteristics appear as opposites. The acceptance of a characteristic from one side requires the denial of its opposite. The collective picture provided by this description suggests that the normative and empirical approaches are in a relationship of antagonistic contradiction.[69]

In a different way, both approaches are intricately bound to one another. The points of contradiction not only express the differences, they also make possible a clearer definition of their own characteristics and boundaries. Each approach relies on the other for its own definition.[70] Their definitions are bound together and so together form a larger unity.[71] . . .

Given the fact that no one in the debate makes his or her paradigmatic context explicit, we are forced to speculate on what is implied and to rely on the literature that deals with the paradigmatic context of the empiricist and normative approaches. I do not claim to have reviewed this literature exhaustively, but instead

Table 1

Characteristics of alternatives to empiricism

Empirical Alternative	Normative Alternative
Prediction	Explanation[52]
Bias limitation (value free)	Bias incorporation (value ladenness)[53]
Separation of knowledge	Integration of knowledge and values[54]
Observation	Understanding[55]
Quantitative	Qualitative[56]
Measurement and testing	Insight and intuition[57]
Objective	Subjective[57]
Detachment	Involvement[57]
Certain knowable world	Relativism – multiperspectives[58]
Focus on content	Focus on process[59]
Aim for certainty	Reliance on faith[60]

Note. — Superscript numbers refer to notes accompanying text.

I have relied on a few authors and on my own impressions to construct the description outlined in table 2.

In considering the paradigmatic context of each research approach, it is important to realize that paradigms are not hard and fast sets of rules, as implied in the static description below. They are, more correctly, loose and evolving frameworks for the ongoing production and resolution of problems. As such, their historical context is important. I have previously characterized those who support the normative approach as revolutionaries and the pragmatic empiricists as reformers, though at other historical points, empiricism has been in the revolutionary position.[78]

From table 2 it is clear that the difference that exists between the empiricist and normativist at the epistemological level is also reflected at the cosmological, ontological, ethical, spiritual, and political levels. Thus the choice between research methods should not be made merely on the basis of epistemological arguments, but it should also be based on the compatibility of the research method with the researcher's own preferred paradigmatic assumptions or worldview, and these should be made explicit so that they can be challenged.

Unfortunately, there is little awareness of the paradigmatic context in the literature under review, hence the choice between approaches is based on narrow rationales, such as the suitability of the method to the research questions being asked.[95] The lack of awareness means that the assumptions operate sub rosa,[96] and that unknowingly, researchers are promoting a particular worldview and its consequent political implications. . . .

STRATEGIES OF CONFLICT

Gyarfas suggests in commenting on the debate between Schuerman and Heineman Pieper that "neither really 'hears' the other."[97] This observation can be applied accurately to the entire debate under review. The style of the debate is similar to that between politically opposed factions, in which each does not want to hear the other. It is difficult to say how conscious the paradigmatic rivalry is, but whether conscious or not, several different political strategies can be identified in the debate that rely on rhetoric rather than on rational discourse. First, each writer tends to criticize specific points rather than to consider the other's complete argument in relation to its objectives. This means points are criticized out of context and

their messages are distorted. It is common for writers to dismiss criticism because it misses the central purpose of their article.[98]

Second, both sides are engaged in what Pepper calls the fallacy of clearing the ground, which assumes that "if a theory is not perfect it is no good, and that if all other suggested theories are no good, then the ground is clear for whatever one's own theory can produce."[99] It appears that authors in this debate assume that support for their own approach can be obtained by drawing attention to the failings of the rival approach. Each author seems to adopt the implicit view that if his or her view is true, all contradictory views must be false.

Third, each side of the debate uses arguments based on assumptions that reflect its own paradigmatic blinders that are different from those of the opponents. Each is playing the game, but each uses different rules. In a similar way both sides try to shift the ground of the debate, redefining the central issues or concerns of the debate to suit their own arguments. This confused logic makes effective communication and cooperative problem solving impossible.

Fourth, both sides polarize and personalize the debate. This strategy captures most vividly the political and ideological nature of the debate. . . . The opponents' arguments are exaggerated to allow for easier criticism and to associate the opposition with unfavorable, extreme, outmoded, or unpopular positions, such as logical positivism and relativism. This leads to a polarization of the debate, encouraging people to take definite sides. The process of polarization encourages increasing personalization of the debate. It is common to identify key people as flag bearers for particular positions, to align with particular authors, and to criticize others. . . .

ATTEMPTS AT SYNTHESIS

At first glance, it seems impossible to escape this conflict. The personalization, polarization, and paradigmatic context of the empiricist-normative debate seems to trap its participants into an ongoing battle that defies resolution. While they remain trapped in this repetitive process, the creative possibilities for social work research and practice will be limited.

One reason why each side remains committed to its own approach is that its own experience has shown that its method is helpful and seems to provide some grasp on the truth. What each side fails to recognize is that both sides might have a grasp on the truth. The

Table 2
The paradigmatic context of empiricism and normativism

	Empiricism	Normative
Cosmological assumptions (the universe as a totality)	Causal deterministic view of reality The world is predictable, knowable, and measurable.[79] Fragmentary view of reality (reality can be understood as separate parts).[80]	Knowledge is contextual and a symbolic social construction. Events can be explained and their meaning for people uncovered. Parts can only be understood in context.
Ontological assumptions (the essence of nature and human nature)	Behavior can be explained in causal deterministic ways. It has a mechanistic quality.[81] People are manipulatable and controllable.[83]	Behavior is intentional and creative.[82] It can be explained but is not predictable. People shape their own reality.
Epistemological assumptions (knowing and how knowledge is generated)	Knowledge arises from experimentation and observation and is grounded in the certainty of sense experience.[84] Rejection of metaphysical knowledge.[86]	Knowledge arises from interpretation and insight and is grounded by empathetic communication with the subjects of the research.[85] Symbols, meanings, and hidden factors are essential to understanding.
Ethical assumptions	A separation between knowledge and values.[87] Science produces knowledge. How it is used is a value, ethical or moral question, and is outside the concern of science.[88]	Values are the subject of research. Moral or ethical relativism. Leads to disinterest in ethical issues or anarchistic individualism.[89]
Spiritual assumptions	Rejection of spiritual explanations or a clear separation between science and religion.	Relativism of spiritual beliefs. Such beliefs are important in the social construction of meaning.
Relationship and political assumptions	The relationship aim between science and society is control.[90] The value-free stance implicitly supports the dominations of the established order.[92] Mutually supportive with both high technology capitalism[94] and centralized industrial socialism.	The relationship aim is empathetic communication.[91] Implicitly conservative since there is no structural or historical analysis of society.[93] Mutually supportive with a liberal society allowing individual freedom and self-determination.

Note. — Superscript numbers refer to notes accompanying text.

fact that they have opposing viewpoints does not nec-essarily mean that one side is wrong. It could mean that each has a partial or an incomplete view. It is my argument that empiricism and normativism are in this position. In such a situation synthesis is required.

A synthesis is a distinctly different viewpoint that can encompass both partial views. It resolves the con-flict and the differences between both partial positions by adopting a broader view that recognizes the truth in each position. A synthesis is not a simple mixture or merger of the characteristics of both sides; it is a com-pletely different unity, with very different implica-tions and conclusions. A synthesis of empiricism and normativism would set a new direction for social work.

Within the literature under review there are vari-ous explicit and implicit indications of a desire to move toward synthesis. Beckerman in 1978 seems to be calling for a synthesis when he argues that both sides of the debate need to be seen as interdependent.[116] Haworth in 1984 again seems to repeat the call by trying to identify an emerging para-digm that leads to wholeness.[117]

I will discuss very briefly three possible syntheses. To explore these in detail and to explain how they pro-vide a synthesis of empiricism and normativism is out-side the scope of this article. Each synthesis represents a different paradigm with its own cosmological, onto-logical, epistemological, ethical, spiritual, and political assumptions. Since each synthesis is not well estab-lished in the social work literature, all of these assumptions would need to be developed in detail to explain adequately each one and to provide a basis for comparing them with the empiricist and normativist paradigms. My intention here is simply to indicate that these syntheses already exist, to show some evi-dence of a movement toward them that can be found in the literature under review, and to provide some guide as to how they could be further explored.

The Critical Paradigm

The critical research approach has its origins in the writings of Marx and Hegel. Central to the critical approach is the notion of the dialectical process and of its universality. Knowledge develops through the dialectical process, which can be described as a move-ment that arises out of the conflict between thesis and antithesis. The conflict or contradiction between these opposites leads to a new synthesis, this new synthesis has its own immediate contradiction, and so the process goes on. The universality of the dialectical process means that everything has its opposite or its contradiction. Conflict is thus a central element of the critical approach; it drives knowledge forward.

The critical paradigm provides a synthesis of empiricism (thesis) and normativism (antithesis). It does this by seeing each of the contradictions listed in table 1 as locked into a dialectical process. Marcuse provides a good account of how the objective and sub-jective are joined in the dialectical process.[118] A useful general introduction to the critical paradigm and its research approach is provided by Fay.[119]

The critical approach is much more evident in British social work literature[120] than it is in the Ameri-can. In the debate under review, Karger would appear to be the most closely associated with this school, as evidenced by his appreciation of the political and structural nature of the debate.[121]

The New Paradigm Research Approach

This approach is associated with the work of Reason and Rowan and the new paradigm research group.[122] The work of Feyerabend,[123] Burrell and Morgan,[124] Morgan,[125] and Pepper[126] is very similar and could also be described as new paradigm research. The essential similarity of these authors is in their rejection of the absoluteness of any one paradigmatic position and their adoption of a relativist standpoint that claims that all positions are necessary and interdependent in the development of knowledge.

In new paradigm research, the empiricist and nor-mative approaches are synthesized as separate compo-nents within a multimethod epistemological approach. While both empiricism and normativism offer differ-ent insights into a field of interest, neither is seen as better than the other. For example, new paradigm research seeks to utilize both subjective and objective insights to make sense of reality.

Given the strong eclectic tradition in social work, new paradigm research could prove very popular. It does not offer a simple mixture but provides a consis-tent relativist philosophy within which the eclectic tradition might find a more secure footing. Evidence of the emergence of this position can be found on the normativist side in the work of Haworth[127] and Heine-man Pieper[128] and on the empiricist side in Fischer's promotion of eclecticism.[129] Though Heineman Pieper's heuristic perspective is very similar, she continually defines it in opposition to the empiricist approach and seems unaware of its possible synthetic nature.[130]

The Creative Paradigm

This approach grows out of the work of David Bohm,[131] Karl Pribram,[132] Ilya Prigogine,[133] and Rupert Sheldrake,[134] whose theories provide a very different way of understanding the universe. The application and development of these ideas for social work is the focus of my own research.[135] The creative paradigm adopts a wholistic view of reality in which parts are not separable but are enfolded in each other. This means that any segment of reality is implicitly enfolded throughout the whole and the whole is implicit in every segment. This cosmological position opens the way for a very different approach to both research and practice. The focus of creative research is to uncover this implicit undivided whole. The fundamental processes for achieving this are synthesis and insight.

Creative synthesis brings together two or more partial views (not necessarily in conflict) to provide a unified view. As an example, the creative paradigm provides a synthesis of empiricism and normativism. The creative view suggests that if we look at the actual practice of empiricism and normativism rather than at how that practice is explicitly described, we will find that elements of each approach are implicit in the other, so that in reality both approaches are inseparable. Problems arise when empiricism or normativism is thought to be a complete view, as it is in the debate under review. When such an approach is adopted, implicit elements of the actual research process are denied (a form of self-deception), which severely limits the utility of the research. Useful findings may be suppressed because the limited methodology cannot justify the means by which they are achieved. Also, a particular methodology may be given false credit for important findings. The creative approach aims at making the implicit explicit, recognizes itself as a partial rather than as a complete view, and in this way avoids self-deception.

However, the creative synthesis that brings different views together may lead to erroneous positions. Insight is the key that ensures that the resultant synthesis has some grasp on the truth. Creative cosmology suggests that the researcher is not separate from the object of research, but that each is enfolded in the other. This means that the object can be understood not only through the researcher's outward experience of the object but also—at the same time—through the researcher's own internal experience. This process of insight is neither subjective nor objective but is a synthesis which could be described as looking in through oneself to the whole.

Methods that encourage the processes of synthesis and insight will need to be found in order to develop the creative approach further. The creative approach is consistent with much of the theory of social work practice, but little evidence of the emergence of this approach is in the debate under review. Haworth's[136] approach, while fitting most consistently within the new paradigm model, does have aspirations that fit closely with the creative paradigm. Though he provides some elements useful to the creative approach, he does not show any evidence of its synthetic nature.

All three paradigms provide a constructive resolution of the empiricist-normative debate, opening up the possibilities for a new debate between the critical, new paradigm, and creative approaches. Each would take social work along a very different path. All three are similar in that each provides an approach to practitioner research. This warrants some mention because there is considerable interest at present in practitioner research in the social work literature.[137] I personally favor the creative approach, as it is consistent with my own moral, political, and philosophical views. However, I would support moves to any of these syntheses because any one of them would free up the debate and move it from its present position of stalemate and polarization.

CONCLUSION

In this essay I have returned to an old debate that is still unresolved in an effort to provide a deeper understanding and to encourage some constructive development. Currently, the debate appears to be at the polarized and personalized stage in which the empiricists have gained the upper hand.

The way forward I have suggested is by means of synthesis. The movement toward synthesis will require a reactivation of the debate, but a reactivation that will enable the participants to give up their own positions in an attempt to understand the opposing position. When both positions are held simultaneously, synthesis is possible.

Various dynamics within the debate create very different possibilities for the future. The outcome will depend on the commitment and actions of those involved in the paradigmatic conflict and in the social, political, and economic context within which social work finds itself. The outcome of the paradigmatic conflict is very important as it directly influences the nature of the whole profession.

I am aware that the emerging syntheses described here have their own paradigmatic qualities that conflict with the empiricist and normative paradigms. Thus, it is not just a change of methods but also a paradigmatic shift that is being sought. How such a shift can be achieved is a very complex matter.[138] However, an open discourse between all positions can only make a positive contribution to the development of all approaches, thus enabling social work research and practice to be more effective and creative.

NOTES

I acknowledge the support and assistance of Emerita Professor Edna Chamberlain, Dr. Allan Halladay, and Dr. Malcolm McCouat in the preparation of this paper.

1. J. Fischer, "The Social Work Revolution," *Social Work* 26 (May 1981): 199–207; M. B. Heineman, "The Obsolete Scientific Imperative in Social Work Research and Practice," *Social Service Review* 55 (September 1981): 371–97; W. H. Hudson, "Author's Reply," *Social Service Review* 57 (June 1983): 340–41; R. W. Imre, "The Nature of Knowledge in Social Work," *Social Work* 29 (January–February 1984): 41–45; H. J. Karger, "Science, Research and Social Work: Who Controls the Profession?" *Social Work* 28 (May–June 1983): 200–205. Their observations are supported by a recent content analysis by T. Tripodi, "Trends in Research Publication: A Study of Social Work Journals from 1956–1980," *Social Work* 29 (1984): 353–59.

2. Heineman, "The Obsolete Scientific Imperative" (n. 1 above), and "Author's Reply," *Social Service Review* 56 (March 1982): 146–48; M. Heineman Pieper, "Author's Reply," *Social Service Review* 56 (June 1982): 312, "The Future of Social Work Research," *Social Work Research and Abstracts* 21, no. 4 (1985): 3–11, and "Letters—the Author Replies," *Social Work Research and Abstracts* 22, no. 2 (1986): 2.

3. W. H. Hudson, "Scientific Imperatives in Social Work Research and Practice," *Social Service Review* 56 (June 1982): 242–58, "Author's Reply" (n. 1 above), and "Letters: The Proof Is in the Pudding," *Social Work Research and Abstracts* 22, no. 2 (1986): 2.

4. L. L. Geismar, "Comments on The Obsolete Scientific Imperative in Social Work Research," *Social Service Review* 56 (June 1982): 311–12.

5. Fischer, "Social Work Revolution" (n. 1 above), and "Revolution, Schmevolution: Is Social Work Changing or Not?" *Social Work* 29 (January–February 1984): 71–74.

6. W. E. Gordon, "Social Work Revolution or Evolution?" *Social Work* 28 (May–June 1983): 181–85, and "Gordon Replies: Making Social Work a Science-based Profession," *Social Work* 29 (January–February 1984): 74–77.

7. R. A. Ruckdeschel and B. E. Farris, "Assessing Practice: A Critical Look at the Single-Case Design," *Social Casework* 62 (1981): 413–19, and "Science: Critical Faith or Dogmatic Ritual: A Rebuttal," *Social Casework* 63 (1982): 272–75.

8. L. L. Geismar and K. M. Wood, "Evaluating Practice: Science as Faith," *Social Casework* 63 (1982): 266–72.

9. M. Rein and S. H. White, "Knowledge for Practice," *Social Service Review* 53 (March 1981): 1–41.

10. J. R. Schuerman, "The Obsolete Scientific Imperative in Social Work Research," *Social Service Review* 56 (March 1982): 144–48.

11. T. P. Holland, "Comments on 'Scientific Imperatives in Social Work Research and Practice,'" *Social Service Review* 57 (June 1983): 337–41.

12. M. G. Gyarfas, The Scientific Imperative Again," *Social Service Review* 57 (March 1983): 149–50.

13. Karger (n. 1 above).

14. Imre (n. 1 above).

15. G. O. Haworth, "Social Work Research: Practice and Paradigms," *Social Service Review* 58 (September 1984): 343–57.

16. R. A. Ruckdeschel, "Qualitative Research as a Perspective," *Social Work Research and Abstracts* 21, no. 2 (1985): 17–21.

17. E. D. Gambrill, "Editorial," *Social Work Research and Abstracts* 21, no. 4 (1985): 2.

18. E. J. Mullen, "Methodological Dilemmas in Social Work Research," *Social Work Research and Abstracts* 21, no. 4 (1985): 12–20.

19. B. A. Thyer, "Letters—on Pseudoscience and Pseudoreasoning," *Social Work Research and Abstracts* 22, no. 2 (1986): 2.

20. Heineman, "Obsolete Imperative" (n. 1 above), p. 371.

21. Gordon, "Social Work: Revolution" (n. 6 above), p. 182.

22. Ruckdeschel and Farris, "Critical Faith" (n. 7 above), p. 275.

23. Imre, "Nature of Knowledge" (n. 1 above), p. 41.

24. Hudson, "Scientific Imperatives" (n. 3 above), p. 256.

25. Fischer, "Social Work Revolution" (n. 1 above), p. 22.

26. Geismar and Wood (n. 8 above), p. 272.

27. Heineman, "Obsolete Imperative," pp. 371–75; Imre, "Nature of Knowledge" (n. 1 above), p. 41; Ruckdeschel and Farris, "Assessing Practice," p. 416.

28. Gordon, "Social Work: Revolution," p. 184; Heineman, "Obsolete Imperative," p. 375.

29. Holland (n. 11 above), p. 337.

30. Heineman, "Obsolete Imperative," p. 371; Imre, "Nature of Knowledge," pp. 41–43; Ruckdeschel and Farris, "Assessing Practice," p. 416; G. O. Haworth (n. 15 above), p. 347.

31. Heineman Pieper, "Future of Social Work" (n. 2 above), p. 3.

32. Heineman, "Obsolete Imperative" (n. 1 above), pp. 377–87.

33. Schuerman, "Obsolete Scientific Imperative" (n. 10 above), p. 145.

34. Hudson, "Scientific Imperatives" (n. 3 above), p. 250.

35. Ibid., pp. 247, 249.

36. Schuerman (n. 10 above), pp. 144–45.

37. Geismar (n. 4 above), p. 311.

38. Geismar and Wood provide a good example of pragmatic science, according to Ruckdeschel and Farris, "Critical Faith" (n. 7 above), p. 278.

39. Hudson, "Scientific Imperatives," p. 252.

40. Ibid., p. 256, tenet 5; however, Hudson ("Author's Reply" [n. 3 above], p. 339), challenges Holland's claim that empiricism cannot deal with love, courage, and hope, suggesting we know these things only through our own experience and through the indirect experience of others who report them.

41. Geismar and Wood (n. 8 above), pp. 271–72.

42. Ibid., p. 271.

43. Ruckdeschel and Farris, "Critical Faith," p. 274; Haworth (n. 15 above), p. 345.

44. While *logical* empiricist or *logical* positivist are not labels that Fischer and Hudson accept, their writings show that they accept the labels, empiricist or positivist. Hudson defines empiricism as "the practice of relying on observation and experiment," in "Scientific Imperatives" (n. 3 above), p. 257. W. C. Young, in *A Christian Approach to Philosophy* (Grand Rapids, Mich.: Baker, 1973), p. 247, defines positivism as "the worldview which rejects the possibility of metaphysical knowledge." However, a central tenet of logicism that propositional logic (which includes mathematics) is truth-preserving (Heineman, "Obsolete Imperative," p. 392, n. 3) is a description Fischer and Hudson do not wish to accept. Positivism and empiricism are terms used interchangeably in the social work literature under review, as they are commonly associated beliefs (e.g., Imre, "Nature of Knowledge" [n. 1 above], p. 41). The trend in social work can be seen as a movement toward a constellation of both beliefs.

45. Heineman, "Author's Reply" (n. 2 above), p. 147; Holland (n. 11 above), p. 338.

46. Hudson, "Scientific Imperatives" (n. 3 above), p. 253.

47. Ruckdeschel, "Qualitative Research" (n. 16 above), p. 20; Heineman Pieper, "Future of Social Work (n. 2 above), p.

8; Ruckdeschel and Farris, "Assessing Practice" (n. 7 above), pp. 416, 419; Haworth, pp. 352–53, 355.

48. Geismar (n. 4 above), p. 147; Schuerman (n. 10 above), p. 146; Hudson, "Letters," p. 340; Mullen (n. 18 above), pp. 8–9.

49. This assessment is in contrast to Karger, who suggests that there is no serious competition to empiricism. Karger denies that the various qualitative models reflect a unified position. See Karger (n. 1 above), p. 202.

50. R. Lecomte, "Basic Issues in the Analysis of Theory for Practice in Social Work" (Ph.D. diss., Bryn Mawr College, 1975).

51. Ruckdeschel, "Qualitative Research."

52. Heineman, "Obsolete Imperative" (n. 1 above), p. 391; Mullen, p. 17.

53. Heineman, "Obsolete Imperative," p. 391; Hudson, "Scientific Imperatives"; Heineman Pieper, "Future of Social Work," p. 5.

54. Imre, "Nature of Knowledge" (n. 1 above), p. 43.

55. Ruckdeschel, "Qualitative Research" (n. 16 above).

56. Ibid., p. 417; Geismar and Wood (n. 8 above); Heineman Pieper, "Future of Social Work," p. 3.

57. Hudson, "Letters" (n. 3 above), p. 340; Heineman Pieper, "Future of Social Work" (n. 2 above), p. 5; Ruckdeschel and Farris, "Assessing Practice," pp. 417–18; Mullen (n. 18 above), p. 14.

58. Heineman, "Author's Reply" (n. 2 above), p. 147, and "Obsolete Imperative" (n. 1 above), p. 391; Ruckdeschel and Farris, "Assessing Practice" (n. 7 above), pp. 417–18.

59. Ruckdeschel and Farris, "Assessing Practice" (n. 7 above), pp. 416–17.

60. Ruckdeschel and Farris, "Critical Faith" (n. 7 above), p. 275.

. . . . .

62. Ibid. For further discussion of this debate in the social sciences see B. Fay and J. D. Moon, "What Would an Adequate Philosophy of Social Science Look Like?" *Philosophy of the Social Sciences* 7 (1977): 209–27; B. Fay, *Social Theory and Political Practice.* (London: Allen & Unwin, 1977); G. Morgan and L. Smircich. "The Case for Qualitative Research," *Academy of Management Review* 5, no. 4 (1980): 491–500; and G. Burrell and G. Morgan, *Sociological Paradigms and Organizational Analysis* (London: Heineman, 1979).

63. Karger (n. 1 above).

64. Rein and White (n. 9 above).

65. Haworth (n. 15 above).

66. Imre, "Nature of Knowledge" (n. 1 above).

67. Mullen (n. 18 above).

68. Heineman Pieper, "Future of Social Work" (n. 2 above), p. 6.

69. Mao Tse-tung, "On Contradiction," in *Selected Works of Mao Tse-tung* (Peking: Foreign Language Press, 1967), 1:343.

70. J. Rowan and P. Reason, "On Making Sense," in *Human Inquiry: A Sourcebook of New Paradigm Research,* ed. P. Reason and J. Rowan (Chichester: Wiley, 1981), p. 130; Reason and Rowan, *Human Inquiry.*

71. Similarly, within each approach there are many divisions. Within, e.g., the empiricist approach, two opposing camps can be identified, the inductivists and the falsificationists. See A. F. Chalmers, *What Is This Thing Called Science?* (Queensland: University of Queensland Press, 1978). The difference between Fischer and Gordon could be explained by this distinction. The divisions within the normative approach are evident in the alternatives offered by Heineman, Ruckdeschel and Farris, Imre, Ruckdeschel, and Haworth. The disunity of the normative approach has been identified as one of its major weaknesses, when it is compared to the empiricist approach. See Karger (n. 1 above).

. . . . .

77. T. S. Kuhn, *The Structure of Scientific Revolutions* (Chicago: University of Chicago Press, 1970).

78. A. Wedberg, *A History of Philosophy* (Oxford: Clarendon Press, 1982), 2:1–6.

79. Morgan and Smircich (n. 62 above), p. 495.

80. Reason and Rowan, eds. (n. 70 above), p. xiv.

81. Morgan and Smircich (n. 62 above), pp. 492, 495.

82. Ibid., p. 495.

83. B. Easlea, *Liberation and the Aims of Science* (Brighton: Sussex University Press, 1973), p. 262.

84. Ibid., p. 74.

85. Fay (n. 62 above), p. 23.

86. J. Habermas, *Knowledge and Human Interests* (Boston: Beacon Press, 1968), p. 78.

87. Fay, p. 23.

88. J. M. Broughton, and M. E. Zahaykevich, "The Peace Movement Threat," *Teachers College Record* 84, no. 1 (1982): 152–73.

89. C. Dandeker, "Theory and Practice in Sociology: The Critical Imperatives of Realism," *Journal for Theory of Social Behaviour* 13, no. 2 (1983): 195–210.

90. Fay, p. 41; Habermas, p. 76.

91. Fay, pp. 81–82.

92. Easlea, p. 173.

93. Fay, pp. 84, 90, 91.

94. Broughton and Zahaykevich, p. 154; Fay, p. 47.

95. Geismar and Wood (n. 8 above), pp. 271–72; Heineman, "Obsolete Imperative" (n. 1 above), p. 391.

96. Imre, "Nature of Knowledge" (n. 1 above), p. 42.

97. Gyarfas (n. 12 above), p. 144.

98. Heineman, "Author's Reply" (n. 2 above), p. 146; Heineman Pieper, "Author's Reply" (n. 2 above), p. 312; Hudson, "Letters" (n. 3 above), p. 339.

99. S. C. Pepper, *World Hypotheses* (Berkeley: University of California Press, 1942), pp. 100–101.

. . . . .

116. Beckerman, p. 14.

117. Haworth (n. 15 above), p. 345.

118. H. Marcuse, *Reason and Revolution* (London: Routledge & Kegan Paul, 1968), pp. 94–120.

119. Fay (n. 62 above).

120. P. Leonard, *Personality and Ideology: Towards a Materialist Understanding of the Individual* (London: Macmillan, 1984).

121. Karger (n. 1 above).

122. Reason and Rowan (n. 70 above).

123. P. Feyerabend, *Against Method* (London: New Left Books, 1975).

124. Burrell and Morgan (n. 62 above).

125. G. Morgan, *Beyond Method* (Beverly Hills, Calif.: Sage, 1983).

126. Pepper (n. 99 above).

127. Haworth (n. 15 above).

128. Heineman, "Author's Reply" (n. 2 above); Heineman Pieper, "Future of Social Work" (n. 2 above).

129. Fischer, "Social Work Revolution" (n. 1 above).

130. An implicit awareness of the synthetic nature of her position is evident in her response to Thyer (n. 13 above). An explicit development of her position as a synthesis would decrease confusion in the debate.

131. D. Bohm, *Wholeness and the Implicate Order* (London: Routledge & Kegan Paul, 1980), and "Insight, Knowledge, Science and Human Values," *Teachers College Record* 82, no. 3 (1981): 380–402; J. Briggs and F. D. Peat, *The Looking Glass Universe: The Emerging Science of Wholeness* (New York: Cornerstone, 1984).

132. Briggs and Peat. See chap. 5 for discussion of Pribram's work.

133. Ibid.; I. Prigogine and I. Stengers, *Order out of Chaos* (Boston: Shambhala, 1984).

134. R. Sheldrake, *A New Science of Life* (London: Paladin, 1985).

135. C. Peile, "Creative Social Work Research: Towards a Synthesis of Empiricism and Normativism" (discussion paper, University of Queensland, 1986).

136. Haworth (n. 15 above).

137. H. Broxmeyer, "Practitioner-Research in Treating a Borderline Child," *Social Work Research and Abstracts* 14 (1978): 5–11; R. P. Barth, "Education for Practice-Research: Towards a Reorientation," *Journal of Education for Social Work* 17, no. 2 (1981): 19–25; Fischer, "Social Work Revolution," p. 201; R.M. Grinnell, *Social Work Research and Evaluation* (Itasca, Ill.: Peacock, 1985).

138. See Kuhn (n. 77 above).

Debate with Authors

COMMENTS ON "RESEARCH PARADIGMS IN SOCIAL WORK: FROM STALEMATE TO CREATIVE SYNTHESIS"

MARTHA HEINEMAN PIEPER   *Chicago, Illinois*
Colin Peile's article, "Research Paradigms in Social Work: From Stalemate to Creative Synthesis" (*Social Service Review* 62 [March 1988]: 1–19), has the worthwhile goal of providing a synthesis of conflicting or partial views of the research paradigm of choice for social work. Peile endorses three distinct paradigms but favors what he terms the "creative paradigm."[1] Unfortunately, Peile rests his argument on a conceptual analysis whose categories are inherently flawed. The problem lies with the unexamined and problematic ontology that regulates his conceptual analysis.

Peile attempts to reach a useful synthesis by relating and synthesizing terms that he says represent the two sides of the current social work debate about research paradigms. However, Peile does not recognize that the terms he attributes to each side are ontologically distinct rather than ontologically isomorphic. Therefore, by definition, he cannot achieve a true synthesis but is limited to a syncretistic mixture that is misleading and, ultimately, divisive. Peile's stated purpose in presenting the categories that are supposed to represent the "empirical" and "normative" alternatives to research is to exemplify the deadlocked nature of the dispute about optimal research paradigms.[2] Never-theless, Peile goes on to make these two categories the basis for his synthesis, in spite of the fact that they rest on mutually exclusive ontologies.

For example, to the extent that Peile identifies the "normative" alternative with the heuristic paradigm that I have advocated, his dichotomous categories are invalid, and I would like to correct this central misconception. First, the heuristic paradigm actually includes many of the characteristics Peile attributes to the other, "empiricist" view. Examples are prediction, observation, quantitative methods, measurement and testing, and the focus on content. Second, many of the characteristics Peile ascribes to the "normative" paradigm are in direct conflict with the tenets of the heuristic paradigm in that they arise from what the heuristic paradigm would consider to be spurious dichotomies. Examples of these untenable dichotomies are: (1) "Bias limitation (value free)"/"Bias incorporation (value ladenness)"; (2) "Separation of knowledge"/"Integration of knowledge and values"; (3) "Objective"/"Subjective"; (4) "Detachment"/"Involvement"; and (4) "Aim for certainty"/"Reliance on faith."[3]

Source: "Comments on 'Research Paradigms in Social Work: From Stalemate to Creative Synthesis'" by M. Heineman Pieper, 1988, *Social Service Review, 62*, 535–536. Copyright 1988 by The University of Chicago. Reprinted by permission.
Social Service Review (1988). © 1988 by The University of Chicago.

In summary, Peile's assertion that the heuristic paradigm I have advanced corresponds even roughly to his "normative" model is entirely unfounded. The heuristic paradigm does not advocate replacing one restrictive paradigm of research with another. For example, as I have repeatedly emphasized, there is ample room in the heuristic paradigm for the experimental model and quantitative data.[4] The heuristic paradigm propounds a flexible, inclusive, open approach to research, which, however, is not equivalent to a paradigm of absolute relativism. The philosophical justification for the breadth of the heuristic paradigm is that there are no sound epistemological or ontological grounds for a more restrictive paradigm of research.

Thus, rather than representing one side of a dialectic, the heuristic paradigm itself represents an inclusive synthesis. It is in opposition to no rational methodology, but only to an inauthentically restrictive and outmoded ontology and epistemology. It is this distinction that Peile does not understand. The heuristic paradigm is at once sufficiently flexible and sufficiently rigorous to end the current factionalism and to satisfy social work's need for productive and relevant research.

NOTES

1. C. Peile, "Research Paradigms in Social Work: From Stalemate to Creative Synthesis," *Social Service Review* (March 1988): 1–19, esp. 2.
2. Ibid., p. 4.
3. Ibid.
4. M. B. Heineman, "The Obsolete Scientific Imperative in Social Work Research," *Social Service Review* 35 (September 1981): 14–15, "Author's Reply," *Social Service Review* 56 (January 1982): 146–48; M. Heineman Pieper, "The Future of Social Work Research," *Social Work Research and Abstracts* 21 (Winter 1985): 6, "Some Common Misunderstandings of the Heuristic Approach," *Social Work Research and Abstracts* 22 (Spring 1986): 2, 22, and "The Author Replies," *Social Work Research and Abstracts* 22 (Summer 1986): 2.

AUTHOR'S REPLY

COLIN PEILE   *Queensland, Australia*
I am thankful that Martha Heineman Pieper has helped to clarify my uncertainty about her relationship to the normative paradigm, and I apologize for any uneasiness such an association may have caused. This association was made early in my paper, "Research Paradigms in Social Work: From Stalemate to Creative Synthesis" (*Social Service Review* 62 [March 1988]: 1–19).* I later went on to suggest that the heuristic paradigm that she promotes is similar to the new paradigm research approach (pp. 12–13).** Her reply to my paper is not explicit about whether this association is more acceptable, although her comments have strengthened my assessment that she would find considerable common ground with this school of thought. Heineman Pieper has been a tireless contributor to the debate, and I trust she will reaffirm her position in the debate if I still have misunderstood.

I am also thankful she has sought to rectify the problematic ontology that she argues undermines my conceptual analysis. Unfortunately, I am confused about the criticisms she proposes and require further clarification if I am going to use them to rework my argument. My first confusion is that Heineman Pieper appears to claim she has achieved what she argues is an impossible task. She claims a true synthesis of empiricism and normativism is not possible because they are mutually exclusive or distinct ontologies. In my reading of her last paragraph, is she not implying that this is exactly what the heuristic paradigm in its inclusiveness is doing?

I agree with Heineman Pieper that the empiricist and normative paradigms are ontologically distinct. In fact I tried to make this very clear in my paper by identifying the paradigmatic assumptions that lie behind each paradigm. Where we differ is that, although I can see their distinct nature, I can also see how inseparable they are and how in many ways they are alike or isomorphic. As opposing paradigms in contradiction with each other they rely on each other for definition, a point I explained in my paper (p. 5). It is the search for these unifying features, to connect what appears disconnected, that is the basis of my approach. This search is informed by a cosmology based on Bohm's work, which says everything is enfolded in every other thing, that everything is connected.[1] This means that even ways of thinking about reality that appear explicitly distinct may at the same time be inseparable from each other at an implicit level. These assumptions must

Source: "Author's Reply" by C. Peile, 1988, *Social Service Review, 62,* 708–709. Copyright 1988 by The University of Chicago. Reprinted by permission.
Social Service Review (1988). © 1988 by The University of Chicago. All rights reserved.
*Editor's Note: See p. 181 in this text.
**Editor's Note: See p. 184–185 in this text.

be understood before deciding whether a synthesis of empiricism and normativism is possible or not within the creative paradigm.

I agree that the heuristic paradigm provides a synthesis, and I would like to better understand the paradigmatic assumptions on which this synthesis is based. This would assist me with a further uncertainty I have with Heineman Pieper's criticism of my paper. She suggests that all I can achieve is a syncretistic mixture. However, in my mind this is far more a danger for the heuristic paradigm, which is inclusive of different approaches, in contrast to the creative approach, which explicitly avoids mixtures seeking a unified wholistic position. My uncertainty is compounded because Heineman Pieper appears to want to avoid the label of absolute relativism, and yet relativism is certainly one of the paradigmatic assumptions that can provide a basis for the sort of synthesis she advocates. In early writings she has appeared more comfortable with the relativist assumptions.[2]

While uncertain about the above elements of Heineman Pieper's criticism, I am very pleased that her comments have focused on the nature of synthesis. The exploration of this area I believe will open up new and creative possibilities for both social work researchers and practitioners. While Heineman Pieper and myself appear to disagree about the means of achieving synthesis, it is reassuring for me that we are both seeking a true synthesis that is neither misleading, divisive, or a syncretistic mixture. I will watch with interest for the development of her ideas in this area.

NOTES

1. D. Bohm, *Wholeness and the Implicate Order* (London: Routledge & Kegan Paul, 1980).
2. M. B. Heineman, "Author's Reply," *Social Service Review* 56 (March 1982): 146-148.

Introduction to "Making Social Work Scientific: Analysis and Recommendations"

In the following selection, a reformulation of a paper first published in 1989, Witkin joins the debates about the best metatheory for social work research, describes some limitations of positivist approaches to social work research, and recommends that social workers adopt a more inclusive philosophy of scientific research. Witkin's position in the debates about the philosophy of social work research is unusual in that he is among the few social work researchers who changed sides: Although he was trained in and initially advanced a positivist approach to social work research, he shifted to a postpositivist approach. Witkin's change of position also illustrates how metatheories of social and behavioral research have implications for practice models. In his early work, Witkin applied the "empirical clinical practice model," a practice model that was developed to conform to a positivist metatheory of research; more recently, Witkin (1991) debunked the empirical clinical practice model and advanced alternatives.[82]

In the following selection, Witkin emphasizes that one of the traditional values of the social work profession is that social problems can be understood and solved rationally. This view denies that social work knowledge is an intuitive and fundamentally irrational "art." Witkin emphasizes that all scientific knowledge is informed by its sociocultural context and that the so-called "neutral" terminology used to describe groups in research often reflects wider sociocultural biases and in fact "implicitly promotes ethnocentrism" (p. 199). Following Weimer (1979), Witkin uses the term "justificationism" to denote the positivist dictum that scientists should focus on the justification rather than the discovery of theories. Witkin advocates an open and inclusive approach to social work research rather than the prescriptive approach advanced by positivist researchers.

Witkin draws on the ideas of the social psychologist Kenneth Gergen, who is among the leading formulators of a social constructionist approach to knowledge (Gergen, 1986, 1991; also called, by others, constructivism, see Lincoln, 1990). The social constructionist approach, which draws in part on the tradition of hermeneutics, emphasizes that meaning is generated and can be understood only in relation to its historical and cultural context (see also the narrative approach advanced by Mishler, 1979, 1986, and Polkinghorne, 1988). In the social constructionist view, language has the central role in determining what counts as an object of study. Language is itself a product of social interaction (Gergen, 1986, p. 150). Gergen says, "it is not the observation that produces the chief constraint over description; it is the form of descriptive discourse itself that constrains. The origins of these forms may, again, be traced to the sphere of social interchange" (1986, p. 150).

Constructionists recognize that to test a theory, scientists first must reach consensus about the criteria used to test theories (Tibbetts, 1986). For example, Gergen asserts that scientists must agree about "how to employ the filter or the lens in a given setting" for "observed variations to correct or sustain a given theory" (1986, p. 150). Constructionists commonly regard themselves as relativists. Relativists assert that because knowledge of reality is biased and is constructed by the knower, the claim that a mind-independent reality can be used to evaluate the veracity of theories has no sound support (Bhaskar, 1989b). They do not, however, believe that all knowledge claims have equal value. For example, a relativist may believe that theories that fulfill the social work profession's aims of social justice are better than those that do not (Witkin & Gottschalk, 1988). As Heineman Pieper points out (see, e.g., the Preface and her responses to Brekke), the heuristic paradigm is not equivalent to relativism. Whereas the heuristic paradigm concurs with relativism that unbiased knowledge of reality does not exist and that knowledge is to some degree a socially constructed phenomenon, the heuristic paradigm is compatible with the position that reality cannot be defined on the basis of what one can know (Bhaskar, 1989b, 1991). In other words, the heuristic paradigm is compatible with the position that, although knowledge is inevitably biased and socially constructed, some theories are truer than others. From the standpoint of the heuristic paradigm, constructionism is a larger-scale heuristic. Many constructionists make the ontological assumption that language is the primary "real" to be known, and that all ways of knowing are structured linguistically, thereby focusing the researcher on the "real" of language.

Witkin applies Karl Weick's (1979) concept of enactment to elaborate the view that heuristics order both thinking and social experience. Witkin's examples of enactment illustrate how an individual's representations of self and other regulate his or her behavior and then create particular experiences with the environment, such as responses in relationships. When one applies these ideas to research design, one can see that the research process "enacts" particular roles between participant/researcher and participant/subject, thus regulating the findings that are obtained. Witkin recommends that researchers be reflective about the meanings they are enacting in the research process so that they can generate research that furthers humanistic values.

DISCUSSION QUESTIONS

1. a. What is enactment?
    b. Give an example of enactment in your own behavior, the behavior of your clients, or organizational behavior in the agencies in which you have worked.
2. What are the two postpositivist criteria for evaluating research that Witkin elaborates?
3. Thomas Kuhn (1970) says that most scientists do not change paradigms and that paradigm shifts occur primarily as students learn the new paradigm. Why might scientists find it difficult to change paradigms?
4. David Harrison (W. D. Harrison, 1987, 1989) described the innovative team approach to practice developed by the National Institute for Social Work in the United Kingdom and termed *community social work* (B. Hearn & Thomson, 1987; Smale, Tuson, Cooper, Wardle, & Crosbie, 1988). Harrison emphasized that

social work appears to be entering a period of new concern for communities, even as social work experiences a psychotherapy boom. The task of increasing commitments to communities . . . appears to be exceptionally difficult. However, social work offers society a way to integrate individual and community aspects of what people seek in life. (1989, p. 75)

What are some ways in which a new, inclusive, postpositivist approach to research can be especially relevant for improving our understanding of how communities function and how we can enhance our communities? (Hint: You may want to look ahead to the selections by Bhaskar and Wimsatt in Chapter 5 and to the introductions to those selections.)

Making Social Work Scientific: Analysis and Recommendations*

Stanley L. Witkin, Ph.D.   *University of Vermont*

The field of social work has been engaged in a long-standing effort to define itself as a scientifically based profession (Zimbalist, 1977). These efforts became more pronounced during the last two decades as resources for social work activities grew increasingly scarce and competitive, and the efficacy of social work services came under serious scrutiny (e.g., Fischer, 1973). In particular, the development of single-case research designs seemed to provide a way for practitioners to utilize the methods of science in their daily practice (e.g., Howe, 1974; Jayaratne and Levy, 1979). Single-case designs were seen as facilitating the merging of the roles of researcher and practitioner (e.g., Bloom and Fischer, 1982) and as a means of developing an empirical knowledge base for practice (Blythe and Briar, 1985). The development of single-case methods is the most salient indicator of a general emphasis on conventional social science research in social work. This emphasis also is evidenced in the development of the empirical clinical practice model (Ivanoff, Robinson, & Blythe, 1987), current textbooks on research (e.g., Dawson et al., 1991; Grinnell, 1988; Royce, 1991; Yegidis & Weinbach, 1991) and the appearance of social work journals that emphasize conventional research (e.g., *Journal of Research in Social Work*). While these developments have helped define the scientific nature of research in social work, they have been the focus of vociferous debate (Peile, 1988b). At issue has been the justification and value to social work of a conventional approach to science (Heineman Pieper, 1981, 1985; Hudson, 1982). The purpose of this paper is to advance critical discussion of this issue by: (1) discussing possible meanings of a scientific social work and explicating its various implications; and (2) proposing that an open approach to inquiry would best serve the profession.

WHAT IS SCIENCE?

Despite the distinction made by some authors, attempts to clearly differentiate between scientific and nonscientific endeavors have met with equivocal results. The most common approach has been to identify criteria which uniquely characterize scientific activity. Although several criteria (e.g., refutability, observation, induction, meaningfulness) have resulted from these analyses (Popper, 1965), their validity has been debated inconclusively for years by philosophers of science. In part this is due to the contrasting views about the nature of phenomena, the form of knowledge this phenomena can take and the methods available for obtaining this knowledge. Within the social or human sciences, the waters get even more muddied (Burrell & Morgan, 1979). For example, Polkinghorne

---

Source: "Making Social Work Scientific: Analysis and Recommendations" by S. L. Witkin, 1993, Unpublished manuscript, University of Vermont. Copyright 1993 by S. L. Witkin. Reprinted by permission.
*Editor's Note: An earlier version of this paper entitled, "Towards a Scientific Social Work," appeared in the *Journal of Social Service Research*, 12, 83–98.

(1983) defines human science as "a science which approaches questions about the human realm with an openness to its special characteristics and a willingness to let the questions inform which methods are appropriate" (p. 289). Similarly, defining science on the basis of scientific activity (i.e., the behavior of scientists), has also met with little success. Despite frequent portrayals of scientists as flawless logicians who, in the pursuit of truth, dispassionately and objectively generate facts, the actual behavior of scientists is often vastly different (Mitroff, 1974; Mahoney, 1976).

Some of the ambiguity about what is and what is not science may be explained by what Kaplan (1964) has labeled, "unreconstructed logic" and "logic-in-use." Reconstructed logic characterizes the way science typically is described in textbooks, for example, equating the conduct of science with the "hypothetico-deductive method." In contrast, logic-in-use refers to the actual manner scientists in a particular discipline go about their business. Such knowledge is implicitly held by the scientific community rather than described in textbooks. Kaplan (1964) admonishes that a "reconstructed logic is not a description but rather an idealization of scientific practice" (p. 10). One consequence of using a reconstructed logic is the tendency to equate science with methodology, i.e., *the* scientific method. Such a view restricts the scope of investigations and denies legitimacy to other forms of inquiry (cf. Haworth, 1984). Given the breadth of interests, applied focus and professional mission of social work, it is important to guard against the over-simplified view of science associated with reconstructed logic.

Historical Trends in Scientific Social Work

The relationship of social work and science has gone from indifference to flirtation to open courtship. Beginning with emancipation from religious authority and the secularization of religious ideas, social work moved from a loosely organized activity to a profession claiming rational knowledge at its core. Philanthropy, institutionalized in charity organizations, became scientifically based "in the sense that it was rational, systematizing, and fact-minded in its guidance of the charitable impulse and it tried to prepare dependents to become self-sufficient in the world of the marketplace as conceived by economic science" (Leiby, 1978b, p. 1518). Separation from religious beliefs permitted development of the view that problems had social origins which could be objectively studied and for which there were rational solutions. This view formed the basis of a new profession whose members required special knowledge and skills.

The development of the medical profession in the early 1900's influenced social workers to adopt a scientific model of practice. The transition in medicine from a profession based on practice wisdom to one based on scientific knowledge through research appealed to many as a desirable path for social work. In 1915, the influential physician Abraham Flexner questioned the professional status of social work because of its lack of a knowledge base founded on the "systematic processes of scientific research" (cited in Austin, 1978, p. 163). Fifty-three years later, Lewis Judd, Director of the National Institute of Mental Health, and a physician, echoed similar sentiments as a prelude to announcing the formation of a Task Force on Social Work Research (Judd, 1988).

The emergence of psychoanalytic theory in the 1920's and its adoption by many social workers was viewed as enhancing the scientific status of the profession, particularly through its association with the medical profession. While characterized as non-scientific in contemporary writing, the psychoanalytic perspective shared many of the same underlying assumptions about behavior research and change, e.g., determinism and reductionism, as its more overtly "scientific" competitors like behaviorism (Goldstein, 1986).

This brief historical overview highlights three aspects of the relationship between social work and science: (1) the long-standing interest of social workers in science; (2) the association of rational knowledge with scientific methods; and (3) the influence of the medical profession and its emphasis on applied science. In other words, rationality as the basis of social work knowledge was located in science and defined by the application of scientific criteria (also, see Gottschalk & Witkin, 1991). In this way, social problems could be identified and solved and, most important, social work could emerge as an independent profession with its own knowledge base. Lubove (1965, cited in Rein & White, 1981) comments:

> The persistent efforts of caseworkers to establish a scientific knowledge base and methodology, to limit the area of intuition, moralism and empirical insight, however much they fell short in practice, showed the extent to which the goal of rationality permeated the subculture. (p. 121)

Thus the foundation for a scientific social work was established.

Current Approaches

Nowhere has the call for a more scientific social work been louder or more frequent than in the practice area. Numerous articles and books have appeared extolling the virtues of practitioner-scientists and describing evaluation methods suitable to the practice setting (e.g., Alter & Evens, 1990; Bloom & Fischer, 1982; Jayaratne & Levy, 1979; Wodarski, 1981). Thomas (1975) enumerates the contributions of a scientific orientation to practice:

> [A] scientific perspective [consisting of] scientific attitudes such as objectivity, parsimony and emphasis on evidence ... scientific precepts [such as] observation, operationism and determinism; and the logic of science, which includes formal logic and the logic of experimental inference. (p. 257)

Jayaratne and Levy (1979), among others, envision a practitioner-researcher using empirically based interventions to alter objectively measured problems in order to establish cause-effect relationships between the two.

Despite these hoped-for benefits, conventional research is neither widespread among social workers nor has it resulted in significant advances in knowledge development. Moreover, increasing criticism has arisen concerning the philosophical basis of the conventional approach, the limits it imposes on the scope of legitimate inquiry and its inconsistency with the values and mission of social work practice (e.g., Heineman Pieper, 1981, 1985, 1989, 1994; Saleebey, 1990; Witkin, 1991). The following section examines the implications of the conventional perspective and examines alternative viewpoints.

IMPLICATIONS AND ALTERNATIVES

All models of science contain various presuppositions about the nature of reality. These models form the context from which theories and methods are developed. Weimer (1979) describes such models of science or "metatheories" as providing:

> an explanation for or a perspective from which to view the occurrence of anything within its domain. It is a framework to which anything that can be conceived or discovered in phenomena can be assimilated. It is thus the ultimate framework that renders intelligible past and present knowledge and provides a rationale for future inquiry. (p. 1)

Weimer (1979) calls the dominant metatheory of science justificationism because it is based on the attempt to justify science as a rational source of knowledge. It does this by identifying knowledge with proof and authority. For the adherent of justificationism, a knowledge claim is considered genuine only if it is proven, and proof in turn depends on the epistemological authority of sense experience.

The Nature of Data and Theories

According to justificationism the ultimate basis of knowledge is sense experience, which provides the "demon proof data of immediate experience" (Will, 1974, p. 37). Factual (observational) data acquired through sense experience can be distinguished from theoretical (abstract) propositions which are derived from these facts. This leads to the doctrine of observational (or experimental) proof: propositions must be factual or observable to be true; they are proven from empirically observable facts (Lakatos, 1970).

This line of reasoning provides one answer to the demarcation problem noted earlier: "a theory is 'scientific' if it has an empirical basis" (Lakatos, 1970, p. 98). It follows that the testing of scientific theories should be a relatively straightforward process of hypothesis formulation and controlled experimentation which yields the crucial data of decision making.

The view of facts as given in sense experience and the related view of the supremacy of concrete entities (facts) over abstract entities (theories) has been discredited. Instead, facts have been shown to be conceptual in nature and direct knowing impossible. For instance, according to the doctrine of factual relativity (Weimer, 1979), empirical knowledge requires prior conceptual knowledge. That is, all observation statements presume knowledge of a conceptual class to which the observed "thing" belongs. This is dramatically illustrated by the arduous learning process which adults who obtained sight after being blind from birth must go through to learn the "rules of seeing." Young (1960, cited in Goldstein & Goldstein, 1978) describes this experience:

> For many weeks and months after beginning to see, the person can only with great difficulty distinguish between the simplest shapes, such as a triangle and a square. If you ask him how he does it, he may say, "Of course if I look carefully I may see that there are three sharp turns at the edge of one patch of light, and four on the other." But he may add peevishly, "What on earth do you mean by saying it would be useful to know this?" (p. 16)

We see the world through the conceptual lenses of beliefs and theories which in turn depend on culture and language. As our lenses change so do our facts. Even "calling the reports of our human eye 'observational' only indicates that we 'rely' on some vague psychological theory of human vision" (Lakatos, 1970, p. 107).

Although various attempts have been made to circumvent the difficulties engendered by the above arguments, it is not possible to create a science free of metaphysics and presuppositions (Phillips, 1974). Social reality may be less a "thing" to be discovered empirically than an "equivocal flow" which is constructed and transformed through the sense-making abilities of human beings. Similarly, researchers' definitions of what is to be studied as well as decisions about measurement and interpretation will be dependent on the social and philosophical perspectives of the scientific community (cf. Austin, 1978).

The complexity of human behavior creates special problems for social work researchers. Human actions cannot be understood simply from a topographical description of the behavioral act. Rather, meaning is inferred by the social context within which the act occurs. For instance, while interobserver agreement concerning whether or not a person has moved his arm upwards may be easy to obtain (although even in this case several conditions must be assumed), agreement on the *meaning* of that action is less facile, e.g., waving to a friend or trying to attract attention (Harré & Secord, 1972). Even when the same words are used to describe actions their meaning may be different. For example, identifying a particular interaction between a husband and wife as a "disagreement" will depend, among other factors, upon knowledge of the cultural context. Whereas disagreements among American couples are related to verbal and physical aggression, Indian couples tend to respond not with aggression, but reasoning (Tellis-Nayak & O'Donoghue, 1982).

No one, not even social scientists, has "immaculate perception" (Hanson, 1958). Observed reality is an interpreted reality arising from a complex and changing social and cultural milieu. To the extent that people act on their perceptions, they shape the very social phenomena they experience. From this perspective, the "reality" which social scientists discover is not "out there," but the product of collective sense-making. Understanding such sense-making and how humans create their realities may be a better use of research energies than attempting to map a purported independent reality. For example, Morawski's (1985) contextual analysis of research on masculinity and femininity demonstrates how the social-historical meaning of these concepts led researchers to conduct studies which would confirm the "reality" of these categories. One way of doing this was to develop measures that defined these gender constructs in a similar, stereotyped manner.

The broadening of social work research to include the above orientation has several potential implications for knowledge use. First, it shifts emphasis from truth as the only basis for action to other considerations. That is, by recognizing the transitory and reflexive nature of truth in the social sciences and its inherently moral and political dimensions, social workers may come to evaluate their theories not only in terms of their veracity, but in their ability to further the liberty, empowerment and social justice of clients (Witkin and Gottschalk, 1988).

Second, common forms of understanding are not taken for granted, but examined in terms of their historical and cultural context and their relationship to dominant social institutions (Gergen, 1985). For example, defining menopause as a deficiency disease, rather than a normal aspect of aging, has important consequences for the medical establishment and pharmaceutical industry (McCrea, 1983). Similarly, investigating wife abuse by focusing on women who choose to stay in their relationships creates a new class of deviants ("battered women who remain with their spouses") for whom services are required and provides professional legitimation for interfering in people's lives. Explanations for remaining in such relationships tend to discredit the competence of these women and influence how professionals perceive and provide services to this population (Loseke & Cahill, 1984).

Third, there is increased sensitivity to how understanding is related to context and, consequently, greater caution in the straightforward use of decontextualized, research-generated information. Context influences understanding in two interrelated ways: (1) by determining the meaning of a message, (2) by providing guidelines for category formation and discriminations.

Actions and context form a figure-ground relationship which determine meaning. Practitioners are sensitive to this relationship and often use it to help clients reinterpret the meaning of their own or others' actions. For example, helping a distressed spouse to see her husband's complaints as belonging to the concept class of "attempts to get attention" rather than "put downs" may facilitate more constructive marital interaction. Similarly, research data may take on new meaning when viewed within an historical or social context. This is most apparent when analyzing research on people occupying relatively low status positions in society such as women (Bleier, 1984), people with disabilities (Gliedman & Roth, 1980), and children (Kessel & Siegel, 1981). The terminology used to describe these groups often obscures these important contextual relationships and implicitly promotes ethnocentrism under the guise of scientific neutrality (cf. Harré, Clarke, & DeCarlo, 1985). Contexts differ in their "psychological availability" depending on whether or not they are occupied and the purposes being pursued within them (Shweder & Miller, 1985). Thus, a researcher conducting an experiment on interpersonal communication may distinguish between blue and white collar occupations, "open" and "closed" body postures, and frequency of eye contact. She/he may also combine these variables into a single category such as "emotional expressiveness." In contrast, the context and activities of persons in the role of subjects in this study may lead to distinctions about public and private expressions, normal and abnormal behavior, and compliance with directives given by authority figures versus persons of equal or lesser status. These distinctions may also be viewed as belonging to a common category, i.e., "what it means to be in a research study." Thus the salient context and meaning of the subjects' actions may be vastly different from that assumed by the investigator.

Enactment as Sense-Making

In the previous section, the notion of sense-making was introduced as important to the development of social research. An interesting illustration of this notion is Weick's (1979) concept of enactment. According to Weick (1979) reality is an equivocal stream of potential information which people act upon in order to reduce uncertainty. Since multiple interpretations of situations are always possible, individuals need a way to restrict the possibilities and provide a functional degree of certainty. The process through which this occurs is termed enactment and it is through this process that people create their social environment. Enactment is action which orders experience. This is done through such means as bracketing and self-fulfilling prophecies. In bracketing, a segment of experience is isolated for further attention. Focusing on some portion of a speech or deciding the "starting point" in an interaction sequence are examples of bracketing. In each case some portion of experience is extracted from its total context and examined. In self-fulfilling prophecies a person acts in a way that produces a reaction which confirms the person's belief about others. For example, people who believe that "everyone's out for themselves" may behave in a manner which keeps others from altruistic behavior in their presence. These individuals may see themselves as reacting to, rather than instigating, this situation and see others' behavior as confirmation of their belief (Watzlawick, Beavin, & Jackson, 1967).

The process of enactment produces "a punctuated and connected summary of a previously equivocal display" (Weick, 1979, p. 131). Equivocality is reduced by imposing structures (causal maps) on these occurrences and selecting meanings and interpretations. Some of this imposed meaning is retained and used to help interpret future situations.

A concept like enactment has several implications for a scientific social work. Conventional researchers who neatly divide the world into distinct entities of people and environments tend to ask certain types of questions and exclude others. For example, an independent environment may be investigated with the aim of identifying its component parts (its "facts"). Once identified, one might look at how these components affect individuals by restricting exposure to one or two of the components and measuring the reaction of the research subjects. Three features of this line of investigation are that: (1) the people serving as subjects are viewed as information-processors rather than information seekers and information-generators (Harré & Secord, 1972); (2) by looking at people as reactors to an independent environment, questions concerning how this environment might be a *product* of individuals are excluded; (3) the picture of the world produced by these studies is static and omits descriptions of the process of individual-environment interaction.

When one's view of "what is out there" is broadened to include enactment processes, distinctions between people and their environment become less clear. Instead of concern solely with environmental variables which produce a response, one might, following Bateson (1972) ask: "What circumstances determine that a given scientist will punctuate the stream of events so as to conclude that all is predetermined, while another will see the stream of events as so regular as to be susceptible to control?" (p. 163). The social environment is often aware it is being observed and understanding differences in information gained as a function of this awareness is an important topic in its own right.

Openness in Social Work Inquiry

The issue here is not the merits of enactment as a metaphor for human behavior, but the degree to which research should be open enough to incorporate such concepts. While a more open approach might lead, in the short run, to a certain amount of confusion, it would also provide an opportunity to broaden the breadth of social work inquiry and, perhaps, forge novel inroads into our understanding of social issues. As illustrated below in Weick's (1979) comment about organizations, social work researchers will have to undergo a cognitive shift if they are to adopt a more open approach to inquiry.

[An organization] that is sensitive to the fact that it produces enacted environments will be less concerned with issues of truth and falsity and more concerned with issues of reasonableness. If environments are enacted then there is no such thing as a representation that is true or false, there simply are versions that are more or less reasonable. Thus, endless discussion of questions about whether we see things the way they really are, whether we are right, or whether something is true will be replaced by discussions that focus on questions such as What did we do? What senses can we make of those actions? What didn't we do? (p. 169)

Openness to new forms of scientific inquiry would affect the questions social work researchers ask and the way outcomes generated by these questions are evaluated. Two examples of alternative evaluation criteria are valuational implications and intellectual generativity (Gergen & Gergen, 1982). Valuational implications arise from the recognition of a valuing component associated with most explanatory forms. For instance, situation versus person-based explanations of human behavior may be linked to values concerning individual versus group benefits. Belief in the benefit of individual action and self-expression and dislike of dependence may be fortified by person-centered explanatory forms. Commitment to aggregate forms of social organization (e.g., community) and suspicion concerning the efficacy of independent expression may be supported by situational forms of explanation.

The valuational implications of explanatory forms extend to the conceptual base of social institutions. For example, political institutions may find different explanatory forms more or less consistent with the forms of governance they advocate. Arguments in favor of one form or the other thus become exercises in ideological justification. Intellectual generativity refers to the assessment of rival interpretations by comparing "their capacity to unsettle or challenge common assumptions within the culture" (Gergen & Gergen, 1982, p. 148; also, see Gergen, 1978). To the extent that dominant explanatory forms restrict options and constrain action, challenging them reduces these constraints.

Enhancement of human welfare is not necessarily an objective of science (Abel, 1976), yet this should be a primary concern of scientific social work. Social research as a value-based endeavor is implicit in the above evaluation criteria. Facts are not discovered and then subject to value judgments; they are already, in part, the product of these judgments. And the resultant understandings about human life are themselves statements about the political and moral condition of people (cf. Harré, 1984). Consideration of alternative criteria facilitates analysis of the underlying moral and political dimensions of social theory and research (Witkin & Gottschalk, 1988). Such analyses can further the development of a model of science consistent with social work values (Haworth, 1984).

A comprehensive approach to social work issues requires multiple perspectives and methodologies. The controversy over the withholding of medical treatment to newborns with congenital disabilities illustrates this point. While it may be important to know the number of infants and the types of medical problems that are subject to treatment/no treatment decisions, it is also necessary to understand how linguistic constraints, theories of childhood, personhood, etc. may restrict our conception of and responses to this situation.

Important value questions such as how *ought* newborn humans be treated do not exist independently of our efforts to study this issue. It is a strength of the social work profession that it can legitimately be involved with all these types of questions. To do this requires a model of science and a method of inquiry flexible enough to recognize and accommodate the complexities of human social life.

Introduction to "The Heuristic Paradigm: A Unifying and Comprehensive Approach to Social Work Research"

In the following paper, Martha Heineman Pieper describes why social work needs a new approach to research, shows how the heuristic paradigm is unifying and comprehensive, offers some examples of applications of the heuristic paradigm in designing research, and clarifies some common misunderstandings of the heuristic paradigm. During the years between 1981, when Heineman Pieper's first paper on the philosophy of research was published, and 1989, when she was invited to give the following paper as the Brown Foundation Lecture on Research at the Smith College School for Social Work, research in social work underwent an important transition. Social work practitioners increasingly became dissatisfied with traditional approaches to research (which we now call the positivist paradigm of social work research), and many studies indicated that students viewed social work research courses as boring and irrelevant (S. Kirk, Osmalov, & Fischer, 1976; Rubin, Franklin, & Selber, 1992; Welch, 1983). Educators, scholars, and practitioners increasingly became concerned about what came to be known as the "gulf" between research and practice in the field of social work. At the same time, many social work scholars became interested in understanding the philosophical bases of research and in applying insights from contemporary philosophy of science to social work research. Heineman Pieper's critique of the positivist research paradigm served as a catalyst for critiques of that paradigm and for the search for alternatives. However, largely because the heuristic paradigm is still so new and most scholars have been educated in positivism, some recent applications of concepts from the heuristic paradigm have been unduly limited in scope (DeRoos, 1990; Zimmerman, 1989).

The movement toward an alternative paradigm steadily gathered momentum in the 1980s (Haworth, 1984; Sherman, 1987; Siporin, 1985). The Philosophical Issues Study Group was founded by a group of social work scholars and educators who shared the goal of examining and formulating conceptual foundations for social work research and practice (Imre, 1991a). By 1989, the Study Group had over 200 members. Members have authored numerous articles critiquing positivist approaches to social and behavioral research and advancing and applying postpositivist alternatives. In 1991, Martha Heineman Pieper was asked to give the keynote address (Heineman Pieper, 1994) at a landmark conference about new approaches to investigating social work practice, organized by Professor Edmund Sherman at the State University of New York at Albany.

Increased enthusiasm for alternatives to the positivist paradigm now has enabled the social work profession to offer its educators, scholars, practitioners, and students a choice of research paradigm. Debates and controversy about the best social work research paradigm occur in many contexts and frequently are quite heated. Different schools of social work tend to adopt different research paradigms; different educators may espouse different research paradigms; and editors of social work journals take either the more restrictive view of research consistent with the positivist paradigm or the more open view of research espoused by researchers who adopt the heuristic paradigm. As Heineman Pieper points out in the following paper and citing her own experience as a student, the choice of research paradigm determines what research is considered acceptable for students, educators, and practitioners to undertake and disseminate (see also Hartman, 1990; A. Weick, 1992). The choice of paradigm also regulates our evaluation of the merit of our work as caseworkers, policymakers, program managers, and researchers. Ultimately, although positivist social researchers conceptualize the choice of paradigm in terms of prescribing the methods that will yield scientific knowledge, researchers who adopt the heuristic paradigm recognize that the debate concerns a choice of the values used in appraising and generating scientific research (Laudan, 1984).

At this point in learning the heuristic approach to research, you may find it most helpful to concentrate on choosing ontological and epistemological assumptions and drawing the environment–system boundary. As Heineman Pieper emphasizes, when researchers choose a system to study, they do so, in part, on the basis of prior ontological assumptions (assumptions about the "real," or object of study). Examine Figure 3–3a. What do you see? Some see an antelope, others a bird. Your assumptions about reality influence what you see. Now look at Figure 3–3b. What do you see? Now look at Figure 3–3c. These illustrations show how, because meaning is contextual, we make assumptions about reality based on familiar contexts. Every researcher necessarily makes ontological and epistemological assumptions. A behaviorist, for example, would assert that the "real" is discrete quantified behaviors. Similarly, the choice of epistemology—or how to know that real, including identifying the allowable sources of evidence—also sets up systematic bias. For example, a neurologist who limits investigation of a child's functioning to the results of an electroencephalogram and a neurological exam will have very different information about that child than a social worker who conducted a psychodynamic diagnostic session using play therapy. The heuristic paradigm encourages you to reflectively examine the ontological and epistemological assumptions you make and to examine the fit between those assumptions. As Heineman Pieper points out, one tenet of the positivist paradigm is that researchers can only determine scientifically those aspects of reality that they can investigate using those methods the positivists deemed scientific. Positivism prescribes epistemological assumptions that in turn delimit ontological assumptions; it therefore endorses an unreflective or "knee-jerk" approach to planning research. In contrast, the researcher who adopts the heuristic paradigm can prioritize analyzing the conceptual consistency and social relevance of the choices being made in designing research as well as the biases introduced by each choice.

Heineman Pieper's description of the environment–system boundary is based on the work of William Wimsatt (see his article in Chapter 5). As Heineman Pieper notes, every researcher, in choosing a system to study, necessarily simplifies the variables not studied by placing them in the environment. You probably can think of many examples of how researchers have made important discoveries by changing the environment–system boundary used to explore a problem. One noted example

Figure 3–3
Context and ontological
assumptions

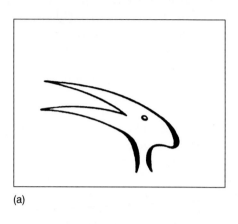

(a)

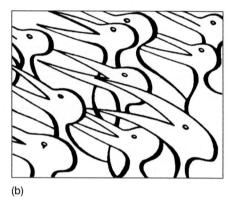

(b)

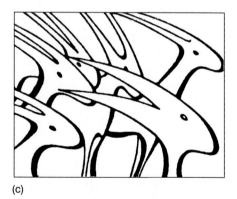

(c)

Source: Adapted from the work of Norwood Russell Hanson
with the permission of Mrs. Fay Hanson

concerns explanations about the interplay between family relationship patterns and schizophrenic symptoms. The bizarre features of schizophrenic communication were often attributed to the patient's neurological dysfunction, limiting the system under study to the patient's neurological tissue and placing family relationships, unstudied, in the environment. When Bateson and his colleagues expanded the environment–system boundary by looking at the family relationships of schizophrenic patients, they made the important discovery that the specific features of schizophrenic communication could be understood as a response to the "double-bind" communication patterns in the family (Bateson, Jackson, Haley, & Weakland, 1956). Examining and changing where one draws the boundary is a very useful way to determine the biases one is generating in planning research.

DISCUSSION QUESTIONS

1. Briefly state five tenets of the heuristic paradigm. What are some common misunderstandings of the heuristic paradigm?

2. What is objectivity according to the heuristic paradigm? Why is reproducibility not a guarantee of the value of a research finding?

3. a. A noted contemporary controversy in geology concerns how the dinosaurs died (Raup, 1986). Some believe that meteors from outer space destroyed the dinosaurs and their environment, and others believe the earth's climate changed and became inimical to dinosaur life. How do those different theories reflect different environment–system boundaries?

   b. How did the following researchers draw the environment–system boundary?

      i. Sigmund Freud, when he decided that the primary cause of psychopathology was intrapsychic conflict rather than traumatic nurture;

      ii. John Broadus Watson, when he recommended that psychologists make "behavior, not consciousness, the objective point of our attack. Certainly there are enough problems in the control of behavior to keep us all working many lifetimes without ever allowing us time to think of consciousness" (1913). How does his delineation of the system under study also reflect his ontological assumptions?

      iii. Jane Addams and Florence Kelley, when they concluded that to remedy the problem of maltreatment of child laborers, reform of the state laws regulating child labor was necessary (see Chap. 2);

      iv. Mary Richmond, when she decided that to study the process of helping Maria Bielowski she should focus on the case process records and talk with the social worker treating Maria (see Chapter 2).

4. What are some of the consequences of a scientific discipline's choice of research paradigm?

5. Take a social or behavioral problem that interests you and practice formulating that problem by drawing the environment–system boundary in different ways.

Look at the information you include and exclude each time you redraw the environment–system boundary.

6. What are some of the biases of experimental designs as outlined by Heineman Pieper?

7. Review Heineman Pieper's discussion of prediction in her 1981 paper and in this 1989 paper. How is a prediction *not* an explanation?

8. What "reals" do scientists in the following disciplines study, and how do they know those "reals"?

   a. astronomy
   b. microbiology
   c. geology
   d. neurology
   e. sociology
   f. psychology
   g. social work
   h. education

9. a. Describe the fit between the problem formulations and ontological and epistemological assumptions in the following examples:

   i. Using a crystal ball that shows graphs of the frequencies of a client's prior violent behaviors to determine the client's potential for violent behavior

   ii. The Cowardly Lion's attempts to overcome his phobias by going to the Wizard of Oz

   iii. The Scarecrow's efforts to gain wisdom by going to the Wizard of Oz

   b. Using the preceding problem formulations, revise the ontological and epistemological assumptions so that a workable solution to the problem would be more likely.

10. Practitioners of both the heuristic and positivist paradigms are concerned with appraising the quality of research designs.

   a. What standards do positivist researchers use to appraise research designs?

   b. What principles can researchers who adopt the heuristic paradigm use to appraise the quality of research designs?

11. a. Try out the heuristic approach by planning a research project on a problem that interests you. Discuss how you formulate the problem, the ontological and epistemological assumptions of your chosen theory, and where you draw the environment–system boundary. Why do you think the choices you have made will provide you with the most useful information about the problem you want to study?

   b. Summarize the biases introduced by each of the choices you have made.

The Heuristic Paradigm: A Unifying and Comprehensive Approach to Social Work Research

MARTHA HEINEMAN PIEPER, PH.D.*

ABSTRACT: Social work should adopt the broad-minded, up-to-date heuristic paradigm of research in place of the overly restrictive, outmoded logical positivist paradigm. In a misguided attempt to become as scientific as the natural sciences, social work has embraced the logical positivist paradigm since the 1950s. But contemporary philosophy of science has undercut conclusively logical positivism's claims and demonstrated that the logical positivist paradigm places unnecessary limitations on scientific endeavors. Unlike the logical positivist paradigm, the heuristic paradigm welcomes the complex, ill-structured, substantively important problems that have been social work's abiding focus. The principles of the heuristic paradigm facilitate rather than obstruct cooperation between researcher and practitioner and between researchers in different fields. Most importantly, the heuristic paradigm makes research user-friendly by expanding rather than restricting the operation of human judgment in the knowledge-building process. The principles, applications, and common misunderstandings of the heuristic paradigm are described.

INTRODUCTION

Today I would like to discuss the heuristic paradigm of social work research (following Kuhn, 1977; Simon, 1966a; Wimsatt, 1986b). *Heuristic* in this usage simply means any problem-solving strategy that appears likely to lead to relevant, reliable, and useful informa-tion. As I have indicated elsewhere (Heineman, 1981; [Heineman] Pieper, 1985), the heuristic approach to research is consistent with mainstream contemporary philosophy of science, which has been accepted by other social sciences to a much greater degree than it has been embraced by social work (see Bhaskar, 1978; Bixenstein, 1976; Blalock, 1979; Bronfenbrenner, 1977; Campbell, 1975; Coser, 1975; Cronbach, 1975, 1986; Mishler, 1979; Noble, 1974; Oldman, 1981; Olshewsky, 1975; Rubenstein, 1984; Rychlak, 1980; Schultz, 1971).

The main obstacle to social work's acceptance of the heuristic paradigm is that the profession has been reluctant to part from the outmoded, logical positivist philosophy of science it espoused in the 1950s (see Blenkner, 1950; Epstein, 1986; Fischer, 1981; Geismar & Wood, 1982; Hudson, 1982; Mullen, 1985).[1] The Social Work Research Group was organized in

*Martha Heineman Pieper is a consultant and private practitioner in Chicago. This paper was given as the Brown Foundation Lecture in Research at the Smith College School for Social Work, July 10, 1989.
Source: "The Heuristic Paradigm: A Unifying and Comprehensive Approach to Social Work Research" by M. Heineman Pieper, 1989, *Smith College Studies in Social Work, 60,* pp. 8–34. Copyright 1989 by Smith College. Reprinted by permission.
Reprint from *Smith College Studies in Social Work,* November 1989, Volume 60 No. 1

[1] There are, of course, social work authors who have questioned the logical positivist hold on social work research (Goldstein, 1986; Heineman [Pieper], 1981, p. 391, n. 2; Pieper, 1985, p. 9, n. 2; Zimmerman, 1989).

1948 in the hope that social work would both enhance its respectability in the scientific community and produce more certain, reliable knowledge by adopting the scientific principles of the so-called hard sciences (Greenwood, 1952, 1955; Kogan, 1960; Macdonald, 1960b). Ironically, by the 1950s the natural sciences were in the process of abandoning logical positivist principles as unworkable and unnecessarily restrictive (see Colodny, 1966; Suppe, 1974). Briefly, logical positivism is a restrictive view of science that arose in Vienna in the 1920s, underwent numerous transformations in a futile attempt to shore up its claim that its prescriptions and proscriptions could produce a superior type of scientific knowledge (Carnap, 1936), and has been abandoned almost entirely by philosophers of science. By 1972, *The Encyclopedia of Philosophy* concluded that logical positivism "is dead, or as dead as a philosophical movement ever becomes" (Hanfling, 1981b, p. 1).[2] Asked in 1979 what he saw as the main defects of logical positivism, one of the foremost advocates of the logical positivist program, A. J. Ayer, replied, "I suppose the most important . . . was that nearly all of it was false" (quoted in Hanfling, 1981b, p. 1). Even so, logical positivism's hold on social work has been tenacious and, even in the other social sciences, the grip of the logical positivist paradigm has been slow to relax. For example, as late as 1979, the psychologist Mishler said that "The philosophical critique of positivist science has not had much effect on psychological and social research" (p. 3).

Like numerous other philosophers since Descartes, the logical positivists' determining value was certainty. They looked for a way to free scientific findings from human error so as to guarantee that scientific results directly mirror reality, concluding that specific observations, namely perceptions of the observable properties of material things brought to us by the five senses, are the preferred means of scientific investigation

because these observations do not distort reality. Further, the logical positivists thought that logical operations could organize these undistorted observations without adding any new information, thereby preserving the purity of the observations.[3] Scientifically meaningful theories, then, are nothing more than abbreviations of empirical observations (see Ayer, 1959; Hanfling, 1981a). It is evident from this brief summary that logical positivism both prescribes and also proscribes specific scientific endeavors. To illustrate, the logical positivist would consider a theory of empathy inappropriate for rigorous scientific study, because empathy cannot be observed in ways the logical positivist considers to be unproblematic. However, because logical positivist prescriptions and proscriptions rest on invalid assumptions, they retard science by placing unnecessary limits on scientific investigation. For example, as contemporary philosophers of science have shown, the study of motor behavior is no less problematic than the study of empathy.

While the prevailing model of social work research does not specifically endorse each and every one of the logical positivist tenets just mentioned, it has adopted the prescriptive and proscriptive viewpoint that accompanies these principles. For example, social work researchers generally accept the logical positivist conclusion that the experimental method is the most scientific way to test theories.

Most of us learned the logical positivist paradigm at some point in our schooling, whether under the name of the scientific method, empirical research, or grounded theory. You have been exposed to the logical positivist research paradigm if: (a) you have learned that the *best* research always follows the experimental method, which is characterized by prediction, operationalized definitions, control groups, randomized subjects, and quantified data, and (b) you have learned that all other research strategies, such as those involving retrospective designs and qualitative data, are inferior or "soft" and are to be used only when the more "rigorous," experimental method is for some reason not feasible (Geismar & Wood, 1982; Hanrahan & Reid, 1984; Howe, 1976; Reid, 1983; Reid & Smith, 1981). In previous articles and lectures, I have presented a systematic critique of the logical positivist research paradigm (Heineman, 1981; [Heineman]

---

[2] An important, less restrictive offshoot of logical positivism is known as logical empiricism, but, following Hanfling (1981b, p. 6), since logical positivism is the most current and generic term, I apply it to the philosophy of research adopted by social work in the 1950s. As used here, then, logical positivism is intended to include logical empiricism. While social work did not adopt the most extreme planks of the logical positivist program, it wholeheartedly accepted logical positivism's prescriptive and proscriptive approach to scientific activity. It is this claim of methodological privilege that is challenged by the heuristic paradigm.

---

[3] Hence the name logical empiricism.

Pieper, 1985). Here, I would like to focus on the heuristic paradigm of research and the advantages it offers social work.

The heuristic paradigm of research is based on the broadminded philosophy of science that has replaced logical positivism and has been generally accepted by the natural sciences. The notion of a "heuristic" was introduced into philosophy of science by the Nobel laureate Herbert Simon (1966b). A heuristic is a problem-solving strategy whose goal is utility rather than certainty. The heuristic researcher takes the realistic view that real life problems are too complex, interactive, and perceiver-dependent to lend themselves to comprehensive analysis and exact solutions. Whether or not they recognize it, *all* problem solvers (including the logical positivists) rely on problem-solving strategies, or heuristics, to make problems manageable and to produce helpful information. To illustrate, we clearly cannot study social dysfunction simultaneously from the perspective of the individual, the family, and socio-economic, political, cultural, and ecological influences. The moment we choose a focus, we choose a heuristic (Wimsatt, 1980b, 1981a). Paradoxically, rather than representing prescriptions for good science, the rules of the experimental method are examples of heuristics. Understood as heuristics, they are potentially useful research tools.

As summarized by Wimsatt (1986b, p. 295), four of the most important properties of heuristics are:

1. In contrast to the logical positivist view of the scientific method as truth preserving, heuristics make no guarantee to produce a correct solution to a problem.

2. Heuristics are short cuts that conserve scientific resources.

3. The errors, or biases, of particular heuristics are systematic. For example, the social worker whose practice is limited to individuals will rarely focus on group dynamics.

4. Heuristics transform the problem to which they are applied to a different, but related problem. Thus, we must always evaluate the appropriateness of our answers to the original problem.

When the question of the appropriate philosophy of research for social work is raised, a frequent reaction is that this issue is esoteric and irrelevant because scientific research, which is seen as down-to-earth and empirical, is not significantly affected by philosophy, which is seen as abstract, bloodless, and metaphysical (Hudson, 1982, p. 250). A related reaction is that good research is atheoretical and, therefore, should be divorced completely from the researcher's philosophy of research. The problem with this view, of course, is that the assertion that research can be atheoretical itself expresses a philosophical viewpoint. Every researcher has a philosophy of research, which he or she may or may not acknowledge and articulate. Once we realize that all research decisions are shaped by the researcher's beliefs, it becomes clear that the choice of a research philosophy is critically important. The philosophy of research we select determines what questions we let ourselves ask, how we go about answering them, what knowledge we consider valid, and the quality of the knowledge we develop. The following brief personal example is offered to illustrate the limitations that social work's choice of the logical positivist philosophy of research has placed on the scope of our professional activities.

In 1977 I chose a dissertation topic which, coincidentally, necessitated a research design that was retrospective and generated qualitative rather than quantitative data. In collaboration with William J. Pieper, I had been working to develop a comprehensive psychodynamic psychology, named *Intrapsychic Humanism* (Pieper & Pieper, in press),* which was being tested in a demonstration project underwritten by the Illinois Department of Children and Family Services. The Department selected the institutionalized adolescents it deemed most incorrigible, and we placed them in a residential program organized by the therapeutic principles of our new psychology. I was treating a homicidal and suicidal fifteen year old, whose behavior was so ungovernable that she had been expelled from every Illinois institution in which she had been placed. . . . In terms of our theory, the data most appropriate for understanding the teenager's treatment process were daily process recordings made over a three-year period, in combination with child care workers' and administrators' comments in the staff log. Outside corroboration that our treatment approach was promising came from the fact that the State Department reviewed the adolescents' progress on a monthly basis and continued to spend thousands of dollars a year to maintain each child in the program.

---

*Editor's Note: Now, Pieper & Pieper, 1990.

I easily obtained three faculty sponsors and prepared my project for the proposal committee, which was a three-member faculty committee that had been established to review all dissertation proposals to ensure that they were sufficiently scientific. To my amazement, the proposal committee decided that my data would not be allowed, first, because they were generated from a project that was already in progress and, therefore, were retrospective and, second, because recollected process recordings were not "empirical," or "hard" data. I was told that only a tape recorder or third party observer could produce acceptable data (Nelson, 1981) and that, in addition, I would have to design a prospective study.

At that point I felt confused. It was clear to me that I would seriously provoke this suicidal and homicidal fifteen year old if I introduced a tape recorder or a note-taking observer into her treatment session. Because it would endanger my client and myself, this method of data gathering was not a feasible way to study the treatment process in which I was interested. When I raised this issue with the proposal committee, they responded that clients usually adjust easily to tape recorders and observers, but that, if I didn't think this girl could tolerate this form of data gathering, I would have to study some other treatment process that could produce "empirical" data. In other words, according to logical positivist tenets, in its natural form my concerted efforts with this client could in principle never be a source of scientific knowledge.

I realized that I would have to learn about philosophy of science in order to understand why my process recordings and the staff log were not considered acceptable data. A day later, I introduced myself to a philosopher of science, William Wimsatt, who generously agreed to take on in individual tutorial a social work student who knew absolutely nothing about his field. As I read the logical positivists of the Vienna Circle, subsequent elaborations of their viewpoints, and contemporary philosophers of science, new vistas appeared. I began to understand that the logical positivist theories and rules I had learned were created from defective arguments and assumptions and, consequently, were unreasonably restrictive. For example, it became clear that, since no facts are privileged, process recordings and staff logs are in principle perfectly valid data and, further, since prediction alone serves no explanatory function, retrospective designs are in principle just as acceptable as predictive ones.

As the proposal committee's decision illustrates, the nature of the research paradigm adopted by social work can determine any aspect of our profession's activities, including what articles are published in social work journals, what is considered good practice, what papers and dissertations are allowed, what questions can be studied, who gets funded, who gets tenured, and, most importantly, whether the field generates a knowledge base that is meaningful to its practitioners. To illustrate, social work's choice of the restrictive, logical positivist paradigm of research has meant that naturalistic interactions (such as the functioning of a large social service agency) and complex problems (such as those presented by multiple-problem families) are often regarded as too untidy and complex to study scientifically, because the variables involved are difficult to isolate, measure and manipulate.

Concomitantly, social work researchers in the logical positivist tradition who investigate clinical methods tend to simplify and manipulate the social work services they study, and often demand that participating clinicians practice *research-determined casework* (Reid, 1977b, 1978). In research-determined casework, investigators believe it is reasonable to choose interventions *solely* for their hypothesized value to produce scientifically acceptable data, and they often fail to consider whether these interventions are congruent with sound practice principles. For example, single-subject researchers frequently ask practitioners to withhold an intervention that seems to be working in order to determine if the client's symptoms will reappear (Hersen & Barlow, 1976, pp. 92—100; Kazdin, 1982, pp. 116-219). Research-determined casework is a heuristic that practitioners do not value. When practitioners are told to make interventions that either have no therapeutic value or may actually be actively antitherapeutic, they understandably become resentful and uncooperative. Practitioners rightly wonder whether knowledge can be helpful to them when it is produced by manipulated treatments that gratuitously cause their clients to regress. Analogously, when researchers artificially limit the length of treatment and simplify interventions in the belief that shorter treatment is better for research purposes, practitioners realize that their clients' needs and their own clinical judgments are being ignored by researchers. Not surprisingly, then, practitioners have largely concluded that research studies are irrelevant to their daily tasks and, therefore, they ignore them. Researchers, in turn, believe that practitioners are alienated from research methods and findings because they are frightened of statistics, and demand that schools of social work increase students' statistical literacy. While everyone should understand quantitative methodology, in my opinion an increased knowledge of statistics will never bridge the current gulf between practitioner and researcher.

The tension between researchers and practitioners and, in academic settings, between research faculty and clinical faculty, results from social work's embrace of the logical positivists' prescriptive and proscriptive view of research. If social work were to adopt the heuristic paradigm, the gulf between the researcher and practitioner would narrow significantly. Researchers and practitioners could collaborate fruitfully, and practitioners would feel motivated to read and engage in research. In other words, the heuristic paradigm makes it possible for researcher and practitioner to cohabit peacefully in one person.

THE HEURISTIC PARADIGM OF RESEARCH

Most importantly, the heuristic paradigm of research attempts to leave behind the outmoded and inappropriately restrictive tenets of the logical positivist paradigm, and to adopt a view of research that embraces the principles of the more inclusive philosophy of science that has been emerging over the last 50 years. I will give you a few examples of fundamental tenets of contemporary philosophy of science that are incorporated into the heuristic paradigm of research. First is the recognition that facts and theories are not distinct; facts are influenced by theories just as theories are shaped by facts (Shapere, 1982). There are no "immaculate perceptions" (Hanson, 1969a, p. 74). In contrast to the logical positivist assumption that the five senses give us direct reports of reality, reality is actually constructed through the interpretation of sensory experience within a preexisting framework of meanings. In other words, knowledge is to some extent perceiver dependent. A dramatic illustration of the constructed nature of sense perception is that when individuals who have been blind since birth have their sight restored, they have to be taught to "see." Initially, they experience only an incomprehensible welter of visual stimuli (Segall, Campbell & Herskovits, 1966, p. 79).

Since no facts are privileged, that is, no one category of facts is inherently better at telling us about reality than another category of facts, the heuristic researcher selects types of data and methods of data gathering for their appropriateness both to the theory chosen to guide the research and also to the problem under study. Every choice of measurement both reflects the philosophical, professional, personal and other biases that the perceiver brings to the measurement, and also *creates* bias by, inevitably, excluding other information. In this context, bias has no pejorative meaning, but rather denotes the inevitable distortions that occur whenever we attempt to describe reality. Because the choice of one type of data is a choice to eliminate other types of data, and because no type of data is more likely to give a privileged report of reality than any other type of data, the choice of data is a crucial aspect of the research design and should not be followed unthinkingly, as though it were a recipe in a cookbook.

For example, let us look at the logical positivists' preference for quantified data. It is certainly true that quantified data can contribute important information abut certain problems. If we are studying the impact of social work services on infant mortality rates, quantitative data may provide the best account of whether the percent of infant deaths is increasing or decreasing. For this purpose, we may not be primarily interested in qualitative data, such as workers' perceptions of change. On the other hand, if we are interested in improving casework services to high school dropouts, we may well choose qualitative data—such as the judgments of the caseworkers who are working with the teenagers as to how to reach them more effectively and, even, suggestions from the teens themselves about how they could be better served. Note that quantifying this data might actually obscure the information we want most to obtain. Because we are interested in the perceptive and creative aspects of the workers' and teens' suggestions, we would not want to use principles of quantification to gather or evaluate them. For example, since the best and most helpful suggestion might be made by only one person, suggestions should not be rated by their frequency, but, rather, each suggestion should be considered seriously in its own right.[4]

---

[4] For the logical positivist, the most important function of clients' and workers' non-quantified suggestions is to generate hypotheses that can be tested experimentally.

I am proposing that when a researcher's chosen theory considers workers' and clients' suggestions to be important data in and of themselves and also considers the researcher's own informed judgment to be adequate to evaluate these suggestions, the researcher can reasonably select those suggestions deemed most appropriate and use them to make program changes without putting them through the wringer of operationalizing definitions, quantification, and predictive designs (Leahey, 1980). Given social work's values and mission, it is surprising that practitioners and clients are so often treated as objects of study rather than as informants. Anthropology, on the other hand, has long recognized that the most valuable data is produced by treating the people it studies as informants rather than as objects (Adair & Spinner, 1981; Levine, 1981). The heuristic paradigm suggests that practitioners' and clients' judgments should be evaluated by the same rules as any other data, namely, by whether they lead to useful knowledge and more effective service.

Because observations are not equivalent to direct reports of reality, no descriptive statistic, or summary of events, ever speaks for itself (Kazdin, 1977). The meaningfulness of any change is always a matter of judgment. If an agoraphobic client who has only been able to come to treatment with a companion travels alone on the bus to her session, her social worker will probably conclude that the symptom-free day is significant. On the other hand, the social worker treating the chronic alcoholic may decide that, although the alcoholic has gone without a drink for one day, this symptom-free time does not represent a significant change. Nothing in the statistic itself tells the investigator how to weigh its importance; only her informed judgment will allow the investigator to make this determination. Once our results are in, whether we conclude that a statistic is meaningful or meaningless, we need to show our thought processes and give others the best possible opportunity for reflective agreement or disagreement.

Since the heuristic paradigm recognizes that every observation is shaped by the observer's presuppositions, it reformulates the logical positivist belief in scientific objectivity. In the heuristic paradigm, objectivity is a heuristic, or problem-solving strategy, rather than a given. One of the most pervasive myths perpetuated by the logical positivist paradigm is that researchers possess greater objectivity than practitioners. But contemporary philosophers of science have argued persuasively that objectivity is not a state of mind but, rather, is simply a species of report in which there is agreement among researchers (Bixenstein, 1976). While the heuristic of objectivity can product a high level of reproducibility, reproducibility can be understood as the result of shared bias and does not establish truth. Reproducibility may result from many factors, including the observer's training, professional allegiance, and area of specialization, as well as personal and cultural influences. The incorrect logical positivist assumption that practitioners' judgments are highly subjective while researchers' judgments are highly objective contributes to the current conflict between researchers and practitioners (Briar, 1980; Karger, 1983; Rein & White, 1981; Saleebeg, 1979). In the heuristic paradigm, the distinction between system (that which is studied) and environment (that which is held constant or, in other words, is not studied) is viewed as a necessary but arbitrary simplification, whose purpose is to manage a sprawling and ill-structured problem.

In contrast, the logical positivist paradigm perpetuates the illusion of researcher objectivity by uniformly drawing an environment-system boundary that excludes the researcher from the system being studied (Wimsatt, 1981a). For example, when investigating treatment, the logical positivist places the client and, often, the practitioner, in the system being studied, while excluding the researcher, who is assumed to be objective. Actually, of course, the researcher is merely out of focus and, therefore, his or her influence goes unnoticed.

The researcher working in the heuristic paradigm draws environment-system boundaries thoughtfully rather than automatically and varies them to yield new information. To illustrate, when the environment-system boundary is drawn to include the researcher in the system being studied, it becomes clear that the researcher and any of her surrogates, such as a videotape, are actively reacted to by the rest of the system (Gadlin & Ingle, 1975; Mishler, 1979; Orne, 1969; Rosenthal, 1980; Rosnow & Davis, 1977; Wachtel, 1980). It goes completely against common sense to think that either the client who is just getting to know the practitioner, or the client who has become comfortable sharing intimate details with a practitioner she or he has come to know, will be unaffected by the presence of either an audio or video recorder or an observing stranger. The researcher who believes that her or his mechanical surrogates are not affecting the practitioner-client interaction displays the bias that results from an unreflective determination of the environment-system boundary. You need only ask yourselves whether you would share a meaningful private experience as freely in the presence of a tape recorder or a note-taking stranger as you would alone with a person you knew and trusted.

As the natural sciences generally recognize, every measurement is influenced by the observer, that is, affects the object being observed (Margenau, 1966). Put differently, every measurement is an interaction. In consequence, subjectivity, or bias, accompanies all scientific endeavors. The heuristic researcher practices bias regulation through bias recognition rather than through the denial of bias. An important step is to recognize that all research strategies, or problem-solving heuristics, introduce systematic bias (Wimsatt, 1981a, 1986b). If we believe that by choosing the "right" research method we can minimize or eliminate bias, then we cease to look for it. One strength of the heuristic paradigm is that it encourages everyone involved in research to try to recognize and manage biases in a nonjudgmental context.

In keeping with the tenet that no facts are privileged, each method of investigation is a heuristic, or common sense rule of thumb and, therefore, no more likely than any other research method to produce useful knowledge. Accordingly, the heuristic paradigm counters the logical positivist claim that the experimental method is *in principle* the best way to test theories. This claim is illustrated by Reid and Smith's assertion that "experimental approaches are the most direct and powerful means that research can provide for improving social work practice" (Reid & Smith, 1981, p. 67).* Like all heuristics, however, the experimental method has its own biases and limitations. Logical positivists distort the experimental method, which is a successful heuristic that has unquestionably advanced scientific understanding, by making inappropriate claims for the superiority of its findings.

One defective assumption that underlies the logical positivist assertion that the experimental method is the best way to test theories is that to predict an event is to explain it. The logical positivist insists that prediction is necessary for optimal science and, correspondingly, proscribes retrospective science except when a prospective study is not feasible. But prediction and explanation serve entirely different functions. We can

predict with a high degree of certainty that if we drop an apple from a tree, it will fall to the ground, but when our prediction comes true we still have not explained the event. Possible explanations are the ripening of the apple, the law of gravity or, as earlier scientists thought, the ground's attraction for the apple. Further, many useful explanatory theories, such as the theory of evolution, have little or no predictive power.

A related flaw in the logical positivist argument for the inherent superiority of the experimental method is that this argument rests on the unwarranted claim that information about cause and effect produced by the experimental method is somehow privileged. Like objectivity, causality is a heuristic. Causality is a useful assumption we make about the world rather than a law of nature. When I kick a stone and it moves, I can only say for sure that the relationship between my kick and the stone's movement is highly correlated. Also, because we can never rule out all alternative hypotheses, no matter how many variables we try to control for, we cannot draw an unproblematic conclusion that the experimental input did or did not cause any change that occurred in the dependent variable.[5] To illustrate, suppose that we develop a theory about the causes of the high incidence of unplanned, unwanted teenage pregnancies. Let us assume further that our theory allows us to predict correctly that if, in addition to a program of peer-group support and individual counseling, we give interested teenagers five dollars a day to avoid pregnancy, fewer of them than before will become pregnant. The experimental method has no privileged way to determine whether the relevant cause is the money, the adolescent's relationship with the worker presenting the money, the peer support generated by the others in the group,

---

*Editor's Note: This citation is from the first edition of Reid & Smith (1989).

---

[5] An interesting parallel to the heuristic approach's reexamination of causality is chaos theory, which is being embraced with increasing enthusiasm by the natural sciences. Chaos theory employs nonlinear data, which were previously viewed as noisy and useless, to understand complex phenomena, such as weather patterns, water turbulence, and population biology, which have not yielded to linear explanations. In linear causality relationships are proportional and can be taken apart and put back together; also, small inputs have correspondingly small effects. In contrast, nonlinear relationships do not repeat themselves (for example, we never have exactly the same weather), partly because small inputs can have amplified effects.

While the experimental method tends to assume that causality is linear or to fit nonlinear data to linear analysis, it is becoming increasingly clear that in nature linear causality is the exception and nonlinear causality is the rule. As the mathematician Stanislaw Ulam remarked, calling chaos theory "nonlinear science" is like calling zoology "the study of nonelephant animals" (Quoted in Gleick, 1987, p. 68).

some combination of these variables, some other variable we don't even know about, or pure coincidence.

When the logical positivists were confronted with the fact that causality could not be demonstrated, they tried to salvage the certainty they had hoped the experimental method could guarantee. They argued that if it could be shown that a theory could predict an event's occurrence with a high probability, the occurrence of the predicted event could be deemed explanatory (could confirm the theory). But as Wesley Salmon points out (1971b), since predictions are not explanatory, a high probability that a prediction will be accurate adds no explanatory power to the occurrence of the event. I can predict that if I tell my dog to keep a secret he won't tell anyone, but the high probability that my prediction will come true neither makes the prediction important nor explains its occurrence. You may well say to my example, "But your theory was trite and led you to predict that something *wouldn't* occur when everyone knows it *couldn't* occur." I would reply that your statement illustrates that the meaningfulness of a prediction is unrelated to its power to predict an event's occurrence, but, rather, is a product of other factors. In order for you to argue that even if my prediction that my dog will keep my secret comes true, it is meaningless, you must be familiar with dogs and their vocalizations.

As this example illustrates, in evaluating our research findings, we cannot substitute the rules of the experimental method for our informed judgment. Unfortunately, however, social work, like the other social sciences, has an aversion to trusting the informed judgment of its own members. One glaring example is the extent to which social science journals, researchers and faculties rely on conceptually untenable "significance tests" to determine the substantive significance of experimental results. As the psychologist Meehl (1986) put it, "Owing to the abusive reliance upon significance testing . . . in the social sciences, the usual article summarizing the state of the evidence on a theory . . . is nearly useless" (p. 325). A significance test is designed to ascertain the probability that, though our sample indicates that the event predicted by our theory occurred, the event did not occur in the population as a whole. But it has been known for decades that significance tests are misnomers in that they tell us nothing about substantive significance (Carver, 1978; Morrison & Henkel, 1970; Nunnally, 1960; Rozeboom, 1960; Smith, 1983). In the first place, significance tests are affected by sample size; large samples skew

the test in the direction of false positives. Further, even if the significance test indicates that it is highly improbable that our sample shows the predicted event when the population does not, for the reasons just discussed, this information will never tell us whether our experimental input caused the correctly predicted event or whether our theory explains it. The sad consequence of social work's unreflective reliance on significance tests is that, instead of learning how to inform, hone and rely on their own capacity for evaluative thinking, students learn to depreciate and bypass their informed judgment when they are faced with the necessity to determine whether their results are substantively important.

Another weakness in the logical positivist assumption that the experimental method is privileged is the notion that when the investigator isolates variables in order to determine their causal importance, he or she has not materially affected the system under study. In actuality, however, if we take the system apart, like Humpty-Dumpty, we may not get it completely back together, because we will be missing small but important pieces. The notion of controlling variables is itself a heuristic, the bias of which is that manipulating interventions only changes the whole in additive and, therefore, easily discernible, ways (Wimsatt, 1986b). To believe that the study of a reduced and manipulated human interaction tells us something significant about natural interactions is not the self-evident conclusion that the logical positivist researcher takes it to be; rather it is an improbable assertion that itself must be demonstrated. If we reduce worker-client interactions to simple, controlled forms, we may produce a lot of information about a strained and artificial sort of human interaction, but we have not necessarily learned much about treatment and life as they naturally occur (Bronfenbrenner, 1977). The heuristic paradigm postulates that the way to understand the complexity practitioners face every day is not reflexively to reduce it to its lowest common denominator, but to embrace it and find ways to learn about it (Wimsatt, 1976).

One reason that the logical positivist researcher ignores complexity, or context, is that he or she believes that the function of the experimental method is to test theories in order to advance those theories that as closely as possible approximate nomothetic, or universal, laws. In contrast, the heuristic researcher recognizes that because every system is contextual, that is, exists in a particular environment, no research method, including the experimental method, can ever justly claim that a theory is universally applicable (Mishler, 1979; Rein & White, 1981). In other words, because all research, including the testing of theories, involves induction, we can never be certain that our conclusions are relevant to any group except our sample. We cannot do research without drawing an environment-system boundary. We need to keep in mind that this boundary is arbitrary and that the environment continues to affect the system. *As a result, any conclusion we draw about a system is, to some extent, determined by environmental influences that we cannot know because, by definition, we are not studying them.* For many years when researchers studied children who did badly or were disruptive in school, they drew the environment-system boundary to include only the child and, occasionally, the family. However, when researchers thought to move the boundary to include the teacher in the system being studied, they found that the child does not just import behavior into the classroom, but that the teacher's personality and teaching style influence the child's classroom behavior (Carrier, 1978). Further, any system we identify is itself not static, but changes over time, which is an important contextual influence. Even highly accurate conclusions about a particular system "decay." For example, the accuracy of psychological tests turns out to be time-limited. Psychological tests describe a specific group of people at a particular moment in time; they do not tell us about human nature itself (Cronbach, 1975).

The heuristic researcher's ideal of selecting research questions solely on the basis of their perceived importance, of selecting data solely for the appropriateness to the research question, and of using informed judgment to evaluate results may seem so commonsensical that some may wonder why it needs to be stressed. Others, however, may feel uneasy about the breadth of the options available to the researcher who applies heuristic principles. The appropriate response to this latter unease is that we cannot exclude complexity in our research efforts because, even more than other professionals, social workers rarely face simple problems. We work not in research laboratories but in agencies or offices that are affected by political, social, economic, and psychological forces. Our clients themselves have multiple and conflicting motives which organize their reactions to their social, cultural, familial, and internal worlds. We ourselves do not go from cocoon to client, but have our own histories and internal and external exigencies. What, then, are we to do? Since the 1950s, when the profession

decided to emulate what it mistook for the natural sciences' approach to knowledge, the determination to simplify complex interactions has caused social work to ignore substantively important information. It is *futile* to simplify complex interactions *solely* with the goal of producing reliable knowledge. The mere act of doing research causes interactive effects we can't even know about. But this does not imply that we should throw up our hands and refuse to act. One primary reason that the heuristic research paradigm is most appropriate for social work is that it encourages the researcher to expect and welcome the surrounding complexities.

APPLICATIONS

By now you are probably wondering how the heuristic paradigm can be applied to your own research interests. Most importantly, the heuristic paradigm will encourage you to examine and elucidate your assumptions, decisions, framework, biases and interests. In contrast, the logical positivist researcher approaches critical research questions, including what problems are important, what solutions are useful, and what designs are appropriate, by unreflectively applying restrictive and outmoded notions of scientific methodology, which are guided by the assumption that the reality most worthy of study is simple, material, and quantifiable.

If you were to take a heuristic approach, you would start by identifying a subject that interested you. Then you would consider a number of possible environment-system boundaries before carefully selecting one, because this choice will have important consequences. For example, the administrative researcher who chooses to study the inefficiency and poor morale of a large public child-placing agency may overlook crucial influences if the court system that decides the fate of state wards is excluded from the field of study. I cannot overemphasize that when we draw the system in, we paint the environment out and never study it.

The logical positivist researcher fails to focus on the environment-system boundary because it is assumed that the investigator is separate from the system being studied and, in turn, that facts will appear the same to every rational investigator. In contrast, the heuristic researcher postulates that different environment-system boundaries will generate different types of data, and, therefore, that a variety of perspectives will tend to reduce rather than perpetuate bias. By spotlighting the choice of environment-system boundary, the heuristic paradigm illuminates a promising avenue of research.

You might choose to study important problems that have been well-researched, but haven't yielded particularly useful results. Simply redraw the environment-system boundary, and restudy the problem. To illustrate, the medical social worker is well aware that, despite his or her best efforts, many patients do not comply with prescribed treatments. The system being studied usually consists of the prescribed regimen, the patient, and, sometimes, the patient's family. By redrawing the system to include the physician, it may be possible to gather significant information about the patient's non-compliance (Lipton & Svarstad, 1977; Mishler, 1984). In other words, including the physician does not merely add a new variable, it creates a new system.

A related research opportunity may present itself if you reexamined the environment-system boundary of a well-researched problem to determine whether the boundaries of the system have been adhered to or whether results that pertain only to the system have been inappropriately extended to the environment. An example is my own research into the phenomenon that is termed the "psychiatric deluge" of social work (Heineman Field, 1980). Historians of social work agreed that social work was deluged by psychodynamic theory in the 1920s. They arrived at this conclusion by studying a system that included only the social work literature. When I expanded the system to include actual practice in a representative, mid-western child-placing agency, I found that there was no psychiatric deluge of social work *practice*, but, on the contrary, that agencies were very slow to accept psychodynamic principles. When social work practice was included in the system defined as the *psychiatric deluge of social work*, it became clear that the spread of ideas from social work journals to social work practice is not something we can take for granted, but, rather, is a process that needs to be studied and facilitated.

Once you have established the system you want to study, you need to decide how you want to investigate it. The heuristic paradigm implies that this choice should be consistent, but that it need *not* meet any specific criteria, such as operationalizing definitions or making quantitative measurements. No specific methods of research can ever correctly claim to produce truth or even to produce the best approximation of truth. The requirement of consistency simply means

that the choice of the problem and the method of investigating it should be compatible and consonant with your theory, assumptions, and aims which, concomitantly, should be reasonable in terms of the phenomena you have chosen to study.

When you adopt a heuristic approach, you will not be dismayed when the problem you are studying appears huge and overdetermined and your research produces conflicting information. You will apply what Simon (quoted in Wimsatt, 1986b, p. 299) terms "bounded rationality." That is, since important problems are so complex that we cannot solve them exactly, we first make them manageable in some way that seems reasonable, and then bring our best, informed judgment to bear on the problem that we have defined and the information we have gathered.

The researcher using the heuristic approach does not accept the myth of researcher objectivity and, therefore, does not fear to get involved with the subject matter. She or he knows that the more reflectively familiar a system and its complexities become, the more patterned and, therefore, useful information can be seen, and the more creative and fruitful ideas developed. The phenomenon that disciplined involvement makes complexity more manageable and patterns more recognizable is frequently illustrated by chess masters, who look at intricate arrangements of pieces on the chessboard and see possibilities that the uninitiated could never begin to imagine (Simon, 1966a, p. 12).

Another advantage of the heuristic paradigm is that investigators in different areas, such as public policy and family therapy, need no longer argue about whose work is more scientific, more valuable, or more empirical. Rather, each researcher can see that no focus is inherently superior and that other researchers legitimately have defined important problems in differing ways. All arguments about whether it is better to study individuals, families, groups, political entities, or public policies are in principle undecidable because, at bottom, they are conflicts about competing values. That is, since we can't know with certainty either the truth or the best way to approximate it, decisions about how to proceed are subjective or value judgments. If we realize the futility of pursuing *the* answer, then we become grateful for any explanation or intervention that promises to help us with the question.

In this way, the heuristic approach facilitates rather than discourages cooperation among investigators. Let us assume that an investigator whose speciality is administration succeeds in improving the delivery of educational services to the high school dropouts we considered in our earlier example. A new problem may now appear, namely, that the teenagers do not make full use of the services. This redefined problem will most likely fall in what the public policy investigator had previously defined as the environment. If the public policy investigator understands this and concludes he or she has neither the training nor inclination to study a system that includes teenagers' motives, there will be more comfort in turning for advice to a clinical colleague whose designated system includes elements of motivation.

The problem of evaluation is often raised when the heuristic paradigm is presented. If we broaden our definition of sound research, how are we to know if a program, service, treatment, or research project has merit? One response is that this problem is not unique to the heuristic paradigm. The logical positivist researcher merely avoids the problem of evaluation through an unwarranted reliance on the mechanics of the experimental method and an unfounded mistrust of human judgments (especially practitioners' and clients' judgments). However, it is well known that statistics can be and, unfortunately, sometimes are tweaked, pulled and bent out of shape by overeager researchers. Also, in contrast to the logical positivist, the heuristic researcher values the informed opinions of those in the trenches, including clients, administrators, and clinicians, as much as he or she values the opinions of researchers. It is supremely irrational to trust social workers with the lives and well-being of clients and then to reason that their conclusions about the service they provide are inherently more biased than the reports of researcher-observers.

In applying heuristic principles of evaluation, you will specify your theory and assumptions as clearly as possible, and analyze the data you gather and organize through the use of your informed judgment rather than through the *mechanical* application of standardized procedures. While standardized procedures may be useful, they are heuristics and, therefore, should be applied with knowledge of their limitations. In evaluating your results, you will do your best to account for biases that accrue, among other sources, from your own personal history and inclinations, and from your choice of assumptions, theory, and type of data. If you conclude that your research results are substantively

significant, then the evaluation process will shift to the true test of any results, namely utility and acceptance by the field over time. Other interested individuals can now try on your suggestions for size. The marketplace of ideas is not perfect, but it is all we have. Deductive logic alone will never tell us whether or not a research conclusion is either useful or true, because it can never eliminate the possibility that causes other than the ones we are considering have brought about the changes we are trying to understand.

How, then, do we choose between competing methods? When different heuristics all produce promising results, as when the behaviorist social worker finds that giving a teenage mother five dollars a day to support her desire to avoid a new pregnancy is effective, and the psychodynamic social worker finds that improving the teenage mother's insight into her unconscious wishes helps prevent a subsequent, consciously unwanted pregnancy, the heuristic paradigm suggests that, like the choice of research problem and method, the choice of treatment methods is multifactorial and contextual. Examples of relevant factors that go into the choice are the worker's training, assumptions, theoretical orientation, professional affiliation, and personal characteristics, as well as the availability of personnel, possibilities of grant money, and current professional, cultural, and social trends. Clearly, a social worker who has had a successful personal experience with insight therapy, whose field work placement was psychodynamically oriented, and whose favorite teachers taught psychodynamic theory is more likely to choose the promising psychodynamic treatment than the promising behavioral treatment.

Unfortunately, as is the case with the other helping professions, the most common criterion that social work uses to choose between competing modalities and interventions has become a narrow type of accountability. The logical positivist preference for simplified, quantified data is one reason that accountability is currently defined almost exclusively in terms of cost and time savings. As a result, practitioners' options are increasingly being curtailed by regulations that ignore clients' individual differences and prescribe a predetermined approach to every client with a similar presenting problem. The burden of proof is on the practitioner who wants to change the rules and lengthen or change treatment plans, just as the doctor who wants to keep the surgical patient in the hospital for a longer than average stay can no longer exercise medical judgment, but must persuade a utilization review committee which, in turn, must satisfy the government or an insurance company. In such a situation, the heuristic researcher would emphasize that cost and time savings are values rather than universal principles and, therefore, that they have to be considered alongside competing values such as the needs of individual clients and social justice, which are equally in keeping with social work's traditional mission.

MISUNDERSTANDINGS OF THE HEURISTIC PARADIGM

In conclusion, I would like to mention three common misunderstandings of the heuristic paradigm (Brekke, 1986; Geismar, 1982; Hudson, 1982; Mullen, 1985; Peile, 1988b; Schuerman, 1982; Thyer, 1986).[6] The first misunderstanding is that the heuristic approach leads to "hopeless relativism" (Schuerman, 1982, p. 146),* that is, provides no way to determine what studies are useful or publishable, or how best to study interactions with clients, to assess the functioning of social agencies, or to know the efficacy of an intervention. Actually, the heuristic approach to research requires more thoughtfulness and rigor than the knee-jerk approach advocated by logical positivism. The heuristic paradigm encourages the investigator to state assumptions, to think about environment-system boundaries, to recognize bias, to select data and methods of data gathering that are appropriate to the research question and the researcher's chosen reality, and to use informed judgment to assess research findings. In contrast, the assumptions and philosophical underpinnings of the logical positivist paradigm of research are almost never examined and explicated by the researcher. Because he or she does not prepackage the research, the researcher using the heuristic approach begins conceptualizing the research and evaluation study much earlier than does the logical positivist researcher.[7]

The experimental method exalted by logical positivism is inherently no more able than any other research method to evaluate theories, because it can never rule out the possibility that hypotheses other than the research hypothesis caused the change observed in the dependent variable. Causality, significance, and relevance cannot be determined by inferential statistics. We do not want to confuse our wish for certainty with the belief that it is possible, and we do not want to be lulled into believing that numbers are unproblematic because we do not examine the assumptions and biases that accompany them.

A second common misconception of the heuristic paradigm is that it rejects the experimental method and quantitative data. The heuristic paradigm is distinguished by its anti-restrictive stance. If the heuristics represented by the experimental method and quantified data are appropriate to the question being studied and the theory used to study it, the heuristic researcher would include and welcome them. The heuristic researcher only rejects the attempt to apply the experimental method and quantified data to all research questions and to exalt them above all other research strategies.

The third and most common misconception of the heuristic paradigm is that the application of its principles will produce knowledge that is neither grounded nor empirical. This misconception rests on the erroneous belief that the information brought to us by our five senses is a direct report of reality. Kant's compelling argument that sense perceptions are perceiver dependent has never been refuted. In this century, authors have shown that both language and vision are shaped by cultural and other influences (Segall, Campbell & Herskovits, 1966; Whorf, 1956). Videotaped interviews are, therefore, inherently no better data than practitioners' informed judgments or clients' self-reports. Researchers should not assume that quantitative measurement always produces valuable data and that non-quantified information always has to be justified. Each choice of data has to make sense in terms of the questions being asked and the reality being studied.

I have suggested a number of reasons why social work should adopt the heuristic paradigm of research in place of the overly restrictive, logical positivist paradigm. Some of these are: (a) contemporary philosophy of science has conclusively undercut logical positivism's claims and demonstrated that the logical positivist paradigm places unnecessary limitations on sci-

---

[6] For further elucidation of these misconceptions, see Heineman, 1982; [Heineman] Pieper, 1982, 1986, 1987, 1988.

[7] Mitroff and Bonoma (1978, p. 236) conclude that "psychology has gone too long between reexaminations of its key ideas regarding the concept of the experiment." They assert (ibid., p. 240) that "the compelling force and power of every controlled experiment is no better than our ability to inspect and to raise challenges to the underlying background assumptions on which it rests."

*Editor's Note: p. 127 in this text.

entific endeavors; (b) unlike the logical positivist paradigm, the heuristic paradigm welcomes the complex, ill-structured, substantively important problems that have been social work's abiding focus (Dunn, Mitroff, & Deutsch, 1981); and (c) the tenets of the heuristic paradigm facilitate rather than obstruct cooperation between researcher and practitioner and between researchers in different fields. Finally and, perhaps, most importantly, the heuristic paradigm makes research user-friendly by expanding rather than restricting the operation of human judgment in the knowledge-building process. Each one of us, whether we specialize in administration, community organization, treatment, or public policy, can and, hopefully, will have a simultaneous identity as a researcher, because each one of us is capable of exercising judgment and creativity in our area of interest so as to advance our knowledge about the important problems that we encounter daily.

Applying the Heuristic Paradigm

CHAPTER 4

Using the Heuristic Paradigm to Design Research

THE VALUE OF APPLYING THE HEURISTIC PARADIGM

In Part I you read about the need for a new approach to research in the social and behavioral sciences, and you learned the central concepts of the heuristic paradigm. Researchers' investment in developing a postpositivist metatheory of research for the social and behavioral sciences has ignited as they increasingly recognize that knowledge can have a transforming impact on society, whether the new knowledge concerns strengthening the immune system against disease, space travel, or caring for children so that they have a stable sense of self-worth. We use the social and behavioral sciences to understand who we are, to define our relationships, our society, and our futures. Accordingly, it is all the more important to develop a science that is explicitly based on humanistic values and that provides a way to search for applicable solutions to pressing social problems. The heuristic paradigm opens the doors to this new science—it affords researchers the freedom to study significant and relevant problems; because it does not include methodological prescriptions but emphasizes conceptual rigor, it challenges you to think through every decision in the research process. You may be wondering, "How do I use this approach?" This chapter presents an overview of how to apply the heuristic paradigm to design research.

Underlying decisions about research design is a crucial epistemological issue that philosophers have discussed for some time, often termed *intersubjectivity* or the "problem of other minds" (see Hull, Chapter 5; see also the Glossary). In brief, *intersubjectivity* can be defined as follows: One cannot know for sure whether one person's communication about his or her experience can be accurately understood by another person (Hanfling, 1981b). For example, if a friend says to you "I feel pain," you cannot determine with certainty whether your interpretation of that statement is an accurate perception of the other person's experience. This problem has many important ramifications for research. To illustrate, if your study states that homeless clients benefited from an outreach program, as I consider applying your findings,

1. How do you define *homeless clients?*
2. How do I know what you mean by *benefited?*
3. How did you arrive at that conclusion?

To respond to the "problem of other minds," positivism has prescribed methodologies such as standardized measurement instruments or a control group. The researcher using the heuristic paradigm, however, recognizes that methodological prescriptions do not solve that problem and unjustifiably devalue other ways of generating scientific knowledge. Because facts cannot be understood outside the context of the process by which they are gathered, the researcher using the heuristic paradigm is concerned about providing the reader with the information necessary for an adequate evaluation of the knowledge. Accordingly, it is the researcher's responsibility to carefully communicate the thought process behind the research design, including conceptual analysis of the biases introduced by the researcher's choices. Karin Knorr Cetina, a prominent sociologist of science who studies scientists at work in laboratories, says that her studies have aimed to illuminate the details in scientists' decision-making processes. Researchers using the heuristic paradigm can apply this aim in research design and writing up their findings: "we should make visible all the processes—including social ones, but *not only* social processes—which bring this scientific finding about" (as quoted in Callebaut, 1993, p. 180).

THE AIM OF RESEARCH DESIGN

Under positivism, the aim of research design has been to test (confirm or disconfirm) theories. Positivist researchers were supposed to formulate problems based on testing predictions deduced from theories (see, e.g., Popper, Appendix; Scriven, Chapter 5). Decisions about data collection and data analysis were supposed to be based on the kinds of evidence positivism prescribed for falsifying or corroborating theoretical propositions. Accordingly, positivist researchers commonly focused theory appraisal and research design on gathering and evaluating the evidence for or against a theoretical proposition (Pieper & Pieper, 1993). However, in fact, no research design is theory-free:

> [T]he application of a particular method entails certain presuppositions about the nature of that to which the method is applied. Moreover, these presuppositions can never be refuted by any application of the method because they constitute an axiomatic basis that is built into the very structure of the method. . . . This is so because a method is a way of ordering observations, of embedding any single observation in a particular network of relationships to other observations. (Danziger, 1988b, p. 89)

There are no completely theory-independent tests of a theory. Therefore, the concepts that positivist researchers regarded as theory-independent evidence for a theory are not.[83] Further, there are no universal pretheoretic criteria that define evidence for a theory. To elaborate, observations cannot be made completely independently of theories. A good theory will explain observations (e.g., will explain why we see the sun come up in the morning). However, even observations that appear to be "robust" (see Glossary; Wimsatt, 1981a) across several theories (e.g., the sun comes up in the morning) support different theories. Ptolemy used the observation of the sunrise to support his theory that the sun revolves around the earth, whereas Copernicus used it to support his theory that the earth spins on its axis during its revolution around the sun. In sum, although a good theory explains observations, observations cannot be completely theory-independent "evidence" for the merit of any single theory. Thus, the concepts that positivist researchers have regarded as independent "evidence" for or against a theory are actually elements of an argument, marshalled for or against a theory:

> When you observe scientists in the laboratory, you find processes of negotiation at work, processes of decision making, which influence what the scientific findings are going to look like. In a sense, the scientific finding is construed in the laboratory by virtue of the decisions and the negotiations it incorporates. (Knorr Cetina quoted in Callebaut, 1993, p. 180)

From a postpositivist standpoint, the aim of research is solving problems. In appraising a theory, postpositivists do *not* focus on which theory is "true" according to some abstract criterion. Rather, they assess whether a given theory is an improvement over alternatives, including whether the researcher regards it as closer to the truth and more useful than the alternatives (Heineman Pieper, 1981, p. 387).* "For scientists to trust an idea is not to give it a claim to infallibility; it is a kind of heuristic judgment" (Wimsatt quoted in Callebaut, 1993, p. 155). A postpositivist approach to showing the support for a theory entails presenting to the reader the breadth and specific details of the researcher's thought process, including the following:

1. The metatheory of research;
2. The problem formulation;
3. The ontological and epistemological assumptions and related theoretical premises;
4. The methodology used to make observations;
5. The resultant observations;
6. The researcher's explanation for the observations.

Because conceptual decisions have a prior, regulatory impact on the specific methods used in research design, this text focuses on conceptual foundations in research design. Readers may also want to refer to the many texts currently available that focus on implementing a specific research method, such as textbooks on descriptive and inferential statistics, ethnography, and qualitative analysis.

---

*Editor's Note: see p. 119 in this text.

DESIGNING RESEARCH THAT ELICITS RESPONSES FROM PARTICIPANT/SUBJECTS

People who are not the researcher(s) and who decide to participate in research typically are called "subjects" (Danziger, 1988b, 1990); however, a subject is something one studies, not an individual one asks to enter into a relationship. Research that elicits responses from people always sets up a relationship between the participants in the research: the researcher (participant/researcher) and the person who has agreed to participate, who often is called the "client," the "subject," or the "informant" (here called the participant/subject). The relationships that social and behavioral participant/researchers set up with participant/subjects have a profound and regulatory impact on the entire research process. The relationship the participant/researcher establishes with participant/subjects both expresses the participant/researcher's values about how other people should be treated and also is a heuristic choice about what data to gather and how to analyze that data.

The relationship between participant/researcher and participant/subject is set up from the beginning of the research process. For example, a participant/researcher may formulate the following research problem: to express the concerns of individuals receiving welfare so that society can better respond to those individuals (e.g., Holbrook, 1986). That participant/researcher will relate with the participant/subjects in her or his research very differently from the participant/researcher whose problem formulation concerns examining a large sample of welfare recipients to see whether a general assistance and employment training program helped more people to reenter the work force. Both problems are valuable and important to pursue; by setting up different relationships with the human participant/subjects, they will yield very different information.

Another illustration of the impact of the relationship the participant/researcher establishes with participant/subjects is that much social and behavioral research occurs in contexts of considerable human need. When a participant/researcher observes people in need but does not help them, the participant/researcher's behavior communicates to the participant/subjects that their (often urgent) needs are unimportant. The participant/subjects' responses often reflect how they feel about being treated inhumanely. For example, some researchers said that it has been difficult to recruit samples of homeless people to study, because potential participant/subjects often respond negatively when approached by researchers with a questionnaire. It is not surprising that people who are hungry and homeless might be angry when, instead of helping them, someone asks them to fill out a questionnaire about their condition. The logical positivist view that researchers can and should be "neutral" and uninvolved with participant/subjects has encouraged researchers to ignore their impact on participant/subjects (Reinharz, 1984). The unfortunate consequence is inhumane treatment of participant/subjects in the name of scientific "objectivity" (see the studies described at the end of this chapter, in Discussion Question 2). This so-called "neutrality" has also led to the collection of unreflectively biased data because the biases inherent in the heuristic choice about the relationship with participant/subjects have not been recognized.

A central consideration in evaluating the relationship that the research design sets up between participants is the participant/subjects' motives. A major problem with interventionist research on clinical practice is that it often does not take into account the fact that when clients come for treatment, their primary motive is to be helped, not to generate knowledge by participating in research. Often, clients are offered the opportunity for treatment in exchange for participation in research. As Heineman Pieper (1994) points out, such a contract exploits disadvantaged clients' lack of access to alternatives and forces them to participate in generating knowledge to meet their need for treatment.

The relationship the participant/researcher sets up with participant/subjects affects the process of data gathering in several respects. The participant/subjects' reactions to the relationship with the participant/researcher influence the data they provide. For example, children labeled with "minimal brain dysfunction" were frightened by the laboratory and the instruments used to study them and resisted the research procedures. The researchers sedated the children so they would comply (Sohmer & Student, 1977). Although the researchers reported that they had sedated the children, they did not discuss the ethical issues inherent in (1) frightening the children with the research procedures and (2) inducing a state of dissociated consciousness for research purposes alone. Furthermore, they did not consider the impact of frightening and drugging the children on the usefulness of the information they would obtain.

Obtaining informed consent is not a straightforward solution to this dilemma (Broadhead, 1984; B. Freedman, 1987; L. Harrison, 1993; Scocozza, 1989). As many authors have noted, the power differential between professionals (practitioners or researchers) and clients, as well as the clients' motive for help and, frequently, mental distress, can compromise the client's freedom to evaluate and reject the request to participate in research (Heatherington, Friedlander, & Johnson, 1989; May, 1979). For example, Broadhead (1984) quotes the experience of an unnamed contributor to the journal *American Sociologist* who was the participant/subject in a research interview with a graduate student researcher:

> In spite of the fact that I was very annoyed at being taped without my permission as well as by the questions and felt increasingly defensive and put down, I did not attempt to terminate the interview. Afterwards I realized how difficult it was to cut off an interview while it is in process. It caused me to reflect on the coerciveness of the interview situation. If as an agency administrator I did not feel free to terminate an interview with a graduate student, it must be almost impossible for the typical subject being interviewed by a "social scientist" to do so when the perceived status differences are reversed. (quoted in Broadhead, 1984, p. 121)

Informed consent is exponentially more problematic if the participant/subjects are extremely vulnerable, such as young children or people requiring medical or psychological treatment, who lack many alternative resources, and cannot critically evaluate the research (Munir & Earls, 1992; Nicholson, 1986). Every researcher has an ethical obligation to treat human subjects in accord with the most highly developed ethical standards. Scientists can, and often have, postponed pioneering research until the community of scientists, ethicists, and the public have established acceptable standards for protecting (1) participant/subjects and (2) society from use of the findings to serve destructive aims (B. Freedman, 1987).

Neither a method nor an observation can be completely theory-free, and the humane treatment of participant/subjects is a prerequisite of research. Accordingly, the belief that "facts" derived from unethical experiments could be useful when separated from the ethical issues is an untenable holdover from positivism. Observations derived from research involving human participant/subjects should not be reported separately from a description of the relationship between the participants (Caplan cited in Kolata, 1994). The many issues involved in the ethics of research with human participant/subjects cannot be elaborated further here; this is an extremely important and multifaceted topic that merits much more extensive study and care.

PROBLEM FORMULATION

Some of the central issues to consider in formulating a research problem follow:

1. What values underlie this problem formulation, especially with regard to social inequalities and improving human relationships?
2. What possible solutions will the problem formulation lead to?
3. Why is this problem formulation important?
4. Who is the client who will use the research, and how can the research be helpful to the client?
5. What are the ontological and epistemological assumptions that underlie the problem formulation?
6. What biases are evident in the problem formulation? For example, where is the environment–system boundary? What data will the problem formulation lead the researcher to collect, and what data will it lead the researcher to exclude?
7. How can biases be regulated through processes such as triangulation and/or the use of controls?

As stated earlier, within a postpositivist framework the aim of scientific research is problem solving (Callebaut, 1993; Laudan, 1984; Nickles, 1987b; Wimsatt, 1981a). Problem formulation is extremely important because it regulates both subsequent design decisions and the possible problem solutions. Because positivism required researchers to reformulate problems to fit into restrictions such as operationism, researchers often found that they could not study the problems they wanted to study (see the examples described by Heineman Pieper, Chapter 3). Using the heuristic paradigm, the researcher no longer must conform to methodological restrictions such as operationalization (see Chapter 5). However, formulating a research problem that leads to important and useful solutions is a challenging task, "not just solving problems but finding good problems in itself is an achievement in science" (Nickles quoted in Callebaut, 1993, p. 55). The problem formulation sets the foundation for the entire research design, and decisions about problem formulation inevitably interact with other decisions a researcher makes. For example, a researcher may begin with a specific problem formulation, discover that the necessary sample is impossible to recruit, and so reformulate the problem.

Herbert Simon points out that many problems researchers want to address are "ill-structured." According to Simon, interesting and useful research begins with a problem formulation that is heuristic in the sense that it is likely to lead to useful and interesting discoveries (see Chapter 5). Many of the most important discoveries occurred when scientists developed new ways to formulate problems. At the same time, researchers' paradigms and guiding theories regulate even the definition of a good problem: "to find a problem and to have the community recognize it as a good problem implies that there is a body of background claims, practices, and constraints that are considered settled by the community" (Nickles as quoted in Callebaut, 1993, p. 56).

To develop the most promising problem formulation, you can explore different ways of formulating problems to investigate the topic that interests you:

1.   Rotate the perspectives you use to define the topic. For example, behaviorists customarily address the topic of a child's aggressive behavior by asking parents and teachers what child behaviors they would like to see change and by teaching those adults how to differentially respond to the child. Another way of formulating the problem is to look at the issue from the child's perspective, which might focus on the parent or teacher behaviors the child would like to see change.

2.   Look at the topic across different explanatory dimensions. As Wimsatt, Goldin-Meadow, and McClintock (1991) point out, explanations can be analyzed across several dimensions (see Discussion Question 6 preceding Simon, Chapter 5). You can reconceptualize your problem formulation using those different dimensions. For example, if you are interested in studying the causes of teenage pregnancy, developing an explanation using a temporal dimension could lead you to focus on the teens' background and history. Alternatively, you can look at the topic from the perspective of a teen's subjective experience, such as, what did it mean to the teen to be pregnant? Yet another alternative is to take a group perspective, for example, by looking at rates of teenage pregnancy within a given neighborhood. Other ways of developing your problem formation are:

3.   Examine the values inherent in your problem formulation.

4.   Examine the theory implicit in the problem formulation, especially the ontological and epistemological assumptions.

5.   Examine the environment–system boundary, including looking at multiple levels of organization (multilevel reductionistic analysis; see Wimsatt, Chapter 5).

6.   Consider triangulation.

7.   Consider possible controls.

Values

Scriven (see Chapter 5) describes how the positivist belief that research can and should be value-free often led researchers to try to eliminate values from the problem-formulation process. As he points out, the elimination of values is impossible; in fact, positivists simply substituted one set of values for another. Consider the following example: A group of students want to investigate the effects of patterns of discrimination against homosexual clients on the clients' feelings of self-worth. The students' aim may be to voice the pain and concerns of the clients to improve clinicians' understanding of the clients. According to the positivist metatheory, research and advocacy are two different enterprises, and as researchers, the students should take a "neutral" position. That "neutral" position, however, commonly requires that students not formulate the problem in terms of social inequalities and the desire to use knowledge to effect social change. Positivism thereby reinforced the status quo (Levins & Lewontin, 1985), in effect substituting one set of values for another. As Bhaskar points out, knowledge is never value-free, and when problem formulation includes a value such as human emancipation, knowledge can have a transforming impact on society (see Chapter 5).

In discussing social planning in the context of complex systems and pervasive uncertainty, Simon brings up a crucial issue for researchers that also is related to the values underlying problem formulation: Who is the client? (Simon, 1981; see also L. Richardson, 1988):

> [I]t may seem obvious that all ambiguities should be resolved by identifying the client with the whole society. That would be a clear-cut solution in a world without conflict of interest or uncertainty in professional judgment. But when conflict and uncertainty are present, it is a solution that abdicates organized social control over the professional and leaves it to him to define social goals and priorities. If some measure of control is to be maintained, the institution of the society must share with the professional the redefinition of the goals of design. (Simon, 1981, p. 177)

Simon's question is especially helpful for approaching some of the complex ethical issues that have plagued research with human participant/subjects. Many research problems have a specific target audience who will use the findings, such as other scholars, an organization interested in subsidizing a program, or parents who want up-to-date approaches to child care. In the context of multiple overlapping social systems, one segment of society may deem pursuit of a research problem crucial. Another group may recommend postponing the research until the ethical issues are articulated and until ways to use the knowledge have been developed with adequate safeguards against harm to human participant/subjects and also against the destructive misuse of the knowledge. For example, scientists have used the argument of long-term benefits to society to justify research harmful to human participant/subjects. Others often object. It is increasingly apparent that the field of research ethics is moving in a direction that opposes deceiving human participant/subjects; researchers are expected to make decisions about research design in accord with society's highest standards for ethical conduct (Caplan, 1978; Kolata, 1994; Zelen, 1979).

Researchers may serve clients whose interests diverge from the commitments of other groups with whom the researcher interacts. For example, sometimes researchers have been in adversarial relationships with agency administrators, especially in the context of program evaluation (e.g., D. Campbell, 1969). However, adversarial relationships with potential consumers of research are not only *not* inevitable, often they are obstructive to the process of knowledge use and dissemination (Cronbach, 1982). As Simon emphasizes, the clients who can use the knowledge need to be motivated by the research contributions: "the members of an organization or a society for whom plans are made are not passive instruments, but are themselves designers who are seeking to use the system to further their own goals" (1981, p. 177). Agencies often seek alliances with researchers to generate knowledge that can be used to improve services. For example, an agency administrator may be concerned that the program does not meet the needs of people of color and may want the researcher to ascertain precursors to the decisions of these clients to abruptly terminate treatment. Given the multiple and often conflicting social systems within which researchers work, research will always serve some client, and the research itself can potentially be a process that serves those most in need. The problem formulation is a crucial point at which the researcher (1) begins to articulate who can benefit from the research and (2) makes a commitment to how the research can be useful.

Choice of Theory: Ontological and Epistemological Assumptions

Postpositivist researchers recognize that decisions about research design are fundamentally regulated by the guiding theory. Because there are no universally accepted definitions of the objects we study (e.g., there is no universal definition of the nature of human consciousness), crucial steps in any research design are (1) defining the objects of study, using ontological assumptions, and (2) defining how those objects of study can be known, using epistemological assumptions (see Heineman Pieper, 1989, Chapter 3; Bhaskar, Chapter 5). Positivist epistemological restrictions sharply limited the ontological assumptions (or theories about reality) deemed acceptable for scientific research. One of the most important contributions of postpositivism is that researchers are no longer required to restrict their ontological assumptions to those that can be studied using a positivist epistemology. Bhaskar (Chapter 5) elaborates the two criteria scientists commonly use to ascribe reality to a posited entity. (1) The entity can be perceived (e.g., as you perceive your notebook). (2) The entity cannot be perceived but can be known by its effects; it is a causal ontology. Examples of the study of a causal ontology include investigating the beautiful Northern Lights to understand the invisible electromagnetic fields that surround the earth and produce the aurora borealis. Social and behavioral researchers can choose theories with causal ontologies, such as motives as defined in intrapsychic humanism (see Chapters 7 and 8); one way to scientifically study those ontologies is by examining their effects.

Another of the most pervasive and underrecognized ways that the researcher's preferred theory influences the research process in the social and behavioral sciences is that it causes the researcher to influence her or his subjects in the direction of supporting the researcher's theory (Orne, 1969). Although according to the positivist approach, methodological solutions such as double-blind designs* reduce or eliminate the impact of the researcher's theory on observations, increasingly, researchers recognize and document the influence of researchers' theories on findings, despite methodological controls.

As the meta-analysis conducted by R. P. Greenberg, Bornstein, Greenberg, and Fisher (1992) illustrates, methodological solutions cannot reduce the impact of the researcher's theory on observations. Greenberg et al. analyzed double-blind studies of the treatment of depressed individuals with newer antidepressants, standard antidepressants, and placebo conditions. Greenberg et al. postulated that the data-gatherers' theoretical preference for antidepressant therapy influenced the data, despite the double-blind methodology and the studies' aim of "objectivity." Specifically, Greenberg et al. were concerned about the "possibility of overreactivity in the clinician ratings because of the clinicians' vested interest in finding treatments superior to the control conditions" (1992, p. 665). They hypothesized that the data gatherers could discern the patients' group memberships; for example, the patients on medication were likely to report common side effects, whereas those on placebo did not. In fact, when Greenberg et al. controlled for data-gatherer bias, they found that, across diagnostic subtypes of depression, data gatherers consistently overestimated the impact of medications in that they rated the outcome of treatment with antidepressants more positively than did the patients. Moreover, "patient ratings of outcome for both standard and new antidepressant medications showed virtually no benefit beyond that obtained from placebo" (Greenberg et al., 1992, p. 666). As this study demonstrates, a design decision cannot eliminate the impact of the researcher's theory on the observations, which in turn underscores the importance of incorporating careful conceptual analysis of the theoretical assumptions in the research design and the presentation of findings.

Figure 3–2 (p. 149) shows one way researchers can compare the theoretical assumptions underlying research about clinical practice. Chapters 7 and 8 include extensive statements of the ontology and the epistemology that guide the research. The sample research project introduced at the end of this chapter also includes a section in which the ontology and epistemology are explicated (see also Chapter 5).

Drawing the Environment–System Boundary and Multilevel Reductionistic Analysis

As Wimsatt describes, every problem formulation defines a system to study and simultaneously leaves other variables out of focus, in the environment. The introduction to Wimsatt's paper (Chapter 5) discusses the use of the environment–system boundary in research. In her 1989 paper (Chapter 3), Heineman Pieper also

---

*Editor's Note: In a double-blind study, both the participant/subjects and the participant/researchers who are collecting data are supposed to be unaware of whether the participant/subjects are in an experimental or a control group.

discusses how redrawing the environment–system boundary illuminates the biases in problem formulation.

Multilevel reductionistic analysis can also be used to analyze problem formulations and recognize bias. Multilevel reductionistic analysis entails moving up and down the levels of organization of the system under study to compare how problems are redefined when the system under study is redefined (see the introduction to Wimsatt, Chapter 5). For example, a researcher may choose to study how to help a child with his hyperactive behavior. The researcher may begin by examining the child's behavior in the context of the relationship between therapist and child. Moving up a level to a larger system, the researcher may decide to examine the child's behavior in the classroom, to see how the behavior labeled hyperactive may express responses to the teacher's and other children's communications. Moving up and down levels of analysis helps the researcher to recognize the diverse variables that impinge on the system under study and to evaluate the way the researcher chooses to draw the environment–system boundary.

Triangulation

The concept of triangulation derives from navigation, and refers to taking multiple perspectives on a given point (LeVine, 1981). Triangulation can help the researcher to recognize the bias inherent in any single perspective:

> If you've only got one way to apply it, detect it, derive it, or measure it, you can't separate out the contribution of the applicator, detector, etc. from the object or property being applied or detected. If you've got multiple ways, you can "triangulate" on the object (D. Campbell, 1975) and simultaneously calibrate the means of detection. (Wimsatt quoted in Callebaut, 1993, p. 155)

Researchers can use triangulation at many points in the research design process, including the following:

1. Select diverse samples.
2. Triangulate the methods used to gather data.
3. Triangulate the methods used for data analysis.

For instance, the design of the history in Chapter 2 triangulated the sample and the methods of data collection (the systematic sample of journal articles as well as the use of other historical materials, e.g., archival records), and also the methods of data analysis (descriptive and inferential statistics as well as qualitative analysis). D. Campbell identified a potential problem with using triangulation: If the means of triangulation are extremely dissimilar, "we again face the paradox of inability to use differences when these so dominate as to make it impossible to match the corresponding aspects of the reports being compared" (1975, p. 190). Conversely, another potential pitfall in using triangulation, as Wimsatt points out (1981a), is that any method of triangulating is a heuristic with inherent biases. If the heuristics used for triangulation are so similar that they share biases, the triangulation process itself will not help the researcher to see those biases, and a "pseudo-robustness" will result.

Controls

When the problem formulation concerns a cause-and-effect relationship (e.g., evaluating the impact of a social service delivery program), the researcher can consider controls as means to recognize bias and develop the conceptual analysis. A control provides a way to examine alternative explanations for the observation. For example, in the social and behavioral sciences, experimental controls have commonly been thought of in terms of the characteristics of a "control group." According to the traditional conceptualizations of experimental control, the control group is selected to match the experimental group (the group that experiences the independent variable, see the Glossary) on variables that the researcher wants to "control" for, or examine and potentially eliminate, as factors in the posited causal relationships between the independent and dependent variables. Positivist researchers incorporated controls into research design in the belief that controls offered significant solutions to the problem of determining which variables are causing an observed effect (e.g., Rubin & Babbie, 1989, p. G2; see the discussion of experimental design in the introduction and discussion questions for Gadlin & Ingle, Chapter 6). For example, Reamer (1993) says, "without a control group it is difficult to know what would have happened to clients without any intervention" (p. 139). However, given the multideter-mined and interactive causal relationships that are the focus of social and behavioral research, controls alone cannot identify cause and effect relationships.

As Sayer (1992) points out, decisions about controls rest on a prior conceptual analysis of the variables that are important to control for and the causal relationship between those variables, as well as with the posited effect. The belief that a matched control group can perform that function assumes that one has an accurate and exhaustive conception of the variables and causal process that lead to the posited effect; in fact, that is rarely the case in science. Compounding the complexity of the problem, with human participant/subjects there is such considerable individual variation that "in categorizing a range of diverse individuals by reference even to a fairly large number of characteristics, it is often not clear to what extent each attribute is causally significant to each individual" (Sayer, 1992, p. 241). Most often, a scientist sets up controls in the face of considerable uncertainty about what variables are involved in the causal process, the nature of those variables, and how they interact. In fact, it is not uncommon that a scientist sets up a control and finds that the control's behavior is unexpected; if the researcher explores reasons for these findings, new discoveries can result. Moreover, despite the most assiduous researchers' efforts, new variables are continually discovered that regulate the causal processes leading to experimental observations (see the discussion of an *artifact* in Chapter 6 and the Glossary).

Although some critics of positivism have rejected the method of experimental design and with it the concept of controls, that solution threatens to throw the baby out with the bathwater. Using the heuristic paradigm, one can use experimental designs when they will generate useful information for the problem one wants to explore. Furthermore, conceptually sound aspects of the notion of a control can be retained and used, for example, when they pertain to the research problem.

A control has been construed broadly in terms of an effort to rule out "the effects of other potential change agents" (D. Campbell, 1969). The concept of experimental control always implies a previously conceptualized theory about the causal relationships between variables, specifically, which types of causes are necessary and sufficient (as opposed to accidental or coincidental) for producing the effect (Bhaskar, 1975). A control can be understood as a variable representing an alternative causal process that the researcher selects because, to the best of the researcher's knowledge, it has important similarities with and also differences from the causal process under study. A control functions comparatively, as a way the researcher can spotlight the causal processes occurring in the experimental intervention. The researcher may implement a control by holding some variables constant. For example, the researcher may want to differentiate the psychological effect of taking a pill from the biochemical impact of the medication and so may set up a control group of individuals who receive a placebo. Sayer identifies three types of controls:

> 1 experimental controls—physically holding something constant which might otherwise vary (e.g., controlling temperature); 2 observational controls—restricting observation to cases where a certain variable or factor happens to be constant, e.g. choosing an ethnically-homogeneous population to study; and 3 mathematical controls—mathematically manipulating some data in order to "control for" the effects of a variable which has not been controlled or constant in practice. (1992, p. 195)

To illustrate further, controls may be introduced in the process of sample selection. Alternatively, they may be used in the process of data analysis, for example, mathematically in an analysis of variance (or ANOVA, see the glossary) when certain variables are "controlled for" (Blalock, 1979b). The use of controls in the social and behavioral sciences occurs within the context of a crucial caveat: Because samples of human participant/subjects are, by definition, open systems that are not only uncontrolled but uncontrollable, and because human action always has uniquely determined and context-dependent causes, the effects produced by the variables under study are always likely to be influenced by a complex, interacting range of alternative variables.

A matched control group may be indicated for specific research problems. For those problems for which a control group is not suited, controls can be incorporated in other ways (Cronbach, 1982). Natural controls also occur in many social service situations. For example, clients customarily seek help because previous efforts to resolve their difficulties have not produced the desired effect. The practitioner/researcher may wonder whether the client's problem would resolve itself without clinical intervention. If the client has struggled for some time, however, the client's prior unsuccessful efforts to resolve his or her difficulties function as a control for the hypothesis that the client would resolve the problem without help. A practitioner/researcher who wants to use that natural control can spotlight it and use it as a comparison in the course of data analysis.

An excellent example of controls in naturalistic, qualitative research in the context of the heuristic paradigm is presented in Chapter 8. Heineman Pieper and Pieper describe the treatment of violent, homicidal teenagers using intrapsychic humanism. An alternative hypothesis for the teens' improvement might be that, rather than intrapsychic treatment, the nonspecific relationship factors purported to be helpful ingredients in any treatment (Frank, 1982) were responsible for the teens' newfound capacity to control their violent behavior. The natural history of the teenagers' prior treatments (documented extensively in their case records and well-known to staff) provided a control for that alternative hypothesis. Each teenager had been treated in numerous prior outpatient, inpatient, and residential facilities that used many other treatment approaches, ranging from behaviorism to psychoanalytically based psychotherapy. The teens had been discharged from the programs and deemed "untreatable" under all prior approaches. Heineman Pieper and Pieper carefully considered the teens' behavior in prior contexts (see Chapter 8); clearly, the teens could not regulate their violent behavior, despite the good intentions of some prior care givers. When the teens received intrapsychic treatment, not only did they prove to be treatable, but they also made such significant progress in controlling their destructive behavior that they could live in open residential settings. Many adapted to mainstream classrooms. The contrast between the results under the antecedent control conditions and the results using intrapsychic humanism is important information for those interested in developing and implementing treatment programs for such clients.

In sum, some of the central issues to consider in problem formulation follow:

1. What are the values that underlie the problem formulation, especially with regard to social inequalities and improving human relationships?
2. What kinds of possible solutions will the problem formulation lead to?
3. Why is this problem formulation important?
4. Who is the client who will use the research, and how can the research help the client?
5. What are the ontological and epistemological assumptions that underlie the problem formulation?
6. What biases are evident in the problem formulation? For example, where is the environment–system boundary?
7. What data will the problem formulation lead the researcher to collect, and what data will it lead the researcher to leave out?
8. How can biases be regulated through processes such as triangulation and/or controls?

DATA GATHERING AND DATA ANALYSIS

The Distinction between a Research Method and a Metatheory

In considering how to gather and analyze data, it is important to keep in mind the distinction between a metatheory of research and a method of data collection and analysis. In the Preface, while outlining the profoundly important and original distinction between naturalistic and interventionist research, Heineman Pieper points out one of the most confusing elements in traditional discussions about "research methods":

> Qualitative research frequently is equated erroneously with new (postpositivist) research paradigms, whereas quantitative research is used mistakenly as a synonym for the standard (positivist) research paradigm (Allen-Meares & Lane, 1990; S. J. Taylor & Bogdan, 1984). This conceptual error occurs when issues that pertain to data analysis are confused with issues that relate to data gathering. (Preface)

A central and enduring confusion in prior approaches to social and behavioral research has been that several distinct heuristic choices, which every researcher makes when designing research, have been conflated into one choice—"research methods."

Decisions about data gathering are extremely important because they regulate the information available to social and behavioral scientists. If a researcher chooses not to gather data about a particular event, in reviewing that research, you may never know that the possibility of such data existed. For example, some researchers assumed that very young children could not benefit from psychotherapy. Accordingly, young children often were not offered individual treatment, and data about their motivation to use psychotherapy could not be collected. With a new approach to treatment (intrapsychic humanism) as well as naturalistic data gathering and analysis, which enables study of the child's experience of treatment without altering the treatment for research purposes, new information has become available about young children's responsiveness to individual psychotherapy (Tyson, 1991b).

In addition to choosing a metatheory of research, other decisions every researcher makes when designing research—which often are not discriminated in standard debates about "research methods"—include the following:

1. Should the data-gathering method be naturalistic or interventionist?
2. What data will I collect and how will I collect them?
3. How will I analyze the data that I have collected?

Recognizing those choices as discrete enables researchers to evaluate how each choice sets up a different heuristic with different biases. Moreover, identifying those choices can increase the flexibility and range of options for research design.

One advantage of the heuristic paradigm as a metatheory is that it does not exclude any research design that promises to yield useful information. The researcher who adopts the heuristic paradigm is free to design research by choosing among all the many ways to collect and analyze data, including gathering quantified data and analyzing data using inferential statistics. For example, researchers often assume that if they conduct an ethnographic study they must gather qualitative data and use qualitative analysis. Similarly, researchers often assume that an experimental design requires quantified data and inferential statistics for data analysis. As Heineman Pieper points out, however, the data collected in a study using an experimental design can be qualitative and can be analyzed qualitatively, and an ethnographer can gather data in quantified form and use a statistical method of data analysis. Chapter 6 focuses on the heuristics established by decisions about data collection and analysis and includes selections that illustrate examination of the biases set up by the heuristics.

Heineman Pieper points out that positivist social work researchers unjustifiably restricted data-gathering methods through their misuse of the term *empirical*. In that positivist paradigm, only "'quantifiable,' simplified, third-party, or mechanically gathered data are accorded the status of being 'empirical'" (1985, p. 4). However, no universal pretheoretic criterion for empirical exists; furthermore, the definition of *observable* or *experience* depends on the researcher's theoretical assumptions. The heuristic paradigm uses the customary definitions of *empirical* and *empiricism*, "the terms empirical and empiricism traditionally refer to knowledge arising from experience that originates extracranially" (Heineman Pieper, Preface). Furthermore, as Heineman Pieper points out, the positivist use of the term *empirical* conflates that term with a misleading notion of accuracy. Because an unbiased record of reality is impossible, the researcher's aim to obtain any form of accuracy always represents a heuristic choice of data.

Naturalistic versus Interventionist Research

In 1991, Heineman Pieper differentiated two major categories of research design within the social and behavioral sciences: naturalistic and interventionist.[84] Before elaborating the implications of her reformulation for research design, it is important to distinguish those research design categories from other uses of the term *naturalistic*. In contemporary philosophy of science, *naturalistic* refers to a new approach to research in that field, which incorporates new ideas from the history and sociology of science as well. As described by Callebaut (1993), three paradigms have evolved in the philosophy of science in the twentieth century. Positivism is paradigm 1. There are two major contemporary paradigms. Paradigm 2 is a version of historicism and relativism that has evolved primarily from Thomas Kuhn's work (e.g., Kuhn, 1970). Paradigm 3 is composed of new versions of realism, also termed *transcendental or critical realism* (see, e.g., Bhaskar, Chapter 5). Callebaut also calls Paradigm 3 the "naturalistic" paradigm. The ideas in each of the paradigms Callebaut describes have been imported into the social and behavioral sciences. The heuristic paradigm accommodates both postpositivist paradigms. Although it excludes the restrictiveness of the logical positivist paradigm, it does not exclude specific methodologies commonly associated with positivist approaches to social and behavioral research (e.g., experimental design or inferential statistical methods of data analysis). Accordingly, the heuristic paradigm has room for the following contemporary beliefs about social and behavioral knowledge:

1. The social constructionist (see Glossary) approaches to social and behavioral research, which build on a relativist philosophy of science. (See the Glossary for a definition of relativism; also see the introduction to Brekke in Chapter 3.)

2. Variants of social constructionism, such as the narrative (Cohler, 1988) and postmodernist (Murphy, 1988; Solomon, 1988) approaches.

3. Derivatives of the new realist metatheories (e.g., Bhaskar, 1989b; Nickles, 1988; Wimsatt, in Chapter 5).

Many concepts of the new naturalistic philosophy of science articulated, for example, by Wimsatt, Nickles, and Lewontin can fit within the heuristic paradigm. As noted previously, the naturalistic paradigm in the philosophy of science follows two prior paradigms, positivism, and Kuhnian relativism. The new naturalistic philosophy of science does not take the positivist position that the social sciences can and should conform to the methodology of the natural sciences (see the Glossary and Bhaskar, Chapter 5). At the same time, the naturalistic paradigm does not hold that there is an unbridgeable chasm between the natural and the social sciences (a belief common in the hermeneutic tradition). Instead, the naturalistic paradigm in the philosophy of science emphasizes that "matters of fact" (observations about science as a process of knowledge generation, as well as accepted observations in discrete fields) are as important in the philosophy of science as they are in any scientific field.

The naturalistic paradigm in the philosophy of science is distinct from the naturalistic method of social and behavioral research, which Heineman Pieper (Preface, 1994) has conceptualized. The naturalistic paradigm in the philosophy of science is a metatheory of knowledge used specifically for the philosophy of science. The concepts of that naturalistic paradigm are conceptual foundations for the heuristic paradigm as a metatheory of research for the social and behavioral sciences.

Within the overarching context of the heuristic paradigm, Heineman Pieper categorized research designs in two broad ways: naturalistic or interventionist. Her distinction responds to a central problem she identified in the relationship between research and treatment in the field of social work:

> Positivist researchers choose and develop the social work treatment modalities they believe to be the most researchable. The treatment methods that fit most easily into the positivist criteria for research are brief, easily standardized, and focus on readily measured overt behavior rather than on the client's subjective experience. On the other hand, treatment modalities that are long term, focus on helping the client to feel better, and take into account the client's unconscious motives as well as the client's manifest behavior are ridiculed as products of a primitive past, which cannot be studied scientifically. (Heineman Pieper, 1994, p. 83)

A naturalistic research design aims to preserve naturally occurring relationships, so that the practitioner can pursue therapeutic aims without compromising the integrity of the treatment and generate knowledge that is free of research-determined alterations.

As Heineman Pieper points out, the researcher's decision about whether the research will be naturalistic or interventionist regulates the data obtained. She differentiates the two approaches according to the researcher's intentions and practices: Whereas "the interventionist researcher intentionally alters clinical practice for research purposes," "the naturalistic researcher is a practitioner who aims to minimize research intrusiveness into practice" (Preface). Accordingly, when designing research, the naturalistic researcher does not introduce into the treatment process data-gathering methods that have research rather than therapeutic aims. Once a researcher decides to implement interventionist research, the researcher will not be able to gather data about the process that would occur without the research-driven intervention. For example, Heineman Pieper points out that once a practitioner introduces a tape recorder into a therapy session, the client's actions in the absence of the tape recorder will never be known. Furthermore, the data include the client's reactions to the tape recorder, and so data are present that would not be if the tape recorder had never been introduced. An implication of Heineman Pieper's distinction between naturalistic and interventionist research is that ethnographic research, as it is commonly described, is interventionist (e.g., Kirk & Miller, 1986; Spradley, 1979). The ethnographer is outside the natural system and enters it to collect data. This is not to argue that ethnographic research is inferior to other kinds of research; rather, acknowledging that ethnography is interventionist rather than naturalistic aids in the process of bias recognition.

Heineman Pieper's delineation of the crucial distinction between naturalistic and interventionist research is an important contribution with pervasive ramifications for social and behavioral research. When she presented this distinction in a keynote address at a national conference about social work practice (Heineman Pieper, 1994), one of the conference participants commented, "I've been collecting data using tape recorders for my whole research career and only now realize that those instruments have affected my data. I'm thinking of throwing out my tape recorder." Several other researchers concurred.[85]

Naturalistic research can occur in many contexts and is not limited to clinical case studies. For example, a consultant to the staff of a treatment program can do naturalistic research about the program's therapeutic services as long as the consultant excludes data-gathering procedures that have research rather than therapeutic purposes. If the staff complete anamnestic process recordings* of their interactions with clients to facilitate the clinical consultation process, that form of data gathering is naturalistic. For therapeutic purposes, staff counselors may design and administer a questionnaire to clients during discharge. This questionnaire helps clients reflect on their feelings about the treatment process and what they would like to accomplish after discharge. In addition to serving a therapeutic function, the completed questionnaires may also be data for naturalistic research (see the "Sample Research Project" at the end of this chapter).

Heineman Pieper's focus on the nature of the relationship between the research participants is very helpful for evaluating the many issues and biases in a research design with human participant/subjects, including the values and ecological validity of the research. Bronfenbrenner advanced the concept of ecological validity because of his dissatisfaction with the problem that "much of developmental psychology, as it now exists, is the science of the strange behavior of children in strange situations with strange adults for the briefest periods of time" (1979a, p. 19). He defined ecological validity as "the extent to which the environment experienced by the subjects

---

*Editor's Note: *Anamnestic process recordings* refers here to the therapist's recollected, detailed description of the interaction between therapist and client(s), presented in a sequential "she said, he said" format that includes nonverbal communications. Many clinical supervisors ask their supervisees to complete anamnestic process recordings and find that the recordings can be very helpful sources of information about therapist–client interaction.

in a scientific investigation has the properties it is supposed or assumed to have by the investigator" (Bronfenbrenner, 1979a, p. 29). He emphasized that, "this means that it becomes not only desirable but essential to take into account in every scientific inquiry about human behavior and development how the research situation was perceived and interpreted by the subjects of the study" (1979a, p. 30).

To apply Heineman Pieper's distinction to this issue, a central and insufficiently recognized aspect of ecological validity is the intent of the participant/researcher. When the relationship is directed by a participant/researcher's intent to generate knowledge, the data yielded will be interventionist. Although that can be helpful for many research problems, it has implications for the ecological validity of that research.

A comprehensive review of the literature conducted by Ceci and Bruck (1993) illustrates the significance of the researcher's intent. They examined the suggestibility of children as witnesses with regard to their experience of child abuse, including whether the child was abused by watching other children being hurt or was physically hurt. The authors recognized and critiqued the use of harassment and terror in interviewing children, such as when a professional interviewing a child victim repeatedly accused the child of lying and told the child that the professional had handcuffs. The vast majority of the research that Ceci and Bruck reviewed consisted of interviews between children and strangers. The participant/researchers did not have a caregiving commitment to the children being studied. In many cases the participant/researchers' behavior toward the children was manifestly inconsistent with a caregiving motive, such as when the participant/researcher intentionally misinformed the child about events the child experienced. This research tradition reflects a particular choice about the kind of information to obtain. Research relationships between strangers are not necessarily ecologically valid with regard to other kinds of relationships. For example, they cannot yield accurate information about children's reactions when the children describe their experience of abuse in the context of a genuine caregiving relationship that also offers the possibility of relief from the abuse. The problems entailed in generalizing from data obtained when the researchers questioning the children are strangers to relationships in which the children are seeking help from a known and trusted caregiver are insufficiently recognized.

Decisions about the Sample(s)

One of the most important decisions in research design is the selection of the sample. In the context of positivism's privileging of statistical methods of data analysis, sampling has been addressed in terms of the type of samples necessary for an experimental design and inferential statistical methods of data analysis. In turn, that emphasis translated into a bias toward large and randomly selected samples. It is not uncommon for positivist researchers to emphasize that a larger sample is a better guarantee of the reproducibility and generalizability of findings. From a postpositivist standpoint, however, "reproducibility is obviously related to the adequacy with which investigative procedures are described . . . if an investigator is explicit about the steps he took, a qualified referee can judge the reproducibility of the findings" (Cronbach, 1982, pp. 121–122; see also Bromley, 1986). With regard to the belief that the generalizability of findings hinges on sample size, Sayer points out that,

> Even in the case of the more modest claim that the generalizations are representative of a unique system, it is not always clear of what they are representative. The most obvious example of this is where a statistical average is found to which no real individuals correspond. (Sayer, 1992, pp. 249–250)

The discussion of sampling in positivist terms has led to the tail wagging the dog in research design. When researchers recognize that restrictive positivist assumptions about sample size and controls are no longer viable criteria for the credibility and utility of a research study, they are free and also enjoined to think through the details of sample selection. Because of the pervasiveness of those prescriptions for research design and sample selection, a postpositivist perspective on the conceptual foundations of sampling needs considerable attention; given space considerations, sampling is only briefly addressed here.

From a postpositivist standpoint, neither the sample type (e.g. random or not) nor size are, in themselves, valid criteria for evaluating scientific merit. Cronbach notes, "randomization may be achieved at the expense of relevance. But relevance is surely the sine qua non in evaluation" (1982, p. 114). Moreover, scientific discoveries consistently have been made using samples of one. In hosts of studies—such as inquiries into the cognitive abilities of dolphins or gorillas—only a few subjects customarily are studied. Decisions about the sample concern the kind of observations one wants to make to develop solutions to the problem. This book contains examples of research using the heuristic paradigm with a sample of one client (e.g., Pieper & Pieper, Chapter 8) and also a systematically selected sample of 2,884 journal articles (Chapter 2).

From a postpositivist standpoint, sampling entails selecting (given the researcher's ontological and epistemological assumptions) the specific objects or individuals who will be included in the research. In the course of designing the research, postpositivist researchers evaluate and reevaluate sampling decisions in relation to the problem formulation and the definition of the "real" under study (see, e.g., the process of "structural analysis" detailed by postpositivist realist researchers, Manicas and Secord in Chapter 5; Sayer, 1992).

Consider the following examples of the problems that can arise if a researcher does not pay careful attention to the "real" being studied in selecting a sample. In a highly publicized study, Zametkin et al. (1990) investigated possible physiological causes of childhood hyperactivity. Yet, their sample consisted of adults who had been diagnosed as having attention deficit hyperactivity disorder in childhood. When one takes into account the many psychological and physiological changes that occur in the course of development, one can see that a sample of adults cannot support conclusions about the brain functioning of children.

Heineman Pieper critiqued the often-cited Minnesota study of monozygotic twins and triplets (Bouchard, Lykken, McGue, Segal, & Tellegen, 1990) and illustrated how errors in the conceptualization of the sample can undercut the researchers' conclusions (1991). The researchers claimed to have a sample of children "reared apart" and concluded that their observation that the children's IQ scores varied in relation to their parentage reflected genetic influences on intelligence, rather than the effects of nurture. An unfortunate consequence of that conclusion is that it can reinforce beliefs that interventions such as education or psychotherapy cannot significantly bolster cognitive development. Heineman Pieper pointed out, however, that the children in the sample were not actually "reared apart" but instead that "they lived together for a mean period of 5.1 months, with a standard deviation of 8.5 months, and that some siblings lived together as long as 48.7 months, or until they were over four years old" (Heineman Pieper, 1991, p. 14). Many theories of child development emphasize that the major psychological structures regulating cognitive function have been established by the age of four years. Therefore, the characteristics of the authors' own sample undercut their conclusions; the findings can be used to argue for the enduring regulatory impact of early childhood nurture on IQ (Heineman Pieper, 1991, p. 15).

When the research involves human participant/subjects, the participant/researcher's decisions about sampling derive in part from his or her decision about the relationship with participant/subjects. Sample size influences the extent to which the participant/researcher can become involved with participant/subjects and understand their distinctive points of view (Skrtic, 1985). For example, a sample size of one person affords the participant/researcher the opportunity for more intensive involvement with the participant/subject than can occur with a sample size of 100. Researchers who want to gain insight into the opinions of a large group of people will need a sample of sufficient size and that is selected to be representative of the target population (e.g., via random or systematic sampling).

Different types of samples are a consequence of different heuristics. Often, a researcher will choose more than one sample. Increasingly, qualitative researchers choose a second sample of informants to evaluate and give the researcher feedback about conclusions based on the first sample. For example, during their extensive qualitative research about innovations in school settings, Huberman and Miles (1985) chose two samples—the initial informants and a group of informants who evaluated the preliminary findings of the researchers' qualitative analysis. In choosing the second group, Huberman and Miles looked for individuals who were "1) . . . reasonably knowledgeable about the phenomena we are studying, non-defensive, and articulate; 2) come from several different roles and perspectives; 3) are themselves of an inquiring, curious turn of mind" (1985, p. 378).

Another important consideration that has an impact on all aspects of the design, including sample selection, concerns the allocation of resources. Some designs are much more costly than others. Regarding the use of a control group, for example, Cronbach points out that when resources for educational and social services are scarce "the burden of proof falls, I would say, on anyone proposing to invest substantial evaluation resources in a no-treatment group" (1982, p. 329).

Choosing Forms of Measurement

The heuristic paradigm accommodates diverse forms of measurement. Positivist researchers mistakenly assumed that quantification exhausted the category of measurement, and so the decisions inherent in measuring have not been examined adequately (Fashing & Goertzel, 1981; Gigerenzer, 1987). Every scientist ultimately relies on her or his informed judgment in choosing the standard to use for measurement. Accordingly, requiring researchers to use a specific form of measurement to generate scientific knowledge is unwarranted. Scientists in other disciplines do not follow positivist restrictions on measurement. For example, in genetic research, a biologist commonly measures deviations in an organism's growth in relation to a qualitative standard—the expected growth pattern.

In the context of postpositivism, measurement can be understood as a repeated observation made with reference to a constant standard. There are many types of measurement, both qualitative and quantified. The practitioner's use of informed clinical judgment in relation to a clinical standard of comparison represents an important form of measurement that positivist social and behavioral researchers have overlooked or disparaged. For example, a practitioner analyzing process recordings can measure a client's progress using qualitative standards such as the change indices described in Chapter 7.

Some of the most crucial priorities in measurement do not involve quantification, but rather concern the standard of comparison used for the measurement and the specific type of observations to measure. Each standard of measurement introduces its own systematic biases, and the researcher chooses standards for measurement in relation to the research problem and her or his assumptions. To illustrate, one can measure health psychologically or physiologically. The standard used regulates the information that will be obtained about the object. A standard can quantify information (e.g., an IQ test); a standard can also be qualitative (Siporin, 1985). For example, a student may enter treatment because he habitually responds to academic examinations with panic attacks. The therapist and the client may measure the client's progress in relation to the standard of the client's habitual response to the test situations. If after a period of psychotherapy the client takes an examination without a panic attack, the therapist and client may conclude that, according to that standard of measurement, progress has occurred.

For a research design to be sound, decisions about measurement need to be consistent with the problem formulation and ontological and epistemological assumptions. Achieving this aim is challenging because it requires careful conceptual analysis, including analysis of what one is measuring. Consider the following example: One of the most commonly cited studies of the development of children's temperament and the relation of temperament to child psychopathology is the longitudinal study by Chess and Thomas (Chess & Thomas, 1984; Chess, Thomas, & Birch, 1972). The researchers concluded that diverse innate child temperaments exist and that a "difficult" temperament, characterized primarily by irritability and "overactivity," predisposes children to develop behavior disorders.

However, the researchers' decisions about data gathering, including their measurement of temperament, resulted in data that do not support their conclusions.

Although the authors sought to measure an inborn characteristic they termed "temperament," in fact they measured temperament using parents' behavioral descriptions of their children. The researchers did not interview the children until the children had become adolescents or young adults, because they found interviewing the children to be difficult (Chess & Thomas, 1984, p. 38). In other words, the researchers measured the parents' perceptions of the child's behavior. Accordingly, the researchers' conclusions that there is an entity such as an inborn temperament that has a causal role in psychopathology are unsupported by the data. In fact, observation of an association between the parents' descriptions of the children and the children's acting-out behavior could suggest that parents' negative perceptions of a child are related to the child's negative behavior, which supports an hypothesis about the influence of nurture, not innate factors, on the child's psychosocial development.

In addition to analyzing what to measure (ontological assumptions), researchers decide about measurement in relation to their beliefs about how the object of study can be scientifically known (epistemological assumptions). In pursuing "objectivity," positivist social and behavioral researchers devised "standardized instruments" (e.g., behavioral rating scales) that often quantify information. They believed that such measures could reduce the impact of researcher bias on the data gathered. "Standardized instruments," however, also reflect the researcher's choices and biases (Lincoln & Guba, 1985; Reinharz, 1984). For example, such instruments are standardized in relation to a population the researcher defines and selects. This is not to argue that such instruments should never be used but to emphasize that methods cannot eliminate researcher subjectivity from the measurement process. Unfortunately, the positivist assumption that data gathered using "standardized instruments" are "objective" encourages researchers to overlook the effects of their choice of heuristics on the data.

Requiring participant/subjects to limit their responses to structured questionnaires may be useful for some problems. However, it also rules out another potentially useful type of data—the participant/subjects' reflections about the problem and their opinions about the data-gathering methods. The point is not that one form of questionnaire is inherently superior to another. Rather, decisions about data gathering should not be based on irrelevant conventions but should be regulated by a focus on the information that will best help the researcher develop a solution to the problem.

Consider the example of a researcher studying the psychotherapy process with a depressed male client. A common psychotherapy research strategy in the context of positivism's prescriptions that researchers use quantified measurements is to require clients to fill out scales about the severity of their symptoms. This design decision represents interventionist research. It also is a decision to quantify information that omits potentially important qualitative information. When the client is not made to complete a research-motivated scale but instead is allowed to describe his pain in his own words, he may begin to cry and experience comfort. In this case, the client is helped, and the clinician-researcher then furthers the therapy and also learns about the quality and depth of the client's pain. The clinician-researcher also gathers information about the client's response to the comfort of being able to share that pain in the way he chooses. By contrast, when the client is asked to fill out a research-motivated questionnaire, information about how the client would react without the introduction of the instrument into the treatment relationship will not be gathered. Furthermore, the client's reactions to the research-motivated intervention will influence the data. For example, the client's depression may appear greater because he has to fill out the questionnaire instead of proceeding in a way that feels helpful to him.

In sum, because measurements will always introduce bias, the researcher adopting the heuristic approach chooses measurements reflectively, according to such standards as their consistency with the researcher's assumptions about reality and how reality can be known, and the relevance of the information they are likely to yield. Consider how researchers measuring intelligence have used different scales over time, including standards derived from craniometry, such as the circumference of the skull, and more recently, IQ tests (Gould, 1981). Present-day theories about intelligence and cognitive functioning do not support using skull size as a standard for measuring intelligence. A more recent example of ill-suited measurement standards is the use of IQ tests to represent the complex changes that occur in a reading program for disadvantaged children (Block & Dworkin, 1974; Seitz, Rosenbaum, & Apfel, 1985). A measurement affords only one perspective on the object measured. Multiple measures, a form of triangulation (see preceding discussion and Fiske, 1982; LeVine, 1981), can enrich the information and allow the researcher to diversify bias. As Wimsatt points out, however, researchers need to evaluate whether the multiple measures may share the same biases and so will yield a "pseudo-robustness" (1981a).

Qualitative Analysis

All research, even research relying on statistical analysis of quantified data, begins with qualitative decisions about data analysis. Any method of data analysis in effect transforms the research problem into another problem. Wimsatt (Chapter 5) points out how challenging it is for researchers to recognize that transformation and to evaluate whether the solutions to the problem—as transformed by data analysis—will be useful for the original research problem. For example, Dixon (1988) points out that political scientists often have used multiple regression models (an inferential statistical procedure) to analyze data about the actions of alienated nations. Multiple regression models, however, can conceptualize time as though it is not continuous, but metric or segmented. Furthermore, because such models aggregate isolated incidences, they treat interactive events (in this case, nations' reactions to each other) as though they are discontinuous rather than causally related. Consequently, when used for data analysis, those models of international behavior in effect transform an interactional process between nations into static aggregates of specific behaviors. Thus, the researchers could not adequately capture sequential, interactive relationships between nations (Dixon, 1988).

Once researchers recognize that any method of data analysis functions as a heuristic that will set up biases, they can then consider the many available ways of analyzing data and reflectively recognize the biases that each sets up. Often, researchers make fresh decisions about data analysis after data collection. Also, researchers may share data, and one researcher may analyze the same data in a very different way, leading to very different results. Because the researcher adopting the heuristic approach recognizes that no one way of analyzing data is inherently superior, she or he is free to make decisions about data analysis on the basis of standards such as generating the most usable solutions to the problem.

Many different methods of qualitative data analysis are currently used, and the methods draw from different metatheories of knowledge. Strauss and Corbin's "grounded theory" (1990) draws heavily from the positivist tradition. It assumes a sharp distinction can be made between theories and observations. An interpretive, hermeneutical approach to qualitative analysis draws from Ricoeur and Gadamer (e.g., Sherman, 1991), and "begins with the assumption that facts are a construction, a part of a whole." The interpretation of facts occurs in the context of a dialogue between the interpreter and the text (L. E. Thomas & Chambers, 1989, p. 285). Mishler's (1990) work on narrative is another example of an approach to qualitative analysis that is consonant with the tradition of hermeneutics. Huberman and Miles (1985) present an approach to qualitative analysis developed in the context of Bhaskar's critical realism. Finally, the ethnographic tradition has made very important contributions to the development of qualitative analysis (Geertz, 1973; Spradley, 1979). A brief overview of how a researcher using the heuristic paradigm can analyze data qualitatively follows (see also Chapters 7 and 8 for examples).

The coding categories in a qualitative analysis can be understood in the light of Levins's (1966) concept of the sufficient parameter: The categories are variables derived from the researcher's theoretical assumptions and reflect regular patterns of meaning that are apparent in the data. Categories can capture patterns at different levels of abstraction. For example, in the history of the field of social work in Chapter 2, one set of categories used for coding the sample of journal articles specifically differentiated between seven types of research design heuristics, whereas a set of categories at a less specific level differentiated studies that used quantified or qualitative data. Qualitative data analysis can incorporate forms of measurement. For example, Heineman Pieper points out that a clinician's anamnestic process recordings can be analyzed using qualitative indices (see Chapters 7 and 8).

The researcher inevitably uses constructs derived from her or his theory to generate coding categories. Even the position that the categories are atheoretical reflects a theory. For example, one might ask, "What would I expect to observe, given this theory?" and generate categories based on answering that question. Two examples of coding categories that might be derived from theories of family treatment are the patterns of intimacy and distance between family members and how family members allow different points of view to be expressed, as opposed to sanctioning different opinions (Hartman & Laird, 1983; Walsh, 1983). Hollis's famous typology of social worker interventions is another classic example of qualitative analysis, which can be a helpful model for examining interventions using process recordings as data (Woods & Hollis, 1990). Researchers usually develop a coding manual that defines and summarizes the major coding categories used. A coding manual is a touchstone for sharing one's ideas and getting feedback, is essential for ascertaining reliability, systematizes observations, and is one way to develop theory.

Qualitative analysis proceeds as the researcher examines the data and sees patterns that are instances of the researcher's theoretical premises. The patterns include both particular constructs and dynamic interactions between the constructs (e.g., see the change indices in Chapter 7). Initial coding categories come to mind, as the researcher explores whether the patterns appear consistently in the data and under what conditions. At the same time, the researcher begins to see examples that are counter to her or his expectations and initial formulations. Although the researcher can experience inconsistencies between the data and her or his initial categories as a loss, in fact, they represent the most fruitful opportunity for developing an understanding of the patterns that appear. With careful analysis of the exceptions, the researcher refines the categories, revises the patterns, and may refine or revise the theoretical premises.

Qualitative researchers have developed many strategies for checking the validity of coding categories and the causal links one posits between them. For example, Huberman and Miles (1985) describe at length the steps they took in defining their coding categories. Initially, they developed patterns they termed "causal fragments" and observed regularities between "chunks" of data, which they evaluated, refined, and pieced together. They recommend "trying out the causal fragments on those being researched" (Huberman & Miles, 1985, p. 368). The techniques they recommend for checking conclusions in qualitative research include triangulating, making contrasts and comparisons, checking for extreme cases or cases that contradict the patterns one is examining, evaluating alternative explanations for the observations, determining whether a finding is repeated, and getting feedback from informants (Huberman & Miles, 1985, p. 369).

When the researcher no longer assumes that the methodological prescriptions of positivism will guarantee the scientific value of the findings, he or she can delve more deeply into credibility—an issue that Heineman Pieper describes as fundamental for research (see Preface). Many decisions in research design result in a project that generates credible information. Decisions about the reliability of observations affect credibility. However, as Heineman Pieper points out, reliability, when defined as agreement between observers, does not guarantee the credibility of research (see Preface). A research study can meet many criteria for reliability and yet still be invalid (see the Glossary definitions of reliability and validity). Using the heuristic paradigm, the researcher recognizes that the impact of the researcher's judgment cannot be avoided. The researcher works hard so that the data reflect a finely tuned judgment process that other observers can understand.

Reliability is one indicator of the credibility of the researcher's judgments about recording, reporting, and interpreting the meaning of the data. Researchers have defined many types of reliability and have used the term in diverse ways. Reliability can be evaluated in many ways, e.g., qualitatively and also by using a quantified index. Decisions about criteria for evaluating reliability are heuristic choices, and should be made in relation to the aims and methods chosen for the research design, as well as standards in the field. Two examples of evaluating reliability in the context of a study that entails coding process recordings follow. First, a student learning clinical practice typically reviews her or his process recordings with a clinical supervisor who evaluates the student's collection of data and also the student's interpretation of the meaning of the data. Together, student and supervisor evaluate the value and meaning of the process recording. A researcher whose data consist of process recordings that have been carefully reviewed in supervision can present that supervisory process as one indicator of reliability. A traditional quantified measure of the reliability of coders' judgments about a coding category is the number of agreements between coders divided by the total number of judgments made in implementing that coding decision

Heineman Pieper and Pieper's report of the demonstration project using intrapsychic humanism (Chapter 8) is an excellent example of qualitative analysis. The authors examine the clinical results of residential care and psychotherapy of a violent adolescent client named Andrew. The paper sets forth a new understanding of the proximal causes, or triggers, of the violent behavior of clients who were forced by traumatic nurture to develop motives for the pain of violent acting-out. (The learned motives for pain are, of course, the ongoing and underlying causes of the clients' violent behavior.) Those triggers are experiences of loss and aversive reactions to pleasure.* The authors' qualitative coding categories reflect these theoretical constructs.

For example, Andrew's response to loss is a coding category that Heineman Pieper and Pieper derived from their theory and that formed one measurement of change. The authors noticed that Andrew habitually became violent in response to loss, seriously hurting himself or others. His behavior ranged from homicidal attacks such as strangling his therapist, to swallowing objects such as open safety pins. By examining Andrew's response to loss, they measured changes in Andrew's capacity to regulate his violent behavior. During residential care that included intensive individual psychotherapy, one of the measurable changes that occurred was:

> Andrew developed a new resilience to caregiving lapses by the staff and to the losses caused by other residents' aggressiveness. In an incident that directly paralleled the earlier time when he had strangled Dr. L, a fight broke out in the house and one of the residents started hitting one of the staff. Andrew intervened and shepherded the boy into the staff room and talked to him until he calmed down. (Heineman Pieper & Pieper, p. 468 in Chapter 8)

Using Statistical Methods of Data Analysis

This discussion cannot cover the many statistical methods of data analysis. You will want to refer to textbooks that focus specifically on the models you are interested

---

*Editor's Note: An aversive reaction to pleasure occurs when the individual's motives for genuine self-caretaking pleasure are gratified, which in turn signifies a loss to the part of the individual with learned motives for pain; those motives for pain rebound with increased intensity. (See Chapters 7 and 8 for elaboration.)

in using. Statistical methods are discussed here briefly, however, and some considerations in choosing statistical methods follow.

In general, statistical methods can be used to compile and describe data (descriptive statistics), and for inference such as from a sample to a population (inferential statistics). Although positivists hoped that statistical methods would settle differences between rival theories (e.g., Carnap, 1963/1991b), scientists rarely calculate the probability of a theory's veracity:

> The idea that by means of a statistic one could mechanically derive a degree of certainty for a hypothesis is an old dream. Many a solution has been proposed, and all of them failed in a scientific context. Physics, which many social scientists took as a model, in fact rarely if ever uses null hypothesis testing. Whether light is composed of particles or of waves—physicists never seriously believed they could assign numerical probabilities to such theories or discover the "true" theory by significance testing. Social scientists, in contrast, seem to be strongly susceptible to the idea that statistics is indispensable for deciding between hypotheses. (Gigerenzer et al., 1989, p. 211)

In the course of analyzing data, some scientists may calculate probabilities of hypotheses, but findings about human judgment indicate a considerably more complex process goes into how scientists evaluate hypotheses: "Satisficing is a crude theory of what else they might be doing" (Giere cited in Callebaut, 1993, p. 177; for the definition of *satisficing*, see the glossary).

All statistical methods require informed judgment throughout their application. After one has chosen a statistical method,

> judgment must intervene again to set the decision criterion, in the case of Neyman-Pearson theory, or the level of significance in Fisherian null hypothesis testing, or the prior probabilities in Bayesian inference. No amount of mathematical legerdemain can transform uncertainty into certainty, although much of the appeal of statistical inference stems from just such great expectations. (Gigerenzer et al., 1989, p. 288)

The many statistical tools available can be divided into descriptive and inferential statistics. Descriptive statistics serve to summarize and compile data, such as in frequencies, means, and modes. Descriptive statistics are the foundation for any meaningful statistical analysis, in that they set forth the distribution of variables for the reader to examine and interpret. Even if researchers use other statistics to interpret the meaning of the information (e.g., a chi-square statistic or a correlation coefficient), the meaning of those statistics can be discerned only in reference to the distributions of the data. Increasingly, social and behavioral researchers are moving away from inferential statistics and toward descriptive statistics, and in particular focus on the visual display of information (Gigerenzer, personal communication, March 1, 1994). Bar charts and other graphics are helpful for interpreting the meaning of the numbers and summarizing trends for the reader. The visual display of information is an art in itself, and reference texts are available that explore the considerable impact of various visual heuristics on how readers process information (e.g., Tufte, 1990).

As the name suggests, inferential statistics aim to derive inferences, such as using a sample to make inferences about a much larger population. In that example, the researcher estimates parameters of a population and tests hypotheses about the population based on data obtained in a sample drawn from that population. Procedures have been developed to maximize the representativeness of the sample (e.g., using a random numbers table to select a "random" sample) and to estimate the representativeness of the sample obtained. Every inferential statistical procedure is the consequence of an underlying theory of probability (Danziger, 1988b; Gigerenzer et al., 1989). According to some texts, inferential statistics is a unified theory; in fact, however, that is not the case:

> In statistical reasoning it has not (yet) proven possible to come to an all-encompassing theory, of which the current positions are special cases. . . . In fact, some working statisticians advocate an ecumenism in which one should apply different approaches to the same set of data. (Gigerenzer et al., 1989, p. 90)

Each statistical method rests on different assumptions and sets up different frameworks for data analysis. For example, each method makes specific assumptions about the sample being studied, the type of data being used, and finally yields different information about the data. As is the case in other fields, statisticians using different methods disagree passionately about fundamental concepts. Those interested in reading more about the evolution and impact of probability theories, including the development of diverse statistical methods, will benefit from the comprehensive history by Gigerenzer et al. (1989).

In choosing a method of statistical analysis, it is important to refer to the complexity of the problem one is addressing and the kinds of data one wants to analyze, including the forms of measurement one has implemented. To illustrate, a bivariate inferential statistical method such as a chi-square may be the most helpful way to ascertain whether Republicans are inclined to oppose, and Democrats to support, legislation that enforces equal rights for gays and lesbians. However, a multivariate inferential statistical method such as discriminant analysis may offer a better way to determine resident characteristics that predict residents' capacity to make productive changes in the course of their treatment in a program for the homeless mentally ill (Walsh, 1986). Predicting how the residents will use the treatment program is a relatively more complex problem than ascertaining voting patterns with regard to two variables (political party and voting yes or no on a piece of legislation). Discriminant analysis assumes multiple levels of measurement, and so it is more appropriate for the problem and the variables as formulated in the treatment outcome study. In sum, the researcher considers both the complexity of the problem and the nature of the variables used to study it in deciding on the level of measurement. Those decisions in turn lead to the decision about the method of data analysis.

The "practical adequacy" of statistical methods "depends in part on the type of object to which they are applied" (Sayer, 1992, p. 194), which in turn is defined via a nonstatistical, conceptual analysis. An important illustration of the problems that can result when a statistical method is misapplied because the researcher did not analyze the theoretical assumptions of the statistical method is provided by Lewontin, Chapter 6. During the 1970s a researcher conducted a highly publicized study which concluded that some racial minority groups are genetically less able to benefit from educational enrichment programs than persons who are not members of racial minority groups. From a humanistic standpoint, such findings are spurious as well as racist. Lewontin points out why, from a methodological and conceptual standpoint, those conclusions were unwarranted. Social and behavioral practitioners and researchers need to be able to recognize and critique such unfortunate misuses of statistical methods.

The statistics used in an inferential statistical analysis reflect contemporary (and often-changing) agreements among statisticians, and their interpretations vary considerably according to the field of study and the problem being studied. Gigerenzer (1993) points out that many social and behavioral researchers have made enduring and substantial contributions without testing their hypotheses via statistical significance tests. Consider, for example, Piaget, Erikson, Kohut, Simon, and Bronfenbrenner. However, the mistaken emphasis on tests of statistical significance for scientific inference has been a serious and far-reaching problem in the social and behavioral sciences. Today close to 100% of psychology journal articles use null hypothesis testing (Gigerenzer, 1993). A misinterpretation of statistical significance tests occurs when the researcher believes:

> that the level of significance by itself determines 1) the magnitude of the effect, 2) the probability that the null hypothesis is true or false, 3) the probability that the alternative hypothesis is true or false, and 4) the degree of confidence that the experimental result is repeatable. (Gigerenzer et al., 1989, p. 209)

Gigerenzer et al. emphasize that "Wishful thinking did its part in making the level of significance seem an answer to all these questions" (1989, p. 209). They also point out that misuses of null hypothesis testing and the misunderstandings of the meaning of statistical significance have been widespread and have occurred in textbooks as well as journals. To illustrate, Gigerenzer (1993) describes how in a study of 70 academic psychologists, 60% mistakenly thought that the level of statistical significance could be interpreted to indicate the probability of replicating the findings (Oakes, 1986).

Fortunately, researchers increasingly are concerned about the erroneous beliefs about the meaning of statistical significance tests. There is a growing trend toward descriptive statistics and the use of figures for displaying information. An illustration of this trend is the editorial by Geoffrey R. Loftus, editor-elect of the psychology journal *Memory and Cognition*. In discussing very flexible and broad guidelines for aspiring authors, Loftus said, "over the years an overreliance on the impoverished binary conclusions yielded by the hypothesis-testing procedure has subtly seduced our discipline into insidious conceptual cul-de-sacs that have impeded our vision and stymied our potential" (1993, p. 3). He recommended that authors use alternative means of displaying data, such as "figures depicting sample means along with standard error bars" (1993, p. 3).

Robert Rosenthal's (1990a) description of how to evaluate a statistic termed *effect size* exemplifies the judgment process entailed in using statistics. Opinions about the magnitude of an effect necessary to imply importance vary widely among fields. For example, Rosenthal refers to two studies of medications, both of which used control groups. The studies were discontinued because the preliminary effect size obtained was evaluated as sufficiently important that the researchers decided it would be unethical to deprive the control group, and others, of the treatment. However, that effect size was considerably smaller than the effect sizes obtained in studies of the outcome of psychological treatment, which some psychotherapy researchers had evaluated as so small that it "sounded the death knell for psychotherapy" (1990a, p. 776). Further, the effect sizes obtained in the medical studies were also considerably smaller than the effects Rosenthal obtained in examining the results of experimenters' experimentally induced expectancies on their research findings in seven different areas of research (1990a). In sum, the use of statistics such as effect size varies widely according to the field of study and the problem addressed (1990a, 1990b). Researchers' interpretations of statistics such as effect size result from the researchers' heuristics, and the criteria for interpreting the statistic need to be examined and described for the reader (1990a, 1990b).

EXAMPLES

Because the heuristic paradigm does not prescribe fixed steps to follow to design scientific research, and because it emphasizes the use of informed judgment and thinking through every decision, you may be concerned that "all bets are off" and there are no standards for judging a promising and valid research design. In the preceding discussion, however, many standards have been described that can be used to evaluate research designs. Moreover, developing a conceptually sound research design follows logically once the researcher formulates the problem and consistent initial assumptions.

For illustration, two examples of potential research designs follow. Given space limitations, the designs are not as fully developed as they would be in actual practice.

Example 1

A psychological consultant had just begun to work with a multidisciplinary rehabilitation team that treated children with head injuries. A typical patient was an eight-year-old child who was hiking with her family, slipped, and fell several feet onto rocks, which resulted in permanent cognitive and perceptual impairment. Initially, the child had been comatose, finally recovered consciousness, and participated in intensive rehabilitation for several months before being discharged. The psychologist was new to the hospital and the team, and was interested in understanding the crisis intervention services that would be useful for the patients and their families. Following the psychologist's suggestion, the team decided to pursue that question using a naturalistic research design.

From a psychological standpoint, rehabilitation consisted primarily of intensive crisis intervention services for the children and their families, ranging from helping them to mourn the loss of the child's injury, to facilitating the most adaptive and highest level of functioning possible. The psychologist used psychosocial crisis intervention theory as her guiding modality (Rapoport, 1970; Parad & Parad, 1980), and proposed to the team that those theoretical assumptions should serve as initial guides for the research process as well. The advantages of that theory are that its ontology is not limited to physiological tissue variables, but includes subjective experience. Further, it does not make the pessimistic assumption that an organic injury (e.g., head injury) precludes a child's capacity to respond to psychological help, and so it could be used to explore the children's response to individual psychological counseling as well as to help the families with the guilt and anguish they almost invariably experienced. Based on a review of the literature, the psychologist decided to offer and study four primary service modalities:

1. A family support group;
2. A support group for the children;
3. Family crisis intervention counseling; and
4. Individual counseling for the children.

Once the decisions had been made about the problem and the theory to use and the team had decided that the research would be naturalistic, the research design began to fall into place. The researchers decided that the sample would be systematic: No child or family would be excluded from the sample, and data would be gathered on an ongoing basis for one year. This resulted in a sample of forty children and families. The treatment team members recognized that a significant problem that they hoped the psychological services would remedy was the anger of patients and their families toward the treatment staff. Sometimes the anger culminated in families removing their children from the unit against medical advice. Although, clearly, some of the anger could be understood as expressions of frustration with lapses in care, most often, the families' anger seemed to be reactions to the very devastating losses that they and the children were experiencing. The staff also hoped that crisis intervention care would result in an improved recovery process. They formulated two central issues for the research to explore:

1. Identify the helpful features of a counseling process for the children and families, including, for example, understanding what prompted the families' anger.
2. Examine the impact of the counseling program on the undesirable treatment outcome of the families' requesting discharge against medical advice.

To respond to the first concern, the staff needed to have a way to understand what kinds of services the children and the families found to be helpful. The decision that the methods would be naturalistic meant that the staff would not use any data-gathering methods that were not in accord with their therapeutic practices. This immediately ruled out investigatory tools that were not used for therapeutic aims.

Alternative sources of data were plentiful. The psychologist kept careful records of her work with her patients, which could serve as one data source about counseling. She also planned to start training two interns, who normally also completed process records as part of the supervisory process, which expanded the available data and provided a natural research group for developing coding categories. The hospital commonly offered quality management questionnaires to all patients on discharge. The team examined the questionnaires and incorporated those into the design as another source of data that would provide feedback from the families about their experience of the quality of the care. The staff's chart notes, which were considerable, offered another perspective on the process of care and the patients' progress in coping with the crisis. The charts could be analyzed qualitatively and also were used to compile quantified data about the families' precipitous requests for discharge against medical advice. The multiple sources of data triangulated perspectives on the problems. For example, staff were most concerned that the evaluation of service include the children's and families' perspectives on the care they received as well as the psychologist's ongoing assessment and the staffs' assessments, as recorded in their chart notes.

In analyzing the biases in their design, the psychologist recognized that because the environment–system boundary was drawn around the immediate hospital care process, information such as the children's functioning at school after discharge was not obtained. The decision that the research would be naturalistic also meant that the staff would not gather follow-up information from the families, except in the informal ways that occurred as the families kept in touch with staff members with whom they had developed especially deep relationships.

Decisions about data analysis followed from the prior decisions. Qualitative analysis could be used to develop initial coding categories in examining the process recordings, the qualitative responses to the questionnaires, and the descriptions of patient discharges in the charts. Examples of the initial categories that the research team derived using crisis intervention theory include the patient's and the family's understanding of the causes of the crisis event. The team formulated a process category to capture the variety of ways the families responded to the loss. At a higher level of abstraction, the team hypothesized that families respond to the crisis event in three major ways: (1) with increased appetitive longings for care from the hospital staff, (2) with anger toward each other and the hospital staff, and (3) with blame directed toward themselves, isolation, and increased distance.

The researchers wanted to look for correlations between the families' patterns of responding to loss, and the families' satisfaction with different forms of service as measured by the questionnaires. The research team decided to use a chi-square analysis to test their hypothesized connections. For example, the staff thought that the families who responded to loss with intensified isolation were more likely to attend only one family support group meeting and then to call on staff on an as-needed basis, rather than establishing regular counseling appointments, as did the families who responded to loss with increased longings for care. The staff planned to compile the number of discharges against medical advice from the year before the psychologist's institution of services, and to compare these figures with those from the year of the initiation of the psychologist's services.

Example 2

A child guidance team in an urban school system was interested in understanding the dynamics that lead to teenage pregnancy. Team members offered voluntary counseling services to teenagers at eight high schools in a large metropolitan area. Team members wanted to improve their understanding of the causes of teenage pregnancy as a step toward developing better services. Rather than using an educational model for explaining teen pregnancy in terms of the teens' knowledge about contraception, the team wanted to examine the impact of social, gender, and racial inequalities on patterns of teenage pregnancy (see Heineman Pieper, 1994).

The team used theoretical assumptions developed from ecological systems, feminist, and ethnic-sensitive models of human development and clinical practice (e.g., Bricker-Jenkins & Hooyman, 1986; Bronfenbrenner, 1979b; Devore, 1983; Gibbs et al., 1989; Gilligan, 1982; Lum, 1992). They postulated that social deprivation, the lack of adequate employment and educational opportunities, experiences of racial and gender discrimination, and consequent feelings of inferiority and hopelessness organized around gender and race would be associated with higher rates of teenage pregnancy. They thought that teenagers who were disempowered might experience the pregnancy as the only avenue open to them to experience a sense of strength and purpose in their lives. The researchers wanted to use their findings to convince funding sources of the importance of providing special preventive counseling services to the teens and to pinpoint the most important areas to focus on in designing preventive services.

The guidance team decided that their research approach would be interventionist, in part because they wanted to gather data using a focus group method that was not part of the high schools' standard services. Because they wanted to have maximal flexibility in using inferential statistical methods of data analysis, they decided to set up random samples: one group of teens who were or had recently been pregnant, and another group, matched for age, ethnicity, and socioeconomic status, who had never been pregnant. Initially, the researchers wanted to include young men in their sample, so that they would also have a group of teenage fathers and another of nonfathers. A significant problem, however, was that the researchers did not have adequate resources to obtain the sample sizes they preferred, 1,600 in all, with 400 for each group. They could afford a total sample of only 400.

In thinking through their method of data analysis, the researchers were concerned about whether they would be able to carry out their preferred method of statistical analysis, which was log-linear analysis. They foresaw that the possibility of low return rates on their questionnaires—along with splitting the sample into different ethnic minority groups for data analysis— meant that if they also had to split the sample into gender categories for data analysis, their cell sizes might be inadequate for log-linear analysis. Accordingly, until they received further funding, they decided to include only young women in their first samples.

The guidance team wanted to gather the data in the context of offering support. They therefore decided to organize the data gathering around focus groups. The focus groups consisted of five weekly sessions in which the teens could share their feelings about their relationships, their schools, their families, and their future plans. The team did not want the teens to feel inhibited by tape recorders, so they decided to use anamnestic process records of the group sessions. Three researchers conducted each group. From prior clinical experience, the researchers knew they could develop process recordings that were very detailed and reflected each researcher's recollections as well as their shared agreement about the final product. The teens were also asked to complete questionnaires that the team developed to triangulate the methods of data collection. The questionnaire included qualitative as well as quantified indicators that covered a range of variables, including the teens' career interests, family socioeconomic status, and neighborhood.

The inferential statistical method of data analysis the researchers wanted to use—log-linear modeling—is designed to test the statistical significance of the relationship between categorical variables, such as the teens' experiences of racial and gender inequalities and the variable of pregnancy. Log-linear models were developed specifically to analyze relationships between categorical variables and have been increasingly used by social and behavioral scientists (Norusis, 1988, p. 298). One of the advantages of this statistical technique for data analysis is that it allows the investigator both to examine the statistical significance of relationships between many variables and to ascertain the effects of interactions between the variables. To illustrate, log-linear modeling can indicate whether the number of teens who became pregnant and expressed distress at racial and gender discrimination is greater than what one would expect given chance alone (Kennedy, 1992; Norusis, 1988).

From their prior clinical experience, the team anticipated that their research might have the following effects. They thought that the young women would be intensely responsive to the discussion of gender issues and might immediately begin to discuss their fears for their safety and their feelings of alienation and anger about inequalities they experienced, both in the classroom and on the streets. The team posited that they would find a statistical interaction between those variables (sensitivity to gender issues, fears for safety, and feelings of alienation and anger about social inequalities). The staff also thought that the data they collected in the first session might begin to shift significantly by the fifth session. For example, they thought that some young women who might be reticent about their career interests in the first session might, by the fifth group, share their aspirations to become lawyers and doctors, but also their conviction that they could never attain those goals. The research team recognized that the data-gathering process could have a substantial effect on the participant/subjects in the research, and they decided that in addition to the other variables developed for the coding process, they needed to develop coding categories that would reflect the teens' increased availability to sharing their feelings in the focus groups. Even more importantly, the team realized that their research could stimulate hopes and expectations and start a unique change process for these young women. In addition to using their research findings to improve services, the team arranged for additional counselors to be available to the young women who participated in the focus groups, so that they would have continued support in pursuing their goals after the research project concluded.

KEY TERMS

Descriptive statistics	**Inferential statistics**
Reliability	**Research design**
Triangulation	**Validity**

DISCUSSION QUESTIONS

1. Examine the research conducted by the early social workers described in Chapter 2.

    a. Was the clinical research that Mary Richmond conducted and reported in *What Is Social Casework?* (1922) naturalistic or interventionist?

    b. Did Florence Kelley use naturalistic or interventionist methods to study the impact of the Illinois legislation regulating child labor?

    c. If Charlotte Towle (from the diagnostic school of casework) interviewed a child named Jim, and Jessie Taft (from the functionalist school of casework) also interviewed Jim, why might they collect very different data about him?

2. a. Select three clinical research studies conducted in the last ten years and reported in a contemporary journal. Show how that research is either naturalistic or interventionist.

    b. What kinds of data did the researchers collect?

    c. What kinds of data might have been left out, given the researchers' choices of data-collection strategies?

    d. What procedures did the researchers use to analyze their data?

    e. What alternative strategies for data analysis might you use with those researchers' data?

3. The scientific standards Heineman Pieper advocates include: (1) a focus on substantive rather than primarily methodological criteria (exalting "substance over method," 1985, p. 4); (2) evaluating the utility of the study's explanations and/or problem solutions ("whether a particular study or methodology has a chance to help us better understand our difficult and complex problems," 1985, p. 4); (3) bias recognition ("the attempt to recognize and allow for bias is of much greater value than the attempt to eradicate it," 1985, p. 4); and (4) whether the research draws upon such valuable resources as practitioners', clients' and informants' judgments (which Heineman Pieper regards as "useful and even indispensable," e.g., in research about treatment and program effectiveness, 1985, p. 4). Apply those standards to appraise the clinical research studies you selected to answer question 2.

4. a. Consider the following types of data a researcher can use. Are they empirical (according to the definition cited by Heineman Pieper in the Preface)?

    i. A contemporary study of the theory Freud advances in *The Interpretation of Dreams* (1953–1974).

    ii. A therapist's process recordings of psychotherapy sessions.

    iii. A chart kept by a client suffering from anorexia and mental health staff that tracks the client's weight changes during the course of treatment.

    iv. The opinions of clients in a case management program for the severely mentally ill in response to an open-ended question about the usefulness of the program, as written by the clients on a questionnaire.

    v.   Audiotape recordings of a psychotherapy session.

   vi.   Clients' opinions about the type of employment rehabilitation program they might find helpful, as reported to and transcribed by a caseworker in that program.

  vii.   Client responses to a questionnaire comprising structured questions and rating scales.

 viii.   Einstein often thought through and supported his theories using "thought experiments." He used a "thought experiment" to illustrate the principle of simultaneity in his famous 1905 paper on relativity, in which he examined assumptions about time and observed that, "every statement about the 'objective' time of an event is, in reality, a statement about the simultaneous occurrence of two events; namely, the simultaneous occurrence of the event in question and, say, the superposition of the 'hands' of a clock on the numbers painted on the dial" (J. Bernstein, 1973, p. 58). According to Einstein's principle of simultaneity:

> if we think about it, we realize that because the speed of light is not infinite it takes a certain amount of time for the light that is illuminating the event in question to reach our eyes, and hence, strictly speaking, we are comparing an event that has already occurred with our watches. As a rule we can ignore this because light travels so fast and the distances involved are so small that this 'delay' is irrelevant. However, if we want to time events on the moon with clocks on the earth, say, the delay is very significant. (J. Bernstein, 1973, p. 59)

> Einstein's thought experiment was that "he imagined two identical clocks, one at the North Pole and one on the equator. He then pointed out that the clock on the equator would have a rate a tiny fraction of a per cent slower, as measured by the clock on the pole, because of the earth's rotation" (J. Bernstein, 1973, p. 65). Are Einstein's "thought experiments" empirical as Heineman Pieper defines it? *Hint:* Just because something is not empirical does not mean that it is not indebted to empirical experience or that it cannot be tested empirically.

   b.   Reconsider the preceding example from Einstein's work. How is any way of measuring time a heuristic?

5. Practice formulating a research problem and selecting the variables you would like to study. Evaluate the variables you have included in your study and some you have left out according to the standard of whether or not studying such variables will yield a relevant and useful solution to the problem.

6. Suppose you are a researcher who wants to study how people who have a quadriplegic disability can retain autonomy and control over their care in their relationships with the people they hire to help them. Consider the following ways of gathering data:

    i.   Interviews with the disabled person and the helper using open-ended questions and ascertaining what is important to them.

    ii.   Asking the disabled person to fill out a questionnaire with answers quantified in the form of scales.

    iii.   Enlisting an observer who will count the frequency of behaviors between the partners (the disabled person and the person hired as a helper) that may signify the disabled person's control and autonomy in the relationship (e.g., when the disabled person makes a request that the helper gratifies).

    a.   Are the preceding approaches naturalistic or interventionist?

    b.   What kind of information is likely to be obtained using each form of data gathering?

    c.   How does each approach to data gathering, in effect, transform the research question into another question?

7. For the history in Chapter 2, qualitative data were collected; for the content analysis, specific characteristics of social work journal articles were tabulated. Data analysis included a statistical method of data analysis, the chi-square test. What are the particular advantages of content analysis for responding to the hypothesis as it was formulated? What are the biases engendered by the use of content analysis?

8. At present, humans are included in research if they consent to participate. For children and other people viewed as incapable of giving informed consent, parents or guardians provide the informed consent. Some ethically problematic or obviously harmful research has been conducted. To deter unethical research, all research on humans in this country must be reviewed by "Institutional Review Boards," whose job is to protect the participant/subjects from potential harm caused by research procedures. Using the standard that the research should not harm the participant/subject, how would you evaluate the following research studies?

    i.   Milby and Weber (1991) described as an important contribution a research study that was an experimental trial of a "treatment" for obsessive-compulsive disorder, called "faradic disruption." Adult patients were asked "to reproduce obsessive ideation or imagery. This cognitive event is followed by a painful electric shock administered until the client signals that the ideation has terminated" (Milby & Weber, 1991, p. 23).

    ii.   In a study that some authors regarded as a landmark in research on hyperactivity, Laufer, Denhoff, and Solomons (1957) gave children they had labeled "hyperkinetic" Metrazol (a drug that induces convulsions) intravenously while the children were connected to an early version of the electroencephalogram. A light much like a strobe light was flashed repeatedly in front of their eyes. The dosage of intravenous Metrazol was increased until the children's brain waves changed to a convulsive pattern.[86]

    iii. Children labeled hyperactive were subjected to radioactive inhalants (Lou, Henriksen, Bruhn, Borner, & Nielsen, 1989).

    iv. Adult participant/subjects were made to believe that they could administer electric shocks to other people at the orders of the participant/researcher (in fact, they could not administer the shocks). The participant/subjects were pressured in various ways and generally agreed to administer the shocks to others (Milgram, 1963, 1965).

  a. Did you include in your criterion for evaluating research with humans the standard that research should not cause the participant/subject a psychological or emotional loss? If not, how would adding that criterion to your standards for evaluating research with humans lead you to reappraise the preceding examples?

  b. Is it possible to eliminate informed judgment and values from the evaluation of scientific research designs?

  c. What standards would you recommend as guidelines for designing research with human participant/subjects?

9. Seitz, Rosenbaum, and Apfel (1985) describe how the initial measures used to evaluate the impact of a multidisciplinary intervention for disadvantaged teenage mothers indicated that within the first few years after services were provided, those services had an impact on the mothers and their children that was at best questionable. When Seitz et al. used different measures ten years later, however, they found that the impact of the services provided was profound and enduring. Look up that study to answer the following questions:

  a. What forms of measurement were used initially? What biases did those measurements set up?

  b. What forms of measurement were used after ten years? What biases did those measurements set up?

  c. Where did the researchers draw the environment–system boundary?

  d. What impact did the choices of measurement, and the choices of where to draw the environment–system boundary, have on evaluations of the efficacy of the program?

10. Consider the problem you formulated in answering question 11 in the Discussion Questions for Heineman Pieper's 1989 paper in Chapter 3.

  a. Choose a research design to investigate that problem and describe the kind of relationship that design sets up with the participant/subjects in the research.

  b. Will your research be naturalistic or interventionist?

  c. Decide what data to gather and describe the biases your choice sets up.

  d. Plan how you will analyze the data.

  e. How do your choices about design, data collection, and data analysis influence the problem formulation and potential solutions to the problem?

▼ ▼ ▼ ▼ ▼ ▼ ▼ ▼ ▼ ▼ ▼ ▼ ▼

SAMPLE RESEARCH PROJECT: DEVELOPING RESIDENTIAL TREATMENT SERVICES FOR HOMELESS, MENTALLY ILL, AND SUBSTANCE-ABUSING CLIENTS

Part 1: Introduction

To further illustrate the use of the heuristic paradigm in designing research, central elements of a sample research project design are presented following each set of Discussion Questions in Chapters 5 and 6. It is impossible to address every aspect of this project, given space limitations, but the key decisions in planning research are highlighted.

The central problem the research project addresses is, *What services are helpful for homeless, mentally ill clients? What do the clients tell us about why those services are helpful?*

It is widely known that homeless mentally ill clients often reject the available shelters and treatment programs. Some researchers and laypersons respond to this problem by assuming that those clients are unmotivated and/or irremediably incapable of improving their capacity for self-caretaking (Chafetz, 1990; Holmes, 1991; Rossi, 1989). However, that assumption about the clients' dejective motivation has not been tested. Clients' reluctance to use such programs may not inhere in the clients but may result, at least in part, from the way in which care is provided. In accord with that possibility, to support homeless mentally ill clients' self-caretaking motivation, service providers need a better understanding of the kinds of services those clients find helpful (Leete, 1988; Mulkern & Bradley, 1986; Susser, Goldfinger, & White, 1990).

This problem formulation entails a prior decision to involve the clients in evaluating the program from which they receive care. That decision is in itself a departure from the most common approach to research with severely mentally ill and homeless clients. The most common research tradition with this population develops and evaluates services using indicators such as client diagnosis (Levine & Huebner, 1991; Minkoff, 1989), rehospitalization (Drake & Wallach, 1988), employment status (Abbott & Blake, 1988), continuance in aftercare (Hiday & Scheid-Cook, 1989), or changes in symptom severity as measured by standardized scales, arrests, medication noncompliance, or substance abuse (Hogarty, 1991; Levine & Huebner, 1991). Although such indicators have some usefulness in relation to some research problems, they share a common bias in that they do not focus on clients' opinions about the services they receive. In part that bias against scientifically studying clients' subjective experience of services reflects the long-standing positivist tradition in social and behavioral research, a tradition based on the impracticable aim of cleansing scientific knowledge of subjectivity (e.g., Carnap, 1963/1991a).

Choosing a guiding theory is part of the process of problem formulation. For this project, one needs a theory that allows the researcher to study the clients' subjective experience, especially their subjective experience of the relationship with those providing care. The theory chosen to guide the research—intrapsychic human-ism—focuses specifically on the clients' subjective experience of the relationship with their caregivers. Ways in which the guiding theory is applied in the research design are discussed in subsequent parts of this sample research project (see Chap-ters 5 and 6). The research project compensates for the bias against understanding these clients' subjective experience via both the guiding theory and the methodol-ogy. With regard to the method, because researchers in this field generally have not asked clients what kinds of services they find helpful, using a data-collection method that elicits these clients' concerns about their care is an important first step toward developing and offering services that homeless mentally ill clients regard as helpful (Carscaddon, George, & Wells, 1990; Chamberlin, 1990; Goering, Paduchak, & Durban, 1990).

Because two other examples of research in the context of the heuristic para-digm use naturalistic methods and intrapsychic humanism as the guiding theory (in Chapters 7 and 8), it is important to underscore that research based on the heuristic paradigm need not use naturalistic methods or the theory of intrapsychic humanism. This book emphasizes the theory of intrapsychic humanism and naturalistic methods to compensate for biases in the social and behavioral research tradition, biases that have been against the study of participants' subjective experience of the caregiving relationship and in favor of interventionist research. The heuristic paradigm accom-modates the diverse theories and methods researchers and practitioners use today. The focus of the heuristic paradigm is not on any single theory or method but rather on careful conceptualization of the problem formulation, theoretical assumptions, and decisions about the data to gather, how data will be analyzed, and how the research will be useful.

Problem Formulation

This chapter presents readings that have been very influential in postpositivist approaches to research. The authors—Michael Scriven, David Hull, Herbert Simon, William Wimsatt, Roy Bhaskar, Peter Manicas, and Paul Accord—are among the leaders in the contemporary postpositivist movement. Although these selections offer useful insights into all aspects of the research process, they are especially applicable to formulating research problems. As Heineman Pieper (1994) points out, one of the most important steps when using the heuristic paradigm to design research is problem formulation. The researcher's problem formulation is a heuristic that guides the entire research process. Two of the major changes resulting from postpositivist approaches to problem formulation are (1) postpositivist researchers no longer have to wedge their research problems into the restrictive guidelines of positivism, and (2) the new ideas about generating knowledge can help researchers to evaluate and improve problem formulations.

Beyond Operationism in Problem Formulation: Introduction to "Logical Positivism and the Behavioral Sciences" and "The Operational Imperative: Sense and Nonsense in Operationism"

In the following papers, Michael Scriven and David Hull critique logical positivism and introduce well-founded principles about scientific knowledge that are especially pertinent to problem formulation in the social and behavioral sciences.[87] Researchers who adopt the heuristic paradigm can use their ideas as a basis for a more open and reflective approach to problem formulation than has been the norm under the positivist metatheory. Scriven emphasizes that logical positivism has had an "enormous" influence on the social and behavioral sciences, especially with regard to three tenets: operationism (also called operationalism), "the value-free ideal," and "deductivism" (1969, p. 197).* He and Hull outline some of the major problems with these ideas and depart from the logical positivists' prescriptive approach to generating knowledge. Rather than establishing requirements for problem formulation in generating scientific knowledge, they focus on understanding how scientists think and generate knowledge (see also Hull, 1985). Scriven emphasizes that values inevitably inform all acts of knowing, that scientists use both inductive and deductive reasoning, and that empathy is a natural way of knowing that can also be used in generating scientific knowledge. Hull shows how the terms used in research cannot be completely operational and are inevitably theory-laden. He concludes that the nonoperational character of theoretical terms is an essential wellspring for the growth of scientific knowledge, rather than a disadvantage.

As Hull notes, operationism in particular was proposed as a way to guarantee "the intersubjectivity and repeatability so important to the objectivity of science" (1968, p. 439). The primary problems with operationism as a solution are:

1.   Operationism is impracticable: because many different measurement operations are available, when a separate concept is reserved for each one, the concepts proliferate "beyond comprehension."

2.   Hull emphasizes that researchers cannot avoid using theories to interpret and integrate observations. Although the social and behavioral sciences now have numerous instruments for measuring constructs that range from self-esteem to child behavior, Hull notes that the findings obtained with those measurements still require theoretical interpretation and integration. Operationism cannot protect scientific knowledge from the bias introduced both by observational procedures and by theories.

3.   A final irony is that although positivist social and behavioral researchers prescribed operationism in the belief that it would render their knowledge more like knowledge in the natural sciences, Hull points out that operationism is not and never could be used as a requirement for generating knowledge in physics or other natural sciences.

Even so, Scriven and Hull find some "sense" in operationism. Scriven believes that it is a good idea for scientists to put their hypotheses in forms they can evaluate and test. He also recommends that the concepts in scientific theories and the processes of scientific research be formulated so that others can understand and apply them. Hull points out that modifications of operationism can be used in processes of discovery as scientists evaluate which aspects of their hypotheses are most strongly supported by observational evidence.

Building on such postpositivist foundations, the researcher who adopts the heuristic paradigm recognizes that all problem formulations are theory- and value-laden and that the requirement that problems must be operationalized is

---

*Editor's Note: The citations used here refer to pages of the original article. You can find the material quoted from this article in the reprint that follows this introduction.

unfounded. Every problem formulation entails different ways of gathering and analyzing data and sets up paths that lead to different potential solutions. Researchers who adopt the heuristic approach can include the following considerations when examining potential problem formulations:

1. Implicit theoretical assumptions and values
2. The information needed to address each problem
3. The solutions each particular formulation is likely to contribute
4. Researchers can use the "sense" in operationism to examine how the theoretical assumptions in their problem formulation lead them to gather some forms of data and exclude other data.

For example, a cognitive behavioral researcher may want to investigate whether low self-esteem is related to depression. The researcher's problem formulation may assume that self-denigrating thoughts cause low self-esteem and depression. The researcher therefore may decide that the best data-gathering methods are questionnaires about clients' thoughts about themselves. One bias that problem formulation sets up is that because the researcher is prioritizing the depressed individual's thought content, the researcher is not focusing on the quality of the interchange between the interviewer and the client. Although the researcher then has data derived from the questionnaires, she or he has omitted data that some practice theories would regard as indispensable, including data about how the interviewer's communications have defined the client–worker relationship.

In short, the researcher who has "operationalized" her or his self-esteem variables and who relies on those instruments for data collection will not gather the data that are potentially valuable to a researcher who formulates the problem using different assumptions and values. For example, a psychodynamic researcher may formulate a hypothesis about the role of self-esteem and depression as follows: some depressed individuals withdraw from gratifying relationships because they believe that others would agree with their own self-denigration. The investigator examining support for that hypothesis might prefer to gather data concerning whether clients respond stably to the worker's offers of help or instead respond with alternating expressions of trust and mistrust. A detailed process recording of the interaction between client and therapist would yield information about the quality of their relationship. The researcher's decision about which form of data to collect stems from his or her formulation of the research problem and the kind of information available. To respond to the enduring desideratum that scientific knowledge should be intersubjective and replicable, the researcher who adopts the heuristic paradigm can elucidate his or her thinking about the research process (the heuristics used and the biases those heuristics generate) to help other researchers to understand, appraise, and potentially use the knowledge generated.

KEY TERMS

Determinism
Intersubjectivity
Phenomenalism

Intension and extension
Occam's (or Ockham's) razor

DISCUSSION QUESTIONS

1. a.   How does Schlick (see Appendix) define the demarcation principle, and
         how does Scriven critique that?

    b.   Do you agree with Scriven's statement that a major implication of the cri-
         tiques of logical positivism is that "it is not possible to state a principle that
         will sharply demarcate meaningful (or 'scientifically meaningful') state-
         ments from others" (1969, p. 196)? Why or why not?

2. a.   How does Bridgman (see Appendix) define operationism, and what is the
         problem with this view according to Scriven?

    b.   Describe the main ideas in Hull's critique of operationism.

    c.   Do you have critiques of your own to add?

    d.   What is the "sense" in operationism according to Hull and Scriven?

3. Review the conceptual steps that lead Scriven to conclude: "'Ultimate values'
    are as elusive as 'ultimate facts.' Hence, all value claims can be given support or
    rejected for lack of it" (1969, p. 201).

4. a.   What is *Verstehen* theory?

    b.   Empathy is one of the principles of practice that clinicians use most. As
         Scriven notes, the logical positivists believed that empathy was not a reli-
         able tool for obtaining knowledge.

         i.   What are the criticisms of empathy as a tool for obtaining reliable
               knowledge that have been advanced (consider also those Scriven him-
               self advances)?

         ii.   Do you have any other criticisms of empathy as a tool for obtaining reli-
               able knowledge? You may be interested in the critique of empathy
               advanced by Martha Heineman Pieper and William Joseph Pieper
               (1990).

         iii. Do you agree with Scriven's contention that "empathy is, in principle, a
               reliable tool for the historian and the physical scientist" (1969, p. 201)?

5. Scriven says, "Classical mechanics, the basic law of economics, the ideal gas
    laws, and many others are not demonstrably empirical, and it is not very impor-
    tant whether they are or not. . . . [L]aws in science may or may not be empiri-
    cal; the only defensible version of this requirement is that they be *informative*—
    a nasty subjective requirement indeed" (1969, pp. 205–206).

    a.   What are the implications of Scriven's statement for positivist social and
         behavioral researchers' prescription that social and behavioral science theo-
         ries must be based on confirmed propositions?

    b.   What makes a class informative as opposed to boring? Why is "informative-
         ness" a "more subtle concept than the positivists supposed" (Scriven, 1969,
         p. 207)?

6. According to Hull, what is one of the thorny issues that an adequate psychologi-
    cal theory should explain but that behaviorists never have resolved?

▼ ▼ ▼ ▼ ▼ ▼ ▼ ▼ ▼ ▼ ▼ ▼

SAMPLE RESEARCH PROJECT: DEVELOPING RESIDENTIAL TREATMENT SERVICES FOR HOMELESS, MENTALLY ILL, AND SUBSTANCE-ABUSING CLIENTS

Part 2: Context and Initial Statement of Values

The context for this research project is the researcher's relationship as consultant to the program, since the researcher offers a consultation group for staff. The group's aim is to help staff with the staff–resident interactions that staff find to be the most difficult. One of the most important problems in mental health care today is "compassion fatigue," also called burnout in its more extreme forms (Heineman Pieper, 1994). Staff who care for the homeless, mentally ill, and substance-abusing population face particularly intense challenges. They often want help in conceptualizing their treatment plans and with their reactive feelings to helping the clients. Intrapsychic humanism differentiates caregiving motives (caregivers' motives to help their clients or children to develop the capacity for a stable, autonomous self-regulation of inner well-being) and personal motives (all other motives) (Heineman Pieper, 1994; Pieper & Pieper, 1990). Help in differentiating their caregiving and personal motives can enable caregivers to provide more compassionate, stable care. A consultation and support group for staff is one way to accomplish that aim.

Other approaches to evaluation have focused on the potentially adversarial nature of the relationship between the program evaluator and the administrators and/or sponsors of the research when the evaluator does *not* have a consulting relationship with the administrators or staff (Bogdan, 1976; D. Campbell, 1969). An entirely different set of issues is raised in the context of a consultant's commitment (Raber, 1984). First and foremost, the consultant's primary aim is to foster the growth of the staff in their capacity as caregivers, an aim that supersedes and regulates other intentions (e.g., research-based motives) that the consultant might have. An adversarial relationship not only is counterproductive to the consultant's aim but can be hurtful to the staff as well as the clients. This context means that the methodology used in the research needs to be naturalistic, so that research-based motives do not distort the consultant's caregiving process.

Second, the context of the consulting relationship sets up a particular response to the research design question of "who is the client?" (see Chapter 4). The information to be gathered in the research responds to staff interests and concerns. The consultant's guiding theory (intrapsychic humanism) holds that responding to and strengthening the staff's caregiving motives will help the staff to provide better care for the clients. The research also aims to be helpful to other practitioners and researchers interested in learning more about how to help clients who are severely mentally ill and homeless. For instance, people commonly experience homeless mentally ill individuals as an alien or frightening "other" (Gibson, 1991). That alienation has an analogue in how people experience individuals with other types of disabilities. Bogdan and Taylor (1989) described four factors that characterized nondisabled individuals' capacity to retain the experience of severely disabled individuals as "valued and loved human beings": "1) attributing thinking to the other, 2) seeing individuality in the other, 3) viewing the other as reciprocating, and 4) defining social place for the other" (p. 135). A research project can aim to begin to remedy the problem of alienation and dehumanization of the homeless mentally ill population by generating knowledge that stimulates the kind of understanding that Bogdan and Taylor identify; it can help people to understand the unique thoughts and feelings of homeless mentally ill clients. Similarly, Sullivan (1992) argues that we need to redefine the problem of severe mental illness and focus on how to integrate people with that problem into the community. In sum, the aims of the research are to improve the services provided to those who are homeless, mentally ill, and substance abusing; to develop understanding of this population and their needs and strengths; and to reduce their social alienation.

The research project as a whole includes several facets:

1. A study of the consultation group process with the staff;
2. A survey of the clients' opinions about services and their understanding of their needs;
3. Analysis of indicators in the chart notes of the clients' behavior and the outcome of the treatment.

This sample research design focuses on one element of the larger project: the survey of the residents about the services provided. A survey was already being conducted by staff when the consultant/researcher joined the program. Subsequently, the survey can be developed in concert with the staff's interests and experiences in administering the survey for therapeutic purposes.

Staff and residents will all sign informed consent documents, which include the information that normal program services will not be altered for research purposes. Staff will complete a survey at bi-yearly intervals about their experience of the consultation group. The process of administering and coding the survey will protect the staff's anonymity and confidentiality.

Staff were interested in tracking whether their work led to improvements for the clients along several dimensions, most importantly, the clients' obtaining stable funding and/or employment, housing, ongoing psychiatric care and counseling, and involvement in other social supports. Accordingly, data will be collected from the chart notes about changes in the clients' status along those variables as well.

Logical Positivism and the Behavioral Sciences

MICHAEL SCRIVEN

The Vienna Circle or *Wiener Kreis* was a band of cut-throats that went after the fat burghers of Continental metaphysics who had become intolerably inbred and pompously verbose. The *kris* is a Malaysian knife, and the *Wiener Kreis* employed a kind of Occam's Razor called the Verifiability Principle. It performed a tracheotomy that made it possible for philosophy to breathe again, and one cannot rightly object to the imperfections of instruments that save lives . . . at the time that they serve that purpose. Only later, when the populace begins to show signs of worshiping the device of deliverance, is it appropriate to point out that we can go on to better devices, indeed, that to fail to do so is to risk an infection that might prove just as fatal as choking to death on a mess of verbiage.

It really is not very interesting for a literate audience to read once again about the nicks on the blade of the *Wiener Kreis*, because they have been exhibited so well by others, notably by Hempel in the work now published as "Empiricist Criteria of Cognitive Significance: Problems and Changes," in *"Aspects of Scientific Explanation*.[1] What I shall do is look at the situation in the post-positivist period and see if we really have met or can meet the charges that were brought against pre-positivist philosophy, especially philosophy of the social sciences, in the same way that one might do this with respect to post-Humean philosophy. Russell, in his *History of Western Philosophy*, remarks that it has been a favorite pastime of metaphysicians since Hume to refute him; but, he says, "for my part, I find none of their refutations convincing; nevertheless, I cannot

but hope that something less sceptical . . . may be discoverable." We must ask whether the situation is as bad with respect to the logical positivists. Have we really met their objections, or have we merely gone soft?

This surely is a much more important question than that of whether the particular instrument they introduced to remedy the defects, the "empiricist criterion of meaning" (the principle of verification), was itself satisfactory as they formulated it. This is not to say that the logical questions about the possibility of salvation by revision of that formula are not interesting in their own right; on the contrary, they are not only interesting but also valuable in several ways. However, one can sum up the results that seem to emerge from such a discussion quite simply: it is not possible to state a principle that will sharply demarcate meaningful (or "scientifically meaningful") statements from others. One must concede that there is a matter of degree involved; that the borderline between sense and "nonsense," in this sense of "nonsense," is not

---

Source: "Logical Positivism and the Behavioral Sciences" by M. Scriven in *The Legacy of Logical Positivism* (pp. 195–209) edited by P. Achinstein and S. Barker, 1969, Baltimore, MD: Johns Hopkins University Press. Copyright 1969 by Johns Hopkins University Press. Reprinted by permission.
1. (New York: Macmillan [The Free Press], 1965). Reference can also be made to the two dozen other citations in J. Passmore, *One Hundred Years of Philosophy*, 3d ed. (New York: Basic Books, 1966), p. 371n, who curiously omits the Hempel paper.

sharp. But now let us ask instead whether the positivists' specific objections to the philosophy and quasi-science of their time have been or can now be met. In this paper I am concerned only with the social sciences, and I am going to restrict myself still further (for reasons of space and time) to a fairly thorough discussion of only one issue, namely, the analysis of "understanding" (*Verstehen*) in the social sciences, a target of particular interest to the logical positivists. I shall, however, have *something* to say about several other aspects of the methodology of the social sciences on which positivism had some bearing.

It is, of course, essential to remember that when we talk about the "logical positivists"—a name apparently due to Feigl—we are not talking about the *original* "positivists," such as Comte (who invented *that* term). The line of descent is clear, from Comte to Mach to Schlick, but there were important changes. In particular, with respect to our topic here, Comte thought that there *was* a special method of the social sciences, the application of the criterion of harmony to our understanding of human nature. But the logical positivists rejected this, or something quite like this (Comte's position is not very clear), for reasons which I shall examine shortly. Hereafter, where I use the term "positivists," however, I am referring to the Vienna Circle and its descendants or disciples from A. J. Ayer to W. C. Salmon.

Impressionistically speaking—and in this area of the history of thought I do not believe we can be very precise—one thinks of the logical positivists as *attacking* nineteenth-century German metaphysics and what they called psychologism in the sciences (which sometimes included Gestalt theory and always included *Verstehen* theory), and as *upholding* the analytic-synthetic distinction, the distinction between the context of discovery and that of verification, the facts-value distinction, operationalism, verificationism, phenomenalism, conventionalism, and formalism (especially in the philosophy of mathematics and in the reconstruction of scientific theories in terms of an uninterpreted calculus and correspondence rules).

The relevance of logical positivism to the behavioral sciences is the result of the influence of these methodological positions on behavioral scientists—and this influence has been enormous, especially with respect to the doctrines of (1) operationalism, (2) the value-free ideal of the behaviorists, and (3) deductivism (i.e., the doctrine that scientific explanation properly consists in deduction of descriptions of, or statements asserting the likelihood of, the phenomenon-to-be-explained from general empirical laws and antecedent conditions).

I shall say only a word about the effect of operationalism, which has been treated by others on many occasions. This is a doctrine whose heart is in the right place, but whose head is in the wrong place. It is good advice to scientists to recommend that they put their claims in testable form, and a very natural extension of this is to suggest that they should make sure that their concepts can be applied in an interjudge-reliable way.[2] The operationalist thought that he saw a nice, neat formula for expressing this recommendation, but unfortunately the formula is considerably too stringent a requirement. It demands that definitions of concepts be expressed as equivalences to sets of operations, but unfortunately there are grave problems about the definition of *operation* and, in particular, grave problems about (1) whether an operational definition of this can be given, (2) what is to count as *one* operation, (3) what is to count as *an* operation. (1) If *operation* cannot be defined operationally, then an important concept in the methodology of science cannot be defined in a way which meets the requirements of operationalism, which certainly appears to restrict its universality and raises the question of whether there may not be other serious exceptions to it. (2) If we measure temperature in one range using a liquid-in-glass thermometer, and in another range using a bolometer, then this would appear to be two different operations, and thus it would be improper to refer to it as the same physical quantity in both cases. In such an instance, operationalism gives a result which is incompatible with standard scientific practice. But, if we interpret these two operations as referring to the *same* concept, it becomes difficult to see how operationalism is true, and especially difficult to see how the claimed master example of operationalism—namely, the introduction of the relativity theory via questioning of the meaning of distant simultaneity—in fact supports the position at all. (3) And, finally, if the notion of an operation is not only not operationally definable, not only plagued by problems of unity identity, but also not very clear itself—as is the case when we try to pin it down—

---

2. This is essentially G. Mandler and W. Kessen's doctrine in *The Language of Psychology* (New York: John Wiley & Sons, 1959).

then the rubric becomes somewhat less valuable than appeared at first sight.

Operationalism, which was supposed to have its foundations in physics—although there are grave doubts as to whether it did in any way reflect the thinking that led to the introduction of the relativity theory—never had much success there but was far more significant in the area of psychology. Here it all too often became the war cry of an avid empiricism, although for reasons implicit in the above discussion there is nothing about it that intrinsically would require this.

The second major doctrine of the positivist and positivist-associated movements is that of value-free social science. I have discussed this at length elsewhere, most recently (in a forthcoming volume edited by R. Lichtman) in a paper entitled "Value Claims in the Social Sciences." The doctrine now seems to me to be an incredible *gaffe* based on not one but a series of logical mistakes. One of these was the transfer of a distinction which makes sense in a given context—the distinction between the facts in the case and the evaluations that we base on them—into a context-free distinction. But this fallacy is something to which we have become particularly sensitive, and it now seems difficult to imagine that it was plausible. Our sensitivity has been aroused particularly in connection with another position that the positivists at times espoused, the doctrine of reductionism or phenomenalism, which maintained that theoretical statements could be reduced to observation statements and that those of one level of science could be reduced to those of a more fundamental level, culminating in the grand reduction to the observation language of physics. But it has become quite clear that the concept of the observation language makes sense only in a particular context; and the observation language of one epoch in physics, or of one part of physics, is the theoretical language of another. There is no "ultimate observation language" any more than there is an ultimate sensedatum language. Analogously, there is no ultimate factual language. And the more interesting side of this coin is that many statements which in one context clearly would be evaluational are, in another, clearly factual. Obvious examples include judgments of intelligence and of the merit of performances such as those of the runners at the Olympic Games.

Another crucial logical error that had to be made in order that one could recommend the avoidance of value judgments developed as follows: The early advocates of value-free science readily conceded that preferences are factual matters and that the performance of particular entities (e.g., theories or people) with respect to preferred qualities are matters of fact; but somehow they supposed that these could not be combined to yield judgments about the superiority of something for someone without a kind of ineradicable subjectivity coming into the picture. But of course it is simply a fact that certain kinds of medicine are good for certain kinds of disease condition, even if this is also a value judgment. And the underlying "value premise" which involves an assertion that, when such and such needs or wants are fulfilled, good has been done, is itself just a fact about human health, although also a value statement. There is nothing in the least dubious about such assertions by comparison with the other assertions of empirical science that are required for the application of any theory. For example, one cannot explain the elliptical orbits of the planets merely by appealing to facts about the pull of gravitation and the masses of the sun and other planets. One must also have a premise which asserts that only these factors need to be taken into consideration. This kind of "adequacy guarantee" can be supported in astronomy, and the corresponding one can be supported in the social sciences, where it has valuational impact and reference.

Yet a third kind of logical mistake was sometimes involved, that of failing to distinguish moral value statements from value statements in general. There are certainly special difficulties about validating moral claims, but the positivists usually did not make a distinction between these and other value claims. Thus their view, which might be given some semblance of plausibility with respect to morality, became a travesty when completely generalized. I believe that morality can be given an entirely objective foundation, but I concede that doing so is more difficult than supporting a claim about the greater merit of the special theory of relativity by comparison with Newtonian dynamics, or about the greater merit of one kind of tax structure over another. Of course, positivists have often thought that the latter kinds of claim could be constructed as instrumental claims, and this, they were quick to point out, could be entirely factual. What they failed to see was that there are no good grounds for thinking that any claims are not instrumental. "Ultimate values" are as elusive as "ultimate facts." Hence, all value claims can be given support or rejected for lack of it.

It was also very common for positivists to suggest that the frequency of disputes about value issues somehow supported their view that these were subjective matters. Yet, in connection with arguments about the existence of God, they were not in the least hesitant to claim that such disputes, which surely are as frequent, were simply signs of poor logical training, poor scientific training, or the interference of emotions with reason.

The final horror in the chamber of bad arguments on the values issue was the suggestion that value claims were not really statements at all, but simply expressions of an attitude with no cognitive content, or with some but only an incidental cognitive component. The emotive theory, with its gradual refinement by Charles L. Stevenson, was the sophisticated version of this idea, and, as is well known, it has been modified to the point where its distinguishability from cognitivism is now in question. To summarize, there is no possibility that the social sciences can be free either of value claims in general or of moral value claims in particular, and the arguments which suggested that, for their own good they should be, were themselves meta-scientific value claims.

The topic of special interest for us here is the nature of our understanding of people. On this issue the positivists reacted against the school of historians proposing the *"Verstehen* theory," that is, the doctrine that empathic insight was a special and valuable tool in the study of human behavior which was without counterpart in the physical sciences. This view did not die with them, for it is explicit in Collingwood's philosophy of history and implicit in the practice of many other historians.

The positivists argued that empathy was not a reliable tool at all, and that the methods of obtaining knowledge, especially knowledge in history, were just the same as those used in the physical sciences. In particular, understanding was possible only via subsumption under established laws.

I shall argue that empathy is, in principle, a reliable tool for the historian *and* the physical scientist. The methods are thus the same throughout the various fields of knowledge, but are not restricted to those traditionally associated with physics.

This is one of those instructive cases where a little historical research yields big dividends simply because we come to the materials with a fresh eye, one not bloodshot with the battles of that day. Let us consider one of the classical attacks on the empathy theory, under one or another of the latter's aliases.

Here is Edgar Zilsel writing on "Physics and the Problem of Historico-Sociological Laws," a deservedly famous paper:[3]

On the other hand the method of "understanding" ("insight") which has often been recommended for social science is not sufficient when investigating historical laws. "Understanding" means psychological empathy: psychologically a historical process is "understood" if it is evident or plausible. The main objection to this criterion of the correctness of a historical assertion is that virtually always opposite historical processes are equally plausible. . . . When a city is bombed it is plausible that intimidation and defeatism of the population result. But it is plausible as well that the determination to resist increases. It would not be plausible, on the other hand, if the bombing changed the pronunciation of consonants in the bombed city. Which process actually takes place can not be decided by psychological empathy but by statistical observation only. In the final analysis the method of understanding is equivalent to the attempts to deduce historico-sociological laws from laws of introspective psychology. However, before regularities are established it is premature to attempt to deduce them. In the construction of new empirical sciences the predeductive stage can not be skipped.

Let us consider what Zilsel calls "the main objection to this criterion of the correctness of a historical assertion." To cut through the brush of preliminary analysis let me suggest that he is assuming that an event cannot be explained by appealing to facts from which it could not have been predicted. He is right that from the occurrence of bombing (B) we cannot in general tell whether defeatism (D) or resistance (R) will be the major effect. But this is not of concern to a historian or a social scientist trying to explain or understand an event or series of events. He *knows* which particular outcome did occur, for *that is precisely what he has to explain;* his task is only to find the antecedent circumstance that caused this outcome, and to help him he has a record from which he discovers the fact of bombing. He also knows, "empathetically" if you like, the simple fact that bombing can very well and often does cause this outcome. There is only one other check required; he must

---

3. *Philosophy of Science,* 8 (1941).

assure himself that no other potential causes are present. If there are none, he can rightly be sure that the bombing was *the* cause. If one or more are present, he must check further to see if the causes co-operated or whether one beat the others to the punch. In simpler cases there is often a certain quality or configuration about the effect which is a sure sign that one particular cause is responsible, and, even without checking that such an antecedent did occur, the historian often is entitled to claim that he *knows* what the cause was. He has seen the key, solved the riddle, diagnosed the condition, and in this kind of case the solution is sometimes so clearly self-identifying that it allows its perceiver to qualify as a knower. "Who is this?" we say, when we are confronted with a picture of some great man as an infant, or hear a few bars from a lesser work, or see a heavily disguised friend, or listen to a strange voice on the telephone at 3 A.M. And then sometimes the answer hits us with eureka-like impact; we spot the giveaway; we *know* the answer. This is like the historian's experience at times, and like the economist's and the psychotherapist's.

There is nothing weaker about our recognition of Sandy through his disguise because of the fact that if the eyes had been blue instead of near-black we would have guessed it was Walter or perhaps not have known whom to guess. Similarly, the fact that we cannot say from $n - 1$ items in a spatio-temporal configuration what the nth will be in no way undercuts the reliability with which we identify the set of n when all are present. The test of identification is whether we *then* can infer an $(n + 1)$th item which checks out.

So empathy is a fine provider of knowledge; that does not mean it is any *more* reliable than observation or inference, from neither of which it is *entirely* (although it is *typically*) distinct. In the well-trained social scientist or historian it is simply one kind of judgment, and a well-trained man can call by the name of knowledge the judgments of which he is certain.

It appears that Zilsel's argument might well refer only to the search for *laws*. In the traditional positivist view, laws were atemporal universal claims of functional dependency involving no essential reference to particular names, a definition which involves inadequacies by some accounts and redundancies by others. In my view, elaborated elsewhere,[4] that definition is

better thought of as an attempt to characterize the most abstract laws of theoretical physics, and is absurdly restrictive as a general account. Just about any non-accidental, relatively simple and useful generalization will be called a law if it is needed badly enough. In particular, laws may be limited in scope by invoking essential reference to particular regions of space-time while weakened in force to express qualitative relative probability; they may be time dependent, and non-predictive, and still be the sweetest sight a scientist ever saw and called a law. The fact that bombing a city will be likely to cause D or R but unlikely to cause a change in the pronunciation of consonants (P) is a fine example of a law—not exactly the pope himself, but a prominent layman or perhaps even a parish priest. This law has no essential time dependency, no particular references—almost no venial sin. Then how do we discover it? By a statistical analysis of bombing studies? No indeed. Just by thinking about the likely effects of B on me, or perhaps instant perception of its likely effects on you—in short, empathy: estimating our own reactions and their transferability, seeing the inside of events in others' lives.

So Zilsel and the many who agreed with him were wrong in saying that empathy could not yield laws or verify them. They were wrong, not only because they had an overly restrictive concept of law as it is used *and is useful* in the sciences, but also because their argument simply did not entail their conclusion. For they certainly were not going to exclude a putative law on the ground that it involved a compound predicate; hence the empirical law "If B then either R or D" would have qualified under their strictest requirements. And just that law is conceded by Zilsel to be attainable by empathy. It is remarkable that he should then deny the value of empathy in divining laws. Thus their ultimate criterion, regardless of logic, is indeed that an event cannot be understood or explained unless it *alone* is predictable for the putative explanation. Now why was that criterion appealing?

I suspect that there were two reasons, both unsound. The first was some vague feeling that it was equivalent to, or guaranteed, the requirement that laws must have empirical content. But Zilsel's own reference to the improbable consequence undermines this point. For, if P is even logically possible, then the disjunctive prediction "R or D" is falsifiable, hence empirical in content. Thus the "empathizable" law "Whenever B then R or D" is empirical. I suspect that Zilsel never thought of the disjunctive-predicate kind of law, or he would not have overlooked this point.

4. "The Key Property of Physical Laws—Inaccuracy," in *Current Issues in the Philosophy of Science*, ed. H. Feigl and G. Maxwell (New York: Holt, Rinehart & Winston, 1961).

And I suppose that this oversight could be attributed to the context, which is one that focuses our attention on the explanation of a *particular* outcome and therefore—perhaps it seemed plausible to say—on laws which have that outcome as the sole dependent variable. I must add a further point, although it rather smacks of hitting a man when he's down. The reason just mentioned does not support the criterion in the way that Zilsel apparently supposed it would, but it also happens to be intrinsically unsound. That is to say, it is not necessary for historical laws to be empirical in order that they be valuable both for expressing knowledge and for generating understanding. Classical mechanics, the basic law of economics, the ideal gas laws, and many others are not demonstrably empirical, and it is not very important whether they are or not. The functions of laws are to simplify and to summarize, to compress and to extend our explicit knowledge, and even when they express a definitional truth they may be just as informative as Pythagoras' theorem is to a man who knows the definitional truths with which Euclid began. It is tempting simply to state that historical (or existing) laws must be empirical, but that is the kind of temptation which leads you to mystical contemplation of your own marvelous system, whose relation to anyone else's conceptual scheme is lost in mists of wonder. In short, laws in science may or may not be empirical; the only defensible version of this requirement is that they be *informative*—a nasty subjective requirement indeed.

The second reason for this criterion is somewhat more cogent, but still unsound. I believe it is the argument on which Hempel now relies; certainly he has often fallen back on this criterion of "symmetry" between explanation and prediction. Perhaps it is best called the "inferribility requirement." The expansion of the original deductive model of explanation to include inductive (statistical) explanations was accomplished within the framework of this same requirement, and, indeed, it is hard to find any other true and non-trivial requirements with which to identify the model today. For the requirement that propositions contained in the explanation be true is either false or trivial: false if *true* is taken precisely, trivial if *true* means "believed to be near enough right to be relevant." The same applies to the requirement that explanations involve general laws. And the requirement of empirical content in laws is, as we have just indicated, false.

This second reason is the desire to avoid *ad hoc* explanations. If we can invoke B to explain D only

when we know that D has already occurred, the suspicion arises that we are simply committing the *post hoc ergo propter hoc* fallacy. Mere succession is not causal sequence. The difference, since Hume's day (according to the positivists), has been the knowledge of a general law that invariably connects the antecedent with the consequent. And an immediate consequence of having that law has been that, given the antecedent, one could predict the consequent. This is a nice, neat solution, but too nice to be good. Without repeating the lengthy and disordered analysis of cause which I have given elsewhere,[5] I can only propose some nonfundamental criticisms. It could hardly be denied that the cause or causes of some phenomena have been discovered. If, for example, it has been found that the cause of a disease X is a particular virus A, then we can be sure that whenever X occurs it is because of infection with A—that is, A caused X. But there are carriers of A who do not develop X; therefore, we cannot say that the presence of A enables one to infer the (possibly future) occurrence of X. Thus X, when it occurs, is explicable in terms of A; but X is not predictable from A, that is, from that which explains it. This, then, ruins the inferribility thesis. But A is *not* an *ad hoc* explanation. For it is an empirical claim that A and not some other antecedent Q was the cause of X, and we support this claim by showing how A and not Q can lead to the symptoms of X. At the crude level of statistics, this means that infection with A increases the incidence of X in a population when compared with a control population, whereas the introduction of Q leads to no such change. But this crude observation normally can be followed up with a micro-account of the development of the virus' attack on the host which culminates in Q. The story is incomplete in many respects: we do not know what gives the carriers their immunity, or the mechanics of many of the stages we observe under the electron microscope. Those details are the answers to other questions, however. We have found the answer to the question we asked at the beginning of our research, namely, what kind of agent causes X and, in particular, exactly what agent.

Such discoveries are therefore most valuable in identifying the cause of a particular event (or series of events), but they are not prediction-generating expres-

---

5. "Causes, Connections, and Conditions in History," in W. H. Dray, ed., *Philosophical Analysis and History* (New York: Harper & Row, 1966).

sions. Once again, informativeness turns out to be a more subtle concept than the positivists supposed.

In recent discussions some positivists have argued that causal explanations of the kinds mentioned above really do implicitly refer to laws in a way which salvages the original thesis. It is true, they say, that the law may not be known, but that there *is* a law connecting the alleged cause with the effect certainly is implicitly asserted, given the explanation. In my view, this claim is simply a result of commitment to determinism, and determinism is false. It is not required by a causal explanation at all. But, even if it were, those who put forth this argument fail to see that they have abandoned precisely the reasons for its plausibility in its original form. As long as one could require the *production* of a true general law connecting cause with effect, one could repudiate the claim that one was confusing succession with causation; the minute that one moves to the view that some law must be present, although it cannot be stated, this refutation of the *ad hoc* nature of the causal claim is no longer possible.

Thus there is a way around the pitfalls of *ad hoc* explanation, lack of informational content, and circularity which does not capitulate to the inferribility model. And there is nothing odd about explanations that appeal to a factor which could have been appealed to equally well if the outcome had been different from what it was, or about explanations that appeal to a factor which is necessarily connected with the outcome that occurs. (Only if the outcome was necessarily connected with the antecedent could it be suggested that the causal explanation was redundant, given the occurrence of the effect.)

What, then, of the *Verstehen* theory? It is a simple, though important, special case of the general procedure of modeling, the special feature being that the model in this case is oneself. But a good electrician experiences the same sense of insight when he hits upon the explanation of a circuit deficiency, and a good theoretical mathematician has corresponding moments of "understanding." The *Verstehen* theorists were right in supposing that there was something special about the behavioral sciences—but it was only that here alone the model of *one's own* behavior can be employed. They were wrong in supposing that this gave them some deeper understanding than could be obtained by the expert wholly imbued with the workings of a mechanical model of the operation of the human fingers, for example. *Verstehen* has its own pitfalls arising from the erroneous transfer of the idiosyncrasies of the observer to the subject of observation, pitfalls which have led to the errors of cultural egocentrism in anthropology and corresponding mistakes in the attempts of clinical psychologists to understand the motivations of hereditarians or minority-group patients. But the positivists were quite wrong in supposing that the *Verstehen* approach could not provide knowledge and that it was essentially different from the procedures of physical scientists in understanding the phenomena of interest to them.

To conclude: there comes a time in the affairs of science and philosophy when nothing is so valuable as hardheadedness. Positivism brought that hardheadedness to philosophy, and perhaps to some parts of science, at a time when it was needed. Hard heads usually have to be thick heads, and it is no surprise to discover in the cool of later years that the issues were not quite so simple as they then appeared. Nevertheless, revolutions are fought by men who lack finesse, and without them we would still be in a rather primitive state. We must pay tribute to the revolutionary while avoiding the mistake of deifying his doctrine.

The Operational Imperative: Sense and Nonsense in Operationism

DAVID L. HULL

ABSTRACT: Several important terms in biology have recently been criticized for not being "operational." In this paper the course of operationism in physics, psychology and genetics is sketched to show what effect this particular view on the meaning of scientific terms had on these disciplines. Then the biological species concept and the concept of homology are examined to see in what respects they are or are not "operational." One of the primary conclusions of this investigation is that few terms in science are completely operational or completely nonoperational. Some scientific terms, especially theoretical terms, are a good deal less operational than others; but, far from being regrettable, this situation is essential if theoretical terms are to fulfill their systematizing function and if scientific theories are to be capable of growth.

Biologists frequently assert that the need in biology for operational definitions, concepts and procedures is imperative. However, what these biologists mean by "operational" ranges from admirable good sense to utter nonsense. At one end of the spectrum, a concept is operational if in some instances there are ways of discovering if the concept is applicable. At the other end, the meaning of the concept is supposedly equivalent to the set of operations used to test its applicability. Surreptitious vacillation between these two extremes has been characteristic of the movement termed "operationism"[1] since its very inception. The purpose of this paper is first, to describe the role played by operationism in physics and psychology, and then to examine various biologists' notions of operationism to see exactly how appropriate they are for actual biological practice.

OPERATIONISM IN PHYSICS

In 1927 P. W. Bridgman in his famous treatise *The Logic of Modern Physics* suggested that a fruitful way of looking at Einstein's special theory of relativity was to regard the theory as substituting "operational definitions" of concepts like length and non-local simultaneity for definitions in terms of properties:

> We may illustrate by considering the concept of length: what do we mean by the length of an object? We evidently know what we mean by length if we can tell what the length of any and every object is, and for the physicist nothing more is required. To find the length of an object, we have to perform certain physical operations. The concept of length is therefore fixed when the operations by which length is measured are fixed: that is, the concept of length involves as much as and noth-

Source: From "The Operational Imperative: Sense and Nonsense in Operationism" by D. L. Hull, 1968, *Systematic Zoology, 17,* pp. 438–457. Copyright 1968 by the Society of Systematic Zoology. Reprinted by permission.

1. The terms "operationism" and "operationalism" are used interchangeably to refer to the thesis made popular by P. W. Bridgman. Bridgman himself abhorred the terms.

ing more than the set of operations by which length is determined. In general, we mean by any concept nothing more than a set of operations; *the concept is synonymous with the corresponding set of operations.*

Bridgman's thesis is both radical and poorly expressed. Synonymy is a relation which holds between linguistic entities. Two words or two statements can be synonymous, but a concept cannot be synonymous with a set of operations. Bridgman might have expressed himself better had he said that a concept such as length denotes a set of operations, not a property of the objects being measured. And what is more, the meaning of the concept is this set of operations. Bridgman's thesis is radical because usually the intension of a concept is considered to be its meaning.

One of the main reasons for trying to formulate operational definitions is to insure the objectivity of science. If a scientific concept is synonymous with a set of operations, and if these operations are such that they can be performed publicly by any qualified person, then the intersubjectivity and repeatability so important to the objectivity of science are guaranteed. If a physicist could restrict himself to just those operations connoted by the term—meter readings, manipulations of various instruments, and the like—then operationism *would* insure intersubjectivity, repeatability and objectivity; but from the start Bridgman had to admit the necessity of paper-and-pencil operations, mental operations, verbal operations—in short, symbolic operations. The introduction of such notions *does not automatically exclude* intersubjectivity, repeatability, and objectivity; but it certainly lessens the guarantee initially connoted by the term "operational definition."

Another reason for wanting operational definitions is to promote clarity and precision. If a scientific concept is synonymous with a *uniquely specified* set of operations, and if these operations in turn can be performed unequivocally to obtain precise results, then the concept itself will be clear and precise. For example, the common notion of length is far from precise. Even Newtonian physicists assumed all sorts of things about length which, independent of their acceptance of Newtonian theory, they had no unquestionable right to assume. For instance, they assumed that the results of measuring length by laying measuring rods end to end would be the same as those of light triangulation. This did not always turn out to be the case. If the

meaning of a concept is completely specified by the results of a unique set of operations, then when two physicists use this concept each knows precisely what the other means. As Bridgman (1927) put it:

> In *principle* the operations by which length is measured should be *uniquely* specified. If we have more than one set of operations, we have more than one concept, and strictly there should be a separate name to correspond to each different set of operations.

Physicists, including Einstein,[2] soon realized that the cost of this way of obtaining precision was too high. The most obvious objection to the strict one to one correspondence between every set of operations and a separate concept is that it multiplies concepts beyond comprehension. There are too many ways of measuring length. No physicist could reserve a special concept of length for each. These concepts must be somehow integrated. Bridgman sees only a practical justification for treating two operationally different concepts as the same concept:

> Strictly speaking, length when measured in this way by light beams should be called by another name, since the operations are different. The practical justification for retaining the same name is that within our present experimental limits a numerical difference between the results of the two sorts of operations has not been detected.

Two operations are said to define the same concept if the results are the same, otherwise not. For example, measuring rods come in various colors. To test whether measuring length with a yellow rod is the same operation as measuring with a brown rod, a physicist must compare the results to see if they are the same within the limits of experimental error. But perhaps the color of the object being measured matters. Or perhaps there is a significant relation between the colors of the rod and the object *ad infinitum.*

---

2. Historically Einstein was affected by the work of Ernst Mach, who tried to formulate operational definitions of all the concepts of Newtonian mechanics and succeeded only in making hash of the theory (Mach, 1960), but nothing in the special theory of relativity requires operationism. See Lindsay (1961), Bridgman (1961) and Grünbaum (1961).

Obviously, the procedure suggested by Bridgman is not and can not be the one actually used in physics. There is a more fundamental justification for considering various operationally different concepts the same concept, namely, physical theory. According to Newtonian theory, certain circumstances (e.g., the movement of the measuring rod from place to place) were thought to be irrelevant to the measurement of length. As it turned out, Newton was mistaken. According to relativity theory, some of these circumstances must be taken into account; but *some* circumstances are still thought to be irrelevant (e.g., the color of the measuring rod). In fact, the whole notion of a *set* of operations defining a concept presupposes some way of deciding when the *same* operation is being repeated and when two operations are *different* operations. In actual practice, such decisions are made in the context of an interplay between theory and the outcome of experimentation and observation. And with the intrusion of theory comes the possibility of other than observational error.

Two of the underlying themes of operationism have been the essential superfluity of scientific theory and the desirability of making science "safe." If all scientific terms are given operational definitions, then all theoretical terms would be replaceable by observation terms and none but observational error would be possible (Hempel, 1965). Bridgman (1927) expressed himself as follows:

> It is evident that if we adopt this point of view toward concepts, namely that the proper definition of a concept is not in terms of its properties but in terms of actual operations, we need run no danger of having to revise our attitude towards nature. For if experience is always described in terms of experience, there must always be correspondence between experience and our description of it, and we never need be embarrassed, as we were in attempting to find in nature the prototype of Newton's absolute time.

Bridgman hoped to spare us the need for any future Einsteins. This is not possible. The only reason that operationism initially looked attractive to physicists was that physics had a strong theoretical foundation. The lack of such a foundation will have serious consequences for operationism in psychology.

At this point an operationist might object as did Bridgman (1959, 1961) that operationism is not a full-fledged philosophy of science. It is merely an attitude, a point of view. The unavoidable reply to this objection is that *the operational point of view depends for what success it does have on the very element of science which it is designed to eliminate.* Operationism was intended as a cathartic to purge physics of all non-empirical wastes, but it proved to be so strong that the viscera were eliminated as well. Physics as a theoretical science is possible only on a more liberal notion of operationism; but any notion of "operational definition" sufficient to permit theoretical terms fails to accomplish the end which served initially as the primary motivation for operationism—the desire to make physics strictly and rigidly empirical.

OPERATIONISM IN PSYCHOLOGY

Because of the strong theoretical foundations of physics, extreme versions of operationism were never very influential in physics, and more moderate versions were able to function with some success. The poverty of operationism was not so immediately apparent in psychology. Traditional psychology was fragmented into introspectionists, physiologists and Freudians. The method of the introspectionists was to analyze consciousness itself, by examining either the verbal reports of a subject or one's own feelings and perceptions. The results were seldom either uniform or comparable. The numerous schools of introspectionist psychology were in constant, unresolvable conflict, with precision, clarity, objectivity, intersubjectivity and repeatability appearing notable for their absence. Freud built a theoretical structure on such data and turned his attention to therapy. As illuminating as Freudian theory may be for the therapist, it is hardly more than a metaphor. No part can be taken literally, and it seems to be suspiciously insulated against disproof.[3] The physiologists tried the opposite tack from that of the introspectionists and Freudians. They concentrated on understanding the central nervous system; but the complexities of their subject

---

3. To discover the latitude that is given the term "operationism," see Ellis (1956) in which "operational definitions" are provided for some of the basic terms in psychoanalytic theory. In addition Else Frenkel-Brunswick (1961) claims that in defining such concepts as the unconscious and instinct, "Freud pursues an essentially operational course."

matter proved to be beyond their capabilities, and little progress was made.

It was in the midst of such factionalism that John B. Watson (1913) introduced behaviorism. He called for retrenchment. In his own work with rats, neither reconstructions of the subject's consciousness nor knowledge of its physiology played a part. The subject was viewed as a black box. All that mattered was input and output. Watson maintained that, in order for psychology to become an objective, exact science, psychologists had to turn their attention to that aspect of animals, including man, which is open to intersubjective, repeatable observation—behavior. Anticipating Bridgman by more than a decade, Watson called for "operational definitions" of the traditional mentalistic terms of psychology. Perhaps each of us has direct access to his own conscious states, but in all other instances the only thing we have to go on is behavior.[4] Thus, such mentalistic terms as "thirst" and "intelligence," if they are to be acceptable scientific terms, must be operationally defined by objective indices like time-lapsed-since-drinking and intelligence tests. One's own feeling of thirst or common sense notions of intelligence cease to be relevant to the psychological concepts of thirst and intelligence. In short, Watson wanted to purge science of Bridgman's "mental operations."

Periodically, in their enthusiasm, behavioral psychologists went even further and denied the actual existence of mind or consciousness. Although the major objections raised by the behaviorists to the existence of minds concerned only the *substantial* minds of classical philosophers like Descartes, at times they seemed to be arguing against self-awareness itself, as if the only way to decide whether you were angry was by looking in the mirror. Certainly *sometimes* our behavior leads us to re-evaluate our introspective estimations of our feelings, but these instances are the exceptions. Behaviorists were tempted to make them the rule. Conversely, what of

those cases in which we all know that we are thinking, but there is no apparent behavior? In his original (1913) paper, Watson suggested that perhaps the so-called higher thought processers were really faint reinstatements of the original muscular act, imperceptable movements in the larynx!

The complete denial of mind was unnecessary bravado on the part of the behaviorists. They needed only to establish that any reference to the results of introspection was unnecessary in the science of psychology (Bergmann, 1961). Knowledge of behavior and the antecedent conditions were sufficient. The advances of behavioral psychology in the last fifty years have been impressive; but the major stumbling block remains—symbolic operations. This was precisely the obstacle confronting Bridgman in physics. It is one thing to define mass in terms of balances, but the moon, which cannot be put in a balance, also has mass. Fairly complicated mathematical manipulations are necessary. Similarly, it is one thing to define fear in terms of trembling, facial expressions and the like; but the subject can also say, "I'm afraid." To avoid the apparent introspective character of such utterances, behaviorists had to treat them as meaningless noises. Any meaning eventually associated with them had to be derived from behavioral studies. In short, behaviorists were faced with the task of giving a behavioral account of language (Skinner, 1957). Even the most evangelical behaviorist cannot claim that such attempts have been very successful.

Disregarding the controversial issue of a behavioral analysis of symbolic operations, let us recall the difficulties which confronted operationism in physics. If a term is to be defined by a set of operations, what is to determine the membership of the set? When are two operations the same operation? Which circumstances are relevant and which irrelevant? For example, there are numerous ways to determine what is commonly thought of as intelligence—in depth interviews, I.Q. tests, and so on.[5] Each of these is in an obvious sense a

---

4. This argument presupposes the underdeveloped state of physiology. Physiological evidence fulfills all the requirements for acceptable scientific data. To protect themselves against any possible future advances in physiology, some behaviorists (e.g., B. F. Skinner, 1953) have contended that even if physiological data were available, it would be redundant. Behavioral studies alone would be sufficient. For a survey of the present state of physiological psychology, see Stellar and Sprague (1966).

5. In my discussion of what is commonly thought of as intelligence, I do not intend to imply that there is a single, unitary, tight cluster of attributes which can be termed "intelligence." It may be the case that under careful analysis, several largely independent factors may emerge. The point is that if a scientist is going to use something as informal as common everyday beliefs about intelligence to guide both the formulation and interpretation of his experiments, he should do so explicitly.

different kind of test. The associated concepts, hence, should be different. But even if we restrict ourselves to a single kind of test, say the Stanford-Binet, there are problems. The questions on the test are under constant revision. New versions of the "same" test are periodically issued. Further, is a particular version of the Stanford-Binet test given in the morning on a sunny day in June to a group of fifteen in a small room the same test when it is given in the late afternoon of a somber day in January to a group of over a hundred in a huge auditorium? A tentative answer to the question of what is to count as the same test can be given by comparing results. If, by and large, the same people do well on two different types of I.Q. test, then there is some reason to claim that these tests are measuring the same thing. Further, if results from giving the same test in the morning and the afternoon do not vary appreciably, then this consideration can be considered irrelevant, and so on.

Though correlation in results is necessary to establish what is to count as the same test and to integrate several different types of tests to form a more general concept, it is not sufficient. For example, if a psychologist were to find a close correlation in the results of the Stanford-Binet intelligence test, the Kuhlmann-Anderson intelligence test and a palmar sweating test, it is unlikely that he would integrate them into a single concept. When the actual practice of behavioral psychologists is studied, one discovers that all sorts of considerations enter in which are not justified on strict operational grounds. For example, when I.Q. tests are formulated, the questions must be selected, but on what grounds? How do we know antecedently which factors are relevant and which irrelevant? In point of historical fact, one consideration which psychologists thought was irrelevant is sex. Any question which distinguished between the sexes was eliminated. We know that certain attributes are correlated with sex in people; for example certain diseases. What right has an operationist to assume in advance that sex is an irrelevant consideration in forming the concept associated with the cluster of attributes commonly termed "intelligence"?

Far from arguing that such operationally unwarranted decisions should be eliminated from psychology, I believe that such considerations are *necessary* in order for operationism to get off the ground. In physics these decisions were made on the basis of a highly articulated theory. Einstein did not *discover*

that length when measured by different means gave different results. Rather, the theory he devised *required* that the results of certain types of measurement not agree. In psychology there was no such theory. About all psychologists had to go on was the accumulated knowledge of everyday experience, some rudimentary psychological theories and a little knowledge of physiology. They were put in the position of developing a theory and formulating definitions simultaneously. In these circumstances, attempts at operational definitions are more often a hindrance than a help. It is one thing to argue for or against operational definitions as the ideal in a finished science; it is another to show the advantages and shortcomings of operational definitions in the process known as science. Operationism does not provide a principle of meaning adequate for an acceptable reconstruction of science as a finished product, but might it not function fruitfully in the logic of discovery? . . .

It is certainly true that some observations are a good deal more direct and free from inference and interpretation than others, but no "fact" is sufficiently brute and pristine to be infallibly insulated against the possibility of error. For example, no observation seemed more direct and free from inference than the observation that the earth did not move. The arguments of Copernicus and Galileo that it both rotated and revolved were extremely complex and required considerable interpretation. Nothing like observational confirmation was obtained for the revolution of the earth until the 19th century—long after all scientists accepted it as an indubitable fact. . . .

There is a continuum of terms in science which stretches from those at one extreme which are relatively free of theoretical import, such as, hard, slick, spot, irregular, and invagination, to those at the other which are intimately associated with a particular scientific theory, such as, electron, atom, inertial gravity, castration complex, cell, gene and species. Often this continuum is treated as if it stretched from observables to unobservables or from real things to mere abstractions. The relation is not that simple. The key property of theoretical terms is the role they play in theories. Observations mark the occasion of their application but do not fully supply their meaning. The surest sign that "species" functions in evolutionary theory as a theoretic term is that if evolutionary theory were abandoned or greatly modified, the meaning of the term "species" would be altered accordingly. . . .

In order for a concept to be operational, must it be applicable in *all* cases, in *most* cases, or in *some* cases? The answer, in all cases, can be shown to be too strong for most scientifically significant terms. If the answer is in some cases, only the most metaphysical terms fail to fulfill this requirement. If the answer is somewhere between all and some, the question remains, "Where?" . . .

CONCLUSION

I would like to conclude this paper with a parable. So the story goes, early date farmers noticed that only half their trees produced dates. To increase their yield they began to weed out the "sterile" trees. For a while they were successful, until the last sterile male tree was cut down. Then all the other trees stopped producing. Theoretical terms are like the male trees. They are not completely operational, but they are necessary for the progress of science. Operationism is fruitful only when it is not total. Strict operationism is incompatible with theory and more moderate versions impossible without it.

ACKNOWLEDGMENTS

The number of people who have heard or read this paper and offered criticisms of it is large. Among these I wish especially to thank Helen Heise, Mortimer Starr and the members of their seminar in philosophical problems in taxonomy, Theodore Crovello, P. H. A. Sneath, Robert R. Sokal, Paul Ehrlich, Donald Holm, David Luce, and Ernst Mayr. My appreciation of the phenetic position on operational homology was greatly heightened by a lengthy correspondence with Donald Colless. Several ideas presented in this section were developed jointly. Considering the nature of the paper and the diversity of opinion and background of those who have commented on it, the inevitable disclaimer that not everyone cited agreed with all the views expressed becomes even more superfluous than usual.

Problem Formulations as Heuristics: Introduction to "Scientific Discovery and the Psychology of Problem Solving"

Herbert Simon, a Nobel laureate, has authored influential books about organization and management in addition to his work on heuristics (1957a, 1957b, 1977, 1981). In the following selection, which was first published in 1966, one of Simon's most important points is that, rather than describing the actual behavior of scientists, philosophy of science tended to be "normative." The "traditional philosophy of science" to which he refers was, at that time, a descendent of logical empiricism. At the time of Simon's writing, the works of Stephen Toulmin (1953), Norwood Hanson (*Patterns of Discovery*, 1958), and Thomas Kuhn (*The Structure of Scientific Revolutions*, 1962, 1970)—which were among the first postpositivist descriptions of science—had already begun to change how philosophers conceptualized science and scientific activity.[88]

Simon advances his problem-solving theory to explain scientific problem solving. He points out that humans think by using heuristics. Heuristics both facilitate problem solving, by organizing information, and set up bias, because heuristics help problem solvers focus on some variables and disregard others. As Simon describes them, heuristics are used in everyday problem solving as well as in scientific research.

In "Thinking by Computers," (1966b) Simon identifies four prominent "heuristic schemes:" means–end analysis, factorization, planning and abstraction, and satisficing (see the Glossary). These heuristics constrain (and so make tractable) the problem-solver's search and also point toward next steps that may yield promising solutions. Simon argues that heuristics are the basis of problem solving by showing that he can use his theory to explain how he developed his theory. For example, he emphasizes how superior methods of observation and representation generate new discoveries. Simon describes how he and his colleagues used digital computers (which were then innovative technologies) to simulate problem-solving strategies and to test their ideas.

Simon emphasizes the importance of processes of discovery in scientific research. He elaborates some other processes he believes may be involved in scientific discovery: incubation and illumination. He develops the concepts of a mental blackboard that stores information, and a goal tree, which is the mental representation of the step-by-step process in the trial-and-error search. He shows how one aspect of discovery is finding a new method of observation; that method of observation can lead to significantly new discoveries. Kuhn (1962, 1970) also describes another form of discovery that occurs during research: when the researcher's findings are unexpected. One of the challenges, of course, is to perceive the unexpected findings; unfortunately, a researcher can experience an unexpected finding as a loss and disregard it or minimize its significance. Simon illustrates how very important it is for researchers to listen and look for data that do not fit their expectations, because those data can be the seed of radically new knowledge.

Scientific problem solving can be conceptualized as a dialogue, as Galileo said, "A question put to Nature" (as cited in Koyre, 1968, p. ix). Heuristics organize how we can know nature's responses. At the same time, reality responds in ways researchers may not expect, which may cause researchers to revise their initial heuristics. Research therefore is a process of continual revision and rethinking. Only rarely will a research process seem to end. Most often, it leads to new questions and opens up new paths, especially if the heuristics are good in terms of engendering both creative thought and systematic analysis.

An essential implication of Simon's paper is that "scientific development involves not only solving problems, but posing them as well" (1966a, p. 36). As Simon says, problem formulation is itself a problem-solving process: The researcher searches for a problem that will be the best representation of the issues at stake and will lead to the most useful solutions. Drawing from Simon's ideas, researchers who adopt the heuristic paradigm consider various ways of representing the problem ("reformulation of questions—more generally, modification of representations—is one of the problem solving processes," 1966a, p. 36).

One way to explore different representations of a problem is to look at the problem using various theoretical perspectives. For example, if one wanted to investigate a particular mental disorder in children, one might begin by looking at how different theories (e.g., behaviorism, neuropsychology, and psychoanalysis) yield very different definitions of and explanations for the constellation of symptoms.

Simon also shows how problem formulation and choice of a method of observation are necessarily interactive decisions. The available methods of observation influence how the researcher will formulate a research problem. Simon gives several examples from the natural sciences. Consider an example from the history of social work: When the settlement house social workers moved into the neighborhoods, they created a new way of finding out about their neighbors' strengths and difficulties, which in turn changed how they formulated problems for social research.

In advancing postpositivist approaches to problem formulation, Mitroff and Featheringham define the "error of the third kind," which is "the error, or probability, of having solved the wrong problem, choosing the wrong problem representation, when one should have solved the right problem, chosen the right representation" (1974, p. 383). They emphasize, "what good does it do to minimize the errors of the first and second kinds, EI and EII,* if the basic conceptualization on which EI and EII are founded is defective?" (p. 393).

Scientists pursue problems they find puzzling and for which they want an explanation. The formulation of the research problem will lead to some kinds of explanations and steer the researcher away from others. Although, as noted previously, the logical positivists defined scientific explanations restrictively, postpositivist philosophers describe many forms of scientific explanation. A key postpositivist criterion for a good scientific explanation is how informative it is (Scriven, 1959 in this chap-

---

*Editor's Note: Statisticians define a Type I error as "rejecting a true hypothesis" (Blalock, 1979b, p. 110), and a Type II error as, "the error of failing to reject an hypothesis when it is actually false" (Blalock, 1979b, p. 109). When discussing how inferential statistics can be used to analyze data and test hypotheses, Blalock says that "the major advantage of statistical procedures over intuitive methods is in the knowledge they provide about these risks of error" (1979b, p. 112).

ter). A good explanation often introduces new discoveries for which new concepts are necessary. As Roy Bhaskar points out, to explain something is:

> to resolve some agent's perplexity about it: it is to render the unintelligible intelligible— by the elucidation, extension, modification or replacement of that agent's existing conceptual field. In particular, scientific explanations do not resolve problems by subsuming some particular problem under a more general one, but by locating such (normally already generalized) problems in the context of a new cognitive setting; it is (new) *concepts*, not (universal) *quantifiers* which accomplish explanatory problem-resolution in science. (Bhaskar, 1989b, p. 90; italics in original)

KEY TERMS

Algorithm	**Ceteris paribus**
Factorization	**Means–end analysis**
Planning and abstraction	**Satisficing**

DISCUSSION QUESTIONS

1. What reasons does Simon give for why heuristics are necessary and useful? Can you think of more reasons?

2. Norwood Hanson says that the logical empiricist, hypothetico-deductive accounts of scientific explanation espoused by Popper (see Appendix) and Hempel (e.g., 1965b) assume that inductive inference can be left out; they

    > begin with the hypothesis as given, as . . . recipes begin with the hare as given. A preliminary instruction in many cookery books, however, reads "First catch your hare." The H-D [hypothetico-deductive] account tells us what happens after the physicist has caught his hypothesis; but it might be argued that the ingenuity, tenacity, imagination and conceptual boldness which has marked physics since Galileo shows itself more clearly in hypothesis-catching than in the deductive elaboration of caught hypotheses. (Hanson, 1958, p. 72)

    Drawing in part from Hanson's work, Simon also focuses on aspects of the process of scientific discovery, such as "hypothesis catching." How does Simon define the following aspects of discovery and problem-solving processes?

    Familiarization
    Selective forgetting
    Goal tree
    Blackboard

3. Notice how, in his conclusion, Simon discusses some "objections" that can be raised to a theory of problem solving. What are the objections, and how does Simon respond to each one? Can you think of any further objections? How do you think Simon might respond to them?

4. Simon argues that the most creative scientists, like the best chess players, have superior heuristics. Those heuristics render their problem solving more efficient and lead them to better solutions. The heuristics may be "a superior technique of observation or of representation" (1966a, p. 27).

   a. Take two different theories of clinical practice and describe how each is a method of observation as well as a method of representation.

   b. Choose two different research methods. Show how each is a method of observation that also regulates the researcher's possible findings.

5. Although my commitment to women's issues led me to include the variable of gender in the content analysis presented in Chapter 2, I was quite surprised when I saw Figure 2–2. I had not expected such a clear association between shifts in the approaches to research in the field of social work and changes in the relative proportions of women and men first authors. When I saw that data, I realized that I had to take a closer look at gender roles and the interface between the women's movement and the history of the social work profession. Such unexpected findings often surprise researchers, and as Herbert Simon says, unexpected findings are part of the research process. Yet, I never would have made that discovery if I had not already been interested in the possible influence of the roles of women and men on research. Can you think of any techniques to help yourself remain open to the possibility of findings that surprise you? How can you help yourself and your colleagues if your findings run counter to what you expect or believe to be true?

6. Explanations can be analyzed along different dimensions. William Wimsatt, Martha McClintock, and Susan Goldin-Meadow outline five dimensions of explanation*:

   1. Explanations of a phenomenon can be given on different time scales (*Temporal* dimension).

   2. A phenomenon can be explained or described at different levels of abstraction or organization (Dimension of *levels of analysis*).

   3. One can explain a phenomenon either in terms of the function it serves ("*Why* it's there," or "*why* explanations") or in terms of the mechanisms which produce it ("*How* it works" or "*how* explanations") (*Causal mode* dimension).

   4. One may explain a phenomenon from a subjective perspective, a group perspective, or from the objective perspective (*perspectival* dimension).

   5. One may explain either how a phenomenon *should* have occurred (*normative* or *rational* explanation) or how it *did* occur (*descriptive* explanation) (*Evaluative* dimension).

Source: Unpublished lecture outline by W. Wimsatt, S. Goldin-Meadow, and M. McClintock, revised July 19, 1991. Emphasis in original. Copyright 1991, Professor William Wimsatt, Susan Goldin-Meadow, and Martha McClintock. Reproduced with permission.

    i. Choose three theories that offer different explanations for the same problem. Evaluate each explanation according to the dimensions outlined by Wimsatt, McClintock, and Goldin-Meadow. Show how each theory also formulates the problem differently.

   ii. Take the research problem you have generated as you have been practicing problem formulation, and use Wimsatt, Goldin-Meadow, and McClintock's dimensions to evaluate the explanation that your problem formulation will produce.

  iii. Try rotating your problem formulation so that it focuses more on one of those dimensions rather than another. For example, suppose you want to study the problem of homelessness. If you formulate the problem as finding out how people experience being homeless, the resulting explanation will be from a subjective perspective. If you reformulate the problem to address how homelessness should be managed by society, the explanation will be normative.

▼ ▼ ▼ ▼ ▼ ▼ ▼ ▼ ▼ ▼ ▼ ▼

SAMPLE RESEARCH PROJECT: DEVELOPING RESIDENTIAL TREATMENT SERVICES FOR HOMELESS, MENTALLY ILL, AND SUBSTANCE-ABUSING CLIENTS

Part 3: Alternative Problem Formulations

An extensive review of the literature indicates that naturalistic studies of services for the homeless mentally ill are almost nonexistent. The most common research methods are interventionist. Data generally are collected by asking homeless and mentally ill clients to participate in structured interviews that are not intended to be therapeutic (e.g., Fischer & Breakey, 1991; Fowler, 1991; Sosin, Colson, & Grossman, 1988; Test & Burke, 1985). Little systematic research has been conducted to determine how staff can be helped to care for this population—although burnout issues often are mentioned—and the research does not use naturalistic methods.

The reliance on interventionist methods in research about helping this population has caused researchers to study only certain kinds of problems. Furthermore, problems related to the caregiving process as it occurs naturally with this population have not been systematically studied. Instead, knowledge about the outcome of services is derived from versions of change processes that have been altered to meet research priorities.

Interventionist methods can lead to other types of problems that also have not been studied. They can engender unfortunate and often unrecognized effects for the caregivers as well as for the clients in the program. For example, interventionist researchers commonly ask program line staff to implement sorting clients into experimental and control groups (Test & Burke, 1985). Staff who had participated in such projects reported that they found it confusing to be asked to provide compassionate care yet also to sit by while those clients in the control group did not get the treatment they needed.

Studying the change process as it occurs naturally is challenging in many respects. The change process is an ongoing series of interactions between client and staff. The helpfulness and outcomes of that process are manifested in very diverse ways, both throughout the caregiving process and after the resident is discharged. For the purposes of study, this complex domain is necessarily reduced to manageable units. Research has been conducted that investigates specifics of the change process that occurs in clinical interviews with clients with other kinds of difficulties (Rice & Greenberg, 1984), but not with homeless, mentally ill, and substance-abusing clients. Research about services for this population has typically focused on atomized, partialized indicators of client change, such as changes in the clients' scores on symptom severity scales. One consequence of this bias has been that very little is known about how to help these clients form, sustain, and benefit from attachments to helping professionals.

Finally, in the context of extremely limited resources, a common research priority has been to define "accountability solely in terms of the value of spending the smallest amount of time and money with any given client" (Heineman Pieper, 1994, p. 84). An example of that bias in research is the assumption that inpatient care should be avoided and that when clients are rehospitalized, it is a negative indicator about the impact of services. By contrast, when short-term cost reduction does not regulate conceptualization of the issues, a client's request to be rehospitalized can be seen to reflect the client's increased trust and reduced alienation from care providers, which in fact is a sign of progress. To illustrate, one client had lived in consistently life-threatening circumstances, on the street, for over a year. She entered the program voluntarily, but within two weeks, she left immediately after provoking a serious, almost physical conflict with another resident. Her friends in the program were so concerned about her well-being that within two days they found her on the street and took her on the bus, at their own expense, to the public mental health hospital.

Another problem resulting from the bias toward defining accountability in terms of reducing expenditures is that data about clients' responsiveness to more comprehensive and sustained care are not gathered. The extent to which the supposed untreatability of this population is an artifact of the lack of sustained and comprehensive services is a very important topic for further investigation. In sum, although allocating scarce resources is an extremely difficult problem, it is not solved when researchers adopt a bias toward briefer and sparser treatments whose effectiveness for this population is highly questionable.

One advantage of formulating a research problem in terms of clients' experience of services is that it draws on the reflective capacities of human participant/subjects. For example, one resident in the program said that she was concerned that homeless people did not realize that there could be a program that would help them and also respect them. On several occasions, she returned to talk with her friends on the street and tried to help them come to the program to get help for themselves. Clearly, the participants in the program could (1) compare the program to other forms of service they had received and (2) evaluate the program's contribution in helping them to improve their condition.

Scientific Discovery and the Psychology of Problem Solving

Herbert A. Simon   *Carnegie Institute of Technology*

The very fact that the totality of our sense experiences is such that by means of thinking (operations with concepts, and the creation and use of definite functional relations between them, and the coordination of sense experiences to these concepts) it can be put in order, this fact is one which leaves us in awe, but which we shall never understand. One may say "the eternal mystery of the world is its comprehensibility." It is one of the great realizations of Immanuel Kant that the setting up of a real external world would be senseless without this comprehensibility.

—Albert Einstein
Out of My Later Years

In the previous chapter a theory of human problem solving was put forward with references to some of the evidence for its validity. The theory has been formalized and tested by incorporating it in programs for digital computers and studying the behavior of these programs when they are confronted with problem-solving tasks.

The thesis of the present chapter is that scientific discovery is a form of problem solving, and that the processes whereby science is carried on can be explained in the terms that have been used to explain the processes of problem solving. In particular, I shall undertake to show how the theory of problem solving described in the previous chapter can account for some of the principal reported phenomena of scientific discovery.

For a description of these phenomena, the analysis will draw heavily upon previously published accounts. Discussions of scientific discovery have always been highly anecdotal, most of our specific information on the subject deriving from reports of specific examples, recorded in some instances by historians and philosophers of science, in some instances by psychologists, but often by the discoverers themselves. The classics in the latter category are Henri Poincaré's celebrated lecture, translated as "Mathematical Creation" (New York: The Science Press, 1913), and the delightful essay by Jacques Hadamard, *The Psychology of Invention in the Mathematical Field* (Princeton: Princeton

U. Press, 1945). Chapter 10 of Max Wertheimer's *Productive Thinking* (New York: Harper & Row, enlarged ed., 1959) reports a series of interviews with Albert Einstein on the course of events that led to the invention of the theory of special relativity.

The literature on the topic produced by philosophers of science is substantial, but has been for purposes of this analysis, on the whole, less useful. (I will mention two important exceptions in a moment.) The reason is that philosophers of science tend to address themselves to the normative more than to the descriptive aspects of scientific methodology. They are more concerned with how scientists *ought to* proceed, in order to conform with certain conceptions of logic, than with how they *do* proceed. Notions of how they ought to proceed focus primarily on the problem of induction: on how generalizations might validly arise from data on particulars and on the degree to which a corpus of data logically confirms a generalization. These are interesting questions of philosophy, but they turn out to have relatively little relation to the actual

Source: "Scientific Discovery and the Psychology of Problem Solving" by H. Simon in *Mind and Cosmos* (pp. 22–40) edited by R. Colodny, 1966, Pittsburgh: University of Pittsburgh Press. Copyright 1966 by the University of Pittsburgh. Reprinted by permission of the Center for the Philosophy of Science, University of Pittsburgh.

291

behavior of scientists—and perhaps less normative value than has been supposed.

In the past few years, two philosopher-historians of science, both originally trained in physics, have made particularly significant contributions to the psychology and sociology of scientific discovery. Both have been quite explicit in distinguishing the processes of discovery from the traditional canons of "sound" scientific method. I shall make considerable use of their work and ideas. One of these men, Norwood Russell Hanson, has set forth his views most extensively in *Patterns of Discovery* (Cambridge: Cambridge University Press, 1958). The other, Thomas S. Kuhn, has produced an original and stimulating account of *The Structure of Scientific Revolutions* (Chicago: University of Chicago Press, 1962).

To explain scientific discovery is to describe a set of processes that is sufficient—and *just* sufficient—to account for the amounts and directions of scientific progress that have actually occurred. For a variety of reasons, perhaps best understood by psychoanalysis, when we talk or write about scientific discovery, we tend to dwell lovingly on the great names and the great events—Galileo and uniform acceleration, Newton and universal gravitation, Einstein and relativity, and so on.[1] We insist that a theory of discovery postulate processes sufficiently powerful to produce these events. It is right to so insist, but we must not forget how rare such events are, and we must not postulate processes so powerful that they predict a discovery of first magnitude as a daily matter.

On the contrary, for each such event there is an investment of thousands of man-years of investigation by hundreds of talented and hard-working scientists. This particular slot machine produces many stiff arms for every jackpot. At the same time that we explain how Schrödinger and Heisenberg, in 1926, came to quantum mechanics, we must explain why Planck, Bohr, Einstein, de Broglie, and other men of comparable ability struggled for the preceding twenty years *without* completing this discovery. Scientific discovery is a rare event; a theory to explain it must predict innumerable failures for every success.

The great events do not, of course, represent sudden leaps forward, unrelated to previous exploration. While modern quantum mechanics clearly did not exist in 1924, and clearly did in 1926, the approach to it was gradual and steady, involving all the illustrious scientists mentioned in the previous paragraph and many hundreds more. And the particular advance that we identify as "the discovery" was followed by many man-years of exploitation and consolidation, just as it was preceded by man-years of exploration and anticipation. The central point remains: scientific discovery, when viewed in detail, is an excruciatingly slow and painful process.

Related to the rarity of great discoveries—and relevant to our understanding of the process—is the rarity of great discoverers. If there are only a few great discoveries, and if a great discoverer is someone who makes a great discovery, then such persons must be rare by definition. But there is a substantive question too. Does science depend, for its major progress, upon heroes who have faculties not possessed by journeymen scientists? Or are the men whose names we associate with the great discoveries just the lucky ones—those who had their hands on the lever at the precise moment when the jackpot showered its rewards?

A case could be made for either view, and my own hunch is that the truth lies somewhere between. If it is luck, a few men in each generation appear more skillful in wooing the goddess than are their fellows. On the other hand, I have encountered no evidence that there exist significant differences between the processes that great scientists use in achieving their discoveries and the processes used by those men we regard merely as "good" scientists.

The theory of scientific discovery I propose to set forth rests on the hypothesis that there are no qualitative differences between the *processes* of revolutionary science and of normal science, between work of high creativity and journeyman work. I shall not claim that the case can be proven conclusively. My main evidence will be data indicating that the processes that show up in relatively simple and humdrum forms of human problem solving are also the ones that show up when great scientists try to describe how they do their work. How convincing the evidence is can better be judged at the end of the chapter.

Let us return, then, to the problem-solving theory proposed in the last chapter and confront that theory with the recorded phenomena of scientific discovery.

The problem-solving theory asserted that thinking is an organization of elementary information processes, organized hierarchically and executed serially. In overall organization, the processes exhibit large amounts of highly selective trial-and-error search using rules of thumb, or heuristics, as bases for their selectivity. Among the prominent heuristic schemes are means-end analysis, planning and abstraction, factorization, and satisficing. Our task is to show how a system with these characteristics can behave like a scientist.

SELECTIVE TRIAL-AND-ERROR SEARCH

The prominence of selective trial-and-error processes in accounts of scientific discovery makes an extended discussion of this phenomenon unnecessary.[2] Examples of such accounts that come immediately to mind, out of a multitude that could be cited, are Hanson's analysis of the development of Kepler's theories (*Patterns of Discovery*, pp. 73–84), and Wertheimer's report of his conversations with Einstein on the theory of special relativity (*Productive Thinking*, Chapter 10).

Wertheimer's book is particularly interesting in this connection, because he can be regarded as a hostile witness. As a Gestaltist he maintains the greatest skepticism about the processes, like trial-and-error, postulated by associationists to account for problem solving. In fact, he almost never uses the phrase "trial and error" without prefixing the adjective "blind." His chapter certainly provides no evidence that Einstein engaged in "random" search. It does provide ample evidence that he made many attempts at solutions that failed—that a great deal of *selective* trial and error took place over the decade or more during which Einstein struggled with the problem of the velocity of light.

Hadamard (*The Psychology of Invention in the Mathematical Field*, p. 48) has expressed the point metaphorically: "It is well known that good hunting cartridges are those which have a proper scattering. If this scattering is too wide, it is useless to aim; but if it is too narrow, you have too many chances to miss your game by a line. I see quite similar circumstances in our subject."

The theory and empirical explorations described above call for precisely this kind of mixture of search and aim. Except where an algorithm is available—that is, in areas that are already well structured, hence, well behind the frontiers of discovery—some amount of trial and error is essential. On the other hand, the sizes of the problem spaces encountered even in relatively simple laboratory tasks show that without powerful heuristics, principles of selectivity, the search could only rarely reach its object.

The theory has a further implication. Evidences of trial and error should be most prominent in those areas of problem solving where the heuristics are least powerful, least adequate to narrow down the problem space. Hence, the paths leading to discoveries we would call creative might be expected to provide even more visible evidences of trial and error than those leading to relatively routine discoveries. We have no quantitative evidence to test this prediction. Moreover, it rests implicitly on a somewhat doubtful *ceteris paribus* assumption: that the heuristics of persons who make creative discoveries are no more powerful than those of their contemporaries who do not.

Let us examine the question more closely. One characteristic of a discovery that marks it as creative is its unexpectedness. To say that it is "surprising" or "unexpected" is to say that it would not readily be chanced upon. But chanced upon by whom? Presumably by scientists working at the time of the discovery. Since it was, by definition, chanced upon or found by the actual discoverer, we must conclude (1) that he was lucky, (2) that he searched longer and harder than his contemporaries, or (3) that he had more powerful selective heuristics than they did. The most plausible hypothesis is that all three conditions are generally met, in varying proportions. Of these three conditions conducive to discovery, the first, luck, implies nothing about the amount of trial and error, or its selectivity.[3] To the extent that the second condition, persistence, is present, trial-and-error search should be prominently visible. If the third condition, superior heuristics, is chiefly responsible for the discovery, no more trial-and-error search will be present than would appear normal in cases of less creative activity.

The evidences of a high degree of persistence in pursuing fundamental problems are numerous in the biographies of creative scientists. Persistence does not always mean continual conscious preoccupation with the problem, or orderly, organized pursuit, but concern with the problem over a considerable period of years, indicated by recurrent attention to it. One could conjecture that while the biographies of "journeyman" scientists might reveal persistent attention to a problem *area* over comparable periods of time, the activity would more likely than in the case of highly creative scientists represent attacks upon, and solutions of, a whole series of relatively well-structured problems within the general area (e.g., determinations of structures of a number of molecules, or of the parameters of a system under a range of experimental conditions). However, the data on this point remain to be gathered.

A good deal less conjectural is the hypothesis that superior problem solvers in a particular area have more powerful heuristics and that they will produce adequate solutions with less search, or better solutions with equivalent search as compared with less competent persons. A. de Groot, for example, compared the searches of grandmasters and ordinary chess players for a good move in a middle-game position. Both classes of players searched for about the same length of time (which was partly an artifact of the laboratory situation), and examined approximately the same number of branches of the game tree. In fact, it was impossible to distinguish, from the statistics of the search, between the grandmasters and the ordinary players. They were easily distinguished by one datum, however: in the particular position examined, all five grandmasters attained better solutions to the problem (chose moves that could be shown to be objectively better) than any of the solutions attained by the ordinary players. While the grandmasters did not engage in more search than the others, their superior selective heuristics allowed them to search more significant and relevant parts of the game tree.[4]

Whence do the superior heuristics, the secret weapons, of the creative scientist come? Frequently, they derive from his possession of a superior technique of observation or of representation. Examples of the former are commonplace: Leeuwenhoek and his microscope, Galileo and his telescope, Lawrence and his cyclotron, and so on. God is on the side of the highest resolutions. The classic example of the interaction between apparatus for symbolizing or representation and scientific discovery is the relation of the calculus to the birth and growth of Newtonian mechanics. One might ask how the creative scientist comes to possess superior techniques. The answer would again be in terms of luck, persistence, and superior heuristics. The answer is not really circular, for it is quite legitimate, in dynamic systems, to explain chickens by the hatching of eggs, and eggs by the laying processes of chickens.

The theory of problem solving set forth in these two chapters itself provides an example of apparatus and representation as sources of heuristics. The idea that problem solving is a process of selective trial and error is an old one. The idea remained vague and largely untested until a formalism became available (list-processing language for computers) that was powerful enough to state the theory formally and precisely and until an instrument became available (the digital computer) that was powerful enough to draw out the implications and predictions of the theory for human problem-solving behavior. The scientists who have been active in developing and testing this theory were all in one way or another—sometimes in very "accidental" ways—thrown into contact with computers soon after these instruments were invented.

INCUBATION AND UNCONSCIOUS PROCESSES IN DISCOVERY

The phenomena of incubation and sudden illumination have held immense fascination for those who have written on scientific discovery. Poincaré's experience on boarding the bus at Coutances takes its place in the annals of illumination along with Proust's madeleine dipped in tea:

> Just at this time I left Caen, where I was then living, to go on a geological excursion under the auspices of the school of mines. The changes of travel made me forget my mathematical work. Having reached Coutances, we entered an omnibus to go some place or other. At the moment when I put my foot on the step the idea came to me, without anything in my former thoughts seeming to have paved the way for it, that the transformations I had used to define the Fuchsian functions were identical with those of non-Euclidean geometry.[5]

Hadamard places particular emphasis on the role of the unconscious in mathematical invention. While he proposes no specific theory of the processes that go on during incubation, he argues strongly that these are active processes and not merely a forgetting of material generated during conscious work that is inhibiting the problem solution.

The theory of problem solving proposed in the last chapter does not assign any special role to the unconscious—or, for that matter, to the conscious. It assumes, implicitly, that the information processes that occur without consciousness of them are of the same kinds as the processes of which the thinker is aware. It assumes, further, that the organization of the totality of processes, conscious and unconscious, is fundamentally serial rather than parallel in time.

Our examination of the phenomena of incubation and illumination and their explanation will proceed in several stages. First, I shall describe briefly the phenomena themselves. Second, I shall consider the question of why the phenomena should be regarded as surprising and in what sense they require special explanation. Finally, the information-processing theory of problem solving will be applied to provide an explanation of the main features of incubation and illumination.

The phenomena themselves are relatively simple, and their occurrence is well documented. In the case of many important scientific discoveries (we do not know in what proportion of all cases), the discoverer reports three main stages in the progress of his inquiry. The first stage, which Hadamard calls "preparation," involves conscious, prolonged investigation that is more or less unsuccessful in solving, or sometimes even satisfactorily framing, the problem. Ultimately, frustration becomes intense, and the problem is dropped from conscious attention. Some time later, often suddenly and with little or no warning (as in the instance reported by Poincaré), or immediately upon awakening from sleep, the central idea for the solution presents itself to the conscious mind, only the details remaining to be worked out. The period between this illumination and the preceding preparation is the incubation period.

While there is little question about the phenomena, they provide no clues as to what goes on during incubation. In the absence of a full-fledged theory of problem solving, one can fill that period with almost any imaginable activity. Illumination is a vivid experience for the person who experiences it, because he is given no hint as to what occasioned the problem solution. Worse, since the incubation processes apparently go on independently of his conscious efforts to solve the problem (and best after these efforts have ceased), the experience gives him few cues as to what he should do when he next encounters a difficult problem—other than to "sleep on it." He must wait until the god decides to seize him.

We can see readily why the phenomenon should be puzzling and surprising to the illuminatee. The solution to a problem that has resisted his hardest efforts suddenly, and without further work, reveals itself to his conscious mind. The notions of continuity in space and time are intrinsic to most of our ideas of causation, and illumination appears to violate this continuity. One must say "appears" because, of course, the laws are only violated in the way they are violated when a magician produces a rabbit from a hat. When we watch the magician, we do not cease to believe in the spatial and temporal continuity of causation, but only in our ability to observe the connections. The same distinction applies to illumination.

If illumination is surprising to a scientist who experiences it, it is less easy to see why it should surprise a psychologist.[6] It is commonplace that many, if not most, of the processes of the central nervous system are inaccessible to consciousness. The subconscious plays a major role in modern theories of motivation, emotion, and psychopathology. There is no a priori reason, then, to assign the problem-solving processes to the conscious rather than the unconscious. From the phenomenal evidence, they in fact belong to both.

I have been using the terms "conscious" and "unconscious" (or "subconscious"—for present purposes, no distinction is made between unconscious and subconscious) to distinguish between what a person is aware of and can report, and what he is not aware of and cannot report. The reports of illumination contain numerous instances that occurred immediately on awakening, but also numerous others that occurred when the discoverer had been awake for some time. Hence, "unconscious" is a more comprehensive term than "asleep." For the sake of parsimony, we shall assume that unconscious processes of the same kinds can occur both in the sleeping and waking states.

It has sometimes been argued that the evidence for unconscious processes is evidence that the information processing in the brain is parallel rather than serial. This argument only has force, of course, for unconscious processes that occur in the waking state when, presumably, they are operating in parallel with the conscious processes and are capable (viz., the Poincaré episode) of interrupting the latter. One can show, however, that a serial system is capable (through a "time-sharing" organization of its processing) of behaving in the observed manner, and the explanation I shall propose for illumination is compatible with either a serial or a parallel organization of cognitive processing.

With these preliminaries out of the way, let us return to incubation and illumination. I should like to describe two mechanisms currently employed in the information-processing theories that appear to go a long way toward accounting for these phenomena. The first of these mechanisms is called *familiarization*, the second is called *selective forgetting*. The familiarization mechanism emerged in the course of constructing a theory of human rote memory, the forgetting mechanism in the course of trying to discover why the organization of the first theorem-proving program, the

Logic Theorist, was more effective in solving problems than the organization of early versions of the General Problem Solver. Neither mechanism was devised, then, with incubation and illumination in mind; they were introduced into the theory to meet other requirements imposed by the data on problem solving.

1. *Familiarization.* Thinking processes make use of certain means in the central nervous system for holding symbols in short-term or "immediate" memory. Little is known of the neurophysiological substrate of immediate memory, but a good deal is known about its phenomenal characteristics. Most important, the number of symbols that can be stored in immediate memory is severely limited—in George Miller's words, "seven, plus or minus two." But a "symbol" can serve as the name for anything that can be recognized as familiar and that has information associated with it in permanent memory. Thus "*a*" is a symbol; so is "Lincoln's Gettysburg Address." For most native speakers of English "criminal lawyer" is a symbol, but for a person just learning the language, the phrase may constitute a pair of symbols denoting a lawyer with certain antisocial tendencies.

The important facts are (1) that only about seven symbols can be held and manipulated in immediate memory at one time and (2) that anything can become a symbol through repeated exposure to it, or familiarization. Familiarization involves storing in *permanent* memory information that allows the symbol to be recognized and a single symbol or "name" to be substituted for it.

Since immediate memory can only hold a few symbols at a time, complex structures can only be acquired by gradually building them up from substructures which are formed, in turn, from still smaller substructures. As each substructure is learned and stored in permanent memory, the symbol that serves as its "name" internally can be used in immediate memory as a single chunk when combining it with other substructures. Thus, a total structure of unlimited size can be assembled without the need for holding more than a few symbols in immediate memory at any given moment. Lincoln's Gettysburg Address is memorized by assembling phrases out of words (which are already familiar units), sentences out of phrases, paragraphs out of sentences, and so on.

Familiarization processes, for reconciling the limits of immediate memory with the needs for storing information structures of unlimited size and complexity in permanent memory, are incorporated in the information-processing theory of memorization called EPAM (Elementary Perceiver and Memorizer), a program that has successfully accounted for a wide range of laboratory data on human memorizing.[7] We will assume here that these same processes go on during complex problem solving, so that in later stages of problem solving complex units are available that existed only as disconnected particulars at an earlier stage.

In proving mathematical theorems it is common first to introduce and prove some subsidiary theorems, or lemmas, which then enter as premises in the proof of the final theorem. The lemma serves to sum up a whole segment of the proof so that the name of the lemma can be used as premise in place of that segment. It should not be assumed that all or most familiarization is as deliberate or conscious as this use of lemmas by mathematicians, but the processes are analogical and perform the same function.

2. *Selective Forgetting.* A second mechanism to be found in information-processing theories of problem solving that is essential to our proposed explanation of incubation and illumination involves more rapid forgetting of some memory contents than of others. The selective forgetting rests, in turn, on the distinction between forms of short-term and long-term memory.

In the typical organization of a problem-solving program, the solution efforts are guided and controlled by a hierarchy or "tree" of goals and subgoals. Thus, the subject starts out with the goal of solving the original problem. In trying to reach this goal, he generates a subgoal that will take him part of the way (if it is achieved) and addresses himself to that subgoal. If the subgoal is achieved, he may then return to the now-modified original goal. If difficulties arise in achieving the subgoal, sub-subgoals may be erected to deal with them.

The operation of such a process requires the goal hierarchy to be held in memory. If a subgoal is achieved, it can be forgotten, but the tree of unattained goals must be retained. In human problem solvers this retention is not always perfect, of course. When part of the structure is lost, the subject says, "Where am I?" or "Now why was I trying to get that result?" and may have to go over some of the same ground to get back into context—i.e., to locate himself in that part of the tree that has been retained in memory. If we were designing such a system, instead of probing the one that human beings possess, we would specify that the goal tree be held in some kind of temporary memory, since it is a dynamic structure, whose function is to guide search, and it is not needed (or certainly not all of it) when the problem solution has been found. Our hypothesis is that human beings are also constructed in this way—that the goal tree is held in a relatively short-term memory.

During the course of problem solving, a second memory structure is being built up. First of all, new complexes are being familiarized, so that they can be handled by the processing system as units. In addition, the problem solver is noticing various features of the problem environment and is storing some of these in memory. If he is studying a chess position, for example, in the course of his explorations he may notice that a particular piece is undefended or that another piece is pinned against the queen.

This kind of information is perceived while the problem solver is addressing himself to particular subgoals. What use is made of it at the time it is noted depends on what subgoal is directing attention at that moment. But some of this information is also transferred to more permanent forms of memory and is associated with the problem environment—in this example, with the chess position. This information about the environment is used, in turn, in the processes that erect new subgoals and that work toward subgoal achievement. Hence, over the longer run, this information influences the growth of the subgoal tree. To have a short name for it (since it is now a familiar unit for us!), I will call the information about the task environment that is noticed in the course of problem solution and fixated in permanent (or relatively long-term) memory the "blackboard."

The course of problem solving, then, involves continuous inter-action between goal tree and blackboard.[8] In the course of pursuing goals, information is added to the blackboard. This information, in turn, helps to determine what new goals and subgoals will be set up. During periods of persistent activity, the problem solver will always be working in local goal contexts, and information added to the blackboard will be used, in the short run, only if it is relevant in those contexts.

What happens, now, if the problem solver removes himself from the task for a time? Information he has

been holding in relatively short-term memory will begin to disappear, and to disappear more rapidly than information in long-term memory. But we have hypothesized that the goal tree is held in short-term memory, the blackboard in long-term memory. Hence, when the problem solver next takes up the task, many or most of the finer twigs and branches of the goal tree will have disappeared. He will begin again, with one of the higher level goals, to reconstruct that tree—but now with the help of a very different set of information, on the blackboard, than he had the first time he went down the tree.

In general, we would expect the problem solver, in his renewed examination of the problem, to follow a quite different path than he did originally. Since his blackboard now has better information about the problem environment than it did the first time, he has better cues to find the correct path. Under these circumstances (and remembering the tremendous differences a few hints can produce in problem solution), solutions may appear quickly that had previously eluded him in protracted search.

There is almost no direct evidence at the present time for the validity of this explanation of incubation and illumination. (I have been able, introspectively, to account for my most recent illumination experience quite simply in these terms, but perhaps my introspections are compromised as witnesses.) It invokes, however, only mechanisms that have already been incorporated in problem-solving theories. It does leave one aspect of the phenomena unaccounted for—it does not explain how the problem that the problem solver has temporarily (consciously) abandoned is put back on the agenda by unconscious processes. It does, however, account for the suddenness of solution without calling on the subconscious to perform elaborate processes, or processes different from those it and the conscious perform in the normal course of problem-solving activity. Nor does it postulate that the unconscious is capable of random searches through immense problem spaces for the solution.

It is difficult, in brief compass, to give an actual example of the tree-blackboard scheme in operation, but a schematized hypothetical example will show in general how the mechanism operates. Suppose that we assign "values" to nodes on the goal tree, the values representing estimates of the reward that could be achieved by searching further from the corresponding nodes. The purpose of the search is to find a node with a value of at least 20—such a node represents a solution of the problem (Figure 1).

A reasonable search rule, starting from any given node, would be to search next from the subbranch with the highest value. Thus, if the problem solver were at node G he would pick up branch J, with value 12, next, then the subbranch P (value 15) of that branch, the sub-subbranch Q (value 8), and so on.

Suppose that, in addition, each time a new node was generated, its name and value were added to a list on a blackboard, and that as soon as the subnodes of that node had been generated, the name and value of the node was erased. The blackboard would then contain, at any moment, the names and values of all nodes that had been generated but had not yet been explored. A possible search rule, different from the one previously mentioned, would be always to pick for next exploration the node on the blackboard with the highest value.

Using the first search rule, the search of this particular hypothetical tree would proceed: A-B-E-G-J-P-Q-... Using the second search rule, the search of the tree would proceed: A-B-E-C-F-I-M, reaching the solution. The branch C with value 11, generated at the same time as B, but not immediately investigated, would be selected from the blackboard in preference to the subgoal G, with value only 9, of goal E.

Now our theory of incubation and illumination derives from the hypothesis that during continued attention to a problem, search tends to be context-determined and to follow something like the first rule. During incubation, the tree disappears, leaving the blackboard, and when search resumes, it begins on the basis of the second rule.

Experiments with programs for discovering mating combinations in chess have shown that very different exploration trees are generated in game situations by the two rules, and that the second rule usually finds the mating combinations with far less search than the first. It would be easy, then, to reproduce incubation and illumination phenomena with these programs—by starting a search with a program using the first rule, but maintaining a blackboard, then at some point switching for a short time to the second rule.

As was mentioned earlier, the same point is demonstrated by comparison of the problem-solving power of the Logic Theorist with the power of early versions of the General Problem Solver. Without going into detail, it can simply be stated that the Logic Theorist used a form of the tree-and-blackboard scheme, while search in the General Problem Solver was always determined in the local context of current goals.[9]

PROBLEM FORMULATION IN SCIENTIFIC DISCOVERY

The theories described in the previous section postulate organized systems of processes which, when a problem of an appropriate kind is posed, will go to work on that problem and attempt to solve it. Scientific development involves not only solving problems, but posing them as well. In some discussions of creativity, asking the right questions is regarded as the crucial creative act; answering questions, in this view, is a relatively routine activity once the questions have been properly posed.

The view that question asking rather than question answering is the critical part of the creative process would be hard to defend in its extreme form. Perhaps it even illustrates itself, for in implying a sharp boundary between question asking and question answering, it may be posing the wrong question. If the issue were properly stated, we would see, first, that reformulation of questions—more generally, modification of representations—is one of the problem-solving processes; second, that the task of formulating a prob-

Figure 1

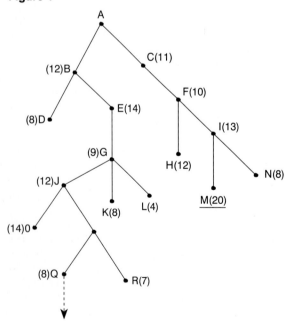

lem can itself be posed as a problem to a problem-solving system.

In exploring the relation of question asking to question answering, Thomas Kuhn's distinction between normal and revolutionary science becomes relevant. Normal science, he argues, does not have to pose its own questions. These questions have already been formulated for it by previous scientific revolutions. The textbooks and classics of science, incorporating the revolution, served "for a time implicitly to define the legitimate problems and methods of a research field for succeeding generations of practitioners." They can do this for two reasons: "Their achievement [is] sufficiently unprecedented to attract an enduring group of adherents away from competing modes of scientific activity. Simultaneously, it [is] sufficiently open-ended to leave all sorts of problems for the redefined group of practitioners to resolve."

Kuhn refers to achievements that share these two characteristics as "paradigms," and he defines normal science as scientific activity within the framework of received paradigms, revolutionary science as scientific activity that establishes new paradigms.[10] Within Kuhn's theory, it is easy to state who poses the problems for investigators engaged in normal science: Their problems come from the paradigms themselves. We must either define "creativity" so that it does not imply question asking as well as question answering, or we must conclude that creativity is not involved in normal science. The choice is one of definition.[11]

Is it necessary to adduce entirely new mechanisms to account for problem formulation in revolutionary science? Kuhn argues that it is not, for the paradigms of any given revolution arise out of the normal science of the previous period. Normal science, in Kuhn's account, leads to the discovery of anomalies, of facts that are difficult or impossible to reconcile with the accepted paradigms. The new problem then—the problem to which the prospective revolutionists address themselves—is to modify the paradigm, or replace it with another that is consistent with the facts, including the new anomalous ones.

In sum, we do not need a separate theory of problem formulation. A problem-solving system of the kind we have been considering—capable of generating subproblems from an initial problem, and capable of testing the adequacy of its solutions by generating new data about the environment—such a system will continue indefinitely to create new problems for itself. Problem formulation in science is to be understood by looking at the continuity of the whole stream of scientific endeavor.

A theory of scientific discovery adequate to explain revolutionary as well as normal science must account not only for the origins of problems, but for the origins of representations, of paradigms, as well. I do not underestimate the importance of this topic, but I shall not undertake to deal with it at any length here. In a previous paper, my colleagues A. Newell and J. C. Shaw, and I have made some general observations about it to which I refer the reader.[12] I shall add just a few more comments.

New representations, like new problems, do not spring from the brow of Zeus, but emerge by gradual—and very slow—stages. The caution stated in the opening pages of this chapter may be recalled: We must not overestimate the capacity of the human mind to invent new representations. The number of such inventions in human history has been very small.

Problem solvers use representations of the spatial relations of objects (engineering drawings are a relatively sophisticated and formalized example). They use representations of the abstract relations of objects (as, for example, in flow charts, genealogical charts, and chemical formulae). They use representations of programs (for example, systems of differential equations, computer programs). One can list a small number of other basic forms of representation and a somewhat larger number of specialized formats within each of these basic forms. The list is not long, and it is hard to find items for it whose history does not go back beyond the Christian era. (The *program* is probably the most recently developed broad form of representation, but it must not be forgotten that a recipe is a program, as is an algorithm like Eratosthenes' sieve. The differential equation represents a highly important subclass within this broad class of representations.)

Thus, our general answer to the question, "Where do representations come from?" is the same as our answer to the question, "Where do problems come from?" Representations arise by modification and development of previous representations as problems arise by modification and development of previous problems. A system that is to explain human problem solving and scientific discovery does not need to incorporate a highly powerful mechanism for inventing completely novel representations. If it did contain such a mechanism, it would be a poor theory, for it would predict far more novelty than occurs.

CONCLUSION

Theories are now available that incorporate mechanisms sufficient to account for some of the principal phenomena of problem solving in at least certain relatively well-structured situations. The aim of this chapter has been to ask how much these theories need to be modified or extended in order to account for problem solving in science. The general tenor of the argument has been that problem solving in science, like problem solving in the psychological laboratory, is a tedious, painstaking process of selective trial and error. Our knowledge of it does not suggest the presence of completely unknown processes far more powerful than those that have been observed in the laboratory.

Several kinds of objections can be raised, and have been, against this "minimalist" theory. One objection is that it does not account for striking phenomena like incubation and illumination. To meet this objection, a mechanism has been proposed that is believed sufficient to produce exactly these kinds of phenomena.

Another objection is that the theory only explains how problems are solved that have already been stated and for which there exist well-defined representations. This objection has not been answered in detail, but an answer has been sketched in terms of the broader social environment within which scientific work takes place. Most scientific activity goes on within the framework of established paradigms. Even in revolutionary science, which creates those paradigms, the problems and representations are rooted in the past; they are not created out of whole cloth.

We are still very far from a complete understanding of the whole structure of the psychological processes involved in making scientific discoveries. But perhaps our analysis makes somewhat more plausible the hypothesis that at the core of this structure is the same kind of selective trial-and-error search that has already been shown to constitute the basis for human problem-solving activity in the psychological laboratory.

NOTES

The preparation of this chapter has been aided by research grants from The Carnegie Corporation and the National Institutes of Health (MH-07722-01).

Most of the ideas in it have been developed in collaboration with my colleague Allen Newell. See his "Some Problems of Basic Organization in Problem-Solving Programs," in *Self-Organizing Systems*, eds. Yovits, Jacobi, and Goldstein (New York: Spartan Press, 1962).

1. Obviously, I am not immune to this tendency.

2. For further discussion, see the previous chapter and A. Newell, J. C. Shaw, and H. A. Simon, "The Processes of Creative Thinking" in Gruber *Contemporary Approaches to Creative Thinking*, eds. Gruber, Terrell, and Wertheimer (New York: Atherton Press, 1962).

3. There are numerous anecdotes, some true, some fictitious, about the role of luck in invention. It is clear, however, that chance events played a role in: discovering vulcanization of rubber, the sweetening power of saccharine, developers in photography, and many other discoveries. See Joseph Rosman, *The Psychology of the Inventor* (Washington: The Inventors Publishing Co., 1931), Chap. 7.

4. A. de Groot, *Thought and Choice in Chess* (Amsterdam: Mouton, 1965).

5. Henri Poincaré, *Mathematical Creation*, reprinted in *The World of Mathematics*, ed. James R. Newman, IV, 2041–50.

6. Mary Henle begins her essay on "The Birth and Death of Ideas" with the sentence, "Perhaps the most astonishing thing about creative thinking is that creative thinkers can tell us so little about it" (in *Contemporary Approaches to Creative Thinking*, Chap. 1). Why astonishing? Would we say: "Perhaps the most astonishing thing about neurotic behavior is that persons suffering from neuroses can tell us so little about it?" Why would we expect, a priori, self-consciousness to be more characteristic of the one than of the other?

7. For an introduction to EPAM see E. A. Feigenbaum, "The Simulation of Verbal Learning Behavior," pp. 297-309 in *Computers and Thought*, eds. Feigenbaum and Feldman (New York: McGraw-Hill, 1964).

8. The roles of goal tree and blackboard in the organization of problem solving have been discussed by Allen Newell, in "Some Problems of Basic Organization."

9. See A. Newell, J. C. Shaw, and H. A. Simon, "Empirical Explorations of the Logic Theory Machine," and A. Newell and H. A. Simon, "GPS, A Program that Simulates Human Thought," in Feigenbaum and Feldman, eds., pp. 109–33, 279–93.

10. Kuhn, pp. 10–12.

11. This account elides some important details. Generating subgoals from a more general goal is a form of question asking also, which is a part both of normal science and of our problem-solving theories. Since this process has already been considered, our only present concern is with problems whose generation cannot be explained in this way.

12. "The Processes of Creative Thinking," pp. 98–104.

Delineating the System under Study: Introduction to "Heuristics and the Study of Human Behavior"

William Wimsatt is a contemporary philosopher of science whose expertise spans many fields, including philosophical issues associated with the mind–body problem (Wimsatt, 1976a), the implications of recent debates in biology and genetics for the philosophy of science (Wimsatt, 1980a, 1980b, 1981b, 1987), and issues in the philosophy of the social and behavioral sciences (Wimsatt, 1981a). His outstanding contributions render the philosophy of science relevant for problems in the social and behavioral sciences, and a thorough understanding of his work will be excellent preparation for conducting social and behavioral research. In this particular article, he sets forth the ideas that serve as cornerstones of the heuristic paradigm, including the following:

1. The problem of generating useful scientific knowledge;
2. The portrayal of the scientist as a problem solver and decision maker;
3. The concepts of heuristics, bias recognition, and the environment–system boundary.[89]

One of Wimsatt's first points is that although social and behavioral science has been viewed by some as less "scientific" than the "hard" sciences (because the social and behavioral sciences necessarily address problems of human interaction and subjectivity), issues such as point of view, problem formulation, and bias also confront scientists in the "hard" sciences. Hence, Wimsatt asserts that the differences between the "hard" and the social and behavioral sciences are more a matter of "degree" than of "kind." An important implication is that social and behavioral scientists can learn from advances in physics and other sciences.

Wimsatt refers to one such advance, chaos theory—an important innovation that has influenced many fields, from physics to economics. Excellent and accessible resources for learning more about chaos theory are *Chaos* by James Gleick (1987), and *Does God Play Dice?* by Ian Stewart (1989). One of the chaos theorists' most important contributions is the discovery that phenomena that appeared irrational and unpatterned (and therefore were long ignored by scientists, who preferred to focus on more understandable phenomena) in fact do have patterns that can be discerned if one develops and uses different heuristics, such as nonlinear causal models. Wimsatt points out that the central defining condition of chaos is not pseudorandomness or unpredictability, but sensitive dependence on initial conditions, so that "initial uncertainties will increase in time if we demand a deterministic account of the behavior of a system" (1986b, p. 293).* The chaos theorists point out that the universe can be deterministic but also entirely unpredictable, because deviations (ascertained in relation to what one would predict using one level of description) accumulate over time exponentially.

---

*Editor's Note: The citations used here refer to pages of the original article. You can find the material quoted from this article in the reprint that follows this introduction.

Wimsatt describes how traditional philosophy of science, including logical positivism, entails norms for scientific activity that are derived from "impossibly idealized" circumstances and so are impossible to fulfill. For example, in his first paragraph, he alludes to the "covering law" model. This is an aspect of logical empiricism in which the philosophers asserted that the aim of science was to derive "covering laws." These laws (with the appropriate information about the system, including initial and boundary conditions) entail the phenomena to be explained. Yet restricting explanation to such "covering laws" is problematic for many reasons. Explaining phenomena in terms of a "covering law" does not provide the kind of information we often would like to know. For example, saying a train is late because it is always late does not tell us why the train is late (Flew, 1984). As Wimsatt describes (1981a), through the use of multiple heuristics that have different biases, we can improve the robustness of our explanations.

Wimsatt reformulates a central problem facing social and behavioral scientists. Rather than asking "How do we generate certain knowledge?" he wonders, "What we do when the complexity of the systems we are studying exceeds our powers of analysis." (1986b, p. 294; see also Simon, 1966b). The conception of the scientist as discovering broadly applicable and exceptionless laws is too idealized and not a useful way to examine scientists' activity. Instead, Wimsatt depicts the scientist as a problem solver and decision maker who seeks to develop information that can be useful for current problems. As Wimsatt notes, we possess "dinky and error-prone equipment" and "a more realistic model of the scientist as problem solver and decision maker includes the existence of such limitations and is capable of providing real guidance and better fits with actual practice in all of the sciences" (1986b, p. 296). As he mentions, Wimsatt draws some of his concepts from Herbert Simon's research on problem-solving methods and organizational decision making, which Simon has applied to the philosophy of science as well (see Simon's articles in this volume). Whereas philosophers of science such as Karl Popper had assumed that discovery processes are not amenable to understanding, Simon's elaboration of the use of heuristics has given us a way to conceptualize the discovery process. Rather than prescribing impossible norms, Wimsatt recommends studying science as it is to understand and improve scientific problem-solving processes. Wimsatt's approach to understanding science is inherently more compatible with the humanistic values that inform the social and behavioral sciences (e.g., the social work profession's traditional value of "starting where the client is") than is the prescriptive approach of logical positivism.

Most important, because we necessarily simplify any problem to solve it, Wimsatt explores how our problem-simplifying tools, or heuristics, affect problem-solving processes. He emphasizes that we can derive considerable insight about scientific activity from the many studies of commonsense thinking patterns (Gigerenzer, 1991b; Kahneman, Slovic, & Tversky, 1982; see also the introduction to Tversky & Kahneman in Chapter 6). Those cognitive researchers have explored both how rationality can be conceptualized and the ways that people approach decision making and problem solving. Given that people inevitably use heuristics, it is irrational for a researcher to proceed as though people do not use heuristics or are omniscient and computationally omnipotent Laplacean demons (see Glossary). Further, most problem solvers work under conditions of uncertainty, with no norms for ascertaining a 'correct' answer and uncertain conditions amplifying the effects of heuristics. To illustrate, a problem solver often needs to use a heuristic to transform an "ill-structured problem" that is not amenable to solution into a problem that can be solved (Simon, 1977).

Although problem-solving heuristics are necessary and often extremely useful, the heuristics themselves necessarily create systematic bias or errors. Through bias recognition, the problem solver can become aware of the impact of the heuristics he or she is using and begin to compensate for the effects of their biases. Wimsatt says that because heuristics with the same biases "hide each others' tracks," one of the greatest challenges for any problem solver is to recognize the "footprint" of a heuristic, and to "calibrate" the heuristics so as to understand their limitations, determine when they can be safely used, and correct for their biases in problem solving.

One of the most important ideas Wimsatt advances in this paper concerns levels of organization and the environment–system boundary. In an earlier paper, Wimsatt says that the metaphor— "the aim of science is to cut Nature at its joints"—is one useful way to approach how scientific theories focus on different levels of organization:

> it implies that Nature *has* joints, or natural units of organization. If so, then explanatory ontological, systematic, and controlling aims of science all coincide at the importance of finding these 'joints,' and of describing the units in between and how they articulate. (1976a, p. 237)

Wimsatt shows how theories address different levels of organization. "[T]he theories at different levels might be thought of as sieves of different sizes, which sift out entities of the appropriate size and dynamical characteristics" (1976a, p. 237). Levels of organization can be differentiated according to scale. For example, a bacterium and a human clearly reflect different levels of organization (Figure 5–1). A single human may be viewed as a lower level of organization by comparison with a larger-scale system such as a community (Bronfenbrenner, 1979a, 1986). The human, however, may be viewed as a larger-scale system by comparison with smaller-scale variables such as the cells that make up the person's skin.

Levels of organization can be distinguished using many other variables besides scale. Wimsatt (1976a) has pointed out, for example, that some theories of the origin of the universe suggest the possibility of the creation of black holes that are only a fraction of a millimeter in size but behave like much larger entities, having a tremendously strong force field that is many, many times their size. Accordingly, the power of the force field is an alternative to size as a way to differentiate levels of organization. Understanding levels of organization illuminates another way that the researcher's theory organizes the researcher's perspective on entities in nature, which is the degree of regularity and predictability that occurs in the interactions between the entities under study (see Figure 5–1). The different wave forms shown in Figure 5–1 illustrate variances in the regulatory and predictability of interactions.

Theories can encourage researchers to focus on a system at a particular level of organization and to assume that "the system is isolated (in effect, that it has no envi-

Figure 5–1
Levels of organization: some conceivable waveforms

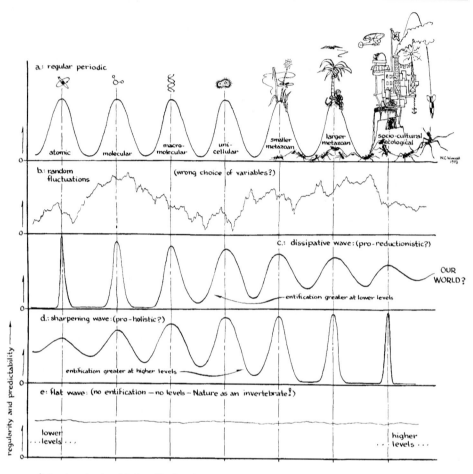

Source: From "Reductionism, Levels of Organization, and the Mind–Body Problem" by W. Wimsatt in *Consciousness and the Brain: Scientific and Philosophical Strategies* (pp. 199–267) edited by G. G. Globus, G. Maxwell, and I. Savodnik, 1976, New York: Plenum. Copyright 1976 by William Wimsatt. Adapted by permission.

ronment) or that its environment is constant in space and time" (Wimsatt, 1986b, p. 300). In fact, however, the environment–system boundary can be redrawn so that the variables under study are redefined in terms of a higher or lower level of organization. For example, one may draw the environment–system boundary around an individual teenager and explain the teenager's gang activities in terms of needs for companionship and outlets for feelings of rage. One can also redraw the environment–system boundary to include the community and view the teenager's gang activities in terms of influences in the community, such as cutbacks in positive recreational activities at the teenager's school and community center. Wimsatt shows how redrawing the environment–system boundary is one very useful way to recognize the biases set up by using any one level of explanation. You can redraw the environment–system boundary to explore various problem formulations as well as to examine the biases researchers set up in choosing the variables to study. Wimsatt terms the analytic procedure used by moving up and down levels of organization "multilevel reductionistic analysis," and he emphasizes that he is describing a form of reductionism that includes moving from a lower to a higher level of organization as well as moving from a higher to a lower level (1986b, p. 309).

KEY TERMS

Covering law model
Monadic versus relational properties

Laplacean demon
Reductionism

DISCUSSION QUESTIONS

1. Summarize the four important properties of heuristics Wimsatt describes.

2. Explain in your own words why the assumption of the "context independence" of a system under study can generate serious problems.

3. Summarize two strategies, triangulation and changing the environment–system boundary, which Wimsatt advances here as ways of recognizing and regulating reductionistic biases.

4. What is *pseudorobustness*? Can you give some examples of how pseudorobustness might occur in social and behavioral research? Can you think of any ways that these examples might break down?

5. Look at the eight types of heuristics Wimsatt describes. Find examples of each heuristic in social and behavioral theories and research procedures. Some examples follow:

   a. "Descriptive localization": Learning disabilities are often described as though they are properties caused by a child's organic defect, which can be viewed as a "monadic" or lower-level description of what may well be a "relational property." For example, others view learning disabilities as a product of the relationship between the child and factors in the learning environment (e.g., as the relationship with the teacher or cultural differences between the child and the teacher).

   b. "Meaning reductionism": Behaviorist practitioners may assume that a client's complaint of depression can be redefined nonproblematically in terms of a lower-level concept, such as the frequency of reported self-critical thoughts, whereas redefining depression as a response to a loss in a relationship (as a "disguised relational property" in Wimsatt's terms) is less "scientific" or valid.

c.   "Modeling localization": If the social workers in an agency suffer from burnout, it is common to look for the cause of the burnout in agency management rather than to consider that the problem may be related to how larger systems—such as the government's commitment to the human services—have an impact on the agency (e.g., the size of the caseloads).

d.   "Context simplification": In child welfare, a child, although removed from the parental home because of abuse, is often placed with her or his grandparents. The fact that the parents probably developed their abusive patterns because their parents mistreated them is ignored in such a placement decision, because the environment (the grandparents' family relationship patterns) may be studied less stringently than were the parents' relationship patterns.

e.   "Generalization": In research on childhood hyperactivity, failures to find organic causes for behavioral symptoms have prompted most researchers to look harder for organic causes (to improve the internal structure of the model) rather than to consider that higher level processes (e.g., family relationship patterns) have been oversimplified and should be explored.

f.   "Observation": Wimsatt gives the example that when a clinician gathers a case history, he or she may not consider family relationships if the observational procedures ignore those variables.

g.   "Control": In research on childhood hyperactivity, experimenters frequently try out various drugs on the children to see if they alter the children's symptoms. They hold the children's environment constant and so do not find out what other researchers who have changed the child's environment discover—that the children's symptoms respond dramatically to environmental changes.

h.   "Testing": Urie Bronfenbrenner's critique of the biases of laboratory-generated knowledge is an excellent example: "it can be said that much of developmental psychology, as it now exists, is the science of the strange behavior of children in strange situations with strange adults for the briefest periods of time" (1979a, p. 19).

6.   In choosing a system to study and the variables to use to describe that system, a researcher inevitably makes a decision about the level of organization from which to address that system. For example, psychoanalytically based theories traditionally have focused on intrafamily relationships and have explained juvenile delinquency in terms of the effects of family relationships on the child's ego functions. The researcher who wants to look at neighborhood influences on juvenile delinquency, and who adopts the heuristic paradigm, can see that, in focusing on how communities influence delinquent behavior, the researcher is redefining the system at a higher level of organization than when looking at intrafamilial relationship patterns. Instead of assuming that a psychoanalytically based theory continues to be the best heuristic for a problem when it is redefined at a higher level of organization, the researcher may use a heuristic from community organization theory and find that children are more likely to adopt

violent delinquent behavior when they are exposed to gang warfare, police brutality, and discriminatory educational and vocational systems. Each level of organization defines the system's variables differently and puts the system in a different context. One aspect of an individual's context is the reference groups to which the person belongs. For example, readers of this book may belong to reference groups such as teachers, students, owners of Toyotas, and aficionados of Swiss chocolate.

To get a clearer idea of the complexity inherent in defining a system and the variables to be studied, consider yourself as a system and name all of the reference groups to which you belong.*

▼ ▼ ▼ ▼ ▼ ▼ ▼ ▼ ▼ ▼ ▼ ▼

SAMPLE RESEARCH PROJECT: DEVELOPING RESIDENTIAL TREATMENT SERVICES FOR HOMELESS, MENTALLY ILL, AND SUBSTANCE-ABUSING CLIENTS

Part 4: Drawing the Environment–System Boundary

For the purposes of this study, the environment–system boundary is drawn around the staff, the consultant/researcher, and the resident in the program. The consultant/researcher is included in the system under study because he is part of the program's normal operations. There is a considerable tradition of regarding client opinions about the services they receive as suspect. Although one may disagree with the assumptions of that tradition, examining some central ideas can facilitate recognizing biases in the proposed research design. D. Campbell (1969) criticized the use of data obtained from clients for the purpose of program evaluation and regarded such data as "grateful testimonials." Following his point, because few resources are available from which this client population can choose, the clients, out of desperation, may be biased to evaluate positively any program that responds to their condition.

Some natural controls for this alternative hypothesis are available in the clients' own histories. For example, even though few alternative services are available, clients in the program under study do compare the program's services with the mental hospitals and shelters that are their other options. Furthermore, many of the clients have chosen not to participate in any program and have a long history of residing on the street.

Moreover, the assumption that client evaluations of a program will inevitably be in a flattened, testimonial form do not fit the preliminary data from the residents. For example, although in preliminary surveys the great majority of residents evalu-

---

Source: Unpublished teaching notes by W. Wimsatt. Copyright 1991, Professor William Wimsatt. Adapted by permission.

ated the services they received positively, residents also frankly expressed their mixed feelings about getting help, including negative opinions about the program. For example, when asked who would help him when he left the program, one resident wrote, "just me, and that's the way I like it, I don't want to have to depend on anyone else."

With regard to the issue of perspective that Wimsatt raises in the following selection,* this research project clearly draws on the subjective perspective, the staff members' experience of their relationship with the residents and the consultation group process, as well as the clients' subjective experience of the program. This has an important advantage. Assuming clients' opinions are unscientific sources of data for program evaluation (Kidder, 1982) rules out a crucial topic: how service providers *can* take client evaluations of services into account.

---

*Editor's Note: See also Discussion Question #6, p. 287.

Heuristics and the Study of Human Behavior

WILLIAM C. WIMSATT

Frank Richter [1986] has argued that many social scientists misunderstand the paradigm that the physical sciences provide; predictability and simple lawlike behavior are frequently as elusive (or nearly so) in the natural sciences as they are in the social sciences.[1] As the recent explosion of interest in chaotic behavior in various scientific disciplines suggests, the phenomenon of detailed unpredictability is quite common (and for quite simple nonlinear systems) throughout all of the natural sciences and, I would argue, in the biological and social sciences as well (e.g., Wimsatt 1980a). To the extent that the misleadingly named "covering law" model applies in the natural sciences, it is only because we can more frequently get away with our simple idealizations there, more simply isolate our systems (in the human sciences, most importantly from our own unintended interventions), more readily treat their relevant properties as context independent, and through it all, focus on questions and parameter ranges that yield simple equilibrium behavior. I don't want to suggest that there are no qualitative differences between the physical, biological, and social sciences—I think that Roy D'Andrade's 1986 picture is fine as a first approximation—but I do believe that many of the things touted as differences in kind are merely differences in degree.

Does this mean that we are doomed to unpredictability everywhere? Chaotic behavior does not imply total unpredictability, but only that initial uncertainties will increase in time if we demand a deterministic account of the behavior of a system. At other levels of description, chaotic behavior is quite regular in its properties (see Feigenbaum 1980 or Hofstadter 1981). The lack of total predictability raises no new epistemological problems that we did not already have with theories of decision making under uncertainty (Luce & Raiffa 1957; Kaufmann 1968). Indeed, one natural response to deterministic complexity that exceeds our capabilities of analysis is to treat the behavior as "random" (Wimsatt 1980a). Chaotic systems, for the purposes of prediction, are simply pseudo-random number generators in which, because they are real systems, rather than computer algorithms, we don't know the "seed" or initial conditions (or often the algorithm) exactly.

I wish to turn to another matter that receives little attention in this book and that seems to me to be an important new direction in the social sciences. This is the question of what we do when the complexity of the systems we are studying exceeds our powers of analysis. This too is an old problem in social science methodology, but it does not indicate a cause for despair, since exactly the same thing has happened frequently in the natural and biological sciences. Roughly, the therapy is the same in both cases: intro-

Source: "Heuristics and the Study of Human Behavior" by W. Wimsatt in *Metatheory in Social Science* (pp. 293–314) edited by D. W. Fiske & R. A. Shweder, 1986, Chicago: University of Chicago Press. Copyright 1986 by the University of Chicago. Reprinted by permission.

duce idealizations, approximations, or other devices that, perhaps artificially, reduce the complexity of the problem. Here, however, we needn't be looking only to the natural sciences for guidance, for the best developed theory of such devices has arisen in psychology and the social sciences. I have in mind the work of Simon, Lenat, Tversky and Kahneman, and others on problem-solving heuristics. (While it might be argued that this is a part of cognitive psychology or artificial intelligence, it is worth noting that Simon's interest in heuristics springs from his "satisficing" theory of decision making, which in turn was motivated jointly by his interest in decision making, in administrative organizations [1957a, and his dissatisfaction with rational decision theory [1955, 1981].)

It is important to note that to regard a system as using heuristics is to regard it as a kind of engineering system. This is implicit in Simon's characterization of the scope of "the sciences of the artificial" (1981)—artificial things are products of design processes or, more generally, of selection processes. In this, I am also following Campbell, who has argued the same point from a somewhat different perspective (see, for example, Campbell 1974). A similar view has been advocated by Dennett (1979) in his characterization of the "design stance" as a perspective for analyzing functionally organized systems. To the extent that heuristics are important in the analysis of our reasoning processes and action or behavior, the boundary between D'Andrade's second and third perspectives (or Dennett's analogous ones) is at least blurred; I think it becomes a matter of degree. I will return to this after I say something more about the nature of heuristics.

HEURISTICS

"Heuristic" has become one of the most widely used terms in artificial intelligence and cognitive psychology and, as with other such terms, shows wide variance in its use. To my knowledge, it was introduced in its present context by Herbert Simon, who borrowed it from the mathematician, George Polya, who used it to describe "rules of thumb" used in solving mathematical problems. For a recent rich and constructive discussion of the nature of heuristics in artificial intelligence work, see Lenat 1982. As I understand them, heuristic procedures, or heuristics, have four important properties that between them explain a number of characteristics of their use:

1. By comparison with truth-preserving algorithms or with other procedures for which they might be substituted, heuristics make no guarantees (or if they are substituted for another procedure, weaker guarantees) that they will produce a solution or the correct solution to a problem. A truth-preserving algorithm correctly applied to true premises must produce a correct conclusion. But one may correctly apply a heuristic to correct input information without getting a correct output.

2. By comparison with the procedures for which they may be substituted, heuristics are very "cost-effective" in terms of demands on memory, computation, or other resources in limited supply (this of course is why they are used).

3. The errors produced by using a heuristic are not random but systematically biased. By this, I mean two things. First, the heuristic will tend to break down in certain classes of cases and not in others, but not at random. Indeed, with an understanding of how the heuristic works, it should be possible to predict the conditions under which it will fail. Second, where it is meaningful to speak of a direction of error, heuristics will tend to cause errors in a certain direction, which is again a function of the heuristic and of the kinds of problems to which it is applied.

4. The application of a heuristic to a problem yields a transformation of the problem into a non-equivalent but intuitively related problem. Most important this means that answers to the transformed problem may not be answers to the original problem. (This property of heuristics was pointed out to me by Robert McCauley, see McCauley, in press).

Traditional philosophy of science is a philosophy of deductive structures and algorithms for computationally omnipotent computers—LaPlacean demons for which computation has a negligible cost. Theories are assumed to have an axiomatic structure, and they are assumed to be closed under entailment; that is, anything that follows from a set of axioms is a part of that theory. Thus, for example, discussions of reductionism are full of talk of in-principle analyzability or in-principle deducibility, where the force of the in-principle claim is something like, "If we knew a total description of the system at the lower level and all of the lower-level laws, a sufficiently complex computer could generate the analysis of all of the upper-level terms and laws and predict any upper-level phenomenon." Of course, we don't have such a complete lower-level description of higher-level systems in any science, we are not even sure that we have all of the relevant lower-level laws, and we have not yet succeeded in producing any such apocalyptic derivations of the total behavior of any higher-level systems—but these are supposed to be merely "technical" difficulties.

I have criticized this unattainable picture of reductive explanation elsewhere (Wimsatt 1976a, 1976b), and I have suggested an alternative account that dovetails naturally with the "heuristic" picture. But the original picture persists widely in philosophical analyses and in "rationalistic" theories in the social sciences, particularly in decision theory, linguistics, and other areas where algorithmic models are found. Its persistence is aided by regarding such theories as "normative"—as specifying what is the optimal behavior, usually under impossibly idealized circumstances (when we have no computational limitations and make no errors in our calculations). The search for larger computers, which can calculate faster, and for various technical improvements to increase reliability (such as doing computations in parallel and cross-checking regularly) shows that our best equipment falls short of this ideal. The gap is far larger if we note that all of our models of phenomena involve simplifications and approximations done to increase analytical tractability, so that the problems we are solving are already less complex than the real world they are designed to mimic.

We are not LaPlacean demons, and any image of science that tells us how to behave as if we were still fails to give useful guidance for real scientists in the real world. In fact it may suggest viewpoints and methods that are less than optimal for the dinky and error-prone equipment we possess. A more realistic model of the scientist as problem-solver and decision-maker includes the existence of such limitations and is capable of providing real guidance and better fits with actual practice in all of the sciences. In this model, the scientist must consider the size of computations, the cost of data collection, and must regard both processes as "noisy" or error-prone. A central feature of it is the use of "cost-effective" heuristic procedures for collecting data, simplifying problems, and generating solutions.

Although a growing number of philosophers and cognitive psychologists have become interested in heuristics, the two groups have focused on different properties of heuristics. Philosophers for the most part have focused on their computational efficiency (property 2 above) and argued the heuristics play an important role in scientific inference and discovery. Note that essentially all "inductive" and discovery procedures in science are heuristic principles, failing as algorithms in part because they do not represent logically valid argument forms. Indeed, psychologists have focused on this fact and gloried in the "irrationality" of our everyday heuristics, by which they mean that we will in the appropriate circumstances draw erroneous conclusions using them (see, e.g., Tversky & Kahneman 1974; Nisbett & Ross 1980; Shweder 1977).

Both of these properties need to be examined together. It is not irrational to use a procedure that may under some circumstances lead you into error if you take pains to avoid those circumstances and if using it saves you a great deal of effort. All instruments in the natural, biological, and social sciences are designed for use in certain contexts and can produce biased or worthless results if they are used in contexts that may fail to meet the conditions for which they were designed. A fair amount of effort in these sciences is devoted to determining the conditions under which instruments can be used without bias or to "calibrating" them to determine their biases so that they can be corrected for. This is one of the major activities of statistical methodologists—either constructing new instruments or calibrating or criticizing the use of existing ones.

Campbell's notion of a "vicarious selector" (1974) is employed widely by him to explain and characterize a hierarchy of selection processes in perception, learning, and cultural evolution. It follows from his characterization of vicarious selectors that they are heuristic procedures (see Wimsatt 1981a, p. 155). I believe that Campbell's conception of a hierarchy of selection processes acting to produce structures' "fit," whether physical or ideational, with their relevant environments is the most productive form for functionalist theories in the social sciences. It lacks their panfunctionalist tenor and also has a much closer connection with evolutionary ideas in the biological sciences, which have recently begun to move toward productive models for the microevolution of culture (see Boyd & Richerson 1985).

Biological adaptations (and in Campbell's scheme, social and psychological ones as well) all meet the defining characteristics of heuristic procedures. First, it is a commonplace among evolutionary biologists that adaptations, even when functioning properly, do not guarantee survival and production of offspring. Second, they are nevertheless cost-effective ways of contributing to this end. Third, any adaptation has systematically specifiable conditions under which its employment will actually decrease the fitness of the organism. These conditions are, of course, seldom found in the "normal" environments of the organism, or the adaptation would be maladaptive and selected against. Fourth, these adaptations serve to transform a complex computational problem about the environment into a simpler problem, the answer to which is usually a reliable guide to the answer to the complex problem. Thus, shorter day length is a good predictor of oncoming winter and is used by a variety of plants and animals to initiate appropriate seasonal changes in morphology and behavior—even though heavy cloud cover or artificial conditions in the laboratory can "fool" this adaptation. Similarly, rapid decreases in general illumination in the frog's visual field are taken to indicate the approach of a predator. Though the frog may be fooled frequently by this adaptation (e.g., cows are not predators but may be frequent parts of the frog's environment), the cost of being wrong is sufficiently great that this is a "cost-effective" solution.

The third property, that the errors produced in using a heuristic are systematic, is widely exploited in the analysis of organic adaptations. It is a truism of functional inference that studying how a system breaks down (and the conditions under which it does) is a powerful tool for determining how it functions normally and the conditions under which it was designed to function. This fact can also be used systematically in the study of our reasoning processes. First, from an analysis of the heuristic, we can determine the conditions under which (and how) it will break down, thus "calibrating" the heuristic. This, as already pointed out, is the task of the methodologist, but it should be applied to our heuristic reasoning processes no less than to the study of our machines or to organic adaptations. But a more interesting insight, first employed by Tversky and Kahneman (1974), is that the widespread occurrence of systematic errors is to be recognized as the "footprint" of a heuristic procedure or procedures. Different heuristics leave characteristically different footprints, so an analysis of the biases can lead to plausible inferences about the character of the reasoning processes that produced them. Usually, we need some knowledge of these reasoning

processes in order to pare down the field of appropriate candidates, but this can be done. For example, I conducted a study of the systematic biases in mathematical models of group selection, a heated controversy in evolutionary biology, and was able to trace the origin of these biases to heuristics for problem simplification characteristic of reductionistic problem-solving strategies. I will discuss this in the next section since reductionistic problem-solving methods are widely used and just as widely criticized in the social sciences (more details of this specific case can be found in Wimsatt 1980b, 1981a).

REDUCTIONIST RESEARCH STRATEGIES AND THEIR BIASES

If reductionistic problem-solving heuristics have a generic bias, it is to ignore, oversimplify, or otherwise underestimate the importance of the context of the system under study. A number of writers (including several in this volume) have complained about the frequency with which properties of the systems they study are assumed to be independent of context, when in fact they are disguised relational properties. Context dependence is a frequent problem of translation for linguists. I have argued that context dependence of biological fitness components at a lower level is a necessary (but not sufficient) condition of the existence of higher-level units of selection (Wimsatt 1980b, 1981b). If reductionistic problem-solving heuristics lead to illegitimate assumptions of context independence, there is a prima facie case for believing that biases of reductionistic problem-solving strategies are extremely pervasive in the social sciences.

How these biases arise can be easily seen from a general characterization of the problem-solving context of a reductionistic problem-solver. First, assume that a scientist starts by choosing, designating, or constructing a system for analysis. This immediately partitions his world of study into that system and its environment (see Star [1983a] for relevant simplification processes here; Griesemer's concept [1983] of the "conceptual map" as fixing the environment in which problem solving takes place is relevant at this stage of analysis.) Second, we must make Simon's "assumption of bounded rationality" that any real-world system is too complex to study in all of its complexity, so we must make simplifications—through selection of properties or objects for study, simplified assumptions about relationships between these properties or objects, assumptions about what variables must be controlled or randomized, and the like. Third, I will assume a very general characterization of what it is to be a reductionist; that is, a reductionist is interested in understanding the character, properties, and behavior of the studied system in terms of the properties of its parts and their interrelations and interactions. (This is a sufficiently inclusive description that it probably captures any analytic methods in general, even those of many who would not call themselves reductionists. It should in any case be acceptable to any reductionist.) This means that the reductionist is primarily interested in the entities and relations internal to the system of study. But this fact, together with the assumption of bounded rationality, has an interesting consequence. While simplifications will in general have to be made everywhere, the focus of the reductionist will lead him to order his list of "economic" priorities so as to simplify first and more severely in his description, observation, control, modeling, and analysis of the environment than in the system he is studying.

Any reductionist who began with the assumption that his system was totally homogeneous in structure and constant through time would have nothing to study: there would be no parts or relations between them. But commonly found in simple models of systems (and even in not-so-simple ones) is the assumption that the system is isolated (in effect, that it has no environment) or that its environment is constant in space and time. This asymmetry in simplifications is indicative of the kinds of biases induced by using reductionistic problem-solving strategies.

Below I outline reductionistic problem-solving strategies. Each one is used in some circumstances because its adoption transforms the initial problem into one that is easier to analyze and to solve. Each of them can be seen as an application of the general schema for making simplifications to a specific scientific activity, whether conceptualizing the system for study and analysis, building or modifying models of its behavior, observing its behavior, designing controlled experiments (or looking for natural data sets that meet desired control conditions), or testing the models. This partial list should suggest a variety of relevant cases in various disciplines. I have somewhat arbitrarily divided the heuristics into heuristics of conceptualization, model building and theory construction, and observation and experimental design, though these activities are seldom as separable as this division might suggest.

Heuristics of Conceptualization

1. *Descriptive localization.* Describe a relational property as if it were monadic or a lower-order relational property. Note that if a property is a function of system properties and environment properties, keeping the environment constant will make the property look as if it is a function only of system properties. Thus, for example, fitness is a relational property between organism and environment. Keeping the environment constant makes it look as if fitness can be treated as a monadic property of organisms. Many context dependencies are hidden in this fashion.

2. *Meaning reductionism.* Assume that new redescriptions of a property at a lower level or an account of that property in terms of the intrasystemic mechanisms that produce it can result in meaning changes (through redefinition) of scientific terms, whereas higher-level redescriptions (or an account of the property in terms of intersystemic mechanisms) cannot. Result: Since philosophers regard themselves as concerned with meaning relations, they are inclined to a reductionistic bias. Note that this is not a bias when it is applied to properties that are "correctly" regarded as monadic at the level of analysis in question, that is, that are context independent for wide ranges of conditions like those normally studied. But if the property in question is a disguised relational property or a functional property (both of which impose conditions on properties or entities outside of the system under study), this assumption can lead to serious mistakes.

Heuristics of Model Building and Theory Construction

3. *Modeling localization.* Look for an intrasystemic mechanism rather than an intersystemic one to explain a systematic property, or if both are available, regard the former as "more fundamental." As derivative corollaries, structural properties are regarded as more important than functional ones, and mechanisms as more important than context (see, e.g., discussions of the assumed stability of personality traits in Shweder 1979a, 1979b, 1980a).

4. *Context simplification.* In reductionistic model building simplify the description of the environment before simplifying the description of the system. This

strategy often legislates higher-level systems out of existence or leaves no way of describing intersystemic phenomena appropriately. This is, in effect, a redescription of the account given above of the origin of reductionistic biases against the importance of context but even at this general level of description has been exceedingly important in some areas. This is perhaps the most striking bias in mathematical models of group selection (see Wimsatt 1980b).

5. *Generalization.* When setting out to improve a simple model of the behavior of a system in its environment, focus on generalizing or elaborating the internal structure of the system at the cost of ignoring generalizations or elaborations of external structure. Because a number of simplifications will have been made both internal and external to the system, there will always be room for improving its internal description and analysis. In effect, this strategy involves the following working maxim: If a model fails to work or predict adequately, it must be because of oversimplifications in the description of internal structure, not because of oversimplified descriptions of external structure (see Star 1983a, 1983b for a sociological perspective on this).

Heuristics of Observation and Experimental Design

6. *Observation.* The reductionist will tend not to model environmental variables and will thus fail to record data necessary to detect interactional or larger-scale patterns. Note that this can apply on a temporal as well as on a spatial scale. Thus one who studies patients without having taken appropriate case histories may be committing this error, as well as one who does not record appropriate contextual variables of the experiment.

7. *Control.* The reductionist in experimental design will construct experimental arrangements so as to keep environmental variables constant (or will often merely assume that they are constant!). He then tends to miss dependencies of system variables on them. This heuristic is particularly interesting, since it follows straightforwardly from an application of Mill's canon—"Vary the factors one at a time, keeping all others constant"—to the context of reductionistic problem solving. If the reductionist is interested in determining causal relations among intrasystemic vari-

ables, he will try to vary the intrasystemic variables one at a time, keeping all of the other intra- and extrasystemic variables constant. As he studies different intrasystemic variables, he will be keeping the other intrasystemic variables constant in different combinations and will thus tease out the various intrasystemic causal relations. But the extrasystemic variables will also be kept constant in each of these experiments, so he will never have done an experiment appropriately designed to determine effects of any extrasystemic variables on system properties. One can imagine a reductionist replying to the claim of the causal importance of some extrasystemic variable "But we have been studying these systems for years, and no one has ever reported any effect of that variable!" But of course not—it has always been kept constant! This is another instance of the old maxim that there are no "universal" control setups. What one must control is a function of what relationships one is studying.

8. *Testing.* Make sure that a theory works out locally (or in the laboratory) rather than testing it in appropriate natural environments or doing appropriate robustness analyses to suggest what are important environmental variables and what are relevant ranges of these parameters for study. (This is such a frequent criticism of experimental studies that I won't even attempt to illustrate or document it. I am sure that you can provide your own favorite examples.)

AN EXAMPLE OF REDUCTIONISTIC BIASES: MODELS OF GROUP SELECTION

I have studied in detail the use of these heuristics in model building in population biology. It may help to illustrate how they operate if I provide a partial description of one case of their operation in the development of models of group selection in evolutionary biology. In recent evolutionary biology, group selection has been the subject of widespread attack and general suspicion. Most of the major theorists have argued against its efficacy. A number of mathematical models attempting to assess the relative efficacy of individual and group selection have been constructed, and virtually all of them seem to support this skepticism: it appears that group selection could be significant only rarely and under very special conditions on the relevant parameter values.

Wade undertook an experimental test of the relative efficacy of individual and group selection—acting in concert or opposition—in laboratory populations of the flour beetle, *Tribolium*. This work produced surprising results. Group selection was a significant force in these experiments, capable of overwhelming individual selection in the opposite direction for a wide range of parameter values. The conflict between his findings and the then known mathematical models of the process led him to a closer analysis of these models (Wade 1978).

The models surveyed made a variety of simplifying assumptions. Although most of them were different, Wade found that five of the assumptions were widely held in common. (Of the twelve models surveyed, each made at least three of them, and five of the models made all five assumptions.) Crucial for present purposes, all of the assumptions were biologically unrealistic and incorrect, and each independently had a strong negative effect on the possibility or efficacy of group selection. Furthermore, these assumptions were made by friends and foes of group selection alike, so one could not argue they were making those assumptions that would buttress their favorite conclusions. Why, then, did they all make assumptions strongly inimical to group selection? Such a coincidence cries out for explanation: We have found a systematic bias suggesting the use of problem-solving heuristics.

These assumptions are analyzed more fully elsewhere (Wade 1978; Wimsatt 1980b), and I will discuss only one of them here. It was first introduced by Richard Levins, an advocate of group selection, and is known as the "migrant pool" assumption. This is the assumption that all of the migrants from any groups (the "offspring" of these groups) go into a common pool from which new groups are drawn at random. It won ready acceptance for two reasons. First of all, it provided substantial analytic simplifications (the need to keep track only of gene frequencies in a single migrant population, rather than recording the independent gene frequencies of the migrants from each parent group). Second, it was equivalent to a time-honored simplifying assumption of population genetics, "panmixia," the assumption that all members of a population have an equal probability of mating with any one member.

Unfortunately, when the process of reproduction is examined at the group level (rather than the individual level at which most theorists conceptualize the problem), this assumption is seen to be equivalent to the assumption of a particularly strong form of "blending inheritance," which (as R. A. Fisher pointed out in 1931 at the individual level) results in a rapid loss of variance, leaving evolution with little variation to act upon. The striking thing is that while all population geneticists know that "blending inheritance" is a thing to avoid (it is avoided at the individual level by the processes of Mendelian segregation), they were unable to recognize that they had made assumptions equivalent to introducing it at the group level in their models of group selection. To put the point in another way, to assume panmixia is the same as assuming that with respect to probability of mating, there are no groups! It is thus not surprising that reductionists should have found little effect of group selection in their models.

A particularly crucial factor in explaining the inability to see the consequences of this assumption is what I have called "perceptual focus" (Wimsatt 1980b, 248–49). If groups are thought of as merely "collections of individuals," as they are by most of these people—a hypothesis that has since been confirmed by interviews with some of the protagonists—then the description of processes is referred to the individual level, and one cannot see that assumptions that appear benign at that level may be dangerous oversimplifications when viewed at a higher level. This phenomenon appears to explain, not only the ready acceptance of the "migrant pool" assumption, but also some of the other assumptions Wade discusses. It also suggests a technique for correcting the systematic biases of the reductionistic problem-solving strategies that I will discuss further on.

HEURISTICS CAN HIDE THEIR TRACKS

One of the remarkable things about the case just discussed is that the biases in these models had not been discovered—in spite of the fact that a variety of models of the processes of group selection had been investigated. One would hope that this "sampling from a space of possible models" (Levins 1968) would be an unbiased sampling and would turn up models with different conclusions if the conclusions were artifacts of the simplifying assumptions that were made (see Wimsatt 1981a). But in this case, it clearly was a biased sample. The question is, Why?

The answer resides in the fact that all of the modelers were using a variety of reductionistic modeling strategies and assumptions. While they approached their models in somewhat different ways, this commonality of generic approach constrained the results. Each of the heuristics in the list of reductionistic modeling strategies independently biases the models against the inclusion or proper consideration of environmental variables. If one then cross-checks these models as a way of validating the results, one will get an apparent robustness of the conclusions, but a spurious one, a case of pseudorobustness. It is tempting to suggest that much of the appearance of success (I do not want to deny that there have been real successes as well) of reductionistic methodologies comes from this phenomenon—that different reductionistic methods hide their mutual inadequacies by covering each others' tracks.

Another important means through which methodologies (regarded as related bundles of heuristics and practices) can "hide their tracks" (and this applies not just to reductionistic methodologies) is through the fourth property of heuristics—that use of a heuristic causes a redefinition or transformation of the problem to which it is applied. If a transformation yields an analytically tractable, and therefore successful, problem, there will be a tendency to act as if the new problem (to which there is now a solution) captures the core issues of the old problem and thus to argue that the old problem is "really" solved by the solution to the new problem. With one step further, the new problem may be taken as defining the proper formulation of the original, and thus it has replaced the old in a manner rendered largely invisible since it is now regarded as a "clarification of the old problem" that preserves the spirit of the research tradition while removing "confusions" that had earlier prevented solution of the problem. This is a "hidden revolution," a more modest paradigm shift masquerading as none at all. The philosopher Ludwig Wittgenstein (1960) has argued that this kind of phenomenon characterizes rule-following behavior and the use of concepts in general. We assimilate new kinds of application of a rule to its original domain of interpretation and thus have the anomalous phenomenon that before it is applied to the new situation, it looks as if we have a real choice as to whether to apply the rule or not, but after the fact, it appears as if we had no other choice!

This kind of invisible paradigm shift has many of the properties Kuhn (1970) ascribes to paradigm shifts in general, except for those connected with the explicit recognition of a revolutionary change. It is still true that the new paradigm carries with it valuational judgments and defines explanatory standards; but instead of arguing that this represents a rejection of the old paradigm, the reductionist will argue that this is the proper interpretation of the old problems and theory, that this was "contained in the old view all along." When this kind of paradigm shift is accompanied by the acceptance of a new formal model, it will result in a bias of over-simplification—often accompanied by the reification of the abstract system to define a kind of (Weberian?) ideal type, which is talked about as if it existed in the real world. Thus thermodynamicists talk about "ideal gases" or "van der Waal's gases," denoting gases whose behavior fits the ideal gas law and van der Waal's equation of state respectively. Biologists, similarly, talk about "Mendelian genes," "Mendelizing traits," "Lotka-Volterra communities," and "panmictic populations," in each case indicating a supposed conformity of a real-world system with the abstract conditions of the model.

While one may decry this kind of reification, the tendency to do it indicates a real and often ignored function of theoretical models. Although we sometimes set out to test our models, far more often we use them as patterns to organize phenomena and to classify results as fitting or not fitting the model. Using the model as a pattern-matching template in this way enormously simplifies the task of finding order in the data, but it also introduces a kind of inertia (or as Tversky and Kahneman would say, an "anchoring" bias), which opposes change in the system. When the results don't fit, we do not throw away the model but instead redescribe the system: the population is *not* panmictic, the gene is *not* Mendelian, the community *not* Lotka-Volterra. The only problem with this activity is that if such pattern matching is mistaken for genuine testing, it can lead advocates of the model to believe that the model has been confirmed, and critics to accuse the advocate of ad hoc-ery and of converting the model into a "meaningless schema" or "covert tautology." The difference between this kind of activity and a real test of the model is that in pattern matching, there often is no attempt to determine the values of the parameters of the model independently. Values are chosen so that the model fits the data, producing a kind of sophisticated curve fitting, rather than a legitimate test of the model. (See Tribe's excellent discussion [1972] of the misuse of the assumptions of rational decision theory in attempts to make real-world decisions.)

A parallel kind of thing can happen when the paradigm is an experimental system rather than a theoretical model. If an experimental system is highly successful, it can become a normative paradigm for how a class of studies should be pursued. "Drosophila genetics" and "Tribolium ecology" mark off, not only model organisms, but sets of procedures for studying them and preferred questions for consideration that were extended as paradigms for studying other organisms in other situations because they represented ideal conceptions of how to study genetics and ecology respectively. When these conceptions are attacked, they elicit spirited defenses of the general methodological approach (see, e.g., Mertz & MacCauley 1980). The bias introduced here is one of overgeneralization—whether of the limited model or of the experimental protocol and design or of the questions asked.

Both of these kinds of promotion of a theoretical or experimental model to a paradigm can reinforce the biases of the other problem-solving techniques by hiding the need to reconceptualize the system or the formulation of the problem of analyzing it. They can defer for a long time the noticing or analyzing of questions that were far more obvious at the start of this line of investigation. This phenomenon—the increasing entrenchment of a theoretical or experimental paradigm—in part serves to explain why disciples of an approach are often far less flexible and far less methodologically conscious than the originators of that approach. I have attempted to model and to explore the consequences of this kind of entrenchment in a variety of contexts, in biological evolution and development, cognitive development, and in models of scientific and cultural change (see Glassman & Wimsatt 1984; Wimsatt 1984, 1985).

TWO STRATEGIES FOR CORRECTING REDUCTIONISTIC BIASES

I know of two general strategies for correcting for the artifacts and biases of problem-solving heuristics. The first is truly general but is subject to specific problems when applied to reductionistic problem solving. The second can be regarded as a specific application of the general approach to reductionistic problem solving, with an eye to addressing the special problems of a reductionistic approach.

The general approach is what Campbell has called "triangulation," which Campbell and Fiske have incorporated in the now classic "multitrait-multimethod" matrix (1959). I have discussed the variety of functions and applications of this method, which I call

"robustness analysis," in a general review of the topic (Wimsatt 1981a). By using a variety of different models, approaches, means of detection, or of derivation and comparing the results, we can hope to detect and correct for the biases, special assumptions, and artifacts of any one approach.

But we have already seen that this approach does not guarantee success. It too is a heuristic procedure. The models of group selection display an ingenious variety of assumptions and approaches, but they all share biasing assumptions in common, assumptions whose biasing effects were not apparent before Wade's review (1978). How can we prevent our array of models and approaches from being a biased sample? To this question, there is no general answer, but there is an answer derived from the character of the biases in this specific case. Recall that the effect of each reductionistic bias is to ignore or to underestimate the effects of variables in the environment. But is this attached unalterably to the variables in question? No—it occurs merely because of where they are located. This bias would be removed for anything that could be brought within the system, and this can be accomplished merely by changing the boundaries of the system being investigated. Thus the strategy for eliminating biases in the description and analysis of groups as collections of individuals is to build models in which the groups are treated as individuals in a larger system in which they are parts and in which we focus on modeling intergroup relations. (This strategy is deliberately exploited in Wimsatt 1981b in the development of models of group inheritance.) The biases of the reductionistic heuristics will still apply, but because the system boundaries have changed, they will have different effects. The comparison of intragroup with intergroup models is the right comparison for testing the robustness or artifactuality of lower-level reductionistic assumptions. A comparable strategy should be equally appropriate for analogous problems in the social sciences.

Similarly, going down a level is the right medicine for testing more holistic models, which may ignore microlevel details. Geneticists regularly (and rightly) complain when higher-level optimization models predict optimal states that may not be genetically possible or that may take some time to attain so that the "equilibrium state" cannot be assumed (see, e.g., the last chapter of Oster & Wilson 1979 for a detailed critique of optimization modeling in population biology). I have called this approach "multilevel reductionistic analysis"

(Wimsatt 1980b), though it is misleading to regard it as reductionistic when the move is from a lower to a higher level. It is reductionistic only in that the approach uses reductionistic problem-solving techniques at any given level. It is not reductionistic in the suggestion that one should go to a higher level of analysis to correct for the biases induced at a lower level.

THE IMPORTANCE OF HEURISTICS IN THE STUDY OF HUMAN BEHAVIOR

I have argued that the study of our heuristics, of the nature of our real reasoning processes, their "cost-effective" advantages, and their systematic biases should be a major topic on the agenda for the human sciences. Let me summarize the reasons why I think this is important. It is important first of all because these heuristics of reasoning are part of our equipment, and as with any equipment, they must be calibrated and used as tools for evaluating hypotheses and experimental and observational studies. This has already been done, for example, in the original investigation of Tversky and Kahneman (1974), as well as their more recent work (Kahneman, Slovic & Tversky 1982; see also Mynatt, Doherty & Tweney 1977; Tweney, Doherty & Mynatt 1981; Shweder 1977, 1979a, 1979b, 1980; and Wimsatt 1980b).

Second, as part of our equipment, these heuristics are part of our subject matter, one of our objects of study. This is true of us, not only as individual problem solvers, but also as social beings. I should at this point confess that I have fallen prey to my own reductionistic biases with my limited focus on the processes of individuals. We should focus also on the heuristics of group processes and upon the biases of groups on the social processes of science. There are, for example, group identification processes that suppress intragroup disagreement, processes of competition that exacerbate disagreements between groups and restrict flow of information and recruits between them, disciplinary and subject-matter biases that lead us to overestimate the importance of and to overextend the subject matter and theories that we know well and to take insufficient account of those we do not. I have formulated these as processes in the sociology of science, but they obviously apply more broadly to other spheres of human action. We need to understand these biases, both for their own sake and also to learn how to correct for their effects.

The new movements in sociology of science (e.g., Latour & Woolgar 1979) are making useful progress in this direction, but from a determinedly "externalist" perspective. Campbell and I agree strongly that a more appropriate approach would be to try to integrate internalist and externalist perspectives. Two recent studies that have taken important and productive steps in this direction are those of Star (1983a, 1983b) and Griesemer (1983). Star focuses on the development of the localizationist perspective in neurophysiology from 1870 through 1906 and has important new analyses of the individual and social processes for handling anomalies and other processes used for legitimizing data and methodological approaches (Star & Gerson, 1983a, 1983b). Griesemer focuses on the recent macroevolution controversy in evolutionary biology and develops tools for analyzing "conceptual maps" (a scientist's models of the relationship between subject areas in his domain and the resultant structure of the problem to be solved) and for tracking the changes in these maps in the conceptual life history of individual scientists or in the diffusion of ideas and research problems from one research group to another.

Third, we need to take stock of and to incorporate an understanding of our reasoning heuristics and their biases into our accounts of human action. These act as constraints on our decision processes, and can lead to a variety of unintended suboptimal consequences, as is documented in the theory and case studies of Janis and Mann (1977). On the positive side, things of which we cannot take account are things we can afford to ignore in an explanatory theory of human behavior. It is a truism that it is not the way the world is but how we conceive of and conceptualize it that determines our actions. If we do conceive it in various oversimplified ways, this can lead us into various sorts of error, but if these ways are indeed simpler than the way the world is, our explanatory tasks should be correspondingly simpler as well. We must be careful to correct for these biases in studying human action, but at the same time we must expect to find them in our accounts of it.

For these reasons, I do not see D'Andrade's third world of meanings and intentions as being quite so different from the engineering and functional systems studied in the biological sciences as he supposes. If I am right in believing that meanings, intentions, plans, strategies, decisions, beliefs, and the like are basically engineered structures, then we should expect them to have the same mix of strengths and weaknesses as any of our artifacts and to be best studied with tools that have at least a family resemblance to the conceptual tools of the other engineering disciplines. Less predictable they may be, but complex machines have always been less predictable than simpler machines—and our cognitive and social worlds are nothing if not complex.

If this sounds like facile reductionism, it is not: if our cognitive structures share design principles with evolutionary and engineering artifacts, this does not (by itself) make them biological or hardware entities. It rather reflects principles of optimal or "satisficing" design common to all three areas. I fully expect that elucidation of some of our social and cognitive heuristics—as studied by social scientists—will provide insights that will be useful in these other disciplines, just as work in them has provided (for better or worse) metaphors and paradigms for social scientists. Before the rise of Darwinism, genetics, and molecular biology gave biology distinctive well-established theories, biologists borrowed freely from psychology and theories of society, and they are now doing so again. Thus evolutionary biologists have recently adopted the theory of games and claim that much more is to be mined for application to biological problems from economics and learning theory (Maynard-Smith 1983), and at least two computer scientists argue that large parallel-processing computers should be developed with an architecture modeled on the structure of the scientific research community (Kornfeld & Hewitt 1981). I suspect that much more is soon to follow.

Note

1. I would like to thank Donald Fiske, Jim Griesemer, and Leigh Star for very useful comments on an earlier draft of this paper. This work was supported by the Systems Development Foundation, Grant no. 6357.

Problem Formulation and the Value of Emancipation: Introduction to "On the Possibility of Social Scientific Knowledge and the Limits of Naturalism"

Roy Bhaskar is a leading contemporary philosopher whose ideas have been applied in fields ranging from intellectual history (e.g., I. Shapiro, 1982) to education (Corson, 1991) to psychology (Manicas & Secord, later in this chapter). His books (1975, 1989a, 1989b, 1991) advance a new philosophy of science—a reformulation of scientific realism he terms *transcendental realism*, which includes a new application of Marxist principles and aims to "illuminate and empower the project of human self-emancipation" (1989b, p. vii). His philosophy of science is especially relevant for social and behavioral researchers who have adopted the values of empowerment and advocacy. Bhaskar has focused on the theory of reality (ontology) that undergirds the philosophy of the natural and social and behavioral sciences. He has criticized many aspects of positivism. One of Bhaskar's most important critiques is that positivism defines being in terms of knowing. By unjustifiably constraining the ways of knowing (or epistemological assumptions) that researchers can use, positivism also constrains the "reals" (the objects of study defined by the researcher's ontological assumptions) that can be studied scientifically.

A question Bhaskar addresses in the following selection is "To what extent can society be studied in the same way as nature?" (1989b, p. 66)* He summarizes how this question has been considered. The positivist tradition has advanced scientism, "which denies that there are any important differences in the methods appropriate to studying societies and nature" (1989b, p. 67). The hermeneutical tradition (derived from *Verstehen* theory, see also Scriven's selection) took the position that there were inalienable differences between the natural sciences and the social and behavioral sciences and emphasized the role of empathy. Bhaskar disagrees with that basis for a distinction between the human and the natural sciences because it rests on the positivist misconception that the natural sciences formulate general laws using observations that nonproblematically mirror reality.

Social and behavioral sciences are unique, according to Bhaskar, in part because they do not exist independently but instead are a part of what they study: "social science is affected or conditioned by developments in, as it patently cannot exist independently of, the rest of society" (1989b, p. 84). Bhaskar defines naturalism as "the thesis that there is (or can be) an essential unity of method between the natural and the social sciences" (1989b, p. 67). Whereas positivist approaches to social and behavioral research have focused on method, Bhaskar regards such a focus as misleading. He points out the importance of articulating assumptions about what is (ontology). He emphasizes that "it is the nature of the object that determines the form of its science" (1989b, p. 67). Further, "without some prior specification of an object of inquiry, any discourse on method is bound to be more or less arbitrary" (1989b, p. 69). Accordingly, the central differences between social and behavioral

---

*Editor's Note: The citations used here refer to pages of the original article. You can find the material quoted from this article in the reprint that follows this introduction.

science and natural science occur because the social and behavioral sciences study humans (rather than, e.g., stars or fossils). One implication of Bhaskar's ideas is that there is no reason why the social and behavioral sciences should aim to emulate physics, because the objects of study are so different. Bhaskar advances a "qualified anti-positivist naturalism," based on a realist view of science in which it is

> possible to give an account of science under which the proper and more or less specific methods of both the natural and social sciences can fall. But it does not deny that there are important differences in these methods, grounded in the real differences that exist in their subject matters. (1989b, p. 67)

In describing how scientists define the objects of scientific knowledge, Bhaskar points out that science uses "two criteria for the ascription of reality to a posited object: a perceptual and a causal one" (1989b, p. 69). In other words, we make onto-logical assumptions about the existence of some objects based on sense perception. An example of such an object is the one you are looking at—this book. We make ontological assumptions about the existence of other objects of knowledge based on perceiving their effects. Examples of such causal ontological assumptions are the con-cepts that describe gravity, electricity, and, as Bhaskar explains, societies or cultures. In the new psychology, intrapsychic humanism, the motives that regulate an individ-ual's self-esteem are defined as a causal ontology (Pieper & Pieper, 1990).

Bhaskar makes another distinction between different objects of scientific knowledge. He shows that objects such as the stars the astronomer studies or the rabbits a biologist studies "exist and act independently of" scientific knowledge (1989b, p. 68). Another object of knowledge is knowledge itself, which is mind-independent in the sense that, for example, the writings of the logical positivists exist independently of what we may think about them. Any researcher always begins from "antecedently existing cognitive materials," such as prior theories (1989b, p. 68). As the researcher examines that prior knowledge, the knowledge itself becomes an object of study (as in a literature review). At the same time, knowledge is a product of sociohistorical processes. For example, it is influenced by political priorities or the interpersonal dynamics that occur on research teams (Pop-kewitz, 1984; Toulmin, 1972). In addition, Bhaskar emphasizes that social and behavioral scientists can produce knowledge that, in practice, can transform social structures.

The positivist bias in favor of oversimplification and smaller and smaller units led to a prescription Bhaskar calls "methodological individualism," which is the requirement that social and behavioral phenomena be explained in terms of facts about individuals. Although, as Bhaskar says, methodological individualism reflects an important truth—that society is made up of individuals—it is misleading as a pre-scription for scientific knowledge, because it overlooks the many implications of the fact that human life always occurs in the context of relationships. For example, Bhaskar emphasizes that "the real problem appears to be not so much that of how we could give an individualistic explanation of social behavior, but that of how we could give a non-social (or strictly individualistic) explanation of individual, at least characteristically human, behaviour!" (1989b, p. 70) Further, methodological indi-vidualism elides the complexity of social systems. Bhaskar's approach to science critiques "individualist and collectivist conceptions of the subject-matter of social science" and instead advances

> a relationist conception, on which its subject matter is conceived as, paradigmatically, the enduring relationships between individuals and groups and their artefacts and nature and functions of them—relationships such as those between parents and children, employer and employees, employees and the unemployed. (1991, p. 147)

Bhaskar emphasizes that the social and behavioral sciences have the potential to transform social structures: "the human sciences are necessarily non-neutral. . . they are intrinsically critical (both of beliefs, and of the objects of beliefs), self-critical and value-impregnating; and in particular . . . they both causally motivate and logically entail value judgments" (1989b, pp. 98–99). Because knowledge and values infuse the motivations that guide our actions, they potentially can guide us to transform society. Actions reciprocally influence knowledge and values. "Of course there is feedback between values and actions, mediated by practices" (1989b, pp. 98–99).

Bhaskar elaborates how scientific knowledge can be grounded in the value of human liberation. He sees knowledge in the social and behavioral sciences "as essentially critical (and self-critical), and as having, through its explanatory power, emancipatory implications for substantive social life itself" (1991, p. ix). Social and behavioral knowledge can either reproduce or transform our social reality (1991, p. 71). To produce knowledge that can transform social structures, the researcher recognizes that both the knowledge with which he or she begins and also the objects of study are already to some degree "pre-interpreted and conceptualized prior to and irrespective of any enquiry;" "the *subject matter* of the human, but *not* the non-human, sciences, is already at least partially meaningful or conceptually/linguistically constituted" (1991, p. 12). This is one reason why it is important for the researcher to take a critical stance toward scientific knowledge.

Bhaskar advances new criteria for theory appraisal. As noted previously, the positivist requirement that scientific explanations should be in the form of predictions is unwarranted. Bhaskar points out that because human systems are open systems ("systems where invariant empirical regularities do not obtain," 1989b, p. 82), focusing on a theory's predictive power is not suitable. Instead, evaluations of social and behavioral science theories can focus on their explanatory power. Another criterion for theory appraisal concerns the values that infuse theories (see Heineman Pieper, Chapter 3; Reinharz, 1992; Witkin & Gottschalk, 1988). Researchers can examine the values that infuse ideologies and social and behavioral theories to produce knowledge that serves human emancipation. Ultimately, as Heineman Pieper points out, reliance on the informed judgment of the researcher and the consumer of research cannot be avoided.

To apply Bhaskar's ideas to research problem formulation, one can consider how the research problem is pre-interpreted or conceptualized, especially in relation to social systems. Do ideologies support the customary definition of the problem? What assumptions about human relationships infuse traditional formulations of the problem? Researchers can ask whether the problem formulation reproduces or can transform both knowledge and social structures. To be transforming, the problem formulation will reflect a critique of the prevailing knowledge about the problem and of how that knowledge informs social structures and relationships. Virtually any social or behavioral science problem entails relationships, and most of those relationships include differences in power (e.g., status or access to resources). One consequence of power differentials is that the concerns of those in power more often are attended to and taken more seriously than the concerns of those who are relatively disempowered (Bricker-Jenkins & Hooyman, 1986; L. Davis, 1985, 1986; Hartman, 1991; MacKinnon, 1985; Martin, 1987; Star, 1979). For example, the saying "children should be seen and not heard" illustrates the extent to which a pervasive belief system disempowers children and silences their voices. Analyzing the different types of power in the problem situation is an essential aspect of problem formulation when researchers want the research to enact the values of advocacy and empowerment:

> The identification of an experienced injustice in social reality, necessary for changing or remedying it, involves much more than redescription, even if it depends on that too centrally. It is a matter of finding and disentangling webs of relations in social life, and engaging explanatory critiques of the practices that sustain them. This may indeed often involve the detection of various types of false and otherwise unhappy consciousness (and more generally being). And this in turn may lead on to critiques of the vocabularies and conceptual systems in which they are expressed, and the additional social practices with which they are implicated. Moreover, such explanatory critiques will lead, *ceteris paribus*, to action rationally directed to transforming, dissolving or disconnecting the structures and relations which explain the experience of injustice and the other ills theoretically informed practice has diagnosed. (Bhaskar, 1991, p. 72)

Researchers can analyze which individuals involved in the problem are the most disadvantaged and most in need of empowerment. Then, the research problem can be formulated in ways that will voice the concerns of the disadvantaged group and be most likely to lead to solutions that begin to correct the inequality. For example, if researchers are evaluating a program that aims to protect children and to help families that have abused or neglected their children, there are several layers of relationships for the researcher to consider. The parents of the children typically have less authority or status than the social worker, and researchers have recognized that such parents often need special assistance and empowerment in relation to the social systems. The children, however, are by far the most powerless, both in relation to their parents and to the social service system. Therefore, a researcher evaluating such a program, who wants to take an empowering approach (e.g., Hegar, 1989; Pieper & Pieper, Chapter 8), would consider whether his or her knowledge can voice the concerns of the children and how potential problem formulations lead to solutions that empower the children. Using such criteria, rather than judging the efficacy of the program based solely on the opinion of the program staff and parents, the researcher would find ways to help the children to describe their opinions about the interventions.

KEY TERMS

Causal ontology   Historicism
Methodological individualism

Discussion Questions

1. Give Bhaskar's definitions for the following terms:

   Naturalism
   Scientism
   Reductionism

2. How is naturalism different from naturalistic research?

3. a. According to Bhaskar, what criteria does science use in ascribing reality to a posited entity?

   b. What are some other examples of a causal ontology besides gravity and magnetic fields?

4. Bhaskar says that positivism is an incorrect account of the natural sciences as well as of the social and behavioral sciences. How so?

5. What are some of the distinctive differences between the natural and the human sciences, according to Bhaskar?

6. Summarize Bhaskar's critique of methodological individualism.

7. a. Why are the social and behavioral sciences "denied, in principle, decisive test situations for their theories" (Bhaskar, 1989b, p. 83. See p. 332 in this volume.)?

   b. Why is the reliance on prediction for theory appraisal (and thereby, experimental design as a privileged test of theories), particularly inapplicable to social systems?

8. What is the "full development of the concept of ideology" as Bhaskar outlines it (p. 334 in this volume)?

9. How does Bhaskar define society?

10. Practice taking three social and/or behavioral theories and articulating the ontological assumptions that undergird each. Some theories to try: behaviorism, psychoanalysis, intrapsychic humanism, ecological systems theory, Marxism.

11. If you agree with Bhaskar that the value-neutrality of social and behavioral science is a shibboleth, you might also agree that values enter into theory appraisal. If so, what values would you use in appraising theories in the social and behavioral sciences?

12. Bhaskar claims that, "values themselves can be false" (p. 334 in this volume). Consider the values and ideologies that have informed the following problem definitions, and explain why you do or do not believe the problem definitions reflect false values:

    a. Problem definition: Many scientists believe that to know a treatment is effective, one must have a group that does not receive the treatment (the control group) for comparison with the group that does receive the treatment. Consider the protests of terminally ill individuals (e.g., people with AIDS) who are being placed in control groups and would prefer to receive the experimental treatments.

b. Problem definition: Rape often has been defined as a crime of lust. Accordingly, rapists have been prescribed medications or behavioral interventions designed to reduce their sexual desires. How might that definition of rape influence the treatment of rape victims in courts of law? How does that differ from the treatment of victims of theft (Brownmiller, 1975; MacKinnon, 1985)?

c. Problem definition: The situation of people with physical disabilities (e.g., quadriplegia) has been construed in dehumanizing ways (Bogdan & Taylor, 1989; S. J. Taylor & Bogdan, 1989). Often it has been defined as dependency on those who help the disabled person with self-care. By contrast, consider how people with disabilities are asserting that they should hire and supervise the people who help them with self-care.

13. Using a social or behavioral problem that you would like to study,

a. Describe the power differentials in the relationships among people involved in the social problem. Whose voices would be least likely to be heard in research about that problem?

b. Review some of the most important research on that problem to see whether the voices of those you identified in 13a have been heard. How might you design research on that problem to call attention to the needs of people who have not been heard?

▼ ▼ ▼ ▼ ▼ ▼ ▼ ▼ ▼ ▼ ▼ ▼

SAMPLE RESEARCH PROJECT: DEVELOPING RESIDENTIAL TREATMENT SERVICES FOR HOMELESS, MENTALLY ILL, AND SUBSTANCE-ABUSING CLIENTS

Part 5: Assumptions of the Guiding Theory

One of the core contemporary problems in conceptualizing care for this population is developing a theory of care that can accommodate and respond to two seemingly disparate issues: (1) How to offer care and advocacy to remedy the pervasive discrimination, disenfranchisement, and disadvantage this population has experienced and continues to experience and (2) simultaneously recognize that these clients have histories of extremely traumatic familial abuse and rejection as well as manifestly self-destructive motives accompanying their self-caretaking motives. Most approaches to care address only one of these issues. Care providers who focus on the environmental oppression of clients find themselves perplexed and dismayed by clients' self-defeating motives, such as when clients refuse food or shelter. Care providers who exclude environmental oppression have been criticized for ignoring those clients' crucial needs for advocacy and improved social supports.

As noted previously, the theory used to guide this research is intrapsychic humanism. Central assumptions of intrapsychic humanism, especially the ontology and epistemology, are described more fully in chapters 7 and 8. Intrapsychic human-ism is unique in that it addresses both issues (1) and (2) above. It leads to an approach to care that combines advocacy and case management with psychotherapy. It recognizes the crucial impact of both current social supports and the client's intrapsychic conflict (e.g., motives for genuine self-caretaking and self-defeating motives). Intrapsychic humanism helps the practitioner/researcher to see both the strengths and potential of the clients and to recognize the extent and effects of the trauma and deprivation that many people who are both homeless and mentally ill have experienced in their distant and recent past relationships (Susser, Struening, & Conover, 1987). One of the most problematic effects of the trauma is that the resi-dents often manifest deep and persistent self-destructive motives. For example, many are overtly suicidal or involved in extremely abusive relationships. Or resi-dents might wait several months to receive funding and then divest themselves of much of it on a spending spree (e.g., buying a stereo rather than paying rent). The data about the clients' status with regard to housing, funding, social supports, and ongoing mental health care and counseling are behavioral expressions of the shifts in the clients' self-caretaking motives.

One of the greatest challenges for staff is helping the residents with their self-destructive motives so that the residents can regain stable housing, funding, and even employment. Progress is complicated by aversive reactions to pleasure, which cause the residents to react with paradoxical alienation, dysphoria, or hostility to positive events (see Chapters 7 and 8). In an example of an aversive reaction to pleasure, one resident who had lived on the streets for several years and had been getting her meals out of garbage cans eagerly came to dinner, took several helpings of food, and yet complained the entire time about everything, from the plates to the food.

On the Possibility of Social Scientific Knowledge and the Limits of Naturalism

Roy Bhaskar

1 INTRODUCTION

In this chapter I want to discuss an old question that refuses to lie down. It is a question that continually resurfaces in philosophical discussions on the social sciences and reappears, in one guise or another, in methodological discussions within them: *to what extent can society be studied in the same way as nature?* Without exaggerating, I think one could call this question the primal problem of the philosophy of the social sciences. For the history of that subject has been dominated by a dispute between two traditions. The first—a naturalistic tradition—has typically seen science as (actually or ideally) unified in its concordance with *positivist* principles, based in the last instance on the Humean notion of law. The second—a rival anti-naturalist tradition, of *hermeneutics*—has posited, by contrast, a radical distinction in method between the natural and social sciences, flowing from and grounded in the idea of a radical distinction in their subject matters. The philosophical lineage of this tradition is traceable back through Weber and Dilthey to the transcendental idealism of Kant. Within the Marxist camp an exactly parallel dispute has occurred, with the so-called 'dialectical materialists' on one side and Lukács, the Frankfurt school and Sartre on the other.

Now, with the possible exception of the 'dialectical materialists' (whose specificity I do not want to discuss here), the great error that unites these disputants is their acceptance of an essentially positivist account of natural science, and more generally of an empiricist

ontology. This is very evident if one looks at Peter Winch's *The Idea of a Social Science*, perhaps the most influential tract written within the so-called 'analytical' school. Winch, it will be remembered, wants to argue that there is an essential identity between philosophy and social science, on the one hand, and a fundamental contrast between the latter and the natural sciences, on the other. When we turn to his arguments for such a contrast we find that they boil down to two. The first is an argument to the effect that constant conjunctions of events are neither sufficient nor (contrary to Weber, for instance) even necessary for social scientific explanation, which is achieved instead by the discovery of intelligible connections in its subject matter.[1] This may be granted. But the required contrast is only generated if we assume that the discovery of intelligible connections in *its* subject matter is not equally the goal of natural scientific explanation. The second is an argument to the effect that social things have no existence, other than a purely physical existence, i.e. as social things, apart from the concepts that agents possess of them.[2] Besides leaving the ontological status of concepts unclear, once more the assumed contrast only gets off the ground if we tacitly assume that, with the privileged exception of

Source: From "On the Possibility of Social Scientific Knowledge and the Limits of Naturalism" in *Reclaiming Reality: A Critical Introduction to Contemporary Philosophy* (pp. 66–69, 70–74, 82–87) by R. Bhaskar, 1989, London: Verso Publications. Copyright 1989 by Verso Publications. Reprinted by permission.

thought itself, only material objects can properly be said to be 'real', that in natural science *esse est percipi*. Winch's anti-naturalism thus depends entirely on empiricist theories of existence and causality. By in effect ceding natural science to positivism, Winch precludes himself from locating the true differences between the natural and the social sciences. Lukács in the Marxist tradition makes an exactly parallel mistake.

Now I think that recent developments in the philosophy of science allow,[3] as the current crisis in the social sciences necessitates, a reconsideration of the problem of naturalism. *Naturalism* may be defined as the thesis that there is (or can be) an essential unity of method between the natural and the social sciences. It must be straightaway distinguished from two species of it: *reductionism*, which posits an actual identity of subject matter as well; and *scientism*, which denies that there are any important differences in the methods appropriate to studying societies and nature, whether or not they are actually (as in reductionism) identified. In contrast to both these forms of naturalism I want to argue for a qualified anti-positivist naturalism. Such a naturalism holds that it is possible to give an account of science under which the proper and more or less specific methods of both the natural and social sciences can fall. But it does not deny that there are important differences in these methods, grounded in the real differences that exist in their subject matters. In particular we shall see that *ontological, epistemological* and *relational* considerations reveal differences that place limits on the possibility of naturalism, or rather qualify the form it must take in the social sciences. Moreover these differences all carry methodological import. However, it will transpire that it is not in spite of, but rather just in *virtue of*, the real differences that distinguish the subject matter of the social from the natural sciences that social science is possible; that here, as elsewhere, it is the nature of the object that determines the form of its science. So that to investigate the limits of naturalism is *ipso facto* to investigate the conditions which make social science, whether or not it is actualized in practice, possible.

I want first to sketch the elements of an adequate account of natural science, in relation to which the possibility of social scientific knowledge can be reappraised.

2   TRANSCENDENTAL REALISM AND THE PROBLEM OF NATURALISM

I have argued elsewhere that it is a condition of the intelligibility of the experimental establishment and the practical application of our knowledge that its objects are real structures which exist and act independently of the patterns of events they generate.[4] It follows from this that causal laws must be analysed as tendencies, which are only necessarily manifest in empirical invariances under relatively special closed conditions.[5] Thus, contrary to the specific claims of Popper and Hempel and the tacit presupposition of Winch, deducibility from empirical invariances, depending upon the availability of constant conjunctions of events, can be neither necessary nor sufficient for a natural scientific explanation. There is an ontological gap between causal laws and their empirical grounds, which both parties to the naturalist debate have hitherto ignored. This not only renders standard positivist methodological injunctions patently inapplicable, it also vitiates the most familiar hermeneutical contrasts. Thus just as a rule can be broken without being changed, so a natural mechanism may continue to endure, and the law it grounds be both applicable and true (that is, not falsified), though its effect, the consequent, be unrealized.[6]

Knowledge, then, has 'intransitive' objects which exist and act independently of it. But it is itself a social process, whose aim is the production of the knowledge of such objects, that is, of the mechanisms of the production of phenomena in nature. Now if we are to avoid the absurdity of the assumption of the production of such knowledge *ex nihilo* it must depend on the utilization of antecedently existing cognitive materials (which I have called the 'transitive' objects of knowledge). Typically, then, the construction of an explanation for some identified phenomenon will involve the building of a model, making use of such cognitive materials and operating under the control of something like a logic of analogy and metaphor,[7] of a mechanism, which *if* it were to exist and act in the postulated way would account for the phenomenon in question.[8] The reality of the posited explanation must then, of course, be subjected to empirical scrutiny (for in general more than one explanation will be consistent with the phenomenon concerned). Once done, it must then itself in principle be explained. And so we have in science a three-phase schema of development, in which in a continuing dialectic, science identifies a phenomenon (or range of phenomena), constructs explanations for it and empirically tests its explanations, leading to the identification of the generative mechanism at work, which now becomes the phenomenon to be explained, and so on. On this view of science its essence lies in the move at any one level from manifest phenomena to the structures that generate them. The question of naturalism can thus be posed as follows: to what extent is it possible to suppose that a comparable move can be made in the domain of the social sciences?

Now our analysis of science immediately pinpoints an internal difficulty in this project. For the objects of scientific inquiry are neither empirically given nor even actually determinate chunks of the world, but rather real structures, whose actual presence and appropriate concept have to be produced by the experimental and theoretical work of science. Thus it would seem that we must first know what kinds of things societies are before we can consider whether it is possible to study them scientifically. Indeed without some prior specification of an object of inquiry, any discourse on method is bound to be more or less arbitrary. The question to which this chapter aspires to make a contribution may therefore be set as follows: what properties do societies possess that might make them possible objects of knowledge for us?

In considering this question it is essential to establish that these properties, and *a fortiori* their bearers, societies, are real. For unless this is done our analysis of science entails that the possibility of a non-reductionist naturalism must straightaway collapse. Now, in this respect, it is important to note that science employs two criteria for the ascription of reality to a posited object: a perceptual and a causal one. The latter turns on the capacity of the entity whose existence is in doubt to bring about changes in material things. It should be noticed that a magnetic or gravitational field satisfies this criterion, but not a criterion of perceivability. On this criterion to be is not to be perceived, but (in the last instance) just to be able to do.[9] The standard hermeneutical fork, turning on a conceptual/perceptible dichotomy, which we have already seen invoked by Winch, ignores of course just the possibilities opened up by a causal criterion for ascribing reality.

. . . . . .

3 AGAINST METHODOLOGICAL INDIVIDUALISM

Methodological individualism asserts that facts about society and social phenomena are to be explained solely in terms of facts about individuals. For Popper, for example, 'all social phenomena, and especially the functioning of social institutions, should be understood as resulting from the decisions etc. of human individuals . . . we should never be satisfied by explanations in terms of so-called "collectives".[10] Social institutions are merely 'abstract models' designed to interpret the facts of individual experience. As Jarvie has put it: '"army" is just the plural of "soldier" and all statements about the army can be reduced to statements about the particular soldiers comprising it.'[11] Watkins concedes that 'there may be unfinished or half-way explanations of large-scale phenomena in terms of other large-scale phenomena (such as inflation in terms of full employment)',[12] but contends that we will not have arrived at so-called 'rock-bottom' (ultimate?) explanations of such phenomena until we have deduced them from statements about the dispositions, beliefs, resources and inter-relations of individuals.[13] Specifically, social events are to be explained by deducing them from the principles governing the behaviour of the 'participating' individuals,[14] together with statements of their situations. In this way, methodological individualism stipulates the *material* conditions for adequate explanation in the social sciences to complement the *formal* ones laid down by the deductive—nomological model.

Now when we consider the range of predicates applicable to individuals and individual behaviour—from those that designate properties, such as shape and texture, that people possess in common with other material objects, through those that pick out states, such as hunger and pain, that they share with other higher animals, to those that designate actions that are, as far as we know, uniquely characteristic of them—the real problem appears to be not so much that of how we could give an individualistic explanation of social behaviour, but that of how we could give a non-social (or strictly individualistic) explanation of individual, at least characteristically human, behaviour![15] For the predicates designating properties special to persons all presuppose a social context for their employment. A tribesman implies a tribe, the cashing of a cheque a banking system. Explanation, whether by subsumption under general laws, advertion to motives and rules, or by redescription (identification), always seems to involve irreducibly social predicates.

Moreover it is not difficult to show that the arguments adduced in support of methodological individualism will not bear the weight placed upon them. For example, a comparison of the motives of a criminal with the procedures of a court is sufficient to show that facts about individuals are neither necessarily more observable nor necessarily easier to understand than social phenomena. Again, a comparison of the concepts of love and war shows that concepts applicable to individuals are not necessarily either clearer or easier to define than those that designate social phenomena.

Significantly, the qualifications and refinements proposed by the advocates of methodological individualism weaken rather than strengthen the case for it. Thus, the admission of ideal types for instance weakens the force of the ontological considerations in favour of it, while allowing 'half-way' and statistical explanations undermines the epistemological ones. Moreover the examples cited of supposedly genuinely 'holistic' behaviour, such as riots and the biological union of mating couples,[16] merely reveal the poverty of their implicit conception of the social. For, upon analysis of their writing, it is clear that most methodological individualists regard 'the social' as a synonym for 'the group'. The issue for them, then, becomes that of whether society, the whole, is greater than the sum of its constituent parts, individual people. Social behaviour, on this view, then becomes explicable as the behaviour of groups of individuals or of individuals in groups.

Now I think that this definition of the social is radically misconceived: sociology is not concerned, as such, with large-scale, mass or group behaviour, conceived as the behaviour of large numbers, masses or groups of individuals, but (paradigmatically) with the persistent *relations* between individuals (and groups), and with the relations between these relations. Relations such as between capitalist and worker, MP and constituent, student and teacher, husband and wife. Now such relations are general and relatively enduring but they do not involve collective or mass behaviour as such in the way in which a strike or a demonstration does (though of course they may help to explain the latter). Mass behaviour is an interesting social psychological phenomenon, but it is not the subject matter of sociology.

Now what makes this situation particularly ironical is that the more sophisticated methodological individualists formally concede that relations must play some role in explanation. What then accounts for the polemics and the passion? I think that it can only be explained in terms of their desire to defend a particular form of substantive social scientific explanation, which they mistakenly hold to be uniquely consistent with political liberalism. As Watkins himself has put it: 'Since Mandeville's *Fable of the Bees* was published in 1714, individualistic social science with its emphasis on unintended consequences has largely been a sophis-

ticated elaboration on the simple theme that, in certain situations, selfish private motives [i.e. capitalism] may have good social consequences and good political intentions [i.e. socialism] bad social consequences'.[17] There is in fact one body of social doctrine, whose avatars are utilitarianism, liberal political theory, pre-Ricardian classical and neo-classical economic theory, that does conform to individualistic prescriptions, on the assumption that what is in effect a generalized aggregation problem can be solved: According to this model reason is the efficient slave of the passions[18] and social behaviour can be seen as the outcome of a simple maximization problem or its dual, a minimization one: the application of reason, the sole identifying characteristic of man, to desires (appetites and aversions, in Hobbes) or feelings (pleasure and pain, in Hume, Bentham and Mill) that may be regarded as neurophysiologically given. Relations play no part in this model; and this model, if it applies at all, applies as much to Crusoe as to socialized man, and to men whatever (i.e. wherever and whenever) their socialisation—with the corollary expressed by Hume that 'mankind is much the same at all times and places'.[19]

The limitations of this approach to social science should by now be well known. To say that human beings are rational does not explain *what* they do, but only at best (that is, supposing that an objective function could be reconstructed for their behaviour and empirically tested independently of it) *how* they do it. Rationality, purporting to explain everything, ends up explaining nothing. To explain a human action by reference to its rationality is like explaining some natural event by reference to its being caused. Rationality is, in this sense, a presupposition of investigation. As for neo-classical economic theory, the most developed form of this tendency in social thought, it may best be regarded as a normative theory of efficient action, generating a set of techniques for achieving given ends, rather than as an explanatory theory capable of casting light on actual empirical episodes. That is, as a praxiology,[20] not a sociology.

Aside from its championship of a particular explanation form, methodological individualism derives plausibility from the fact that it seems to touch on an important truth, awareness of which accounts for its apparent necessity: namely the idea that society is made up of or consists of and only of people. In what sense is this true? In the sense that the material presence of social effects consists only of changes in people and changes brought about by people on other material things—objects of nature, such as land, and artefacts produced by work on objects of nature. We could express this truth as follows: *the material presence of society = persons and the (material) results of their actions*. It is this truth that the methodological individualists have glimpsed, only to shroud it with their apologetic shifts.

It is clear that there is, in methodological individualism, a sociological reductionism and psycho- (or praxio-) logical atomism at work, exactly paralleling with respect to the content of explanation, the theoretical reductionism and ontological atomism determining its form. In the philosophy of social science, the sociology of individualism plays as important a role in defining the object of investigation as the ontology of empiricism does in defining its method. Together I think that they must be held largely responsible (or rather, they theoretically reflect whatever is responsible) for the social scientific malaise.

The *relational* conception of the subject matter of sociology advocated here may be contrasted not only with the *individualist* conception, exemplified by utilitarian social theory, but with what I shall call the *collectivist* conception, best exemplified perhaps by the work of Durkheim, with its heavy emphasis on the concept of the group. Durkheim's group is not of course the same as Popper's. It is to use a Sartrean analogy more of the nature of a fused group than a series.[21] In particular, as definitive of the social, it is characterized by the possession of certain emergent powers, whose justification I will consider below. Nevertheless the key concepts of the Durkheimian corpus, such as conscience collective, organic *vs.* mechanical solidarity, anomie and so on, all derive their meaning from their relationship to the concept of the collective nature of social phenomena. Thus, for Durkheim, to the extent at least that he is to remain committed to positivism, enduring relationships must be reconstructed from collective phenomena; whereas on the realist and relational view advanced here, collective phenomena are seen primarily as the expressions of enduring relationships. Note that on this conception sociology is not only not essentially concerned with the group, it is not even essentially concerned with behaviour.

If Durkheim combined a collectivist conception of sociology with a postivist methodology, Weber combined a neo-Kantian methodology with a still essentially individualist conception of sociology. His break from utilitarianism is primarily at the level of the forms of action or types of behaviour he is prepared to recognize, not at the level of the unit of study. It is significant that just as the thrust contained in Durkheim's isolation of the emergent properties of the group is constrained by his continuing commitment to an empiricist methodology, so the possibilities opened up by Weber's isolation of the ideal type are constrained by his continuing commitment to an empiricist ontology.[22] In both cases a residual empiricism holds back, and ultimately annuls, a real scientific advance. For it is as futile to attempt to sustain a concept of the social on the basis of the category of the group, as it is to attempt to sustain a concept of natural necessity on the basis of the category of experience. Marx, I think, did make the attempt to combine a realist ontology and a relational sociology.[23] One can thus schematize four tendencies in social thought as in Table 1.

It should be noted that as the relations between the relations that constitute the proper subject matter of sociology may themselves be *internally related* only the category of *totality* can express this.

. . . . . .

7   THE LIMITS OF NATURALISM

How, given that societies exist, and have the kinds of properties that they do, might they become possible objects of knowledge for us?

Table 1

	Method	Object
Utilitarianism	empiricist	individualist
Weber	neo-Kantian	individualist
Durkheim	empiricist	collectivist
Marx	realist	relational

Note: concepts of method (social epistemology) underpinned by general ontology; concepts of object (social ontology) underpinned by general epistemology.

The major ontological limits on the possibility of naturalism, turning on the activity-, concept-, and space-time-dependence of social structures, have already been isolated. Before considering how social scientific knowledge is possible, despite or as I shall try to show because of these features, I want to consider two other kinds of limits on naturalism, which I shall characterize as epistemological and relational respectively.

Society, as an object of inquiry, is necessarily 'theoretical' in the sense that, like a magnetic field, it is necessarily unperceivable; so that it cannot be empirically identified independently of its effects. It can only be known, not shown, to exist. However in this respect it is no different from many objects of natural scientific inquiry. What does differentiate it is that society not only cannot be empirically identified independently of its effects, but it does not *exist* independently of them either. But, however strange this is from an ontological point of view,[43] it raises no special epistemological difficulties.

The chief epistemological limit on naturalism is not raised by the necessarily unperceivable character of the objects of social scientific investigation, but by the fact that they only manifest themselves in 'open systems'; that is, in systems where invariant empirical regularities do not obtain. Now the real methodological import of this point must be distinguished most carefully from its significance for the doctrines of received philosophy of science. It is as easy to exaggerate the former, as to underestimate the latter. For, as I have shown in detail elsewhere,[44] practically all the theories of orthodox philosophy of science, and the methodological directives they secrete presuppose closed systems. Because of this, they are totally inapplicable to the social sciences—which is not of course to say that the attempt cannot be made to apply them, with disastrous results. Humean theories of causality and law, deductive—nomological and statistical models of explanation, inductivist theories of scientific development and criteria of confirmation, and Popperian theories of scientific rationality and criteria of falsification, together with the hermeneutical contrasts parasitic upon them, must all be totally discarded. The only concern of social science with them is as objects of substantive explanation.

The real methodological import of the absence of spontaneously occurring, and the impossibility of artificially creating, closed systems is strictly limited: it is that the social sciences are denied, in principle, decisive test situations for their theories. This means that the criteria for the rational confirmation and rejection of theories in social science *cannot be predictive*, and so must be *exclusively explanatory*. Particularly important here will be the capacity of a theory to be developed in a non-*ad hoc* way so as to situate, and preferably explain, without strain, a possibility, once (and perhaps even before) it is realized, when it could never, given the openness of the social world, have predicted it. It should be stressed that this difference has in itself no ontological significance whatsoever. It does not affect the form of laws, which in natural science too must be analysed as tendencies; only the form of our knowledge of them. Because the mode of application of laws is the same in open and closed systems alike,[45] the mode of application of laws is the same in society as in nature. And although the necessity to rely exclusively on explanatory criteria *may* affect the subjective confidence with which we hold social scientific theories, if we have *independently* validated claims to social scientific knowledge (on explanatory criteria) then we are just as warranted in applying our knowledge as in natural science. Or rather, given that the problem is not typically whether or not to apply some theory, T, to the world, but rather *which* out of two or more theories, T, T´ . . . etc. to apply, the degree of our preference for one theory over another will not be affected by a limitation on the grounds with which that preference must be justified.

In addition to allowing (relatively)[46] decisive test situations, experimental activity in the natural sciences, in enabling access to the otherwise latent structures of nature, may provide an invaluable component of the process of scientific discovery that the social sciences, in this respect, will be denied. However, our discussion of the relational and ontological limits will generate an analogue and a compensator respectively for this role in discovery.

The chief relational difference is that the social sciences are part of their own field of inquiry, in principle susceptible to explanation in terms of the concepts and laws of the explanatory theories they employ; so that they are *internal* with respect to their subject matter in a way in which natural science is not. This qualifies the sense in which the objects of social scientific investigation can be said to be intransitive, or exist and act independently of it. For it is possible and indeed likely, given the internal complexity and interdependence of social activities, that its objects do not exist independently of, and may be causally affected by, social science; just as one might expect that social science is affected or conditioned by developments in, as it patently cannot exist independently of, the rest of society. So far the argument has turned merely on the possibility of a relatively undifferentiated society/social science link. But the case for such a link may be strengthened by noting that just as a social science without a society is impossible, so a society without some kind of scientific, protoscientific, or ideological theory of itself is inconceivable (even if it consists merely in the conceptions that the agents have of what they are doing in their activity). Now if we denote the proto-scientific set of ideas P, then the transformational model of social activity applied to the activity of knowledge-production would suggest that social scientific theory, T, requiring cognitive resources is produced, at least in part, by the transformation of P. The hypothesis under consideration is that this transformation will be vitally affected by developments in the rest of society, S.

It might be conjectured that in periods of transition or crisis generative structures, formerly opaque, become more visible to men and women.[47] And that this, though it never yields the epistemic possibilities of a closure, does provide a partial analogue to the role that experimental activity plays in natural science. The social conditions for the production and emergence of a social scientific theory must of course be distinguished from the conditions for its subsequent development and (though there are evident connections between the two) from the conditions for its wider societal influence or assent.[48] Thus it is surely no accident that Marxism was born in the 1840s or stunted in the East under Stalin and in the West during the Cold War and post-war boom. Or that sociology, in the narrow sense, was the fruit of the two decades before the First World War.[49]

It should be noted that because social systems are open historicism (in the sense of deductively justified prediction) is untenable. Moreover, because of the historical (transformational) character of social systems, qualitatively new developments in society will be occurring which social scientific theory cannot be expected to anticipate. Hence for ontological, as distinct from purely epistemological, reasons, social scientific, unlike natural scientific, theory is *necessarily* incomplete. Moreover, as the possibilities inherent in a new social development will often only become apparent long after the development itself, and as each new

development is, in a sense, a product of a previous one, we can see why it is that history must be continually rewritten. There is a relational tie between the development of the object of knowledge and the development of knowledge that any adequate theory of social science, and methodology of social scientific research programmes, must take account of. In particular, Lakatosian judgements about the progressive or degenerating nature of research programmes[50] in the social sciences cannot be made in isolation from judgements about factors in the rest of society, S, conditioning work in particular programmes.

Once a hypothesis of a causal mechanism has been produced in social science it can then be tested quite *empirically*, though exclusively by reference to its explanatory power. But I have so far said nothing about how the hypothesis of the generative mechanism is produced, or indeed about what its status is. It is to these questions that I now turn.

In considering theory construction in the social sciences it should be borne in mind that the putative social scientist would, in the absence of some prior theory, be faced with an inchoate mass of social phenomena, which he or she would somehow have to sort out and define. In systems, like social ones, which are necessarily open, the problem of constituting an appropriate (i.e. explanatorily significant) object of inquiry becomes particularly acute. Fortunately most of the phenomena with which the social scientist has to deal will already be identified, thanks to the *concept-dependent* nature of social activities, under certain descriptions. In principle the descriptions or nominal definitions of social activities that form the transitive objects of social scientific theory may be those of the agents concerned or theoretical redescriptions of them. The first step in the transformation P → T will thus be an attempt at a real definition of a form of social life that has already been identified under a particular description. Note that in the absence of such a definition, and failing a closure, any hypothesis of a causal mechanism is bound to be more or less arbitrary. Thus in social science attempts at real definitions will in general precede rather than follow successful causal hypotheses—though in both cases they can only be justified empirically, that is, by the revealed explanatory power of the hypotheses that can be derived from them.

The problem, then, is shifted from that of how to establish a non-arbitrary procedure for generating causal hypotheses to that of how to establish a non-arbitrary procedure for generating real definitions. And here a second differentiating feature of the subject-matter of the social sciences should be recalled—the *activity-dependent* nature of social structures, such that the mechanisms at work in society exist only in virtue of their effects. In this respect society is quite distinct from other objects of scientific knowledge. But note that, in this, it is analogous to the objects of philosophical knowledge. For just as the objects of philosophical knowledge do not exist as objects of a world apart from the objects of scientific knowledge, so social structures do not exist apart form their effects. So I suggest that in principle as philosophical discourse stands to scientific discourse, so a discourse about society stands to a discourse about its effects. Moreover, in both cases we are dealing with conceptualized activities, whose conditions of possibility or presuppositions the second-order discourse seeks to explicate. However, there are also important differences. For in social scientific discourse we are concerned not to isolate the general conditions of knowledge as such, but the particular mechanisms and relations at work in some identified sphere of social life. Moreover, its conclusions will be historical, not formal; and subject to empirical test, as well as to various a priori controls.[51]

It is here that the hermeneutical tradition, in highlighting what may be called the conceptual moment in social scientific work, has made a real contribution. But it makes two mistakes. Its continuing commitment to the ontology of empirical realism prevents it from seeing (1) that the conditions for the phenomena, namely social activities as conceptualized in experience, may be *real*; and (2) that the phenomena themselves may be *false* or in an important sense inadequate.

Thus what has been established, by conceptual analysis, as necessary for the phenomena may consist precisely in that extra-conceptual reality which consists of the real relations and processes in which people stand to each other and nature, of which they may or may not be aware; which is really generative of social life and yet unavailable to direct inspection by the senses. Moreover, such a transcendental analysis in social science in showing the historical conditions under which a set of categories may be validly applied *ipso facto* shows the conditions under which they may not be applied. This makes possible a second-order critique of consciousness, best exemplified perhaps by Marx's analysis of commodity fetishism.[52] Value rela-

tions, it will be remembered, for Marx, are real but they are historically specific social realities. And fetishism consists of their transformation in thought into the natural, and so ahistorical, qualities of things. But, as Norman Geras has pointed out,[53] Marx employed another concept of mystification. This is best exemplified by his treatment of the wage form, in which the value of labour power is transformed into the value of labour. This Marx declares to be an expression 'as imaginary as the value of the earth', 'as irrational as a yellow logarithm'.[54] Here he engages in what we may call a first-order critique of consciousness—in which, to put it bluntly, he identifies the phenomena themselves as false; or, more formally, shows that a certain set of categories are not properly applicable to experience at all. Thus, contrary to what is implied in the transcendental idealist tradition, the transformation P $\rightarrow$ T both (1) isolates real but non-empirical conditions and (2) consists essentially, as critique, in two types of conceptual criticism and change.

Now the appellation 'ideology' to the set of ideas P is only justified if their *necessity* can be demonstrated; that is, if they can be explained, as well as criticized.[55] This involves something more than just being able to say that the beliefs concerned are false (or superficial) and being able to say why they are false or superficial, which normally entails of course having a superior explanation for the phenomenon in question. It involves, in addition, being able to give an account of the *reasons* why the false or superficial beliefs are *held*—a mode of explanation clearly without parallel in the natural sciences. For beliefs, whether about society or nature, are clearly social objects.

Once this step is taken then conceptual criticism and change passes over into social criticism and change. For, in a possibility unique to social science, the object that renders illusory beliefs necessary comes, at least in the absence of any overriding considerations, to be criticized in being explained. So that the point now becomes, *ceteris paribus*, to change it. In the full development of the concept of ideology, theory fuses into practice, as facts about values, mediated by theories about facts, are transformed into values about facts.[56] The rule of value-neutrality, the last shibboleth of the philosophy of social science, collapses, when we come to see that values themselves can be false.

To sum up, then, society is not given in, but presupposed by, experience. But it is precisely its peculiar ontological status, its transcendentally real character, that makes it a possible object of knowledge for us. Such knowledge is non-natural but still scientific.

As for the law-like statements of the social sciences, they designate tendencies operating at a single level of the social structure only. Because they are defined only for one relatively autonomous component of the social structure and because they act in systems that are always open, they designate tendencies (such as for the rates of profit on capitalist enterprises to be equalized) which may never be manifested. But they are nevertheless essential to the understanding and the changing of, just because they are really productive of, the different forms of social life.

As for society itself it is not, as the positivists would have it, a mass of separable events and sequences. Nor is it constituted, as a rival school would have it, by the momentary meanings that we attach to our physiological states. Rather it is a complex and causally efficacious whole—a totality, whose concept must be constructed in theory, and which is being continually transformed in practice. As an object of study, it cannot be read straight off the empirical world. But neither can it be reconstructed from our subjective experiences. But, though positivism would have had us forget it, that much at least is the case with the objects of study in natural science too.

[Notes]

1. See P. Winch, *The Idea of a Social Science*, Routledge & Kegan Paul, London, 1958, esp. pp. 114–15.

2. Ibid., esp. pp. 108, 124–5.

3. Especially R. Harré, *The Principles of Scientific Thinking*, Macmillan, London 1970; R. Harré & E.H. Madden, *Causal Powers*, Blackwell, Oxford 1975; and R. Bhaskar, *A Realist Theory of Science*, 2nd Edition, Harvester Press, Hassocks, Sussex, and Humanities Press, New Jersey 1978. Cf. R. Keat, 'Positivism, Naturalism and Anti-naturalism in the Social Sciences', *Journal for the Theory of Social Behaviour*, 1971, I. pp. 3–17; R. Harré & P.F. Secord, *The Explanation of Social Behaviour*, Blackwell, Oxford 1972; and R. Keat & J. Urry, *Social Theory as Science*, Routledge & Kegan Paul, London 1975.

4. See my *A Realist Theory of Science*, esp. chs 1 & 2.

5. Ibid., ch. 2, sect. 4.

6. Ibid.

7. See R Harré, *Principles of Scientific Thinking*, esp. ch. 2; and M. Hesse, *Models and Analogies in Science*, University of Notre Dame Press, Indianapolis, 1966, esp. ch. I.

8. Cf. N.R. Hanson, *Patterns of Discovery*, Cambridge University Press, Cambridge, 1965, esp. pp. 85ff.

9. See *A Realist Theory of Science*, p. 182.

10. K.R. Popper, *The Open Society and its Enemies*, Vol. II, Routledge & Kegan Paul, London, 1962, p. 98.

11. I. Jarvie, *Universities and Left Review*, 1959, p. 57.

12. J.W.N. Watkins, 'Historical Explanation in the Social Sciences', *British Journal of the Philosophy of Science*, 1957, 8, reprinted as 'Methodological Individualism and Social Tendencies', *Readings in the Philosophy of the Social Sciences*, ed. M. Brodbeck, Macmillan, New York, 1968, p. 271.

13. Ibid.

14. J.W.N. Watkins, 'Ideal Types and Historical Explanation', *British Journal of the Philosophy of Science*, 1952, 3, reprinted in *The Philosophy of Social Explanation*, ed. A. Ryan, Oxford, 1973, p. 88.

15. Cf. A. Danto, *Analytical Philosophy of History*, Cambridge University Press, Cambridge, 1965, ch. XII, and S. Lukes, 'Methodological Individualism Reconsidered', *British Journal of Sociology*, 1968, 19, reprinted in A. Ryan, *The Philosophy of Social Explanation*.

16. J.W.N. Watkins, 'Ideal Types', p. 91 and 'Methodological Individualism', p. 273.

17. Ibid., p. 278.

18. D. Hume, *A Treatise on Human Nature*, ed. L.A. Selby-Bigge, Oxford, 1968, p. 415.

19. D. Hume, *Essays Moral and Political*, Vol. II, ed. T.H. Green & T.H. Grose, London, 1875, p. 68.

20. Cf. S. Kotarbinski, 'Praxiology', *Essays in honour of O. Lange*, Warsaw, 1965.

21. J.P. Sartre, *Critique of Dialectical Reason*, New Left Books, London, 1976, Book II, ch. I and Book I, ch. 4.

22. There are, of course, non-, and even anti-individualist tendencies in Weber's thought (see e.g. R. Aron, *Philosophie Critique de l'histoire*, NRF, Paris, 1969); just as there are non-, and (especially in *The Elementary Forms of Religious Life*) anti-positivist strains in Durkheim's (see e.g. R. Horton 'Levy-Bruhl, Durkheim and the Scientific Revolution', *Modes of Thought*, eds. R. Finnegan & R. Horton, Faber & Faber, London, 1973).

23. Cf. R. Keat & J. Urry, *Social Theory*, ch. 5, and B. Ollman, *Alienation*, Cambridge University Press, Cambridge, 1971, esp. chs. 2 & 3 respectively.

. . . . . .

43. But is the notion of a 'field' that exists only in virtue of its effects any stranger, or *prima facie* more absurd, than the combination of principles of wave and particle mechanics in elementary micro-physics, now reckoned a common-place?

44. *A Realist Theory of Science*, Appendix to ch. 2.

45. Ibid., ch. 2, sect. 4.

46. Cf. P. Duhem, *The Aim and Structure of Physical Theory*, Atheneum, New York, 1962, pp. 180–90.

47. If true, this would have an analogue to the domain of social psychology in the conscious technique of 'Garfinkelling' (see e.g. H. Garfinkel, *Essays in Ethnomethodology*, Prentice-Hall, New Jersey, 1967), and perhaps in the role played by psychopathology in the development of a general psychology.

48. Consider, for example, the way in which the mass unemployment of the 1930s not only provided the theoretical dynamo for the Keynesian innovation, but facilitated its ready acceptance by the relevant scientific community.

49. Cf. e.g. A. Giddens, *Capitalism and Modern Social Theory*, Cambridge University Press, Cambridge, 1971, Postscript; and G. Therborn, *Science, Class and Society*, New Left Books, London, 1976, ch. 5, part III.

50. See e.g. I. Lakatos, 'Falsification and the Methodology of Scientific Research Programmes', *Criticism and the Growth of Knowledge*, eds. I. Lakatos & A. Musgrave, Cambridge University Press, Cambridge, 1970.

51. Thus the transformational model of social activity implies that it is a necessary condition for any adequate theory of a social system that the theory be capable of showing how the system reproduces or transforms itself. A priori considerations of this sort can be used to criticize particular social theories. See, for example, M. Hollis and E. Nell, *Rational Economic Man*, Cambridge University Press, Cambridge, 1975, esp. ch. 8 for a criticism of neo-classical economic theory along these lines.

52. K. Marx, *Capital*, Vol. I, ch. 1.

53. N. Geras, 'Essence and Appearance: Aspects of Fetishism in Marx's *Capital*' *New Left Review*, 1971, 65, reprinted as 'Marx and the Critique of Political Economy', *Ideology in Social Science*, ed. R. Blackburn, Fontana, London, 1972, p. 291.

54. See *Capital*, Vol. 1, p. 537 and *Capital*, Vol. III, p. 798 respectively.

55. Cf. N. Geras, in *Ideology in Social Science*, ed. Blackburn, and J. Mepham, 'The Theory of Ideology in Capital', *Radical Philosophy* (1972), 2.

56. C. Taylor 'Neutrality in Political Science', *Philosophy, Politics and Society*, 3rd series, eds. P. Laslett & W. Runciman, reprinted in A. Ryan, *The Philosophy of Social Explanation*, shows clearly how theories (or 'explanatory framework') do in fact secrete values. Unfortunately, however, by not specifying any criterion for choosing between theories, he leaves himself open to the interpretation that one should choose that theory that most satisfies our conception of what 'fulfils human needs, wants and purposes' (p. 161); rather than that theory which, *just because it is explanatorily most adequate*, and capable *inter alia* of explaining illusory beliefs about the social world, best allows us to situate the possibilities of change in the value-direction that the theory indicates. Taylor thus merely displaces, rather than transcends, the traditional fact/value dichotomy.

Problem Formulation, Ontological Assumptions, and Causality: Introduction to "Implications for Psychology of the New Philosophy of Science"

In the following paper, Manicas and Secord show how Bhaskar's philosophy of scientific realism (also called critical or transcendental realism) addresses "many of the tensions and conflicts which have plagued modern psychology from its beginnings" (1983, p. 400).* They summarize how Bhaskar's scientific realism addresses four major unresolved questions in the philosophy of psychology:

1. What are the objects of scientific knowledge?
2. What is scientific knowledge, and how do the objects of knowledge help us understand the similarities and differences between the sciences?
3. What is causality?
4. What is explanation?

In responding to those questions, Manicas and Secord cover many of the important topics in postpositivist philosophies of science that have been introduced in prior selections. These topics include the debates about realism versus relativism, the criteria used to appraise scientific theories, reductionism, the symmetry thesis, and scientific explanation. They emphasize that "our proposals for psychology are integrative and result from a radically new understanding of the nature of science and of the world as we know it" (1983, p. 400).

Manicas and Secord begin by summarizing two conceptualizations of psychological knowledge they regard as inadequate: the "standard view of science," which corresponds to logical positivist beliefs about science (or "the received view") and the "Kuhnian or paradigmatic critique." In discussing the "foundationist" or logical positivist view of science, Manicas and Secord raise a question that the logical positivists also addressed: "what are the criteria of truth?" They argue that the standard or logical positivist metatheory rested on an oversimplified approach to theory appraisal, which assumed that hypotheses can be simply "tested against the 'facts'" (1983, p. 400). However, "facts" for one theorist often are not "facts" for another theorist, as Thomas Kuhn pointed out cogently in *The Structure of Scientific Revolutions* (1970). Further, different scientific paradigms will differently define a "test" and sufficient evidence for a hypothesis (Laudan, 1984). Although Kuhn's argument is powerful, according to Manicas and Secord, a problem with Kuhn's beliefs about science is that they apparently lead to "a consensus theory of truth in which, in fact, there are no independent checks on the nature of the consensus" (1983, p. 401). Manicas and Secord, by contrast, emphasize that working scientists develop rational criteria for appraising their theories; scientists also assume their empirical findings will be checks that help them correct their theories (see also Wimsatt, 1987). Therefore, Kuhn's depiction of science excludes important elements of the scientist's experience of research.

---

*Editor's Note: The citations used here refer to pages of the original article. You can find the material quoted from this article in the reprint that follows this introduction.

Manicas and Secord show how Bhaskar's scientific realism includes Kuhn's premise that scientific knowledge is a social and historical product: "there is no preinterpreted 'given' and . . . the test of truth cannot be 'correspondence'" (Manicas & Secord, 1983, p. 401). In the new scientific realism, the conceptualization of scientific knowledge as a sociohistorical product does *not* mean that there are no criteria against which theories can be evaluated. In fact, "it is precisely the task of science to invent theories that aim to represent the world" and also to generate "rational criteria in terms of which theory is accepted or rejected" (Manicas & Secord, 1983, p. 401). Because there are mind-independent objects of knowledge, rational criteria can be used to assess theories. "Since our theories are constitutive of the known world but *not* of the *world*, we may always be wrong, but *not* anything goes" (Manicas & Secord, 1983, p. 401). In other words, to recognize the limitations and biases that theories introduce, one must recognize that a reality exists independent of those theories—a reality to which the theories respond and that offers researchers corrections for theories. In the realist view, "the 'things' of the world are complex composites" (p. 401). Accordingly, the sciences that aim to explain the structures and properties of diverse objects of knowledge are necessarily autonomous and cannot be unified as the logical positivists had prescribed. In other words, an important reason why psychology should not aim to emulate physics is because a different science is needed to study human consciousness than to study light, gravity, or atoms. According to Manicas and Secord, Bhaskar's assumptions about reality also lead to a new conception of causality in which the world is comprised of multilevel, complex structures and organized interactional processes. Although there is regularity, that is not homologous with predictability. In open systems (most notably, human systems), constant conjunctions of events do not occur. Therefore, although we experience patterns, probabilities, and tendencies, determinism does not hold, and causal processes may have surprising, unpredictable outcomes (Bhaskar, 1989b).

This new view of causality also affords a new view of scientific explanation. Manicas and Secord reject the logical positivist covering law model of scientific explanation. To be scientific, according to the logical empiricist metatheory, an explanation had to treat the event to be explained as an instance subsumed under a covering law. In other words, explanation was a process of "subsumption." To illustrate, if a positivist social scientist wanted to explain how a client progressed in treatment, the explanation would consist of viewing that event (of progress) as an outcome that could be predicted, given the initial conditions and a covering law. By contrast, the new realist metatheory described by Manicas and Secord does not assume that a general law can yield an explanation of any event. Instead, scientific explanation is a causal explanation that requires both a definition of the properties of the objects involved and historical understanding of the specific situation:

> ... [E]xplanation requires the resolution of the event into its components and a theoretical redescription of them: It requires causal analysis. As part of this process, it requires retrodiction to possible causes and the elimination of alternatives that might have figured into the particular configuration. Explanation thus requires knowledge of the causal properties of the configured structures *and* a historical grasp of the particular and changing configuration. (1983, p. 403)

Manicas and Secord define scientific explanation as a form of "causal analysis" in which "we show how in each particular case a particular causal configuration occurred that had just the achieved result" (1983, p. 403).

Because the new scientific realist account of scientific explanation focuses on the complexity and uniqueness of the contextual factors that influence any event, the focus is relational, unlike the positivists' bias toward "methodological individualism" (see Bhaskar's critique in the previous selection). According to Manicas and Secord, "the acts of persons are open-systemic events in which a wide variety of systems and structures are involved" (1983, p. 405). Manicas and Secord think that perhaps "every psychologist" has always known that the complexities of people and their behavior could not be explained by subsumption under a general law. The explanation of human behavior ultimately requires a multidisciplinary effort. The authors note that they may be misunderstood as advocating the use of inferential statistical models of data analysis that use multiple variables (e.g., multiple regression). Methodologically based solutions, however, cannot be adequate for explaining behavior, because such solutions overlook the crucial step of defining the objects of knowledge. This step can be accomplished only by theoretical analysis: "identification of structures and their dynamics can only be accomplished by the multilevel application of imaginative theory that simultaneously guides observation, analysis, and experiment" (1983, p. 405).

One of the salient problems in psychology and the other social and behavioral sciences is that some social-psychological theories tend to emphasize subjective meaning in their explanations of behavior, while disregarding the impact of social structures. Other theories focus on social structures but fail to recognize the causal role of human agency. Manicas and Secord believe scientific realism can "wed" those perspectives. They claim that "social structure is simultaneously the relatively enduring product but also the medium of motivated human action" (1983, p. 408). Social structures, which are "reproduced and transformed by action," "preexist for individuals" (1983, p. 408). Manicas and Secord conclude by distinguishing between the tasks of scientists and the tasks of clinicians. As Martha Heineman Pieper has pointed out, however, such a distinction cannot hold. She shows how clinicians are scientists who can generate new knowledge based on naturalistic research about their practice (see the Preface).

KEY TERMS

Correspondence theory of truth   Deductive-nomological explanation

DISCUSSION QUESTIONS

1. a.   Why might critics of Kuhn's views have been concerned that his "paradigm account of science precipitously courted irrationalism" (Manicas & Secord, 1983, p. 401; see p. 345 in this volume; see also Gholson & Barker, 1985)?

    b.   Some scientific realists emphasize that practicing scientists regard themselves as making rational decisions among competing theories and that they plan their research process according to rational criteria. Do you agree with the view that Manicas and Secord ascribe to Kuhn, that scientists' choices among competing theories are fundamentally influenced by irrational socio-logical and psychological factors? Why or why not?

c.   Consider yourself and your co-workers as scientists. When you are helping clients, are your actions based on judgments that you can explain rationally?

d.   What experiences have you had in trying to introduce a new approach or theory? Have you found that if you challenge a prevailing belief system your colleagues' responses are rational? How do you think scientists react when they are faced with a new theory that challenges their assumptions?

2.   Following Bhaskar, Manicas and Secord emphasize the importance of defining the objects of our study. Norwood Hanson gives the following wry illustration of the many factors that can contribute to definitions of theoretical terms in science:

> Suppose that when that first black swan was discovered in Australia (in the late 18th Century) a certain American zoologist behaved badly. Having just returned the page proofs of a book in which he had remarked several times that "All swans are white," he refused to accord the name "swan" to those birds which were swan-like in all respects save their color. His colleagues, of course, would have found it much more convenient to speak of two species of swan. But no, this zoologist-fellow persists, arguing, "It is improper to call those, or any, black birds 'swans' because all swans are white!" In this way he transforms an inductive generalization into a definitional truth. (1969b, p. 37)

a.   What connection does Hanson make between definitions and inductive generalizations?

b.   How does Hanson's story illustrate why a definition of a theoretical term is always a heuristic?

c.   What do you think Hanson means when he says the zoologist's definition is a kind of "truth"?

3.   Manicas and Secord say that "on the realist view, 'things' of the world never operate under conditions of complete closure" (see p. 347 in this volume).

a.   Review the discussions of the symmetry thesis and the deductive method of theory-testing (in the introduction to "The Obsolete Scientific Imperative in Social Work Research," in Chapter 3 and also in the introduction to the selection by Popper in the Appendix). What does the observation that human systems are not closed mean for the symmetry thesis and the deductive method of testing social and behavioral theories?

b.   What are the implications of that point (human systems are open) for the use of experimental designs as ultimate tests of theories?

c.   What are some implications of that point for how one would approach clinical assessment, for example, of a client's potential for violence?

d.   What are some implications of that point for evaluating the effects of an intervention?

4. Manicas and Secord argue that "for the standard view of science, the world is a determined concatenation of contingent events; for the realist, it is a contingent concatenation of real structures" (see p. 348 in this volume). According to this realist understanding of causality, why is the future not determined? Why does a realist recognize that we may be able to explain the past and yet not be able to predict the future?

5. Manicas and Secord, citing Bhaskar, say, "one must be a realist ontologically to be a fallibilist epistemologically"(see p. 346 in this volume).

    a. What do they mean?

    b. Why does that comment represent a postpositivist point of view?

6. There has been an ongoing debate about similarities and differences among the sciences. As Bhaskar emphasized in his selection, it is the object of inquiry that determines the nature of the science. What do Manicas and Secord say are key differences between the natural and the social and behavioral sciences?

7. Manicas and Secord say, "Unless human action and social structure constitute radically different levels of description and conceptualization, with neither reducible to the other, their articulation and integration within a single system cannot be accomplished" (see p. 353 in this volume). According to Manicas and Secord, how does the realist theory of science view society as both a product of and an ongoing influence on human action?

8. Extra credit: ". . . all our perceptions, categories, and frames of meaning are mediated and are culturally and historically loaded." However, Manicas and Secord regard objectivity, redefined as "warranted assertibility," as an attainable value (see p. 353 in this volume). In the realist's view, what are some criteria according to which knowledge can be appraised as having "warranted assertibility"?

▼ ▼ ▼ ▼ ▼ ▼ ▼ ▼ ▼ ▼ ▼ ▼

SAMPLE RESEARCH PROJECT: DEVELOPING RESIDENTIAL TREATMENT SERVICES FOR HOMELESS, MENTALLY ILL, AND SUBSTANCE-ABUSING CLIENTS

Part 6: The Epistemology and Sample Selection Process

The epistemology of intrapsychic humanism addresses the client's subjective experience of intrapsychic agency, or the capacity to bring about a stable sense of self-worth. Only the client's intrapsychic therapist can perceive the clients' intrapsychic agency, because only in that relationship does a caregiver have a nonpathological motive to have caregiving motives regulate personal motives; also, only in that relationship does a client make a commitment to develop a more stable well-being via psychological caregiving. The ways of knowing the client's motives used in this research project cannot access the client's intrapsychic agency reality, because they do not occur in the context of an intrapsychic caregiving relationship. In other words, in intrapsychic treatment, the therapist and ultimately the client can know the client's experience of intrapsychic agency, but that aspect of agency cannot be captured by a way of knowing such as a survey. The survey that is part of this project's data collection process with the residents addresses an aspect of interpersonal agency, specifically, that aspect of their agency that the clients can introspect and verbalize.

Intrapsychic humanism is especially applicable for this research problem for several reasons. Researchers in the field of services for the severely mentally ill have emphasized that an approach to care is needed that recognizes the client's strengths and that integrates the counseling process with case management and community care. Intrapsychic humanism offers a way to understand and respond to the client's developmental motives* in the context of caregiving relationships with therapists, staff counselors, and other residents in the program.

One of the advantages of seeking the opinions of the participant/subjects in the research is that the researcher benefits from their reflectiveness. The sample to be selected is purposive and systematic in that no resident in the program will be excluded. Thus, biases in the sample will be those of the program admission process. Briefly, salient characteristics of the sample are that the residents are seeking help voluntarily when they complete the questionnaire, although many have a history of resisting housing and other forms of mental health care. The sample spans multiple ethnic and racial groups; the income levels of the residents' families also are diverse.. Many residents have a history of suicide attempts, violence against others, chronic substance abuse, and serious medical problems. For a resident to be treated in the program, however, his or her problems need to be controllable in an outpatient setting with a high patient/staff ratio and relatively little security. Very few residents declined to complete the preliminary versions of the survey; those who declined gave reasons based on deep feelings of mistrust. One stated, "I don't want to put anything down in writing."

Another advantage of this naturalistic process of sample selection is that the clients can respond to the survey about their opinions and needs when they are relatively more comfortable and functional. These clients often are without social services for long periods of time; talking with them about their opinions and needs on a street corner, when they might be hungry or ill, would, most importantly, be inhumane. Secondarily, it would reduce the detail and reflectiveness of the information.

---

*Editor's Note: Motives for better, genuine self-caretaking, see chapters 7 and 8.

Implications for Psychology of the New Philosophy of Science

PETER T. MANICAS   *Queens College, City University of New York*

PAUL F. SECORD   *University of Houston*

ABSTRACT: Polarities reflecting conflicts and tensions between approaches to psychology are attributed to an older, mistaken view of the nature of science. Salient features of a new philosophy of science that has developed over the past few decades are identified and their implications for psychology drawn. All science only approaches closure in the laboratory; outside of the laboratory, the world is radically open. Although scientific theory is equally valid in and out of the laboratory, it is not sufficient to explain behavior, nor is it easily applied. Neither natural nor social science has as its central role the explanation and prediction of individual behavior. Just as the application of physics requires engineering technology, explaining the behavior of particular individuals requires not only psychological theory but also situational, biographical, and historical information.

This article provides psychologists with an overview of exciting developments in the philosophy of science that have occurred during the last two decades or so and briefly points up their implications for psychology as a science, a discipline, and a profession. These new philosophical developments provide a framework for psychology and the social sciences that will help to reconcile conflicting views and approaches within psychology and in its relations to the various biological and social science disciplines.

In the monumental *Psychology: A Study of a Science*, edited by Sigmund Koch (Volumes 1–6,

1959–1963), one eminent psychologist after another, after many years—or even a lifetime of research—admitted to strong doubts about where they had been and what had been achieved, and some suggested that our most basic assumptions about the nature of psychology as a science and a method had to be questioned. They were right, although at that time new directions were not at all clear.

Koch's diagnosis was incisive. He argued that psychology was unique insofar as

> its institutionalization preceded its content and its methods preceded its problems. . . .
>
> The "scientism" that many see and decry in recent psychology was thus with it from the start. . . . From the earliest days of the experimental pioneers, man's stipulation that psychology be adequate to science outweighed his commitment that it be adequate to man. (1959, Vol. 3, p. 783)

Even more crucially, Koch went on to point out that psychology bases "its understanding of vital questions of method on an extrinsic philosophy of science which (in some areas) is twenty years or more out of date" (p. 788).

Source: "Implications for Psychology of the New Philosophy of Science" by P. T. Manicas and P. F. Secord, 1983, *American Psychologist*, *38*, pp. 399–413. Copyright 1983 by the American Psychological Association, Inc. Reprinted by permission.

Psychology has become far more sophisticated in its methodologies and procedures and has generated a large body of knowledge in the decades since then, but the philosophy of science that is implicit in contemporary psychology has not changed all that much. Moreover, in the last decade or so, we find Taylor in 1973 and Toulmin in 1978 observing (here in Taylor's words) that "psychology is a vast and ramified discipline [containing] many mansions, [yet] intellectually divided against itself." The past decade or so has seen the fragmentation of psychology into "dozens of highly specialized, and largely non-interacting sub-disciplines" (Toulmin, 1978). Toulmin attributed this, rightly, in our view, to the still dominating neopositivist theory of the behavioral sciences that succeeded the old positivism of the 1930s and 1940s.

But if, as these writers have argued, the root issue remains the very conception of science, of its methods, tasks, and limits, then the time may be ripe for a resolution. In recent decades a virtual Copernican Revolution has taken place in the philosophy of science, a radical change that has profound implications for the human sciences. We see these changes arriving at an extraordinary convergence on a new heuristic for the human sciences. This heuristic, which derives from a wide variety of disparate quarters—from continental hermeneutics, post-Wittgensteinian action theory and philosophy of mind, phenomenology, structuralism, and neo-Marxism—is not merely consistent with the new philosophy of science, but as we shall argue, is firmly grounded in the fundamental insights of that new philosophy (Bhaskar, 1975, 1989a).

What follows is a sketch of the main features of the new theory of science and its implications for psychology. We believe that adopting this new perspective would resolve many of the tensions and conflicts which have plagued modern psychology from its beginnings. What we suggest is not some arbitrary and ecumenical redistribution of labor; our proposals for psychology are integrative and result from a radically new understanding of the nature of science and of the world as we know it.

THE NEW THEORY OF SCIENCE

To minimize misunderstanding, it may be helpful to begin with what, in our view, is the dominating philosophy of science. Called the "standard view" by Scheffler (1967), it remains widely held among psychologists and other social scientists.

The Standard View of Science

1.   A *foundationist* epistemology, although made relative in practice, sees scientific propositions as founded on "data." The test of the truth of propositions is "correspondence" between theory and data in the sense proposed by Carnap (1956) and later modified. In other words, while perhaps no one any longer supposes that there is a preinterpreted "given" or even some transhistorical, theory-neutral data base, it is generally held that some propositions at least, are basic in that they constitute the test sentences for scientific theory. More roughly stated, hypotheses are to be tested against the "facts."

2.   Theories are understood to be *interpreted calculi* or *hypothetico-deductive systems*. Theoretical terms, or *hypothetical constructs*, gain their meaning implicitly through their systemic relations to other terms in the theory, or explicitly by being connected to observations (through "operational definitions," "correspondence rules," or a "dictionary").

3.   Research is more or less atheoretical, with many researchers avoiding theory as far as possible and seeking to test only hypotheses related to variables that can be closely tied to observations. Few investigators attempt to develop full-blown theories. Hypothetical constructs may or may not be understood realistically—as representing real mechanisms productive of predictive outcomes or not. In this regard the use of *model* is ambiguous. Sometimes a model is taken to be a representation of real mechanisms; sometimes models are understood heuristically or instrumentally, as purely mathematical, or as "convenient fictions" (Achinstein, 1969). Both views share in emphasizing predictability as the acid test of theory.

4.   A Humean conception of causality and of lawfulness is taken for granted. On this view, causal relations are regular contingent relations between events. When strict universality is not possible, "reliable regularities between independent and dependent variables" or "probabilistic relationships among complex, interacting variables" may be all that can be achieved.

5.   Attending the Humean conception of lawfulness, the standard view holds to a conception of explanation as subsumption under law. On this view explanation and prediction are exactly symmetrical. A full, complete (or ideal) explanation is *deductive-nomologi-*

cal. In research practice, explanations are inductive-statistical, so that one achieves a better explanation when the probability statement "predicts the dependent variable more accurately by identifying additional independent variables, by better defining the relationship among these independent variables (and) by specifying more accurately the relationship of each of the dependent variables. . . ." (Hempel, 1965b).

The foregoing ideas are strongly identified with recent logical empiricism (Scriven, 1969). But some of them have a much longer history, a fact of considerable relevance in explaining their place as the conventional wisdom about science. As more recent empiricism developed, from the late 1920s on, a number of problems and issues came to a head. Key doctrines came under attack; some were clarified, some amended, and some were dropped altogether (Brown, 1977; Suppe, 1974). One example may suffice here. In 1958, Hempel amended the "received view" of scientific theories in articulating the theoretician's dilemma: If theoretical terms are defined in terms of observations, they cannot function as explanatory; if, on the other hand, they are not, then how did they have empirical support? Attempts to resolve this dilemma culminated in the notion of theories sketched as Point 2 above (Hempel, 1965b).

The Kuhnian or Paradigmatic Critique

By the late 1950s, alternatives to the standard view were available and included books by Stephen Toulmin (1953, 1961), David Bohm (1957), Mario Bunge (1959), and Norwood Hanson (1958), but these were largely ignored by psychologists. Not until Kuhn's *The Structure of Scientific Revolutions* (1962/1970) was read and absorbed did "paradigms" become the rage and key themes in logical empiricist philosophy of science come under scrutiny by the larger community, especially in psychology and the social sciences.

Kuhn attacked empiricist epistemology, the received view of theory, and logical empiricist ideas about scientific change and development (Brown, 1977). He argued, along with Toulmin, Hanson, and many others, that observation was "theory laden" and that science must be understood as a social activity in which disciplines develop their own rules of practice. These philosophers made clear that observations were not "given" but were profoundly shaped by the observer's preconceptions and theoretical notions.

They demonstrated convincingly that scientific meanings could not be found in observations alone, as the logical empiricists had maintained. And the idea that there could be unambiguous logical connections between theory and observation was overthrown. Finally, that scientists were human observers was demonstrated to make science a social activity, which subjected it to normative or paradigmatic influences operating apart from the internal criteria of science.

All this was salutary, as far as it went; but as its critics saw, the paradigm account of science precipitously courted irrationalism (Feyerabend, 1975; Lakatos & Musgrave, 1970). The problem was clear enough: If there is no theory-neutral data base (foundationism) and if disciplines constitute their own scientific practice, what are the criteria of truth? Does the paradigm view lead to a consensus theory of truth in which, in fact, there are no independent checks on the nature of the consensus? Indeed, as one social scientist put it, "working scientists . . . continue to be skeptical about this new interpretation of how science develops. . . . Even if Kuhn's view turns out to be correct, it is possible that it might be necessary for scientists to believe in the more traditional view in order to proceed with the work of science" (Cole, 1980). This suggestion—that in order to do science one must have a false view of it—is bizarre on its face, and it powerfully suggests a confused understanding of science. In our view, not only has logical empiricism not been exorcized, perhaps for the reasons which Cole indicated, but as well, the paradigm alternative is itself seriously deficient.

The Realist Critique

An alternative to the standard and paradigmatic views of science is now available. Whereas its origins lie in another philosophical line critical of the standard view, the *realist* theory constitutes a constructive alternative view of science. The earliest anticipations are to be found in the various writings of Michael Scriven (1956, 1962, 1964), Michael Polanyi (1964, 1967), and in Bunge, Bohm, and Toulmin, already mentioned. The decisive advance was taken, in our judgment, by Rom Harré (1970, 1972; Harré & Madden 1975) and as influenced by Harré and others, by Roy Bhaskar (1975, 1978, 1982, 1989a).

Our characterization of this view is necessarily brief and thus is put forth virtually without the supporting arguments available in the extensive literature.

Nevertheless, since we believe that this new view has profound implications for psychology and the social sciences, it is important to try to convey its substance. This third view, variously called simply, *the realist theory of science* (Bhaskar, 1975), *transcendental realism* (Bhaskar, 1989a), or as suggested by Donald Campbell (Note 1), *fallibilist realism*, has the following essential features.

1.   It agrees with Kuhn and those epistemologies influenced by hermeneutics (Gadamer, 1975) that foundationism, even in its recent weakened forms, must be categorically rejected. Instead, it argues that knowledge is a social and historical product; hence the inevitability of a nonvicious hermeneutic circle (Bhaskar, 1989a). This means that there is no preinterpreted "given" and that the test of truth cannot be "correspondence." Epistemologically, there can be nothing *known* to which our ideas (sentences, theories) can correspond. But versus the unknowable Kantian thing-in-itself, it is precisely the task of science to invent theories that aim to represent the world. Thus, in the spirit of Kuhn (but as more cogently argued by Toulmin, 1972), the practices of the sciences generate their own *rational* criteria in terms of which theory is accepted or rejected. The crucial point is that it is possible for these criteria to be rational precisely because on realist terms, there is a world that exists independently of cognizing experience. Since our theories are constitutive of the known world but *not* of the *world*, we may always be wrong, but *not* anything goes. As Bhaskar has noted, one must be a realist ontologically to be a fallibilist epistemologically.

2.   The realist theory holds naturalism to be nonreductive or emergent; both the world and science are stratified. The basis for this view is the idea that the "things" of the world are complex composites. A simple if crude example may be helpful. Ordinary table salt is not, usually, *just* NaCl, since the purest of it contains other "things." But more important, at another *level*, the compound NaCl is a complex of elements, Na and Cl. Sodium and chlorine each have causal properties, and NaCl has causal properties that are not true of either sodium or of chlorine. But at still another level, sodium and chlorine are themselves complexes of electrons, neutrons, quarks, and so on. Later we will see, analogously, that the activities of persons in society may be seen as a set of interacting, interwoven structures at different levels. Establishing

the existence and properties of these novel "things"— the theoretical things of science—is the product of theoretical and experimental work in precisely the sense that science demands the construction of confirmable explanatory theories about such structures and their properties (Harré, 1970).

Accepting a realist view of science allows us to see the problem of reduction in three different senses (Bhaskar, 1975, pp. 115ff.):

1.   A lower-order domain provides the basis for the existence of some higher-order attribute; for example, our speech apparatus is the basis for the power of speech.

2.   The principles of a higher-order science are explained in terms of a lower-order science; at least a partial translation is possible. For example, certain perceptual capacities may be explained in terms of the neurophysiological properties of the visual system.

3.   From a knowledge of principles in a lower-order science, behavior in the higher-order domain is predicted. For example, behavioral experience involving mental processes may be predicted from the principles of brain chemistry alone.

Clearly the third sense makes the strongest claim; yet it has many supporters among behavioral scientists, at least as a promissory note. Senses 2 and 3 are often confused: Evidence supporting Sense 2 is often erroneously offered in support of Sense 3. Bhaskar notes that the principles and laws of chemistry can be explained in terms of those of physics, but the latter cannot be used to predict the next eruption of Mt. Vesuvius. It is the failure of reduction in this third sense that allows sciences to remain autonomous. Mitosis and growth cannot be predicted without biological laws, even if some principles of biology can be reduced to chemistry. A parallel issue in psychology is whether behavior can be predicted without invoking mental processes, a question we will return to shortly.

3.   In contrast to logical empiricism and to Kuhnian views, in the new heuristic the Humean analysis of causation and of lawfulness is rejected. Instead of the usual characterization, $R_i = f(S_i)$ or $R_i = f(S_i \cdots S_n)$, where R is the dependent variable that is some function of an independent variable S or set of S's, we write, "If S_i, then *ceteris paribus*, i necessarily acts in

virtue of its structure *N*." That is, given the "independent variable" *S* as a condition, *i* necessarily acts in a certain fashion because of its structure. In other words, scientific laws in this non-Humean framework are *not* about events or classes of events, regularly or stochastically conjoined, but are about the causal properties of structures that exist and operate in the world. This difference is crucial.

On the Humean conception, a dispositional property, for example, the solubility of salt, should manifest itself when "triggered," in this case, when put in water. If it does not, of course, the implicit *ceteris paribus* clause may be invoked. But within Humean strictures, this move is objectionable: Unless the *ceteris paribus* clause can be definitely specified, the "law" becomes a tautology—true no matter what obtains. This problem cannot arise under the realist view, because, to be specific about the conditions of the *ceteris paribus* clause, one *must* have a theory about the causal properties of the structure under conditions of closure, spelling out when the conditions of the *ceteris paribus* clause are satisfied (Sellars, 1961). That is, one must have a theoretical understanding of the nature of the structure such that one can specify the conditions under which the dispositional property will *not* be realized.

That is why we say a law has the form, "If S_i then *ceteris paribus*, necessarily *i* phi's in virtue of its structure *N*." If *theoretical* salt, NaCl, is put in theoretical water, H_2O, then *ceteris paribus*, it must dissolve—it cannot do otherwise. Theory tells us quite precisely that this is a causal property of NaCl (and of H_2O), and it tells us why. To be sure, *actual* salt (any concrete instance of salt) only *tends* to dissolve in actual water. This is because, of course, the conditions of the *ceteris paribus* clause are not always met. Thus, not only is the world stratified but it is a complex of structures and structured processes. On the realist view, "things" of the world never operate under conditions of complete closure. This explains why we have the experience of *patterns*, of tendencies, and of probabilities. Events are the conjunctures of structured processes and are always the outcome of complex causal configurations at the same and at many different levels.

If this is the case, then we can also say that causal processes may have surprising effects. They need not, for example, yield the outcomes which they usually do. Thus, if *S* is followed by non-*R* then, on the realist view, there may still be some structure whose causal properties may be having effects. There is no reason to suppose what is implied in the Humean doctrine; namely, that in the absence of predictable outcomes, the "law" does not apply, that once initiated by S_i, the causal property did not play a role in the outcome, or that the *theoretical* relation between S_i and *N* is for that reason false.

These considerations also allow us to see the significance and rationale of experiment in science. Since the structures of the world never operate under conditions of complete closure, we can test our theories about them by intervening to create (as far as possible) closures. To do this, of course, we need theories about the structures and their causal properties. The patterns of experience are where we begin. Led by a hypothesis that there is some causally efficacious mechanism at work, we construct theory about it. The theory tells us what we can expect if with ingenuity, we can isolate the theorized mechanism. A good experiment confirms a theory precisely because if it establishes the right conditions and eliminates interfering causal mechanisms, the experiment yields what would *not* have been observed without the experiment. In contrast to the standard Humean view, we experiment not because we are interested in getting more reliable, more precise, and more probable empirical regularities but rather because we believe that the laws of nature apply and operate even in the absence of experimental closure.

More generally, then, the dominating views of science, logical empiricism, and the newer Kuhnian perspective cannot sustain the distinction, implicit in the practices of the well-established natural sciences, between the development of theories representing the structures of nature (including the experimental test of our theories about the structures of nature) and the application of these theories to explain, diagnose, and predict those particulars and events of interest to us. But the realist theory can sustain this distinction. These considerations suggest a fourth crucial contrasting feature of the new view of science versus the old.

4. The realist theory of science rejects in toto the covering law model of scientific explanation and the attending instrumentalist idea that explanation and prediction are symmetrical. On the realist view, events such as the collapse of a bridge or the cancerous growth of an organ are the conjunctions of causal processes operating in open systems. Such outcomes are the result of different mechanisms of very different kinds combining in many different ways. But if so, the covering law model is, at best, seriously misleading.

Scientific explanation is not subsumption. Rather, it is causal explanation, and it demands that we show how in each particular case a particular causal configuration occurred that had just the achieved result. In general, explanation requires the resolution of the event into its components and a theoretical redescription of them: It requires causal analysis. As part of this process, it requires retrodiction to possible causes and the elimination of alternatives that might have figured into the particular configuration. Explanation thus requires knowledge of the causal properties of the configured structures *and* a historical grasp of the particular and changing configuration.

Accordingly, we may often be in a position to explain some event once it has occurred, when it would have been impossible—even in principle—to predict it. Although the relatively enduring structures of the world have definite (and knowable) causal properties, it is only under closure that explanation and prediction are symmetrical. In an open world, the configurations of structures and structured processes are not predictable. Indeed, for the standard view of science, the world is a determined concatenation of contingent events; for the realist, it is a contingent concatenation of real structures. And this difference is monumental. The past is, in a sense, "determined." That is, what happened can be causally *explained*. But the future is *not* determined precisely because the complexly related structures and systems of the world are constantly being reconfigured.

It would be easy to miss the force of the radical contrast we are drawing and to suppose that what we have put forth is, perhaps in other words, a reformulation of the standard view. Thus, it may be said that everyone recognizes uncertainty in prediction, that interaction hypotheses are widely employed, and that the typical effort of psychology (and the social sciences) is to aim at discovering reliable explanatory relationships between a wide variety of variables. These statements are doubtless true, but it is exactly these activities and the ideas that support them that we are here challenging and contrasting with the new heuristic.

One way to clarify further is to suggest why the alternative view is easily missed. One important reason is the uncritical collapse of the distinction, crucial for realist theory, between so-called empirical laws (generalizations) and causal laws. Roughly, empirical laws are statements of regularities, strict or probabilistic, between terms that are more or less readily available to direct empirical confirmation. A familiar example from learning theory of the 1930s is the various lawlike statements about the learning curve, plotted in terms of number of errors on successive trials. This was so often in such a great variety of situations found to take a negatively accelerated form that it was generally regarded as a "law of learning." Now, in hindsight, and with a better understanding of learning mechanisms, it is obvious that such a "law" has no explanatory power whatsoever. Another type of regularity is probabilistic, for example, "the probability of emitting the response will increase with the number of reinforcements." Or consider the probabilistic formulae in decision theory. Typically these probabilistic descriptions require analysis at a deeper, structural level to be fully understood.

Most methodology books in psychology and the social sciences recognize (rightly) that philosophers have repeatedly struggled to find an effective way to conceptualize causal laws in a manner distinct from contingent correlations (generalizations). Most methodological books also call attention to the fact that one cannot, without further justification, assume that a high correlation is a causal relation.

The standard view holds that, for explanation, certain conditions must be fulfilled; for example, that there must be a contiguity of time and place between the independent and dependent variables and that "the third variable problem" must be solved: Some unspecified variable must not have produced the relationship. Given that such constraints are satisfied (to the best of our ability), such regularities are, in the standard view, thought to be explanatory. Of course, in predicting particular instances, it is readily acknowledged that regularities are but "relational tendencies."

Consider the best candidate for this sort of account, $pv = k$. The correlation is perfect, but what does it explain? To explain (say) exploding gas chambers or the explosion of some particular chamber filled with gas, one would need more than—indeed, *other* than—$pv = k$, which is merely descriptive. One would need to show (at least) that, for example, the temperature of the gas in the chamber was increased *sufficiently* where "sufficiently" would be relative to the tensile strength (a causal property!) of the container. This sort of objection (important to the covering-law model of explanation) is not, however, the present problem. Rather, one should notice that $pv = k$ is *itself* a consequence of what is needed to explain the explosions of containers, that *because* gases are clouds of molecules that behave in certain theoretically defined ways, that is, because there are causal laws about gases (in addition to empirical laws about them), gases have the *tendencies* they have, and that indeed, the empirical laws about them hold to the extent that they do.

In other words, we can say that gases, in general, have a tendency to maintain a constant relation between pressure and volume *and* to explode their containers when they are heated. Both of these are tendencies because both assertions contain *ceteris paribus* clauses. We can say that they are tendencies because, as theory tells us, if the CP clauses *were* satisfied, it is necessary that $pv = k$, and quite impossible that containers of such and such a tensile strength *not* explode when the gas is sufficiently heated.

A similar analysis is available for every empirical law or generalization. Consider *sulphur is yellow*. The optical properties of sulphur, emitting photons of such and such a frequency, together with the (less-well-understood) mechanisms of human percipience, will generally result in our experiencing sulphur as yellow. On the present analysis, laws give us the optical properties of material substances *and* the perceptual properties of percipients, and these explain both generalizations familiar to experience and why these generalizations hold to the extent that they do. Thus, we see the cruciality of the distinction between the discovery of the causal properties of the generative mechanisms (structures) of the world and the application of this knowledge to analyze, explain, and predict.

We are mistakenly led into collapsing this distinction because the patterns of ordinary experience do obtain: They are patterns that allow for generalization. So we are quite content to explain the saltiness of water by noting that salt was put into it and it dissolved, sulphur is usually yellow in appearance, that guilty people often comply more readily, revolutionary upheavals seem reasonably related to differences in the rates of expectation and satisfaction, and so on. Nevertheless, these tendencies become intelligible only insofar as causal laws are natural necessities and are sharply distinguished from the empirical regularities they generate. Still, it may yet be thought that empirical regularities *explain* events. If so, it may be because it is still supposed that events may be explained by showing them to be the outcomes of a single law or set of laws of one science; that, for example, there is an economic explanation of a recession, a psychological explanation of a divorce, and so on.

But it seems that there is only one science in which such a view is even plausible. That science is celestial mechanics. And this is because the events of interest to us, the position and velocity of some planet, are governed by laws operating under relative *closure*. That is, there is a sense in which we explain these events by simply instantiating variables into a deterministic system under closure. Even so, we presuppose some very theoretical and *explanatory* properties of space/time structures in our "explanation." In any case, it is hard to imagine how much damage has been done by taking celestial mechanics as the paradigm of a scientific explanation. We take it that no one would be fooled into thinking that the explanation of a collapsed bridge, a cancerous growth in an organ, or a volcanic eruption would take the same form. But if so, it is puzzling that one should suppose that the laws of economics or history should explain recession and revolutions (Manicas 1981).

IMPLICATIONS FOR PSYCHOLOGY

The implications of the realist view for psychology are enormous. One implication may be emphasized at this point. Undoubtedly, persons are complex particulars and the events of interest to us, for example, instances of behavior or kinds of behavior are the result of complex transactions of many different kinds of structures at many different levels including (as we shall next argue) those particular structures of interest to psychology. But if so, it would surely be a vain hope to suppose that behaviors might be explained merely by appeal to anything that can usefully be described as a psychological law. But let us emphasize that this conclusion does not depend upon the special powers that distinguish persons as agents from other animals—or indeed from hurricanes. It is as true of complex physical events as of behavioral episodes.

It may be that every psychologist has always known this, however persistent has been the hope (fear, on the part of some) that psychology could, in principle, explain behavior by identifying (under some description) its lawfully conjoined antecedents. Consider here the exactly appropriate illustration by Campbell and Misanin:

> Few, if any psychologists now believe that those conditions once labelled basic drives, such as

hunger, thirst, sex, and maternal behavior, are pre-dominantly governed by some common underlying generalized drive state. Even if there is some acti-vating or energizing state common to many basic drives, it is clear that the specified behaviors elicited by those drives are controlled by a complex of interactions among environmental stimuli, hor-monal states, physiological imbalance, previous experience, etc., and that the basic drive concept is of little value in unravelling these complexities (Campbell & Misanin, 1969).

The point here is precisely that specific behav-iors—like most events in the world—cannot be explained as the simple manifestations of some single law or principle. What we have is interacting levels of stratification. Indeed, the acts of persons are open-sys-temic events in which a wide variety of systems and structures are involved, systems that are physical, bio-logical, psychological, and, as we shall argue, sociologi-cal as well. This posture leads to the conclusion that laboratory psychology should not be aimed at explain-ing behavior—action in the word; its purpose is far more circumscribed. The explanation of behavior, as we shall see, is properly a multidisciplinary effort and, though based on the behavioral sciences, necessarily transcends them to involve both biology and the social sciences.

Our stress on openness and the multiplicity of sys-tems may easily be misunderstood. Psychologists might say, "What else is new? We've known all along that there are complex interactions among variables. That's why we've developed ANOVA, multiple regres-sion analysis, and path analysis." But that complaint would miss the point. These techniques are unques-tionably valuable tools, especially in a descriptive sense, but their routine application is unlikely to zero in on natural mechanisms that underlie behavior. Nor are such results by themselves properly considered explanations. Identification of structures and their dynamics can only be accomplished by the multilevel application of imaginative theory that simultaneously guides observation, analysis, and experiment.

Rejection of a misguided ideal for psychology does not make psychology as a science impossible. On the contrary, once we are clearer about the nature of the sciences, we can see that psychology is best construed as a family of related sciences with different tasks and different methodologies. But psychology in this sense

is autonomous, in that there is an important difference between the subject matters of psychological and physical sciences.

Whether a science is autonomous in the present sense is a direct function of the nature of stratification in the world. That is, if from a knowledge of the causal properties and antecedent conditions of struc-tures in one domain of science we cannot explain events at the next level, then that level defines another science with an irreducible subject matter. As Bhaskar (1989a) writes, even if we could explain organic life in terms of physical and chemical elements out of which organic things are formed, and perhaps even reproduced this process in laboratories, biology would not be otiose. Living things do not cease to be real; knowledge of biological structures and processes would still be necessary to account for the world as we know it.

The Problem of Consciousness

It is hardly a novelty to assert that the problem of con-sciousness continues to bedevil inquiry in psychology and the human sciences (Taylor, 1982; Toulmin, 1982). In experimental psychology, one manifestation among many is the ongoing debate over whether imagery plays an essential part in certain cognitive skills, or whether it is a mere epiphenomenon (Cooper & Shepard, 1973; Pylyshyn, 1973). But, more tellingly, at the level of social behavior, it is surely dif-ficult to deny that consciousness, along with agency, intention, and action (as against movement) constitute the crucially relevant difference in the subject matter of the human sciences (Boden, 1973).

Psychologists have adopted various strategies for coping with consciousness, but it may not be unfair to classify these under two main heads. One strategy is to minimize consciousness, either by a behaviorist end-run (Skinner, 1969, pp. 156ff.; Gibson, 1979) or by reductionist strategies—for example, arguing that conscious phenomena may be in principle reducible to brain chemistry (Churchland, 1981). The other strat-egy assigns to consciousness a central role, but in effect often rejects the causal model altogether. Humans are to some extent self-determining, accord-ing to this move, supported by some clinicians, humanists, and existentialists.

Our intention is not to assess the many arguments and conclusions in the recent literature. In our view, both sides are right and both sides are wrong, but more interestingly, this is because both sides of the argument have been infected by the mistaken assumption that it is the aim of a scientific psychology to explain our everyday actions by showing that they can be derived from a single set of laws or principles of behavior as discovered in the experimental laboratory. However, once, this assumption is dropped, we can see how both sides are right and both are wrong.

Humanistically oriented psychology is correct in insisting that because the phenomena of consciousness are real, psychology constitutes a different level of stratification from the physical sciences. Moreover, from this they rightly see that to explain action, one has to include those phenomena in any explanation. But they are mistaken in supposing that this is incompatible with the existence of psychological laws, construed here, let us emphasize, as statements about the causal properties of psychological structures.

On the other hand, the other side is correct in arguing that as a science, psychology should study the causal properties of psychological structures and processes but is mistaken in construing these as statements of invariance between antecedents and specific behaviors. Indeed, if we take our clue from the new heuristic and keep clearly in mind the distinction between discovering the causal properties and relations of structures in complex entities and applying this knowledge to explain, predict, and diagnose the particulars of the world, we can readily identify a resolution.

Experimental Psychology

In the history of psychology, "experimental psychology" has been used to refer to various and not necessarily compatible enterprises. And this is one of the problems in resolving the disputes among protagonists of widely varying approaches. We shall argue, as the foregoing account of science implies, that experimental psychology is necessarily a theoretical science. To be sure, there are experimentalists in psychology who are antitheoretical. But if we are correct, they radically misinterpret their experimental efforts. Such experimental work is, of course, closely associated with versions of positivism, especially versions of behaviorism; thus, it is not surprising that if we reject positivist understandings of science, this conception of experimental work as atheoretical should also fall. Positivistically oriented experimentation aims at establishing functional relationships between variables, and is not concerned with underlying causal mechanisms.

On the realist view, however, causal mechanisms are at the core of science. And the areas to which psychology has devoted its major effort during its century-long history are precisely the appropriate ones: memory, learning, perception, and the relation of such cognitive processes to their biological underpinnings. But whether these topics are approached from a positivist or from a realist perspective makes a crucial difference.

As Bhaskar (1975) writes, natural science aims at producing knowledge of "real structures which endure and operate independently of our knowledge, our experience, and the conditions which allow access to them" (p. 25). Science aims at discovering lawful processes, but such laws are not about events but about the causal powers of those structures which exist and operate in the world. In cellular biology, the physico-chemical properties of cells are a case in point; cells have certain structures that are reflected in the power of cells to perform certain functions.

The description of relational, structural processes is a description of natural powers or mechanisms that are the core of scientific theory. Dynamite has the power to explode by virtue of its structures; only when we can describe these dynamically can we grasp its nature. Thus, this philosophical view turns logical empiricism upside down. Theoretical entities are not hypothetical, but real; observations are not the rock bottom of science, but are tenuous and always subject to reinterpretation.

To bring this closer to the concerns of psychologists, a familiar example from linguistics may be helpful. Chomsky's generative grammar is seen (rightly or wrongly) as a theoretical structure that enables persons to generate sentences, and that thus provides a core explanation of linguistic competence. But explaining linguistic performances requires a host of other variables, including many situational ones. Every linguistic performance is different from every other; no two are the same. We believe that psychology as an experimental science is best understood in analogous terms—as concerned with the structure of our competencies and not our realization of them in our everyday behavior.

Psychologists who misread us here are apt to be startled. We are not proposing to disenfranchise psychologists whose specialty is clinical, child, industrial, organizational, social, or whatever. If the new heuristic is taken seriously, then, as an experimental science, psychology can deal only with what we are calling competencies or powers. Explaining their actualization requires more than experimental science provides, and thus there is a place for the other psychological sciences that pertain to human action in life settings. And practitioners would ideally specialize in putting the findings of psychological science together with information about concrete individuals and their social settings in order to gain understanding of their behavior. But the same is true of physics, which provides the theoretical knowledge for an atomic bomb. It takes engineering technology to construct one and make it explode.

So experimental psychology is experimental for precisely the reasons that physics or chemistry is experimental. It aims at knowledge of those structures that in complex interaction give humans the special powers they have (acquire and develop) and that they exercise in acting in the world (Taylor, 1971; Harré & Secord, 1972, esp. chap. 12). So conceived—and let us stress this—experimental psychology does not explain everyday behavior, even though, of course, it is capable of shedding light on the complex mechanisms (neurophysiological, perceptual, cognitive, etc.) that taken together, underlie performances by individuals acting in the world.

The acts of persons in life settings are open-systemic events that involve an enormous range of codetermining structures and systems. One needs knowledge only of physics to account for the fall of a person from a precipice; one needs knowledge of biological structures and processes to comprehend birth or death; one needs psychology to have an understanding of the structures and processes that underlie performances—and of course, this is made more difficult by the fact that the relevant intrinsic structures of persons are complexly related and causally codetermining. But before proceeding further we need briefly to discuss statistical and probabilistic explanations.

Statistical and Probabilistic Explanations

The use of statistical probabilities in quantum mechanics is often cited as a justification for using probabilities in psychology. In fact, probabilities are used in psychology in a considerable variety of ways. But none of these are like their usage in quantum mechanics. There, the nature of electrons in principle requires that nothing can be said concerning the microparticles in a collection of electrons that goes beyond what is said of the macrobehavior of the collection itself. This principal constraint does not apply to psychology, however. Sets of actions by a single individual, or a set of actions by many individuals, *can* in principle be broken down into their constituent unities.

In effect, the statistically significant difference between the mean performance of two or more sets of individuals so common to experiments is a kind of probability usage. What it amounts to is making a crude generalization by attributing individual variances to "error" when, in fact, there are usually real differences between individuals. Another use of statistics is at the macrolevel, as in economics, demography, or educational sociology.

Do findings based on such methods constitute explanations? This question has been frequently debated, but the answer depends on what one takes as a scientific explanation. From the perspective of the new philosophy of science, however, they clearly do not constitute explanations. For from that viewpoint, explanations must be based on a dynamic structure/process that has causal force. Mere description is insufficient. Yet, this does not mean that statistical methodologies and probabilistic approaches are useless. Far from it. Often they are an earlier necessary stage in the process of description and discovery, and they may, for example, lead to the discovery of powers or competencies that are at first understood only at the macrolevel, but that later may be explained in terms of generative mechanisms.

Not all of psychology, however, is experimental psychology, and not all psychologists need to have the same tasks and methods. In the remainder of this article, three additional tasks and three commensurate methodologies are distinguished, each logically associated with specialties within the behavioral sciences. These specialties include psychologists whose concern is the understanding of concrete persons, of individual personalities and their life histories. Another group is the social psychologists, focusing on the actions of individuals in the social contexts and structures of the world. This takes us into the realm of the sociological, which is concerned with persons or aggregates of persons acting in life situations. But first we must discuss what Bhaskar (1982) has called the new heuristic in the social sciences.

The New Heuristic in the Social Sciences

Parallel and often complementary to the debate in the theory of the natural sciences has been a violent debate in the social sciences. This is probably less familiar to psychologists, but it is nevertheless crucial to the understanding of social behavior. Although phenomenology, ethnomethodology, dramaturgy, action theory, structuralism, critical theory and neo-Marxism, and the new heuristics constitute an enormously mixed bag, it is not untrue to say that each has contributed key elements to the new heuristic, preserving what was of central importance to mainstream conceptions and integrating them into a roomier and more critically defensible posture. Again, this story is much too large to tell here, but as before, it is possible to identify the central insights. (See especially, Bhaskar, 1975, 1982, 1989a; Giddens, 1976, 1977, 1979; Bourdieu, 1977).

Perhaps the most important feature of the new heuristic is the new integration of central themes of the "subjectivist" versus "objectivist" approaches in social theory. The opposition between these terms is resolved by drawing a radical distinction between human action and social structure. Unless human action and social structure constitute radically different levels of description and conceptualization, with neither reducible to the other, their articulation and integration within a single system cannot be accomplished. But this, too, is of a piece with the new realist theory of science. As above, we held that psychology must be an autonomous science if we are to account for the world as we know it, so too must we reject reductionism in the social sciences. This means that methodological individualism is false; social phenomena cannot be explained solely in terms of knowledge about individuals (Bhaskar, 1989a).

Action theory, phenomenology, ethnomethodology, and "interpretive sociologies" in general have emphasized the idea that action is meaningful and intentional and have insisted, rightly, that such behavior is social behaviour, that "meanings" are always social meanings, and that intentionality necessarily involves "ongoing reflexive monitoring of conduct" in a socially managed milieu. Nevertheless, these orientations have tended, if subtly, to deny the "objective" character of society.

An opposite tendency has prevailed in the "objectivist" camp. Structural functionalism (Durkheim, Parsons) and recent continental structuralism (e.g., Levi-Strauss, 1966; Althusser, 1969; Godelier, 1972) have rightly emphasized the "reality" of society, but have tended to deny, again, if subtly, the efficacious causal role of agency.

The new heuristic weds these perspectives by arguing that social structure is simultaneously the rela-

tively enduring product but also the medium of motivated human action. This conception allows both views to flourish without contradiction. Thus, social structures (e.g., language) are reproduced and transformed by action, but they preexist for individuals. They enable persons to become persons and to act (meaningfully and intentionally), yet at the same time, they are "coercive," limiting the ways we can act. It is thus that action is social, for, as acquiring the particular skills, competencies, habits, and forms of thought presuppose human capacities, they also presuppose society in the double sense that in acting we use and we express social structures. Social structures are, accordingly, constituted by the motivated human acts that either reproduce or transform the very structures that are its medium. Spoken language is reproduced through its use; it is also changed in use. But social structure is rarely intentionally reproduced; social change and history is the cumulative product of the largely unintended consequences of our intentional acts. People marry for psychological reasons, not to reproduce the structural form that the family takes, an unintended consequence of their acts.

This way of viewing the matter allows us to see clearly both the strengths and limitations of the subjectivist and objectivist views. As Bhaskar writes:

> Society is not the unconditioned creation of human agency (voluntarism), but it does not exist independently of it (reification). And individual action neither completely determines (individualism) nor is completely determined by (determinism) social forms. [On the transformational model of social activity] unintended consequences, unacknowledged conditions, and tacit skills . . . limit the actor's understanding of the social world while acknowledged (unconscious) motivation limits one's understanding of oneself (Bhaskar, 1982, p. 286).

Social Psychology

This new heuristic leads to a very clear distinction between the social sciences and social psychological science (Bhaskar, 1982). The social sciences focus on the structures produced by human agency, studying how these relate to each other and to enduring practices. Thus, economists abstract the economic aspects of behavior to build functional models of how the economic system works; sociologists study the structures of social institutions and their interlocking with other aspects of society.

Social psychological science focuses on individuals in their interaction with one another and with social institutions and on how this activity relates to the larger social structures. Engagements in social activities (practices) may be described and analyzed either from the point of view of the agent—in hermeneutic terms involving her or his motivations, beliefs, competencies, understandings, and so on, or in terms of her or his place (function) in the social structures. Social psychology has, as it were, the onerous task of joining these two perspectives. In this sense social psychology is generally thought of as an interdisciplinary inquiry concerned at once with the insights and contributions of psychology and the social sciences. This theoretical and empirical task has been neglected by most social psychologists, including many with sociological backgrounds (e.g., symbolic interactionism, ethnomethodology, Goffman's microsociology; see Layder 1981, 1982; Secord, 1982). But the power of analyses by those few who have seen this clearly, like Kurt Lewin, Solomon Asch, and Muzafer Sherif, lies in just this perspective.

Social psychology, then, is ideally a mediating discipline between general psychology, on the one hand, and the social sciences, on the other. There is nothing new in this; it is reflected in the fact that both psychology and sociology have long claimed it as their own discipline. But from the point of view of the new heuristic, social psychology has not served this mediating role very well. The most popular practice of social psychologists whose discipline is psychology has been to detach individuals from their social world and to study them in relative isolation. Consider many of the dominant research themes of both past and present: attitudes and attitude change, perceptual defense, person perception, cognitive consistency theory, dissonance theory, equity theory, and currently, attribution theory.

In all of these, the focus is usually on looking inward at cognitive processes rather than outward at situations and social structures. Of course such research is a perfectly legitimate scientific endeavor and, in principle, is even consistent with the new heuristic, in that it can be seen as focused on social competencies. Since all human powers are realized socially, their particular forms and contents will be culturally and historically variable. As Mead so well put it, "social psychology presupposes an approach to experience from the standpoint of the individual, but undertakes to determine in particular that which belongs to this experience because the individual himself belongs to a social structure" (1934, p. 1).

Lest we paint too one-sided a picture, some research topics in social psychology roughly fit its mediating role: taken in a different way, equity theory falls here as well as under the previous heading. Other candidates, past and present, are small group behavior (once perhaps the dominant concern of the discipline), social exchange processes, interpersonal attraction, social roles, conformity to social norms, social power, altruistic behavior, ecological psychology, and environmental psychology.

But topics alone do not give the whole picture. Social psychologists have largely followed the standard line in their methodological approaches, and this adherence has often blocked any possibility of gaining knowledge of the links between social behavior and social structure. Thus, endless experiments on "bargaining" or on the "prisoner's dilemma" have only the most tenuous connection to negotiation in life settings: Structuring these investigations in the standard experimental paradigm has virtually eliminated the essential features of negotiation.

More central to the new heuristic is the concept of the person as we know and understand persons in our everyday lives (Harré & Secord, 1972, p. 87), and in this respect social psychology is not an experimental science in the way that experimental psychology is, since it must look to actual life situations. But beyond that, a truly mediating discipline would spell out the articulation between individual behavior, on the one hand, and social structure, on the other (Layder, 1981, 1982; Secord, 1982).

Our view of experimentation in social psychology may seem at odds with common consensus, so further comment is required. From midcentury onward social psychology has commonly been regarded as an experimental discipline (at least by those trained in psychology, if not in sociology). And, as already noted, if general psychologists experiment to discover and detail the competencies that are (one hopes) species-universal, social psychologists can legitimately experiment by introducing social variables into the laboratory or the field, especially those pertinent to the society native to the participants.

But it is important to recognize that social variables enormously complicate experimentation, making closure extraordinarily difficult to achieve, and further,

that even when their experiments are technically successful, in the realist view of science social psychologists have no more warrant than general experimenters
for believing that their experiments explain everyday
behavior. The fruits of such experimentation provide
only partial knowledge and understanding of social
behavior in life situations. Phenomena in open systems
require knowledge of additional conditions and contexts, and frequently biographical/historical knowledge as well. This is why many astute observers from
other areas of psychology (e.g., Neisser, 1980), from
sociology (e.g., Giddens, 1979), and from philosophy
and political theory (e.g., Bernstein, 1978) see experimental social psychologists as looking in the wrong
place at the wrong phenomena. These observers, we
assume, have at the very least an implicit grasp of
what we have described as the central role of social
psychology.

Psychology as Biographical and Diagnostic

The professional activities of a great many psychologists have only been briefly referred to so far, and
much of our discussion has only been indirectly
related to their concerns. Their fields of interest
include clinical, humanist, developmental, personality,
along with many related psychological specialties that
are sometimes referred to as applied psychologies
(e.g., industrial, personnel, medical psychology). Most
of these perspectives can be seen as bringing to bear all
of the foregoing discussion in the attempt to understand individual persons and their behavioral patterns
as they occur in the concrete social world.

Consider the conflict within psychology over the
problem of consciousness and the explanation of behavior. Humanistic psychological orientations rejected
behaviorist and reductionist strategies pertaining to consciousness and put the concept of the person in the center of their frame. They thus urged, rightly, we think,
that to understand persons we need to adopt a
hermeneutical approach, that we must seek "to define
correctly the interpretations of the agent" (Taylor,
1973). This insight, shared by phenomenology, action
theory, and interpretive sociologies, argues that to
understand a person we must grasp the person's meanings and understandings, the agent's vision of the world,
his or her plans, purposes, motivations, and interests.
This is not to say that once this is accomplished, behavior is fully understood; such knowledge provides only
one piece of the puzzle, but a necessary one.

Except as a counter to the claims of those with a
radical behaviorist orientation, this idea does not
demand esoteric philosophical argument, although a
great deal of recent philosophy, from Wittgenstein to
existential phenomenology and critical theory, has provided pertinent philosophical arguments. We know a
great deal about one another; otherwise, it would be
hard to imagine how we could get along at all. What
might be surprising to a Martian investigator—some
real discovery about human motivation or desire—will
not be a discovery to us. This knowledge is reflected
in human languages, whose concepts and distinctions
are the product of a long evolutionary and historical
experience, an experience in which, as Scriven has
noted, "the easy material" regarding human understanding has been "winnowed out" and where the
"nonsense" has not survived the press of continued
experience (Scriven, 1964).

Put in simple terms, the insight of the hermeneutical perspective is this: If our aim is to explain behavior
as it occurs in ordinary life there is no escaping the
ordinary description of behavior and experience. Certainly causal mechanisms and structures discovered by
experimental psychology or other sciences apply to
such behavior, but by themselves they do not provide
sufficient explanation, and they certainly do not
enable us to dispense with ordinary language and to
substitute a pure scientific language of behavior. We
hasten to add that the reverse cannot be done either:
Ordinary language cannot substitute for the language
of causal mechanisms and structures.

Of course, our ordinary concepts and distinctions
remain revisable; some might be abandoned or modified, others added through insights made by remarkable individuals, poets, novelists, philosophers, and
psychologists. Consider here the impact of Freud on
our ordinary self-understandings. Moreover, to say
that we know a great deal about one another is not to
say that our understandings are perfect, or even as
adequate as we might like. And no doubt, a too characteristic narrowness and provinciality is to some
extent, at least, broken down by humanist education
(Joynson, 1974).

Finally, our everyday understandings or interpretations can in any particular instance be wrong. There
are two aspects to this fallibility. The first regards the
entire shift of modern epistemology and its rejection
of the idea of "brute data". It is by now commonplace
that there is no such thing as a noninterpreted "given"
that can serve as the foundation of knowledge. This

applies not only as regards our knowledge of the other person as agent, but also to our understanding of the natural world as well. That is, all our perceptions, categories, and frames of meaning are mediated and are culturally and historically loaded. But this does not eliminate the possibility of objectivity, construed here as warranted assertibility. Nor are we accordingly driven to a morass of relativism.

The other aspect of our fallibility stems from the continuous possibility of self-deception, so that as there is no chance for incorrigible knowledge of others, neither is there the possibility of incorrigible self-knowledge (Solomon, 1974).

These points raise some very crucial questions for psychology as a science. But the question that defined the conflict between humanists and their opponents is not one of these. The question is not whether some hermeneutic psychological science might replace our ordinary understandings of ourselves and others, understandings we regularly if imperfectly have available to us. Rather the question is, what would be involved in achieving a better understanding, a better account of our acts and the acts of others? Put bluntly, it is a question of what is the character of hermeneutical science?

Much depends, of course, on what one means by science. Science functions honorifically, and thus important political (institutional) dimensions are involved. Scientific knowledge is too frequently thought of as the only kind of knowledge, or at least as the best—truest, surest. At the same time, having the credentials associated with the acquisition of such knowledge gives us access not otherwise available, to research monies, to authority, to status. These political dimensions are too complex to pursue here. But the scientific dimensions are clear. The entire drift of current reexaminations of science and its epistemology makes the claims of science much less secure than empiricists' demands would ever have allowed. In the new heuristic, whether palatable or not, scientific knowledge is much closer to knowledge that is more familiarly accessible, through common sense, literature, and other modes of experience (Bernstein, 1978, esp. Part IV).

To be sure, the idea of science as a mode of controlled inquiry remains and is important. The public, critical, and systematic character of scientific inquiry must be acknowledged, and in this sense, hermeneutical science differs from the sort of hermeneutical understanding we take for granted and with which it is continuous. But more can be said.

On the view of science sketched earlier, we distinguished between sciences that aim at discovering the structures and mechanisms at work in the world, and on the other hand, sciences that apply this knowledge to explain, predict, and diagnose the phenomena of the world.

Meteorology applies knowledge derived from physics, astronomy, geology, and other sciences to offer explanations and predictions of concrete meteorological phenomena, for example, the cause of some drought. Many systems are involved in this event, including often, the past activities of human actors as, for example in the Sahel. And we recognize that meteorology is not an exact science. History, similarly, seeks to explain historical events as concrete episodes involving particular persons in society, in particular times and places. It uses knowledge derived from the special social sciences, a host of auxiliary sciences, for example, numismatics, paleography, and knowledge drawn from common experience as well.

A hermeneutic science of individual persons is then the psychological analogue to history or to meteorology. It is engaged in understanding the concrete person and his or her life history and particular patterns of behavior, including as reflexively applied, self-understanding. But evidently, although the task remains hermeneutic and close to our common task as social beings, as a scientific effort it requires also that the inquirer use whatever special knowledge is available regarding implicated psychological structures and mechanisms as these operated in the individual biography. And since the person is born and matures in a social world, this understanding inevitably also includes references to what is known about social structures pertinent to that biography. Finally, in contrast to our prescientific mode of understanding, hermeneutic inquiry as a science would be constrained by the systematic, public demands of establishing the evidential credibility of its accounts. Although this picture may seem somewhat idealized, it conforms closely, we believe, to the best actual practices of the various person-oriented psychologies. Moreover, it helps to explain both the fallibility and uncertainty that characterize such practice, and the feeling, sometimes hostilely expressed by experimental psychologists, that such psychology is more like a critically informed and systematic application of common sense than a radically unique and special "science." But given the correctness of the view of science defended here, no other more rigorous person-oriented science is possible.

One must also distinguish between the explanatory, diagnostic, and therapeutic aspects of such science. As an explanatory science, the parallel to history is extremely close. Insofar as history seeks to explain some particular event, it offers an account that traces and connects the complicated conjunctions of motivated acts and their intended and unintended consequences within a structurally limited arena of space and time. The account generally takes the form of a narrative, and the explanation requires also the ability of the historian to enter that situation and to communicate to an audience not only what happened, but what it was like (Hexter, 1971, pp. 208–221). The appeal of a psychoanalytic account (whether valid or not) lies in just this feature.

The relation between common sense and hermeneutic science parallels the relation between Everyman the historian versus the professional historian. Hexter (1971) argues that in writing history, the historian appeals to two "records": first, to the record of the past in concrete evidence, "whatever is publicly accessible to examination and evaluation" (pp. 66ff.), and to the second record, namely, "everything that historians bring to their confrontation with the record of the past" (p. 79). This second record, of course, every inquirer brings when confronting the world, whether of nature, of society, or of individual persons. For Hexter, however, a key difference between Everyman the historian and the professional concerns the treatment of the first record, "a difference in grounds on which they expect and receive credence" (p. 65). And so it is with laypersons and their professional analogue, clinicians, who must be far more critical than laypersons with respect to what is taken as descriptive fact or evidence.

Similar considerations apply to the diagnostic aspect except that emphasis has now shifted to what is wrong or amiss. This still demands an understanding of causes. Diagnoses, of course, are called for when, from an ordinary point of view, others are enigmatic, their behaviors (beliefs, etc.) are anomalous, bizarre, and unintelligible, or when they seek or need help. It is thus also that therapy enters.

Of course it may be that we shall not be able to achieve a significantly better grasp of the psychological structures implicated in such cases, and that in a real sense, these remain, from a theoretical point of view, intractable. Nevertheless, even under these conditions, it may be desirable to have persons specifically qualified to help persons deal with such problems. Participation in self-knowledge, use of behavioral techniques

proved efficacious in practice, and other strategies and technologies are surely legitimate to the extent that they are ameliorative.

More optimistically, as we learn more about basic human powers and competencies and the structures that underlie them, we may learn more about the causes of incompetencies, disabilities, and the like. Some of these (e.g., aphasia) are manifestly neurological in form, but some may not be. In any case, the diagnostic and therapeutic sciences, like medicine, require knowledge both of the concrete individual and of the relevant structures, even if, unlike medicine, the problems that call for psychological amelioration need not be physiologically manifest or even physiological at all.

CONCLUSION

Summarizing what we have said in a succinct and intelligible fashion is virtually impossible. But perhaps we can draw a few conclusions. Philosophy of science has most commonly been the work of philosophers, not scientists. Both epistemology and ontology are central concerns in such philosophy, and these topics have a long history spanning many centuries. A few philosophically oriented scientists may perhaps be partly influenced in their choice of criteria by philosophical writings, but more commonly, scientists contrast with philosophers in generating their own criteria for validity out of their daily practices in scientific research. With this framework in mind, we may ask about the relative compatibility between scientific practices and logical positivism/empiricism versus a realist view of science.

It seems clear that the appeal to scientists of positivism/empiricism has rested on its emphasis on the senses, on observation as a "factual" basis for science. The hard-nosed scientist, like the proverbial Missourian, wants to be shown the evidence. But other themes of that philosophy perhaps only appeared palatable, or their full implication might not have been grasped. The idea of a rigorous logical linkage between observations, hypotheses, and theory sounds fine in principle, but had scientists become aware of the paradoxes and dilemmas created by that idea (eventually pointed out by philosophers), they might have been less ready to accept it.

As for the ontology of logical positivism, which emphasizes hypothetical entities rather than real ones, philosophers have had centuries of argument and practice in convincing others that we cannot know the real world, and perhaps scientists found this idea especially convenient when they were criticizing the work of other scientists (while secretly believing that their own postulated entities were real enough). With respect to Humean causation, few scientists should really feel comfortable with the idea that cause is at bottom illusory, nothing more than the concomitance of events. The idea of necessary and sufficient cause—causal or generative mechanisms or structures—would seem to be something that hard-nosed scientists would dearly love to have at the basis of their science.

What this leads up to is the conclusion that the realist theory of science should be more palatable to the working scientist than positivism or neopositivism. It allows scientists to believe that they are grappling with entities that, although often not observable directly, are real enough. And scientists know that they do not follow rules in jumping from observations or empirical generalizations to theoretical propositions, and further, that even in the confirmatory stage, spelling out a theory (even if in mathematical language) is a slippery and hazardous process.

Finally, the realist theory as presented here, following Bhaskar, provides a means of sharply distinguishing between the task of the scientist and the task of the clinician or technician. The former practices science by creating at least partially closed systems; the latter uses the discoveries of science, but in order to bring about changes in the everyday world, also employs a great deal of knowledge that extends beyond science. This principle defines their respective roles more clearly, and certainly has no unfavorable connotations for either side. It would seem that once they understand it, scientists would happily adopt a realist theory of science.

Data Collection and Data Analysis

The selections in this chapter address decisions about data collection and data analysis by examining some common heuristics that regulate those processes. The first two readings point out two fundamental types of heuristics that often are taken for granted and that inform every research design. Whorf shows how every act of knowing relies on the heuristic of language. The language that researchers use in relating with their informants, and for gathering and analyzing data, has a profound and regulatory impact on the information the researcher generates. Then, Tversky and Kahneman show how cognitive heuristics organize complex information and structure all judgments and decision-making processes, including decisions that influence the kind of information used to solve a problem (data collection) and how those data are interpreted (data analysis). Gadlin and Ingle and Lewontin illustrate how all methods of gathering and analyzing data are heuristics that simultaneously set up systematic biases and are useful for solving certain kinds of problems.

Language as a Heuristic: Introduction to "Science and Linguistics"

Language is an example of a large-scale heuristic that is so familiar and taken for granted that its biases are very difficult to recognize. We tend to not notice our language's effects on understanding and communication unless we compare it with another language. Whorf describes how language organizes many aspects of our thought process and how language inevitably biases all aspects of knowing and communication.

One of the most important distinctions Whorf makes is between two different types of ontological assumptions:

1. The "real" of the subject matter about which one is communicating, or the objects to which language refers

2. The "real" of language, or the particular grammatical structures and terms we use to communicate and conceptualize our experience

As Whorf says,

> the world is presented in a kaleidoscopic flux of impressions which has to be organized by our minds—and this means largely by the linguistic systems in our minds. We cut nature up, organize it into concepts, and ascribe significances as we do, largely because we are parties to an agreement to organize it in this way. ... (1956, p. 213)*

Because our conceptualization depends on the structures of language, "no individual is free to describe nature with absolute impartiality" (1956, p. 214).

Thoughts shape language and at the same time, language shapes thought. Different terms may not be readily translatable into another language, because they refer to different experiences. To illustrate, Tshabalala (1991) described how the social work concept of respect for clients' right to self-determination has implicitly individualistic overtones in American culture, whereas the concept of respect in the Nguni culture of South Africa, which is not readily translatable into English, draws from a community- and kinship-based idiom. In another example, Paolo Freire's concept of *conscientizacao* often has been translated as *consciousness-raising*. However, *consciousness-raising* has hierarchical connotations that are foreign, and in fact antithetical, to Freire's meaning. Whereas some usages of *consciousness-raising* can imply moving from a lower to a higher form of consciousness, *conscientizacao* refers to "learning to perceive social, political, and economic contradictions, and to take action against the oppressive elements of reality" (Freire, 1970, p. 19). *Conscientizacao* occurs through a communal process in which participants discover and transform their view of the world and how they relate to it, rather than being passive recipients of knowledge from outside the community.

One of the most important implications of Whorf's statements for the way we understand science is that there is a "new principle of relativity": "all observers are not led by the same physical evidence to the same picture of the universe, unless their linguistic backgrounds are similar, or can in some way be calibrated" (1956, p. 214). This is one reason why "pure empiricism" and theory-free observations are impossible. Scientists cannot use "facts" to build generalizations or axioms that hold true across contexts, because all communications are already structured by a crucial aspect of context: the linguistic system of the knower, which then biases the knower's conceptualization. That process of influence is not simply unidirectional, however. As William Wimsatt points out, there is an interactive relationship between language and the objects of study:

> Linguistic analyses of the structure of theories have failed to capture the modes of organization of complex systems, for although language structures our view of reality, it ultimately is structured in response to it. Although our conceptual structures tend to come in strata (corresponding to levels of organization) or perspectives (which cross-cut these

---

*Editor's Note: The citations used here refer to pages of the original article. You can find the material quoted from this article in the reprint that follows this introduction.

levels), a realist analysis of the underlying causal structures and the changing forms that they take for systems of increasing complexity is necessary to understand how our linguistic structures take the forms that they do. (1990)*

Leaving behind the restrictiveness of positivism has especially important implications for generating research that reflects the cultural diversity of society. Like language, ways of knowing vary across cultures. For example, in some cultures, the most valuable heritage of information is passed from generation to generation primarily through an oral rather than a written tradition. The heuristic paradigm makes room for old as well as new methods for studying those traditions, such as a researcher's recollected notes of stories told by the informants (Jones & Thorne, 1987; Martin, 1987). Furthermore, positivism's emphasis on generating universally applicable propositions has the effect of flattening out contextual variations. By emphasizing the importance of context, the heuristic paradigm allows for a greater focus on culturally specific meanings and cultural variations.

DISCUSSION QUESTIONS

1. What are the two fallacies of "natural logic" that Whorf outlines?

2. In this paper, Whorf focuses on the impact of linguistic systems across cultures. Within a society, however, diverse dialects and jargons also have a profound impact on how we communicate and know each other.

    a. Describe how a researcher from one English-speaking ethnic tradition may use language that differs considerably from the tradition of her or his informants. One example of this difference is the way the word *bad* is defined by different cultural subgroups in the United States. If the researcher says "that is a bad boy" to a group of teenage girls, how might the researcher's comment be differentially interpreted?

    b. As an example of how terms can have radically different meanings even within the social and behavioral sciences, compare how the term *triangulation* is used by an ethnographer (e.g., see Glossary) and by a family systems therapist.

    c. Suppose you wanted to construct a new theory about human relationships. If you use the same terminology that other theorists have used, what problem is that likely to create for your readers? For a theory that uses radically new language to describe new discoveries about human nature, psychopathology, and treatment, see *Intrapsychic Humanism: An Introduction to a Comprehensive Psychology and Philosophy of Mind* (Pieper & Pieper, 1990).

---

3. Whorf emphasizes that in human relationships "agreement is reached by linguistic process, or else it is not reached" (1956, p. 212).

   a. What does his statement imply about whether there can be a basis for a relationship if the participants do not share the same language?

   b. Some recent child development research has studied how infants "babble" before they speak words. That research also shows that the "baby talk" adults commonly use when communicating with infants has some common linguistic features. Even deaf babies babble by using their hands (Petitto & Marentette, 1991). What are some implications of Whorf's statement for how we can understand the "baby talk" linguistic process that occurs between caregivers and infants?

4. Elsewhere in your education, you may have heard the false claim that the Eskimo language has many more words for snow than English does. The anthropologist Laura Martin (1986) has shown how Whorf's statement that the Eskimo language has three words for snow is inaccurate. Whorf's claim has been picked up and misused repeatedly, resulting in what another anthropologist termed "the great Eskimo vocabulary hoax" (Pullum, 1989). According to Martin, the myth began with Franz Boas; Whorf used Boas's example. Martin emphasizes that there are many Eskimo words for snow, but that the multiple words for snow do not represent an unusual or special case in the Eskimo language. There are also many versions of other root words in Eskimo language simply because of the grammatical structures of the language. There is nothing at all peculiar about the behavior or distribution of "snow words" in these languages. The structure of Eskimo grammar means that the number of "words" for snow is literally incalculable, a conclusion that is inescapable for any other root as well (Martin, 1986, p. 419). Further, Eskimo has about as much differentiation as English does for 'snow' at the monolexemic level: snow and flake. That these roots and others may be modified to reflect semantic distinctions not present in English is a result of gross features of Eskimo morphology and syntax and not of lexicon (Martin, 1986, p. 422). In their critiques of Whorf, Martin and Pullam overlook Whorf's extensive discussion about how different linguistic patterns refer to different experiences and organize thinking in different ways. How do Whorf's comments about the different Hopi and English linguistic patterns indicate that differences between languages are much greater than mere variations in the number of words for particular objects?

5. One implication of Whorf's views is that the principles that underlie social and behavioral theories have culturally specific meanings that we do not recognize unless we compare them with another linguistic system. Find examples of differences in the meanings for common concepts in the social and behavioral sciences. (It may be helpful to refer to dictionaries or books that describe the life of people in cultures other than your own.) As a start, find different meanings for *human, community, family,* and *therapy.*

6. The definition of *language* itself depends on language and thus is changeable rather than fixed. Stephen Toulmin writes: "A language is a Protean thing: it is subject to synchronic diversity in its local dialects and specialized usages, while

a continual influx of neologisms and syntactical novelties leads to diachronic diversity also" (1972, p. 342). To define language, Toulmin says, we can "make it a condition for acknowledging the continued 'unity' of the language, at any time, that members of the various speech-communities employing it should be capable of making themselves sufficiently intelligible to one another" (1972, p. 343). Consider the language with which you are familiar as well as different dialects in your chosen language today and in the past. Is Toulmin's definition of language satisfying to you?

▼ ▼ ▼ ▼ ▼ ▼ ▼ ▼ ▼ ▼ ▼ ▼

SAMPLE RESEARCH PROJECT: DEVELOPING RESIDENTIAL TREATMENT SERVICES FOR HOMELESS, MENTALLY ILL, AND SUBSTANCE-ABUSING CLIENTS

Part 7: Data Collection

Many homeless and mentally ill clients are members of ethnic minority groups, and this population as a whole is multicultural (Campinha-Bacote, 1991; Carter, 1991). To generate an instrument that can best address the diverse experiences of a multi-cultural population, it is even more important *not* to rely on preformatted instruments developed for other populations. It is especially important to develop an instrument that helps these clients to share their subjective experiences, as Jones and Thorne emphasize,

> By failing to include the subject's viewpoint in various aspects of assessment and psycho-logical inquiry, we have often obscured the meaning of our findings and have promoted the attitude that cultural differences are boundaries to be crossed rather than relation-ships to be entered into. (1987, p. 494)

In concert with the naturalistic aims of the research project, the survey given to the patients will be developed with the staff during the sustained process of working with the residents. Developing the instrument in this way has the advantage of making it more relevant and helpful for this staff group and resident population. For example, another important characteristic of this population is that many are illiterate and experience considerable discomfort about being illiterate. To help the residents to voice their opinions, the data collection process needs to be flexible and also to avoid stimulating residents' feelings of embarrassment. The staff have developed a workable process by which they help illiterate residents to write out their opinions during a counseling interview. Some residents also answer questions by working on the questionnaires alone or with the help of friends. The decision that the research will be naturalistic means that this process, which is already occurring, can be the means for collecting the data for research.

Jones and Thorne (1987) elaborate the improvements in ecological validity that result via such a process of instrument development, especially when the research involves multicultural and minority group populations. The data collection methods "are not applied from an entirely different context and set of experiences, and they are not an imposed ethic" (Jones & Thorne, 1987, p. 493).

Examples of this collaborative process of instrument development follow. The staff have already drafted and are using a survey, which helps them to discuss the residents' concerns and feelings during the process of discharge from the program. Suggestions for expanding and revising the survey have been taken from staff, discussed, and incorporated into the draft of the survey. Staff are interested in finding out what kind of aftercare activities the residents want to pursue, including recreational activities and a support group for residents after discharge from the program. During application of the preliminary draft of the survey, some problems have been identified, and the survey has been revised. One of the problems that exemplifies how a data-gathering method always influences the participant/subjects in the research is that some residents reacted to the preliminary survey with intense worry about the impending discharge. This was true even for patients for whom a specific discharge date had not been set. For example, a resident was worried that taking the questionnaire meant that she was being "kicked out" of the program for some offense unknown to her. To facilitate the therapeutic process, the survey was revised to exclude any implication of pending discharge.

Science and Linguistics

Benjamin Whorf

Every normal person in the world, past infancy in years, can and does talk. By virtue of that fact, every person—civilized or uncivilized—carries through life certain naïve but deeply rooted ideas about talking and its relation to thinking. Because of their firm connection with speech habits that have become unconscious and automatic, these notions tend to be rather intolerant of opposition. They are by no means entirely personal and haphazard; their basis is definitely systematic, so that we are justified in calling them a system of natural logic—a term that seems to me preferable to the term common sense, often used for the same thing.

According to natural logic, the fact that every person has talked fluently since infancy makes every man his own authority on the process by which he formulates and communicates. He has merely to consult a common substratum of logic or reason which he and everyone else are supposed to possess. Natural logic says that talking is merely an incidental process concerned strictly with communication, not with formulation of ideas. Talking, or the use of language, is supposed only to "express" what is essentially already formulated nonlinguistically. Formulation is an independent process, called thought or thinking, and is supposed to be largely indifferent to the nature of particular languages. Languages have grammars, which are assumed to be merely norms of conventional and social correctness, but the use of language is supposed to be guided not so much by them as by correct, rational, or intelligent THINKING.

Thought, in this view, does not depend on grammar but on laws of logic or reason which are supposed to be the same for all observers of the universe—to represent a rationale in the universe that can be "found" independently by all intelligent observers, whether they speak Chinese or Choctaw. In our own culture, the formulations of mathematics and of formal logic have acquired the reputation of dealing with this order of things: i.e., with the realm and laws of pure thought. Natural logic holds that different languages are essentially parallel methods for expressing this one-and-the-same rationale of thought and, hence, differ really in but minor ways which may seem important only because they are seen at close range. It holds that mathematics, symbolic logic, philosophy, and so on are systems contrasted with language which deal directly with this realm of thought, not that they are themselves specialized extensions of language. The attitude of natural logic is well shown in an old quip about a German grammarian who devoted his whole life to the study of the dative case. From the point of view of natural logic, the dative case and grammar in general are an extremely minor issue. A different atti-

Source: From "Science and Linguistics" by B. L. Whorf in *Language, Thought, and Reality: Selected Writings of Benjamin Lee Whorf* edited by J. B. Carroll, 1956, Cambridge, MA: MIT Press. Copyright 1956 by MIT Press. Reprinted by permission.

Reprinted from *Technol. Rev.,* 42:229–231, 247–248, no. 6 (April 1940).

365

tude is said to have been held by the ancient Arabians: Two princes, so the story goes, quarreled over the honor of putting on the shoes of the most learned grammarian of the realm; whereupon their father, the caliph, is said to have remarked that it was the glory of his kingdom that great grammarians were honored even above kings.

The familiar saying that the exception proves the rule contains a good deal of wisdom, though from the standpoint of formal logic it became an absurdity as soon as "prove" no longer meant "put on trial." The old saw began to be profound psychology from the time it ceased to have standing in logic. What it might well suggest to us today is that, if a rule has absolutely no exceptions, it is not recognized as a rule or as anything else; it is then part of the background of experience of which we tend to remain unconscious. Never having experienced anything in contrast to it, we cannot isolate it and formulate it as a rule until we so enlarge our experience and expand our base of reference that we encounter an interruption of its regularity. The situation is somewhat analogous to that of not missing the water till the well runs dry, or not realizing that we need air till we are choking.

For instance, if a race of people had the physiological defect of being able to see only the color blue, they would hardly be able to formulate the rule that they saw only blue. The term blue would convey no meaning to them, their language would lack color terms, and their words denoting their various sensations of blue would answer to, and translate, our words "light, dark, white, black," and so on, not our word "blue." In order to formulate the rule or norm of seeing only blue, they would need exceptional moments in which they saw other colors. The phenomenon of gravitation forms a rule without exceptions; needless to say, the untutored person is utterly unaware of any law of gravitation, for it would never enter his head to conceive of a universe in which bodies behaved otherwise than they do at the earth's surface. Like the color blue with our hypothetical race, the law of gravitation is a part of the untutored individual's background, not something he isolates from that background. The law could not be formulated until bodies that always fell were seen in terms of a wider astronomical world in which bodies moved in orbits or went this way and that.

Similarly, whenever we turn our heads, the image of the scene passes across our retinas exactly as it would if the scene turned around us. But this effect is background, and we do not recognize it; we do not see a room turn around us but are conscious only of having turned our heads in a stationary room. If we observe critically while turning the head or eyes quickly, we shall see, no motion it is true, yet a blurring of the scene between two clear views. Normally we are quite unconscious of this continual blurring but seem to be looking about in an unblurred world. Whenever we walk past a tree or house, its image on the retina changes just as if the tree or house were turning on an axis; yet we do not see trees or houses turn as we travel about at ordinary speeds. Sometimes ill-fitting glasses will reveal queer movements in the scene as we

Figure 9.
Languages dissect nature differently. The different isolates of meaning (thoughts) used by English and Shawnee in reporting the same experience, that of cleaning a gun by running the ramrod through it. The pronouns 'I' and 'it' are not shown by symbols, as they have the same meaning in each language. In Shawnee ni- equals 'I'; -a equals 'it.'

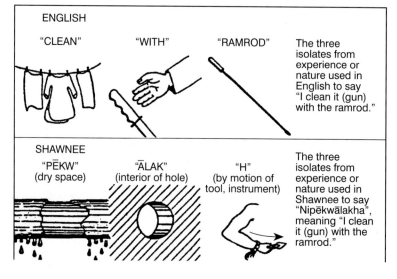

Figure 10.
Languages classify items of experience differently. The class corresponding to one word and one thought in language A may be regarded by language B as two or more classes corresponding to two or more words and thoughts.

Hopi – one word (Masa´ytaka)
English – three words

English – one word (Snow)
Eskimo – three words

Hopi – Pāme
English – one word (Water); Hopi – two words

Hopi – Kēyi

look about, but normally we do not see the relative motion of the environment when we move; our psychic makeup is somehow adjusted to disregard whole realms of phenomena that are so all-pervasive as to be irrelevant to our daily lives and needs.

Natural logic contains two fallacies: First, it does not see that the phenomena of a language are to its own speakers largely of a background character and so are outside the critical consciousness and control of the speaker who is expounding natural logic. Hence, when anyone, as a natural logician, is talking about reason, logic, and the laws for correct thinking, he is apt to be simply marching in step with purely grammatical facts that have somewhat of a background character in his own language or family of languages but are by no means universal in all languages and in no sense a common substratum of reason. Second, natural logic confuses agreement about subject matter, attained through use of language, with knowledge of the linguistic process by which agreement is attained: i.e., with the province of the despised (and to its notion superfluous) grammarian. Two fluent speakers, of English let us say, quickly reach a point of assent about the subject matter of their speech; they agree about what their language refers to. One of them, A, can give directions that will be carried out by the other, B, to A's complete satisfaction. Because they thus under-

stand each other so perfectly, A and B, as natural logicians, suppose they must of course know how it is all done. They think, e.g., that it is simply a matter of choosing words to express thoughts. If you ask A to explain how he got B's agreement so readily, he will simply repeat to you, with more or less elaboration or abbreviation, what he said to B. He has no notion of the process involved. The amazingly complex system of linguistic patterns and classifications, which A and B must have in common before they can adjust to each other at all, is all background to A and B.

These background phenomena are the province of the grammarian—or of the linguist, to give him his more modern name as a scientist. The word linguist in common, and especially newspaper, parlance means something entirely different, namely, a person who can quickly attain agreement about subject matter with different people speaking a number of different languages. Such a person is better termed a polyglot or a multilingual. Scientific linguists have long understood that ability to speak a language fluently does not necessarily confer a linguistic knowledge of it, i.e., understanding of its background phenomena and its systematic processes and structure, any more than ability to play a good game of billiards confers or requires any knowledge of the laws of mechanics that operate upon the billiard table.

The situation here is not unlike that in any other field of science. All real scientists have their eyes primarily on background phenomena that cut very little ice, as such, in our daily lives; and yet their studies have a way of bringing out a close relation between these unsuspected realms of fact and such decidedly foreground activities as transporting goods, preparing food, treating the sick, or growing potatoes, which in time may become very much modified, simply because of pure scientific investigation in no way concerned with these brute matters themselves. Linguistics present a quite similar case; the background phenomena with which it deals are involved in all our foreground activities of talking and of reaching agreement, in all reasoning and arguing of cases, in all law, arbitration, conciliation, contracts, treaties, public opinion, weighing of scientific theories, formulation of scientific results. Whenever agreement or assent is arrived at in human affairs, and whether or not mathematics or other specialized symbolisms are made part of the procedure, THIS AGREEMENT IS REACHED BY LINGUISTIC PROCESSES, OR ELSE IT IS NOT REACHED.

As we have seen, an overt knowledge of the linguistic processes by which agreement is attained is not necessary to reaching some sort of agreement, but it is certainly no bar thereto; the more complicated and difficult the matter, the more such knowledge is a distinct aid, till the point may be reached—I suspect the modern world has about arrived at it—when the knowledge becomes not only an aid but a necessity. The situation may be likened to that of navigation. Every boat that sails is in the lap of planetary forces; yet a boy can pilot his small craft around a harbor without benefit of geography, astronomy, mathematics, or international politics. To the captain of an ocean liner, however, some knowledge of all these subjects is essential.

When linguists became able to examine critically and scientifically a large number of languages of widely different patterns, their base of reference was expanded; they experienced an interruption of phenomena hitherto held universal, and a whole new order of significances came into their ken. It was found that the background linguistic system (in other words, the grammar) of each language is not merely a reproducing instrument for voicing ideas but rather is itself the shaper of ideas, the program and guide of the individual's mental activity, for his analysis of impressions, for his synthesis of his mental stock in trade.

Formulation of ideas is not an independent process, strictly rational in the old sense, but is part of a particular grammar, and differs, from slightly to greatly, between different grammars. We dissect nature along lines laid down by our native languages. The categories and types that we isolate from the world of phenomena we do not find there because they stare every observer in the face; on the contrary, the world is presented in a kaleidoscopic flux of impressions which has to be organized by our minds—and this means largely by the linguistic systems in our minds. We cut nature up, organize it into concepts, and ascribe significances as we do, largely because we are parties to an agreement to organize it in this way—an agreement that holds throughout our speech community and is codified in the patterns of our language. The agreement is, of course, an implicit and unstated one, BUT ITS TERMS ARE ABSOLUTELY OBLIGATORY; we cannot talk at all except by subscribing to the organization and classification of data which the agreement decrees.

This fact is very significant for modern science, for it means that no individual is free to describe nature with absolute impartiality but is constrained to certain modes of interpretation even while he thinks himself most free. The person most nearly free in such respects would be a linguist familiar with very many widely different linguistic systems. As yet no linguist is in any such position. We are thus introduced to a new principle of relativity, which holds that all observers are not led by the same physical evidence to the same picture of the universe, unless their linguistic backgrounds are similar, or can in some way be calibrated.

This rather startling conclusion is not so apparent if we compare only our modern European languages, with perhaps Latin and Greek thrown in for good measure. Among these tongues there is a unanimity of major pattern which at first seems to bear out natural logic. But this unanimity exists only because these tongues are all Indo-European dialects cut to the same basic plan, being historically transmitted from what was long ago one speech community; because the modern dialects have long shared in building up a common culture, and because much of this culture, on the more intellectual side, is derived from the linguistic backgrounds of Latin and Greek. Thus this group of languages satisfies the special case of the clause beginning "unless" in the statement of the linguistic relativity principle at the end of the preceding para-

Figure 11.

Contrast between a "temporal" language (English) and a "timeless" language (Hopi). What are to English differences of time are to Hopi differences in the kind of validity.

Objective Field	Speaker (Sender)	Hearer (Receiver)	Handling of Topic, Running of Third Person
Situation 1a.			English . . . "He is running" Hopi . . . . . ."Wari" (Running, Statement of fact)
Situation 1b. Objective field blank Devoid of running			English . . . "He ran" Hopi . . . . . ."Wari" (Running, Statement of fact)
Situation 2			English . . . "He is running" Hopi . . . . . ."Wari" (Running, statement of fact)
Situation 3 Objective field blank			English . . ."He ran" Hopi . . . . . ."Era wari" (Running, statement of fact from memory)
Situation 4 Objective field blank			English . . . "He will run" Hopi . . . . . ."Warikni" (Running, statement of expectation)
Situation 5 Objective field blank			English . . . "He runs" (e.g., on the track team) Hopi . . . . . ."Warikngwe" (Running, statement of law)

graph. From this condition follows the unanimity of description of the world in the community of modern scientists. But it must be emphasized that "all modern Indo-European-speaking observers" is not the same thing as "all observers." That modern Chinese or Turkish scientists describe the world in the same terms as Western scientists means, of course, only that they have taken over bodily the entire Western system of rationalizations, not that they have corroborated that system from their native posts of observation.

When Semitic, Chinese, Tibetan, or African languages are contrasted with our own, the divergence in analysis of the world becomes more apparent; and, when we bring in the native languages of the Americas, where speech communities for many millenniums have gone their ways independently of each other and of the Old World, the fact that languages dissect nature in many different ways becomes patent. The relativity of all conceptual systems, ours included, and their dependence upon language stand revealed. That American Indians speaking only their native tongues are never called upon to act as scientific observers is in no wise to the point. To exclude the evidence which their languages offer as to what the human mind can do is like expecting botanists to study nothing but food plants and hothouse roses and then tell us what the plant world is like!

.   .   .   .   .   .

What surprises most is to find that various grand generalizations of the Western world, such as time, velocity, and matter, are not essential to the construction of a consistent picture of the universe. The psychic experiences that we class under these headings are, of course, not destroyed; rather, categories derived from other kinds of experiences take over the rulership of the cosmology and seem to function just as well. Hopi may be called a timeless language. It recognizes psychological time, which is much like Bergson's "duration," but this "time" is quite unlike the mathematical time, T, used by our physicists. Among the peculiar properties of Hopi time are that it varies with each observer, does not permit of simultaneity, and has zero dimensions; i.e., it cannot be given a number greater than one. The Hopi do not say, "I stayed five days," but "I left of the fifth day." A word referring to this kind of time, like the word day, can have no plural. The puzzle picture (Fig. 11, page 213) will give mental exercise to anyone who would like to figure out how the Hopi verb gets along without tenses. Actually, the only practical use of our tenses, in one-verb sentences, is to distinguish among five typical situations, which are symbolized in the picture. The timeless Hopi verb does not distinguish between the present, past, and future of the event itself but must always indicate what type of validity the SPEAKER intends the statement to have: (a) report of an event (situations 1, 2, 3 in the picture); (b) expectation of an event (situation 4); (c) generalization or law about events (situation 5). Situation 1, where the speaker and listener are in contact with the same objective field, is divided by our language into the two conditions, 1a, and 1b, which it calls present and past, respectively. This division is unnecessary for a language which assures one that the statement is a report.

Hopi grammar, by means of its forms called aspects and modes, also makes it easy to distinguish among momentary, continued, and repeated occurrences, and to indicate the actual sequence of reported events. Thus the universe can be described without recourse to a concept of dimensional time. How would a physics constructed along these lines work, with no T (time) in its equation? Perfectly, as far as I can see, though of course it would require different ideology and perhaps different mathematics. Of course V

(velocity) would have to go too. The Hopi language has no word really equivalent to our 'speed' or 'rapid.' What translates these terms is usually a word meaning intense or very, accompanying any verb of motion. Here is a clue to the nature of our new physics. We may have to introduce a new term I, intensity. Every thing and event will have an I, whether we regard the thing or event as moving or as just enduring or being. Perhaps the I of an electric charge will turn out to be its voltage, or potential. We shall use clocks to measure some intensities, or, rather, some RELATIVE intensities, for the absolute intensity of anything will be meaningless. Our old friend acceleration will still be there but doubtless under a new name. We shall perhaps call it V, meaning not velocity but variation. Perhaps all growths and accumulations will be regarded as V's. We should not have the concept of rate in the temporal sense, since, like velocity, rate introduces a mathematical and linguistic time. Of course we know that all measurements are ratios, but the measurements of intensities made by comparison with the standard intensity of a clock or a planet we do not treat as ratios, any more than we so treat a distance made by comparison with a yardstick.

A scientist from another culture that used time and velocity would have great difficulty in getting us to understand these concepts. We should talk about the intensity of a chemical reaction; he would speak of its velocity or its rate, which words we should at first think were simply words for intensity in his language. Likewise, he at first would think that intensity was simply our own word for velocity. At first we should agree, later we should begin to disagree, and it might dawn upon both sides that different systems of rationalization were being used. He would find it very hard to make us understand what he really meant by velocity of a chemical reaction. We should have no words that would fit. He would try to explain it by likening it to a running horse, to the difference between a good horse and a lazy horse. We should try to show him, with a superior laugh, that his analogy also was a matter of different intensities, aside from which there was little similarity between a horse and a chemical reaction in a beaker. We should point out that a running horse is moving relative to the ground, whereas the material in the beaker is at rest.

One significant contribution to science from the linguistic point of view may be the greater development of our sense of perspective. We shall no longer be able to see a few recent dialects of the Indo-European family, and the rationalizing techniques elaborated from their patterns, as the apex of the evolution of the human mind, nor their present wide spread as due to any survival from fitness or to anything but a few events of history—events that could be called fortunate only from the parochial point of view of the favored parties. They, and our own thought processes with them, can no longer be envisioned as spanning the gamut of reason and knowledge but only as one constellation in a galactic expanse. A fair realization of the incredible degree of diversity of linguistic systems that ranges over the globe leaves one with an inescapable feeling that the human spirit is inconceivably old; that the few thousand years of history covered by our written records are no more than the thickness of a pencil mark on the scale that measures our past experience on this planet; that the events of these recent millenniums spell nothing in any evolutionary wise, that the race has taken no sudden spurt, achieved no commanding synthesis during recent millenniums, but has only played a little with a few of the linguistic formulations and views of nature bequeathed from an inexpressibly longer past. Yet neither this feeling nor the sense of precarious dependence of all we know upon linguistic tools which themselves are largely unknown need be discouraging to science but should, rather, foster that humility which accompanies the true scientific spirit, and thus forbid that arrogance of the mind which hinders real scientific curiosity and detachment.

The Framing of Information and Judgments Under Uncertainty: Introduction to "The Framing of Decisions and the Psychology of Choice"

Economic theories and legal reasoning have often been based on the concept of the "rational man," the belief that when faced with the same problem rational people will find the same solution. For example, the "rational man" is used as a standard against which "criminal intent" can be evaluated (Dascal & Wroblewski, 1991). In economic theory, the individual is regarded as a "rational utility maximizer," and organizations are "rational profit maximizers" (Ulen, 1990, describes and critiques that position; see also Rhoads, 1985). However, since the early 1970s researchers have studied patterns of human decision making and reasoning and have found that people often reason and make decisions in ways that are unexpected and that differ from those definitions of rationality. In the next selection, the cognitive researchers Amos Tversky and Daniel Kahneman examine decision making in the uncertain situations that confront most problem solvers. Other psychologists, most notably Gerd Gigerenzer (1991a, 1991b), are currently studying human reasoning and the standards used for conceptualizing human reasoning. The contributions of these cognitive researchers are important because research design, data collection, and data analysis can be regarded as problem-solving processes, and the cognitive heuristics that inform other problem-solving processes regulate research decisions as well. By understanding cognitive heuristics and their biases, researchers can examine the decisions they make in designing research and can better regulate the biases inevitably introduced by the heuristics they choose.

Tversky and Kahneman have been leaders in the study of the cognitive heuristics that regulate decision making. The authors' interest in looking at judgment and decision making grew out of their review of prior research on decision making in the 1950s and 1960s, from which they concluded that there was "a substantial discrepancy between the objective record of people's success in prediction tasks and the sincere beliefs of these people about the quality of their performance." They recognized that "people's impressions of how they reason, and of how well they reason, could not be taken at face value" (Kahneman et al., 1982, p. xi).

Tversky and Kahneman explore the effects of problem framing on people's inclination to take risks. Various problem frames are analogous to taking multiple visual perspectives on a given point. Tversky and Kahneman assume that for a judgment (e.g., an estimate of the height of a mountain) to be veridical, that judgment should not alter with a change in perspective. They investigate whether decision-making processes are veridical or whether judgments shift with changes in perspective. In presenting their subjects with problems, they retain the same logical structure of a problem but frame it differently to see whether a different frame leads people to make different judgments. The first problem concerned the choice of treatments, and the participant/subjects were initially asked to choose between a treatment that offered certainty that "200 people will be saved" and another treatment that offered one-third "probability that 600 people will be saved, and 2/3 probability that no people will be saved" (p. 453).* The majority of subjects chose the solution that promised certainty, which Tversky and Kahneman interpreted to be risk-averse behavior. Retaining the same logical structure of the problem, they then changed the frame and again asked their participant/subjects to choose between two treatments. With one treatment it would be certain that "400 people will die" and with the other, there was "1/3 probability that nobody will die, and 2/3 probability that 600 people will die." The majority of participant/subjects chose the latter alternative, which the authors regarded as "risk-taking" behavior. They summarized people's behavior as "risk aversion in choices involving gains and risk seeking in choices involving losses" (1981, p. 454). This study has relevance for many aspects of the research process. To illustrate, it underscores the effects of research problem framing on the information (or data) that the researcher chooses to gather. The study also shows that question framing has a profound, regulatory impact on the data collected.

To explain their findings, Tversky and Kahneman propose that to simplify complex information about a problem situation, people use a mental account, against which they evaluate the potential outcomes of their acts. In most situations, they evaluate their acts "in terms of a minimal account, which includes only the direct consequences of the act" (p. 456). However, if the outcomes of a potential act are likely to have consequences for "an account that was previously set up by a related act," such as if a potential consequence represents a loss, people will evaluate the act in a more inclusive way, and they typically incorporate more of the context in their evaluation.

Tversky and Kahneman's work on heuristics and biases has been extremely influential. Recently, however, an important controversy has begun that focuses on the assumptions that have guided their research on heuristics and biases. Tversky and Kahneman's conceptualization of heuristics and biases is narrow and restrictive compared with the formulation of these terms by Herbert Simon and William Wimsatt and in the heuristic paradigm. In Tversky and Kahneman's work, a *heuristic* refers to a very specific cognitive reasoning process that can lead to solutions that are correct according to selected standards of probabilistic reasoning. A heuristic also sets up biases. In their view, a bias sets up the problem solver to arrive at incorrect answers. Inherent in Tversky and Kahneman's definitions of heuristic and bias is the assumption that ascertaining whether an answer is correct or incorrect according to the researcher's standards is an appropriate regulatory value for research about human reasoning.

The contemporary controversy about Tversky and Kahneman's work centers around the ideas they developed in a 1974 paper, "Judgment under Uncertainty: Heuristics and Biases," in which they delineated what they regarded as systematic biases in lay persons' and researchers' judgments of frequencies and probabilities. Tversky and Kahneman described three heuristics (availability, representativeness, and adjustment from an anchor), which they believed led their participant/subjects to make those errors. They emphasized that, although those cognitive heuristics may lead to irrational judgments in some situations with some problems, the heuristics

---

*Editor's Note: The citations used here refer to pages of the original article. You can find the material quoted from this article in the reprint that follows this introduction.

are neither intrinsically fallacious nor designed for irrationality. On the contrary, cognitive heuristics facilitate problem solving in most decision-making situations (see also Kahneman & Tversky, 1983).

Researchers have explored the three heuristics elaborated in Tversky and Kahneman's 1974 paper and have investigated how those heuristics might be present in decision making in many fields, including education and medical diagnosis (Kahneman et al., 1982). Fagley (1988) used the heuristics that Tversky and Kahneman defined to illuminate school psychologists' decisions and the psychologists' interpretations of information about student behavior. Hollon and Kriss (1984) applied research about processing heuristics and biases to theories of psychological change. Hackman (1983) applied information about the heuristics Tversky and Kahneman defined to generate maxims for improving the collection, analysis, and presentation of information so that it is more useful for decision makers. Other researchers investigated the impact of cognitive frames and heuristics on conversations between family doctors and their patients. The researchers concluded that to help patients understand and find solutions for their difficulties, doctors need to understand the heuristics that patients use to conceptualize their difficulties (D. A. Evans, Block, Steinberg, & Penrose, 1986). The heuristics Tversky and Kahneman (1974; Kahneman et al., 1982) identified also underlie the process of stereotyping that can lead to racial and ethnic bias in many situations, such as decision making about punishments for crimes (Bodenhausen & Wyer, 1985). Further research has indicated that when people are educated about those cognitive heuristics, they can compensate for them to some extent (Fischhoff, 1982).

The formulations of heuristics and biases that Tversky and Kahneman advanced in their 1974 paper, as well as the assumptions about human rationality that underlie those formulations, have become increasingly controversial. The most important critique, by Gerd Gigerenzer, is that Tversky and Kahneman's approach to studying decision making "takes the uncertainty out of judgment under uncertainty."[90] Gigerenzer shows how Tversky and Kahneman's formulation of heuristics and biases is influenced both by the positivist belief in prescriptiveness as a value to regulate scientific research and by the positivist neglect of the impact of subjectivity. Gigerenzer says that Tversky and Kahneman define a "bias" normatively, as an incorrect answer by contrast with the researchers' chosen standards (Gigerenzer, 1991b). In other words, Tversky and Kahneman assume that the most valuable approach to human decision making is evaluative, using categories such as correct and incorrect answers, which in turn are based on norms the researchers have chosen. Although for some problems there clearly are correct answers (e.g., 2 + 2 = 4), the most difficult (and the most common) problems facing decision makers occur under conditions of uncertainty. An inherent aspect of those uncertain conditions is that no norms can be mechanically applied for ascertaining a correct answer. In other words, no formal norms can be applied independently of the content of a problem. Moreover, people have extremely diverse subjective experiences and attach different meanings to different aspects of a problem; they frame a problem in different ways and respond to it in reference to different contexts. An aspect of Gigerenzer's argument builds on the postpositivist recognition that there is no justification for privileging researchers' preferences for the norms or context that should be used to obtain an answer to a problem. Further, Gigerenzer emphasizes that Tversky and

Kahneman have not examined sufficiently the merit of the norms they have chosen to evaluate judgment under uncertainty, and that in fact the norms they used as standards for correct answers to the decision-making problems are flawed:

> the probabilistic rules against which cognitive and social psychologists have measured the proficiency of their subjects are in fact a highly (and, I shall argue, often misleadingly) selected sample of those routinely used, consulted, and discussed by working probabilists and statisticians. When claiming "errors" and "fallacies", cognitive and social psychologists have largely ignored conceptual and technical distinctions fundamental to probability and statistics. (Gigerenzer, 1991b, p. 86)

The findings from Gigerenzer's studies indicate how some of the biases Tversky and Kahneman identify, such as overconfidence, do not hold up. For example, when researchers frame questions concerning people's confidence in the accuracy of their own guesses differently from the frames Tversky and Kahneman used—that is, in terms of frequencies rather than Tversky and Kahneman's emphasis on single events—"comparing their estimated frequencies with actual frequencies of correct answers made 'overconfidence' disappear" (Gigerenzer, 1991b, p. 89).

In addition to the normative critique of the heuristics and biases program led by Tversky and Kahneman, Gigerenzer and his colleagues have critiqued the program descriptively. Gigerenzer and co-workers examine the use of probabilistic reasoning and the conceptualization of rationality (Gigerenzer, 1991a, 1991b; Gigerenzer, Hoffrage, & Kleinbolting, 1991; Gigerenzer & Hug, 1992). In critiquing Tversky and Kahneman's work on descriptive grounds, Gigerenzer argues for a broader understanding of human rationality and a broader conception of heuristics and of their role: "although they [Tversky and Kahneman] repeatedly asserted that these heuristics are useful, almost all of their work focused on how they lead to 'errors'" (1991b, p. 101). He believes that the narrow conceptualization of Tversky and Kahneman's use of the terms *heuristics* and *biases* has led to a "conceptual dead end" (1991b, p. 101):

> In artificial intelligence research one hopes that heuristics can make computers smart; in the "heuristics and biases" program one hopes that heuristics can tell why humans are not smart. The fundamental problem with the latter is that most "errors" in probabilistic reasoning that one wants to explain by heuristics are in fact not errors. . . . Thus heuristics are meant to explain what does not exist. Rather than explaining a deviation between human judgment and allegedly "correct" probabilistic reasoning, future research has to get rid of simplistic norms that evaluate human judgment instead of explaining it. (Gigerenzer, 1991b, p. 102)

Gigerenzer and Hug succinctly formulate the questions that arise when one begins to consider the conceptualization of cognitive heuristics and human reasoning:

> What counts as human rationality: reasoning processes that embody content-independent formal rules, such as propositional logic, or reasoning processes that are well designed for solving important adaptive problems, such as social contracts or social regulations? Second, how specific are the laws of reasoning? Do they consist of rules that are general pur-

pose and can be applied to any problem, or rules that are domain specific and designed for a limited class of problems? (1992, p. 129)

Gigerenzer argues that human rationality should not be conceptualized in terms of context-independent standards such as those of formal logic, but that it is more reasonable to conceptualize rationality in relation to social context and in terms of finding domain-specific solutions.

In concert with the work of Simon and Wimsatt, the heuristic paradigm described in this book defines the terms *heuristic* and *bias* more broadly than the restrictive definitions used by Tversky and Kahneman. Furthermore, the heuristic paradigm does not prescribe specific norms to delineate heuristics and biases. An important implication of the reformulation of human rationality advanced by Gigerenzer and his colleagues is that it underscores how unreasonable it is to conceptualize science as a search for explanations based on immutable, formal laws. Instead, in understanding rationality it is more helpful to recognize that rationality can be regarded as "domain-specific" (Gigerenzer & Hug, 1992) or "bounded" (Simon, 1981). Accordingly, an aim of research is to find solutions that are applicable within particular contexts. One implication of extending those formulations to the research process means that it is not reasonable to expect that all scientific research should yield findings that are generalizable across multiple contexts. Instead, evaluations of research can focus on whether the study offers workable solutions to problems in specific domains.

KEY TERMS

Risk assessment   Uncertainty

DISCUSSION QUESTIONS

1. To better appreciate the contributions of cognitive researchers, try the following tasks that have been used in experiments about human reasoning:

   a. You see four cards, each of which has one of the following letters on its face: E, K, 4, 7. You know that each card has a letter on one side and a number on the other. Evaluate the truth of the following rule: "If a card has a vowel on one side, then it has an even number on the other." To evaluate that rule, you can turn over two and only two cards. Which cards will you turn over? (Johnson-Laird & Wason cited in Gardner, 1985, pp. 361—362; Answer is in note 91).

   b. Which of the following sequences of heads and tails is less likely to occur?

      HHHTTT

      HTHHTT[92]

2. Tversky and Kahneman illustrate another deviation from the "rational man" theory of decision making: People typically experience a "temporary devaluation of

money which facilitates extra spending and reduces the significance of small discounts in the context of a large expenditure, such as buying a house or a car".(See p. 386 in this volume.) What are some other examples of context-dependent variations in the values attributed to goods or services?

3. In reconceptualizing judgment under uncertainty, Gigerenzer writes, "judgment under uncertainty occurs in a social environment in which there are other 'players' who make a person's response more or less rational." He recounted an anecdote to illustrate his point. A Welsh villager "once was offered the choice between a pound and a shilling, and he took the shilling. People came from everywhere to witness this phenomenon. They repeatedly offered him a choice between a pound and a shilling. He always took the shilling. Seen as a single choice (and by all monotone utility functions), this choice would seem irrational" (1991b, p. 108).

   a. Gigerenzer also points out, however, that when seen in the context of how others are responding, the villager's behavior is quite rational. What rational aim does the villager accomplish by repeatedly choosing the shilling?[93]

   b. Describe how you changed the environment–system boundary to answer (a).

4. Tversky and Kahneman state:

   > Individuals who face a decision problem and have a definite preference (i) might have a different preference in a different framing of the same problem , (ii) are normally unaware of alternative frames and of their potential effects on the relative unattractiveness of options, (iii) would wish their preferences to be independent of frame, but (iv) are often uncertain how to resolve detected inconsistencies. (1981, p. 458. See p. 386 in this volume.)

   Researchers face decision problems whenever they formulate a problem, choose a theory, decide what data to collect, and conceptualize data-analysis methods. Given what you have learned about the impact of different frames on decision makers' judgments, how might a researcher maximize the opportunity to look at those decisions from multiple perspectives?

5. Baruch Fischhoff, one of the leading researchers investigating heuristics and decision making, found that people are subject to a "knew it all along" bias (1977). Once people are told a correct answer to a question, the "knew it all along" bias leads people to overestimate how much they would have known about the answer had they *not* been told the correct answer, as well as how much they actually knew about the answer *before* they were told.

   a. How might the "knew it all along" bias influence people's ability to appraise the originality of a new theory?

   b. How might that bias influence students' capacity to appraise what they still need to learn for a test?

   c. How might that bias influence researchers who need to consider what they do *not* know in formulating the research problem?

▼ ▼ ▼ ▼ ▼ ▼ ▼ ▼ ▼ ▼ ▼ ▼ ▼

SAMPLE RESEARCH PROJECT: DEVELOPING RESIDENTIAL TREATMENT SERVICES FOR HOMELESS, MENTALLY ILL, AND SUBSTANCE-ABUSING CLIENTS

Part 8: Framing Questions

A significant aspect of developing the survey for residents and interpreting the data obtained is considering how questions are framed and the meaning of the respondents' answers in light of how questions are framed. One of the initial issues seems to result from the impaired cognitive functioning that is due to episodes of psychosis in some respondents. The psychosis affects how some residents responded to questions. Certain types of questions are more difficult than others for residents with episodic psychoses.

For example, one question on the preliminary survey asks the residents to check those services they find to be helpful and lists seven services. The next question asks the respondents to list those services they find to be *not* helpful and lists the same seven services. Some residents checked both questions in exactly the same way, clearly not noticing that their answers were inconsistent. This problem could be handled by reframing the question or by developing a code to use in data analysis that would capture this problem. To make this decision while developing the instrument, the researchers looked at how many residents had that kind of problem in responding and noticed that it was only a very small percentage. Rather than change the way questions were framed, the researchers created a code for the coding manual to indicate the cases for which the answers to those questions are contradictory.

The Framing of Decisions and the Psychology of Choice

Amos Tversky   *Stanford University*

Daniel Kahneman   *The University of British Columbia*

SUMMARY: The psychological principles that govern the perception of decision problems and the evaluation of probabilities and outcomes produce predictable shifts of preference when the same problem is framed in different ways. Reversals of preference are demonstrated in choices regarding monetary outcomes, both hypothetical and real, and in questions pertaining to the loss of human lives. The effects of frames on preferences are compared to the effects of perspectives on perceptual appearance. The dependence of preferences on the formulation of decision problems is a significant concern for the theory of rational choice.

Explanations and predictions of people's choices, in everyday life as well as in the social sciences, are often founded on the assumption of human rationality. The definition of rationality has been much debated, but there is general agreement that rational choices should satisfy some elementary requirements of consistency and coherence. In this article we describe decision problems in which people systematically violate the requirements of consistency and coherence, and we trace these violations to the psychological principles that govern the perception of decision problems and the evaluation of options.

A decision problem is defined by the acts or options among which one must choose, the possible outcomes or consequences of these acts, and the contingencies or conditional probabilities that relate outcomes to acts. We use the term "decision frame" to refer to the decision-maker's conception of the acts, outcomes, and contingencies associated with a particular choice. The frame that a decision-maker adopts is controlled partly by the formulation of the problem and partly by the norms, habits, and personal characteristics of the decision-maker.

It is often possible to frame a given decision problem in more than one way. Alternative frames for a decision problem may be compared to alternative perspectives on a visual scene. Veridical perception requires that the perceived relative height of two neighboring mountains, say, should not reverse with changes of vantage point. Similarly, rational choice requires that the preference between options should not reverse with changes of frame. Because of imperfections of human perception and decision, however, changes of perspective often reverse the relative apparent size of objects and the relative desirability of options.

We have obtained systematic reversals of preference by variations in the framing of acts, contingencies, or outcomes. These effects have been observed in a variety of problems and in the choices of different groups of respondents. Here we present selected illustrations of preference reversals, with data obtained from students at Stanford University and at the University of British Columbia who answered brief ques-

Source: "The Framing of Decisions and the Psychology of Choice" by A. Tversky and D. Kahneman, 1981, *Science, 211,* pp. 453–458. Copyright © 1981 AAAS. Reprinted by permission.

tionnaires in a classroom setting. The total number of respondents for each problem is denoted by N, and the percentage who chose each option is indicated in brackets.

The effect of variations in framing is illustrated in problems 1 and 2.

> Problem 1 [N = 152]: Imagine that the U. S. is preparing for the outbreak of an unusual Asian disease, which is expected to kill 600 people. Two alternative programs to combat the disease have been proposed. Assume that the exact scientific estimate of the consequences of the programs are as follows:
>
> If Program A is adopted, 200 people will be saved. [72 percent]
>
> If Program B is adopted, there is 1/3 probability that 600 people will be saved, and 2/3 probability that no people will be saved. [28 percent]
>
> Which of the two programs would you favor?

The majority choice in this problem is risk averse: the prospect of certainly saving 200 lives is more attractive than a risky prospect of equal expected value, that is, a one-in-three chance of saving 600 lives.

A second group of respondents was given the cover story of problem 1 with a different formulation of the alternative programs, as follows:

> Problem 2 (N = 155):
>
> If Program C is adopted 400 people will die. [22 percent]
>
> If Program D is adopted there is 1/3 probability that nobody will die, and 2/3 probability that 600 will die. [78 percent]
>
> Which of these programs would you favor?

The majority choice in problem 2 is risk taking: the certain death of 400 people is less acceptable than the two-in-three chance that 600 will die. The preferences in problems 1 and 2 illustrate a common pattern: choices involving gains are often risk averse and choices involving losses are often risk taking. However, it is easy to see that the two problems are effectively identical. The only difference between them is that the outcomes are described in problem 1 by the number of lives saved and in problem 2 by the number of

lives lost. The change is accompanied by a pronounced shift from risk aversion to risk taking. We have observed this reversal in several groups of respondents, including university faculty and physicians. Inconsistent responses to problems 1 and 2 arise from the conjunction of a framing effect with contradictory attitudes toward risks involving gains and losses. We turn now to an analysis of these attitudes.

THE EVALUATION OF PROSPECTS

The major theory of decision-making under risk is the expected utility model. This model is based on a set of axioms, for example, transitivity of preferences, which provide criteria for the rationality of choices. The choices of an individual who conforms to the axioms can be described in terms of the utilities of various outcomes for that individual. The utility of a risky prospect is equal to the expected utility of its outcomes, obtained by weighting the utility of each possible outcome by its probability. When faced with a choice, a rational decision-maker will prefer the prospect that offers the highest expected utility (1, 2).

As will be illustrated below, people exhibit patterns of preference which appear incompatible with expected utility theory. We have presented elsewhere (3) a descriptive model, called prospect theory, which modifies expected utility theory so as to accommodate these observations. We distinguish two phases in the choice process: an initial phase in which acts, outcomes, and contingencies are framed, and a subsequent phase of evaluation (4). For simplicity, we restrict the formal treatment of the theory to choices involving stated numerical probabilities and quantitative outcomes, such as money, time, or number of lives.

Consider a prospect that yields outcome x with probability p, outcome y with probability q, and the status quo with probability $1 - p - q$. According to prospect theory, there are values $v(.)$ associated with outcomes, and decision weights $\pi(.)$ associated with probabilities, such that the overall value of the prospect equals $\pi(p) v(x) + \pi(q) v(y)$. A slightly different equation should be applied if all outcomes of a prospect are on the same side of the zero point (5).

In prospect theory, outcomes are expressed as positive or negative deviations (gains or losses) from a neutral reference outcome, which is assigned a value of zero. Although subjective values differ among individuals and attributes, we propose that the value function is commonly S-shaped, concave above the reference point and convex below it, as illustrated in Fig. 1. For example, the difference in subjective value between gains of $10 and $20 is greater than the subjective difference between gains of $110 and $120. The same relation between value differences holds for the corresponding losses. Another property of the value function is that the response to losses is more extreme than the response to gains. The displeasure associated with losing a sum of money is generally greater than the pleasure associated with winning the same amount, as is reflected in people's reluctance to accept fair bets on a toss of a coin. Several studies of decision (3, 6) and judgment (7) have confirmed these properties of the value function (8).

The second major departure of prospect theory from the expected utility model involves the treatment of probabilities. In expected utility theory the utility of an uncertain outcome is weighted by its probability: in prospect theory the value of an uncertain outcome is multiplied by a decision weight $\pi(p)$, which is a monotonic function of p but is not a probability. The weighting function π has the following properties. First, impossible events are discarded, that is, $\pi(0) = 0$, and the scale is normalized so that $\pi(1) = 1$, but the function is not well behaved near the endpoints. Second, for low probabilities $\pi(p) > p$, but $\pi(p) + \pi(1-p) \leq 1$. Thus low probabilities are overweighted, moderate and high probabilities are underweighted, and the latter effect is more pronounced than the former. Third, $\pi(pq)/\pi(p) < \pi(pqr)/\pi(pr)$ for all $0 < p, q, r \leq 1$. That is, for any fixed probability ratio q, the ratio of decision weights is closer to unity when the probabilities are low than when they are high, for example, $\pi(.1)/\pi(.2) > \pi(.4)/\pi(.8)$. A

Figure 1.
A hypothetical value function.

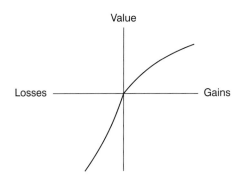

Value

Losses ——————————— Gains

Figure 2.
A hypothetical weighting function.

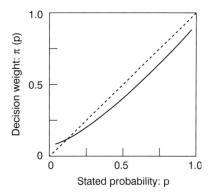

Decision weight: $\pi(p)$

Stated probability: p

hypothetical weighting function which satisfies these properties is shown in Fig. 2. The major qualitative properties of decision weights can be extended to cases in which the probabilities of outcomes are subjectively assessed rather than explicitly given. In these situations, however, decision weights may also be affected by other characteristics of an event, such as ambiguity or vagueness (9).

Prospect theory, and the scales illustrated in Figs. 1 and 2, should be viewed as an approximate, incomplete, and simplified description of the evaluation of risky prospects. Although the properties of v and π summarize a common pattern of choice, they are not universal: the preferences of some individuals are not well described by an S-shaped value function and a consistent set of decision weights. The simultaneous measurement of values and decision weights involves serious experimental and statistical difficulties (10).

If π and v were linear throughout, the preference order between options would be independent of the framing of acts, outcomes, or contingencies. Because of the characteristic nonlinearities of π and v, however, different frames can lead to different choices. The following three sections describe reversals of preference caused by variations in the framing of acts, contingencies, and outcomes.

THE FRAMING OF ACTS

Problem 3 [N = 150]: Imagine that you face the following pair of concurrent decisions. First examine both decisions, then indicate the options you prefer.

Decision (i). Choose between:
  A. a sure gain of $240 [84 percent]
  B. 25% chance to gain $1000, and
       75% chance to gain nothing [16 percent]

Decision (ii). Choose between:
  C. a sure loss of $750 [13 percent]
  D. 75% chance to lose $1000, and
       25% chance to lose nothing [87 percent]

The majority choice in decision (i) is risk averse: a riskless prospect is preferred to a risky prospect of equal or greater expected value. In contrast, the majority choice in decision (ii) is risk taking: a risky prospect is preferred to a riskless prospect of equal expected value. This pattern of risk aversion in choices involving gains and risk seeking in choices involving losses is attributable to the properties of v and π. Because the value function is S-shaped, the value associated with a gain of $240 is greater than 24 percent of the value associated with a gain of $1000, and the (negative) value associated with a loss of $750 is smaller than 75 percent of the value associated with a loss of $1000. Thus the shape of the value function contributes to risk aversion in decision (i) and to risk seeking in decision (ii). Moreover, the underweighting of moderate and high probabilities contributes to the relative attractiveness of the sure gain in (i) and to the relative aversiveness of the sure loss in (ii). The same analysis applies to problems 1 and 2.

Because (i) and (ii) were presented together, the respondents had in effect to choose one prospect from the set: A and C, B and C, A and D, B and D. The most common pattern (A and D) was chosen by 73 percent of respondents, while the least popular pattern (B and C) was chosen by only 3 percent of respondents. However, the combination of B and C is definitely superior to the combination A and D, as is readily seen in problem 4.

Problem 4 [N = 86]. Choose between:

A & D. 25% chance to win $240, and
         75% chance to lose $760. [0 percent]

B & C. 25% chance to win $250, and
         75% chance to lose $750. [100 percent]

When the prospects were combined and the dominance of the second option became obvious, all respondents chose the superior option. The popularity of the inferior option in problem 3 implies that this problem was framed as a pair of separate choices. The respondents apparently failed to entertain the possibility that the conjunction of two seemingly reasonable choices could lead to an untenable result.

The violations of dominance observed in problem 3 do not disappear in the presence of monetary incentives. A different group of respondents who answered a modified version of problem 3, with real payoffs, produced a similar pattern of choices (11). Other authors have also reported that violations of the rules of rational choice, originally observed in hypothetical questions, were not eliminated by payoffs (12).

We suspect that many concurrent decisions in the real world are framed independently, and that the preference order would often be reversed if the decisions were combined. The respondents in problem 3 failed to combine options, although the integration was relatively simple and was encouraged by instructions (13). The complexity of practical problems of concurrent decisions, such as portfolio selection, would prevent people from integrating options without computational aids, even if they were inclined to do so.

THE FRAMING OF CONTINGENCIES

The following triple of problems illustrates the framing of contingencies. Each problem was presented to a different group of respondents. Each group was told that one participant in ten, preselected at random, would actually be playing for money. Chance events were realized, in the respondents' presence, by drawing a single ball from a bag containing a known proportion of balls of the winning color, and the winners were paid immediately.

Problem 5 [N = 77]: Which of the following options do you prefer?

  A. a sure win of $30 [78 percent]
  B. 80% chance to win $45 [22 percent]

Problem 6 [N = 85]: Consider the following two-stage game. In the first stage, there is a 75% chance to end the game without winning anything, and a 25% chance to move into the second stage. If you reach the second stage you have a choice between:

  C. a sure win of $30 [74 percent]
  D. 80% chance to win $45 [26 percent]

Your choice must be made before the game starts, i.e., before the outcome of the first stage is known. Please indicate the option you prefer.

Problem 7 [N = 81]: Which of the following options do you prefer?

E. 25% chance to win $30 [42 percent]
F. 20% chance to win $45 [58 percent]

Let us examine the structure of these problems. First, note that problems 6 and 7 are identical in terms of probabilities and outcomes, because prospect C offers a .25 chance to win $30 and prospect D offers a probability of .25 x .80 = .20 to win $45. Consistency therefore requires that the same choice be made in problems 6 and 7. Second, note that problem 6 differs from problem 5 only by the introduction of a preliminary stage. If the second stage of the game is reached, then problem 6 reduces to problem 5; if the game ends at the first stage the decision does not affect the outcome. Hence there seems to be no reason to make a different choice in problems 5 and 6. By this logical analysis, problem 6 is equivalent to problem 7 on the one hand and problem 5 on the other. The participants, however, responded similarly to problems 5 and 6 but differently to problem 7. This pattern of responses exhibits two phenomena of choice: the certainty effect and the pseudocertainty effect.

The contrast between problems 5 and 7 illustrates a phenomenon discovered by Allais (14), which we have labeled the certainty effect: a reduction of the probability of an outcome by a constant factor has more impact when the outcome was initially certain than when it was merely probable. Prospect theory attributes this effect to the properties of π. It is easy to verify, by applying the equation of prospect theory to problems 5 and 7, that people for whom the value ratio $v(30)/v(45)$ lies between the weight ratios $\pi(.20)/\pi(.25)$ and $\pi(.80)/\pi(1.0)$ will prefer A to B and F to E, contrary to expected utility theory. Prospect theory does not predict a reversal of preference for every individual in problems 5 and 7. It only requires that an individual who has no preference between A and B prefer F to E. For group data, the theory predicts the observed directional shift of preference between the two problems.

The first stage of problem 6 yields the same outcome (no gain) for both acts. Consequently, we pro-pose, people evaluate the options conditionally, as if the second stage had been reached. In this framing, of course, problem 6 reduces to problem 5. More generally, we suggest that a decision problem is evaluated conditionally when (i) there is a state in which all acts yield the same outcome, such as failing to reach the second stage of the game in problem 6, and (ii) the stated probabilities of other outcomes are conditional on the nonoccurrence of this state.

The striking discrepancy between the responses to problems 6 and 7, which are identical in outcomes and probabilities, could be described as a pseudocertainty effect. The prospect yielding $30 is relatively more attractive in problem 6 than in problem 7, as if it had the advantage of certainty. The sense of certainty associated with option C is illusory, however, since the gain is in fact contingent on reaching the second stage of the game (15).

We have observed the certainty effect in several sets of problems, with outcomes ranging from vacation trips to the loss of human lives. In the negative domain, certainty exaggerates the aversiveness of losses that are certain relative to losses that are merely probable. In a question dealing with the response to an epidemic, for example, most respondents found "a sure loss of 75 lives" more aversive than "80% chance to lose 100 lives" but preferred "10% chance to lose 75 lives" over "8% chance to lose 100 lives," contrary to expected utility theory.

We also obtained the pseudocertainty effect in several studies where the description of the decision problems favored conditional evaluation. Pseudocertainty can be induced either by a sequential formulation, as in problem 6, or by the introduction of causal contingencies. In another version of the epidemic problem, for instance, respondents were told that risk to life existed only in the event (probability .10) that the disease was carried by a particular virus. Two alternative programs were said to yield "a sure loss of 75 lives" or "80% chance to lose 100 lives" if the critical virus was involved, and no loss of life in the event (probability .90) that the disease was carried by another virus. In effect, the respondents were asked to choose between 10 percent chance of losing 75 lives and 8 percent chance of losing 100 lives, but their preferences were the same as when the choice was between a sure loss of 75 lives and 80 percent chance of losing 100 lives. A conditional framing was evidently adopted in which the contingency of the non-critical virus was eliminated, giving rise to a pseudocertainty effect. The certainty effect reveals attitudes toward risk that are inconsistent with the axioms of rational choice, whereas the pseudocertainty effect violates the more fundamental requirement that preferences should be independent of problem description.

Many significant decisions concern actions that reduce or eliminate the probability of a hazard, at some cost. The shape of π in the range of low probabilities suggests that a protective action which reduces the probability of a harm from 1 percent to zero, say, will be valued more highly than an action that reduces the probability of the same harm from 2 percent to 1 percent. Indeed, probabilistic insurance, which reduces the probability of loss by half, is judged to be worth less than half the price of regular insurance that eliminates the risk altogether (3).

It is often possible to frame protective action in either conditional or unconditional form. For example, an insurance policy that covers fire but not flood could be evaluated either as full protection against the specific risk of fire or as a reduction in the overall probability of property loss. The preceding analysis suggests that insurance should appear more attractive when it is presented as the elimination of risk than when it is described as a reduction of risk. P. Slovic, B. Fischhoff, and S. Lichtenstein, in an unpublished study, found that a hypothetical vaccine which reduces the probability of contracting a disease from .20 to .10 is less attractive if it is described as effective in half the cases than if it is presented as fully effective against one of two (exclusive and equiprobable) virus strains that produce identical symptoms. In accord with the present analysis of pseudocertainty, the respondents valued full protection against an identified virus more than probabilistic protection against the disease.

The preceding discussion highlights the sharp contrast between lay responses to the reduction and the elimination of risk. Because no form of protective action can cover all risks to human welfare, all insurance is essentially probabilistic: it reduces but does not eliminate risk. The probabilistic nature of insurance is commonly masked by formulations that emphasize the completeness of protection against identified harms, but the sense of security that such formulations provide is an illusion of conditional framing. It appears that insurance is bought as protection against worry, not only against risk, and that worry can be manipulated by the labeling of outcomes and by the framing of contingencies. It is not easy to determine whether people value the elimination of risk too much or the

reduction of risk too little. The contrasting attitudes to the two forms of protective action, however, are difficult to justify on normative grounds (16).

THE FRAMING OF OUTCOMES

Outcomes are commonly perceived as positive or negative in relation to a reference outcome that is judged neutral. Variations of the reference point can therefore determine whether a given outcome is evaluated as a gain or as a loss. Because the value function is generally concave for gains, convex for losses, and steeper for losses than for gains, shifts of reference can change the value difference between outcomes and thereby reverse the preference order between options (6). Problems 1 and 2 illustrated a preference reversal induced by a shift of references that transformed gains into losses.

For another example, consider a person who has spent an afternoon at the race track, has already lost $140, and is considering a $10 bet on a 15:1 long shot in the last race. This decision can be framed in two ways, which correspond to two natural reference points. If the status quo is the reference point, the outcomes of the bet are framed as a gain of $140 and a loss of $10. On the other hand, it may be more natural to view the present state as a loss of $140, for the betting day, and accordingly frame the last bet as a chance to return to the reference point or to increase the loss to $150. Prospect theory implies that the latter frame will produce more risk seeking than the former. Hence, people who do not adjust their reference point as they lose are expected to take bets that they would normally find unacceptable. This analysis is supported by the observation that bets on long shots are most popular on the last race of the day (17).

Because the value function is steeper for losses than for gains, a difference between options will loom larger when it is framed as a disadvantage of one option rather than as an advantage of the other option. An interesting example of such an effect in a riskless context has been noted by Thaler (18). In a debate on a proposal to pass to the consumer some of the costs associated with the processing of credit-card purchases, representatives of the credit-card industry requested that the price difference be labeled a cash discount rather than a credit-card surcharge. The two labels induce different reference points by implicitly designating as the normal reference the higher or the lower of the two prices. Because losses loom larger than gains, consumers are less willing to accept a surcharge than to forego a discount. A similar effect has been observed in experimental studies of insurance: the proportion of respondents who preferred a sure loss to a larger probable loss was significantly greater when the former was called an insurance premium (19, 20).

These observations highlight the lability of reference outcomes, as well as their role in decision-making. In the examples discussed so far, the neutral reference point was identified by the labeling of outcomes. A diversity of factors determine the reference outcome in everyday life. The reference outcome is usually a state to which one has adapted; it is sometimes set by social norms and expectations; it sometimes corresponds to a level of aspiration, which may or may not be realistic.

We have dealt so far with elementary outcomes, such as gains or losses in a single attribute. In many situations, however, an action gives rise to a compound outcome, which joins a series of changes in a single attribute, such as a sequence of monetary gains and losses, or a set of concurrent changes in several attributes. To describe the framing and evaluation of compound outcomes, we use the notion of a psychological account, defined as an outcome frame which specifies (i) the set of elementary outcomes that are evaluated jointly and the manner in which they are combined and (ii) a reference outcome that is considered neutral or normal. In the account that is set up for the purchase of a car, for example, the cost of the purchase is not treated as a loss nor is the car viewed as a gift. Rather, the transaction as a whole is evaluated as positive, negative, or neutral, depending on such factors as the performance of the car and the price of similar cars in the market. A closely related treatment has been offered by Thaler (18).

We propose that people generally evaluate acts in terms of a minimal account, which includes only the direct consequences of the act. The minimal account associated with the decision to accept a gamble, for example, includes the money won or lost in that gamble and excludes other assets or the outcome of previous gambles. People commonly adopt minimal accounts because this mode of framing (i) simplifies evaluation and reduces cognitive strain, (ii) reflects the intuition that consequences should be causally linked to acts, and (iii) matches the properties of hedonic experience, which is more sensitive to desirable and undesirable changes than to steady states.

There are situations, however, in which the outcomes of an act affect the balance in an account that was previously set up by a related act. In these cases, the decision at hand may be evaluated in terms of a more inclusive account, as in the case of the bettor who views the last race in the context of earlier losses. More generally, a sunk-cost effect arises when a decision is referred to an existing account in which the current balance is negative. Because of the nonlinearities of the evaluation process, the minimal account and a more inclusive one often lead to different choices.

Problems 8 and 9 illustrate another class of situations in which an existing account affects a decision:

Problem 8 (N = 183): Imagine that you have decided to see a play where admission is $10 per ticket. As you enter the theater you discover that you have lost a $10 bill.

Would you still pay $10 for a ticket for the play?

Yes [88 percent]   No [12 percent]

Problem 9 [N = 200]: Imagine that you have decided to see a play and paid the admission price of $10 per ticket. As you enter the theater you discover that you have lost the ticket. The seat was not marked and the ticket cannot be recovered.

Would you pay $10 for another ticket?

Yes [46 percent]   No [54 percent]

The marked difference between the responses to problem 8 and 9 is an effect of psychological accounting. We propose that the purchase of a new ticket in problem 9 is entered in the account that was set up by the purchase of the original ticket. In terms of this account, the expense required to see the show is $20, a cost which many of our respondents apparently found excessive. In problem 8, on the other hand, the loss of $10 is not linked specifically to the ticket purchase and its effect on the decision is accordingly slight.

The following problem, based on examples by Savage (2, p. 103) and Thaler (18), further illustrates the effect of embedding an option in different accounts. Two versions of this problem were presented to different groups of subjects. One group (N = 93) was given the values that appear in parentheses, and the other group (N = 88) the values shown in brackets.

Problem 10: Imagine that you are about to purchase a jacket for ($125) [$15], and a calculator for ($15) [$125]. The calculator salesman informs you that the calculator you wish to buy is on sale for

($10) [$120] at the other branch of the store, located 20 minutes drive away. Would you make the trip to the other store?

The responses to the two versions of problem 10 were markedly different: 68 percent of the respondents were willing to make an extra trip to save $5 on a $15 calculator; only 29 percent were willing to exert the same effort when the price of the calculator was $125. Evidently the respondents do not frame problem 10 in the minimal account, which involves only a benefit of $5 and a cost of some inconvenience. Instead, they evaluate the potential saving in a more inclusive account, which includes the purchase of the calculator but not of the jacket. By the curvature of v, a discount of $5 has a greater impact when the price of the calculator is low than when it is high.

A closely related observation has been reported by Pratt, Wise, and Zeckhauser (*21*), who found that the variability of the prices at which a given product is sold by different stores is roughly proportional to the mean price of that product. The same pattern was observed for both frequently and infrequently purchased items. Overall, a ratio of 2:1 in the mean price of two products is associated with a ratio of 1.86:1 in the standard deviation of the respective quoted prices. If the effort that consumers exert to save each dollar on a purchase, for instance by a phone call, were independent of price, the dispersion of quoted prices should be about the same for all products. In contrast, the data of Pratt *et al.* (*21*) are consistent with the hypothesis that consumers hardly exert more effort to save $15 on a $150 purchase than to save $5 on a $50 purchase (*18*). Many readers will recognize the temporary devaluation of money which facilitates extra spending and reduces the significance of small discounts in the context of a large expenditure, such as buying a house or a car. This paradoxical variation in the value of money is incompatible with the standard analysis of consumer behavior.

DISCUSSION

In this article we have presented a series of demonstrations in which seemingly inconsequential changes in the formulation of choice problems caused significant shifts of preference. The inconsistencies were traced to the interaction of two sets of factors: variations in the framing of acts, contingencies, and outcomes, and the characteristic nonlinearities of values

and decision weights. The demonstrated effects are large and systematic, although by no means universal. They occur when the outcomes concern the loss of human lives as well as in choices about money; they are not restricted to hypothetical questions and are not eliminated by monetary incentives.

Earlier we compared the dependence of preferences on frames to the dependence of perceptual appearance on perspective. If while traveling in a mountain range you notice that the apparent relative height of mountain peaks varies with your vantage point, you will conclude that some impressions of relative height must be erroneous, even when you have no access to the correct answer. Similarly, one may discover that the relative attractiveness of options varies when the same decision problem is framed in different ways. Such a discovery will normally lead the decision-maker to reconsider the original preferences, even when there is no simple way to resolve the inconsistency. The susceptibility to perspective effects is of special concern in the domain of decision-making because of the absence of objective standards such as the true height of mountains.

The metaphor of changing perspective can be applied to other phenomena of choice, in addition to the framing effects with which we have been concerned here (*19*). The problem of self-control is naturally construed in these terms. The story of Ulysses' request to be bound to the mast of the ship in anticipation of the irresistible temptation of the Sirens' call is often used as a paradigm case (*22*). In this example of precommitment, an action taken in the present renders inoperative an anticipated future preference. An unusual feature of the problem of intertemporal conflict is that the agent who views a problem from a particular temporal perspective is also aware of the conflicting views that future perspectives will offer. In most other situations, decision-makers are not normally aware of the potential effects of different decision frames on their preferences.

The perspective metaphor highlights the following aspects of the psychology of choice. Individuals who face a decision problem and have a definite preference (i) might have a different preference in a different framing of the same problem, (ii) are normally unaware of alternative frames and of their potential effects on the relative attractiveness of options, (iii) would wish their preferences to be independent of frame, but (iv) are often uncertain how to resolve detected inconsistencies (*23*). In some cases (such as problems 3 and 4 and perhaps problems 8 and 9) the advantage of one frame becomes evident once the competing frames are compared, but in other cases (problems 1 and 2 and problems 6 and 7) it is not obvious which preferences should be abandoned.

These observations do not imply that preference reversals, or other errors of choice or judgment (24), are necessarily irrational. Like other intellectual limitations, discussed by Simon (25) under the heading of "bounded rationality," the practice of acting on the most readily available frame can sometimes be justified by reference to the mental effort required to explore alternative frames and avoid potential inconsistencies. However, we propose that the details of the phenomena described in this article are better explained by prospect theory and by an analysis of framing than by ad hoc appeals to the notion of cost of thinking.

The present work has been concerned primarily with the descriptive question of how decisions are made, but the psychology of choice is also relevant to the normative question of how decisions ought to be made. In order to avoid the difficult problem of justifying values, the modern theory of rational choice has adopted the coherence of specific preferences as the sole criterion of rationality. This approach enjoins the decision-maker to resolve inconsistencies but offers no guidance on how to do so. It implicitly assumes that the decision-maker who carefully answers the question "What do I really want?" will eventually achieve coherent preferences. However, the susceptibility of preferences to variations of framing raises doubt about the feasibility and adequacy of the coherence criterion.

Consistency is only one aspect of the lay notion of rational behavior. As noted by March (26), the common conception of rationality also requires that preferences or utilities for particular outcomes should be predictive of the experiences of satisfaction or displeasure associated with their occurrence. Thus, a man could be judged irrational either because his preferences are contradictory or because his desires and aversions do not reflect his pleasures and pains. The predictive criterion of rationality can be applied to resolve inconsistent preferences and to improve the quality of decisions. A predictive orientation encourages the decision-maker to focus on future experience and to ask "What will I feel then?" rather than "What do I want now?" The former question, when answered with care, can be the more useful guide in difficult decisions. In particular, predictive considerations may be applied to select the decision frame that best represents the hedonic experience of outcomes.

Further complexities arise in the normative analysis because the framing of an action sometimes affects the actual experience of its outcomes. For example, framing outcomes in terms of overall wealth or welfare rather than in terms of specific gains and losses may attenuate one's emotional response to an occasional loss. Similarly, the experience of a change for the worse may vary if the change is framed as an uncompensated loss or as a cost incurred to achieve some benefit. The framing of acts and outcomes can also reflect the acceptance or rejection of responsibility for particular consequences, and the deliberate manipulation of framing is commonly used as an instrument of self-control (22). When framing influences the experience of consequences, the adoption of a decision frame is an ethically significant act.

REFERENCES AND NOTES

1. J. Von Neumann and O. Morgenstern, *Theory of Games and Economic Behavior* (Princeton Univ. Press, Princeton, N. J., 1947): H. Raiffa, *Decision Analysis: Lectures on Choices Under Uncertainty* (Addison-Wesley, Reading, Mass., 1968): P. Fishburn, *Utility Theory for Decision Making* (Wiley, New York, 1970).

2. L. J. Savage, *The Foundations of Statistics* (Wiley, New York, 1954).

3. D. Kahneman and A. Tversky, *Econometrica* 47, 263 (1979).

4. The framing phase includes various editing operations that are applied to simplify prospects, for example by combining events or outcomes or by discarding negligible components (3).

5. If $p + q = 1$ and either $x > y > 0$ or $x < y < 0$, the equation in the text is replaced by $v(y) + \pi(p) [v(x) - v(y)]$, so that decision weights are not applied to sure outcomes.

6. P. Fishburn and G. Kochenberger, *Decision Sci.* 10, 503 (1979); D. J. Laughhunn, J. W. Payne, R. Crum, *Manage. Sci.*, in press: J. W. Payne, D. J. Laughhunn, R. Crum, *ibid.*, in press: S. A. Eraker and H. C. Sox, *Med. Decision Making*, in press. In the last study several hundred clinic patients made hypothetical choices between drug therapies for severe headaches, hypertension, and chest pain. Most patients were risk averse when the outcomes were described as positive (for example, reduced pain or increased life expectancy) and risk taking when the outcomes were described as negative (increased pain or reduced life expectancy). No significant differences were found between

patients who actually suffered from the ailments described and patients who did not.

7. E. Galanter and P. Pliner, in *Sensation and Measurement*, H. R. Moskowitz *et. al.*, Eds. (Reidel, Dordrecht, 1974), pp. 65–76.

8. The extension of the proposed value function to multiattribute options, with or without risk, deserves careful analysis. In particular, indifference curves between dimensions of loss may be concave upward, even when the value functions for the separate losses are both convex, because of marked subadditivity between dimensions.

9. D. Ellsberg, *Q. J. Econ.* 75, 643 (1961): W. Fellner, *Probability and Profit—A Study of Economic Behavior Along Bayesian Lines* (Irwin, Homewood, Ill., 1965).

10. The scaling of v and π by pair comparisons requires a large number of observations. The procedure of pricing gambles is more convenient for scaling purposes, but it is subject to a severe anchoring bias: the ordering of gambles by their cash equivalents diverges systematically from the preference order observed in direct comparisons [S. Lichtenstein and P. Slovic, *J. Exp. Psychol.* 89, 46 (1971)].

11. A new group of respondents ($N = 126$) was presented with a modified version of problem 3, in which the outcomes were reduced by a factor of 50. The participants were informed that the gambles would actually be played by tossing a pair of fair coins, that one participant in ten would be selected at random to play the gambles of his or her choice. To ensure a positive return for the entire set, a third decision, yielding only positive outcomes, was added. These payoff conditions did not alter the pattern of preferences observed in the hypothetical problem: 67 percent of respondents chose prospect A and 86 percent chose prospect D. The dominated combination of A and D was chosen by 60 percent of respondents, and only 6 percent favored the dominant combinations of B and C.

12. S. Lichtenstein and P. Slovic, *J. Exp. Psychol.* 101, 16 (1973); D. M. Grether and C. R. Plott, *Am. Econ. Rev.* 69, 623 (1979); I. Lieblich and A. Lieblich, *Percept. Mot. Skills* 29, 467 (1969); D. M. Grether, *Social Science Working Paper No. 245* (California Institute of Technology, Pasadena, 1979).

13. Other demonstrations of a reluctance to integrate concurrent options have been reported: P. Slovic and S. Lichtenstein, *J. Exp. Psychol.* 78, 646 (1968); J. W. Payne and M. L. Braunstein, *ibid.* 87, 13 (1971).

14. M. Allais, *Econometrica* 21, 503 (1953): K. McCrimmon and S. Larsson, in *Expected Utility Hypotheses and the Allais Paradox*, M. Allais and O. Hagan, Eds. (Reidel, Dordrecht, 1979).

15. Another group of respondents ($N = 205$) was presented with all three problems, in different orders, without monetary payoffs. The joint frequency distribution of choices in problems 5, 6, and 7 was as follows: ACE, 22; ACF, 65; ADE, 4; ADF, 20; BCE, 7; BCF, 18; BDE, 17; BDF, 52. These data confirm in a within-subject design the analysis of conditional evaluation proposed in the text. More than 75 percent of respondents made compatible choices (AC or BD) in problems 5 and 6, and less than half made compatible choices in problems 6 and 7 (CE or DF) or 5 and 7 (AE or BF). The elimination of payoffs in these questions reduced risk aversion but did not substantially alter the effects of certainty and pseudocertainty.

16. For further discussion of rationality in protective action see H. Kunreuther, *Disaster Insurance Protection: Public Policy Lessons* (Wiley, New York, 1978).

17. W. H. McGlothlin, *Am. J. Psychol.* 69, 604 (1956).

18. R. Thaler, *J. Econ. Behav. Organ.* 1, 39 (1980).

19. B. Fischhoff, P. Slovic, S. Lichtenstein, in *Cognitive Processes in Choice and Decision Behavior*, T. Wallsten, Ed. (Erlbaum, Hillsdale, N. J., 1980).

20. J. C. Hershey and P. J. H. Schoemaker, *J. Risk Insur.*, in press.

21. J. Pratt, A. Wise, R. Zeckhauser, *Q. J. Econ.* 93, 189 (1979).

22. R. H. Strotz, *Rev. Econ. Stud.* 23, 165 (1955); G. Ainslie, *Psychol. Bull.* 82, 463 (1975); J. Elster, *Ulysses and the Sirens: Studies in Rationality and Irrationality* (Cambridge Univ. Press, London, 1979); R. Thaler and H. M. Shifrin, *J. Polit. Econ.*, in press.

23. P. Slovic and A. Tversky, *Behav. Sci* 19, 368 (1974).

24. A. Tversky and D. Kahneman, *Science* 185, 1124 (1974); P. Slovic, B. Fischoff, S. Lichtenstein, *Annu. Rev. Psychol.* 28, 1 (1977); R. Nisbett and L. Ross, *Human Inference: Strategies and Shortcomings of Social Judgment* (Prentice-Hall, Englewood Cliffs, N. J., 1980); H. Einhorn and R. Hogarth, *Annu. Rev. Psychol.* 32, 53 (1981).

25. H. A. Simon, *Q. J. Econ.* 69, 99 (1955); *Psychol. Rev.* 63, 129 (1956).

26. J. March, *Bell J. Econ.* 9, 587 (1978).

27. This work was supported by the Office of Naval Research under contract N00014-79-C-0077 to Stanford University.

A Procedure for Gathering Data Is a Heuristic: Introduction to "Through the One-Way Mirror: The Limits of Experimental Self-Reflection"

In the following selection, Gadlin and Ingle point out the biases that inform experimental designs. They were among the first to publish a critique of the overwhelmingly prevalent belief that experimental design is a privileged way to collect data. As Gadlin and Ingle suggest, the scientific method had come to be associated with the specific version of experimental design they critique. When they wrote their article in 1975, experimental design had become so prevalent and accepted in psychology that the assumptions underlying it were rarely questioned (Bronfenbrenner, 1979a; Rossi & Wright, 1984). A similar trend took place in the field of social work, as noted in Chapter 2, when researchers who adopted positivist beliefs about social work research did not include the quality of the relationship between participant/researcher and participant/subject as a central issue in their formulations of the social work profession's approach to research. Gadlin and Ingle's analysis is helpful for recognizing some central biases in experimental designs whether or not you choose to use such designs.

Many different experimental methodologies have been developed. "Experiments," in the sense of hypothesis-testing, have been used since the dawn of humankind. The experiment as the test of a theory traditionally is based on a prediction that is deduced from the theory. The experimenter predicts that, given certain initial conditions, the introduction of the experimental variable will yield particular results. Scientists from many disciplines conduct an 'experiment' using just one instance of the problem they want to study. One famous single-case educational experiment occurred when Jean-Marc Gaspard Itard took custody of Victor, known as "the Wild Child of Aveyron." Victor had lived by himself in a forest from early childhood until he was twelve years old. Itard wanted to determine the impact of his program of education and nurture on Victor (Itard, 1805/1962).

In another form of experiment, the experimenter sets up two groups. The experimental group receives the impact of the experimental variable. A matched control group, which does not receive the experimental intervention, is set up in the effort to discern and rule out potential causes of change in the experimental group other than the experimental variable. Then changes in both groups over time are recorded and compared. For example, the pioneering French scientist Louis Pasteur demonstrated the impact of vaccine against anthrax by vaccinating one group of sheep and not vaccinating another group. The vaccinated group did not succumb to the anthrax that was devastating sheep. The townspeople observing the experiment were convinced of the vaccine's efficacy when they could compare the reactions of the sheep that had received the vaccine with those that had not (Latour, 1988).

A particular type of experimental design has developed in psychology during this century (Danziger, 1985). In experiments conducted by Wilhelm Wundt, during the last part of the nineteenth century, the participant/subjects often were fellow psychologists, and their introspected cognitive processes were respected as important data. However, as psychologists such as Edmund Boring disseminated positivist beliefs about science (Boring, 1929/1950), it became increasingly important to study and report those characteristics of participant/subjects in experimental studies that were regarded as representative of most people (and so ahistorical and not unique to one person)(Danziger, 1979). With the impact of behaviorism, experimenters increasingly focused on observations of neuromuscular behavior rather than the introspective experience of participant/subjects.

Rosenthal's landmark studies on the many ways in which experimenters influence the participant/subjects in the research, and thereby influence the data they collect (Rosenthal, 1969), helped to convince many researchers that experimental controls in fact cannot control for many relevant variables and always introduce new biases (see also Bronfenbrenner, 1979a). As Gadlin and Ingle (1975) point out, following Orne (1969), a crucial element of any experimental research is discerning the effects of the experimental situation on the participant/subject. Experimenter effects on human participant/subjects have been noticed for some time. One of the first comments about experimenter effects was made during the 1880s, when members of the Society for Psychical Research in London were investigating "thought-transference" in hypnosis (Alvarado, 1987).

Martin Orne's investigations of experimenter effects, which he termed "demand characteristics," have been very influential:

> Subjects are never neutral toward an experiment . . . because subjects are active, sentient beings, they do not respond to the specific experimental stimuli with which they are confronted as isolated events but rather they perceive these in the total context of the experimental situation. Their understanding of the situation is based upon a great deal of knowledge about the kind of realities under which scientific research is conducted, its aims and purposes, and, in some vague way, the kind of findings which might emerge from their participation and their responses. (Orne, 1969, p. 144)

The "demand characteristics" of an experiment are the cues that govern the participant/subject's perception of the experiment. Orne described many assumptions participant/subjects commonly make about the experimental situation:

1. Participant/subjects comply and perform seemingly dangerous activities, assuming the experimenter has taken precautions to protect them.
2. Participant/subjects try to produce data characteristic of a "good subject."
3. Participant/subjects want to believe that the experiment is meaningful and will provide useful information to further human knowledge. (Orne, 1969, p. 145)

Cues that affect participant/subjects' behavior vary from

> scuttlebutt about the experiment, its setting, implicit and explicit instructions, the person of the experimenter, subtle cues provided by him, and, of particular importance, the experimental procedure itself . . . although the explicit instructions are important, it appears that subtler cues from which the subject can draw covert or even unconscious inference may be still more powerful. (Orne, 1969, p. 146)

KEY TERMS

Artifact   **Dependent variable**
Independent variable   Placebo

DISCUSSION QUESTIONS

1. Designing and evaluating an experiment involves many complex judgments. In the following example, some complex issues are simplified because the participant/subjects are not human. The participant/researchers wanted to find out whether octopuses can learn by watching other octopuses. The experimenters divided up their sample of octopuses into "demonstrators" and "observers." The demonstrators were conditioned to choose a ball of a particular color. The experimenters ruled out the possibility that color preference might account for the octopuses' selections by training half the octopuses to prefer red balls and half to prefer white balls. Then untrained, "observer" octopuses watched the demonstrators perform the task of selecting the balls. The researchers found that

    > after being placed in isolation, the observers, in a similar test, consistently selected the same object as did the demonstrators. This learning by observation occurred irrespective of the object chosen by the demonstrators as the positive choice and was more rapid than the learning that occurred during the conditioning of animals. The task was performed correctly without significant errors and further conditioning for 5 days. (Fiorito & Scotto, 1992)

    a. What are the dependent variables? What are the independent variables?

    b. What are the two comparison groups?

    Researchers in a hurry may look at the abstracts of articles without reading the entire articles. The abstract of the article contained the preceding information. Now consider the following information reported in the article: The demonstrator octopuses learned to choose specific colors through a classical conditioning process that combined reward and punishment. When the octopuses chose the ball of the correct color, they received a fish reward; when they chose the incorrect color ball, they were punished with an electric shock. Recall that the authors say that the observer octopuses (who did not receive classical conditioning, e.g., they did not experience the rewards or punishments) learned simply by watching the demonstrator octopuses, and in fact, the observers learned more quickly. We are only beginning to find out about how octopuses learn, although researchers suspect their brains are fairly developed. Accordingly, we do not know about the effects of electric shocks on how octopuses process and retain information.

    c. What are the ethical implications of subjecting octopuses to electric shocks?

    d. What impact might electric shocks conceivably have on octopus learning?

    e.   In the preceding experiment, how might electric shocks have functioned as an artifact?

2. Take a theory that interests you and:

    a.   Deduce a prediction from that theory.

    b.   Based on that prediction, describe an experiment that would test it.

3. Practice thinking through how you might investigate a problem that interests you in the following two ways:

    a.   Design a single-case study.

    b.   Use an experimental group design in which there is a control group and an experimental group.

    c.   How do the different choices of design lead you to revise the problem formulation?

    d.   Articulate the biases you have set up using both methods, with a particular focus on the kind of relationship you have established between yourself as participant/researcher and your participant/subjects.

4. a. What are some implications of the "evaluation apprehension" Gadlin and Ingle describe for clinical practice evaluation research?

    b.   How might it affect the client to be told that his or her treatment would be included in a research study? If it is a single-case study, what might Gadlin and Ingle say about the effect of the participant/subject's knowledge that she or he was being studied on the kind of data the participant/subject reports?

5. Social welfare policies may be viewed as "social experiments." For example, in developing new policies for the administration of public welfare benefits, a new program that combines job training with cash benefits may be tried as an "experiment" in one state and the findings used to determine whether it should be implemented in the country as a whole. Find some examples of social welfare "experiments" and evaluate both the methodology and the results.

6. Following is a recent example of an experimental design that did not cause human participant/subjects a loss. To see whether the decline in fertility that occurs with aging could be reversed, researchers examined the impact of in vitro fertilization with donated oocytes on the outcomes of pregnancy for women over age forty. They set up two matched comparison groups of women who wanted to undergo in vitro fertilization, one with women under forty, and one with women over forty, and they also compared the outcomes of the in vitro fertilization for those groups with outcomes of a matched group of women forty years and older who sought to become pregnant and used their own oocytes. The researchers found that the groups of women who underwent in vitro fertilization with donated oocytes conceived and gave birth to healthy children in almost equal proportions. With regard to fertilization rates in vitro, clinical pregnancy rates, and successful pregnancy completion rates, women of all ages who underwent oocyte donation had better outcomes than women over forty who used their own oocytes. The researchers concluded:

> The age-related decline in female fertility may be reversed in couples electing to use donated oocytes from a younger woman, and women of advanced reproductive age may conceive, carry, and give birth to infants with success rates similar to those of their younger counterparts using assisted reproductive methods. (Sauer, Paulson, & Lobo, 1992, p. 1320)

Consider that model, and then describe how a researcher using the heuristic paradigm might use an experimental design to test the following common (but mistaken) assumption: Disadvantaged clients are less able to benefit from psychotherapy and change than clients from more privileged backgrounds.

▼ ▼ ▼ ▼ ▼ ▼ ▼ ▼ ▼ ▼ ▼ ▼ ▼

SAMPLE RESEARCH PROJECT: DEVELOPING RESIDENTIAL TREATMENT SERVICES FOR HOMELESS, MENTALLY ILL, AND SUBSTANCE-ABUSING CLIENTS

Part 9: Qualitative Analysis

To begin to capture the residents' subjective experiences of the services, data analysis will begin with qualitative analysis. Cronbach emphasizes, "Evaluative conclusions are descriptive. They may be elaborated into explanatory or causal propositions, but the elaboration comes second. For evaluators, the validity of descriptive information is of prime importance" (1982, p. 115). Accordingly, a prime aim of the coding manual will be to generate codes that reflect the diverse array of experiences the residents report. Each code needs to be carefully developed and its validity examined in relation to the guiding theory, to the overall data, and to the other codes. The details of that process are summarized briefly.

The coding manual will be developed using central concepts of intrapsychic humanism, especially the focus on client's motives for relationship pleasure and improved self-caretaking. For instance, the coding manual can consistently focus on relationship experience. On the survey, residents are asked what they believed caused them to enter the program. One code will be "relationship problems with family" and another, "relationship problems with friends." Codes differentiate various responses to all the survey questions asking clients about their relationships, including a question about who the residents can rely on after leaving the program. This elicits further information about the residents' relationships. For example, one resident answered that she could rely on "my brother, and that isn't very good because we have never really gotten along." Another set of codes will focus on the residents' feelings about themselves, their core sense of self-worth. One survey question asks what the residents would prefer *not* to have to deal with on leaving the program. A resident answered, "my inner self."

In designing a coding manual, a researcher aims to consider possible sources of bias in interpreting the meaning of the data. Intrapsychic humanism points out that individuals with psychopathology have learned motives to idealize unstable caregiving. One implication of this unfortunate state is that clients may be compelled to idealize services that are, from another perspective, inadequate or even iatrogenic. At the same time, aversive reactions to pleasure can cause a patient in treatment to signify as negative an experience that in fact represents genuine caregiving because that experience is a loss to the part of the person that needs abusive forms of caregiving (see chapters 7 and 8). These biases constitute a problem when using patient evaluations of any treatment process. Thus, if the problem formulation focuses on evaluating the program per se (by contrast with also voicing the clients' concerns, as is the case with this problem formulation), the researcher would not want this information to be the sole perspective used in an evaluation of the usefulness of a program. Triangulation of perspectives is crucial in compensating for those forms of bias. Other perspectives that can be brought to bear in evaluating services include a clinical supervisor's perspective on the nature of the treatment process or comparative studies of the results obtained using different forms of services with a similar population (see also Chapter 7). This is another reason why additional data about changes in the residents' housing, funding, employment, and social and medical support systems will be obtained.

The coding manual will be developed as coders systematically read and conceptualize common themes in the residents' survey responses. As coding categories are developed, the categories will be systematically refined and described in a coding manual. The reliability of each category will be measured in a quantified form, via the number of agreements divided by the total number of judgments made. Then, after obtaining satisfactory initial quantified measures of the reliability of the coding manual as a whole, the reliability of the coding will be evaluated throughout the coding process as two coders will code every fifth set of data and compare their coding.

Through the One-Way Mirror: The Limits of Experimental Self-Reflection

HOWARD GADLIN   *University of Massachusetts—Amherst*

GRANT INGLE   *University of Massachusetts—Amherst*

I wished, by treating Psychology like a natural science, to help her become one.

William James (1892)

E. G. Boring (1929/1950) once said that the application of the scientific method to the study of human behavior would count as mankind's greatest achievement. Few people today would unhesitatingly agree with such a statement; still fewer could share its optimism. Even those who think that the wish of William James has been fulfilled are uncertain about the consequences. For a multiplicity of reasons, psychologists are questioning the natural science methodology that has dominated the field since its inception. Much of this inquiry has focused on the laboratory experiment. Specifically, there are three major areas of concern:

1. The ethics of experimentation are in question. Psychologists have been worried about the use of coercion and deception in research and uncertain of the limits of "legitimate" scientific inquiry.

2. The applications of scientific knowledge are a second source of uncertainty. Psychologists have raised questions about the interests served by psychological experimentation and the purpose for which the resulting knowledge is employed.

3. The limits of experimentally derived knowledge are a further concern. Psychologists have come to question the experiment[1] as a means to describe and comprehend reality.

Although we believe that these issues are interconnected, we shall concentrate on the third concern. Items 1 and 2 are generally considered matters of political or ethical preference rather than issues of scientific import. For most psychologists, such considerations are probably peripheral to their commitment to experimental methodology. By contrast, questions about the validity of the knowledge that comes from experimentation strike at the core of scientific activity. Basically, psychologists have begun to wonder about the external validity of the results of laboratory experimentation. Included among these doubts is the concern that perhaps people behave in significantly different ways in the laboratory than they do in "real life." Indeed, many suspect that people behave as they do in experiments because of direct or indirect features of the experimenter-subject relationship. To these critics, the experiment does not fulfill its own criterion of objectivity (Rosenberg, 1969; Rosenthal, 1969). Defenders of the experimental method have tried to demonstrate that the results obtained in human research are not artifactual. Although acknowledging that features of the experiment or of the experi-

---

Source: "Through the One-Way Mirror: The Limits of Experimental Self-Reflection" by H. Gadlin and G. Ingle, 1975, *American Psychologist, 30,* pp. 1003–1009. Copyright 1975 by the American Psychological Association. Reprinted by permission.

[1] Throughout this article, we are specifically talking about the *laboratory* experiment, which examines dependent variables in light of manipulations performed upon independent variables. Still, we realize that much of the discussion oversimplifies complex and multifaceted issues; however, space considerations limit the development of our arguments.

menter-subject relationship *can* influence results, they assert that "neither logical consideration nor the empirical data warrant much concern about . . . artifacts" (Kruglanski, in press).

A METHODOLOGICAL PROBLEM IN ASSESSING METHOD

Ironically, both critics and paladins of the experiment have based their arguments largely on the results of experiments. Neither those who would exonerate nor those who would convict the experiment of charges of bias have questioned the suitability of the experimental method to evaluate itself. Obviously, it could be argued that an experimental demonstration of the inadequacies of experiments is self-contradictory and an experimental demonstration of the objectivity of the experiment is self-serving. The experimental method necessarily presumes its own appropriateness and cannot adequately handle questions of its own efficacy. The experimentalist attempting to answer questions about the experimental method is in the precarious position of attempting to assess "objectively" the mode of inquiry he or she, as experimenter, accepts and trusts to be objective and value free. Furthermore, the experimenter has the peculiarly complex task of attempting to understand and explain his or her own behavior. We must recall that it is precisely around the recognition that one cannot always accurately understand and explain one's own behavior that psychology has been able to build its current credibility. Among other reasons, it was in the face of the "apparent" limitations of self-consciousness that introspection was dropped as the primary tool of psychological investigation (Boring, 1929/1950). In this sense, the experimental investigation of experiments amounts to the functional equivalent of employing introspection to validate introspection and therefore represents a direct contradiction of the spirit underlying the prevailing interpretation of what constitutes "good" science. Additionally, such work finds the psychologist attempting to step outside of the psychologist's usual role into the role of participant observer. Fortunately, this position is one quite familiar to sociologists and anthropologists who often investigate the role-determined behavior of others. For example, the words of one anthropologist (Turner, 1967) describing the epistemological situation of his native informants would seem equally apt when applied to psychologists attempting to investigate the experiment as a method of investigation:

His vision is circumscribed by his occupancy of a particular position, or even of a set of situationally conflicting positions, both in the persisting structures of his society and also in the role structure of the given ritual. Moreover, the participant is likely to be governed in his actions by a number of interests, purposes, and sentiments, dependent upon his specific position, which impair his understanding of the total situation. An even more serious obstacle against his achieving objectivity is the fact that he tends to regard as axiomatic and primary the ideals, values, and norms that are overtly expressed or symbolized in the ritual. (p. 27)

This description[2] should serve as a further warning of the limitations of self-analysis even by scientists. We need to attempt to understand the "interests, purposes, and sentiments" dependent upon our specific positions. We would suggest that it is more than a role that is shared by the participants in the current controversy; the critics and defenders of the experiment lie closer together than they had imagined—they share a common paradigm. From an understanding of that paradigm we hope to recognize currently implicit dimensions of the scientific role.

THE PARADIGM IN PSYCHOLOGY

T. S. Kuhn (1962), investigating the historical development of science, developed the idea of paradigm which he first defined as "universally recognized scientific achievements that for a time provide model problems and solutions to a community of practitioners" (p. viii). Kuhn developed the notion of paradigm by showing how scientists share a way of looking at the world, a method for inquiring further about what is seen, and a means of evaluating the answers obtained to the questions asked. This is the paradigm. The paradigm specifies the scientist's relation to the world he or she investigates as well as the investigation itself. In addition, the paradigm specifies the way the scientist understands both that relationship and those investigations.

Fortunately, recent concern about the appropriateness and adequacy of the laboratory experiment in

---

[2] Although it may not be immediately obvious that Turner's observations are relevant to an understanding of the experimental situation, the appropriateness of this perspective will appear clearer as the article proceeds.

psychology has resulted in a large body of literature that examines this method's historical development and rationale (Bakan, 1972; Giorgi, 1967, 1970; Koch, 1969; Kvale, 1973; Lyons, 1964; Romanyshyn, 1971; Schultz, 1969). Generally, the consensus of these writers is that emerging 20th-century psychology closely mirrored 19th-century physics, in both method and assumptions, and that the then-prevailing tenets of natural science were isomorphically transposed to the study of human behavior. The resulting development of psychology as a science, as Koch (1969) pointed out, "was unique in the extent to which its institutionalization preceded its content and its method preceded the problem" (p. 64). The prescriptions of this paradigm not only affected the empirical investigation of various psychological phenomena but also specified, however inadvertently, the relationship of psychologists to their human subject matter.

In short, the experimental method has been paradigmatic in psychology: From this paradigm, psychologists have seen both the subject matter and the method of investigating that subject matter, the experiment, in the same light. In this light, however, subject matter and method of investigation are seen as independent of one another; this independence of subject matter and method constitutes one cornerstone of the dominant paradigm. With the experiment seen only as method, the subject-experimenter relationship is prescribed as a person-thing relationship in which, as noted above, subjects are manipulable objects; that is, the experimenter-subject relationship is depersonalized because the "objectivity" of the experimental method requires it.

The literature of the social psychology of the laboratory experiment is particularly instructive. Clearly, almost all social psychology experiments depend on some kind of interaction between experimenter(s) and subject(s). Thus, the social psychology experiment is itself representative of the phenomena that constitute the subject matter of social psychology. We would expect, then, that the experimentally derived understanding of social behavior developed by social psychologists would be amply employed in the analysis of the experimental situation. In actuality, this is not the case. The literature examining the social psychology of the experiment only vaguely refers to the general social psychology literature for an understanding of the experimenter-subject relationship: Subject matter and method are seen as separate and independent. This separation has existed since the early days of experimental social psychology.

Thus, beginning with the works of Floyd Allport (1919, 1924) and continuing through J. F. Dashiell (1935) and up to the "discovery" of experimenter and subject "artifacts" toward the end of the 1950s, the social nature of human experimentation has seemed more a procedural difficulty (e.g., Bergum & Lehr, 1963; Fraser, 1953; Howes & Solomon, 1950; Meddock, Parsons, & Hill, 1971; Milgram, 1965) than an indicator of a broad methodological problem or a general conceptual crisis. There was little change in the actual practice of social psychology or other areas dominated by the experimental investigation of human behavior even in the 1960s, when a variety of revisions were suggested in the experimental method (e.g., Argyris, 1968; Brown, 1965; Darroch & Steiner, 1970; Freedman, 1969; Giorgi, 1970; Greenberg, 1967; Jourard, 1967; Kelman, 1967) and when some researchers went as far as Lyons (1964) in suggesting:

> I would insist that a way out of our present dilemma in psychology is to be found only by stepping out of the experimental situation, so to speak. One should start by suspecting the orientation toward the psychologist's work which is embalmed in our current experimental methodology. (p. 100)

Of course, from a paradigmatic point of view, this unchanging situation is quite understandable: Abandoning the experiment would be much more than the abandonment of a prevailing method; it would be desertion of a paradigm. Kuhn's (1962) own words explain quite eloquently why psychologists do not reject the paradigm when confronted with anomaly:

> Once a first paradigm through which to view nature has been found, there is no such thing as research in the absence of any paradigm. *To reject one paradigm without simultaneously substituting another is to reject science itself.* That act reflects not on the paradigm but on the man. Inevitably, he will be seen by his colleagues as "the carpenter who blames his tools." (p. 79; italics added)

DEFENDING THE EXPERIMENT

Clearly, although social psychologists have not stopped experimentation, the experimental studies of artifact have created a conceptual crisis. Recently, believers in the experimental method have begun to counter much of the criticism. In social psychology, Kruglanski (in press) has emerged as one of the prime defenders of the laboratory experiment.

Kruglanski reveals the paradigmatic nature of his commitment to the experimental method in the very terms with which he chooses to discuss the problem of the experiment. His article is entitled "The Human Subject in the Psychology Experiment: Fact and Artifact." The key word here is *artifact*, which Kruglanski says

> denotes an error of inference regarding the cause of an observed effect. Specifically, a factor covariant with the experimental independent variable or with the background conditions of the research might constitute a condition for the invalid interpretation of an effect, or the denial of a true effect. This fundamental notion of covariance (or confounding) has the important implication that a propaedeutic condition for the detection of an artifact is its clear conceptual discriminability from the essential variable of theoretical interest.

Clearly, to conceptualize a problem in terms of fact or artifact, as does Kruglanski, one must assume a world already divided into independent and dependent variables.[3] Once we define the problem of the experiment in terms of fact or artifact, we accept the experimental method. From within that context, there is a good and a bad research method, and a correct and an incorrect inference based upon that method, but there are never questions about experiments as method. Consequently, on the basis of a particularistic reading of the literature or subject artifacts, Kruglanski can critically observe

> cases in which loose conceptualizations of an alleged source of bias (affording poor discriminability) obscured the inference whether the obtained results were artifact or essence of the phenomena involved.

We arrive at a position from which Kruglanski's criticisms of "artifact" studies can be perfectly correct and still be irrelevant to questions of the suitability and desirability of the experimental method.

Lyons (1964, p. 99) recalls that Jerome Bruner (1951) once stated the basic requirement of the experimental situation in the following manner:

> It is of the essence in any given experiment that we define in advance what we as experimenters mean by relevant information and do not depend upon the subject's response to do it for us; otherwise we would be in a complete circle. (p. 131)

What holds for questions phrased within the language of experimentation does not necessarily hold for questions phrased about experimentation. It is precisely around this characteristic of experimentation and the experimenter-originated definitions that some of the doubts about experimental research originated. It is because questions about experiments phrased in experimental language are circular that such experiments are self-contradictory. Kruglanski's critique of the artifact-based criticisms of the experimental method exemplifies, within the language of the experimental paradigm, our initial assertion—that a direct experimental refutation or proof of the validity of experimental results is self-contradictory.[4]

The debate about the experiment then becomes less than an empirical inquiry: We never see an empirical comparison of two alternative methodologies, nor even an attempt to create the terms for such a comparison. Rather, the debate is transformed into another experimental investigation. Questions about the experimental method and questions about the information resulting from that method are understood only as questions of "artifact." For this transformation, both the critics and the defenders of the experimental method must share the responsibility. From within the context of his paradigm, Kruglanski responds quite appropriately to the criticisms raised. These criticisms stem from allegations that experiments are not working correctly, rather than from the suspicion that the laboratory experiment, as currently conceptualized, is unworkable.

---

[3] Thibaut and Kelly (1959, p. 2) have criticized this commonplace assumption, especially in regard to the investigation of dyadic relationships.

[4] In order to evaluate experiments, one needs absolute values regarding the effects of that setting, etc. These values cannot be obtained solely on the basis of laboratory experiments; one must necessarily step outside the laboratory experiment in order to generate the appropriate comparisons.

It is still possible, however, that within the body of general psychological literature there are empirically investigated and theoretically formulated phenomena that have direct relevance for an understanding of the experimental situation.

EVALUATION APPREHENSION

Certainly, we might expect some of the findings accumulated within this universalistic tradition to bear directly upon the experimental situation. As was observed earlier, there are few references to the general social psychology literature within either the critical or defensive discussions of experimentation. This omission becomes understandable when we recall the paradigmatic nature of the psychologists' commitment to the experiment, particularly in the paradigm's separation of method and content. The social psychology literature is not seen as having relevance for an understanding of the social psychology of the experimental situation. This is most clear when we examine the social psychologists' treatment of "evaluation apprehension." Evaluation apprehension appears concurrently within two literatures in social psychology, the discussions of the experiment and the treatment of social facilitation.

In the studies of subject artifacts, evaluation apprehension is described as "active, anxiety-toned concern that he [the subject] win a positive evaluation from the experimenter, or at least that he provide no grounds for a negative one . . . " (Rosenberg, 1969, p. 281). As it appears in the contemporary literature on social facilitation, the influence of the presence of others on a subject's behavior, that is, evaluation apprehension, conceived originally in Hullian terms, is described as "anticipation of performance evaluation which increases drive level or behavioral arousal" (Henchy & Glass, 1968, p. 453).

Without question, the similarity between the two independently developed conceptions is striking. In the social facilitation literature, it is one of the competing hypotheses offered to explain social facilitation. In the literature that examines the so-called subject artifacts, evaluation apprehension is used as both a descriptive term for the phenomenon and an explanation of the phenomenon. What is most interesting is the fact that none of the studies of evaluation apprehension (as artifact) cites any of the studies on social facilitation. Similarly, none of the studies of social facilitation cites any of the studies of evaluation appre-

hension (as artifact). It is difficult to imagine a stronger confirmation of the hypothesis that within the dominant psychological paradigm, method and subject matter are perceived independently. This separation keeps the critics of the experimental method from exploring a vast store of empirical work relevant to an understanding of the experiment, and the separation allows the defenders of the experimental method to ignore evidence that would require a reexamination of that method.

Overall, the experimental results of social facilitation research converge on the conclusion that the experimenter, whether physically present or electronically represented, functions as an audience (spectator) who influences the behavior of his or her subject in ways that extend well beyond the structure of the experiment and the manipulation of variables.

CONCLUSIONS

Invariably, we must confront the question, What does it all mean? Even if one is convinced that we have demonstrated the existence of a paradigm in psychology and that that paradigm is a behavioristic version of the experimental method, what implications might there be for scientific practice and scientific education? We begin with a negative injunction. Defenders of the experimental method would have us believe all is well in the laboratory. For example, Kruglanski (in press) asserts:

> The absence of acceptable evidence for subject-artifacts renders *unnecessary* the various techniques aimed at their elimination. In addition, a detailed examination of these techniques suggests that they may contain several serious difficulties, which render them *undesirable* as substitutes for current modes of experimentation. (italics added)

We could not agree less with this position. By implication, it suggests a continued adherence to the experimental method and a continued emphasis on that method in the education of future psychologists. By contrast, we would support, in both education and "actual" research, an intensive exploration of alternative methodologies. Certainly, it would be, as Kuhn so clearly shows, scientific suicide to simply abandon the experimental method. That is not being suggested here. We desire a movement toward a new paradigm. We consider the recognition of the existing paradigm a necessary first step toward that development in psychology.

At the same time, we are reluctant to propose an "alternative" paradigm (as was suggested by many readers of an earlier draft of this article). True, Kuhn has argued that old paradigms are replaced by more promising paradigms rather than abandoned in the face of criticism. Yet we share Koch's opinion that many of the current problems in psychology were a consequence of "method preceding content." Certainly, we are wary of prescribing *the* alternative methodology that would lead to the "real" scientific paradigm in psychology. At the same time, we recognize that there ought to be some lessons to be learned from past omissions and errors. At the least, a critical examination of the past and present should suggest some new directions in which psychology could develop. The following suggestions, then, are not meant to indicate a systematic program, but rather some general guidelines for further exploration.

Phenomena Should Precede Method

We ought to begin with a reversal of the present emphases: Psychology should initially address itself to phenomena, not methodology. Rather than selecting for research those phenomena suited to our methods, we ought to shape and develop our methods to fit phenomena. This is not to argue that considerations of scientific methodology are insignificant. Indeed, at times methodological developments can be crucial for paradigm change. Method is essential to science, but it can emerge from confrontation with phenomena rather than being applied to them. Such was the case in the natural sciences, but those particular methods may not be appropriate to psychological phenomena. Movements toward the development of methods suited to previously excluded phenomena are in fact underway, and in many different areas of psychology (e.g., field research in social psychology and the new interest in ESP).

The last several years have seen, if not a flight from the laboratory, at least an increased willingness to leave its confines for brief excursions. Ultimately, however, it is not the laboratory itself we are criticizing. Instead, it is the conception of the experimenter-subject relationship as it was institutionalized by the laboratory experiment. If one brings to field research the same notions of science that were born in the laboratory, then only the setting for research will have

changed. It is not the setting of research that needs to be changed, but the nature of the research relationship, on the one hand, and our consciousness of that relationship, on the other.

Psychological Research Should Be Reflexive

Conducting research means entering into relationships with people, and these relationships significantly affect the outcome of the research. Our present methodology prescribes these relationships as impersonal ones, leads us to minimize the effects of "personal" factors, turns our attention away from a consideration of the relationships, and facilitates treating our subjects as objects. Alternatively, we are suggesting that there is no way in which human research cannot be relational and that psychological methodology must attend to the relational quality of research; this is the beginning of reflexivity.

Our current idea of science directs our attention away from developing a consciousness about the research relationship. We are suggesting that we abandon what we consider a futile attempt to control, inhibit, or deny the relational aspect of research. Rather, we suggest that the relational quality of research be attended to, that it be developed and investigated. Harold Raush (Note 1) has described this process as one in which

> the relationship between investigator and subject is overtly recognized as influencing the data. The relationship is seen as establishing conditions for the data to emerge, and examination of the relationship between investigator and subjects becomes part of the data analysis itself.

One of the more interesting alternatives that incorporates this perspective would involve considering and treating our subjects as informants (in the anthropological sense) rather than as uninformed objects. This does not mean, as Victor Turner's (1967) remarks earlier in this article indicate, that we need to take our subjects at their word. It does mean, however, developing the means whereby we can learn from our subjects as well as from their performance. This particular approach promises a tremendous increase in the information available to us and a new depth to our understanding of psychological events. It also suggests some possibilities for a whole new range of research, in which those we formerly considered our subjects are now our collaborators in research endeavors. Experimentation, when its relational nature is acknowledged, can become a social project rather than a laboratory exercise. The research relationship might be developed as one in which both researchers and participants mutually explore psychological phenomena. Clearly, the implications and problems associated with such a reorientation are beyond the scope of this article. Among the issues it raises is the question of scientific methodology: What is it to become, or what is to become of it (e.g., see Tart, 1973)? Obviously, we cannot answer such a question in advance of attempting the type of explorations we suggest.

Additionally, reflexivity can be created by acknowledging that the study of human behavior necessarily includes the behavior of psychologists. This recognition implies, of course, that the psychologist is as prone to psychological processes as anyone else and should be especially self-conscious of this fact when acting as a scientist. This self-consciousness includes the psychologist's awareness of his relationship to and with his subject matter and the awareness of his own role with respect to his inquiry. The knowledge that derives from such reflexivity is a tripartite knowledge—about the subject, about the researcher, and about the knowledge itself. Little has been written about such matters in the psychological journals, but there does exist a small if obscure literature known as critical social science theory. The works of Habermas (1971), Ratner (1971), and Horkheimer (1972) can provide an introduction for those interested. Understandably, we have only hinted at the possible contents of an alternative paradigm for psychology.

Hopefully, unlike the currently dominant paradigm, the next one will develop along with the emergence of an authentically psychological subject matter and the investigation of problems within that domain. At the very least, even those who are wholehearted supporters of the experimental method can support the creation of environments conducive to the development of paradigm disputes. Kuhn has noted that the first efforts of a developing paradigm are often clumsy and incomplete and that there will be many things that the dominant paradigm can explain which the developing paradigm will not:

> But paradigm debates are not really about relative problem-solving ability, though for good reasons they are usually couched in those terms. Instead, the issue is which paradigm should in the future guide research on problems many of which neither competitor can yet claim to resolve completely. A decision between alternative ways of practicing science is called for, and in the circumstances that decision must be based less on past achievement than on future promise. The man who embraces a new paradigm at an early stage must often do so in defiance of the evidence provided by problem-solving. He must, that is, have faith that the new paradigm will succeed with the many problems that confront it, knowing only that the older paradigm has failed with a few. A decision of that kind can only be made on faith. (pp. 158–159)

It is our hope that if enough psychologists can develop such a faith, then we can in turn develop a science that in fact gives us the ability to reason. Perhaps then we can contribute to the accomplishment of Floyd Allport's goal of solving the "most vital problems of the social order."

Reference Note

1. Raush, H. Personal communication, May 1974.

A Procedure for Analyzing Data Is a Heuristic: Introduction to "The Analysis of Variance and Analysis of Causes"

Richard Lewontin is one of the leading evolutionary biologists in the world. He has authored several books, including, with co-authors Rose and Kamin, *Not in Our Genes: Biology, Ideology, and Human Nature* (1984) and, with Richard Levins, *The Dialectical Biologist* (1985). Lewontin's books are especially informative with regard to analyzing and critiquing contemporary theories about the genetic causes of mental disorders.

The following selection is a complex, multifaceted paper that illustrates a form of research design that can be termed *conceptual analysis*. Although it may be difficult on first reading, mastering Lewontin's analysis will help you to understand many issues in contemporary debates about the environmental and genetic causes of human behavior, conceptualizations of causal interactions between organisms and their environments, and the uses and misuses of the analysis of variance (ANOVA). You may find it helpful to study the analysis of variance, covariance, and path analysis as you read this paper. An excellent and accessible source for more introductory information about the analysis of variance is a series by Marija Norusis (e.g., *The SPSS Guide to Data Analysis*, 1988).

Any procedure for data analysis is a heuristic that in effect reformulates the original research problem into another problem. Lewontin demonstrates the biases that result when the heuristic of ANOVA is applied to study the problem of genetic and environmental influences on human behavior. ANOVA is useful for addressing one aspect of the problem of environmental and genetic causation of behavior. However, in effect, ANOVA transforms the research problem, and systematic errors result if ANOVA is used for other aspects of the same problem. In other words, Lewontin describes two research problems: (1) distinguishing two mutually exclusive causes for variation in the phenotype (environment versus genotypic variation) and (2) assessing the different contributions of two causes (environment versus genotypic variation) that interact in producing variations in the phenotype. Lewontin emphasizes that in the second research problem, it is conceptually impossible to assign quantitative values to the contributions of interacting causes. Nonetheless, researchers often misuse ANOVA for precisely that purpose. In other words, ANOVA transforms the original problem as follows:

> [I]f we cannot ask how much of an individual's height is the result of his genes and how much a result of his environment, we will ask what proportion of the deviation of his height from the population mean can be ascribed to deviation of his environment from the average environment and how much to the deviation of this genetic value from the mean genetic value. (Lewontin, 1974, p. 402)*

---

*Editor's Note: The citations used here refer to pages of the original article. You can find the material quoted from this article in the reprint that follows this introduction.

The consequence of reformulating the problem using the heuristic of the ANOVA is that "a totally different object has been substituted as the object of investigation, almost without noticing it" (Lewontin, 1974, p. 403). When ANOVA transforms one problem into another problem, two prominent biases are set up. First, the linear model used in ANOVA can describe only occurrences in a specific place and time; it cannot be used to explain functional relations in general. As Lewontin says, ANOVA cannot solve the problem of functional relations between environment and genotype in the production of a phenotypic variation, because it is "too specific in that it is spatiotemporally restricted in its outcome" (1974, p. 403). The second major bias set up by ANOVA is that it "confounds different causative schemes in the same outcome," and so it is too general to give a veridical account of distinctive, interacting causal relationships (1974, p. 403).

According to Lewontin, the biases set up by the treatment of interacting causation by ANOVA have been invisible in part because of the following misapprehension:

> [T]hings can be broken down into parts without losing any essential information and . . . in any complex interaction of causes, main effects will almost always explain most of what we see while interactions will tend to be of a smaller order of importance. But this is a pure a priori prejudice. (Lewontin, 1974, p. 408)

Lewontin points out how a thoroughgoing reductionism leads to analyses of the complex interactions between organisms and their environments that are so over-simplified as to be incorrect. To elaborate, when applied to understandings of human behavior, a thoroughgoing reductionism causes researchers to overlook important interactive effects. For example, research on the constellation of child behaviors commonly termed *childhood hyperactivity* has been dominated by expla-nations that focus on the child's neurological functioning, even though no neurologi-cal defect has been found that is common to children labeled hyperactive. Instead, consistent evidence has shown that the children's behavior varies in relation to how adult care givers (parents and teachers) treat the child (Tyson, 1991a).

Lewontin's analysis responds to a significant social problem. In his conclusion, Lewontin suggests that ideologies may influence how scientists pursue problems and that scientists' findings can support specific political aims as well. When Lewontin wrote this paper, a major problem was that some researchers had concluded that environmental factors cannot modify what they regarded as genetic influences on students' academic performance; their research, in effect, supported the political goal of cutting back funds for educational programs. Other researchers who have pointed out that ideologies influence arguments about the relative impact of genes and environment on behavior include Block and Dworkin (1974), who showed how IQ tests, because they are culturally biased, have been used to support policies that perpetuate social inequalities. They connected the reliance on IQ tests with psy-chology's effort to conform to logical empiricist standards: "bad philosophy of sci-ence has played an important role in the construction of IQ tests and has served to keep many psychologists and educators from seeing the inadequacies of IQ tests as measures of intelligence" (Block & Dworkin, 1974, p. 333). Richardson (1984) used the debate over the genetic basis of IQ as one example of issues in theory appraisal. Specifically, he emphasized that because science cannot be value-free one criterion to use in evaluating a scientific theory is the ideology that the theory implicitly or explicitly supports.

KEY TERMS

Additivity

ANOVA (analysis of variance)

Interactive effects

Allele

Genotype

Phenotype

DISCUSSION QUESTIONS

1. Why is there an appearance of separation of causes in ANOVA, and why is that an illusion?

2. Why does Lewontin call the nature versus nurture debate a "pseudoquestion"(see p. 409 in this volume)?

3. Suppose a researcher analyzed data using ANOVA and argued that environmental enrichment differentially affects people with different genotypes. Use Lewontin's conceptual analysis to critique that researcher's argument.

4. a. Norwood Hanson writes:

> We say that where there is boiling there is heat, where there is smoke there is fire, where there are swamps there are mosquitoes. But while we might say that the heat causes the water to boil, we need not say that the fire causes the smoke. (The brakes on my car usually smoke, but they have never yet broken into flames.) And would we say that the swamp causes the mosquitoes? Not always, surely. Still less would we say that the swamp causes our insect bites. (1969b, p. 271)

Hanson distinguishes between observed conjunctions between events and causal relationships and shows that observed conjunctions often are confused with causal relationships. Lewontin points out that pervasive ideologies encourage researchers to draw incorrect conclusions about causal connections and to confuse conjunctions with causal relationships. Show how the following arguments represent a confusion of observed conjunctions and causal connections and also manifest the impact of discriminatory ideologies:

  i. From the observation that a higher proportion of physically disabled than nondisabled children are abused, some researchers have argued that physically disabled children cause the abuse.

  ii. From the observation that most social workers are female and that more women than men suffer from discrimination in the workplace (Mason, 1992; Sancier, 1992b), some suggest that a solution to social workers' low pay and status is to recruit more male social workers.

  b. Hanson shows how when we are looking for causes we may want to prevent an effect or produce an effect (1969b, p. 272). Describe how a clinician seeks to do both in the treatment process.

5. In understanding causal relationships, a distinction traditionally has been drawn between a necessary cause and a sufficient cause. "A necessary cause is a variable in the absence of which the event cannot occur but in the presence of which the event may or may not occur, and a sufficient cause is a variable in the presence of which the event will occur but in the absence of which the event may or may not occur" (Heineman Pieper & Pieper, 1990, p. 120).

   a. In a famous episode in the children's television series about the adventures of Spanky and Alfalfa, Alfalfa (a 7-year-old child who tends to be timid) is trying to hang onto a curtain rod that, from a child's point of view, is quite high. A big black spider dangles down from the ceiling in front of his eyes and spins around in front of his face, tickling his nose. Alfalfa goes cross-eyed and then, in distress, first loosens one hand and then the other, falling from the curtain rod. Keeping in mind that with regard to human systems we cannot formulate causal laws but only probabilities, is the spider the necessary or sufficient cause of Alfalfa's fall?

   b. Langston Hughes writes, "Hold on to your dreams, for if dreams die, life is a broken-winged sparrow that cannot fly" (from "Dreams," 1986, p. 7). In Hughes's view, are dreams necessary or sufficient causes of human happiness?

6. With regard to the distinction between necessary and sufficient causes, Hanson writes:

   > Not all, not even most, of the important causes in science fall easily into either category. The causes of cancer or of sleep, of life and death, of the arrangement of the solar system and the galaxies—all of these are enormously complex. . . . For instance, the elimination of cancer . . . probably requires far more than just the discovery of a necessary cause. (1969b, p. 274)

   a. Take two theories of psychopathology and summarize how those theories outline necessary and sufficient causes for psychological symptoms (e.g., psychoanalysis, behaviorism, intrapsychic humanism, family systems). What are the implications of determining the causes of psychopathology for treatment planning?

   b. Some researchers concluded that the learning problems of disadvantaged children are entrenched early in life and are so exacerbated by their deprived environments that providing enriched educational programs cannot make substantive improvements in the children's academic accomplishments. Consider the two variables of (1) a deprived (nonacademic) environment and (2) educational resources. Distinguish which are the necessary and sufficient causes of disadvantaged children's educational achievements. Why does the argument that remedial programs should not be implemented, because they will not influence the children's nonacademic environmental deprivations, reflect a conflation of the necessary and sufficient causes of the children's educational achievements?

7. Consider how different theories of treatment conceptualize the mechanism of cure in psychotherapy differently. What are some implications of Lewontin's

discussion of interactive causes for conceptualizing the potential curative impact of psychotherapy?

▼ ▼ ▼ ▼ ▼ ▼ ▼ ▼ ▼ ▼ ▼ ▼

SAMPLE RESEARCH PROJECT: DEVELOPING RESIDENTIAL TREATMENT SERVICES FOR HOMELESS, MENTALLY ILL, AND SUBSTANCE-ABUSING CLIENTS

Part 10: Plan for Data Analysis Using Inferential Statistics

After the coding categories are developed and coding is completed for data derived from the surveys, the chart notes, and staff feedback, descriptive statistics will be used to compile the responses. The inferential statistical method of log-linear analysis will be used to address specific subquestions. One important question to address will be the interaction between the residents' positive evaluations of the program and behavioral indicators of change (e.g., obtaining stable funding).

Log-linear models were developed specifically to analyze relationships between categorical variables and have been increasingly used by social and behavioral scientists: "These models are useful for uncovering the potentially complex relationships among the variables in a multiway crosstabulation" (Norusis, 1988, p. 298). One of the advantages of this statistical technique for data analysis is that it allows the investigator both to examine the statistical significance of relationships between many variables and also to ascertain the effects of interactions between the variables. Using log-linear analysis, the researcher can divide clients into groups based on the type of substance they abuse (e.g., alcohol, prescription drugs, and nonprescription drugs) and then to compare their differential responses about the usefulness of individual and group counseling services. Because all residents are included in the sample, and none are excluded, the sample meets the criteria for statistical data analysis using log-linear modeling (Kennedy, 1992).

Log-linear modeling will also be used to focus on particular subgroups of the sample, including breakdowns by gender, race, and ethnicity. For instance, a significant concern in the field has been whether residential milieu treatment programs can be helpful to clients with dual diagnoses, specifically mental illness and substance abuse (MISA) (Bond, McDonel, Miller, & Pensec, 1991; Levine & Huebner, 1991). Researchers note that "in the sparse literature on treatment for persons with MISA there is little evidence on the efficacy of group modalities" (Bond et al., 1991, p. 33). Often, staff trained to help severely mentally ill clients are less familiar with working with people with chronic substance abuse problems. Previous ways of handling substance abuse problems have been to relegate clients with such problems into different programs (Drake, Teague, & Warren, 1990; Kline, Harris, Bebout, & Drake, 1991). This is increasingly difficult to implement in practice, however. For example, when a person becomes more available to receiving help, often the person will reveal previously concealed chronic substance abuse problems. Currently, this is a subject at the forefront of practitioner concern. An analysis of the survey responses that compare respondents along the dimension of substance abuse problems will be conducted using log-linear modeling. Log-linear analysis will be used to take a closer look at this particular subgroup, specifically, the statistical relationships between substance abuse/nonsubstance abuse and clients' satisfaction and dissatisfaction with specific services and the types of services that clients with substance abuse problems want.

The Analysis of Variance and the Analysis of Causes

RICHARD C. LEWONTIN   *Harvard University*

This issue of the *American Journal of Human Genetics* contains two articles by Newton Morton and his colleagues (1,2) that provide a detailed analytic critique of various estimates of heritability and components of variance for human phenotypes. They make especially illuminating remarks on the problems of partitioning variances and covariances between groups such as social classes and races. The most important point of all, at least from the standpoint of the practical, social and political applications of human population genetics, occurs at the conclusion of the first paper [1] in which Morton points out explicitly the chief programmatic fallacy committed by those who argue so strongly for the importance of heritability measures for human traits. The fallacy is that a knowledge of the heritability of some trait in a population provides an index of the efficacy of environmental or clinical intervention in altering the trait either in individuals or in the population as a whole. This fallacy, sometimes propagated even by geneticists, who should know better, arises from the confusion between the technical meaning of heritability and the everyday meaning of the word. A trait can have a heritability of 1.0 in a population at some time, yet could be completely altered in the future by a simple environmental change. If this were not the case, "inborn errors of metabolism" would be forever incurable, which is patently untrue. But the misunderstanding about the relationship between heritability and phenotypic plasticity is not simply the result of an ignorance of genet-

ics on the part of psychologists and electronic engineers. It arises from the entire system of analysis of causes through linear models, embodied in the analysis of variance and covariance and in path analysis. It is indeed ironic that while Morton and his colleagues dispute the erroneous programmatic conclusions that are drawn from the analysis of human phenotypic variation, they nevertheless rely heavily for their analytic techniques on the very linear models that are responsible for the confusion.

I would like in what follows to look rather closely at the problem of the analysis of causes in human genetics and to try to understand how the underlying model of this analysis molds our view of the real world. I will begin by saying some very obvious and elementary things about causes, but I will come thereby to some very annoying conclusions.

DISCRIMINATION OF CAUSES AND ANALYSIS OF CAUSES

We must first separate two quite distinct problems about causation that are discussed by Morton. One is

Source: "The Analysis of Variance and the Analysis of Causes" by R. C. Lewontin, 1974, *American Journal of Human Genetics, 26,* pp. 400–411. Copyright © 1974 by the American Society of Human Genetics. All rights reserved. Reprinted by permission of The University of Chicago Press.

to discriminate which of two alternative and mutually exclusive causes lies at the basis of some observed phenotype. In particular, it is the purpose of *segregation analysis* to attempt to distinguish those individuals who owe their phenotypic deviation to their homozygosity for rare deleterious gene alleles from those whose phenotypic peculiarity arises from the interaction of environment with genotypes that are drawn from the normal array of segregating genes of minor effect. This is the old problem of distinguishing major gene effects from "polygenic" effects. I do not want to take up here the question of whether such a clear distinction can be made or whether the spectrum of gene effects and gene frequencies is such that we cannot find a clear dividing line between the two cases. The evidence at present is ambiguous, but at least *in principle* it may be possible to discriminate two etiological groups, and whether such groups exist for any particular human disorder is a matter for empirical research. It is possible, although not necessary, that the form of clinical or environmental intervention required to correct a disorder that arises from homozygosity for a single rare recessive allele (the classical "inborn error of metabolism") may be different from that required for the "polygenic" class. Moreover, for the purposes of genetic counseling, the risk of future affected offspring will be different if a family is segregating for a rare recessive than if it is not. Thus, the discrimination between two *alternative* causes of a human disorder is worth making if it can be done.

The second problem of causation is quite different. It is the problem of the *analysis* into separate elements of a number of causes that are interacting to produce a single result. In particular, it is the problem of analyzing into separate components the interaction between environment and genotype in the determination of phenotype. Here, far from trying to discriminate individuals into two distinct and mutually exclusive etiological groups, we recognize that all individuals owe their phenotype to the biochemical activity of their genes in a unique sequence of environments and to developmental events that may occur subsequent to, although dependent upon, the initial action of the genes. The analysis of interacting causes is fundamentally a different concept from the discrimination of alternative causes. The difficulties in the early history of genetics embodied in the pseudoquestion of "nature versus nurture" arose precisely because of the confusion between these two problems in causation. It was supposed that the phenotype of an individual could be the result of *either* environment *or* genotype, whereas we understand the phenotype to be the result of *both*. This confusion has persisted into modern genetics with the concept of the phenocopy, which is supposed to be an environmentally caused phenotypic deviation, as opposed to a mutant which is genetically caused. But, of course, both "mutant" and "phenocopy" result from a unique interaction of gene and environment. If they are etiologically separable, it is not by a line that separates environmental from genetic causation but by a line that separates two kinds of genetic basis: a single gene with major effect or many genes each with small effect. That is the message of the work by Waddington [3] and Rendel [4] on canalization.

QUANTITATIVE ANALYSIS OF CAUSES

If an event is the result of the joint operation of a number of causative chains and if these causes "interact" in any generally accepted meaning of the word, it becomes conceptually impossible to assign quantitative values to the causes of that *individual event*. Only if the causes are utterly independent could we do so. For example, if two men lay bricks to build a wall, we may quite fairly measure their contributions by counting the number laid by each; but if one mixes the mortar and the other lays the bricks, it would be absurd to measure their relative quantitative contributions by measuring the volumes of bricks and of mortar. It is obviously even more absurd to say what proportion of a plant's height is owed to the fertilizer it received and what proportion to the water, or to ascribe so many inches of a man's height to his genes and so many to his environment. But this obvious absurdity appears to frustrate the universally acknowledged program of Cartesian science to analyze the complex world of appearances into an articulation of causal mechanisms. In the case of genetics, it appears to prevent our asking about the relative importance of genes and environment in the determination of phenotype. The solution offered to this dilemma, a solution that has been accepted in a great variety of natural and social scientific practice, has been the *analysis of variation*. That is, if we cannot ask how much of an individual's height is the result of his genes and how much a result of his environment, we will ask what proportion of the deviation of his height from the population mean can be ascribed to deviation of his environment from the average environment and how much to the deviation of this genetic value from the mean genetic value. This is the famous linear model of the analysis of variance which can be written as

$$Y - \mu_Y = (G - \mu_Y) + (E - \mu_Y) + (GE) + e, \quad (1)$$

where μ_Y is the mean score of all individuals in the population; Y is the score of the individual in question; G is the average score of all individuals with the same genotype as the one in question; E is the average score of all individuals with the same environment as the one in question; GE, the genotype-environment inter-action, is that part of the average deviation of individuals sharing the same environmental and genotype that cannot be ascribed to the simple sum of the separate environmental and genotypic deviations; and e takes into account any individual deviation not already consciously accounted for, and assumed to be random over all individuals (measurement error, developmental noise, etc.).

I have written this well known linear model in a slightly different way than it is usually displayed in order to emphasize two of its properties that are well known to statisticians. First, the environmental and genotypic effects are in units of *phenotype*. We are not actually assessing how much variation in environment or genotype exists, but only how much perturbation of phenotype has been the outcome of average difference in environment. The analysis in expression (1) is completely *tautological*, since it is framed entirely in terms of phenotype and both sides of the equation must balance by the definitions of GE and e. To turn expression (1) into a contingent one relating actual values of environmental variables like temperature to phenotypic score, we would need functions of the form

$$(E - \mu_Y) = f(T - \mu_T) \quad (2)$$

and

$$GE = h[(g - \mu_g), (T - \mu_T)], \quad (3)$$

where g and T are measured on a genetic and a temperature scale rather than on a scale of phenotype. Thus, the linear model [equation (1)] makes it impossible to know whether the environmental deviation ($E - \mu_Y$) is small because there are no variations in actual environment or because the particular genotype is insensitive to the environmental deviations, which themselves may be quite considerable. From the standpoint of the tautological analysis of expression (1), this distinction is irrelevant, but as we shall see, it is supremely relevant for those questions that are of real importance in our science.

Second, expression (1) contains population means at two levels. One level is the grand mean phenotype μ_Y and the other is the set of so-called "marginal" genotypic and environmental means, E and G. These, it must be remembered, are the *mean* for a given environment averaged over all genotypes in the population and the *mean* for a given genotype averaged over all environments.

But since the analysis is a function of these phenotypic means, it will, in general, give a different result if the means are different. That is, the linear model is a *local analysis*. It gives a result that depends upon the actual distribution of genotypes and environments in the particular population sampled. Therefore, the result of the analysis has a historical (i.e., spatiotemporal) limitation and is not in general a statement about *functional* relations. So, the genetic variance for a character in a population may be very small because the functional relationship between gene action and the character is weak for any conceivable genotype or simply because the population is homozygous for those loci that are of strong functional significance for the trait. The analysis of variation cannot distinguish between these alternatives even though for most purposes in human genetics we wish to do so.

What has happened in attempting to solve the problem of the analysis of causes by using the analysis of variation is that a totally different object has been substituted as the object of investigation, almost without noticing it. The new object of study, the deviation of phenotypic value from the mean, is not the same as the phenotypic value itself; and the tautological analysis of that deviation is not the same as the analysis of causes. In fact, the analysis of variation throws out the baby with the bath water. It is both too specific in that it is spatiotemporally restricted in its outcome and too general in that it confounds different causative schemes in the same outcome. Only in a very special case, to which I shall refer below, can the analysis of variation be placed in a one-to-one correspondence in the analysis of causes.

NORM OF REACTION

The real object of study both for programmatic and theoretical purposes is the relation between genotype, environment, and phenotype. This is expressed in the *norm of reaction*, which is a table of correspondence between phenotype, on the one hand, and genotype-environment combinations on the other. The relations between phenotype and genotype and between phenotype and environment are many-many relations, no single phenotype corresponding to a unique genotype or vice versa.

In order to clarify the relation between the two objects of study (i.e., the norm of reaction and the analysis of variance, which analyzes something quite different), let us consider the simplified norms of reaction shown in figures 1a–h. We assume that there is a single well ordered environmental variable E, say temperature, and a scale of phenotypic measurement P. Each line is the norm of reaction, the relationship of phenotype to environment, for a particular hypothetical genotype (G_1 or G_2).

The first thing to observe is that the phenotype is sensitive to differences in both environment and genotype in every case. That is, there is a reaction of each genotype to changing environment, and in no case are the two genotypes identical in their reactions. Thus in any usual sense of the word, both genotypes and environment are *causes* of phenotypic differences and are necessary objects of our study.

Figure 1a is in one sense the most general, for if environment extends uniformly over the entire range and if the two genotypes are equally frequent, there is an overall effect of genotype (G_1 being on the average superior to G_2) and an overall effect of environment (phenotype gets smaller on the average with increasing temperature). Nevertheless, the genotypes cross so that neither is always superior.

Figure 1b shows an overall effect of environment, since both genotypes have a positive slope; but there is no overall effect of genotype, since the two genotypes would have exactly the same *mean* phenotype if all environments are considered equally. There is no a priori way from figure 1b of ranking the two genotypes. However, if because of particular circumstances the distribution of environments were heavily weighted toward the lower temperatures, the G_1 would be consistently superior to G_2 and an analysis of variance would show a strong effect of genotype as well as of environment, but very little genotype-environment interaction. Thus the analysis of variance would reflect the particular environmental circumstances and give a completely incorrect picture of the general relationship between cause and effect here, where there is overall no effect of genotype but a strong genotype-environment interaction.

Figure 1c is the complementary case to that shown in figure 1b. In figure 1c there is no overall effect of environment, but G_1 is clearly superior to G_2 overall. In this case a strong environmental component of variance will appear, however, if either one of the genotypes should be in excess in the population. So the

Fig. 1.—a–h.

Examples of different forms of reaction norms. In each case the phenotype (*P*) is plotted as a function of environment (*E*) for different genotypes (*G₁, G₂*).

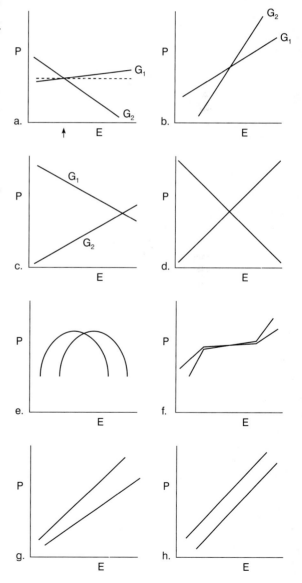

historical events that mold the genotypic distribution of a population will have an effect on the judgment, from the analysis of variance, of the importance of environment.

The overall lack of genetic effect in figure 1*b* and of environmental effect in figure 1*c* can both appear in a trait like that shown in figure 1*a*, which overall has both effects if the distribution of environments or of genotypes is asymmetric. Thus if environments are distributed around the arrow in figure 1*a*, there will *appear* to be no average effect of genotype, while if the population is appropriately weighted toward an excess of G_1, the average phenotype across environments will be constant as shown by the dashed line. Here real overall effects are obscured because of spatiotemporal events, and the analysis of variance fails to reveal significant overall differences.

These last considerations lead to two extremely important points about the analysis of variance. First, although expression (1) appears to isolate distinct causes of variation into separate elements, it does not because the amount of *environmental* variance that appears depends upon the *genotypic* distribution, while the amount of *genetic* variance depends upon the *environmental* distribution. Thus the appearance of the separation of causes is a pure illusion. Second, because the linear model appears as a sum of variation from different causes, it is sometimes erroneously supposed that removing one of the sources of variation will reduce the total variance. So, the meaning of the genetic variance is sometimes given as "the amount of variation that would be left if the environment were held constant," and the environmental variance is described as "the amount of variance that would remain if all the genetic variation were removed," an erroneous explanation offered by Jensen [5], for example. Suppose that the norms of reaction were as in figure 1*a* and a unimodal distribution of environments were centered near the arrow, with a roughly equal mixture of the two genotypes. Now suppose we fix the environment. What will happen to the total variance? That depends on which environment we fix upon. If we choose an environment about 1 SD or more to the right of the mean, there would actually be an *increase* in the total variance because the difference between genotypes is much greater in that environment than on the average over the original distribution. Conversely, suppose we fix the genotype. If we chose G_2 to be our pure strain, then, again we would *increase* the total variance because we had chosen the more environmentally plastic genotype.

The apparent absurdity that removing a source of variance actually increases the total variance is a consequence of the fact that the linear model does not really effect a separation of causes of variation and that it is a purely local description with no predictive reliability. Without knowing the norms of reaction, the present distribution of environments, the present distribution of genotypes, and without then specifying which environments and which genotypes are to be eliminated or fixed, it is impossible to predict whether the total variation would be increased, decreased, or remain unchanged by environmental or genetic changes.

In figure 1*d* there is neither an overall effect of genotype or environment, but both can obviously appear in a particular population in a particular environmental range as discussed above.

Case 1*e* has been chosen to illustrate a common situation for enzyme activity, a parabolic relation between phenotype and environment. Here genotypes are displaced horizontally (have different temperature optima). There is no overall superiority of either genotype nor is there any general monotone environmental trend for any genotype. But for any distribution of environments except a perfectly symmetrical one, there will appear a component of variance for genotypic effect. Moreover, if the temperature distribution is largely to either side of the crossover point between these two genotypes, there will be very large components of variance for both genotype and environment and a vanishingly small interaction component; yet over the total range of environments exactly the opposite is true!

Figure 1*c* also shows a second important phenomenon, that of differential phenotypic sensitivity in different environmental ranges. At intermediate temperatures there is less difference between genotypes and less difference between the effect of environments than at more extreme temperatures. This is the phenomenon of canalization and is more generally visualized in figure 1*f*. Over a range of intermediate phenotypes there is little effect of either genotype or environment, while outside this zone of canalization phenotype is sensitive to both [4]. The zone of canalization corresponds to that range of environments that have been historically the most common in the species, but in new environments much greater variance appears. Figure 1*f* bears directly on the characteristic of the analysis of variance that all effects are measured in phenotypic units. The transformations [equations (2) and (3)] that express the relationship between the phenotypic deviations ascribable to genotype or environment and the actual values of the genotypes or environmental variables are not simple linear proportionalities. The sensitivity of phenotype to both environment and genotype is a function of the particular range of environments and genotypes. For the programmatic purposes of human genetics, one needs to know more than the components of variation in the historical range of environments.

Figures 1a–f are meant to illustrate how the analysis of variance will give a completely erroneous picture of the causative relations between genotype, environment, and phenotype because the particular distribution of genotypes and environments in a given population at a given time picks out relations from the array of reaction norms that are necessarily atypical of the entire spectrum of causative relations. Of course it may be objected that any sample from nature can never give exactly the same result as examining the universe. But such an objection misses the point. In normal sampling procedures, we take care to get a representative or unbiased sample of the universe of interest and to use unbiased sample estimates of the parameters we care about. But there is no question of sampling here, and the relation of sample to universe in statistical procedures is not the same as the relation of variation in spatiotemporally defined populations to causal and functional variation summed up in the norm of reaction. The relative size of genotypic and environmental components of variance estimated in any natural population reflect in a complex way three underlying relationships: (1) they reflect the actual functional relations embodied in the norm of reaction; (2) they reflect the actual distribution of genotype frequencies, and this distribution, a product of long-time historical forces like natural selection, mutation, migration, and breeding structure, changes over periods much longer than a generation; and (3) they reflect the actual structure of the environments in which the population finds itself, a structure that may change very rapidly indeed, especially for human populations. The effects of historical forces and immediate environment are inextricably bound up in the outcome of variance analysis which thus is not a tool for the elucidation of functional biological relations.

EFFECT OF ADDITIVITY

There is one circumstance in which the analysis of variance can, in fact, estimate functional relationships. This is illustrated exactly in figure 1h and approximately in figure 1g. In these cases there is perfect or nearly perfect additivity between genotypic and environmental effects so that the differences among genotypes are the same in all environments and the differences between environments are the same for all genotypes. Then the historical and immediate circumstances that alter genotypic and environmental distributions are irrelevant. It is not surprising that the assumption of additivity is so often made, since this assumption is necessary to make the analysis of variance anything more than a local description.

The assumption of additivity is imported into analyses by four routes. First, it is thought that in the absence of any evidence, additivity is a priori the simplest hypothesis and additive models are dictated by Occam's razor. The argument comes from a general Cartesian world view that things can be broken down into parts without losing any essential information and that in any complex interaction of causes, main effects will almost always explain most of what we see while interactions will tend to be of a smaller order of importance. But this is a pure a priori prejudice. Dynamic systems in an early stage in their evolution will show rather large main effects of the forces acting to drive them, but as they approach, equilibrium the main effects disappear and interactions predominate. For example, that is what happens to additive genetic variance under selection. Exactly how such considerations apply to genotype and environment is not clear.

Second, it is suggested that additivity is a first approximation to a complex situation, and the results obtained with an additive scheme are then a first approximation to the truth. This argument is made by analogy with the expansion of mathematical functions by Taylor's series. But this argument is self-defeating since the justification for expanding a complex system in a power series and considering only the first-order terms is precisely that one is interested in the behavior of the system in the neighborhood of the point of expansion. Such an analysis is a local analysis only, and the analysis of variance is an analysis in the neighborhood of the population mean only. By justifying additivity on this ground, the whole issue of the global application of the result is sidestepped.

Third, it is argued that if an analysis of variance is carried out and the genotype-environment interaction turns out to be small, the assumption of additivity is justified. Like the second argument, there is some circularity. As the discussion of the previous section showed, the usual outcome of an analysis of variance in a particular population in a restricted range of environments is to underestimate severely the amount of interaction between the factors that occur over the whole range.

Finally, additivity or near additivity may be assumed without offering any justification because it suits a predetermined end. Such is the source of figure 1*g*. It is the hypothetical norm of reaction for IQ taken from Jensen [5]. It purports to show the relation between environmental "richness" and IQ for different genotypes. While there is not a scintilla of evidence to support such a picture, it has the convenient properties that superior and inferior genotypes in one environment maintain that relation in all environments, and that as environment is "enriched," the genetic variance (and therefore the heritability) grows greater. This is meant to take care of those foolish egalitarians who think that spending money and energy on schools generally will iron out the inequalities in society.

Evidence on actual norms of reaction is very hard to come by. In man, measurements of reaction norms for complex traits are impossible because the same genotype cannot be tested in a variety of environments. Even in experimental animals and plants where genotypes can be replicated by inbreeding experiments or cloning, very little work has been done to characterize these norms for the genotypes that occur in natural populations and for traits of consequence to the species. The classic work of Clausen et al. [6] on ecotypes of plants shows very considerable non-additivity of the types illustrated in figures 1*a–d*.

As an example of what has been done in animals, figure 2 has been drawn from the data of Dobzhansky and Spassky [7] on larval viability in *Drosophila pseudoobscura*. Each line is the reaction norm for larval viability at three different temperatures for a fourth chromosome homozygote, where the chromosomes have been sampled from a natural population. As the figure shows, there are a few genotypes that are of uniformly poor viability, probably corresponding to homozygosity for a single deleterious gene of strong effect. However, most genotypes are variable in their expression, and there is a great deal of genotype-environment interaction with curves crossing each other and having quite different environmental sensitivities.

PURPOSE OF ANALYSIS

Just as the objects of analysis are different when we analyze causes and when we analyze variance, so the

purposes of these analyses are different. The analysis of causes in human genetics is meant to provide us with the basic knowledge we require for correct schemes of environmental modification and intervention. Together with a knowledge of the relative frequencies of different human genotypes, a knowledge of norms of reaction can also predict the demographic and public health consequences of certain massive environmental changes. Analysis of variance can do neither of these because its results are a unique function of the present distribution of environment and genotypes.

The legitimate purposes of the analysis of variance in human genetics are to predict the rate at which selection may alter the genotypic composition of human populations and to reconstruct, in some cases, the past selective history of the species. Neither of these seems to me a pressing problem since both are academic. Changes in the genotypic composition of the species take place so slowly as compared to the extraordinary rate of human social and cultural evolu-

Fig. 2.
Actual reaction norms for viability of fourth chromosome homozygotes of *Drosophila pseudoobscura*. Data from Dobzhansky and Spassky [7].

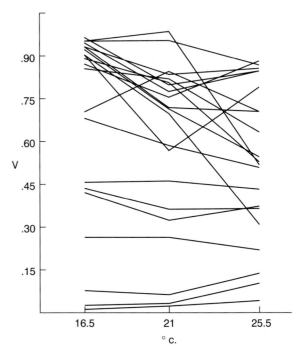

tion that human activity and welfare are unlikely to depend upon such genetic change. The reconstruction of man's genetic past, while fascinating, is an activity of leisure rather than of necessity. At any rate, both these objectives require not simply the analysis into genetic and environmental components of variation, but require absolutely a finer analysis of genetic variance into its additive and nonadditive components. The simple analysis of variance is useless for these purposes and indeed it has no use at all. In view of the terrible mischief that has been done by confusing the spatiotemporally local analysis of variance with the global analysis of causes, I suggest that we stop the endless search for better methods of estimating useless quantities. There are plenty of real problems.

REFERENCES

1. Morton NE: Analysis of family resemblance. I. Introduction. *Am J Hum Genet 26*:318–330, 1974

2. Rao DC, Morton NE, Yee S: Analysis of family resemblance. II. A linear model for familial correlation. *Am J Hum Genet 26*:331–359, 1974

3. Waddington CH: Genetic assimilation of an acquired character. *Evolution 7*:118–126, 1953

4. Rendel JM: Canalization of the scute phenotype of Drosophila. *Evolution 13*:425–439, 1959

5. Jensen AR: How much can we boost IQ and scholastic achievement? *Harvard Educ Rev 39*:1–123, 1969

6. Clausen J, Keck DD, Heisey WM: Experimental studies on the nature of species. I. Effects of varied environments on western North American plants. *Carnegie Inst Washington Publ 520*:1–452, 1940

7. Dobzhansky T, Spassky B: Genetics of natural populations. XI. Manifestation of genetic variants in *Drosophila pseudoobscura* in different environments. *Genetics 29*:270–290, 1944

Using the Heuristic Paradigm to Evaluate Practice

It is easy to be pleased with the results of social service when we measure them just after the first changes for the better, or when we see them from one angle and no more. But when we dare to examine them from the point of view of life as a whole, with the permanent welfare of the individual and society in mind, we are applying a much severer test of values. (Mary Richmond, 1922, p. 90)

Mary Richmond describes an enduring problem in the social and behavioral sciences: How can we conduct evaluative research about practice that will facilitate lasting and beneficial change and contribute to knowledge? As Richmond emphasizes, superficial measurements of initial changes taken from one perspective cannot do justice to the complexity of human change processes, and they do not meet the "severer test of values," which aims for enduring changes with constructive ramifications for human welfare as a whole.

An unnecessary obstruction to developing ways of evaluating practice, which Richmond could not have foreseen but which Heineman Pieper has identified, is that positivist researchers generally overlooked or devalued naturalistic approaches to research. Instead, they emphasized interventionist methods that alter the natural change process for research rather than therapeutic aims. As Heineman Pieper points out in the Preface, because naturalistic research has the advantage of preserving the change process as regulated by the practitioner's therapeutic intentions, it offers a unique type of accuracy. Since the social and behavioral sciences adopted positivist beliefs about science, knowledge about the natural processes of change that occur in every practitioner's daily experience—processes that are not affected by interventionist research methods—has been neglected. Richmond, like other early social workers such as Jane Addams, recognized that the study of practice, as it occurs naturally, can enhance our capacity to engender constructive social changes. Two of the most unfortunate consequences of the chasm that widened between

417

practitioners and researchers when researchers prescribed interventionist approaches were that: (1) researchers generated knowledge that practitioners found irrelevant, and (2) the wisdom that only a practitioner's informed judgment can yield often was discounted as "unscientific" (Heineman Pieper, Preface, 1981, 1989 in this volume, see also 1994; Polkinghorne, 1988; Saleebey, 1979, 1989).

To begin to respond to the need for naturalistic approaches to evaluating practice, this chapter begins with a historical overview of evaluation research implemented by social workers and then presents an approach to naturalistic evaluations of practice based on the heuristic paradigm.

HISTORICAL OVERVIEW OF EVALUATIVE RESEARCH IN SOCIAL WORK

Before discussing approaches to evaluations of practice, it is important to briefly conceptualize evaluation. *Evaluation* entails a comparison between the object of the evaluation and a standard or precept. In the social and behavioral sciences, the object of an evaluation of practice is invariably a change process that occurs in the context of one or more human relationships. The standards used to evaluate practice define the ideals toward which practitioners strive and regulate the quality of the social and behavioral sciences' contributions to knowledge, social reform, and individual services. Social and behavioral researchers use diverse standards for evaluation, including responsiveness to community needs (Whitaker, 1974), cost-effectiveness, expectations for employee competence, the feasibility of the program in relation to the resources allocated, professional values (Ruckdeschel, in press), and participant satisfaction (Rossi & Freeman, 1985). Every evaluator implicitly or explicitly chooses at least two types of standards when evaluating practice:

1. Standards for scientific research, articulated in the assumptions of a research paradigm;
2. Standards for the practice of a particular intervention model.

One of the most common recommendations researchers have made is that an evaluation of one form of service should include at least one comparison group, using clients who receive other types of services as standards (D. T. Campbell & Stanley, 1963), or control groups, using clients who receive no services (Blenkner, 1962; Thyer, 1991). Practitioners, however, often express ethical reservations about setting up control or comparison groups (Saleebey, 1979). An evaluator who does not want to set up comparison or control groups can incorporate comparison with other service models in other ways (see also Chapter 4). For example, in conducting a literature review, a practitioner commonly selects a treatment approach from among other models of service and makes comparative judgments about the value of the diverse service models. The evaluator can describe her or his judgments. Then, changes that the evaluator finds in looking at the service under study can be compared with changes reported in other interventions with clients who had similar strengths and difficulties.

Social and behavioral researchers have approached evaluation of practice in different ways, depending in part on their discipline and their historical context. The following historical overview illustrates some central issues in evaluation by chronicling practice evaluation by social work researchers from 1920 through 1989. As part of the content analysis of 2,884 social work journal articles published in *Social Casework, Social Service Review,* and *Social Work* from 1920 to 1989 described in detail in Chapter 2, the articles were coded according to whether they addressed the topic of evaluation and, if so, according to the way they addressed evaluation.

For coding purposes, evaluation was defined broadly because there is no conceptual justification for methodological restrictions in defining evaluation (Scriven, 1983). The coding categories were designed to comprehensively include previous research. Studies were coded as evaluative if they:

1. Advanced an approach to evaluation of practice or social programs;
2. Described explicitly evaluative research about social work practice or social programs;
3. Presented case materials as a paradigm of good practice such that the evaluation was implicit.

For example, some articles included an extensive description of an intervention as one part of the research; such studies also were coded as evaluative. If an article described a particular problem (e.g., in child psychopathology) and reviewed contemporary theories about the origins and treatment of the problem, but did not include a comprehensive description of an intervention as an exemplar of a helpful treatment, the study would not have been coded as evaluative. Other articles that were not coded as evaluative include those that applied theories of human development and studies analyzing the traits of a particular client group.

Once a study was coded as evaluative, it was then coded as implementing one of the following aims:

1. Advancing (but not implementing) a model for evaluating social work programs;
2. Advancing (but not implementing) a model for evaluating social casework practice;
3. Compiling evaluative studies of social work programs (e.g., a meta-analysis);
4. Compiling evaluative studies of social casework practice;
5. Evaluating educational practices (e.g., clinical supervision);
6. Evaluating social work programs;
7. Evaluating social casework practice.[94]

A substantial proportion of the entire sample of social work journal articles was evaluative (1,115 of 2,884, or 39%). These findings undercut positivist researchers' claims that social workers did not produce evaluations (Blenkner, 1950; Briar & Miller, 1971; Weber & Polansky, 1960/1975). As was the case with social work research as a whole (see Chapter 2), authors of evaluative articles chose a review/commentary research design heuristic more often than any other single format (see Table 7–1, p. 421 and Figure 7–1, p. 422). Most studies examined social service programs in the United States, but some addressed services in other countries. Even though experimental designs were prescribed by positivist researchers, only 3% of all evaluative studies used an experimental design.

Although positivist researchers prioritized one research design heuristic for all evaluative research (their version of experimental design), in fact, social work researchers used very different research design heuristics, depending on whether their purpose was to evaluate social work programs (Figure 7–2, p. 422) or casework practice (Figure 7–3, p. 423). The research design heuristic used most often for evaluating social programs was the review/commentary (43%). For evaluating casework practice, the great majority of researchers (81%) chose research design heuristics that relied solely on qualitative data. By contrast, program evaluators chose designs with quantified data more often than qualitative analyses (32% and 22%, respectively). Almost half of all evaluators of casework practice (49%) chose qualitative single-case studies, and almost one-third (32%) conducted large-scale analyses using qualitative data. By contrast, less than 11% of studies (including experimental designs) with evaluations of practice used quantified data. The proportion of studies that included original evaluations of practice or programs and used an experimental design was very small (3%). In prescribing the use of quantified data and experimental designs as criteria for good science, and endorsing only those studies for publication, positivism devalued the design heuristics that social workers preferred to use for evaluation. That unfortunate consequence of the positivist approach was directly opposed to a stated aim of positivist social work researchers—to stimulate evaluative studies of practice.

The history in Chapter 2 identified changes in the roles of women and men in the profession as a salient factor in changes in social work research. Those gender-related patterns persist in evaluative research as well. Whereas 600 of 1,340 (46%) of articles first-authored by women were evaluative, only 400 of 1,353 (33%) of articles first-authored by men were evaluative. One explanation for this pattern may be that most social work practitioners have been women, whereas men were more likely to hold faculty and administrative positions, especially after the 1950s. Accordingly, as practitioners, the women would be more inclined to collect data about casework practice and social programs as part of their daily work. By contrast, researchers who were not practitioners might have other interests; furthermore, they might have more difficulty collecting data about practice. Both of those factors might encourage researchers in nonpractice positions to prefer nonevaluative research topics.

In historical context, the data indicate that social work researchers' inclusion of evaluative topics in their research changed with the adoption of positivism. Positivist researchers hoped that the adoption of positivism would yield more evaluative research about social work practice. Many positivists believed that if social work researchers conformed with their methodological prescriptions, social workers would more readily discern whether or not they were offering helpful services (Blenkner, 1950). However, the introduction of positivism did not increase the proportion of evaluative research. The high point of evaluative research occurred before the 1950s, before social work researchers adopted positivism (Figure 7–4, p. 424).

Table 7-1
Distribution and percentages of seven research design heuristics in evaluative and nonevaluative articles, 1920 to 1989

Research Design Heuristics

Evaluative Articles	Reviews/ commentaries		Histories		Case studies- Qualitative data		Large-scale analyses- Qualitative data		Case studies- Quantified data		Large-scale analyses- Quantified data		Experimental designs		Totals	
	#	%	#	%	#	%	#	%	#	%	#	%	#	%	#	%
Advancing (but not implementing) a model for evaluating social programs	15	79	0	0	0	0	0	0	0	0	4	21	0	0	19	100
Advancing (but not implementing) a model for evaluating social casework practice	22	82	0	0	0	0	0	0	1	4	4	15	0	0	27	101
Compiling evaluative studies of social programs	22	82	0	0	0	0	0	0	0	0	5	19	0	0	27	101
Compiling evaluative studies of social casework practice	15	60	0	0	0	0	1	4	0	0	9	36	0	0	25	100
Evaluating educational practices	51	58	1	1	11	13	16	18	0	0	8	9	1	1	88	100
Evaluating social programs	212	43	18	4	0	0	106	22	0	0	138	28	18	4	492	101
Evaluating social casework practice	40	9	0	0	213	49	138	32	3	<1	30	7	13	3	437	100
Subtotal	337	34	19	2	224	20	261	23	4	<1	198	18	32	3	1115	100
Non-Evaluative Articles	1270	72	101	6	0	0	95	5	0	0	293	17	10	<1	1769	100
Total	1647	57	120	4	224	8	356	12	4	<1	491	17	42	2	2884	100

Percentages have been rounded and so may not add up to 100 in some cases.

Figure 7–1

Distribution of seven research design heuristics used in social work journal articles that included evaluation, 1920 to 1989

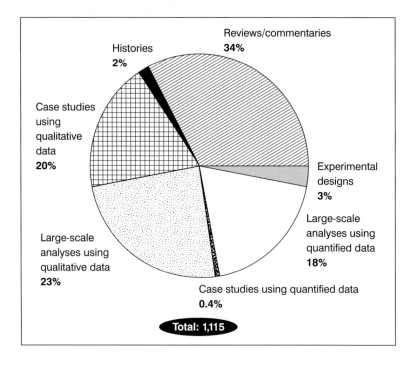

Reviews/commentaries
34%

Histories
2%

Case studies using qualitative data
20%

Experimental designs
3%

Large-scale analyses using quantified data
18%

Large-scale analyses using qualitative data
23%

Case studies using quantified data
0.4%

Total: 1,115

Figure 7–2

Distribution of seven research design heuristics used in social work journal articles that included evaluation of social programs, 1920 to 1989

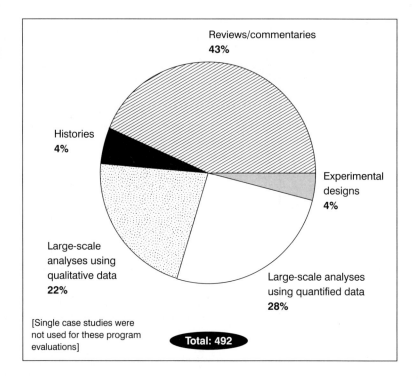

Reviews/commentaries
43%

Histories
4%

Experimental designs
4%

Large-scale analyses using qualitative data
22%

Large-scale analyses using quantified data
28%

[Single case studies were not used for these program evaluations]

Total: 492

422

Figure 7–3
Distribution of seven research design heuristics used in social work journal articles that included evaluation of casework practice, 1920 to 1989

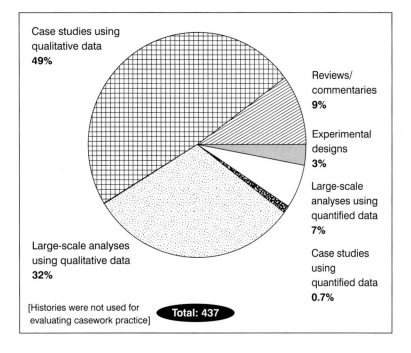

Case studies using qualitative data
49%

Reviews/commentaries
9%

Experimental designs
3%

Large-scale analyses using quantified data
7%

Case studies using quantified data
0.7%

Large-scale analyses using qualitative data
32%

[Histories were not used for evaluating casework practice]

Total: 437

The early social workers ascribed great importance to evaluating practice, as is illustrated by Edith Abbott's comments:

> If we have a profession three things are true: 1) there are basic principles; 2) these basic principles can be taught; and 3) they must come from two sources—a critical examination of the methods used to produce certain results and a searching equally for the causes of apparent failure and apparent success. (E. Abbott, 1931, p. 45)

Similarly, the American Association of Social Workers recommended, in their report of the Milford Conference held in 1929, that "every social case work agency should be constantly analyzing its own problems and methods" (American Association of Social Workers, 1929/1931, p. 41). Social workers such as Mary Richmond, Porter Lee, Mary Jarrett, and Jessie Taft analyzed their own practice and that of others to improve practice methods and to conceptualize the elements of helpful practice (see also Adie, 1939; Claghorn, 1927; Lee & Kenworthy, 1929; Reed, 1931). The adoption of positivism, however, had an especially discouraging impact on evaluations of practice. Evaluations of casework practice fell from a high of 25% of all articles published in the 1940s to 15% in the 1950s, 1960s, and 1980s, and a low of 10% in the 1970s (Figure 7–5, p. 425).

Although evaluative research declined overall after the 1940s (see Figure 7–4), the high point for evaluations of social work programs occurred in the 1970s (see Figure 7–5). The surge of program evaluations in the 1970s corresponds with the observations of evaluation researchers, who generally attribute the 1970s focus on

Figure 7–4
Social work journal articles that included evaluation by decade, 1920 to 1989

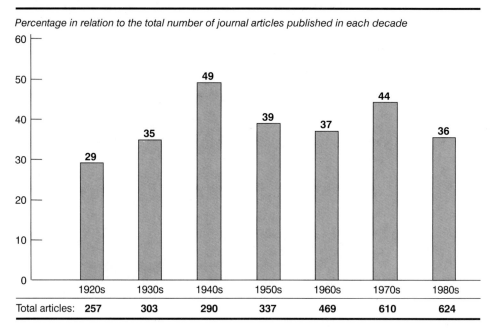

Percentage in relation to the total number of journal articles published in each decade

	1920s	1930s	1940s	1950s	1960s	1970s	1980s
	29	35	49	39	37	44	36
Total articles:	257	303	290	337	469	610	624

program evaluation to federal initiatives to evaluate War on Poverty programs, many of which were published in the 1970s (Rossi & Wright, 1984; Scriven, 1983).[95]

Although the adoption of positivism did not increase the proportion of evaluative studies, it did spawn treatment models based on behaviorism (Fischer & Gochros, 1975; A. Schwartz, 1983; Thyer & Hudson, 1987). *Behaviorism* is a clinical theory that was generated largely to conform to positivist criteria for scientific acceptability (Buckley, 1989; Ehrenwald, 1976). The combined influences of positivist requirements for research and behaviorist clinical precepts aggravated a problem that had festered in evaluation: the conflation of practice model precepts with precepts for good science. In effect, the precepts of behaviorism (e.g., the variables studied must be observable, behavior must be measurable) and the unwarranted, restrictive standards of the positivist philosophy of research (e.g., theoretical constructs must be operationalized) have jointly dominated subsequent evaluation research (Bloom & Block, 1977; Howe, 1974; J. Nelson, 1988; Thyer, 1991). Only recently have these precepts begun to be disentangled (Meyer, 1984; E. A. R. Robinson, Bronson, & Blythe, 1988; Ruckdeschel & Farris, 1981; Witkin, 1991). The requirement that single-case designs operationalize variables (Bloom & Fischer, 1982; Howe, 1974; J. Nelson, 1985; Rabin, 1981; Thyer, 1991) is another example of how the theoretical assumptions of behaviorism were prescribed as necessary for evaluation research under the umbrella of positivist criteria for scientific meaningfulness. However, positivist researchers' beliefs that evaluative research on practice would be dominated by a single-case design using quantified data (Bloom & Fischer,

1982; Fischer, 1981), which they mistakenly believed could enact experimental principles, were not realized.

Another reason the positivist approach to social work research may have obstructed the growth of evaluative research is that many positivist researchers prescribed that practice evaluators should be researchers, not practitioners (Blenkner, 1950), because they believed that researchers' observations of practice were freer of distortion than those of practitioners (McVicker Hunt, 1959). They devised scales to collect quantified data about client movement, which they believed remedied "defects in caseworker judgments as a measuring instrument" (D. G. French, 1952; McVicker Hunt, 1948, p. 344). In addition, positivist researchers defined evaluation restrictively: the use of an experimental design. Many practitioners commented that they did not want to use experimental designs, leading positivist researchers to conclude incorrectly that practitioners did not evaluate their practice (Blenkner, 1950, 1962; Briar, 1979). For example, Weber and Polansky stated:

> Testing the results of one's interventions may seem like an obvious step in the direction of excellence, but it is not universally welcomed, of course. The practitioner often has

Figure 7–5
Social work journal articles that included evaluation of casework practice or evaluation of social programs, by decade, 1920 to 1989

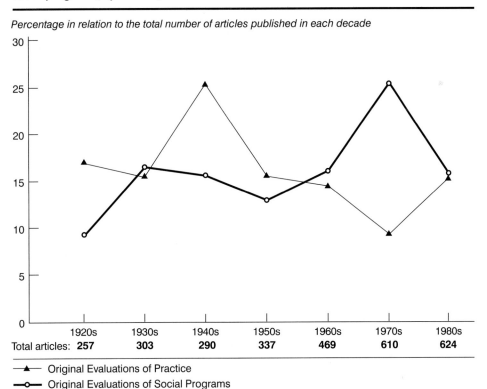

Percentage in relation to the total number of articles published in each decade

	1920s	1930s	1940s	1950s	1960s	1970s	1980s
Total articles:	257	303	290	337	469	610	624

—▲— Original Evaluations of Practice
—○— Original Evaluations of Social Programs

enough trouble with the daily effort he is making to offer help without raising fundamental doubt in his mind about the efficacy of his whole undertaking. (1960/1975 pp.
183–184)

In reviews of the efficacy of casework, some positivist researchers restricted their
sample of social work practice research to studies using experimental design (Fischer,
1973; Wood, 1978). Based on that small and unrepresentative sample of evaluative
research, those researchers then concluded that social work practice is ineffective.

Throughout the 1980s, many researchers increasingly recognized that social
workers were not adopting the behaviorist single-case designs that positivist
researchers prescribed for evaluating practice. Positivist researchers responded to
this problem in several ways. They often handled the irrelevance of their prescriptions for practitioners by writing textbooks mandating that students adopt positivist
prescriptions for practice research, implying that the students would be unethical
practitioners if they did not subscribe to positivist tenets (e.g., Grinnell, 1981;
Ivanoff, Robinson, et al., 1987; Rubin & Babbie, 1989; see Siporin, 1985, for a critique of that view). When they became practitioners, however, most students did
not follow those authoritarian positivist prescriptions (Rubin & Zimbalist, 1981;
Welch, 1983).

Other contemporary positivist approaches to research about practice adhere to
the Social Work Research Group's distinction between "practice wisdom" and "scientific knowledge": Practitioner knowledge is not regarded as scientific until it is
"tested" by research designs endorsed under positivism (Reid, 1994). Some positivist psychotherapy researchers have extended the scope of evaluation beyond the
narrow confines of the "study of results" emphasized by the Social Work Research
Group (Blenkner, 1950). They have sought to remedy the problem of the irrelevance of research to practice by studying change processes, rather than focusing on
outcome alone (Elliott, 1983; Mahrer, 1988; Orlinsky & Howard, 1986; Rice &
Greenberg, 1984). However, change process research, as it has been adapted for
social work research (Berlin, 1990b; I. Davis, 1990; Reid, 1990), reflects positivist
beliefs, including:

1. The prescription that process variables must be quantified (Reid, 1990, pp. 131,
   136);
2. The belief that change process research can generate theory-free data, from
   which practice theories will be developed (Reid, 1990, pp. 144-145; Videka-
   Sherman, Reid, & Roseland, 1990);
3. Context stripping (Mishler, 1979, 1986), whereby the meaning of interactions
   with the client is interpreted apart from contexts such as the evolving practitioner–client relationship (Reid, 1990).

Further, change process research incorporates interventionist biases by introducing
data-gathering methods that lack a therapeutic rationale into the natural change
process (Berlin, Mann, & Grossman, 1991; Davis, 1990).

In sum, positivist approaches to studying social work practice have not solved the problem Mary Richmond articulated in 1922: How can we conduct evaluative research about practice that will facilitate lasting and beneficial change and contribute to knowledge? Because positivist research standards were incompatible with many social work practice models (Heineman Pieper, 1981, 1985, 1989), most practitioners have rejected or ignored positivist approaches to evaluation of practice (Rabin, 1981; E. A. R. Robinson et al., 1988; Saleebey, 1979; Welch, 1983).

Increasingly, social workers have emphasized the importance of finding alternative ways to study and evaluate practice that make use of practitioners' informed judgment and are compatible with the social work profession's traditional humanistic values. Naturalistic approaches to practice research promise to be more fertile ground for generating new solutions to this perennial dilemma. Some guidelines for such evaluations are presented next.

Because the practice illustrations used in the following discussion all concern evaluations of psychotherapy with children, a brief overview of the evaluation of treatment of children is pertinent. Evaluation of practice with children mirrored many of the trends in evaluation described previously. The early social workers were advocates for the needs and rights of children (Addams, 1910/1990; Muncy, 1991). Social workers treated or collaborated in the treatment of children during the Child Guidance Movement, developed principles for practice with children (Hamilton, 1947; Lee & Kenworthy, 1929), and found that case studies containing explicit or implicit evaluations of treatment of children were useful educational tools (Towle, 1941a).

With social work's adoption of the positivist approach to social work research, some evaluators of social services for children adopted positivist tenets such as that the researcher must use an experimental design to ascertain the impact of services (Beck, 1958). Following Patterson's lead, behavioral therapists monitored change using teacher and parent logs of those child behaviors the adults had defined as problematic (Ayllon, Layman, & Kandel, 1975; Patterson, Jones, Whittier & Wright, 1965; Walker & Buckley, 1968). Behavioral researchers developed the single-case design (Pinkston & Herbert-Jackson, 1975), which some (incorrectly) believed could apply the principles of experimental design to single-case evaluation (Benbenishty, 1989; Bloom, 1978; Flowers, 1990; Howe, 1974; Kazdin & Tuma, 1982; Nuehring & Pascone, 1986; Orcutt, 1990; Rabin, 1981). Some researchers have combined outcome studies in meta-analyses that have reported that diverse models of child treatment have some positive effects (Casey & Berman, 1985; Weisz, Weiss, & Alicke, 1987).

Although the examples in the following discussion draw from individual psychotherapy with children, a naturalistic approach to evaluation can be used by evaluators who use any practice model, including diverse treatment theories and interventions in education, community organizations, and program management. In accord with the heuristic paradigm's nonrestrictive stance, evaluators can use a naturalistic approach to evaluation and collect both quantified and qualitative data. A strategy for data analysis built on the use of change indices also is presented, which can be applied with both qualitative and quantified data.

DESIGNING NATURALISTIC EVALUATIONS OF PRACTICE

Problem Formulation

A Problem Formulation Is a Heuristic

The logical positivist philosophers of science largely overlooked the important question "what is a problem?" They advanced a "Spartan" conceptualization of scientific problems as "experimental data plus the demand that data be explained/ predicted/ controlled according to the accounts of explanation, prediction, and instrumental control which they set forth" (Nickles, 1988, p. 53). Positivist approaches to evaluating clinical practice and social programs prescribed restrictive rules for formulating evaluation problems, such as requiring researchers to oversimplify and operationalize problems (Bloom & Fischer, 1982; Howe, 1974; J. Nelson, 1981; Rossi & Freeman, 1985).

By contrast, postpositivist researchers such as Dunn, Mitroff, and Deutsch (1981) emphasize that "the enterprise of evaluation is a messy, squishy, or ill-structured problem, that is, a problem whose complexity demands that the researcher take an active part in defining the problem" (quoted in Heineman Pieper, 1985, p. 8). Evaluation entails "multiple methodologies, multiple functions, multiple impacts, multiple reporting formats—evaluation is a multiplicity of multiples" (Scriven, 1983, p. 257; see also Brower & Garvin, 1989). The researcher who adopts the heuristic paradigm examines how a possible problem formulation guides the evaluator through the multiple alternatives toward particular theories and decisions about gathering and analyzing data and then toward different solutions to the problem (see also Chapter 5).

The diversity of potential problem formulations represents an advantage. One way to recognize the biases engendered by any single problem formulation is to consider various ways of formulating the evaluation problem and to examine how the different problem formulations lead to the generation of different data and different solutions. Drawing from Wimsatt's description of the properties of heuristics, Heineman Pieper states, "heuristics transform the problem to which they are applied to a different, but related problem. Thus, we must always evaluate the appropriateness of our answers to the original problem" (1989, p. 11). One way to assess a potential problem formulation is to examine whether the evaluation problem as formulated will lead to workable solutions (Heineman Pieper, 1989). For example, an evaluation may be used to generate a report for policy analysts or for an administrator making staff allocation decisions, or it may be used to appraise interventions. Assessing the potential usefulness of the evaluation data at the outset forestalls generating studies that do not help policymakers (Rein & White, 1977), program administrators (M. Weiss & Rein, 1970), or clinicians (Heineman Pieper, 1989).

Most clinical examples in this chapter come from aspects of an evaluation of the individual treatment of a child named Bobby.[96] Bobby was a six-year-old boy whose Italian-American family was well-educated and from an upper-middle-class income bracket. He came for help with a protracted and relentless experience of self-hatred, which was so severe that he had on several occasions expressed a desire to die. His parents and teacher reported that he had fought violently with peers in several contexts including a preschool classroom, an after-school puppet-making workshop, and a children's soccer league. Bobby's other symptoms included enuresis, and his teacher reported that he was disorganized, easily frustrated, and did not follow directions. The treatment plan for Bobby consisted of individual child psychotherapy and parental counseling for his parents, which involved helping Bobby's parents to collaborate with his school in setting up a more supportive classroom environment.

To evaluate Bobby's treatment, the researcher who adopts the heuristic paradigm could formulate the evaluation research problem in many ways, such as, Did Bobby's symptoms diminish or remit? Were the practitioner's interventions with Bobby consistent with the precepts of the practitioner's chosen treatment model? Each problem formulation causes the researcher to focus on different aspects of the case and will generate very different information.

What Causes the Client to Change?

Any evaluation problem contains assumptions about the factors that cause clients to change and about the nature of the change process itself. Positivist approaches to single-case evaluation of practice assume that the impact of treatment on the client can be represented accurately by a linear model, for example, as links on a cause-and-effect chain in which the intervention is the cause examined and change in the client's behavior is the effect (Bloom & Fischer, 1982; Howe, 1974; J. Nelson, 1988; Orcutt, 1990; Thyer, 1991). As the physicist and philosopher Norwood Hanson said about such causal models, "this simplicity is unreal" (1958, p. 51). Such oversimplified views of the cause-and-effect processes at work in clinical practice, along with unrealistic expectations that experimental design can definitively isolate the causal variables influencing clients, have contributed to positivist prescriptions that researchers must use experimental designs to understand the factors that produce client changes (Bloom, 1978; Rossi & Wright, 1984; Tripodi, 1981).

By contrast, postpositivist researchers do not construe causation as linear but as complex, multifactorial, and interactive (Heineman Pieper, 1989; Kim, 1981; Levins & Lewontin, 1985; Lincoln, 1985; Margenau, 1966; Zimmerman, 1989).[97] Because human systems are open systems, multiple unforeseeable influences can affect a clinical change process. Accordingly, prediction (and thus, experimental design) cannot serve as a privileged criterion for appraising theories in the human sciences (Bhaskar, 1978, 1989b, 1991). Postpositivist social and behavioral scientists emphasize that all knowledge is contextual, that we experience contiguous events as patterned or random depending on our heuristics, and that the causal relationships we perceive are generated by complex interactions (Bhaskar, 1989b; Bronfenbrenner, 1979a; Cronbach, 1975; Mishler, 1979). Levins and Lewontin elaborate that their postpositivist, dialectical approach to causality "stresses system properties as the primary objects of study, as opposed to the conventional emphasis on separate elements, to which are added as a secondary refinement the interactions between them" (1985, p. 194; see also Lincoln & Guba, 1985).

Child therapists have long recognized that the assessment of the impact of interventions with children is extremely complex, because many variables affect the child, including the child's natural maturational process, changes within the child's family, and the child's experiences at school (A. Freud, 1965). Similarly, many practice models conceptualize client problems as multifactorial and interactional, and many practitioners plan interventions that aim to change several client problems.

Complex practice problems and broad treatment goals necessitate an inclusive analytic description of the change process and an unrestrictive approach to formulating evaluation problems. Researchers who adopt the heuristic paradigm are not limited by the positivist assumptions that researchers can observe only contiguous events and cannot understand underlying causal processes (Sayer, 1992; see also Manicas & Secord, Chapter 5). Rather, researchers can aim to understand the causal mechanisms in the change processes they study. For example, a central evaluation issue can be framed as "what happened?" (M. Weiss & Rein, 1970, p. 104). Positivism artificially excludes from study diverse influences on the change process in the belief that they have been controlled for (Howe, 1974). The heuristic paradigm, however, welcomes complex problems without sacrificing conceptual rigor, because the researcher can address the biases introduced when using a heuristic to make the problem manageable (Heineman Pieper, 1989). As noted in Chapter 6, regardless of the specific type of data-gathering method used, the researcher using the heuristic paradigm prioritizes providing sufficient information so the reader can evaluate the causal factors that might produce change.

Drawing the Environment–System Boundary

Every problem formulation focuses the researcher's attention on a system of variables and their interactions. The researcher necessarily simplifies the context, or environment, of that system (Heineman Pieper, 1989; Mishler, 1979). Hence, an "asymmetry in simplifications" results from the researcher's chosen environment–system boundary (Wimsatt, 1986b, p. 300). When formulating problems, the researcher who adopts the heuristic paradigm considers "a number of possible environment–system boundaries before carefully selecting one, because this choice will have important consequences" (Heineman Pieper, 1989, p. 23). One of the most important initial questions to be answered in drawing the environment–system boundary is whether the evaluator and the practitioner will be the same person. If not, and if the evaluator introduces data-gathering procedures into the practitioner's change process, the evaluation will be interventionist rather than naturalistic.

By varying the environment–system boundaries, the researcher who adopts the heuristic paradigm can examine how each delineation of the environment–system boundary rotates the perspective on the problem under investigation and generates different biases (Heineman Pieper, 1989; Wimsatt, 1980b, 1986b). To illustrate, in some positivist approaches to single-case evaluation, the client's relationship with the therapist is commonly excluded from study (left in the environment) (Bloom & Block, 1977; Howe, 1974; Slonim-Nevo & Vosler, 1991). However, therapist variables such as competence, experience, and theory preference, as well as unique qualities of the therapist–client relationship, have very powerful influences on treatment outcome (Marziali & Alexander, 1991). Although the researcher may choose not to focus on those variables, she or he can recognize that, by leaving those variables in the environment, the nature of their effects on the outcome cannot be known. Two types of systems are delineated whenever an evaluator formulates the research problem

1. The practitioner chooses the client system to be treated.
2. The evaluator (who may be the practitioner) chooses the system to use to evaluate the treatment.

The System to Be Treated In addition to defining the evaluation research problem (e.g., did the client's symptoms improve?) an evaluator of practice always defines the client's problem. To illustrate, in evaluating Bobby's treatment, the practitioner–evaluator defined Bobby's primary problem as acquired self-defeating motives that were expressed in symptoms of self-directed rage. (See Chapter 8 for a more extensive description of intrapsychic humanism's account of how an individual acquires such motives.) Heineman Pieper emphasized that positivist evaluation research, in its "preoccupation with simplicity and control," has required that the complex, "ill-structured" problems experienced by clients be distorted so that they fit into the positivists' "misguided definitions of scientific rigor" (Heineman Pieper, 1985, p. 7). Rather than imposing methodological restrictions on how client problems can be formulated, the researcher who adopts the heuristic paradigm recognizes that a client's problem can be formulated in several different ways.

To illustrate, when parents ask for help for their child, family therapists commonly "reframe" the problem by defining it in terms of the family relationships (Hartman & Laird, 1983) and treat the family. On the other hand, child psychoanalysts commonly view the child's behavior as symptomatic of the child's intersystemic conflict and focus on treating the individual child (Glenn, 1978). Each delineation of the environment–system boundary results in a very different intervention. For instance, clinicians who treat children commonly must decide whether to interview the child about her or his difficulties or whether to expand the system under study and interview the entire family and the child's teachers. If the clinician interviews the child with the family or observes the child with the teacher, the clinician will gather information about those interpersonal relationship patterns. If the clinician interviews the child individually, she or he will not observe those specific interpersonal relationship patterns but will observe different variables. For example, a sexually abused young child who has been intimidated into silence by her father will be more likely to disclose the abuse in the context of individual play therapy than if she is asked to discuss her difficulties in her father's presence.

The System Used to Evaluate the Treatment The evaluator's environment–system boundary delineates the sources of data the evaluator will use, which can range from therapist–client interactions to information derived from family members or other collaterals, such as school staff or the clinician's supervisor. In many contemporary evaluations of child treatment, the children's opinions about the treatments they experience are excluded, that is, are "drawn" out of the system used to evaluate the treatment. Instead, evaluators seek the opinions of adults about the child's progress

(Tyson, 1991b).[98] In addition to setting up an ethically questionable bias against children, excluding the children from the system used to evaluate the treatment has resulted in a loss of important information. For example, in a meta-analysis that was unusual in that children's self-report measures were included in some evaluation studies, Casey and Berman (1985) found that children's self-report measures of treatment efficacy showed smaller effect sizes* than did observer ratings of changes in child behaviors. In a more recent evaluation of a family preservation program treating families reported for abuse and neglect, the parents reported increased satisfaction following the interventions but the children did not (K. Nelson, 1992). Researchers who investigate practice often find that different individuals perceive problems and the change process differently (Devore, 1983; Kidder, 1982; McCord, 1978), even if they are part of the same family system (Slonim-Nevo & Vosler, 1991; Witkin & Harrison, 1979). Postpositivist evaluation researchers, such as Scriven, emphasize that the evaluation researcher has a moral responsibility to take the perspective of everyone involved in the change process into account, although whether or not individuals are sources of data for a given evaluation depends on how the evaluation problem is formulated (1983, p. 249; see also Lincoln & Guba, 1985; Parlett, 1981; Reinharz, 1992). Another consideration in delineating the system used to evaluate treatment is that therapeutic precepts, such as preserving confidentiality, may preclude going outside the treatment relationship to obtain evaluative data. In such a case, the naturalistic evaluator would use only data derived from therapeutic interactions with the client to evaluate the treatment, because naturalistic research always preserves the integrity of the system under study (e.g., in this case, the treatment).

The positivist approach to social and behavioral research assumed that the practitioner's involvement with clients impaired her or his judgment about treatment efficacy. However, the heuristic approach regards the practitioner's informed judgment as a valuable resource for evaluating practice. The clinician's informed judgment is a helpful resource in an evaluation of practice, because the worker knows the entire context of the treatment, knows the client, can interpret the client's feedback about the accuracy of the practitioner's communications, and can distinguish what changes are occurring. The following example illustrates how the meaning of a client response can be understood only with the help of the practitioner's informed judgment.

For three sessions, Bobby spent much of the time vehemently "bombing" toy soldiers with the gummy bears the therapist gave him as a snack. If the therapist had misunderstood something Bobby had shared, Bobby could have been communicating that he feels the therapist "bombed" him. On the other hand, Bobby initially had great difficulty sharing vulnerable feelings with the therapist. If the "bombing" sessions were preceded by Bobby becoming unusually trusting and sharing new feelings

---

*Editor's Note: An effect size is a calculation commonly used in the approach to reviewing studies of treatment termed "meta-analysis." The effect size is a compilation of quantified outcome indices reported in several studies and is regarded as one way to quantify the change believed to be produced by an intervention. See Chapter 4 for reference to some issues in evaluating the meaning of an effect size statistic.

with the therapist for the first time, the "bombing" could signify his reactive motives to punish himself for having done so. A third possibility is that the therapist had just told Bobby she was planning a vacation, and he was saying he felt "bombed" by that news. Only the therapist who knows the context of the ongoing treatment can discern the significance of Bobby's "bombing."

Client opinions can be a rich source of evaluative data (Ellwood, 1988; Geismar, Lagay, Wolock, Gerhart, & Fink, 1972; F. Hollis, 1976; Hougland, 1987; Powell, 1988; Rodriguez & Cortez, 1988), and children often spontaneously communicate their evaluations of the treatment (Haworth, 1990). For example, a three-and-a-half-year-old African-American child named Sheila originally came for therapy because her parents were engaged in a protracted custody battle, and she wanted help with her intense, self-directed angry feelings about her parents' conflicts. After four months of therapy, Sheila drew a "fire," told the therapist that her father had recently been very angry, and that his angry feelings made her feel like she had been set on fire. She then showed how a fire engine came quickly and put the fire out. When the clinician asked her "what is the fire engine?" she commented that "the house is me, the fire engine is us." Such a statement could indicate either that she feels the therapist is stifling her expressions of anger or that she feels the therapy helps her to protect herself from her angry feelings about her parents' conflicts and treatment of her. Several factors can be taken into consideration in evaluating the significance of Sheila's statements: Sheila was increasingly able to share her deep feelings of anger with the therapist; both the therapist and the therapist's supervisor thought that the therapist had not discouraged Sheila from sharing her anger; and there were other indicators that Sheila felt the treatment was helpful. All these factors led the therapist to conclude that Sheila's statement meant that Sheila felt the therapy was helping her with the anger generated by the custody battles. This example also illustrates how the significance of client evaluations of practice cannot be understood apart from the context of the ongoing treatment relationship.

Values and Problem Formulation

One crucial step in evaluations based on the heuristic paradigm is evaluating how the researcher's values regulate the research (Heineman Pieper, 1981, 1985, 1989). The practitioner's values influence his or her role in relation to clients, such as whether the worker is an advocate, mediator, or resource provider (Goldstein, 1987). As Mishler said, "how the interviewer's role is to be taken into account is of course a difficult problem, but it is not solved by making the interviewer invisible and inaudible, by painting her or him out of the picture" (1986, pp. 82–83). Dunn, Mitroff, and Deutsch emphasized that "The main problem in evaluation research is not so much to avoid reactivity and proactivity, which is impossible and even undesirable in many circumstances, but to systematically monitor their positive and negative impact on performance" (1981, p. 214). Ethnographic research has a tradition of "researcher self-monitoring" termed "disciplined subjectivity": The validity of the research hinges on the researcher's intensive involvement with and reflexive awareness of her or his interactions with the participant/subjects (Erickson, 1973, cited in LeCompte & Goetz, 1982, p. 43; Parlett, 1981). Only the researcher's "immersion" (D'Andrade cited in Spradley, 1979, p. 190) in the field setting facilitates the ethnographer's assessment of those factors that are stable, those that change, and the diverse influences on change (LeCompte & Goetz, 1982; Parlett, 1981; P. Rosenblatt, 1981).

Evaluation approaches that focus only on outcome measures overlook the utility of evaluations in which the evaluator compares the intervention with professional values. An illustration can be drawn from the contemporary empowerment approach to practice with children, which emphasizes that children are disempowered in relation to social systems and recommends that the clinician be an advocate in practice with children (Hegar, 1989). Drawing from that empowerment model, a value-based problem an evaluator might address is, Did the intervention enact the value of child protection? For example, a clinician who interviews an abused child may report the abuse to the Department of Children and Family Services, assiduously gather supporting data, and aggressively try to protect the child. Despite the worker's best efforts, however, the child may be returned to an abusive family that refuses services.[99] In such cases, although practitioners may not always accomplish the outcomes they desire, they may find it helpful to recognize that their actions have upheld their professional values.

Ontological and Epistemological Assumptions

Ontological and epistemological assumptions regulate any act of knowing, and accordingly they inform the evaluator's problem formulations. An evaluator of practice necessarily makes at least three choices that set up her or his ontological and epistemological assumptions:

1. The choice of a paradigm, or metatheory, of research;
2. The choice of a practice theory;
3. The choices about gathering and analyzing data for studying the implementation of that practice theory.

The evaluator's choice of practice theory governs the meanings the evaluator ascribes to the data. The assumptions of social and behavioral theories often are so different as to be fundamentally incompatible. Even the so-called "eclectic" or "research-based" practice models (O'Hare, 1991) represent a theoretical approach that is incompatible with many clinical practice models. Although some clinicians say they do not adhere to any one theory and instead make practice decisions on the basis of "what works," they still use standards (which often are unarticulated and so are an implicit practice theory) in arriving at their judgment about "what works." Every practice theory has ontological assumptions that define and regulate the practitioner's observations (Heineman Pieper, 1981, 1985, 1989; Tyson, 1993; Wimsatt, 1986b). For example, in understanding the behavioral symptoms of childhood hyperactivity, the clinician oriented toward biological explanations for human behavior focuses on the central nervous system as the ontology, or "real," to be studied (Johnson, 1988). The clinician who adopts behavioral theories assumes neuromuscular behavior is the real to be studied (Pinkston, Levitt, Green, Linsk, & Rzepnicki,

1982) and defines hyperactivity as a behavior in response to environmental contingencies. The clinician using intrapsychic humanism focuses on the subjective experience of purposiveness (also termed *agency*, or *motives*) as the real to be studied. According to intrapsychic humanism, hyperactive behaviors are motivated (though not necessarily chosen) by the child in the pursuit of an inner esteem based on a sense of effective purposiveness. The experiences that signify this esteem have been distorted in a dysfunctional way due to the child's early experiences (Pieper & Pieper, 1990; Tyson, 1991a, 1991b).

Each theory also makes very different assumptions about epistemology (Dean & Fenby, 1989), or how to know the ontology under study, and so leads to very different ways of generating data. The behaviorist clinician counts behavioral fluctuations in reaction to the reinforcement schedule (Pinkston et al., 1982). A biologically oriented clinician may draw from the many neurological and neuropsychological tests available (Johnson, 1988). A clinician using intrapsychic humanism uses the practitioner's understanding of the client's subjective experience of the therapeutic relationship to apprehend the real under study (Pieper & Pieper, 1990).

Different practice theories formulate therapeutic goals differently. The goal of psychodynamic treatment according to Michael Basch is a capacity for self-scrutiny (1980, p. 178). By contrast, the goal of a behavioral treatment is a reduction or increase in targeted behaviors. The goal of structure-building treatment using intrapsychic humanism is the autonomous self-regulation of inner well-being. The goal of intrapsychic supportive treatment is the ability for an increasingly stable capacity to forego self-destructive or self-defeating motives (Pieper & Pieper, 1990). To illustrate further, researchers define "good moments" in psychotherapy differently, in relation to the outcome criteria of their theories (Mahrer & Nadler, 1986).

In short, given the same client, proponents of different practice models observe radically different variables, formulate client problems differently, generate different data, define change differently, set different goals, and evaluate their practice according to different standards. The incompatible assumptions of practice models pose a significant and insufficiently recognized problem for reviewers who want to compile a meta-analysis of evaluation studies that use different practice models. For example, when Casey and Berman reviewed seventy-five studies of the outcome of psychotherapy with children, one of the questions they asked was, "How effective were different kinds of therapy for different reported problems?" They found that "the results permitted no clear answer because there was a strong tendency for behavioral and non behavioral studies to examine different kinds of target problems" (Casey & Berman, 1985, p. 393). Researchers sometimes do not recognize the incompatibility between practice models, and do not differentiate the assumptions of the metatheory of research from practice precepts. Those researchers then conflate the practice precepts with the assumptions of a metatheory of research, prescribe the precepts of the practice model as the basis for evaluation research, and criticize practitioners who do not adhere to that practice model for not evaluating their practice (Briar, 1979; Fischer, 1981; Thyer, 1989).

The incompatibility of theoretical precepts often has been discussed under the rubric of the "incommensurability" of theories. A strict version of the incommensurability of theories, consonant with the radical assumptions of relativism, assumes that proponents of different theories cannot address each others' research problems and observations, because they do not share common assumptions, methods, concepts, or observations. In effect, they see different worlds (Guba, 1990; Kuhn, 1962, 1970; see also Manicas & Secord, Chapter 5). If competing theories do not share any meanings, "this renders the notion of a rational choice between such incommensurable theories problematic; and even encourages skepticism about the existence of a mind-independent world" (Bhaskar, 1985, p. 363). Contemporary realist philosophers of science advance a modified view of incommensurability and assert that competing scientific theories are "alternative descriptions of the same world" (Bhaskar, 1985, p. 363; see also Manicas & Secord, 1983; Shapere, 1989). One consequence of a realist standpoint is that a researcher using one practice theory can evaluate the work of a practitioner who uses a different practice theory. For the researcher who adopts the heuristic paradigm, the incompatible precepts of practice models represent an advantage, because comparing those different precepts aids in recognizing the biases engendered by using any single practice model (see Figure 3–2).

The Compatibility between the Evaluator's and the Practitioner's Theories

One of the most important decisions an evaluator makes is whether or not to use the same practice model as the practitioner used. The researcher who adopts the heuristic paradigm always addresses the implications of that decision. The practitioner and the evaluator may or may not agree on how to define the client's problem. If they do not agree, the researcher who adopts the heuristic paradigm must address the implications of those different definitions. During the first session, Bobby defined his problem by drawing a picture of a dot, saying, "Sometimes I feel like a dot." He then stabbed the dot with his pencil. When asked if part of him caused him to feel badly about himself, he said "a lot," and when asked if he wanted help with those feelings, he nodded and said "yes." The practitioner targeted Bobby's most urgent problem as his feelings of pain caused by his self-directed rage; the practitioner also focused on Bobby's motive for help with that pain. By contrast, an evaluator using behavioral theory might focus on the frequency of the problem behavior, such as the incidence of Bobby's self-harming gestures. The evaluator and the practitioner who target different aspects of Bobby's problem then view the entire treatment differently and will conceptualize the evaluation in totally different terms.

If the evaluator's practice model differs from the practitioner's, one consequence is that the evaluator's explanations of treatment events will differ from the practitioner's. For example, Bobby came to a therapy session and described as fact an incident that was obviously greatly exaggerated. He told the therapist a "whopper." According to some behavioral theories, the practitioner should modify Bobby's whopper-telling behavior to make the therapeutic situation as close to the environment outside the treatment relationship as possible (Kendall & Braswell, 1985; Rzepnicki, 1991). From the standpoint of ego psychology, the practitioner should interpret and thereby confront Bobby's "whopper" in the interest of strengthening his reality-testing ego functions (Lieberman, 1979). From the standpoint of intrapsychic humanism (the theory used for Bobby's treatment), Bobby's "whopper" could be understood as a reaction to two possible experiences: a loss that he is trying to restitute by making up the "whopper," or an aversive reaction to the pleasure he experiences in wanting to share his experiences. According to intrapsychic humanism, an aversive reaction occurs because people develop motives to seek unpleasure, of which they may or may not be aware, which compel them to withdraw from or sabotage pleasure (Pieper & Pieper, 1990, pp. 218–220). A pleasurable experience that gratifies the part of the self that has conscious motives for pleasure simultaneously signifies a loss to the part of the self that has unconscious motives for pain, which then rebounds with the increased intensity manifested in the aversive reaction. The intrapsychic therapist decides whether to address Bobby's whopper-telling reaction on the basis of whether at that moment the therapist thinks an interpretation will help Bobby to identify his self-defeating motives and thereby enhance his motivation for conflict-free self-caretaking. Because the therapist may perceive that Bobby is not ready to discern the self-defeating motives that cause the "whopper"-telling reaction, she would not necessarily bring it to his attention, even though she would recognize the "whopper" and its implications. Each practice model prescribes different guidelines for the clinician's response to Bobby's "whopper," and so each will lead to a different evaluation of the intervention conducted.

In addition to examining the compatibility between the evaluator's and the practitioner's practice theories, the researcher who adopts the heuristic paradigm examines the compatibility between the evaluator's approach to research and his or her practice theory. Clinicians have found positivist approaches to practice evaluation to be irrelevant in part because the positivists' restrictive epistemology proscribed the study of aspects of reality that are the focus of many clinical theories, such as subjective experience or unconscious motives (Heineman Pieper, 1981, 1985, 1989). The positivists' restrictive epistemological assumptions (e.g., the requirement for operationalization) are incompatible with the epistemological assumptions of many practice models (Heineman Pieper, 1981, 1985, 1989). To illustrate further, social constructionism is a heuristic that defines a linguistic ontology, such as discourse, as the real to be studied (Gergen, 1986; see also Mishler, 1986). That ontological assumption is compatible with such practice theories as the hermeneutic (D. Scott, 1989) and narrative models (Cohler, 1988). However, social constructionism does not focus on other ontologies that practitioners may want to address, such as the metacognitive, metalinguistic "real" of an infant's motive for self-regulating inner esteem, or intrapsychic agency, in which gratification is signified, for example, by the infant's smile (Pieper & Pieper, 1990). As emphasized previously, the heuristic paradigm does not restrict the researcher's choices of ontology or epistemology. The researcher who adopts the heuristic paradigm can choose practice theories that focus on variables as diverse as the flickers of communication in the initial phase of the treatment of a severely autistic child, to patterns of relationships among children in a therapy group, to changes in the weight of an obese child.

Decisions about Data Collection and Data Analysis

Postpositivist researchers have conceptualized alternative standards for naturalistic research, such as dependability, credibility, and trustworthiness (Lincoln & Guba, 1985; Mishler, 1986; Reason, 1981; Ruckdeschel, 1985). Those standards entail making the assumptions that guide decisions about data collection and analysis as explicit and available to the reader as possible (LeVine, 1981). For example, the researcher who adopts the heuristic paradigm might attempt to maximize the intercoder reliability of a rating scale but would also recognize that those procedures for enhancing reliability cannot substitute for the researcher's explication of the biases inherent in even the most reliable scale. Because every intervention process is unique, researchers should not expect specific coding procedures to be equally applicable across varying interventions (Lincoln & Guba, 1985; Ruckdeschel & Farris, 1981; Schein, 1987).

As described in Chapter 6, the researcher who adopts the heuristic paradigm plans data gathering and analysis in relation to the problem formulation, potentially useful solutions, and consistency with the researcher's ontological and epistemological assumptions (Parlett, 1981, p. 222; see also Nickles, 1987a). The content analysis of social work journal articles indicated that evaluators made very different decisions about data gathering and analysis in relation to the aim of their evaluation (see Figures 7–2 on p. 422 and 7–3 on p. 423).

Data Collection

All data-collection strategies are heuristics that prioritize one form of accuracy at the expense of others. To elaborate, evaluators of the War on Poverty programs often collected data using measures that were not designed to elicit client opinions about program services but instead measured aspects of client functioning that researchers deemed important (e.g., IQ tests) (Geismar & Krisberg 1967; Kidder, 1982; Rossi & Wright, 1984). Limiting data collection to such indicators set up a systematic bias in which client opinions about the need for and effectiveness of the programs were overlooked (Kidder, 1982; McDill, McDill, & Sprehe, 1969; Scriven, 1983) or devalued (McCord, 1978).

Drawing from the positivist tenet that it is possible to gather bias-free data, some approaches to single-case design recommend that the practitioner ask clients to record their problem behaviors (Berlin, 1983; Bloom & Block, 1977; Bloom & Fischer, 1982; J. Campbell, 1990) and use audiotapes or videotapes of the treatment (J. Nelson, 1981, 1985). However, research on experimenter effects has demonstrated that there is no basis for assuming that such procedures produce distortion-free data (Orne, 1969; Webb, Campbell, Schwartz, Sechrest, & Grove, 1981). As Heineman Pieper has pointed out (Preface, 1981, 1985, 1989, 1994), audiotapes and videotapes produce data that are biased in a different way, because the taping introduces a variable into the treatment situation that has no therapeutic rationale. The client invariably reacts to this variable, which thereby alters the treatment process. The researcher who adopts the heuristic paradigm considers which form of accuracy is most important to address the problem.

Anamnestic process recordings are an alternative, often overlooked data-collection strategy for naturalistic evaluations of practice. Although biased by the practitioner's selective recollection of the events, anamnestic process recordings avoid the biases introduced by audiotape or videotape recordings or other instruments (Heineman Pieper, 1985), because they do not introduce any nontherapeutic instruments into the treatment relationship. Further, they have the advantage of providing the reader with an experience-near description of the practitioner's view of the client and the therapeutic process. The process recording should give sufficient detail about the interactions between client and therapist to inform the reader about the client, the nature of the interventions conducted, and the impact of the interventions on the client (Ruckdeschel & Farris, 1981, 1982). For example, in her book *Play Therapy*, Virginia Axline (1969) appends detailed verbatim descriptions of therapeutic interactions with children, many of which afford the reader a firsthand understanding of the child, how she related with the child, and how the child responded to her interventions. The detail and scope of the recordings help the reader to reflectively agree or disagree with her judgments about the treatment.

Data Analysis

One of the greatest challenges the researcher faces is the organization and interpretation of data. An evaluator who collects many long and detailed process recordings will have a great deal of data that needs to be interpreted and reduced. One way the evaluator organizes the data is by drawing an environment–system boundary around the time frame from which the data will be selected. The evaluator can select from time frames that range from within-session interactions, as Florence Hollis did when she conducted her classic qualitative analysis of practitioner communications (Woods & Hollis, 1990), to the process over several sessions, or the entire length of the treatment. Wimsatt notes that one common bias resulting from the heuristics of "observation" occurs when the context of a system is oversimplified, so that data that would allow the researcher to recognize "interactional or larger-scale patterns" is not recorded. "This can apply on a temporal as well as on a spatial scale" (Wimsatt, 1986b, p. 302). An illustration of the influence of a temporal environment–system boundary on an evaluation of practice is that a child whose prior relationships had caused her to feel very fearful was in treatment for six months before she tasted the snacks the clinician had available for her. The significance of the child's tentative trial of the snacks would not be understood adequately unless the environment–system boundary included the time span of the full six months, when the child did not even touch the snacks.

An environment–system boundary also is drawn when the evaluator decides the level at which to analyze the data. Positivist approaches to single-case design have assumed that "ideal explanations will always be about smaller and smaller units" (Heineman Pieper, 1985, p. 5). Because the researcher who adopts the heuristic paradigm is not biased toward smaller units, he or she determines the level (or levels) of analysis to use when approaching the data in relation to the problem to be addressed. Each level of data analysis produces different types of evidence and documentation for the evaluator's conclusions (Scriven, 1983, p. 257). For example, the evaluator may want to focus on very specific statements made by the client, or may want to examine larger patterns in the therapeutic relationship, or both. Any specific client behavior may be regulated by factors at a higher level of analysis, such as the client's experience of the ongoing relationship with the therapist. A reductionistic environment–system boundary precludes examination of higher-order influences that in fact may be very significant.

Because the evaluator using the heuristic paradigm recognizes that, as Scriven says, "evaluation is a multi-level enterprise" (1983, p. 257), she or he selects levels of analysis and recognizes the biases introduced by those selections. One way to address the biases set up by any one level of analysis is to evaluate the practice using multiple levels of data analysis (LeVine, 1981; Scriven, 1983). To illustrate, a researcher may choose to analyze the specific communications of the therapist of a children's group (Costantino, Malgady, & Rogler, 1986). Yet very potent effects of the intervention may be connected to factors at a higher level of organization, such as the therapist's ethnicity and social role in relation to the participants (Devore, 1983; LeCompte & Goetz, 1982). For example, in a group treatment program for minority children, group therapists who are themselves members of minority groups, and who have succeeded despite the obstacles of discrimination, may exert very powerful influences on the children. The children find it easier to identify with members of their own minority group, and such leaders help the children to believe they can fulfill their aspirations (Devore, 1983; Lum, 1992).

A Change Index

Virtually every evaluation of practice includes measures of change that are either implicit or explicit. Positivist social and behavioral researchers commonly limited measures of change to those that yield quantified data. As noted previously, many mistakenly assumed that such measures could be "objective" or theory-free. Positivist researchers also commonly regarded their methods of data analysis as theory-free, as Gigerenzer points out (1991a). Rather than assuming that theory-free data exist and can be examined atheoretically, the researcher who adopts the heuristic paradigm can select the theoretical assumptions to incorporate into data analysis. A measure of change that can be used in evaluations can be termed a *change index*. The concept of the change index is derived from the "sufficient parameter," first advanced by Levins (1966) and then applied to the social and behavioral sciences by Wimsatt (1981a). The change index is a heuristic defined on a given level of analysis that the researcher generates to index and organize data that are, by definition, at a lower level of abstraction. Wimsatt describes the sufficient parameter as follows:

> [It is] an index which, either for most purposes or merely for the purposes at hand, captures the effect of significant variations in lower-level or less abstract variables (usually only for certain ranges of the values of these variables) and can thus be substituted for them in the attempt to build simpler models of the upper-level phenomena. (1981a, p. 149)

According to Wimsatt (1981a), the history of science includes many examples of the uses of sufficient parameters because such parameters are central to scientific explanations. The evaluator's change index can be context-sensitive and embrace the complex, interactive properties of systems. For example, the evaluator can develop the change index based on aspects of the client's problem and treatment goals that signify the problem is being resolved. As noted previously, the evaluator's theory informs both the formulation of the client's problem and the definition of the treatment goals. An intrapsychic practitioner may recognize that a child's chronic fighting with peers represents a core conflict. The practitioner then may formulate one goal of the treatment as helping the child to forego motives for unpleasurable relationships and to pursue motives for pleasurable relationships. Accordingly, that problem formulation and goal can inform one change index used to evaluate treatment progress.

To organize some lower-level information (in these examples, data from the treatment process), a change index generates systematic bias because it is selective and necessarily leaves out other lower-level information. As Levins (1966) notes, the researcher who recognizes those biases then can generate multiple change indices with different biases. In naturalistic evaluations of practice, the researcher can generate one or more change indices to focus on aspects of the client's problem, treatment goals, and theoretical assumptions that are particularly relevant to how the evaluator wants to study the change process.

Generating a change index. As described earlier, Bobby's therapist, together with Bobby, identified Bobby's self-destructive reactions to loss as the top-priority problem to be treated. As evaluator of the practice, the practitioner also wanted to ascertain whether that problem improved and so formulated the evaluation problem as whether the goal of helping Bobby control his self-destructive motives was being reached. Soon after the therapy began, the therapist saw that Bobby's most acute episodes of self-destructive self-rage occurred in reaction to losses Bobby experienced, such as getting a below-average grade on a test, having to go out of town to visit relatives when he preferred to stay home, or being bullied by an older child (Pieper & Pieper, 1990, pp. 212–216). According to intrapsychic humanism, in intrapsychic treatment the client will become increasingly able to respond to loss by turning to the therapeutic relationship for help with feelings about the loss rather than by pursuing motives for pain in the form of isolated rage against the self or conflict with others (Pieper & Pieper, 1990). Building on one aspect of the problem formulation, one goal of the treatment, and a tenet of the practice theory, the clinician defined Bobby's response to loss as one change index.

Accordingly, the evaluator selected for analysis process recordings of the treatment sessions that followed a loss, such as when the bus Bobby took with his parents was delayed, and caused them to arrive late for the session. That change index helped the evaluator focus on 35 of the 100 process recordings and, within those 35, to analyze those interactions that represented the child's responses to loss. The evaluator then could see that Bobby's motives for isolated, self-destructive self-rage in response to loss gradually were accompanied by, and then often subordinated to, motives to experience the support of the care-giving relationship for help with the loss.

For example, in the second month of treatment, when Bobby's bus was delayed and he was late to a session, Bobby reacted with acute self-depreciation and shame. He suggested that he and the therapist play hide and seek, and then tried to hide in the garbage can. The therapist interpreted this action for Bobby, asking him if perhaps one part of Bobby wondered if the therapist missed him and had been looking for him and also that another part of him made him feel like garbage that should be thrown out. In response to that interpretation, Bobby said, "yeah." He came out from behind the garbage can and asked the therapist if he could have one of the popsicles he had asked the therapist to provide for him as a snack. Eight months later, Bobby responded to a similar loss by initiating the hide and seek game, but this time he hid under the chair where, at his request, the therapist was counting with her eyes closed. The therapist suggested that perhaps he was experiencing a motive to be close to help himself with the loss, but also a feeling that he should hide his feelings about the loss. As Bobby grew increasingly able to respond to loss by sharing the painful, self-raging reactions, he also became more able to pursue his motives for care-getting pleasure in the therapeutic relationship. For example, after eighteen months of treatment, when he again missed some treatment time because his family was stuck in traffic, he came in and exclaimed, "I was really looking forward to coming today, too!" Bobby's growing ability to handle loss by turning to the pleasure of the therapeutic relationship rather than to the soothing provided by his self-rage (Pieper & Pieper, 1990) coincided with Bobby's describing, in other moments, more pleasurable relationships with peers and also pursuing motives for pleasurable closeness with the therapist, such as asking for her collaboration in painting a brightly colored picture of a very happy bear and his bear friend at the beach.

Although it was not necessary to obtain another perspective on Bobby's responses to loss, and although it might even be countertherapeutic, the treatment plan for Bobby included the therapist's availability to confer with his parents at their request. After the first year of treatment, Bobby's mother reported that there had been only one incident of suicidal ideation. During the therapist's vacation, the family had to cancel a trip to an amusement park that Bobby had been looking forward to for some time; at the same time, an argument had arisen between Bobby's grandparents that provoked Bobby to tearful remonstrations and a statement that he felt like dying. By the end of the second year of treatment, Bobby's mother spontaneously reported that she was "amazed" when she realized a year had gone by and Bobby had never talked about wanting to die. She said that Bobby's new teacher had been very surprised to learn that in the past Bobby had been combative with peers, because he was one of the top students in the class, related very positively with peers, and some other students had enlisted his help in teaching them spelling.

Like all heuristics, every change index focuses on some information but leaves out other important information. The researcher who adopts the heuristic paradigm addresses that bias, most importantly, by recognizing it and acknowledging its effects on the conclusions drawn from the data. More than one change index may be used to round out an evaluation of practice. For example, the therapist noticed that in the initial phase of treatment Bobby experienced intense self-criticism and frustration when he could not perform a new activity (e.g., doing a simple crossword puzzle) up to his expectations. At those moments, he often became so frustrated that he relinquished his motives to pursue the new activity. For example, he would crumple up the crossword and throw it out in exasperation. Therefore, Bobby's reactions to the experience of learning were used as another change index to evaluate client change. As the treatment progressed, Bobby became more able to share his feelings of frustration and worry about his ability when he was learning something new, and he became more able to pursue his motives to learn. For example, after one year of treatment, he entered the session and said, "We're learning cursive." Then he practiced the new handwriting with the clinician, clearly feeling he could tolerate his mistakes more comfortably in her presence.

Using change indices can help practitioners reflect on the changes they aim to accomplish and to determine whether those changes are taking place. A major problem with attempting to evaluate change in open systems is that many variables impinge on the system under study. Also, there are many potential explanations for observed changes. Although the complexity of evaluating change has pushed some researchers toward positivist methodological prescriptions in the belief that such prescriptions will ascertain the impact of treatment, the researcher who adopts the heuristic paradigm recognizes that such methodologically based solutions are both unwarranted and unjustifiably restrictive. The researcher who adopts the heuristic paradigm prizes examining and explicating her or his assumptions and diversifying heuristics with the aim of diversifying bias. For example, when the evaluator uses multiple change indices, he or she can rotate the perspective on changes that occur within the system and can gain a more complete picture of events in the system over time. The evaluator then has various perspectives on the changes, which offer touchstones for reexamining how practice theories conceptualize change processes.

While reflecting on the value of the services provided, the evaluator also can compare the observed changes in relation to changes reported by practitioners using other approaches with clients with similar problems. For example, another perspective on the value of Bobby's treatment can be gained by comparing the changes that occurred during his treatment with changes reported by practitioners using other practice models. Others have reported that children with Bobby's severe presenting symptoms often do not manifest any significant improvement in their social and family relationships or in their academic performance, despite traditional psychiatric counseling and pharmacologic management (Chess & Thomas, 1984; G. Weiss & Hechtman, 1986). Thus, in relation to other available approaches to practice, the treatment approach used with Bobby—intrapsychic humanism—shows unusual promise.

CONCLUSION

One of the most challenging problems facing the human services today is evaluating the quality of services provided. This has been an enduring and extremely difficult problem, partly because of the complexity of the systems and causal mechanisms that social and behavioral evaluators address. Positivist social work researchers assumed that the early social workers had not addressed the issues entailed in evaluating social work practice. However, data reported here indicate that the early social workers *did* contribute evaluative research about practice to improve practice models. Further, the adoption of positivism did *not* lead to more evaluative research about social work practice, as positivist researchers had hoped. In fact, social work researchers' adoption of positivist prescriptions and proscriptions was followed by a decline in naturalistic, qualitative evaluations of practice. Even more important, the positivist prescriptions for evaluation research were incompatible with the values espoused by practitioners, because positivism prescribed research-driven interventions into the treatment process that were incompatible with the treatments that practitioners wanted to conduct. Consequently, a chasm developed between researchers and practitioners that began to be bridged only when Heineman Pieper advanced the heuristic paradigm as an approach to research that is inherently compatible with practitioners' aims and values.

Through naturalistic methods, the heuristic paradigm enables research about practice to be both scientific and compatible with the tenets of practice theories. The heuristic paradigm embraces practitioners' informed judgment as an inherent, essential aspect of the evaluative process; it regards clients' opinions as central for understanding any change process. Unlike positivist single-system designs, naturalistic approaches based on the heuristic paradigm do not require manipulation or deception of clients, nor do they cause clients additional losses by requiring that they subsume their concerns and natural forms of self-expression to the priorities of a research agenda. The heuristic paradigm offers guidelines to help evaluators explicate the assumptions that underlie their research. Moreover, the heuristic paradigm can facilitate communication about the services provided, so that practitioner–researchers can communicate to their colleagues their process of thinking through practice decisions and nurture the dialogue that can improve and perfect our knowledge.

DISCUSSION QUESTIONS

1. Deciding which individuals are chosen as sources of data for the evaluation is a major issue in designing evaluation research.

   a. After presenting the powerful story of a man named Ed who was labeled mentally retarded, Bogdan and Taylor write, "Devaluing an individual's perspective by viewing it as naive, unsophisticated, immature, or a symptom of some underlying pathology can make research one-sided and service organizations places where rituals are performed in the name of science" (1976, p. 51). What are some implications of omitting clients as sources of data for evaluating programs and clinical practice?

   b. What might be some consequences of obtaining client evaluations of practice through an interventionist rather than a naturalistic approach?

    c.   Find a study that evaluates a social program. Show how the evaluator drew the environment–system boundary so that you can see who is included as a source of data about the change processes the program implements. How does that environment–system boundary influence the findings of the evaluation?

    d.   Redraw the environment–system boundary by including other sources of data about the impact of the program. Consider how that might alter the findings.

2.   Design two evaluations of practice using the conceptual foundations of the heuristic paradigm:

    a.   An evaluation of the services that an agency you are familiar with offers;

    b.   An evaluation of practice with one client.

3.   In the Preface, Martha Heineman Pieper defines science as "a systematic inquiry into some aspect of reality that is communicated in a way that will allow an interested person to make an informed evaluation of the process of inquiry and its conclusions." Evaluate the research designs you planned in answering question 2, as follows:

    a.   Are the assumptions that you have made in designing the research clearly outlined, and are they consistent with each other?

    b.   How might you present your research so as to provide a reader with sufficient information to judge both the process of the inquiry, and your findings?

4.   In his article called, "Do Photographs Tell the Truth?" Howard Becker addresses some problems that also confront any researcher:

> Photographers know perfectly well that their pictures represent a small and highly selected sample of the real world about which they are supposed to be conveying some truth. They know that their selection of times, places, and people, of distance and angle, of framing and tonality, have all combined to produce an effect quite different from the one a different selection from the same reality would produce. (1979, p. 99)

    a.   In the preceding statement, is Becker's position more akin to realism, relativism, or skepticism, and why?

    b.   How are the photographer's choices of times, places, people, and so on similar to choices a researcher makes in designing research?

    c.   What are some similarities between the influences of a photographer on his or her participant/subjects and the effects of social and behavioral researchers on their participant/subjects? What are some differences?

In discussing truth, Becker says,

> Every photograph, because it begins with the light rays something emits hitting film, must in some obvious sense be true; and because it could always have been made differently than it was, it cannot be the whole truth and in that obvious sense is false. (1979, p. 101)

    d. How does that statement summarize the way a heuristic always sets up biases?

    e. What central issues in a metatheory of knowledge for the social and behavioral sciences is Becker alluding to in the following points?

        i. "Most of us . . . do worry about whether the pictures we make and look at are 'true' and can be seen to be true by others who look at them" (Becker, 1979, p. 100).

        ii. Rather than ask "is it true," it makes more sense to ask, "is this photograph telling the truth about what?" (p. 101) "We must first specify what we are getting the truth about" (p. 101).

        iii. "Pictures can ordinarily contain enough information that we can use them to give us evidence about more than one topic" (p. 101).

        iv. "More than one true thing can be said on the basis of a single image" (p. 106).

        v. "We can never be absolutely sure of the truth of an assertion. Our knowledge is always partial and therefore fallible; we may find a new piece of evidence tomorrow which will show us that the assertion we thought true is, after all, false" (p. 106).

        vi. "No single standard of truth is acceptable for all social groups and all purposes" (p. 107).

5. In discussing issues of "truth and practical adequacy" in his book about a realist approach to the generation of social and behavioral science knowledge, Andrew Sayer (1992) makes two points that are especially relevant for evaluations of practice:

> It is precisely because the world does not yield to just any kind of expectation that we believe it exists independently of us and is not simply a figment of our imagination. If there were no cases of our statements being confounded, if wishful thinking worked, there would be no reason for being a realist, and we could say that truth was purely relative to our conceptual scheme. (p. 67)

    a. How can a practitioner–researcher enhance his or her ability to perceive and consider practice experiences that confound his or her expectations and be most available to the seeds of new discoveries?

    b. What are the implications of the following statement with regard to the incommensurability of practice theories? "From the fact that knowledge and the material world are different kinds of things it does not follow that there can be no relationship between them; and second, the admission that all knowledge is fallible does not mean all knowledge is equally fallible" (Sayer, 1992, p. 68).

    c. What standards can the researcher who adopts the heuristic paradigm use to assess the robustness of knowledge generated in naturalistic evaluations of practice?

Discovering New Solutions in the Context of the Heuristic Paradigm

Introduction to "Treating Violent 'Untreatable' Adolescents: Applications of Intrapsychic Humanism in a State-Funded Demonstration Project"

The following selection by Martha Heineman Pieper and William Joseph Pieper illustrates how the heuristic paradigm broadens the domain of scientifically acceptable research and offers you the opportunity to use the naturalistic approach that Martha Heineman Pieper describes in the Preface. You will find it helpful to review the ideas in the Preface as you consider the research applications the selection exemplifies. Heineman Pieper defines naturalistic clinical research as "the systematic study of clinical practice that is not intentionally altered for research purposes" (Preface). As she points out, one source of confusion about naturalistic research is that its opposite is never mentioned: The term *naturalistic* has often been used to refer to research designs that are interventionist. For example, investigators studying educational programs have assumed that an ethnographic study by a researcher who enters the program as a participant-observer is naturalistic research (Skrtic, 1985). However, when researchers were not already part of the system (e.g., as educators), then the researcher's data gathering was driven by research rather than service aims. Using Heineman Pieper's demarcation, that research is interventionist rather than naturalistic. By contrast, in the following study, the participant/researchers were directing the program's services and treating the patients in the program. To conduct their research, they did not alter any of the program's services.

Heineman Pieper's reconceptualization of naturalistic research also redresses positivist misconceptions about the roles of practitioners and researchers. Positivist researchers often defined practitioner and researcher roles according to their invalid assumption that the process of theory generation could be sharply distinguished from the process of theory testing. For example, Hudson commented in his "Author's Reply" to Holland (Chapter 3) that there are theory developers and "empiricists"; he regarded the "empiricists" as theory testers. Postpositivist researchers recognize that such a dichotomy is untenable. For example, there is no theory-free way to test theories, and scientists repeatedly test their theories in the course of developing them (e.g., see Simon, Chapter 5).

In the following study, Martha Heineman Pieper and William Joseph Pieper aim to "minimize research intrusiveness into practice" (Preface). They exemplify the role of naturalistic clinical researchers, who operate within the broad definition of scientific activity advanced by the heuristic paradigm. They generate new theory, apply it, and report the findings, without modifying their commitment to humanistic values and to maintaining the integrity of the therapeutic process.

Heineman Pieper and Pieper describe how they applied their revolutionary, comprehensive psychology and philosophy of mind—intrapsychic humanism—to an extremely serious and important problem: helping homicidal and suicidal teenage state wards who are so beset by violent rage that no treatment program will take them, including the most protective and advanced inpatient psychiatric treatment facilities. As Heineman Pieper and Pieper emphasize, the problem they addressed has far-reaching implications, both for the violent teenagers who were rejected by all other treatment programs and for those who wanted to care for them but did not know how.

Despite the pressing need to find ways to treat such clients, and also the fact that the Piepers' research is in accord with social work's traditional mission and values, Heineman Pieper was prevented from using the study as a dissertation topic because a committee established to evaluate the "scientific" merits of dissertation proposals prohibited it (see Heineman Pieper, Chapter 3). From another perspective, the fact that the research applying Heineman Pieper and Pieper's discoveries about human nature and treatment (articulated fully in their book, Pieper & Pieper, 1990, and summarized in the following selection) was considered "unscientific" raises important questions about research in the social and behavioral sciences. Heineman Pieper and Pieper's research was not excluded because of reservations about whether their work was humane or useful. Further, the committee that excluded that research did not focus on the merit of the new psychology the Piepers were developing. In other words, the committee did not use the standard of substantive importance in evaluating Heineman Pieper's proposal. Instead, they focused on methodology. The research was excluded solely because the naturalistic research methods did not conform to the positivist prescriptions for science that the committee favored. Specifically, the study did not use third-party data-collection methods; it was underway at the time of the proposal and therefore could not be prospective;[100] and clients were neither chosen randomly nor placed in control groups. A definition of "science" so restrictive that it excludes from the domain of legitimate inquiry theoretically anchored, systematic, and humane research that seeks to solve our most pressing social problems not only is obsolete but also obstructs the realization of the values that motivate most scientists.

In May 1992, Martha Heineman Pieper was invited back to the University of Chicago School of Social Service Administration by the Alumni Association to give a

Centennial Lecture. This invitation to present her research on the demonstration project applying the principles of intrapsychic humanism to violent adolescent state wards was extended by the schools' alumni, who are largely practitioners. Thus, her invitation did not signify that the gap between researchers and practitioners in social work had narrowed. Instead, her invitation reflected the persistence of practitioners in advocating the dissemination of scientific knowledge that is relevant to the human problems they address every day.

The following paper illustrates research constructed within the heuristic paradigm. In concert with the heuristic paradigm's aim of relevance, Heineman Pieper and Pieper address a social problem that is acutely important, and their research explores a workable therapeutic and programmatic solution. They describe the theoretical assumptions that underlie both their treatment program and the process of their research about that program. They describe their decisions about data collection and analysis, and they support their qualitative analysis with plentiful illustrations from the data. In the interest of recognizing and addressing bias, they use multiple criteria to evaluate the progress of the client who is the central focus of study. As emphasized previously, the selection of this material does not indicate that a researcher using the heuristic paradigm must be restricted to naturalistic methods and qualitative data analysis. A researcher adopting the heuristic paradigm can choose from among all the contemporary methods of collecting and analyzing data, including using experimental design, an interventionist approach to gathering data, or data quantification.

Heineman Pieper's distinction between naturalistic and interventionist research is based on the "intentions and practices of the researcher" (Preface), which emphasizes that the practitioner–researcher's motives have a powerful regulatory impact on the treatment. As emphasized in Chapter 4, the participant/researcher's motives also have a powerful impact on the participant/subject, the research design, and the data. Heineman Pieper's distinction between naturalistic and interventionist research can be applied to understand the process of generating new approaches to treatment. To illustrate, historically, some practitioners developed theories of treatment using naturalistic research approaches, such as the model of crisis intervention advanced by Lydia Rapoport (1970). Others advanced practice models regulated by research rather than therapeutic aims, such as the "empirical clinical practice model" that was developed to meet positivist requirements for data gathering (Bloom & Fischer, 1982). Heineman Pieper points out that if a practice model prescribes interventions because they facilitate data gathering for research purposes, the research is interventionist rather than naturalistic. In the following selection, Heineman Pieper and Pieper describe why they chose a naturalistic approach to research:

> The most compelling of the several reasons for choosing a naturalistic method of data collection over an interventionist methodology was that, since the therapeutic action of a treatment process informed by the psychology of intrapsychic humanism depends on the therapist's ability to subordinate personal motives to caregiving motives, and since research-determined interventions are driven by personal motives, research-determined interventions are by definition iatrogenic and contraindicated in intrapsychic treatment. (page 460)

In sum, the primary objective of the naturalistic participant/researcher is not disturbing her or his natural relationships with the participant/subjects in the study. Usually, the naturalistic participant/researcher is providing a form of service; the research process occurs in the context of that helping process and does not modify it. The naturalistic participant/researcher may provide help in many forms, such as psychotherapy, education, community organization, or management of human services. An intrapsychic therapist who also is a naturalistic participant/researcher will conceptualize herself or himself as a caregiver in relation to the participant/subjects in the research. In concert with intrapsychic humanism, the intrapsychic clinician's caregiving motives regulate any other motives the participant/researcher may have (e.g., to generate a publishable study). Any research procedure that requires the participant/researcher to subsume service aims under research purposes represents interventionist research, even if the data were gathered using a nonintrusive procedure such as anamnestic process recording. An example of naturalistic research by a program manager is that a naturalistic participant/researcher who directs a program for the homeless mentally ill may decide to incorporate community organization and may enlist a consultant to help staff develop skills in community organizing. While providing the consultation group, the program director may examine whether the training opportunity has led staff to change the way they help clients. The program director may gather data by examining staff's written reports about their services and clients' responses to services and also by keeping anamnestic notes about staff's discussions of their interactions with clients.

One important implication of Heineman Pieper's conceptualization of naturalistic research is that social and behavioral scientists no longer need to experience conflict between two primary aims: helping and generating scientific research. The naturalistic participant/researcher can generate scientific research without disrupting the process of caring for participant/subjects. For example, researchers videotaping disadvantaged families to study child development sometimes witness a child crying. To continue the videotaping and conform to positivism's prescription for researcher "objectivity," the researchers may not comfort the child and may find such restraint difficult. That uncomfortable and ethically questionable dilemma would never occur in a naturalistic research process using the heuristic paradigm, because with Heineman Pieper's new formulation, the naturalistic participant/researcher's entire research process could be regulated by the aim of helping. Accordingly, the naturalistic participant/researcher would not be torn between research protocols and the wish to offer help and would be free to comfort the child. The following selection illustrates how the heuristic paradigm opens up new avenues for scientific research, so that we can retain the integrity of therapeutic and service processes, study the complexity of practice, and develop relevant solutions to our pressing human problems.

DISCUSSION QUESTIONS

1. The ontological assumptions (the "real" to be known) of intrapsychic humanism focus on the client's subjective experience of purposiveness, that is, motives or

agency. Within the category of agency reality, intrapsychic humanism focuses particularly on an experience of agency that Heineman Pieper and Pieper discovered, intrapsychic regulatory agency. Each individual's experience of intrapsychic agency (or each individual's intrapsychic motive) regulates that person's self-esteem and all the individual's other motives. To illustrate, an individual who experiences the paradigmatic caretaking the Piepers describe will not need to use interpersonal experience as a source of self-worth. By contrast, if an individual does not experience nurture that allows him or her to develop autonomous, self-regulatory self-esteem, the choice of which interpersonal motives to gratify will be dictated to a greater or a lesser extent by the need for pain relief (delusional soothing).

The epistemology (the way of knowing the "real") of intrapsychic humanism is conceptualized as intrapsychic caregiving—an activity in which caregivers have the potential to know the subject's intrapsychic regulatory agency experience (Pieper & Pieper, 1990, p. 12 ff.). With regard to treatment, to apprehend their patients' experience of intrapsychic agency reality, an intrapsychic therapist offers the patient an intrapsychic caregiving relationship. The patient's motive to be a partner in that relationship, and the therapist's motive to confirm and strengthen the patient's capacity for self-regulating, stable inner esteem (intrapsychic regulatory agency), are the unique factors that construct the epistemology used to know the patient's intrapsychic regulatory agency. The therapist attends to the process meaning of the patient's associations to apprehend the patient's intrapsychic agency motives. The process meaning of a patient's communication is "its significance in relation to the patient's movement toward or away from the pleasure of the intrapsychic caregiving relationship" (Pieper & Pieper, 1990, p. 277; Pieper & Pieper, 1991, 1992a).

    a.   What are some of the central therapeutic principles that Heineman Pieper and Pieper used in applying intrapsychic humanism to treat the teenagers?

    b.   What are some of the principles of program operation and management that were derived from intrapsychic humanism?

    c.   Why, given the assumptions of intrapsychic humanism, would an interventionist approach to research not be appropriate for their study?

    d.   Given the assumptions of intrapsychic humanism, how is the design of the research the authors present in this selection appropriate to their theory?

2. How, given their theory, do the authors conceptualize the client's core problem?

3. a.   How do the authors formulate the research problem?

    b.   How do the authors gather their data?

    c.   How do the authors analyze the data?

4. Look at the section where Heineman Pieper and Pieper use change indices to assess the client's progress.

    a.   One of the change indices they use is Andrew's ability to control his self-destructive motives. How does Andrew's capacity to regulate his self-destructive motives change during treatment?

    b.   How does Andrew's capacity to regulate his homicidal motives change during treatment?

    c.   Notice that at the onset of the treatment, Andrew used his self-destructive and homicidal motives to soothe himself in response to loss. What other ways does he develop for soothing himself in response to loss?

5.   If a researcher focuses only on measuring changes in initial symptomatic behaviors, the researcher may overlook important, qualitatively new changes. Sometimes, client change occurs in the form of new capabilities and motives. What new motives and capabilities does the patient experience in the therapeutic relationship?

6.   Anamnestic data should allow readers to make their own judgment about the process. Someone using a different modality (e.g., behaviorism) might criticize this treatment process and say, "they should have taught the teenagers concrete skills." Yet, the mechanism of the therapeutic action according to intrapsychic humanism is the therapist's response to and respect for the patient's developmental, self-caretaking motives. Why would the preceding criticism be irrelevant, given the theoretical assumptions of intrapsychic humanism?

7.   Evaluate this research using the following standards for research advanced by the heuristic paradigm:

    a.   Addressing a substantively important problem and presenting solutions;

    b.   Basing the research on humanistic values, including advancing social justice;

    c.   Explicating theoretical assumptions (especially ontological and epistemological assumptions);

    d.   Systematically presenting the decisions about research design for the reader to evaluate;

    e.   Ensuring consistency between the ontological and epistemological assumptions and the research design.

8.   Heineman Pieper and Pieper point out that when they authored their study many other clinicians concluded that the teenagers they treated were inherently "untreatable." Their study thus presents the important finding that teenagers with such severe problems can use treatment based on the principles of intrapsychic humanism.

    a.   What are positivist requirements for using research findings and their implications (often termed the "generalizability" of findings)? (For an example, refer to the paper by Hudson, in Chapter 3.)

    b.   Rather than generalizability, the heuristic paradigm's standard of relevance leads to a concern for the applicability of research findings. What might a researcher who adopts the heuristic paradigm consider in evaluating the applicability of the findings of a research study?

    c.   Using the principles you articulated in (b), describe some implications of the findings of Heineman Pieper and Pieper's study for clinical practice.

    d. What are some of the ramifications of this demonstration project for policy decisions about the allocation of resources for helping teenagers such as those the Piepers treated?

9. This study can be used as a model for a naturalistic approach to clinical interventions. Select a case from your own clinical practice and design a research project using a naturalistic approach. Remember to:

    a. Consider multiple possible problem formulations.

    b. Examine the bias introduced by the environment-system boundaries.

    c. Describe your ontological and epistemological assumptions.

    d. Reflect on the values underlying your research.

    e. Specify how you will collect data and analyze data.

    f. Evaluate the consistency between your decisions about data collection and analysis and your ontological and epistemological assumptions.

    g. Use other procedures for recognizing bias, such as triangulation and multi-level reductionistic analysis.

10. Extra-extra-credit question: In discussing a postpositivist, realist, "ontic" conception of scientific explanation, the philosopher of science Wesley Salmon comments,

> our efforts at finding causal relations and causal explanations often if not always take us beyond the realm of observable phenomena. Such knowledge is empirical knowledge, and it involves descriptive knowledge of the hidden mechanisms of the world, but it does go beyond descriptive knowledge of the observable phenomena. There is no logical necessity in the fact that causal mechanisms involve unobservables; that is just the way our world happens to work. (1989, p. 133)
>
>   For the proponent of the ontic conception of scientific explanation, realism provides a straightforward answer to the question of the distinction between descriptive and explanatory knowledge. Taking "description" in the narrower sense which includes only description of appearances, the realist can say that explanatory knowledge is knowledge of the underlying mechanisms, causal or otherwise, that produce the phenomena we want to explain. To explain is to expose the inner workings, to lay bare the hidden mechanisms, to open the black boxes nature presents to us. (1989, p. 134)

Consider the ontological assumptions of intrapsychic humanism (look again at question 1 and the Piepers' discussion of consciousness, pp. 457–458).

    a. What are the "hidden" or "unobservable" causal mechanisms that explain human behavior according to intrapsychic humanism?

    b. Use the ontological assumptions you described in (a) to summarize the scientific explanation that intrapsychic humanism offers for the mechanism of the therapeutic action in intrapsychic treatment (notice that the causal mechanisms you include will explain the changes in Andrew's behavior that you discussed in question 4).

    c. Salmon's "ontic" conception of scientific explanation is an alternative to positivist models of scientific explanation, such as Hempel and Oppenheim's deductive-nomological model of scientific explanation.[101] As Salmon says in the preceding quote, the ontic conception of scientific explanation offers a way to distinguish simple description of observable phenomena from scientific explanation. According to that ontic model, scientific explanation focuses on uncovering what it is in the nature of the entities being studied that produces the phenomena we want to explain. If a positivist researcher were to say to you that the case study presented in Chapter 8 is "only" descriptive and not scientific knowledge, how could you use the "ontic" conception of scientific explanation to rebut that critique?

d. Salmon also says that scientific explanations increase our understanding,

> 1) when we obtain knowledge of the hidden mechanisms, causal or other, that produce the phenomena we seek to explain, 2) when our knowledge of the world is so organized that we can comprehend what we know under a smaller number of assumptions than previously, and 3) when we supply missing bits of descriptive knowledge that answer why-questions and remove us from particular sorts of intellectual predicaments. (1989, p. 135)

You addressed criterion 1 in your answer to (c). Now state how intrapsychic humanism meets Salmon's second and third criteria for scientific explanations.

Treating Violent "Untreatable" Adolescents: Applications of Intrapsychic Humanism in a State-Funded Demonstration Project

MARTHA HEINEMAN PIEPER

WILLIAM JOSEPH PIEPER

The dual aims of this paper are to describe and impart a concrete sense of an innovative state-sponsored residential treatment program that existed between 1974 and 1977, and to give an illustration of naturalistic research.* The program applied a new treatment approach based on the principles of intrapsychic humanism to severely emotionally disturbed, homicidally violent, poverty-level adolescents who were considered untreatable by any other method. Intrapsychic humanism is a recent, nonderivative, comprehensive depth psychology that represents a unified theory of child development, psychopathology, and treatment. This new psychology is comprehensively explicated in *Intrapsychic Humanism: An Introduction to a Comprehensive Psychology and Philosophy of Mind* (Pieper & Pieper, 1990). Since the theory is fully presented in that volume, this paper will address only those aspects of intrapsychic humanism that are most pertinent to an understanding of the treatment of violent adolescents.

In the tradition of Aristotle, but in contrast to Freud, the object relations theorists, Bowlby, Kohut, Stern and Alice Miller, intrapsychic humanism asserts that every baby is born with an innate motive for and capacity to experience the pleasure of a conflict-free caregiving relationship. Therefore, the term normal development acquires a specific and unique meaning. It refers to a caregiving process that brings about an attainable type of childhood and adulthood in which the subjective experience of personal existence consists of a consciously self-regulated and conflict-free inner well-being. The psychic pain that other psychologists and philosophers take as unalterable normality, while typical, in fact represents a heretofore unrecognized form of (alterable) mental illness; conversely, true normality, while not typical, i.e., not widespread, is an attainable state of stable inner well being that is neither associated with internalized conflicts nor vulnerable to the influence of external stresses and losses. Even more radically, intrapsychic humanism asserts that the unshakable well-being that characterizes true normality can be established as a result of intrapsychic treatment, which is the form of treatment based on the view of human nature and development explicated by intrapsychic humanism.

While intrapsychic humanism asserts that the psychic pain that Freud and others assume to be the inevitable unhappiness of everyday living not only can be treated, but can also be prevented, intrapsychic humanism is not utopian. It does not suggest that a structural improvement in the human condition can be attained by social reform or cognitive understanding

Source: A version of this paper was presented by Martha Heineman Pieper at the University of Chicago, School of Social Service Administration, for the Alumni Centennial lecture, May 2, 1992. Copyright 1992 by Martha Heineman Pieper and William Joseph Pieper. Reprinted by permission of the authors.

*Editor's Note: See the Preface and Chapter 4 for a discussion of naturalistic research. See also the methodology section later in this paper for a discussion of the application of the principles of naturalistic research to this project.

alone (although clearly both are necessary, neither is sufficient). And, just as importantly, intrapsychic humanism neither ignores the individual's interaction with her/his environment, nor concludes that situational effects are insignificant.

After Freud abandoned his trauma theory of mental illness, he unswervingly promulgated a view of human nature that continues to be prevalent in our culture: that psychopathology is only an extension of endemic psychic pain, that is, that mental illness is an exaggerated but qualitatively unchanged state of the normal mind. From the perspective of intrapsychic humanism, however, the cause of mental illness is trauma. Conflicted human nature is not innately determined, but represents the developing human's attempt to maintain a viable sense of inner well-being in the face of unstable parenting. Our view that the etiology of psychopathology is trauma is reflected in the aim and action of intrapsychic treatment. The goal of intrapsychic treatment is not the completion of an incomplete developmental process that commenced in infancy, but rather the completion of a developmental intrapsychic process that commences within the therapeutic relationship. Other clinical theories mistake what Freud called the common unhappiness of every day life for essential human nature and assert that even the most successful treatment will leave the client with an intractable type of existential incompleteness. This is illustrated by the quote attributed to Freida Fromm-Reichmann which Hannah Green chose as emblematic of her treatment: "I Never Promised You a Rose Garden."

The therapeutic action in intrapsychic treatment is the caregiving act of nurturing the client's heretofore unengaged motives for the conflict-free pleasure of intrapsychic caregiving intimacy. Intrapsychic caregetting pleasure refers not to an affect, but to a meaning structure of effective self-regulatory agency nurtured by the act of regulating the caregiving relationship. Accordingly, the therapeutic action in intrapsychic treatment is not hermeneutic; it does not have the primary goal of conflict resolution (it does not rely on transference interpretations of dynamically unconscious psychosexual conflicts) (Freud, 1953-1974); it does not have the primary focus of constructing a coherent narrative of the client's life (Cohler, 1988); and it does not aim for the restoration of the self by means of strengthening compensatory sectors of the self through transmuting internalizations that restitute defects accrued from unavoidable lapses in parental

empathy (Kohut, 1971). Just as importantly, intrapsychic treatment does not advocate any type of unreflective caregiving, specifically, the practice of intrapsychic caregiving never entails indiscriminate transference gratification, nor does it represent a process of reparenting (e.g., it is not a 'corrective emotional experience,' Soth, 1986). Also, it should be noted that intrapsychic caregiving does not depend on empathy, either as perception (vicarious introspection) or as the mode of therapeutic action. It is manifestly demonstrable that because of the solipsistic nature of introspection, empathy as vicarious introspection represents at best a figure of speech. That is, the act of introspection is not open to the knowing act of another; therefore empathy cannot reliably distinguish between delusion and actuality. In consequence, there are conceptual flaws in theories that posit empathy either as the basis of therapeutic action or as a mode of perception,* because there is no way to know when the therapist's experience of affective attunement represents her/his wish fulfillment or compliance with the client's wishes.

The mechanism of therapeutic change in intrapsychic humanism is not insight but the intrapsychic caregetting pleasure produced by the client's experience of effective self-regulatory agency with regard to being the regulating cause of the caregiving s/he receives from the therapist. Over time, the superiority of this type of relationship-based self-regulation causes the client to recognize that the type of self-regulation that depends on motives for pain which have the unconscious meaning of pleasure represents an unnecessary and unwanted loss. Because it does not rely on insight, intrapsychic humanism is an appropriate treatment for infants and psychotic and/or violent clients, as well as for the type of relatively mature and well functioning client who is considered most appropriate for traditional psychodynamic treatment.

THE PROJECT

In the middle 70's, a concatenation of circumstances affecting the Illinois Department of Child and Family Services, hereafter called DCFS, gave us the opportunity to use the principles of intrapsychic humanism to treat the Department's "most difficult," violent, anti-

---

*Editor's Note: For example, self-psychology (Kohut, 1959, 1971); see also Pecukonis, 1990.

social adolescents. The problem presented by DCFS's violent adolescents was and is a staggering one. In the State of Illinois, as in most other heavily urban states, there is a large number of homicidally violent and self-destructive adolescent state wards for whom there exist no treatment programs. In the past these adolescents were restrained and medicated in state mental hospitals. However, one result of the Civil Rights movement was a changed interpretation of the rights of children and the mentally ill, which resulted both in stringent restrictions on the commitment of adolescents to mental hospitals and also in the requirement that restriction of liberty for mental illness be accompanied by a corresponding right to treatment. As a result, in the late 1960s and early 1970s, DCFS suddenly found itself saddled with a group of adolescents for whom it was responsible but for whom it had no available resources or programs. Attempts to send these adolescents out of state to custodial and quasi-treatment institutions resulted in well-publicized disasters and law suits.

In February of 1974 we approached DCFS with a proposal to treat its "most difficult" adolescents.[1] DCFS funded our project and referred us those adolescents who, by DCFS' own determination, fit into the "most difficult" category. The numbers of these "most difficult" adolescents, the lack of resources for them, and the high per capita cost of the program ($150–$200 a day per adolescent—remember, this was the 1970s) insured that our Project was not being given adolescents who could be placed elsewhere.

RELEVANT CONSTRUCTS OF INTRAPSYCHIC HUMANISM

This brings us, then, to a brief description of the key principles and constructs of intrapsychic humanism and the specifics of how they informed our program. One central tenet of intrapsychic humanism is that within every human there are two distinct but interrelated and interacting forms of consciousness, interpersonal and intrapsychic. Interpersonal consciousness refers to the diverse motives and self-experiences that are immediately accessible by introspection. It corresponds both to the consciousness of cognitive psychology and also to the psychoanalytic topographic and structural constructs of conscious and unconscious consciousness. Interpersonal motives are cognitive (e.g., to learn), social (e.g., to make friends), and physiological (e.g., to eat). Motives to regulate the

choice and pursuit of interpersonal motives also exist in interpersonal consciousness.

Intrapsychic consciousness, which is the new type of consciousness identified by intrapsychic humanism, is unlike interpersonal consciousness, in that it exclusively refers to a unitary motive—the motive to have an effective agent-self that stably regulates one's core well being. In development, the intrapsychic motive for effective self-regulatory agency is focused on the pleasure of being the regulating cause of the caregiving motives of the primary caregivers. One of the key discoveries of intrapsychic humanism is that the intrapsychic motive is the basis for the capacity for self-regulation: that is, what makes each of us human is truly defined not, as is usually thought, by the attributes that set us apart from other species, the cognition and language manifested in our capacity for sophisticated symbolic thinking, but rather by the need we share with many other species for caregiving intimacy. Further, we demonstrate (Pieper & Pieper, 1990) that cognitive and linguistic motives are under the hegemony of the intrapsychic motive.

A child will develop intrapsychic psychopathology when the parents' own conflicts about intimacy render them unable to respond to the child with stable caregiving pleasure. The experience of inconsistent caregiving causes the child to develop motives for a form of caregiving mutuality that an external observer would recognize as unstable, but which to the child represents an ideal (stable) type of caregetting pleasure. This motive for a pain-based mode of self regulation of core well-being is the defining characteristic of intrapsychic psychopathology. In addition, intrapsychic psychopathology prevents one's core well-being from ever becoming autonomously self-nurturing, but rather one's inner well-being remains fixated in its original state of vulnerability to the vicissitudes of interpersonal motive gratification. In the presence of intrapsychic psychopathology, intrapsychic motive gratification (pathological core well-being) can result either from the gratification of pathological interpersonal motives, such as motives for compulsive gambling, or from the gratification of interpersonal motives that are not pathological in themselves, such as making a new, positive friendship. To reiterate, optimally core (intrapsychic) self-esteem is unaffected by the events of everyday life. It becomes autonomously self-regulating only through the developmental gratification of intrapsychic motives for genuine caregetting pleasure. In contrast, the clinical hallmark of intrapsychic psychopathology is that the individual's core self-esteem never becomes stable, but remains vulnerable to the ups and downs of everyday successes and failures, and, in addition, it can be generated by the gratification of motives for pain with the meaning of pleasure.

What differentiates the "most difficult" adolescents from individuals with intrapsychic psychopathology who manage to have successful careers and satisfying family lives is the degree to which their interpersonal consciousness is regulated by pathological motives, and, specifically, the degree to which their conscious sense of contentment derives from the gratification of motives for aggression toward others or themselves. Violence as a way of life can become an object of desire when intrapsychic psychopathology becomes interpersonally organized in a volatile combination of highly self-destructive and paranoid interpersonal identifications. In the case of the State wards, these identifications occurred within the corrosive socioeconomic privation of unrelieved poverty.

REGULATORY PRINCIPLES OF THE RESIDENTIAL MILIEU

The structural difference between intrapsychic and interpersonal forms of psychopathology was directly reflected in the structure of the program's milieu. While the intensive individual intrapsychic treatment, the part of our therapeutic program which aimed at effecting structural change in the nature of the adolescents' intrapsychic motive gratification process (core self-esteem), was essentially the same for the "most difficult" adolescents as for a well-functioning outpatient, the residential milieu was designed to respond therapeutically to the destructive interpersonal motives which were used as the ongoing fuel of the adolescents' pathological core self-esteem.

The challenge for the milieu was to make it possible for the residents to discover that nurturing, relationship-based ways of regulating themselves were superior to the destructive patterns of self-regulation which were deeply entrenched at the time they entered our program. Therefore, we tried never to leave any adolescent without a therapeutic relationship to turn to; all residents had 'round the clock one-to-one milieu staff called, fittingly, their 1-1's. This intensive interpersonal coverage had two aims: (1) to make it possible for the adolescents to experience their motives for violence in the context of a caregiving relationship, and (2) to enhance the adolescents'

abilities to recognize the superior pleasure of a self-esteem based on genuine intrapsychic relationship pleasure by providing abundant opportunities for interpersonal relationship pleasure (socializing with the workers, cooking good food, getting help with homework).

Because the pleasure of true caregiving intimacy is incompatible with the type of pain-based intimacy that is intrinsic to psychopathology, the residents periodically experienced the therapeutic relationship offered by the 1-1's as threatening (consequently, the 1-1's were in constant danger of being attacked). As a result, in carefully selected, critical instances, psychotropic medications and physical isolation were used to protect both the staff and resident. However, to facilitate the goal of helping the residents turn to the experience of caregiving intimacy rather than to destructive motives for soothing, when residents needed to be separated from other residents or staff, their 1-1's would stay with them. The Program Director would make a contract with the affected adolescent as to what behavior the adolescent needed help with controlling and what forms of control would be appropriate. Such a contract is entirely different from the contracts used in milieus organized by the principles of behaviorism, such as token economies (Agee, 1979; Edwards & Roundtree, 1981; Feindler, 1987; Kupfersmid, Mazzarins, & Benjamin, 1987). Our contract focused on preventing behaviors (such as hitting others) that endangered the resident's ability to continue in the program. Our contract was designed neither to induce or coerce compliance with specific programmatic aspects of the milieu therapy (e.g., attending a scheduled group meeting) nor to foster behaviors that were merely socially desirable (such as having good table manners or being polite, e.g. Burdsal, Force, Klingsporn, 1989). When a resident was not able to maintain her/his agreement not to attack staff, the consequences (such as some time in the quiet room, or, later when the program was no longer located in a hospital site, a few days on an inpatient unit at the Illinois Department of Mental Health's Read Zone Center) were chosen only because they promised to allow the resident to continue in the program by protecting the staff and residents from the resident's lack of regulatory control. In intrapsychic humanism, therapeutic change is seen as a function of the intrapsychic caregetting pleasure generated within the client's therapeutic relationships, not of behavioral inducements.

While in most residential programs, the therapist makes or participates in many of the management decisions about her/his client (Piersma, 1985; Scavo & Buchanan, 1989; Soth, 1986), our program administrators were assigned total responsibility for decisions about the residents' daily lives, such as the granting of passes. Because the engine in intrapsychic therapy is intrapsychic caregiving pleasure, it is important for the therapist not to bear responsibility for the resident's interpersonal world, e.g., not to be associated with milieu decisions resulting in interpersonal losses, such as the decision that it would be dangerous to allow a resident a field trip. When the residents know that therapists do not make these decisions, they are free to turn to the therapeutic relationship with pain-regulated reactions of anger, hurt, and paranoia, thus furthering their dawning awareness of the superiority of the pleasure of therapeutic involvement over the soothing pleasure of pain relief based on meanings of self or other-directed rage.

It should be clear both that the child care workers were an integral and valued component of our program, and also that our approach to the milieu placed them under tremendous stress. In most programs, when residents break the rules or hurt staff or other residents, they are expelled from the program, so that although staff may occasionally feel themselves in danger, they know that if a resident erupts, s/he will be gone (Colson et al., 1991; Gentilin, 1987). We knew that the nature of the adolescents we had accepted meant that initially they were likely to become violent in response to facilitative staff responses as well as in reaction to staff errors and other externally imposed losses. In fact, in the course of this demonstration project there was much property damage, and the staff incurred many bruises, cuts requiring sutures, serious eye injuries, and, on one occasion, a broken nose. One psychotherapist required emergency room treatment as the result of the residents' actions. A focus of this paper concerns the principles for managing violent behavior in a residential setting, and, particularly, for helping staff work with violent adolescents without a loss of morale in a therapeutic program that does not permit total isolation or aversive or punitive measures. The programmatic issue of how to protect clinical staff from violent patients in ways that are not antitherapeutic is rarely addressed because therapeutic concerns tend to be submerged in the presence of violence (Allen et al., 1986; Colson et al., 1986; Colson & Coyne, 1978); the violent patient is typically expelled from a program or responded to solely with the goals of enforced acceptable behavior, deterrence, or containment (Feindler, 1987; Gentilin, 1987; Scavo & Buchanan, 1989). In order to support the staff and help them understand the process of treating the teenagers, we provided them with a weekly, hour-long, supportive and educational inservice training session in which they discussed their interactions with residents.

In addition to helping staff cope with their reactions to client violence, we faced what was often the equally difficult challenge of helping staff to keep their positive feelings for the clients within therapeutic bounds. One regulatory principle of the clinical theory of intrapsychic humanism is the importance of distinguishing between personal and caregiving motives. The etiology of psychopathology as we define it is that the parents' psychic pain prevents them from giving the child the stable well-being that arises from the experience of being the ongoing regulating cause of the parents' caregiving motives. By definition, the individual with intrapsychic pain uses interpersonal experience for intrapsychic well-being. Unstable parenting itself falls into this category, so that, in spite of their best efforts to give their child optimal parenting, parents with intrapsychic pain use their child to gratify personal as well as caregiving motives. A relatively benign example of this phenomenon is the parent who encourages a child to excel at something in order to gratify the parent's needs. A more psychotoxic example is the parent who creates and fosters conflict with the child in order to satisfy a personal need for conflicted relationships.

Thus, central to both intrapsychic treatment and also to milieu treatment regulated by the principles of intrapsychic humanism is the therapist's and child care worker's capacities to be free from the need to use the client for the gratification of personal motives, which include the need to feel helpful, to be liked, etc. Much of our inservice training was devoted to helping the staff distinguish between positive impulses toward residents based on personal motives (such as to take a resident home) and positive impulses based on caregiving, professional motives.

THE DIAGNOSTIC PROCESS IN INTRAPSYCHIC HUMANISM

Intrapsychic humanism takes a unique approach to diagnosis. Whereas other treatment modalities use static categorizations (Grellong, 1987; Lochman, 1984;

Meeks, 1985; Place, Framrose, & Willson, 1985a; Reis & Resnick, 1984) which often overlap and do not lead straightforwardly to therapeutic interventions, the only nosological categories in intrapsychic humanism are treatable and untreatable. The explanation is that the foundational, determining type of all psychopathology, intrapsychic psychopathology, is unitary, in that it represents the use of interpersonal motive gratification (including the gratification of motives for interpersonal pain) to produce a delusional type of core (intrapsychic) well-being. There is only one criterion for treatability in intrapsychic humanism: the conscious motive to become less regulated by psychic pain through a commitment to a treatment relationship. The sole criterion for admission into our program was that the adolescent make at least a one-time expression of the motive to be helped in the program (if she or he disavowed this motive soon after or steadily for the next three years, this did not disqualify her or him).

METHODOLOGY

The Choice of a Naturalistic Research Methodology

The most compelling of the several reasons for choosing a naturalistic method of data collection over an interventionist methodology was that, since the therapeutic action of a treatment process informed by the psychology of intrapsychic humanism depends on the therapist's ability to subordinate personal motives to caregiving motives, and since research-determined interventions are driven by personal motives, research-determined interventions are by definition iatrogenic and contraindicated in intrapsychic treatment. Randomization of subjects was out of the question, since it would have interfered with one of the program's objectives—to treat adolescents who were carefully selected by DCFS as their "most difficult." While it was also not possible to establish a control group (without treatment these adolescents would have been even more dangerous to themselves and others), we did have a standard of comparison already available since each adolescent came to us with a long baseline history of being untreatable by any other method and in any other setting. The behavior problems of all the adolescents referred to us had been chronic since an early age and had been steadily worsening in spite of

the efforts of those programs which had tried and failed to treat these teens.

The Dependent Variables

Although there were no research-determined interventions in our project, a full anamnestic record was kept by all therapists for supervisory purposes and by all child care staff for purposes both of communicating with other shifts and also of bringing to inservice training sessions.[2] From this very full record, the variables that were chosen to indicate client change were the very behaviors that had made these adolescents untreatable by any other method, namely violence toward themselves and others. In assessing the effectiveness of the treatment process for helping these teenagers to gain self-regulatory control over their violent behavior, we chose two types of events as markers: the nature of the teens' aversive reactions to pleasure, and the nature of their response to losses. Examples of losses are therapist and 1-1 vacations, and caregiving lapses by staff.

The *aversive reaction to pleasure* is a key construct in intrapsychic humanism. The aversive reaction to pleasure represents the reactive peremption of an individual's motives for genuine, self-caretaking pleasure by nurture-induced motives for pain, which have the unconscious meaning to the subject of (delusional) self-caretaking pleasure.[3] Aversive reactions to pleasure are not limited to the therapeutic relationship, but characterize all psychopathology, which, you will remember, we define more broadly than any other theory, to include the common unhappiness of everyday life. An example of a relatively benign aversive reaction to pleasure is the otherwise successful individual who feels unaccountably depressed or dissatisfied after achieving a sought-for recognition. Although never before recognized, the phenomenon of the aversive reaction to pleasure is pervasive. Further, clinicians' failure to understand their clients' aversive reactions to pleasure is probably the most unseen and common source of clinicians' dissatisfaction with their work.

The advantage of using violent behavior as the dependent variable is that arguments over whether or not intrapsychic change occurred can be avoided—either an adolescent hits someone or swallows glass or s/he does not. Without exception, in the initial stage of treatment each resident's aversive reactions to pleasure and reactions to externally imposed loss involved violence directed at others and/or themselves.

The dependent variable was studied at certain recurring times: 1) before and after the occurrence of major stresses (losses), such as therapist and child care worker vacations, program relocations, caregiving lapses by program staff, provocative or hostile acts by family members, and all significant events of chance (death, serious illness) and 2) at those times when an aversive reaction could be anticipated. In addition, any time that there was an unanticipated episode of violent behavior, an effort was made to ascertain whether the primary stimulus was a loss or an aversive reaction to pleasure.

CLINICAL RESULTS

Due to limitations of space, we cannot give the milieu process the same attention as the psychotherapy process will receive. The following example is meant to illustrate the important function served by the child care workers. This milieu process involved a resident we will call Carol. Carol came to us with the dual diagnosis of brain damage associated with mental retardation and schizophrenic reaction. She related to the world as an aggressively unsocialized, retarded individual. Carol had been severely abused by her mother, who was diagnosed as both schizophrenic and as a substance abuser. The mother beat the children, and did not feed them regularly, so that Carol reported that they were forced to eat roaches, suck on plaster, and borrow, beg or steal money and food. The mother would also take Carol and her siblings far from home and drop them off like dogs to be gotten rid of.

Carol's 1-1 worker, Adrian, mentioned during an inservice meeting that she had been worried by Carol's behavior the day before. What confused and concerned Adrian was that Carol, who had been reacting to beginning psychotherapy, had approached her insisting that she (Carol) was Carol's sister and that Carol was at home. As Carol described the sister's characteristics, they were all positive and sociable. Carol said she was going to get Carol, left and then came back as Carol, which meant she came back with a lot of negative and aggressive feelings. Adrian wanted to know how to help Carol recover from what she understood to be a delusional state. She was also concerned that Carol might have a multiple personality disorder. The inservice leader suggested that it was more helpful to see Carol's behavior as representing the beneficial effects of her treatment—that it was a communication to staff that she was starting to feel there was another Carol who she had never known was there, who was an unretarded beautiful person. Carol could not feel yet that she owned this sense of self, so she experienced it as an attribute of a sibling, and was trying it out experimentally with the staff. She was soliciting positive feedback from her 1-1 about the good feelings that were emerging from her psychotherapy. This incident also provides a contrast with the prevailing approach to aggressive impulsive adolescents (Agee, 1979; Davis & Raffe, 1985; Edwards & Roundtree, 1981; Feindler, 1987; Scavo & Buchanan, 1989), which is to discourage fantasy and to focus on helping the adolescent become more in touch with "reality." In other modalities (Davis & Raffe, 1985; Feindler, 1987; Grellong, 1987; Lochman, 1984), Carol's statement about being her own sister would have been seen as a process of ego regression or fragmentation of the self. In intrapsychic humanism, regression is defined very differently—as the client's movement away from the use of the therapeutic relationship for genuine self-esteem. By this definition, Carol's sharing of her fantasy was the opposite of regression—it was an attempt to try on a new, more positive self identity in the context of the caregetting intimacy with her 1-1. Adrian was able to apply her newfound understanding of Carol's fantasy the next day, when Carol once again asserted that she was her own sister. Adrian reported that she felt very comfortable making positive responses to Carol's description of the "good sister," and that Carol seemed very pleased with their interchange.

The clinical results from the psychotherapy process will be the focus of the remainder of this paper. To return to Carol, the following psychotherapy interview represents Carol's aversive reaction to pleasure and the therapist's facilitative response.

Initially, Carol had tremendous outbreaks of hostility in which she hit staff and destroyed property. Carol's treatment had been complicated by the fact that her first therapist left the program after another resident hit her with a chair, opening up a gash in her leg that required 100 stitches to close. Over the course of a year Carol made dramatic progress with her new therapist, to the point that it became obvious that she was not in fact retarded. When this interview occurred, Carol had just transferred to a school for children with normal intelligence.

When the therapist arrived, Carol was waiting at the door.

Carol: I got my glasses and went to school.
Therapist: You look marvelous.
Carol: Thanks. She drew a picture and talked about what happened at school and how much she liked it.
Therapist: That's great, I'm so happy you have a school that is just right for you.
Carol: Yes, I'm proud of myself. Proud of you too.
Therapist: Yes, I'm proud of us too—we've done good work.
Carol: I'm glad to have you. She drew a chicken.

This was the first aversive reaction to pleasure. The therapist remained attentive but silent. Then Carol asked the therapist if she had seen the news, that there was a three year old baby who had been beaten severely by her father. The baby didn't die, but everyone said she was retarded. They thought the father had done it, but he was crazy. To this second aversive reaction to pleasure, the therapist responded,

Therapist: He must have been crazy to do that. It must have been terrible for the baby.
Carol: Yes. And my mother died of a drug overdose.
Therapist: You are telling me your parents weren't able to care for you the way you deserved.
Carol: Yes. I took care of me and them, cooked, cleaned, gave all the money I earned to them.

She had a look of great pain and was silent for a moment. Then, assertively,

Carol: I love my parents, we did a lot of things together.
Therapist: I can hear you have a lot of different feelings about them.
Carol: Draw a picture of me before you go.

As you can see from this process, Carol's aversive reaction to the dual pleasures of possessing a conscious experience of core well being that was apart from the identity of being retarded, and of being helped to achieve this through the therapeutic relationship, took the form of bringing to her therapist feelings of love for the parents who had been so abusive towards her. This expression was thoroughly constructive, in that though the need for the experience of self-rage was overriding, in stark contrast to her established pattern of destructive acting out, this time Carol was able to gratify her motive for self-rage within the safety of the caregiving mutuality with the therapist.

This process illustrates that the aversive reaction to pleasure represents a singular opportunity for deepening the therapeutic caregiving mutuality (which is yet another way in which this construct is categorically different from the psychoanalytic notion of negative therapeutic reaction). The aversive reaction to pleasure advances the therapeutic process by bringing to the surface, that is, to the caregiving mutuality, previously invisible manifestations of the pathogenic intrapsychic process in which the significance of caregiving love is attached to experience that objectively represents pain.

AN EXTENDED EXAMPLE OF INTRAPSYCHIC TREATMENT

The focus on the process of one client—Andrew—will be used to concentrate not only on identifying change (outcome) but also on the principles and techniques associated with that change (process). Our dual aims are to describe how change is brought about, and also to indicate that positive change in fact occurred.

The large file that DCFS had on Andrew revealed that in the first 10 years of his life Andrew was in the care of five sets of people. Both his parents were addicted to drugs and alcohol. At age three Andrew's father described his affect storms as "demonic." Andrew was abused by his parents and siblings. For example, one of the parents' disciplinary methods was to make him eat garbage. From his 10th year, he was placed in and expelled from a long series of foster homes and Illinois institutions. When no other Illinois program could be found to accept him, he was sent to an out-of-state institution.

As had happened in each of his in-state failed placements, following a honeymoon period in which the out-of-state institution began to feel that it was getting somewhere with Andrew, he became unmanageably aggressive. Notwithstanding the various types of restraints, including psychotropic medications, administered by the institution, Andrew began to attack, bite and bruise staff members. He also swallowed objects, such as paper clips, straight pins, and buttons. As a result, he had to have abdominal surgery, which the institution took as the opportunity to perform a punitive sterilization. The institution never informed Andrew about the nature of the surgery.

After the surgery, Andrew's attacks on staff continued, and the institution expelled him. He was transferred to a residential treatment center in Illinois, where the familiar pattern of a calm period followed by aggression and expulsion repeated itself. At first, his new therapist noted that Andrew was developing a positive paternal transference to him and that he was trying to provide Andrew with the warm early developmental experiences he had lacked. Two weeks later, when this therapist told Andrew to stop writing on a wall, Andrew picked up a knife and grabbed him. He held the knife at his throat and threatened to kill him. Andrew then made the worker get down on his knees and beg. He hit him in the face, threw him against a chair, and ran out of the room.

Andrew was transferred to a private hospital where a senior child psychiatrist with broad expertise in treating regressed antisocial adolescents advised the Court that he was unable to keep him even in a specialized hospital setting and that he knew of no program anywhere in the United States that would accept him. The psychiatrist said that Andrew was constantly either suicidal or homicidal and that he no longer had any motive to engage positively with anyone. DCFS chose Andrew as one of the "most difficult" adolescents being referred to the intrapsychic humanism project.

Andrew was to remain in his current inpatient unit until mid May, when he was to transfer to our program. However, in late April, Dr. L, the therapist who was to have begun therapy with Andrew, manifested a health problem that required surgery. That fact plus the therapist's impending vacation in August suggested that it would be better to delay Andrew's therapy until September. However, the waiting period he was already undergoing was beginning to unhinge the little self-regulation Andrew could muster, and he began seriously to decompensate. He told our program director that he had rabies and verbalized other manifestations of psychotic soothing, and it was decided that the gain of offering him an immediate therapeutic relationship experience outweighed the loss he would experience from the two premature interruptions.

The first interview went as follows:

Andrew walked down the hall rolling his eyes wildly and singing in a loud, aggressive voice. He had a wild disorganized look, and was barely relating through a dissociative haze.

Andrew: Can I bring some of those toys in from the playroom?

Dr. L: Sure. (Andrew made no move to do so)

Andrew: What do you want to know?

Dr. L: Whatever you feel like telling me.

Andrew: (very defensively) I don't know anything about myself. (Pause) Well, what do you want to know?

Dr. L: Whatever you feel comfortable telling me.

Andrew: I don't have anything to say.

Dr. L: Sometimes you will feel like just being silent in here. I know it is difficult to begin because we are just beginning to get to know each other. And I don't need to know anything at all. I just want to be of help to you.

Andrew: I know all about you.

Dr. L: What do you mean?

Andrew: You are going to be my psycho. . . (he got stuck)

Dr. L: Psychotherapist. Yes. (Explained he would see him twice a week, and what the times were.)

Andrew then related how he liked to play with soldiers, especially Green Beret dolls. Suddenly, he said, "They" did an operation on me.

Dr. L: They did?

Andrew: Yes. They sterilized me. I can't ever have children not ever. (He told the story. How he had swallowed coins at the out-of-state institution, and was told that the surgery he had was merely to remove them. He hadn't known until he got back to Chicago and was examined at another hospital what they had actually done.)

Dr. L: That's criminal and shocking.

Andrew: What they did to me was important.

Dr. L: *Very* important.

Andrew: My father was really mad—but I am madder—they did it to *me.* They were trying to suicide me. I know it—I was the only one who was sterilized. How much time do we have?

Dr. L: Andrew, we have to stop for today. I'll see you Friday at 9:30.

Andrew: Goodbye. It's been nice talking to you.

Dr. L: Goodbye.

In the second interview Andrew was very frustrated at not finding toys he liked and he requested a soldier doll, which the therapist said he would provide. He then sang a song which included the words, "I have a Doctor Feelgood." Shortly after this interview, Dr. L decided that he must tell Andrew both that he had to have minor surgery in the near future and also that he would be taking some vacation time in August. Andrew was extremely distressed by the impending operation and convinced that Dr. L's experience with the medical profession would be similar to his.

In the month and a half before Dr. L's surgery, Andrew was very edgy. He continued to relate Dr. L's upcoming surgery to his own experience, and he tried to kill a pigeon that sat on the window sill. However, he was also able to express concern for his therapist and to recognize that he was going to miss him.

During the time Dr. L was in the hospital, Andrew went on a destructive rampage: he hit another therapist with a chair, kicked in a glass door, and in general was totally out of control. Beginning the first postoperative day, Dr. L called Andrew daily.

Upon his return, Dr. L found Andrew angry, regressed, and regulating his sense of self almost entirely through destructive and self-destructive forms of pain relief. He became upset easily and met every frustration by hitting someone. Over the next few days, Andrew broke the nose of one worker and sent two others to the hospital with eye injuries so severe they could not return to work for a month. Our staff at this point refused to have anything to do with Andrew, and our only hope of keeping him in the program was to put him in a quiet room. His 1-1's remained with him at all times. Dr. L assented to Andrew's request that the frequency of therapy times be increased to every other day. Andrew talked about being lonely and scared and manifestly leaned on Dr. L for help.

In the middle of July, the program director took a five day vacation and Andrew swallowed coins and had to have his stomach pumped at a general hospital. The radiologist said his colon looked "like a junk shop."

The days before Dr. L's vacation were spent trying to work with the staff around letting Andrew out of the quiet room. For the first time Andrew was able to reduce the tension he experienced between therapy interviews by bringing his discomfort to the therapeutic mutuality. For example, when he became upset about something that had happened on the unit, Andrew sat down and wrote Dr. L a note telling him about it. In one interview, he told Dr. L he didn't want to see him anymore, and when Dr. L suggested that those feelings stemmed from his imminent vacation, Andrew broke down and sobbed. The day Dr. L left, Andrew arranged a party for him.

In September, Andrew found the reunion with Dr. L very difficult and brought a friend to many therapy sessions as a way of regulating his tension. There was a tumultuous period when it seemed that two different Andrews were deadlocked in a fierce battle for control, but occasionally he was able to regulate his violent impulses in a new way as the following interview indicates.

Dr. L was meeting with the program director just before therapy time, when Andrew stormed upstairs and began hitting Dr. L, saying that he would teach him to go away.

Dr. L: I can understand your feeling that way, but you don't have to hit me for me to hear you.

Andrew: (Then began hitting the program director. After a minute it became clear that part of the problem was that his friend had asked Andrew to go somewhere with him at a time that would conflict with Andrew's therapy.)

Dr. L: That's a real problem being pulled in two different directions by divided loyalties—I bet we can get a staff person to take your friend where he wants to go and you can meet him after therapy is over.

Andrew: I need to be in the quiet room.

Dr. L: O.K.

Andrew: No. (He looked very sad. Suddenly he took a huge desk and turned it upside down on himself so he couldn't move, creating his own external restraints.)

The staff did transport Andrew's friend, and when it was time for the actual therapy to begin, Andrew studied his baseball cards contentedly for the duration of the session. While the episode began with violence, Andrew also managed to convey the problem to his therapist—his fear of missing his therapy time—thus exhibiting trust that the program would solve that problem for him.

At the end of September, Andrew was subjected to an acute, unexpected loss when the hospital administration abruptly reclaimed our unit. Andrew alternated between fury and desperate closeness. When he first heard the news, he slapped Dr. L hard a number of times, then in a menacing manner vowed to keep him imprisoned in the therapy room. Dr. L made no move to force Andrew to let him out, and in time Andrew relented and told the staff he had hit his therapist. He then spent the rest of the session expressing regret for what he had done. Dr. L said, "Both of us wish we could be locked in in the sense of being able to continue to have therapy here."

In the last interview in the hospital unit, Andrew sang a song about there being "a thin line between love and hate." He asked Dr. L to write something to him on his mattress which he was using like a yearbook, asking people to inscribe notes to him on it. Dr. L wrote, "To Andrew: For all we have done together in the past and can do together in the future."

Andrew was very pleased and thanked him. But as the end of the therapy time neared, and the magnitude of the loss sank in, Andrew began hitting Dr. L very hard. Dr. L reminded him of what he had sung, that there was a thin line between love and hate. Andrew allowed Dr. L to leave the therapy room, but then lunged at him again. Dr. L knew he appeared upset. Later Dr. L was in his office on the unit and Andrew came in and hugged him and said he was very sorry.

Andrew: You're upset.

Dr. L: Yes, it's a sad day.

Andrew: Because I hit you?

Dr. L: No, because we have to leave here before we are ready.

Andrew initially had a difficult time adjusting to the group home to which we relocated. He would beg Dr. L not to leave at the end of the session, and hit him a number of times. At this point, at Andrew's request, Dr. L was seeing him seven days a week and calling him every night. In the middle of October, a staff member failed to get Andrew back in time for his therapy hour, and that night Andrew hit the staff person and broke his glasses. Andrew called Dr. L, who said he knew he was upset about missing therapy and that everyone still wanted him there. Andrew ran out the door and around the block, and, with his child care worker chasing him, he raced back in the door and went to sleep. When Dr. L came in the next day, Andrew was waiting at the door for him with some poems he had written. Andrew said one of them was about his resolution not to hit people anymore, but to try to talk to them. This was an example of the fact that Andrew's motives to feel better through inflicting pain were becoming consciously unattractive to him, even though he couldn't always control them.

In the interviews immediately following, Andrew was elusive and unpredictable, and clearly having an aversive reaction both to the closeness he had felt and to his new wish to control his aggressiveness. In the grip of an aversive reaction to pleasure, clients unknowingly attach the meaning of loss (pain) to each

experience of care-getting pleasure with the therapist, because conscious caregetting pleasure interferes with their unconscious use of internalized relationship unpleasure for delusional inner well-being. As a result, the client consciously experiences the therapist as a source of pain and trouble rather than as a recognized and available ally. Swept up in this dynamic, two days later Andrew slapped Dr. L hard enough that the next day the program director told Andrew that he would only be seeing Dr. L with someone else in the room. Andrew looked very depressed and promised he would never hurt Dr. L again and that, if he ever did, then Dr. L could always have someone else sit in on the therapy. The program director assented to his plea. The next two days he maintained regulatory control, but then, in the face of staff errors, he blew up, hit two staff, and ran off. The staff called the police, who found Andrew and took him to a hospital emergency room. The program director and Dr. L spent the night with him there, making arrangements for him to go to the State adolescent inpatient unit because our staff adamantly refused to have him back. Dr. L continued the treatment at the hospital during the interval needed to help the group home staff accept him back.

One day after he returned Andrew told Dr. L he had gotten a girl pregnant and showed him lots of pictures of pregnant women. He told Dr. L he liked him a lot, and then had an immediate aversive reaction and took a tack, put it in his mouth and claimed to have swallowed it. Dr. L told him that there were better ways to help himself feel better, expressed his concern for him, and declared that Andrew would have to go to the emergency room. After ten minutes of listening to Dr. L's concerns, Andrew confessed that he hadn't swallowed the tack. Dr. L realized Andrew was telling him the truth, and praised him for having shared the pain of the need to hurt himself and just as importantly, for the self-restraint it took to keep his self-rage on the level of fantasy instead of actually swallowing something harmful. For the duration of Andrew's stay in the program, there were only two further episodes of acting out the need to hurt himself, and in neither instance did he have to go to the emergency room. Increasingly, his need for self-rage was gratified solely on the level of fantasy, to the point where motives that at one time resulted in physical self-abuse now presented as a form of banter. He would tell his therapist or the staff that he had harmed himself, would listen to their concerned response, and then would laugh and say the story was untrue.

It took Andrew a longer time to gain regulatory control over his aggression toward others. During Andrew's therapy hour a week or two later a terrific fight erupted in the group home and one of the other adolescents put his hand through a window and had to go to the hospital. Andrew was very upset by this and declared that he was leaving the house. He turned on Dr. L and began seriously strangling him, saying he was going to kill him. He relented to the point of being able to call the program director to announce that he was hitting his therapist. Hanging up, he said with clenched teeth that if Dr. L made a sound Andrew would break his nose, then finish him off before anyone could rescue him. He talked about wanting to stab Dr. L in the groin. He said he had never actually killed anyone, but that maybe he would tonight. He called another staff member and told him that he was hitting Dr. L. He kept telling Dr. L to stay silent. He turned out the lights and said he was going to kill Dr. L in the dark. After what seemed to Dr. L like an endless time, Andrew said he was sorry. He let go of Dr. L and walked him downstairs. Then he burst into tears and again told Dr. L how important he was to him. Dr. L told him he would stick with him. He helped Dr. L on with his coat. (From this interview on, Dr. L was never again alone with Andrew—Andrew's one-to-one staff person and sometimes a third person sat in on every therapy hour.)

The subsequent therapy sessions were very difficult for Andrew both because he was faced with the self-imposed loss that he would never again be able to see Dr. L alone, and also because the presence of the third person interfered with Andrew's delusional belief that he was capable of controlling his violent outbursts. In a representative hour, Andrew saw Dr. L coming and ran into the bathroom saying he was going to jump out the window. Then he started hitting at Dr. L. His primary 1-1, *Bert*, held him.

Dr. L: Talk to me, don't hit me.
Andrew: I can't talk to you with Bert there.
Dr. L: It's necessary, Andrew.
Andrew: You're afraid of me.
Dr. L: Yes.
Andrew: Hit me back.
Dr. L: That won't help—I can't help you by hitting back.

(Andrew began talking about how he was going to kill Dr. L. He was getting so agitated that Dr. L felt he should leave, that at any moment he might break away from Bert.)

Dr. L: Can I say two things?
Andrew: Go ahead.
Dr. L: I know that part of you feels very angry, given the betrayals you experienced with people in your past. . .
Andrew: (screaming) I know what you are talking about don't ever say "past" to me again.
Dr. L: The other thing is that in terms of your saying you don't want me for a therapist, I have to be fair to all parts of you and they aren't all talking, so I am going to keep coming.
Andrew: (consumed by the murderous rage) GET OUT!

With child care workers holding him Andrew would recite lists of ways in which he was going to murder Dr. L. He said he never wanted Dr. L to come back, and he demanded that he leave. Dr. L would stay as long as he felt the child care workers could tolerate the strain of restraining Andrew, and he kept saying to Andrew that he had to be fair to all parts of him. Over the next week and a half, Andrew came to accept the reality of the third person(s) and thus began to relinquish his own delusions of having regulatory control over his violent impulses. At the end of this time he brought a problem to Dr. L about a friend of his, and when Dr. L helped him find a solution, he hugged Dr. L and told him he valued him and that he would never really kill him.

A week later, after a fight broke out between two residents, Andrew blew up, grabbed a kitchen knife and hit one of the staff. However, when the staff indicated that they were afraid to wrestle him for the knife, Andrew ran out the door and two blocks directly to the fire station, where he allowed the firemen to take the knife away and call the police, who arranged his commitment to Read Zone Center, where he remained for three days.

A scheduled physical examination provided the stimulus for Andrew's beginning the process of mourning the punitive sterilization he had undergone at the out of state institution. On the day he was to see his physician, he talked seriously about killing himself. When Dr. L made the connection between his suicidal feelings, the visit to the doctor, and his operation, he broke down and sobbed in terrible pain. The next interview he ran into the kitchen and got a knife, saying he was going to kill Dr. L because he was the only reason he ever felt upset. As the child care work-ers held Andrew, Dr. L repeated over and over that the pain did not originate with him, but was inside Andrew. (This pattern in which the pain of Andrew's aversive reaction to the pleasure of turning to Dr. L for help was first manifested as negative feelings about himself, and then was reorganized in a paranoid shift in which Andrew externalized the source of his painful feelings onto Dr. L, continued for the next two months. However, the duration of his regulation by paranoid rage progressively shortened until finally he would permit himself to have a reunion with Dr. L in the same interview.)

Although he never actually needed to go to Read Zone Center again, in the following months, Andrew began saying he wanted to go there whenever he was upset to the point that he feared losing control. He also began to realize that when he was upset he would hit out at anyone to reduce his tension.

In December 1974 the therapy process afforded evidence of a beginning change in Andrew's capacity for self-regulation. Dr. L told Andrew of his plan to take a week's vacation. Andrew became very angry, but, in contrast to the previous summer, he did not pursue a soothing based on the pain produced by harmful acting out. Instead, his motive to pursue core well-being through the pleasure of the therapeutic caregiving relationship remained hegemonious, even though Dr. L's motives were the source of a significant loss. In one session, he ran into the kitchen and grabbed a knife, but he was able to put it down him-self without needing to go to the firehouse, and then he returned to go back to playing cards with a staff member.

After Dr. L's Christmas vacation, some things began coming together for Andrew. He was able to go to his physician without being paralyzed by pain, and, most importantly, he was able to start school. Andrew had been diagnosed as retarded, but the staff had no ques-tion that Andrew possessed above average intelligence. However, Andrew's reactive pride in response to his relentless experience of self-denigration had always prevented him from admitting that he was not up to grade level. In fact, he was such a talented story teller that he could fake reading, making up stories as he recognized a word or two, and it was a long time before the staff and Dr. L realized that he could only read at a first grade level. His increasing reflectiveness made it possible for him to recognize both that the therapeutic relationship could help him with his anxi-eties about going to school, and also that he could reg-ulate that relationship to make it even more facilita-tive. Accordingly, he worked with Dr. L to rearrange the times of the therapy so that he could leave for school immediately afterward, drawing on the caregiv-ing relationship to enable him to stay in balance until school was to begin.

At the beginning of March, Dr. L had to change the time of a therapy hour. The next day when Dr. L went in, Andrew was very angry. He called his father and said he had a terrible therapist. His father obviously told him to hit Dr. L, because Andrew's reply was "That wouldn't work because he would just tell me to stop hitting him." Andrew hung up, ran down the stairs and out the door and, grabbing a brick from the alley, smashed in the windshield of Dr. L's car. Later, he was very apologetic and Dr. L told Andrew he knew that part of him had felt very betrayed when the time was changed.

As Andrew became more consciously positive about his therapeutic relationships, he decreasingly needed to turn to his parents as a source of pain with the meaning of pleasure. But his aversive reactions to relinquishing this source of self-rage meant that he was constantly on edge and the slightest loss from the milieu was more than he could bear. One day, his 1-1, Bert, failed to come in. Andrew called Bert and stayed on the phone for 3/4 of the therapy time, using his relationship with him for regulatory control. While he was on the phone he was quite friendly to Dr. L, but the moment the call ended, he threw the phone at him. Andrew said he was sorry and that he had promised Bert he wouldn't hurt Dr. L. He said Dr. L could sit down, that he would be O.K. Dr. L did sit down because Andrew had recently demonstrated a newly won capacity for a self-regulation that enabled him to keep this sort of short-term promise. A moment later Andrew hurled a plastic case at Dr. L, blackening his eye.

Andrew: (immediately) I'm really sorry.
Dr. L: That pain is inside you, Andrew, it stays with you; it's not left behind by hitting me.

From that day forward, Andrew was not allowed to bring hard objects into his therapy.

In early April, 1975, Andrew was faced with another tragic event when an older sister died in a car accident. Andrew was able to get through this wrench-ing experience without destructive acting out by drawing on his caregiving relationship with the staff and Dr. L to help shore up his capacity for self-regulation. He was able to ask Dr. L not only to come to the funeral, but also to come with him to his father's house before the service, which Dr. L did.

The structural shift in Andrew toward a pain-free type of self regulatory agency continued so that increasingly he was regulated by the ideal of anchoring his sense of core well-being in the caregiving relationship rather than in the gratification of pain-regulated motives. When Andrew missed a therapy hour, instead of hitting someone or swallowing something, he would go to bed. If Dr. L had to change a therapy hour, Andrew asked him to bring him some candy rather than breaking his windshield or blackening his eye. Increasingly, Andrew's aversive reactions occurred in the form of fantasies and associations. One day, Dr. L brought him a toy racing car he had asked for, and he reacted with manifest pleasure, showing it to everyone in the house, and thanking Dr. L profusely. He said he wanted to take a picture of the racing car with Dr. L and his 1-1. Then he immediately began to sing "On shaky ground."

Andrew: You know what Bert told me? Bert told me about this paranoid schizophrenic girl who wanted Nelly (a child care worker) to take her out to the Y and when her request was granted, she became totally paranoid and said she hadn't wanted to go and demanded that she be returned home immediately or she would attack the 1-1.

Andrew's story of the girl who reacted negatively to getting what she wanted was an aversive reaction to the pleasure of Dr. L's responsiveness to his request, but it occurred in the form of associations conveyed within the intimacy of the therapeutic relationship and indicated that he was beginning to recognize that he could be angry in reaction to feelings of closeness.

Andrew developed a new resilience to caregiving lapses by the staff and to the losses caused by other residents' aggressiveness. In an incident that directly paralleled the earlier time when he had strangled Dr. L, a fight broke out in the house and one of the residents started hitting one of the staff. Andrew intervened and shepherded the boy into the staff room and talked to him until he calmed down.

Instead of getting angry at Dr. L for purposes of pain relief whenever he felt badly, he began to turn to

the therapeutic caregiving relationship and specifically, would ask Dr. L to help him understand his discomfort. The following interview also illustrates the helpful role the milieu staff played vis a vis the psychotherapy. Near the end of the therapy session, Andrew told his 1-1 that he had had a good dream the night before. He and his sister-in-law had been stuck in an elevator together and they were laughing and smoking marijuana. He asked Bert curiously why he would dream about being stuck in an elevator when that had never happened to him.

Bert: Ask Dr. L.

Andrew: Why would I Dr. L?

Dr. L: You can dream about anything you have ever known or could imagine or that has ever happened to you.

Andrew: My sister in law died three years ago—she was stuck in an elevator once (silence).

Dr. L: I have a hunch that in your sleep last night you were dreaming about your sister.

Andrew: (angry) If I wanted to dream about her I would dream about her.

Andrew: (suddenly very soft) I was thinking a lot about her last night. I miss her so much. Remember when you went to tell me she was dead, and I already knew. It's just not the same without her. I don't like my family so much any more. We used to crack up and joke and play. It's not as much fun. What's wrong with you, Dr. L?

Dr. L: It's just so sad about your sister.

Andrew: I want to go to the cemetery and bring some flowers to her grave, O.K. Bert?

Bert: Yes.

Dr. L: I'm sorry, but I have to leave for today.

Andrew: I won't be here tomorrow—I'm going to my friend's house and I'm not coming back for therapy (an aversive reaction that he shared within the therapeutic relationship).

Dr. L: I'll be here, though and I'll hope to see you. Bye.

Andrew: Bye.

Andrew began to have sustained times of enjoyment without dysfunctional types of aversive reactions. For the first time he would call Dr. L and tell him he had had a good day and relate his activities.

The balance between Andrew's motives had shifted to the point that he would manifestly worry about slipping back to a reliance on the old, destructive forms of soothing, and he used Dr. L as an ally to try to help him decide how to take care of himself.

Dr. L's second summer vacation came and went, and Andrew did not become violent toward himself or others. One of the most significant changes Andrew manifested was his increasing willingness to allow Dr. L to enhance his self-awareness of forms of his pain that were invisible to him, and his capacity to avoid destructive aversive reactions to this potent type of therapeutic pleasure. Whereas in the beginning of therapy Andrew consistently soothed himself every time he felt badly by blaming Dr. L for his dysphoria and becoming enraged if Dr. L mentioned motives he was not feeling at the moment, now he often welcomed Dr. L's comments and worked hard to understand them. The day after Dr. L returned from vacation, the following interview occurred.

Andrew spent a long time saying he was going to kill himself, drink dye, swallow aspirins, run out in the street and get hit by a car, etc. After about fifteen minutes of this Dr. L said that he thought that some of this pain was coming from the interruption caused by his vacation, from the fact that they hadn't seen each other for so long.

Andrew's mood seemed to change after Dr. L said this and he played cards.

Andrew was fine the rest of that day and evening.

Andrew was also increasingly receptive to hearing about his aversive reactions to pleasure. This interview took place ten days after the one just mentioned.

Andrew called Dr. L from his father's house before therapy and said he wasn't coming and hung up.

Dr. L: (Called him back). I think I can help you with what is happening, if you could listen to me for a minute.

Andrew: O.K.

Dr. L: You are really learning to be good to yourself—for weeks you have been taking fantastic care of yourself, but the old part of you that tried to feel better by not being good to yourself is really reacting to that good care.

Andrew: (very sadly) I sent the 1-1 back—I can't make therapy now.

Dr. L: He should have waited anyway as Bert would have, but he's new.

The next day Andrew was clearly struggling to understand the pain-motivated part of himself, which

was becoming more and more alien. He puzzled: "You know, I don't understand something. There's this lake near where my father lives where children are always drowning when they try to skate on it, but they still go back and skate and drown."

Even when Dr. L had to cancel a therapy hour, which was a stimulus that had led to disaster in the past, Andrew was able to keep his anger on the level of fantasy, and to use both the 1-1 sitting in on therapy and Dr. L to bolster his desire to keep the relationship pleasure intact.

Andrew occasionally became violent after this, though he never caused any significant injury, and his aggressive behavior only occurred in response to chaos caused by other residents or significant caregiving lapses by staff. He himself wondered at the change. In March, 1976, on the anniversary of his sister's death, a time he would normally have become violent, he said, "You know what? I haven't broken any windows in a long time." His 1-1 said, "Yes. You are really learning there are better ways to deal with the pain." Andrew had an aversive reaction and said, "but I am today," but immediately added, "No I'm not. I don't feel like breaking windows." On days that were difficult for him, he began to report having dreams of hitting people, but would remain calm during his waking hours.

His attitude toward school continued to undergo a metamorphosis. Whereas initially his shame made him hide his inadequacies, he was now able to spend thirty minutes of sustained work doing difficult multiplication problems and asking for help when he got stuck. Within a few months he was reading at a seventh grade level.

Another important aspect of Andrew's progress was his sustained effort to mourn his punitive sterilization—that is, to respond to his pain about it by turning to the therapeutic relationship rather than by becoming violent or self-destructive. In an interview that occurred in March of 1976, Andrew appeared wearing a new pair of pants and a shirt and feeling pleased about how he looked. The compliments he received stimulated him to think about his loss. Characteristically, he began by denying the fact of the loss.

Andrew: I went to the doctor and he told me my sterilization was reversed.

Dr. L: Wow.

Andrew: I can be a father (pause). Can't I?

Dr. L: Any baby you care for and love becomes yours.

Andrew: But I don't want someone else to go through all the work of having it and giving it up, that isn't right.

Dr. L: If they can't take care of it and give it to someone who can, whoever loves and cares for a baby is the father or mother.

Andrew: But I can have my own. (pause deadly serious) Can they reverse it? (pause) Can they?

Dr. L: Probably not, Andrew.

Andrew: Why not?

Dr. L: Because it is difficult under the best circumstances and your surgery was done badly, which makes it even harder.

Andrew: If they can. . .I'm going to stop talking about it (he left the room but came back in minutes). Can't they fix it?

Dr. L: No, they should be able to, but they probably can't.

Andrew: But they can transplant hearts.

Dr. L: I know.

Andrew: By the time they figure it out, I'll be dead.

As time went on, Andrew was able to call the out-of-state institution himself and ask them why they had done this to him, and, even, to make an appointment to see our medical consultant to have him explain the exact nature of the surgery he had undergone. A few months later, Andrew made an appointment with someone at a local adoption agency to discuss the possibility of adopting a baby in the future.

Andrew's relationship with Dr. L continued to evolve into a stable and conscious source of pleasure. After the program director had told him he could never be alone with Dr. L again, he had a sustained aversive reaction to the pleasure of being prevented from following his motives to harm the therapeutic relationship, and he would either studiously ignore Dr. L, or he would try to attack him. While the 3rd person held him back, Andrew would describe in detail all the sadistic things he intended to do to Dr. L when he got the chance.

Subsequently, he would talk to his 1-1 about private and important things knowing Dr. L was listening. However, because the 1-1's lack of training often meant that his responses were inadequate, Andrew would leave the room, allow Dr. L to tell the 1-1 what to say, then return, listen to the 1-1, and calm down, knowing full well where the response had originated. Finally, he was able not only to address questions to Dr. L directly, but also to turn to him as a source of superior caregiving when the 1-1 let him down in some way.

The worst and, ultimately, insuperable problem Andrew (and all of us) faced was DCFS's abrupt insistence on rewriting its contract with the program and reducing the per diem it was paying for the adolescents, which in effect meant closing the program. When we first agreed to accept these "most difficult" clients, we set only one condition—that as long as things went well, the state would leave the residential component of the program intact for a minimum of five years. We explained that the clients' symptoms would be much improved after a year or two, but that the clients would continue to need the same level of support they had been receiving for some time after their symptoms improved or many of the gains that had been made would be lost. DCFS accepted our conditions, but two years later, when the residents had improved demonstrably, it concluded that either the adolescents had not been as ill as it had thought, or, alternatively, that they were so much better they did not require the same level of support. The nature of the clients' personal histories and relations with DCFS was so chaotic that they were all represented by the public defenders' office, and the public defender, an ally of the program, managed to use the courts to stave off the State's desire to cut back the clients' treatment services from January until October 1976. At that point, DCFS forced the program to move out of the home in which it had been located. One of the adolescents reacted by stealing money and running away. Shortly thereafter, Andrew hit one of the staff in the face, sending him to the hospital. It was clear that, although for a year he had been able to tolerate staff and therapist vacations, caregiving lapses from the milieu staff, the constant violence in his family, chaos in the residential setting, and aversive reactions without seriously hurting anyone or himself or needing hospitalization, the threat of the program ending overwhelmed his newly won capacity for self-regulatory control.

Andrew chose to live with his father rather than to accept temporary quarters in another program. When this arrangement predictably failed, Andrew was very reflective and said that Dr. L had been right, that it hadn't worked out at his father's.

Dr. L: There are some things you can only really find out by going through.

Andrew: Well next time I'll listen.

Dr. L: But if you can listen next time, it will be because you went through it this time.

Andrew: (somberly and prophetically) I'll tell you what I do know now. I know that the day will come when I will be well enough to live on my own, but that I have to take my time and not rush it.

Dr. L: That's exactly right.

Unfortunately, this story does not have the happy ending that Andrew was reaching for with increasing stability and determination. In spite of heroic efforts on the part of the public defenders' office, DCFS managed to reduce the residents' per diem to the point that, in spite of our assiduous private fund raising efforts, our program was forced to close altogether. Although DCFS was convinced that the adolescents would continue to improve as outpatients, it was clear to us that this was not true. We knew that the residents still needed a milieu that could support their newfound capacities for self-regulation, especially given their intense aversive reactions to the pleasure of their progress. In our judgment, if the residents were confronted with a milieu that was both less supportive and also exposed them to new losses, they would not continue to improve and would be unable to maintain the gains they had made. The only question in our minds was the extent to which they would return to violence as a source of self-soothing. As the program directors emphatically told DCFS, in Andrew's case, at least, we were convinced that he would not be alive in two years if his treatment were prematurely terminated.

Dr. L said goodbye to Andrew with great sorrow and regret. We knew that Andrew had not reached the point at which it would be safe for him to be seen as an outpatient, although it was equally clear that that day would have come if DCFS had not prematurely ended the residential component of the program. Dr. L never saw Andrew again after the program closed, although Andrew called him occasionally. From his calls, Dr. L knew that Andrew was in and out of foster homes and was hospitalized a number of times at a state facility.

Though foreseen, it was still a terrible shock to all of us when eighteen months after we were forced to close, a call came from the public defender telling us that Andrew had died playing "chicken" on a motorcycle.

CONCLUSION

Since space considerations preclude a full discussion of the clinical implications of our program, we will focus on the question most readers may have, namely, given the numbers of troubled, acting out adolescents, what is the real significance of a treatment approach that is so expensive and necessitates such high staffing patterns? The answer is twofold. First, it is meaningful to know that even the "most difficult" adolescents are not beyond help—that if these adolescents do not receive treatment, it is because a decision has been made about the allocation of scarce resources, not because they are incorrigibly feral. Second, many adolescents—who are not driven to enact this degree of interpersonal violence and who could be treated in a less intensive setting—currently are pronounced hopeless or handled with repressive measures unlikely to result in lasting change because of the failure to understand their true dynamics (Gilliland-Mallo & Judd, 1986; Grellong, 1987; Grey & Dermody, 1972; York, York & Wachtel, 1983). To give but one example, a recognition of the existence of aversive reactions to pleasure can help mental health professionals treating troubled adolescents to maintain their commitment and effectiveness in the face of behavior that otherwise appears to signify the adolescents' imperviousness to dedicated therapeutic caregiving.

Notes

1. Not only were there no therapeutic programs that could either contain or help these teens, but, more fundamentally, there was no other theory that led straightforwardly to treating them (Cornsweet, 1990; Place, Framrose, & Willson, 1985b; Rinsley, 1990). The theories that were available for treating aggressive or self-destructive teenagers were developed and implemented with teens who were much less disturbed and violent than this population (Aichhorn [1965] worked with adolescents who were "lazy" or involved in petty thievery; Redl and Wineman [1957] worked with latency age children in residential care; others implemented behavioral programs with incarcerated teens). Further, we were very uncomfortable with the authoritarian and intrusive nature of many of the behavioral approaches, such as the token economies that were being used with less aggressive populations (for recent examples of behavioral approaches, see Kupfersmid, Mazzarins, & Benjamin, 1987; a similarly authoritarian model is the 'tough love' approach, e.g. Newton, 1985).

2. In order to protect the confidentiality of the patient and family in conformity with statutory law and the social

work code of ethics, we have disguised both identifying information and the specifics of the case process.

3. Freud's notion of negative therapeutic reaction and our construct of aversive reaction to pleasure differ in cause, scope, and perceived significance. Freud posited that the negative therapeutic reaction occurred only in treatment, and he ascribed it to his construct of the death instinct, which he advanced as an incorrigible instinctual drive derivative that aims for self-defeat and destruction (Freud, S., 1953-1974 *The Ego and the Id, Standard Edition, vol. 19*, pp. 49-50).

Conclusion

The kind of future that social and behavioral scientists can build depends in part on how we understand our past. The social and behavioral sciences have been influenced profoundly by the logical positivist approach to research. Positivism was a prescriptive and proscriptive approach to generating scientific knowledge that assumed that scientific knowledge could and should be relatively context-free and comprised of static universal propositions whose truth was guaranteed. Under those requirements, knowledge about the intricacies of human cultures and relationships and knowledge that explicitly served the aims of social justice—forms of knowledge that are the wellspring of human community—often were devalued as inherently unscientific.

The history of the influence of logical positivist beliefs on the approaches to research in the field of social work illustrates that those beliefs are contrary to efforts to realize scientific aims important to social workers and other social and behavioral scientists: potent human services and reflective social change. For too long, the social and behavioral sciences have been hampered by inordinately restrictive positivist assumptions about scientific knowledge and the knowledge-generation process.

The social and behavioral sciences are unique in that the subjects scientists often want to know about are humans and their societies. Accordingly, the process of scientific research can engage both the knower (the participant/researcher) and the known (the participant/subject) in discovering new facts about human nature and human society as well as in formulating and trying out new solutions for social problems. In turning away from the false security offered by the restrictiveness of positivism, social and behavioral scientists turn towards the rich ideas offered by the postpositivist researchers whose contributions form the basis for the heuristic paradigm. The early postpositivist philosophers, such as Kuhn, Hanson, and Simon, began by assuming that studying how scientists actually work would yield promising insights about generating scientific knowledge. In concert with that respect for working scientists, the heuristic paradigm has been developed as an approach to knowledge that can be used by those who work actively to solve our pressing human problems—clinicians, program administrators, policymakers, community organizers, and educators—so that we can benefit from the informed judgment that can accrue only from practical experience.

The knowledge of the social and behavioral sciences is not limited to an arcane set of principles that are known by and influence only a select few; it infuses culture at all levels. Humans understand themselves according to how they are understood by each other. Therefore, the social and behavioral sciences have a direct impact on human society and self-understanding. Examples abound of ways in which scientific knowledge continually transforms how human beings know each other and create their societies, ranging from theories of child development to which parents refer in caring for their children, to social policies for providing elderly people with adequate resources. Because the common objects of inquiry in the social and behavioral sciences—humans and their societies—are complex, reflective, and relational, the overly reductionistic assumptions of positivism have had unfortunate consequences for how human nature, relationships, and communities have been conceptualized and engendered. Fortunately, a community of social and behavioral scientists now has emerged that eagerly embraces and contributes scientific knowledge that is free of positivism's restrictions and that actively promotes human welfare. The knowledge of the social and behavioral sciences is in itself a change process that can be developmental and growth-enhancing. As the new community of scientists builds on humane, postpositivist foundations for knowledge, they can discover and realize a fresh potential for using science to enrich and transform human society.

Appendix: Selections from Logical Positivism and Its Derivatives

The following selections present the original formulations of some of the most important ideas associated with the logical positivist metatheory that subsequently were imported into the social and behavioral sciences:

1. Operationism;
2. The verification theory of meaning;
3. The belief that induction can be eliminated from theory testing and that scientific theories can be tested using only deductive reasoning;
4. The belief that scientific knowledge can be demarcated from all other forms of knowledge using falsification.

Percy Bridgman, a physicist at Harvard University, advances operationism in the following selection from his 1927 book, *The Logic of Modern Physics*. Moritz Schlick advances the verification theory of meaning in the selection included here. A professor at the University of Vienna, Schlick held the chair of the physicist and positivist philosopher Ernst Mach. Schlick was one of the leaders of the group of philosophers known as the Vienna Circle, which began meeting in 1924 (Hanfling, 1981b). The Vienna Circle disbanded after Schlick was killed in 1936 and other members emigrated because of the political upheavals of World War II. Many members of the Vienna Circle continued to have widespread, international influence. They sponsored conferences and authored the journal *Erkenntnis* as well as many books, among them the beginning sections of a work initially conceived by the logical positivist philosopher Otto Neurath, the *International Encyclopedia of Unified Science* (Hanfling, 1981b, p. 103). Schlick's selection is from a series of lectures Schlick gave between 1925 and 1936 entitled "Form and Content. An Introduction to Philosophical Thinking." Sir Karl Popper is a noted German philosopher of science, currently a professor at the London School of Economics. In this selection from his

1934 book, *Logik der Forschung* (*The Logic of Scientific Discovery*, 1959), he addresses the logical positivists' questions and aims, issues that, in his opinion, they had not resolved satisfactorily.

Although contemporary philosophers of science disagree with the prescriptions of the logical positivists (Suppe, 1977), the questions the positivists raised are still important, particularly their concern with the nature of scientific knowledge. The logical positivists believed that the knowledge of the natural sciences and the social and behavioral sciences could be appraised and systematized using essentially the same principles; they believed in the unity of the sciences and aimed to formulate all scientific knowledge in the mathematical language of physics. As noted in Chapter 1, positivism traditionally was associated with the belief that ideas not grounded in specific types of observation obscure scientific knowledge and that scientists should aim to describe observable phenomena and formulate general laws to predict events in nature. The logical positivists took a distinctive tack: Rather than defining philosophical problems in terms of being (focusing on ontological assumptions), they formulated issues by focusing on language. More specifically, in their philosophy of science, they focused on demarcating scientifically meaningful statements. The earlier positivists, by contrast, were not preoccupied with restricting what counted as scientifically meaningful statements, and they did not aim to excise metaphysical ideas from the philosophy of science. In fact, Auguste Comte, who is generally regarded as the founder of positivism, extended his metatheory of knowledge into a religion complete with a temple, sacraments, and venerable individuals (positivist philosophers) in which the worship of humanity substituted for the worship of God.

Logical positivism was a reaction against British and German idealism. Philosophers have developed many distinct versions of idealism over time, but idealism traditionally is regarded as the view that reality is or depends on mind or ideas. Idealist philosophers disagreed with the realist belief that there are mind-independent objects of knowledge. The logical positivists reacted, in particular, against the idealism of Georg Hegel (1770–1831), who argued most notably that the world is a manifestation of absolute mind or spirit. Hegel's philosophical system elaborated the knowledge of absolute mind.

The logical positivists aimed to excise from the philosophy of science those ideas they believed to lack empirical consequences. They termed such ideas "metaphysical." Since the time of Aristotle, metaphysics has been a multifaceted term that refers to discussions about the nature of reality that go beyond purely factual or scientific issues. Contemporary philosophers recognize that metaphysics informs all philosophy to some degree, including such topics as whether space and time are real. The logical positivists used the term *metaphysics* in a pejorative sense; they labeled "metaphysical" those propositions they considered scientifically meaningless. They included statements about subjective experience, such as feelings, in their category of metaphysical propositions (Carnap, 1963/1991a). They conceptualized the aim of philosophy of science as appraising and systematizing scientific knowledge, and they thought that by proscribing metaphysical (or scientifically meaningless) ideas they could arrive at a superior form of scientific knowledge. In effect, the logical positivists formulated prescriptions about what scientists should and should not investigate, based on their beliefs about the ways of knowing that were scientifically acceptable. Schlick wrote:

The chaotic state in which philosophy has found itself throughout the greatest part of its history is traceable to the unlucky fact that firstly it has accepted certain formulations with far too much naivete, as genuine problems, without first carefully testing whether they really possessed a sound meaning; and secondly, that it has believed the answers to certain questions to be discoverable by particular philosophical methods that differ from those of the special sciences. (1925–1936/1981, p. 87)

SCHLICK'S VERIFICATION PRINCIPLE

Following Ludwig Wittgenstein's early work, Schlick wanted to find a way to con-nect the meaning of propositions with something more than language, in part because he recognized that language was so context-dependent that it could not be a secure basis for the lawlike system of scientific knowledge the logical positivists hoped to generate (some of the other logical positivists, including Rudolf Carnap, disagreed with Schlick on this point; see Hanfling, 1981a, p. 16). For example, Schlick said:

> In order to arrive at the meaning of a sentence or proposition we must go beyond propo-sitions. For we cannot hope to explain the meaning of a proposition merely by presenting another proposition . . . I could always go on asking "But what does this new proposition mean?" You see there would never be any end to this kind of inquiry, the meaning would never be clarified if there were no other way of defining it than by a series of proposi-tions. (quoted in Hanfling, 1981b, p. 19)

In the following selection, Schlick claims that a proposition is scientifically meaningful if it is verifiable, that is, "if we are able to describe a way of verifying it, no matter whether the verification can be carried out or not" (1938/1979, p. 35). Like Bridgman, Schlick tied meaning directly to procedures or methods: "the dis-covery of the meaning of any proposition must ultimately be achieved by some act, some immediate procedure" (quoted in Hanfling, 1981b, p. 19). The logical posi-tivists believed that the verification criterion constituted a revolution in philosophy. It was an all-or-nothing criterion that they wanted to use to excise many thorny, unsolved problems from philosophy by labeling them metaphysical, or scientifically meaningless (see the selection by Scriven in Chapter 5).

One criticism of the verification theory of meaning as a way to demarcate scien-tific from nonscientific knowledge was that to implement a method of verifying a proposition, one must *already* know its meaning (Hanfling, 1981b). To illustrate, one must already know the meaning of the terms used in a proposition such as "the sun is the center of the solar system" to implement a procedure to verify that proposition. Further, in any act of knowing, one necessarily makes ontological assumptions, although the logical positivists branded ontological assumptions as sci-entifically meaningless. In his landmark critique of the tenets of logical empiricism, including the verification principle, Quine observed that even to talk about the objects of knowledge requires that one assume such objects exist such that they can be experienced by others: "the positing of physical objects is . . . coeval, I expect, with language itself. For language is social and so depends for its development upon intersubjective reference" (1948, p. 42).

The verification principle did not withstand the criticism it aroused, so the logical positivists revised it. As Rudolf Carnap, a prominent logical positivist, wrote in 1936, the verification theory of meaning was so restrictive that it eliminated many significant propositions of science and history from the category of scientific meaningfulness (p. 421). Carnap said his most stringent criterion of scientific meaning, testability, was roughly equivalent to Bridgman's concept of operationism (Carnap, 1963/1991a). However, because he recognized that many scientific terms were not testable, Carnap revised his views and advanced a less stringent criterion, confirmability, for scientific meaningfulness. A proposition was confirmable (and hence was scientifically meaningful) if one knew what empirical evidence could be used to support or contradict it. Carnap recognized that "if by verification is meant a definitive and final establishment of truth, then no [synthetic] sentence is ever verifiable." He concluded that "we can only confirm a sentence more and more" (1936, p. 420).

BRIDGMAN'S OPERATIONISM

Bridgman was not a member of the Vienna Circle, yet in the following selection, published in 1927, he also sets forth a view of scientific knowledge that focuses on defining scientifically meaningful statements. Like the logical positivists, Bridgman uses the category of "meaninglessness" to describe concepts that do not meet his criteria for scientific meaning (1927, p. 6). Bridgman centers his discussion on the definition of a scientific concept. Writing in the context of the overturn of classical physics by Einstein's discoveries, Bridgman recognizes that new experiments will always uncover new facts that differ completely from our experience and that they will transform what we conceive of as experience. He aims to prevent scientists from accepting concepts that later can be shown to be false. (As Bridgman says, Newton's concept of absolute time had been accepted for some time, only to be overturned by Einstein's conclusions.) Bridgman recommends the following to accomplish his aim of ensuring more certain scientific knowledge:

1.   Although our understanding of "external nature" may change as new facts are uncovered, there is a path to understanding that does not have to be "subject to future change, namely that part which rests on the permanent basis of the character of our minds" (1927, pp. 1–2). By delimiting how we know the objects we study, Bridgman hopes to make knowledge more secure in the face of the continuing flux of external nature.

2.   The scientist should adopt an attitude of "pure empiricism," devoid of a priori ideas that could "determine or limit the possibilities of new experience" (1927, p. 3). Bridgman assumes that the researcher can engage in acts of knowing without using a preliminary conceptual framework (or heuristic).

3.   The two preceding positions led Bridgman to formulate his most famous recommendation: Scientists should define the meaning of concepts in methodologi-

cal terms: "the concept is synonymous with the corresponding set of operations" (1927, p. 5). This is the "operationism" (also called "operationalism") that became prevalent in positivist approaches to social and behavioral science (Leahey, 1980). Bridgman uses the example of Newton's concept of absolute time, saying that if Newton had applied operationism to absolute time, he might have recognized that the concept was scientifically meaningless (1927, p. 6). He says that operationism recognizes that concepts are always relative to context and that methods of knowing, such as an experimental design and specific measuring instruments, are part of that context. Bridgman's formulations are both prescriptive and proscriptive. For example, he says, "*In principle* the operation by which length is measured should be *uniquely* specified. If we have more than one set of operations, we have more than one concept" (1927, p. 10). This prescription highlights one of the most important assumptions underlying the logical positivist philosophy: the assumption that prescriptions and proscriptions will yield a superior form of scientific knowledge.

David Hull outlines some of the problems with operationism in the paper included in Chapter 5. Bridgman defines operationism as the belief that a concept can be synonymous with a set of operations. Hull critiques that belief: "synonymy is a relation which holds between linguistic entities. Two words or two statements can be synonymous, but a concept cannot be synonymous with a set of operations" (Hull, 1968, p. 438). He recognizes that one of Bridgman's aims in formulating operationism was to ensure "the objectivity of science." For example, "if the operations are such that they can be performed publicly by any qualified person, then the intersubjectivity and repeatability so important to the objectivity of science are guaranteed" (Hull, 1968, pp. 438–439). However, as Hull says, Bridgman had to acknowledge that operational definitions cannot be free of symbolic operations (e.g., values and theoretical assumptions), which "certainly lessens the guarantee initially connoted by the term 'operational definition'" (1968, p. 439).

The following illustration shows some of the difficulties with operationism. If you want to estimate a child's potential for educational achievement, you necessarily make a subjective determination about the measuring instrument you will use. If you use an IQ test, as often has been done, you will obtain a very different measurement than if you watch the child learn new ideas in class and evaluate the child's responses to the teacher. How do you decide which instrument to use? How do you determine the accuracy of a given measurement? (e.g., see the Preface.) Even if you use the same instrument, is it always the same observation? If not, what counts as the same observation? As Hull (1968) points out, because some subjectivity is always involved in all decisions about how to know anything, operationism cannot free the measurement process of subjectivity.

POPPER'S DEDUCTIVE METHOD OF THEORY TESTING AND FALSIFICATION

Popper distinguished his views from those of the logical positivists, yet he wanted to address some of the same issues they raised. For example, although he also wanted to find a methodological criterion to demarcate scientific from nonscientific knowledge, he strongly disagreed with the use of verification as a criterion for meaningfulness.

> The repeated attempts made by Carnap to show that the demarcation between science and metaphysics coincides with that between sense and nonsense have failed. The reason is that the positivistic concept of "meaning" or "sense" (or of verifiability, or of inductive confirmability, etc.) is inappropriate for achieving this demarcation—simply because metaphysics need not be meaningless even though it is not science. In all its variants demarcation by meaninglessness has tended to be *at the same time too narrow and too wide:* as against all intentions and all claims, it has tended to exclude scientific theories as meaningless, while failing to exclude even that part of metaphysics which is known as "rational theology." (Popper, 1963/1991, p. 183)

Popper emphasized that conclusive confirmation of a proposition was impossible, yet he wanted to find a method for appraising the correctness of scientific theories. In the following selection, Popper begins to address that problem by describing an aspect of the problem of induction—"how to establish the truth of universal statements which are based on experience" (p. 28). Popper distinguishes between inductive and deductive inference. *Deductive inference* is inference from universal premises to singular instances. Deductive inference is often believed to be truth preserving because if the premises of a deductive inference are true, then its conclusion also must be true.[102] For example, if I know for sure that all students like Swiss chocolate, and I know for sure that you are a student, I can deduce for sure that you like Swiss chocolate. By contrast, as was noted in Chapter 3, inductive inferences can never be certain. For example, I may observe that your entire class enjoys Swiss chocolate, and I may infer that students enjoy Swiss chocolate; however, I may be surprised and encounter a student who abhors Swiss chocolate, thereby disconfirming my inference. Unlike deductive inference, inductive inference cannot be truth preserving; as Popper emphasizes, "any conclusion drawn in this way may always turn out to be false: no matter how many instances of white swans we may have observed, this does not justify the conclusion that *all* swans are white" (1934/1959, p. 27). Popper points out that scientists and nonscientists use inductive reasoning all the time and that philosophers have long debated about principles that can be used to justify inductive inferences. Popper, however, believes that "a principle of induction is superfluous" and "must lead to logical inconsistencies" and that the problems associated with inductive logic are "insurmountable" (1934/1959, p. 29).

Instead Popper recommends a "deductive method of testing . . . the view that a hypothesis can *only* be empirically *tested* . . . and only after it has been advanced" (1934/1959, p. 30). He thus separates theory testing from discovering and generating theories. He outlines four standards for testing theories:

1. "Internal consistency;"
2. The "logical form of the theory" (e.g., ruling out tautological theories);
3. Comparison with other theories to determine whether or not the theory is a scientific advance;

4. "[T]he testing of the theory by way of empirical applications of the conclusions which can be derived from it," primarily through testing predictions deduced from the theory (1934/1959, pp. 32–33). Popper asserts that such standards avoid the use of inductive logic (1934/1959, p. 33).

In the following selection, Popper rejects the logical positivists' approach to demarcating scientific from nonscientific knowledge. He anticipates the criticism that the theory-testing standards he advocates do not demarcate scientific from non-scientific knowledge sufficiently, and he recommends falsification as a criterion that can be used for this purpose: "I shall require [of a scientific system] that its logical form shall be such that it can be singled out, by means of empirical tests, in a negative sense: *it must be possible for an empirical scientific system to be refuted by experience*" (1934/1959, p. 41). In Popper's view, for a proposition to be scientifically meaningful, it must be stated in such a way that it can be falsified. Popper's criterion has been applied by philosophers such as Adolf Grunbaum (1984), who argued that Freud's theories are not scientific, because his propositions are not stated so that they can be refuted. For example, if the analyst's interpretations do not tally with the patient's subjective experience, the analyst may interpret the patient's reports of her or his experience as a manifestation of defense mechanisms. Accordingly, if the patient disagrees with the analyst's interpretation, the analyst may view the patient's disagreement *not* as a disconfirmation of the analyst's interpretation but as the patient's denial of a fact. Because under such conditions Freud's propositions could not be falsified, Grunbaum argued that they were unscientific.

Postpositivist philosophers of science have criticized Popper's beliefs. They have noted, for instance, that one cannot avoid using induction in theory testing, in part because multiple theories can explain a given observation, and one must use induction to choose a theory (Rychlak, 1980). For example, a child's overactive behavior may be explained as a learned response to a stimulus, as a manifestation of a neurological abnormality, or as the child's search for a pathological form of self-soothing. Choosing a particular explanation for the child's behavior requires inductive inference (see also Heineman Pieper, 1981). Other philosophers have argued that prescribing falsification as a criterion for demarcating scientific from nonscientific knowledge is as flawed as the logical positivists' use of confirmation. For example, Ian Mitroff said, "falsification can never be more certain than confirmation because the act of falsification involves judgments which are no more certain than those involved in confirmation" (1973, p. 273).

Ironically, one of the implications of logical positivism was that its restrictive epistemological assumptions undercut the position that there is a mind-independent reality that can serve as a standard for appraising the truth of theories. For instance, Carnap believed that propositions about the nature of reality were metaphysical and therefore scientifically meaningless (1963/1991a). As Copleston wrote, because "empiricism started with the demand for respect for facts and then went on to resolve facts into sensations," it arrived at "the odd conclusion that though science is purely descriptive, there is really no world to be described, apart from the contents of consciousness" (1966/1985, p. 117). Einstein, in a letter to Schlick, disagreed with that implication of the logical positivists' position:

In general your presentation fails to correspond to my conceptual style insofar as I find your whole orientation so to speak too positivistic . . . I tell you straight out: Physics is the attempt at the conceptual construction of a model of the real world and its lawful structure. . . . In short, I suffer under the unsharp separation of Reality of Experience and Reality of Being. . . . You will be astonished about the "metaphysicist" Einstein. But every four- and two-legged animal is *de facto* in this sense a metaphysicist. (quoted in Manicas, 1987, p. 188)

KEY TERMS

A priori and a posteriori   **Analytic and synthetic statements**
Fact   **Proposition**

DISCUSSION QUESTIONS

1. What does Popper mean when he says that he eliminates "psychologism" from an account of scientific knowledge?

2. Define Bridgman's operationism. Refer to Hull's critique of Bridgman's operationism (see the selection by Hull in Chapter 5), and formulate the central points of Hull's critique.

3. a. Operationism has had an important and often overlooked influence on how we know other humans. For example, positivist social and behavioral researchers often have assumed that to obtain reliable knowledge about other people we must operationalize theoretical terms and so use standardized instruments to measure attributes of the people we want to know about. What are some of the instruments that you have seen used to measure different human characteristics?

    b. Humans are sensitive and changeable, and so researchers using the same measurements often obtain very different data about the same person. The problem is compounded if the person is seen in a different context or at a different point in his or her development (Bronfenbrenner, 1979a; Ceci & Bronfenbrenner, 1991). To illustrate, a child's potential for learning varies considerably depending on the quality of nurturing relationships available to the child. In their study in Chapter 8, Heineman Pieper and Pieper describe how intrapsychic humanism was used to treat two teenagers whom educational diagnosticians had evaluated as uneducably mentally retarded. During intrapsychic treatment, the teenagers attained normal educational achievement for their age. To begin to learn, the teenagers had to overcome a major obstacle: the view of themselves as retarded that had been imposed on them. What information might *not* be collected when data about a child are limited to operationalized indicators?

4. What happens to the use of single-case studies as one method of generating scientific knowledge if you accept Popper's view that inductive inference is not an acceptable way to generate scientific knowledge?

5. **a.** Select a behavioral or social science theory. Using a problem related to that theory, show how you can use (i) deductive inference and (ii) inductive inference.

   b. Using a particular research finding as an example, show how there are many possible explanations for that finding.

6. **a.** Wesley Salmon (1989) says that in the first half of this century, a common view in the philosophy of science was that science cannot provide explanations and that explanations belong in the realms of theology and metaphysics. Instead, science aimed simply to describe. How do those views stem from logical positivism? Hint: Consider how any explanation entails ontological assumptions.

   b. Positivist social and behavioral researchers often eschew causal explanations (why) in the belief that they can at best describe correlations between phenomena. Yet, "at present," says Salmon, "virtually all philosophers of science of widely diverse persuasions agree that science can teach us, not only that, but also why" (1989, p. 181). Do you think an important task of the social and behavioral sciences is to tell us why as well as to describe? Why or why not?

7. Consider Copleston (1966/1985), quoted earlier.

   a. How do the epistemological assumptions of both positivism and relativism in effect rule out some ontological assumptions?

   b. How does Hudson's statement "if you can't measure the client's problem, it doesn't exist" (1978, p. 65) illustrate how restrictive epistemological assumptions circumscribe the "reals" that can be studied scientifically?

Meaning and Verification

MORITZ SCHLICK

... In the preceding arguments we have often made use of the principle that the meaning of a statement can be given only by indicating the way in which the truth of the statement is *tested*. What is the justification of this principle? There has been a great deal of dispute about this question in modern philosophy, and certainly it deserves our full attention, for if I am not mistaken it is *the* fundamental principle of philosophizing, and neglect of it is the cause of all serious troubles in metaphysics.

The object of every proposition is to express a fact. It seems, then, that in order to state the meaning of the proposition we have to indicate the fact which it expresses. But how strange! Is not the fact in question already indicated by the proposition itself? In fact, we have convinced ourselves long ago . . . that a proposition expresses its own meaning, it does not stand in need of an explanation. An explanation which said *more* than the proposition itself would not be a correct explanation of it, and if it said the same thing as the proposition it would be superfluous. As a matter of fact, when we hear somebody make a statement and ask him 'What do you mean by it?' we usually get and expect as an answer a mere repetition of the first statement, only in different words, and very often we are actually satisfied by this procedure which is nothing but a translation from one language into another one. Why are we satisfied? Evidently because we did not *understand* the first expression, but do understand the second one.

This last remark gives us the clue to solve the paradox. We can ask for a meaning only as long as we have not understood a statement. And as long as we have not understood a sentence it is actually nothing but a series of words; it would be misleading to call it a proposition at all. A series of words (or other signs) should be regarded as a proposition only when it is understood, when its meaning is comprehended. If we agree to use our terms in this way there will be no sense in asking for the meaning of a proposition, but we may very well inquire (and that was our actual problem) after the meaning of a *sentence* or any complex of signs which we suppose to express something.

Now there is not the slightest mystery about the process by which a sentence is given meaning or turned into a proposition: it consists in defining the use of the symbols which occur in the sentence. And this is always done by indicating the exact circumstances in which the words, according to the rules of the particular language, should be used. These rules must be taught by actually applying them in definite situations, that is to say, the circumstances to which

Source: From "Meaning and Verification" in *Philosophical Papers* (Vol. 2, 1925–1936, pp. 309–312, 361–369) by M. Schlick and edited by H. L. Mulder and B. van de Velde-Schlick, 1979, Boston: D. Reidel. (Original work published 1938, "Form and Content. An Introduction to Philosophical Thinking" in *Gesammelte Aufsätze 1926–1936* by M. Schlick, Vienna: Gerold & Co.) Copyright 1979 by G. M. H. van de Velde. Reprinted by permission.

they fit must actually be *shown*. It is of course possible to give a verbal description of any situation, but it is impossible to *understand* the description unless some kind of connection between the words and the rest of the world has been established beforehand. And this can be done only by certain *acts*, as for instance gestures, by which our words and expressions are correlated to certain experiences.

Thus, if I utter a sentence, and you ask me what I mean by it (perhaps by shrugging your shoulders or by looking at me with a vacant stare), I shall have to answer you by translating the sentence into a language you understand, or, if you do not understand any language yet, I shall have to teach you one; and this involves certain acts on our part, I have to make you undergo certain experiences. All your future understanding will be by virtue of these experiences. In this way all meaning is essentially referred to experience.

It must be clear by this time that there is only one way of giving meaning to a sentence, of making it a proposition: we must indicate the rules for how it shall be used, in other words: we must describe the facts which will make the proposition 'true', and we must be able to distinguish them from the facts which will make it 'false'. In still other words: The Meaning of a Proposition is the Method of its Verification. The question: 'What does this sentence mean?' is identical with (has the same answer as) the question: 'How is this proposition verified?'

It is one of the most serious errors in philosophy to think of a proposition as possessing meaning independently of the possible ways of its verification. People have fallen into hopeless confusion because they believed they knew the meaning of a phrase, and yet had to declare themselves unable *in principle* to define any circumstances in which it would be true. As long as it is logically impossible for me to indicate a method of ascertaining the truth or falsity of a proposition, I must confess I do not know what is actually asserted by the proposition.

After you have once seen this clearly you will no longer understand even the possibility of a different opinion: you will recognize that no opinion can even be formulated without admitting the truth of the preceding remarks. The view contained in these remarks has, it is true, found many opponents, but the very name by which it is usually called shows that it has not been properly understood. It is known as the 'experimental theory of meaning'. But it is not a theory; there can be no 'theory' of meaning. A theory is a set of

hypotheses which may be either true or false and have to be tested by experience. It is not necessary to make hypotheses about meaning, and they would come too late, because we must presuppose meaning in order to formulate any hypothesis. We have not made any assumptions, we have done nothing but formulate the rules which everybody always follows whenever he tries to explain his own meaning and whenever he wants to understand other people's meaning, and which he never actually violates—except when he begins to philosophize.

In establishing the identity of meaning and manner of verification we are not making any wonderful discovery, but are pointing to a mere truism. We are simply maintaining that a proposition has meaning for us only if it makes *some* kind of difference to us whether it is true or false, and that its meaning lies entirely in this difference. Nobody has ever explained the meaning of a sentence in any other way than by explaining what would be different in the world if the proposition were false instead of true (or vice versa).

This, I am sure, cannot be denied. But the great objection usually raised against the view I have been defending consists in maintaining that the 'difference in the world' expressed by the proposition may not be observable or in any way discoverable. In other words: if a sentence is to have meaning for us we must, of course, know which fact it expresses, but it may be absolutely impossible for us to find out whether the fact actually exists. In this case the proposition could never be verified, but it would not be meaningless. Therefore, our adversaries conclude, meaning is distinct from verifiability, and not dependent upon it.

This argument is faulty on account of an ambiguity of the word 'verifiability'. In the first place, one might call a proposition verifiable, if the actual facts are such as to permit our finding out its truth or falsity whenever we feel like it. In this sense it would be impossible for me to verify the statement: 'There is gold to be found in the earth 300 feet below my house', for there are many empirical circumstances which absolutely prevent me from discovering its truth; and yet the assertion was certainly not nonsensical. Or take the statement: 'On the back side of the moon there are mountains 10,000 feet high'. It is not improbable that no human being will ever be able to verify or falsify it, but which philosopher would be bold enough to declare the sentence to be devoid of meaning! I think it must be clear that we have nothing to do with this use of the term 'verifiability', and that we must have had something else in mind when we said that the Meaning of a Proposition was its Method of Verification.

As a matter of fact, we call a proposition verifiable if we are able to *describe* a way of verifying it, no matter whether the verification can actually be carried out or not. It suffices if we are able to *say* what must be done, even if nobody will ever be in a position to do it. . . .

Every proposition is essentially verifiable. This is the most fundamental principle of philosophizing; we shall do well to devote the rest of our time to its elucidation.

Whenever we assert anything we must, at least in principle, be able to say how the truth of our assertion can be tested; otherwise we do not know what we are talking about; our words do not form a real proposition at all, they are mere noises without meaning. This must be admitted by everyone who asks himself sincerely and carefully how he becomes aware of the *meaning* of a proposition. What criterion have we to find out whether the meaning of a sentence has been grasped? How can I assure myself, for instance, that a pupil has properly understood the sense of a proposition which I try to explain to him?

There is only one answer, and it is this: a person knows the meaning of a proposition if he is able to indicate exactly the circumstances under which it would be true (and distinguish them from the circumstances which would make it false). This is the way in which Truth and Meaning are connected (it is clear that they must be connected in some way). To indicate the meaning of a proposition and to indicate the way in which it is verified *are identical procedures*.

Every proposition may be regarded as an answer to a question, or (if the question is difficult) as the solution of a problem. A sentence which as the grammatical form of a question (with an interrogation mark at the end) will have meaning only if we can indicate a method of answering it. It may be technically impossible for us to do what the method prescribes, but we must be able to point out some way in which the answer could be found. If we are, in principle, unable to do this, then our sentence is no genuine question at all. And where there is no question, there can be no answer; we are confronted with an 'insoluble problem'. This is the only case of an 'absolutely unanswerable question': it is unanswerable, because it is no question. It may look like one, because outwardly it has the grammatical form of a question, but in reality it is a meaningless series of words, followed by a question mark.

Now we understand the nature of the so-called insoluble problems about which philosophers have worried so much: they are insoluble not because their solution lies in a region forever inaccessible to the knowing mind, not because they pass the power of our understanding, but simply because they are no problems. Unfortunately—no, fortunately—all genuine 'metaphysical questions' turn out to be of this kind. Metaphysics, as we stated before, consists essentially in the attempt to express content, i.e., in a self-contradictory enterprise, but it is by no means easy to see that a question inquiring into the nature of content is nothing but a meaningless arrangement of words. The difficulty of perceiving this is the real cause of all the troubles from which philosophical speculation has been suffering for about twenty-five centuries. If the nonsense in the typical metaphysical issues had been as easy to detect as the lack of meaning (say) in the question, 'is time more logical than space?', most of the futile discussions of our great thinkers would have been avoided . . .

The question of metaphysics is so important that I may perhaps be permitted to give another illustration of the way in which it disappears from our philosophy.

Descartes, as is well known, maintained the view that only human beings were endowed with 'consciousness' and that we must look upon animals as mere automata behaving exactly 'as if' they were 'conscious' creatures, but in reality being condemned to a 'souless' existence. One may easily and justly point out that Descartes' argument might be extended to our human fellow beings. How can I ever be sure that my human brothers and sisters are more than mechanical automata and possess a consciousness similar to my own?

Most philosophers, I believe, are inclined to regard this question as a genuine question, and to answer it in this way: the behavior of all human beings, and also the behavior of all animals down to insects and worms, is, in the most important respects, so similar to my own behavior that I must infer the existence of consciousness 'within' them; it is an inference by analogy, it is true, but based on such striking correspondence that it must be regarded as valid with a degree of probability which can hardly be distinguished from certainty. Nevertheless these philosophers admit that the probability is not exactly equal to 1, that it is not absolute certainty, and that here we are confronted with a case where absolute certainty can never be gained. According to their opinion the existence of consciousness in beings other than myself is a typical insoluble problem. There is no imaginable way of deciding it.

What are we to think of it? Our verdict is simple: if the question is really definitely unanswerable it can be only because there is no meaning in it. And if this is so, if there is no problem at all, there can be no *probable* answer either, it must be nonsense to assert that animals and human beings 'very likely' possess consciousness. We can speak of probability only where there is at least a theoretical possibility of discovering the truth.

The fact is that our question is actually meaningless because it is interpreted in a metaphysical way: the word 'consciousness' (one of the most dangerous terms in modern philosophy) is supposed to stand for content, and this is the reason why it was declared that we could not be absolutely sure of its existence except in our own ego, for did not content require intuition, and was not intuition restricted to our own consciousness? I know that most people find it very difficult to admit that there is no sense in this reasoning, but I must insist that without admitting it we cannot even take the first step in philosophy.

Our 'problem' is meaningless, because the word 'consciousness' occurs in it in such a way that we cannot possible express what we mean by it. It is used in such a way that it makes no discoverable difference in the world whether my fellow creatures are 'conscious' beings or not. Whether the answer is 'yes' or 'no', it cannot be verified, and this means that we did not know what we were talking about when we put the question.

It is one of the most important tasks of philosophy to analyze how the word 'consciousness' must be interpreted in order to make sense in different contexts. We know, of course, that some structure must be indicated by it. Keeping this in mind we can easily give a non-metaphysical interpretation to our question: 'Are animals conscious beings?' If it is to be a real, legitimate question it can mean nothing but: 'Does the behavior of animals show a certain structure?' Now it has become a genuine problem and can receive a definite answer. The answer is, of course, not given by the philosopher but by the biologist. It is his business to define carefully the kind of structure which comes into question (he will probably describe it in terms of 'stimuli' and 'response'), and to state by observation in each case whether a particular animal or human being under particular circumstances exhibits this particular structure. This is an entirely empirical statement to

which truth or probability may be ascribed in the same way as to another expression of a fact. It must be noted that wherever the phrase 'a person is conscious (or unconscious)' is used in everyday life it has a perfectly good meaning and is verifiable because it expresses nothing but observable facts (which a physician, for instance, may enumerate). It is only on the lips of the metaphysician that the word is employed in a different way, in a 'philosophic' way, which he believes to be a consistent interpretation, but which actually is a metaphysical abuse.

Our discussion of the 'problem' of other peoples 'consciousness' or 'soul' has shown that the confusion is due not only to a careless use or lack of analysis of the terms 'consciousness' or 'self', but that a misunderstanding of 'existence' has also something to do with it. For clearly our question could have been formulated by asking: 'Does "consciousness", or "a soul", or "a mind" *exist* in other living beings?' The same misunderstanding is the cause of the nonsensical problem concerning the 'existence of an External World'. In order to get rid of such meaningless questions we need only remember, once for all, that, since *every* proposition expresses a fact by picturing its structure, this must also be true for propositions asserting the 'existence' of something or other. The only meaning such a proposition can have is that it pictures a certain structure of our experience. This was seen quite clearly even by Kant. He expressed it in his own way by saying that 'reality' was a 'category', but from his explanation of his own thought we can infer that what he had in mind practically coincides with the interpretation we have to give to the term 'existence'. According to this interpretation such questions as, 'does the inside of the sun exist?', 'did the earth exist before it was perceived by any human beings?' etc., have a perfectly good sense, and must, of course, be answered in the affirmative. There are certain ways of verifying these positive answers, certain scientific reasons for believing them to be true, and they assure us of the reality of mountains and oceans, stars, clouds, trees and fellow men by the same methods of observation or experience by which we learn the truth of any proposition. If by 'external world' we mean this empirical reality, its existence is no problem, and if a philosopher means something else, if he is not satisfied with empirical reality, he must tell us what he does mean. He says he is concerned with 'transcendent' reality. We do not understand this word and ask him for an explanation, which he may give by saying that 'transcendent' refers to genuine metaphysical Being, not to merely empirical reality. If we ask him what is meant by this distinction and how a proposition asserting transcendent existence of anything can be verified, he must answer that there is no way of ever testing the truth of such a proposition definitely. We must inform him that, if this is the case, there is no meaning in his propositions about a metaphysical external world, and that we must continue to use this phrase in the good old innocent sense in which it stands for stars, mountains, trees as contrasted with dreams, feelings and wishes which form the 'internal' world. We must inform the philosopher that it is not his business to tell us what is real and what is unreal—this must be left to experience and science, but it is his business to tell us what we *mean* when we judge of a certain thing or event that is 'real'. And in every case he can answer the question concerning the sense of such a judgment only by pointing to the operations by which we should actually verify its truth. If I know exactly what I have to do in order to find out whether the shilling in my pocket is real or imagined, then I know also what I mean by declaring that the shilling is a real part of the external world, and there is no other meaning of the words 'real' or 'external world'.

For, let us repeat it once more: the complete and only way of giving the meaning of a proposition consists in indicating what would have to be done in order to find our whether the proposition is true or false (no matter whether we are actually able to do it). This insight is often called 'the experimental (or operational) theory of meaning', but I should like to point out that it would be unjust to call it by such an imposing name. A 'theory' consists of a set of propositions which you may believe or deny, but our principle is a simple triviality about which there can be no dispute. It is not even an 'opinion', since it indicates a condition without which no opinion can be formulated. It is not a theory, for its acknowledgement must precede the building of any theory. A proposition has no meaning unless it makes a discoverable difference whether it is true or false; a proposition whose truth or falsity would leave the world unchanged does not say anything about the world, it is an empty sentence without meaning. 'Understanding' a proposition means: being able to indicate the circumstances which would make it true. But we could not describe these circumstances if we were not able to recognize them, and if they are recognizable it means that the proposition is, in principle, verifiable. Thus, understanding a statement and knowing the way of its verification is one and the same thing.

This principle is nothing surprising or new or wonderful: on the contrary, it has always been followed and used by scientists as a matter of course, at least unconsciously, and in the same way it has always been acknowledged by common sense in everyday life; the only place where it has been neglected is in philosophical discussions. Science could not possibly act otherwise, because its whole business consists in testing the truth of propositions, and they cannot be tested except on the strength of our principle.

Now and then it happens in the development of science that a concept is used in a vague manner so that there is no absolute clarity about the verification of the propositions in which the concept occurs. Within certain limits of accuracy the ordinary tests of their truth may suffice for years or centuries, and then suddenly some contradiction will show up and force the scientists to inquire carefully into the signification of his symbols. He will have to stop and think. He will pause in his scientific investigations and turn to philosophic meditation until the meaning of his propositions has become perfectly clear to him.

The most famous instance of this kind, and one which will forever be memorable, is Einstein's analysis of the concept of Time. His great achievement, which is the basis of the Restricted Theory of Relativity, consisted simply in stating the *meaning* of assertions that physicists used to make about the simultaneity of events in different places. He showed that physics had never been quite clear about the signification of the term 'simultaneity', and that the only way of becoming clear was to answer the question: 'How is the proposition "two distant events happen at the same time" actually verified?' If we show how this verification is done, we have shown the *complete* sense of the proposition and of the term, and it has no meaning besides. All those philosophers who have condemned Einstein's ideas and theory (and some are condemning it even to this day) do it on the ground that there is a simultaneity the significance of which is understood without verification. They call it 'absolute simultaneity'. This sounds very well, but unfortunately those philosophers have failed to tell us how their simultaneity can actually be distinguished from that of Einstein; they have not been able to give us the slightest hint how anyone can ever find out whether two distant events occur 'absolutely simultaneously' or not. Considering this, I think we must take the liberty of regarding their assertion as meaningless.

I have just alluded to the difference between the scientific attitude and the philosophical attitude. We can formulate it by saying: Science is the pursuit of Truth, and Philosophy is the pursuit of Meaning.

Of course the two cannot actually be separated. It is impossible to discover the truth of a proposition without being acquainted with its meaning. No one can essentially contribute to the progress of science without having before his mind the genuine and final sense of the truths he is investigating. That is why all great scientists have also been philosophers. They have been inspired by the philosophic spirit. Nevertheless the distinction must be made, and it has the advantage of giving a satisfactory answer to the endless questions concerning the nature and task of philosophy. Our definition of philosophy gives a clear and full account of its relationship to science and makes it easy to understand the historical development of this relationship.

Philosophy is most certainly not a science, not even the Science of the sciences, and it has been one of its greatest misfortunes that it has been mistaken for one and that philosophers have, in outward appearance, adopted scientific methods and language. It often makes them a little ridiculous, and there is a good deal of truth in the way in which Schopenhauer describes the contrast between the genuine philosopher and the academic scholar who regards philosophy as a sort of scientific pursuit.

A science is a connected system of propositions which form the result of patient observation and clever combination. But philosophy, as Wittgenstein has put it,[1] 'is not a theory, but an activity. The result of philosophy is not a number of "philosophical propositions", but to make propositions clear.' As a matter of fact, the results of the pursuit of meaning cannot be formulated in ordinary propositions, for if we ask for an explanation of a meaning, and the answer is given in a sentence, we should have to ask again, 'but what is the meaning of this sentence?' and so on. If we are to arrive at any sense at all, this series of questions and definitions cannot go on forever, and the only way in which it can end is by some prescription that will tell us what to *do* in order to get the final meaning. You want to know what this particular note here signifies? Well, strike this particular key of the piano! That puts an end to your questions.

Thus a teacher of philosophy cannot provide us with certain true propositions which will represent the solution of the 'philosophical problems': he can only teach us the activity or art of thinking which will enable us for ourselves to analyze or discover the meaning of all questions. And then we shall see that the so-called philosophical problems are either meaningless combinations of symbols, or can be interpreted as perfectly sound questions. But in the latter case they have ceased to be philosophical and must be handed over to the scientists, who will try to answer them by his methods of observation and experiment.

Kant, who in spite of his complicated philosophy had many bright moments of profound insight, has said that he could teach philosophizing, but not philosophy. That was a very wise statement, and it implies that philosophy is nothing but an art or activity, that there are no philosophical propositions, and consequently no system of philosophy. Another great thinker who seems to have been well aware of the nature and place of philosophy was Leibniz. When he founded the Prussian Academy of Science in Berlin and sketched out the plans for its constitution, he assigned a place in it to all the sciences, but philosophy was not one of them. He must have felt somehow that it could not be regarded as the pursuit of a particular kind of truth, but that the determination of meaning must pervade *every* search for truth.

When we look for the most typical example of a philosophical mind we must direct our eyes towards Socrates. All the efforts of his acute mind and his fervent heart were devoted to the pursuit of meaning. He tried all his life to discover what it really was that men had in their minds when they discussed about Virtue and the Good, about Justice and Piety; and his famous irony consisted in showing his disciples that even in their strongest assertions they did not know what they were talking about and that in their most ardent beliefs they hardly knew what they were believing.

As long as people speak and write so much more than they think, using their words in a mechanical, conventional manner, disagreeing about the Good (in Ethics), the Beautiful (in Aesthetics) and the Useful (in Economics and Politics), we shall stand in great need of men with Socratic minds in all our human pursuits. And since also in science the great discoveries are made only by those superior minds who in the routine of their experimental and theoretical research keep wondering what it is all about and therefore remain engaged in the pursuit of meaning, the philosophical attitude will be recognized more than ever as the most powerful force and the best part of the scientific attitude.

---

[1]*Tractatus Logico-Philosophicus*, London 1922, 4.112.

Broad Points of View

Percy Bridgman

Whatever may be one's opinion as to our permanent acceptance of the analytical details of Einstein's restricted and general theories of relativity, there can be no doubt that through these theories physics is permanently changed. It was a great shock to discover that classical concepts, accepted unquestioningly, were inadequate to meet the actual situation, and the shock of this discovery has resulted in a critical attitude toward our whole conceptual structure which must at least in part be permanent. Reflection on the situation after the event shows that it should not have needed the new experimental facts which led to relativity to convince us of the inadequacy of our previous concepts, but that a sufficiently shrewd analysis should have prepared us for at least the possibility of what Einstein did.

Looking now to the future, our ideas of what external nature is will always be subject to change as we gain new experimental knowledge, but there is a part of our attitude to nature which should not be subject to future change, namely that part which rests on the permanent basis of the character of our minds. It is precisely here, in an improved understanding of our mental relations to nature, that the permanent contribution of relativity is to be found. We should now make it our business to understand so thoroughly the character of our permanent mental relations to nature that another change in our attitude, such as that due to Einstein, shall be forever impossible. It was perhaps excusable that a revolution in mental attitude should occur once, because after all physics is a young sci-

490

ence, and physicists have been very busy, but it would certainly be a reproach if such a revolution should ever prove necessary again.

NEW KINDS OF EXPERIENCE ALWAYS POSSIBLE

The first lesson of our recent experience with relativity is merely an intensification and emphasis of the lesson which all past experience has also taught, namely, that when experiment is pushed into new domains, we must be prepared for new facts, of an entirely different character from those of our former experience. This is taught not only by the discovery of those unsuspected properties of matter moving with high velocities, which inspired the theory of relativity, but also even more emphatically by the new facts in the quantum domain. To a certain extent, of course, the recognition of all this does not involve a change of former attitude; the *fact* has always been for the physicist the one ultimate thing from which there is no appeal, and in the face of which the only possible attitude is a humility almost religious. The new feature in the present situation is an intensified conviction that in reality new orders of experience do exist, and that we may expect to meet them continually. We

Source: From "Broad Points of View" in *The Logic of Modern Physics* (pp. 1–32) by P. Bridgman, 1927, New York: Macmillan. Reprinted by permission.

have already encountered new phenomena in going to high velocities, and in going to small scales of magnitude: we may similarly expect to find them, for example, in dealing with relations of cosmic magnitudes, or in dealing with the properties of matter of enormous densities, such as is supposed to exist in the stars.

Implied in this recognition of the possibility of new experience beyond our present range, is the recognition that no element of a physical situation, no matter how apparently irrelevant or trivial, may be dismissed as without effect on the final result until proved to be without effect by actual experiment.

The attitude of the physicist must therefore be one of pure empiricism. He recognizes no *a priori* principles which determine or limit the possibilities of new experience. Experience is determined only by experience. This practically means that we must give up the demand that all nature be embraced in any formula, either simple or complicated. It may perhaps turn out eventually that as a matter of fact nature can be embraced in a formula, but we must so organize our thinking as not to demand it as a necessity.

THE OPERATIONAL CHARACTERS OF CONCEPTS

Einstein's Contribution in Changing Our Attitude Toward Concepts

Recognizing the essential unpredictability of experiment beyond our present range, the physicist, if he is to escape continually revising his attitude, must use in describing and correlating nature concepts of such a character that our present experience does not exact hostages of the future. Now here it seems to me is the greatest contribution of Einstein. Although he himself does not explicitly state or emphasize it, I believe that a study of what he has done will show that he has essentially modified our view of what the concepts useful in physics are and should be. Hitherto many of the concepts of physics have been defined in terms of their properties. An excellent example is afforded by Newton's concept of absolute time. The following quotation from the Scholium in Book I of the *Principia* is illuminating:

I do not define Time, Space, Place or Motion, as being well known to all. Only I must observe that the vulgar conceive those quantities under no other notions but from the relation they bear to sensible objects. And thence arise certain prejudices, for the removing of which, it will be convenient to distinguish them into Absolute and Relative, True and Apparent, Mathematical and Common.

(I) Absolute, True, and Mathematical Time, of itself, and from its own nature flows equably without regard to anything external, and by another name is called Duration.

Now there is no assurance whatever that there exists in nature anything with properties like those assumed in the definition, and physics, when reduced to concepts of this character, becomes as purely an abstract science and as far removed from reality as the abstract geometry of the mathematicians, built on postulates. It is a task for experiment to discover whether concepts so defined correspond to anything in nature, and we must always be prepared to find that the concepts correspond to nothing or only partially correspond. In particular, if we examine the definition of absolute time in the light of experiment, we find nothing in nature with such properties.

The new attitude toward a concept is entirely different. We may illustrate by considering the concept of length: what do we mean by the length of an object? We evidently know what we mean by length if we can tell what the length of any and every object is, and for the physicist nothing more is required. To find the length of an object, we have to perform certain physical operations. The concept of length is therefore fixed when the operations by which length is measured are fixed: that is, the concept of length involves as much as and nothing more than the set of operations by which length is determined. In general, we mean by any concept nothing more than a set of operations; *the concept is synonymous with the corresponding set of operations*. If the concept is physical, as of length, the operations are actual physical operations, namely, those by which length is measured; or if the concept is mental, as of mathematical continuity, the operations are mental operations, namely those by which we determine whether a given aggregate of magnitudes is continuous. It is not intended to imply that there is a hard and fast division between physical and mental concepts, or that one kind of concept does not always contain an element of the other; this classification of concept is not important for our future considerations.

We must demand that the set of operations equivalent to any concept be a unique set, for otherwise there are possibilities of ambiguity in practical applications which we cannot admit.

Applying this idea of "concept" to absolute time, we do not understand the meaning of absolute time unless we can tell how to determine the absolute time of any concrete event, *i.e.*, unless we can measure absolute time. Now we merely have to examine any of the possible operations by which we measure time to see that all such operations are relative operations. Therefore the previous statement that absolute time does not exist is replaced by the statement that absolute time is meaningless. And in making this statement we are not saying something new about nature, but are merely bringing to light implications already contained in the physical operations used in measuring time.

It is evident that if we adopt this point of view toward concepts, namely that the proper definition of a concept is not in terms of its properties but in terms of actual operations, we need run no danger of having to revise our attitude toward nature. For if experience is always described in terms of experience, there must always be correspondence between experience and our description of it, and we need never be embarrassed, as we were in attempting to find in nature the prototype of Newton's absolute time. Furthermore, if we remember that the operations to which a physical concept are equivalent are actual physical operations, the concepts can be defined only in the range of actual experiment, and are undefined and meaningless in regions as yet untouched by experiment. It follows that strictly speaking we cannot make statements at all about regions as yet untouched, and that when we do make such statements, as we inevitably shall, we are making a conventionalized extrapolation, of the looseness of which we must be fully conscious, and the justification of which is in the experiment of the future.

There probably is no statement either in Einstein or other writers that the change described above in the use of "concept" has been self-consciously made, but that such is the case is proved, I believe, by an examination of the way concepts are now handled by Einstein and others. For of course the true meaning of a term is to be found by observing what a man does with it, not by what he says about it. We may show that this is the actual sense in which concept is coming to be used by examining in particular Einstein's treatment of simultaneity.

Before Einstein, the concept of simultaneity was defined in terms of properties. It was a property of two events, when described with respect to their relation in time, that one event was either before the other, or

after it, or simultaneous with it. Simultaneity was a property of the two events alone and nothing else; either two events were simultaneous or they were not. The justification for using this term in this way was that it seemed to describe the behavior of actual things. But of course experience then was restricted to a narrow range. When the range of experience was broadened, as by going to high velocities, it was found that the concepts no longer applied, because there was no counterpart in experience for this absolute relation between two events. Einstein now subjected the concept of simultaneity to a critique, which consisted essentially in showing that the operations which enable two events to be described as simultaneous involve measurements on the two events made by an observer, so that "simultaneity" is, therefore, not an absolute property of the two events and nothing else, but must also involve the relation of the events to the observer. Until therefore we have experimental proof to the contrary, we must be prepared to find that the simultaneity of two events depends on their relation to the observer, and in particular on their velocity. Einstein, in thus analyzing what is involved in making a judgment of simultaneity, and in seizing on the act of the observer as the essence of the situation, is actually adopting a new point of view as to what the concepts of physics should be, namely, the operational view.

Of course Einstein actually went much further than this, and found precisely how the operations for judging simultaneity change when the observer moves, and obtained quantitative expressions for the effect of the motion of the observer on the relative time of two events. We may notice, parenthetically, that there is much freedom of choice in selecting the exact operations; those which Einstein chose were determined by convenience and simplicity with relation to light beams. Entirely apart from the precise quantitative relations of Einstein's theory, however, the important point for us is that if we had adopted the operational point of view, we would, before the discovery of the actual physical facts, have seen that simultaneity is essentially a relative concept, and would have left room in our thinking for the discovery of such effects as were later found.

Detailed Discussions of the Concept of Length

We may now gain further familiarity with the operational attitude toward a concept and some if its implications by examining from this point of view the concept of length. Our task is to find the operations by which we measure the length of any concrete physical object. We begin with objects of our commonest experience, such as a house or a house lot. What we do is sufficiently indicated by the following rough description. We start with a measuring rod, lay it on the object so that one of its ends coincides with one end of the object, mark on the object the position of the other end of the rod, then move the rod along in a straight line extension of its previous position until the first end coincides with the previous position of the second end, repeat this process as often as we can, and call the length the total number of times the rod was applied. This procedure, apparently so simple, is in practice exceedingly complicated, and doubtless a full description of all the precautions that must be taken would fill a large treatise. We must, for example, be sure that the temperature of the rod is the standard temperature at which its length is defined, or else we must make a correction for it; or we must correct for the gravitational distortion of the rod if we measure a vertical length; or we must be sure that the rod is not a magnet or is not subject to electrical forces. All these precautions would occur to every physicist. But we must also go further and specify all the details by which the rod is moved from one position to the next on the object—its precise path through space and its velocity and acceleration in getting from one position to another. Practically of course, precautions such as these are not mentioned, but the justification is in our experience that variations of procedure of this kind are without effect on the final result. But we always have to recognize that all our experience is subject to error, and that at some time in the future we may have to specify more carefully the acceleration, for example, of the rod in moving from one position to anther, if experimental accuracy should be so increased as to show a measurable effect. In *principle* the operations by which length is measure should be *uniquely* specified. If we have more than one set of operations, we have more than one concept, and strictly there should be a separate name to correspond to each different set of operations.

. . . . . .

It is interesting to observe that any increased accuracy in knowledge of large scale phenomena must, as far as we now can see, arise from an increase in the accuracy of measurement of small things, that is, in the measurement of small angles or the analysis of minute differences of wave lengths in the spectra. To know the very large takes us into the same field of experiment as to know the very small, so that operationally the large and the small have features in common.

This somewhat detailed analysis of the concept of length brings out features common to all our concepts. If we deal with phenomena outside the domain in which we originally defined our concepts, we may find physical hindrances to performing the operations of the original definition, so that the original operations have to be replaced by others. These new operations are, of course, to be so chosen that they give, within experimental error, the same numerical results in the domain in which the two sets of operations may be both applied; but we must recognize in principle that in changing the operations we have really changed the concept, and that to use the same name for these different concepts over the entire range is dictated only by considerations of convenience, which may sometimes prove to have been purchased at too high a price in terms of unambiguity. We must always be prepared some day to find that an increase in experimental accuracy may show that the two different sets of operations which give the same results in the more ordinary part of the domain of experience, lead to measurably different results in the more unfamiliar parts of the domain. We must remain aware of these joints in our conceptual structure if we hope to render unnecessary the services of the unborn Einsteins.

The second feature common to all concepts brought out by the detailed discussion of length is that, as we approach the experimentally attainable limit, concepts lose their individuality, fuse together, and become fewer in number, as we have seen that at dimensions of the order of the diameter of an electron the concepts of the length and the electric field vectors fuse into an amorphous whole. Not only does nature as experienced by us become different in character on its horizons, but it becomes simpler, and therefore our concepts, which are the building stones of our descriptions, become fewer in number. This seems to be an entirely natural state of affairs. How the number of concepts is often kept formally the same as we approach the horizon will be discussed later in special cases.

A precise analysis of our conceptual structure has never been attempted, except perhaps in very restricted domains, and it seems to me that there is room here for much important future work. Such an analysis is not to be attempted in this essay, but only some of the more important qualitative aspects are to be pointed out. It will never be possible to give a clean-cut logical analysis of the conceptual situation, for the nature of our concepts, according to our operational point of view, is the same as the nature of experimental knowledge, which is often hazy. Thus in the transition regions where nature is getting simpler and the number of operationally independent concepts changes, a certain haziness is inevitable, for the actual change in our conceptual structure in these transition regions is continuous, corresponding to the continuity of our experimental knowledge, whereas formally the number of concepts should be an integer.

The Relative Character of Knowledge

Two other consequences of the operational point of view must now be examined. First is the consequence that all our knowledge is relative. This may be understood in a general or a more particular sense. The general sense is illustrated in Haldane's book on the *Reign of Relativity*. Relativity in the general sense is the merest truism if the operational definitions of concept is accepted, for experience is described in terms of concepts, and since our concepts are constructed of operations, all our knowledge must unescapably be relative to the operations selected. But knowledge is also relative in a narrower sense, as when we say there is no such thing as absolute rest (or motion) or absolute size, but rest and size are relative terms. Conclusions of this kind are involved in the specific character of the operations in terms of which rest or size are defined. An examination of the operations by which we determine whether a body is at rest or in motion shows that the operations are relative operations: rest or motion is determined with respect to some other body selected as the standard. In saying that there is no such thing as absolute rest or motion we are not making a statement about nature in the sense that might be supposed, but we are merely making a statement about the character of our descriptive processes. Similarly with regard to size: examination of the operations of the measuring process shows that size is measured relative to the fundamental measuring rod.

The "absolute" therefore disappears in the original meaning of the word. But the "absolute" may usefully return with an altered meaning, and we may say that a thing has absolute properties if the numerical magnitude is the same when measured with the same formal procedures by all observers. Whether a given property is absolute or not can be determined only by experiment, landing us in the paradoxical position that the absolute is absolute only relative to experiment. In some cases, the most superficial observation shows that a property is not absolute, as, for example, it is at once obvious that measured velocity changes with the motion of the observer. But in other cases the decision is more difficult. Thus Michelson thought he had an absolute procedure for measuring length, by referring to the wave length of the red cadmium line as standard;[1] it required difficult and accurate experiment to show that this length varies with the motion of the observer. Even then, by changing the definition of the length of a moving object, we believe that length might be made to reassume its desired absolute character.

To stop the discussion at this point might leave the impression that this observation of the relative character of knowledge is of only a very tenuous and academic interest, since it appears to be concerned mostly with the character of our descriptive processes, and to say little about external nature. [What this means we leave to the metaphysician to decide.] But I believe there is a deeper significance to all this. It must be remembered that all our argument starts with the concepts as given. Now these concepts involve physical operations; in the discovery of what operations may be usefully employed in describing nature is buried almost all physical experience. In erecting our structure of physical science, we are building on the work of all the ages. There is then this purely physical significance in the statement that all motion is relative, namely that no operation of measuring motion have been found to be useful in describing simply the behavior of nature which are not operations relative to a single observer; in making this statement we are stating something about nature. It takes an enormous amount of real physical experience to discover relations of this sort. The discovery that the number obtained by counting the number of times a stick may be applied to an object can be simply used in describing natural phenomena was one of the most important and fundamental discoveries ever made by man.

Meaningless Questions

Another consequence of the operational character of our concepts, almost a corollary of that considered above, is that it is quite possible, nay even disquiet-

---

[1] A.A. Michelson, Light Waves and Their Uses, University of Chicago Press, 1903, Chap. V.

ingly easy, to invent expressions or to ask questions that are meaningless. It constitutes a great advance in our critical attitude toward nature to realize that a great many of the questions that we uncritically ask are without meaning. If a specific question has meaning, it must be possible to find operations by which an answer may be given to it. It will be found in many cases that the operations cannot exist, and the question therefore has no meaning. For instance, it means nothing to ask whether a star is at rest or not. Another example is a question proposed by Clifford, namely, whether it is not possible that as the solar system moves from one part of space to another the absolute scale of magnitude may be changing, but in such a way as to affect all things equally, so that the change of scale can never be detected. An examination of the operations by which length is measured in terms of measuring rods shows that the operations do not exist (because of the nature of our definition of length) for answering the question. The question can be given meaning only from the point of view of some imaginary superior being watching form an external point of vantage. But the operations by which such a being measures length are different from the operations of our definition of length, so that the question acquires meaning only by changing the significance of our terms—in the original sense the question means nothing.

To state that a certain question about nature is meaningless is to make a significant statement about nature itself, because the fundamental operations are determined by nature, and to state that nature cannot be described in terms of certain operations is a significant statement.

It must be recognized, however, that there is a sense in which no serious question is entirely without meaning, because doubtless the questioner had in mind some intention in asking the question. But to give meaning in this sense to a question, one must inquire into the meaning of the concepts as used by the questioner, and it will often be found that these concepts can be defined only in terms of fictitious properties, as Newton's absolute time was defined by its properties, so that the meaning to be ascribed to the question in this way has no connection with reality. I believe that it will enable us to make more significant and interesting statements, and therefore will be more useful, to adopt exclusively the operational view, and so admit the possibility of questions entirely without meaning.

This matter of meaningless questions is a very subtle thing which may poison much more of our thought than that dealing with purely physical phenomena. I believe that many of the questions asked about social and philosophical subjects will be found to be meaningless when examined from the point of view of operations. It would doubtless conduce greatly to clarity of thought if the operational mode of thinking were adopted in all fields of inquiry as well as in the physical. Just as in the physical domain, so in other domains, one is making a significant statement about his subject in stating that a certain question is meaningless.

In order to emphasize this matter of meaningless questions, I give here a list of questions, with which the reader may amuse himself by finding whether they have meaning or not.

1. Was there ever a time when matter did not exist?

2. May time have a beginning or an end?

3. Why does time flow?

4. May space be bounded?

5. May space or time be discontinuous?

6. May space have a fourth dimension, not directly detectible, but given indirectly by inference?

7. Are there parts of nature forever beyond our detection?

8. Is the sensation which I call blue really the *same* as that which my neighbor calls blue? Is it possible that a blue object may arouse in him the same sensation that a red object does in me and *vice versa*?

9. May there be missing integers in the series of natural numbers as we know them?

10. Is a universe possible in which $2 + 2 \neq 4$?

11. Why does negative electricity attract positive?

12. Why does nature obey laws?

13. Is a universe possible in which the laws are different?

14. If one part of our universe could be *completely* isolated from the rest, would it continue to obey the same laws?

15. Can we be sure that our logical processes are valid?

GENERAL COMMENTS ON THE OPERATIONAL POINT OF VIEW

To adopt the operational point of view involves much more than a mere restriction of the sense in which we understand "concept," but means a far-reaching change in all our habits of thought, in that we shall no longer permit ourselves to use as tools in our thinking concepts of which we cannot give an adequate account in terms of operations. In some respects thinking becomes simpler, because certain old generalizations and idealizations become incapable of use; for instance, many of the speculations of the early natural philosophers become simply unreadable. In other respects, however, thinking becomes much more difficult, because the operational implications of a concept are often very involved. For example, it is most difficult to grasp adequately all that is contained in the apparently simple concept of "time," and requires the continual correction of mental tendencies which we have long unquestioningly accepted.

Operational thinking will at first prove to be an unsocial virtue; one will find oneself perpetually unable to understand the simplest conversation of one's friends, and will make oneself universally unpopular by demanding the meaning of apparently the simplest terms of every argument. Possibly after every one has schooled himself to this better way, there will remain a permanent unsocial tendency, because doubtless much of our present conversation will then become unnecessary. The socially optimistic may venture to hope, however, that the ultimate effect will be to release one's energies for more stimulating and interesting interchange of ideas.

Not only will operational thinking reform the social art of conversation, but all our social relations will be liable to reform. Let any one examine in operational terms any popular present-day discussion of religious or moral questions to realize the magnitude of the reformation awaiting us. Wherever we temporize or compromise in applying our theories of conduct to practical life we may suspect a failure of operational thinking.

A Survey of Some Fundamental Problems

Sir Karl Popper

A scientist, whether theorist or experimenter, puts forward statements, or systems of statements, and tests them step by step. In the field of the empirical sciences, more particularly, he constructs hypotheses, or systems of theories, and tests them against experience by observation and experiment.

I suggest that it is the task of the logic of scientific discovery, or the logic of knowledge, to give a logical analysis of this procedure; that is, to analyze the method of the empirical sciences.

But what are these 'methods of the empirical sciences'? And what do we call 'empirical science'?

I. THE PROBLEM OF INDUCTION.

According to a widely accepted view—to be opposed in this book—the empirical sciences can be characterized by the fact that they use 'inductive methods', as they are called. According to this view, the logic of scientific discovery would be identical with inductive logic, i.e. with the logical analysis of these inductive methods.

It is usual to call an inference 'inductive' if it passes from singular statements (sometimes also called 'particular' statements), such as accounts of the results of observations or experiments, to universal statements, such as hypotheses or theories.

Now it is far from obvious, from a logical point of view, that we are justified in inferring universal statements from singular ones, no matter how numerous; for any conclusion drawn in this way may always turn out to be false: no matter how many instances of white swans we may have observed, this does not justify the conclusion that *all* swans are white.

The question whether inductive inferences are justified, or under what conditions, is known as *the problem of induction*.

The problem of induction may also be formulated as the question of how to establish the truth of universal statements which are based on experience, such as the hypotheses and theoretical systems of the empirical sciences. For many people believe that the truth of these universal statements is '*known by experience*'; yet it is clear that an account of an experience—of an observation or the result of an experiment—can in the first place be only a singular statement and not a universal one. Accordingly, people who say of a universal statement that we know its truth from experience usually mean that the truth of this universal statement can somehow be reduced to the truth of singular ones, and that these singular ones are known by experience to be true; which amounts to saying that the universal statement is based on inductive inference. Thus to ask whether there are natural laws known to be true appears to be only another way of asking whether inductive inferences are logically justified.

Source: "A Survey of Some Fundamental Problems" in *The Logic of Scientific Discovery* (pp. 27–42) by K. R. Popper, 1959, New York: Basic Books. (Original work published 1934.) Copyright 1959 by Sir Karl Popper. Reprinted by permission.

Yet if we want to find a way of justifying inductive inferences, we must first of all try to establish a *principle of induction*. A principle of induction would be a statement with the help of which we could put inductive inferences into a logically acceptable form. In the eyes of the upholders of inductive logic, a principle of induction is of supreme importance for scientific method: '. . . this principle', says Reichenbach, 'determines the truth of scientific theories. To eliminate it from science would mean nothing less than to deprive science of the power to decide the truth or falsity of its theories. Without it, clearly, science would no longer have the right to distinguish its theories from the fanciful and arbitrary creations of the poet's mind.'[1]

Now this principle of induction cannot be a purely logical truth like a tautology or an analytical statement. Indeed, if there were such a thing as a purely logical principle of induction, there would be no problem of induction; for in this case, all inductive inferences would have to be regarded as purely logical or tautological transformations, just like inferences in deductive logic. Thus the principle of induction must be a synthetic statement; that is, a statement whose negation is not self-contradictory but logically possible. So the question arises why such a principle should be accepted at all, and how we can justify its acceptance on rational grounds.

Some who believe in inductive logic are anxious to point out, with Reichenbach, that 'the principle of induction is unreservedly accepted by the whole of science and that no man can seriously doubt this principle in everyday life either'.[2] Yet even supposing this were the case—for after all, 'the whole of science' might err—I should still contend that a principle of induction is superfluous, and that it must lead to logical inconsistencies.

That inconsistencies may easily arise in connection with the principle of induction should have been clear from the work of Hume;[*1] also, that they can be avoided, if at all, only with difficulty. For the principle of induction must be a universal statement in its turn. Thus if we try to regard its truth as known from experience, then the very same problems which occasioned

its introduction will arise all over again. To justify it, we should have to employ inductive inferences; and to justify these we should have to assume an inductive principle of a higher order; and so on. Thus the attempt to base the principle of induction on experience breaks down, since it must lead to an infinite regress.

Kant tried to force his way out of this difficulty by taking the principle of induction (which he formulated as the 'principle of universal causation') to be '*a priori* valid'. But I do not think that his ingenious attempt to provide an *a priori* justification for synthetic statements was successful.

My own view is that the various difficulties of inductive logic here sketched are insurmountable. So also, I fear, are those inherent in the doctrine, so widely current today, that inductive inference, although not 'strictly valid', can *attain some degree of 'reliability' or of 'probability'*. According to this doctrine, inductive inferences are 'probable inferences'.[3] 'We have described', says Reichenbach, 'the principle of induction as the means whereby science decides upon truth. To be more exact, we should say that it serves to decide upon probability. For it is not given to science to reach either truth or falsity . . . but scientific statements can only attain continuous degrees of probability whose unattainable upper and lower limits are truth and falsity'.[4]

At this stage I can disregard the fact that the believers in inductive logic entertain an idea of probability that I shall later reject as highly unsuitable for their own purposes (see section 80, below). I can do so because the difficulties mentioned are not even touched by an appeal to probability. For if a certain degree of probability is to be assigned to statements based on inductive inference, then this will have to be justified by invoking a new principle of induction, appropriately modified. And this new principle in its turn will have to be justified, and so on. Nothing is gained, moreover, if the principle of induction, in its turn, is taken not as 'true' but only as 'probable'. In short, like every other form of inductive logic, the logic of probable inference, or 'probability logic', leads

---

[1] H. Reichenbach, *Erkenntnis* I, 1930, p. 186 (cf. also p. 64 f.).
[2] Reichenbach *ibid.*, p. 67.
[*1] The decisive passages from Hume are quoted in appendix *vii, text to footnotes 4, 5, and 6; see also note 2 to section 81, below.

[3] Cf. J. M. Keynes, *A Treatise on Probability* (1921); O. Külpe, *Vorlesungen über Logic* (ed. by Selz, 1923); Reichenbach (who uses the term 'probability implications'), *Axiomatik der Wahrscheinlichkeitrechnung, Mathem, Zeitschr.* 34 (1932); and in many other places.
[4] Reichenbach, *Erkenntnis* I, 1930, p. 186.

either to an infinite regress, or to the doctrine of *apriorism*.*[2]

The theory to be developed in the following pages stands directly opposed to all attempts to operate with the ideas of inductive logic. It might be described as the theory of *the deductive method of testing*, or as the view that a hypothesis can only be empirically *tested*—and only *after* it has been advanced.

Before I can elaborate this view (which might be called 'deductivism', in contrast to 'inductivism'[5]) I must first make clear the distinction between the *psychology of knowledge* which deals with empirical facts, and the *logic of knowledge* which is concerned only with logical relations. For the belief in inductive logic is largely due to a confusion of psychological problems with epistemological ones. It may be worth noticing, by the way, that this confusion spells trouble not only for the logic of knowledge but for its psychology as well.

2. ELIMINATION OF PSYCHOLOGISM.

I said above that the work of the scientist consists in putting forward and testing theories.

The initial stage, the act of conceiving or inventing a theory, seems to me neither to call for logical analysis nor to be susceptible of it. The question how it happens that a new idea occurs to a man—whether it is a musical theme, a dramatic conflict, or a scientific theory—may be of great interest to empirical psychology; but it is irrelevant to the logical analysis of scientific knowledge. This latter is concerned not with *questions of fact* (Kant's *quid facti?*), but only with questions of *justification or validity* (Kant's *quid juris?*). Its questions are of the following kind. Can a

statement be justified? And if so, how? Is it testable? Is it logically dependent on certain other statements? Or does it perhaps contradict them? In order that a statement may be logically examined in this way, it must already have been presented to us. Someone must have formulated it, and submitted it to logical examination.

Accordingly I shall distinguish sharply between the process of conceiving a new idea, and the methods and results of examining it logically. As to the task of the logic of knowledge—in contradistinction to the psychology of knowledge—I shall proceed on the assumption that it consists solely in investigating the methods employed in those systematic tests to which every new idea must be subjected if it is to be seriously entertained.

Some might object that it would be more to the purpose to regard it as the business of epistemology to produce what has been called a '*rational reconstruction*' of the steps that have led the scientist to a discovery—to the finding of some new truth. But the question is: what, precisely, do we want to reconstruct? If it is the processes involved in the stimulation and release of an inspiration which are to be reconstructed, then I should refuse to take it as the task of the logic of knowledge. Such processes are the concern of empirical psychology but hardly of logic. It is another matter if we want to reconstruct rationally the *subsequent tests* whereby the inspiration may be discovered to be a discovery, or become known to be knowledge. In so far as the scientist critically judges, alters, or rejects his own inspiration we may, if we like, regard the methodological analysis undertaken here as a kind of 'rational reconstruction' of the corresponding thought-processes. But this reconstruction would not describe these processes as they actually happen: it can give only a logical skeleton of the procedure of testing. Still, this is perhaps all that is meant by those who speak of a 'rational reconstruction' of the ways in which we gain knowledge.

It so happens that my arguments in this book are quite independent of this problem. However, my view of the matter, for what it is worth, is that there is no such thing as a logical method of having new ideas, or a logical reconstruction of this process. My view may be expressed by saying that every discovery contains 'an irrational element' or 'a creative intuition', in Bergson's sense. In a similar way Einstein speaks of '. . . the search for those highly universal . . . laws from which a picture of the world can be obtained by pure deduc-

---

*[2]See also chapter x, below, especially note 2 to section 81, and chapter *ii of the *Postscript* for a fuller statement of this criticism.
[5]Liebig (in *Induktion und Deduktion*, 1865) was probably the first to reject the inductive method from the standpoint of natural science; his attack is directed against Bacon. Duhem (in *La Théorie physique, son objet et sa structure*, 1906; English translation by P. P. Wiener: *The Aim and Structure of Physical Theory*, Princeton, 1954) held pronounced deductivist views. (*But there are also inductivist views to be found in Duhem's book, for example in the third chapter, Part One, where we are told that only experiment, induction, and generalization have produced Descarte's law of diffraction: *cf.* the English translation, p. 455.) See also V. Kraft, *Die Grundformen der Wissenschaftlichen Methoden*, 1925; and Carnap, *Erkenntnis* 2, 1932, p. 440.

tion. There is no logical path', he says, 'leading to these . . . laws. They can only be reached by intuition, based upon something like an intellectual love ('*Einfühlung*') of the objects of experience'.[1]

3. DEDUCTIVE TESTING OF THEORIES.

According to the view that will be put forward here, the method of critically testing theories, and selecting them according to the results of tests, always proceeds on the following lines. From a new idea, put up tentatively, and not yet justified in any way—an anticipation, a hypothesis, a theoretical system, or what you will—conclusions are drawn by means of logical deduction. These conclusions are then compared with one another and with other relevant statements, so as to find what logical relations (such as equivalence, derivability, compatibility, or incompatibility) exist between them.

We may if we like distinguish four different lines along which the testing of a theory could be carried out. First there is the logical comparison of the conclusions among themselves, by which the internal consistency of the system is tested. Secondly, there is the investigation of the logical form of the theory, with the object of determining whether it has the character of an empirical or scientific theory, or whether it is, for example, tautological. Thirdly, there is the comparison with other theories, chiefly with the aim of determining whether the theory would constitute a scientific advance should it survive our various tests. And finally, there is the testing of the theory by way of empirical applications of the conclusions which can be derived from it.

The purpose of this last kind of test is to find out how far the new consequences of the theory—whatever may be new in what it asserts—stand up to the demands of practice, whether raised by purely scientific experiments, or by practical technological applications. Here too the procedure of testing turns out to be deductive. With the help of other statements, previously accepted, certain singular statements—which we may call 'predictions'—are deduced from the theory; especially predictions that are easily testable or applicable. From among these statements, those are selected which are not derivable from the current theory, and more especially those which the current theory contradicts. Next we seek a decision as regards these (and other) derived statements by comparing them with the results of practical applications and experiments. If this decision is positive, that is, if the singular conclusions turn out to be acceptable, or *verified*, then the theory has, for the time being, passed its test: we have found no reason to discard it. But if the decision is negative, or in other words, if the conclusions have been *falsified*, then their falsification also falsifies the theory from which they were logically deduced.

It should be noticed that a positive decision can only temporarily support the theory, for subsequent negative decisions may always overthrow it. So long as theory withstands detailed and severe tests and is not superseded by another theory in the course of scientific progress, we may say that it has 'proved its mettle' or that it is '*corroborated*'.[*1]

Nothing resembling inductive logic appears in the procedure here outlined. I never assume that we can argue from the truth of singular statements to the truth of theories. I never assume that by force of 'verified' conclusions, theories can be established as 'true', or even as merely 'probable'.

In this book I intend to give a more detailed analysis of the methods of deductive testing. And I shall attempt to show that, within the framework of this analysis, all the problems can be dealt with that are usually called '*epistemological*'. Those problems, more especially, to which inductive logic gives rise, can be eliminated without creating new ones in their place.

4. THE PROBLEM OF DEMARCATION.

Of the many objections which are likely to be raised against the view here advanced, the most serious is perhaps the following. In rejecting the method of induction, it may be said, I deprive empirical science of what appears to be its most important characteristic; and this means that I remove the barriers which

---

[1]Address on Max Planck's 60th birthday. The passage quoted begins with the words, 'The supreme task of the physicist is to search for those universal laws . . . ," etc. (quoted from A. Einstein, *Mein Weltbild*, 1934, p. 168; English translation by A. Harris: *The World as I see It*, 1935, p. 125). Similar ideas are found earlier in Liebig, *op. cit.*; cf. also Mach, *Principien der Wärmelehre* (1896), p. 443 ff. *The German word '*Einfühlung*' is difficult to translate. Harris translates: 'sympathetic understanding of experience'.

[*1]For this term, see note *1 before section 79, and section *29 of my *Postscript*.

separate science from metaphysical speculation. My reply to this objection is that my main reason for rejecting inductive logic is precisely that *it does not provide a suitable distinguishing mark* of the empirical, non-metaphysical, character of a theoretical system; or in other words, that *it does not provide a suitable 'criterion of demarcation'*.

The problem of finding a criterion which would enable us to distinguish between the empirical sciences on the one hand, and mathematics and logic as well as 'metaphysical' systems on the other, I call the *problem of demarcation*.[1]

This problem was known to Hume who attempted to solve it.[2] With Kant it became the central problem of the theory of knowledge. If, following Kant, we call the problem of induction 'Hume's problem', we might call the problem of demarcation 'Kant's problem'.

Of these two problems—the source of nearly all the other problems of the theory of knowledge—the problem of demarcation is, I think, the more fundamental. Indeed, the main reason why epistemologists with empiricist leanings tend to pin their faith to the 'method of induction' seems to be their belief that this method alone can provide a suitable criterion of demarcation. This applies especially to those empiricists who follow the flag of 'positivism'.

The older positivists wished to admit, as scientific or legitimate, only those *concepts* (or notions or ideas) which were, as they put it, 'derived from experience'; those concepts, that is, which they believed to be logically reducible to elements of sense-experience, such as sensations (or sense-data), impressions, perceptions, visual or auditory memories, and so forth. Modern positivists are apt to see more clearly that science is not a system of concepts but rather a system of *statements*.[*1] Accordingly, they wish to admit, as scientific or legitimate, only those statements which are reducible to elementary (or 'atomic') statements of experience—to 'judgments of perception' or 'atomic propositions' or 'protocol-sentences' or what not.[*2] It is clear that the implied criterion of demarcation is identical with the demand for an inductive logic.

Since I reject inductive logic I must also reject all these attempts to solve the problem of demarcation. With this rejection, the problem of demarcation gains in importance for the present inquiry. Finding an acceptable criterion of demarcation must be a crucial task for any epistemology which does not accept inductive logic.

Positivists usually interpret the problem of demarcation in a *naturalistic* way; they interpret it as if it were a problem of natural science. Instead of taking it as their task to propose a suitable convention, they believe they have to discover a difference, existing in the nature of things, as it were, between empirical science on the one hand and metaphysics on the other. They are constantly trying to prove that metaphysics by its very nature is nothing but nonsensical twaddle—'sophistry and illusion', as Hume says, which we should 'commit to the flames'.[*3]

If by the words 'nonsensical' or 'meaningless' we wish to express no more, by definition, than 'not belonging to empirical science', then the characterization of metaphysics as meaningless nonsense would be trivial; for metaphysics has usually been defined as non-empirical. But of course, the positivists believe they can say much more about metaphysics than that some of its statements are non-empirical. The words 'meaningless' or 'nonsensical' convey, and are meant to convey, a derogatory evaluation; and there is no doubt that what the positivists really want to achieve is not so much a successful demarcation as the final overthrow[3] and the annihilation of metaphysics. However

---

[1] With this (and also with sections 1 to 6 and 13 to 24) *cf.* my note: *Erkenntnis* 3, 1933, p. 426; *It is now here reprinted, in translation, as appendix *i.

[2] *Cf.* the last sentence of his *Enquiry Concerning Human Understanding*. *With the next paragraph, compare for example the quotation from Reichenbach in the text to note 1, section 1.

[*1] When I wrote this paragraph I overrated the 'modern positivists', as I now see. I should have remembered that in *this respect* the promising beginning of Wittgenstein's *Tractatus*—'The world is the totality of facts, not of things'—was cancelled by its end which denounced the man who 'had given no meaning to certain signs in his propositions'. See also my *Open Society and its Enemies*, chapter 11, section ii, and chapter *i of my *Postscript*, especially sections *11 (note 5), *24 (the last five paragraphs), and *25.

[*2] Nothing depends on names, of course. When I invented the new name 'basic statement' (or 'basic proposition'; see below, sections 7 and 28) I did so only because I needed a term *not* burdened with the connotation of a perception statement. But unfortunately it was soon adopted by others, and used to convey precisely the kind of meaning which I wished to avoid. *Cf.* also my *Postscript*, *29.

[*3] Hume thus condemned his own *Enquiry* on its last page, just as later Wittgenstein condemned his own *Tractatus* on its last page. (See note 2 to section 10.)

[3] Carnap, *Erkenntnis* 2, 1932, p. 219 *ff.* Earlier Mill had used the word 'meaningless' in a similar way, *no doubt under the influence of Comte; *cf.* Comte's *Early Essays on Social Philosophy*, ed. by H. D. Hutton, 1911, p. 223. See also my *Open Society*, note 51 to chapter 11.

this may be, we find that each time the positivists tried to say more clearly what 'meaningful' meant, the attempt led to the same result—to a definition of 'meaningful sentence' (in contra-distinction to 'meaningless pseudo-sentence') which simply reiterated the criterion of demarcation of their *inductive logic*.

This 'shows itself' very clearly in the case of Wittgenstein, according to whom every meaningful proposition must be *logically reducible*[4] to elementary (or atomic) propositions, which he characterizes as descriptions or 'pictures of reality'[5] (a characterization, by the way, which is to cover all meaningful propositions). We may see from this that Wittgenstein's criterion of meaningfulness coincides with the 'inductivists' criterion of demarcation, provided we replace their words 'scientific' or 'legitimate' by 'meaningful'. And it is precisely over the problem of induction that this attempt to solve the problem of demarcation comes to grief: positivists, in their anxiety to annihilate metaphysics, annihilate natural science along with it. For scientific laws, too, cannot be logically reduced to elementary statements of experience. If consistently applied, Wittgenstein's criterion of meaningfulness rejects as meaningless those natural laws the search for which, as Einstein says,[6] is 'the supreme task of the physicist': they can never be accepted as genuine or legitimate statements. This view, which tries to unmask the problem of induction as an empty pseudo-problem, has been expressed by Schlick[*4] in the following words: 'The problem of induction consists in asking for a logical justification of *universal statements* about reality . . . We recognize, with Hume, that there is no such logical justification:

there can be none, simply because *they are not genuine* statements.'[7]

This shows how the inductivist criterion of demarcation fails to draw a dividing line between scientific and metaphysical systems, and why it must accord them equal status; for the verdict of the positivist dogma of meaning is that both are systems of meaningless pseudo-statements. Thus instead of eradicating metaphysics from the empirical sciences, positivism leads to the invasion of metaphysics into the scientific realm.[8]

In contrast to these anti-metaphysical stratagems— anti-metaphysical in intention, that is—my business, as I see it, is not to bring about the overthrow of metaphysics. It is, rather, to formulate a suitable characterization of empirical science, or to define the concepts 'empirical science' and 'metaphysics' in such a way that we shall be able to say of a given system of statements whether or not its closer study is the concern of empirical science.

My criterion of demarcation will accordingly have to be regarded as a *proposal for an agreement or convention*. As to the suitability of any such convention opinions may differ; and a reasonable discussion of these questions is only possible between parties having some purpose in common. The choice of that purpose must, of course, be ultimately a matter of decision, going beyond rational argument.[*5]

Thus anyone who envisages a system of absolutely certain, irrevocably true statements[9] as the end and

---

[4]Wittgenstein, *Tractatus Logico-Philosophicus* (1918 and 1922), Proposition 5. *As this was written in 1934, I am dealing here of course *only* with the *Tractatus*.

[5]Wittgenstein, *op. cit.*, Proposition 4.01; 4.03; 2.221.

[6]*Cf.* note 1 to section 2.

[*4]The idea of treating scientific laws as pseudo-propositions—thus solving the problem of induction—was attributed by Schlick to Wittgenstein. (*Cf.* my *Open Society*, notes 46 and 51 *f.* to chapter 11.) But it is really much older. It is part of the instrumentalist tradition which can be traced back to Berkeley, and further. (See for example my paper 'Three Views Concerning Human Knowledge', in *Contemporary British Philosophy* 1956; and 'A Note on Berkeley as a Precursor of Mach', in *The British Journal for the Philosophy of Science* iv, 4, 1953, pp. 26 *ff.*, now in my *Conjectures and Refutations*, 1959. Further references in note *1 before section 12 (p. 59). The problem is also treated in my *Postscript*, sections *11 to *14, and *19 to *26.)

[7]Schlick, *Naturwissenschaften* 19, 1931, p. 156. (The italics are mine.) Regarding natural laws Schlick writes (p. 151), 'It has often been remarked that, strictly, we can never speak of an absolute verification of a law, since we always, so to speak, tacitly make the reservation that it may be modified in the light of further experience. If I may add, by way of parenthesis', Schlick continues, 'a few words on the logical situation, the above-mentioned fact means that a natural law, in principle, does not have the logical character of a statement, but is, rather, a prescription for the formation of statements.' *('Formation' no doubt was meant to include transformation or derivation.) Schlick attributed this theory to a personal communication of Wittgenstein's. See also section *12 of my *Postscript*.

[8]*Cf.* Section 78 (for example note 1). *See also my *Open Society*, notes 46, 51, and 52 to chapter 11, and my paper 'The Demarcation between Science and Metaphysics', contributed in January 1955 to the planned Carnap volume of the *Library of Living Philosophers*, edited by P. A. Schilpp.

[*5]I believe that a reasonable discussion is always possible between parties interested in truth, and ready to pay attention to each other. (*Cf.* my *Open Society*, chapter 24).

purpose of science will certainly reject the proposals I shall make here. And so will those who see 'the essence of science . . . in its dignity', which they think resides in its 'wholeness' and its 'real truth and essentiality'.[10] They will hardly be ready to grant this dignity to modern theoretical physics in which I and others see the most complete realization to date of what I call 'empirical science'.

The aims of science which I have in mind are different. I do not try to justify them, however, by representing them as the true or the essential aims of science. This would only distort the issue, and it would mean a relapse into positivist dogmatism. There is only *one* way, as far as I can see, of arguing rationally in support of my proposals. This is to analyze their logical consequences: to point out their fertility—their power to elucidate the problems of the theory of knowledge.

Thus I freely admit that in arriving at my proposals I have been guided, in the last analysis, by value judgments and predilections. But I hope that my proposals may be acceptable to those who value not only logical rigour but also freedom from dogmatism; who seek practical applicability, but are even more attracted by the adventure of science, and by discoveries which again and again confront us with new and unexpected questions, challenging us to try out new and hitherto undreamed-of answers.

The fact that value judgments influence my proposals does not mean that I am making the mistake of which I have accused the positivists—that of trying to kill metaphysics by calling it names. I do not even go so far as to assert that metaphysics has no value for empirical science. For it cannot be denied that along with metaphysical ideas which have obstructed the advance of science there have been others—such as speculative atomism—which have aided it. And looking at the matter from the psychological angle, I am inclined to think that scientific discovery is impossible without faith in ideas which are of a purely speculative kind, and sometimes even quite hazy; a faith which is completely unwarranted from the point of view of science, and which, to that extent, is 'metaphysical'.[11]

---

[9]This is Dingler's view; *cf.* note 1 to section 19.

[10]This is the view of O. Spann (*Kategorienlehre*, 1924).

[11]*Cf.* also: Planck, *Positivismus und reale Aussenwelt* (1931) and Einstein, *Die Religiosität der Forschung*, in *Mein Weltbild* (1934), p. 43; English translation by A. Harris: *The World as I See It* (1935), p. 23 *ff*. *See also section 85, and my *Postscript*.

Yet having issued all these warnings, I still take it to be the first task of the logic of knowledge to put forward a *concept of empirical science*, in order to make linguistic usage, now somewhat uncertain, as definite as possible, and in order to draw a clear line of demarcation between science and metaphysical ideas—even though these ideas may have furthered the advance of science throughout its history.

5. EXPERIENCE AS A METHOD.

The task of formulating an acceptable definition of the idea of empirical science is not without its difficulties. Some of these arise from *the fact that there must be many theoretical systems* with a logical structure very similar to the one which at any particular time is the accepted system of empirical science. This situation is sometimes described by saying that there are a great many—presumably an infinite number—of 'logically possible worlds'. Yet the system called 'empirical science' is intended to represent only *one* world: the 'real world' or the 'world of our experience'.[*1]

In order to make this idea a little more precise, we may distinguish three requirements which our empirical theoretical system will have to satisfy. First, it must be *synthetic*, so that it may represent a non-contradictory, a *possible* world. Secondly, it must satisfy the criterion of demarcation (*cf.* sections 6 and 21), *i.e.* it must not be metaphysical, but must represent a world of possible *experience*. Thirdly, it must be a system distinguished in some way from other such systems as the one which represents *our* world of experience.

But how is the system that represents our world of experience to be distinguished? The answer is: by the fact that it has been submitted to tests, and has stood up to tests. This means that it is to be distinguished by applying to it that deductive method which it is my aim to analyze, and to describe.

'Experience', on this view, appears as a distinctive *method* whereby one theoretical system may be distinguished from others; so that empirical science seems to be characterized not only by its logical form but, in addition, by its distinctive *method*. (This, of course, is also the view of the inductivists, who try to characterize empirical science by its use of the inductive method.)

[*1]*Cf.* appendix *x.

The theory of knowledge whose task is the analysis of the method or procedure peculiar to empirical science, may accordingly be described as a theory of the empirical method—*a theory of what is usually called experience*.

6. FALSIFIABILITY AS A CRITERION OF DEMARCATION.

The criterion of demarcation inherent in inductive logic—that is, the positivistic dogma of meaning—is equivalent to the requirement that all the statements of empirical science (or all 'meaningful' statements) must be capable of being finally decided, with respect to their truth *and* falsity; we shall say that they must be '*conclusively decidable*'. This means that their form must be such that *to verify them and to falsify them* must both be logically possible. Thus Schlick says: ' . . . a genuine statement must be capable of *conclusive verification*'[1]; and Waismann says still more clearly: 'If there is no possible way to *determine whether a statement is true* then that statement has no meaning whatsoever. For the meaning of a statement is the method of its verification.'[2]

Now in my view there is no such thing as induction.[*1] Thus inference to theories, from singular statements which are 'verified by experience' (whatever that may mean), is logically inadmissible. Theories are, therefore, *never* empirically verifiable. If we wish to avoid the positivist's mistake of eliminating, by our criterion of demarcation, the theoretical systems of natural science,[*2] then we must choose a criterion which allows us to admit to the domain of empirical science even statements which cannot be verified.

But I shall certainly admit a system as empirical or scientific only if it is capable of being *tested* by experience. These considerations suggest that not the *verifiability* but the *falsifiability* of a system is to be taken as a criterion of demarcation.[*3] In other words: I shall not require of a scientific system that it shall be capable of being singled out, once and for all, in a positive sense; but I shall require that its logical form shall be such that it can be singled out, by means of empirical tests, in a negative sense: *it must be possible for an empirical scientific system to be refuted by experience.*[3]

(Thus the statement, 'It will rain or not rain here tomorrow' will not be regarded as empirical, simply because it cannot be refuted; whereas the statement, 'It will rain here tomorrow' will be regarded as empirical.)

Various objections might be raised against the criterion of demarcation here proposed. In the first place, it may well seem somewhat wrong-headed to suggest that science, which is supposed to give us positive information, should be characterized as satisfying a negative requirement such as refutability. However, I shall show, in sections 31 to 46, that this objection has little weight, since the amount of positive information about the world which is conveyed by a scientific statement is the greater the more likely it is to clash, because of its logical character, with possible singular statements. (Not for nothing do we call the laws of nature 'laws': the more they prohibit the more they say.)

Again, the attempt might be made to turn against me my own criticism of the inductivist criterion of demarcation; for it might seem that objections can be raised against falsifiability as a criterion of demarcation similar to those which I myself raised against verifiability.

---

[1]Schlick, *Naturwissenschaften* 19, 1931, 1931, p. 150.

[2]Waismann, *Erkenntnis* 1, 1930, p. 229.

[*1]I am not, of course, here considering so-called 'mathematical induction'; what I am denying is that there is such a thing as induction in the so-called 'inductive sciences'; that there are either 'inductive procedures' or 'inductive inferences'.

[*2]In his *Logical Syntax* (1937, p. 321 f.) Carnap admitted that this was a mistake (with a reference to my criticism); and he did so even more fully in 'Testability and Meaning', recognizing the fact that universal laws are not only 'convenient' for science but even 'essential' (*Philosophy of Science* 4, 1937, p. 27). But in his inductivist *Logical Foundations of Probability* (1950), he returns to a position very like the one here criticized: finding that universal laws have zero probability (p. 511), he is compelled to say (p. 575) that though they need not be expelled from science, science can very well do without them.

[*3]Note that I suggest falsifiability as a criterion of demarcation, but *not of meaning*. Note, moreover, that I have already (section 4) sharply criticized the use of the idea of meaning as a criterion of demarcation, and that I attack the dogma of meaning again, even more sharply, in section 9. It is therefore a sheer myth (though any number of refutations of my theory have been based upon this myth) that I ever proposed falsifiability as a criterion of meaning. Falsifiability separates two kinds of perfectly meaningful statements: the falsifiable and the non-falsifiable. It draws a line inside meaningful language, not around it. See also Appendix *i, and chapter *i of my *Postscript*, especially sections *17 and *19.

[3]Related ideas are to be found for example, in Frank, *Die Kausalität und ihre Grenzen* (1931), ch. 1 §10 (p. 15 f.); Dubislav, *Die Definition* (3rd edition 1931), p. 100 f. (*Cf.* also note 1 to section 4, above.)

This attack would not disturb me. My proposal is based upon an *asymmetry* between verifiability and falsifiability; an asymmetry which results from the logical form of universal statements.[*4] For these are never derivable from singular statements, but can be contradicted by singular statements. Consequently it is possible by means of purely deductive inferences (with the help of the *modus tollens* of classical logic) to argue from the truth of singular statements to the falsity of universal statements. Such an argument to the falsity of universal statements is the only strictly deductive kind of inference that proceeds, as it were, in the 'inductive direction'; that is, from singular to universal statements.

A third objection may seem more serious. It might be said that even if the asymmetry is admitted, it is still impossible, for various reasons, that any theoretical system should ever be conclusively falsified. For it is always possible to find some way of evading falsification, for example by introducing *ad hoc* an auxiliary hypothesis, or by changing *ad hoc* a definition. It is even possible without logical inconsistency to adopt the position of simply refusing to acknowledge any falsifying experience whatsoever. Admittedly, scientists do not usually proceed in this way, but logically such procedure is possible; and this fact, it might be claimed, makes the logical value of my proposed criterion of demarcation dubious, to say the least.

I must admit the justice of this criticism; but I need not therefore withdraw my proposal to adopt falsifiability as a criterion of demarcation. For I am going to propose (in sections 20 *f.*) that the *empirical method* shall be characterized as a method that excludes precisely those ways of evading falsification which, as my imaginary critic rightly insists, are logically admissible. According to my proposal, what characterizes the empirical method is its manner of exposing to falsification, in every conceivable way, the system to be tested. Its aim is not to save the lives of untenable systems but, on the contrary, to select the one which is by comparison the fittest, by exposing them all to the fiercest struggle for survival.

The proposed criterion of demarcation also leads us to a solution of Hume's problem of induction—of the problem of the validity of natural laws. The root of this problem is the apparent contradiction between what may be called 'the fundamental thesis of empiricism'—the thesis that experience alone can decide upon the truth or falsity of scientific statements—and Hume's realization of the inadmissibility of inductive arguments. This contradiction arises only if it is assumed that all empirical scientific statements must be 'conclusively decidable', i.e. that their verification and their falsification must both in principle be possible. If we renounce this requirement and admit as empirical also statements which are decidable in one sense only—unilaterally decidable and, more especially, falsifiable—and which may be tested by systematic attempts to falsify them, the contradiction disappears: the method of falsification presupposes no inductive inference, but only the tautological transformations of deductive logic whose validity is not in dispute.[4]

---

[4]For this see also my paper mentioned in note 1 to section 4, *now here reprinted as appendix *i; and my *Postscript*, esp. section *2.

Glossary*

A priori and a posteriori: An a priori proposition is a proposition that can be known to be true without reference to any experience aside from what is necessary to understand the meaning of the words in the proposition. An a posteriori proposition is a proposition whose justification requires reference to experience. *A posteriori* and *empirical* are often regarded as synonymous. Although some philosophers, such as Plato and Leibniz, contended that some very important ideas such as cause, substance, likeness, and difference cannot be derived from experience and so must be a priori, the British empiricists, notably Locke and Hume, stated that all knowledge stems from experience. Immanuel Kant's revolutionary insight is that some a priori concepts are necessary for, and even assumed in, the very possibility of human experience.

Additivity: To make a two-way analysis of variance test (to examine how more than one independent variable influences the dependent variable), one assumes the property of additivity. *Additivity* means that the interaction between two variables does not produce a different result from what would be expected by combining their separate influences. When significant interaction effects occur in an analysis of variance (ANOVA), the two variables interacting produce an effect over and above that of each variable alone (see *interactive effects*).

Algorithm: A formal problem-solving procedure that systematically locates the solution using a specific, constant, step-by-step procedure. Common algorithms are mathematical formulas, used, for example, in calculating percentages.

Allele: One of various mutational forms of a gene.

Analytic and synthetic statements: Significant philosophical discussion of analytic and synthetic statements began with Kant. The distinction Kant made is based on the nature of the evidence needed to assess whether the statement is true or false. In an analytic statement, the concept of the predicate is included in the subject, and so the statement is a priori, true. "All students are human" is an analytic statement. By contrast, in a synthetic statement, the predicate is not included in the subject, by definition. "All students like research" is a synthetic statement, in that it adds to the subject (students) attributes that are not entailed in it by definition. The logical positivists

---

I am indebted to Stuart Glennan and Deborah Zuskar for their assistance with this Glossary.

Editor's Note: A Glossary is inevitably very limited because these terms have been (and are) used in diverse ways. Short definitions cannot reflect the actual diversity of meaning. Where possible, readers are referred to specific works for further elaboration of the meanings of the terms. Other helpful resources are Bynum, Brown and Porter (1985), Jones (1969), and Flew (1984).

reformulated Kant's analytic–synthetic distinction, defining analytic statements as those whose truth can be ascertained only by logical means and defining synthetic statements as those whose truth can be ascertained only by other means (e.g., experience). One of the most important criticisms of logical positivism was that no sharp distinction can be made between analytic and synthetic statements, because many analytic statements rely on definitions of terms, which in turn rest on language. Because language assumes knowledge of the objects of experience, such analytic statements also ultimately refer to experience (Quine, 1948).

ANOVA, or analysis of variance: An inferential statistical method of data analysis used to test the null hypothesis that two or more population means are equal by examining the variability within samples derived from the population. For example, one might compare the differences between two samples, composed of one group of people who received a treatment, and another group that did not (an experimental group and a control group, although one is not limited to using only two groups). If the null hypothesis is rejected as highly improbable, traditionally, one infers a difference between the population means. ANOVA partitions the variability within the sample into two parts: (1) the variability around the mean, within each group, and (2) the variability between the means of the groups. One-way (using one independent variable) and two-way (using two independent variables) ANOVAs can be conducted. A "higher-order" ANOVA means more than two independent variables are used (Norusis, 1988).

Artifact: An aspect of an experimental variable with effects on the dependent variable that are not recognized by the experimenter, that therefore cannot be controlled for in the experimental situation, and that considerably influence the results of the inquiry (Boring, 1969). There are patterns in the recognition of artifacts. At first, scientists resist recognizing them. Then, although the patterns are recognized, their implications often are not taken seriously. Finally, their implications may be recognized, and the artifacts themselves become a subject for scientific research (McGuire, 1969).

Causal ontology: Bhaskar points out that scientists use two types of criteria to ascribe realness to a posited object: perceptual and causal (see Chapter 5). Some objects of knowledge are ascribed realness (ontological status) because we perceive them; for example, you see this book. A causal ontology is a "real" that is known not because we perceive it but because it brings about changes, and we perceive those changes. The examples Bhaskar gives are magnetic fields and gravity. An example of a causal ontology as defined in the new psychology, intrapsychic humanism, are the motives that regulate one's self-esteem (Pieper & Pieper, 1990).

Ceteris paribus: A Latin phrase that means "other things being equal," or "other things corresponding." It is often used to refer to the initial (or background) conditions in a prediction. "Other things being equal" means assuming the initial conditions are stable from situation to situation.

Correspondence theory of truth: A theory of truth that holds that "true propositions are copies of whatever in the world makes them true" (Hacking, 1983, p. 133). A correspondence theory of truth assumes that a reality exists, against which the phenomenon that is being evaluated as true can be compared. The pragmatists have developed other theories of truth. Pierce believed that truth is "whatever hypothesizing, inducing and testing settled down upon," that is, a set of "stable conclusions reached by that unending community of inquirers" (quoted in Hacking, 1983, p. 60). Other pragmatists viewed truth as "whatever answers to our present needs," or as Dewey said, truth is "warranted acceptability" (cited in Hacking, 1983, p. 61).

Covering law model: See *deductive-nomological explanation.*

Deductive-nomological explanation: A model of scientific explanation that consists of a derivation of a statement of the fact to be explained from general laws (covering laws) and statements describing initial or background conditions (Hempel & Oppenheim, 1948). The explanation is a valid deductive argument that concludes with the statement that an event to be explained (the explanandum) occurred. The explanation of the event, or the premises of the statement together with the rest of the deduction (the explanans), must include at least one general law under which the occurrence of the event can be subsumed. That is the "covering law." The most noted expositors of deductive-nomological explanations are the logical empiricist philosophers of science Carl Hempel and Paul Oppenheim (1948). This model of explanation has been criticized chiefly on two grounds: (1) that many explanations (e.g., functional explanations) are not of this form; and (2) that many arguments of this form do not seem to be explanatory. For example, in everyday life, we explain phenomena without requiring such laws, and also the laws may not in themselves provide adequate explanations.

Dependent variable: The variable that the experimenter predicts will change as a result of the action of the independent variable.

Descriptive statistics: Used to summarize quantified data so that they can be understood more easily. Common descriptive statistics are frequency distributions and percentages.

Determinism: The belief that for every event there are conditions that inevitably cause that event to take place and that in effect rule out any other event from occurring. Hobbes, Laplace, Hume, Kant, and Mill all developed different understandings of determinism. In psychology, determinism commonly refers to the belief that human actions are not freely chosen but are regulated by motives that are external constraints (outside the individual's conscious control) on the individual's capacity to choose. Bhaskar argues that the common view of determinism is flawed because it assumes that "because an event was caused to happen, it had to happen before it was caused" (Bhaskar, 1985, p. 96).

Empiricism: Refers to the belief that all knowledge is based on experience. Typically, empiricism denies that humans are born with innate ideas and holds instead (as Locke said) that only experience provides the mind with ideas. Empiricism has sometimes (incorrectly) been equated with knowledge derived from experimentation and is associated with skepticism about metaphysical claims.

Epistemology: The study of knowledge—the ways it occurs and the bases for knowing. Every theory rests on assumptions about how to know the reality the theory describes and explains. For example, a method of clinical interviewing is based on assumptions about how to know the reality that the clinical theory addresses.

Extension: The extension of a concept refers to the set of things to which the concept applies, or the set of objects that fall under the concept (by contrast, see *intension*).

Fact: Different philosophical systems regard the nature of facts in different ways. Positivist philosophers hold that facts can be theory-free. Following Mach, the positivists viewed facts as clusters of relatively uncomplicated and stable sensations. Positivist social and behavioral scientists defined facts as data derived from experimentation, which are contrasted with values, intuitions, or a priori assumptions. The pragmatist philosopher John Dewey emphasized that facts

> are not self-sufficient and complete in themselves. They are selected and described, as we have seen, for a purpose [and] in regulated inquiry facts are . . . the particular facts and kinds of facts that will link up with one another in the definite ways that are required to produce a definite end. . . . [T]heir function is to serve as evidence and their evidential quality is judged on the basis of their capacity to form an ordered whole in response to operations prescribed by the ideas they occasion and support. (1938, p. 113)

Postpositivist philosophers of science recognize that facts cannot be either theory-free or value-free. According to sociologists of science, such as Stephen Shapin (1982), data that scientists who use one scientific theory accept as fact during a given historical period may be regarded as highly questionable (or be given an entirely different meaning) by scientists who use a different theory or who live during a different time period. For example, for Ptolemaic astronomers, the observation that the sun rises indicated that the sun revolves around a stable planet earth; however, the sunrise indicates to us that the earth spins on an axis.

Factorization: According to Simon (1966b), factorization is a heuristic in which the problem solver factors a large problem into a smaller number of problems and then begins solving the smaller problem that has the least number of unknowns. This heuristic is similar to "partializing" problems in social work practice.

Genotype: The genetic constitution of an organism.

Heuristic: From the Greek word, *heuriskein,* meaning "to discover or to find." Herbert Simon uses the term to signify a problem-solving strategy, including techniques of observation and representation (1966a, in Chapter 5). Simon argues that the scientist who makes creative discoveries employs superior heuristics, which enable the scientist engaging in trial-and-error problem-solving searches to explore "more significant and relevant" aspects of the problem (1966a, p. 27). Every heuristic both facilitates problem solving and also sets up systematic biases. As Wimsatt says, heuristics "hide their tracks," so the biases can be difficult to recognize (1986b, in Chapter 5). According to the heuristic paradigm, the term refers to many different forms of problem-solving strategies including, for example: (1) a theory, (2) a way of collecting data, and (3) a linguistic system. Heuristics range in scope from smaller-scale heuristics, such as a mental status exam or a particular research design, to larger-scale heuristics, such as a theory of human development or a metatheory of knowledge.

Historicism: Historicism has traditionally been associated with the view that all social phenomena are determined by historical events and so can be understood only relative to their historical context. Two of the most important versions of historicism follow: (1) History is a valid explanatory principle, and historical epochs are distinctive and need to be understood on their own terms. (2) Social science should be concerned with discovering laws that govern historical developments and that can be used to predict sequences of historical events. Karl Popper's (1964) critique of the latter version of historicism has been very influential.

Ideology: Traditionally refers to a systematic body of ideas that justifies, or functions to uphold, a political position or state of society. An ideology also includes implicit and pervasive assumptions. The term often refers to false ideas that mobilize political and social actions. Ideologies can infuse scientific knowledge; they are so pervasive in the sociohistorical context that they can become the scientist's accepted assumptions about reality. For example, beliefs associated with misogyny guided medical practices that were destructive of women's sexual functioning (Pieper & Pieper, 1992b). Critiques of ideologies generally expose both the lack of evidence for the beliefs composing the ideology and also the social functions that such false beliefs serve (Bhaskar, 1991; Bricker-

Jenkins & Hooyman, 1986; Outhwaite, 1987; Richardson, 1984).

Independent variable: The variable introduced by the experimenter in the effort to discern its effects. Also called the *experimental variable* (see by contrast, *dependent variable*).

Inferential statistics: The aim of inferential statistics is to derive generalizations, such as about a population based on knowledge about a sample. Commonly, the researcher estimates parameters of a population and tests hypotheses about the population based on data obtained in a sample drawn from that population. The researcher uses procedures to estimate and maximize the representativeness of the sample, including selecting a "random" sample using a random numbers table. The wide variety of inferential statistical methods include analysis of variance (or ANOVA, see Lewontin, Chapter 6) and multiple regression. An illustration of the use of inferential statistics for data analysis is drug testing. A sample's response to the medication can be used as the basis for generalizing about the medication's utility for a similar population. Every inferential statistical method of analysis requires that the sample meet certain assumptions, but researchers vary in the extent to which they follow those standards. How statisticians think about the use of inferential statistics depends on whether they are positivist or postpositivist. To illustrate, postpositivist researchers emphasize that the meaning of any statistic always needs to be evaluated using substantive criteria. Postpositivists also recognize that statistical inferences based on a sample are not necessarily statements about the probability that corresponding events will recur in the future with other samples and populations (see Gigerenzer et al., 1989). Statistical analyses often have been misused, as Heineman Pieper (1981, 1985) points out, and as Lewontin describes (see Chapter 6; see also Gigorenzes, 1993).

Instrumentalism: The antirealist position that scientific theories are only instruments or tools for deriving predictions from data, or for describing phenomena, and that the truth or falsity of theories is irrelevant. Dewey called his philosophy "instrumentalism" to distinguish it from earlier pragmatist theories. In his view, terms were defined in relation to their function, and the truth of concepts was defined in terms of their efficacy.

Dewey's beliefs differ substantially from those of contemporary instrumentalists.

Intension: The intension of a concept refers to the set of properties that make up the concept or the attributes contained in it (also called its "sense") (by contrast, see *extension*).

Interactive effects: In analysis of variance (ANOVA), an interaction effect occurs when the assumption of additivity does not hold. An example of when the assumption of additivity does not hold is that when hydrogen and oxygen are combined, they yield water, which differs from what one would expect if the two elements were examined separately (Blalock, 1979b, p. 356). In Chapter 6, Lewontin points out that because of the nature of the causal processes at work in the interaction between the genotype and the environment, these processes have an interactive effect on the phenotype; accordingly, one cannot use ANOVA to quantify the separate influences of the two independent variables (genotype and the environment) on the dependent variable (the phenotype).

Intersubjective knowledge: Commonly refers to knowledge that exists between (conscious) minds. For example, it is available to and validated by more than one person. As Hull points out (Chapter 5), intersubjectivity has long been regarded as both problematic and as a fundamental characteristic of scientific knowledge. Logical positivist philosophers of science and those who sought to realize logical positivist aims prescribed methodological solutions as guarantees of the intersubjectivity of scientific knowledge (e.g., operationism as outlined by Bridgman in the Appendix). To illustrate, Rudolf Carnap said that one of the major advantages that accrues when social and behavioral scientists use the "physicalist" language is that "the events described in this language are in principle observable by all users of the language" (1963/1991a, pp. 51–52). As Hull points out, however (see Chapter 5), all methodologies are theory and value-laden, and so methodological prescriptions cannot guarantee intersubjective knowledge. Heineman Pieper and Pieper include an up-to-date discussion of the problem of intersubjective knowledge when they present their new psychology and philosophy of mind, intrapsychic humanism. They define intersubjectivity as, "the sharing of subjective states of meaning that originate in cranially distinct centers

of solipsistic consciousness"; they point out that "there has been no general agreement about when and in what manner intersubjectivity occurs (i.e., whether it is fundamentally innate, constructed, or learned)" (Pieper & Pieper, 1990, pp. 342–343).

Laplacean demon: A computer with unlimited computational power and complete knowledge of every fact of fundamental physics. Pierre Simon de Laplace was a French mathematician and philosopher who lived from 1749 to 1827 and who proved the mechanical stability of the solar system, drawing primarily from Newtonian mechanics. Laplace developed a position called *mechanical determinism*. He believed that with a sufficiently powerful algorithm and computational ability, he could describe the mechanics of the universe.

Logical empiricism: The members of the Vienna Circle initially called themselves logical positivists. However, they adopted the term logical empiricist very quickly, as they began to revise their views in response to criticism from other philosophers. Rudolf Carnap and Carl Hempel were two of the leading logical empiricists. In the 1981 selection, Heineman Pieper uses the term "logical empiricism" to designate the philosophy of research that stemmed from logical positivism; see footnote 3 to that paper.

Means–end analysis: A heuristic in which the problem solver defines differences between the present situation and the desired situation, considers various ways of reducing those differences, and then selects a method to reduce the difference (Simon, 1966b, p. 14).

Mentalism: Some positivist philosophers and behaviorists use this term to refer to concepts about mental experience, such as the terms *motive* or *emotion*. The term often has pejorative connotations.

Methodological individualism: An assumption that has regulated how positivist social researchers defined the objects of their study, namely, that "facts about society and social phenomena are to be explained largely in terms of individuals" (Bhaskar, 1989b, p. 70).

Monadic versus relational properties: A monadic property is a property of an individual entity or part of a system. A relational property is a property that an entity has only in virtue of its relation to other entities. The color of one's hair is a monadic property, whereas whether or not one is married is a relational property. A relational property does not say something about the individual intrinsically, but it describes how one stands in relation to others.

Naturalism: At present, the term *naturalism* has three primary meanings. (1) The first meaning is close to materialism—the belief that all that is real, including apparently nonmaterial entities such as minds, can be understood in terms of interactions of material elements. (2) Human and social life can, in principle, be explained scientifically, as can other natural phenomena. However, this is not to say there is or should be an identity of subject matter and method between the social and natural sciences, as the logical positivists prescribed (see Bhaskar, Chapter 5). (3) Statements of fact and value are not completely distinct. In contrast to beliefs that value-free facts are possible, contemporary naturalism includes the recognition that there are no value-free facts. For example, in Bhaskar's concept of naturalism, scientific knowledge serves either to reinforce the status quo, including oppressive systems, or to further human emancipation. He describes science as part of a transformational conception of human activity (Bhaskar, 1989b). Callebaut uses the term the "naturalistic turn" to describe a new paradigm in contemporary philosophy of science (see Chapter 4). There are divergences of opinion within that paradigm. One of the central ideas, according to Callebaut, is that humans are both a part of nature and also help to construct the specific objects of our knowledge and knowledge itself, the means by which those objects can be known. Further, "our knowledge is uncertain and fallible, but also corrigible" (Callebaut, 1993, p. 3). As Heineman Pieper points out, naturalism is distinct from naturalistic research (see the Preface).

Normative: Traditionally means prescribing a norm or standard.

Occam's (or Ockham's) razor: Although this term is not found in the works of William of Ockham, it has come to refer to a principle applied in theory appraisal, that is, that the theorist should refer to no more "reals" (or ontological assumptions) than are necessary.

Ontology: The study of being; the assumptions about "what is" on which any theory is based.

Paradigm: Thomas Kuhn, a physicist who also became a historian and philosopher of science, first elaborated the concept of a scientific paradigm as part of his theory about how scientific ideas evolve and change in his landmark book, *The Structure of Scientific Revolutions* (1962, 1970). The concept of "paradigm" is very inclusive and varies (Masterman, 1970). In its most common usage in the history and philosophy of science, and as coined by Kuhn, it refers to a set of assumptions about reality and how to know that reality that members of a scientific community generate and share (Kuhn, 1962, 1970; Shapere, 1964). A paradigm includes values, such as what kinds of explanations and research procedures are acceptable. A paradigm also can be viewed as a large-scale heuristic.

Phenomenalism: A theory of knowledge, stemming in part from empiricism, that holds that all statements about the world are statements about actual or possibly actual experiences and that experience can be understood only as a succession of conscious ideas, impressions, or sense data. The logical positivist assumption that statements referring to anything other than sense data are scientifically meaningless is one form of phenomenalism.

Phenotype: The observable behavioral and physiological characteristics of an organism, that reflect the combined influences of genotype and environment.

Placebo: As defined in medicine, a placebo is a substance or intervention that a researcher believes does not have a therapeutic effect but that the researcher gives to subjects who are told they are receiving an intervention that has or may have a therapeutic effect. The rationale for the use of placebos in research is to differentiate the effects of an independent variable from other effects of the experimental situation. Some placebo trials have involved deception; the experimenter does not tell the participant/subjects that they may be receiving a placebo. In other research designs, the participant/subjects are informed that they will receive either a placebo or a treatment, but the participant/subjects, by definition, do not know which alternative they are receiving. The "placebo effect," or the impact on the participant/subjects of their belief that the intervention is therapeutic, is very powerful. Orne describes one of the most telling examples of the power of placebo effects: "in battlefield situations saline solution by injection has 90 per cent of the effectiveness of morphine in alleviating the pain associated with acute injury" (Orne, 1969, p. 165). Aspects of the experimental situation interact with and influence the strength of the placebo effect.

Planning and abstraction: A heuristic in which the problem solver abstracts the essential features of a problem, which necessarily entails omitting some aspects of the problem; solves the simplified problem; and then uses that solution as a guide in solving the full problem (Simon, 1966b, pp. 14–15).

Proposition: An indicative sentence such as a claim or an assertion; often refers to a claim that is set forth as the basis of an argument. The logical positivists distinguished between sentences and propositions, using the term *proposition* to indicate a particular kind of sentence that is "describable as true or false" (Hanfling, 1981a, p. 16). As Schlick says, "every proposition may be regarded as an answer to a question" (1938/1979, p. 36).

Realism: A philosophical position that has many variants, all of which claim the existence of a mind-independent reality that is knowable in some way, even though ways of knowing reality may be irrevocably biased (Leplin, 1984). Although philosophers espouse various forms of scientific realism, Wimsatt describes how

> on certain grounds (usually, for example, that the existence of an entity or property is known, derivable, or detectable through a variety of independent means . . .) scientists would argue that an entity or property is real, and they cannot imagine plausible or possible theoretical changes that would undercut this conclusion. Furthermore, they might argue that their experimental and problem solving approaches require them to presuppose the existence of that entity, property, or phenomenon—a heuristic argument. (1987, pp. 23–24)

Wimsatt says that even many opponents of scientific realism "could accept this kind of local and

heuristic realism" (1987, pp. 23–24; see also Heineman Pieper's definition in her 1987 response to Brekke, in Chapter 3). One of the most thought-provoking contemporary presentations of a realist philosophy of science is Bhaskar's transcendental (also called critical) realism (1975, 1989a, 1989b, 1991). With regard to transcendental realism's new emphasis on ontology and its implications for demarcating science and nonscience, Bhaskar says,

> whereas transcendental realism asks explicitly what the world must be like for science to be possible, classical philosophy asked merely what science would have to be like for the knowledge it yielded to be justified. It was presumed that our knowledge was justified; science was not viewed as a process in motion; and doing away with ontology left philosophy without any critical purchase on science. (1975, p. 43)

Bhaskar elaborates how a focus on ontology is one way of demarcating scientific and nonscientific knowledge:

> For the transcendental realist it is the nature of the object that determines the possibility of a science. Thus he can allow, without paradox, that there may be no humanly intelligible pattern to be discovered in the stars or politically intelligible pattern in voting behavior. So that no science of astrology or psephology is possible, no matter how scrupulously 'scientific method' is adhered to. (1975, p. 44)

Reductionism: Generally refers to describing a phenomenon in terms of another phenomenon that is regarded as more fundamental or basic. The logical empiricist view of reductionism was that the statements of higher level theories (including entities, properties, and laws, e.g.) should be deducible in terms of lower-level theories without any loss of information. Bhaskar defines logical positivist reductionism as the assertion that there is "an actual identity of subject matter" between the human and natural sciences (1989a, p. 2). Wimsatt emphasizes that the logical empiricist view of reductionist explanation is "unattainable" (1986b). Another view of reduction that Wimsatt addresses is that it concerns explanatory relationships between different levels of phenomena, which does not sacrifice the information or meaning available at either level (1976a). Accordingly, although reduction may be thought of as reducing the more complex to the less so, in fact, reduction may increase complexity rather than reduce it. This is because explanations for lower-level phenomena are not necessarily less complex than explanations for higher-level phenomena (see also Wimsatt, 1980b).

Relativism: Philosophers have elaborated several different types of relativism. Relativists typically recognize the importance of the social environment in influencing values and assumptions about reality. They emphasize that given the diversity of social environments, there is great diversity in values and knowledge. Epistemological relativists characteristically maintain that because unbiased knowledge is impossible, no sound arguments can be made for the existence of a mind-independent reality that can be used as a standard for evaluating the veracity of theories. In contrast, some contemporary realists (e.g., Bhaskar and Wimsatt) believe both that there can be no unbiased knowledge and also that there is a mind-independent reality that is the basis for correcting theories and developing truer theories.

Reliability: Traditionally refers to an assessment of the quality of judgment in research, and more commonly addresses an important aspect of the problem of intersubjectivity, for example, How do I know that your judgments about a given observation would accord with my own, and unless I know that, how can I evaluate the utility of your observations? Researchers traditionally find ways to show other researchers that their observations are reliable. Ways of demonstrating reliability range from using multiple coders to judge the same material and report the judgments about which they agree and disagree, to using audiotapes or videotapes, to conducting comprehensive process recordings of a treatment session for another reader to evaluate. Bias is present in all of those approaches. As with validity, researchers have identified different aspects of reliability, and the customary procedures for ascertaining reliability vary. A common way of quantifying the reliability of coders' judgments is to have coders code the same material and then calculate the percentage of agreements out of the total of disagreements and agreements. As Heineman Pieper points out in the Preface, positivist social and behavioral researchers often have confused reliability and credibility:

[R]eliable observations are not necessarily credible; no matter how many people tell us they saw a Martian, we are unlikely to find them credible. Clinical credibility—our conviction of the scientific value, i.e., fundamental correctness, of the practitioner-researcher's interventions and theoretical understanding—can rest on the comprehensive, detailed, well conceptualized presentation by a single practitioner of her/his conduct and understanding of a specific treatment process.

Research design: A research design is a heuristic the researcher reflectively sets up to solve the research problem. A researcher makes several distinct choices when designing research, including: choosing a philosophy of research, formulating the research problem, selecting ontological and epistemological assumptions and regulating values, delineating a system to study and drawing the environment–system boundary, planning whether the research will be naturalistic or interventionist, and deciding how to collect and analyze data. The heuristic approach to designing research does not proscribe, prescribe, or privilege any research method. It prioritizes reflective analysis of the biases set up by each choice. A research design based on principles of the heuristic paradigm can be satisficing, in that it can lead to workable solutions to the researcher's problem, be compatible with humanistic values, and be conceptually consistent.

Risk assessment: Entails judgments about perceived hazards. It is an inherently subjective process, although assessment of risks also is informed by information from the general public and experts. Risk assessment is significantly affected by heuristics, and understanding those heuristics can improve decision making.

Robustness: A concept formulated primarily by William Wimsatt, robustness is an important concept for philosophers of science using the naturalistic paradigm (see Chapter 4). Robustness refers (1) to a characteristic of some aspects of scientific knowledge and (2) to an analysis of how elements of knowledge are observed or generated, termed "robustness analysis." Observations or other elements of knowledge that are "robust" are those that hold up, or are relatively invariant, when multiple ways of knowing are used. Robustness is a criterion scientists use in evaluating a knowledge claim,

I believe that we ought to be looking for *what crite-ria scientists use in deciding whether to trust an entity, or claim, or whatever*—rather than wondering what happens in the long run, as traditional scien-tific realists did, or whether our terms really refer. . . . And if you ask what criteria they use, it turns out that they use robustness—the detection or derivation of an entity or result in a number of inde-pendent ways. (Wimsatt, quoted in Callebaut, 1993, p. 155; italics in original)

Robustness analysis is a process in which diverse models, methods of observation, or means of derivation are used in order to compensate for the biases of any single way of knowing (see Wim-satt, 1981a, and the selection by Wimsatt in Chapter 5). Wimsatt points out a central caveat: Any robustness analysis is a heuristic, and if the diverse approaches used in the analysis share sim-ilar biases, one will not be able to detect them or their consequences; such an analysis results in "pseudo-robustness."

Satisficing: An extremely important heuristic, because although some algorithms will yield the best solutions for some problems, there are no such algorithms for most problems, and the prob-lem solver has limited resources for finding potential problem solutions. The researcher must decide which solutions are "good enough" accord-ing to some criterion: "heuristics that proceed on this basis are sometimes called 'satisficing' heuris-tics" (Simon, 1966b, p. 16).

Skepticism: A philosophical position that began with early Greek philosophers and that questions the reliability of all knowledge claims. Skeptics typi-cally construct their arguments to raise doubts. More extreme versions of skepticism question any knowledge that is not logical or mathematical and claim that there are no standards for evaluat-ing scientific knowledge.

Social constructionism: Refers to a theory of knowl-edge advanced by many contemporary social and behavioral researchers. Kenneth Gergen (1985) links the term to Berger and Luckmann's *The Social Construction of Reality* (1967). According to Gergen, a social constructionist focuses on explaining the processes by which people explain their world, including themselves and their inter-actions. The emphasis is on how humans, through

language, jointly construct reality both in the pre-sent as well as the past. There is also a future ori-entation in the sense that our constructions have a creative impact on ourselves, others, and our society. Social constructionism has a critical focus, "it begins with radical doubt in the taken-for-granted world—whether in the sciences or in daily life—and in a specialized way acts as a form of social criticism. . . . It invites one to challenge the objective basis of conventional knowledge" (Gergen, 1985, pp. 266–267).

Statistical significance testing: Tests of the level of statistical significance refer to the degree of prob-ability that the findings would occur if the null hypothesis is correct. As Heineman Pieper points out, "statistical significance has nothing directly to do with the research hypothesis. It is only rele-vant to the rejection of a null hypothesis, which is usually untrue anyway" (1985, p. 7; see also Rozeboom, 1960; Salmon, 1971a, 1989). Further, other factors that do not relate to the validity of the researcher's hypothesis, such as the size of the sample, can affect the level of statistical sig-nificance. For example, simply enlarging the sam-ple may yield statistically significant findings, even though previously the same procedure led to findings that were not statistically significant. Sta-tistical significance has often been confused with substantive significance (Heineman Pieper, 1985; K. Smith, 1983). (See Gigerenzer et al., 1989, for a comprehensive discussion.)

Syllogism: A form of reasoning from the general to the specific. In logic, a syllogism is a deductive argument with a major premise, a minor premise, and a conclusion. For example: All students want to learn about research to contribute to and improve the knowledge base of the social and behavioral sciences (major premise). You are a student (minor premise). You want to learn about research to contribute to and improve the knowl-edge base of the social and behavioral sciences (conclusion).

Triangulation: Derives, as Robert LeVine (1981) sug-gests, from astronomy and navigation, and refers to taking a measurement of a point from different perspectives. It has also come to refer to using different instruments to arrive at a final determi-nation.

Uncertainty:

> Uncertainty is a fact with which all forms of life must be prepared to contend. At all levels of biological complexity there is uncertainty about the significance of signs or stimuli and about the possible consequences of actions. At all levels, action must be taken before the uncertainty is resolved, and a proper balance must be achieved between a high level of specific readiness for the events that are most likely to occur and a general ability to respond appropriately when the expected happens. (Kahneman & Tversky, 1982, pp. 590–510)

Uncertainty is commonly attributed to one of two loci: the external world, or our own state of knowledge. To illustrate, people are inclined to experience uncertainty about past events as being due to ignorance but uncertainty about future events as being due to conditions in the external world (Kahneman & Tversky, 1982, pp. 515–516).

Validity: The distinction between truth and validity has a well-developed rationale in logic. Validity is a standard used to assess an argument. If an argument is valid, its conclusion follows logically from its premises. If the premises of a valid argument are true, it is impossible for its conclusion to be false. An illustration of how truth and validity can be distinguished is that an argument may have a false premise and still be valid if its conclusions follow logically from the premise; moreover, an invalid argument may have true premises and a true conclusion. In much social and behavioral research, validity has also come to have an unrelated meaning; it commonly refers to whether or not data collection procedures capture the phenomena the researcher aims to study (Brinberg & Kidder, 1982). For example, scales that claim to measure patient depression may measure patients' reactive feelings about having to fill out a questionnaire before being able to share their pain in the way they feel most comfortable. Such scales can be criticized as lacking in validity. Researchers have identified and defined various forms of validity: content, criterion, construct (Cronbach & Meehl, 1955), concurrent, internal, external (Bronfenbrenner, 1979a; Rosenthal, 1982), predictive, convergent, discriminant (D. T. Campbell & Fiske, 1959; Fiske, 1982), and "face"

validity (Kidder, 1982; Lather, 1986a). Definitions of the various forms of validity tend to vary among researchers.

One way that social and behavioral researchers often have determined validity is by correlating one data collection procedure with another data collection procedure (a form of validity that is often termed *criterion validity*). Over time, if researchers do not analyze whether the data collection procedures capture the phenomenon they are intended to capture, and instead rely only on comparing the data collection procedure with data collection procedures, a pervasive illusion of validity can result. For example, some researchers claimed the Bender Gestalt could measure organic brain damage in children when they "validated" the instrument by comparing Bender Gestalt findings with electroencephalogram (EEG) findings. Then, the Bender Gestalt was used to validate other tests that purported to measure organicity, such as certain scales on IQ tests (Koppitz, 1964). However, Herbert Birch (1964) emphasized that over time such processes of validation resulted in an illusion of validity. In fact, the Bender Gestalt and the EEG could at best only record functional symptoms and could not record what many researchers claimed they were measuring—structural brain damage. Through conceptual analysis and examining the history of the validation of a data collection procedure, one can begin to evaluate validity.

Two of the most important types of validity are internal and external validity. Internal validity refers to the extent to which the data collection procedures used are internally consistent and consistent with the researchers' theoretical concepts. External validity addresses whether the results obtained through the research correspond to experience outside the research situation. For example, Urie Bronfenbrenner (1979a) said that laboratory-based studies of humans lack external or ecological validity. He emphasized that the laboratory is an artificially constructed environment that induces entirely different effects on participant/subjects in the research than what they would experience in their native environments. Furthermore, in a laboratory the researcher cannot study the diverse interactions between the environment and the participant/subject in the research that one can observe in a natural setting.

Notes

1. "A value judgment, including one of truth, typically incorporates a descriptive or evidential component alongside its prescriptive, imperatival or practical component" (Bhaskar, 1989b, p. 159).

2. Orcutt's recent (1990) description of an "alternative" heuristic paradigm in social work research does not represent the heuristic paradigm as advanced by Martha Heineman Pieper. Moustakas's (1981) elaboration of "heuristic research" differs entirely from Heineman Pieper's.

3. See Grob (1983) and M. Fraser et al. (1991). Briar and Miller said that the early social workers did not "stop to take stock" but frantically accumulated knowledge (1971, p. 7).

4. The authors who have stated such assumptions are so numerous that they cannot all be cited here. They include, however, Austin (1978, 1983), Briar (1979), Fischer (1978, 1981), W. E. Gordon (1951), Reid (1977a), Richan & Mendlesohn (1973), Trattner (1989, see p. 150), Wood (1980), and Zimbalist (1977).

5. Among those who viewed the Social Work Research Group's formulation of an approach to research as an innovative commitment to "pure" science are W. E. Gordon (1951), Greenwood (1955), Kahn (1954), Polansky (1960/1975), and Zimbalist (1977).

6. Many histories of social work did not address social work research. Leiby (1978a), for example, omits the Social Work Research Group, although his chronicle does encompass the 1950s. Ehrenreich (1985) and Woodroofe (1962) do not address social work research. Some significant exceptions include Germain (1970) and Chambers (1963/1980, 1986b). F. Hollis (1983), in her comments about "the way it really was," emphasized that the early social workers did use a "valid scientific approach" (cited in Siporin, 1985, p. 206).

7. For example, M. Fraser et al. (1991). Some (including Briar, 1979; Greenwood, 1955; Hoffman, 1956; Shyne, 1967) went further, stating that the knowledge the early social workers produced should be rejected.

8. See also the historian Gerald Grob (1983) and the sociologist Amitai Etzioni (1969).

9. While commenting that the early social workers' research was not "scientific" for several reasons, including that "questions or hypotheses were not often posed in formal, observable terms," Zimbalist also recognized that he was imposing his own philosophy of research on the researchers of the past rather than re-creating their views of research (1977, pp. 33–34). One historian who did not depreciate social work research of the past using positivist beliefs about science is Carel Germain (1970), who, for example, described Mary Richmond's formulations of "scientific charity."

10. Some histories that omit the significance of the women's rights movement for the social work profession are Bruno (1957), N. Cohen (1958), Trattner (1989), and Leiby (1978a). William Berleman said the movement for women's suffrage was an "unusual cause" and linked it with "spiritualism" and "anti-vivisection" (1968, p. 396). Arthur Schlesinger, in his influential chronicle of the Roosevelt era, noted the exceptional influence of the Hull House reformers yet also called them "dedicated old maids" (1956, p. 24). In his (1955) history, *The Age of Reform*, R. Hofstadter barely mentions the early social workers and the movement for women's rights.

11. Horn commented, "families were not as easily manipulated as some historians have assumed" (1984, p. 26). Other exceptions to the oversimplified history of the work of the early social workers include Garrett (1949) and Germain (1970). Recently, Edleson (1991) studied case records to chronicle how social workers counseled and advocated for battered women between 1907 and 1945.

12. Woodward comments: "History will never be free of bias, nor should it expect to be . . . historians in general prefer to maintain a pluralistic methodology" (1980, p. 36).

13. For further critique of the "new sociology of science," see Bunge (1991, 1992) and Richards (1981, 1987). One of Bunge's critiques is that the new sociology of science "does not go far enough in investigating the social circumstances of scientific research, for in most cases it restricts its interest to investigating what it calls 'local accounting procedures' . . . such as particular laboratories, as if the particular site were more important than both the generic features of scientific research and the structure of society at large. . . . In this regard, NSS [new sociology of science] is a retreat from Marxist SS [social science]" (1992, p. 71). In his view, the new sociology of science misses such important topics as "the deliberate underfunding of social science research by the U.S. conservative governments and of scientific research in general by the British conservative government" (p. 71).

14. In other words, the content analysis compiles the frequency of occurrence of variables, disregarding the specific context in which those variables appear. By contrast, the historical analysis examines how the sociohistorical context influences variables such as the researcher's choice of research method.

15. The coding manual used for the content analysis is available from the author.

16. Gender was ascertained on the basis of the first author's name. Names commonly used for both men and women (e.g., Leslie) were coded as "unknown"; only 6% of the entire sample was coded "unknown." Based on a reliability check of 100 cases, reliability of coders' judgments of gender was 98% (percent of agreements divided by total). The decision to use the first author for coding purposes was based on an analysis of a subsample of 311 articles. That analysis indicated that 89% of articles were single-authored. In the 11% of multiple-authored articles, authors were listed either alphabetically, or, one assumes, in the order of the significance of their contribution to the study. Accordingly, only for those articles in which there are multiple authors of different genders who are listed alphabetically is it possible that the gender of the first author *might not* be the most reliable indicator of the gender of the author who made the most significant contribution. Because only 3% of the 311 articles had authors of different genders who were ordered alphabetically, I assumed that the gender of the first author is a reliable indicator of the gender of the author(s) who made the most significant contribution(s) to the study.

17. I defined *evaluation* broadly so that it would encompass studies that described and commented on interventions conducted, because unless stated otherwise, the implication of such studies is that the intervention is helpful. With regard to the study of evaluation research, the coding procedures and categories used are described further in Chapter 7.

18. Book reviews, editorial comments, poetry, and letters to the editor were excluded from the sample. Several procedures were undertaken to evaluate and improve reliability. Three coders (the author and two research assistants) developed the coding categories by coding articles and discussing the codes. The categories were refined until coding resulted in 90% or better interrater reliability over several different coding episodes. Then, each article was coded by two different coders. The first coder coded the article for all the different codes used (first-author gender, research design heuristic, presence or absence of evaluative content, and approach to evaluation). The second coder, whose function was to provide a check for the first coder, coded each study for (1) whether the author(s)

used primarily qualitative or quantified data to support their conclusions and 2) the two evaluation coding categories used (see Chapter 7). When the two coders disagreed, the disagreement was resolved by a third coder. In the very rare event that there were three disagreements, a fourth coder was used. As a result, the evaluation codes arrived at for each article always represented an agreement between two coders, and the discrimination between qualitative and quantified data also reflected agreement between two coders.

19. Taber and Shapiro (1965) examined a sample of 124 articles published from 1920 to 1963; Howe and Schuerman (1974) examined a sample of 286 articles published from 1957 to 1972; Rosenblatt, Turner, Patterson, and Rollosson (1970) examined a sample of 938 articles published from 1964 to 1968; Weinberger and Tripodi (1969) chose a sample of 1,894 articles published from 1956 to 1965; M. Fraser et al. (1991) examined articles published from 1985 to 1988, defined 817 articles as "other," and analyzed 269 articles for the type of research design used (pp. 11–12). Tripodi (1984) categorized 4,856 journal articles, only 1,051 of which he coded and analyzed as "research" articles, using the classification of Weinberger and Tripodi (1969).

20. M. Fraser et al. had similar findings in their content analysis from 1985 to 1988 (1991, p. 12).

21. Dewey also regarded the positivists' conceptualization of facts and the process of scientific inquiry as misguided (1938).

22. Jessie Taft summarized the painful psychological effects of discrimination against women: "For the alert modern woman, conscious to her finger tips, knowing in her heart that she could give a lifetime of happy associations to the man she loved, and to society, healthy, normal children, the deadlock into which the present social order forces her is a cruel, blighting thing—a choice between a crippled life in the home or an unfulfilled one out of it" (Taft, 1915, p. 3). The experiences of Sophonisba Breckinridge and Florence Kelley exemplify the discrimination these women experienced. Breckinridge was initially appointed to teach home economics at the University of Chicago (despite her J.D. and Ph.D. in another academic field); Kelley was denied admission to one law school in this country, because of her gender (Sklar, 1985). Nonetheless, Breckinridge became a tenured faculty member at the School of Social Service Administration at the University of Chicago, and Kelley obtained

her law degree at Northwestern and became a member of the Bar Association in Illinois.

23. The "three r's" of the settlement house movement were "residence, research, and reform" (Chambers, 1963/1980).

24. Settlements varied in the extent to which they aggressively pursued the aims of the women's movement as well as other reforms, and indeed some settlements pursued conservative political aims (Karger, 1987; Mohl & Betten, 1974; E. Shapiro, 1978). However, Hull House was regarded as the leading settlement and, especially with regard to the development of social research, was profoundly influential. The Hull House settlers developed an approach to research that was adopted, to various degrees, by many other settlements and that influenced several other institutions as well, as will be shown.

25. Addams contributed to the monumental work, U.S. Congress, Senate Report of 1910–1911, *Report on Conditions of Woman and Child Wage-Earners in the United States*, Vols. 1–18. S. Doc. 645, 61st Congress, 2nd Session.

26. One of the SSA students who later co-authored the influential Hollis-Taylor report, Alice Taylor Davis, described her first impression of Sophonisba Breckinridge in 1939 as she entertained students at a tea: "A frail older Southern lady who was gracious, courteous, and feminine. Later, I sensed that she was the embodiment of a pioneer suffragette—a person of keen intellect and tenacious courage, with the capacity for brilliant strategy, a strong will, and tensile strength" (1988, p. 170). Davis described Edith Abbott in one of her lectures on the history of public welfare: "She walked into the large, crowded amphitheater with a determined step, always wearing a hat. She placed her briefcase firmly on the desk and began without referring to notes. Through her lectures, we students lived vicariously the history of public welfare in England and the United States—local, state, and federal. The principles of governmental responsibility from colonial times to the present were dramatized with references to people and successful policies or legislation; inadequacies were made clear from factual data or by sharp thrusts at public officials who failed to live up to their trust and responsibility. Her dry sense of humor and commitment to public welfare in words and actions promoted learning through identification" (1988, p. 171).

27. That particular legislation was subsequently modified, as a consequence of political party shifts, much to the disappointment of the Hull House settlers. Even so, it remained an influential foundation for more permanent protections for workers.

28. See also Pollock (1983) with regard to improvements in conditions for child workers.

29. Rossiter (1982) documents the discrimination against women that pervaded federal agencies at the time.

30. Research on the Philadelphia Charity Organization Society led Rauch to conclude that, "by expanding the limits of women's participation in the organized charity system, visitors blazed a trail for women superintendents, a positive gain for educated women in need of employment" (1975, p. 255).

31. Richmond's formulations have been further supported by the many more recent findings about the importance of empathy, warmth, and genuineness in the therapeutic process.

32. For example, Trattner wrote about social workers' response to Flexner, "[A]ccepting the verdict as pronounced by this expert on the subject social workers . . . [social workers] desperately began trying to define and perfect techniques they could call their own." Trattner also implied that Richmond derived the standards for the research in *Social Diagnosis* (1917) from Flexner's remarks (Trattner, 1989, p. 235).

33. Jarrett said that the very first psychiatric social worker was Edith Burleigh, who worked with Dr. James J. Putnam in the Neurological Clinic of the Massachusetts General Hospital in Boston, in 1905 (Southard & Jarrett, 1922, p. 519).

34. For a notable exception, see Chambers (1963/1980).

35. Graham Taylor (who led the Chicago Commons settlement) pointed to the debilitating impact of the repression of reform movements for the settlements (1936). In addition, in a 1934 message to Taylor to commemorate the 40th anniversary of the settlement, Jane Addams alluded to the settlements' advocacy for many different points of view, the settlements' commitment to political movements that conservatives increasingly perceived as radical, and also to the repression of free speech. Addams said, "only Graham Taylor's valiant defense of free speech saved the

Settlements from defeat in performing what seemed to them an important function" (G. Taylor, 1936, p. 302).

36. In a later book, Witmer expressed different views: "A distinguishing characteristic of modern social work, in contrast to older systems of charity and philanthropy, is that it has a body of scientific rules based on observation and research and on the findings of other disciplines" (1942, p. 55–56).

37. Porter Lee also said that social work was not "scientific." For Lee, the meaning of "scientific" contrasted with the meaning of the term "empirical":

> The derivation of the competence of the social worker has thus far been almost wholly empirical. It is almost entirely the product of experience and only to a limited extent is it scientific or scholarly. We begin to see the possibilities of incorporating science into our knowledge and methods but in the practical work of every day we have not begun to equip ourselves with the science and scholarship characteristic of many of the older professions. Empirical experience is an entirely valid basis for practice. It is indeed an important factor in the practice of the professions much more highly endowed with science and scholarship than ours. True professional work, however, can never become stable, its fundamental conceptions can never be clear, its relationship to the whole web of life can never be established until the equipment of its practitioners is marked by growth in science and scholarship as well as in technical proficiency. (1935/1937c, p. 253)

38. I am indebted to Dr. Gloria Cunningham (personal communication, October 1992) for suggesting this interpretation of some effects of psychoanalytic theory on social workers' beliefs about research. In this regard, it is perhaps not an accident that Charlotte Towle, who was one of the leading educators in psychiatric social work and a prolific author, both emphasized that clinical social work was a science and also was one of the few leading clinical social work educators who did not undergo a Freudian-based psychoanalysis (Posner, 1986).

39. This emphasis persisted through the 1940s. For example, the very diverse subjects that were con-

sidered legitimate foci for scientific inquiry are reflected in a content analysis of the articles published in *The Family* from 1939 to 1942 (LaBarre, 1942).

40. George Herbert Mead, whose ideas were influential for Jane Addams, Mary Richmond, and Jessie Taft, said that behaviorism represented the philosophy of the Queen of Hearts in *Alice in Wonderland*: "Off with their heads!" (cited in R. Rosenberg, 1982).

41. Manicas (1987) describes how the discipline of sociology adopted operationism as well as the logical positivist belief that scientific research could and should be value-free, and he chronicles how the discipline discouraged dissenting views.

42. See also Lee (1937a, 1935/1937b, 1935/1937c) for his perspective as part of the faculty of the New York School of Social Work.

43. The educational problems posed by the sudden need for new social workers were in themselves very challenging. Edith Abbott summarized the problem in her "Report to the President, 1930–1933": "To try to provide some training for the hastily recruited staffs of the great public relief services has been perhaps our most discouraging and, at the same time, most useful work. No special short course or special 'emergency courses' of any kind have been offered, for it has been our experience in the past that such courses provide only the 'little learning' that in a professional field is indeed 'a very dangerous thing.' Every possible effort, however, has been made to make available the regular courses at hours when untrained recruits engaged for the emergency work could attend" (1930–1933, p. 7).

44. See Rossiter (1982) for a description of how the reforms in employment discrimination that women scientists in other fields accomplished during the 1920s had begun to erode by the 1940s.

45. Jane Addams (1910/1990) and Franklin Roosevelt (Schlesinger, 1956) had met with the Webbs, and Edith Abbott (1931) also cited their work.

46. J. Fisher wrote, "Their economic consciousness sharpened by daily contact with the more extreme aspects of poverty-ridden America, they could not at the same time but relate their own needs to those of their clients and incorporate in their program the insistent cry for adequate relief, for work, for social security, which beat against them on all sides" (1936/1990, p. 96).

47. Towle had written, "Social security and public assistance programs are a basic essential for attainment of the socialized state envisaged in a democratic ideology, a way of life which so far has been realized only in slight measure" (1945, p. 57, as quoted in Sutter, 1980; see also Towle, 1945/1987).

48. In describing the impact of psychology's adoption of positivism, Buckley commented, "the prestige formerly afforded to scientific theories came to be given to scientific methods. The successful model for the development of a science was physics. Psychologists tried as much as possible to conform to that model in an effort to raise their discipline's status within the scientific community. Behaviorism was a logical development of this trend in that it sought to make the procedure of investigation in psychology as close as possible to that in physics. Ironically, Watson and his colleagues, like most of the scientific community, were ignorant of the revolution that was transforming physics. . . . It was the physics of Ernst Mach, not Einstein, that provided the model for scientific achievement" (1989, p. 80).

49. "After reaching a low point in 1935, the fertility rate of both black and white women began a steep rise, peaking in 1957" (Abramovitz, 1988, p. 320).

50. In 1944–1945, only 5% of the graduates of master's programs were men. The percentage of male graduates increased steadily for several years until by 1950, 39% of graduates were men. From 1953 to 1957, the percentage of male graduates decreased very slightly. From 1959 to 1969, 40% or more of the graduates of master's programs were men. The proportion of male graduates then began to drop again until it reached 21% in 1981 (National Association of Social Workers, 1983–1984).

51. This problem began in the 1930s (Chambers, 1986b) but became increasingly apparent in the 1950s. For example, Harry Hopkins's biographer commented about Hopkins's rapid rise through administrative positions in the social work profession during the late 1920s: "He had entered a profession founded principally by women, but which in a male-dominated society was quick to reward the talents of the comparatively few men who entered it. This was particularly true of the Red Cross, where men held all the top management jobs" (McJimsey, 1987, p. 27).

52. In 1960, Mary Macdonald wrote, "Fourteen schools of social work offer doctoral programs. The

number of degrees awarded has increased sharply over the past four years, from twelve in 1955–1956 to twenty-six in 1958–1959." Moreover, at that time few graduates of social work doctoral programs pursued research careers, "Some years ago a follow-up of students revealed that very few moved from doctoral programs to positions in research . . . few doctoral candidates prepare themselves to be career research workers, and indeed the schools even in their doctoral programs have had limited resources for research training" (1960a, p. 513).

53. The members of the Steering Committee of the Social Work Research Group represented many social and behavioral science disciplines in addition to social work, including economics, anthropology, psychology, and sociology. Some of the most influential researchers who studied social work practice were listed as representing other disciplines (e.g., Kogan from psychology and Pollak from sociology).

54. For similar comments, see Blenkner (1959), Greenwood (1955), Hoffman (1956), and Maas and Varon (1949).

55. Maas's misuse of "empirical" is characteristic of the way the term came to be misused by the Social Work Research Group and its followers. For further elaboration of how the term was misused, see the selections by Heineman Pieper in this volume.

56. For example, at the School of Social Service Administration at the University of Chicago, students were required to take a total of four research courses to complete their master's degree (Macdonald, 1957).

57. Some of the most influential social work practice theorists (including Towle, 1954, and Hamilton in the "Foreword" to Stein & Cloward, 1958) read the work of SWRG members, but they did not critique the SWRG's distinction between "social workers" and "social scientists."

58. D. G. French (1952) stated that out of ninety studies funded by the National Institute of Mental Health in 1951, only "four were focused on problems of specific concern to social work." Moreover, he said that social workers submitted very few proposals, and of the social work proposals submitted, "most of these did not meet the standards set up by the National Advisory Mental Health Council" (p. 119).

59. The "Minutes of the Annual Meeting of the Social Work Research Group, May 17, 1951" describe findings from the SWRG's survey of social work jour-nals; one conclusion drawn was that a significant problem is "stimulating the writing of research papers," as though the articles that were published in the journals were not research (Social Work Research Group, 1951a).

60. Further examples of this emphasis come from the minutes of the Research Section of NASW (the name the SWRG adopted when the NASW was established and became their parent organization). Members were planning for a conference about child welfare sponsored by the Elizabeth McCormick Fund. They recommended specifically that "consideration should be given to research into the process of helping people rather than the person receiving help" (Research Section, NASW, October 24–25, 1955). Another example is Shyne's 1967 comment: "traditionally, certain descriptive data about the characteristics of clients, as well as about the volume of service, have been collected as part of agency administration. Although it is doubtful whether such data-collecting should be termed 'research,' data are the stuff of research, and the data needed for immediate administrative purposes may bring into focus questions that call for study in more analytical fashion" (p. 468).

61. Einstein wrote to Sir Karl Popper, "altogether I really do not at all like the now fashionable . . . 'positivistic' tendency of clinging to what is observable. I regard it as trivial that one cannot, in the range of atomic magnitudes, make predictions with any desired degree of precision, and I think (like you, by the way) that theory cannot be fabricated out of the results of observation, but that it can only be invented" (Einstein, 1934/1959, p. 458).

62. Reichenbach (1891–1953) was not a member of the Vienna Circle, in part because he resided in Berlin rather than Vienna. However, he agreed with many of the logical positivists' ideas and collaborated actively with members of the Vienna Circle. For example, he edited *Erkenntnis* with Rudolf Carnap. Like Carnap and Hempel, he emigrated to the United States. A prominent scholar who lectured widely in the United States, he held a chair at the University of California at Los Angeles, which was given to Carnap following Reichenbach's death. Peter Achinstein noted that Reichenbach "would have given the William James lectures at Harvard in 1953, but was prevented from doing so by his untimely death" (quoted in Edwards, 1967, p. 115).

63. For similar formulations, see also Kahn (1954) and Maas and Wolins (1954).

64. The reader may want to see the Appendix for the selection from Bridgman (1927), in which he first set forth the concept of an operational definition; Hull's critique of operationism is included in Chapter 5.

65. The instruments developed by positivist social researchers to evaluate casework often were not used by practitioners. Positivist researchers expressed surprise that their instruments were not used but did not alter the premises of that approach to research. For example, an early instrument used to evaluate casework was the movement scale, which was "not used by the Family Service Department of the Community Service Society under whose auspices it was developed" (French, 1952, p. 149–150).

66. This distinction was reflected in W. E. Gordon's title, "Toward Basic Research in Social Work" (1951).

67. "We should make deliberate use of practitioner 'lore.' If we listen to what the practitioner says works as distinguished from why he says it works, we may get valuable leads and hunches to be tested through research" (Blenkner, 1959, p. 105).

68. One set of reviewers found his ideas to be, "to say the least, debatable" (Cambria & Day, 1952, p. 203).

69. A major reason for this particular aggregation is that the research design heuristics grouped together share trends over time, so that although such groupings always obscure some distinctions, these groupings reflect common trends. For example, the percentage of articles with all three of the research design heuristics using quantified data (case studies, large-scale analyses, and experimental designs) increased following the adoption of positivism.

70. The chi-square test evaluates the probability that the relationships between the variables found in the sample would occur if there were no relationship between the variables in the population of journal articles as a whole, for example, if the variables were statistically independent (Norusis, 1988, p. 246). "Two values are independent whenever knowing the value of one variable tells you nothing about the value of the other variable" (Norusis, 1988, p. 245). Findings of statistical significance are not equivalent to substantive significance (Norusis, 1988, p. 252; Kennedy, 1992; Rozeboom, 1960), so percentages are reported as well.

71. The chi-square statistic can be calculated by examining each cell in the crosstabulation table, finding the difference between the observed frequency and the expected frequency in each cell, squaring that difference, dividing the squared difference by the expected frequency, and summing the results of that calculation for each cell in the table. The sum is the chi-square statistic. Statisticians have developed procedures for evaluating whether chi-square statistics are statistically significant, in relation, for example, to the number of cells in a crosstabulation (Kennedy, 1992; Norusis, 1988).

72. "The standardized residuals are the residuals divided by the square root of the expected values . . . large standardized residuals indicate cells with either considerably more or considerably fewer observations than you would expect if the variables were independent" (Norusis, 1988, p. 252). Adjusted standardized residuals have been adjusted for a normal distribution.

73. Some social workers disagreed with Fischer's conclusions. For example, in a letter to the editor, David Hallowitz (1973) critiqued Fischer's premise that the research designs used in the studies Fischer cited could reflect the changes that often occur in casework. He emphasized, "Some clients in the research projects reviewed by Fischer may have been profoundly helped; the lives of others might have been totally wasted if help had not been given; still others may not have changed but their suffering was relieved and they were made to feel like worthwhile human beings. Are you going to tell a depressed mother who is totally immobilized and unable to take care of her four children and who just tried to kill herself: 'I'm sorry, I can't help you. Research has shown that you will come out just as well without my help!' . . . [L]et us engage in research endeavors that aim not to justify our existence as a profession but to strengthen and improve the good work we have been doing" (p. 107).

74. The gulf was so pervasive by 1960 that an educator in a school of social work who was also a psychoanalyst wrote about clinical research and assumed that "social scientists" and "social work practitioners" were two entirely distinct groups of social workers (Friend, 1960, p. 13). He went on to say, "[T]he practitioner should not expect, at least at this stage, to be a unified interdisciplinary scientist with all technical means at his disposal" (Friend, 1960, p. 15).

75. Dressel (1987) observed, "Patriarchy operates in the work place not only through men and women performing different jobs, but also through male supervision of female employees, [and] male production of knowledge for women's work" (p. 295).

76. Although some researchers believe that innate predispositions or very early socialization cause women to be more inclined than men to author qualitative research (Belenky et al. [1986]), the findings with regard to that issue are far from conclusive (Riger, 1992; Star, 1979).

77. Some women (and feminists) espouse positivist beliefs about social work research, see for example, Ivanoff, Robinson, and Blythe (1987).

78. See also Goldstein (1963), who cites Nagel (1961), as a source for defining scientific explanation; Miller (1970).

79. Two analyses of published social work research were conducted, in which the authors used an incorrect and methodologically based definition of "empirical" research: "included ethnographic and clinical case studies that had a clear methodology and identifiable variables, as well as studies that employed quantitative forms of analysis" (Task Force on Social Work Research, 1991, p. 42). For the discussion about the correct usage of the term "empirical," see the selections by Heineman Pieper and Chapter 4. One analysis the Task Force commissioned concluded that published research about practice was problematic because "the two designs that are able to control for the most threats to internal validity, experimental and quasi-experimental designs, account for only 13% of the reported studies. This finding is bothersome in light of the emphasis in these articles on direct practice and on outcome and effectiveness" (Glisson [1990], cited in Task Force on Social Work Research [1991], p. 43). The other analysis criticized contemporary social work research for "little mastery of basic scientific methods, especially the use of experimental design and advanced statistics. For a practice-oriented profession, we find the dearth of experimental and quasi-experimental methods puzzling" (Fraser & Taylor [1990], quoted in Task Force on Social Work Research [1991], p. 43). Like the Social Work Research Group, the Task Force Report emphasized that social work practice is of questionable effectiveness because it is not "research-based," in other words, not based on that unjustifiably restrictive positivist definition of research.

80. There were few exceptions; one was Zimbalist (1964).

81. The powerful influence of the combination of an ideology with institutional changes on the growth of a discipline has been noted by other historians. For example, in his history of how biochemistry became a distinctive academic discipline, Kohler (1979) observed that institutional changes in schools of medicine produced new roles for biochemists. Also, a new ideology adopted within medicine (in the case of biochemistry, the ideology was "scientific medicine," imported primarily from Germany at the turn of the century) had a regulatory impact on both knowledge and standards of service, which enhanced the importance of the new academic specialty.

82. Debates are continuing on that topic, see D. F. Harrison, Hudson, and Thyer (1992) and Witkin (1992).

83. This statement is not intended to represent a position with regard to whether science is realist or not; it is not a statement that there can be no facts that are "robust" across theories (see Wimsatt, 1981a, 1987).

84. Heineman Pieper's delineation of naturalistic research methods differs from (1) descriptions of naturalistic research by authors with a positivist orientation and (2) how *naturalistic* has been used to refer to the most contemporary paradigm of research in the philosophy of science (e.g., Callebaut [1993]). For an example of the first, Reid and Smith (1981/1989) include in the category of naturalistic those research designs that represent interventions into the therapeutic process for research rather than therapeutic aims. In other words, they include in the category of naturalistic research designs that are excluded using Heineman Pieper's definition. Furthermore, Reid and Smith subcategorize naturalistic research into designs that are "Exploratory-descriptive" and those that are "explanatory-predictive." Their unwarranted dichotomy between exploratory-descriptive, and explanatory studies reflects their debt to the restrictive positivist definitions of scientific explanation (see the introduction to Heineman Pieper's 1981 paper in Chapter 3). With regard to the second use of naturalistic, the term *naturalism* has had a long tradition in the philosophy of science. The new, third paradigm Callebaut (1993) identifies in the philosophy of science is termed the

naturalistic paradigm. It is based on a reformulation of naturalism and is a metatheory that philosophers, historians, and sociologists of science apply to the study of the sciences. (See also the Glossary and the paper by Bhaskar in Chapter 5.)

85. Personal communication, August 24, 1991.

86. Convulsive patterns do not necessarily equal convulsive behavior.

87. Scriven has written prolifically about the evaluation of social programs. The reader may be especially interested in his 1983 paper, "Evaluation ideologies," in which he critiques how evaluation has been addressed in the past and advances a postpositivist approach to program evaluation. He has been one of the leading critics of the restrictive logical positivist account of explanation in the natural and social sciences and in history (Scriven, 1959). David Hull is one of the foremost historians and philosophers of science today. One of Hull's most important recent works presents his intensive research about the influence of social processes, such as patterns in professional relationships among scientists, in the generation of knowledge in biology (1988).

88. The following selection was part of a compendium of papers in the philosophy of science edited by Colodny (1966).

89. This paper was part of a symposium conducted at the University of Chicago in 1983 (Fiske & Shweder, 1986).

90. Gerd Gigerenzer, personal communication, December 16, 1992.

91. Gardner (1985) summarizes the answer:

Most subjects realize that there is no need to select the card bearing the consonant, since it is clearly irrelevant to the rule; they also appreciate that it is essential to turn over the card with the vowel, for an odd number opposite would infirm the rule. The difficulty inheres in deciding which of the two numbered cards to pick up. There is a strong temptation to pick up the card with the even number, because the even number is mentioned in the rule; and this temptation proves fatal to a majority of subjects. But, in fact, it is irrelevant whether there is a vowel or a consonant on the other side, since the rule does not actually take a stand on what must be opposite to even

numbers. On the other hand, it is essential to pick up the card with the odd number on it. If that card has a consonant on it, the result is irrelevant. If, however, the card has a vowel on it, the rule in question has been infirmed, for the card must (according to the rule) have an even (and not an odd number) on it. (p. 362)

92. Apparently, individuals judge frequencies of samples on the basis of their similarity to the features of the "parent" population. Because irregularity is an essential feature of randomness, irregular samples are judged more likely than regular samples, even though both series are equally likely to occur. (Gardner, 1985 p. 371)

93. "Seen in its social context, where a particular choice increases the probability of getting to choose again, this behavior looks different" (Gigerenzer, 1991b, p. 108).

94. The coding manual is available from the author. All coding decisions were based on an agreement between two coders.

95. The results of a chi-square test of the statistical significance of the relationships between research design heuristics using three types of data and decade of publication for the subsample of articles that included evaluation ($N = 1,115$) were chi-square = 70.15 ($p < .00005$).

96. To protect the confidentiality of the patient and family in conformity with statute and the social work code of ethics, I have disguised both identifying information and the specifics of the case process.

97. Bhaskar (1989b) shows how universal causal laws, such as gravity, operate independently of human agency, and that causal laws cannot be conflated with the patterns of contiguous events that humans perceive. Furthermore, patterns of contiguous events cannot be conflated with the researcher's experience of those events, because each researcher's experience is organized in part by the cognitive constructions of her or his sociohistorical context and knowledge base.

98. Kidder (1982) described how researchers' conclusions about treatment efficacy often differed from the opinions of the program's clients.

99. The following is an example of such a problem: A social worker in the outpatient mental health clinic of a community hospital interviewed a five-year-

old child whose parents brought her to the clinic because she suffered from daytime enuresis. The child's mother had stated she had no problems taking care of the child but was concerned about the child's enuresis. In the first interview, the child revealed that her mother and grandmother commonly beat her with a spatula, that she slept in a bedroom with a roof that often leaked on her, that frequently she did not have enough to eat, and that she was often left home alone. The child showed the social worker a bruise on her head that she said resulted from being hit with a spatula. The social worker recognized that he had to notify the Department of Children and Family Services (DCFS) about the alleged abuse, and he cleared the decision with the child psychiatrist who was the clinical and administrative supervisor of the clinic. He contacted the DCFS, who conveyed that taking protective custody of the child was not indicated. The social worker documented the child's report of abuse in a written report to the DCFS and contacted the child abuse hotline. Following hospital policy, the social worker discussed with the parents the fact that DCFS was being notified. Despite the social worker's careful and tactful discussion, the child's family was furious, threatened to sue the hospital, and refused to come back to discuss the problem with the worker. Four days later, the DCFS investigator said that the abuse case had to be dropped because the state's attorney believed that the child's report and the bruise were insufficient evidence to merit indicating the case for trial. Although the DCFS offered services, the child's family refused them.

100. See discussion of prediction and explanation in Chapter 3, pp. 104–106, 112, 115–116, 209–211.

101. Although in his 1989 book, Wesley Salmon briefly alludes to the need for controlled experimentation to ascertain the effects of psychotherapy, in a personal communication, he clarified his position in that regard. Salmon emphasized that he endorses an approach to evaluating the effects of treatment that is nonrestrictive with regard both to the methodologies for evaluation and the ontological assumptions of the theories of treatment that are being tested (personal communication, December 2, 1992).

102. Universal instantiation is one type of deductive inference that is particularly important in the debate between Popper and the logical positivists. In universal instantiation, one can infer from a general statement, such as "all students find research useful," a singular statement, such as "you (a student) find research useful."

References

Abbott, E. (1910). *Women in industry: A study in American economic history.* New York: Appleton.

Abbott, E. (1915). Field-work and the training of the social worker. *Proceedings of the National Conference of Charities and Corrections, 42nd annual session* (pp. 615–621). Madison, WI: Midland Publishing.

Abbott, E. (1923, October 25). Letter to Dean James H. Tufts. In *School of Social Service Administration Papers.* Box 1, Folder 1, Department of Special Collections, Regenstein Library, University of Chicago.

Abbott, E. (1930–1933). Report to the president, 1930–1933. In *School of Social Service Administration Papers.* Box 1, Folder 2, Department of Special Collections, Regenstein Library, University of Chicago.

Abbott, E. (1931). Some basic principles in professional education for social work (an address delivered at the National Conference of Social Work, Memphis, 1928). In E. Abbott (Ed.), *Social welfare and professional education* (pp. 44–80). Chicago: University of Chicago Press.

Abbott, E. (1936). *The tenements of Chicago, 1908–1935.* Chicago: University of Chicago Press.

Abbott, E. (1937). *Some American pioneers in social welfare.* Chicago: University of Chicago Press.

Abbott, E. (1940). Unemployment relief: A federal responsibility. *Social Service Review, 14,* 438–452.

Abbott, E. (1952). The Hull House of Jane Addams. *Social Service Review, 26,* 334–338.

Abbott, G. (1909). *Legal position of married women in the United States.* Unpublished master's thesis, University of Chicago.

Abbott, M., & Blake, G. (1988). An intervention model for homeless youth. *Clinical Sociology Review, 6,* 148–158.

Abel, R. (1976). *Man is the measure: A cordial invitation to the central problems of philosophy.* New York: Free Press.

Abramovitz, M. (1988). *Regulating the lives of women: Social welfare policy from colonial times to the present.* Boston: South End Press.

Achinstein, P. (1969). Approaches to the philosophy of science. In P. Achinstein & S. Barker (Eds.), *The legacy of logical positivism: Studies in the philosophy of science.* Baltimore: Johns Hopkins University Press.

Adair, J., & Spinner, B. (1981). Subjects' access to cognitive processes: Demand characteristics and verbal report. *Journal of the Theory of Social Behaviour, 11,* 31–52.

Addams, J. (1895, December 19). Letter from Jane Addams to President Harper. In *President's Papers.* Box 1, Folder 9, Department of Special Collections, Regenstein Library, University of Chicago.

Addams, J. (1897). Social settlements. In *Proceedings of the National Conference of Charities and Cor-*

rections, 24th annual session, Toronto, Canada (pp. 338–346). Madison, WI: Midland Publishing.

Addams, J. (1899). Function of the social settlements and the labor movement. *Annals of the American Academy of Political and Social Science, 13,* 323–345.

Addams, J. (1907). *Newer ideals of peace.* Chautauqua, NY: Chautauqua Press.

Addams, J. (1909). *The spirit of youth and the city streets.* New York: Macmillan.

Addams, J. (1912). *A new conscience and an ancient evil.* New York: Macmillan.

Addams, J. (1916). *The long road of woman's memory.* New York: Macmillan.

Addams, J. (1930). *The second twenty years at Hull House, September 1909 to September 1929, with a record of a growing world consciousness.* New York: Macmillan.

Addams, J. (1935a). Julia Lathrop's services to the state of Illinois. *Social Service Review, 2,* 191–211.

Addams, J. (1935b). *My friend, Julia Lathrop.* New York: Macmillan.

Addams, J. (1960). Why women should vote. In E. Cooper Johnson (Ed.), *Jane Addams: A centennial reader* (pp. 104–113). New York: Macmillan.

Addams, J. (1983). *Peace and bread in time of war.* Silver Spring, MD: National Association of Social Workers. (Original work published 1922)

Addams, J. (1990). *Twenty years at Hull-House. With autobiographical notes by Jane Addams.* Urbana: University of Illinois Press. (Original work published 1910)

Adie, D. (1939). Responsibility of the state in the supervision of public welfare programs. *Social Service Review, 13,* 611–625.

Adler, P., & Adler, P. (1987). The past and the future of ethnography. *Journal of Contemporary Ethnography, 16,* 4–24.

Agee, V. L. (1979). *Treatment of the violent incorrigible adolescent.* Lexington, MA: Lexington Books.

Aichhorn, A. (1965). *Wayward youth.* New York: Viking Press. (Original work published 1935)

Alkin, M. C., & Fitz-Gibbon, C. T. (1975). Methods and theories of evaluation programs. *Journal of Research and Development in Education, 8,* 2–15.

Allen, J. G., Colson, D. B., Coyne, L., Dexter, N., Jehl, N., Mayer, C. A., & Spohn, H. E. (1986). Problems to anticipate in treating difficult patients in a long-term psychiatric hospital. *Psychiatry, 49,* 350–358.

Allen-Meares, P., & Lane, B. (1990). Social work practice: Integrating qualitative and quantitative data collection techniques. *Social Work, 35,* 452–458.

Allport, F. H. (1919). Behavior and experiment in social psychology. *Journal of Abnormal and Social Psychology, 14,* 297–300.

Allport, F. H. (1924). *Social psychology.* Boston: Houghton Mifflin.

Alter, C., & Evens, W. (1990). *Evaluating your practice: A guide to self-assessment.* New York: Springer.

Althusser, L. (1970). *For Marx* (B. Brewster, Trans.). New York: Random House, Vintage Books.

Alvarado, C. S. (1987). Note on the use of the term subject in pre-1886 discussions of thought-transference experiments. *American Psychologist, 42,* 101–102.

American Association of Social Workers. (1931). *Social case work: Generic and specific. (an outline; report of the Milford Conference).* New York: American Association of Social Workers. (Original work published 1929)

Amsterdam, S. (1982). The National Women's Trade Union League. *Social Service Review, 56,* 259-272.

Anderson, S. B., & Ball, S. (1978). *The profession and practice of program evaluation.* San Francisco: Jossey-Bass.

Andrews, J. L. (1990). Female social workers in the second generation. *Affilia, 5,* 46–59.

Aptekar, H. (1941). *Basic concepts in social case work.* Chapel Hill: University of North Carolina Press.

Aptheker, H. (1966). DuBois on Florence Kelley. *Social Work, 11,* 98–100.

Argyris, C. (1968). Some unintended consequences of rigorous research. *Psychological Bulletin, 70,* 185–197.

Aronson, S., & Sherwood, C. (1967). Researcher versus practitioner: Problems in social action research. *Social Work, 12,* 89–96.

Atherton, C. (1993). Empiricists versus social constructionists: Time for a cease-fire. *Families in Society: The Journal of Contemporary Human Services, 74,* 617–624.

Austin, D. (1978). Research and social work: Educational paradoxes and possibilities. *Journal of Social Service Research, 2,* 159–176.

Austin, D. (1983). The Flexner myth and the history of social work. *Social Service Review, 57,* 357–377.

Axline, V. (1969). *Play therapy.* New York: Ballantine Books. (Original work published 1947)

Ayer, A. J. (Ed.). (1959). *Logical positivism. The library of philosophical movements.* New York: Free Press.

Ayllon, T., Layman, D., & Kandel, H. J. (1975). A behavioral-educational alternative to drug control of hyperactive children. *Journal of Applied Behavior Analysis, 8,* 137–146.

Back, E. (1969). Technocracy and the ethic of social work. *Social Service Review, 43,* 430–438.

Bakan, D. (1972, March). Psychology can now kick the science habit. *Psychology Today,* pp. 26, 28, 86–88.

Basch, M. (1980). *Doing psychotherapy.* New York: Basic Books.

Bateson, G. (1972). *Steps to an ecology of mind.* New York: Ballantine.

Bateson, G., Jackson, D., Haley, J., & Weakland, J. (1956). Toward a theory of schizophrenia. *Behavioral Science, 1,* 251–264.

Beck, D. F. (1958). Research relevant to casework treatment of children: Current research and study projects. *Social Casework, 39,* 105–123.

Becker, H. (1979). Do photographs tell the truth? In T. Cook & C. Reichardt (Eds.), *Qualitative and quantitative methods in evaluation research.* Sage Research Progress Series in Evaluation. Beverly Hills, CA: Sage.

Beckerman, A. (1978). Differentiating between social research and social work research: Implications for teaching. *Journal of Education for Social Work, 14,* 9–15.

Belenky, M., Clinchy, B., Goldberger, N., & Tarule, J. (1986). *Women's ways of knowing: The development of self, voice and mind.* New York: Basic Books.

Benbenishty, R. (1989). Combining the single-system and group approaches to evaluate treatment effectiveness on the agency level. *Journal of Social Service Research, 12,* 31–48.

Benzer, S. (1959). On the topology of the genetic fine structure. *Proceedings of the National Academy of Sciences, 45,* 403-406.

Berger, P. L., & Luckmann, T. (1967). *The social construction of reality: A treatise in the sociology of knowledge.* Garden City, NY: Doubleday, Anchor.

Bergmann, G. (1961). Sense and nonsense in operationism. In P. G. Frank (Ed.), *The validation of scientific theories* (pp. 46–56). New York: Collier. (Original work published 1954–1955)

Bergum, B. O., & Lehr, D. J. (1963). Effects of authoritarianism on vigilance performance. *Journal of Applied Psychology, 47,* 75–77.

Berk, R. A., & Rossi, P. H. (1976). Doing good or worse: Evaluation research politically reexamined. *Social Problems, 23,* 337–349.

Berkman, T. (1952). Letter to the editor: Response to Zimbalist's "Organismic social work versus partialistic research," *Social Casework, 33,* 163–164.

Berleman, W. C. (1968). Mary Richmond's *Social Diagnosis* in retrospect. *Social Casework, 49,* 395–402.

Berlin, S. (1983). Single case evaluation: Another version. *Social Work Research and Abstracts, 19,* 3–11.

Berlin, S. (1990a). Dichotomous and complex thinking. *Social Service Review, 64,* 46–59.

Berlin, S. (1990b). The utility of change-process research for the education of practitioners and single-case evaluation. In L. Videka-Sherman & W. J. Reid (Eds.), *Advances in clinical social work research.* Silver Spring, MD: National Association of Social Workers Press.

Berlin, S., Mann, K., & Grossman, S. (1991). Task analysis of cognitive therapy for depression. *Social Work Research and Abstracts, 27,* 3–11.

Bernard, J. (1973). My four revolutions: An autobiographical history of the ASA. *American Journal of Sociology, 78,* 773–791.

Bernstein, I. N. (1978). Social control in applied social science: A study of evaluative researchers' conformity to technical norms. *Social Science Research, 7,* 24–47.

Bernstein, J. (1973). *Einstein.* New York: Viking Press.

Bernstein, R. J. (1978). *The restructuring of social and political theory.* Philadephia: University of Pennsylvania Press.

Bhaskar, R. (1975). *A realist theory of science.* Leeds, England: Leeds Books.

Bhaskar, R. (1978). On the possibility of social scientific knowledge and the limits of naturalism. *Journal for the Theory of Social Behavior, 8,* 1–28.

Bhaskar, R. (1982). Emergence, explanation and emancipation. In P. F. Secord (Ed.), *Explaining social behavior: Consciousness, human action, and social structure.* Beverly Hills, CA: Sage.

Bhaskar, R. (1985). Realism. In W. F. Bynum, E. J. Browne, & R. Porter (Eds.), *Dictionary of the history of science* (pp. 362-363). Princeton, NJ: Princeton University Press. (Original work published 1981)

Bhaskar, R. (1989a). *The possibility of naturalism: A philosophical critique of contemporary human sciences* (2nd ed.). New York: Harvester Wheatsheaf.

Bhaskar, R. (1989b). *Reclaiming reality: A critical introduction to contemporary philosophy*. London: Verso.

Bhaskar, R. (1991). *Philosophy and the idea of freedom*. Oxford: Basil Blackwell.

Billingsley, A. (1970). Black families and white social science. *Journal of Social Issues, 26*, 127–142.

Birch, H. (1964). *Brain damage in children: The biological and social aspects*. Baltimore: Williams & Wilkins.

Bixenstine, E. (1976). The value-fact antithesis in behavioral science. *Journal of Humanistic Psychology, 16*, 35–57.

Blackwell, J. E. (1981). *Mainstreaming outsiders: The production of black professionals*. Bayside, NY: General Hall.

Blalock, H. M. (1979a). Presidential address: Measurement and conceptualization problems: The major obstacle to integrating theory and research. *American Sociological Review, 44*, 881–894.

Blalock, H. M. (1979b). *Social statistics* (2nd ed., rev.). New York: McGraw-Hill.

Bleier, R. (1984). *Science and gender: A critique of biology and its theories on women*. New York: Pergamon.

Blenkner, M. (1950). Obstacles to evaluative research in casework: Parts I and II. *Social Casework, 31*, 54–60, 97–105.

Blenkner, M. (1959). Comments. In A. Shyne (Ed.), *Use of judgments as data in social work research, proceedings* (p. 105). New York: National Association of Social Workers.

Blenkner, M. (1962). Control groups and the "placebo effect" in evaluative research. *Social Work, 7*, 52–58.

Block, N. J., & Dworkin, G. (1974). IQ: Heritability and inequality, Part 1. *Philosophy and Public Affairs, 3*, 331–409.

Bloom, M. (1969). The selection of knowledge from the behavioral sciences and its integration into social work curricula. *Journal of Education for Social Work, 5*, 15–27.

Bloom, M. (1978). Challenges to the helping professions and the response of scientific practice. *Social Service Review, 52*, 584–595.

Bloom, M., & Block, S. (1977). Evaluating one's own effectiveness and efficiency. *Social Work, 22*, 130–136.

Bloom, M., & Fischer, J. (1982). *Evaluating practice: Guidelines for the accountable professional*. Englewood Cliffs, NJ: Prentice-Hall.

Bloor, D. (1976). *Knowledge and social imagery*. London: Routledge & Kegan Paul.

Blythe, B. J., & Briar, S. (1985). Developing empirically based models of practice. *Social Work, 30*, 483–488.

Boden, M. (1973). The structure of intentions. *Journal for the Theory of Social Behavior, 3*, 23–46.

Bodenhausen, G. V., & Wyer, R. S. (1985). Effects of stereotypes in decision making and information-processing strategies. *Journal of Personality and Social Psychology, 48*, 267–282.

Boeckmann, M. E., & Lengermann, P. M. (1978). Evaluation research: System, functions, future. *Sociological Focus, 11*(4), 329–340.

Boehm, W. W. (1961). Social work: Science and art. *Social Service Review, 35*, 144–152.

Bogdan, R. (1976). Conducting evaluation research—Integrity intact. *Sociological Focus, 9*(1), 63–72.

Bogdan, R., & Taylor, S. (1976). The judged, not the judges. *American Psychologist, 31*, 47–52.

Bogdan, R., & Taylor, S. (1989). Relationships with severely disabled people: The social construction of humanness. *Social Problems, 36*(2), 135–147.

Bohm, D. (1957). *Causality and chance in modern physics*. London: Routledge & Kegan Paul.

Bond, G. R., McDonel, E. C., Miller, L. D., & Pensec, M. (1991). Assertive community treatment and reference groups: An evaluation of their effectiveness for young adults with serious mental illness and substance abuse problems. *Psychosocial Rehabilitation Journal, 15*, 31–43.

Borenzweig, H. (1971). Social work and psychoanalytic theory: A historical analysis. *Social Work, 16*, 7–16.

Boring, E. G. (1950). *A history of experimental psychology* (2nd ed.). New York: Appleton-Century-Crofts. (Original work published 1929)

Boring, E. G. (1969). Perspective: Artifact and control. In R. Rosenthal & R. Rosnow (Eds.), *Artifact in behavioral research*. New York: Academic Press.

Bouchard, T. J., Jr., Lykken, D. T., McGue, M., Segal, N., & Tellegen, A. (1990). Sources of human psychological difference: The Minnesota study of twins reared apart. *Science, 250*, 223–228.

Bourdieu, P. (1977). *Outline of a theory of practice* (R. Nice, Trans.). In *Cambridge Studies in Social Anthropology* (Vol. 16). Cambridge, England: Cambridge University Press.

Boyd, R., & Richerson, P. (1985). *Culture and the evolutionary process.* Chicago: Univ. of Chicago Press.

Brandl, J. E. (1978). Evaluation and politics. *Evaluation and Change,* Special issue, 6–7.

Breckinridge, S. P. (1910). Introduction. In E. Abbott, *Women in industry: A study in American economic history.* New York: Appleton.

Breckinridge, S. P. (1913). The color line and the housing problem. *Survey, 29,* 575–576.

Breckinridge, S. P. (1924). *Family welfare work in a metropolitan community: Selected case records.* Chicago: University of Chicago Press.

Breckinridge, S. P. (1930). Separate domicil for married women. *Social Service Review, 4,* 37–52.

Breckinridge, S. P. (1931). The scope and place of research in the program of the family society. *Proceedings of the National Conference of Social Work, 58,* 223–231.

Breckinridge, S. P. (1936). The new horizons of professional education for social work. *Social Service Review, 10,* 437–449.

Breckinridge, S. P. (1938). Social workers in the courts of Cook County. *Social Service Review, 12,* 230–250.

Breckinridge, S. P., & Abbott, E. (1912). *The delinquent child and the home: A study of the delinquent wards of the Juvenile Court of Chicago.* New York: Russell Sage.

Brekke, J. (1986). Scientific imperatives in social work research: Pluralism is not skepticism. *Social Service Review, 60,* 538–544.

Brekke, J. (1987). Author's reply. *Social Service Review, 61,* 370–373.

Briar, S. (1979). Incorporating research into education for clinical practice in social work: Toward a clinical science in social work. In A. Rubin & A. Rosenblatt (Eds.), *Sourcebook of research utilization* (pp. 132–140). New York: Council on Social Work Education.

Briar, S. (1980). Toward the integration of practice and research. In D. Fanshel (Ed.), *The future of social work research.* Washington, DC: National Association of Social Workers.

Briar, S., & Miller, H. (1971). *Problems and issues in social casework.* New York: Columbia University Press.

Brickell, H. M. (1978). The influence of external political factors on the role and methodology of evaluation. In T. D. Cook (Ed.), *Evaluation studies review annual* (Vol. 3). Beverly Hills, CA: Sage.

Bricker-Jenkins, M., & Hooyman, N. (Eds.). (1986). *Not for women only: Social work practice for a feminist future.* Silver Spring, MD: National Association of Social Workers.

Bridgman, P. W. (1927). *The logic of modern physics.* New York: Macmillan.

Bridgman, P. W. (1959). "The Logic of Modern Physics" after thirty years. *Daedalus, 88,* 518–526.

Bridgman, P. W. (1961). The present state of operationalism. In P. G. Frank (Ed.), *The validation of scientific theories* (pp. 75–80). New York: Collier.

Brinberg, D., & Kidder, L. (Eds.). (1982). *Forms of validity in research. New directions for methodology of social and behavioral science* (No. 12). San Francisco: Jossey-Bass.

Broadhead, R. S. (1984). Human rights and human subjects: Ethics and strategies in social science research. *Sociological Inquiry, 54,* 107–123.

Broadhurst, B. (1982). Review of James Leiby, "A history of social welfare and social work in the United States." *Journal of the History of the Behavioral Sciences, 18,* 83–85.

Bromley, D. B. (1986). *The case-study method in psychology and related disciplines.* New York: John Wiley & Sons.

Bronfenbrenner, U. (1977). Toward an experimental ecology of human development. *American Psychologist, 32,* 513–531.

Bronfenbrenner, U. (1979a). *The ecology of human development: Experiments by nature and design.* Cambridge, MA: Harvard University Press.

Bronfenbrenner, U. (1979b). The laboratory as an ecological context. In *The ecology of human development: Experiments by nature and design* (pp. 109–131). Cambridge, MA: Harvard University Press.

Bronfenbrenner, U. (1986). Ecology of the family as a context for human development: Research perspectives. *Developmental Psychology, 22,* 723–742.

Bronfenbrenner, U., Kessel, F., Kessen, W., & White, S. (1986). Toward a critical social history of developmental psychology: A propaedeutic discussion. *American Psychologist, 41,* 1218–1230.

Brower, A. M., & Garvin, C. D. (1989). Design issues in social group work research. *Social Work with Groups, 12,* 91–102.

Brown, H. (1977). *Perception, theory and commitment: The new philosophy of science.* Chicago: University of Chicago Press.

Brown, R. (1965). *Social psychology.* New York: Free Press.

Brownmiller, S. (1975). *Against our will: Men, women and rape.* New York: Bantam.

Brumberg, J. J. (1988). *Fasting girls: The emergence of anorexia nervosa as a modern disease.* Cambridge, MA: Harvard University Press.

Brumberg, J. J., & Tomes, N. (1982). Women in the professions: A research agenda for American historians. *Reviews in American History, 10,* 275–296.

Bruner, E. M. (1956). Primary group experience and the processes of acculturation. *American Anthropologist, 58,* 605–623.

Bruner, J. S. (1951). Personality dynamics and the process of perceiving. In R.R. Blake & G. Ramsey (Eds.), *Perception, an approach to personality.* New York: Ronald.

Bruno, F. (1957). *Trends in social work 1874–1956: A history based on the proceedings of the National Conference of Social Work.* New York: Columbia University Press.

Brush, S. (1989). Prediction and theory evaluation: The case of light bending. *Science, 246,* 1124–1129.

Buck, R., & Hull, D. L. (1966). The logical structure of the Linnaean hierarchy. *Systematic Zoology, 15,* 97–111.

Buckley, K. W. (1989). *Mechanical man: John Broadus Watson and the beginnings of behaviorism.* New York: Guilford.

Bunge, M. (1959). *Causality: The place of the causal principle in modern science.* Cambridge, MA: Harvard University Press.

Bunge, M. (1991). A critical examination of the new sociology of science: Part 1. *Philosophy of the Social Sciences, 21,* 524–560.

Bunge, M. (1992). A critical examination of the new sociology of science, Part 2. *Philosophy of the Social Sciences, 22,* 46–76.

Burdsal, C., Force, R. C., & Klingsporn, M. J. (1989). Treatment effectiveness in young male offenders. *Residential Treatment for Children and Youth, 7,* 75–88.

Burrell, G., & Morgan, G. (1979). *Sociological paradigms and organizational analysis: Elements of the sociology of corporate life.* London: Heinemann.

Callebaut, W. (1993). *Taking the naturalistic turn, or how real philosophy of science is done.* Chicago: University of Chicago Press.

Cambria, S., & Day, F. (1952). Research newsnotes: Recent publications. *Smith College Studies in Social Work, 23,* 203.

Campbell, D. A., & Misanin, J. R. (1969). Basic drives. In P. H. Mussen & M. R. Rosenzweig (Eds.), *Annual review of psychology* (Vol. 20). Palo Alto, CA: Annual Reviews.

Campbell, D. T. (1955). The informant in quantitative research. *American Journal of Sociology, 60,* 339–342.

Campbell, D. T. (1961). The mutual methodological relevance of anthropology and psychology. In F. L. K. Hsu (Ed.), *Psychological anthropology: Approaches to culture and personality.* Homewood, IL: Dorsey.

Campbell, D. T. (1966). Pattern matching as an essential in distal knowing. In K. R. Hammond (Ed.), *The psychology of Egon Brunswik.* New York: Holt, Rinehart & Winston.

Campbell, D. T. (1967). Stereotypes and the perception of group differences. *American Psychologist, 22,* 817–829.

Campbell, D. T. (1969). Reforms as experiments. *American Psychologist, 24,* 409–429.

Campbell, D. T. (1974). Evolutionary epistemology. In P. A. Schilpp (Ed.), *The philosophy of Karl Popper* (Vol. 1). LaSalle, IL: Open Court Press.

Campbell, D.T. (1975). Degrees of freedom and the case study. *Comparative Political Studies, 8,* 178–193.

Campbell, D. T., & Fiske, D. W. (1959). Convergent and discriminant validation by the multitrait-multimethod matrix. *Psychological Bulletin, 56,* 81–105.

Campbell, D. T., & LeVine, R. A. (1961). A proposal for cooperative cross-cultural research on ethnocentrism. *Journal of Conflict Resolution, 5,* 82–108.

Campbell, D. T., & Stanley, J. C. (1963). *Experimental and quasi-experimental designs for research.* Boston: Houghton Mifflin.

Campbell, J. (1990). Ability of practitioners to estimate client acceptance of single-subject evaluation procedures. *Social Work, 35,* 9–14.

Campinha-Bacote, J. (1991). Community mental health services for the underserved: A culturally specific model. *Archives of Psychiatric Nursing, 5,* 229–235.

Caplan, A. L. (Ed.). (1978). *The sociobiology debate: Readings on ethical and scientific issues.* New York: Harper & Row.

Carlson, E. A. (1966). *The gene: A critical history.* Philadelphia: W. B. Saunders.

Carlton-La Ney, I. (1983). Notes on a forgotten black social worker and sociologist: George Edmund Haynes. *Journal of Sociology and Social Welfare, 10,* 530–539.

Carnap, R. (1936). Testability and meaning. *Philosophy of Science, 3,* 420–471.

Carnap, R. (1956). The methodological character of theoretical concepts. In H. Feigl & M. Scriven (Eds.), *The foundations of science and the concepts of psychology and psychoanalysis. Minnesota studies in the philosophy of science: Vol. 1.* (pp. 38–76). Minneapolis: University of Minnesota Press.

Carnap, R. (1991a). Intellectual autobiography. In P. A. Schlipp (Ed.), *The philosophy of Rudolf Carnap. Library of living philosophers: Vol. 11.* LaSalle, IL: Open Court Press. (Original work published 1963)

Carnap, R. (1991b). R. Carnap, replies and expositions. In P. A. Schlipp, (Ed.), *The philosophy of Rudolf Carnap. Library of living philosophers: Vol. 11.* LaSalle, IL: Open Court Press. (Original work published 1963)

Carrier, J. (1978). Misrecognition and knowledge. *Inquiry, 22,* 321–342.

Carscaddon, D., George, M., & Wells, G. (1990). Rural community mental health consumer satisfaction and psychiatric symptoms. *Community Mental Health Journal, 26,* 309–318.

Carter, J. (1991). Chronic mental illness and homelessness in black populations: Prologue and prospects. *Journal of the National Medical Association, 83,* 313–317.

Carver, R. (1978). The case against statistical significance testing. *Harvard Educational Review, 48,* 378–399.

Casey, R., & Berman, J. (1985). The outcome of psychotherapy with children. *Psychological Bulletin, 98,* 388–400.

Casselman, B. L. (1971). On the practitioner's orientation toward research. *Smith College Studies in Social Work, 42,* 211–233.

Castle, W. E. (1916). Is selection or mutation the more important agency in evolution? *Scientific Monthly, 2,* 91–98.

Caute, D. (1978). *The great fear: The anti-communist purge under Truman and Eisenhower.* New York: Simon & Schuster.

Ceci, S. J., & Bronfenbrenner, U. (1991). On the demise of everyday memory: "The rumors of my death are much exaggerated" (Mark Twain). *American Psychologist, 46,* 27–31.

Ceci, S., & Bruck, M. (1993). Suggestibility of child witnesses: A historical review and synthesis. *Psychological Bulletin, 113,* 403–439.

Chafetz, L. (1990). Withdrawal from the homeless mentally ill. *Community Mental Health Journal, 26,* 449–461.

Chamberlin, J. (1990). The ex-patients' movement: Where we've been and where we're going. *Journal of Mind and Behavior, 11,* 3–4.

Chambers, C. (1980). *Seedtime of reform: American social service and social action, 1918–1933.* Westport, CT: Greenwood Press. (Original work published 1963)

Chambers, C. (1986a). Toward a redefinition of welfare history. *Journal of American History, 73,* 407–433.

Chambers, C. (1986b). Women in the creation of the profession of social work. *Social Service Review, 60,* 1–33.

Chess, S., & Thomas, A. (1984). *Origins and evolution of behavior disorders: From infancy to early adult life.* New York: Brunner/Mazel.

Chess, S., Thomas, A., & Birch, H. G. (1972). Behavior problems revisited: Findings of an anterospective study. In S. Harrison & J. F. McDermott (Eds.), *Childhood psychopathology.* New York: International Universities Press.

Churchland, P. M. (1981). Eliminative materialism and propositional attitudes. *The Journal of Philosophy, 78,* 67–89.

Churchland, P. (1985). *Images of science: Essays on realism and empiricism, with a reply from Bas C. Van Fraassen.* Chicago: University of Chicago Press.

Claghorn, K. (1927). The problem of measuring social treatment. *Social Service Review, 2,* 181–193.

Clague, E. (1935). Research in social work. In *Social Work Year Book 1935* (3rd issue). New York: Russell Sage Foundation.

Clausen, J., Keck, D., & Heisey, W. (1940). *Experimental studies on the nature of species: I. Effects of varied environments on western North American plants. Carnegie Institution of Washington Publication, 520,* 1–452.

Cohen, I. B. (1963). Science in America: The nineteenth century. In A. M. Schlesinger, Jr., & M.

White (Eds.), *Paths of American thought*. Boston: Houghton Mifflin.

Cohen, I. B. (1977). History and the philosopher of science. In F. Suppe (Ed.), *The Structure of scientific theories* (pp. 308–344). Champaign-Urbana: University of Illinois Press.

Cohen, N. (1956). A changing profession in a changing world. *Social Work, 1,* 12–19.

Cohen, N. (1958). *Social work in the American tradition: Field, body of knowledge, process, method, point of view*. Dryden Press: New York.

Cohler, B. (1988). The human studies and the life history: The *Social Service Review* lecture. *Social Service Review, 62,* 552–575.

Cole, S. (1980). *The sociological method: An introduction to the science of sociology*. Boston: Houghton Mifflin.

Coles, G. (1987). *The learning mystique*. New York: Pantheon Books.

Colless, D. H. (1967a). An examination of certain concepts in phenetic taxonomy. *Systematic Zoology, 16,* 16–27.

Colless, D. H. (1967b). The phylogenetic fallacy. *Systematic Zoology, 16,* 289–295.

Colodny, R. (Ed.). (1966). *Mind and cosmos: Essays in contemporary science and philosophy*. Pittsburgh: University of Pittsburgh Press.

Colson, D. B., Allen, J. G., Coyne, L., Dexter, N., Jehl, N., Mayer, C. A., & Spohn, H. (1986). An anatomy of countertransference: Staff reactions to difficult psychiatric hospital patients. *Hospital and Community Psychiatry, 37,* 923–928.

Colson, D. B., Cornsweet, C., Murphy, T., & O'Malley, F. (1991). Perceived treatment difficulty and therapeutic alliance on an adolescent psychiatric hospital unit. *American Journal of Orthopsychiatry, 61,* 221–229.

Colson, D. B., & Coyne, L. (1978). Variation in staff thinking on a psychiatric unit: Implications for team functioning. *Bulletin of the Menninger Clinic, 42,* 414–422.

Cook, T., & Campbell, D. (1979). *Quasi-experimentation: Design and analysis issues for field settings*. Boston: Houghton Mifflin.

Cook, T., & Reichardt, C. (1979). *Qualitative and quantitative methods in evaluation research*. Beverly Hills, CA: Sage.

Cooper, L. A., & Shepard, R. N. (1973). Chronometric studies of the rotation of mental images. In W. G. Chase (Ed.), *Visual information processing, proceedings*. New York: Academic Press.

Cooper, M. (1990). Treatment of a client with obsessive-compulsive disorder. *Social Work Research and Abstracts, 26,* 26–32.

Copleston, F. (1985). *A history of philosophy: Vol. 8. Bentham to Russell*. New York: Doubleday. (Original work published 1966)

Cornsweet, C. (1990). A review of the research on hospital treatment of children and adolescents. *Bulletin of the Menninger Clinic, 54,* 64–77.

Corson, D. (1991). Bhaskar's critical realism and educational knowledge. *British Journal of Sociology of Education, 12,* 223–241.

Coser, L. (1975). Presidential address: Two methods in search of a substance. *American Sociological Review, 40,* 691–700.

Costantino, G., Malgady, R., & Rogler, L. (1986). Cuento therapy: A culturally sensitive modality for Puerto Rican children. *Journal of Consulting and Clinical Psychology, 54,* 639–645.

Costin, L. (1983a). Edith Abbott and the Chicago influence on social work education. *Social Service Review, 57,* 94–111.

Costin, L. (1983b). *Two sisters for social justice: A biography of Grace and Edith Abbott*. Urbana: University of Illinois Press.

Coyle, G. (1952). New insights available to the social worker from the social sciences. *Social Service Review, 26,* 289–304.

Cravens, H. (1985). History of the social sciences. In S. Kohlstedt & M. Rossiter (Eds.), *Historical writing on American science: Perspectives and prospects*. Baltimore: Johns Hopkins University Press.

Cronbach, L. J. (1975). Beyond the two disciplines of scientific psychology. *American Psychologist, 30,* 116–127.

Cronbach, L. J. (1982). *Designing evaluations of educational and social programs*. San Francisco: Jossey-Bass.

Cronbach, L. J. (1986). Social inquiry by and for earthlings. In D. W. Fiske & R. A. Shweder (Eds.), *Metatheory in social science: Pluralisms and subjectivities*. Chicago: University of Chicago Press.

Cronbach, L. J., & Meehl, P. (1955). Construct validity in psychological tests. *Psychological Bulletin, 52,* 281–302.

Cronbach, L. J., & Suppes, P. (1969). *Research for tomorrow's schools: Disciplined inquiry for education*. New York: Macmillan.

Cullen, Y. T. (1983). An alternative tradition in social work: Bertha Capen Reynolds, 1885–1978. *Catalyst, 4,* 315), 55–73.

D'Andrade, R. (1986). Three scientific world views and the covering law model. In D. W. Fiske & R. A. Shweder (Eds.), *Metatheory in social science: Pluralisms and subjectivities.* Chicago: University of Chicago Press.

Danziger, K. (1979). The positivist repudiation of Wundt. *Journal of the History of the Behavioral Sciences, 15,* 205–230.

Danziger, K. (1985). The origins of the psychological experiment as a social institution. *American Psychologist, 40,* 133–140.

Danziger, K. (1987). Social context and investigative practice in early twentieth century psychology. In M. G. Ash & W. R. Woodward (Eds.), *Psychology in twentieth-century thought and society.* New York: Cambridge University Press.

Danziger, K. (1988a). A question of identity: Who participated in psychological experiments? In J. Morawski (Ed.), *The rise of experimentation in American psychology.* New Haven, CT: Yale University Press.

Danziger, K. (1988b). On theory and method in psychology. In W. J. Baker, L. P. Mos, H. V. Rappard, & H. J. Stam (Eds.), *Recent trends in theoretical psychology.* New York: Springer-Verlag.

Danziger, K. (1990). *Constructing the subject: Historical origins of psychological research.* Cambridge: Cambridge University Press.

Darroch, R., & Steiner, I. D. (1970). Role-playing: An alternative to laboratory research? *Journal of Personality, 38,* 302–311.

Dascal, M., & Wroblewski, J. (1991). The rational law-maker and the pragmatics of legal interpretation. *Journal of Pragmatics, 15,* 421–444.

Dashiell, J. F. (1935). Experimental studies of the influence of social situations on the behavior of individual human adults. *A Handbook of Social Psychology, 2,* 1097–1158.

Davenport, J., & Reims, N. (1978). Theoretical orientation and attitudes toward women. *Social Work, 23,* 306–309.

Davies, P., & Gribbin, J. (1992). *The matter myth: Dramatic discoveries that challenge our understanding of physical reality.* New York: Simon & Schuster.

Davis, A. F. (1973). *American heroine: The life and legend of Jane Addams.* New York: Oxford University Press.

Davis, A. T. (1988). *The making of a teacher: 50 years in social work.* Silver Spring, MD: National Association of Social Workers.

Davis, I. (1990). Microanalysis of intervention-client change loops: The heart of change-process research. In L. Videka-Sherman & W. J. Reid (Eds.), *Advances in clinical social work research.* Silver Spring, MD: National Association of Social Workers.

Davis, I., & Reid, W. J. (1988). Event analysis in clinical practice and process research. *Social Casework, 69,* 298-306.

Davis, L. (1985). Female and male voices in social work. *Social Work, 30,* 106–113.

Davis, L. (1986). A feminist approach to social work research. *Affilia, 1,* 32–47.

Davis, M., & Raffe, I. H. (1985). The holding environment in the inpatient treatment of adolescents. *Adolescent Psychiatry, 12,* 434–443.

Dawson, B. G., Klass, M. D., Corey, R. F., & Edgley, C. K. (1991). *Understanding social work research.* Needham Heights, MA: Allyn & Bacon.

Dean, R. (1989). Ways of knowing in clinical practice. *Clinical Social Work Journal, 17,* 116–127.

Dean, R., & Fenby, B. (1989). Exploring epistemologies: Social work action as a reflection of philosophical assumptions. *Journal of Social Work Education, 25,* 46–54.

Dean, R., & Reinherz, H. (1986). Psychodynamic practice and single system design: The odd couple. *Journal of Social Work Education, 22,* 71–81.

Deegan, M. J. (1981). Early women sociologists and the American Sociological Society: The patterns of exclusion and participation. *American Sociologist, 16,* 14–24.

Deegan, M. J. (1986). *Jane Addams and the men of the Chicago school.* New Brunswick, NJ: Transaction Books.

Dennett, D. C. (1979). *Brainstorms: Philosopical essays on mind and psychology.* Cambridge, MA: Bradford Books, MIT Press.

DeRoos, Y. S. (1990). The development of practice wisdom through human problem-solving processes. *Social Service Review, 64,* 276–287.

Deutsch, A. (1937). *The mentally ill in America: A history of their care and treatment from colonial times.* New York: Doubleday.

Devore, W. (1983). Ethnic reality: The life model and work with black families. *Social Casework, 64,* 525–531.

Dewey, J. (1938). *Logic: The theory of inquiry.* New York: Henry Holt.

Dewey, J. (1970). John Dewey: A selection from "Ethics." In G. Grob & R. Beck (Eds.), *Ideas in America: Source readings in the intellectual history of the United States.* New York: Free Press. (Original work published 1900–1901)

Diner, S. J. (1970). Chicago social workers and blacks in the Progressive Era. *Social Service Review, 44,* 393–410.

Dixon, W. (1988). The discrete sequential analysis of dynamic international behavior. *Quality and Quantity, 22,* 239–254.

Dobzhansky, T., & Spassky, B. (1944). Genetics of natural populations. *Genetics, 29,* 270–290.

Dore, M. (1990). Functional theory: Its history and influence on contemporary social work practice. *Social Service Review, 64,* 358–374.

Drake, R. E., Teague, G. B., & Warren, S. R. (1990). Dual diagnosis: The New Hampshire program. *Addiction and Recovery, 10,* 35–39.

Drake, R. E., & Wallach, M. (1988). Mental patients' attitudes toward hospitalization: A neglected aspect of hospital tenure. *American Journal of Psychiatry, 145,* 29–34.

Dressel, P. (1987). Patriarchy and social welfare work. *Social Problems, 34,* 294–309.

Drew, P. (1983). *A longer view: The Mary E. Richmond legacy.* Baltimore: School of Social Work and Community Planning, University of Maryland.

DuBois, E. C. (Ed.). (1992). *The Elizabeth Cady Stanton–Susan B. Anthony reader: Correspondence, writings, speeches* (rev. ed.). Boston: Northeastern University Press.

Dunn, W., Mitroff, I., & Deutsch, S. (1981). The obsolescence of evaluation research. *Evaluation and Program Planning, 4,* 207–208.

East, E. M. (1912). The Mendelian notation as a description of physiological facts. *American Naturalist, 46,* 633–655.

Edgerton, R. E. (1971). *The individual in cultural adaptation.* Berkeley: University of California Press.

Edleson, J. (1991). Social workers' interventions in woman abuse: 1907–1945. *Social Service Review, 65,* 304–313.

Edwards, D., & Roundtree G. (1981). Assessment of a behavior modification program for modifying disruptive behavior of emotionally disturbed adolescent males in a residential facility. *Corrective and Social Psychiatry Journal of Behavior Technology, Methods and Therapy, 27,* 171–180.

Edwards, P. (Ed.). (1967). *The encyclopedia of philosophy.* New York: Macmillan.

Ehrenreich, J. (1985). *The altruistic imagination: A history of social work and social policy in the United States.* Ithaca, NY: Cornell University Press.

Ehrenwald, J. (Ed.). (1976). *The history of psychotherapy: From healing magic to encounter.* New York: Jason Aronson.

Ehrlich, P. (1961). Has the biological species concept outlived its usefulness? *Systematic Zoology, 10,* 167–176.

Ehrlich, P. (1964). Some axioms of taxonomy. *Systematic Zoology, 13,* 109–123.

Ehrlich, P., & Holm, R. W. (1962). Patterns and populations. *Science, 137,* 652–657.

Ehrlich, P., & Holm, R. W. (1963). Reply to Webster. *Science, 139,* 237–242.

Einstein, A. (1959). Letter to Sir Karl Popper. In K. Popper, *The logic of scientific discovery.* New York: Basic Books. (Original work published 1934)

Eisner, E. (1984). Can educational research inform educational practice? *Phi Delta Kappa, 65,* 447–452.

Elliott, R. (1983). "That in your hands": A comprehensive process analysis of a significant event in psychotherapy. *Psychiatry, 46,* 113–129.

Elliott, R. (1984). A discovery-oriented approach to significant change events in psychotherapy: Interpersonal process recall and comprehensive process analysis. In L. N. Rice & L. S. Greenberg (Eds.), *Patterns of change: Intensive analysis of psychotherapy process.* New York: Guilford.

Ellis, A. (1956). An operational reformulation of some of the basic principles of psychoanalysis. In *Minnesota studies in the philosophy of science, Vol. 1,* (pp. 131–154). Minneapolis: University of Minnesota Press.

Ellwood, A. (1988). Prove to me that MELD makes a difference. In H. B. Weiss & F. H. Jacobs (Eds.), *Evaluating family programs* (pp. 303–313). New York: Aldine de Gruyter.

Epstein, W. (1986). Science and social work. *Social Service Review, 60,* 145–160.

Etzioni, A. (Ed.). (1969). *The semi-professions and their organization.* New York: Free Press.

Evans, D. A., Block, M. R., Steinberg, E. R., & Penrose, A. M. (1986). Frames and heuristics in doctor-patient discourse. *Social Science and Medicine, 22,* 1027–1034.

Evans, S. (1989). *Born for liberty: A history of women in America.* New York: Free Press.

Fagley, N. S. (1988). Judgmental heuristics: Implications for the decision making of school psychologists. *School Psychology Review, 17,* 311–321.

Fashing, J., & Goertzel, T. (1981). The myth of the normal curve: A theoretical critique and examination of its role in teaching and research. *Humanity and Society, 5,* 14–31.

Fay, B. (1988). Review of "A history and philosophy of the social sciences," by Peter Manicas. *History and Theory, 27,* 287–296.

Fee, E. (1983). Women's nature and scientific objectivity. In M. Loew & R. Hubbard (Eds.), *Woman's nature: Rationalizations of inequality.* New York: Pergamon.

Feigel, H. (1945). Operationalism and scientific method. *Psychological Review, 52,* 250–259.

Feigenbaum, M. (1980). Universal behavior in non-linear systems. *Los Alamos Science, 1,* 4–27.

Feindler, E. L. (1987). Clinical issues and recommendations in adolescent anger control training. *Journal of Child and Adolescent Psychotherapy, 4,* 267–274.

Feyerabend, P. K. (1978). *Against method.* London: NLB, Verso. (Original work published 1975)

Field [Heineman Pieper], M. (1979). *The impact of psychodynamic theory on casework, 1917–1949.* Unpublished doctoral dissertation, School of Social Service Administration, University of Chicago.

Field [Heineman Pieper], M. (1980). Social casework practice during the "psychiatric deluge" *Social Service Review, 54,* 482–507.

see also Heineman (Pieper), M., and Pieper, M. Heineman.

Fiorito, G., & Scotto, P. (1992). Observational learning in Octopus vulgaris. *Science, 256,* 545–547.

Fischer, J. (1973). Is casework effective? A review. *Social Work, 18,* 5–20.

Fischer, J. (1978). *Effective casework practice: An eclectic approach.* New York: McGraw-Hill.

Fischer, J. (1980–1981). Do research reviews contribute to knowledge development? The case of *Social Service Research*: Reviews of studies. *Journal of Social Service Research, 4,* 69–83.

Fischer, J. (1981). The social work revolution. *Social Work, 26,* 199–207.

Fischer, J. (1984). Revolution, schmevolution: Is social work changing or not? *Social Work, 29,* 71–75.

Fischer, J., & Gochros, H. (1975). *Planned behavior change: Behavior modification in social work.* New York: Free Press.

Fischer, P., & Breakey, W. (1991). The epidemiology of alcohol, drug, and mental disorders among homeless persons. *American Psychologist, 46,* 1115–1128.

Fischhoff, B. (1977). Perceived informativeness of facts. *Journal of Experimental Psychology: Human Perception and Performance, 3,* 349–358.

Fischhoff, B. (1982). Debiasing. In D. Kahneman, P. Slovic, & A. Tversky (Eds.), *Judgment under uncertainty: Heuristics and biases.* Cambridge, MA: Cambridge University Press.

Fish, V. K. (1983). Feminist scholarship in sociology: An emerging research model. *Wisconsin Sociologist, 20,* 43–56.

Fisher, J. (1990). The rank and file movement 1930–1936. *Journal of Progressive Human Services, 1,* 95–99. (Original work published 1936)

Fisher, R. A. (1931). *The genetical theory of natural selection.* Cambridge, MA: Cambridge University Press.

Fiske, D. (1982). Convergent-discriminant validation in measurements and research strategies. In D. Brinberg & L. Kidder (Eds.), *Forms of validity in research. New directions for methodology of social and behavioral science: No. 12.* San Francisco: Jossey-Bass.

Fiske, D., & Shweder, R. A. (Eds.). (1986). *Metatheory in social science: Pluralisms and subjectivities.* Chicago: University of Chicago Press.

Fletcher, R. C. (1947). Research and statistics in social work. In *Social Work Year Book.* New York: Russell Sage.

Fletcher, R. C. (1949). Research and statistics in social work. In *Social Work Year Book, 1949* (10th issue). New York: Russell Sage.

Flew, A. (1984). *A dictionary of philosophy* (2nd ed., rev.). New York: St. Martin's Press.

Flexner, A. (1915). Is social work a profession? *Proceedings of the National Conference of Charities and Corrections,* pp. 576–590. Madison, WI: Midland Publishing.

Flowers, L. C. (1990). An example of clinical inquiry in practice: The direct influence treatment model. In B. Orcutt (Ed.), *Science and inquiry in social work practice*. New York: Columbia University Press.

Foucault, M. (1980). *Power/knowledge: Selected interviews and other writings 1972–1977*. (C. Gordon, Ed.; C. Gordon, L. Marshal, J. Mepham, & K. Soper, Trans.). New York: Pantheon.

Fowler, R. D. (Ed.). (1991). Special issue: Homelessness. *American Psychologist, 46*(11), 1113–1255.

Fraiberg, S. (1970). The muse in the kitchen: A case study in clinical research. *Smith College Studies in Social Work, 40*, 101–104.

Frank, J. (1982). Therapeutic components shared by all psychotherapies. In J. Harvey & M. Parks (Eds.), *Psychotherapy research and behavior change* (pp. 9–37). Washington, DC: American Psychological Association.

Franklin, D. (1986). Mary Richmond and Jane Addams: From moral certainty to rational inquiry in social work practice. *Social Service Review, 60*, 504–525.

Franklin, J. H. (1989). *Race and history: Selected essays, 1938–1988*. Baton Rouge: Louisiana State University Press.

Fraser, D. C. (1953). The relation of an environmental variable to performance in a prolonged visual task. *Quarterly Journal of Experimental Psychology, 5*, 31–32.

Fraser, M., Taylor, M. J., Jackson, R., & O'Jack, J. (1991). Social work and science: Many ways of knowing? *Social Work Research and Abstracts, 27*, 5–15.

Freedman, B. (1987). Scientific value and validity as ethical requirements for research: A proposed explication. *IRB, 9*, 7–10.

Freedman, J. (1969). Roleplaying: Psychology by consensus. *Journal of Personality and Social Psychology, 13*, 107–114.

Freire, P. (1970). *Pedagogy of the oppressed* (M. B. Ramos, Trans.). New York: Herder and Herder.

French, D. G. (1952). *An approach to measuring results in social work. Report on the Michigan Reconnaissance Study of Evaluative Research in Social Work sponsored by the Michigan Welfare League*. With analyses of four evaluative studies prepared by John Hill, Leon Festinger, Helen Witmer, & Alfred Kahn. New York: Columbia University Press.

French, L. (1940). *Psychiatric social work*. New York: Commonwealth Fund.

Frenkel-Brunswick, E. (1961). Confirmation of psychoanalytic theories. In P. G. Frank (Ed.), *The validation of scientific theories* (pp. 95–110). New York: Collier.

Freud, A. (1965). *Normality and pathology in childhood: Assessments of development*. New York: International Universities Press.

Freud, S. (1953–1974). Project for a scientific psychology. In J. Strachey (Ed. and Trans.), *The standard edition of the complete psychological works of Sigmund Freud* (Vol. 1). London: Hogarth. (Original work published 1895)

Freud, S. (1953–1974). J. Strachey (Ed. and Trans.), *The standard edition of the complete psychological works of Sigmund Freud*. London: Hogarth.

Freud, S. (1963). Three case histories. In P. Rieff (Ed.), *The collected papers of Sigmund Freud*. New York: Collier.

Friend, M. (1960). The historical development of family diagnosis. *Social Service Review, 34*, 2–16.

Furumoto, L. (1987). On the margins: Women and the professionalization of psychology in the United States, 1890–1940. In M. Ash & W. Woodward (Eds.), *Psychology in twentieth century thought and society*. Cambridge: Cambridge University Press.

Gadamer, H. G. (1975). *Truth and method* (G. Barden & J. Cumming, Trans.). New York: Seabury.

Gadlin, H., & Ingle, G. (1975). Through the one-way mirror: The limits of experimental self-reflection. *American Psychologist, 30*, 1003–1009.

Gallagher, J. (1952). A commentary on research (response to Zimbalist). *Social Casework, 33*, 255–257.

Gardner, H. (1985). *The mind's new science: A history of the cognitive revolution*. New York: Basic Books.

Garrett, A. (1941). *Casework treatment of a child*. New York: Family Welfare Association of America.

Garrett, A. (1949). Historical survey of the evolution of casework. *Social Casework, 30*, 219–229.

Garvin, C. D., & Reed, B. G. (1983). Gender issues in social group work: An overview. *Social Work with Groups, 6*, 5–18.

Gay, P. (1988). *Freud: A life for our time*. New York: W. W. Norton.

Gebhardt-Taylor, M. (1982). Educational training programs for social service workers: A quantitative and qualitative evaluation. *Journal of Social Service Research, 5,* 85–93.

Geddes, A. (1941). Public welfare research and the schools of social work. *Social Service Review, 15,* 55–65.

Geertz, C. (1973). *The interpretation of cultures: Selected essays.* New York: Basic Books.

Geertz, C. (1983). *Local knowledge: Further essays in interpretive anthropology.* New York: Basic Books.

Geismar, L. L. (1982). Comments on "The obsolete scientific imperative in social work research." *Social Service Review, 56,* 311–312.

Geismar, L. L., & Krisberg, J. (1967). *The forgotten neighborhood: Site of an early skirmish in the War on Poverty.* Metuchen, NJ: Scarecrow Press.

Geismar, L. L., Lagay, B., Wolock, I., Gerhart, U. C., & Fink, H. (1972). *Early supports for family life: A social work experiment.* Metuchen, NJ: Scarecrow Press.

Geismar, L.L., & Wood, K. (1982). Evaluating practice: Science as faith. *Social Casework, 63,* 266–272.

Gentilin, J. (1987). Room restriction: A therapeutic prescription. *Journal of Psychosocial Nursing and Mental Health Services, 25,* 12–16.

Gergen, K. J. (1978). Toward generative theory. *Journal of Personality and Social Psychology, 36,* 1344–1360.

Gergen, K. J. (1985). The social constructionist movement in modern psychology. *American Psychologist, 40,* 266–275.

Gergen, K. J. (1986). Correspondence versus autonomy in the language of understanding human action. In D. W. Fiske & R. A. Shweder (Eds.), *Metatheory in social science: Pluralisms and subjectivities* (pp. 136–162). Chicago: University of Chicago Press.

Gergen, K. J. (1991). *The saturated self: Dilemmas of identity in contemporary life.* New York: Basic Books.

Gergen, K. J., & Gergen, M. M. (1982). Explaining human conduct: Form and function. In P. F. Secord (Ed.), *Explaining human behavior: Consciousness, human action and social structure.* Beverly Hills, CA: Sage.

Germain, C. (1970). Casework and science: A historical encounter. In R. Roberts & R. Nee (Eds.), *Theories of social casework.* Chicago: University of Chicago Press.

Germain, C., & Hartman, A. (1980). People and ideas in the history of social work practice. *Social Casework, 61,* 323–331.

Gershonson, C., MacDonald, M., Perlman, H., & Ripple, L. (1952). Letter to the editor (response to Zimbalist). *Social Casework, 33,* 257–258.

Ghiselin, M. (1966). On psychologism in the logic of taxonomic controversies. *Systematic Zoology, 15,* 202–205.

Gholson, B., & Barker, P. (1985). Kuhn, Lakatos, and Laudan: Applications in the history of physics and psychology. *American Psychologist, 40,* 755–769.

Gibbs, J. T., & Huang, L. N. (1989). *Children of color: Psychological interventions with minority youth.* San Francisco: Jossey-Bass.

Gibbs, L. (1983). Evaluation research: Scientist or advocate? *Journal of Social Service Research, 7,* 81–92.

Gibbs, L. E. (1990, March). *Reasoning for social workers: Bridging the gap between research and practice.* Paper presented at the Council on Social Work Education Annual Program Meeting.

Gibson, J. J. (1979). *The ecological approach to visual perception.* Boston: Houghton Mifflin.

Gibson, R. (1991). Broken brothers and breaking stereotypes: How can we respond to homeless people as they are instead of as they "ought" to be? *Public Welfare, 49,* 34–41.

Giddens, A. (1976). *New rules of sociological method: A positive critique of interpretive sociologies.* New York: Basic Books.

Giddens, A. (1977). *Studies in social and political theory.* London: Hutchinson.

Giddens, A. (1979). *Central problems in social theory: Action, structure, and contradiction in social analysis.* Berkeley: University of California Press.

Gigerenzer, G. (1987). Probabilistic thinking and the fight against subjectivity. In L. Kruger, G. Gigerenzer, & M. Morgan (Eds.), *The probabilistic revolution: Vol. 2. Ideas in the sciences* (pp. 11–34). Cambridge, MA: MIT Press.

Gigerenzer, G. (1991a). From tools to theories: A heuristic of discovery in cognitive psychology. *Psychological Review, 98,* 254–267.

Gigerenzer, G. (1991b). How to make cognitive illusions disappear: Beyond "Heuristics and biases." *European Review of Social Psychology, 2,* 83–115.

Gigerenzer, G. (1993). The superego, the ego, and the id in statistical reasoning. In G. Keren & C. Lewis (Eds.), *A handbook for data analysis in the behavioral sciences: Methodological issues.* Hillsdale, NJ: Lawrence Erlbaum.

Gigerenzer, G., Hoffrage, U., & Kleinbolting, H. (1991). Probabilistic mental models: A Brunswikian theory of confidence. *Psychological Review, 98,* 506–528.

Gigerenzer, G., & Hug, K. (1992). Domain-specific reasoning: Social contracts, cheating and perspective change. *Cognition, 43,* 127–171.

Gigerenzer, G., Swijtink, Z., Porter, T., Daston, L., Beatty, J., & Kruger, L. (1989). *The empire of chance: How probability changed science and everyday life.* Cambridge, MA: Cambridge University Press.

Gilligan, C. (1982). *In a different voice: Psychological theory and women's development.* Cambridge, MA: Harvard University Press.

Gilliland-Mallo, D., & Judd, P. (1986). The effectiveness of residential care facilities for adolescent boys. *Adolescence, 21,* 311–321.

Gilmour, J. S. L. (1940). Taxonomy and philosophy. In J. Huxley (Ed.), *New systematics* (pp. 461–474). London: Oxford University Press.

Giorgi, A. (1967). The experience of the subject as a source of data in a psychological experiment. *Review of Existential Psychology and Psychiatry, 7,* 169–176.

Giorgi, A. (1970). *Psychology as a human science—a phenomenologically based approach.* New York: Harper & Row.

Glassman, R., & Wimsatt, W. C. (1984). Evolutionary advantages and limitations of early developmental plasticity. In C. R. Almli & S. Finger (Eds.), *The behavioral biology of early brain damage: Vol. 1. Research orientations and clinical observations.* New York: Academic Press.

Gleeson, J. P. (1990). Engaging students in practice evaluation: Defining and monitoring critical initial interview components. *Journal of Social Work Education, 26,* 295–309.

Gleick, J. (1987). *Chaos: Making a new science.* New York: Penguin.

Glenn, J. (1978). General principles of child analysis. In J. Glenn & M. Scharfman (Eds.), *Child analysis and therapy.* New York: Jason Aronson.

Gliedman, J., & Roth, W. (1980). *The unexpected minority: Handicapped children in America.* New York: Harcourt Brace Jovanovich.

Glisson, C., & Fischer, J. (1987). Statistical training for social workers. *Journal of Social Work Education, 23,* 50–58.

Godelier, M. (1972). System structure and contradiction in capital. In R. Blackburn (Ed.), *Ideology in social science; readings in critical social theory.* London: Fontana.

Goering, P., Paduchak, D., & Durbin, J. (1990). Housing homeless women: A consumer preference study. *Hospital and Community Psychiatry, 41,* 790–794.

Goldstein, H. (1963). *Research standards and methods for social workers.* New Orleans: Hauser.

Goldstein, H. (1983). Starting where the client is. *Social Casework, 64,* 267–275.

Goldstein, H. (1986). Toward the integration of theory and practice: A humanistic approach. *Social Work, 31,* 352–357.

Goldstein, H. (1987). The neglected moral link in social work practice. *Social Work, 32,* 181–186.

Goldstein, H. (1990). The knowledge base of social work practice: Theory, wisdom, analogue, or art? *Families in Society, 71,* 32–43.

Goldstein, M., & Goldstein, I. F. (1978). *How we know: An exploration of the scientific process.* New York: Plenum.

Goodrich, T. J. (1978). Strategies for dealing with the issue of subjectivity in evaluation. *Evaluation Quarterly, 2,* 631–645.

Gordon, L. (1989). *Heroes of their own lives: The politics and history of family violence, Boston 1880–1960.* New York: Penguin.

Gordon, W. E. (1951). *Toward basic research in social work.* Paper delivered at the fiftieth anniversary meeting of the Missouri Association for Social Welfare, October, 1950, St. Louis. Published by the George Warren Brown School of Social Work.

Gottschalk, S., & Witkin, S. L. (1991). Rationality in social work: A critical examination. *Journal of Sociology and Social Welfare, 18,* 121–135.

Goudge, T. A. (1961). *The ascent of life; a philosophical study of the theory of evolution.* London: Allen & Unwin.

Gould, S. J. (1981). *The mismeasure of man.* New York: W. W. Norton.

Green, H. (1964). *I never promised you a rose garden.* New York: Holt, Rinehart & Winston.

Greenberg, M. S. (1967). Role playing: An alternative to deception? *Journal of Personality and Social Psychology, 7,* 152–157.

Greenberg, R. P., Bornstein, R. F., Greenberg, M. D., & Fisher, S. (1992). A meta-analysis of antidepressant outcome under "blinder" conditions. *Journal of Consulting and Clinical Psychology, 60*(5), 664–669.

Greenwood, E. (1957). Social work research: A decade of reappraisal. *Social Service Review, 31,* 311–320.

Greenwood, E. (1955). Social science and social work: A theory of their relationship. *Social Service Review, 29,* 20–33.

Greenwood, E. (1958). Social work research: The role of the schools. *Social Service Review, 32,* 152–166.

Greenwood, E., & Massarik, F. (1950). Some methodological problems in social work research. *American Sociological Review, 15,* 546–550.

Gregg, J. R. (1950). Taxonomic language and reality. *American Naturalist, 84,* 421–433.

Grellong, B. A. (1987). Residential care in context: Evolution of a treatment process in response to social change. *Residential Treatment for Children and Youth, 4,* 59–70.

Grey, A., & Dermody, H. (1972). Reports of casework failure. *Social Casework, 53,* 534–543.

Griesemer, J. L. (1983). *Communication and scientific change: The role of conceptual maps in the macroevolution controversy.* Unpublished doctoral dissertation, University of Chicago.

Grinker, R. R., MacGregor, H., Selan, K., Klein, A., & Kohrman, J. (1961). The early years of psychiatric social work. *Social Service Review, 35,* 111–126.

Grinnell, R. (Ed.). (1981). *Social work research and evaluation.* Itasca, IL: F. E. Peacock Press.

Grinnell, R. (Ed.). (1985). *Social work research and evaluation* (2nd ed.). Itasca, IL: F. E. Peacock Press.

Grinnell, R. (Ed.). (1988). *Social work research and evaluation* (3rd ed.). Itasca, IL: F. E. Peacock Press.

Grob, G. (1983). *Mental illness and American society: 1875–1940.* Princeton, NJ: Princeton University Press.

Grünbaum, A. (1961). Operationism and relativity. In P. G. Frank (Ed.), *The validation of scientific theories* (pp. 84–96). Boston: Beacon.

Grünbaum, A. (1984). *The foundations of psychoanalysis: A philosophical critique.* Berkeley: University of California Press.

Guba, E. (1985). The context of emergent paradigm research. In Y. Lincoln (Ed.), *Organizational theory and inquiry: The paradigm revolution.* Beverly Hills, CA: Sage.

Guba, E. (1990). The alternative paradigm dialog. In E. Guba (Ed.), *The paradigm dialog* (pp. 17–27). Newbury Park, CA: Sage.

Guba, E. G., & Lincoln, Y. S. (1983). Epistemological and methodological bases of naturalistic inquiry. In G. Madaus, M. Scriven, & D. Stufflebeam (Eds.), *Evaluation models: Viewpoints on educational and human services evaluation.* Boston: Kluwer-Nijhoff.

Gyarfas, M. G. (1983). The scientific imperative again. *Social Service Review, 57,* 149–150.

Habermas, J. (1971). *Knowledge and human interests* (J. J. Shapiro, Trans.). Boston: Beacon Press.

Hacking, I. (1983). *Representing and intervening: Introductory topics in the philosophy of natural science.* Cambridge, England: Cambridge University Press.

Hackman, J. D. (1983). Seven maxims for institutional researchers: Applying cognitive theory and research. *Research in Higher Education, 18,* 195–208.

Hale, N. (1971). *Freud and the Americans: The beginnings of psychoanalysis in the United States, 1876–1917.* New York: Oxford University Press.

Hallowitz, D. (1973). Letter to the editor. *Social Work, 18,* 106–108.

Hamilton, G. (1947). *Psychotherapy in child guidance.* New York: Columbia University Press.

Hanfling, O. (Ed.). (1981a). *Essential readings in logical positivism.* Oxford, England: Blackwell.

Hanfling, O. (1981b). *Logical positivism.* New York: Columbia University Press.

Hanrahan, P., & Reid, W. (1984). Choosing effective interventions. *Social Service Review, 58,* 244–258.

Hanson, N. R. (1958). *Patterns of discovery: An inquiry into the conceptual foundations of science.* Cambridge, England: Cambridge University Press.

Hanson, N. R. (1969a). Logical positivism and the interpretation of scientific theories. In P. Achinstein & S. Barker (Eds.), *The legacy of logical positivism: Studies in the philosophy of science*. Baltimore: Johns Hopkins University Press.

Hanson, N.R. (1969b). *Perception and discovery: An introduction to scientific inquiry*. W. Humphreys (Ed.). San Francisco: Freeman, Cooper.

Hanson, N. R. (1971). *Observation and explanation: A guide to philosophy of science*. New York: Harper & Row.

Harré, R. (1970). *The principles of scientific thinking*. Chicago: University of Chicago Press.

Harré, R. (1972). *The philosophies of science; an introductory survey*. New York: Oxford University Press.

Harré, R. (1984). *Personal being: A theory for individual psychology*. Cambridge: Harvard University Press.

Harré, R., Clarke. D., & DeCarlo, N. (1985). *Motives and mechanisms: An introduction to the psychology of action*. London: Methuen.

Harré, R., & Madden, E. H. (1975). *Causal powers: A theory of natural necessity*. Oxford, England: Basil Blackwell.

Harré, R., & Secord, P. F. (1972). *The explanation of social behavior*. Oxford, England: Basil Blackwell.

Harrison, D. F., Hudson, W., & Thyer, B. (1992). On "A critical analysis of empirical clinical practice": A response to Witkin's revised views. *Social Work, 37*, 461–464.

Harrison, L. (1993). Issues related to the protection of human research participants. *Journal of Neuroscience Nursing, 25*(3), 187–193.

Harrison, W. D. (1987). Reflective practice in social care. *Social Service Review, 61*, 393–404.

Harrison, W. D. (1989). Social work and the search for postindustrial community. *Social Work, 34*, 73–75.

Hartman, A. (1990). Editorial: Many ways of knowing. *Social Work, 35*, 3–4.

Hartman, A. (1991). Words create worlds. *Social Work, 36*, 275–276.

Hartman, A., & Laird, J. (1983). *Family centered social work practice*. New York: Free Press.

Hawking, S. (1988). *A brief history of time: From the big bang to black holes*. New York: Bantam Books.

Haworth, G. (1984). Social work research, practice, and paradigms. *Social Service Review, 58*, 343–357.

Haworth, M. (1990). *A child's therapy: Hour by hour*. Madison, CT: International Universities Press.

Hearn, B., & Thomson, B. (1987). *Developing community social work in teams: A manual for practice*. London: National Institute for Social Work.

Hearn, G. (1958). *Theory building in social work*. Toronto: University of Toronto Press.

Hearnshaw, L. S. (1987). *The shaping of modern psychology: An historical introduction*. New York: Routledge & Kegan Paul.

Heatherington, L., Friedlander, M. L., & Johnson, W. F. (1989). Informed consent in family therapy research: Ethical dilemmas and practical problems. *Journal of Family Psychology, 2*, 373–385.

Hegar, R. (1989). Empowerment-based practice with children. *Social Service Review, 63*, 372–383.

Hegner, H. (1897). Scientific value of social settlements. *American Journal of Sociology, 3*, 171–182.

Heilbrun, C. (1991). The politics of mind: Women, tradition, and the university. In S. Gabriel & I. Smithson (Eds.), *Gender in the classroom: Power and pedagogy*. Urbana: University of Illinois Press.

Heineman [Pieper], M. (1981). The obsolete scientific imperative in social work research. *Social Service Review, 55*, 371–397.

Heineman [Pieper], M. (1982). Author's reply. *Social Service Review, 56*, 146–148.

see also Pieper, M. Heineman.

Hempel, C. G. (1945). Studies in the logic of confirmation. *Mind, 54*, 1–26; 97–121.

Hempel, C. G. (1958). *The theoretician's dilemma: A study in the logic of theory construction. Minnesota studies in the philosophy of science: Vol. 2*. Minneapolis: University of Minnesota Press.

Hempel, C. G. (1965a). Fundamentals of taxonomy (A prior version of the paper was presented at the Work Conference on Field Studies in the Mental Disorders, American Psychopathological Association, New York, February, 1959). In *Aspects of scientific explanation and other essays in the philosophy of science*. New York: Free Press.

Hempel, C. G. (1965b). *Aspects of scientific explanation and other essays in the philosophy of science*. New York: Free Press.

Hempel, C. G., & Oppenheim, P. (1948). Studies in the logic of explanation. *Philosophy of Science, 15*, 135–175.

Henchy, T., & Glass, D. C. (1968). Evaluation apprehension and the social facilitation of dominant and subordinate responses. *Journal of Personality and Social Psychology, 10,* 446–454.

Hersen, M., & Barlow, D. (1976). *Single-case experimental designs: Strategies for studying behavior change.* New York: Pergamon.

Herzog, E., & Frings, J. (1952). A proposed next step in the diagnostic-functional issue. *Social Casework, 33,* 140–146.

Hexter, J. H. (1971). *The history primer.* New York: Basic Books.

Hiday, V., & Scheid-Cook, T. (1989). A follow-up of chronic patients committed to outpatient treatment. *Hospital and Community Psychiatry, 40,* 52–59.

Higham, J. (1954). Intellectual history and its neighbors. *Journal of the History of Ideas, 15,* 339–347.

Hill, R. (1980). Social work research on minorities: Impediments and opportunities. In D. Fanshel (Ed.), *The future of social work research* (pp. 188–198). New York: National Association of Social Workers.

Himmelfarb, G. (1989). Some reflections on the new history. *American Historical Review, 94,* 661–670.

Himmelfarb, G. (1992, October, 16). Telling it as you like it: Post-modernist history and the flight from fact. *Times Literary Supplement, 4672,* 11–16.

Hoffman, I. (1952). *Toward a logic for social work.* Unpublished memorandum. St. Paul, MN: Amherst H. Wilder Charity, Department of Research and Statistics.

Hoffman, I. (1956). Research, social work, and scholarship. *Social Service Review, 30,* 20–32.

Hofstadter, D. (1981, November). Metamagical themas: Strange attractors. *Scientific American,* pp. 22–43.

Hofstadter, R. (1955). *The age of reform: From Bryan to F. D. R.* New York: Alfred A. Knopf.

Hogarty, G. E. (1991). Social work practice research on severe mental illness: Charting a future. *Research on Social Work Practice, 1*(1), 5–31.

Holbrook, T. (1986). Current renewed interest in personal document research. *Social Casework, 67,* 403–409.

Holland, T. (1983). Comments on "Scientific Imperatives in Social Work Research and Practice." *Social Service Review, 57,* 337–339.

Hollis, E., & Taylor, A. (1951). *Social work education in the United States: The report of a study made for the National Council on Social Work Education.* New York: Columbia University Press.

Hollis, F. (1939). *Social casework in practice: Six case studies.* New York: Family Welfare Association of America.

Hollis, F. (1949). *Women in marital conflict: A casework study.* New York: Family Welfare Association of America.

Hollis, F. (1976). Evaluation: Clinical results and research methodology. *Clinical Social Work Journal, 4,* 204–212.

Hollis, F. (1983). The way it really was. *Smith College Studies in Social Work, 10,* 3–9.

Hollon, S. D., & Kriss, M. R. (1984). Cognitive factors in clinical research and practice. *Clinical Psychology Review, 4,* 35–76.

Holmes, S. A. (1991, December 25). Homelessness rises, but not as issue. *New York Times, CXLI (48825)* p. 10.

Hook, S. (Ed.). (1959). *Psychoanalysis, scientific method and philosophy.* New York: New York University Press.

Horkheimer, M. (1972). *Critical theory* (M. J. O'Connell, Trans.). New York: Herder and Herder.

Horn, M. (1984). The moral message of child guidance, 1925–1945. *Journal of Social History, 18,* 25–36.

Hornstein, G. A. (1988). Quantifying psychological phenomena: Debates, dilemmas, and implications. In J. Morawski (Ed.), *The rise of experimentation in American psychology.* New Haven: Yale University Press.

Hougland, J. (1987). Criteria for client evaluation of public programs: A comparison of objective and perceptual measures. *Social Science Quarterly, 68,* 386–394.

House, E. R. (1983). Assumptions underlying evaluation models. In G. Madaus, M. Scriven, & D. Stufflebeam (Eds.), *Evaluation models: Viewpoints on educational and human services evaluation.* Boston: Kluwer-Nijhoff.

Howard, G. S. (1985). The role of values in the science of psychology. *American Psychologist, 40,* 255–265.

Howe, M. W. (1974). Casework self-evaluation: A single subject approach. *Social Service Review, 48,* 1–23.

Howe, M. W. (1976). Using clients' observations in research. *Social Work, 21,* 28–32.

Howe, M. W., & Schuerman, J. (1974). Trends in the social work literature: 1957–72. *Social Service Review, 48,* 279–285.

Howes, D. H., &. Solomon, R. L. (1950). A note on McGinnies' "Emotionality and Perceptual Defense." *Psychological Review, 57,* 229–234.

Huberman, A. M., & Miles, M. B. (1985). Assessing local causality in qualitative research. In D. Berg & K. Smith (Eds.), *Exploring clinical methods for social research.* Beverly Hills, CA: Sage.

Hudson, W. (1978). First axioms of treatment. *Social Work, 23,* 65–66, 518–519.

Hudson, W. (1982). Scientific imperatives in social work research and practice. *Social Service Review, 56,* 246–258.

Hudson, W. (1983). Author's reply. *Social Service Review, 57,* 339–341.

Hudson, W. (1986). The proof is in the pudding [Letter to the editor]. *Social Work Research and Abstracts, 22,* 2.

Hughes, L. (1986). *The dream keeper and other poems.* New York: Alfred A. Knopf.

Hull, D. (1968). The operational imperative: Sense and nonsense in operationism. *Systematic Zoology, 17,* 438–457.

Hull, D. (1985). Openness and secrecy in science: Their origins and limitations. *Science, Technology and Human Values, 10,* 4–13.

Hull, D. (1988). *Science as a process: An evolutionary account of the social and conceptual development of science.* Chicago: University of Chicago Press.

Hull House Residents. (1906–1935). *Hull House Yearbooks, 1906–1935.* In Jane Addams Memorial Collection, Department of Special Collections, University of Illinois Library.

Hurlin, R. G. (1941). From the point of view of research. *The Family, 21,* 288–291.

Imre, R. W. (1982). *Knowing and caring: Philosophical issues in social work.* Washington, DC: University Press of America.

Imre, R. W. (1984). The nature of knowledge in social work. *Social Work, 29,* 41–45.

Imre, R. W. (1991a, March). *Understanding understanding.* Paper presented at the Annual Program Meeting of the Council on Social Work Education, New Orleans.

Imre, R. W. (1991b). What do we need to know for good practice? *Social Work, 36,* 198–200.

Inglis, W. G. (1966). The observational basis of homology. *Systematic Zoology, 15,* 219–221.

Ishibashi, N. (1991). Multicultural students: What do they want? *School Social Work Journal, 16,* 41–45.

Itard, J.-M. Gaspard. (1962). *The wild boy of Aveyron* (G. Humphrey & M. Humphrey, Trans.). New York: Appleton-Century-Crofts. (Original work published 1805)

Ivanoff, A., & Blythe, B. (1989). Response to R. G. Dean & B. L. Fenby, (1989). Exploring epistemologies: Social work action as a reflection of philosophical assumptions. *Journal of Social Work Education, 25,* 176–177.

Ivanoff, A., Blythe, B., & Briar, S. (1987). The empirical clinical practice debate. *Social Casework, 68,* 290–298.

Ivanoff, A., Robinson, E. A. R., & Blythe, B. J. (1987). Empirical clinical practice from a feminist perspective. *Social Work, 32,* 417–423.

Jackson, P. (1978). Black charity in Progressive Era Chicago. *Social Service Review, 52,* 400–417.

Jackson, P. (1990). *Life in classrooms.* New York: Teacher's College Press.

Jacob, F., Perrin, D., Sanchez, C., & Monon, J. (1960). L'operon: Groupe de genes a expresssion coordinnie par un operateur. *Comptes Rendus Academie des Sciences, 250,* 1727–1729.

James, J. W. (1979). Isabel Hampton and the professionalization of nursing in the 1890s. In M. Vogel & C. Rosenberg (Eds.), *The therapeutic revolution: Essays in the social history of American medicine.* Philadelphia: University of Pennsylvania Press.

James, W. (1907, February 12). Letter to Jane Addams. In *Jane Addams Memorial Collection.* Reel 5/0060-6, Special Collections, University Library, University of Illinois at Chicago.

James, W. (1970). Pragmatism. In G. Grob & R. Beck (Eds.), *Ideas in America: Source readings in the intellectual history of the United States.* New York: Free Press.

Janis, I. L., & Mann, L. (1977). *Decision making: A psychological analysis of conflict, choice, and commitment.* New York: Macmillan.

Jarrett, M. (1919). The psychiatric thread running through all social case work. In *Proceedings of the National Council of Social Work.* Chicago: Rogers & Hall.

Jarrett, M. (1925). The need for research in social case work by experienced social workers who are themselves doing the case work. *Journal of Social Forces, 3,* 668–669.

Jarrett, M. (1927). Present conditions in education for psychiatric social work. *Social Forces, 6,* 221–229.

Jayaratne, S., & Levy, R. (1979). *Empirical clinical practice.* New York: Columbia University Press.

Jensen, A. (1969). How much can we boost IQ and scholastic achievement? *Harvard Educational Review, 39,* 1–123.

Johannsen, W. (1909). *Elemente der Exakten Erblichkeitslehre.* Jena, Germany: G. Fisher.

Johnson, H. (1988). Drugs, dialogue, or diet: Diagnosing and treating the hyperactive child. *Social Work, 33,* 349–355.

Johnson, H. (1989). Disruptive children: Biological factors in attention deficit and antisocial disorders. *Social Work, 34,* 137–144.

Jones, E. E., & Thorne, A. (1987). Rediscovery of the subject: Intercultural approaches to clinical assessment. *Journal of Consulting and Clinical Psychology, 55,* 488–495.

Jones, W. T. (1969). *A history of Western philosophy* (2nd ed., Vols. 1–5). New York: Harcourt Brace Jovanovich.

Jourard, S. M. (1967). To be or not to be: Existential-psychological perspectives on the self. *University of Florida Monographs, Social Sciences,* No. 34. Gainsville: University of Florida Press.

Joynson, R. B. (1974). *Psychology and common sense.* London: Routledge & Kegan Paul.

Judd, L. (1988). Paper presented at the annual meeting of the Group for the Advancement of Doctoral Education, Columbus, OH.

Kadushin, A. (1976). Men in a women's profession. *Social Work, 21,* 440–447.

Kahn, A. (1954). The nature of social work knowledge. In C. Kasius (Ed.), *New directions in social work.* New York: Harper & Brothers.

Kahneman, D., Slovic, P., & Tversky, A. (1982). *Judgment under uncertainty: Heuristics and biases.* Cambridge, England: Cambridge University Press.

Kahneman, D., & Tversky, A. (1982). Variants of uncertainty. In D. Kahneman, P. Slovic, & A. Tversky (Eds.), *Judgment under uncertainty: Heuristics and biases.* Cambridge, England: Cambridge University Press.

Kahneman, D., & Tversky, A. (1983). Can irrationality be intelligently discussed? *Behavioral and Brain Sciences, 6,* 509–510.

Kaplan, A. (1964). *The conduct of inquiry: Methodology for behavioral science.* New York: Chandler.

Karger, H. J. (1983). Science, research and social work: Who controls the profession? *Social Work, 28,* 200–205.

Karger, H. (1987). *The sentinels of order: A study of social control and the Minneapolis Settlement House Movement, 1915–1950.* New York: University Press of America.

Karpf, M. (1931). *The scientific basis of social work: A study in family case work.* New York: Columbia University Press.

Kasanin, J. (1935). A critique of newer trends. *The Family, 16,* 36–37.

Kaufmann, A. (1968). *The science of decision making: An introduction to praxeology.* New York: McGraw-Hill.

Kaufman, I., & Makkay, E. S. (1956). Treatment of the adolescent delinquent. *Case Studies in Childhood Emotional Disabilities, 2,* 316–352.

Kazdin, A. (1977). Assessing the clinical or applied importance of behavior change through social validation. *Behavior Modification, 1,* 427–452.

Kazdin, A. (1981). Drawing valid inferences from case studies. *Journal of Consulting and Clinical Psychology, 49,* 183–192.

Kazdin, A. (1982). *Single-case research designs.* New York: Oxford University Press.

Kazdin, A., & Tuma, A. H. (1982). *Single-case research designs. New directions for methodology of social and behavioral science. Number 13.* San Francisco: Jossey-Bass.

Keith, G. (1941). Research: A tool of the administrator. *Social Service Review, 15,* 328–335.

Kelley, D. (1990). Horizons of intellectual history: Retrospect, circumspect, prospect. In D. Kelley (Ed.), *The history of ideas: Canon and variations. Library of the history of ideas (Vol. 1).* Rochester: University of Rochester Press.

Kelley, F. (1969). *Some ethical gains through legislation.* New York: Arno. (Original work published 1905)

Kelley, F. (1986). *The autobiography of Florence Kelley: Notes of sixty years* (with an introduction by Kathryn Kish Sklar; K. K. Sklar, Ed.). Chicago: Charles H. Kerr.

Kellogg, P. (1914). *The Pittsburgh district: Civic frontage.* New York: Russell Sage Foundation.

Kelman, H. (1967). Human use of human subjects: The problem of deception in social psychological experiments. *Psychological Bulletin, 67,* 1–11.

Kendall, P. C., & Braswell, L. (1985). *Cognitive-behavioral therapy for impulsive children.* New York: Guilford Press.

Kennedy, J. (1992). *Analyzing qualitative data: Log-linear analysis for behavioral research* (2nd ed.). New York: Praeger.

Kessel, F. S., & Siegel, A. (Eds.). (1981). *The child and other cultural inventions.* New York: Praeger Scientific.

Key, K. H. L. (1967). Operational homology. *Systematic Zoology, 16,* 275–276.

Kidder, L. (1982). Face validity from multiple perspectives. In D. Brinberg & L. Kidder (Eds.), *Forms of validity in research. New directions for methodology of social and behavioral science, No. 12.* San Francisco: Jossey-Bass.

Kim, J. (1964). Inference, explanation and prediction. *Journal of Philosophy, 61,* 360–368.

Kim, J. (1981). Causes as explanations: A critique. *Theory and Decision, 13,* 293–309.

Kimmel, A. (1981). *Ethics of human subject research. New directions for methodology of social and behavioral science.* San Francisco: Jossey-Bass.

Kirk, J., & Miller, M. (1986). *Reliability and validity in qualitative research. Qualitative research methods series, no. 1.* Newbury Park, CA: Sage.

Kirk, S., & Fischer, J. (1976). Do social workers understand research? *Journal of Education for Social Work, 12,* 63-70.

Kirk, S., Osmalov, M., & Fischer, J. (1976). Social workers' involvement in research. *Social Work, 21,* 121–124.

Klein, P., & Merriam, I. (1948). *The contribution of research to social work.* Papers presented at the 1948 National Conference of Social Work under the auspices of the Committee on Social Work Research. New York: American Association of Social Workers.

Kline, J., Harris, M., Bebout, R., & Drake, R. (1991). Contrasting integrated and linkage models of treatment of homeless, dually diagnosed adults. *New Directions for Mental Health Services, 50,* 95–106.

Klopfer, P. H. (1981). Origins of parental care. In P. J. Gubernick & P. H. Klopfer (Eds.), *Parental care in mammals* (pp. 1–12). New York: Plenum.

Knorr-Cetina, K. (1981). *The manufacture of knowledge: An essay on the constructivist and contextual nature of science.* Oxford: Pergamon.

Koch, S. (1959–1963). *Psychology: A study of a science.* (6 Vols.). New York: McGraw-Hill.

Koch, S. (1969, September). Psychology cannot be a coherent science. *Psychology Today,* pp. 14, 64, 66–68.

Kogan, L. (1960). *Social science theory and social work research.* Proceedings of an institute held by the Social Work Research Section of the National Association of Social Workers, June 8–12, 1959.

Kogan, L. (1975). Principles of measurement. In N. Polansky (Ed.), *Social work research* (pp. 68–92). Chicago: University of Chicago Press. (Original work published 1960)

Kohler, R. (1979). Medical reform and biomedical science: Biochemistry: A case study. In M. Vogel & C. Rosenberg (Eds.), *The therapeutic revolution: Essays in the social history of American medicine.* Philadelphia: University of Pennsylvania Press.

Kohut, H. (1959). Introspection, empathy and psychoanalysis: An examination of the relationship between mode of observation and theory. *Journal of the American Psychoanalytic Association, 7,* 459–483.

Kohut, H. (1971). *Analysis of the self: A systematic approach to the psychoanalytic treatment of narcissistic personality disorders. The psychoanalytic study of the child, No. 4.* New York: International Universities Press.

Kolata, G. (1994, January 1). Experts try to look at era in judging radiation tests. *New York Times,* pp., 1, 7.

Koppitz, E. (1964). *The Bender Gestalt test for young children.* New York: Grune & Stratton.

Kornfeld, W., & Hewitt, C. (1981). The scientific community metaphor. *IEEE Transactions of Systems, Man, and Cybernetics,* SMC-11, 24–33.

Koroloff, N. M., & Anderson, S. C. (1989). Alcohol-free living centers: Hope for homeless alcoholics. *Social Work, 34,* 497–504.

Koyré, A. (1968). *Metaphysics and measurement: Essays in scientific revolution.* Cambridge, MA: Harvard University Press.

Kravetz, D. (1976). Sexism in a woman's profession. *Social Work, 21,* 421–427.

Kruglanski, A. W. (in press). The human subject in the psychological experiment: Fact and artifact. In *Advances in Social Psychology.* (as cited in Gadlin & Ingle, 1975)

Kupfersmid, J., Mazzarins, H., & Benjamin, R. (1987). Programming as a means of assault prevention. *Child and Youth Services, 10,* 49–83.

Kuhn, T. S. (1962). *The structure of scientific revolutions.* Chicago: University of Chicago Press.

Kuhn, T. S. (1970). *The structure of scientific revolutions* (2nd ed.). Chicago: University of Chicago Press.

Kuhn, T. S. (1977). *The essential tension: Selected studies in scientific tradition and change.* Chicago: University of Chicago Press.

Kvale, S. (1973). The technological paradigm of psychological research. *Journal of Phenomenological Psychology, 3,* 143–159.

LaBarre, M. (1942). Editing. *The Family, 23,* 193–196.

Lakatos, I. (1970). Falsification and the methodology of scientific research programmes. In I. Lakatos & A. Musgrave (Eds.), *Criticism and the growth of knowledge.* Cambridge, England: Cambridge University Press.

Lakatos, I. (1978). Methodology of scientific research programmes. In J. Worrall & G. Currie (Eds.), *Philosophical papers.* Cambridge, England: Cambridge University Press.

Lakatos, I., & Musgrave, A. (Eds.). (1970). *Criticism and the growth of knowledge.* Cambridge, England: Cambridge University Press.

Lather, P. (1986a). Issues of validity in openly ideological research: Between a rock and a soft place. *Interchange, 17,* 63–84.

Lather, P. (1986b). Research as praxis. *Harvard Educational Review, 56,* 257–277.

Lathrop, J. (1905). *Suggestions for institution visitors.* Chicago: Public Charities Committee of the Illinois Federation of Women's Clubs.

Latour, B. (1987). *Science in action: How to follow scientists and engineers through society.* Cambridge, MA: Harvard University Press.

Latour, B. (1988). *The pasteurization of France.* Cambridge: Harvard University Press.

Latour, B., & Woolgar, S. (1979). *Laboratory life: The construction of scientific facts.* Beverly Hills, CA: Sage.

Laudan, L. (1981). The pseudo-science of science? *Philosophy of the Social Sciences, 11,* 173–198.

Laudan, L. (1984). *Science and values: An essay on the aims of science and their role in scientific debate.* Berkeley: University of California Press.

Laufer, M., Denhoff, E., & Solomons, G. (1957). Hyperkinetic impulse disorder in children's behavior problems. *Psychosomatic Medicine, 19,* 38–49.

Layder, D. (1981). *Structure, interaction and social theory.* London: Routledge & Kegan Paul.

Layder, D. (1982). Grounded theory: A constructive critique. *Journal for the Theory of Social Behavior, 12,* 103–123.

Leahey, T. (1980). The myth of operationism. *Journal of Mind and Behavior, 1,* 127–143.

LeCompte, M. D., & Goetz, J. P. (1982). Problems of reliability and validity in ethnographic research. *Review of Educational Research, 52,* 31–60.

Lee, P. (1937a). Social work as cause and function. (Address given at the National Conference of Social Work, 1929.) In P. Lee (Ed.), *Social work as cause and function and other papers.* New York: Columbia University Press.

Lee, P. (1937b). The social worker and social action. (Address delivered before the New York State Conference on Social Work, 1935.) In P. Lee (Ed.), *Social work as cause and function and other papers.* New York: Columbia University Press.

Lee, P. (1937c). What is the basis of public confidence in social work? (Address delivered at the Conference of the Association of the New York School of Social Work, 1935.) In P. Lee (Ed.), *Social work as cause and function and other papers.* New York: Columbia University Press.

Lee, P., & Kenworthy, M. (1929). *Mental hygiene and social work.* New York: Commonwealth Fund.

Leete, E. (1988). A consumer perspective on psychosocial treatment. *Psychosocial Rehabilitation Journal, 12,* 45–52.

Leiby, J. (1978a). *A history of social welfare and social work in the United States.* New York: Columbia University Press.

Leiby, J. (1978b). Social welfare: History of basic ideas. In J. B. Turner (Ed.), *Encyclopedia of social work.* Washington, DC: NASW.

Leighninger, L. (1975). Social workers, immigrants, and historians: A re-examination. *Journal of Sociology and Social Welfare, 2,* 326–344.

Lenat, D. B. (1982). The nature of heuristics. *Artificial Intelligence, 19,* 189–249.

Leplin, J. (Ed.). (1984). *Scientific realism.* Berkeley: University of California Press.

Levi-Strauss, C. (1966). *The savage mind.* Chicago: University of Chicago Press.

Levine, I., & Huebner, R. (1991). Homeless persons with alcohol, drug, and mental disorders. *American Psychologist, 46,* 1113–1114.

LeVine, R. A. (1966). Outsiders' judgments: An ethnographic approach to group differences in personality. *Southwestern Journal of Anthropology, 22,* 101–116.

LeVine, R. D. (1981). Knowledge and fallibility in anthropological field research, In M. Brewer & B.

Collins (Eds.), *Scientific inquiry and the social sciences.* San Francisco: Jossey-Bass.

Levins, R. (1966). The strategy of model-building in population biology. *American Scientist, 54,* 421–431.

Levins, R. (1968). *Evolution in changing environments: Some theoretical explorations.* Princeton, NJ: Princeton University Press.

Levins, R., & Lewontin, R. (1985). *The dialectical biologist.* Cambridge, MA: Harvard University Press.

Levitt, E. E. (1959). The basic philosophy of experimentation. *Smith College Studies in Social Work, 30,* 63–72.

Lewontin, R. C. (1974). The analysis of variance and the analysis of causes. *American Journal of Human Genetics, 26,* 400–411.

Lewontin, R., Rose, S., & Kamin, L. (1984). *Not in our genes: Biology, ideology, and human nature.* New York: Pantheon Books.

Lieberman, F. (1979). *Social work with children.* New York: Human Sciences Press.

Lincoln, Y. (Ed.). (1985). *Organizational theory and inquiry: The paradigm revolution.* Beverly Hills, CA: Sage.

Lincoln, Y. S. (1990). The making of a constructivist: A remembrance of transformations past. In E. Guba (Ed.), *The paradigm dialog.* Newbury Park: Sage.

Lincoln, Y. S., & Guba, E. G. (1985). *Naturalistic inquiry.* Newbury Park: Sage.

Lindsay, R. B. (1961). Operationalism in physics. In P. G. Frank (Ed.), *The validation of scientific theories* (pp. 69–75). New York: Collier.

Lipton, F. R., Nutt, S., & Sabatini, A. (1988). Housing the homeless mentally ill: A longitudinal study of a treatment approach. *Hospital and Community Psychiatry, 39,* 40–45.

Lipton, H., & Svarstad, B. (1977). Sources of variation in clinicians' communications to parents about mental retardation. *American Journal of Mental Deficiency, 82,* 155–161.

Lochman, J. (1984). Psychological characteristics and assessment of aggressive adolescents. In C. Keith (Ed.), *The aggressive adolescent: Clinical perspectives* (pp. 17–62). New York: Free Press.

Loeb, M. (1960). The backdrop for social research: Theory-making and model-building. In L. Kogan (Ed.), *Social science theory and social work research.* New York: National Association of Social Workers.

Loftus, G. (1993). Editorial comment. *Memory and Cognition, 21,* 1–3.

Loseke, D. R., & Cahill, S. E. (1984). The social construction of deviance: Experts on battered women. *Social Problems, 31,* 296–310.

Lou, H., Henriksen, L., Bruhn, P., Borner, H., & Nielsen, J. (1989). Striatal dysfunction in attention deficit and hyperkinetic disorder. *Archives of Neurology, 46,* 48–52.

Lovaas, O. I., & Bradley, B. (Eds.). (1974). *Perspectives in behavior modification with deviant children.* Englewood Cliffs, NJ: Prentice-Hall.

Lowry, F. (Ed.). (1939). *Readings in social case work 1920–1938: Selected reprints for the case work practitioner.* New York: Columbia University Press.

Lubove, R. (1968). *The professional altruist: The emergence of social work as a career, 1880–1930.* Cambridge, MA: Harvard University Press. (Original work published 1965)

Luce, R. D., & Raiffa, H. (1957). *Games and decisions.* New York: Wiley.

Lucente, R. (1987). N=1: Intensive case study methodology reconsidered. *Journal of Teaching in Social Work, 1,* 49–64.

Lum, D. (1992). *Social work practice and people of color: A process-stage approach* (2nd. ed.). Monterey, CA: Brooks/Cole.

Lyons, J. (1964). On the psychology of the psychological experiment. In C. Scheerer (Ed.), *Cognition: Theory, research, promise.* New York: Harper & Row.

Maas, H. S. (1991). Still dancing: Review of Helen Harris Perlman's "Looking back to see ahead" and "The dancing clock and other memories." *Readings: A Journal of Reviews and Commentary in Mental Health, 6,* 18–22.

Maas, H. S., & Varon, E. (1949). The case worker in clinical and socio-psychological research. *Social Service Review, 23,* 302–314.

Maas, H. S., & Wolins, M. (1954). Concepts and methods in social work research. In C. Kasius (Ed.), *New directions in social work.* New York: Harper & Brothers.

MacDonald, M. (1951). The curriculum in social work at the University of Chicago. *Social Service Review, 25,* 459–465.

MacDonald, M. (1957). Research in social work. In *Social Work Year Book, 1957* (13th Issue, pp. 489–500). New York: National Association of Social Workers.

MacDonald, M. (1959). Compatibility of theory and method: Analysis of six studies. In A. Shyne (Ed.), *Use of judgments as data in social work research.* New York: National Association of Social Workers.

MacDonald, M. (1960a). Research in social work. In *Social Work Year Book, 1960* (14th Issue, pp. 507–517). New York: National Association of Social Workers.

MacDonald, M. (1960b). Social work research: A perspective. In N. Polansky (Ed.), *Social work research.* Chicago: University of Chicago Press.

Mach, E. (1960). *The science of mechanics* (6th ed.). Chicago: Open Court.

MacKinnon, C. (1985). Pornography, civil rights, and speech. *Harvard Civil Rights—Civil Liberties Law Review, 20,* 1–70.

Mahoney, M. J. (1976). *Scientist as subject: The psychological imperative.* Cambridge, MA: Ballinger.

Mahrer, A. (1988). Discovery-oriented psychotherapy research: Rationale, aims, and methods. *American Psychologist, 43,* 694–702.

Mahrer, A. R., & Nadler, W. P. (1986). Good moments in psychotherapy: A preliminary review, a list, and some promising research avenues. *Journal of Consulting and Clinical Psychology, 54,* 10–15.

Manicas, P. T. (1981). Review of "States and social revolutions." *History and Theory, 20,* 204–208.

Manicas, P. T. (1987). *A history and philosophy of the social sciences.* Oxford: Basil Blackwell.

Manicas, P. T., & Secord, P. F. (1983). Implications for psychology of the new philosophy of science. *American Psychologist, 38,* 399–413.

Margenau, H. (1966). The philosophical legacy of quantum theory. In R. Colodny (Ed.), *Mind and cosmos: Essays in comtemporary science and philosophy* (pp. 330–356). Pittsburgh: University of Pittsburgh Press.

Martin, L. (1986). "Eskimo words for snow": A case study in the genesis and decay of an anthropological example. *American Anthropologist, 88,* 418–423.

Martin, R. (1987). Oral history in social work education: Chronicling the black experience. *Journal of Social Work Education, 23,* 5–10.

Martinez-Brawley, E. (1987). From countrywoman to federal relief administrator: Josephine Chapin Brown, a biographical study. *Journal of Sociology and Social Welfare, 14,* 153–185.

Marziali, E., & Alexander, L. (1991). The power of the therapeutic relationship. *American Journal of Orthopsychiatry, 61,* 383–391.

Mason, M. A. (1992). Standing still in the workplace: Women in social work and other female-dominated occupations. *Affilia, 7,* 23–43.

Masterman, M. (1970). The nature of a paradigm. In I. Lakatos & A. Musgrave (Eds.), *Criticism and the growth of knowledge.* Cambridge, England: Cambridge University Press.

May, K. A. (1979, January). The nurse as researcher: Impediment to informed consent? *Nursing Outlook,* pp. 36–39.

Maynard-Smith, J. (1983). *Evolution and the theory of games.* London: Cambridge University Press.

Mayr, E. (1963). *Animal species and evolution.* Cambridge, MA: Belknap Press.

McCauley, R. M. (in press). Competence, heuristics, and scientific discovery. *British Journal for the Philosophy of Science* (as cited in Wimsatt, 1986).

McCord, J. (1978). A thirty-year follow-up of treatment effects. *American Psychologist, 33,* 284–289.

McCrea, F. B. (1983). The politics of menopause: The "discovery" of a deficiency disease. *Social Problems, 31,* 111–123.

McDill, E. L., McDill, M. S., & Sprehe, J. T. (1969). *Strategies for success in compensatory education: An appraisal of evaluation research.* Baltimore: Johns Hopkins University Press.

McGuire, W. J. (1969). Suspiciousness of experimenter's intent. In R. Rosenthal & R. Rosnow (Eds.), *Artifact in behavioral research.* New York: Academic Press.

McJimsey, G. (1987). *Harry Hopkins: Ally of the poor and defender of democracy.* Cambridge, MA: Harvard University Press.

McVicker Hunt, J. (1948). Measuring movement in casework. *Social Casework, 29,* 343–351.

McVicker Hunt, J. (1959). On the judgment of social workers as a source of information in social work research. In A. Shyne (Ed.), *Use of judgments as data in social work research* (pp. 38–54). New York: National Association of Social Workers.

McVicker Hunt, J., & Kogan, L. (1950). *Measuring results in social casework: A manual on judging movement.* New York: Family Service Association of America.

Mead, G. H. (1934). *Mind, self, and society: From the standpoint of a social behaviorist* (C. W. Morris, Ed.). Chicago: University of Chicago Press.

Meddock, T. D., Parsons, J. L., & Hill, K. T. (1971). Effects of an adult's presence and praise on young children's performance. *Journal of Experimental Child Psychology, 12,* 197–211.

Meehl, P. (1986). What social scientists don't understand. In D. W. Fiske & R. A. Shweder (Eds.), *Metatheory in social science: Pluralisms and subjectivities* (pp. 315–338). Chicago: University of Chicago Press.

Meeks, J. E. (1985). Inpatient treatment of the violent adolescent. *Adolescent Psychiatry, 12,* 393–405.

Meier, E. (1951). Parallels in development: Student and profession. *Social Casework, 32,* 407–413.

Mencher, S. (1959). *The research method in social work education.* New York: Council on Social Work Education.

Mertz, D. B., & MacCauley, D. (1980). The domain of laboratory ecology. *Synthese, 43,* 95–110.

Messing, K. (1983). The scientific mystique: Can a white lab coat guarantee purity in the search for knowledge about the nature of women? In M. Lowe & R. Hubbard (Eds.), *Woman's nature: Rationalizations of inequality.* New York: Pergamon.

Meyer, C. (1984). Integrating research and practice [Editorial]. *Social Work, 29,* 323.

Milby, J. B., & Weber, A. (1991). Obsessive compulsive disorders. In T. Kratochwill & R. Morris (Eds.), *The practice of child therapy* (2nd ed.). New York: Pergamon.

Milgram, S. (1963). Behavioral study of obedience. *Journal of Abnormal and Social Psychology, 67,* 371–378.

Milgram, S. (1965). Some conditions of obedience and disobedience to authority. *Human Relations, 18,* 57–76.

Mill, J. S. (1974). A system of logic; ratiocinative and inductive: Being a connected view of the principles of evidence and the methods of scientific investigation. In J. M. Robson (Ed.), *Collected works of John Stuart Mill* (Vol. 8, IV–VI, appendices). Toronto: University of Toronto Press and Routledge Kegan Paul.

Miller, R. (1958). An experimental study of the observational process in casework. *Social Work, 3,* 96–102.

Miller, R. (1970). Discussion: Response to Fraiberg's "The muse in the kitchen." *Smith College Studies in Social Work, 40,* 135–139.

Minkoff, K. (1989). An integrated treatment model for dual-diagnosis of psychosis and addiction. *Hospital and Community Psychiatry, 40,* 1031–1036.

Mishler, E. (1979). Meaning in context: Is there any other kind? *Harvard Educational Review, 49,* 1–19.

Mishler, E. (1984). *The discourse of medicine: Dialectics of medical interviews.* Norwood, NJ: Ablex.

Mishler, E. (1986). *Research interviewing: Context and narrative.* Cambridge, MA: Harvard University Press.

Mishler, E. G. (1990). Validation in inquiry-guided research: The role of exemplars in narrative studies. *Harvard Educational Review, 60*(4), 415–442.

Mitroff, I. (1973). Systems, inquiry, and the meanings of falsification. *Philosophy of Science, 40,* 255–276.

Mitroff, I. (1974). *The subjective side of science: A philosophical inquiry into the psychology of the Apollo moon scientists.* New York, Amsterdam: Elsevier.

Mitroff, I., & Bonoma, T. (1978). Psychological assumptions, experimentation and real world problems: A critique and an alternate approach to evaluation. *Evaluation Quarterly, 2,* 235–260.

Mitroff, I., & Featheringham, T. (1974). On systemic problem-solving and the error of the third kind. *Behavioral Science, 19,* 383–393.

Mitroff, I., & Kilmann, R. (1978). *Methodological approaches to social science.* San Francisco: Jossey-Bass.

Mohl, R., & Betten, N. (1974). Paternalism and pluralism: Immigrants and social welfare in Gary, Indiana, 1906–1940. *American Studies, 15,* 5–30.

Montagu, J. D. (1975). The hyperkinetic child: A behavioral, electrodermal and EEG investigation. *Developmental Medicine and Child Neurology, 17,* 299–305.

Morawski, J. G. (1982). Assessing psychology's moral heritage through our neglected utopias. *American Psychologist, 37,* 1082–1095.

Morawski, J. G. (1985). The measurement of masculinity and femininity: Engendering categorical realities. *Journal of Personality, 53,* 196–223.

Morawski, J. G. (Ed.). (1988). *The rise of experimentation in American psychology.* New Haven: Yale University Press.

Morgan, G., & Smircich, L. (1980). The case for qualitative research. *Academy of Management Review, 5,* 491–500.

Morgan, T. H. (1914). The mechanism of heredity as indicated by the inheritance of linked characters. *Popular Science Monthly, 84,* 5–16.

Morrison, D., & Henkel, R. (Eds.). (1970). *The significance test controversy: A reader.* Chicago: Aldine.

Morton, N. (1974). Analysis of family resemblance: I. Introduction. *American Journal of Human Genetics, 26,* 318–330.

Moustakas, C. (1981). Heuristic research. In P. Reason & J. Rowan (Eds.), *Human inquiry: A sourcebook of new paradigm research* (pp. 207–208). New York: Wiley.

Mullen, E. (1985). Methodological dilemmas in social work research. *Social Work Research and Abstracts, 21,* 12–20.

Muller, H. J. (1940). An analysis of the process of structural change in chromosomes of Drosophila. *Journal of Genetics, 40,* 1–66.

Mulkern, V., & Bradley, V. (1986). Service utilization and service preferences of homeless persons. *Psychosocial Rehabilitation Journal, 10,* 23–30.

Muncy, R. (1991). *Creating a female dominion in American reform, 1890–1935.* New York: Oxford University Press.

Munir, K., & Earls, F. (1992). Ethical principles governing research in child and adolescent psychiatry. *Journal of the American Academy of Child and Adolescent Psychiatry, 31*(3), 408–414.

Murphy, J. (1988). Making sense of postmodern sociology. *British Journal of Sociology, 39,* 600–614.

Mynatt, C., Doherty, M., & Tweney, R. (1977). Confirmation bias in a simulated research environment: An experimental study of scientific inference. *Quarterly Journal of Experimental Psychology, 29,* 85–95.

Nagel, E. (1961). *The structure of science: Problems in the logic of scientific explanation.* New York: Harcourt Brace.

National Association of Social Workers [N.A.S.W.]. (1983–1984). *Supplement to the Encyclopedia of Social Work* (17th ed.). Silver Spring, MD: National Association of Social Workers.

Neisser, U. (1980). On "social knowing." *Personality and Social Psychology Bulletin, 6,* 601–605.

Nelson, J. (1981). Issues in single-subject research for non-behaviorists. *Social Work Research and Abstracts, 17,* 31–37.

Nelson, J. (1985). Verifying the independent variable in single-subject research. *Social Work Research and Abstracts, 21,* 3–8.

Nelson, J. (1988). Single-subject research. In R. Grinnell (Ed.), *Social work research and evaluation* (pp. 362–399). Itasca, IL: F. E. Peacock.

Nelson, K. (1992, March). *Assessing interventions: Beyond the "Black Box" in social work research.* Paper presented at the Annual Program Meeting of the Council on Social Work Education, Kansas City.

Newton, B. (1985). Tough love: Help for parents with troubled teenagers—reorganizing the hierarchy in disorganized families. *Pediatrics, 76,* 691–694.

Nicholson, R. H. (Ed.). (1986). *Medical research with children: Ethics, law, and practice.* Oxford, England: Oxford University Press.

Nickles, T. (1987a). Methodology, heuristics, and rationality. In J. C. Pitt & M. Pera (Eds.), *Rational changes in science: Essays on scientific reasoning* (pp. 103–132). Boston: D. Reidel.

Nickles, T. (1987b). 'Twixt method and madness. In N. J. Nersessian (Ed.), *The process of science.* Dordrecht, Netherlands: Kluwer Academic Publishers.

Nickles, T. (1988). Questioning and problems in philosophy of science: Problem-solving versus directly truth-seeking epistemologies. In M. Meyer (Ed.), *Questions and questioning.* New York: Walter de Gruyter.

Nietzsche, F. (1972). *The portable Nietzsche* (W. Kaufmann, Ed.). Princeton, NJ: Princeton University Press. (Original work published 1888)

Nisbett, R., & Ross, L. (1980). *Human inference: Strategies and shortcomings of social judgment.* Englewood Cliffs, NJ: Prentice-Hall.

Noble, C. (1974). Philosophy of science in contemporary psychology. *Psychological Reports, 35,* 1239–1246.

Norusis, M. (1988). *The SPSS guide to data analysis.* Chicago: SPSS.

Nuehring, E., & Pascone, A. (1986). Single-subject evaluation: A tool for quality assurance. *Social Work, 31,* 359–365.

Nunnally, J. (1960). The place of statistics in psychology. *Educational and Psychological Measurement, 20,* 641–650.

Oakes, M. (1986). *Statistical inference: A commentary for the social and behavioral sciences.* New York: Wiley.

Odencrantz, L. C. (1929). *The social worker in family, medical, and psychiatric social work.* New York: Harper & Brothers.

O'Donnell, J. M. (1979). The crisis of experimentalism in the 1920s: E.G. Boring and his uses of history. *American Psychologist, 34,* 289–295.

O'Hare, T. (1991). Integrating research and practice: A framework for implementation. *Social Work, 36,* 220–223.

Oldman, D. (1981). Sources of antagonism to "qualitative" research. *Social Science Information Studies, 1,* 231–240.

Olshewsky, T. (1975). Dispositions and reductionism in psychology. *Journal of the Theory of Social Behavior, 5,* 129–144.

Oppenheimer, R. (1930). Domestic relations courts—A study in Americana. *Social Service Review, 4,* 17–22.

Orcutt, B. (1990). *Science and inquiry in social work practice.* New York: Columbia University Press.

O'Reilly, C. (1969). Race in social welfare. In R. Miller (Ed.), *Race, research, and reason: Social work perspectives: Report* (pp. 89–98). New York: National Association of Social Workers.

Orlinsky, D. E., & Howard, K. I. (1986). Process and outcome in psychotherapy. In S. L. Garfield & A. E. Bergin (Eds.), *Handbook of psychotherapy and behavior change: An empirical analysis* (3rd ed., pp. 311–381). New York: Wiley.

Orne, M. (1969). Demand characteristics and the concept of quasi-controls. In R. Rosenthal & R. Rosnow (Eds.), *Artifact in behavioral research* (pp. 143–179). New York: Academic Press.

Oster, G., & Wilson, E. O. (1979). *Caste and ecology in the social insects.* Princeton, NJ: Princeton University Press.

O'Toole, M. (1991). "Margot O'Toole's record of events." *Nature, 351,* 180–183.

Outhwaite, W. (1987). *New philosophies of social science: Realism, hermeneutics and critical theory.* New York: St. Martin's Press.

Parad, H., & Parad, L. (Eds.). (1980). *Crisis intervention, book II.* Milwaukee, WI: Family Service America.

Parlett, M. (1981). Illuminative evaluation. In P. Reason & J. Rowan (Eds.), *Human inquiry: A sourcebook of new paradigm research.* New York: Wiley.

Patterson, G. R., Jones, R., Whittier, J., & Wright, M. A. (1965). A behavior modification technique for the hyperactive child. *Behavior Research and Therapy, 2,* 217–226.

Patton, M. (1990). *Qualitative evaluation and research methods.* Newbury Park, CA: Sage.

Pecukonis, E. V. (1990). A cognitive/affective empathy training program as a function of ego development in aggressive adolescent females. *Adolescence, 25,* 59–76.

Peebles-Wilkins, W., & Francis, E. A. (1990). Two outstanding black women in social welfare history: Mary Church Terrell and Ida B. Wells-Barnett. *Affilia, 5,* 87–100.

Peile, C. (1988a). Author's reply. *Social Service Review, 62,* 708–709.

Peile, C. (1988b). Research paradigms in social work: From stalemate to creative synthesis. *Social Service Review, 62,* 1–19.

Perlman, H. H. (1957). Freud's contribution to social welfare. *Social Service Review, 31,* 192–202.

Perlman, H. H. (1989). *Looking back to see ahead.* Chicago: University of Chicago Press.

Petitto, L., & Marentette, P. (1991). Babbling in the manual mode: Evidence for the ontogeny of language. *Science, 251,* 1493–1496.

Phillips, D. L. (1974). The madness in our methods: A three-author exchange, in four parts. *Sociology and Social Research, 58,* 225–236.

Phillips, D. L. (1990). Postpositivistic science: Myths and realities. In E. Guba (Ed.), *The paradigm dialog.* Newbury Park, CA: Sage.

Pieper, M. Heineman. (1982). Author's reply. *Social Service Review, 56,* 312.

Pieper, M. Heineman. (1985). The future of social work research. *Social Work Research and Abstracts, 21,* 3–11.

Pieper, M. Heineman. (1986a). The author replies. *Social Work Research and Abstracts, 22,* 2.

Pieper, M. Heineman. (1986b). Some common misunderstandings of the heuristic approach. *Social Work Research and Abstracts, 22,* 2, 22.

Pieper, M. Heineman. (1987). Comments on "Scientific imperatives in social work research: Pluralism is not skepticism." *Social Service Review, 61,* 368–370.

Pieper, M. Heineman. (1988). Comments on "Research paradigms in social work: From stalemate to creative synthesis." *Social Service Review, 62,* 535–536.

Pieper, M. Heineman. (1989). The heuristic paradigm: A unifying and comprehensive approach to social work research. *Smith College Studies in Social Work, 60,* 8–34.

Pieper, M. Heineman. (1991). *Science, not scientism: The robustness of naturalistic clinical research.* [Keynote address given at the Conference on Qualitative Methods in Social Work Research, State University of New York at Albany, August 1991.] Manuscript copy.

Pieper, M. Heineman. (1994). *Science, not scientism: The robustness of naturalistic clinical research.*

[Keynote address given at the Conference on Qualitative Methods in Social Work Research, State University of New York at Albany, August 1991.] In E. Sherman & W. J. Reid (Eds.), *Qualitative research in social work*. New York: Columbia University Press.

see also Field [Heineman Pieper], M., and Heineman [Pieper], M.

Pieper, M. Heineman, & Pieper, William J. (1990). *Intrapsychic humanism: An introduction to a comprehensive psychology and philosophy of mind.* Chicago: Falcon II Press.

Pieper, M. Heineman, & Pieper, W. J. (1991, September). *The privilege of being a therapist: A new psychology, intrapsychic humanism, offers a fresh perspective on caregiving intimacy and the development of the professional self.* Keynote address presented at the 20th Anniversary Conference of the National Federation of Societies of Clinical Social Work.

Pieper, M. Heineman, & Pieper, W. J. (1992a). It's not tough, it's tender love. *Child Welfare, 71,* 369–377.

Pieper, M. Heineman, & Pieper, W. J. (1992b, May 27). *A new psychology challenges the misogyny and misanthropy of Freud's legacy.* Invitational paper presented at the Chicago Association for Psychoanalytic Psychology.

Pieper, M. Heineman, & Pieper, W. J. (1992c). *Treating violent untreatable adolescents: Applications of intrapsychic humanism in a state-funded demonstration project.* Alumni Centennial Invitational Lecture Series, University of Chicago School of Social Service Administration.

Pieper, M. Heineman, & Pieper, W. J. (1993). Response to "Psychoanalytic fallacies: Reflections on Martha Heineman Pieper and William Joseph Pieper's Intrapsychic Humanism." *Social Service Review, 67,* 651–654.

Piersma, H. L. (1985). "Mom and Dad": Views on the relationship between direct-care staff and therapists in residential, adolescent treatment facilities. *Adolescence, 20,* 975–979.

Pinkston, E. M., & Herbert-Jackson, E. (1975). Modification of irrelevant and bizarre verbal behavior using parents as therapists. *Social Service Review, 49,* 46–63.

Pinkston, E. M., Levitt, J. L., Green, G. R., Linsk, N. L., & Rzepnicki, T. L. (1982). *Effective social work practice: Advanced techniques for behavioral intervention with individuals, families, and institutional staff.* San Francisco: Jossey-Bass.

Pinsof, W. (1989). A conceptual framework and methodological criteria for family therapy process research. *Journal of Consulting and Clinical Psychology, 57,* 53–59.

Place, M., Framrose, R., & Willson, C. (1985a). The difficult adolescents who are referred to a psychiatric unit: I. Classification. *Journal of Adolescence, 8,* 297–306.

Place, M., Framrose, R., & Willson, C. (1985b). The difficult adolescents who are referred to a psychiatric unit: II. Clinical features and response to treatment. *Journal of Adolescence, 8,* 307–320.

Platt, A. (1977). *The child savers: The invention of delinquency* (2nd ed.). Chicago: University of Chicago Press.

Polansky, N. (1952). Why research in the social work curriculum? *Smith College Studies in Social Work, 22,* 147–154.

Polansky, N. (1971). Research in social work. In *Encyclopedia of Social Work* (16th ed., Vol. 2). New York: National Association of Social Workers.

Polansky, N. (1975). *Social work research.* Chicago: University of Chicago Press. (Original work published 1960)

Polanyi, M. (1964). *Personal knowledge: Towards a post-critical philosophy.* New York: Harper & Row, Harper Torchbooks/Academy Library.

Polanyi, M. (1967). *The tacit dimension.* London: Routledge & Kegan Paul.

Polkinghorne, D. E. (1983). *Methodology for the human sciences.* Albany: State University of New York Press.

Polkinghorne, D. E. (1988). *Narrative knowing and the human sciences.* Albany: State University of New York Press.

Pollak, O. (1956). *Integrating sociological and psychoanalytic concepts: An exploration in child psychotherapy.* New York: Russell Sage.

Pollak, O. (1963). Worker assignment in casework with marriage partners. *Social Service Review, 37,* 41–53.

Pollock, L. (1983). *Forgotten children: Parent–child relations from 1500 to 1900.* New York: Cambridge University Press.

Popkewitz, T. (1984). *Paradigm and ideology in educational research: The social functions of the intellectual.* New York: Falmer Press.

Popper, K. R. (1959). *The logic of scientific discovery* (original title, Logik der Forschung, trans. author). New York: Basic Books (Original work published 1934)

Popper, K. R. (1964). *The poverty of historicism.* New York: Harper & Row, Harper Torchbooks.

Popper, K. R. (1965). *Conjectures and refutations: The growth of scientific knowledge* (2nd ed.). New York: Basic Books.

Popper, K. R. (1991). The demarcation between science and metaphysics. In P. Schilpp (Ed.), *The philosophy of Rudolf Carnap. Library of living philosophers. Vol. 11.* LaSalle, IL: Open Court Press.

Posner, W. B. (1986). *Charlotte Towle: A biography.* Unpublished doctoral dissertation, School of Social Service Administration, University of Chicago.

Powdermaker, F., Levis, H. T., & Touraine, G. (1937). Psychopathology and treatment of delinquent girls. *American Journal of Orthopsychiatry, 7,* 58–71.

Powell, D. R. (1988). Toward an understanding of the program variable in comprehensive parent support programs. In H. B. Weiss & F. H. Jacobs (Eds.), *Evaluating family programs* (pp. 267–285). New York: Aldine De Gruyter.

Pullum, G. (1989). Topic comment: The great Eskimo vocabulary hoax. *Natural Language and Linguistic Theory, 7,* 275–281.

Pumphrey, M. (1957). The first step—Mary Richmond's earliest professional reading, 1889–1891. *Social Service Review, 31,* 144–163.

Pumphrey, M. (1961). Mary E. Richmond—the practitioner. *Social Casework, 42,* 375–385.

Purpura, D., & Reaser, G. (1974). *Methodological approaches to the study of brain maturation and its abnormalities: Summary report.* Baltimore: University Park Press.

Pylyshyn, Z. W. (1973). What the mind's eye tells the mind's brain: A critique of mental imagery. *Psychological Bulletin, 80,* 1–24.

Quine, W. V. O. (1948). Two dogmas of empiricism. *Philosophical Review, 60,* 20–43.

Raber, M. F. (1984). Management of consultation and education programs in the community mental health center. *Adminstration in Mental Health, 12,* 89–109.

Rabin, C. (1981). The single-case design in family therapy evaluation research. *Family Process, 20,* 351–366.

Rank, O. (1936). *Will therapy: An analysis of the therapeutic process in terms of relationships* (J. Taft, Trans.). New York: W. W. Norton.

Rank, O. (1978). *Truth and reality* (J. Taft, Trans. Introduction by J. Taft). New York: W. W. Norton. (Original work published 1936)

Rao, D., Morton, N., & Yee, S. (1974). Analysis of family resemblance: II. A linear model for familial correlation. *American Journal of Human Genetics, 26,* 331–359.

Rapoport, L. (1970). Crisis intervention as a mode of brief treatment. In R. Roberts & R. Nee (Eds.), *Theories of social casework.* Chicago: University of Chicago Press.

Ratner, C. (1971). Totalitarianism and individualism in psychology. *Telos, 3,* 2–72.

Rauch, J. (1975). Women in social work: Friendly visitors in Philadelphia, 1880. *Social Service Review, 49,* 241–259.

Raup, D. M. (1986). *The Nemesis affair: A story of the death of dinosaurs and the ways of science.* New York: W. W. Norton.

Reamer, F. (1993). *The philosophical foundations of social work.* New York: Columbia University Press.

Reason, P. (1981). Issues of validity in new paradigm research. In P. Reason & J. Rowan (Eds.), *Human inquiry: A sourcebook for new paradigm research.* New York: Wiley.

Reason, P., & Rowan, J. (1981). *Human inquiry: A sourcebook for new paradigm research.* New York: Wiley.

Redl, F., & Wineman, D. (1957). *The aggressive child.* New York: Free Press.

Reed, E. (1931). A scoring system for the evaluation of social case work. *Social Service Review, 5,* 214–236.

Reed, J. (1979). Doctors, birth control, and social values: 1830–1970. In M. Vogel & C. Rosenberg (Eds.), *The therapeutic revolution: Essays in the social history of American medicine.* Philadelphia: University of Pennsylvania Press.

Reichenbach, H. (1938). *Experience and prediction: An analysis of the foundations and the structure of knowledge.* Chicago: University of Chicago Press.

Reid, W. J. (1966). Use of laboratory devices to investigate caseworkers' activities. In National Association of Social Workers (Eds.), *Trends in social work practice and knowledge: N.A.S.W Tenth Anniversary Symposium* (pp. 238–245). New York: National Association of Social Workers.

Reid, W. J. (1977a). A journal for research: An editorial. *Social Work Research and Abstracts, 13,* 2–3.

Reid, W. J. (1977b). Social work for social problems. *Social Work, 22,* 374–381.

Reid, W. J. (1978). The social agency as a research machine. *Journal of Social Service Research, 2,* 11–23.

Reid, W. J. (1983). Developing intervention methods through experimental designs. In A. Rosenblatt & D. Waldfogel (Eds.), *Handbook of clinical social work.* San Francisco: Jossey-Bass.

Reid, W. J. (1990). Change process research: A new paradigm? In L. Videka-Sherman & W. J. Reid (Eds.), *Advances in clinical social work research.* Silver Spring, MD: National Association of Social Workers Press.

Reid, W. J. (1994). Reframing the epistemological debate. In E. Sherman & W. J. Reid (Eds.), *Qualitative research in social work.* New York: Columbia University Press.

Reid, W. J., & Epstein, L. (1972). *Task-centered casework.* New York: Columbia University Press.

Reid, W. J., & Smith, A. (1989). *Research in social work (2nd ed.).* New York: Columbia University Press.

Rein, M., & White, S. (1977). Policy research: Belief and doubt. *Policy Analysis, 3,* 239–271.

Rein, M., & White, S. (1981). Knowledge for practice. *Social Service Review, 55,* 1–41.

Reinharz, S. (1984). *On becoming a social scientist.* New Brunswick, NJ: Transaction.

Reinharz, S. (1992). *Feminist methods in social research.* New York: Oxford University Press.

Reinherz, H., Regan, J., & Anastas, J. (1983). A research curriculum for future clinicians: A multimodel strategy. *Journal of Education for Social Work, 19,* 35–41.

Reis, K., & Resnik, D. (1984). Adolescent suicidal behavior: A residential treatment center view. *Residential Group Care and Treatment, 2,* 21–34.

Reisch, M. (1986). From cause to case and back again: The reemergence of advocacy in social work. *Urban and Social Change Review, 19,* 20–24.

Rendel, J. (1959). Canalization of the scute phenotype of Drosophila. *Evolution, 13,* 425–439.

Rescher, N., & Oppenheim, P. (1955). Logical analysis of gestalt concepts. *British Journal for the Philosophy of Science, 6,* 89–106.

Research Section, N.A.S.W. (1955, October 24–25). *Minutes. N.A.S.W. Collection.* Folder 1357. Social Welfare History Archives, University of Minnesota at Minneapolis.

Reynolds, B. C. (1932). An experiment in short-contact interviewing. *Smith College Studies in Social Work, 3,* 3–107.

Reynolds, B.C. (1965). *Learning and teaching in the practice of social work.* New York: Russell & Russell.

Rhoads, S. E. (1985). *The economist's view of the world: Government, markets, & public policy.* Cambridge, England: Cambridge University Press.

Rice, L. N., & Greenberg, L. S. (Eds.). (1984). *Patterns of change: Intensive analysis of psychotherapy process.* New York: Guilford Press.

Richan, W., & Mendelsohn, A. (1973). *Social work: The unloved profession.* New York: New Viewpoints.

Richards, R.J. (1981). Natural selection and other models in the historiography of science. In M. Brewer & B. Collins (Eds.), *Scientific inquiry and the social sciences.* San Francisco: Jossey-Bass.

Richards, R. J. (1983). Why Darwin delayed, or interesting problems and models in the history of science. *Journal of the History of the Behavioral Sciences, 19,* 45–53.

Richards, R. J. (1987). *Darwin and the emergence of evolutionary theories of mind and behavior.* Chicago: University of Chicago Press.

Richardson, L. (1988). The collective story: Postmodernism and the writing of sociology. *Sociological Focus, 21,* 199–208.

Richardson, R. (1984). Biology and ideology: The interpenetration of science and values. *Philosophy of Science, 51,* 396–420.

Richmond, M. (1897a). Comments, discussion on social settlements. In *Proceedings of the National Conference of Charities and Corrections, 24th Annual Meeting, Toronto* (pp. 473–474). Madison, WI: Midland Publishing.

Richmond, M. (1897b). The need of a training school in applied philanthropy. In *Proceedings of the National Conference on Charities and Corrections, 24th Annual Meeting, Toronto* (pp. 181-188). Madison, WI: Midland Publishing.

Richmond, M. (1912). *Friendly visiting among the poor: A handbook for charity workers.* New York: Macmillan. (Original work published 1899)

Richmond, M. (1917). *Social diagnosis.* New York: Russell Sage.

Richmond, M. (1922). *What is social casework? An introductory description.* New York: Russell Sage.

Richmond, M. (1930). *The long view: Papers and addresses by Mary E. Richmond.* New York: Russell Sage.

Richter, F. (1986). Non-linear behavior. In D. W. Fiske & R. A. Shweder (Eds.), *Metatheory in social science: Pluralisms and subjectivities.* Chicago: University of Chicago Press.

Riger, S. (1992). Epistemological debates, feminist voices: Science, social values, and the study of women. *American Psychologist, 47,* 730–740.

Rinsley, D. B. (1990). The severely disturbed adolescent: Indications for hospital and residential treatment. *Bulletin of the Menninger Clinic, 54,* 3–12.

Robinson, E. A. R., Bronson, D. E., & Blythe, B. J. (1988). An analysis of the implementation of single-case evaluation by practitioners. *Social Service Review, 62,* 285–301.

Robinson, V. (1934). *A changing psychology in social case work.* Chapel Hill: University of North Carolina Press. (Original work published 1930)

Robinson, V. (1960). The University of Pennsylvania School of Social Work in Perspective: 1909–1959. *Journal of Social Work Process, 11,* 11.

Robinson, V. (1962). *Jessie Taft: Therapist and social work educator, a professional biography.* Philadelphia: University of Pennsylvania Press.

Rodriguez, G. G., & Cortez, C., P. (1988). The evaluation experience of the Avance Parent–Child Education Program. In H. B. Weiss & F. H. Jacobs (Eds.), *Evaluating family programs* (pp. 287-301). New York: Aldine De Gruyter.

Rodwell, M. K. (1987). Naturalistic inquiry: An alternative model for social work assessment. *Social Service Review, 61,* 231–246.

Roland, A. (1985). Science and war. In S. G. Kohlstedt & M. W. Rossiter (Eds.), *Historical writing on American science: Perspectives and prospects.* Baltimore, MD: Johns Hopkins University Press.

Romano, J. (1975). *American psychiatry: Past, present, and future.* Keynote address presented on the occasion of the 200th anniversary of the establishment of the first state-supported mental hospital in America. Charlottesville, VA: University Press of Virginia.

Romanyshyn, R. D. (1971). Method and meaning in psychology. *Journal of Phenomenological Psychology, 2,* 93–114.

Rorty, Richard. (1979). *Philosophy and the mirror of nature.* Princeton: Princeton University Press.

Rosenberg, C. (1976). *No other gods: On science and American social thought.* Baltimore: Johns Hopkins University Press. (Original work published 1961)

Rosenberg, M. J. (1969). The conditions and consequences of evaluation apprehension. In R. Rosenthal & R. L. Rosnow (Eds.), *Artifact in behavioral research.* New York: Academic Press.

Rosenberg, R. (1982). *Beyond separate spheres: Intellectual roots of modern feminism.* New Haven: Yale University Press.

Rosenblatt, A., Turner, E., Patterson, A., & Rollosson, C. (1970). Predominance of male authors in social work publications. *Social Casework, 51,* 421–430.

Rosenblatt, P. (1981). Ethnographic case studies. In M. Brewer, & B. Collins (Eds.), *Scientific inquiry and the social sciences.* San Francisco: Jossey-Bass.

Rosenthal, R. (1969). Interpersonal expectations: Effects of the experimenter's hypothesis. In R. Rosenthal & R. L. Rosnow (Eds.), *Artifact in behavioral research.* New York: Academic Press.

Rosenthal, R. (1980). *Experimenter effects in behavioral research.* New York: Oxford University Press.

Rosenthal, R. (1982). Valid interpretation of quantitative research results. In D. Brinberg & L. Kidder (Eds.), *Forms of validity in research. New directions for methodology of social and behavioral science: No. 12.* San Francisco: Jossey-Bass.

Rosenthal, R. (1990a). How are we doing in soft psychology? *American Psychologist, 45,* 775–777.

Rosenthal, R. (1990b). Some differing viewpoints on doing psychological science. *Zeitschrift fur Padogogische Psychologie, 4,* 161–165.

Rosenthal, R., & Rosnow, R. (1969). *Artifact in behavioral research.* New York: Academic Press.

Rosnow, R., & Davis, D. (1977). Demand characteristics and the psychological experiment. *Etc, 34,* 301–313.

Ross, H., & Johnson, A. (1946). The growing science of casework. *Journal of Social Casework, 27,* 273–278.

Rossi, P. H. (1989). The family, welfare, and homelessness. *Notre Dame Journal of Law, Ethics, and Public Policy, 4,* 281–300.

Rossi, P., & Freeman, H. (1985). *Evaluation: A systematic approach.* Beverly Hills, CA: Sage.

Rossi, P., & Wright, J. (1984). Evaluation research: An assessment. *Annual Review of Sociology, 10,* 331–352.

Rossiter, M. (1982). *Women scientists in America: Struggles and strategies to 1940.* Baltimore: Johns Hopkins University Press.

Rothman, D. (1971). *The discovery of the asylum: Social order and disorder in the New Republic.* Boston: Little, Brown.

Rothman, S. (1978). *Woman's proper place: A history of changing ideals and practices, 1870 to the present.* New York: Basic Books.

Royse, D. (1991). *Research methods in social work.* Chicago: Nelson-Hall.

Rozeboom, W. (1960). The fallacy of the null-hypothesis significance test. *Psychological Bulletin, 57,* 416–428.

Rubenstein, R. (1984). Epidemiology and anthropology: Notes on science and scientism. *Communication and Cognition, 17,* 163–185.

Rubin, A., & Babbie, E. (1989). *Research methods in social work.* Belmont, CA: Wadsworth.

Rubin, A., Franklin, C., & Selber, K. (1992). Integrating research and practice into an interviewing skills project: An evaluation. *Journal of Social Work Education, 28,* 141–152.

Rubin, A., & Zimbalist, S. (1981). Issues in the MSW research curriculum, 1968–1979. In S. Briar, H. Weissman, & A. Rubin (Eds.), *Research utilization in social work education.* New York: Council on Social Work Education.

Ruckdeschel, R. (1985). Qualitative research as a perspective. *Social Work Research and Abstracts, 21,* 17–22.

Ruckdeschel, R. (1994). The qualitative case study and evaluation: Issues and methods. In E. Sherman & W. J. Reid (Eds.), *Qualitative research in social work.* New York: Columbia University Press.

Ruckdeschel, R., & Farris, B. (1981). Assessing practice: A critical look at the single-case design. *Social Casework, 62,* 413–419.

Ruckdeschel, R., & Farris, B. (1982). Science: Critical faith or dogmatic ritual? *Social Casework, 63,* 272–275.

Ruel, M. (1972). *Women's caucus resolution for CSWE Annual Program Meeting, 1972 (unpublished memorandum).* Women's Commission of the Council on Social Work Education.

Rychlak, J. (1980). The false promise of falsification. *Journal of Mind and Behavior, 1,* 183–195.

Rzepnicki, T. (1991). Enhancing the durability of intervention gains: A challenge for the 1990s. *Social Service Review, 65,* 92–111.

Salasin, S. (1978). Linking knowledge to social policymaking. An interview with Amitai Etzioni. *Evaluation and Change, special issue,* 54–62.

Saleebey, D. (1979). The tension between research and practice: Assumptions of the experimental paradigm. *Clinical Social Work Journal, 7,* 267–284.

Saleebey, D. (1989). The estrangement of knowing and doing: Professions in crisis. *Social Casework, 70,* 556–563.

Saleebey, D. (1990). Philosophical disputes in social work: Social justice denied. *Journal of Sociology and Social Welfare, 17,* 29–40.

Salmon, W. (Ed.). (1971a). *Statistical explanation and statistical relevance.* Pittsburgh: University of Pittsburgh Press.

Salmon, W. (1971b). Statistical explanation. In W. Salmon (Ed.), *Statistical explanation and statistical relevance.* Pittsburgh: University of Pittsburgh Press.

Salmon, W. (1989). *Four decades of scientific explanation.* Minneapolis: University of Minnesota Press.

Salomon, E. (1967). Humanistic values and social casework. *Social Casework, 48,* 26–32.

Sancier, B. (1991). Notes for the next generation. *Affilia: Journal of Women and Social Work, 6,* 5–7.

Sancier, B. (1992a, March). *Retrospective on women's "place" in social work education: Roots, responses, and renewal.* Invitational presentation at the Council on Social Work Education Annual Program Meeting.

Sancier, B. (1992b). Whose backlash is it, anyway? *Affilia: Journal of Women and Social Work, 7,* 5–7.

Sanders, M. (1957, March). Social work: A profession chasing its tail. *Harpers,* 56–62.

Sattler, R. (1967). Petal inception and the problem of pattern detection. *Journal of Theoretical Biology, 17,* 31–39.

Sauer, M. V., Paulson, R. J., & Lobo, R. A. (1992). Reversing the natural decline in human fertility: An extended clinical trial of oocyte donation to women of advanced reproductive age. *Journal of the American Medical Association, 268,* 1275–1279.

Sayer, A. (1992). *Method in social science: A realist approach* (2nd ed). London: Routledge.

Scavo, R., & Buchanan, B. (1989). Group therapy for male adolescent sex offenders: A model for residential treatment. *Residential Treatment for Children and Youth, 7,* 59–74.

Scheffler, I. (1967). *Science and subjectivity.* New York: Bobbs-Merrill.

Schein, E. (1987). *The clinical perspective in fieldwork* (Sage Qualitative Methods Series 5). Newbury Park, CA: Sage.

Schlesinger, A. J. (1956). *The age of Roosevelt: The crisis of the old order, 1919–1933*. Boston: Houghton Mifflin.

Schlick, M. (1979). Meaning and verification. In H. L. Mulder & B. van de Velde-Schlick (Eds.), *Philosophical papers* (Vol. 2, 1925–1936, pp. 309–312, 361–369). Boston: D. Reidel. (Original work published 1938)

Schlick, M. (1981). Positivism and realism. In O. Hanfling (Ed.), *Essential readings in logical positivism* (pp. 83–110). Oxford: Basil Blackwell. (Original work published 1925–1936)

Schneir, M. (Ed.). (1972). Declaration of sentiments and resolutions, Seneca Falls. In *Feminism: The essential historical writings*. New York: Random House.

School of Social Service Administration, University of Chicago (1925–1932). *Collected papers*. Regenstein Library, University of Chicago, Department of Special Collections.

Schriver, J. (1987). Harry Lurie's assessment and prescription: An early view of social workers' roles and responsibilities regarding political action. *Journal of Sociology and Social Welfare, 14*, 111–127.

Schuerman, J. (1982). The obsolete scientific imperative in social work research. *Social Service Review, 56*, 144–146.

Schultz, D. P. (1969). The nature of the human data source in psychology. In D. Schultz (Ed.), *The science of psychology: Critical reflections*. New York: Appleton-Century-Crofts. (as cited in Gadlin & Ingle, 1975)

Schultz, D.P. (1971). Psychology: A world with man left out. *Journal of the Theory of Social Behaviour, 1*, 99–107.

Schwartz, A. (1967). The southern New Jersey chapter of N.A.S.W.: A study in the sociology of the profession. *Social Service Review, 41*, 401–410.

Schwartz, A. (1983). Behavioral principles and approaches. In D. Waldfogel & A. Rosenblatt (Eds.), *Handbook of clinical social work* (pp. 202–208). San Francisco: Jossey-Bass.

Schwartz, M. C. (1973). Sexism in the social work curriculum. *Journal of Social Work Education, 9*, 65–70.

Scocozza, L. (1989). Ethics and medical science. On voluntary participation in biomedical experimentation. *Acta Sociologica, 32*(3), 283–293.

Scotch, C. B. (1971). Sex status in social work: Grist for women's liberation. *Social Work, 16*, 5–11.

Scott, D. (1989). Meaning construction and social work practice. *Social Service Review, 63*, 39–51.

Scott, J. (1989). History in crisis? The others' side of the story. *American Historical Review, 94*, 680–692.

Scriven, M. (1956). A possible distinction between traditional scientific disciplines and the study of human behavior. In *Minnesota studies in the philosophy of science* (Vol. 1). Minneapolis: University of Minnesota Press.

Scriven, M. (1959). Truisms as the grounds for historical explanation. In P. Gardiner (Ed.), *Theories of history: Readings from classical and contemporary sources* (pp. 443–471). New York: Free Press.

Scriven, M. (1962). Explanations, predictions and laws. In *Minnesota studies in the philosophy of science* (Vol. 3). Minneapolis: University of Minnesota Press.

Scriven, M. (1964). Views of human nature. In T. W. Wann (Ed.), *Behaviorism and phenomenology: Contrasting bases for modern psychology*. Chicago: University of Chicago Press.

Scriven, M. (1969). Logical positivism and the behavioral sciences. In P. Achinstein & S. Barker (Eds.), *The legacy of logical positivism: Studies in the philosophy of science* (pp. 195–209). Baltimore: Johns Hopkins University Press.

Scriven, M. (1976). Evaluation bias and its control. In G. V. Glass (Ed.), *Evaluation studies review annual* (Vol. 1, pp. 119–139). Beverly Hills, CA: Sage.

Scriven, M. (1983). Evaluation ideologies. In G. Madaus, M. Scriven, & D. Stufflebeam (Eds.), *Evaluation models: Viewpoints on educational and human services evaluation*. Boston: Kluwer-Nijhoff.

Secord, P. F. (1982). Integrating the personal and the social. In P. F. Secord (Ed.), *Explaining human behavior: Consciousness, human action and social structure*. Beverly Hills, CA: Sage.

Segall, M., Campbell, D., & Herskovits, M. (1966). *The influence of culture on visual perception*. New York: Bobbs-Merrill.

Seitz, V., Rosenbaum, L., & Apfel, N. (1985). Effects of family support intervention: A ten-year follow-up. *Child Development, 56*, 376–391.

Sellars, W. (1961). The language of theories. In H. Feigl & G. Maxwell (Eds.), *Current issues in the philosophy of science. Symposia of scientists and philosophers. Proceedings of Section L of the American Association for the Advancement of Science, 1959.* New York: Holt, Rinehart & Winston.

Shakespeare, W. (1972). *The complete Signet classic Shakespeare.* (S. Barnet, Ed.). New York: Harcourt, Brace Jovanovich.

Shapere, D. (1964). The structure of scientific revolutions (review). *Philosophical Review, 73,* 383–394.

Shapere, D. (1982). The concept of observation in science and philosophy. *Philosophy of Science, 49,* 293–299.

Shapere, D. (1989). Evolution and continuity in scientific change. *Philosophy of Science, 56,* 419–437.

Shapin, S. (1982). History of science and its sociological reconstructions. *History of Science, 20,* 157–211.

Shapiro, E. (1978). Robert A. Woods and the settlement house impulse. *Social Service Review, 52,* 215–226.

Shapiro, I. (1982). Realism in the study of the history of ideas. *History of Political Thought, 3,* 535–578.

Sheinfeld, S. N. (1978). The evaluation profession in pursuit of value. *Evaluation and Program Planning, 1,* 113–115.

Sheinfeld, S. N., & Lord, G. L. (1981). The ethics of evaluation researchers: An exploration of value choices. *Evaluation Review, 5,* 377–391.

Sherman, E. (1987). Hermeneutics, human science, and social work. *Social Thought, 13,* 34–41.

Sherman, E. (1991). Interpretive methods for social work practice and research. *Journal of Sociology and Social Welfare, 18,* 69–81.

Shweder, R. A. (1977). Likeness and likelihood in everyday thought: Magical thinking in judgments about personality. *Current Anthropology, 18,* 637–648.

Shweder, R. A. (1979a). Rethinking culture and personality theory: Part 1. *Ethos, 7,* 255–278.

Shweder, R. A. (1979b). Rethinking culture and personality theory: Part 2. *Ethos, 7,* 279–311.

Shweder, R. A. (1980a). Rethinking culture and personality theory: Part 3. *Ethos, 8,* 60–94.

Shweder, R. A. (Ed.). (1980b). *Fallible judgment in behavioral research. New Directions for Methodology of Social and Behavioral Science, No. 4.* San Francisco: Jossey-Buss.

Shweder, R. A., & Miller, J. G. (1985). The social construction of the person: How is it possible? In K. Gergen & K. Davis (Eds.), *The social construction of the person.* New York: Springer-Verlag.

Shyne, A. (1959). A prologue: Purpose and plan of the conference. In A. Shyne (Ed.), *Use of judgments as data in social work research: Proceedings.* New York: National Association of Social Workers.

Shyne, A. (1967). Casework research: Past and present. *Social Casework, 43,* 467–473.

Sieber, J. E., & Sanders, N. (1978). Ethical problems in program evaluation: Roles not models. *Evaluation and Program Planning, 1,* 117–120.

Siegel, D. (1985). Effective teaching of empirically based practice. *Social Work Research and Abstracts, 21,* 40–48.

Simkhovitch, M. (1938). *Neighborhood: My story of Greenwich House.* New York: W. W. Norton.

Simon, H. A. (1955). A behavioral model of rational choice. *Quarterly Journal of Economics, 69,* 99–118.

Simon, H. A. (1957a). *Administrative behavior.* New York: Macmillan.

Simon, H. A. (1957b). *Models of man: Social and rational. Mathematical essays on rational human behavior in a social setting.* New York: Wiley.

Simon, H. A. (1966a). Scientific discovery and the psychology of problem solving. In R. Colodny (Ed.), *Mind and cosmos: Essays in contemporary science and philosophy.* Pittsburgh: University of Pittsburgh Press.

Simon, H. A. (1966b). Thinking by computers. In R. Colodny (Ed.), *Mind and cosmos: Essays in contemporary science and philosophy.* Pittsburgh: University of Pittsburgh Press.

Simon, H. A. (1977). *Models of discovery and other topics in the methods of science.* Boston: Dordrecht-Reidel.

Simon, H. A. (1981). *The sciences of the artificial* (2nd ed.). Cambridge, MA: M.I.T. Press.

Simons, R. (1987). The impact of training for empirically based practice. *Journal of Social Work Education, 23,* 24–30.

Siporin, M. (1985). Current social work perspectives on clinical practice. *Clinical Social Work Journal, 13,* 198–217.

Siporin, M. (1989). Metamodels, models, and basics: An essay review. *Social Service Review, 63,* 474–480.

Skinner, B. F. (1953). *Science and human behavior.* New York: Macmillan.

Skinner, B. F. (1957). *Verbal behavior.* New York: Appleton-Century-Crofts.

Skinner, B. F. (1969). *Contingencies of reinforcement: A theoretical analysis.* New York: Appleton-Century-Crofts.

Sklar, K. K. (1985). Hull House in the 1890s: A community of women reformers. *Signs, 10,* 658–677.

Skrtic, T. (1985). Doing naturalistic research into educational organizations. In Y. Lincoln (Ed.), *Organizational theory and inquiry: The paradigm revolution.* Beverly Hills, CA: Sage.

Slonim-Nevo, V., & Vosler, N. (1991). The use of single-system design with systemic brief problem-solving therapy. *Families in Society: The Journal of Contemporary Human Services, 72,* 38–44.

Smale, G., Tuson, G., Cooper, M., Wardle, M., & Crosbie, D. (1988). *Community social work: A paradigm for change* (Practice and Development Exchange, National Institute for Social Work). Todmorden, England: Waddington & Sons.

Smith, D. (1974). Women's perspective as a radical critique of sociology. *Sociological Inquiry, 44,* 7–13.

Smith, K. (1983). Tests of significance: Some frequent misunderstandings. *American Journal of Orthopsychiatry, 53,* 315–321.

Smith, V. (1891). Women in charity and reform. In *Proceedings of the National Conference on Charities and Corrections, Indianapolis, Indiana.* (pp. 231–241). Madison, WI: Midland Publishing.

Sneath, P. H. A. (1961). Recent developments in theoretical and quantitative taxonomy. *Systematic Zoology, 10,* 118–139.

Social Work Research Group. (Nov. 1949–May, 1955). *Newsletter.* Nos. 1–20. *NASW Supplement 2,* Box 3 (12J-1a), Folder 3. Social Welfare History Archives, University of Minnesota at Minneapolis.

Social Work Research Group. (1951a, May 17). Minutes of the Annual Meeting. In *NASW Supplement 2,* Box 3 (12J-1a), Folder 7. Social Welfare History Archives, University of Minnesota at Minneapolis.

Social Work Research Group. (1951b, September 13–14). Minutes of the Steering Committee. In *NASW Supplement 2,* Box 3 (12J-1a), Folder 1. Social Welfare History Archives, University of Minnesota at Minneapolis.

Social Work Research Group. (1951c, March 19). Transmittal letter. In *Appendix to Research Projects, 1950. NASW Supplement 2,* Box 3 (12J-1a), Folder 1. Social Welfare History Archives, University of Minnesota at Minneapolis.

Social Work Research Group. (1955). *The function and practice of research in social work* (unpublished reports, 1951, 1952, 1953, by the Social Work Research Group, with introduction by Margaret Blenkner, Chairman in 1955). Research Section, National Association of Social Workers.

Sohmer, H., & Student, M. (1977). Auditory nerve and brain stem evoked responses in normal, autistic, minimal brain dysfunction and psychomotor retarded children. *Electroencephalography and Clinical Neurophysiology, 44,* 380–388.

Sokal, R. R. (1964). Numerical taxonomy and disease classification. In J. A. Jacques (Ed.), *The diagnostic process* (pp. 51–79). Ann Arbor: University of Michigan Press.

Sokal, R. R., & Camin J. H. (1965). The two taxonomies: Areas of agreement and conflict. *Systematic Zoology, 14,* 175–195.

Sokal, R. R., & Sneath, P. H. A. (1963). *Principles of numerical taxonomy.* San Francisco: W. H. Freeman.

Solomon, R. C. (1974). Freud and unconscious motivation. *Journal for the Theory of Social Behavior, 4,* 191–216.

Solomon, R. C. (1988). Supplement: The end of the self: Structuralism, post-modernism, Foucault, and Derrida. In K. Thomas, A. Ryan, & W. Bodmer (Eds.), *A history of Western philosophy 7: Continental philosophy since 1750: The rise and fall of the self* (pp. 194–203). Oxford: Oxford University Press.

Sosin, M. R., Colson, P., & Grossman, S. (1988). *Homelessness in Chicago: Poverty and pathology, social institutions and social change.* Chicago: The University of Chicago.

Soth, N. (1986). Reparenting and deparenting as a paradigm for psychiatric residential treatment. *Child Care Quarterly, 15,* 110–120.

Southard, E. E., & Jarrett, M. C. (1922). *The kingdom of evils: Psychiatric social work presented in one hundred case histories together with a classification of social divisions of evil.* New York: Macmillan.

Sperry, R. (1983). *Science and moral priority: Merging mind, brain, and human values.* New York: Columbia University Press.

Spradley, J. P. (1979). *The ethnographic interview.* New York: Holt, Rinehart and Winston.

Sroufe, L. A., Jacobvitz, D., Mangelsdorf, E. D., & Ward, M. J. (1985). Generational boundary dissolution between mothers and their preschool children: A relationship systems approach. *Child Development, 56,* 317–325.

Stadler, L. J. (1954). The gene. *Science, 120,* 811–819.

Stanley, L., & Wise, S. (1983). *Breaking out: Feminist consciousness and feminist research.* Boston: Routledge & Kegan Paul.

Star, S. L. (1979). Sex differences and the dichotomization of the brain: Methods, limits and problems in research on consciousness. In R. Hubbard, & M. Lowe (Eds.), *Genes and gender: II. Pitfalls in research on sex and gender.* Staten Island, NY: Gordian Press.

Star, S. L. (1983a). *Scientific theories as going concerns: The development of the localizationist perspective in neurophysiology, 1870–1906.* Unpublished doctoral dissertation, University of California, Berkeley.

Star, S. L. (1983b). Simplification in scientific work: An example from neuroscience research. *Social Studies of Science, 13,* 205–228.

Star, S. L., & Gerson, E. (1983a). *Management of anomalies in scientific research: Part 1. Varieties of anomaly.* Unpublished manuscript.

Star, S. L., & Gerson, E. (1983b). *Management of anomalies in scientific research: Part 2. Properties of artifacts.* Unpublished manuscript.

Starr, P. (1982). *The social transformation of American medicine.* New York: Basic Books.

Stein, H., & Cloward, R. (Eds.). (1958). *Social perspectives on behavior: A reader in social science for social work and related professions.* Glencoe, IL: Free Press.

Steinberg, M. L. (1988). *Career stages and the professional attitudes and behaviors of social workers: A study of the graduates of the School of Social Service Administration of the University of Chicago, 1908–1983.* Unpublished doctoral dissertation, School of Social Service Administration, University of Chicago.

Stellar, E., & Sprague, J. M. (Eds.). (1966). *Progress in physiological psychology* (Vol. 1). New York: Academic Press.

Stetson, E. (1983). Black feminism in Indiana, 1893–1933. *Phylon, 44,* 292–298.

Stevens, W. (1971). *The collected poems of Wallace Stevens.* New York: Alfred A. Knopf.

Stewart, I. (1989). *Does God play dice? The mathematics of chaos.* New York: Basil Blackwell.

Still, G. (1902). The Coulstonian lectures on some abnormal psychical conditions in children. *Lancet, 1,* 1008–1012, 1077–1082, 1163–1168.

Strauss, A., & Corbin, J. (1990). *Basics of qualitative research: Grounded theory procedures and techniques.* Newbury Park, CA: Sage.

Straussner, S., & Phillips, N. (1988). The relationship between social work and labor unions: A history of strife and cooperation. *Journal of Sociology and Social Welfare, 15,* 105–118.

Stricker, F. (1976). Cookbooks and law books: The hidden history of career women in twentieth century America. *Journal of Social History, 10,* 1–19.

Strom, S. H. (1983). Challenging "woman's place": Feminism, the left, and industrial unionism in the 1930s. *Feminist Studies, 9,* 359–386.

Suchman, E. A. (1967). *Evaluative research: Priniciples and practice in public service and social action programs.* New York: Russell Sage.

Sullivan, W. P. (1992). Reclaiming the community: The strengths perspective and deinstitutionalization. *Social Work, 37*(3), 204–209.

Suppe, F. (Ed.). (1974). *The structure of scientific theories.* Urbana: University of Illinois Press.

Suppe, F. (1977). Introduction: The search for philosophic understanding of scientific theories. In F. Suppe (Ed.), *The structure of scientific theories* (pp. 3–232). Urbana: University of Illinois Press.

Susser, E., Goldfinger, S. M., & White, A. (1990). Some clinical approaches to the homeless mentally ill. *Community Mental Health Journal, 26,* 463–480.

Susser, E., Struening, E. L., & Conover, S. (1987). Childhood experiences of homeless men. *American Journal of Psychiatry, 144,* 1599–1601.

Sutter, S. C. (1980). *Guide to the Charlotte Towle papers (1915–1968).* Department of Special Collections, Regenstein Library, University of Chicago.

Suzuki, P. T. (1986). The University of California Japanese evacuation and resettlement study: A prolegomenon. *Dialectical Anthropology, 10,* 189–213.

Sze, W. C., & Hopps, J. G. (1974). *Evaluation and accountability in human service programs.* Cambridge, MA: Schenkman.

Taber, M., & Shapiro, I. (1965). Social work and its knowledge base: A content analysis of the periodical literature. *Social Work, 10,* 100–107.

Taft, J. (1915). *The woman movement from the point of view of social consciousness.* Unpublished doctoral dissertation, Graduate School of Arts and Literature, University of Chicago.

Taft, J. (1918). The limitations of the psychiatrist. *Medicine and Surgery, 2*, 365–369.

Taft, J. (1937). The relation of function to process in social case work. *Journal of Social Work Process, 1*, 1–18.

Taft, J. (1962). *The dynamics of therapy in a controlled relationship.* (With an introduction by V. Robinson. New York: Dover. (Original work published 1933)

Talbot, M., & Rosenberry, L. K. M. (1931). *The history of the American Association of University Women, 1881–1931.* Cambridge, MA: Houghton Mifflin.

Tart, C. (1973). Status of consciousness and state-specific sciences. *Science, 176*, 1203–1210.

Task Force on Social Work Research. (1991, November). *Building social work knowledge for effective services and policies: A plan for research development* (Report, with assistance provided by the National Institute of Mental Health). Austin, TX: Capital Printing.

Taylor, C. (1971). Interpretation and the sciences of man. *Review of Metaphysics, 25*(1), 3–51.

Taylor, C. (1973). Peaceful coexistence in psychology. *Social Research, 40*(1), 55–82.

Taylor, C. (1982). Consciousness. In P. H. Secord (Ed.), *Explaining human behavior: Consciousness, human action and social structure.* Beverly Hills, CA: Sage.

Taylor, G. (1936). *Chicago commons through forty years.* Chicago: Chicago Commons Association.

Taylor, L. (1954). The social settlement and civic responsibility: The life work of Mary McDowell and Graham Taylor. *Social Service Review, 28*, 31–40.

Taylor, S. J., & Bogdan, R. (1984). *Introduction to qualitative research methods: The search for meanings* (2nd ed.). New York: Wiley.

Taylor, S. J., & Bogdan, R. (1989). On accepting relationships between people with mental retardation and non-disabled people: Towards an understanding of acceptance. *Disability, Handicap and Society, 4*, 21–36.

Tellis-Nayak, V., &. O'Donoghue, G. (1982). Conjugal egalitarianism and violence across cultures. *Journal of Comparative Family Studies, 13*, 277–290.

Test, M. A., & Burke, S. S. (1985). Random assignment of chronically mentally ill persons to hospital or community treatment. In R. F. Boruch & W. Wothke (Eds.), *Randomization and field experimentation: New directions for program evaluation, No. 28.* San Francisco: Jossey-Bass.

Thibaut, J. W., & Kelley, H. H. (1959). *The social psychology of groups.* New York: Wiley.

Thomas, E. J. (1975). Use of research methods in interpersonal practice. In N. Polansky (Ed.), *Social work research: Methods for the helping professions.* Chicago: University of Chicago Press.

Thomas, E. J., Walter, C., & O'Flaherty, K. (1974). Computer-assisted assessment and modification possibilities and illustrative data. *Social Service Review, 48*, 170–183.

Thomas, L. E., & Chambers, K. O. (1989). Phenomenology of life satisfaction among elderly men: Quantitative and qualitative views. *Psychology and Aging, 4*(3), 284–289.

Thyer, B. (1986). On pseudoscience and pseudoreasoning. *Social Work Research and Abstracts, 22*, 2.

Thyer, B. (1989). Response to R. G. Dean, and B. L. Fenby, "Exploring epistemologies: Social work action as a reflection of philosophical assumptions." *Journal of Social Work Education, 25*, 174–176.

Thyer, B. (1991). Guidelines for evaluating outcome studies on social work practice. *Research on Social Work Practice, 1*, 76–91.

Thyer, B., & Hudson, W. W. (1987). Progress in behavioral social work: An introduction. *Journal of Social Service Research, 10*, 1–6.

Tibbetts, P. (1986). The sociology of scientific knowledge: The constructivist thesis and relativism. *Philosophy of the Social Sciences, 16*, 39–57.

Torres, L. B. (1973). The participants in social science research. *Professional Psychology, 4*, 209–248.

Toulmin, S. (1953). *The philosophy of science: An introduction.* New York: Harper & Row.

Toulmin, S. (1961). *Foresight and understanding: An enquiry into the aims of science.* New York: Harper & Row.

Toulmin, S. (1972). *Human understanding.* Princeton, NJ: Princeton University Press.

Toulmin, S. (1978). Wittgenstein: The Mozart of psychology. *New York Review of Books, 25*(14).

Toulmin, S. (1982). The genealogy of "consciousness." In P. H. Secord (Ed.), *Explaining human behavior: Consciousness, human action and social structure.* Beverly Hills, CA: Sage.

Towle, C. (1928, April). How to know a foster family: Part 1. *Child Welfare League of America Bulletin*, 2–3.

Towle, C. (1936). Factors in treatment. In *Proceedings of the National Conference on Social Work 63rd*

Annual Session, Atlantic City (pp. 179–191). Chicago: University of Chicago Press.

Towle, C. (1940). A social case record from a psychiatric clinic with teaching notes. *Social Service Review, 14,* 523–540.

Towle, C. (1941a). *Social case records from psychiatric clinics; with discussion notes.* Chicago: University of Chicago Press.

Towle, C. (1941b). Some basic principles of social research in social case work. *Social Service Review, 15,* 66–80.

Towle, C. (1948). The classroom teacher as practitioner. *Social Service Review, 22,* 312–323.

Towle, C. (ca 1950s). *Looking ahead in the fields of orthopsychiatric research.* Box 12, Folder 5, Charlotte Towle Papers, Regenstein Library, University of Chicago, Department of Special Collections.

Towle, C. (1954). *The learner in education for the professions: As seen in education for social work.* Chicago: University of Chicago Press.

Towle, C. (1958, October 17). *Letter to Ms. Kathleen Woodroofe.* Box 2, Folder 4, Charlotte Towle Papers, Regenstein Library, University of Chicago, Department of Special Collections.

Towle, C. (1961). Social work: Cause and function, 1961. *Social Casework, 42,* 385–397.

Towle, C. (1987). *Common human needs* (rev. ed.). Silver Spring, MD: National Association of Social Workers. (Original work published 1945)

Trattner, W. (1989). *From poor law to welfare state: A history of social welfare in America* (4th ed.). New York: Free Press.

Tribe, L. (1972). Policy science: Analysis or ideology? *Philosophy and Public Affairs, 2,* 66–110.

Tripodi, T. (1981). The logic of research design. In R. Grinnell (Ed.), *Social work research and evaluation* (pp. 198–225). Itasca, IL: Peacock Press.

Tripodi, T. (1984). Trends in research publication: A study of social work journals 1956–1980. *Social Work, 29,* 353–359.

Trolander, J. (1987). *Professionalism and social change: From the settlement house movement to neighborhood centers, 1886 to the present.* New York: Columbia University Press.

Tshabalala, M. (1991). *Social work practice in South Africa: Prospects for developing anti-racist social work practice.* Paper presented at the Council on Social Work Education, Annual Program Meeting, New Orleans, LA.

Tufte, E. (1990). *Envisioning information.* Cheshire, CT: Graphics Press.

Turner, V. W. (1967). *The forest of symbols: Aspects of Ndambu ritual.* Ithaca, NY: Cornell University Press.

Tversky, A., & Kahneman, D. (1974). Judgment under uncertainty: Heuristics and biases. *Science, 185,* 1124–1131.

Tversky, A., & Kahneman, D. (1981). The framing of decisions and the psychology of choice. *Science, 211,* 453–458.

Tweney, R., Doherty, M., & Mynatt, C. (1981). *On scientific thinking.* New York: Columbia University Press.

Tyson, K. (1991a, September). *New solutions for enduring problems in the treatment of young children.* Paper presented at the 20th Anniversary Conference of the National Federation of Societies of Clinical Social Work.

Tyson, K. (1991b). The understanding and treatment of childhood hyperactivity: Old problems and new approaches. *Smith College Studies in Social Work, 61,* 133–166.

Tyson, K. (1992). A new approach to relevant and scientific research for practitioners: The heuristic paradigm. *Social Work, 37,* 541–556.

Tyson, K. (1993, May 27–29). *Advancing clinical social work: Prior approaches and a view toward the future based on intrapsychic humanism.* Keynote address presented at the Conference on Clinical Social Work, What is the Present Status of Clinical Social Work in the United States? Co-sponsored by the Scuola per Assistenti Sociali, L.U.M.S.A., Rome, Scuola Diretta a Fini Speciali per Assistenti Sociali, Universita Cattolica del Sacro Cuore, Milan, and School of Social Work, Loyola University of Chicago. Rome.

Tyson, K. (1994). Heuristic guidelines for naturalistic qualitative evaluations of child treatment. In E. Sherman & W. J. Reid (Eds.), *Qualitative research in social work.* New York: Columbia University Press.

Ulen, T. S. (1990, December). The theory of rational choice, its shortcomings, and the implications for public policy decision making. *Knowledge, 12,* 170–198.

Van Kleeck, M. (1934). The common goals of labor and social work. *Proceedings of the National Conference of Social Work, 61,* 284–303.

Videka-Sherman, L., Reid, W. J., & Roseland, R. W. (1990). Themes, issues, and prospects. In L. Videka-Sherman, & W. J. Reid (Eds.), *Advances in clinical social work research.* Silver Spring, MD: National Association of Social Workers.

Vigilante, J. (1974). Between values and science: Education for the profession during a moral crisis or is proof truth? *Journal of Social Work Education, 10*, 107–115.

Wachtel, P. (1980). Investigation and its discontents: Some constraints on progress in psychological research. *American Psychologist, 35*, 399–408.

Waddington, C. (1953). Genetic assimilation of an acquired character. *Evolution, 7*, 118–126.

Wade, M. J. (1978). A critical review of the models of group selection. *Quarterly Review of Biology, 53*, 101–104.

Wagner, D. (1986). Collective mobility and fragmentation: A model of social work history. *Journal of Sociology and Social Welfare, 13*, 657–700.

Wald, L. (1915). *The house on Henry Street.* New York: Holt.

Walker, H. M., & Buckley, N. K. (1968). The use of positive reinforcement in conditioning attending behavior. *Journal of Applied Behavior Analysis, 1*, 245–250.

Walsh, F. (1983). Family therapy: A systematic orientation to treatment. In D. Waldfogel & A. Rosenblatt (Eds.), *Handbook of clinical social work.* San Francisco: Jossey-Bass.

Walsh, S. F. (1986). Characteristics of failures in an emergency residential alternative to psychiatric hospitalization. *Social Work in Health Care, 11*, 53–64.

Watson, J. B. (1913). Psychology as the behaviorist views it. *Psychological Review, 20*, 158–177.

Watson, J. B. (1970). *Behaviorism.* New York: W. W. Norton. (Original work published 1912)

Watson, J. D., & Crick, F. H. C. (1953). Molecular structure of nucleic acid. *Nature, 171*, 964–967.

Watts, P. (1964). Casework above the poverty line: The influence of home service in World War I on social work. *Social Service Review, 38*, 303–315.

Watzlawick, P., Beavin, J., & Jackson, D. (1967). *The pragmatics of human communication: A study of interactional patterns, pathologies, and paradoxes.* New York: W. W. Norton.

Webb, E. J., Campbell, D. T., Schwartz, R. D., Sechrest, L., & Grove, J. B. (1981). *Nonreactive measures in the social sciences* (2nd ed.). Boston: Houghton Mifflin.

Weber, R., & Polansky, N. (1975). Evaluation. In N. Polansky (Ed.), *Social work research: Methods for the helping professions* (pp. 182–201). Chicago: University of Chicago Press. (Original work published 1960)

Webster, G. L. (1963). Population biology. *Science, 139*, 236–237.

Weick, A. (1983a). A growth-task model of human development. *Social Casework, 64*, 131–137.

Weick, A. (1983b). Issues in overturning a medical model of social work practice. *Social Work, 28*, 467–471.

Weick, A. (1986). The philosophical context of a health model of social work. *Social Casework, 67*, 551–559.

Weick, A. (1987). Reconceptualizing the philosophical perspective of social work. *Social Service Review, 61*, 218–230.

Weick, A. (1992). Should scholarly productivity be the primary criterion for tenure decisions? No! *Journal of Social Work Education, 28*, 135–138.

Weick, K. E. (1979). *The social psychology of organizing.* Reading, MA: Addison-Wesley.

Weimer, W. B. (1979). *Notes on the methodology of scientific research.* Hillsdale, NJ: Erlbaum.

Weinberger, R., & Tripodi, T. (1969). Trends in types of research reported in selected social work journals, 1956–65. *Social Service Review, 43*, 439–447.

Weiss, C. H. (1972). *Evaluation research: Methods for assessing program effectiveness.* Englewood Cliffs, NJ: Prentice-Hall.

Weiss, G., & Hechtman, L. (1986). *Hyperactive children grown up: Empirical findings and theoretical considerations.* New York: Guilford.

Weiss, M., & Rein, R. (1970). The evaluation of broad-aim programs: Experimental design, its difficulties, and an alternative. *Administrative Science Quarterly, 1*, 97–109.

Weisz, J., Weiss, B., & Alicke, M. (1987). Effectiveness of psychotherapy with children and adolescents: A meta-analysis for clinicians. *Journal of Consulting and Clinical Psychology, 55*, 542–549.

Welch, G. J. (1983). Will graduates use single-subject designs to evaluate their casework practice? *Journal of Education for Social Work, 19*, 42–47.

Westkott, M. (1979). Feminist criticism of the social sciences. *Harvard Educational Review, 49*, 422–430.

Wexler, A. (1984). *Emma Goldman: An intimate life.* New York: Pantheon.

Whitaker, G. P. (1974). Who puts the value in evaluation? *Social Science Quarterly, 54*, 759–761.

White, M. (1963). Pragmatism and the scope of science. In J. Schlesinger, M. Arthur, & M. White (Eds.), *Paths of American thought* (pp. 190–202). Boston: Houghton Mifflin.

White, M., & Epson, D. (1990). *Narrative means to therapeutic ends.* New York: W. W. Norton.

White, R. C. (1930). The relative value of case study and statistics. *The Family, 10*, 259–265.

White, R. C. (1956). The problem of knowing in social work. *Social Work, 1*, 94–99.

Whorf, B. (1956). Science and linguistics. In J. B. Carroll (Ed.), *Language, thought and reality: Selected writings of Benjamin Lee Whorf.* New York: MIT Press and John Wiley & Sons.

Will, F. L. (1974). *Induction and justification: An investigation of Cartesian procedure in the philosophy of knowledge.* Ithaca, NY: Cornell University Press.

Williams, W., & Evans, J. W. (1969). The politics of evaluation: The case of Head Start. *Annuals of the American Academy of Political and Social Science, 385*, 118–132.

Wimsatt, W. C. (1976a). Reductionism, levels of organization, and the mind-body problem. In G. G. Globus, G. Maxwell, & I. Savodnik (Eds.), *Consciousness and the brain: A scientific and philosophical inquiry.* New York: Plenum.

Wimsatt, W. C. (1976b). Reductive explanation: A functional account. In C. A. Hooker (Ed.), *Proceedings of the Meeting of the Philosophy of Science Association.* Dordrecht, The Netherlands: D. Reidel.

Wimsatt, W. C. (1980a). Randomness and perceived-randomness in evolutionary biology. *Synthese, 43*, 287–329.

Wimsatt, W. C. (1980b). Reductionistic research strategies and their biases in the units of selection controversy. In T. Nickles (Ed.), *Scientific discovery: Vol. 2. Case studies* (pp. 213–259). Dordrecht, The Netherlands: D. Reidel.

Wimsatt, W. C. (1981a). Robustness, reliability, and overdetermination. In M. Brewer & B. Collins (Eds.), *Scientific inquiry and the social sciences* (pp. 124–163). San Francisco: Jossey-Bass.

Wimsatt, W. C. (1981b). Units of selection and the structure of the multilevel genome. In P. D. Asquith & R. N. Giere (Eds.), *PSA-1980* (Vol. 2). East Lansing, MI: Philosophy of Science Association.

Wimsatt, W. C. (1984, May). *Generative entrenchment, developmental constraints, and the innate-acquired distinction.* Paper presented at the conference entitled Integrating scientific disciplines, Georgia State University.

Wimsatt, W. C. (1985). *Von Baer's law, generative entrenchment, and scientific change.* Unpublished manuscript.

Wimsatt, W. C. (1986a). Forms of aggregativity. In A. Donagan, A.N. Perovich, Jr., & M. Wedin (Eds.), *Human nature and natural knowledge: Essays presented to Marjorie Greene on the occasion of her seventy-fifth birthday* (pp. 259–291). Dordrecht, The Netherlands: D. Reidel.

Wimsatt, W. C. (1986b). Heuristics and the study of human behavior. In D. W. Fiske & R. A. Shweder (Eds.), *Metatheory in social science: Pluralisms and subjectivites* (pp. 293–314). Chicago: University of Chicago Press.

Wimsatt, W. C. (1987). False models as means to truer theories. In M. H. Nitecki & A. Hoffman (Eds.), *Neutral models in biology* (pp. 23–55). New York: Oxford University Press.

Wimsatt, W. C. (1990, October 25). *Abstract: Complexity and organization revisited—mapping the joints of nature: Levels of organization, perspectives, and causal thickets.* Unpublished manuscript.

Wimsatt, W., Goldin-Meadow, S., & McClintock, M. (1991, July 19). *Lecture outline revised.* Unpublished manuscript.

Wimsatt, W. C. (1990–1991). *Teaching notes.* Unpublished manuscript.

Windle, C., Molnar, S. F., & Neigher, W. (1978). Ethical problems in program evaluation: Advice for trapped evaluators. *Evaluation and Program Planning, 1*, 97–108.

Witkin, S. L. (1993). *Making social work scientific: Analysis and recommendations.* Unpublished manuscript, University of Vermont.

Witkin, S. L. (1989). Towards a scientific social work. *Journal of Social Service Research, 12*, 83–98.

Witkin, S. L. (1991). Empirical clinical practice: A critical analysis. *Social Work, 36*, 158–163.

Witkin, S. L. (1992). Empirical clinical practice or Witkin's revised views: Which is the issue? *Social Work, 37*, 465–468.

Witkin, S. L., & Gottschalk, S. (1988). Alternative criteria for theory evaluation. *Social Service Review, 62*, 211–224.

Witkin, S. L., & Harrison, D. (1979). Single-case designs in marital research and therapy. *Journal of Social Service Research, 3*, 51–66.

Witmer, H. (1930). By way of introduction. *Smith College Studies in Social Work, 1*, 1–5.

Witmer, H. (1942). *Social work: An analysis of a social institution.* New York: Farrar & Rinehart.

Witmer, H. (1943). Science and social work. *Smith College Studies in Social Work, 14*, 222–230.

Wittgenstein, L. (1960). *Remarks on the foundations of mathematics.* London: Blackwell.

Wodarski, J. S. (1981). *The role of research in clinical practice: A practical approach for the human services.* Baltimore: University Park Press.

Wolters, R. (1975). The New Deal and the Negro. In J. Braeman (Ed.), *The New Deal: The national level* (pp. 170–217). Columbus: Ohio State University Press.

Wood, K. (1978). Casework effectiveness: A new look at the research evidence. *Social Work, 23,* 437–458.

Wood, K. (1980). Experiences in teaching the practitioner-researcher model. In R. W. Weinbach & A. Rubin (Eds.), *Teaching social work research.* New York: Council on Social Work Education.

Woodroofe, K. (1962). *From charity to social work in England and the United States.* Toronto: University of Toronto Press.

Woods, M., & Hollis, F. (1990). *Casework: A psychosocial therapy* (4th ed.). New York: McGraw-Hill.

Woodward, W. R. (1980). Toward a critical historiography of psychology. In J. Brozek & L. Pongratz (Eds.), *Historiography of modern psychology: Aims, resources, approaches.* Toronto: C. J. Hogrefe.

Woolgar, S. W. (1976). The identification and definition of scientific collectivities. In G. Lemaine, R. Macleod, M. Mulkay, & P. Weingart (Eds.), *Perspectives on the emergence of scientific disciplines.* Chicago: Aldine.

Wye, C. (1972). The New Deal and the Negro community: Toward a broader conceptualization. *Journal of American History, 59,* 621–639.

Yegidis, B. L., & Weinbach, R. W. (1991). *Research methods for social workers.* White Plains, NY: Longman.

Yin, R. K. (1989). *Case study research: Design and methods.* Newbury Park: Sage. (Original work published 1984)

York, P., York, D., & Wachtel, T. (1983). *Toughlove.* New York: Bantam.

Young, P. (1939). *Scientific social surveys and research: An introduction to the background, content, methods, and analysis of social studies.* Englewood Cliffs, NJ: Prentice-Hall.

Zametkin, A., Nordahl, T., Gross, M., King, C., Semple, W., Rumsey, J., Hamburger, S., & Cohen, R. (1990). Cerebral glucose metabolism in adults with hyperactivity of childhood onset. *The New England Journal of Medicine, 323,* 1361–1366.

Zelen, M. (1979). A new design for randomized clinical trials. *The New England Journal of Medicine, 300,* 1242–1245.

Zigler, E., & Gordon, E. (Eds.). (1982). *Day care: Scientific and social policy issues.* Boston: Auburn House.

Zimbalist, S. (1952). Organismic social work versus partialistic research. *Social Casework, 33,* 3–10, 393–395.

Zimbalist, S. (1964). Research in the service of a cause: The changing context of community welfare research. *Social Service Review, 38,* 130–136.

Zimbalist, S. (1977). *Historic themes and landmarks in social welfare research.* New York: Harper & Row.

Zimmerman, J. (1989). Determinism, science, and social work. *Social Service Review, 63,* 52–62.

Name Index

Subject Index